MÁLAGA

A Comprehensive Guide to Spain's Most Hospitable City

THOMAS MARTIN

FAROLA BOOKS

For my parents, who love Málaga

*In none of the Spanish towns have I been
so happy, so entirely at home, as here in Málaga.
I like the manners of the people. Good scenery,
and the open sea, both indispensable to me,
I have found here, and, what is still of more
consequence, I have found most amiable people.*

Hans Christian Andersen
(In Spain, *1863*)

Published by Farola Books
farolabooks@gmail.com

First published 2023
Copyright © Thomas Martin, 2023

ISBN: 978-1-7395074-0-4

Cover image: © Nick Kenrick, flickr.com/photos/zedzap
Title page illustration: freepik.com

Contents

To The Reader

I hope you enjoy this book. More importantly, I hope you find it **useful**. If it helps convince you that Málaga is a great destination for a city-break or holiday, then it will have done its job. If you visit Málaga and this book helps you make the most of your trip, then even better.

I wrote this book because Málaga is one of my favourite cities in Spain, yet when I told friends about my visits some would express surprise, or even incredulity, imagining a Benidorm-esque hellscape of British sports bars and all-day full English breakfasts. Wanting to recommend Málaga to others, I tried to find a decent guidebook (in English) and found none. There were a few self-published guides, but the quality and value for money seemed poor (double-spaced with wide margins to maximize the page count). Even from the sample pages available to view on the Amazon website, it was obvious that many contained errors. The most amusing example of this is a book which informs the reader that 'one of the symbols of Málaga is an ashtray'. That took me a while to work out. The Spanish word for an ashtray is *cenicero*. One of the symbols of Málaga is the *cenachero*, or fish seller.

I'm sure there are errors in my book, too, but they are inadvertent, and I'd like to take this opportunity to apologize for them. Information goes out of date, but I'm genuinely sorry if you waste an afternoon looking for a bar that closed two months ago, or had trouble finding a bus because the route changed.

Because this book is self-published, to have included sumptuous full-colour photographs would have almost doubled the cost of printing the paperback edition. I preferred to keep the cost down instead. Similarly, although maps and 'phrase book' sections used to be *de rigueur* for any guidebook, these days people mainly use their smartphones instead. Think of this book, then, as a companion to your mobile phone.

If you have enjoyed this book and would like to recommend it to others, I should be enormously grateful if you would consider leaving a review on the website of the store from which you bought it.

Please also feel free to contact me at farolabooks@gmail.com if you would like to send any comments, corrections or suggestions. I'd be delighted to hear from you.

Acknowledgements

There are many people whom I want to thank for helping this book come to fruition. First of all, Jean and Charlie. This book began life as a modest list of recommendations for their holiday in Málaga. I'd also like to thank Philip and Jane who used my guide to Sevilla, Córdoba and Granada and provided useful comments, and James who read an early draft of this book.

I have been hugely encouraged by people I 'know' through Twitter whose interest in the book has been a great source of encouragement. I should mention in particular Christian M, Steven D, Val S, Asoka K, Guy S, Paul K, Martin S and Andrew M. I am thankful to Gillian L for casting her eye over the section on Judaism and helping me not to put my foot in my mouth, and to Cara who helped explain the intricacies of bringing a book to publication.

I have dedicated this book to my parents. My happiest times in Málaga have been spent with them.

I have also been able to spend more time in Málaga thanks to the generosity of my friend Peter, whom I had the pleasure of accompanying upon his first visit to Málaga. He has been a consistent support to me and I shall be forever grateful.

I am grateful, too, to those Hispanophile journalists who not only encouraged me but also expressed an interest in reading the text — in particular Tim Parfitt, Christopher Howse and Graham Keeley. Do read their excellent writing about Spain (and other topics) at: timothyparfitt.com, twitter.com/BeardyHowse and twitter.com/grahamkeeley.

Most of all, though, my thanks are due to the wonderful people of Málaga, who have made me welcome in their city on so many occasions.

barrio		breakfast/*almuerzo*	
address		sweet bakery	
restaurant		ice cream	
bar		website	
tasting menu		tickets	
reservations		Spanish	
reserve on thefork		English	
reserve on Google		date	
menú del día		opening hours	
children's menu		closed	
tapas		information	
raciones/½ *raciones*		price range	
wine list		entry charge	
Málaga wine/*vermú*		free	
cocktails		free audio guide	
beers		gallery	
coffee		museum	
take away		email	
delivery		WhatsApp	
traditional dishes		Android	
world/fusion cuisine		iOS	
steaks or grill		note	
vegetarian options		Facebook/Meta	
salads		phone	
fish		Instagram	
seafood		summer hours	
sandwiches/*tostadas*		off–season hours	
egg dishes		family friendly	
cheese		guided tour	
soup/stews		Metro	
rice dishes		bus	
homemade puddings		bus stop ID	
fast food		*Cercanías*	

Introduction

'A couple of days is enough for Málaga.' (Hand-book for Travellers in Spain, *Richard Ford, 1845*)

I hope that this book will persuade you that Richard Ford — who was as enamoured with Spain as he was (often) contemptuous of it — was wrong about Málaga. Every year, more than 18 million travellers (a quarter of them from the United Kingdom) touch down at Málaga–Costa del Sol Airport. The overwhelming majority then hire a car, take a coach, or board a local train to head for the resorts of Torremolinos, Benalmádena, or Fuengirola. Holidaymakers seeking somewhere more glamorous venture further west to Marbella. Those who turn their noses up at beach resorts might head inland to one of the famed white villages (*pueblos blancos*) of southern Andalucía, or further inland to Granada or even Sevilla. Very few of the almost five million Brits who pass annually through Málaga airport visit the city after which it is named, or if they do, stay for no more than an hour or two.

Málaga is often overlooked as a destination in its own right, just as the charming city of Alicante is ignored in the stampede towards Benidorm. The sun-worshippers heading towards the all-inclusive hotels of Fuengirola don't think of Málaga as a 'resort'. The stag and hen parties bound for Torremolinos no doubt consider it staid and unexciting. The TOWIE wannabes making for 'Marbs' presumably think Málaga unsophisticated (oblivious to the irony of that judgement). Maybe those *en route* to the *pueblos blancos* or the great city of Granada with its magnificent Alhambra imagine Málaga to be uncultured, dull and mercantile. And many more snootily ignore the Costa del Sol entirely, preferring the well-worn charms of hip Barcelona, romantic Sevilla, or elegant Madrid.

In fact, Málaga has something to offer all of these 'types' (except stag and hen parties, who can, and should, go elsewhere). If you're the sort of person who likes the beach but wants to enjoy some local culture and cuisine as well, then Málaga is ideal. If culture is your thing, then Málaga's dozens of museums could keep you busy for several days. History buffs will find evidence of Phoenician, Roman and Moorish civilizations alongside baroque and Renaissance churches, ghosts of the Civil War, and reminders of the city's industrial past. If it's culinary culture you're after, then Málaga offers some of the finest food and wine in Spain. If you're an *aficionado* of the city-break, then whilst Málaga may not be in quite the same league as Venice, Prague or Sevilla, it's no provincial backwater either.

Excellent transport links (by air, road and rail) mean that it is also easy to combine a stay in Málaga with another destination. If you are visiting Gaucín, Granada or Torremolinos, then why not spend a day or two in Málaga as well? Flights between the United Kingdom and Málaga are frequent and, due to the popularity of the Costa del Sol, relatively cheap, even from regional airports. Although it is possible to find direct flights to cities like Granada and Sevilla from some UK airports, they are often expensive, less than daily, and rarely available outside high season. Get a cheap flight to Málaga instead and approach these cities by rail. Combining a visit to Málaga with cities even further afield is also possible. You can leave Málaga after breakfast and, thanks to Spain's network of high-speed trains, be in Barcelona (or Madrid) in time for lunch (or elevenses).

Whatever sort of traveller you are, I hope this guide will encourage you to consider Málaga as more than simply an airport — either as a holiday destination in itself or as a place to spend an enjoyable day (or a few days) as part of a longer holiday.

¡Buen viaje!

T. Martin

Antes de Viajar (Before You Go)

This book is not intended to be a volume to be clutched as you wander around Málaga and its environs. I hope, rather, that it will whet your appetite concerning what Málaga has to offer and help you to plan and make the most of your trip. I also hope that the background information and history will help you to gain a deeper understanding of Málaga's 'soul'.

When planning your trip, you should be aware that a number of the attractions mentioned in this guide are extremely popular and some will be fully booked weeks ahead.

Booking ahead — as far ahead as possible — is **essential** if you want to visit the **Alhambra** (p. 580ff.) or the **Caminito del Rey** (p. 548f.). If you want to visit **Córdoba** (p. 564ff.), then it's advisable to book your train ticket ahead of time to get the cheapest price and book a timed-entry ticket for the **Mezquita-Catedral** (p. 569ff.) at the same time. Booking ahead is also strongly advised if you wish to visit any fine-dining restaurants (the sort that serve tasting menus).

Finally, when planning your itinerary, bear in mind that **all municipal** museums and galleries in Spain are closed on Mondays.

 Every location (sightseeing attraction, restaurant, bar, shop, etc.) mentioned in this guide is shown on a companion Google Map. Scan the QR code or consult it here: **bit.ly/MalagaMap**

On a mobile device, you will need to use the **LEGEND** label to display the relevant 'layers' (travel, restaurants, shopping, etc. — day trips outside Málaga city also have their own layers).

⊕ Websites and Online Resources

A very useful website is **malagatop.com** 🔊 ⊕ run by Alejo Tomás, a native of Málaga. His site is comprehensive and regularly updated. Alejo is a great ambassador for his city and a trustworthy source of information (the website is in Spanish and English).

One of the most comprehensive non-commercial websites about the city and province of Málaga is **viajerosencortomalaga.com** 🔊 maintained by Francisco Jurado. It contains a wealth of information. (Spanish only)

facebook.com/muelleuno 🔊 is the best way to keep informed about the many seasonal events that take place on Muelle Uno, especially events for families and children and monthly craft markets (*zocos*).

guidetomalaga.com ⊕ is one of the most comprehensive — and certainly the best-known — websites about Málaga in English. The creation of Joanna Styles, a British travel writer living and working in Málaga, it is frequently updated with information about upcoming events and festivals.

genmalaga.com ⓐ is, alas, only in Spanish, but it maintains a very useful listing of current events and exhibitions.

visita.malaga.eu ⓐ ✤ is the official tourist information website for Málaga. ⚠ Although most information is available in English, some of the 'news' and 'events' listings are only in Spanish.

malagadestino.es ⓐ ✤ is a scheme that began in 2023: a kind of loyalty card for locals and tourists in the form of smartphone apps (see p. 5). Sign-ups are limited, so if you can't register at first, try again later. The scheme is free and the 'card' will get you discounts of 5%–25% at participating restaurants, hotels, shops, museums and leisure services. With each purchase, users earn points which can increase the level of discount.

malaga.es/en/laprovincia ⓐ ✤ is the tourism section of the website of the *Diputación* (Provincial Government) and it has a wealth of information about patrimony, traditions, gastronomy, natural features, flora and fauna of the province (all available in English). This excellent website is well worth studying if you plan to explore beyond the city of Málaga.

blog.fuertehoteles.com ⓐ ✤ The Fuerte Hotel Group has four hotels in Andalucía, one in the Province of Málaga (in Marbella). Their company blog has well-written, interesting and helpful articles about places in the Málaga Province, local traditions, foods and festivals. Well worth a look.

visitcostadelsol.com ⓐ ✤ This is another tourism website maintained by the Provincial Government (*Diputación*) of Málaga.

andalucia.com ✤ Founded in 1996 by Chris Chaplow, few independent tourism information websites are so comprehensive or impressive. Despite the huge quantity of information, it manages to stay up-to-date thanks to its use of a team of contributors. There is also a lively forum.

malagafoto.com ✤ A collection of lovely photos of Málaga taken by Christian Machowski.

𝕏 Twitter

@turismodemalaga	✤	The city's official *turismo* account (some tweets in English).
@DisfrutaMalaga	ⓐ	Event listings from the *Diario Sur* newspaper: cinema, theatre, concerts, exhibitions, hiking, activities for children and more.
@Christian_ESEM	ⓐ ✤	Beautiful photos of Málaga (and tweets about soccer) from Christian Machowski (many of his tweets are in English).
@Malaga_AyerYHoy	ⓐ	Contemporary and historic photos of Málaga.
@malaga	ⓐ	The official account of the *Ayuntamiento* (Town Hall).
@ZappaplayZappa	ⓐ	A personal account. Mixed content but featuring lots of stunning photos of the city and province.
@Storm_Malaga	ⓐ	An amateur account focusing on local weather.
@opiniondemalaga	ⓐ	Málaga's *Opinión de Málaga* newspaper.
@CarnavalMLG	ⓐ	A dedicated account for the Málaga *Carnaval*.

@cofradiasmalaga   ⊕   A shared account for the Málaga Holy Week Fraternities.

@feria_malaga   ⊕   The official account of the August *feria* (fair). The hashtag is **#FeriaMLG**

@SaboraMalaga   ⊕ ⊕   A food and drink-focused account maintained by the *Diputación* (Provincial Government).

@malagademuseos   ⊕ ⊕   An account bringing together Málaga's museums.

@culturamalaga   ⊕   The cultural account of the *Ayuntamiento* (Town Hall).

@alcazabamlg   ⊕   Shared account of the Alcazaba and Castillo de Gibralfaro.

@festivalmalaga   ⊕   The account of the Málaga Film Festival.

@DiarioSUR   ⊕   Málaga's *Diario SUR* newspaper.

@mPICASSOm   ⊕   Málaga's jewel-in-the-crown Picasso Museum.

@GuidetoMalaga   ⊕   The account of the 'Guide to Málaga' blog and guide.

@DiocesisMalaga   ⊕   The official account of the Catholic Diocese of Málaga.

@diputacionMLG   ⊕   The Provincial Government (*Diputación*) official account.

@MalagaCF_en   ⊕   Málaga Football (Soccer) Club (in English).

@unicajaCB   ⊕   Málaga's Basketball Team Account.

📱 Apps

Arca

The Arca App is a project of the Municipal Archives of Málaga that links to dozens of historical photos via a GPS-enabled map (in English) enabling users to scan QR codes around the city:

  Android   iOS

Málaga in Your Pocket

A free and multilingual app (Spanish, English, French and German) developed by the Málaga *Diputación* (Provincial Government) covering 103 towns and villages in the Province of Málaga.

  Android   iOS

Málaga Destino

 A new scheme (launched in 2023) to give (primarily) tourists discounts in participating attractions and businesses. Sign-ups are limited, so if you're unable to register, try again later. You can also use the **Málaga In Your Pocket** app (above) to register for and use the scheme. malagadestino.es.

Callejero (City Street Map)

 This is a web page rather than an app, but it works well on a smartphone (tip: if you lose the layers menu, swipe right from the left-hand side of the screen and select **GeoPortal**). **Callejero** is an official street map maintained by the *ayuntamiento* that you can use to find all sorts of amenities (🖥 only) from taxi ranks to drinking fountains to markets. It is especially useful if you are staying in an apartment because it shows the locations of communal refuse collection points. Under the '*Medio ambiente*' heading, select '*Envases*' (tins — yellow), '*Papel y cartón*' (paper & cardboard — blue), '*Residuos sólidos urbanos*' (general waste — brown), or '*Contenedores de vidrio*' (glass — green).
🌐 sig.malaga.eu/territorio/callejero/?gp=0

📅 Mondays in Málaga?

Throughout Spain, municipal museums and galleries are closed on Mondays, but there are so many places to visit in Málaga that one hardly notices. However, if your time is limited, especially over a long weekend, you will need to plan. The **Museum of Málaga**, **CAC** and **MUPAM** (p. 248ff.) are both closed on Mondays, as is the **Carmen Thyssen** (p. 247). The **Pompidou** (p. 244) is closed on Tuesdays. The **Cathedral** and both **Picasso museums** are open every day. However, although the **Alcazaba** (p. 236) is open to visit on Monday, the lift is not in operation.

🎒 Useful things to bring with you

🐷 If you are going to be staying in an *hostal* or an apartment, have a look at the 'Money Saving Tips' section on p. 49.

💳 Using a euro-denominated debit card (see p. 49) will save you money.

💊 Over-the-counter medicines (like Aspirin or Paracetamol) are comparatively expensive in Spain (and can only be purchased from pharmacies, not supermarkets), so bring a supply.

➕ Nationals of EU member states should bring a current EHIC (European Health Insurance Card), and UK citizens should make sure they have an up-to-date 'GHIC', as well as health insurance.

🧳 If you normally travel with hand luggage only, consider whether it's worth checking in luggage for the return journey. There are no great bargains in the airport Duty-Free, but wine, spirits, olive oil, ham, charcuterie, cheese etc. are all cheaper in Spain than in the UK. You could bring back quite a hamper of delicacies.

🎧 Since the COVID pandemic, audio guides are now mostly free because they are accessed on your smartphone rather than requiring a handheld unit. Bring headphones or earbuds with you to enable you to use them.

Comunicación (Language)

This book is not a guide to the Spanish language, but it contains many Spanish words and phrases, especially those relating to food and drink. Spain has one of the lowest levels of English proficiency in the European Union (11.7%), lagging just behind the Czech Republic and Bulgaria. By way of comparison, a quarter of the population of France speaks English, as do a third of Greeks, over half of all Swedes and the majority of Netherlanders. Many Spaniards working in the hospitality industry speak English, as well as around 20% of citizens under 35, but on the whole, especially outside the larger hotels and well-worn tourist spots, most *malagueños* you meet are unlikely to speak much more than rudimentary English.

A little knowledge of Spanish (also called *caſtellano*[1], or 'Castilian') is helpful when it comes to finding your way around (understanding signs), choosing what to eat and drink (decoding menus), making the most of bars and restaurants, and simply being polite and friendly. But if languages aren't your thing, don't worry too much. Spanish isn't Hungarian and is one of the easiest foreign languages for English speakers to learn. Many words are similar to English (useful should you have an *accidente* and need to go to *el hospital* in an *ambulancia* to see a *médico*, who'll give you a *prescripción* to take to a *farmacia*), and if you know any French, Italian or Latin, then Spanish should be a piece of cake (or 'eaten bread' as they say in *caſtellano*).

Another reason not to fear a lack of linguistic ability is that Spaniards are generally polite, hospitable and friendly. Certainly, their manner is direct and no-nonsense, and 'please', 'thank you', and 'sorry' are not used as frequently as in the UK, but this is not on account of rudeness. They are likely to be just as apologetic for their lack of ability in English as you may be about your inability to speak Spanish. More often than not, they will be happy to take time to communicate in 'Spanglish', especially when it comes to transactions in hotels, bars, and the like. Indeed, even if you hope to practise your Spanish, you may find that people reply to you in English. This is not, however, because they have judged your language skills and found them wanting. It is more likely to be because they want to practise their English and are trying to be helpful. Most Spaniards are fiercely proud of their home town, their culture and their cuisine. They will do whatever they can to ensure that you enjoy it too.

With the exception of Spain (*España*) itself, the place names in this book are written with Spanish spellings. In most cases, these are no different to English spellings, but a few British archaisms remain. In English it is still common to refer to the river Tajo by its Latin name 'Tagus' and the city of Córdoba is often called 'Cordova' by older people. The reason for my using local spellings is that these help with recognition (*e.g.* reading signs), and with pronunciation. The English pronunciation of 'Cordova' is '**kor-doh**-vah' (stress on the second syllable), whereas in Spanish the stress is on the first syllable of Córdoba (indicated by

---

1   Spanish is very different to English and German in that it tends not to capitalize any word that is not strictly speaking a proper noun, or at the beginning of a sentence. So days of the week, months and titles like '*señor*' take lower case initial letters, for example. Oddly, however, '*Internet*' is always capitalized.

the accent over the 'o') so it is '**kor**-doh-bah'. It's not a huge difference, but a useful one to be aware of if you are listening attentively for an announcement at a railway station. This is particularly the case in the south of Spain, where people tend to swallow the ends of words and some consonants disappear entirely. The first (or penultimate) syllable may be all you may hear!

I have also used Spanish demonyms and adjectives because there is often little agreement about their English versions. It's quite common to read 'Malagan' (or even 'Malagasy') nowadays, yet the OED prefers 'Malagenean'. And what about a native of Ronda? I have seen 'Rondan', 'Rondanese' and the curious half-transliteration 'Rondeno'. It seems more consistent, therefore, to stick with '*malagueño*' and '*rondeño*' (and their feminine and plural forms).

💬 Transliteration

I have transliterated many of the Spanish words and phrases that you might need to pronounce, and have done so in a rather basic (and probably somewhat inconsistent) way. I hope the pronunciations are fairly obviously phonetic (although I have not used IPA). I have used the small capitals KH to express the velar fricative (the **ch** of the Scots loch — IPA χ). I've also used RR in some words as a reminder that although the Spanish /r/ is almost always a flap/tap (slightly 'rolled'), in certain positions (*e.g.* in the initial position and before certain vowels) and when doubled, it is stressed with considerable 'rolling'. In the pronunciation examples, **bold** type is used to indicate stress (*e.g.* Málaga = **ma**-la-gah; café = ka-**fay**).

🗣 Pronunciation

The beauty of (standard) Spanish is that its pronunciation is extremely regular and perfectly phonetic. Consonants are consistently pronounced, although a handful depend upon the following vowel. Vowels are highly regular and diphthongs are in reality only pseudo-diphthongs. That is, diphthongs are treated as sequential vowels regarding pronunciation, but usually as a single vowel regarding stress. The precise pronunciation depends upon the pairing of weak/strong vowels, but if you pronounce diphthongs quickly as two regular vowels then you will not go far wrong.

Unlike 'stress-timed' languages like English and German, Spanish is a 'syllable-timed' language like French and Italian in which stress is regular, except only more so. This is why listening to a Spaniard speaking ten to the dozen can feel like being under machine gun fire — rat-a-tat, rat-a-tat... Take the sentence:

How do you say 'apples' in English? / *¿Cómo se dice «manzanas» en inglés?*

In English, you'll hear (phonetically) something like:

how-ja say appalzin inglish

In Spanish, every syllable is the same length (though not the same stress):

*ko-moh say **dee**-thay man-**than**-nass en een-**glayss***

Aá Accents and Stress

Spanish diacritics (accents) are of two kinds. The *tilde*, which looks like an acute accent (ˊ) and the *diéresis* which looks like an umlaut (¨) and only occurs above **u** (**ü**). There is also what looks like a third kind of accent — what in English is called a tilde but which in Spanish is called a *virgulilla*: **ñ**. This is actually a distinct letter of the Spanish alphabet, pronounced

/ny/.

To take the *diéresis* (**ü**) first. The letter **u** is pronounced as 'oo' before a consonant (*museo* = moo-**say**-o) and as 'w' before a vowel (*suelo* = **sway**-loh). When it occurs after **g**, its function is to modify the pronunciation of the preceding consonant and it is silent: *e.g. guitarra* = gee-**tarr**-ah; *guerra* = **geh**-rrah. That is, it makes the **g** like the **/g/** in 'gas' not the **/ch/** in 'loch'. With the *diéresis*, **ü** is pronounced as **/w/**: *e.g. pingüino* = pin-**gween**-oh; *vergüenza* = bair-**gwen**-thah). It occurs very rarely. The letter **u** (without *diéresis*) also occurs after **q**, but unlike in English where it forms a **/kw/** sound, it forms a simple **/k/** sound: *e.g.* **queso** = **kay**-soh). In Spanish, the **/kw/** sound is made by **cu** (before a vowel, *e.g. cuando* = **kwan-doh**).

The *tilde* (ˊ) is even more straightforward and regular and it does not affect pronunciation. It only occurs over vowels. In writing, although it is also used to differentiate interrogative pronouns, its main use is to indicate where the **stress** falls. As an inflected language, stress is crucial. For example, *hablo* (**ab**-loh) means 'I speak' (present tense), whereas *habló* (ab-**loh**) means 'he/she/it spoke' (past tense).

The regular stress pattern is fairly straightforward. If a word of more than one syllable ends in a **vowel**, **s**, or **n**, then the stress falls on the penultimate syllable:

banco	bank	**ban**-koh
bancos	banks	**ban**-koss
viven	they live	**bee**-ben
farmacia	pharmacy	far-**math**-yah
periodista	journalist	peh-ree-oh-**dee**-stah

When a word ends in a **consonant** (other than **s** or **n**), then the stress falls on the final syllable:

azul	blue	ath-**ool**
tenedor	fork	teh-neh-**dor**
español	Spanish	ess-pan-**yol**
estoy	I am	ess-**toy**

When a vowel has an accent, then that syllable is stressed, wherever it occurs:

celebre	he/she celebrates	thay-**lay**-bray
celebré	I celebrated	thay-lay-**bray**
célebre	famous	**thay**-lay-bray

📖 Simplified Pronunciation Key

Letter	IPA	Pronunciation (English approximation)
Aa	**a**	Like **a** in **a**pple
Bb	**b**	Like **b** in **b**ad
	β	Between vowels the lips should not be fully closed, similar to the **v** in **v**alue
Cc	**θ** (TH)	Before the vowels **e** and **i**, like **th** in **th**in

	k	Everywhere else, like **c** in **c**offee
	s	In parts of Andalucía you'll also hear it pronounced like the **c** in **c**entre
Ch	tʃ	Like **ch** in **ch**urch
Dd	d, ð	Very similar to **d** in **d**ay. Between vowels and after a vowel at the end of a word, similar to the **th** in **th**en
Ee	e	Midway between the **e** in t**e**n and the **ay** in s**ay** (or like the **ai** in **ai**r)
Ff	f	Like **f** in **f**our
Gg	g	Like **g** in **g**et
	χ (κн)	Before the vowels **e** and **i**, like the **ch** in the Scots lo**ch**
Hh	–	Silent, except in some loanwords, but sometimes aspirated in Málaga
Ii	i	Like **e** in h**e**. Before other vowels, it's like the **y** in **y**ou (when unaccented)
Jj	χ (κн)	Like **ch** in the Scots lo**ch**, although it can sometimes sound like the English **h**
Kk	k	Like **k** in as**k**, and only in loanwords — Spanish prefers **c** and **qu**
Ll	l	Similar to the **l** in **l**ine, but shorter, somewhat clipped
Ll ll	ʎ, y	Similar to the **y** in **y**awn or the **ll** in mi**ll**ion, but in some accents closer to the **s** in plea**s**ure
Mm	m	Like **m** in **m**ore
Nn	n, ŋ	Like **n** in **n**o, or like the **ng** in si**ng** before **c** or **g**
Ññ	ɲ	Like the **ny** in ca**ny**on
Oo	o	Like **o** in d**o**g
Pp	p	Like **p** in **p**ort
Qq	k	Like **k** in **k**in (for the **qu** sound of **qu**een, Spanish prefers **cu**)
Rr	ɾ	When soft, like **tt** in the U.S. pronunciation of bu**tt**er
	r (rr)	When hard (initial position, or doubled) it is rolled as in Scots English
Ss	s	Like **s** in **s**ix — sometimes slightly more aspirated, but never like the **sh** in **sh**erry. Spaniards do not say 'Ssshh!' but 'Ssssss!'
Tt	t	Like **t** in **t**en, but dental not palatal
Uu	w	Before another vowel (especially after **c**) like **w** in t**w**ig.
	u	Everywhere else like **oo** in p**oo**l, but a bit shorter
Vv	b, β	Identical to Spanish **b** in almost all cases
Ww	g, w	Used only in words of foreign origin (Spanish prefers **u**). Pronunciation varies from word to word.
Xx	ks	Like the **x** in extra. In some cases it may be pronounced like **gs** or **s**
Yy	i	Like the vowel **i** when a word on its own (*i.e.* *y* = 'and') or at the end of a word
	j	Between the **y** in **y**ellow and the **s** in plea**s**ure when in any other position.
Zz	θ, s	Always the same sound in standard Spanish — like the **th** in **th**in (but often like **s** in **s**ale in Andalucía)

⏰ Telling the Time

Not the time, exactly, but the time of day and the days of the week. If you spot a bar or restaurant you fancy trying later, or another day, it's helpful to be able to understand the opening times displayed. The most useful vocabulary is:

lunes	**Monday**
martes	**Tuesday**
miércoles	**Wednesday**
jueves	**Thursday**
viernes	**Friday**
sábado(s)	**Saturday(s)**
domingo(s)	**Sunday(s)**
festivos	**feast days (or holidays)**
fin de semana	**weekend**
laborales	**weekdays**
cerrado	**closed**
hoy	**today**
mañana	**tomorrow**
mañana(s)	**morning(s)**
tarde(s)	**afternoon(s)/evening(s)**
noche(s)	**late evening(s)/night(s)**

🧳 *Guiris* vs. *Extranjeros*

As noted above, Spaniards are generally very forgiving of foreigners who cannot speak Spanish. In Spain, I have never encountered even a suggestion of the condescending disdain that one might receive from a *maître d'hôtel* in a Parisian bistro. However, you should be aware that there are broadly two classes of tourist, as far as Spaniards are concerned. The *castellano* catch-all word for 'foreigner' is '*extranjero*' ('stranger'). Indeed, some natives of Málaga would probably regard people from Madrid as *extranjeros*.

But '*guiri*' denotes a rather different sort of foreigner, or stranger. The etymology of the term is uncertain and probably goes back to the 19th-century Carlist Wars, but nowadays a *guiri* denotes a coarse, uncouth foreign visitor. The word refers to a foreign tourist who stands out because of the way he or she behaves.

An *extranjero* may want to drink wine and sample the *tapas*, whereas a *guiri* will demand a pint of Stella and a fry-up. Spain makes a lot of money from both kinds of tourists, and people working in Benidorm or Fuengirola can hardly afford to look down upon the *guiris* who pay their wages, but Málaga has set its sights upon attracting *extranjeros* (and *viajeros*), rather than *guiris*. And be warned, plenty of *extranjeros* are only a pitcher of *sangría* or a plate of substandard *paella* away from achieving *guiri* status.

👣 Learning Spanish

There are many ways to learn Spanish. The Spanish cultural institute, the *Instituto Cervantes* (**cervantes.org**), has 86 centres in 45 countries and offers high-quality programmes of tuition from beginner level right upwards. If you can spare the time to spend a couple of weeks or more in Spain, then an intensive course offered by a language school or university (search **bit.ly/LearnSpanishMLG**) is a very effective and enjoyable way to make very quick progress, even from a baseline of *nada* ('nothing', *i.e.* as an absolute beginner). The internet has made it far easier to learn foreign languages online and via smartphone apps, as well as to practise speaking and listening with both native speakers and other learners using Skype and Zoom.

🔠 Learning the Basics

But what if you just want to dust off some rusty Spanish once learned at school or on a trip to Ibiza in the 90s, or learn 'just enough' of the basics to feel that you belong in the 'traveller' (not 'tourist') category? Two quick and basic Spanish courses that I can recommend are:

Quickstart Spanish (by Nuria Hervás; published by BBC Active) First published in 2003 and revised in 2008, this remains — in my opinion — the best short audio course to learn the basics of the language that will actually be useful to travellers. The 2 CD version is still on sale, but there is also an Audible® audiobook version. The teaching is done in the form of a number of slightly cheesy but sweetly entertaining dialogues covering all of the basics (greetings, directions, eating, drinking, etc.) in 2 hours and 20 minutes.

I used it in preparation for my first visit to Spain more than two decades ago, when the only Spanish words I knew were *hola, sí, gracias, vino* and *sombrero*. I worked my way through the course a couple of times (so about 5 hours of listening) in a single week and it proved genuinely useful once I got to Spain, not least because it familiarized me with the sound and pronunciation of the language. Simply being able to order a beer or a cup of coffee, ask how much something costs, or ask for the bill (all things you will do frequently in Spain) makes one feel like an *extranjero*, not a *guiri*.

Talk Spanish 1 (by Almudena Sanchez and Aurora Longo; published by BBC Active) is a more recent (2014), mainly audio, course from the BBC. The book comprises about 100 pages of lessons originally accompanied by a CD but is now available as a Kindle audio version.

Phrase Books are probably relics of a bygone age, though two good ones are published by the **BBC (by Carol Stanley and Phillippa Goodrich, 2005)** and by **DK Eyewitness (2017)**. A better plan is to try to master the pronunciation of Spanish using a quick audio course, and then rely on your smartphone's Google Translate app. Remember that, assuming your phone supports it, you can take a photo of a page of a Spanish menu or sign and Google will translate it for you. It won't always do so entirely accurately, but it should give you the gist. For example, *calamares del campo* is translated by Google as 'field squid' but actually means 'onion rings'; so as useful as Google is, beware!

🗣 *Intercambios de idiomas*

If you already speak some *castellano* and want to practise your language skills with locals while in Málaga then you could perhaps spend an evening at an *'intercambio'* — an event, usually held in a bar, where native Spanish speakers and non-native learners spend time in conversation. The usual pattern is that Spanish is spoken for an hour, then a non-Spanish language for an hour (with English and German being the most common). These events charge a nominal fee of a couple of euros or so with participants expected to buy some drinks because venues agree to reserve space for the *intercambio* and often need to hire extra bar staff.

By their nature, such events tend to come and go because they are generally organized by students and young people. Searching Google (**bit.ly/IntercambiosMLG**) is probably your best bet. Also, check out: **pachange.net/malaga**. When registering, you will be asked to indicate your level of proficiency. There are lots of free online tests that will tell you roughly where you are.

💬 *Ceceo, seseo y el idioma malagueño*
(Lisping, Not Lisping, and the Vernacular of Málaga)

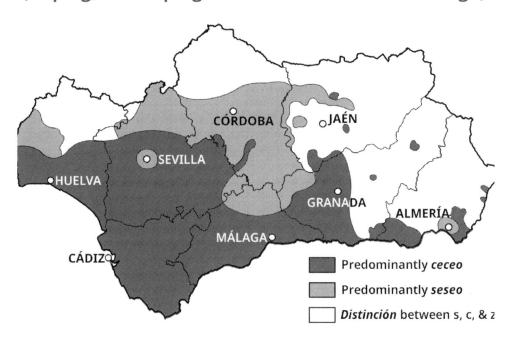

▓	Predominantly *ceceo*
▒	Predominantly *seseo*
☐	*Distinción* between s, c, & z

As the title suggests, this section is likely to interest readers who already speak *castellano* as it's concerned with regional differences in both pronunciation and vocabulary.

The pronunciation of standard and regional varieties of Spanish is fairly consistent and far more regular than that of English. The most notable differences concern the pronunciation of **c** (before **i** or **e**), **s** and **z**. In standard Spanish, **s** is always pronounced like the **s** in salt, while **c** (before **i** or **e**) and **z** are pronounced like the **th** in thin. This is called *diſtinción* (dees-teen-тнее-**on**) and is what you hear across most of Spain. In South America and parts of Andalucía, you will hear *seseo* (say-**say**-oh) where the **c** (before **i** or **e**), **s** and **z** are all pronounced like the **s** in salt. This is the form that Duolingo® teaches. But it is not as common in Peninsular Spain as many suppose, being found in the Province of Córdoba and the cities of Sevilla and Almería (indeed South American pronunciation may be explained by the prominence of Sevilla during the age of exploration, and the use of *seseo* in parts of Extremadura from whence came many *conquiſtadores*).

Less well-known is *ceceo* (тнау-тнау-oh), where **c** (before **i** or **e**), **s** and **z** are all pronounced like the **th** in thin; a sort of 'over-lisping'. (Incidentally, the story that the Spanish incorporated the **/th/** sound in deference to a lisping medieval king is nothing but an urban myth.) As the map of the historic distribution shows, *ceceo* is most commonly found in the provinces of Cádiz and Málaga, the southern parts of Huelva and Sevilla, and pockets of Granada and Almería. It has traditionally been associated with rural mountain dwellers and is considered by educated people as distinctive of 'lower class usage', like H-dropping or glottal stops in English. It has also been more typical of male speech, with more women adopting *seseo*.

A cultured city like Antequera with its wealth of religious houses (and therefore schools) has always preferred *seseo*, but the fishermen and dockers of Málaga clung to *ceceo*. However, things are changing, and in the city of Málaga *diſtinción* now predominates, especially amongst the young, with Cádiz and Huelva following suit. *Ceceo* is now largely a rural phenomenon. What you will hear in Málaga, however, is a distinctive form of *andaluz* Spanish, including the tendency to 'swallow' final **/s/** sounds, so that *la casa* (the house) and *las casas* (the houses) sound identical. Another 'swallowed' (elided) consonant is the intervocalic **/d/** which is lost in most instances: for example **pesáo** for *pesado* ('heavy'), **a menúo** for *a menudo* ('often') and — now common throughout Spain — **pescaíto** for *pescadito* (little fish).

Sometimes so many consonants (and even entire words in some phrases) are elided that the result is likely to flummox even proficient *caſtellano* speakers. Talking about being in someone's house, '*en casa de...*' becomes '**ancá**'. The interjection '*claro*' ('of course', or 'indeed') loses its initial sound to become just '**aro**' (which elsewhere in Spain means 'hoop'). The common filler word '*pues*' is reduced to **pué** or even **po**. '*Vamos a ver*' ('let's see') loses three consonants and becomes the barely recognisable '**amové**'. To ask 'Where are you going?' ('*¿Andónde vas?*'), *malagueños* enquire, '**¿Andevá?**'. To stress the truth of what one asserts, a Spaniard might add a rhetorical '*¿es o no es?*' ('isn't it?') whereas a *malagueño* reduces this to '**¿eonoé?**'. A *malagueño* waiter may show you to your table with the invitation, '**Ven pacá**', which elsewhere in Spain would be '*Ven por acá*' ('Come this way'). Some words even change gender. If you visit Málaga in July, you might want to complain about '*el calor*' (the heat). *Malagueños*, on the other hand, moan about '*la caló*'.

A very typically *malagueña* word originally formed in a similar way is **pechá**, an elision of *pechada* that means 'to put up with' something. In Málaga, however, it is also commonly used to mean 'a lot' of something. So in addition to the differences between *diſtinción*, *seseo* and *ceceo* and the disappearing consonants of Andalucía, you will encounter something else: the distinctive vocabulary of Málaga. Some of these words are *andaluz* manglings (as above), while others are local colloquialisms, and many are borrowed from Caló (the language of the Roma in Spain) or are corruptions of English or Arabic (reflecting Málaga's importance as a port). Thus, **aliquindoi** (to be in the know or up to speed) is an assimilation of '(take) a look and do i(t)' — a phrase once used by English-speaking foremen. From Arabic, you will hear *malagueños* calling a 'bedroom' (normally *habitación* or *dormitorio*) an *alcoba*, and using *alhaja* instead of the more standard *joya* ('jewel'). The use of Arabic-derived terms is probably not a remnant of Moorish colonial occupation and is more likely due to the significant presence of North African merchants in the city throughout the 19th century.

From Caló we get *chavea* for 'boy' and, by extension, any male of any age (just as women are referred to as '*niña*' ('girl') and '*rubia*' ('blonde') regardless of their age or hair colour). Other common ways to refer to a man are '*canío*' ('canine', 'dog') and '*compadre*' ('one's child's godfather'). Staying with dogs, *malagueños* don't feel *hambre* ('hunger') but *canina* (which can also mean 'skull'), whereas the state of having no money is *canino*. Some *malagueño* colloquialisms are very curious, such as *piños* ('pine trees') for 'teeth', and *haba* ('bean') for 'foot'.

As a visitor, you will mostly encounter these localisms when it comes to eating and drinking. A café menu blackboard offering '*tejeringos o pitufo y mitad*' would be auto-translated by your phone as 'knitting or smurf and half', whereas in fact what is on offer is '*churros* or a toasted roll and a white coffee'. Likewise a '*campero*' is not a 'camper van' but a large soft muffin filled with ham, cheese, lettuce, tomato, mayonnaise and ketchup.

📶 Wifi & 🔤 Postage

Even very basic *hostales* (see p. 47) now offer free Wifi, and you should be able to connect to free Wifi while out and about, which is good news if you don't have a cheap data roaming plan. The *ayuntamiento* (city council) offers free public Wifi, but the access points are mainly located in or near municipal buildings (*e.g.* the tourist information office, museums, the town hall, etc.) so the signal is strongest near these locations and can be pretty weak in other parts of the *centro histórico* (the Callejero GeoPortal street map shows the locations — see p. 5). There are also plenty of apps (*e.g.* wifimap.io) that can help you to find other public Wifi hotspots. Most of the trendier coffee shops have customer Wifi, as do chains like McDonald's, Starbucks, VIPs, etc. Other establishments are increasingly likely to have Wifi available. You may need to ask the staff for the password — '*la clave del wifi*' (lah **kla**-bay del **wee**-fee).

Free Wifi is also available in shopping centres (*e.g.* **Centro Comercial Larios Centro**), **El Corte Inglés**, the **María Zambrano** railway station, on an increasing number of urban buses, almost all intercity buses and on AVE trains. If your plan makes data roaming prohibitively expensive but you'd rather not bother with constantly connecting to new free networks, then another option is to buy a prepaid ('*prepago*') data SIM (Movistar, Vodafone, Orange and Yoigo are the main Spanish operators) or use an 'eSIM' service like airalo.com.

If you want to send a postcard (*postal* — **poh-stal**), you can buy a stamp (*sello* — **seh**-lyo) from a post office (*correos*), but it is quicker and easier to visit an *estanco* (tobacconist). To post the postcard you just need to find a yellow postbox (*buzón* — scan the QR code to visit the official 'postbox finder').

Málaga is a great pearl, chief ornament of a necklace, the abode of well-being, the polar star; it is the rival of planets, the halo of the moon; a beckoning treasure, the throne of ancient dominion; musk-scented vase and watch-tower of eagles; beauty unveiled, refuge in misfortune, consolation in grief.

Lisan ad-Din Ibn al-Khatib (1313–1374),
Excelencias de Málaga y Salé

¿Por qué? (Why should you visit?)

'Málaga is a fine, but purely commercial city: one day will suffice. It has
few attractions beyond climate, almonds and raisins, and sweet wine.'
(Handbook for Travellers in Spain, *Richard Ford,* 1845)

⌛ Importance and History

The first points to make are that Málaga is a relatively large city (in Spanish terms), and an old city. With a population of just over half a million people (about the same as Sheffield in the UK), it is the second most populous city in Andalucía (after Sevilla), and the sixth largest in Spain. When it comes to economic activity, Málaga ranks fourth in Spain (after Barcelona, Madrid and Valencia). The port, crucial to the *malagueña*[2] economy for millennia, has ten wharves and is one of the largest in the Mediterranean, handling almost half a million containers and 40,000 vehicles annually. Between four and five cruise ships dock in Málaga each week, carrying almost half a million passengers, and two ferries per day link Málaga to Melilla, one of Spain's two North African autonomous cities. The two wharves nearest the city centre have recently been redeveloped with shops, restaurants and parks and are now used by super-yachts and small cruise ships, rather than commercial freight.

Málaga is a spring chicken compared to Cádiz (founded 1100 BC), but it was still founded a decade or so before Rome, which makes it impressively old. When the Phoenicians established a trading post at 'Malaka' around the year 770 BC, they discovered a settlement of Ancient Iberians slightly to the west of modern Málaga (near what is now the airport). After the Phoenicians, Málaga was perhaps controlled by the Greeks (briefly), the Carthaginians, and the Romans. After falling to the Visigoths, the Byzantine emperor Justinian I recaptured the city for the Empire.

The territory passed back and forth between the Byzantines and the Visigoths until the city fell to the Moors in 743 AD, after a hundred years of skirmishes and incursions. For the next 744 years, it was a Moorish city and for a while the capital of a *taifa* (a semi-independent principality). In 1487, Málaga was reconquered by *los Reyes Católicos* (the Catholic Monarchs) Fernando and Isabel after a long, arduous and bloody siege. Being the last significant seaport under Moorish control, its fall was the final nail in the coffin of the Nasrid Kingdom of Granada, which would come only three years later in 1492 — a big year for Spanish history.

Málaga's status as an important port on the southern seaboard of Spain (the now much larger port of Algeciras only developed after the loss of Gibraltar, and even at the end of the 19th century was still just a single wooden jetty) meant that its history has been marked by

---

2   *malagueño/malagueña* is an adjective means 'pertaining to Málaga'. It is also a noun meaning an inhabitant or native of Málaga. In some contexts the Latin term *malacitano* (or *malacitana*) is used.

upheaval. After a period of reconstruction in the centuries following the *reconquista* there came a series of 17th and 18th-century disasters, including earthquakes and industrial explosions. And yet Málaga, like Bilbao in the north, became a centre of economic free trade doctrine and political liberalism (much like Manchester and Newcastle in the north of England).

☀ Climate

We tend to think of Spain as a warm and sunny country, and this perception is borne out by Málaga, which enjoys 320 days of sunshine a year and fewer than 40 days of rain. Winters are mild, while summers are warm and dry. Between June and August, the average temperature is 25° C (77° F) with an average maximum of 30° C (86° F). This means that it is warm enough to sit outside a café at midnight, but not (usually) so unbearably hot during that day that you have to seek refuge in your air-conditioned hotel room until dusk.

♨ Food and Drink

'This is sweet Málaga, known as the beautiful, from whence hail the famous raisins, the famous women, and the wine preferred for Communion'
(Nicaraguan poet and diplomat Rubén Darío, in La Nación, *c.1904)*

As the late chef-turned-culinary-globetrotter Anthony Bourdain put it, 'If you're looking for the best food in the Western world, forget France. Come to Spain.'[3] The Basque Country in northern Spain has more Michelin stars per capita than any other region of the world and Catalonia's El-Bulli is still regarded by many adoring foodies as the world's best restaurant, despite its having closed at almost the height of its popularity in 2011. But Bourdain was talking not so much of the gels and foams of *haute cuisine* or molecular gastronomy, but of the everyday food of Spain — parchment-thin slices of *jamón*, salads drizzled with grass-green olive oil, and fat, juicy prawns sizzling in garlic infused oil so rich that it tastes more buttery than butter. The British restaurant critic Giles Coren wrote in 2015 that he ate the best meal of his life, not at The Ivy or Noma, but at an ordinary bar-restaurant in Pedraza, a Spanish town of fewer than 440 people.[4]

The bread and potatoes stodge of northern Europe does not suit the climate of Spain (although Spaniards love stews and pulses) and unlike in the French classical tradition, there is little reliance upon rich or clever sauces. In Spain, the quality and freshness of the ingredients take centre stage. A simple salad of tomatoes, mottled green and red, is a revelation — nothing more than oil, coarse salt and pepper is necessary because the tomatoes themselves are so intensely flavoured. Enjoying a tasting menu at one of Málaga's best res-

---

3   'Spain' *Anthony Bourdain: No Reservations*, Travel Channel, Series 4, Episode 17 (TV), 18 August 2008.

4   'Giles Coren eats the best lunch in the world', *The Times* (Newspaper), 23 May, 2105. bit.ly/GilesCorenSpain

taurants, one of the courses consisted of a single '*Fea de Tudela*' tomato with Ibiza salt and a dressing made with bright green olive oil from Jaén and sweet Málaga wine vinegar; just four ingredients. And it was phenomenal. The bar food staple of *huevos rotos* ('broken eggs') — fried chunks of potato with slivers of *jamón* topped with a runny-yolked fried egg — takes ham, egg and chips to a new level of deliciousness.

Just as appealing as the quality of food is the manner of its eating. Service *à la russe* (starter, main course, and dessert served sequentially) is the norm at lunchtime and in more expensive restaurants, but in the evening, the unfailingly sociable Spaniards prefer to share a selection of dishes (called *raciones*) — perhaps some fried peppers, a plate of anchovies, a platter of prawns, squid or lamb cutlets, maybe a salad, or some slices of barnyardy sheep's cheese. As well as these heartier *raciones* (full, or sharing, portions), are *tapas*. A *tapa* is a small serving of food to accompany a drink, because you will rarely see a Spaniard drinking without eating. The *tapa* might be very modest and handed over for free when you order a drink — a couple of *escabeche* mussels, a triangular slice of slightly crystalline *manchego* cheese, a saucer of fat, green olives or just a handful of potato crisps. A small dish of crisps, by the way, is not quite as dull as it sounds. These crisps are not Walkers (or Lay's, as Walkers is known outside the UK). They will most probably have been fried that day, in local olive oil, at a nearby *freiduría* and delivered to the bar in huge paper sacks.

Tapas menus (or *cartas* in Spanish — *menú* refers to a prix fixe set menu) offer richer fare — crisp *croquetas* with an interior of molten *béchamel*, sliced *chorizo* braised in red wine, sizzling garlic prawns, chickpea and spinach stew, fried potato with gently piquant *brava* sauce, or a medallion of pork tenderloin flambéed in whisky. Some bars specialize in 'gourmet *tapas*', marrying the venerable staples of Spain with the culinary wizardry of Ferran Adrià or the flavours of Southeast Asia. For the visitor, the great advantage of this mode of eating (*tapas* and *raciones*) is that it's possible to sample an enormous variety of dishes. There's no need to feel torn between the meat and the fish: ordering *tapas* and small plates means that you can have both (and more besides) without feeling like a glutton.

In Málaga, you will find all the familiar Spanish favourites as well as quite a few local specialities. Fish and seafood are an obsession even in Madrid, which is as far from the sea as it's possible to be in Spain. On the coast — and Málaga is no exception — the bounty of the sea is front and centre. Many local dishes, especially those involving dried fruit, aubergines and molasses, have their origins in Moorish times and many have links to Sephardic (Jewish) cuisine. The province to the east, Almería, is the centre of Spanish market horticulture, and Málaga is famed for its subtropical fruit, which means that the salad vegetables and fruit available in Málaga are of exceptional quality and freshness. Andalucía is the largest olive-growing region on earth, accounting for 40% of all olive oil produced worldwide. Even if you only ever purchase 'Italian' olive oil, some proportion of what you buy will almost certainly have originated in Andalucía.

As well as olives, the Province of Málaga is known for almonds and grapes. Málaga is the only region of Spain to have a separate *Denominación de Origen* for its grapes in their dried form as well as in their fermented liquid form. While every wine list features the familiar Rioja, Navarra, and Rueda regions, the Province of Málaga produces excellent wine of its own, both table wine and fortified wine in 'sherry' and dessert styles. Sir John Falstaff was fond of 'Sherris Sack' — the fortified wines now known as 'Sherry' (*i.e.* Jerez) — but some 70 years after Henry IV Part 1 was performed, Samuel Pepys would write in his diary that:

> '*Malago Sack... [is] excellent wine, like a spirit rather than wine.*'[5]

---

5   The Diary of Samuel Pepys, Monday 20 July 1663. bit.ly/PepysMalagaSack

It is for sweet white wines made from Moscatel (Muscat) grapes that Málaga is most famous, but nowadays the region's red, rosé and dry white wines are becoming much better-known. As well as wine, Málaga is also home to a variety of spirits. Most famous is probably Resoli — a rich anisette embellished with coffee, cinnamon and cloves. There is also a local premium brandy (1886 Gran Reserva), and rum (a spirit first exported from Andalucía to the Caribbean, rather than vice versa). The undisputed king of *malagueño* spirits, however, is gin. It comes as a surprise to many to learn that Spain is the third largest consumer of gin in the world (after The Philippines and the USA). When it comes to per capita consumption, Spain outdrinks everywhere else at a fraction under 70 centilitres (*i.e.* a bottle) per person annually, with the UK (48 cl) and even the largest gin market of The Philippines (39 cl) trailing considerably behind. Much of that gin is produced by Larios, a distillery founded in Málaga (though now located in Madrid). Like Cadbury in Birmingham, the name Larios is intertwined with the history and geography of its home city.

Gin is produced in several areas of Málaga province. In 2017, in the eastern region of Axarquía, they began producing Gin Ballix flavoured with local variety 'Osteen' mangoes. The Vélez-Málaga neighbourhood is home to Alborán Gin. The village of Cuevas Bajas is famous for its purple carrots, and since 2016 the taste of this unique carrot is also found in the gin Simbuya, produced by Esalui. Oxén Spiritus is produced in Ojén just outside Marbella. And Málaga's oldest functioning distillery, El Tajo, in Ronda, launched its gin onto the market in 1895 (which is also the name of the gin). As for Málaga city, in 2015, the gin connoisseur and manager of the 'Gin Tonic' bar, Carlos Villanueva, launched two gins. He named both gins after Málaga: Malaka London Dry contains classic botanicals, whilst Malaka Premium has a Mediterranean profile with a faint note of jasmine.

🛉 Culture

Málaga is neither the capital of Spain nor of Andalucía, but of the Province of Málaga. It is, then, 'provincial' by definition, and for many years was regarded as the less sophisticated sibling of Sevilla, once the wealthiest and grandest city in all of Europe. Partly thanks to Washington Irving, the Dan Brown of his day, millions flock to the Moorish Alhambra of Granada, and rightly so (though in my opinion, the Alcázar of Sevilla is in some ways even more impressive). What few people know is that Málaga has a Moorish citadel (Alcazaba) of its own. Though rather less grand than the Alhambra and not a royal residence like the palace in Sevilla, it is older than either. Many architectural historians agree that only the Krak des Chevaliers in Syria is better preserved.

The Alcazaba was built on a hill to protect the strategic port of Málaga, and in due course, a second Moorish fortification — the Castillo de Gibralfaro — was constructed on the summit of a slightly higher hill to protect the Alcazaba. Hard against the walls of the Alcazaba is a Roman theatre built in the first century BC. Although quarried by the Moors when building the Alcazaba, much of the *cavea* remains. It was only rediscovered in 1951, ironically enough beneath Málaga's Cultural Centre. Restoration was completed in 2011 and it is now open to visitors and used for open-air concerts.

After the *reconquista*, churches were built upon the sites of mosques (that had themselves displaced far older Visigothic churches, that had, in turn, displaced Roman temples) including a fine, though unusual, Renaissance cathedral. Patches of the medieval footprint of Málaga's old city remain, as do many buildings, but successive wars, sieges, revolutions and even earthquakes have also left their mark. Much of central Málaga was renewed in the 19th century during the period of confidence that followed the Napoleonic wars, and many of Málaga's most beautiful streets are pure *Belle Époque* (albeit in the markedly Spanish style of Eduardo Strachan Viana-Cárdenas). Yet more devastation came with the Civil War and a period of deep economic decline, but visiting Málaga today, one would hardly know.

The centre is largely and mercifully free of the sort of monstrosities that filled the lacunae of many other European cities. A few high-rise blocks were built in the 1960s and 1970s near the Malagueta Beach, but are contained within the space of a few streets. Across the river in the other direction, towards the railway station, the no doubt picturesque hovels of Roma and working-class *barrios* have been demolished and replaced with decidedly unpicturesque tenements. But whilst nineteenth-century slums might be 'colourful' for tourists to explore, they were not as much fun for the people who had to live in them. Also, in the hands of the fanatically house-proud Spanish, tenement flats manage to seem far brighter than those in the UK. The biggest change, though, has come about in the last couple of decades. Residential, commercial and ecclesiastical buildings have been restored and cleaned. Sixteenth-century urban palaces have been tastefully converted into galleries, museums and boutique hotels. The scruffy port area of El Ensanche ('the expansion'), once home to dosshouses, brothels and sex shops, has been transformed into Málaga's most vivacious, arty district.

Málaga has always had a 'respectable' and sophisticated side that has charmed visitors, but in the past, there was a louche underbelly — the seedy Mr Hyde emerging at night to eclipse Dr Jekyll. Nicholas Luard wrote in the 1960s of Málaga's 'stately old-fashioned feel,' describing how '[h]orse-drawn carriages clop slowly in the shadow along the broad leafy boulevardes, and jacarandas blossom violet against crumbling façades with windows covered by ornate wrought-iron grilles.' At night, however, the city 'changes and becomes a sailors' town. Prostitutes patrol the streets, and the bars, together with the little satellite businesses that circle round them, the boot-blacks, lottery tickets sellers, cigarette ladies and pinchito stalls, stay open until the early hours.'[6] The prostitutes have gone (or at least moved online or out of town), though Málaga continues to be a city that continues until the early hours, and lottery ticket sellers are still a feature, raising funds for the charitable foundation 'ONCE' that does magnificent work to improve the lives of blind and disabled people.

Nothing symbolizes the transformation of Málaga from faded port to buzzing city destination quite so much as the recent proliferation of new museums and galleries. Claims vary regarding the number of museums and galleries in Málaga, but 'around 40' is a phrase one often hears. It's true that some of these museums are very small and somewhat niche, but for a city of its size, it's an impressive number. My favourite example of the niche is the Wine Museum, which regularly receives excoriating one-star reviews on TripAdvisor. Admittedly there is very little on display apart from infographic displays (in Spanish) and a lot of wine labels. On the other hand, the ticket price also includes a tasting of two local wines meaning that you 'get back' most of the admission charge. It is probably not a 'must-see' attraction for everyone, but for anyone interested in the wine of the region, it is not to be missed.

The building the museum occupies is, in fact, the headquarters of the *Consejo Regulador* (regulatory authority) for the two Málaga wine regions (Málaga, and Sierras de Málaga) as well as for Málaga Raisins. The museum is meant to showcase and explain their work. It is lov-

---

6   Nicholas Luard, *Andalucia: A Portrait of Southern Spain* (London, Century, 1984)

ingly curated, the staff are kind, enthusiastic, knowledgeable and friendly (they faithfully respond to all their TripAdvisor reviews, thanking patrons for their visit — always a good sign of a well-run attraction), and if you make use of the free audio guide you will learn quite a lot about winemaking in the Málaga region. Sure, it might be far more interesting to visit a vineyard in the hills, but one can't do that in an hour and a half on a (rare) rainy day.

Many of the city's museums are fairly recent foundations. Even the Picasso Museum, devoted to Málaga's most famous son, only opened its doors in 2003. Málaga is home to the first branch of the Centre Georges Pompidou outside France. Other sites are planned — in the Middle East, Mexico and Brussels — but securing the gallery's first expansion outside Paris was a huge feather in Málaga's *sombrero*. Another accolade for the city was winning the competition to host the first museum outside Madrid to exhibit works from the collection of Doña Carmen Thyssen-Bornemisza. A number of cities vied for the honour and Málaga won, much to the chagrin of her native Barcelona. The third big jewel in the crown was another satellite — that of the Russian State Museum (though the invasion of Ukraine in 2022 has strained the cultural relationship between Málaga and St Petersburg, to say the least).

🏮 *Ambiente*

'The natives of the better classes in Málaga are gay and hospitable; the ladies graceful, beautiful, and sprightly.' (Hand-book for Travellers in Spain, *Richard Ford, 1845*)

You don't need to speak *castellano* to understand this word. 'Ambience', for Spaniards, is enormously important and refers to something more than the vibe or atmosphere of a place. A Spaniard may not be able to put her finger upon exactly what makes for *'buen ambiente'* (because it will be a *'no sé qué'*) but she will know it when she feels it. A particular bar may have excellent wine and stunning food, but without *'buen ambiente'* it will never thrive. *Ambiente* is the totality of the place and the people that occupy it; both are necessary. Nowhere empty has *ambiente*. The place might be a bar, a square, a beach, or even a shop, but the presence of people is what gives it its *ambiente*. In Spanish, the word *ambiente* can also simply mean a room, as in *'mi piso tiene cinco ambientes'* ('my flat has five rooms'). This is appropriate insofar as gauging *ambiente* is basically the ability to 'read a room'.

Foreigners often complain that Spaniards have no concept of 'private space'. They throng, rather than queue; they are tactile and stand very close when speaking to you; they tend to speak loudly; and if they see a bar that is already so packed that movement is impossible, they will conclude that this is the place to be. In fact, it is the Spanish conception of **public** space that is different to that of Anglo-Saxons. Spaniards guard the private space of their homes more closely, perhaps, than we do. On the other hand, they do not try to create pockets of privacy in the public square. A couple wishing to enjoy a romantic dinner *à deux* had better visit another part of town or, better, another town, where they will not run into any friends or relatives. When Paco and María want to invite their friends for dinner, it is more likely to mean dining at a restaurant than at home. Spaniards are endlessly sociable. Meeting for dinner in a restaurant is preferable because it increases the likelihood of bumping into other friends. The only thing better than a quiet dinner with a couple of friends is a very noisy dinner with a dozen friends. 'Let's go somewhere quieter,' said no Spaniard ever. Indeed it's often suggested that the inability of Spaniards to arrive anywhere on time is a consequence of their polite and sociable nature, rather than the opposite as one might suppose.

The reason that María arrives at 8.30 pm for the drinks you arranged for 8 pm is not that she is disorganized or lazy, but simply that when she left work, one of her colleagues asked her to go for a coffee. Being a typically sociable Spaniard, she accepted the invitation. In the café, she bumped into her husband's cousin's neighbour who insisted that she accompany him and his friends to a nearby bar for a beer. As she prepared to leave that bar, she met a group of friends from her schooldays who told her quite firmly that she could not possibly leave until she had shared a *tapa* and a glass of wine with them. And that was all before she nipped back to her apartment to change into something more suitable for the evening (Spain is a country where people will still dress up to go to a bar).

If you are seeking solitude, then Spain (or rather, a Spanish city) is probably not the best destination. If, on the other hand, you enjoy being among people or enjoy people-watching, then nowhere is better. Málaga has *ambiente* by the bucketload. Being smaller, it is more relaxed than cities like Barcelona or Madrid and there is no shortage of places to find peace and quiet (though not necessarily solitude) in a city full of Spaniards intent upon having a good time. Between the old city and the quayside is a subtropical park where people go to escape from the heat and bustle of the town. There are plenty of noisy bars and lively squares, but there are also silent museums and peaceful churches. But even the hustle and bustle of Málaga's centre is a far cry from Friday night in any UK town. The volume may be raised because people are enjoying themselves, but you are unlikely to see anyone falling over drunk, vomiting into a bin or behaving in an obnoxious fashion. It's not unusual to see, at almost midnight, toddlers playing happily beneath the outdoor tables of a bar as their parents enjoy postprandial drinks.

Many elements combine to create the distinct *ambiente* of Málaga — its history, its trading links, its culinary traditions, its popular culture, the built environment and architecture, the character of its people, and the storms — political and meteorological — that it has weathered. Yet what is immediately obvious to any visitor who stays more than a day or two here is the role played by geography. Spaniards love to observe that 'Africa begins at the Pyrenees,' and although this overstates the case somewhat, it is hard to escape the feeling that Málaga, geologically and meteorologically at least, belongs as much to Africa as to Europe. The city is sheltered to the north by mountains that form a vast horseshoe-shaped arc running through southern Andalucía, curving south at Gibraltar to sweep into Africa and form the Atlas Mountains. Palm trees are found all over Spain, but the flora of Málaga feels even more exotic: cacti proliferate, as do jacaranda trees with their vivid mauve blossom. These are reminders of Málaga's status as a port, for these plants came from the Americas and the Caribbean.

The *leveche* wind from the Sahara (called the sirocco in the eastern Mediterranean) brings sand in the form of dust ('*calima*'), turning the sky orange, although the hotter wind is the *terral* — cold air from the north that gathers heat over the central Spanish plain before dropping down into the Málaga basin and out to sea. This wind results in a decrease in humidity and, thus, an increase in the risk of wildfires. Another peculiar climatic phenomenon is the *taró*: a type of fog observed locally from Málaga to Ceuta when the (cold) water that comes from the Atlantic evaporates upon contact with the hot, dry winds that come from the south. It is typical of the month of August and visibility is usually reduced significantly.

The combination of high temperatures and fog is quite disorientating.

The sea which Málaga faces is not the Atlantic of the Algarve, nor the Mediterranean of Alicante, but the *mar de Alborán* — a gyre that funnels cooler water from the Atlantic into the Mediterranean and saltier, warmer water from the Mediterranean over the Gibraltar sill to the ocean beyond. Perhaps more than anything, it is this sea that contributes most to the unique *ambiente* of Málaga.

One might think that Torremolinos — a 'former fishing village' that swapped lobster pots for lobster-coloured Brits — would have a greater affinity with the sea, but in Málaga, the connection runs far deeper. For almost 2,800 years, maritime trade has been conducted here; the garum shipped to Rome in antiquity and then the raisins, the wine and the oil, right up to nineteenth-century steel and the petrochemicals (and wine and oil) of today. The sea is never far away, not only physically, but spiritually too. *Malagueños* enjoy the beach as much as any other Spaniard but would regard an entire week of 'soaking up the rays' as an unsociable waste of time. Going to the beach is not squeezed into a single week. It is an after-work relaxation or a family afternoon out, an opportunity to meet friends for an *espeto* (skewer) of sardines and some cold beer, as well as a swim and a spot of sunbathing.

The sea, in a city like Málaga, is a constant presence. It is the sea that has historically connected Málaga to Europe, to Africa, and to the world. As it laps constantly against the shore it provides the rhythm for the lives of *malagueños*. They may be less inclined to strip off and dive in than their northern European visitors, but it is a constant in their lives. It shapes and enriches their city. The US poet Walt Whitman was almost obsessed with the sea, but he realized that it was fruitless to try to capture it in verse. Instead, he resolved to show in his writing that 'we have really absorbed each other and understand each other.' That is a good description of the people of Málaga and the Alborán Sea.

The *ambiente* of Málaga is, by definition, impossible to describe in words. It can only be experienced, and thus the only way to understand it is through experience. In 1862, Hans Christian Andersen wrote, 'Málaga, charming town, I feel myself at home in thee!'[7] Many others have found themselves saying the same thing ever since.

🎭 *La Gente*

La Gente — the people — are of course an important element of any city and perhaps the most significant factor in determining the *ambiente* of a place. A huge part of the enjoyment we derive from staying in a lovely hotel or eating and drinking in a gourmet restaurant or a buzzing bar, is due to the people we encounter in those places, both members of staff and fellow patrons and guests.

In the 1960s, the Ministry of Information and Tourism under the Franco regime came up with the slogan 'Spain is Different'. For those early British tourists, Spain must have seemed very different indeed, not just in terms of heat and sun, but in its enjoyment of wine, garlic and olive oil. However, being different to the UK is not the same thing as homogeneity. I suspect that if one asked the man on the Clapham Omnibus what 'Spain' suggested to him, he might mention garlic, flamenco, bullfighting, beaches, and *paella*, among other things. Yet bullfighting is popular in some regions of Spain and proscribed in others, *paella* is jealously guarded by the people of Valencia and flamenco is seen as an *andaluz*, rather than simply a Spanish, art form. Spain is as 'different' from region to region and city to city as anywhere else in the world.

Spain is not a federation, properly speaking, but it is a 'decentralized unitary country' with

---

7   Hans Christian Andersen, *In Spain and a Visit to Portugal* (New York: Hurd and Houghton, 1870)

significant devolution of power from Madrid to the regions (called Autonomous Communities or *comunidades autónomas*) which are in turn divided into provinces and further into *comarcas* (somewhat like counties) and municipalities. Often referred to as 'asymmetrical federalism', the differences between Spain's autonomous communities are not only cultural, but political; for example, the governments of Catalonia and the Basque Country wield more devolved powers than other communities do. However, the cultural differences are the most obvious.

As is so often the case, regional stereotypes tend to contain a grain of truth and find their way into the jokes that people tell. Thus, people from Asturias are thought to be patriotic heavy drinkers, Catalans are hard-working, industrious and stingy, the people of Madrid are louche and cocky, and so forth. The natives of Andalucía, in the view of many Spaniards, are fun-loving, passionate, happy, and funny, but also lazy. That said, most of the jokes about Andalucía are actually based on puns that turn on the local accent and the tendency to drop the final consonants in many words.

The Spanish equivalent of the 'Irish' joke, by the way, targets the people of Lepe, a beautiful small town in the *andaluz* province of Huelva. This is probably because of a legend that a sailor from Lepe made a fool of himself on one of Columbus's voyages by claiming to have spotted land during the night. Pleasingly, however, the municipality of Lepe has, in recent years, become a centre of strawberry cultivation and one of the wealthiest towns in Huelva, growing almost half of all strawberries sold in Europe. In 2011, in the Parliament of Andalucía, it was even suggested that the *chiste lepero* (the Lepe joke) be declared a *Bien de Interés Cultural* (Asset of Cultural Interest).

Spaniards from Galicia to Valencia, Barcelona to Huelva, do tend to share a number of traits. The first thing one notices is their sociability; a *joie de vivre* enriched by the fellowship of others. They tend to be stylish and smart, taking pride in their appearance. They relish good food and love to drink, but disapprove of gluttony or drunkenness. The passionate 'Latin temperament' is no myth — their enjoyment of flamenco, folk songs, dancing, religious processions and, for many, bullfighting, is visceral. And they love to party. Every city, town and village has at least one major annual *feria* (fair) and usually a couple of minor ones, and these are celebrated at full throttle by young and old. Everyday life is put on hold for a weekend (or for an entire week) and everything is about the party.

Malagueños — the people of Málaga — exhibit all these attractive qualities, though perhaps even more keenly than people from other parts of Spain, or of Andalucía. They even have their own word to describe themselves — '*malaguita*'. Simply being from Málaga is not the same as being *malaguita*. Anyone born in Málaga is a *malagueño* or a *malagueña*, but only those who are passionate about all the typical traditions of the city — Holy Week, carnival, the *feria*, the bulls, Málaga Football Club, anchovies, smooth shell clams with lemon and black pepper, Moscatel wine — will be *malaguitas*

This fierce pride in, and identification with, their city manifests itself in the language they use. Málaga is Spanish speaking, but they speak it in a *malaguita* way. In Sevilla, a sandwich roll and a coffee with milk is a *bocadillo* and a *café con leche*, just as it is in the rest of Spain. In Málaga, though, it is a *pitufo* and a *mitad*. In the rest of Spain, during Holy Week, large floats called *pasos* (often mistranslated as 'steps', but derived from the Latin *passus* meaning 'having suffered') are carried through the streets, but in Málaga they are known as *tronos* (thrones). Málaga prides itself in being different, and yet the wonderful thing is that this sense of pride and distinctiveness does not make the locals aloof or unwelcoming in the slightest. If anything, the opposite is true.

One of the things that strikes the first-time visitor to Málaga is the kindness and hospitality

23

of its denizens. This can be seen very clearly at the annual *feria* held in August. Perhaps the most famous, and probably the most impressive, *feria* in Spain is the April Fair in Seville, a week-long party involving music, dancing and drinking. The fairground is composed of *casetas* (hospitality tents) filled with the great and the good of *sevillana* society. However, apart from a handful of *casetas* hosted by the municipality, a couple of trades unions, and the Communist Party, they are all private and you need an invitation to gain entry. At the Málaga *feria*, however, all the *casetas* are public. If there is room, anyone is welcome to come in (though there is an admission charge for some), buy a drink, have something to eat, and dance. To modify a well-known Spanish phrase, it is very much a case of '*Mi caseta es tu caseta*'.

Malagueña hospitality extends easily to visitors and tourists. Large-scale tourism is a fairly recent phenomenon for the city of Málaga, and despite occasional grumbles in the letters pages of the newspapers about new hotels and the number of apartments being offered as holiday rents, most *malagueños* I have spoken to think that growth in the tourist sector has been positive overall for the city. Local politicians will have to keep an eye on the situation, however, if Málaga is not to go the same way as Sevilla and Barcelona, where one frequently sees graffiti urging tourists to 'Go Home!'

The *Ayuntamiento* (Town Hall) promoted the motto, '*Málaga: Ciudad Genial*' to market the city, and it is an apt moniker. In Spanish, '*genial*' nowadays tends to mean 'great' or 'cool', but its more literary meaning is closer to the English word, viz. 'friendly; causing delight or happiness'. Any city may evoke delight or happiness through its appearance, but only its people can make it actually 'friendly'. Málaga is justly proud of its beautiful buildings, fine museums and delicious food and drink, but its greatest treasure is its people.

🦎 Duende

El duende is perhaps best described as 'the spirit of evocation'. Every *andaluz* is obsessed with it, yet few can quite explain what it is. It's a bit like Aristotle's definition of Justice (*i.e.* what the just man practices). *Duende* is what *los andaluces* have. It comes from inside as a physical and emotional response to art, and it is a necessary pre-condition for creating such powerful art in the first place. It is what gives you chills and makes you smile or cry as a bodily reaction to an artistic performance that is particularly expressive. Folk music in general, especially flamenco, tends to embody an authenticity that comes from a people whose culture is enriched by diaspora and hardship; *vox populi*, the human condition of joys and sorrows. Drawing on popular usage and Spanish folklore, the *granadino* poet Federico García Lorca attempted to develop the aesthetics of *duende* in a lecture he gave in Buenos Aires in 1933: *Juego y teoría del duende* ('Play and Theory of the *Duende*').

At least four elements can be isolated in Lorca's vision of *duende*: irrationality, earthiness, a heightened awareness of death, and a hint of the diabolical (or at least the mysteriously supernatural). The *duende* (literally) is an earth spirit (somewhat goblin-like) who helps the artist see the limitations of intelligence, reminding him that 'ants could eat him or that a great arsenic lobster could fall suddenly on his head'; who brings the artist face-to-face with death, and who helps him create and communicate memorable, spine-chilling art. The *duende* is seen, in Lorca's lecture, as an alternative to style, to mere virtuosity, to God-given grace and charm (what Spaniards call '*ángel*'), and to the classical, artistic norms dictated by the muse. Not that the artist simply surrenders to the *duende*; they have to battle it skilfully, 'on the rim of the well', in 'hand-to-hand combat'. Lorca writes: 'The *duende*, then, is a power, not a work. It is a struggle, not a thought. I have heard an old maestro of the guitar say, "The *duende* is not in the throat; the *duende* climbs up inside you, from the soles of the feet." Meaning this: it is not a question of ability, but of true, living style, of blood, of the most ancient culture, of spontaneous creation.'

Duende might be found in any art, but particularly in poetry and music. A technically flaw-less performance of a piece of music might be impressive, yet have no *duende*. Whereas a street guitarist, slightly out of tune and not fretting every note to perfection, may still dis-play the sort of passion and soul that reeks of *duende*. Even those of us who are not *andaluces* are aware of this phenomenon. Your grandmother's steak and kidney pudding may have a vitality and authenticity that a far more polished *Filet de Bœuf en Croûte* at a fine dining restaurant lacks. A Palestrina motet sung at Mass by a choir who believe the words they are singing may have more power and credibility than a recording by a professional choir. The crooning of a folk singer may move you more than a world-class tenor's aria. And so forth.

The two art forms, par excellence, where the *an-daluces* encounter the most profound *duende* are flamenco and the *co-rrida* (erroneously called a 'bullfight' in English). Flamenco is essentially a professionalized form of *andaluz* folk music, song and dance; it is opera and ballet rolled into one. It is at once earthy and pri-mal, and yet also highly stylized and complex. It combines guitar music, singing, dancing, clapping, finger-snapping and other-worldly ululations known as *jaleo*. The *corrida*, too is the professionalized display form of the sport of horseback bull hunting, made into an art form on foot. Foreigners tend to imagine that the aim of a bullfight is to kill a bull, but while that might be the inevitable end result, it is not why people still flock to watch it in such huge numbers.

The Iberian fighting bull is effectively a wild animal. The closest we have in the UK are the Chillingham Cattle in Northumberland — barely domesticated, and potentially dangerous. In the space of about 20 minutes, the matador and his assistants use short barbs and colour-ed cloths (over three acts) to dominate a wild animal. The final movement of the *corrida* is often the most profound expression of *duende*. A man and a bull move closely together, en-gaged in a sort of dance. By necessity, it is not a dance that can have been choreographed, for until some ten minutes before this moment, the bull had never in its five-year life encoun-tered a human being (they are herded on horseback or by motor vehicle).

Sometimes (depressingly often for *aficionados*) it can seem formulaic and workmanlike, but when touched by *duende* then it is magical, mysterious, almost religious. Zoological experts apparently claim that if a fighting bull were put into an arena with a tiger, the tiger might come off worse. So the spectacle of a man engaged in a kind of dance with a bull should be impossible. It conforms to Lorca's categories. It is irrational for a man to go into an arena with a dangerous animal, it is earthy insofar as the world of nature is brought into the heart of the city, and death is only ever a few inches, or few seconds, away. That is *duende*.

What is typical of both flamenco and the *corrida* in Spain is that although both are regarded as the zenith of an art, the practitioners of both art forms (only ignorant foreigners would call bullfighting a 'sport') have often come from the working classes. Almost all flamenco virtuosi are of Roma heritage. Historically speaking, aristocratic bullfighters dominated the bull from upon horseback, and although they displayed skill and bravery, they rarely summoned much *duende*. Similarly, if you go to the April Fair in Sevilla, you will see the cream of *sevillana* society dancing what looks very much like flamenco, but it's not. It is a related dance called the *sevillana* — elegant certainly, and often moving and beautiful, but lacking in *duende*. Only a Romani can achieve that.

洲 *Paseo*

The late afternoon *paseo* (stroll) can be witnessed in every part of Spain, and it is indulged in by every age and class, although it is often the retired who seem most in evidence. At one level, it is a constitutional, a stroll to take the air and to wake from the afternoon nap. It is also an opportunity to meet friends, partake of the first alcoholic drink of the afternoon/evening, or have *merienda* — a cup of coffee and a snack — because dinner time in Spain is not until at least 9 pm and more likely 10 pm. Even in suburban residential areas, parents stroll and chat while children play. Whether you are in a large  city, a modest town, or a tiny village, you will see people taking an afternoon walk. And this is partly what it is all about: to see and be seen. Few Spaniards undertake the *paseo* in a T-shirt and jogging bottoms: this is something to dress up for, especially for older people.

The time of the *paseo* varies. It was traditionally taken after waking from the siesta, but these days fewer than 16% of Spaniards sleep each afternoon. Spain's daily timetable is changing slowly, but since the Second World War it has maintained an uneasy compromise between its time zone (Central European Standard Time) and its longitude (most of Spain is west of the Greenwich Meridian). When one considers this, Spain's 'late' meals make more sense. The *malagueño* who has lunch at 2 pm is dining at the same time as a Glaswegian (on the same longitude) who sits down at 1 pm. Similarly, beginning dinner at 9 o'clock seems rather late to a British visitor, but in Plymouth (again on the same longitude) it is only 8 o'clock. The summer afternoon heat, and the siesta that developed to cope with it, are also factors.

Thirty years ago, all shops and offices closed for a few hours in the afternoon to allow time for lunch and a siesta. Now only a few do, but the divided day persists, as do its consequences. Beginning dinner at 9 or 10 o'clock was the only option when most people worked until two, had a siesta, and then went back to work for three hours afterwards. So two *paseos* persist, too. One is after the notional siesta, around 4 or 5 o'clock, while the other is 'after work', around 7 or 8 o'clock.

The *paseo* can feel odd to the visitor at first. Where did all these people suddenly come from? Why are they so smartly dressed? Where are they going? But soon it becomes a familiar part of the daily routine. Every day, families venture outdoors, and elderly Spanish men put on a crisp shirt and a natty tie to walk a few hundred yards at a stately pace. Old ladies, similarly, don their best frocks and jewellery and squeeze their bunions into their most stylish sandals (gold ones, usually — no one wears gold sandals with the aplomb of a diminutive Spanish octogenarian).

The reasons for the endurance of the *paseo* are several. As noted above, while Spaniards may call on relatives, they rarely call on friends — they are sociable in public. It is also something common to all classes. Out in the suburbs, on estates of tightly-packed social housing, people still emerge from their flats in the late afternoon, to watch their children play, have coffee or a beer, and chat to their neighbours. The *paseo* is about far more than exercise. Without the *paseo*, how would one learn that the Rodríguezes have a new baby, that *señor* Díaz is out of hospital, that Mari-Luz has a new boyfriend, or that *señora* Mendoza has lost an alarming amount of weight?

🛡 Safety

Spain is the only country where I have had my pocket picked (in Barcelona) — quite an achievement given how much time I have spent in Africa, Asia and the Middle East. This unfortunate fact notwithstanding, I have always felt very safe in Spain; something that is reflected in the statistics. Police-recorded assaults in Spain as a whole average around 60 per 100,000. By way of comparison, Italy and Germany record around twice as many, France five times as many, and England and Wales a staggering 12 times as many (though this may, of course, simply reflect greater efficiency with paperwork in the UK).

There are certainly areas in some Spanish cities with the same sorts of crime problems as in the UK (drugs, gangs, theft, illegal prostitution, etc.) and Málaga is no exception. However, city centres are pretty safe at any time of the day or night for a number of reasons. One is that Spaniards are very keen on 'public space' and they like to occupy it — parks, streets, pavements, squares, etc. — and therefore nowhere in any city centre is ever really 'deserted' (save for what Spaniards call the *madrugada*, *i.e.* the hour or two just before dawn). Spaniards rarely sit down for dinner before 9 pm, very few bars close before midnight, and many stay open until 2 or 3 am. Another reason, as I outlined above, is that Spaniards don't really understand 'personal space', at least not in the public sphere. It would be unkind to say that they are 'nosey', but they certainly take an interest in what is going on around them. That means keeping a look out for thieves and pickpockets. You might find that a man peddling novelty key rings is angrily chased from a bar by its owner, while the guy selling other trinkets is unmolested. This is probably because the former is a known swindler or thief whilst the latter is trusted.

Even so, the usual advice holds true. Use the safe in your room (or, in smaller guest houses, in reception) and do not carry all your cash and cards with you. The easiest way to spend euros in Spain is by using a pre-paid currency card (bit.ly/WhichCurrencyCards) which can be topped up online or via a smartphone app. You tend to get a better exchange rate and will not be at the mercy of the often eccentric conversion charges levied on non-euro card transactions. It may also be used for withdrawing cash from ATMs. Keep the currency card on your person, and your main bank card back at your accommodation; then, in the unlikely event of your pocket being picked, you will be able to cancel the currency card and still have a means of accessing money and making purchases.

Try to keep money and valuables in a zipped or buttoned pocket, and better still, separate pockets. Women can use a small handbag which they should keep to the front, rather than slinging behind (with three branches in Málaga, the Spanish chain Misako — misako.com — sells quite stylish small handbags and bum bags at bargain prices). Some men might feel confident enough to use a 'man bag' too, of course. Never hook handbags or jackets over chair backs in bars or restaurants. Know where your phone is, and never place it on the table. Be alert when you use an ATM.

Make sure you have a made note of your credit card numbers and relevant emergency phone numbers. Also, keep a note of your phone's model name and IMEI number, serial number, etc. If your phone is stolen, the police will ask for this information when you report the theft.

It is a **legal requirement** to carry ID in Spain. For UK citizens, that means a passport. In practice, however, most tourists are unaware of this law, and the police probably realize this. Even those who do know of the existence of Article 4 of *La Ley Orgánica 4/2000* do not usually cart their passports around with them, understanding the nightmare that a lost passport would initiate. Anecdotally, the only people I have heard of falling foul of this law are tourists who make trouble in other ways (drunken stag weekenders, for example).

On the other hand, a number of museums and galleries are free for EU citizens, so if you have an EU passport, there will be occasions when you will need to have it with you. Increasingly, ID is required for entry to pre-booked attractions and for train and long-distance bus travel. My advice, in accordance with Spanish law, must therefore be to keep your passport with you at all times. I merely observe that many foreign visitors to Spain keep about their person either a photocopy of their passport, or a colour photo of it on their smartphones.

🏃 Pickpocket Tricks

Professional pickpockets tend to work in teams and, unfairly or not, certain groups in society are regarded with more suspicion. Spain is probably a little less racially tolerant than the UK, especially where Africans and North Africans are concerned, but recent governments have done little to address the flood of migrants crossing the Alborán Sea and the Western Mediterranean. Madrid wins brownie points for their generosity in accepting refugees, yet does little to help them find work or assimilate, or support the cities and provinces along the coast that receive the largest influxes. Migrants too often end up in poor-quality housing in ghettoes and, with legal employment barred to them, turn to petty crime.

You will often see young men (mostly sub-Saharan Africans) selling handbags and other 'designer' goods of dubious origin and doubtful quality on the street. These *manteros* (so-called because they display their wares on a large blanket or *manto*) are usually 'illegals' and they are routinely moved on by the police. The stationary tourists gawping at the fake Gucci handbags are sitting (or rather, standing) targets for pickpockets who are often, but not always, in cahoots with the *manteros*.

Matronly Roma women may try to sell you sprigs of herbs (usually *romero* — rosemary) or flowers. Mostly these women are absolutely genuine and simply trying to earn a little money, but like the *manteros*, they sometimes work in teams to pickpockets (if you want to support Roma families, which are generally pretty low down the socio-economic ladder, you could take a carriage ride; see p. 100). I have also heard reports of fake 'chuggers', complete with clipboards, whose aim is to distract you while an accomplice rifles through your pockets. In general, then, keep your wits about you in such situations or when anything causes you to stand still (*e.g.* watching a street entertainer).

It should be noted that although Málaga has a relatively high immigrant population (overwhelmingly Moroccans) in comparison to other Spanish cities of comparable size, it experiences little in the way of social disaffection or ethnic strife. An example of good relations in the city was seen in the 2022 World Cup when Morocco beat Spain on penalties and knocked them out of the competition. Although following other Moroccan victories there were violent scenes in France, Belgium and The Netherlands, Moroccan *malagueños* celebrated open-ly in the main streets of Málaga city centre without any incident at all.

You will also encounter entirely genuine street vendors selling high-quality handmade items. These people do deserve your attention if you like the look of their wares. Many of them were victims of the 2008–2014 economic downturn that was particularly keenly felt in Andalucía, which at one point had the highest unemployment rate in the EU. The COVID pandemic and subsequent cost of living squeeze cannot have helped people already struggling to get back on their feet. The other situation in which you're likely to come across ped-lars is when you are sitting on a *terraza* enjoying a drink. Here the goods for sale tend to be flowers, novelty items or pseudo-ethnic artefacts or jewellery. A simple '*no gracias*' (**noh grath**-yass) is usually enough to send them on their way if you aren't interested.

In Málaga, the other vendors commonly encountered are the *biznagueros* who sell traditional jasmine bloom corsages called *biznagas* and are thus regarded as a venerable part of *mala-gueña* culture. They wear a distinctive uniform of black trousers, white shirt and red sash. The *biznaga* is made from cut fresh flowers and does not last long. Putting it in water will do nothing because the jasmine blooms are threaded onto a dried thistle stem. You are meant to present it to your inamorata there and then!

As tourist numbers increase, so does street begging. Most beggars tend to occupy a place on the street and do not pes-ter passers-by. Like some of the street vendors, many of these begging have very sad stories to tell bound up with the post-2008 economic downturn in Spain and the almost unbelievable unemployment rates which followed. Another group of people seen begging are the disabled. A very con-crete way of helping disabled people in Spain is by buying an ONCE (**on**-thay) lottery ticket. The *Organización Nacional de Ciegos Españoles* (ONCE) was founded in 1938 to support the blind and visually impaired, but now supports people with all kinds of disabilities. Partly, this is through social projects, but one of the chief means of support is through providing jobs as ticket sellers (ONCE lottery tickets are not sold in shops, but by registered street sellers from ONCE kiosks).

In the UK over 60% of the blind are unemployed. In Spain, the figure is around 5% and this held steady even during recent economic turbulence. Since 2014, ONCE has developed its commercial arm, known as Ilunion — a network of companies covering around 50 business lines, including a chain of excellent hotels (there have a 4-star one in Málaga on the Paseo Marítimo Antonio Machado) and various services for the hospitality sector. Ilunion employs over 32,000 people, around 40% of whom are blind or disabled. Between ONCE and Ilunion, some 38,000 blind and disabled people are directly employed, with a further 95,000 work-ing for projects and companies supported by the ONCE Foundation. By any metric, ONCE is an extremely effective charitable endeavour and often seems to do a far better job of caring for people with disabilities than does the state. Public trust in ONCE is extremely high.

Tickets are sold every day. Monday to Thursday, the ticket is called a *cupón* (and cost €2 in 2023) with over 408,000 prizes from the €500,000 top prize, right down to the €2 prize (your money back). On Fridays, the slightly more expensive *cuponazo* has prizes up to €6,000,000. On Saturdays and Sundays the *sueldazo* ('salary') ticket has a top prize of €300,000 plus €5,000 per month for 20 years. These prizes give an indication of how many tickets are sold on a daily basis. It seems to me rather wholesome that the top levels of prize money are generally enough to make winners comfortably off, rather than suddenly insanely wealthy in ways that might ruin their lives.

Very few ONCE vendors speak English, but you can just ask for *un cupón* (oon koo**pon**), *un cuponazo* (oon kupon-**ah**-THO) or *un sueldazo* (oon swell-**dah**-THO), perhaps adding *para hoy* (for today: para oiy) for good measure. You can check your results each day (after 10 pm) online: bit.ly/onceresults If you win a small prize, just take your *cupón* to a kiosk and collect your winnings. When buying or redeeming a *cupón* you will need to be patient — many vendors rely upon strong spectacles or need to use a magnifying glass or text-to-speech app to check tickets and some are hard of hearing. Larger wins will be paid directly into your bank account, but as a foreigner, you will be liable for tax!

♿ Accessibility

Málaga is a pretty easy city to visit. It has beautiful buildings, interesting museums and galleries, fascinating history, delicious food and drink, and lovely people, as well as excellent direct air connections with most European airports. But it is also a very compact city. Most of the main sights are in the *centro histórico* (historic city centre) and around the port redevelopment, an area of less than a square mile. The *centro histórico* and the port are also almost completely pedestrianized, making both relatively easy for visitors with disabilities or limited mobility to access.

The daily *paseo*, though enjoyed by families and people of all ages, is *par excellence* the preserve of elderly *malagueños*, strolling through the park or along the quay. Older people are valued and respected in Spanish society and deference is rightly shown to them. Even the Spanish word for 'retired' ('*jubilado*') is rather sweet. You would say, '*Mi padre no trabaja, está jubilado*' ('My father doesn't work, he is retired'), but what it literally means is, 'My father doesn't work, he is rejoicing.' Wherever older people go for the *paseo* (the quayside, the park, the Alameda, etc.) one tends to find abundant benches upon which to rest weary bones (though too few have backs and arms). Málaga, then, is generally an elderly-friendly city, which means that it takes accessibility seriously too.

Only two of the main attractions might be challenging or unsuitable for people with mobility problems — the Gibralfaro Castle (but you can still take the bus and admire the unequalled view of Málaga), and the Alcazaba. However, in the case of the latter, there is a lift on the Calle Guillén Sotelo to enable visitors to at least visit the main Nasrid buildings in the heart of the complex, though not the rest of the citadel which has some steep paths and steps — look for 'Ascensor a la Alcazaba' on the companion Google map. **This lift does not operate on Mondays.** There is a ticket machine in the vestibule of the lift where you can purchase your admission ticket. According to the website of the Málaga City Council, all of the main museums are adapted for the disabled, as is the Cathedral (though not the '*cubiertas*' or roof). Even the Botanical Gardens, a short bus ride from the city centre, has an extensive 'wheelchair route' which could equally be used by anyone wishing to avoid uneven paths.

All hotels, of any star rating, must have a lift, and most of the larger ones will have some suitably adapted rooms. *Hostales* and apartments are not legally required to have lift access, so always check when booking. Bars and restaurants have been encouraged to provide disabled access through the city council's 'Accessible Málaga' campaign but, to be honest, the picture is mixed. The new establishments on the quayside and in 'Soho' tend to have very good accessibility and facilities, whilst some of the older establishments in the centre are somewhat limited when it comes to space. Many bars and cafés in the centre have easily accessible outdoor terraces ('*terrazas*'), but you should ask about lavatory facilities if you have difficulty with steps.

Lavatories are a problem for many older and smaller venues. Many of the more ancient bars are very small, with loos up or down a flight of stairs. Not that it is any comfort, but the provision of public lavatories is a challenge for most visitors to Spain. If you have mobility issues, then my advice is broadly the same as in the 'Lavatories' section (p. 293f.) — basically, use the loo whenever you encounter one, whether you need to or not! Museums all have accessible toilets, as do El Corte Inglés, the Larios Shopping Centre and the railway station. All new buildings and new reforms of buildings must include accessible lavatories. Some facilities are out of date, while others are way ahead of the game. For example, the accessible facilities on Muelle Uno have recently been adapted to the needs of people who are ostomized.

 Málaga Airport offers assistance to adult travellers (and accompanied children) with disabilities and/or limited mobility. Information about these services, with links to smartphone apps can be found here: bit.ly/AGPAirportAccessibility (QR code left).

The Spanish National Rail operator, RENFE, offers similar assistance, also with smartphone apps: bit.ly/MalagaRailAssistance (QR code right). All stations on the local ◉ *Cercanías* train network are fully accessible, with lifts and escalators when the station is underground.

The /W\ Málaga Metro is fully adapted, not only for those who use wheelchairs or have limited mobility but also for those with sensory impairment. If you want to head out of the city centre, the Málaga bus network ('EMT') has reserved seats for the elderly and disabled, and the main routes are served by vehicles that have been fully adapted with wheelchair ramps (*e.g.* 🚌 19 serving the airport, as well as 🚌 1, 3, 4, 10, 11, 16, 24, 33, 34, 35 and C2). You can book a specially adapted taxi by calling: 📞+34 952 333 333, 📞+34 952 320 000, or 📞 +34 952 040 805.

Remember, too, that although the centre of Málaga is largely pedestrianized, taxis have access to all but a few streets, so wherever you want to go, you will be able to take a taxi almost to the door for a few euros.

 As part of the *Málaga Ciudad Accesible* (Accessible City Málaga) initiative, the Town Hall offers guided visits, tailored to the needs of visitors. Booking is essential, at least three days ahead. More information (in Spanish) here: bit.ly/AccessMalaga (QR code left). You could also ask at the *turismo* (*oficina de turismo* or tourist information office).

Another project of the city council is *Disfruta La Playa* (Enjoy the Beach), a support service for people with disabilities and reduced mobility, to facilitate their enjoyment of the beach and help them access the sea through the use of amphibious chairs, flotation materials, etc. It is available from 23 June to 15 September (when the beaches are manned by lifeguards) and information and the phone numbers to book the services are to be found on the '*Málaga Ciudad Accesible*' web page above.

A Brief History
Phoenicians

The region around Málaga has been inhabited since ancient times. In the Nerja Caves, paintings of seals have been dated that could well be the first known work of art in the history of mankind, dating back 42,000 years. The Phoenicians arrived in the 9th century BC to trade with the Bastetani people (an ancient Iberian tribe). They first established an enclave at Cerro de Villar at the mouth of the Guadalhorce River (close to where the airport is now located). Gradually the centre of commercial activity moved towards the area of the city of Málaga as we now know it due to the natural harbour at the foot of Mount Gibralfaro and plentiful silver and copper deposits. The colony of Mlk (𐤌𐤋𐤊) or Malaka was founded, again by the Phoenicians, in the 8th century BC. The name is almost certainly derived from the Phoenician word for 'salt', probably because fish was salted near the harbour. The most significant economic activity was fish processing (salting and fermenting) and the production of Tyrian Purple, the enormously costly dye extracted from sea snails. A sign of the importance of Malaka was the existence of its own mint (there is a clear connection between the Old Castilian and Phoenician words for a mint: **ceca** and **sikka**).

Greeks?

There is no consensus about whether Malaka became a Greek colony (Μαινάκη/Mainákē) for a time. The sources are scant — little more than a reference in the *Ora Maritima* of the 4th c. Roman author Rufius Festus Avienus who claims that 'Malacha' used to be called 'Menace' and many of the features of the mountain near the harbour were named in 'the Greek tongue'.[8] Most archaeologists and historians think that the Greek colony, if it existed, was more likely to have been on the site of the abandoned Phoenician town of Cerro de Villar (at the mouth of the Guadalhorce River, near the modern-day airport). It is true that a great deal of Greek pottery has been unearthed in Huelva, Sevilla and Málaga, but that is only evidence of a trading relationship. Either way, following the Siege of Tyre by Nebuchadnezzar II (585–572 BC), the centre of power moved west and Malaka became a Carthaginian colony in about 573 BC.

Roman Hispania

'Málaga, like Cádiz, a city of selfish merchants, deserted Tyre for rising Carthage, and then deserted Carthage for rising Rome. It made terms with Scipio, became a **municipium,** *and was embellished with an amphitheatre, part of which was laid open in digging the foundations of the* **Convento de la Paz,** *and re-buried, as usual.'* (Hand-book for Travellers in Spain, Richard Ford, 1845)

---

8   *Ora Maritima*, Rufius Festus Avienus, 420–431

The Romans conquered the city, like other regions under the rule of Carthage, in the year 218 BC after the Punic wars. Unlike the Phoenicians, who were primarily interested in trade, rather than building a unified empire with common citizenship, the Romans unified the people of the coast and the interior under a common power. They introduced Latin as the language of the ruling classes and popularized customs that would gradually change the lives of the indigenous population. Malaka was integrated into the Roman Republic as Malaca, part of Hispania Ulterior. The *municipium Malacitanum* was a transit point on the Via Herculea, revitalizing the city both economically and culturally by connecting it with other developed enclaves of Hispania Interior and with the other ports of the Mare Nostrum (Mediterranean). Like the Phoenicians before them, the Romans continued to prize Málaga as a source of Imperial Purple dye and of salted and fermented fish (garum).

When the Republic fell, and gave way to the Principate, the territories of Malaca, which had already by then been occupied by the Romans for two centuries, were administratively included within Baetica, one of the four provinces into which Hispania was divided. According to the Greek geographer Strabo, the city had an irregular plan, in the style of Phoenician cities. The Romans began the construction of several important works. The Flavian dynasty improved the port and under Augustus, the *Teatro Romano* was built. Converted from a federated city into a municipality, it was governed by the *Lex Flavia Malacitana*. This grant of citizenship materialized between the years 81 and 96 AD and was recorded on five bronze tablets, of which only one is preserved. Towards the end of the period of Roman rule, Malaca emerged as a centre of Christian belief, something we know about partly due to the wave of persecution that took place under the emperor Diocletian. The first known bishop of Malaca, San Patricio (Patrick) attended the Council of Elvira in c. 305, one of 19 bishops from the province of Baetica. Under the Hispano-Roman Emperor Theodosius (379–395 AD), Christianity became the official creed of the Empire.

Vandals, Goths, Byzantines, and Goths again

The Western Roman Empire, mired in decadence, gave way to the dominance of the Vandals, who around the year 411 AD devastated the coast of Malaca. After the division of the Roman Empire and its definitive crisis, Malaca fell within the areas of the Peninsula affected by the great migrations and settlements of the Silingi Vandals who, during the 5th century, imported the Arian heresy to the West. The fractured remnants of the Western Empire were consumed by ill-considered land grabs and infighting between various Germanic tribes. In 552 AD the Byzantine Emperor Justinian I conquered Malaca, among other territories, with the intention of rebuilding the Roman Empire (the 'Recuperatio Imperii').

The city was sacked and conquered again for the Visigoths by King Sisebut in the year 615 AD, but it would be in 624 AD, during the reigns of the Visigoth Suintila and the Emperor Heraclius, when the Byzantines definitively abandoned their hold on cities in the area of the strait. It is known that the Visigothic king Sisebut razed a large part of the city, and although it maintained its episcopal rank and was the location of a mint for King Sisenand (631–636 AD), its population was decimated and commercial activity declined. Such was the devastation that the first Islamic invaders of the old Visigothic county of Malacitano initially located their capital inland, in Archidona.

Conquista

The beginning of the 8th century AD saw the collapse of the Gothic monarchy and the penetration of Islam into the Iberian Peninsula from the coasts of North Africa (though directed by the Caliphate in Damascus). The Umayyad invasion represented an imperial expansion, but it was also a colonial adventure bringing large numbers of Arab and Berber settlers. After the Arab conquest, the city became part of the Muslim polity of al-Andalus and was known as Mālaqa (مالقة). In 743 Mālaqa definitively entered the area of Arab influence, after years of uprisings by its Hispano-Gothic inhabitants. By 750, the Umayyads were overthrown in Damascus by the Abbasids and moved the seat of the caliphate to Córdoba.

Mālaqa became a city surrounded by walls with five large gates and a number of suburbs and neighbourhoods (also walled), dotted with orchards on the banks of the Guadalmedina. Next to the Muslim medina were neighbourhoods of Genoese merchants, Jews, and 'Mozarabs' (Christians). After an unsettled existence under the Visigoths, the beginning of Arab rule was undoubtedly a period of stability and progress. The Arabs brought with them fresh ideas about town planning and administration and advanced agricultural technology, particularly irrigation. In the 11th century, in the Jewish quarter of the medina of Mālaqa, the Hebrew philosopher and poet Solomon ibn Gabirol rhapsodized his natal town as the 'City of Paradise'. In this long period, Mālaqa grew to a population of more than 20,000 inhabitants and became one of the most densely populated cities in the entire Iberian Peninsula.

The Taifa of Mālaqa

When the Umayyad Caliphate of Córdoba dissolved into several kingdoms, the Hammudid Dynasty made Mālaqa the capital of its own independent kingdom between the years 1026–1057. Mālaqa was a quasi-independent *taifa* at various points, including under the dynasties of Zirid from 1073 to 1090, Hassoun from 1145 to 1153, and Zannun from 1229 to 1238.

A 'taifa' was a semi-independent, or reasonably autonomous principality (from the Arabic word for 'sect' or 'division'), but its power would ultimately depend upon a caliphate of some sort, either in Hispania (Al-Andalus) or North Africa. A good analogy might be the princely states of the Indian subcontinent — ruled by all those Nizams, Nawabs and Walis who wielded genuine power and prestige, but as vassals of a greater power (whether the Mughal Emperor, the British Queen Empress or the post-1947 Federal Government).

A short time-line of Málaga under Muslim rule may be useful at this point:

- Muslim conquest (711–732)
- (Umayyad) Emirate (later Caliphate) of Córdoba (756–1031)
- First Taifa period (1009–1110)
- Almoravid rule (1085–1145)
- Second Taifa period (1140–1203)
- Almohad rule (1147–1238)
- Third Taifa period (1232–1287)
- (Nasrid) Emirate of Granada (1238–1492)
- *Reconquista* by the forces of Fernando and Isabel (1492)

On the death of Ibn Zannun, the last king of the *Taifa* of Mālaqa, in 1238, the city became part of the Nasrid Kingdom of Granada under Muhammad ibn Yusuf ibn Nasr, remaining under the rule of this dynasty until the conquest of the Catholic Monarchs. In 1279, the Republic of Genoa signed an economic and commercial treaty with Muhammad II, making Mālaqa the principal port of the Nasrid kingdom and therefore the main link between the Mediterranean, the Atlantic and the North Sea, also establishing routes with the Far East.

The traveller Ibn Battuta, who passed through around 1325, described Mālaqa as 'one of the largest and most beautiful towns of al-Andalus [uniting] the conveniences of both sea and land, and abundantly supplied with foodstuffs and fruits'. He praised its grapes, figs, and almonds; and claimed that 'its ruby-coloured Murcia pomegranates have no equal in the world.' Another exported product was its 'excellent gilded pottery'. The town's mosque he described as 'large and beautiful', with 'exceptionally tall orange trees' in its courtyard.

Reconquista

The *reconquista* of the Nasrid kingdom by the Spanish Crown began with the capture of the rather insignificant town of Alhama de Granada in February 1482. A few months later, the former Emir of Granada Abu'l-Hasan Ali ibn Sa'd took refuge in Mālaqa after being overthrown by his son Muhammad XII (Boabdil). Following this loss, the Arabs built a large number of defensive towers for the city — Torre Molinos to the west, Puerto de la Torre to the north (on the old road to Antequera), the 11 towers of Alhaurín de la Torre, the tower of Alhaurín el Grande to the north-west, and to the east, the Torre de Benagalbón.

The conquest of the city of Málaga by the *Reyes Católicos* in August 1487 was a bloody episode in the final effort to conquer the Nasrid kingdom. A powerful Castilian army made up of 12,000 cavalrymen, 25,000 infantry and 8,000 more soldiers in support advanced on a city defended by 15,000 Nasrid soldiers and Ghomara Berbers. The siege of the city was one of the longest of the *reconquista*, lasting six months. The city fell on 13 August 1487 and the *Reyes Católicos* entered the medina on 19 August. The conquest of the city was a harsh and definitive blow to the Nasrid kingdom of Granada, which had now lost its main seaport. Determined to make Málaga an example of the futility of resistance, Fernando granted only 25 families permission to remain, enslaving (or executing) thousands of the vanquished.

Land was granted as part-payment to the troops who accompanied the *reconquistadores*, between five and six thousand Christians from Extremadura, León, Castilla, Galicia and the Levante repopulated the province, of whom about a thousand settled in the capital. At first, four parishes were erected in the city: the churches of El Sagrario, San Juan, Santiago and Santos Mártires. The city later extended beyond the walls with the creation of the convents of La Trinidad, Capuchinos, Los Angeles and the Royal Sanctuary of La Victoria.

The Modern Age

New communities coalesced around the churches and convents built outside the walled enclosure of the old medina, giving rise to the formation of *barrios* outside the walls, such as La Trinidad and El Perchel, and the so-called '*Málaga conventual*' (Málaga of the Convents). The main crafts and industries were textiles, leather, ceramics, metal, wood, construction, wine and agriculture. Málaga became the main point of departure for agricultural exports from the kingdoms of Córdoba, Jaén and Granada.

From the 16th to the 18th century, the city underwent a period of instability, partly due to frequent and devastating epidemics, floods caused by the Guadalmedina River (often in years of bad harvests), earthquakes, explosions of gunpowder mills, Berber slaving raids and relentless military conscription campaigns. Despite all these challenges, the population increased from 3,616 to 4,296 families within 100 years.

In 1585, Felipe II ordered a new study of the Port, leading to the construction of a new dock in 1588 overseen by the Italian engineer Fabio Bursoto. In the following two centuries, the Port was extended both west and east. In the 17th century, wine and raisins were the backbone of Málaga's exports and constituted the main source of income. In the textile field, silk stood out (an inheritance from the Moors). Málaga attracted a significant influx of foreign merchants largely from Flanders, England, and France. Málaga had become one of the most important and strategic ports in Spain. Its importance only grew after 1704 when Spain ceded Gibraltar to the British.

During the second half of the 18th century, the chronic water supply problems suffered by Málaga were solved with the completion of one of the most important engineering projects yet carried out in Spain: the San Telmo Aqueduct. The construction of this infrastructure project, plus a new extension of the port, the reactivation of the construction of the Cathedral and a new Customs building, were some of the milestones of that century. The *malagueño* bourgeoisie was already beginning to germinate and would lay the foundations for the economic boom of the 19th century.

19th Century

In many ways, events of the 19th and early 20th centuries militated against what should have been a Golden Age. Málaga has always thrived when she has traded. She was established as a trading post by the Phoenicians, was prized by the Romans because of trade, and under Moorish rule the *de facto* port of Granada. After the 'discovery' of the Americas, Sevilla was in the ascendant due to her geographical position, but industrialization brought new opportunities for Málaga. However, unlike in the United Kingdom, Switzerland and The Netherlands, 'Free Trade' in Spain was only championed locally by municipalities (such as Barcelona, Bilbao and Málaga), and rarely by the national government.

The Whigs and Peelites had no real Spanish counterpart and although the 18th century had seen the formation of '*Sociedades Económicas de los Amigos del País*' (Economic Societies of Friends of the Country) to promote economic development, the reform movement could not be sustained without the patronage of Carlos III, and it did not survive him. Spain returned to what she knew best, namely a centralized, bureaucratic state. The 'Liberals' may have been keen to smash the vested interests of the aristocracy and the Church, but did little to ensure that these interests weren't simply transferred to an exclusive cadre of fellow 'liberals'. As a result, Spanish trading practices had a poor reputation. In his concisely titled *Spain* of 1830, the Scots businessman Henry David Inglis took a dim view of the corruption he witnessed at the Port of Málaga, such as unexplained reductions in the size of consignments before shipping, though he adds, 'I relate this, not of course as an example of government oppression of injustice, but as a proof of the lax and unhinged state of the government and total want of integrity.'

Ultimately, however, it was the French invasion, the ignominious abdication of the Spanish Royal House, the Spanish War of Independence and the continual tug of war between the forces of autocracy and liberalism that all conspired to hold Málaga back in comparison with other European cities. Málaga was a pioneer at the beginning of the Industrial Revolution, becoming the first genuinely industrial city in Spain and holding second place after Barcelona for much of the 19th century. Due to its enterprising bourgeoisie and its strong desire for modernity, Málaga was one of the most rebellious cities in Spain during the nineteenth century and the scene of various uprisings. This revolutionary activity earned the city the title 'Always intrepid' and the motto 'The first when freedom is endangered' from Isabel II.

Industry

For all of the radical politics of 19th century Málaga, this was also the period that saw the rise of the great bourgeois families of Málaga, many of them with influence in national politics — the Larios family, the conservative politician Antonio Cánovas del Castillo, the industrialist Manuel Agustín Heredia, the Loring family, the Marqués de Salamanca, and many more. Under their influence, Málaga had two well-defined sectors, both located outside the historic centre. To the west, the urban landscape began to industrialize, while to the east, villas and hotels began to appear. In 1834, the foundry of Manuel Agustín Heredia — 'La Constancia'— opened. Between 1860 and 1865, communications received a significant boost with the construction of the Málaga–Álora, Málaga–Cártama and, most importantly, Málaga–Córdoba railway lines, linking the city with the rest of Spain. Towards the end of the 19th century, the tram transformed travel within the city. From 1860, working-class neighbourhoods like El Bulto and Huelin were created to house workers employed by the nearby factories.

The end of this century of prosperity was visible over the horizon in the 1880s due to the high tariffs on British coal and the lack of competitiveness that this generated in the Málaga steel industry compared to other industrial complexes in the north of the country (unlike in Britain, Spanish liberalism was idealistic and uninterested in doctrines such as Free Trade). Arguably more catastrophic was the phylloxera plague that all but annihilated Málaga's vineyards and thus the agricultural production of this basic sector of the provincial economy. In addition, it also brought with it significant deforestation of the slopes where the vineyards were formerly cultivated, which in turn] caused an increase in flooding along virtually the entire coastal zone.

This serious crisis and its aftermath, the loss of employment, the collapse of companies, the rise in poverty and a general decline in economic activities, led many people from Málaga to seek other sources of wealth to replace what had been lost, founding in 1897, for example, the *Sociedad Propagandística del Clima y el Embellecimiento de Málaga* (Society for the Promotion of the Beautification of Málaga), an initiative aimed at promoting tourism and a distant antecedent of the tourist boom that arrived in earnest in the 1950s.

20th Century

In May 1931, after the proclamation of the Second Republic, convents, churches and religious buildings were burned in Málaga, destroying a large part of the historic, artistic and architectural heritage of the city. Agitators took to the streets at dawn on 11 May 1931, damaging or destroying over 40 religious buildings. In 1933, the first deputy of the Spanish Communist Party, Cayetano Bolívar, was elected for Málaga. Due to its association with anticlerical, republican, radical and socialist politics for many years, the city was known as '*Málaga la roja*' (Red Málaga), even though Catholic, liberal and conservative interests have always had important representation and are well-rooted in the city. This is perhaps not unusual. Many British towns and cities with reputations for radical liberalism also have deep-rooted conservative elements. It is less the case today, but in the past, Newcastle was not Newton Aycliffe, and Manchester was not Mansfield.

La Guerra Civil

In 1936, at the outbreak of the Spanish Civil War, the military *coup d'état* was put down in Málaga thanks to the intervention of (mainly anarchist) workers' militias. However, the province was soon practically isolated from the rest of the region loyal to the Republic, being connected only by the Almería highway. For this reason, during the first months of the war, Málaga acted on many occasions outside the government of the Republic. On 7 February 1937, the Francoist army, in collaboration with soldiers from the Italian *Corpo Truppe Volontarie*, launched an offensive against the city that was met with little resistance.

The occupation of Málaga led to an exodus of civilians and soldiers along the Almería highway, where they were subjected to air and sea bombardment causing multiple deaths. This

37

episode is known as The Crime of the Málaga–Almería Highway. In Málaga, the repression of the Francoist military dictatorship was one of the harshest of the war, with an estimated 20,000 shot and buried in common graves such as those in the San Rafael cemetery (the largest mass grave in Spain and now an urban park).[9]

El Caudillo

After the Civil War, recovery was slow. A trickle of foreign visitors wrote about the grinding poverty they encountered. At Almuñecar — just along the coast from Nerja — Laurie Lee related the sad spectacle of malnourished villagers struggling to land a net containing 'a pink mass of glutinous jellyfish and … quivering sardines,' a haul too meagre to go for auction, being shared out instead, after which 'the children and the workless poor were left to scratch in the sand for the small fry which had passed unnoticed, and these they ate raw on the spot'.[10] When Shirley Deane, an Australian living in Nerja with her family set off for the beach in her bathing costume, she was chastised by the mayor — not only for her indecent attire, but because 'the women of Nerja did not swim', and only on the Feast of St John the Baptist were they even permitted to walk on the beach. The ban was not an arbitrary restriction upon the freedom of 'respectable' women, but an attempt to save their dignity — the beach was primarily a communal latrine, there being no lavatories in the homes of the poor.

Spain was a basket case, impoverished by years of unrest, revolution and then Civil War, yet with an authoritarian government that presided over an unproductive, centralized economy. Even Sheila O'Callaghan, the strongly pro-Franco author of *Cinderella of Europe*[11] admitted that half of the national budget was spent on the armed forces and police and only one fifteenth on education. Barely half of Spanish children attended school despite supposed 'universal provision'. Even now one still sees the occasional example of what used to be a very common sight in Spain — an elderly Spaniard, a child of the Civil War years, short in stature and bow-legged — not the effects of old age so much as childhood malnutrition and rickets. V. S. Pritchett tells how he was repeatedly asked, 'Do you eat well in England?' Adding, '"*No se come*" — there is nothing to eat, how many times have I heard those words!'[12]

As late as 1963, the writer and satirist Nicholas Luard (husband of the food writer Elisabeth Luard) found the Avenida de Generalissimo Franco (as the Alameda Principal had been renamed) in a pitiful state. The government had graciously given the war-wounded permission to hawk cigarettes and matches and Luard recalls seeing 'black bundles tied up with string'. As he explains, 'The bundles were people and the string held their clothes around their battered bodies ... Many of either sex, with both of their legs amputated, perched knee-high to the passer-by on little wheeled sleds ... They were simply the *andaluz* who, innocent or complicit, had been crippled alike in the country's orgy of insanity.'[13]

Spain and the Black Legend

The mid-twentieth century was a watershed between the 'foreign' Spain of the 'Black Legend' and the 'familiar' Spain of package holidays and *paella*. Throughout the Middle Ages, Britain and Spain were bound together through royal marriages (four queens consort and one king of England were Spaniards, and three English women were queens consorts of Spanish kingdoms) but after the Protestant Reformation and the death of Queen Mary of England and Spain and the departure of her husband King Felipe of Spain and England (*jure uxoris*),

9   vscw.ca/en/node/34
10   Laurie Lee, *A Rose for Winter* (Hogarth Press, 1955)
11   Sheila M. O'Callaghan, *Cinderella of Europe* (London, Skeffington, 1950)
12   V. S. Pritchett, *The Spanish Temper* (London, Chatto and Windus, 1954)
13   Nicholas Luard, *Andalucía: A Portrait of Southern Spain* (London, Century, 1984)

relations soured. Anti-Spanish feeling ran high in both England and The Netherlands (two royal houses that would later be briefly joined), but not simply because Spain was, at times, an actual military foe. The implication was that there was something more fundamental. The Spaniard was seen as untrustworthy, superstitious, deceitful and 'unenlightened'.

Almost all writing by English travellers to Spain until Laurie Lee and Gerald Brenan (with a few exceptions) displayed these prejudices. Spain is seen as uncivilized, but excitingly so. The bandits, adventurers and murderous lovers are feared, but also admired. The charms of Spanish women are celebrated not because of their beauty or accomplishments, but because they are *femmes fatales* with the power to bewitch. Derwent Conway, writing under the pseudonym 'Henry David Inglis', claimed to have met in Málaga the Spanish wife of a 'respectable Scotch merchant' who told him that 'she did not know one Spanish woman who had always led a virtuous life'.[14] The implication may be superficially disapproving and moralizing, but the inference on the part of many readers would surely have been more titillating: not only are Spanish women exotically beautiful, but they have lax sexual morals. If those women happen to be Gypsies, then the exoticism is multiplied, as in Hans Christian Andersen's unsettling description of a young Romani girl who despite her tender years is 'fully developed' and 'scantily clad'. The fabulist Madame d'Aulnoy writes with typical French condescension about an imagined journey through Spain, telling her reader that 'even youths of quality begin at the age of 12 or 13 years to entertain a concubine' and claims that syphilis is so common that it is taken for granted. The Spanish, then, are sexually dissolute, but also sexually exciting. Anyone familiar with Edward W. Said's account of 'Orientalism' — a Western view of 'The East' which is simultaneously fearful and romanticizing — should be able to see something similar happening with respect to Spain.

The food, moreover, is usually described as barely edible. Mrs William Pitt Byrne allows that the bread passes muster, but protests that the oil and garlic turned her stomach. The wine, on the other hand, has a 'pitchy taint of undressed goatskins' and that from Málaga 'has a physicky taste'.[15] Almost every travel writer mentions with disgust the oil, garlic and wine, and for most of the 16th century, the Spanish consumption of tomatoes was considered suspect as many people in Britain believed them to be unfit for eating, if not actually poisonous.[16] The food and drink, then, is exotic, pungent, and even dangerous — a far cry from the plain, mild dishes of England. Strongly flavoured and rich food helped explain the Spanish character because it inflamed the passions. Even sympathetic commentators, like Ann, Lady Fanshawe (wife of the British Ambassador to Madrid in the 1660s and the first person in Europe to write down a recipe for 'icy cream') stress how different the food is in Spain: 'Their water tastes like milk and their wheat makes the sweetest and best bread in the world; bacon beyond belief good, Segovia veal much larger and fatter than ours [...] The cream is much sweeter and thicker than any I ever saw in England; their eggs much exceed ours, and so all sorts of salads and roots and fruits'.[17]

Suspicion of Spain was not simply a Protestant prejudice against Catholics, but an English, or Anglo-Saxon one. Some English Protestants, such as the Revd Edward Clarke (a chaplain to the British Embassy in the 18th century) and Richard Ford became quite Hispanophile in their views, whereas the recent convert to Catholicism Evelyn Waugh was sniffily dismissive on his visit, writing only a year before being received into the Church. Though he praised Barcelona, he was disgusted by Málaga, reporting: 'very little to see or do [...] smells strongly of olive oil and excrement [...] In the Cathedral a riotous group of begging choirboys, paralyzed old women, and a dull verger'. As for the wine, so admired by Pepys and the Empress

---

14   Henry D. Inglis, *Spain in 1830* (London, Whitaker, Treacher, and Co, 1831)
15   Mrs William Pitt Byrne, *Cosas de España: Illustrative of Spain and the Spaniards as they are* (London, 1866)
16   A. F. Smith, *The Tomato in America: Early History, Culture, and Cookery* (University of South Carolina Press, 1994
17   Lady Fanshawe, *Memoirs* (Published 1839 but written in the 1670s)

Catherine the Great, he found it 'a species of dark, sweet sherry which I had drunk and disliked in England'. Sampling it in Málaga, he found it no better, pronouncing it to be 'very nasty'.[18]

But what really set Spain apart — Catholicism aside — was the bullfight. Almost every literary traveller to Spain mentions it, disapproves of it, and yet is clearly fascinated by it. Some, like Richard Ford, make an effort to understand what is going on (as did Ernest Hemingway much later), but for most, the *corrida* is evidence of the congenital bloodthirstiness and cruelty of the Spanish race, but also of their thrilling, almost superhuman, bravery. Bullfighting was primitive, but due to its association with the bull-leaping of Mycenaean Greece and the tauroctony of the Roman cult of Mithras, also undeniably 'civilized'. Most of all, it was evidence that Spain was not just 'different' but **utterly** different. Their food might be laced with garlic and dripping with oil, unlike the milk puddings and roast beef of England, but it was still food; their religion might be ostentatious and superstitious unlike the comfortingly undemonstrative Anglicanism of England, but it was still recognisably religion; yet bullfighting had no British analogue. It was evidently not a form of hunting, nor was it pitting animals against each other (as in cock-fighting), nor was it a kind of sport with 'winners and losers'. Most of all, foreigners lacked the vocabulary even to speak about the 'bullfight' *[sic]*. Culturally, it was an unintelligible language.

Málaga moderna

For all that writers like Laurie Lee and Gerald Brenan wrote movingly about the grinding poverty of Spain in the first half of the 20th century, it was clearly part of Spain's appeal for them, at least early in their writing careers. As David Mitchell in his anthology *Travellers in Spain* (Fuengirola, Ediciones Santana, 1988) puts it, they were 'struck by a crackling intensity'. Suffering and poverty were facets of that 'intensity'. Gerald Brenan wrote that Málaga 'charges the air with real desires and cravings' which is exhilarating to someone from 'the dull hurry of London streets and their sea of pudding faces — which often seem to have known no greater grief than that of having arrived late in the chocolate or cake queue'.[19] In his 1949 preface to *The Face of Spain*, Brenan is keen to encourage his countrymen to visit 'one of the most beautiful countries in the world ... unlike any other'.[20]

His plea was heeded. *Everybody's Travel Guide to Spain* was published in 1954, promising to appeal to those who, 'seeking new and rewarding experiences, have decided to give Spain a trial'. Spain was open for tourist business, but it was still as distant and exotic as the 'Hippy Trail' through Iran and Afghanistan to India which was taking off at the same time. Paris and Venice were for conventional travellers — Spain was for the adventurous 'explorer'. All that changed only a couple of years later when the London-based travel agent Horizon Holidays operated the first charter flights to the Costa Brava. In 1951, just over a million tourists visited Spain. In 1961, 7.4 million did, and by 1973 that figure had grown to 35 million — a number greater than the population of Spain at the time. No wonder that in the preface to the 1959 second edition of *The Face of Spain*, Brenan was able to write, 'the face of Spain has changed almost out of recognition'. With the benefit of hindsight, tourism has perhaps been a mixed blessing, but there can be no doubt that it was a huge engine of — mostly positive — change.

The Province of Málaga experienced the demographic and economic expansion and upheaval caused by the boom in the tourism sector on the Costa del Sol, and while many Spaniards flocked to the area looking for work, almost an equal number left for other parts of Spain.

18   Evelyn Waugh, *Labels: a Mediterranean Journal* (Duckworth 1974, first published 1930)
19   Gerald Brenan, *The Face of Spain* (Turnstile Press, 1950)
20   *Idem.*

The *Cercanías* local train network was inaugurated in 1968 and in 1972 the University of Málaga was founded. On 27 September 1988, a decision by the *Junta de Andalucía* (Government of Andalucía) deprived the city of Málaga of 10% of its population by unilaterally approving the segregation of the then *barrio* of Torremolinos. Arguably, however, it was the loss of the tourism-wealthy district of Torremolinos that ultimately led the city councillors of Málaga to begin thinking about how they might better exploit their own patrimony in the promotion of tourism, leading to the situation in which we find ourselves today.

Málaga looked on as her neighbours on the Costa del Sol attracted huge amounts of foreign income through tourism, while at the same time observing how these former coastal villages were transformed into seas of concrete. Málaga set out to attract a different sort of tourist. Not the sun-worshipper looking for an all-inclusive bargain, but the sort of traveller who might normally visit Sevilla, Barcelona, Venice or Prague. As lovely as Málaga's beaches are, the city's real appeal lies in its well-preserved Moorish citadel, Roman theatre, attractive old town, trendy 'Soho' district, lively bars and wonderful food. In 2023, the global NGO 'Future of Tourism Coalition' announced that it would establish its headquarters in Málaga.

The *Ayuntamiento* set out to develop the city as a whole, not as a typical tourist 'resort' but as a lively, attractive, culturally-rich destination that people will not only want to visit but also move to. They have also worked hard to attract business. The Andalucía Technology Park, in the west of the city, is home to 646 companies employing almost 20,000 workers. In November 2022, Google's announcement that it would be setting up its main cybersecurity hub in the city was a symbolic boost, bringing with it an investment of $650 million. They follow many other multinationals that have discovered that plenty of job applicants would rather work for a lower wage in Málaga (with better quality of life) than for a higher salary in an office in London or New York.

I hesitate to engage in crystal ball gazing, but it is clear to any observer that there are both opportunities and dangers as Málaga looks to the future. The growth of tourism has been a success insofar as tourism has grown (faster than anywhere else in Spain, in fact). In 2023, the ruling Partido Popular was re-elected with a majority in every municipal district (under a first-past-the-post, rather than D'Hondt, system, there would have been no opposition councillors at all). This is perhaps a sign that Mayor Francisco de la Torre's pro-tourism policies, despite considerable criticism from many sides, are at least not universally unpopular with voters. The issue of 'too much tourism' has, however, become neuralgic in both Barcelona and Sevilla. The government of Málaga will need to find the 'Goldilocks Zone' for tourism, *viz.* neither too little nor too much. The difficulty lies in agreeing on what level is 'just right'.

Another challenge is achieving the right balance between tourism and the oft-mentioned drive to promote 'innovation, technology and sustainability'. In 2022, Málaga unveiled a new logo featuring the motto '*la ciudad redonda*' ('the all-round city'). Its bid to host the 2027 BIE Expo was entitled 'The Urban Era: towards the sustainable city'. They lost out to Belgrade in the final vote, but no doubt the search for the 'sustainable city' will continue.

Símbolos de Málaga (Symbols of Málaga)

The banner or flag of Málaga is vertically divided into two equal parts, *purpure* (purple) on the flagpole and *vert* (green) on the wing, with the coat of arms (tinctures reversed) in the centre. It was awarded by the *Reyes Católicos* after the taking of the city in the 15th century.

The coat of arms of the city was created by a Royal Decree of the Catholic Monarchs on 30 August 1494. The motto reads, in my translation: 'The First When Freedom is in Danger, the Very Noble, Very Loyal, Very Hospitable, Very Beneficent, Very Illustrious and Always

Daring, the City of Málaga'. In the documents of the Catholic Monarchs, Málaga had already been given the title of 'Very Noble'. Felipe IV, in 1640, granted the city the title of 'Very Loyal' for the services provided by the city, especially the large amounts of money contributed to the Crown.

The title of 'Very Illustrious' was granted in 1710 by Felipe V for the services rendered to the Crown by the city during the War of Succession. 'Always Daring' and 'The First When Freedom is in Danger' were granted by Queen Isabel II in a Royal Decree of 21 August 1843, in thanks to the struggles that caused the fall of General Espartero (Regent of Spain during the minority of Queen Isabel II). The title of 'Very Hospitable' was granted by King Alfonso XIII in a Royal Decree of 1 January 1901 for the noble and selfless conduct of the people of Málaga on the occasion of the sinking of the German war frigate Gneisenau. And in 1922 and as proof of Royal appreciation for the city, recognizing the charitable help given to the soldiers of the Army of Africa and support of a hospital for them, Málaga was awarded the title of 'Very Beneficial'. The motto 'Tanto Monta' is a quotation of the motto of the Catholic Monarchs, 'Tanto monta, monta tanto' ('They amount to the same, the same they amount to').

The principal patrons of Málaga are the martyrs Ciriaco and Paula, and the Virgin (Mary) of Victoria. The first were two young people who lived at the end of the 3rd century and who, on the occasion of the tenth persecution decreed by the Emperor Diocletian against the Christians, were arrested and required to offer sacrifices to the Roman divinities. Ciriaco and Paula refused to engage in pagan worship and they were therefore sentenced to death by stoning on 18 June 303 AD on the bank of the Guadalmedina in a place today called Martiricos (near the football stadium). After the reconquiŝta, King Fernando gifted Málaga the image of the Virgen de la Viĉtoria, a sculpture of German origin given to the monarchs by Emperor Maximilian I, and she has been patron of the city ever since. In the place where the camp of los Reyes Católicos was located, the church of Nueŝtra Señora de la Viĉtoria was founded and the image is enthroned here. Her feast day is 8 September (The Nativity of Mary), a local holiday.

One of the most popular emblems of Málaga is the statue of El Cenachero (the fish seller) made by the sculptor Jaime Fernández Pimentel in 1968 and located in the Plaza de la Marina. The flower that symbolizes Málaga is the biznaga, a jasmine flower corsage. The biznaguero (biznaga seller) is another iconic character immortalized in a statue in the Pedro Luis Alonso Gardens. The other popular symbol is the boquerón (anchovy) — the favourite fish of the city and the nickname of both the local football team and of malagueños in general. Another symbol is La Farola — the lighthouse. There are many more unofficial and more recent symbols like the perspiring, red-faced German beer drinker of the Victoria beer advert and the sweet Moscatel 'Cartojal' wine drunk during the feria. Málaga also has its own favoured Holy Week images of Jesus and Mary. The Criŝto Cautivo from the La Trinidad neighbourhood and the Esperanza (María Santísima de la Esperanza Coronada) from neighbouring El Perchel are known as the 'Lords of Málaga'.

¿Cuándo visitar? (When to visit?)

Unlike Madrid or Sevilla, which can both be uncomfortably hot in high summer, and unlike cities in central Spain like Burgos and Albacete which can both get very cold, Málaga has a pretty pleasant climate all year round. It cannot be said to be hot all year round but even in winter, the mercury rarely dips below the mid-teens Celsius during the day.

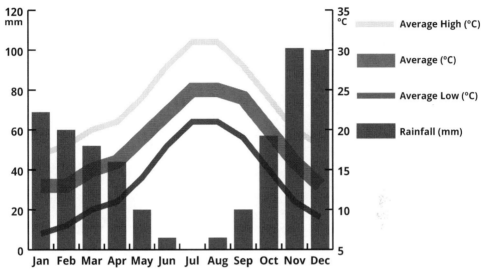

As the chart shows, average temperatures fall in the 'pleasant' and 'pleasantly warm/hot' zone between the mid-teens and high twenties. Apart from a handful of freak weather events, it is rare to experience sustained temperatures of much more than 30°C. And while the rainfall figures may look alarming in the Winter, the number of rainy **days** is low. Although almost 100 mm of rain on average falls in November, it does so over just five or six days, meaning that 24–25 days are a sunny 15°–20°C. So for any given day in November, the odds of its being dry are 5:1. Hans Christian Andersen wrote that Málaga's 'warm sunshine was a magic veil' and Málaga is a very sunny city: the second sunniest in Spain after Alicante, with just under 3,000 annual hours of sunshine. Even in dark December, which manages 'only' 160 hours of sunshine, Málaga still manages to be more than 100 hours sunnier than London or Paris.

While towns that roast in the summer can often be extremely cold in the winter due to their elevation or inland position, Málaga rarely feels truly cold. In former times the entire episcopate (bishops) of the Spanish Church used to meet in Málaga every January on account of the city's pleasant climate. Indeed, Málaga is the warmest city in mainland Europe between December and February. Frosts are not unknown, and in the far northern suburbs there can be snow, but the last recorded snowfall in the *centro histórico* — in fact, the **only** recorded snowfall — was on 2 February 1954. Two days later came the lowest temperature ever recorded: –3.8°C (25.2°F) on 4 February 1954. The temperate winter climate of Málaga was noted by Sir John Talbot Dillon, (1734–1806), an Anglo-Irish naval officer, traveller and historian who wrote extensively on the geography of Spain. Writing about Málaga, he observed that 'the dreary month of January in a northern climate is here a source of delight; the fields are full of perriwinkle [sic], myrtle, oleander and lavender, with many other flowers in bloom.'[21]

21   John Talbot Dillon, *Travels through Spain ... in a series of Letters, including the most interesting subjects contained in the Memoirs of Don G. Bowles and other Spanish writers* (London, 1780)

¿Dónde alojarse? (Where to Stay?)

Where you choose to stay will depend on many factors. Luckily, Málaga has many and varied options, from five-star luxury hotels with Michelin Star quality food, as well as chain hotels, family-run hotels, bed and breakfasts, boarding houses, self-catering apartments and Airbnb lets, all the way down to budget hostels with dormitories and shared bathrooms. This section contains no listing of recommended hotels partly because accommodation is a very personal choice. Hotels tend to be very effective when it comes to providing information online. Almost by definition, there are no 'hotels that only the locals know about'. Also, the hotel landscape in Málaga is changing **very quickly**. Hotel growth in the capital of Málaga has been spectacular in the last couple of decades as the city has gone from being a transit area for the coast to becoming a destination in itself. In 2008, the hotels of Málaga attracted 779,847 travellers and in 2018, a decade later, 1.39 million guests stayed in their rooms, an increase of 78%. But although I give no specific recommendations, I hope that the information in this section will help you to choose overnight accommodation that is perfect for you.

For some people, what matters is the place (the town, city, or locality) visited and a hotel is just somewhere to shower and sleep. For others, though, the hotel is a big part of the experience. The buffet breakfast, the room service, spa treatments and the services of a concierge are all indispensable aspects of any holiday. For many travellers to the all-inclusive resorts of the *costas*, the hotel is everything. A running joke of the UK sitcom TV series 'Benidorm' concerned holidaymakers who stay in the same hotel year after year, yet have never visited the town's beach less than 500 metres away.

Unlike the beach-side developments of Torremolinos or Fuengirola, in Málaga, the primary attraction is the city — its museums, bars and restaurants. So think carefully about what you want from your accommodation. Do you enjoy staying somewhere sleek and modern, or do you prefer the appeal of a historic building? Do you like a little luxury to be part of the experience, or do you really only need somewhere to sleep? If the former, then you will want to book into a hotel with a 4 or 5-star rating or a 'boutique' hotel and, if the latter, then a modest hotel or an '*hostal*' (not to be confused with a 'hostel' — see below!) may be a better choice. If you are looking for a measure of independence with the use of a fridge, microwave and washing machine, or if you want a more 'homely' vibe, then look for an Airbnb let or an apartment.

You'll no doubt have your preferred website through which to make accommodation bookings (I have mainly, though not exclusively, used booking.com quite happily for well over a decade) so I make no specific recommendations. Websites can rise and fall with alarming speed. A decade ago, **venere.com** was a market leader, but now it no longer exists. TripAdvisor, Google and Skyscanner have all entered the hotel aggregator (websites offering services from multiple providers) market in recent years, so the situation will no doubt continue to change, year by year. But here follow some general tips, regardless of which booking website you choose to use.

Make a flexible booking if you can

If you absolutely **must** stay in a 5-Star hotel within 200 metres of the Cathedral, or in an apartment with a roof terrace in Soho, then **book early**. If you are more flexible, then booking three months ahead will still give you plenty of choice. But even in this case, I strongly recommend using a 'book now pay later' option. You will pay a modest premium — usually a few euros per room/property per night — for making a booking that can be cancelled at no cost and there are a couple of very good reasons to consider this. The first is our experience of COVID. We have seen how easily travel plans can be disrupted by events beyond our control. But another reason is that you can often find something better at the last minute.

Let's say that in March, for a trip in July, you find a hotel with double rooms for €200 per night. It's perfect, but frankly a bit more than you want to pay. So you book another hotel for €120 per night on a 'book now, pay later' basis. A few weeks before your trip, check the website again. You might find that your dream hotel still has rooms available, but now for only €150 per night. You can now cancel the original booking and book with your preferred hotel. How does this work? Hotels advertise rooms with aggregators (like **booking.com**, **expedia.com**, **hotels.com**, etc.) at full price. But no hotel wants empty rooms, ever, because for hotels, costs (energy, staffing, etc.) are largely fixed. The running costs of a fully booked hotel are not disproportionately greater than for an empty hotel. The lights are on, the bar and kitchen are open, and domestic staff continue to turn up for their shifts. A hotel might prefer to rent a room for €200, but it is better to rent it for €150, €100, or even €50, than not to rent it at all.

Properties also pay a percentage of the room rate to the aggregator site. The precise percentage varies but it will often be between 10% and 20%. Therefore, if you see a hotel or *hostal* you like the look of, there is no harm in contacting the property directly to see if you can get a better rate by booking direct. If a hotel is paying an 18% commission to an aggregator on a €100 per night room, then they might only be receiving €82. Thus, if they deal directly with you and sell you the room for €91, then you are both €9 per night better off.

Don't Ignore the Suburbs

When deciding where to stay, a stone's throw from the Cathedral, or somewhere in the centre of the old city (*centro histórico*) might seem like the best option, but bear in mind that you will pay a premium for the location, and central locations are often quite noisy at night. The tourist centre of Málaga is made up of the *barrios* of *centro histórico* and 'Soho' (see p. 56ff.). But accommodation in the *barrios* of El Perchel, Mármoles, La Goleta, La Merced and parts of La Trinidad near the river is unlikely to be more than a 10–20 minute (up to one kilometre) walk from the centre, or a short bus ride costing less than a euro. It is also likely to be considerably cheaper. Also, if your plans include making a day trip from Málaga, or travelling to another destination, then a hotel close to the rail and bus stations might be a convenient choice.

Hosteles

There are quite a few real hostels in Málaga, catering mainly for backpackers, young people, and (*horribile dictu*) stag and hen parties. They can be extremely cheap — less than €20 per person per night — but you will have to share a (same-sex) dormitory and you won't have your own bathroom (which usually means jostling for position in the morning queue). Out-of-term, rooms in university halls of residence are often available for rent. These tend to be in the north of the city (in the university district) and while you will have your own room, bathrooms are often, but not always, shared. They can be excellent value.

Apartamentos

Apartments (and even entire houses) can be rented through Airbnb and most aggregator sites. Some are owned and operated by private landlords, others are managed by property companies and travel agents. They range from the rather small and basic all the way up to luxurious penthouse apartments with Scandinavian mattresses, hot tubs, roof terraces and an option to pay extra to have staff clean your rooms and make your beds every day.

If you are travelling as a group (for example a family, two couples or a group of friends), an apartment is almost always a far more cost-effective option than a hotel. Read the reviews carefully, of course, but in my experience, the standard of apartments available in Málaga for holiday rent is pretty high as long as you book using a reputable website. Whereas an international hotel brand can trade on its reputation, a single apartment is its own brand, so owners and agents will usually work hard to give excellent service.

There are still a few things to bear in mind. First, apartment bookings usually require a deposit against damage, which is charged to your debit or credit card upon arrival, and returned after check out. This means that a fair chunk of money (either from your bank account or towards your monthly credit card limit) is not going to be available to you during

your stay. Second, unlike hotels and most *hostales*, which have 24-hour front desks, apartments will often add a surcharge if you arrive late at night. Last, unlike hotels, they will not have facilities to look after your luggage after you check out, so you will need to make other arrangements, though this is easily done: visit bit.ly/LuggageMLG or scan the QR link.

Hoteles

These are regular hotels with a front desk, foyer, usually a bar and/or dining room (even if only for breakfast), and rooms with *en suite* bathrooms (or what the French — to whom '*en suite*' is a strange Anglicism — would call '*avec salle de bains attenante*'). Facilities vary depending on size. Hotel star ratings in Spain are partly determined by hotel facilities as in the UK but also by room size and features; so a boutique hotel with a bar, restaurant, concierge and rooftop terrace could in theory have only one or two stars if its rooms are on the small side. A four-star hotel might be rather faded and tatty, while a two or three-star hotel might be chic and luxurious with hydromassage showers and original art on the walls. All hotels, of any star rating, must have private bathrooms, central heating and a lift.

Hotel ratings are determined regionally, so a 4-star hotel in Andalucía needs to satisfy different criteria than a 4-star in La Mancha or Asturias. In 2020, the Government of Andalucía introduced new norms for awarding star ratings, partly based on minimum requirements and partly based on the accumulation of points (awarded, for example, when the hotel is a historic building, had original artwork on the walls or fresh flowers in reception). These new regulations come fully into force in 2025, so the picture remains mixed at the time of publication.

Some of the distinctions are quite subtle. Four and five-star hotels must employ 'multilingual' staff in reception, while 2 and 3-star establishments only need bilingual employees. The second language is not specified, however. The new regulations will cover apartments, *hostales* (see below), hostels and *pensiones* as well as hotels, and also reintroduce the '*gran lujo*' (luxury) category for 5-star hotels. Again, the distinctions are fine. For example, all 5-star hotels must have an *à la carte* (or buffet) restaurant open daily and provide a 'pillow menu', but a *gran lujo* 5-star hotel can earn points for having a resident sommelier or famous head chef, and for extending its pillow menu to cover all bed linen.

In summary, while star ratings are a reasonable guide to the level of comfort, service and luxury, it is far more useful to read recent reviews (though see the advice on p. 48).

Hostales

An *hostal* (pronounced oss-**tal**), is NOT a hostel! Although '*hostal*' is the most common term, an *hostal* might also be called a *pensión, posada, casa de huéspedes* or *albergue*. *Hostales* are (usually) family-run and are similar to *pensions/pensioni* found in France and Italy. Some of the more basic *hostales* are not too far from (British) bed and breakfasts, but nowadays many are closer to small hotels in quality. Many are even rather luxurious, but cannot call themselves hotels because they have rooms of different sizes (most being converted townhouses and apartments rather than purpose-built hotels) and lack dining facilities and/or a ground-floor reception. *Hostales* also used to follow a star rating system (1 to 3 stars) which was as variable as that for hotels. But as a general rule: *hostales* occupy the upper floor(s) of a building, not the whole site; they must have heating and air-conditioning; rooms must be cleaned daily; at least some rooms must have en-suite lavatories and bathrooms. *Hostales* with 2 or 3 stars must have a lift. From 2025, *hostales* will be star rated according to the same points-based system as hotels and will be categorized as 1 or 2 stars. Once again, look at the reviews!

Pros and Cons of *Hostales*

The cons are few. As most *hostales* are converted apartments, many of the rooms can be quite dark. Some will be street-facing, even with balconies, but some will be 'interior', arranged around a central patio or courtyard (sometimes little more than a ventilation shaft). This is no bad thing in the heat of summer as it means that your room stays relatively cool. The relative gloominess of such rooms can be a distinct advantage when sleeping during the siesta or at night, unmolested by neon street lighting or people leaving a noisy bar at 2 am. When you use your room for little more than sleeping and washing, interior rooms are probably preferable. Small and family-run *hostales* tend to maximize their number of beds, from tiny single rooms right up to rooms sleeping 6 or more. You just need to book the right room!

Some of the very cheapest rooms do not have a private bathroom (a requirement for a hotel, but not an *hostal*); so you always need to look carefully at the room description. One-star *hostales* are not required to have a lift, so if mobility is an issue, please check. Some *hostales* offer simple breakfasts or have a deal with a nearby bar, and many have vending machines in reception with hot drinks, chilled soft drinks and snacks, but there may be no food or drink at all. Larger *hostales* have 24-hour reception, but an increasing number are completely un-staffed, with check-in conducted entirely online and entry controlled by keypads.

The pros are rather more, *ceteris paribus*. *Hostales* are usually family-run and, sexist though it may sound, Spanish women (we could perhaps just say Spaniards in general) are fanatically house-proud and so even the most old-fashioned *hostales* will probably be spotless. In many decades of staying in some very low-cost accommodation, I have never stayed in an *hostal* that was even mildly grubby — a bit frayed around the edges, yes; but dirty, never.

Hostales do not (usually) have bars or restaurants, but in Spain, this hardly matters as there will always be about a dozen bars (probably more) within a hundred metres. If you want a massive buffet breakfast, that means staying in a 3 to 5-star hotel and paying upwards of €15 per day for the privilege. The biggest 'pro', however, is that an *hostal* is likely to be around half the price of a 3-star hotel. While some *hostales* are quite basic — a clean room and bathroom, a desk and a comfortable bed — some are quite luxurious. I have stayed in *hostales* where rooms have come equipped with power showers, irons and ironing boards, Nespresso® coffee makers, fridges and even mini-kitchens. Some, in short, are more like boutique hotels, but because they are on the first or second floor they cannot call themselves 'hotels'.

🦉 Being Review–Savvy

Reading hotel and *hostal* reviews is an art in itself. A lot of small hotels will offer a typical Spanish breakfast: tomato bread, olive oil toast (*tostada*), pastries, juice, coffee, etc. Spanish guests might judge such provision as 'excellent' whereas British (and especially US) guests will describe it as 'disappointing' because it lacks the huge variety of UK/US breakfast buffet troughs. Other common complaints from British/American guests often concern the fact that staff 'do not speak English' and 'noise' from the street.

Spain has a relatively low level of proficiency in English at around 22% (in the EU, only Bulgaria and Hungary have lower levels), but while Spaniards in the hospitality industry may sometimes struggle with English (particularly in some family-run establishments), they are likely to be polite and make great efforts to communicate. The occasionally encountered 'French experience', where a Parisian *maître d'hôtel* who can speak faultless English refuses to do so on principle, is unknown. But the 'noisy' complaint is my personal favourite. After raving about how such-and-such a hotel is 'right in the centre of the city', the reviewer then complains about noise, as if the centre of a city packed with bars, restaurants and clubs should be expected to be deathly quiet after a British person's 'bedtime' (a time at which many Spaniards are just sitting down to dinner). Another amusing niggle is the number of British guests who bemoan the lack of tea and coffee-making facilities in the room, not realising that this is almost entirely a British obsession. Why anyone would want sachets of instant coffee, artificial milk, and a miniature kettle in their room when a decent *café con leche* in the bar across the road costs less than a couple of euros is beyond me. Admittedly, tea is more of an issue. If you have a serious addiction to 'proper tea' then bring your own travel kettle, or book an apartment (or a hotel with room kettles) and bring your own tea from home, or else limit your overseas holidays to Ireland, Gibraltar, Malta and Cyprus. What I mainly look for are comments about cleanliness, location, staff helpfulness and the quality of the Wifi signal. Most smaller establishments don't have websites, so check the Google reviews. As a rule of thumb, if an owner takes the time to thank guests for positive reviews (and politely engage with negative ones), that's usually a sign that they take good service seriously.

Tips for booking.com and other aggregator booking sites

First, open an 'incognito' or 'private' browser window. A booking site will use your IP address and cookies to record the fact that you are looking for accommodation in a particular location on particular dates. It is then possible for the algorithm to increase the quoted prices for that place and time. So, browse in private until you are ready to log in and book.

Search for your location and dates, number of people and number of rooms. The top results will be the 'top picks' or 'recommendations'. These may be the most popular places, or they may be those that have paid a fee to be placed higher in the results. If money is no object and your aim is luxury, then you might want to rank the results according to review score (generally more instructive than the star rating). However, if you are looking to find the best value 'bang for buck' accommodation, then use the filters to exclude shared accommodation, stipulate private bathrooms (if you like) and display in price order.

When it comes to 'room type' look out for 'balcony' if you want an outside/street-facing room.

A 'balcony', by the way, doesn't mean a balcony you can sit out on; it just means a window opening onto the street. To see what kind of balcony it is, you'll need to peruse the photos. When given the list of accommodation options, start clicking on properties and look first at the location (most sites have a map feature). Study the room and hotel/*hostal* facilities.

To keep track of your expenditure and limit transaction fees, pay for accommodation using a euro-denominated payment card. Known as 'Forex' or 'FX' cards, these are prepaid travel cards that you can load using your regular credit or debit card, converting it to the foreign currency of your choice. You can use a Forex card just like a debit card to pay for your expenses in a local currency. You can also withdraw local cash from ATMs (though some charge a fee, so you may need to try a few to find one that doesn't). The advantage of using a Forex card is that when paying for goods and services in euros, the conversion to euros has already been done so you won't need to pay the often considerable conversion fees on individual transactions. In the UK, the main euro prepaid cards are from CaxtonFX, FairFX and The Post Office. There is also Currensea, which is not prepaid but linked to your bank account. Have a look at comparison sites (*e.g.* **bit.ly/WhichCurrencyCards**) to see which one would work best for you. You can also use your prepaid card for other online transactions ahead of your trip, such as ticket purchases and train and bus journeys.

🏵 Money Saving Tips When Staying in *Hostales*

If you are going to be staying in a top-end hotel then this section is not for you, but if you are staying in a basic hotel or in an *hostal* and want to make your holiday budget go a little further, then read on!

One can easily spend more than a week in Málaga, especially if you plan a day trip or two, but if you are visiting for a weekend, a long weekend, a few nights midweek, or even up to a week, then save money on your flight by bringing only hand luggage if you can.

Unless you have very particular requirements when it comes to the shower gel and hair products you use, then buy these in Málaga, especially if you are spending more than a couple of nights. Those 100 ml 'travel miniatures' on sale in the UK are very poor value for money (though you can invest in a set of small bottles and fill them from your own stock of gels and lotions). Even the cheapest *hostales* provide complimentary shower gel and shampoo, but often in rather miserly sachets (though do remember that you can always ask for more). Unless you are going to arrive late at night, or on a Sunday or public holiday, the best plan is to buy your toiletries when you arrive. There is a well-stocked branch of the Mercadona supermarket at the main railway station (María Zambrano). Here you'll be able to buy shower gel, shampoo, conditioner, deodorant, toothpaste etc. in full sizes for less than the cost of the travel-size equivalent purchased in the UK. There are also several branches of Lidl, Aldi and other supermarkets dotted around the city (see p. 295ff.).

Unless you are renting an apartment, bring with you:

A corkscrew — almost all Spanish wine is sealed with corks, rather than screw tops. With excellent wine on sale in supermarkets at considerably under €5, it is useful to be able to open it. If you are travelling with hand luggage only (which makes a corkscrew a potentially offensive weapon), the Eroski supermarket in the Larios Shopping Centre near the bus station sells decent quality corkscrews for €1 (in an aisle containing 'bargain' goods on sale for €1 or €2). The word in *castellano* is '*sacacorchos*' (**sakka-kor**-choss).

A knife, fork and spoon — supermarkets (and other shops, see p. 297f.) sell prepared salads, fruit salads, pastries, snacks, yoghurts and desserts. Having basic cutlery will enable you to enjoy some cheap snacks and make up a picnic if the mood takes you. If you are travelling with hand luggage only, bring plastic picnic cutlery — available from IKEA or eBay.

Travel Wash — Dr Beckmann, Stergene and Dylon are the well-known brands. All are packaged in travel-friendly 100 ml sizes. This is a handy product to have with you in case you stain an article of clothing, or need to wash some underwear or a T-shirt. Be aware that your bathroom may not have a sink plug, so you will need to be creative if you want to soak any articles of clothing. Seasoned travellers will bring their own one-size-fits-all travel plug — 'Trekmates' produce a very effective silicone travel plug: **bit.ly/TMTravelPlug**. There are also a few self-service laundrettes in the centre of Málaga — search for '*lavandería*' on Google Maps: **bit.ly/MLGLaunderettes**

If you are travelling with hand luggage only but want to bring back wine, spirits, olive oil, vinegar or other liquid goods from Málaga, then you could check in luggage for the return flight only. Make room in your case by packing your 'small cabin bag' as tightly as possible with heavier non-liquid items. The choice of wines, spirits and foodstuffs available at the post-security 'Duty-Free' section at Málaga airport is fairly limited and relatively expensive so it's far cheaper to buy these items from a supermarket or *ultramarinos* and put them in your checked-in luggage if you can. As late as 2023, there were no restrictions upon bringing food (*e.g.* charcuterie, cheese, etc.) from an EU country into the UK (though not vice versa). See the 'Gifts' section on p. 302 for ideas of things to bring back from Málaga.

Whether you are staying in a grand hotel or a humble *hostal* (but not in an apartment), you will always be able to leave your luggage at reception if you arrive before check in, or need to check out before heading for the airport. Ask, '*¿Puedo dejar mi equipaje?*' (**pway**-do day-**khar** mee ayk-ee-**pakh**-ay). If you are staying in an apartment this is not (usually) an option, but there are 'left luggage' lockers that you can use for a few euros. Search on Google Maps for '*consignas*' (see the '*Apartamentos*' section on p. 46).

🍾 Forgotten Something?

It's easily done. You arrive in Málaga, eager to head out for some *tapas* and a glass of wine and, as you unpack, you realize that you have forgotten to bring something quite important. Top of your packing checklist should be: passport, credit/debit cards, smartphone (and other devices if you need them), AC plug adapter(s), charging cables, and essential medication. If you've forgotten to bring any items of clothing, then Primark (in the Larios Shopping Centre) is the cheapest place to buy emergency replacements. They also sell charging cables, hats and inexpensive sunglasses. If you have forgotten to bring an AC plug adaptor, try MediaMarkt (in the main railway station), FNAC (in the Larios Shopping Centre) or El Corte Inglés.

If you forget your medication, then visit a pharmacy ('*farmacia*' — supermarkets do not sell medicines, even aspirin). They will either be able to provide you with what you need or tell you if you need to visit a doctor (and help you find one). It's a good idea to take photos of your medicine bottles and packets, and your prescription(s), and keep them on the camera roll of your smartphone. Many drugs are available '*sin receta*' (without a prescription) in Spain. However, some very basic medications, such as paracetamol and antihistamines, are far more expensive than in the UK and can only be purchased from pharmacies.

Keep a photo of your passport information page on your smartphone too, and print out a hard copy. If you use smartphone apps for boarding passes and travel tickets, bring hard copies of these too, in case you lose or damage your phone, or it runs out of charge. Use a euro currency prepaid travel card and keep it separate from your main credit or debit card. Take the euro card out and about and leave your other card(s) in the room or reception safe. That way, if you lose one, you will still have the other as back up. Put the 'Report Lost Card' emergency phone numbers in your phone, and keep a separate paper note.

🧍Tourist Taxes?

At the time of publication, there were rumours of an imposition of a *tasa turística* (tourist tax). The mayor, Paco de la Torre, had a well-publicized discussion with his opposite number in Sevilla about it in 2022 and the main left-wing parties have also made it a manifesto commitment. Málaga has certainly been enriched economically as its popularity as a tourist destination has grown over the last decade, but not all have felt the benefit. The benefits for a city centre bar owner may be obvious, but people in jobs apparently unconnected with hospitality feel that they have missed out. Many protest that the *ayuntamiento* has lavished funds upon the *centro histórico* to the neglect of the *afueras* (suburbs).

Málaga is not Torremolinos. Before it attracted tourists, Torremolinos wasn't much more than a village and if the flow of tourists dried up tomorrow it is hard to see how it could survive, let alone prosper. But Málaga is a provincial capital and, although not in the major league of Spanish seaports, is it one that has seen the strongest recovery since COVID. As noted in the previous section, the challenge for the city authorities is to find the 'Goldilocks' point for the number of tourists — not so few that the hospitality trade suffers, nor so many that the city feels swamped, more like an exhibit in a museum than a functioning metropolis. At the moment, Málaga is popular; a city that people want to move to rather than escape from. Interviewing a senior manager at Citigroup, the newspaper *El País* reported that many employees preferred to stay in, or return to, Málaga and enjoy walking to work and having sunshine in November rather than working in London where they could earn 30% to 40% more.[22]

The current mayor is a member of the Partido Popular, a traditionally pro-free market party (similar, historically at least, to the UK Conservative Party), and one might guess that he would be opposed to the imposition of a tax on tourism. On the other hand, in his more than 20 years at the helm, he has been at the forefront of Málaga's development as a tourist destination and, now in his 80s, he will be thinking about his legacy. What Málaga needs to avoid is the '*turismofobia*' experienced by cities like Sevilla and Barcelona where large sections of the press, not to mention graffiti artists, regularly rail against the 'invasion' of tourists. These complaints are not the normal gripes about drunken, sunburnt Brits, either. They simply feel that there are too many tourists and this has a negative impact on the life of the city overall.

Despite de la Torre's party allegiance, he is well-known as a pragmatic and independently-minded politician, so my guess is that Málaga will have imposed a (modest) tourist tax by 2024 or 2025. It is unlikely to reach the levels seen in Barcelona, where tourists staying in top-end hotels pay up to €5 per night, and is more likely to be around €1 for cruise passengers and those staying overnight, and possibly a little more for those staying in 4 and 5-star hotels. Even so, if the average stay is 3 nights, this would raise around €4 million given current visitor numbers. That is not a great deal of money, but as José Damián Ruiz Sinoga (an academic at the University of Málaga) argued recently, 'A tourist tax is also a mechanism to make visitors aware that they are consuming resources that we do not have in excess, and generating an extra cost in the maintenance of urban infrastructures and services.'[23] It would also help to calm the complaints of local ratepayers. As with so many issues, the economic benefits may be meagre, but the political case is strong.

---

22   Pablo Ordaz, 'Málaga, en boca de todos', *El País Semanal*, 4 December 2022
23   José Damián Ruiz Sinoga, 'La tasa turística', *Málaga Hoy*, 14 October 2022

Lo básico (The Basics)

City:	**Málaga**
Province:	**Málaga**
Autonomous Community:	**Andalucía**
City rank (Spain):	**6th**
City rank (Andalucía):	**2nd**
Airport rank (Spain):	**4th**
Airport rank (Andalucía):	**1st**
Port rank (Spain):	**13th**
Port rank (Andalucía):	**3rd**
Foundation:	**Phoenician, c.770 BC (as Malaka)**
Population (City):	**579,076**
Population (Municipality):	**987,813**
Population (Province):	**1,717,504**
Highest point (Municipality):	**Cresta de la Reina 1,032 metres**
Highest point (Province):	**La Maroma (2,066 metres)**
Government:	***Ayuntamiento* (City) *Diputación* (Province)**
Head of Government:	***Ayuntamiento: Alcalde* (Mayor) *Diputación: Presidente***
Budget (2023):	**€976 million *(Ayuntamiento)* €374 million *(Diputación)***
GDP growth (Province)	**2.2% (2023) 7.7% (2022)**
Diocese (Catholic)	**Málaga (1st c. AD, re-founded 1486)**
Demonyms:	***malagueño, -a*	*malacitano, -a***
Primary Patron:	**Our Lady of Victory**
Patrons:	**Holy Christ of Health (*Santo Cristo de la Salud*) Saints Ciriaco and Paula**

Directory

ⓘ *Oficinas de turismo* (Tourist Information)

The main office is located at **Plaza de la Marina 11**, but there is also a small kiosk near the **Alcazaba** (p. 236), and a useful information point on the main concourse of the **María Zambrano railway station** (where, for example, you can purchase a bus pass (*'bonobús'*).

British Consulate Málaga:
  📍 Calle Mauricio Moro Pareto 2 (opposite the bus station)
  📞 +34 952 352 300

Pharmacy (24 hours): Farmacia Caffarena
  📍 Alameda Principal 2

Emergency Services: 📞 112

Health Emergency: 📞 061

Police Emergency: 📞 092

Fire Brigade: 📞 080

Emergency assistance for tourists (S.A.T.E.):   📞 +34 951 92 61 61

Defibrillators: 🌐 bit.ly/DefibMLG

Taxis: 📞 +34 952 333 333
📞 +34 952 040 804 📞 +34 952 040 090
📱 pidetaxi.es (see p. 99)

Responsible Tourism

The pro-tourism policies of the Málaga *Ayuntamiento* are not without their critics. Tourism contributed around €7.4 million to the local economy in 2022 (a figure set to rise considerably judging by current growth), but while it is undoubtedly good for hotels, bars and museums, many ordinary residents feel that it does little to improve their lives. Indeed, some claim that the growing number of tourists impinges upon them negatively. Unsurprisingly, the authorities have been at pains to point out that their tourism strategy is targeted at 'responsible tourists' — the sort attracted by art galleries, Renaissance churches and fine dining, rather than bottomless brunches, cut-price cocktails and the club scene.

The antics of British stag weekenders, hen party-goers and the like are well-known to the residents of Torremolinos and even Marbella, but in recent years the denizens of Málaga have taken to social media to post photos of revellers and to express their utter confusion regarding their behaviour. In 2022, new by-laws were passed to impose fines for the possession of 'novelty' inflatable dolls, headbands featuring genitalia or megaphones, among other nuisances. The *ayuntamiento* also launched a campaign in collaboration with the main hoteliers setting out the sort of behaviour they expected of visitors (**bit.ly/ImproveYourStay**).

It's not just boozed-up young people who behave badly, however. I am often shocked by how casually many British visitors drop litter, despite the excellent provision of bins. Northern European tourists probably do not quite grasp how precious a resource water is in southern Spain (more rubbish on the streets requires more water for cleaning). In July 2023 one of the reservoirs supplying the east of the Province was at only 7% of its usual capacity. I will add, if I may, three other suggestions for being a better tourist:

- If you visit a municipal market (and you definitely should), please buy something!
- Traditional grocers (*'ultramarinos'*, see p. 297ff.) are great treasures and your custom will help to keep them in business. They are usually excellent places to buy snacks and sandwiches.
- Venture outside the *centro histórico* to have a drink, some *tapas* or even a meal in a local bar, café or restaurant. It's far too easy to stick to the same city centre streets and go back to the same haunts. Explore a little!

¿Cómo llegar? (Arriving)
✈ By Air

It's easy and cheap to get from the airport to the city centre. In 2023, a taxi from the airport to the centre of Málaga cost around €28, while taking a train and a bus cost less than €4. Even if you take a taxi to your hotel or apartment, you will lose little time and save up to €20 by first catching the ◉ '*Cercanías*' train into town and picking up a taxi at the railway station.

Leaving the airport terminal through the main exit, turn to your left. Follow the building until you come to a zebra crossing (*cruce peatonal*). Cross and walk straight ahead. The distance between the airport and the train station is no more than 250 metres.

You can pay at the barrier with a contactless payment card, 'touching out' at the end of your journey. You can also buy a ticket if you prefer (or want to use cash). The ticket machines are on your right as you enter the station and are touch-screen controlled, offering a choice of languages. Your destination will be **Málaga-María Zambrano** (main rail station) if you want to pick up a taxi, or **Málaga-Centro-Alameda** if you want to walk across the river into the city centre. To buy more than one ticket, press the **+** sign to select the quantity you require. Use your ticket to go through the barriers and go down the escalator on your left for trains to the city centre (or right if you are heading to Torremolinos and points west). You'll need to adapt these instructions if you are not staying in the centre of Málaga.

Trains are every 20 minutes at 14', 34' and 54'. The journey to María Zambrano takes 8 minutes (3 stops). In front of María Zambrano station there will be dozens of taxis to take you on the rest of your journey or, if you want to take the bus, then read the guide to Málaga's bus system on p. 96ff. Alternatively, you could switch to the Metro (follow signs inside the railway station to **Perchel** metro station) and catch the subway to **Atarazanas**. There is more information on p. 98f.

Alternatively, you can take the bus (🚌 **A at 00' and 30'**) all the way to the city centre.

Returning to the airport is just as easy. From the centre of Málaga, travel to María Zambrano station from whence trains to the airport leave at similar times past the hour: 13', 33', 53'. Málaga–Costa del Sol is a small but very busy airport, so allow yourself enough time, especially if you need to check in yourself and/or your luggage. Experience has taught me that the later in the day your return flight is, the higher the likelihood of its being delayed.

🚢 By Cruise Liner

There are four passenger terminals in the Port of Málaga. Muelle 3 is the berth for Trasmediterranea and Balearia ferries to and from Melilla (Spain's autonomous exclave in North Africa) and it is a short walk from the *centro histórico*. The cruise liner terminals are not operated by the Port Authority but by a company called 'Cruceros Málaga' (**malaga.globalportsholding.com**). Terminal Palmeral is on Muelle Dos (see p. 69) and is used by smaller and luxury craft. If you dock here then you will probably have concierges and personal shoppers at your disposal.

Large cruise liners dock at Terminals A and B (located on the Muelle de Zona de Levante). There is a shuttle bus (every 15 minutes or so) operated by Cruceros Málaga which costs a few euros and there are usually plenty of taxis waiting. An alternative is to walk to the Farola lighthouse and take the Bus (🚌14) from the Paseo de la Farola (🅑1301). In the city centre, there are stops on the Paseo del Parque (near the Cathedral) and on the Alameda Principal (near the Atarazanas Market).

🚆 By Train

One of the great advantages of Málaga is that because its airport serves the entire Costa del Sol, it is very easy to fly to, quite cheaply, from practically every airport in Europe. However, it is also possible to reach by train or even intercity coach. If your local airport has flights to Sevilla or Granada, you can easily travel to or from Málaga by coach or train.

If you love trains or fear flying, then it is certainly possible to travel to Málaga from pretty much anywhere in Europe, including the UK. For up-to-date information about how to do so, consult the European rail guru par excellence, 'The Man in Seat 61' **bit.ly/MalagaSeat61**.

🚗 By Car

How you arrive by car depends upon where you are travelling from, of course. As long as your satnav has the latest data downloaded you should be directed along suitable roads (remembering that there are a lot of toll roads in Spain, so make sure that you decide whether to include this option or not). For more detailed route planning, involving meal, fuel or charging stops, give **abetterrouteplanner.com** a try.

Most hotels (and all 4 and 5-star hotels) offer parking and most *hoŝtales* and apartments can arrange it for you. There is a certain amount of free on-street parking in Málaga (outside the historic centre, mainly on the western side of the river). You may have to spend quite a long time searching for it. In general, yellow lines always mean no parking, green means residents' parking, blue means paid-for parking (look for a ticket machine nearby) and white boxes mean free parking spaces (though there may be a time restriction). Although Málaga has a number of underground car parks totalling over 5,000 spaces (**smassa.eu**), they are only affordable for short stays (but some hotels have 'abono' permits for the use of guests). The cheapest long-term parking option in central Málaga is the María Zambrano railway station. Search online for a provider and compare deals, which can be competitive: **bit.ly/LTParkingMalaga**.

🚲 By Bicycle

If you are on a bicycle touring holiday, one challenge will be storing your bicycle. May sure you have insurance that covers Europe (**eta.co.uk** is excellent). Even with insurance, there will be a time limit for on-street bicycle storage. A lot of cyclists opt for apartments with balconies on which they can store their bikes. For other types of accommodation, enquire with the hotel or property. Even small *hoŝtales*, for example, may have access to a private '*patio interior*'. Málaga's very modest, but slowly growing, network of cycle paths (*carriles bici*) can be seen here: **bit.ly/MalagaBici**. The open cycle map is also useful: **cyclosm.org**.

¿Dónde? (Finding Your Bearings)

The outline map below shows the extent of the Málaga municipality, an area of approximately 22 km by 15 km, divided into eleven districts (*distritos*). The urban area of Málaga, extends north to the Autovía del Mediterráneo, a 1,300-kilometre-long non-toll motorway that runs from the French border all the way down the Mediterranean coast before sweeping west as far as Algeciras in the Bay of Gibraltar. The airport is only 5 miles south-west of the city centre, a journey of less than 10 minutes by train. Between the Airport and Málaga proper is the Guadalhorce River and its estuary (now a beautiful, if somewhat wild, nature reserve). This is where Phoenicians first encountered Ancient Iberians, later moving the embryonic port north-east to a more sheltered position in the bay that forms a natural harbour.

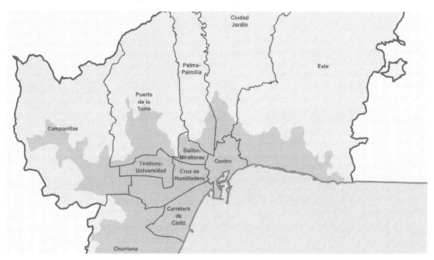

Almost everything that a visitor to Málaga would wish to see is to be found in the centre ('*Distrito Centro*' — see opposite for more detail). The Gibralfaro Castle and Alcazaba, the Cathedral and *Teatro Romano*, the historic centre and Market, the trendy 'Soho' *barrio*, the quayside development and most of the galleries and museums are all found here and the rail and coach stations are just a few metres outside it. Outside this couple of square miles are the suburbs — old residential districts to the south-west, north, and east; newer settlements, including the university, to the north-west.

The map on the next page zooms in on part of a single municipal district — '*Centro*' — which is made up of 35 *barrios* (wards), some amounting to no more than a few streets, and in the following pages I describe those of most interest to visitors. '*Centro*' is approximately 3 km by 3 km, meaning that almost any point on the map is less than 1.5 km from the centre point (the Plaza de la Constitución). To simplify matters, I have further divided some areas likely to be of interest to visitors and combined some of the more far-flung *barrios*. For example, I have combined Perchel Norte, Perchel Sur and Plaza de Toros Vieja under the single designation 'El Perchel', and I have separated 'Alameda' from 'El Ensanche' (aka 'Soho').

What counts as a *barrio* is a matter of some debate in any case, as it is the world over. There are people living in London's Battersea who call it 'South Chelsea' to make it sound more select, while some in Belsize Park will say that they live in Camden to sound less rarefied. Also, people know what is meant by 'Blackfriars', even though there hasn't been a Blackfriars (*viz.* a Dominican priory) at Blackfriars since 1538. So it is in Málaga. Places disappear but names remain. The picturesque but insanitary *barrio* of La Coracha was demolished in 1990, and the fishermen's hovels of El Bulto were razed ten years, yet both names survive. The convent of La Merced was confiscated in the 1830s and the church of the same name demolished in 1963, but the name of the *barrio*, market and square survives.

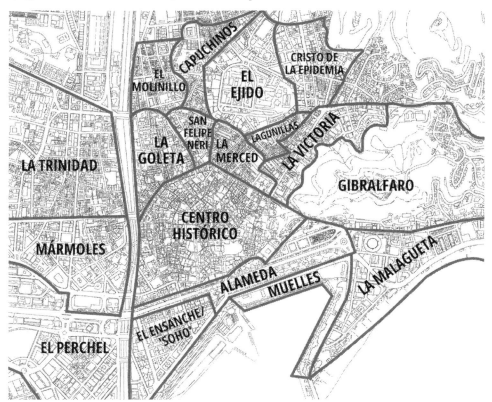

Centro Histórico

This *barrio* of around 45 hectares corresponds to the area within the Nasrid defensive walls before 1487. Little is known for certain about the size and shape of Phoenician and Roman Málaga, but the excavations that have been carried out suggest that they were of similar dimensions to the Moorish *medina*. As a typical medieval Nasrid city, Moorish Málaga comprised a citadel (the Alcazaba) with a compact network of mosques, baths and markets around it (the *centro histórico*) and, beyond the walls, the suburbs. Higher up, the fortified castle of Gibralfaro provided protection.

After the *reconquista*, the *medina* was Christianized, with mosques converted into churches and bath houses closed. Medieval Europeans were not known for their personal cleanliness, with Elizabeth I of England boasting that she bathed once a month 'whether she needed it or not'. Elizabeth's self-indulgent cleanliness would have scandalized her namesake Isabel of Castilla whose piety meant that she reputedly only bathed twice in her entire life. She was horrified to learn from Cristóbal Colón (Christopher Columbus) that Caribbean natives bathed every day and she commanded that her new subjects must cease this irreligious behaviour at once. In Spain, however, poor personal hygiene was not simply a secular fashion, it was a religious and therefore a political, statement. Muslims used public baths and performed ablutions before prayer (and Jews had the mikvah), so frequent washing was regarded as evidence of a 'suspect' religious affiliation. For Christians, bodily filthiness came to be associated with spiritual cleanliness. Later, frequent bathing would be regarded as evidence that someone was a secret Muslim, as would the refusal to eat pork. Spanish enthusiasm for *charcuterie* has survived to the present day. Luckily, aversion to bathing has not and Spaniards find the British habit of taking a bath (rather than a shower) rather disgusting.

Málaga's oldest churches (*i.e.* those founded by Fernando and Isabel) are found within the *centro histórico*. The most important of these is the Cathedral of Our Lady of the Incarnation, built on the plot of land formerly occupied by the principal mosque of the city (which had itself probably supplanted a far earlier Visigothic church). Work on the Cathedral finally began in 1528, 41 years after Málaga was reconquered. It was consecrated in 1588 and completed in 1782 after a succession of vicissitudes and interruptions. Or rather, it was not completed. The first thing anyone notices about Málaga's Cathedral is its lop-sided appearance. The south tower of a façade is unfinished and has an odd, stunted appearance. It is not simply that the tower is missing, but that the building is visibly incomplete; as if the stonemasons clocked off on a Friday afternoon in 1782 and simply forgot to return. As a result, the Cathedral is known locally as *La Manquita* or 'the maimed woman'.

The reason popularly given for the Cathedral's unfinished state, and one that fits with the city's tradition of liberal radicalism, is that the money earmarked for the second tower's construction was diverted to Americans fighting for independence from the British. This story no doubt appealed to a Spain that had recently fought against Britain in the Seven Years' War of 1756–1763, though one suspects public opinion had moved on by the time of the Peninsular War (1808–1814) when Britain was an ally against the French. The truth is almost certainly more prosaic, yet still in keeping with Málaga's mercantile tradition: the money was probably used to build the main road to Antequera. Toward whatever end the money was diverted, U.S. Independence was, and is, a cause close to the *malagueño* hearts. Every year on The 4th of July a celebration takes place in the Plaza del Obispo in front of the Cathedral. Bernardo de Gálvez & Madrid, a soldier from Málaga, fought with the United

States in Pensacola. The town of Galveston (Texas) is named after him.

The *centro histórico* is divided into four parishes established by command of *los Reyes Católicos* (see the 'Churches' section from p. 262ff.). Of these, the church of Our Lady of the Sacristy (*Santa María del Sagrario*) is the oldest, having been constructed at the base of the minaret of the old mosque in 1498. It now forms part of the Cathedral complex, occupying part of the orange tree patio once used for ritual ablutions.

Málaga's antiquity is evident in its street layout. The plan is not orthogonal and many streets are narrow, winding, and intersect at odd angles. However, cutting through this medieval labyrinth, several wide, straight thoroughfares are now found: the result of nineteenth-century urban renewal which meant the demolition of older buildings and streets. A prime example of such a redevelopment is the main shopping street, the Calle Marqués de Larios, more commonly called the Calle Larios. It runs south from the old main square (*plaza mayor*) in the centre of the *centro histórico* to the Alameda Principal and was fully pedestrianized in 2002. Though only 300 metres long and 15 metres wide, Calle Larios is the fifth most expensive street in Spain (in terms of rent), the top four streets being in Barcelona and Madrid.

The former *plaza mayor*, renamed the Plaza de la Constitución in 1812, was the main square in Málaga under Nasrid rule, although the current buildings are far more recent even than those of the *reconquista*. The nineteenth century saw huge changes to the shape of most Spanish cities as a result of the *desamortización española*: the confiscation by the Spanish government of land and buildings belonging to the Church, religious orders and municipalities. In the 18th century, under Carlos III, the rationale for confiscation had largely been economic, but throughout the 19th century, especially under Joseph Bonaparte (José I), the justification was openly ideological and anti-clerical. The reason that Spanish towns have large numbers of modestly sized squares, and the reason that so many of those squares are named after saints, is that they occupy the spaces where convents and religious houses once stood. This was not the case for the Plaza de la Constitución, although some of the religious buildings surrounding the square were seized, demolished and rebuilt.

For every tourist who is delighted by recent urban development in Málaga, there are probably a dozen locals who are not. Plenty of *malagueños* complain about what they see as the wanton destruction of Málaga's historic buildings by the *ayuntamiento* (at least one keyboard warrior gave his now-defunct blog a rather upfront description: 'The purpose of this blog is to denounce the City Council of Málaga'). Whilst some of the buildings constructed in the historic centre of Málaga over the last half century have undeniably been shockers, there is a certain irony in objecting to, for example, the reform/destruction of the Pasaje de Heredia (a lane that leads away from the north-eastern corner of the Plaza de la Constitución) as it could only be constructed in the first place because an older building had been confiscated and demolished by the state (though one might still object to the unsympathetic glass structure currently occupying the site on aesthetic grounds).

Had such ideological objections to new buildings held sway in the nineteenth century, no doubt many fine buildings would have been preserved. On the other hand, the stunning Calle Larios itself would never have been built, and Málaga would have been the poorer for it. Calle Larios is one of the most elegant boulevards in Spain, even in Europe, and a masterpiece of Spanish Belle Époque. The plan to give Málaga a grand thoroughfare first took shape in the 1870s and was the brainchild of the renowned civil engineer José María de Sancha. The *ayuntamiento* lent their support to the project in 1880, creating a public company to oversee the work and selling one million pesetas' worth of shares (over €28 million today). Ninety per cent of the shares were purchased by the Second Marqués de Larios & Larios, giving him effective control of the project. Larios appointed the 32-year-old architect Eduardo Strachan Viana-Cárdenas to oversee the design and construction. The first change was to the trajectory of the street, which had originally been intended to run south-east past the Cathedral. In Strachan's design, the street run due south from the square to the Alameda.

Strachan's inspiration came from Chicago (like Málaga, a 'windy' city) where he saw elegant, symmetrical buildings with rounded corners. The effect in the Calle Larios is harmonious. The individual buildings are not identical, but they are of similar height (four or five storeys) and the balconies and cornices form a single line that ends in a vanishing point when observed from either end of the street. As well as being pleasing to the eye, the curved corners of the buildings have another advantage — they more effectively channel the sea breeze into the streets off the Calle Larios. This must have been a boon in a city which (then) lacked effective sanitation, although the Calle Larios itself had modern sewers and its buildings all had running water and two bathrooms per apartment; unheard of at the time.

Unsurprisingly, because Calle Larios was the creation of a confident bourgeoisie, its official inauguration in 1891 raised the hackles of the many unemployed working class in Málaga. An ill-judged attempt at largesse — throwing sugared almonds to the crowds — spectacularly misfired when the donors were pelted by the sweets being lobbed back. As a symbol of *malagueño* high society, the Calle Larios also suffered much damage during the Civil War and it was renamed Calle Abril 14 (the date of the proclamation of the Second Republic). Another feature of the street that did not last much beyond the turn of the 20th century was its pavements, although here the damage was done by nature rather than Republicans. For some twenty years, the Calle Larios was known as '*el salón de baille*' (the ballroom) because it had pavements of wooden parquet. The *ayuntamiento* banned pet dogs from the street in an attempt to preserve the wooden 'paving' from the effects of their ordure, but in the end, it was the flood of 1907 that put an end to this slightly bizarre feature of urban design.

After the Civil War, the original name of Larios was restored and rebuilding commenced. The task was fittingly entrusted to Strachan's great-nephew, Fernando Guerrero-Strachan Rosado. Although he drew the designs for the restoration, he was unable to oversee the task himself because he was also involved in a project to rehabilitate the *barrio* of La Coracha (a picturesque but insanitary slum between the Castillo de Gibralfaro and the Alcazaba that has since been completely demolished). While visiting La Coracha on reconnaissance, he contracted typhus and died, aged only 34.

Since its reconstruction, the Calle Larios has remained the grand thoroughfare of Málaga; a street that might be named '*Calle Mayor*' or '*Gran Vía*' in other Spanish cities. Sky-high rents mean that independent shops and cafés have largely given way to big high street brands like

Zara, Mango and Oysho. Nonetheless, a couple of cafés and a few independent outlets cling on, none more tenaciously than one of Málaga's best ice cream parlours: Casa Mira. The original Casa Mira was, until a few years ago, to be found on the parallel street, Calle Nueva (New Street), another 19th-century road carved through the medieval tangle of lanes. Severino Mira came to Málaga in 1890 from his native Jijona, near Alicante, with a donkey cart laden with *turrón* (nougat), and like many before and after him, he began making ice cream.

After a brief hiatus during the Civil War, the Mira family recovered their premises (which had been occupied by an anarchist trade union) and went on to open their Calle Larios branch in 1943. The aftermath of the war brought new challenges. In the 1890s, the only way to make ice cream had been to bring snow from the Serranía de Ronda mountains. In the 1940s there was electricity and refrigeration, but now the raw materials were in short supply. Contraband powdered milk from the USA, black-market sugar and ingenious use of doctored ration books ensured that the *malagueños* got their ice cream. Now operated by the fifth generation, Casa Mira still produces *turrón de Jijona* (the soft, chewy kind) but the main business is ice cream. The style, like most Spanish ice cream, is Italian *gelato*, although the flavours are distinctly Spanish. Orange, lemon and citrus are popular flavourings, as is *turrón* (Eva Perón visited Casa Mira during her 1947 European tour and ordered the *turrón* ice cream), and several kinds of chocolate. Alongside the inevitable Oreo®, Toblerone®, and Ferrero Rocher® varieties there are flavours unique to Spain. One that flummoxes many tourists who speak a little Spanish is *mantecado* which sounds alarming when one considers that *manteca* is the Spanish word for lard. In fact, *mantecados* are crumbly shortbread biscuits made with lard — a rather more tempting option. Another typically Spanish flavour is *cuajada con miel* — sharp ewe's milk curd with honey. Málaga also has its own toponymic variety (Málaga) which is essentially a rather superior kind of rum and raisin using sweet Málaga wine and local raisins.

As the city's main thoroughfare, the Calle Larios also forms part of the route for all of the *hermandades* and *cofradías* that take part in the processions of *Semana Santa* (Holy Week). Both *cofradía* and *hermandad* mean 'brotherhood' — the former formed more obviously from the Latin (*cf. confrere*), and the latter from the Spanish word for brother, *hermano* (which itself comes from another Latin word for brother, *germanus*). The brotherhoods are examples of what the Catholic Church calls 'associations of the faithful' (as distinct from religious orders or institutes). According to the description in *The Code of Canon Law*, the purpose of such associations is to 'strive in a common endeavour to foster a more perfect life, to promote public worship or Christian doctrine, or to exercise other works of the apostolate such as initiatives of evangelization, works of piety or charity, and those which animate the temporal order with a Christian spirit.'[24] Being a member of a brotherhood is a year-round commitment, undertaking works of charity and raising funds for social projects. Much of the restoration work in churches damaged before and during the Civil War has been organized and partly financed by the brotherhoods who have their 'canonical headquarters' in those churches. Some brotherhoods have particular apostolates with children, young people, the sick or elderly, and many are associated (at least historically) with hospitals and care homes.

They are most in evidence, however, during the liturgical celebrations of *Semana Santa* in pretty much every town in Spain. Even a small village will have at least one brotherhood. *Semana Santa* celebrations can be quite modest in some places, while in others they can tend towards the opulent (Valladolid, Sevilla and Cádiz are among the best-known for putting on a grand display). Sevilla has around 60 brotherhoods, but Málaga is not far behind with over 40. The most ancient, the Brotherhood of the True Cross (*Vera ✠ Cruz*), was founded in 1505.

---

24   Canon 298. §1, Code of Canon Law (Libreria editrice vaticana, 2000)

Each brotherhood has its own *imágenes* ('images' or painted wooden sculptures); usually one of Jesus and one of the Virgin Mary. Some brotherhoods are custodians of an entire tableau of images, for example depicting Jesus before Pilate, or the Last Supper. These *imágenes* have particular names or dedications, so a statue of Jesus might be 'Jesus of the Great Power', 'Jesus of the Five Words', 'Jesus of Silence', etc. At a particular time on an appointed day, the *imagen*, placed on a bier and surrounded by flowers and candles, will leave the church of the brotherhood and make its stately way to the Cathedral. The processions begin on Palm Sunday and continue until Good Friday, long into the night and small hours.

The platform supporting the figure of Christ or the Virgin is known as a *trono* (throne) in Málaga but elsewhere in Spain it is called a *paso* (usually [mis]translated as 'step'). Some of these *tronos* or floats are frankly enormous; so enormous that a few brotherhoods have to begin their processions from temporary marquees because the doors of their churches are too narrow. The heaviest *tronos* are those carrying *imágenes* of the Virgin Mary because they are so richly decorated. The heaviest of all is the *trono* of the Crowned Our Lady of Sorrows (*La Virgen de Dolores Coronada*), weighing in at 4,200 kg, but few are less than 3,000 kg. Part of the beauty of *Semana Santa* is the way in which some of the *tronos* sway slightly as they move forward, seeming to bring the images of Jesus and Mary to life.

As well as forming one of the main Holy Week routes, Calle Larios has one of the most impressive and elaborate displays of Christmas lights in Spain. Spaniards are fond of decorative lights, and it is a Spanish firm (Iluminaciones Ximénez) which, in addition to designing the Christmas lights in Málaga, has won contracts to provide displays in 40 cities on four continents, including New York, Las Vegas, Hong Kong and Sofia. These are a far cry from illuminated Father Christmas figures. Rather than being strung across the street like banners, the Calle Larios lights are often designed to create a complete canopy; almost a building made of light (a recent display recreated the nave of the Cathedral of Málaga, complete with 'columns', vaulted 'ceilings' and even 'stained glass windows' rendered using 1,806,679 LED bulbs). This light show costs the city around €800,000, making it the most expensive display per capita in the country, although the extra visitors it attracts contribute far more than this to the local economy.

Calle Larios is also the location for celebrations of a more secular kind. It has been used as an open air museum to exhibit works of sculpture, including Rodin's *The Thinker* (or one of them). A significant piece on permanent display (on the corner of Larios and Strachan) is *Points of View*, by the British sculptor, Sir Tony Cragg. It is also the centre of the *feria* (Fair) of Málaga in the city centre. Annual fairs, known as *ferias*, are held all over Spain and the timing is often determined by the feast day of the city's patron saint. The *feria* in Valencia is in March for St Joseph, in Madrid it is in May for St Isidore the Labourer, and in Sevilla the *feria* is effectively an extension of Easter. In Málaga, the *feria* is held in August, to include both the Feast of the Assumption (15 August) and the anniversary of the *reconquista* of Málaga (19 August). Traditionally, *ferias* are held in a *recinto ferial* — a dedicated fairground outside the centre — and tend to come to life after dinner (which is around 10 pm in Spain), continuing into the small hours. Although there are rides and games for children, a Spanish *feria* is principally concerned with eating, drinking (at the Feria de Jerez, 440,000 half bottles of sherry are consumed, as well as other beverages), and dancing. The nocturnal revels in Málaga take place in the *recinto* out towards the airport, but there is also a 'daytime *feria*' and this takes place in and around Calle Larios.

Every September, Calle Larios also hosts Málaga Fashion Week (more accurately a weekend event that attracts 30,000 people) when the street becomes a 350-metre-long couture catwalk. Since 1998, Málaga has hosted an annual film festival in Spring for (mainly) Spanish language cinema. The 'red carpet' is laid along the entire length of Calle Larios.

The *centro histórico* is much more than the Cathedral and Calle Larios, of course. Also, *malagueños* subdivide it into smaller *barrios*, largely reflecting the original division into parishes. The area northwest of the church of Los Mártires Ciriaco y Paula, for example, has quite a different feel in comparison to the streets to the south. Locals call this *barrio* Pozos Dulces ('Sweet Wells') and it is characterized by narrow, winding streets largely consisting of houses with a handful of bars and almost no other commercial enterprises. For a long time, it was assumed that the street layout was Moorish, but more recently historians have concluded that it dates from the early years following the *reconquista* and that in Moorish times there was an orchard here.

The wells that may have given rise to its name postdated the Moors and were sunk to supply the convents in the area. In the 19th century, the *barrio* was one of the poorest in Málaga and the location of many serious epidemics. It was also one of the parts of Málaga worst affected by the great flood of 1907. One little square is worth walking through as you explore, though — the Plaza del Pericón, which for many years was a bleak and almost derelict spot but now has a small 'vertical garden' modelled on the one on the side of Caixa Forum in Madrid, designed by Patrick Blanc. Other streets have been emblazoned with lines from poetry written about Málaga (or by *malagueños*), such as these words by Vicente Aleixandre:

'My eyes always see you, the city of my seabound days.
Perched on a majestic mountain, barely standing still
In your plunge into the wavy blue,
You rule under the sky and above water,
Frozen in mid-air as if a joyous hand
Had kept you there, in a picture of glory,
Before you sink down the loving waves.'

The Moorish citadel of the Alcazaba is in this *barrio*, as is the *Teatro Romano*. Many small museums are found in the compact centre, including the Málaga branch of Madrid's Thyssen-Bornemisza gallery. The Calle Larios, perpendicular to the port, is a useful landmark and you will find yourself criss-crossing it many times as you explore the streets.

El Ensanche ('Soho')

As much as I love Málaga, I am slightly disappointed that *El Ensanche* ('The Expansion') has lately been given the slightly naff moniker 'Soho'. One suspects that the etymology is part New York (South of Houston Street) and part London (edgy and cool former red-light district). Málaga's 'Soho' is south of the historic centre and was formerly an area known for, among other attractions, its brothels and sex shops. Even so, the name grates somewhat, reminding one of etymologically ignorant attempts to rebrand London's Fitzrovia as 'Noho'. In truth, if you are in search of a London comparison, the vibe is rather more hipster Shoreditch than venerable Soho.

Sailors looking for ladies of the night have to venture further afield these days because the new Soho (like its London namesake) is rather cool and upmarket. Establishments that once promised '24-Hour XXX Movies' or tempted mariners with opportunities to 'relax' (a Spanish tabloid euphemism for sexual services) with beautiful women have given way to fusion restaurants, cocktail bars and boutique hotels. This is not a district in which to find venerable bars unchanged by progress, or old-style restaurants serving the heavy Spanish stews of yesteryear. Here it is all about culinary twists and riffs and Spanish dishes 'reimagined'. What you will find, however, is some seriously good food and cool, bijou accommodation. It is also the place to come if you want something more interesting than the usual Spanish lagers found in every bar. The main brewery in Sevilla — Cruzcampo — opened a craft beer brewery-cum-bar in Soho in 2018, and it has proved very popular. Cruzcampo's regular beer is pretty unexciting, truth be told, but the 'craft' offerings in their Málaga branch are rather good. Soho is also home to Málaga's contemporary art museum (CAC) and a 'street exhibition' of urban art (MAUS — '*Málaga Arte Urbano en el Soho*') and the grungy vibe of the district is strangely enhanced by the presence of a couple of former sex shops now boarded up and awaiting gentrification. A link to a dingier past.

The *ensanche* was reclaimed from the sea in the 19th century, a time of relative prosperity for Málaga, and was part of the expansion of the port (which has been moving increasingly southwards ever since). Expansion began in the 1870s according to a plan by Rafael Yagüe, but it would not be until Daniel Rubio's Málaga Ensanche Plan of 1929 that the 'Heredia Ensanche' began to take on its final form.[25] The period of construction explains the orthogonal street layout and the range of architectural styles. The 'Soho' re-brand began to take shape in the early 2000s with the impetus coming from local residents and businesspeople (and this is why I ultimately support the name-change, my pedantic grumbles above notwithstanding) who formed an association to bring about renewal. A logo was chosen by public competition and a plan proposed to the *ayuntamiento*. It's perhaps fair to say that 'El Ensanche' is a locality, while 'Soho' is a concept...

> The Spanish have interesting attitudes towards sex. Spain is still, in many ways, a fairly conservative Catholic country. The drunken promiscuity of young British holidaymakers is regarded with resigned sadness, and both marriage and the family are still important. But, though traditional, Spaniards are not especially prudish. There is a strong sense of the public and private being distinct and separate realms. Prostitution is quasi-legal, but largely conducted out of town in motel brothels on motorways. Prostitutes advertise their services in newspapers ('Relax' may be a gentle euphemism, but the description of services offered is somewhat less euphemistic) and even in provincial towns (like Málaga) the sight of same-sex couples holding hands or kissing attracts no disapproval. Spain, after all, legalized same-sex unions before the UK did.

Alameda

This is the area of the city, par excellence, to witness the daily *paseo*. The main street running parallel to the port, the Alameda Principal is a wide boulevard shaded with 100-year-old fig trees. Travelling east, it becomes the Paseo del Parque. These thoroughfares follow the line of the southern city walls, which Carlos III allowed to be demolished in 1786, and are built

---

25 Daniel Rubio Sánchez (1883–1968) was a *malagueño* architect who worked mainly in Albacete (he designed the building that now houses the Cutlery Museum) and in Málaga. One of his best-known works is the Mercado de Salamanca (just north of the *barrio* of La Goleta), and a striking building on Calle Sagasta (No. 5)

on partly reclaimed land. As the contemporary poet Francisco Bejarano put it, 'She was born, like Aphrodite, from the foam
born from the continuous kissing of the waves on the
beach.'[26]

Throughout the 19th
century, the Alameda
Principal was **the** boulevard. Until the inauguration of the Calle Marqués de Larios in 1891,
this broad thoroughfare was where the cream of *malagueña* society came for the *paseo*; to
see and be seen. It was the location of the finest and most fashionable hotels where German
Pilsners and French wines were served. The commercial bourgeoisie who congregated here
even became known as '*la oligarquía de la Alameda*' ('the Alameda oligarchy'). Until 1925, it
was closed to traffic, so was more like an urban park than the busy road it now is, and was
lined with white poplars, hence its name ('*alameda*' means 'poplar grove'). Standing between
the old, walled *medina* to the north and the Ensanche Heredia (as the reclaimed 'expansion'
was then known) and the port further to the south, the Alameda symbolized a new and open
Málaga — not cowering behind the protective walls the of the medieval city, but looking
outward to the world and its riches.

When Hans Christian Andersen stayed in Málaga in 1862, his hotel overlooked the Alameda,
and his description of it is vivid: 'There were bare-legged Bedouins in their white burnooses,
African Jews in long embroidered kaftans, Spanish women in their becoming black man-
tillas, ladies of higher rank in bright-coloured shawls, elegant looking young men on foot
and on horseback, peasants and porters; all was life and animation.'[27] Andersen saw the
Alameda in its pomp, but a visitor several decades earlier — the English traveller William
Jacob — was less impressed:

> *Like all Spanish cities, Málaga is a most beautiful object from a distance,*
> *but will not bear a near inspection. The Alameyda [sic] is the only part of*
> *the town which is handsome, and that is truly magnificent. It consists of a*
> *footwalk in the middle, about eighty feet wide, with orange and oleander*
> *trees planted on each side : without these are good carriage roads, and on*
> *both sides a row of sumptuous and elegant houses.* [28]

Another 19th-century observer of Málaga was Louisa Tenison, daughter of the Earl of Li-
chfield, who travelled in Andalucía with her husband, the Whig MP and pioneer of photography, Lt. Col Edward King-Tenison. It is likely that Edward took some of the earliest
photographs of Spanish cities. Louisa's book about their travels, *Castilla and Andalucía* (1853)
was beautifully produced and illustrated, but her opinions (though entertaining) are rather
typical of Anglo-Saxons of the time. Like Andersen, she spent some time in a hotel on the
Alameda, observing and recording. Unlike Andersen, she was less than impressed. In a par-
agraph perhaps best described as a 'sideways compliment', she writes:

> *'There is an elegance and a dressy appearance about the mantilla which*
> *create surprise at its not having been adopted by other nations; and if*
> *Spaniards could only be made to feel how unbecoming bonnets are to them,*
> *the rich masses of whose splendid hair prevent the bonnet being properly*

---

26   «*Nació, como Afrodita, de la espuma nacida del continuo besar de las olas en la playa*»

27   H. C. Andersen, *ibid.*

28   William Jacob, *Travels in the South of Spain in Letters Written A.D. 1809 and 1810* (London, 1811) p.225

> *worn, they would cherish the mantilla as conferring on them a particular charm in which they are safe to fear no rivals.'[29]*

Elsewhere in the text she bemoans the 'pretty women' whose beauty is spoiled by their 'gaudy' clothing. One assumes that she was hoping to find a Spain where married women still wore only black and didn't presume to adopt 'non-Spanish' fashions. This is by no means an unusual approach among early 20th-century Hispanists. In other words, 'I should rather that you exotic foreign people conformed more reliably to the exotic foreign picture of you that I have in my head.'

At the beginning of the 20th century, the Alameda was reconfigured and planted with fig trees (so technically it is now the *Higueral* Principal), opening to traffic in 1925 and renamed the Avenida de Alfonso XIII. During the Franco regime, it was renamed again to become the Avenida del Generalísimo, reverting to its original name of Alameda Principal after the restoration of democracy in the late 1970s. The fig trees are now mature and it is almost impossible to imagine Alameda without the dappled shade that their huge canopy provides. The people of Málaga are very attached to these gnarled old trees, perhaps because many have memories of climbing into their branches as children to witness processions (the Alameda is a key thoroughfare for Holy Week processions, and also the parade of the Kings at Epiphany). But, alas, some may soon need to be felled. Quite a few of them are supported with steel cables and according to the botanist José Antonio del Cañizo, poor pruning has led to several becoming infected with fungal blight.

In recent years, much of the northern side of the street has been *'en obras'* (undergoing works) as they sank a new line to bring the Metro into the historic centre. Until recently, a modest metro system inaugurated in 2014 brought *malagueños* from the western suburbs as far as the railway station, but in 2023 the Atarazanas station opened, bringing the metro to the *centro histórico*. The significant works involved provided the *ayuntamiento* with a golden opportunity to increase pedestrian space along the Alameda. Until a few years ago, there were four lanes of traffic, but now the single lanes of traffic that originally ran between the pavements and the fig trees have been pedestrianized (apart from a couple of sections necessary to access underground car parks). The traffic-free promenades were officially opened in late 2019, but have taken some getting used to. Prior to tightening rules about the use of e-scooters, both sides of the street were used as rat-runs, and a poorly marked cycle path (*carril bici*) has meant confusion for both pedestrians and cyclists about who has the right of way. No doubt these teething troubles will soon settle down. The south side of the Alameda is where you will find Málaga's florists, and on both sides of the street vendors of roasted and candied almonds and roast potatoes can often be seen. During *Semana Santa* (Holy Week) and the *feria* (fair) you will also find *buñuelos* (doughnuts) and other seasonal treats on sale.

Although following the enlargement of the pedestrian areas many buses have been rerouted along the Avenida de Manuel Agustín Heredia, the Alameda Principal remains an important bus interchange (see the section about public transport on pages p. 96ff.). The *ayuntamiento* has an ambitious plan to re-route traffic underground (as had been done in Madrid with the M30 ring road, now submerged beneath an urban park), so in the future, you may catch your buses from an interchange beneath the Plaza de la Marina. This is not as unusual as it sounds. Several Spanish cities have underground bus interchanges, and Madrid has several.

At the eastern end of the Alameda is the Parque de Málaga, which despite being tiny (barely

---

29   William Jacob, *Travels in the South of Spain in letters written in 1809 and 1810* (London, J. Johnson and Co., W. Miller, 1811), pp. 225–226, quoted in Blanca Krauel, *Viajeros británicos en Andalucía. De Christopher Hervey a Richard Ford (1760–1845)*, (Málaga, 1986)

40 metres wide and 800 metres long) and next to a busy road, is a surprising oasis of calm. It is more of a botanical garden than a park, with trees and shrubs from all over the world. Created in 1904, as Spain reeled from the phylloxera epidemic that devastated Spanish vines, it was one of the first attempts by the city authorities to create spaces pleasing to tourists. As well as a stunning variety of tropical and sub-tropical plants and trees, it contains children's playgrounds, a small open air theatre and a seasonal café-bar.

Muelles

A *muelle*, in Spanish, is a quay or wharf, and this snippet of the map shows the two quays (out of ten that make up the Port of Málaga) that have been redeveloped for shopping, dining and recreation. The waterfront of Soho (Muelle 4) has not yet been developed and is currently a none-too-picturesque strip of somewhat dilapidated warehouses, customs posts and administrative buildings. However, with the steady gentrification of Soho, work on this area is likely to start in the near future. At the eastern end of this quay, just before Muelle Dos, there used to be a London-Eye-style Ferris wheel known as the Mirador Princess. Having previously travelled around a number of Spanish cities (and to Andorra) the wheel (the second largest in Europe after the London Eye) was initially due to remain in Málaga until 2018. Though there had been spats with the *ayuntamiento* and port authorities in the past (the derelict headquarters of the Catholic mission to sailors, the Apostleship of the Sea, had to be demolished to make space for its construction), most observers expected the contract between the Ferris wheel operators and the city to be extended. They were wrong. The attraction was dismantled in 2019 to make way for, of all things, a car park.

Muelle Uno juts out into the Mediterranean on a mole (spit) between the original commercial port and the passenger port. This quay was the first extension of the Port of Málaga beyond the natural shoreline. *Malagueño* merchants petitioned King Felipe II to begin construction and work began in 1588. It was this expansion which, in the late 18th century, allowed the city of Málaga to reclaim some of the territory of the port and develop what is now the boulevard of the Alameda. A clue to the former geography of Málaga is found in the name of the municipal market, the *Mercado de Atarazanas*, meaning 'Market of the Boatyard'. Once on the shoreline, the site is now more than 700 metres from the sea.

Significant changes came to the Port at the end of the twentieth century when Málaga stopped receiving crude oil, previously one of its major cargoes. For some time, cargo ships had been increasing in size and the docks closest to the city were no longer suitable. Wharves needed to be constructed further away from the shore in deeper waters. In effect, the Port of Málaga steadily moved southwards, leaving the older docks derelict and unused. First came an 'Extension Plan' to enlarge the port. Then, working with the *ayuntamiento* and the Government of Andalucía, the Port authorities worked on a 'Special Port Plan', approved in 1998.

The aim of the 'Special Port Plan' was to redevelop the port interior and to integrate the port and the city. The area that is now shopping malls, restaurants, gardens and esplanades had been a fenced-off commercial port dominated by an enormous grain silo, meaning that the city centre had no seafront, despite being only metres from the sea. Until a decade ago, *malagueños* wishing to enjoy a walk by the sea needed to go to one of the beaches to the east or west of the port. The enlargement of the commercial port has made available around three kilometres of the old port, an area of 20 hectares. The first stage of the plan to be completed was the 700-metre-long Muelle Uno (running north–south), now operated under contract by a commercial company of the same name.

At the city end is the polychrome glass cube of the Centre Pompidou Málaga (the first branch of the gallery outside France), and at the other is the lighthouse: La Farola. Although the Spanish word for lighthouse is *faro*, the Málaga lighthouse is one of only two in Spain to have a feminine grammatical gender (the other is in Tenerife). Constructed in 1817, the current structure replaced a wooden lantern of a century earlier. It once stood at the end of the quay, but successive extensions to the ferry port mean that La Farola is now oddly marooned in the middle of the port area. No longer a working lighthouse, there are plans to use the structure to house a permanent exhibition exploring the history of the Port of Málaga.

The 500-metre-long promenade between the Centre Pompidou and La Farola is now home to dozens of restaurants, cafés, bars and shops, with shaded walkways and palm trees for protection from the sun. This development, which opened in 2011, was one of the first big projects in the transformation of Málaga; the culmination of 13 years of negotiations with the Port authorities and a budget of €80m. Despite having around 25 shops and 30 eateries, the atmosphere is tranquil and it is extremely popular with *malagueños*, especially in the evening and at weekends. The view of the park with the Cathedral and civic buildings behind and the Alcazaba above is quite beautiful, just try not to stare out to sea towards the enormous and far from beautiful cement silos and cranes. Large cruise ships dock further out along the quay, out of sight, and Muelle Uno is now only used by yachts and smaller, luxury craft.

 A majority of the shops along Muelle Uno sell 'personal goods' (clothing, shoes, jewellery, cosmetics or toiletries). There are no branches of Primark here, but neither will you find Manolo Blahnik or LOEWE. Typical stores include a homeware shop called Mandragora, a couple of confectioners and an optician (presumably handy for cruise ship passengers who forgot to pack their prescription sunglasses). Located in a modernist wooden kiosk, qqbikes.com will hire you an electric bike for the day, half day or by the hour. In addition to the permanent shops, there is a very popular *zoco* (open air market, or 'souk') on (most) Sundays, with up to a hundred stalls selling all manner of artisan and hand-crafted goods from jewellery to clothing, toiletries to olive oil.

 Muelle Uno is very popular with families, and there are seasonal events and play clubs for children during the school holidays. The best way to find out what's going on is by consulting their Facebook/Meta page: **@muelleuno**. For grown-ups (and children) there are boat trips several times a day between January and November. Prices for the more luxurious trips can be fairly steep but promise a couple of hours on a modern catamaran and include a meal — either lunch or dinner at one of the restaurants on the quayside. If you just fancy a pootle around the port in a smaller boat, then an hour's tour isn't too expensive. There are a few operators and a variety of craft — some glass-bottomed (see p. 292).

One of the main draws of Muelle Uno — as so often in Spain — is the food and drink, and there is something here to suit every taste and budget. At the basic end is Burger King and KFC — both outlets swarming with children whose parents would probably rather be eating sardines or *tortilla*. A step up from these global fast food giants are branches of Spain's homegrown chains — Foster's Hollywood, Chopp and La Tagliatella (respectively an American diner, a *tapas* bar from Granada, and a pasta restaurant). I wouldn't go out of my way to recommend any of them (though Chopp does inexpensive *tapas*, and the Foster's Hollywood Club Sandwich is of generous proportions) but all are superior to the international chains. For a more modest snack, however, Muelle Uno has branches of the three brands operated by Grupo Restalia, the undisputed king of cheap and tasty Spanish grub — 100 Montaditos, Cervecería Bar Sureña and 'TGB' (The Good Burger).

Apart from cheap 'family restaurants', there are over a dozen mid-range establishments. Actually, 'family restaurant' is not a particularly meaningful designation in Spain, because here every restaurant and bar is a 'family restaurant'. A Burger King meal might be a treat for Spanish children, but you are just as likely to come across Spanish toddlers enthusiastically tucking into garlic prawns in a downtown bar. On Muelle Uno, as well as 'Spanish' restaurants, there is an Indian restaurant, a Sushi restaurant, a Greek restaurant, a number of fish and seafood restaurants and couple of 'Argentine' steakhouses. Many are (Spanish) chains, the Iberian analogues of places like Zizzi, Browns and Prezzo. In other words, not *haute cuisine* but fairly reliable for a reasonably priced meal with an unbeatable view.

There are also ice cream parlours and cafés for *merienda* (afternoon tea). Bodegas Quitapenas offer a more traditional *malagueño* bar experience, stocking a range of *vinos dulces* (sweet wines) alongside their reds and whites. For cocktails try Nusa or La Mar de Vinos. If all you desire is a cool glass of something to slake your thirst, there are several bars occupying waterside wooden kiosks at the city end of the quay. There is no need to worry about the *terraza/mesa/barra* distinction here (see p. 107) — when the whole bar is basically outdoors, the prices are the same.

The great advantage of Muelle Uno is that the majority of customers are Spaniards rather than gullible foreigners hoodwinked by lurid photographs of *paella* and €20 pitchers of *sangría*. Spaniards, including those in search of a bargain, take their food and drink seriously, so use them as a guide to where's hot and where's not. Finally, lest you conclude that Muelle Uno is a strip mall of naff chain restaurants, it is also where you will find Málaga's first Michelin-starred restaurant: Restaurante José Carlos García, which offers a 19-course (mainly, but not exclusively, seafood) tasting menu (see p. 171).

Muelle Dos (Wharf Two) is the second phase of the 'Special Plan' to have been completed and runs along the waterfront (east-west), perpendicular to Muelle Uno and parallel to the Parque de Málaga. Unlike the commercial Muelle Uno, Quay Number Two is a more tranquil, shaded promenade. Expect to see people out for a stroll as well as joggers and runners (cycling is not permitted). The aim here has been to bring together the city and the port by blurring the edges a little. It should be difficult to say where the city becomes the port, and vice versa, because one blends into the other. At the same time, International Maritime Agency rules issued in the wake of the 9/11 attacks, require clear boundaries to berths used by cruise ships. This conundrum — an area that both blends and separates its constituent parts — was the challenge faced by those who entered the public competition to design the project.

The winning entry — a design by the Málaga architects Jerónimo Junquera and Liliana Obal — uses glass, trees and a masonry pergola to provide a barrier between land and sea whilst giving a sense of openness. Visibility is preserved by making the handful of buildings low-rise, and what is effectively a concrete barrier has been fashioned into a canopy of undulating white beams, arranged to recall the swell of the sea and a canopy of palm trees. Even the benches, on closer examination, turn out to do double duty as concrete 'anti-terror' barriers.

There are only five buildings along the 500-metre length of the esplanade, built where a massive 1950s grain silo (constructed to store imported wheat) once stood. At either end are restaurants. The quality of both is fairly good, though neither is cheap. The attraction here is the view, rather than the food — so they are probably places to enjoy a glass of wine and a snack overlooking the bay, rather than splash out on your evening meal. In between are three buildings, owned by the Junta de Andalucía (Regional Government) which operates Muelle Dos. One is used as a maritime station for visiting cruise ships, the second as government offices (with occasional exhibitions) and the third housed the Museo Alboranía — a small museum with an aquarium and various exhibits exploring local marine life. Sadly this closed during the COVID pandemic and it is uncertain whether it will reopen.

Between the promenade and the Parque de Málaga, the *ayuntamiento* has constructed new gardens, children's play areas and water features. The pathways are lined with 420 palm trees and a further 7,400 trees and tropical plants have been planted in the gardens. It will no doubt take several years for this vegetation to 'grow out' but the eventual effect will be the expansion of the Parque de Málaga almost to the water's edge. The palm trees give this *muelle* its slightly pompous name of 'El Palmeral de las Sorpresas'. This translates as 'The Palm Grove of Surprises', which makes it sound like a Carlos Ruiz Zafón novel. The name is taking some time to embed itself and in general the name 'Muelle Uno' is often used to describe both wharves.

Muelles Uno and Dos are the accessible parts of the Port of Málaga, but there are eight other '*muelles*'. Extending into the sea beyond La Farola lighthouse is the Muelle de Levante, or cruise port, while southwest of Muelle Dos are the seven quays of the commercial port. Moving anticlockwise from Muelle Dos, Muelle 3 is the ferry terminal, and Muelle 4 (alongside Soho) is a commercial dock earmarked for further development to become, in effect, an extension of Muelle Dos. Muelle 5 is a floating dry dock ('*Dique Flotante*') and Muelles 6 and 7 (the large silos of which are visible across the bay) are for solids, liquids and dangerous goods. Muelle 8 is a small but busy fishing port and the site of a 2,600 m³ cold storage facility and a plant producing 50 tonnes of ice each day. The largest dock, Muelle 9, is the container port, the fourth largest in Spain by volume.[30]

La Malagueta

This *barrio*, at the eastern end of central Málaga, is a residential district where you will find the bullring of Málaga (also called 'La Malagueta') and the Playa de Malagueta, Málaga's 'city beach'. This is Málaga's 19th-century seaside resort and it has a handful of high-rise apartment blocks built during the early years of the Spanish tourism boom. Nonetheless, slight visual similarities aside, La Malagueta has little in common with Torremolinos. Málaga and the coastal region to the east was really the first 'tourist development' on the Costa del Sol, though it catered more to tourists from Madrid and Sevilla than from Manchester and Southampton.

La Malagueta is largely a residential district these days, even if some of those owning apartments here are residents of Sevilla or Madrid for most of the year. Like British tourists,

---

30   puertomalaga.com/en/

Spaniards love to spend time in Spanish resorts. The difference is that while the British come to escape from damp English summers, Spaniards visit to escape the frying-pan-like heat of the Spanish interior. The other difference is that Spaniards do not holiday in Benidorm or Torremolinos. Some, like the Spanish Royal Family, go to the islands (Mallorca), but others do go to the *costas*. Resort towns like Cádiz, Huelva, El Puerto de Santa María, and Almería are full of tourists during the summer — just not 'foreign' tourists.

Although La Malagueta has a number of 1960s and 1970s tower blocks constructed in the days when Málaga fancied herself as a rival to Torremolinos in attracting tourists, one can still see what a dash it must have cut as a handsome residential area. A fine example of such architecture are the Casas de Félix Sáenz, two blocks of rather striking houses built by the *malagueño* merchant Félix Sáenz for rent. Both blocks, dating from 1922 and designed by Fernando Guerrero Strachan (nephew of Eduardo Strachan Viana-Cárdenas), are structured over several floors and surmounted by towers of different heights, incorporating pavilions, terraces, balconies and glazed windows. Guerrero Strachan combined in the Félix Sáenz Houses the Neo-Renaissance style (in the overall composition and decorative details) with the *neomudéjar* style (in the use of materials and the design of the eaves).

So do not ignore La Malagueta. It's a pleasant part of town with plenty of decent restaurants and agreeable bars. The beach and its promenade are well used, not only by sunbathers and swimmers during the summer, but by walkers, runners and cyclists all year round. After work and at weekends, *malagueños* make for the beach to visit a *chiringuito* — a beach barbecue shack. The *chiringuitos* in Málaga are famous for their *espetos de sardinas* (half a dozen fresh sardines threaded onto a skewer — traditionally cane or olive wood — and grilled over a wood fire), and while they serve mainly fish and seafood some have more extensive menus, including children's options. They are also bars where you can enjoy just a beer or a cup of coffee on the beach (though diners are prioritized at mealtimes).

La Malagueta is the location of St George's Anglican Cemetery, the first non-Catholic burial ground established since the *reconquista*. Prior to its opening in 1831, Protestants were buried (though 'disposed of' might be a more accurate phrase) on the beach under cover of darkness. With the (mainly merchant) British community growing in Málaga, the British Vice Consul William Mark sought to address this undignified (and unsanitary) practice when he was appointed in 1824. He secured a plot of ground from the *ayuntamiento* and the relevant Royal Order was granted on 11 April 1830. The first remains interred in the new cemetery were those of the Ulsterman Robert Boyd, who had accompanied General Torrijos on his ill-fated expedition to foment the overthrow of the authoritarian King Fernando VII. His execution by firing squad led to questions being asked in the British Parliament, though Palmerston's response (as Foreign Secretary) was legalistic: 'The execution took place and ... as far as the Spaniards were concerned, it was quite in accordance with the laws of Spain.' As to Mr Boyd, he was afraid, that however they might lament his fate, his death 'was justifiable according to the laws of nations.'[31] Boyd's monument in the cemetery is inscribed, 'To the memory of Robert Boyd, Esq, of Londonderry, Ireland. The friend and fellow-martyr of Torrijos, Calderón etc. who fell at Málaga, in the sacred cause of liberty, on the 11 December 1831, aged twenty-six years.' In 2004, the *ayuntamiento* named a street in Huelin (not far from the San Andrés beach where the executions took place) 'Calle Robert Boyd'.

---

31   *Hansard*, 27 June, 1834

Other remains interred in the cemetery lived quieter lives and (in the main) met more peaceful ends than Boyd. Robert Mark's family mausoleum is there, as are the graves of the Hispanists Gerald Brenan and Gamel Woolsey, the physician Joseph Noble (who died in 1861 in one of Málaga's frequent cholera epidemics), the Torremolinos hotelier George Langworthy, and the poet of the 'Generation of '27' Jorge Guillén who was not technically a Protestant, but had a rather fraught relationship with the Catholic Church. One of the most moving graves is also one of the smallest — that of a baby girl called Violette who died aged just one month. Her epitaph reads, '*ce que vivent les violettes*', that is, she lived 'as the violets live' — for but a short time.

Another grave is that of the student of Hayek and historian of medieval Spanish economic theory Marjorie Grice-Hutchinson who for many years looked after the cemetery. After her death in 2003, the cemetery became rather run down, but nowadays a well-run board of trustees has made great improvements, tidying the precinct and producing information and educational materials for visitors, even organizing 'family fun days' (see p. 280). Within the cemetery lies St George's Chapel, a former funerary pavilion converted into an Anglican church in 1891 — the first Protestant place of worship in mainland Spain. The cemetery itself is a tranquil and beautiful place to explore. When Hans Christian Andersen visited in 1862, he noted the 'myrtle hedge, covered with flowers sufficient for a thousand bridal wreaths, high geranium-bushes growing round the tomb-stones' and recorded that 'passion flowers flung their tendrils over many grave-stones [and] pepper-trees waved their dropping branches amidst this place of repose.' He could 'well understand how a splenetic Englishman might take his own life in order to be buried in this place.'[32]

La Malagueta is also the site of Málaga's most famous hotel — a hotel which also tells the story of modern Málaga in its own history. Designed by Fernando Guerrero Strachan and standing almost directly opposite the gates to the cemetery, the Gran Hotel Miramar (which translates rather prosaically into English as the 'Grand Seaview Hotel') reopened in 2017 after a €65 million refurbishment and was Málaga's first only true five star or '*gran lujo*' ('great luxury') hotel. Like the Ritz in London and the Negresco in Nice, it is part of the clumsily named 'Leading Hotels of the World Group', an association of hoteliers founded in 1928 and calling to mind the 'Society of the Crossed Keys' in the Wes Anderson film, *The Grand Budapest Hotel* (but presumably without the white-knuckle ski chases and intrigue).

In 1905, King Alfonso XIII stayed in the Ritz in Paris while on his grand tour in search of a wife and keenly felt his own kingdom's lack of luxury hotels. As well as founding the Madrid Ritz, he also decreed that Málaga should have a fine hotel of its own, and in 1926 he officially inaugurated the Hotel Principe de Asturias and spent every winter there until his abdication in 1931 (the Prince of Asturias is the Spanish Prince of Wales, so to speak). In 1926, the Prince of Asturias was Alfonso's eldest son (also called Alfonso), but he renounced his claim to the then-defunct Spanish throne in 1933 in order to marry a Cuban commoner. On the same day, King Alfonso's second son, Jaime, also renounced his claim to the throne on account of his deafness (though he continued to lay claim to the defunct French throne).

The third son, Juan, received the title of 'Prince of Asturias' while serving with the British Royal Navy in Bombay. Francisco Franco, despite claiming to be a royalist, sidelined Juan (in exile) during his dictatorship because he feared that he would favour democracy, preferring Juan's son Juan Carlos, whom he felt would be more likely to continue the *franquista* dictatorship. In fact, Juan Carlos proved to be a stout and brave defender of democracy in Spain after becoming king (one of the reasons that he is still held in high regard by older Spaniards, despite the mistresses, trophy hunting and dodgy financial dealings).

---

32   H. C. Andersen, *ibid.*

During the Civil War, the hotel was commandeered for use as a hospital, re-opening after the war as the Hotel Miramar. During its heyday, it welcomed guests such as Elizabeth Taylor, Orson Welles and Jean Cocteau, as well as — more predictably — the bullfight groupies Ernest Hemingway and Ava Gardner (Hemingway was obsessed with bullfighting while Ava Gardner was more interested in the bullfighters). However, unable to compete with resorts like Torremolinos and Marbella, the hotel closed its doors in 1967 and between 1987 and 2007 the building housed the provincial Palace of Justice (its former prison is now the wine cellar).

If the room rate (€200–€400 in 2023) is outside your budget, the Gran Hotel Miramar is still worth a visit for the *ambiente* alone. The architecture is a slight jumble — part *Belle Époque*, part *neomudéjar* ('*mudéjar*' being the name used to describe a Muslim who remained in Spain after the *reconquista* — in architecture it describes the continuing Arab influence on secular and Christian buildings.) The overall effect is handsome and stylish, though it's fair to say that some of the more recent decorative details, whilst undoubtedly expensive and sumptuous, verge upon the 'Dubai Shopping Mall' aesthetic. The Lobby Bar (also known as the 'Royal Coffee Lounge and Bar') is open to non-residents daily between 9 am and midnight. The Príncipe de Asturias Restaurant is open to non-residents daily for lunch (1–4 pm) and dinner (7–11 pm). The rooftop 'Chill Out Terrace' is open to non-residents from Sunday to Thursday between 6 pm and 1 am and on Fridays and Saturdays until 2 am. Booking is advised for the restaurant (there is a booking form on the website **bit.ly/miramarrestaurant**) and for the roof terrace **hotel.miramar@hsantos.es**). For both restaurant and terrace, 'smart casual' is the minimum dress code, which in Spain usually means a jacket and tie for men, and certainly not shorts.

Gibralfaro

North of La Malagueta is the Monte Gibralfaro, or Gibralfaro Mountain. 'Mountain' is a rather generous description because the summit is only 136 metres above sea level, but because it is so near the centre of Málaga (and the sea) Gibralfaro seems to tower above the city. Monte Gibralfaro, like 'River Avon', is tautological because 'gibralfaro' means 'rock of light', formed from the Arabic word for mountain (*jabal*) and the Phoenician word for light (*faro* — they presumably got it from the Greeks, or vice versa). Monte Gibralfaro literally means, therefore, 'Mountain of Light Mountain', just as 'Rock of Gibraltar' means 'Rock of Tariq's Rock'.

A steep, winding road leads up through the forest of pine and eucalyptus to the summit where we find the castle and, close by, the Parador de Málaga.

Paradores — An Unlikely Success Story

A *parador* (from the verb *parar*, meaning 'to stop' or 'to stay') is a state-run hotel. In most countries, this would be something to avoid at all costs, perhaps reminiscent of the ghastly Intourist hotels of the former Soviet Union. One might think that in bureaucratic and often inefficient Spain this would doubly be the case, but some of the best hotels in Spain are *paradores*, synonymous with luxury and good service. The government-owned (though not government-run) company that operates Spain's almost one hundred *paradores* was a project of that tourism-minded monarch, Alfonso XIII. In 1911, he established a Royal Tourism Commission and in due course appointed The Marqués de la Vega-Inclán as commissioner for tourism.

Many years later, in the 1960s, as part of a new spirit of openness and international engagement, the Franco regime would settle upon the slogan 'Spain is different' to attract tourists. The background to this was the Second Spanish Republic, the ensuing Civil War, and then Spain's half-hearted neutrality during the Second World War. The background of King Alfonso's push to encourage tourism was essentially the backdrop of the nineteenth century, which had been fairly calamitous for Spain, too. It had begun with Napoleon's brother on the Spanish throne, then a return to the House of Bourbon and the reactionary Fernando VII under whom Spain lost most of her colonial possessions. Fernando's daughter Isabel (known in English as Isabella II) may or may not have been a nymphomaniac, but the fact of her sex (rather than sex life) led to the Carlist Wars (the prospect of a female monarch was unacceptable to many). After Isabel was deposed as queen, Spain elected the second son of King Victor Emmanuel II to reign as King Amadeo. He managed this for just over two years before declaring that the Spanish people were not so much 'different' as 'ungovernable'. The short-lived First Spanish Republic gave way to the restoration of the Bourbon monarchy in the person of Alfonso XII, Isabel's son and the father of Alfonso XIII.

After such a long period of continuous upheaval, it is little wonder that Alfonso XIII wanted to bring a sense of openness to the nation he ruled. As well as marrying a granddaughter of Queen Victoria (Princess Victoria Eugenie of Battenberg) he was keen for Spain to hold her own when it came to offering visitors style and luxury. Yet, while Alfonso is usually credited as the founder of Madrid hotels like the Ritz and the Palacio, and the eponymous Alfonso XIII in Sevilla, the real dynamo of the first Spanish tourism boom was the Marquess of Vega-Inclán. During his military and diplomatic career, he visited London, Paris and Berlin indulging his passion for art. His first significant project was the creation of the El Greco museum in Toledo and he would later oversee the restoration of that city's 14th century synagogue. After being named by Alfonso  as tourism commissioner, Vega-Inclán visited the United States, publicizing the cultural riches of Spain. Later projects would include the restoration of the Alhambra of Granada (a near derelict ruin when Irving Washington stayed, or rather squatted, there in the 1820s) and the Royal Alcázar of Sevilla. He also saved another ruin — the house of Miguel de Cervantes in Valladolid — and founded the Museum of Romanticism in Madrid. But perhaps his greatest legacy was the foundation of Spain's *Patronato Nacional de Turismo* (National Tourist Board) in 1928 and the nationwide network of *paradores*.

Many *paradores* are former monasteries, castles or royal palaces, such as the *Hostal de Los Reyes Católicos* in Santiago de Compostela, which began as a place of lodging for pilgrims in 1486 and is therefore often said to be the oldest continuously operating 'hotel' in the world. These historic properties are classed under the invented term '*esentia*' suggesting that even state-owned companies are in thrall to brand consultants. Modern-build *paradores* are categorized as either '*civia*' (city centre) or '*naturia*' (on the coast or in areas of natural beauty), two other faux-Latin neologisms.

The Málaga *parador* is a modern hotel, and because it is in the city centre (albeit surrounded by pines and eucalyptus) it is classed as a *'civia' parador*. The unique selling point of the Málaga *parador* is not that it is a grand Renaissance building, but its commanding position and stunning views. These alone could justify a *'naturia'* designation, whereas a 14th-century castle 30 metres away helps it edge towards *'esentia'*. It opened in 1948, and although it is inconceivable that a modern hotel could be constructed next door to a UNESCO-listed Moorish fort nowadays, the design is restrained and sensitive. Like all *paradores* it has luxurious rooms, superior service, a pool and fine dining (and not many hotels have an original Picasso displayed in reception), but it is the view across the Bay of Málaga which entices the guests. With only 38 rooms, every room has a balcony and a sea-view.

It is largely for the view that tourists make the journey up the hill to the castle. As a building, the castle's interior is less well-preserved than the Alcazaba (it was used as a military fort well into the 20th century), although the double ramparts are impressive. The entrance ticket, purchased from a touch screen machine, will get you into the castle **and** the Alcazaba, so my advice is to visit the castle for the magnificent view of Málaga and visit the Alcazaba for the architecture. The castle has a small terrace café inside which, like the café of any self-respecting historic monument, is run by volunteers. But for classier refreshments, non-residents are welcome to visit the terrace and café of the *parador* just across the road (though your coffee will cost three times as much).

Though not particularly high, Monte Gibralfaro is steep-sided so the easiest way to reach the top is by bus (see the entry on p. 286). You can then return to the city centre on foot, or by bus if your footwear is unsuitable (the path is paved, but the smooth surface of the incline, or rather decline, requires a decent amount of grip). As part of its ambitious and relentless project to develop Málaga, in 2017 the *ayuntamiento* announced a €530,000 plan to develop the area around the castle on the northern side of the mountain. Part of this task involved renewing the forest, felling dead trees and removing non-native species. The small picnic area and *mirador* (viewpoint) were redesigned and modernized, and a children's playground with climbing ropes, climbing walls and a zip-wire created. Three walking trails were due to be renewed and extended. If you have the time, this is a pleasant route to take either up or down the mountain.

Guadalmedina

Now we look not at a *barrio* but at the river that divides modern Málaga in two; though visitors may question the use of the word 'river' for what is, at best, a sluggish stream flowing alongside an empty riverbed of scrubby grass where children kick footballs and people go jogging and dog-walking. A majestic river seems to be an essential feature of any great city (think of the Thames, Seine or Tiber), but in Málaga, the river is almost conspicuous in its absence. The river bed and bridges are still in place, creating a curious effect of a river gone missing. Among Spanish cities, only Madrid has a more disappointing urban watercourse.

The Guadalmedina was once a mighty, albeit sporadic, river. Rather too mighty, in truth. Its name comes from the Arabic '*Wadi 'l Medina*' (River of the City), and if you look at a map of Andalucía, you will notice that many of the rivers begin with '*guadal*' (*i.e. wadi 'l*). Málaga's river is not long — only around 47 kilometres, and it rises in the mountains north of Málaga. More familiar with the *costas*, people often forget that Spain is a very mountainous country (the second most mountainous in Europe after Switzerland, with dozens of ski resorts) and many rivers are highly seasonal, drying almost completely in winter and then surging as the snow melts in the spring. Hans Christian Andersen visited Málaga several decades before the river was dammed and he wrote about an open-air market held on the dry riverbed mentioning the 'horses and donkeys, pots and pans boiling over open fires, counters and tables set out'.[33] The Guadalmedina (formed from five tributaries, or *arroyos*), no more than a trickle in winter, regularly burst its banks when in spate.

A century or so after the *reconquista* many of the mountain forests around Málaga were cleared for agricultural use. The danger in the mountains of Andalucía tends not only to be melting snow in spring but also torrential rains in autumn. These swelled the river, but also further eroded its deforested banks, exacerbating the problem. For hundreds of years, Málaga suffered regular and catastrophic flooding. After a particularly serious flood in 1907, King Alfonso XIII decreed that a solution needed to be found and the building of a dam and reservoir commenced.

It was an ambitious undertaking, resulting in a reservoir (El Agujero) of 4.5 cubic hectometres, but even this proved to be insufficient. Further works were carried out in the decades following, involving reforestation with Aleppo Pines and the construction of 30 stone dykes. Only in 1983, with the construction of a second dam (El Limonero) of 25 cubic hectometres, as well as further reforestation, was the problem of flooding in Málaga finally solved. So while Málaga's once mighty river is nowadays a rather unimpressive spectacle, it is no longer a constant source of fear and danger for *malagueños*.

El Perchel
(Perchel Sur, Plaza de Toros Vieja & Estación)

Most visitors to Málaga city will pass through the *barrio* known as El Perchel because this is where the railway station is located (though technically it lies a few metres outside the 'Centro' district). A *percha* was originally an article of fishing tackle — a kind of pegged frame upon which nets were hung to dry (it is also the word used in Spanish to mean 'coat hanger') — and the name gives a clue to the historical occupation of the inhabitants of this area.

In the sixteenth century, when El Perchel was a dangerous place to live on account of frequent slaving raids from North Africa, it had a reputation as a den of iniquity. An innkeeper tells Don Quixote that '*los Percheles de Málaga*' are known for 'agility of foot, lightness of hand and a deal of base trickery; pleading with widows, ruining of damsels, deception of children in care, and fame at last in every law-court in the land.' The bad reputation of El Perchel was proverbial. There was even a popular saying, 'Kill the king and run to Málaga'. On the other hand, the beauty of *perchelera* women was legendary and often celebrated in verse.

Like Triana in Sevilla, El Perchel was once the Gypsy quarter, but the slums were cleared long ago to be replaced by rather unremarkable and often ugly tenements. However, it is

---

33   H. C. Andersen, *ibid*.

still home to many Romani families. These '*gi-tanos*' are relatively well-integrated and yet still regarded with suspicion, despite their consistent presence in Spain for at least 600 years. Many Spaniards regard Roma as authentically 'Spanish' thanks to their accomplishments in flamenco, their innate understanding of '*duende*' (see p. 24ff.) and their bravery in facing the bulls. But prejudice remains. The Hispanist art critic Michael Jacobs, in his majestic book *Andalucía*, mentions a medical researcher who uncovered three cases of leprosy in a part of the city of Málaga that happened to be populated largely by *gitanos*. Once the research was published, large numbers of Romani children were ostracized from their schools. That *barrio*, though, was not El Perchel but La Palmilla, a bleak neighbourhood of tower blocks in the northernmost suburbs of Málaga. This is where Málaga's poorest Roma now live alongside poorly integrated migrants, in miserable conditions. Skirmishes between drug gangs are frequent, crime is commonplace, children drop out of school to take labouring jobs, and fighting cocks are raised on tower block roofs. Cervantes' phrase, 'lightness of hand and a deal of base trickery,' is not entirely redundant, sadly.

El Perchel, comparatively gentrified though it may be, is probably not a *barrio* that will have you reaching for your camera, but that doesn't mean it should be ignored. There are several modern top-quality hotels and many smaller hotels and *hostales* as well as apartments for holiday rent. Prices here are a bit cheaper than in the very centre even though the Cathedral is only 1.5 km or so from the railway station; less than 25 minutes' walk or a few minutes by bus. The railway and coach stations mean that transport links from El Perchel are very good.

The railway station, Málaga–María Zambrano, is not just a railway station, it also houses a shopping centre. The dining establishments are of the fast-food variety and more likely to be of interest to *malagueño* families who come to visit the multiplex cinema, but the supermarket (Mercadona, closed on Sundays and holidays) is worth knowing about. Not far from the railway station is the Larios Shopping Centre, which is the closest large shopping complex to the centre. It has a very large subterranean supermarket — 'Eroski', which may sound like the Greek god of love reincarnated as a Polish nobleman but is actually a name formed from the Basque words '*erosi*' (to buy) and '*toki*' (place). Larios Centro is also the place to come if you arrive in Málaga to find that you have neglected to pack your underwear or forgotten to bring a T-shirt and need to buy something cheap from Primark to tide you over. Everyday essentials — footwear, clothing, toiletries, groceries, electronics, repairs etc. — will be considerably cheaper in Larios Centro than in the *centro histórico*.

The presence of the railway and coach stations means that El Perchel is a fairly busy part of town, so there are plenty of places to eat and drink. The huge choice of bars and restaurants in the *centro histórico* might make it unlikely that you will want to make a special journey to El Perchel, but if you happen to be staying in the area, or wish to eat before catching a train, there is plenty of choice. Not far from the station is Los Valle Churros — one of the best and most charmingly traditional places to have breakfast in the whole of Málaga (see p. 189).

A little further south-west, about 15 minutes' walk from the railway station, is a bar that is well-known throughout Spain, even throughout Europe: the *Bar Mercado de Huelin* (Huelin Market Bar). The *barrio* of Huelin was one of the first working-class suburbs of Málaga, built by the part-English industrialist Eduardo Huelin Reissig in the 1870s. In the paternalistic fashion of the time, Huelin Reissig wanted to ensure that workers in his sugar processing plants could live in decent houses with separate bedrooms and kitchens, small patios, and enough space to keep chickens or pigs. The area was first called 'Palodú' (from *palo dulce*, sugar cane) but soon became known by the name of its founder, Huelin. A decade after the *barrio* was built, alas, Eduardo Huelin's business interests suffered a number of shocks and his factories were closed. Fortunately, most of his employees were taken on by the Larios company and so the Port Sunlight of Málaga survived.

Although some gentrification has taken place in the last decade or so, Huelin is still largely a working-class *barrio* of blue-collar workers, and when you walk into the Bar Mercado de Huelin at lunchtime, this is plain to see. There are no hipsters or businessmen in suits here, only locals — men in hi-vis gear on their lunch breaks, pensioners, young mothers and pre-school children. It's a typical Spanish bar, the sort that can be found in the suburbs of any Spanish city. It's clean and well cared for and the staff are extremely friendly, but the Formica tables and fruit machines make it clear that this is not a historic and picturesque hostelry in the *centro histórico*.

The lunch menu is simple and popular, and it is the lunchtime set menu that has made the name of this bar known well beyond the environs of Málaga. Like many bars in Spain, the Bar Mercado de Huelin offers a *menú del día* ('menu of the day', see p. 114f.) with a choice of three starters, three mains, dessert (or coffee), a drink (a glass of beer, wine, or water), and bread. Like many bars in Spain, it's a family-run establishment that's been trading for over 50 years. According to a Spanish saw, 'A good cook, when you give her a chicken, makes you a marvel,'[34] and that is the secret of this bar. Indeed, it is the secret of a great many Spanish bars.

The 'good cook' at the Bar Mercado de Huelin is Chiqui. Her sister Mame is the manager and her son Adrián the barman. The *menú* for the day depends upon what is available (and cheap) in the market (so there is never fish on a Monday). This sort of home-cooked *menú del día* is similar to that served in thousands of bars and restaurants all over Spain. What makes the Mercado de Huelin famous is the cost. Your three-course lunch, including a drink, would, until comparatively recently, have set you back an amazing €3, making it the cheapest lunch in the whole of Spain. It would not surprise me if it were the cheapest lunch in Western Europe. Perhaps it would not satisfy the sort of punter who likes to post photos of foams and emulsions on Instagram, but it is delicious, filling and wholesome. It also provides an economic conundrum to mull over during lunch. How can an unsubsidized bar which employs six people serve a tasty three course lunch (with a glass of wine) for less than the cost of a Prêt à Manger sandwich? Moreover, how can they manage this feat six days a week for many years? However, the impact of the COVID pandemic took its toll and a significant reduction in footfall meant that the cost of lunch had to increase. In 2022, the price increased to €5 — still unlikely to break the bank.

Mármoles
(including Perchel Norte)

Mármoles means 'marbles', though do not expect to find this reflected in the architecture. Like most of Málaga west of the Guadalmedina River, the buildings here are mainly 20th-century apartment blocks. The name of the *barrio* comes from the eponymous street — Calle Mármoles — which is itself derived from the marble bollards erected outside the Hermitage of Zamarrilla.

---

34   '*Una buena cocinera, que le das un pollo y te hace una maravilla.*'

The hermitage is an 18th-century wayside chapel on what was once the main road to Antequera, financed by public subscription in 1757. Those setting off on a journey would pray the rosary here (if they recited the Creed as well they would also gain an indulgence of 40 days). Like many churches in Málaga, it was badly damaged by rioters in 1931 and its treasured sculptures of Christ and the Blessed Virgin were destroyed. Now sensitively restored, it sits incongruously among modern blocks of flats and is home to a venerable Holy Week fraternity ('The Royal and Most Excellent Brotherhood of Our Holy Father Jesus of the Holy Scourging, Holy Christ of the Miracles, and Holy Mary Crowned with Bitterness').

The name 'Zamarrilla' is quite secular, however. It is the name of a plant found in southern Spain and North Africa (apparently known as 'Felty Germander' in English), but in the case of the chapel the name comes from the *nom de guerre* of a notorious 19th-century bandit called Cristóbal Ruiz Bermúdez from Igualeja, near Ronda. A number of versions of the legend are in circulation, but the basics are that in 1844, hunted by the Civil Guard, Zamarrilla hid beneath the skirts of the statue of the Virgin in the hermitage. The legend relates that, having evaded the guard, he pinned a white rose to the breast of the statue of Mary (made of wood, in the Spanish style) with his dagger. As he watched, the rose became blood-red and Zamarrilla realized that he had been saved by the redeeming blood of Christ. Like any penitent bandit of legend, he ended his days in a religious community, serving the poor.

The other reason why visitors to Málaga may venture into this *barrio* is for shopping. The nearest branches of Lidl and Aldi to the historic centre are located here, as is the department store El Corte Inglés — the Spanish equivalent of Selfridges (technically, the store is in El Perchel Norte). El Corte Inglés is not the cheapest place to shop, though it does have the virtue of selling almost everything. It even has a newsagent, tobacconist, travel agent and dispensing chemist. Unlike smaller shops, which often close for the siesta, it is open all day.

Spain's First Great Retail Giant

A couple of decades ago, most Brits would have struggled to name any Spanish consumer or financial brands beyond Harveys Bristol Cream. Now, it's a much easier task. The O2 and Virgin mobile networks are part-owned by the Spanish Telefónica group. If you once banked with the Abbey National or TSB, you are probably now with Santander or Sabadell. You can order a pint of San Miguel in your local pub, you probably know someone who drives a Seat Ibiza car, and your nearest city probably has a branch of Zara.

The first big name in Spanish retail, however, is one that has never expanded beyond Spain (save for two stores in Portugal). El Corte Inglés has been Spain's most recognisable high street brand since the days of Franco. While numerous department stores flourished in the UK, Spain only ever really had one, and it was all-conquering. Its smaller competitor, Galerías Preciados, went into receivership in 1995 and El Corte Inglés moved in, acquiring the company and its stores. Six years later, it bought the nine Spanish Marks and Spencer stores following the departure of the British retailer. El Corte Inglés now has 92 branches throughout Spain.

The name may mystify some visitors and it does not mean, as many assume, 'The English Court' (that would be '*La Corte Inglés*'). It means, rather, 'The English Cut' and reflects the

Spanish reverence for Savile Row tailoring. The name, however, is almost accidental, though serendipitous. The original 'El Corte Inglés' was a children's tailor on a street north of the Puerta del Sol in Madrid, founded in 1890. It was acquired in 1934 by César Rodriguez Gonzalez and his nephew Ramón Areces Rodriguez. At the age of 15, in 1920, Ramón had gone to Cuba and learned about the department store business at Almacenes El Encanto in Havana.

The vision of a huge department store came from Pepín Fernández, a cousin of César who, when he declined to hire Ramón for his own store, was persuaded to allow him to manage the El Corte Inglés store. Pepín would go on to found Galerías Preciados, while Ramón and César built up El Corte Inglés. Competition between the two companies, the flagship stores of which were located on the same Madrid street, Calle Preciados, was fierce and sparked a retail revolution in the 1950s and 1960s. Francoist Spain was not an economy in which entrepreneurship thrived, with the government setting production and retail quotas. Shops tended to be small and specialist, clustering together, with stationers on one street, milliners on another, and cobblers on a third, with an alleyway of bakeries in between. A shop, then, that sold stationery, hats, shoes and bread all on the same premises, was a thrilling novelty. Window displays, seasonal sales, loyalty cards, national advertising campaigns, 'own brand' labels, marketing slogans and air-conditioned stores were like something from the future.

At first, El Corte Inglés expanded more slowly than Galerías Preciados due to the policy, imposed by Ramón Areces, of dispensing with external financing as much as possible and expanding only through self-financing. On the other hand, Galerías Preciados was left exposed by its debts, which led to its eventual collapse and acquisition by El Corte Inglés, thus ending a sixty-year family rivalry.

Spaniards complain endlessly about El Corte Inglés's prices and the airs and graces of its sales staff, but they still shop there. In part, this is due to national pride. Primark may be cheaper, but El Corte Inglés is a venerable Spanish brand that accompanied Spaniards through the dreary days of the dictatorship. It may also be about the sort of aspiration and association with quality that lay behind the name of that children's tailor. To borrow the slogan of a well-known British department store, El Corte Inglés is 'reassuringly expensive'. But most of all, the store's popularity comes down to the enormous variety of goods that it sells. Whether you want a child's comic or a set of encyclopaedias, a box of cigars or a match to light them, a Cartier watch or a technician to mend it, a tub of ice cream or a freezer to store it in, El Corte Inglés has them all.

Since 1989, it's also been possible to plan your holiday through one of its 599 Viajes El Corte Inglés travel agencies. You can do your weekly shop at an out-of-town Hipercor hypermarket, or city centre Supercor, or you can buy chocolates and flowers at an Opencor shop on a garage forecourt. The Spanish equivalent of Homebase or B&Q is Bricor — also a division of El Corte Inglés, as is the high street fashion brand Sfera. One of the reasons for the historical popularity of El Corte Inglés was that it was one of the first stores to allow people to purchase goods on credit without having to provide a *nómina* (payslip). Nowadays, customers can spread the cost of purchases with a purchasing card administered by another division of the company, Financiera El Corte Inglés. Insurance, household energy and telecoms are offered by other subsidiaries.

El Corte Inglés is a family-owned private limited company not listed on Ibex, the Spanish stock exchange. It has risen to the top and maintained its position as a result of prudent investment decisions and cautious expansion, as well as its willingness to diversify its range of services. Having led a consumer revolution in the 1960s, it remains to be seen whether it will weather the current challenges that have precipitated the closure of former titans of retail like British Home Stores and Debenhams in the UK. The Las Ramblas branch in Barcelona closed in 2018, and I suspect that there will be further store closures, not least because most stores are enormous (the main Málaga store occupies an entire block and has nine floors), and 16 Spanish cities, including Málaga, have two or more stores (Madrid has twelve). The traditional in-store product range may change as departments like electronics and white goods increasingly move online, but the diverse portfolio of El Corte Inglés — exemplified most recently by its cyber currency arm Bitcor — means that the somewhat antiquated yet curiously reassuring green and white logo will remain a familiar sight for some years to come.

El Corte Inglés is not the cheapest place to shop, but it is reasonably priced by British standards (though clothing is relatively expensive), and the range and quality are impressive. There is a supermarket in the basement (useful if you're staying in an apartment) while the top floor houses 'Gourmet Experience' selling high-quality produce; one of nine such outlets nationally. If the basement *supermercado* is Sainsbury's, then Gourmet Experience is Selfridges Food Hall. It's worth remembering that for items like ham, cheese and tinned delicacies, El Corte Inglés is still cheaper than at the airport. Cured hard cheeses and Spanish ham (*jamón*) are well able to survive out of the fridge for a few hours on the aeroplane. It's also a good place to buy *rabitos* (chocolate dipped figs, which are one of the most delicious chocolates known to man and make an interesting gift), as well as boxes of Málaga raisins. Raisins are cheaper in municipal markets and *ultramarinos*, but if you want to give them as a gift, then you may want to take them home in something more presentable than a paper bag.

Gourmet Experience also boasts a number of food outlets, from pizza to Spanish *alta cocina*, from Vietnamese 'street' food to artisanal ice cream. There is a 'GastroBar' that serves excellent wines and where many of the products on sale in Gourmet Experience may be sampled. Also on the top floor is a roof terrace and a cocktail bar with panoramic views across Málaga. Gourmet Experience is open long after the main store closes, from 10 am until midnight daily, and until 2 am on Friday and Saturday. The top floor of a department store may not seem like the most atmospheric place to eat, but it is an affordable way of eating top-quality food ('*alta cocina*' in more ways than one).

La Trinidad

North of the Calle Mármoles is the *barrio* of La Trinidad, named after the 16th century Trinity Convent, once home to the Calced (shod) Trinitarian Friars (in contradistinction to the Discalced — or unshod — Trinitarian Friars) and dedicated to St Onuphrius (*Onofre*), a rather obscure 4th-century Egyptian saint popular in Spain. This *barrio* is now one of the most populous districts in Málaga. The city's main acute and maternity hospitals are located here. The convent is in a state of near-ruin having been seized by the state in 1835 and subsequently used as a military barracks. The nearby church dedicated to the Trinity is of 19th-century construction. In 2019, the Mayor of Málaga, Francisco de la Torre, floated the idea of restoring the ruined convent for use as Málaga's archaeological museum, but in 2023, work had still not begun.

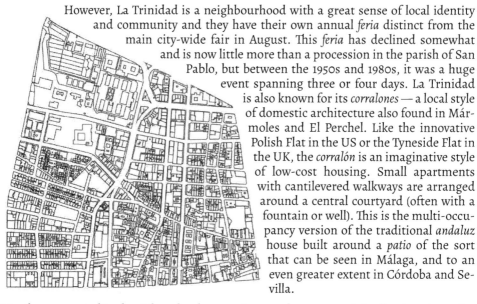

However, La Trinidad is a neighbourhood with a great sense of local identity and community and they have their own annual *feria* distinct from the main city-wide fair in August. This *feria* has declined somewhat and is now little more than a procession in the parish of San Pablo, but between the 1950s and 1980s, it was a huge event spanning three or four days. La Trinidad is also known for its *corralones* — a local style of domestic architecture also found in Mármoles and El Perchel. Like the innovative Polish Flat in the US or the Tyneside Flat in the UK, the *corralón* is an imaginative style of low-cost housing. Small apartments with cantilevered walkways are arranged around a central courtyard (often with a fountain or well). This is the multi-occupancy version of the traditional *andaluz* house built around a *patio* of the sort that can be seen in Málaga, and to an even greater extent in Córdoba and Sevilla.

Mostly constructed in the 18th and 19th centuries, *corralones* were originally a housing solution for poor manual workers and would have been cramped for families having only a couple of bedrooms and a kitchen/dining area opening onto the gallery walkway. The source of water was originally the well or common pumps in the *patio*, where the shared bathroom facilities were also located. Nowadays, *corralones* have mains water and bathrooms, but their reduced size means that they are only really suitable for single people or couples. However, the *ayuntamiento* has poured significant funding into restoration and refurbishment because they see *corralones* as one of the solutions to combating loneliness among the elderly and a way of prolonging their ability to live independently. The flats are small, meaning they are easy to care for, but the key to everything is the patio — a place where neighbours meet; a common project, filled with flowers and lovingly cared for (the city council awards annual prizes for the best kept). The *corralón* could have been swept aside as a relic of a different age, but thanks to a little imagination on the part of politicians, planners and health professionals, it has found a new purpose: enabling elderly people to live in their own homes, not exactly 'independently', but codependently, and without isolation.

Over 65% of Spaniards live in a flat or apartment, four times as many as in the UK. This preference began with the building boom of the 1950s and 1960s. But a much longer historical trajectory is in play too. Urban Spaniards have always lived on top of one another. Partly this is a reflection of their sociability, but it is also facilitated by their attitude towards public space. Perhaps they are happy to live in flats because they spend so much time out of them — taking a walk, meeting friends at a bar, or congregating in shared and public places in preference to private homes. Blocks of flats constructed around a shared space are hardly rare. Examples can be seen in most British cities, after all. The difference is that in Spain they seem to work, and people like them. They are high-density, but relatively low-rise in comparison to some postwar British tower blocks. The shared space, rather than being a wasteland of broken glass and abandoned shopping trolleys, is where families congregate as they emerge from their apartments after the siesta; adults chat, children play, and elderly people don their Sunday best to embark upon that Spanish social convention, the *paseo*.

Semana Popular de los Corralones

Every year in late May and/or early June, residents open their *corralones* to the public and the *ayuntamiento* (town hall) stages exhibitions and events. Generally, around 30 *patios* and *corralones* (there are 106 in Málaga altogether) take part in the annual '*Semana Popular de los Corralones*' (Popular Week of the Corralones) and the '*Barrio Abierto*' (Open Barrio) project. '*La alacena del Corralón*' (The Larder of the *Corralón*) events involve cookery demonstrations and are an opportunity to sample some genuinely home-cooked traditional dishes of Málaga. There are also flamenco concerts, choir recitals and other concerts staged by residents and local religious fraternities. It is not always easy to find information or a detailed programme, but your best bet is to ask at the *turismo* or to search online: bit.ly/CorralonesMLG. This should enable you to find the programme of the latest festival. The best way to visit the *corralones* is with a guided tour (enquire about tours from the *turismo*). Even if your Spanish is poor or non-existent it will only cost a few euros and you will have the reassurance of being part of a group and knowing that your presence is expected! The tour price also includes '*merienda*' (coffee and a snack) at one of the larger *corralones*.

North of the Centro Histórico
La Goleta, San Felipe Neri, El Molinillo & Capuchinos

The *barrios* north of the *centro histórico* are part of the '*Centro*' district but have more of a local (and down-at-heel) feel, with fewer shops and no branches of Zara or The Body Shop in sight. These *barrios* are more residential than the *centro histórico*, but none is short of interesting shops, beautiful churches, shady squares, pleasant bars and good quality restaurants. These were originally the suburbs of Nasrid Málaga, being outside the city walls. The enlargement of the city was constrained to the south by the sea, to the east by the Monte Gibralfaro and to the west by the river (back when it really was a river) so it most naturally expanded north. This, then, is 'old' Málaga — just not quite as old as the *centro histórico*.

La Goleta means 'the schooner' and the area takes its name from a maritime academy that once operated here. In Nasrid times, it was known as the suburb of Funtanalla (or Fontanilla) and was connected to the city proper via the Bab Al-Funtanalla, later Christianized as the Puerta de Granada. The gate itself was demolished in 1821 and the only reminder of it now is found in the name of a street (Calle Granada) that leads north from the Plaza de la Constitución. La Goleta is a somewhat down-at-heel part of town and although perfectly safe for visitors it is known to have had something of a problem in the past with *yonquis* (junkies) and *camellos* (drug dealers). Even so, it is hardly East Harlem and is not somewhere that should be avoided by tourists, any more than a visitor to London should avoid the cannabis-scented attractions of Camden Market.

As in other cities, 'cleaning up' local drug, crime and gang problems tends only to shift the problem into farther-flung suburbs. The densely populated *barrios* of La Palmilla and Los Asperones (in the far north and far west, respectively) both suffer from unusually high levels of crime. Both are failures of urban planning. La Palmilla was built in the 1950s and 1960s to accommodate families from El Perchel displaced by slum clearances. Los Asperones was built as a 'temporary' settlement in 1988 next to the municipal landfill. No tourist is ever likely to stray into either neighbourhood, I should add. Most *malagueños* have never been anywhere near them either which, of course, is part of the problem. Their plight remains invisible.

La Goleta has its fair share of churches and convents. The Convent of San José is still home to nuns who still support their life of cloistered prayer by making items used by churches in Málaga, such as linen and hosts (the 'wafers' used for Mass), so they would probably be surprised to learn that Wikipedia thinks they moved out years ago. Other convents have been converted for different uses. One of these is the Franciscan Friary of San Luis El Real (not St Louis IX of France, but his descendant St Louis, Bishop of Toulouse — the appellation *real* means that the convent enjoyed royal privileges). It was founded in 1489 and survived until its confiscation in 1836. Most of the extensive buildings were demolished and the land given over to public baths, housing and, at one time, a bullring. The convent has not disappeared from the architectural record entirely, however.

The name is recorded in the Plaza San Francisco (another of those Spanish squares created by the destruction of religious buildings). On the Calle Los Cristos ('the crucifixes') just to the north, there is a drinking fountain and water trough. This is one of dozens in Málaga that exist thanks to an initiative of a Bishop of Málaga, José Molina Lario, in 1785. The *fuente* (fountain) on Calle Los Cristos dates from 1789 and is attached to what was once the back wall of the convent of San Luis El Real. It was endowed by the Franciscan friars and there is a stone plaque commemorating the year and depicting the five wounds, or *stigmata*, of St Francis. One of the 15th-century buildings of the convent survives, although the interior is unrecognisable after its rather rococo makeover. In 1871 it became a *liceo* (lyceum); a cultural society of the sort that was becoming popular all over Europe at that time. It was while under the care of the *liceo* that the current decoration was undertaken, not least the painting of its ceiling and the addition of gilded columns and woodwork. The lobby is *neomudéjar* and leads into a small hall (the former choir) decorated in the rococo style, and the main hall (the former chapel) is neoclassical with an exuberant ceiling painting depicting the coronation of Dante. In the early twentieth century, it housed the Royal Music Conservatory named for Queen María Cristina, falling into disrepair when the conservatory built new premises in 1971. In 2009 it was acquired by the Unicaja Foundation, the corporate social responsibility arm of the Unicaja Bank, and reopened in 2014 as the Sala María Cristina: a chamber music concert hall.

The Convent of the Mercederías has also been converted to another use, although the Mercederian nuns only built their convent (or, to be strictly accurate, monastery) in the late nineteenth century, many decades after the confiscation. The sisters themselves remain in Málaga, though in reduced numbers and surviving thanks to overseas members (their Mother Superior in 2023 was from Guatemala). The church is still in use. Based on designs by Eduardo Strachan and completed after his death by Manuel Rivera Valentín, the exterior is painted *sangre de toro* (bull's blood — an understandably popular colour for Spanish buildings) in a restrained style that evokes the Romanesque. The interior, however, is pure nineteenth-century rococo. The attached buildings — the school and old novitiate quarters — have been made into a museum to display the works of the *malagueño* neo-expressionist painter Jorge Rando (b. 1941, see p. 252). The creation of the museum was a joint project of the Jorge Rando Foundation, the *ayuntamiento*, the Mercedarian Nuns, and the Diocese of Málaga, which is the owner of a famous work by Rando depicting the Passion of Christ.

Until the mid-twentieth century, La Goleta was the site of a women's prison (now a district police station) and, from 1896, a coal-fired power station — 'La Purificación'. Despite the economic activity of the port and a certain amount of light industry on the outskirts, it is difficult to get a sense, nowadays, of Málaga's industrial history. Though it never reached the levels of industrialization of port cities like Bilbao in the north or Algeciras in the Bay of Gibraltar, Málaga once hummed with the sounds and smells of processing and manufacturing. A traditional industry was sugar refining (the Marqués de Larios & Larios made his fortune from sugar before branching out into gin), but there was heavy industry too, including smelting works and foundries. In its heyday, La Purificación was the largest power station in Andalucía, despite its city centre location. The availability of power, as well as local ironworks, meant that Málaga was the first city in Andalucía to install an electric street lamp — *El Sonajero* ('the rattle') — in 1902. This was 23 years after Newcastle upon Tyne, the first city in the world to be lit by electricity, but in the Spanish context, it made Málaga a trailblazer. In 1959, *El Sonajero* was removed and 'donated' to the *barrio* of García Grana, north of the main railway station. The *ayuntamiento* was forced to rescue the 13-metre, four-tonne street lamp after an attempt was made to cut it down to sell for scrap. After a thorough restoration, it was returned to García Grana in 2012, finding a new location in the Plaza de la Biznaga. The power station that once supplied it with electricity is long gone, although the station chimney is still visible; a silent reminder of Málaga's industrial past.

East of La Goleta is the tiny *barrio* of San Felipe Neri, named after the parish church at its heart. The church is something of a curiosity in that it was founded neither by a monarch nor by a bishop, but by a nobleman, Antonio Tomás Guerrero Coronado & Zapata, Count of Buenavista, with its construction completed in 1730. Several religious orders expressed interest in occupying it. As Don Antonio had decided that it should be dedicated to Saint Philip Neri, the 16th-century Roman priest and so-called 'Second Apostle of Rome', he decided to accept the approach of the Congregation of the Oratory, seeing it as a sign from God. The Oratorian House was confiscated twice in the 19th century, first by the invading French and later by the Spanish government, and it was badly burned in 1931. It was only fully restored in 2011. Sadly, it is only open during mass, but it is a lovely church in a tasteful and restrained baroque style with a beautiful domed marble baldachin over the altar.

The *barrio* of San Felipe Neri is also home to the Gaona Institute (now officially called the Instituto Vicente Espinel) which was the first public high school in Málaga, inaugurated in 1846 (in the former Oratorian House of Studies), and the only one in existence in the province until 1928, when another was opened in Antequera. Aspiring to be a sort of mini-university, it featured a natural history museum, a botanical garden, a weather station, and a provincial library. Pablo Picasso studied here, as did other luminaries such as the poets Vicente Aleixandre and Emilio Prados, the philosopher José Ortega y Gasset and the crusading Republican lawyer, Victoria Kent. Also in the *barrio* is (for my money) Málaga's most unusual and fascinating museum, the Museo del Vidrio y Cristal (Glass and Crystal Museum), occupying a rather grand 18th-century former inn.

El Molinillo ('The Mill' — a number of mills were established here after the San Telmo aqueduct was completed) is north of La Goleta and San Felipe Neri, and visibly scruffier. Once a thriving local neighbourhood, residents now complain of being left behind as the historic centre grows and thrives. One can see its past glories in the architecture, like the impressive *neomudéjar* Salamanca Market. Tourism is not a panacea, but one may hope that it can play its part in rehabilitating this area without forcing out local residents. Hundreds of Airbnb lets are not what is needed, but tourists spending money wouldn't hurt and might help persuade the *ayuntamiento* to come up with a 'strategic plan' to rehabilitate the area. So if you are nearby (at the Jorge Rando museum, say), visit a local bar and have some lunch or a couple of drinks.

Capuchinos is another *barrio* that grew up after the *reconquista*, around the first convent of the Capuchin Franciscans in Málaga, erected on an extensive hill in the north-west of the old city, where previously a hermitage dedicated to Santa Brigida stood. In 1620, the city council granted the friars the land around the hermitage. In 1636, a new church was built, to which the convent was later added and the square and surrounding streets began to be laid out. During the plague of 1636 and 1637, it served as a hospital for the sick.

During the 19th and 20th centuries, Capuchinos was a lower and middle-class neighbourhood. According to the 1845 census, it seems that Calle Capuchinos was still a road on the northern edge of the city. The area was occupied by orchards and plots growing potatoes, vegetables and flowers, and by dairy farms (the district to the north of 'Centro' is still known as Ciudad Jardín — 'City Garden'). Little by little the orchards began to disappear, although some still remained at the beginning of the 20th century, coexisting with bakeries, pottery factories, tanneries, and other craft industries. A good way to explore these lesser-known (but still very close to the centre) *barrios* is to do one of the walking routes designed by the Holy Week Fraternities (see p. 411).

North-west of the Centro Histórico
La Merced, La Victoria, Lagunillas, Cristo de la Epidemia & El Ejido

La Merced is the *barrio* to the north-east of the *centro histórico* and takes its name from the church and priory of La Merced (dedicated to Our Lady of Mercy) founded by the Mercedarians — a Catholic mendicant order of friars (and later, nuns) founded in 1218 in Barcelona by St Pedro Nolasco. *Merced* is the Spanish word for 'mercy' and Spaniards have traditionally had great devotion to Our Lady of Mercy — the popularity of the name Mercedes attests to this. The full name of the order is 'The Royal, Celestial and Military Order of Our Lady of Mercy and the Redemption of Captives' and as its name suggests, it was founded to redeem Christians taken captive by the Islamic polities of North Africa and Southern Europe.

Recent years have seen the publication of a stream of books celebrating the culture of Southern Spain before 1492, for example María Rosa Menocal's *The Ornament of the World: How Muslims, Jews and Christians Created a Culture of Tolerance in Medieval Spain*. The gist of most of these books is that a flourishing, cosmopolitan and liberal culture fostered by Spain's Moorish rulers was senselessly destroyed by the fundamentalist Catholic forces of Fernando and Isabel who ushered in a period of oppression, typified above all by the Spanish Inquisition. From our twenty-first-century standpoint, we might find much to criticize about the Catholic Monarchs — the forced conversions and the expulsion of Jews to name just two — but it does not follow that the rulers they overthrew were paragons of enlightened virtue.

However attractive the idea of a lost paradise of *convivencia* (living together) under the Moors might be, the truth is probably closer to the '*coexistencia precaria*' suggested by Dario Fernández Morera in his book *The Myth of the Andalusian Paradise: Muslims, Christians, and Jews under Islamic Rule in Medieval Spain*. Muslims, Christians and Jews may indeed have coexisted at times, but it was unlikely to have amounted to a real 'living together'. These groups remained distinct in terms of religion, culture and, crucially, power. The dynamic of Moorish society was one of ruler and vassal at best, and this is borne out by the linguistic record. Spanish (*castellano*) is a language that evolved from Vulgar Latin and the first identifiable written records appeared as late as the ninth century, after the Moorish conquest of much of the peninsula. Had the conquered population and their Moorish rulers genuinely lived together then one might expect to see more of an Arabic influence in modern Spanish. In fact, although calculations vary by a percentage point in either direction, the number of words with an Arabic etymology in Spanish runs at about 7%, whereas over 30% of words in English — a Germanic language — have a French origin. Moreover, those Arabic-origin words overwhelmingly describe nouns relating to food ingredients, farming, commerce and administration (*i.e.* those areas of life where otherwise separate groups would have come into contact) rather than domestic and family life, art, poetry or philosophy.

Even in these areas of vocabulary, we tend to find noun pairs. Thus we have *óleo* and *aceite* for oil, *escorpión* and *alacrán* for scorpion, and *oliva* and *aceituna* for olive, reflecting Latin and Arabic roots respectively. The same thing occurs in English for Germanic and French roots of course: cow/beef, sheep/mutton, dove/pigeon, but these extend far beyond the realms of food and farming. In English we find buy and purchase, blossom and flower, weep and cry, deem and judge, forgive and pardon, grave and tomb, and thousands more. Indeed, many such etymologically distinct noun pairs are familiar from the British use of legal doublets, which suggest a conscious marrying of two linguistic traditions: law and order, kind and nature, goods and chattels, etc. Within 80 years of the Norman Conquest, the grammar of English had already changed significantly, and by the time of the emergence of Middle English not long after that, the assimilation of French vocabulary was more or less complete. The Moors ruled significant portions of Iberia for over 750 years, and many Christians and most Jews would have spoken at least some Arabic, yet it failed to make much of an impact upon either Spanish or Ladino (the version of Spanish spoken by Sephardic Jews).

Raiding parties from North Africa routinely captured slaves from the European coast of the Mediterranean, even penetrating as far as Eastern Europe. The *Saqaliba* or Slavs (from which the English word 'slave' ultimately comes) were highly prized, especially as concubines, and many ended up in Andalucía or were traded through *andaluz* ports. Furthermore, the Moors had taken Southern Iberia by conquest and according to Sharia Law, conquered people were the spoils of war. They could be made to serve as soldiers (like the Ottoman Mamluks), taken into sexual slavery or put to work. Those not enslaved, but unwilling to embrace Islam, were required to pay the *jizyah* — an annual tax levied upon non-Muslim subjects. Jews, who tended to be highly educated and skilled in administration, had it slightly better but were still placed under restrictions as *dhimmi* (non-Muslims).

Those who believe in the existence of a Moorish paradise of tolerance and enlightenment are not wholly mistaken, however. Andalucía was under Muslim rule for almost 800 years, and during this time there were times when various rulers ushered in periods of relaxed, open tolerance. However, in every case, these rulers were overthrown, either by the rulers of the neighbouring taifas or by invading forces from North Africa. In 1090, after 300 years of Muslim rule in Iberia, the Almoravid Sultan of Morocco invaded — ostensibly to assist the rulers of the Spanish taifas to repel the Christian invaders from the north. Whatever *convivencia* had hitherto been achieved was swept away by a far more fundamentalist regime. Less than a century later, in 1147, the Almoravid dynasty itself was judged to have 'gone native' and it fell to the even more hard-line Almohads.

Two biographical examples serve to show that the narrative of Moorish tolerance and *convivencia* is at best flawed, if not entirely fabricated. One of the greatest Jewish scholars of the medieval period, Moses Maimonides, was born in Córdoba in 1135 (or 1138, sources vary). He was not only a religious scholar, but a renowned philosopher, astronomer and physician, revered as a polymath in his own lifetime. However, the Almohad conquerors of Andalucía abolished *dhimmi* status in 1148, meaning that Christian and Jewish communities had a stark choice: conversion, slavery (and forced conversion), exile, or death. It seems that Maimonides' family at first feigned conversion, but as is so often the burden of their people, even supposedly converted Jews were made to wear a distinguishing badge. The family eventually chose exile, and the young Moses first moved around southern Spain before he was forced to flee to Fez in Morocco and thence to Egypt, where he died in 1204. The other great intellectual to fall foul of the Almohads was Maimonides' near contemporary Ibn Rushd, better known by the Latinized form of his name, Averroes. Also born in Córdoba, Ibn Rushd was the pre-eminent philosopher of Moorish Spain and his commentaries on Aristotle were eagerly imbibed by St Thomas Aquinas. In the works of Aquinas, St Paul was given the title 'The Apostle', St Augustine is 'the Doctor', and Aristotle, 'the Philosopher'. Ibn Rushd is honoured with the sobriquet 'The Commentator'. As a Muslim, erstwhile judge of the Sharia tribunals in both Sevilla and Córdoba, and court physician to the caliph, Ibn Rushd might have been expected to be protected, even celebrated, in his native city. However, Ibn Rushd's teachings were judged to be heretical and following a trial in Córdoba, his works were publicly burned and he was exiled; first to Lucena in Spain from whence he fled to Marrakesh. Historians have plausibly claimed that Ibn Rushd was a victim not of the caliph's displeasure but of the scheming of the *ulema* (or scholars) of the royal court. Either way, it is not a tale that fits the popular narrative of tolerant enlightenment.

For much of its time under Moorish rule, Andalucía was a region at war — martial, religious and intellectual — and this was part of the background against which the Mercedarian Order was founded. When they first came to Málaga in 1499, the friars were installed in a small hermitage near the port by a Christian noble called Alonso Fernández de Ribera. He had been gifted the chapel, and an impressive cross to place at its door, by the *Reyes Católicos* in gratitude for the part he had played in the siege of Málaga of 1487. However, the location proved insecure due to frequent raids by Berber pirates and the friars looked for land closer to the city walls.

The royal decree approving the erection of the new convent was issued by Queen Juana of Castilla in 1507 and this was ratified the following year in a bull of Pope Julius II. Receiving papal approval no doubt reassured the friars because Queen Juana was not well-known for her piety. The eldest surviving daughter of Fernando and Isabel (and elder sister of Catalina de Aragón, future Queen of England), Juana had nominally become Queen of Castilla upon her mother's death in 1504 as the crowns of Castilla and Aragón had been united only temporarily in marriage, so her father Fernando continued to occupy the throne of Aragón. By the time of his death, effective control of what would henceforth be the Kingdom of Spain was already in the hands of Juana's son, Carlos I. In popular legend, Juana is '*Juana la Loca*' (Joanna the Mad) — as beautiful as her mother Isabel was plain, and as irreligious as her mother was pious. Juana's supposed religious scepticism and lack of Christian devotion alarmed her mother, but Isabel was known as '*La Católica*' and one suspects that few would have come up to her standards. It is usually a lazy cliché to say of a person that he or she is 'more Catholic than the Pope', but it might have been said truthfully of Isabel (not least because the occupant of the papal throne at the time of the *reconquista* was the Spaniard Roderic Llançol i de Borja, better known as Alexander VI, 'the Borgia pope').

The tragic element of this story is that Juana's presumed madness led to her spending the last fifty years of her life effectively imprisoned in Tordesillas (near Valladolid); first on her father's orders, and then at the behest of her son, Carlos I. Many reasons have been proposed as the cause of Juana's '*locura*'. Clerics were quick to point to her lack of enthusiasm for the faith and her interest in Martin Luther, though if there were 'religious' reasons for her mental health problems perhaps they lay in the manner in which she was 'punished' for her perceived lack of piety — being suspended by ropes with heavy weights tied to her feet. Juana was a highly intelligent young woman, able to speak all four Spanish romance languages (Castilian, Galician-Portuguese, Leonese and Catalan) and proficient in French and Latin. Her other accomplishments were as much as anyone would expect of a nubile princess — dancing, drawing, needlework, horsemanship, singing, and mastery of the clavichord and guitar. She was clearly not — as many of her Habsburg descendants would tragically turn out actually to be — 'feeble minded'.

Modern historians suggest that Juana suffered from depression, a predisposition probably exacerbated or even awakened by episodes of post-partum depression after the births of her six children (Juana and her husband produced between them two future emperors and four future queens). She was also devoted to her husband, Felipe *El Hermoso* (Philip the Handsome) and never recovered from his death. Felipe had been proclaimed King of Castilla and, had he lived, Juana's life as queen may have been very different. Her father, Fernando, had been content for her to marry a Habsburg in order to strengthen an alliance with the Emperor because the heir to the throne was still her elder brother Juan (who, as it happened, was married to Felipe's sister, Margarita of Austria). Juan died in 1497, officially of tuberculosis, though the word on the street was that his demise was due to sexual exhaustion brought on by teenage enthusiasm for his new wife. The new heir became Isabel, the eldest daughter of Fernando and Isabel, who was Queen of Portugal. Alas, she died the following year, which upset Fernando's scheming. Juana as heir would mean a Habsburg on the Spanish throne, *jure uxoris*. With Felipe's death in 1506 at the age of 28, Juana fell victim first to the dynastic machinations of her father, and then of her son.

Whether Queen Juana's decree had legal force or not, the Mercedarians set about building a new church and priory in what is now the Plaza de La Merced (Our Lady of Mercy Square). At the time of the church's construction, it was known as the Plaza del Mercado (Market Square) and had been an open urban space associated with commerce during Moorish rule. There is a persistent legend that beneath the square lie the remains of another Roman theatre. The genesis of this rumour is possibly the Arabic name of the city gate nearby — 'Gate of the Theatre' (Bab Al-Mala'ab). One problem with this theory is that although there have been no archaeological excavations carried out, no evidence of any pre-Moorish structures has been found during periodic building work or the digging of foundations. The theory's proponents aver that this is due to the older 'theatre' of the Merced having been plundered for stone when the 'second' theatre was built, although that structure dates from the first century BC, and Roman rule in Hispania was only properly consolidated under Caesar Augustus after the Cantabrian Wars in 29 BC. More to the point, the 'second theatre' theory relies upon a somewhat loose translation of the Arabic word mala'ab (مَلعَب), which can mean 'theatre', but is just as likely to mean 'playground' or 'pleasure ground' — in other words, an open space where people go to enjoy themselves.

The first Mercedarian church was a modest, *neomudéjar* building about which very little is known because it was demolished and rebuilt in the late eighteenth century. The first church had been hurriedly built and was probably rather small, little more than a chapel. With the benefit of hindsight it is easy to forget that for all the triumphalism of the *reconquista*, no one in 1492 knew for sure that Moorish occupation was at an end in the Iberian Peninsula. Vienna was besieged by the Ottomans in 1529 and the last attempt to restore Islamic rule in Spain was finally put down in 1571 (the Rebellion of the Alpujarras). The Spanish coast, especially the *andaluz* coast, was constantly threatened by Berber pirates and it is estimated that from the 16th to the 19th century between 1 million and 1.5 million Europeans were captured and enslaved by North African corsairs.[35] The Mercedarians themselves had sought a site closer to the heart of the city precisely because they had been attacked by pirates, so it is hardly surprising that they felt time was of the essence in establishing themselves.

Construction of the second, larger, church of the Merced was begun in 1792 in a more austere, neoclassical style. Less than 40 years later the convent was seized by the state as part of the programme of confiscations inaugurated by Juan Álvarez Mendizábal during his tumultuous six-month tenure as Prime Minister of Spain. As a liberal, his fortunes had waxed and waned under King Fernando VII. The King had been restored to the Spanish throne with British help in 1813 (replacing 'King' José Bonaparte, who had deposed him) on condition that he accepted the liberal constitution of 1812. After a promising start, Fernando decided he preferred absolutism and reneged. Mendizábal went into exile. Fernando generally made a mess of being king, although his wife, María Cristina of the Two Sicilies was far more shrewd. María Cristina was Fernando's fourth wife and also his niece (she was also the second of his nieces to become his wife). Although she did not produce a son, as Fernando had presumably hoped, she proved jealous of her own daughters' place in the line of succession. As Fernando lay dying in 1833, María Cristina persuaded him to decree that Sallic Law be put aside (which, as a born-again absolutist, he was able to do). This meant that the heir would

---

35   Robert C. Davis, *Christian Slaves, Muslim Masters: White Slavery in the Mediterranean, the Barbary Coast and Italy, 1500–1800*, (Palgrave Macmillan, 2003)

be their three-year-old daughter Isabel (later Isabel II) and not Fernando's brother Don Carlos. On the one hand, this led to the Carlist Wars, whereas on the other it undoubtedly saved the institution of the Spanish monarchy for a few more decades.

Ruling as Regent following her husband's death, the 'Queen Governor' María Cristina realized that she needed the support of liberals, and so Mendizábal returned from exile. Although a liberal in many ways (he supported the abolition of tithes and supported the freedom of the press), he was also a Freemason in the continental anticlerical tradition and he made the confiscation of church property his priority. No doubt he would have enjoyed considerable public support had he limited himself to reclaiming land owned by the church, especially where it was unproductive or where the clergy extracted unjust rents; but evicting congregations of blameless religious sisters who ran schools and hospitals and prayed for the sick and the dead was not, as we might say nowadays, a 'good look', especially in a period before any functioning welfare state. If you get rid of the friars and nuns who are running schools, clinics and hospitals, taking in foundlings and orphans, and feeding the poor, who takes over their functions? Following his blitzkrieg upon ecclesiastical properties in 1836–1837, a more moderate government came to power and, once again, Mendizábal was forced into exile.

It is reasonable to ask why, if the Spanish Church was so powerful (too powerful, even), how was the confiscation of Church property allowed to succeed? The answer is partly to be found in the internal politics of the Catholic Church. What most people think of as 'the Church' is what is known as the 'secular Church' (oxymoronic as that may sound). The secular clergy are parish priests, under the bishop of a particular place. But many of the clergy, especially in a Catholic country like Spain are not 'secular' but 'religious'. This does not mean that they are more holy ('religious') than their secular colleagues, but simply that they are members of religious orders, like the (*e.g.* Benedictines, Franciscans, Mercedarians, etc.). A continual frustration for Catholic Bishops, who are appointed by the Pope to rule the Church in their local area, is that these 'religious' priests are only partially under their authority. They follow their own rules and owe ultimate obedience to the head of their own religious order, who may well reside in Madrid or even Rome.

A Bishop has authority regarding which priests he permits to celebrate mass or hear confessions in his diocese, but beyond that, he has little power over members of religious orders. The confiscation, therefore, whilst damaging the overall power of the Church, also offered an opportunity for bishops to consolidate their own power. The properties confiscated were overwhelmingly those of religious communities (of monks, nuns or friars), rather than ordinary parish churches. Had it been the latter, then Mendizábal would have had a popular insurrection on his hands. The dissolution of the monasteries in Britain followed a similar policy — Henry VIII did not confiscate ordinary parish churches, but rather priories, convents, monasteries and shrines associated with religious orders.

In 1836 the priory of the Mercedarians was confiscated and the friars evicted. The church was handed over to the Bishop of Málaga. The priory buildings were used as a military barracks until 1889 when it was demolished to make way for a municipal market. Houses were built on the former gardens, along with a theatre. The theatre was demolished in 1869 following a catastrophic fire, and the current Teatro Cervantes was opened near the site in 1870. The church remained open, now served by priests of the Diocese of Málaga rather than Mercedarian Friars. It soon fell into a poor state of repair and there were successive attempts to improve its physical state. In 1881 a new bell was hung — a significant moment because it had been cast in Málaga at the Ferrería Heredia, then one of the most modern ironworks in the world. The bell tower, however, had to be demolished after being damaged in the earthquake of 1884 and, seven years later the furnaces of the Heredia were extinguished when extortionate tariffs on British coal rendered their operation unprofitable. The bell is now on display in the Málaga Museum.

The church was badly damaged in the *quema de conventos* (the Burning of Convents) in 1931. The Second Spanish Republic had been declared on 14th April, following the overthrow of the *de facto* dictator General Miguel Primo de Rivera and the abdication of Alfonso XIII. The new Republican government was committed to a process of secularization but it was not quite as radical as many hoped, and it was certainly not considered sufficiently anti-clerical by many. Both the president, Niceto Alcalá-Zamora, and the Interior Minister, Miguel Maura, were practising Catholics (albeit of a liberal, secular-minded sort) and represented the republican Right as opposed to the radical Left. On 10th May, a church in Madrid was set on fire and others followed. As news of the fires in Madrid spread, so did the burning of ecclesiastical property and the cities affected were mainly in the south — Valencia, Alicante, Sevilla, Granada, Cádiz, Córdoba, Murcia and Málaga. Between 10th and 13th May 1931 around 100 churches were partially or totally destroyed, countless works of art were lost, cemeteries were desecrated and several people lost their lives.

Relative to its size, no city in Spain suffered as much destruction as Málaga, and much of its religious, cultural and artistic heritage was lost. The Republican Governor, Juan García Gómez-Caminero, did little to prevent the conflagrations and even ordered the Civil Guard to stand down. He sent a tersely ambiguous telegram to Madrid reporting, 'Burning of churches begun. Will continue tomorrow.' He was dismissed but soon promoted. In Madrid, 21 churches, convents and schools were damaged or destroyed. In Málaga, 21 churches and religious houses were set alight, and a further 22 attacked and looted, with damage spreading to private residences and businesses. Almost half of the destruction in the whole of Spain occurred in Málaga (which was then a quarter of the size of Madrid). In addition to bricks and mortar, many priceless works of art were lost forever. At least fourteen sculptures by the Baroque master Pedro de Mena (1638–1688) were damaged or lost, accounting for almost a third of his extant works. Even most Republicans were horrified by the violence and saw clearly how such wanton destruction undermined the liberal aims of the new Spanish Republic. In an article published in the Republican newspaper *El Sol* on 11 May, the action was condemned by Spain's foremost writers and philosophers, including Gregorio Marañón, José Ortega & Gasset, and Ramón Pérez de Ayala:

'Burning convents and churches shows neither true republican zeal nor progressive spirit, but rather a primitive or criminal fetishism that leads one both to adore material things and to destroy them.'

For the next 30 years, the church of the Merced stood in ruins, serving as a reminder of the excesses of anti-clerical zeal. Only in 1963 did the diocese of Málaga agree to its demolition to make way for housing. This volte-face almost certainly came about due to the discovery that a local priest, the infamous Hipólito Lucena Morales, had been using the ruined church for irreligious 'liturgies' celebrated with a community of women that had gathered around him. It had come to light that Father Hipólito's 'community' was less a spiritual support group and more a sex-centred cult. The church had ceased to be a reminder of hate-filled anti-clericalism. It had become a symbol of the excesses of the clergy that gave rise to anti-clericalism in the first place. Even so, the final destruction of one of Málaga's most emblematic churches is something still mourned in newspaper articles over 50 years later.

Málaga's history as an epicentre of radicalism is commemorated through a number of monuments and street names throughout the city. For a while in the 19th century, the Plaza de La Merced was renamed the Plaza Riego in honour of the Spanish general and liberal politician Rafael Riego who had been a staunch defender of the 1812 constitution (he had lived for a time in an apartment nearby). Since 1842 the plaza has been dominated by the obelisk monument to another opponent of the absolutism of Fernando VII: General José María Torrijos. After a period of exile in London, Torrijos returned to Spain in 1831 along with 60 men hoping to overthrow the king. He was caught and later executed on the San Andrés beach along with 48 of his fellow revolutionaries.

The most famous former resident of the Plaza de La Merced, however, is undoubtedly Pablo Picasso or, to call him by his baptismal name: *Pablo Diego José Francisco de Paula Juan Nepomuceno María de los Remedios Cipriano de la Santísima Trinidad Ruiz y Picasso*. He was born in a second-floor flat at number 36 in 1881, and shortly afterwards his family moved to the apartment next door. His father José Ruiz & Blasco, also an artist, was professor of drawing at the San Telmo Royal Academy of Fine Art and curator of the Art Museum in Málaga. After landing a more secure position at the Fine Art School in La Coruña, he moved there with the ten-year-old Pablo and the rest of the Ruiz & Picasso family. (Picasso later adopted his mother's surname, perhaps because Ruiz is the eleventh most popular surname in Spain.) Although the Ruiz & Picasso family returned for holidays in the 1890s, Pablo never returned as an adult. Thus, many people find it strange (or even desperate) that the city of Málaga makes such a fuss of its long-absent son.

Yet we know from Picasso's family that he continued to think of himself as a proud *malagueño* and often expressed the hope that a permanent exhibition of his works would one day open in Málaga. Although his first public exhibition was in La Coruña (when he was 13 years old), he pined for Málaga, as did his father, and he lamented that La Coruña was 'Neither Málaga, nor bulls. No friends, no nothing!'. One of Picasso's earliest known works, *La Picador Amarillo*, depicting a mounted bullfighter, was painted after attending a bullfight in the bullring of Málaga in 1890, shortly before his ninth birthday. He enjoyed playing '*toros & toreros*' (bulls and bullfighters) with other children in the square. His friends and family recall that he talked constantly of Málaga and remained convinced that Málaga wine was the secret of his productivity. On his deathbed in the South of France, he called his nephew close and gestured towards the window, saying, '¡Mira, allí, al sur, eśtá Málaga!' ('Look, there, to the south, is Málaga!'). Like many memories of childhood, Picasso's recollection of Málaga was perfect and idyllic — perhaps the reason that he never returned was the fear of discovering that the city was not as he remembered it.

He has returned now, though, in the form of a life-size sedentary bronze statue in the Plaza de La Merced. Tourists and Picasso pilgrims take turns sitting next to him on the marble bench to take selfies as Picasso looks across the square where he played as a child. In his left hand, he holds a sketchbook, in his right, a pencil. There is something fitting about his holding a pencil (and not a brush, as one might expect), for it was in Málaga that he was taught to draw by his father, and his first word is said to have been '*piz*' — a child's word for a *lápiz*: a pencil. His wish for a permanent exhibition has also been fulfilled by the inauguration of

93

the Picasso Museum in the Buenavista Palace, and the Birthplace Museum in the Plaza de La Merced. The museum's connection with Picasso runs far deeper than simply displaying some of his works in a city hoping to cash in on his fame. It is owned and operated by the Picasso family trust and 155 of the almost 300 works on display were eagerly donated by Picasso's relatives.

The oval-shaped *barrio* of El Ejido ('The Common') is occupied by university faculty buildings (though the new campus in Teatinos is where most of the university is now located). In Moorish times, the cattle that provided meat and milk to the city grazed here and later it was a clay-pit and the site of brickworks. The economic crisis suffered by the Province of Málaga as a result of the phylloxera infestation and the collapse of the steel industry at the end of the 19th century turned El Ejido into a shanty town where immigrants from rural areas settled. Because of the soft clay, many of these families dug caves into the hill and there were cave-dwellers in Málaga as recently as the 1950s. Unless you attend a concert at the Music Conservatory or the Cánovas Theatre, there is little of interest to the visitor here.

North-west of El Ejido is the *barrio* of Cristo del Epidemia. This area, with the same clay deposits as El Ejido, was the centre of brickmaking in the Moorish period. The *Reyes Católicos* set up their camp here, which is why the Basilica of Our Lady of Victory (*Nuestra Señora de la Victoria*) is now located here (confusingly, the Church of La Victoria is not technically in the *barrio* of La Victoria.) The name of the *barrio* comes from the area's association with a couple of miracles of deliverance from epidemics. The first and best-known story concerns a statue of Christ at the Column carved by José Micael y Alfaro (1595–1650) commissioned by a Holy Week brotherhood. However, when they moved their headquarters it was to a church that already had an image of the scourging of Christ, so the brotherhood's image ended up in private hands. In 1649, when Málaga had been suffering from plague for almost a year, the widow of the man who bought the sculpture decided to flee the city for the more salubrious countryside. As the cart bearing her belongings reached the Plaza de la Constitución, the oxen pulling it stopped and wouldn't budge. As a crowd gathered, someone spotted the statue of Christ. Some members of a local brotherhood took the sculpture and announced that this was 'the true doctor who would cure Málaga'. The plague was in retreat anyway, but people were quick to attribute the recovery to this miraculous image. Renamed '*El Cristo de la Salud*' (The Christ of Health), he was named co-patron of Málaga and placed in the basilica of Our Lady of Victory.

The precise origin of the name *Cristo del Epidemia* actually comes from a second miracle over 150 years later. This time the epidemic was yellow fever that had arrived on a French warship and quickly spread. The people of Málaga tried to gain access to the Basilica to pray to the *Cristo de la Salud*, but the churches were closed and public worship suspended. The *ayuntamiento* sought to satisfy the people by displaying the sculpture outside the town hall, but the populace demanded a full-blown procession. Numerous attempts to organize a procession were put down all over the city, with only El Perchel managing one at night after breaking into the Convent of San Andrés and taking the image of Our Lady of Mount Carmel.

Then, on 26 November 1804, an elderly nun from the Monastery of La Paz in the *barrio* of La Trinidad died, and in accordance with the public health measures in force, all of her clothing and personal effects were to be burned. Among her possessions was a crucifix and the man taking her belongings to the makeshift crematorium in El Ejido felt uneasy about burning a sacred image, so when his mule stopped to drink at the Tejeros Fountain (located where Calle Rodríguez de Berlanga now is), just south of the Basilica, he seized his opportunity to offload it. People came to pray and, without any access to their beloved images locked inside the locked-down churches, began to proclaim a miracle. The epidemic was officially declared over on 20 December, and the churches reopened. The simple, almost Naïve crucifix, piously saved from the flames in 1804, succumbed to the flames in the rioting of 1931.

Between Cristo de la Epidemia and La Merced are the small *barrios* of Lagunillas and La Victoria. Lagunillas means 'little lagoons' because clay extraction in this area would leave behind water-filled trenches. Another local name for this *barrio* is 'Cruz Verde' because the 'green Cross' (in the sense of living, rather than green-coloured) was the emblem of the Spanish Inquisition and this is where *autos de fe* were held. It is one of the more deprived *barrios* in 'Centro' but, like anywhere in Málaga, there are plenty of interesting little shops and good bars serving excellent food and drink, so do explore!

The *barrio* of La Victoria began to take shape after the *reconquista* when the land located between the old Plaza del Mercado (the current Plaza de La Merced) and the basilica and Royal Sanctuary of the Victory began to be occupied. In the mid-19th century, La Victoria became known as an area of petty bourgeoisie: dressmakers, owners of washing and ironing workshops, small merchants and administrative employees.

The church of San Lázaro, founded by the *Reyes Católicos* in 1491 was initially constructed as a chapel for the hospital that was also located there, intended to treat lepers. Today only the chapel remains since the rest of the facilities suffered extensive damage during the floods of 1628. It was restored under the direction of the architect Enrique Atencia in 1948. It is in the *neo-mudéjar* style, and the main altar is neo-baroque, in gilded wood, inlaid with mother of pearl originally made in the middle of the 18th century for the chapel of the San Estanislao de Kostka School in the neighbourhood of El Palo. The nearby Water Chapel, also known as the Rescue Chapel, the Corner Chapel or the 'Victoria Lighthouse', was commissioned in 1797 by some residents of Calle de la Victoria and designed by Marcos López and José Miranda.

Moverse (Getting Around Town)

📱 Apps & Websites

In my opinion, **moovitapp.com** is the most reliable urban mapping app available (at the time of publication at least). Its coverage and reach are wider than Google's and it generally seems to have the most up-to-date information (though for the app to report accurate information, the local transport companies need to ensure their online feeds are updated). If the ads bother you, it's possible to buy a one-month subscription. The very popular **citymapper.com** app recently added Málaga to its list of locations, but the coverage is not as extensive as Moovit's. It's fine for journeys in the city centre, but patchy beyond.

For travel outside city limits, the website **rome2rio.com** pretty reliably tells you your options to get from **A** to **B** anywhere in the world. However, beware! Sometimes the information updates lag, especially after timetable changes, and Spanish travel timetables vary seasonally, so **always** double-check the information with the transport provider. Even if their information is not up to date, **rome2rio** will usually be able to tell you who the bus providers are. The main operator in Andalucía is **ALSA** (**alsa.com** 🌐), closely followed by **Avanza** (**avanzabus.com** 📱). ALSA is a subsidiary of the UK company National Express, but don't let this put you off. ALSA buses are a very comfortable way to travel and, given that vast tracts of Spain have little railway infrastructure, they are used by 'normal' travellers, not just impecunious students.

busbud.com is also a useful site (and smartphone app) that will allow you to book and buy tickets for most bus journeys in Spain. However, it is usually slightly cheaper to use the ALSA or Avanza smartphone apps for booking tickets where possible. (See also p. 475)

renfe.com (**RRen**-fay) is the Spanish national railway site where you can plan journeys and buy tickets. There is also an app for e-tickets. Most tickets can be purchased on the UK **thetrainline.com** site, which has recently improved considerably and will often give you a wider choice of tickets than the official RENFE website, including options for the **ouigo** (**we**-go) and **iryo** (**eer**-yo) operators. All operators and agencies have smartphone apps that can be used for e-tickets. They also send you a confirmation email which includes links to add tickets to Google or Apple Wallet, or print conventionally.

🚌 Buses

If you are staying in the *centro histórico* or the *barrios* immediately surrounding it, then most of the main sights are easily walkable, but you may want to take the bus to get to and from the railway station, especially if you have luggage to carry. Other sights, such as the Russian and Automobile Museums, are an easy bus journey or rather a long walk. If you fancy a long walk along the beach (either east towards El Palo or south-west towards the Guadalhorce estuary) then taking a bus in one direction might be a good option to save time and shoe leather. Take a bus out and walk back, or walk until you get tired and take a bus back to the centre.

 Android iOS **EMT Málaga** is the local bus company's official app

City buses are operated by a company owned by the *ayuntamiento* called **EMT (Empresa Malagueña de Transportes)** and they are cheap and easy to use. Most of the main bus routes pass along the Alameda Principal or the Avenida de Manuel Agustín Heredia (Soho), which is convenient for the *centro histórico*. Many have stops near the María Zambrano Railway Station if you are staying west of the river. The 'Directions' feature of Google Maps (and of iOS Maps) is linked to the EMT database and gives reasonably accurate results (select 'Public Transport' to see options by bus, train and metro). A free app (EMT Málaga) is available for Android and iOS and provides real-time information and route planning; however, the Moovit app is probably easier to use for tourists who may not know the name of the place they are going to and would rather click a location on a map. The EMT website (**emtmalaga.es**) is in Spanish but offers a Google Translate option in the top-right-hand corner. It gives information about lines and timetables and also features a route planner. Most bus stops in the city centre have live bus information displayed, which is usually accurate to within a couple of minutes.

Bus etiquette is broadly similar to that in the UK, just remember to choose the stop on the correct side of the road for the direction in which you wish to travel! Spaniards often do not stand in a visible queue but they keep a careful mental tally of their own position in the order of travellers. In other words, although it may look like there is no queue, a sharp-eyed *abuelita* (granny) is likely to come out with some very unladylike language if you attempt to push in front of her when the bus arrives. If you want to find the end of the queue just ask someone '*¿Quién es el último?*' (kyenn ess el **ool**-teemoh — 'Who is the last?"). Buses are boarded from the front door, with the middle and rear doors for disembarkation only. Bus drivers are usually able to give change but will refuse notes larger than €5, so try to have coins or, at most, a €5 note. Contactless payments by debit card have become a feature since COVID, with 80% of the fleet already fitted with contactless payment points. A bit of language comes in handy. A phrasebook might advise you to ask for '*un billete sencillo, por favor*', but this will make you sound like an over-eager exchange student. Most people just hand over the money. You could say '*uno*' (**oo**-noh) if you like, though if you want more than one ticket for others in your party then say the number: *dos* (**doss**), *tres* (**tRRayss**), *cuatro* (**kwat-RRoh**), etc. Like English buses, there are seats for the elderly and disabled clearly indicated (mostly towards the front). A digital display shows the next stop (sometimes with a recorded voice announcement and even full-colour maps displayed on a screen) and you should press the 'next stop' button to request your stop. All buses in Málaga are air-conditioned, though older vehicles sometimes struggle to keep cool, especially when impatient passengers insist on opening the windows!

If you (and your travelling companions) are likely to take more than four or five journeys during your visit to Málaga then it is worth buying a ten-journey pre-paid ticket called a *tarjeta bus* (or *bonobús*), dramatically reducing the journey price (it is valid on any EMT bus journey except the Airport bus). You can purchase these from *estancos* (tobacconists) or *quioscos*

(newspaper kiosks). You can also buy them from the information desk on the main concourse of the María Zambrano railway station. A 10-journey ticket is sold as a plastic smart card and includes a deposit for the card itself — just ask for *tarjeta bus* (tar-**khay**-ta booss). If you need more journeys then you can top up the card at any *estanco* or *quiosco*. The minimum top-up amount is 10 journeys. A map of charging points can be viewed here: **bit.ly/MalagaBusCharge**, or scan the QR code. Remember that most *quioscos* and *estancos* close for the siesta (usually 1400–1800).

The *tarjeta bus* has other advantages over buying individual tickets. First, it can be used by multiple travellers. So if you are a couple or a family, you only need one card. To use the card on the bus, tap it against the reader — there is one next to the driver and another pair further inside the bus. If two or more people are travelling on the same ticket, wait for the beep and then tap again, for as many people as are travelling (you can 'tap in' up to 15 travellers providing you have sufficient journeys loaded on the card).

The second advantage is '*transbordo*' (transfer). If you catch another bus within an hour you still need to tap in, but your card will not be charged. This is standard on most bus transport in Spain. *Transbordo* only works when you change buses, so if you take the same number bus again, even in a different direction, you will be charged. So if you catch a bus from the centre to the railway station to buy a ticket or visit the Mercadona supermarket, just make sure you take a different number bus on your return journey and it will probably be free.

The card itself does not expire, though the loaded balance expires 365 days after purchase/top-up. However, these expired journeys will be reactivated at the next top-up. So if you have a card with 4 expired journeys, if you top up with 10 journeys, you will have a new balance of 14 journeys. As the *tarjeta bus* is not personalized, it is transferable, so you can give or lend it to someone you know who is going to be visiting Málaga.

A Bus ticket prices were substantially lowered in September 2022 as part of a government package of measures to help with the 'cost of living crisis', with the cost of ten bus journeys dropping again in 2023 to €4.20 (¢42 per journey). Although this is a temporary 'special offer', the previous price had been less than €10, still representing a significant saving on buying individual tickets. Thus, when the price inevitably increases again, the *tarjeta bus* will still be the cheapest way to travel around Málaga. Scan the QR code for the latest ticket prices. Children under the age of 3 travel free as long as they do not take up a seat.

Ⓜ Metro

It is unlikely that, as a visitor to Málaga, you will need to make much use of the **metromalaga.es**. The line going north-west from the metro station near the María Zambrano Railway Station (**El Perchel**) passes through residential suburbs and through areas where a number of the university faculties are located. The line going south-west might look handy for Málaga's southern beaches (like San Andrés) or attractions such as the Automobile Museum, but buses are usually more convenient from the city centre. The Metro (an urban light railway system, only a small section of which is underground) is a boon for workers who need to travel into the centre (or out to the Technology Park) every day, but visitors are unlikely to notice much of a time saving when compared with a bus for most journeys.

However, with the opening of the **Atarazanas** metro station on the Alameda Principal in 2023 (it was due to open in 2022, but there were delays), visitors may well make greater use of this option, just two stops from **El Perchel** station, which is located between the Bus and Train stations. Eventually, the city centre terminus is due to be located at the Plaza de la Marina, forming a combined Metro and bus subterranean interchange.

 The EMT Bus card cannot currently be used on the Metro, but single and multiple-journey tickets may be purchased from the machines at stations. The simplest ticket is called the **Billete Ocasional**, but if you are likely to make more than a couple of return journeys, then a better option is the **Tarjeta Monedero Metro de Málaga**. As long as there are sufficient funds loaded onto the card then several people can travel together on the same card. For the current ticket prices scan the QR code.

⚠ It might seem like the green **Tarjeta Monedero Consorcio de Transportes** (Málaga Transport Consortium prepaid card, which covers travel on intercity buses, urban buses, ◐ *Cercanías* trains and the Metro) is the best deal of all, but it isn't really suitable for visitors. Unlike London's Oyster card, which is a multi-network pre-paid card, the Consortium card is personalized, like a season ticket. It's only a money-saver if you need to make multiple journeys using the same combination of train, metro and bus on the same route.

🚗 Taxi

Taxis are a fair bit cheaper in Spain than in the UK, and much cheaper than in London. All tax-is have meters and prices are regulated by the *ayuntamiento*. For travelling around town, the standard rate (**in 2023**) was €0.88 per km on weekdays between 0600 and 2200. The higher rate (2200–0600, weekends, and holidays) was €1.07 per km. The standard minimum charge was €3.85, or €4.75 at the higher rate. The same rates apply to journeys to and from the air-port plus a €5.50 supplement (in 2023 the **average** taxi fare from/to the airport was around €28). Check the latest tariffs via the QR code or here: 🌐**free-now.com/es/tarifas-malaga**.

 Taxis are plentiful, so you are unlikely to wait long, wherever you are. To locate the official taxi ranks, consult the '**Callejero**' app (QR code left) and select '**Transporte**' and '**Paradas de Taxi**'. Uber and cabify now operate in Málaga. I would also recommend the PideTaxi App:

The pidetaxi.es app is very useful as it works right across Spain by linking with local ra-dio-taxi and minicab firms. This means that you can use it in Málaga, but also in most other Spanish towns and cities. Non-Spanish bank cards tend not to work with the app, though, so you will probably have to pay cash. Booking with PideTaxi is slightly cheaper than hailing a cab in the street or picking one up from a rank. It's also handy for when you need to pre-book a taxi at a particular time.

🚲 Bicycle

Málaga is a pretty bike-friendly city because, apart from the Monte Gibralfaro, it is mainly on the flat and is fairly compact. There are a few bicycle paths but the network remains, to say the least, 'incomplete'. There are more and more outlets that hire out bicycles, including one on Muelle Uno. Like almost every other city in Europe, Málaga until recently had its own public bicycle hire scheme (called MálagaBici). However, as it was administered by the *ayuntamiento* — by bureaucrats in other words — hiring a bicycle was a lengthy and bureaucratic palaver, involving a complex registration process and lots of form filling. For a tourist with only a couple of days in Málaga, it was totally impractical.

Unsurprisingly, that bicycle hire scheme has now been discontinued and the *ayuntamiento* has invited tenders from private companies to run similar schemes. Exactly which companies are hiring bikes in Málaga when you visit is anyone's guess, so keep your eyes peeled and use the QR codes displayed on hire bikes to visit the relevant app with terms and conditions.

 Serious cyclists who want a high-end road bike to explore the city or even something suitable for the mountains (or anyone wanting to make more than a short journey) should book ahead online with bike2malaga.com (prices are on a sliding scale, getting cheaper the longer the hire period). They also have road bikes, hybrids, e-bike hybrids and both hardtail and full-suspension mountain bikes for hire, all of which are very well maintained. Other bike hire companies in the centre of Málaga include malagabiketours.eu, biketoursmalaga.com, www.rentacarprima.com, labiciclettabikerent.com, alikindoi.org/en/home, and eatsleepcycle.com, all of which are excellent. However, new establishments are opening all the time, so search online for maximum options.

🚶 On Foot

Málaga is a compact city and very easy to explore on foot. Apart from the Botanical Gardens and Russian Museum, none of the main sights is really more than 20 minutes' walk from anywhere else. Another exception to this rule of thumb is the Castillo de Gibralfaro which is not far as the crow flies, but quite a steep climb.

If you are visiting Málaga during the summer (June-August) remember that walking is far more pleasant an activity in the shade than in the full glare of the sun. You'll notice that on a particular street, everyone walks on the same side — locals always choose the shady side! You may want to take a leaf out of the locals' book and make the most of the siesta. It will help you avoid the midday sun and also recharge your batteries so that you can feel refreshed for the evening — no bad thing in a city where most people sit down for dinner well after 9 pm. The siesta, by the way, doesn't necessarily mean a nap; it can just be a rest.

A lot of smaller bars close after lunch (around 4 pm) and reopen in the evening (around 7 pm). Big-name stores remain open all day, but many smaller establishments still close for the siesta. Municipal offices and banks always do. Most churches will also close after the lunchtime mass (which is often at 1 pm or 1.30 pm) and then open up again in the evening. If you don't want to skulk in your hotel room, then the afternoon is a good time to visit museums and galleries. They are often quieter at this time of day and because most are in old buildings, nice and cool.

Other options

Horse and carriage rides are popular throughout Andalucía. The owners and operators are mainly *gitanos* (Romani), many of whom go from town to town according to the cycle of local fairs. During the *feria*, the most stylish way to be seen at the *recinto ferial* or arrive at the bullring is by horse and '*carruaje*' and the carriage drivers will often be wearing full *andaluz* riding gear of high-waisted trousers, short jacket and wide-brimmed hat. But for the rest of the year most customers are tourists and Paco will be in his flat cap and cardigan. The prices are regulated by the *ayuntamiento* and represent good value. The horses are well cared for. The main 'carriage rank' is the Plaza de la Marina, at the city end of the Parque de Málaga.

Segways® can be hired from a number of outlets in Málaga including, for example, **Segway Málaga Experience** on Muelle Uno. Search **bit.ly/SegwaysMLG** for more options. Segways are only hired out as part of a tour (one guide for 8 people). Helmets and high-vis vests (provided) are required, so these tours are not for the self-conscious, or stylish.

🚌 Provincial Buses

Longer bus routes outside the city of Málaga are operated by the *Consorcio de Transporte Metropolitano del Área de Málaga* (Metropolitan Transport Consortium) with their distinctive green and cream livery. They have a user-friendly website in English: **bit.ly/ctmamalaga** (or scan QR code). It's possible to buy a travel card for these buses, but as pointed out above such cards are of little practical use for the visitor. They are designed for commuters who regularly use the same local bus, metro, and provincial bus on the same route.

☂ Tours

As in any city, there are plenty of walking tours on offer every day. Some of the pricier options (*e.g.* those organized by **welovemalaga.com**) start at €45 (2023 prices) for a walking tour, almost doubling if drinks and *tapas* are included, though they are highly rated. As is increasingly the case, many tours on offer are 'free' and last 1.5 or 2 hours. The guide is paid through tips at the end of the tour. You do not have to pay anything at all, but it would be fair to give what you think is reasonable for the length of the tour, taking into account the number of people sharing the same tour. Operators offering both free and paid tours include: '**Explore Málaga**', '**Málaga a Pie**' (Málaga On Foot), and '**Málaga Adventures**'. All the guides are officially registered and speak good English. The websites **freetour.com/malaga** and **guruwalk.com/malaga** list a variety of possibilities as well as the ability to book in advance online.

If you would rather cover a bit more ground by bike then **biketoursmalaga.com** offer very good value guided tours which last for 3 hours, bicycle hire included. Tours run every day, morning and afternoon, and it's possible to book online.

The *ayuntamiento* has a fascinating page on its website, with a map, for a self-guided route showing the main points of archaeological interest (from the Roman, Phoenician/Punic, and Moorish periods) in the old city at **rutasarqueologicas.malaga.eu**. The main site is in Spanish. However, the points of interest all have a link to '*más información*' (more information) and this is provided in Spanish and English. You could use this resource to guide you around a historical route, often past features you might not otherwise notice. A dozen of the more visitable locations are shown on the **MÁLAGA History** layer of the companion Google map (**bit.ly/MalagaMap**).

Málaga in 3 Days! The Top Ten of Everything

Any Google search (other search engines are available) will serve up no end of results for 'Málaga in a Day', 'Málaga in 3 Days', 'A Week in Málaga' etc. Some of these web pages are interesting and useful, written by bloggers who have actually visited and know the city well. Some are written by genuine, resident experts like Alejo Tomás (**malagatop.com**) or Joanna Styles (**guidetomalaga.com**). On the other hand, some of the guides that appear in national newspapers are imaginative works of fiction. One example (claiming to be an 'expert' guide, no less), recently published by a respected UK broadsheet, contains several howlers. The author mentions a shop on Calle Larios that had gone bust two years before the 'expert guide' was published. The reader is encouraged to 'stroll up the Gibralfaro mountain' to visit the Alcazaba (spoiler: the Alcazaba is at the **foot** of the Gibralfaro mountain.) The other suggestions aren't bad, but some are hardly typical of the city — a Moroccan tea shop, an Argentinian restaurant, and a spa experience. The article should perhaps have been titled, 'Some Information About Málaga That I Found On The Internet'.

The other problem with these 'What to Do in Málaga in X-Number-of Days' articles, handy though they may be, is that we are all different. Some travellers are culture vultures, keen to tick off the maximum number of museums and galleries. Others are foodies or *bons vivants*, focusing on bars and restaurants. For some, the pleasure is more ontological and about simply imbibing the *ambiente*. **You can pick up leaflets from the *turismo* that suggest itineraries for 1, 2 or 3-day stays, plus walks, nature routes, food routes, guides to particular neighbourhoods etc. They are all excellent: bit.ly/MalagaRoutes.** But for what it's worth, here's my list of two dozen things to do, see, eat and drink in the City of Málaga:

🐾 Get a good view

A good way to see the lie of the land is to take in the views from the Castillo de Gibralfaro (p. 238). Other locations with commanding views are the Alcazaba (p. 236), the roof (*cubiertas*) of the Cathedral (p. 263) and any one of the many rooftop bars in the city (p. 219).

🏛 Go to market

Spanish municipal markets are always interesting to visit (p. 222) with their beautiful displays of every kind of food imaginable. Try to buy something, though — a smoothie or some fruit, a handful of Málaga's famous almonds or raisins, or a few slices beautiful ham to take home with you.

🐚 Enjoy some *conchas finas*

The *concha fina* is a smooth shell clam eaten raw with lemon juice, salt and pepper and, ideally accompanied by a glass of dry white wine. They are served in dozens of bars, but perhaps the most atmospheric place to enjoy them is the Mercado Atarazanas (p. 225).

🏛 Discover Moorish Málaga

A visit to the Alcazaba (p. 236) is the most obvious way to get a feel for Málaga's Moorish past. Call into the Roman *Teatro* at the same time.

🎨 *Málaga Picassiana*

Pablo Picasso may not have returned to Málaga as an adult, but he never forgot it. You have a couple of options to immerse yourself in the life and work of the great artist: the large Museo Picasso (p. 245), or the more intimate Museo Casa Natal (birthplace museum, p. 246).

🍷 Drink a Very Old Tear

A popular local wine is called *lágrima trasañejo* ('very old tear'). The fortified wines of Málaga were once hugely popular in Britain but are little known these days. The iconic bar in which to sample a good range of wines from the barrel is Antigua Casa de Guardia (p. 197). To find out more about the winemaking of the region, pay the Museo del Vino a visit (p. 250).

🖼 Go to a Gallery

The most famous and high-profile art gallery is the Carmen Thyssen (p. 247), though if you'd prefer to see more contemporary art, try CAC Málaga (p. 249) or the Centre Pompidou (p. 244).

🥄 Breakfast like a *Malagueño*

As in the rest of Spain, *churros* are a popular morning snack, but in Málaga, they are called *tejeringos*. Plenty of cafés serve them, and few feel more authentic than Los Valle (p. 189).

☕ Stop for Coffee

If you didn't have one with your *tejeringos*, make sure you take the opportunity to order a coffee in the traditional fashion (p. 136). Enjoy your *mitad*, *semi largo*, or *sombra* and watch the world go by.

⛪ Go to Church

The Cathedral is well-known, but there are lots of other churches (p. 262ff.) in the city centre, all of which have interesting features. Most are open in the morning and early evening.

🍸 The *Hora del Vermú*

No one sits down for lunch until 2 pm, but the bars are full long before this with people enjoying an aperitif. *Vermú* (vermouth, often spelt '*vermut*' in the Catalan fashion) has enjoyed a resurgence in recent years, shrugging off its formerly fusty reputation. Most traditional bars serve *vermú* (p. 162).

🧑‍🤝‍🧑 And Now Lunch...

You will never be stuck for a lunch stop in Málaga, but a typically Spanish approach is to have a *menú del día* — a great value two or three-course set lunch, including a glass of wine or beer. A few are mentioned in the **Comer y Beber** section (p. 168ff.), but keep your eyes peeled when out and about because *menú del día* options usually appear on blackboards outside bars.

🍦 Have an Ice Cream

Rather than rounding off a meal with one of the rather dull puddings one tends to find on Spanish menus, go for ice cream. Try Casa Mira (p. 192) and enjoy your ice cream in the shadow of the Cathedral or on Calle Larios. Try a flavour that you won't find at home, like *cuajada con miel* (sheep milk curd with honey) or, of course, *Málaga* (wine and raisin).

✈ *Ir a tapear*

If you've had a decent lunch then enjoy Málaga's *tapas* scene in the evening. While you can easily enjoy an entire *tapas*-based meal in a single bar, the authentic way to do it is to go on a crawl (*raſtreo*), sampling the speciality of the house at each stop.

🏛 Take in a Museum

Málaga's largest museum, the Museo de Málaga (p. 248), is near the Alcazaba and has a huge variety of exhibits on display, including works of art. Also in the shadow of the Alcazaba is the more intimate Museo del Patrimonio Municipal (MUPAM, p. 248).

🚶 Enjoy the *Paseo*

The afternoon or early evening stroll (*paseo*) is a Spanish institution when sleepy parks and streets suddenly fill with people. The quayside (Muelle Uno and Muelle Dos) is an ideal place for a pre-dinner perambulation.

🌳 Go to the Park

You could begin your afternoon *paseo* by walking through the quiet and cool Parque de Málaga (p. 287), only metres from the hustle and bustle of the city centre but a real oasis of calm. Alternatively, take a bus to the stunning La Concepción Botanical Gardens (p. 286).

⛱ Go to the Beach

Málaga's 'city centre beach' is La Malagueta, just beyond the bullring, but you could hop on a bus to El Palo or Pedregalejo (p. 283), or walk along the Promenade 'Antonio Banderas' south-west of the railway station (p. 281) where the beaches are busy with local families.

🍢 Try an *Espeto*

Grilled skewers of sardines called '*espetos*' (eaten all year round, but at their juiciest, fattest best from July to September) are enjoyed all along the coast of the Province of Málaga, prepared in beach restaurants known as *chiringuitos* or *merenderos*. Every beach has at least one.

🏛 Visit a Small Museum

As well as the big crowd pullers, Málaga has plenty of small and unusual museums. Two of the most enjoyable are the Glass Museum (p. 250) and the Museo de Artes y Costumbres Populares (Museum of Popular Arts and Customs, p. 250).

🥄 Cool Down with a Cold *Tapa*

Málaga's signature salad (p. 128) is a cool and refreshing mix of cod, potato, orange and olives. If you're not a fish lover, look out for *ajoblanco* (p. 128), a delicious chilled almond soup.

🚶 Venture Beyond the Centre

There's plenty to keep you occupied in the historic centre of Málaga, but there is much to be said for wandering further afield and discovering that fabulous local bar before anyone else.

🍖 Try *Salchichón de Málaga*

Málaga's local sausage is not quite like any other salami you've tasted, being only very mildly cured. Bar Diamante is a good place to order it in a *pifuto* (little sandwich) (p. 114).

🐟 Eat *Boquerones*

Málaga is famous for its fresh anchovies, available from January to November. Enjoy them marinated in lemon or vinegar, or else quickly fried in crunchy batter. Eaten whole.

Gastronomía (Gastronomy)

The variety of establishments devoted to eating and drinking, and the nomenclature thereof, can be confusing. You can order breakfast in a bar, have a beer in a *cafetería*, a three-course meal in a *taberna*, and *tapas* in a *restaurante*; so the following attempt at a taxonomy may be enlightening. **⚠** Throughout this book I have used the terms 'lunch' and 'dinner' to mean, respectively, 'midday meal' and 'evening meal'.

Restaurante

Unsurprisingly, a restaurant, but in a world where McDonald's and The Ivy are both 'restaurants', this is not always a very instructive description. A place that calls itself a *restaurante* should, at least, have a dedicated dining area with table service. It may be the sort of place that has tablecloths and leather-bound menus, or it may be a bare-tables sort of place with the menu written on a blackboard. *Restaurantes*, as in the UK, come in all shapes and sizes. It is worth mentioning at this point that a menu, in Spain, is not a *menú* (meh-**noo**), but a *carta*. A *menú* is a set menu usually, but not always, offered only at lunchtime, Monday to Friday. Some *restaurantes* are filled with dining tables and only visited by people wishing to eat. These are the places that are only open for lunch and dinner. Other *restaurantes* are basically bars with a separate dining area called a *comedor*. Half the patrons might be sitting down for three courses while the rest are standing in the bar scoffing *tapas*.

Asador

An *asador* (ass-a-**dor**) is a *restaurante* specializing in roast meat, which in most of Spain tends to mean lamb or pork (an *asador* is the spit upon which meat is roasted). Most are quite traditional establishments, but not to be overlooked is the *asador de pollos*, or roast chicken shop. Until fairly recently, most home-cooking in Spain was done on the hob, so people would visit an *asador* to buy a roast chicken (or suckling lamb or pig). Most tourists ignore these roast chicken joints because they look, from the outside, like kebab shops, but they are experts at what they do, invariably serving utterly delicious, moist chickens with flavourful skin. Some have a couple of tables and offer meal deals (roast chicken with a side and a beer), but those in the Carretera de Cádiz *barrio* south-west of the railway station are great places to pick up a roast chicken to enjoy as a picnic in the Parque del Oeste or on the beach (see p. 233f.).

Mesón

Mesón (may-**sonn**) is a rather old-fashioned word for an inn. The *mesones* so-called tend to be rather traditional. Do not expect to encounter avocado foams or carrot gels; the vibe here is more Don Quixote than Ferran Adrià.

Parrilla

(pah-**RReel**-ya) The most common cooking techniques in Spain are the stove (soups, stews, *paellas*, etc.), the fryer (*croquetas*, chips, etc.) and the *parrilla* (everything else) — ovens are unusual outside traditional restaurants, although every bar has a '*microondas*' (microwave). *Parrilla* can mean a flat-top grill (more accurately known as a *plancha*), or it can mean a real grill over charcoal. Any restaurant or bar calling itself a *parrilla* is more likely to be cooking on the latter. But even the humble bar cook cooking on a flat top is likely to produce excellent results and Spanish chefs are master grill cooks. There is a reason why the flat top grill is known by the Spanish name '*plancha*' even in British kitchens.

Marisquería

Mariscos is the term used to refer to seafood, so a *marisquería* (mah-riskay-**RRee**-ah) is a fish and seafood restaurant. **A** Although fish are *pescados*, *pescaderías* are fishmongers, not dining establishments.

Chiringuito

A *chiringuito* (chee-reen-**ghee**-toh) is a typically *malagueño* establishment that combines the *marisquería* (seafood restaurant) and the *parrilla* (grill) outdoors. *Chiringuitos* (sometimes called *merenderos*) are near, or on, the beach. Some are little more than shacks with outside seating, while others are smart, air-conditioned restaurants with terraces. What they have in common are their barbecues, or charcoal grills, over which most of their fish dishes are prepared. The most typical and emblematic preparation is the *espeto* — an olive wood, cane or metal skewer of fresh sardines. Going to Málaga and not eating an *espeto* would be like going to Naples and not eating pizza.

The 'Father of the *Espeto*' was Miguel Martínez Soler, also known as '*Migué el de las sardinas*', who developed this method of cooking sardines around 1882. This fisherman from El Palo was probably not the first person to skewer sardines on a piece of olive wood and roast them over a fire on the sand, but he made the technique famous at his bar, La Gran Parada. He not only perfected a way of cooking the fish that intensifies its flavour and preserves its best properties, but his humble restaurant was the precursor of *chiringuitos* all along the Costa del Sol (the word *chiringuito* was borrowed from Cuba, where it refers to any beach bar).

Despite the simplicity of the method, achieving a good sardine *espeto* is not an easy task. The *espetero* (or *amoragador*) must be capable of withstanding the high temperatures of the barbecue even in the most intense summer months and needs to 'listen' to the cooking fish, keeping the embers at the right point to achieve a perfect end result — i.e. a crisp, blistered skin but a soft and juicy interior forming soft flakes. There are basic principles that every self-respecting *espetero* should know, such as ensuring that the spine of the sardine is always below the skewer, otherwise, when turning it over the meat of the loin would soften and fall. It is also important to control the intensity of the embers so that the fish neither remains raw nor becomes dry.

Taberna

A *taberna* (tab-**air**-nah) is a bar, but of a fairly traditional sort — the sort of place that if it were in Britain might have wood panelling and a log fire. Primarily drinking establishments, *tabernas* usually also serve good quality food: *tapas* and sharing plates at the very least, and sometimes full sit-down meals.

Pub

If a place is called a 'pub' (**poob**) it's a pretty safe bet that an attempt has been made to recreate an English (or an Irish) pub, or perhaps someone's idea of an English (or Irish) pub. This may mean that they have a range of beers beyond the standard offer of one sort of lager. It might be called a 'pub' because it is trying to be cool (Spaniards can be curiously Anglophile, conflating Englishness and 'style'), or it might just be slightly grungy. It could be a temple to the gin and tonic or throb to the beat of death metal. There is no way of knowing until you have a look inside. It is likely to be relatively expensive compared to more traditional bars.

Cafetería

A *cafetería* (kaf-ay-tay-**ree**-ah) could be a coffee-shop, a bar or a restaurant. It could be primarily a café selling coffee, cakes, ice cream and snacks, but unlike similar establishments in the UK, it will almost certainly have draught beer and a selection of wines and spirits. Alternatively it might just be a bar with a good kitchen and a reputation for good coffee and breakfasts. A pure coffee and cakes sort of place could also be called a *panadería*, *pastelería*, *confitería*, or just a *café*. The precise boundary between a *cafetería* and a bar is loose and fluid, but a *cafetería* always serves food. *Cafetería* is one of the few *castellano* words to have entered the English language (along with embargo, canyon, cargo, patio, bonanza, breeze, etc.).

Bar

Spain has a LOT of bars. In fact, it has more bars per capita than hospital beds — one bar for every 169 residents (in the UK there is one pub per 1,400 inhabitants). And that is just the average. The town of Mogán near Las Palmas on the island of Gran Canaria has a bar for every 43 people. This is not to say, however, that Spaniards are dipsomaniacs. They drink less alcohol than the Irish, the British or the French. Rather, it reflects the fact that Spanish bars (the plural form in *castellano* is '*bares*', pronounced **bar**-ess) are rarely simply 'boozers'. A bar can be many things, but it always has an actual bar across which drinks are sold. Some tiny bars serve very little apart from drinks, but even the most basic usually offers a few *tapas*. This is the baseline. Perhaps the most basic bar in Spain — a temple to Sherry in Madrid called La Venencia, serves no drinks except sherry (no beer, no wine, or soft drinks), but it does serve olives, *chorizo* and *mojama* (air-dried tuna). Almost every bar serves coffee and those that open in the morning will offer breakfast (coffee or freshly squeezed orange juice and toasted bread with tomato, ham, cheese, or jam). Some offer a *menú* at lunchtime. Some close between lunch and dinner, others are busy in the late afternoon with people enjoying *merienda*. In plenty of bars, it is possible to have a full meal. Some bars have a separate *comedor* which means that they are also *restaurantes*. Most bars are open until midnight (later on Friday and Saturday nights), whereas *cafeterías* tend to close a little earlier.

Spanish bars have at least two, and sometimes three, price categories — *terraza*, outside tables with waiter service; *mesa*, inside tables with waiter service (in some establishments called *sala*, especially where it is a separate dining room), and *barra*, where food and drink are ordered from and consumed at the bar (the word for the establishment is *bar*, but the word for the counter is *barra*). A *tapa* of cheese might cost you €2 at the *barra*, €3 at a *mesa*, and €4 on the *terraza*. *Restaurantes* that have seating inside and outside do not usually charge different rates.

The food offer of many bars changes according to the time of day, especially in bars known for serving good food. At lunchtime (usually from 1.30 or 2 pm) and during the evening meal service (generally from around 9 pm), you will find that many or all of their tables are set aside for customers eating meals. The normal way of indicating this is with tablecloths, even just paper ones. If you want to just have a drink and a *tapa*, then be prepared to stand! Of course, if you intend to order a meal, but you want to begin with some drinks and *tapas*, then that's fine, but bars do not want valuable tables to be occupied by someone nursing a €2 beer and a complimentary saucer of olives when they could have someone spending €18 on a bottle of wine and €20 on steak.

To get a sense of what sort of bar a particular bar is, go inside and have a look, taking your cue from the locals. Are people sitting at tables eating meals? Are they knocking back the *vino* and hoovering up the *tapas*? Or are they sipping little glasses of beer and picking daintily at dishes of olives? This is also a reliable way of choosing the right things to try, especially when it comes to *tapas*. Except in the tourist traps which have worked out that British tourists enjoy nothing more than a plate of chicken nuggets, it's rare to come across bad food in Spain. But every bar will have its own speciality and the locals know what it is. In one bar you might notice that a majority of customers are tucking into slices of *tortilla*. Around the corner, the *tortilla* is untouched because everyone is enjoying the fried *calamares* (squid).

Bodega/Vinoteca

A *bodega* is technically a wine merchant (derived from the Greek word for 'storehouse' — *apotheke* — which also gives us 'boutique'). Until comparatively recently most of the wine sold in Spain was 'bulk wine'. One would take empty bottles to the *bodega* to be filled from the barrel. *Bodegas* and *vinotecas* began offering customers samples of the wine on sale and over time became more like bars than shops. Nowadays almost all *bodegas* in the city are basically bars, but you should expect a decent choice of wines, beyond the house red, white and rosé (*tinto*, *blanco* and *rosado*). Out of town, '*bodega*' is the word used to describe a winery, where wine is made.

Cervecería

(ther-bay-thay-RRee-ah) Technically a brewery (of beer, *cerveza*) but these days often just a bar. Every bar serves draught beer, but a *cervecería* will usually serve more than one variety.

Bar de Copas

This is a cocktail bar and is principally about the consumption of spirits and cocktails. Beyond crisps, olives and nuts, do not expect much in the way of food (though some have great *tapas* menus). Beer is often bottled rather than draught and most customers will be drinking cocktails or spirits with mixers (like the ever-popular 'gin-tonic'). Most *bares de copas* do not open until the evening because cocktails and mixed drinks are a postprandial tipple in Spain, not *apéritifs*. Before a meal, Spaniards will drink beer, wine, sherry or *vermú* (vermouth).

Club

Not everything called a 'club' is a nightclub in the conventional sense. *Malagueño* nightclubs have names like 'Bambú' and 'Cabaret'. If you see an illuminated sign saying simply 'club' then the chances are that it may be what is known in Spain as a *'puticlub'* — a hostess bar or, less euphemistically, a brothel (the last of these in the *centro histórico* closed in 2016, but there are still one or two in the suburbs). The same goes for anything called a *güisquería*. If a *panadería* sells *pan* (bread) and a *cervecería* sells *cerveza* (beer), then one might assume that a *güisquería* sells *güisqui* (whisky), whereas it's just another name for a *puticlub*. Most brothels are out of town, operating out of roadside motels, but if you want to sample the conventional nightlife I would suggest searching online and studying the reviews rather than looking for 'club' signs! I am really no expert, but I am told that the best nightclubs are found in Torremolinos and Marbella, with Málaga's offering rather tame in comparison.

👀 Using TripAdvisor and Other Websites

Google > TripAdvisor: I'm increasingly of the opinion that TripAdvisor has had its day. It's primarily a travel and tourist app so only the most 'touristy' attractions rise to the top. TripAdvisor is unlikely to help you find a bar or restaurant off the tourist track. Google reviews are more reliable as they are more likely to come from locals. For example, one of my favourite spots for a bargain *menú del día* in Málaga is a small cafe near the Parque del Oeste. On Google, it has hundreds of recent reviews (all in Spanish) and a score of 4.5/5, which I would say is fair (though I'd give it 5). On TripAdvisor, it has three reviews (from 8 years ago), a score of 3.5, and is listed (incorrectly) as 'permanently closed'.

Price Categories: The classification of establishments by price is somewhat vague and comparative rather than quantitative. It makes sense not to provide specific prices because this avoids the need continually to update the listings and prevents users from being misled by out-of-date information. Another reason for vagueness is that review sites cannot easily compare like with like. A *tapas* bar may not have anything priced more than €9 on its *carta*, which would put it in the 'cheap eats' category, but that does not necessarily mean it is cheap (that all depends on the size and quality of the dishes).

Remember the online booking feature: Part of the fun of choosing a restaurant is wandering past, having a look at the menu, peering inside and deciding whether you like the cut of its jib. But if you already know where you want to eat, ⊕thefork.co.uk (or ⊕thefork.es) lists many of the restaurants that offer online reservations.

Read between the lines: A handful of bad reviews might set alarm bells ringing, but often they can say more about the diners than the dining establishment. I have seen bars marked down for a 'poor choice of beers' even though almost no bar in Spain has more than one beer on tap. Another common gripe is a 'poor selection of desserts'. Again, this is to be expected. Spain doesn't really do puddings, at least not beyond the usual, rather pedestrian, suspects. Of course, it works the other way around, too. Rave reviews and high scores may be waxing lyrical about burgers and pizza rather than the fresh, local cuisine that you are perhaps looking for.

What do Spaniards think? A sensible rule of thumb is to prioritize the opinions of Spanish reviewers. This is not because Spaniards are more discerning than other nationalities, or have superior palates, but because they have the context necessary to make a fair judgment. You or I might find a dish of *gambas al pil pil* enjoyable (or not), but a Spaniard will have years of experience eating that dish, in dozens of establishments, for comparison. One should, however, resist according Spanish reviews some kind of infallibility. Spaniards are equally able to leave a bad review about 'outrageous prices' simply because a beer cost ¢20 more than in their favourite local bar.

What does the manager say? Look to see whether the bar or restaurant replies to reviews, either to acknowledge a good review or to address an issue raised in a poor review. If the manager or owner is prepared to take the time to respond to plaudits and complaints then it probably suggests an establishment which takes feedback seriously, values its customers and is keen to raise its game where necessary.

Make your own contribution: If you had a great experience, leave a review. In fact, even if you had a poor meal, leave a review (Google is probably best these days). And if the owner invites you back to make amends, take them up on the offer and promise to post an honest review. Even the best places can have off-days and you might get a free drink or meal.

Have a look at the website: A slick, professionally produced website may look impressive, but not if the most recent menu (*carta*) was uploaded four years ago. On the other hand, plenty of smaller establishments have no website, but their Facebook/Meta or Instagram page is frequently updated with the latest *menú del día* and photos of dishes that they are proud of.

Making Bookings

An increasing number of venues have online booking forms on their own websites, **thefork**, and/or **Google**. This makes booking tables very easy. But don't be nervous about booking by email, even if you don't speak *castellano*. As long as your message is simple, Google Translate will probably do a reasonable job of rendering it in Spanish (and translating the reply into English). Obviously, if you are staying in a hotel (rather than a *hostal*), you can ask the concierge or front desk to make bookings for you.

Some great bars in Málaga do not take reservations because they are so small. Others only accept bookings by phone and in person. If you don't speak *castellano* there is no cause for fear. Bars and restaurants take bookings because they want your custom. There are no sniffy Parisian *maître d*'s in Málaga intent upon denying you a table because you used the '*tu*' not the '*vous*' form of the verb. Free movement of labour in the European Economic Area (at least before 2020) meant that a lot of younger people working in hospitality have worked in the UK and speak excellent English. But let's look at how you could book a table in *castellano*.

Do they speak English?

¿habla usted inglés? — **ab**-lah **oo**-sted **een-glayss** (the 'd' of 'usted' is similar to the 'dd' of 'eisteddfod')

If they answer in English, problem solved!

Ask for a reservation

There are politer (i.e. more grammatically complex) and more direct (i.e. grammatically simpler) ways of expressing oneself in *castellano* which largely hinge on the use of the subjunctive and the '*usted*' form of verbs. In English we have to 'confect' a form of 'polite' speech because we lack polite/

familiar forms of verbs and pronouns, so we end up saying things like, 'I wonder if I might book' or 'Would you be so kind as to...' Luckily, Spaniards are pretty direct, so keep it simple. Your question could begin in one of two ways:

¿puedo reservar? — **pway**-doh ray-sayr-**bar** — 'Can I reserve?'

¿Es posible reservar? — ess poh-**see**-blay ray-sayr-**bar** — 'Is it possible to reserve?'

What you want to reserve:

una mesa — **oo**-nah **may**-sah — 'a table'

For how many people:

para una persona — **pah**-rah **oo**nah pair-**soh**-na — 'one person'

para dos personas — **pah**-rah doss pair-**soh**-nass — 'two people'

3 — *tres* — trayss	5 — *cinco* — ᴛʜin-koh	7 — *siete* — **syay**-tay
4 — *cuatro* — **kwat**-ro	6 — *seis* — **say**-ees	8 — *ocho* — **och**-oh

Then at what time:

a las nueve — a lass **nway**-bay — at nine o'clock

a las nueve y media — a lass **nway**-bay ee **may**-dyah — at nine-thirty

(If you want to book a table for lunch at 1 o'clock or at 1.30 — both pretty early by Spanish standards — you'll need to use the singular article: *la una* or *la una y media*.)

If you need to specify the day, then the following vocabulary may be useful:

hoy — oi — today

esta noche — **ess**-tah **noh**-chay — this evening

mañana — man-**yah**-nah — tomorrow

mañana por la noche — man-**yah**-na por la **noh**-chay — tomorrow evening

The table on the next page may help ››

¿Puedo reservar una mesa para

1 una	persona	a la	1 una	hoy?
2 dos			2 dos	esta noche?
3 tres			3 tres	mañana?
4 cuatro			—	
5 cinco	personas	a las	7 siete	(y media) mañana por la noche?
6 seis			8 ocho	
7 siete			9 nueve	
8 ocho			10 diez	

✂ *Tapas,* ⊙ *Raciones* & 🍴 *Menús del Día*

A *tapa* is traditionally a morsel accompanying a drink, of the sort and size that might be given away free — a few olives, a handful of crisps, a single *croqueta*, a slice of ham on a small piece of dry or toasted bread. It is also a tradition that reputedly began in Andalucía, although it reaches its apotheosis in the elaborate *pintxos* of the Basque Country. Buy a beer in Granada and you'll be given a substantial *tapa* to go with it; buy a beer in Barcelona and you'll get nothing. There are still a handful of bars in Málaga that will give you a tiny bite to accompany your drink, but in most places, you will have to pay if you want more than a few olives. The word *tapa* comes from the verb *tapar* 'to cover', and it seems likely that *tapas* were originally placed on the tops of glasses to keep out the dust, flies, and other sources of contagion.

You will also see encounter the *ración*, which is a plate or large portion of *tapas*, enough for a few people to share. In between the *ración* and the *tapa* is the *media ración*. Many options on the *carta* will be available as *tapas, raciones* or *medias raciones*, priced accordingly. There is no hard and fast rule about the proportions, but the bigger the portion the better value and a rough rule of thumb is that a *tapa* is enough for one person, a *media ración* enough for two, and a *ración* is enough for 4 (though some *raciones*, like soups or stews, are intended to be a large portion for one). You should be able to work it out from the menu. A *ración* would be enough for a few people who just wanted something to pick at but might serve 2 people sharing it as a meal, or part of a meal.

Sometimes the *carta* specifies the number of items. For example, dishes like *croquetas* (croquettes) may indicate *unidad/unidades* (unit or units) abbreviated to 'Ud.' and 'Uds.' This can be a cause of confusion: on signs and instructions the polite form of the second person ('you') pronoun (*usted/ustedes*) is most commonly abbreviated as 'Vd./Vds.' (from the old Spanish '*vusted*', a contraction of '*vuestra merced*' - 'your mercy'), but 'Ud./Uds.' is also sometimes used. To confuse you still further, '*ostra (Ud.)*' means one oyster, but '*conchas finas (Ud.)*' usually means two clams.

Raciones always come with a little basket of bread and strangely moreish tiny breadsticks ('breadtwigs', perhaps?) called *picos*. Feel free to order something to share (*para compartir*) — this is how the Spaniards do it. But — and this is important advice — try to resist the temptation to order everything that you want to eat at once. Go with the flow. Order a drink and a *tapa* (or *media ración* if there are more than two of you). That will allow you to make a judgment about the quality of the food. You can then decide to order more or go elsewhere. In a conventional restaurant, you are required to predict that you will want to have the prawns to start and then the steak. When it comes to *tapas*, you order the prawns and then see how you feel once you've eaten them. In Spain, eating is not something to be rushed.

It is perhaps worth saying that the starter/main/dessert shape of the normal restaurant meal in the UK is only loosely adhered to in Spain. Even in restaurants, ordering something to share (*para compartir*) is normal and expected, especially for starters. A lot of restaurant menus (*cartas*) list main courses that are fairly obviously dishes for one person — a duck leg, a burger, a veal steak, etc. The temptation, then, is to assume that the dishes listed in the section before that are conventional 'starters'. '*Entradas*' may literally mean 'starters', but only in the poshest restaurants will they be starters suitable for one person. If there are four people in your party, order two dishes to start, to share. If there are two of you, order one. If you are on your own, order something light, like *gazpacho* or a *tapa*.

Some English translations of menus translate *ración* as 'plate', which should not be confused with *platos combinados* which are dishes meant for one person that combine items on the menu. Menus (that is, *cartas*) of bars that remain open during the day often have an all-day *carta* that will list:

Tapas — Raciones — Platos Combinados — Bocadillos

This allows smaller bars to maintain an impressive-looking menu. There will always be *jamón*, for example, and you can have it as a *tapa*, as a *ración* (or *media ración*), in a bread roll as a *bocadillo* (sandwich), or as a *plato combinado*, where it might come with fried eggs, salad and fried potatoes. *Platos combinados* are not terribly elegant or exciting, but they are good value and filling. They usually combine a main ingredient (eggs, fish, meat), a carbohydrate (potatoes or rice) and a salad or vegetable(s).

🥪 Los Sándwiches

The standard sandwich is the *bocadillo* (or the larger *bocata*); a filled roll or chunk of baguette that should comfortably fill the hand. *Montaditos* are technically tiny open sandwiches that one often sees displayed on bars (those sold by the chain '**100 Montaditos**', are actually tiny *bocadillos* or *bocaditos*). However, if you are in a supermarket, steer clear of anything called a sandwich because it is likely to be made with flabby white bread: tolerable when toasted, otherwise pretty dreadful. The Spanish equivalent of the *croque-monsieur* is the '*sándwich mixto*' — a cheese and ham toastie often with the addition of an egg and also available as a '*sándwich vegetal*'. However, a *sándwich vegetal* is not a vegetarian sandwich! It is usually a cheese and ham sandwich with the addition of lettuce and tomato.

In Málaga, however, the names of sandwiches are slightly different from the standard Spanish names. A *bocadito/mondatido* (tiny sandwich) is called a *pulga* ('flea') or *pulguita* ('little flea'), a *bocadillo* (standard-sized roll) is a *pitufo* ('smurf'), and the large *bocata* is a *viena* ('Vienna'). Just as it comes as a surprise to many people that the incredibly popular Italian bread '*ciabatta*' was invented in 1982, many *malagueños* assume that the *pitufo* has always been a feature of Málaga breakfast menus. In fact, its origin is fairly recent. The Mateo Luque bakery in El Perchel wanted to create a bread roll that would appeal to children — something smaller than the large *viena* that was popular at the time. The palm-sized roll was initially called a '*bollito de viena*' ('little Vienna bun'), but the baker Gonzalo León seized upon the idea of using cartoon characters from the TV show 'The Smurfs' (launched in Spain in 1983). Soon, the roll itself came to be called a 'smurf'.

Málaga's other local sandwich is the *campero* (meaning 'country style'). It probably dates from the 1950s, but it really took off — like the *pitufo* — in the 1980s. It is a large sandwich made in a '*mollete*' (a soft muffin typical of Antequera not unlike the stottie cake of the North East of England), originally containing lettuce, tomato, 'York' ham, cheese, mayonnaise, ketchup, and mustard, though nowadays one can choose from many other fillings. It is prepared like a *panino* on a grill and appropriately enough the restaurateur most widely credited with its invention, Miguel Berrocal Márquez, ran a burger bar on Calle Carretería called 'Los Panin-is'. Well-prepared from good ingredients it can be both tasty and extremely filling.

📖 El menú del día

A *menú*, as we have seen, is not a menu (that is a *carta*) but a set menu or *menú del día*: a daily lunch menu offered by many bars, cafés and even traditional restaurants. The provision of a *menú del día* used to be a legal requirement. In the 1960s, in a move that would warm the hearts of fans of the Big State, the government fixed not only the price but also the content of the *menú* itself, and even stipulated that there should be exactly 80 grams of bread. The *menú del día* is not the daily special. In some establishments, it may be anything but special and just what they want to offload because it was not sold yesterday. However, most *menús del día* are good value, filling and good quality.

You will get a *primer plato* (starter) — very often offering choices like *ensalada mixta*, *espaguetis* (spaghetti with tomato sauce), *sopa* (soup), or simply *verduras* (vegetables) — and a *segundo plato* (main course). The choices for these two courses will be listed on a blackboard or printed menu and there are usually 3 or 4 options for each. Mains will usually include one chicken/meat and one fish/seafood choice. The meat is often *ternera*, which is often translated as veal but is somewhat older and richer/darker than milk-fed veal. A drink (*bebida*) is generally included, as is bread (*pan*). If the menu says *vino*, that usually might mean a glass, but it can be a carafe or half a bottle in some restaurants. It also means that you can choose beer or water instead. Most *menús del día* give you the choice of either pudding or coffee (*postre o café*).

Before 2019, many commentators confidently declared that the days of the *menú del día* were numbered, or even over. However, the COVID pandemic and rising food costs have given the set lunch menu a second wind as restaurateurs have sought to tempt diners back. On the other hand, prices have jumped by a few euros. The average price of a *menú del día* across Spain was reckoned to be €13.50 in 2023. You can usually expect the price of the *menú* to be about the same as the average price of a main course from the *carta*, so in smarter restaurants you might pay over €20, but it will still be far cheaper than going *a la carta*. It's perfectly acceptable for children to share a *menú*, though some places offer a children's *menú*. Unlike the *carta*, a *menú* is usually only available at lunchtime (1 pm at the very earliest) Monday to Friday; and you should be able to see which bars and cafés are heaving with Spaniards (and thus a good bet). However, leave it too late and you won't be able to find a table in the better places. A few places offer a *menú* at weekends, though it will be more expensive.

⚑ Cómo comer (How to Eat)

You may be the sort of person who normally has a very light lunch with a main meal in the evening, in which case the *menú del día* is probably not going to suit you. But if you are prepared to go native, remember that Spanish lunches are long and unhurried and can be followed by a siesta and then a restorative *paseo*. The lunchtime *menú*, providing you find one that appeals, is the cheapest way to eat in the middle of the day, so give it a go if you can. It's also a very cost-effective way of eating in more expensive restaurants. Admittedly the choice at lunchtime will be more limited, but it is also likely to be less than half the price of eating at the same establishment in the evening.

Going to a restaurant in the evening can be a very pleasant experience, but I would recommend giving the pastime of *tapear* (to go for *tapas*, especially bar to bar) a shot too. It will not cost any more than going to a restaurant and enables one to try a greater variety of eateries and dishes. It is also a great way of finding the best places to eat. If a place has fantastic *tapas*, then in all likelihood their sit-down dining will be of good quality too. Start off in a promising-looking bar and order a *tapa* of something that sounds delicious, especially if you see people around you eating it. Move on somewhere else. The walk between the first and second bar will reanimate your appetite. Repeat until you are full, or ready for bed. If the mood takes you, have something more substantial in the form of a *ración* or *media ración*. This is a very enjoyable way of eating, especially in a pair or group. In a restaurant, you might order a steak and it would come with an accompaniment of some kind of potato and some vegetables. In a bar, from the *carta* of *tapas/raciones*, you rather order the elements you fancy separately. A plate of ham, some lamb chops, or *tortilla*; some *patatas*, a salad or griddled mushrooms. Order a couple of dishes to begin with and wait to see if you want more. You do not need to order everything in one go.

Do not ignore salad. Because of the freshness and quality of the ingredients — including the olive oil — salads are an especially delicious option in Spain. Even a very simple green or tomato salad is a very different creature when compared to its insipid and watery British equivalent. Salads can also be quite filling, frequently embellished with nuts, dried fruit, chicken, ham, cheese, seafood, asparagus, artichokes, or pickled spiralized carrot or beetroot (popular in Spain long before the recent spiralizing fad).

100 Montaditos

This is the name of a chain of sandwich shops named after the original branch opened on Instantilla Beach in Huelva in 2000 by the *sevillano* entrepreneur José María Fernández Capitán. In some ways, it is the Pret a Manger of Spain, though crossed with Poundland. The concept is simple — freshly made sandwiches (actually *bocaditos*, or *pulgas* as they would be called in Málaga) in one hundred combinations for around €1 each. The concept spread quickly and there are now 350 franchise outlets in Spain with a further 100 worldwide. A sign of its popularity is that even after the global economic downturn in 2008, 100 Montaditos continued to expand. On the original *carta* everything cost €1, although some options, like those on multigrain bread or with fillings like smoked salmon, now cost more, though on Sundays and Wednesdays, **everything** is €1. It is not a gourmet sandwich bar by any means, and neither does it pretend to be, but it is a very handy place for a cheap and tasty snack offering a massive amount of choice. You can pretty much have any sandwich you want (16 of the 100 are vegetarian, indicated with a green dot), all are made to order and come with a handful of crisps. Most branches are open from late morning until around 11 pm.

First, find your table (there is usually air-conditioned seating inside if the *terraza* is packed) and consult the menu. Since COVID this is mainly online, though sometimes there is a large version displayed at the counter.

Daily Menu in English ‘Euromania’ Menu (Sun & Wed)

Choose your sandwiches (there are also salads and hot snacks) and drinks, making a note of the numbers (a pad and bookie's pens used to be provided for this, but since COVID you'll need to rely on your memory or use your phone's note-taking app). You order at the counter. It can be a struggle to remember what the Spanish for 'one number 24 and two number 48s' is (in case you are wondering it is *'un número veinticuatro, y dos números cuarenta y ocho'* which would get you a *tortilla*, lettuce, tomato and mayonnaise sandwich and two chicken, green pepper and *alioli* sandwiches), so I would recommend assuming a pleading look and showing the server your phone screen. They will ask your name and take your money, handing you your receipt. When your order is ready your name will be announced over loudspeaker

—listen carefully, because unless your name happens to be Thomas or Anna, it will probably be pronounced in a decidedly *castellano* fashion. Go to the kitchen hatch and collect your food, remembering to take your receipt. If you get a seat outside, they may give you a pager that will beep, flash or vibrate when your order is ready.

My advice is to adopt an '*hispano*' form of your name for 100 Montaditos and places like it. For example, if you are called Stephen, Spaniards find the initial /**st**/ sound almost impossible and will say something like 'Esteepen' over the Tannoy. Just translate yourself into '*Esteban*' (ess-**tay**-ban) to make life simpler. There are five branches in the centre of Málaga:

- **María Zambrano Railway Station (upper floor, near the entrance to the cinema) 1200–2300**
- **Larios Shopping Centre 0930–2300**
- **Calle Sagasta 3 (near the Atarazanas Market) 0930–2300**
- **Calle Alcazabilla 12 (near the Roman Theatre) 1200–2300**
- **Muelle Uno 1200–0000**

Those branches that open before noon also serve a cheap *desayuno* (breakfast, available until noon or even later) — fresh coffee and either a *tostada* (usually with tomato *concassé* and *jamón serrano*) or a grilled croissant with butter and jam (*mantequilla y mermelada*) for a few euros. For a supplement, you can add a glass of freshly squeezed orange (where available). The Spanish pronunciation of croissant, by the way, is krua-**sann**.

🍴 *Especialidades*

As noted above, the *menú del día* is not the 'daily special'. The dishes of the day will be called *sugerencias del chef* — 'suggestions of the chef'. Some places also advertise their *especialidad(es) de la casa* — what the restaurant is known for, and unlikely to change seasonally.

🍃 Formal Dining

Tapas is a simple enough concept — simply order a few, and if you need more, order some more. If there's something you particularly enjoy, order a *ración* or a *media ración*. The *menú del día*, too, comes with built-in portion control. You order your '*primer plato*', '*segundo plato*' and then either '*postre*' or coffee. The finest of fine dining restaurants might offer tasting menus, which again make the ordering decisions for you. Simply sit in your chair and wait for the tiny but beautifully crafted courses to arrive.

Things get a little more complicated for foreign visitors when they sit down for an evening meal. Finding a perch in a bar and ordering *tapas* is easy. It's still *tapas*. Instead, I'm talking about sitting at a table (which you may even have booked), with place settings and waiter service. Spanish menus are not quite like British menus. Whether you are dining at The Ivy or a branch of Côte Brasserie, The Travellers Club or Bella Italia, you can navigate the menu in much the same way. You may want something to nibble first, like bread or olives, but then you would usually order a starter and a main, and a pudding if you feel like it. Job done. Spain, however, is different, partly because of the dominance of *tapas*-style eating.

There are two kinds of what I call 'tablecloth restaurants' (*i.e.* establishments with waiter service where you dine seated at a table, ordering from a menu) — the traditional *mesón* and the 'modern Spanish' restaurant. Let's look at the *mesón* type first.

Many of these are primarily *tapas* bars with a separate '*comedor*' (dining room) or primarily restaurants with a *tapas* bar area. A few are tiny bars where for lunch and dinner they put out a few paper tablecloths to indicate that these tables are for meals, not *tapas*. Try to book a table 'just for *tapas*' at 9 pm and you will be politely declined. If you book for dinner instead, when you are handed the *carta* you see that the first thirty items are... *tapas*! This is why it is confusing. But I shall try to explain.

'Tapa' has two meanings. The first, and original, meaning is a small appetizer or snack served to accompany a drink. So four people each enjoying a glass of wine accompanied by a handful of olives and a few *croquetas* are 'having *tapas*'. The second meaning of *tapa* refers to the size of the portion. If *jamón* is on the menu, it might come as a *tapa* (a couple of slices), a *media ración* (a side plate-sized portion) and a *ración* (a dinner plate-sized portion). So according to the latter sense, four people ordering many different *tapas*-sized dishes (and probably a *ración* or two) would be 'having dinner'.

After the list of *tapas*, the *cartas* of the *mesón* type restaurants are usually organized according to main ingredients, so there may be sections for egg, rice, fish and meat dishes. Ordering from such a *carta* is the more formal version of 'going for *tapas*'. You will need to decode the *carta* somewhat. Just because an item is at the top doesn't mean that it is a 'starter' (*e.g.* you may wish to order a *tapa* of cheese to enjoy at the end of the meal instead of a pudding). Quite a few of the dishes are designed to be shared. This is especially the case with salads, which are often huge. Some 'main' dishes are clearly intended for one person (a piece of fish, a steak, or a stew of some kind) while a big plate of prawns, ham or squid is usually shared.

The second kind of restaurant — the 'Modern Spanish' restaurant — can be a false friend because rather than a huge *carta* of *tapas* and *raciones*, it will look more familiar to British and American visitors. You will spot headings like '*Para empezar*' (To start) and '*Entrantes*' (Starters), followed by main courses — '*Pescados*' (Fish), '*Carnes*' (Meat), and maybe '*Arroces*' (Rice) or '*De cuchara*' ('by spoon', *i.e.* stews), and finally '*Dulces*' (Puddings). My advice is to begin with the main course, which is usually a single serving, not designed to be shared, and work backwards to the 'starters'. This is because the 'starters' are not necessarily a single serving. Sometimes the *carta* will be helpful and say '*Para compartir*' (To share), but often one has to infer this from price and description. Many foreigners have been caught out ordering what they thought were individual starters but were actually sharing plates, ending up completely stuffed with ham, cheese and salad long before the steak arrives. A selection of *croquetas* to share might be delicious, but one person ploughing through half a dozen would no doubt find them somewhat monotonous. If in doubt about a particular dish, ask the waiter, '*¿Es para una persona o para compartir?*' (ess para **oo**na pair-**so**-na, oh para kom-paRR-**teer**) — 'Is it for one person, or to share?'

¡¦¦ 🍽 *Cubiertos* (Cutlery) and *Pan* (Bread)

Despite the apparent informality of Spanish dining (*e.g.* courses arriving in the 'wrong' order or being brought all at once, the acceptability of sharing, etc.) and the fact that *tapas* are essentially finger-food, Spaniards can be curiously formal in their eating habits.

If something can be eaten using cutlery, then it is. It's customary to be handed a dinky knife and fork to eat a *tapa* that you would expect simply to be popped into the mouth in one go. The same miniature cutlery accompanies a morning croissant or pastry. Soup, lentils, beans etc. are eaten with a large dessert-spoon, whereas puddings of any size are usually eaten with a teaspoon. For some reason, fried eggs are always eaten with just a fork, though it is acceptable to use bread to help.

Bread is the third item of cutlery after a knife and fork. It is often used in place of a knife to move food onto a fork (though oddly it is never dipped in soup). *Menús del día* and even *raciones* always come with bread, and I sometimes wonder whether Spaniards would actually be able to eat at all if there were no bread on the table. Sometimes, it's not even very good bread (it can range from utterly delicious to slightly dry and powdery), but it is always there. The Spanish obsession with bread helps to explain their love of *picos* — tiny batons of dry bread like midget *grissini* that are consumed by the barrow-load in every Spanish bar, with everything. Even Chinese and Indian restaurants in Spain give you bread rolls. As in France, bread goes on the tablecloth or napkin, not the plate. You will be charged for bread — though usually only a euro or two in most establishments. Bread is part of the *cubierto* or 'cover charge', and whilst some Spaniards complain about what they see as creeping hidden charges, drinking and dining establishments in Spain have had a tough time of things ever since the financial crisis of 2008. Thousands of bars and restaurants closed (though nowhere near as many as experts predicted, or feared) and in 2012 the youth unemployment rate in Spain tipped over 55%. Ten years later, rising energy prices and significant increases in the cost of living exerted another squeeze. Unlike in many other countries, employers cannot rely on low wages being topped up by service charges or tips.

The *cubierto* is a subject of much debate. Although it literally means 'cover', it conventionally refers to the place setting, specifically the cutlery necessary to eat your meal. The confusion with 'cover charge' ('*cargo de entrada*') is because the cutlery and napkin is often delivered to your table along with the bread basket, for which a charge is made. In most establishments (*i.e.* those that do not state on their menu that a charge is made for bread as part of a set menu) you can tell the waiter or waitress that you don't want bread: '*No quiero/queremos pan, gracias,*' (I/we don't want bread, thanks — noh **kyai**-ro/kair-**ay**-moss pan, **grath**yass). And remember, you can also ask them to bring you some olive oil (for which you won't be charged) to mop up.

🛏 *Servilletas* (Napkins)

Nothing odd about napkins you might think, but Spaniards never, ever, eat without them, even at home. If you watch Spaniards eating you will notice them wiping their mouths after practically every mouthful. Even at the bar, where the napkins (*servilletas*) are made from curiously non-absorbent paper a little like Izal lavatory paper, they are used fastidiously and then immediately scrunched up and tossed on the floor. This means that a bar floor littered with discarded paper napkins (and prawn shells) is regarded as a sign of popularity and quality, rather than poor front-of-house cleanliness. There are tales of newly established bars sending waiters around to more popular rivals to 'steal' the litter from the floor.

🍾 *¡Que Aproveche!*

This phrase is formed from the verb *aprovechar* — to take advantage of, to make the most of. This is what your waiter will say when he gives you your food. But unlike *bon appétit* this is no unctuous bit of 'waiter-ese' but rather a widely used greeting. You'll hear it whether you have ordered a slice of omelette or a rich dish of stuffed guinea fowl, and even the Colombian *chico* who serves you in McDonald's will wish you the same, without a hint of irony. If you meet friends who are already eating, the correct greeting is *¡Que aproveche!* (or *¡Buen provecho!*) rather than *buenos días*.

🚶 *Sobremesa*

Spanish restaurants and bars just about manage to serve courses in order when it comes to the *menú del día*, otherwise it is anyone's guess what order the food will arrive in. Generally, it comes when it is ready. This is a good reason to order *tapas* and *raciones* in stages, or you are likely to find that your lamb chops will arrive before the fried peppers you had intended to enjoy as a starter. When eating in courses at 'tablecloth restaurants', though, Spaniards wait for everyone to be served their first course before anyone starts eating. Main courses are eaten as they arrive, without waiting. At the pudding, once again no one begins until all puddings have been served. After everyone has finished eating (after café, and over *digeſti-vos*) comes the *sobremesa* ('at the table') — the period of at least 20 minutes (it can sometimes be hours) sitting at the table that Spaniards evidently need in order to come to terms with the fact that the meal really is over. Once the *sobremesa* is concluded, it will almost be time for *tapas*, or at least *merienda*.

Observing Spaniards eating and drinking at such a leisurely pace, and mindful of their love of the siesta (even though only 16% of Spaniards still get to take one) and putting off until *mañana* what does not need to be done today, one might conclude that it is something of a miracle that the Spanish economy functions at all. It says more, in fact, about the importance attached to social eating and drinking in Spain. Productivity per hour is lower in Spain than in Germany but slightly higher than in the UK. Spaniards also work more hours per year than either the Germans or the British. Most Spaniards aspire to '*trabajar lo juſto*' — work just enough to live. What matters to most is not amassing a huge fortune, but the ability to share in the *disfrutar de la vida* (enjoyment of life).

✋ 'The Embarrassment'

When sharing *tapas* (or more often *raciones*), the last slice of ham, piece of cheese, olive, or whatever, is known as *la vergüenza* (bair-**gwen**-thah) — 'the embarrassment' or shame (the false friend '*embarazada*' is the state of being pregnant). Looking around a bar, you may notice that the last *tapa* is very often left to be cleared away, uneaten, everyone having been too polite even to ask *¿Quiere alguien la vergüenza?* ('Does anyone want the embarrassment?')

🚰 *Agua* (Water)

Sit-down meals are always accompanied by water, and in traditional bars (in summer) you may also receive a glass of water with a *tapa*, even though you have just ordered a beer. Water served with meals is almost always still and you might be offered a choice: *fría* (cold) or *del tiempo* ('of the season', *i.e.* ambient temperature). Spaniards often ask for both so that each diner can mix according to taste. The noun *agua* is an oddity, by the way — it is a feminine noun (most nouns ending in –a, –d, –z, and –ión are feminine, while masculine nouns tend to end in –o, –e, –ma, or a consonant other than –d or –z) which in the singular takes the masculine article **el** for reasons of euphony, so it is *el agua* but *las aguas*.

If you ask for *agua* or *un agua* as part of a drinks order then you are likely to be served bottled mineral water. There are thousands of springs in Spain and hundreds of brands of excellent quality mineral water. This is partly a consequence of the fact that until comparatively recently a great deal of tap water was not potable. If you want tap water, then ask for a glass (*vaso*) or jug (*jarra*) *de agua*. If you want to be sure, then tap water is *agua del grifo*. Since 2022, Spanish bars and restaurants have been required by law to offer tap water to customers. If you are walking around town and need a cold drink, then most bars will sell you a bottle of chilled water to take away. Ask for *agua fría para llevar* (**ag**-wah **free**-ya para yeh-**bar**).

As in France, sparkling water (*agua con gas*) is enjoyed as an aperitif (*aperitivo*) or as a soft drink rather than with food, particularly as it is often very fizzy, like Perrier. Lighter styles which pair well with food are the delicious Aigua Vilajuïga, Vichy Catalan, Mondariz, Sant

Aniol and Pineo brands. Aigua Vilajuïga and Vichy Catalan are both naturally carbonated.

🍴 *Propina* (The Tip)

Although leaving a tip is becoming more common in Spain, especially in restaurants, it is not quite universal. At the venerable Antigua Casa de Guardia bar in Málaga, they still ring a bell every time someone leaves a tip. Unlike in the UK and the USA where many of the people serving you will be students or young, part-time workers, most waiting and bar staff in Spain are full-time employees working in the service industry as a career and do not expect tips to top up their wages. You will probably notice how many barmen (and they usually are men) are middle-aged. Spain has a minimum wage calculated at a full-time monthly salary, rather than an hourly rate. Having said that, both minimum and average monthly income is lower than in the UK and lower than the EU average.

Having a service charge added to your bill is unusual, except in some high-end restaurants, although most customers will probably leave a tip in a restaurant (a 'tablecloth restaurant', that is). Even so, it will not be anything like the 12.5% (or 15%) that is customary in the UK. The American standard of 20% would be regarded as profligate. Hence, the normal practice is to round up or leave a few euros. Tipping is common in bars, but most customers will leave the 'shrapnel' of their change. Your change is always given to you on a small plastic or metal saucer. Let's say that you ordered a coffee and a beer and your bill comes to €3.20, so you hand over a €5 note and your change is €1.80 given as €1/50¢/20¢/10¢ coins. Most Spaniards would probably leave nothing, and those that do tip might only leave 10¢ or 20¢. Leaving 50¢ or €1 would seem like burning money. The same goes for taxis. Rounding up to leave a bit of loose change is appreciated, but tips are not expected. (As we saw above, however, many walking tour guides offer 'free' tours and rely on 'tips' for their daily wage.)

🍴 Tapas Bar Favourites

In Spain, some dishes are ubiquitous. There can hardly be a bar in the country that does not prepare *tortilla española* every day, just as every bar has a *jamón* (cured leg ham) on the go, with others hanging above in readiness for the knife. The *tapas* listed below are likely to be found in almost every bar in Spain:

Croquetas (kro-**kay**-tass) — Crumbed, fried ovoids of flavoured *béchamel* — the main types are cheese, ham and cod (*bacalao*).

Queso (**kay**-soh) — Cheese. It's often *manchego*, a sharp and tasty ewe's milk cheese from La Mancha, but there are many other kinds. The soft and blue varieties are mainly found in the north (where most of the dairy herds are), getting harder as one moves south.

Jamón (кнam-**on**) — Without doubt the finest ham in the world, and very possibly the finest single food item in the world. Smell it, touch it, rub it on your lips and then taste it. Garnet red flesh and rich, yellow fat, three years in the making. British boiled or baked ham (known as *Jamón York* in Spain) can be a fairly insipid product, but *jamón* is rich, unctuous and deeply 'piggy'. The truth is that even the cheap stuff is pretty good, but the very best is *Jamón Ibérico de Bellota* (*bellota* means 'acorn', the main diet of the fattening pigs), often called *pata negra* (black foot). In a bog-standard *bocadillo* you will be given *serrano*, fed on a mix of cereals, but still free-range and delicious.

Bacalao — (bakka-**laow**) Dried salt cod, and tastier than one might think. It is often found in *croquetas*, but as a dish on its own it might be an acquired taste (or texture).

121

Gambas — (**gam**-bass) The most common name by which prawns are known. Prepared in a variety of ways, one of the most popular is *gambas al ajillo* (sizzling in olive oil with garlic).

Mini hamburguesas (**mee**-nee am-bor-**gay**-sass) — These sound faddish, but they are a popular *tapa* and (when well-made) are subtle and delicious. Expect a beautifully tender, well-seasoned veal burger in a tiny soft bun, perhaps with *confit* onions and cheese.

Albóndigas (al-**bonn**-dee-gass) — Small meatballs, usually made from pork and served in a tomato sauce. They take their name from the Arabic *al-bunduq*, meaning 'hazelnut'.

Aceitunas (a-THay-**toon**-ass) — Olives. Mainly green, sometimes stuffed, but always fresher and juicier than anything available in the UK (even those from Waitrose).

Boquerones (bo-kay-**rown**-ayss) — Fresh, white, and grilled or fried; or marinaded in lemon (or wine vinegar) and olive oil (the dark, salted and cured anchovies we are more used to are called *anchoas*). There cannot be a bar in Spain that does not serve *boquerones*, but the natives of Málaga are convinced theirs are the best of the best. The nickname of the local football team, Málaga Club de Fútbol, is '*Los Boquerones*'.

Calamares (calah-**mar**-ayss) — Squid, of course; but often called *rabas* (served in strips, not rings) on *tapas* menus, like battered squid chips with masses of lemon and salt. *Calamares del campo* are not squid, but battered onion rings.

Mejillones rellenos (meh-KHil-**yoh**-naiss rell-**yay**-noss) — Stuffed mussels; taken from their shells, and mixed with a piquant tomato sauce, then put back into the shell and gratinéed with *béchamel* and breadcrumbs. Sometimes called *tigres* because of the (very) slightly spicy sauce.

Patatas bravas (pah-**tah**-tass **brah**-vass) — Fried potato served with a spicy tomato sauce. What passes as 'spicy' (*picante*) in Spain is likely to be fairly mild to English tastes, with the 'heat' coming from paprika (*pimentón*) rather than chilli.

Pimientos de Padrón (pim-**yen**-toss day pad-**ron**) — Mild, green, thumb-sized chilli peppers (sometimes dusted with cornmeal) and either quickly fried or chargrilled. Guidebooks like to tell you that one in every couple of dozen is tongue-scorchingly hot, but I have eaten hundreds over the years and never really encountered a hot one, though it is true some are more peppery than others. Padrón is a small town near Santiago de Compostela, famous for growing these peppers.

Tortilla (tor-**teel**-ya) — Good old Spanish omelette: potatoes and onions cooked very slowly in oil as for a confit, before the addition of eggs. Sometimes *jamón*, *chorizo*, etc. is added.

Paella (pah-**ail**-ya) — Not usually to be recommended outside Valencia or a *valenciano* restaurant. Authentic paella should have beans, rabbit and snails (*caracoles*) but it is more common to encounter seafood paella. Delicious when it is properly prepared, look around to see whether locals are ordering it.

Ensaladilla rusa (en-salla-**deel**-ya RROO-sah) — 'Little Russian Salad'. This embellished potato salad is very popular in Spain and is always based on diced, boiled potatoes, vegetables and mayonnaise. The Spanish version usually contains tuna, prawns or surimi (crab sticks). Since 2022, it has been renamed *ensaladilla ucraniana* in most establishments, for obvious reasons.

Morcilla (mor-**theel**-ya) — Spanish black pudding, of which there are many regional varieties. Most contain paprika and are more highly seasoned than the English kind. In Andalucía, cumin, onions, rice or pine nuts are often added. It is a popular sandwich filling.

Chorizo (choh-**RRee**-thoh) — A pork sausage flavoured with paprika. Like *morcilla*, there are dozens of varieties and it features in many dishes as a way of adding paprika and pork fat. The juicy, fat, soft *chorizos* are added to cooked dishes, whereas the drier, firmer *chorizos* are sliced and eaten like salami. You might occasionally see a particular dish, such as *fabada* — a bean stew — described as '*con todos los sacramentos*' (with all the sacraments). This means 'with all the trimmings', in other words: *morcilla*, *chorizo* and *tocino* (*pancetta*).

The pronunciation of the name of this cured sausage is a frequent obsession of foreign visitors to Spain, who like to show their mastery of *castellano* by making fun of those who pronounce it 'kuritzoh' or 'choritzoh'. The Spanish pronunciation is either 'choh-**RRee**-thoh' or 'choh-**RRee**-soh', but remember: **ch** as in church, with the **r** rolled, **i** as in police (not as in pin), and both **o** sounds as in stop, not as in stone (people often forget about the vowels!).

Empanadillas (em-pa-na-**deel**-yas) — small, hot-water-crust pasties (meat, fish, vegetables or cheese, with tuna being the most popular filling).

Garbanzos con espinacas (gar-**ban**-thos kon ess-pin-**ack**-ass) — chickpeas stewed with spinach, garlic, spices and vinegar. This dish is often ignored by foreigners because it sounds somewhat dull. It's not.

Huevos rotos (**way**-voss **roh**-toss) — literally 'broken eggs': a dish of fried potato and usually one other ingredient (ham, sausage, *morcilla*, baby eels, etc.) topped with a fried egg or two. It sounds naff, but in reality, it is a surprisingly refined and delicious dish.

Tortillitas de camarones (tor-teel-**yee**-tass day kah-mar-**oh**-nayss) — Everyone has a favourite *tapa*, and this is one of mine. Halfway between a pancake and a fritter, these are made from chickpea flour batter enriched with garlic, parsley and tiny shrimp, fried into crisp, lacy galettes. They are a speciality of Cádiz, but are popular throughout Andalucía. Some are made with finely diced prawns, but those made with the tiniest imaginable brown shrimp are the real deal. Nothing accompanies a cold beer quite like *tortillitas de camarones*.

Regional Specialities

Five of the eight provinces of Andalucía are coastal, and one of the other three, Sevilla, extends almost to the sea and effectively has an inland seaport. Unsurprisingly, therefore, fish and seafood loom large in the *andaluz* diet. In the temperate north cuisine is dominated by hearty stews, cured sausages (*embutidos*) and North Atlantic cod. The year-round availability of lush grass means that almost all of the milk and much of the cheese consumed in Spain comes from the north-west. Refrigeration and efficient supply-lines mean that all these products are available throughout Spain, but that does not make them traditional. In the north, the land is used for pasture and the cultivation of maize and wheat. In the south, it is given over to chickpeas, rice, olives, fruit and salad vegetables (under glass). Octopus is popular throughout Spain, but only in Galicia does it approach the status of a staple (though most of the octopus consumed in Spain nowadays is imported from the Falkland Islands).

There are four major influences on the gastronomic culture of Andalucía: the sea, the land, the climate and history. The sea determines the kinds of fish and seafood that are consumed. Anchovies and sardines are more widely consumed in Andalucía than cod (*bacalao*). The Gulf of Cádiz — basically a huge funnel between the Mediterranean/Alborán Sea and the Atlantic Ocean — is an incredibly rich source of fish and shellfish, including bluefin tuna and several kinds of prawn and clam. Another delicacy of the coastal region is the range of *cañadilla* (in Latin *Murex*) or sea-snail. In Italy they are known as *maurice* and in France as *burez* and they look like giant, spiny whelks. These molluscs were known in antiquity and were called *muax* (μύαξ) by Aristotle. Indeed, it is likely that these creatures were what first attracted Phoenician merchants to southern Spain as they were used in the manufacture of costly Tyrian Purple dye.

The land and climate are responsible for the shape of the *andaluz* diet too. The hills are planted with olives, to the extent that the northern *andaluz* province of Jaén is practically a monoculture. The forests of the Sierra Morena (Huelva) and Sierra Nevada (Granada) are suited to the rearing of pigs for ham. Each pig needs one hectare of holm oak or cork forest to develop the appropriate ratio of meat to fat to produce a high-quality product. With much of the land unsuited to traditional animal husbandry, game is more popular in Andalucía than in other *comunidades* (autonomous communities, or devolved regions) of Spain. Wild boar, venison, rabbit, pigeon, quail and partridge are all seen on menus. Across the great *meseta* of central Spain, sheep predominate, meaning ewe's milk cheeses and lamb dishes. In the more mountainous south, one is more likely to encounter goat's milk cheese and dishes made from kid.

The low-lying plain of the Guadalquivir River around Sevilla is the centre of long-grain rice cultivation. Sevilla is 70 miles from the sea but is at sea level — and although its heyday was the seventeenth century (before the pre-eminence of Cádiz) it remains Spain's only commercial river port, handling 4 million tonnes of cargo per year. Instead of cereals, the main farinaceous crop is legumes, predominantly chickpeas. In the local speciality of *pescaíto frito*, small pieces of fish are dredged in flour made from chickpeas or grass peas instead of wheat flour which creates a crisper coating. Although historians are divided, many think that the dish of fish and chips was introduced to Britain by Sephardic (Spanish) Jews. They came, very probably, via the Low Countries where they learned the art of the potato chip from the Belgians and left *pescaíto frito* behind them in The Netherlands as the dish known as 'kibbeling'.

The *pescaíto frito* you eat in Andalucía is a mix of different fish, all in mouthful-sized chunks. There will probably be *adobo* or *rosada*, both common names for some variety of dogfish or small shark (or kingklip — see p. 130), as well as *choco* (cuttlefish) and whatever is cheap at the market that day. In Málaga, *boquerones* (anchovies) are popular, as are *chanquetes* (whitebait). The painter Ignacio Zuloaga memorably described the *chanquetes* of Málaga as 'crisp sea spray'. The landscape of Andalucía also influences, as it does everywhere, the varieties of wine produced by local grapes, with the grapes used to make sherry being cultivated in three distinct kinds of soil the extraordinary properties of which were noted by the Romans.

Finally, the pre-*reconquista* history of Andalucía shaped the cuisine in many ways. The obsession with pork, lard and shellfish probably came about as a means of demonstrating one's Christianity, but former food customs survived in other ways. The first record of a Jewish community in Iberia is found in the Roman era (*e.g.* in the writings of Valerius Maximus and Josephus), but if Iberia is indeed the biblical Tarshish, then the link may be far older. Yoghurt is probably a Hebrew import, as are cucumbers and mint (and all the things that the Judaeans remembered with sorrow in their Babylonian captivity). Culinary practices related to the observation of the Sabbath have also survived, such as the unleavened bread that forms part of the La Mancha version of *gazpacho*, and the *ollas* or stews slow-cooked in embers. These could be prepared ahead of the Sabbath, during which work in the kitchen was forbidden. It was probably also the Jews who introduced the customs of pickling as a way of preparing meat and fish that could not be cooked fresh on the Sabbath.

Few people have written more beautifully about Spanish cuisine than the food writer Claudia Roden (a Sephardic Jew born in Egypt), and as she has observed, the cuisine of the Mediterranean is full of similarities and echoes thanks to its climate, geography and the continual movement of people over centuries. It is perhaps impossible to know whether the Jews brought cumin to Iberia or whether the Arabs brought cinnamon, but they ultimately came from the same region of the world — the fertile crescent of the Middle East. As we have seen, the names of many food items in Spanish are derived from Arabic, including *arroz* (rice), *aceite* (oil), *albaricoque* (apricot), *berenjena* (aubergine), *mazapán* (marzipan), etc.

The olive and the almond are leitmotifs of Spanish cookery. Although olives were first introduced to the Iberian Peninsula by the Phoenicians, cultivation increased greatly after the Arabs brought their knowledge of irrigation with them. Almonds, on the other hand, are additions to the Spanish table for which the Arabs probably can claim responsibility. The quintessential Spanish soup is undoubtedly *gazpacho* (derived from a Mozarabic word meaning 'treasure chest'), although it can only have achieved its current form after the arrival of the tomato from the New World in 1521 (or perhaps 1493, depending upon whom you believe). Its origin is in a far more obviously Moorish dish known today as *ajoblanco* ('white garlic') — a chilled soup of almonds, garlic, and bread puréed with water and a little oil and vinegar (a recipe for a very similar dish is found in *Apicius*). Indeed, food historians suggest that the addition of tomatoes to *ajoblanco* to make the *gazpacho* we know today happened long after the 16th century, possibly as late as the nineteenth century.

Moorish influence is seen in the ingredients themselves — aubergines, artichokes, carrots, dates, figs, citrus fruits — but also in spices and flavourings — cinnamon, cumin, anise, nutmeg, mint, and coriander — as well as their manner of combination. It was from the Arabs that Spaniards discovered the pleasures of 'sweet and savoury'. The Arab influence is also seen, counter-intuitively enough, in the distillation of alcohol, using techniques developed in ninth-century Iraq. Although alcohol was haram if consumed as a beverage, it was licit to use it as medicinally or as a perfume. Non-Muslims, unsurprisingly, turned the technology over to the production of a primitive *orujo*, a *grappa*-like spirit.

Honey predated the arrival of the Moors by millennia. Cave paintings discovered near Valencia showing people foraging for honey have been dated to around 6000 BC. What the Moors did bring, however, was not just a love of honey, but a honey substitute: sugar cane, from which was (and still is) made a kind of light molasses known as *miel de caña* (cane honey). The famously sweet tooth of the Arabs extended also to 'savoury' dishes, especially those involving dried fruits like apricots, raisins, dates and various citrus fruits.

Spain is unlikely ever to be celebrated for its patisserie, however delicious it might be. There are two traditions — an imported French tradition of puff pastry, cream and custard that the Bourbon monarchs introduced in the 18th century; and an older, simpler tradition of biscuits and sweetmeats. This latter tradition is the one most influenced, and partially created, by the sweet-loving Moors and Jewish bakers, and continued by cloistered nuns, who to this day support themselves by selling biscuits, cakes and jam.

One Arab contribution to confectionery that is beyond doubt is *mazapán*, or marzipan. The etymology of *mazapán* is far from certain, with a wealth of likely candidates in Latin, Greek and Arabic. There are two historical trajectories of marzipan — the Northern European line which came via the Ottoman Empire, and the Southern European line, which came from the Levant via North Africa. As well as *mazapán* it is not hard to discern the Arab (and Jewish) origins of *turrón* (nougat), which is clearly related to the *halwa* of the Middle East. It is more difficult to be certain about the origins of other sweets and biscuits because following the *reconquista* their names were vigorously 'de-Islamicized' or 'de-Judaized'. Among food historians, there are two schools of thought regarding the origins of the biscuits and pastries of Spain — positing either a Moorish or Jewish origin. The latter theory seems more likely given that in Moorish Spain, Jews lived more closely with the Mozarabs (Christians). But regardless of which theory one favours, we can agree that the ultimate origin of many of these confections is Middle Eastern.

☕ *La Cocina Malagueña*

In her sumptuous guide to the food of Spain, *Delicioso: A History of Food in Spain*, María José Sevilla advances her compelling theory that to talk of 'Spanish Cuisine' (*cocina española*) is a mistake and that it makes more sense to talk about *cocinas españolas*. Although many dishes are found on menus all over Spain, cooking is still highly regional. A bar in Sevilla may serve *fabada*, the popular pork and bean stew, but on the menu it will be called '*fabada asturiana*' (from Asturias). *Porra*, a version of *gazpacho* thickened with bread, is almost always '*porra antequerana*' (from Antequera) whilst *salmorejo* is '*salmorejo cordobés*' (from Córdoba). *Salmorejo* is also an old-fashioned name for *ensalada malagueña*, which is not a kind of chilled tomato soup at all (see p. 128). Ask for '*una manzanilla*' in Jerez and you will be given a glass of dry Manzanilla sherry, but in a Madrid café, they'll probably bring you a cup of chamomile tea. In the olive-growing interior of Andalucía, people are more likely to think of one of the fourteen varieties of Manzanilla olive that are grown there.

This is of course true of most countries. A person whose knowledge of Italian food does not extend beyond a Bella Pasta restaurant might imagine that all Italians tuck into something called '*spaghetti alla bolognese*' and eat identical kinds of pizza, whereas cuisine is markedly different from region to region. Regional cuisines can become diluted, especially when restaurants cater for large numbers of tourists. Tourists want to eat *paella*, because it is what they know, or what they think they know, so restaurants on the Costa del Sol began putting this dish from Valencia, 650 km away, onto menus. As it happens, there is a very similar dish that is native to Málaga known as *arroz a la parte* ('rice in parts'). A rich broth is prepared with fish and shellfish. The fish is removed and rice is cooked in the same broth, before being thickened with fried bread, garlic, chillies, wine and parsley. Then it is served, rather like *cocido madrileño*, in three courses — the broth, then the fish and shellfish, and finally the rice. The survival and reappearance of these dishes is due in no small part to the efforts of a *malagueño* lawyer called Enrique Mapelli who, in the 1980s, began collecting and publishing traditional local recipes, culminating in a book published in 2009 (*La cocina tradicional de Málaga*).

🌿 *Aceite*

Olive oil is so important in Spanish cuisine that it deserves its own section. Andalucía produces 80% of Spain's olive oil, with the Province of Jaén alone producing more oil than the whole of Greece. Introduced by the Phoenicians, olives have been grown in Spain for over 3,000 years, with serious production developed by the Romans, but it is only since the early 20th century that Spain has been a serious exporter of olives and olive oil. The production of olive oil is still dominated by small village cooperatives that sell direct to local consumers or to larger cooperatives or companies. 'Gourmet' oils are still a fairly new development, with many rural Spaniards buying their 5 litre containers of oil direct from the cooperatives, or purchasing refined oil suitable for frying from supermarkets. In this way, olive oil is following the same trajectory as Spanish wine which a few decades ago was largely being sold in bulk as consumers took their empty bottles to the *ultramarinos* (grocers) to be filled from a barrel (or polypin). But just as winemakers have focused on quality, producing fine wines of export quality where once they made agreeable plonk, so olive producers have an eye on the gourmet market with super-fresh, pure, unblended and 'single-estate' products.

Spain lies beneath the 'Butter Equator' — the dividing line between the butter-loving Northern Europeans and the olive oil-loving Southern Europeans (with a mixed butter/oil zone found in Central France, Northern Italy and the Balkans). The Spanish cooking fats are olive oil and lard, with butter only really used to make 'foreign' patisserie like croissants and puff pastry (traditional Spanish baked goods are made with lard). In general, more refined (technically, 'rectified') lighter olive oil is used for frying and deep frying (because it has a higher smoke point) while virgin and extra virgin oils are used for drizzling, dressings, uncooked chilled soups, etc. If you see AOVE on a menu (*e.g. 'tostada con AOVE y tomate'*) it refers to olive oil ('toast with olive oil and tomato') as it stands for '*Aceite de Oliva Virgen Extra*' (Extra Virgin Olive Oil).

The vocabulary of olives and olive oil comes from both Latin and Arabic sources (*olivum* and *az-zayt* respectively). The Spanish word for (edible) oil is '*aceite*' (a-**thay**-tay), and the related word '*aceituna*' (a-thay-**too**-na) is one of the words for olive, the other being '*oliva*' (o-**lee**-ba). '*Olivo*' (o-**lee**-bo) is the word for olive tree. If you want some olives to snack on, you'd ask for '*unas aceitunas*' but if you ask for olive oil it would not be '*aceite de **aceituna***' but '*aceite de **oliva***' (in actual fact, you would just ask for '*aceite*' because '*oliva*' is taken as read). An olive grower is not an '*aceitunero*' but an '*olivarero*'.

Those of us who remember the 1970s and 1980s will recall that Rioja simply meant a rather rough sort of Spanish red wine taken to student parties (it was exported as 'bulk wine'). Now we know that Rioja can also be white or pink (*rosado*), and we are likely to refer to it by the grape variety: Tempranillo, Garnacha or whatever. In the 1970s, if you wanted to cook with olive oil it meant a trip to the chemist, whereas now every supermarket stocks an array of different oils. However, those of us in non-olive-growing countries are only just learning that there are olive varieties too (around 250 are cultivated in Spain). You might be very proud of your bottle of English cold-pressed rapeseed oil, but do you know whether the variety is Canberra, Picto or Elgar? A Spanish consumer is far more likely to know that the variety used to produce her rather pricey bottle of extra virgin olive oil is Picual (the most widely cultivated), Arbequina (a popular fruity, grassy variety grown in Catalonia) or the more bijou Alfarara (from Albacete). The main varieties grown in the Province of Málaga are:

Hojiblanca (Antequera) — full-bodied, with a buttery consistency. It has a grassy aroma with flavours of hay, apples and nuts. It finishes with a slightly bitter taste of unripe fruits and almonds.

Picual (Antequera) — fruity flavour with hints of almond and an aroma of apple

Picudo (Antequera) — sweet and grassy at first, with a pungent aroma of bitter oranges, followed by light pepper and long, light bitterness.

Arbequina (Antequera) — pleasantly grassy, fruity, and fresh with aromatic notes of green apple, artichoke, and even banana. On the finish, fresh, high-quality Arbequina olive oils have a subtly sweet almond flavour and slightly peppery kick.

Verdial de Vélez-Málaga (Axarquía) — somewhat peppery and with an intensely fruity flavour. It is noted for its ripe, fruity taste.

Aloreña (Álora) — fresh green grass on the nose. On the palate, creamy with a fruity taste reminiscent of apples with a hint of fresh almonds.

Nevadillo (Axarquía) — aromas of green grass and tomato with delicate tinges of fig and apple. On the palate, it has a very mild bitterness and a pleasant medium level of spice.

Lechín (Ronda) — complex aroma of green olives, dried fruits and hints of apricot with a well-balanced flavour of ripe apple, with a delicate spicy finish.

📖 Understanding *cartas*

The days of phrase books and dictionaries are largely over, thanks to the smartphone and cheaper roaming charges. Download the Google Translate (or similar) app for your iOS or Android phone and use it to check translations of items on *cartas* and *menús* in Spanish. If you have a contract that means paying through the nose for data roaming, then try to connect to Wifi. There is some free coverage in Málaga city centre and many bars and restaurants are now connected. You will probably need to ask the barman or waiter for the password — *la clave del wifi* (lah **kla**-bay del **wee**-fee). Many of the bars and restaurants in the *centro histórico* will be able to give you a *carta* in English: *¿Tiene una carta en inglés?* (**tyay**-nay una **kar**-tah en een-**glayss**?).

The following is a list, by no means exhaustive, of typical *andaluz* dishes (if any is associated with a particular province, this is indicated), some of which will probably not be in any phrase book and might flummox a translator app.

🍲 *Entrantes, Sopas & Cocidos* (Starters, Soups And Stews)

Abajao (Cádiz) — Asparagus stir-fried with onions, tomato and garlic and served with eggs.

Aceitunas aliñás — Olives marinated with bitter orange, red pepper, fennel, thyme, oregano, etc.

Ajo harina (Jaén) — A stew of cod and potatoes in a sauce of tomatoes, peppers, paprika, and cumin.

Ajoblanco (Granada & Málaga) — The forerunner of *gazpacho*; chilled garlic and almond soup.

Arroz Caldoso Marinero (Málaga) — Imagine paella in soup form. My advice is to ignore *paella* in Málaga (go to Valencia if you want to try it), but order this if you see it on the menu.

Berza Malagueña (Málaga) — A hearty thick soup with *pringá* as the main flavour, plus green beans and carrots.

Caldillo de pintarroja (Málaga) — A spicy and savoury marine winter soup using dogfish (aka 'Morgay'). Traditionally eaten by Málaga's fishermen to warm up before (or after) sailing out to sea and a favourite in the many traditional taverns.

Cazuela de Fideos (Málaga) — A spicy fish soup made from whichever fish is available (or leftover) that day, with the addition of *fideos* (short noodles).

Ensalada/Ensaladilla malagueña — The signature salad of Málaga is made with potatoes, cod (sometimes tuna), oranges (traditionally *cachorreña* or sour oranges) and green olives. It is sometimes called '*salmorejo*' in Málaga which, confusingly, is also the name of a completely different dish (a thick, chilled tomato soup from Córdoba).

Gachas — A porridge made from wheat or other cereals.

Garbanzos con bacalao — Chickpeas stewed with salt cod.

Gazpacho — A chilled and blended soup of tomatoes, peppers, cucumber, garlic and sherry vinegar.

Gazpachuelo (Málaga) — Quite different from *gazpacho*! A *malagueña* bouillabaisse thickened with mayonnaise served hot or warm, not chilled.

Habas con calzones — Runner beans with ham (*lit.* 'beans in their pods')

Habas fritas con jamón (Granada) — Haricot beans cooked with ham.

Migas (Córdoba, Granada, Málaga, & Almería) — Breadcrumbs fried with garlic and served with one or more toppings — sausage, ham, egg, fish, shellfish, grapes, cheese, etc.

Migas de harina (Granada) — A thick wheat porridge with garlic.

Porra (Málaga) — *Gazpacho* is ubiquitous throughout the Iberian peninsular, but this is the version from Antequera, in the Province of Málaga. A thick *gazpacho* eaten with a spoon rather than drunk from a glass, and often garnished with tuna or cod.

Puchero andaluz — A rich stew (chicken, beef, lamb, pork, etc.) with potatoes, chickpeas and vegetables. Quite similar to *cocido madrileño*.

Remojón/Picadillo de naranjas (Granada, Málaga) — Orange salad, often with onions, olives, cod, etc.

Salmorejo (Córdoba) — A thicker version of *gazpacho*, more like a sauce than a soup and often used as such.

Sopa cachorreña — A cream soup made from *cachorreña* (sour) oranges, garlic, tomato, cumin and paprika. Often garnished with flakes of cod.

🥕 *Verduras* (Vegetables)

Alboronía — The *andaluz* version of ratatouille (or *pisto* as it is known in Spain).

Alcauciles rellenos (Cádiz, Sevilla) — Stuffed artichokes.

Andrajos (Jaén, Almería, Granada) — Tomato, pepper, garlic stew with dumpling strips.

Berenjenas con miel (de caña) — Popular throughout Andalucía, but this dish of fried aubergine slices or batons drizzled with 'cane honey' (*viz.* molasses) really belongs to Málaga because it is the centre of sugar cane production.

Habas a la rondeña (Ronda, Málaga) — A hearty casserole of broad beans and ham or gammon; beautiful with crusty bread.

Pipirrana — Another dish found all over Andalucía, made from finely chopped red pepper, green pepper, tomato, onion, olives, tuna, and mussels or other seafood dressed with extra virgin olive oil and sea salt.

Piriñaca (Cádiz) — This is basically unblended *gazpacho*, more like a salad than a soup.

🐄 *Carnes* (Meat)

Chivo Lechal Malagueño (Málaga) — Roast suckling goat (kid). Málaga is famous for its goats, and the La Axarquía region of the province is famous for this dish. Often served with '*pastoril*' sauce made with bacon and almonds, and accompanied by the offal, either fried with onions or made into a pate.

Flamenquín (Córdoba) — A slice of ham or pork rolled around cheese, crumbed and fried.

Huevos a la flamenca — Eggs cooked in *pisto* (ratatouille).

Manteca colorá (Málaga) — Literally 'coloured lard'; pork loin in lard and paprika enjoyed cold on toast or in a sandwich.

Pan de Pollo (Málaga) — This translates as 'chicken bread' — a *pâté* or terrine of chicken, pig's liver and pork belly.

Pepitoria de Pollo (Málaga) — Chicken with almonds, a kind of non-spicy chicken korma.

Plato de los montes (Málaga) — Pork loin in paprika-flavoured lard, served with fried potato, onions, peppers, black pudding, etc. A very hearty 'mountain' dish.

Pringá — Comes in different forms depending on which meat was used (it can be made from beef, pork, *chorizo* or *morcilla*), but it's what we would call 'pulled' in English; slow cooked and tender, almost rillettes. Similar to *zurrapa*, but more meat than fat.

Tartar de Salchichón (Málaga) — A recent addition to the culinary patrimony of Málaga. '*Salchichón de Málaga*' is a very lightly cured sausage that has the soft mouthfeel almost of raw pork, so this is a take on the classic steak tartare using Málaga's native charcuterie.

Zurrapa (Málaga) — Another pork and lard dish, this time of shredded pork in seasoned lard (without paprika) and spread on toast. Very 'porky' and quite delicious.

🍴 🐟 *Pescados & Mariscos* (Fish & Seafood)

Amoragás — This means 'roasted on a wood (or charcoal) fire' (see *espeto*).

Araña — Not a dish, but a kind of fish (and not a spider as Google will translate it) — the weever. The spines are venomous, but it is a good eating fish, with a flavour similar to sole.

Atún encebollado (Cádiz) — Tuna stewed with tomatoes and onions.

Atún mechado (Málaga) — Tuna braised with white wine and bacon.

Cazuela de arroz a la malagueña (Málaga) — The *malagueño* version of paella. Also known as **Arroz a la Parte**.

Fideos con caballa (Cádiz) — Short noodles with mackerel.

Espeto de sardinas (Málaga) — Up to half a dozen sardines grilled over wood/coals on a skewer. The origin of these sardine skewers is associated with open-air beach bars.

Fritura Malagueña (Málaga) — Every coastal town in Andalucía has its own version, but the basics are the same: small fish and pieces of larger fish, dredged in chickpea flour and quickly fried to achieve a 'good fry' (*viz.* not too greasy or heavy). The difference in Málaga is that you will find more anchovies in your *fritura*. See also *pescaíto frito*.

Erizos de mar (Cádiz) — Sea urchins (the orange roes are eaten raw with lemon juice).

Ortiguillas (Cádiz) — Sea anemones (either fried or made into soup).

Papas con chocos — Potatoes with cuttlefish.

Garbanzos con chocos (Cádiz) — Chickpeas with cuttlefish.

Pescado adobado/Bienmesabe — Fish which has been marinated in vinegar, bay, cumin, paprika and garlic before cooking. ⚠ *Bienmesabe* just means 'it tastes good' and is also the name of a pudding made from honey, egg yolks and almonds!

Pescaíto frito — Fried fish, first dusted in chickpea or pea grass flour. The Spanish word is actually *pescadíto* but because *andaluces* are famous for swallowing their consonants, the 'd' has been completely dropped over time.

Pescado en blanco (Málaga) — A simple country cousin of the *grande bouillabaisses* of the French littoral, made with fish and potatoes.

Rosada — Not the name of a dish, nor of a specific fish, but according to the food writer and seafood expert Alan Davidson, the name given to several kinds of small shark or dogfish, so called because the raw fish has a pale pink hue, though white when cooked. Far be it from me to disagree with the great man, but the reality is probably more complex — *rosada* seems to be a catch-all term for a kind of firm-fleshed white fish that appears regularly on menus but which is rarely seen in markets. The most likely explanation is that it is 'Kingklip' (Cusker Eel), fished in the Southern Atlantic and Indo-Pacific oceans. In other words, it's what Spanish restaurants have in their freezers. Don't let that put you off, though. It's a good-eating fish, a little softer than monkfish with large, firm flakes and a mild, sweet flavour.

Soldaditos de Pavía — 'Soldiers of Pavia'; strips of battered cod with grilled red pepper.

Trucha de Riofrío — Freshwater trout.

Urta a la roteña (Cádiz) — Red-banded sea bream in the style typical of the town of Rota, cooked with tomatoes.

🍸 Postres & Dulces (Puddings & Sweets)

Alfajores — Pastries made from a paste of almonds, nuts and honey.

Bizcochos marcheneros (Sevilla) — Plain macaroons.

Borrachuelos (Málaga) — Especially popular at Christmas and Easter, these pastries are flavoured with wine and *anís*, filled with candied sweet potato or pumpkin jam, and usually dipped in honey syrup.

Candié (Jerez de la Frontera, Cádiz) — Another sugar and egg yolk confection, flavoured with sweet wine.

Entornao (Sevilla) — A cake flavoured with paprika and sesame.

Granizado de almendra (Málaga) — A frozen dessert made from almonds, sugar and cinnamon.

Hojaldrina — A crumbly cookie.

Mostachón (Sevilla) — A cream-covered meringue, usually topped with fruit. A pavlova.

Pan de Cádiz — A kind of *turrón* made in Cádiz from sweet potato and eggs and filled with *mazapán* and crystallized fruits or jam.

Pan de higo — Dried figs pressed into a cake and eaten with cheese.

Pastel cordobés (Córdoba) — A puff pastry cake filled with pumpkin, cider and sometimes ham(!)

Pestiños — Crumbly honey wafers a little like substantial brandy snaps.

Poleá (Cádiz) — A sweet variety of porridge.

Peras estofadas (Málaga) — Pears poached in wine with honey and cinnamon.

Tarta Malagueña (Málaga) — A cake made with ground almonds and Málaga sweet wine, as well as apricot jam.

Tocino de cielo — 'Heaven's bacon'; a tooth-shattering sweet confection of caramelized egg yolks.

Torta inglesa (Sevilla) — 'English cake' [sic] made from puff pastry and filled with pumpkin jam.

Tortas de aceite — Thin, crisp, round wafers made with flour, olive oil, aniseed and sesame.

Tortas Locas (Málaga) — 'Mad Cakes' were invented in the 1950s to bring a little sweet luxury to ordinary *malagueños* who could not afford rich cream cakes. These are sandwiches of puff pastry filled with custard and iced with orange frosting, topped with a glacé cherry.

Turrolate (Córdoba) — A festive kind of *turrón* made from cocoa and almonds or peanuts.

Yemas del Tajo (Málaga) — A version of *Yemas de Santa Teresa* made by nuns in Ronda.

Yemas de San Leandro (Sevilla) — Another local version of *Yemas de Santa Teresa*.

🥬 Vegetarian Options

A decade or so ago, few Spaniards really understood what vegetarianism meant. They could grasp that it involved not eating large pieces of meat, but the avoidance of meat products *per se* was regarded with either suspicion or a total lack of comprehension. In Spain, 'not eating meat' is often understood to mean not eating meat like lamb, beef or pork, because this is what is covered by the word *carne*. Cured pork products like *jamón*, *pâtés*, and even poultry are not readily thought of as 'carnes'. *Jamón* (ham) in particular crops up in a great many dishes which one would otherwise expect to be vegetarian. Very often it is a garnish that could easily be omitted, so you might want to check while ordering, although most establishments are pretty clued up these days, and even the vegan diet is beginning to be understood with symbols starting to appear on menus indicating what particular dishes contain.

If you are a vegetarian who eats and enjoys fish, then Spain will be an Omega-3-rich gastronomic paradise. If you don't eat fish, you'll need to be more careful in your choices, especially in Andalucía. Larger restaurants (the sort with tablecloths and *cartas* in several languages) will be used to dealing with vegetarians and those with other dietary requirements, like gluten-free dishes, but smaller bars might not be so up to speed. The following is a list of some (usually) safe options you are likely to find on many, or even most, *cartas* (Ⅴ denotes vegan):

queso — cheese ▪ **tortilla** — omelette, and just eggs, potatoes (and onion) unless indicated otherwise Ⅴ**gazpacho** — this is vegetarian but sometimes comes with diced ham as a garnish Ⅴ**pisto** — Spanish ratatouille, but check it contains no meat Ⅴ**porra/salmorejo** — the thicker variants of *gazpacho* often come with ham/fish garnishes, so ask for it '*sin guarnición*' (sin gwar-nith-**yon**) ▪ **croquetas** — often just cheese flavoured *béchamel*, but can also contain cod/ham; other popular flavours are *Cabrales* (blue cheese), *espinacas & piñones* (spinach and pine nuts), *roquefort & nuez* (blue cheese and walnuts), and *setas* (wild mushrooms) Ⅴ**zanahorias aliñadas** — carrots marinated in garlic, cumin, oregano and paprika ▪ **espárragos con huevos** — asparagus with diced hard boiled egg (a common alternative term for asparagus is *trigueros*) Ⅴ**espinacas con garbanzos** — spinach and chickpeas Ⅴ**berenjenas** — aubergines, fried and often drizzled with *miel de caña* (molasses) Ⅴ**ajoblanco** — almond and garlic soup Ⅴ**patatas bravas/arrugadas** — sautéed/boiled potatoes with spicy tomato or other sauces ▪ **patatas con alioli** — potatoes with garlic mayonnaise (real *alioli* is actually vegan but rarely encountered) Ⅴ**pimientos de Padrón** — fried/grilled peppers ▪ **pimientos del piquillo** — sweet red peppers, but check if they are stuffed, and with what (it's usually cream cheese) Ⅴ**setas/hongos/champiñones** — generic terms for mushrooms, though *champiñones* are generally button mushrooms Ⅴ**tostada con tomate** — toasted bread with tomatoes, garlic and oil ▪ **huevos** — eggs: *rotos* are fried with potato (but check what else), *revueltos* are scrambled, often with ham or prawns, but also commonly with white *espárragos* or *ajetes* (garlic shoots — especially delicious) Ⅴ**tomates aliñados** — tomato salad, which sounds dull, but in Spain rarely is Ⅴ**ensaladas** — *ensalada mixta* is a plain salad, but check for any other kind of salad as ham and/or fish often creep in.

⚠ Even what looks like a plain lentil stew may be prepared with a base of meat stock, and most traditional Spanish biscuits are made with lard!

⏱ Mealtimes

Desayuno	**Breakfast**	The first meal of the day. Either something very light at home, or more substantial in a bar or café
Almuerzo	**Elevenses**	1000–1200: A more substantial mid-morning snack, usually in a bar. A continuation of breakfast.
Hora del vermú	**Aperitif**	From ≈ 1300: Pre-lunch drinks (traditionally vermouth) and light snacks ('*tapitas*')
Comida	**Lunch**	From ≈ 1400: This is the main meal, eaten in courses in a traditionally leisurely fashion
Sobremesa	**'At table'**	Time spent chewing the fat around the table at the end of the meal (it also follows *cena*)
Siesta	**Nap**	Rest taken after lunch. The daily nap is observed by fewer and fewer Spaniards, but the afternoon rest clings on, largely as a retreat from the scorching summer heat.
Merienda	**Tea**	The antipodes of *almuerzo* — an afternoon snack, usually sweet.
Paseo	**Stroll**	The post-siesta perambulation. Part constitutional, part social institution.
Tapeo	**Pre-dinner**	From ≈ 1900: Pre-dinner drinks (beer, sherry or wine), usually accompanied by *tapas*.
Cena	**Dinner**	When dinner is eaten outside the home, it can be an elaborate affair, but it can just as easily involve a few *tapas*. At home, it might just be a sandwich. Lunch is generally the main meal of the day.

The 'Mediterranean diet' is reckoned to be one of the healthiest ways to eat. But this is only in part due to what is eaten — plenty of fruit, vegetables, nuts and legumes, generous quantities of olive oil, more fish than meat, few rich sauces, puddings as a very occasional treat, and very little processed food of any kind. Other 'lifestyle' factors have an impact too. The fact that the *paseo* is an institution means that most Spaniards walk every day. *Tapas* culture means eating a succession of small portions rather than huge meals. Although Spaniards eat 'dinner' relatively late, it is usually a light meal. Even in restaurants, lunch is the main meal of the day, so most locals take in (or 'frontload') most of their calories in the first half of the day. Meals also tend to be eaten slowly and have a strong social element with the '*sobremesa*', or time spent chatting around the table, almost as important as the food itself.

Another factor is perhaps that rather than three meals a day, Spaniards have several. While this may seem to go against the 'don't snack between meals' advice, these snacks **are** meals. Eating little and often means that one is rarely ravenous and at risk of ordering a massive repast with 'eyes bigger than one's belly'. For breakfast, most Spaniards will have an espresso (*i.e. café solo*) and a biscuit or small piece of cake at home (cereals are consumed by children). The second instalment of breakfast is taken mid-morning and is called *almuerzo*. If you speak South American Spanish, or learned using Duolingo®, then this may be confusing because *almuerzo* is often translated as 'lunch' (etymologically it means 'bite'). The vocabulary varies from country to country (*e.g.* in Mexico '*hora del lonche*' means lunchtime, whereas in Peru it's teatime), but in Spain, *almuerzo* is generally elevenses or round-two of breakfast, and *comida* is lunch (though it also means 'food' or 'meal' in general). In bars and cafés, the menu for *desayuno* and *almuerzo* is the same — coffee, juice, toast (*tostada*) and pastries.

Times of day like 'morning' (*mañana* — meaning both 'morning' and 'tomorrow') and 'afternoon' (*tarde*) are movable feasts in Spain, where the day is divided according to meals. The standard pre-noon greeting is 'good day' (*buenos días*) rather than 'good morning'. For most people, '*la tarde*' only begins at lunch, which can be quite late if you don't sit down until 2 or 3 o'clock. For some older Spaniards, '*la tarde*' doesn't properly begin until after lunch, or even after the siesta.

And to further confuse English speakers, '*tarde*' (*lit.* 'late') is used for both 'afternoon' and 'evening'. Thus, you'll hear the greeting '*buenas tardes*' at 2 pm as well as at 8 pm. At some point, '*tarde*' becomes '*noche*' (night). Again, precisely when this happens varies, but the key moment is usually dinner. The greeting '*buenas noches*' is used as a salutation as well as when taking leave. Visit a bar at 11 pm and the barman who bids you 'good night' is welcoming you, not bidding you farewell. Another period of the day is '*madrugada*', the small hours before dawn — usually experienced by those who have not yet gone to bed rather than early risers.

Spain's odd relationship with times of day is largely due to the fact that it is in the wrong time zone. Geographically, it should use GMT like Portugal (Valencia, on Spain's east coast, is on the Greenwich Meridian). Thus, when a Spaniard sits down for lunch at a rather late 2.30 pm, it is a more reasonable 1.30 pm elsewhere on the same longitude. The disparity goes back to 1940 and a meeting on the Franco-Spanish border between Franco and Hitler. Determined to remain technically neutral, Franco had nothing to offer Germany save for adopting the same time zone. The reason for not correcting the difference subsequently may be to do with the desire to keep the same time as (most of) the rest of the European Union.

🥐 Breakfast

The breakfast (*desayuno*) eaten mid-morning throughout Spain consists of toasted bread (*tostada*), with olive oil (or for more traditional *andaluces*, paprika-infused lard) and topped with tomato and salt. The bread used in Málaga is either a crusty white roll or a *mollete antequerano*, a roll from Antequera with the consistency of an English muffin (the dough is made with milk rather than just water). In most bars it is possible to order your *tostada* with cheese, ham, *chorizo*, pâté ('*foie*') or jam ('*mermelada*') and this 'breakfast' is usually served until lunch so it can make a reasonable midday snack if you can't manage to hang on until the Spanish 'lunchtime' of 2 pm or so.

Most people outside Spain are now familiar with *churros* — deep-fried tubular doughnuts to be dipped into chocolate. These are popular throughout Spain for breakfast, *almuerzo* and *merienda*, as well as a welcome way to soak up the booze at 5 am after a night on the tiles. They are especially popular in Málaga, although they are piped into the oil from a round nozzle instead of a star-shaped one, giving them a smooth but slightly lumpy appearance, and they are eaten with a cup of *café con leche* (coffee with milk) just as often as with the more traditional thick, sweet chocolate. In most of Spain they are called *churros*, which is the sound supposedly made by the batter hitting the oil, but in Málaga they are called *tejeringos* (teh-кнeh-**rin**-goss) after the implement used to pipe the dough into the hot oil, which looks like a syringe ('*jeringa*').

💬 Useful Phrases

Hi! / Hello!	*¡Hola!*	**oh**-la
Excuse me / Sorry	*Disculpe*	diss-**kool**-peh
Yes / No	*Sí / No*	see / noh
Do you have ...?	*Tiene ...?*	**tyen**-neh ...?
Does it have ... in?	*Lleva ...?*	**yay**-ba...?
Fish	*pescado*	pes-**ka**-doh
Meat	*carne*	**kar**-nay
Dairy	*lácteos*	lak-**tay**-oss
Nuts	*frutos secos*	**froo**-toss **say**-koss
I'm allergic to ...	*Soy alérgico a ... (m)*	soy al-**air**-kheeko ah ...
	Soy alérgica a ... (f)	soy al-**air**-kheeka ah ...
Without ...	*sin ...*	sin...
I can't eat...	*No puedo comer...*	noh **pway**-do kom-**air**
Do you have a menu (in English)?	*Tiene una carta (en inglés)?*	**tyen**-neh **oo**-na **kar**-ta (enn een-**glayss**)?
How much does it cost?	*¿Cuánto cuesta?*	**kwan**-toh **kwess**-tah?
The bill, please	*La cuenta, por favor*	la **kwen**-tah, por fav-ORR
Thank you (very much)	*(Muchas) Gracias*	(**moo**-chass) **grath**-yass
You're welcome	*De nada.*	day **nah**-dah
Where is ...?	*Dónde está ...?*	**donn**-day ess-**stah** ...?
Goodbye	*Adiós*	add-**yoss**
I don't know	*No sé*	noh say

🍖 Cooking of Meat

Useful vocabulary for ordering steaks, burgers, etc.:

Very rare/blue	*muy poco hecho*	moy **poh**-ko **ech**-oh
Rare	*poco hecho*	**poh**-ko **ech**-oh
Medium rare	*en punto*	enn **poon**-toh
Medium	*punto pasado*	**poon**-toh pah-**sah**-doh
Medium well	*hecho*	**ech**-oh
Well done	*bien hecho*	byenn **ech**-oh

Bebidas (Drinks)

☕ Café

Visitors to Spain either love the coffee or hate it. The two main kinds encountered are '*natural*' and '*mezcla*' (a mix of natural and '*torrefacto*'), the latter being the more traditional and widely consumed of the two. *Mezcla* blends are a result of the '*torrefacto*' process in which the raw beans are sprayed with a fine mist of sugar solution before roasting. The sugar is burnt off leaving a dark roasted bean with a hint of caramel to create a deep rich coffee without bitterness. These *torrefacto* beans are blended with 'natural' beans in different ratios, ranging from mostly natural with a hint of *torrefacto*, half-and-half, right up to 100% *torrefacto*. Most bars favour a *mezcla*. The only people who favour 100% *torrefacto* these days are older men (usually) who probably regard brandy and a cigar as a 'light breakfast'.

The *torrefacto* process was invented during the coffee shortages of the Civil War as a method of preservation, and Spaniards developed a taste for it. If you find the coffee too strong, ask for an Americano, and if that is still too strong for you, ask for it '*poco cargado*' (**poh**-ko kaRR-**gah**-do). If you don't like the caramelized, rather punchy flavour of *torrefacto* at all, either look for 'natural' (the trendier bars advertise the kind of coffee they use) or drink coffee in the more modern coffee shops (which tend not to use *torrefacto* blends), or even Starbucks, where you can guarantee that your coffee will taste of almost nothing at all.

The most common coffee orders in Spain are:

café solo — an espresso/lungo shot; if you ask simply for '*un café*' this is what you will get.

café con leche — espresso topped up with milk, but stronger than an Italian latte. You may be asked whether you want cold (*fría*), room-temperature (*templada*), or hot (*caliente*) milk. If they don't give you enough milk, ask for more: '*más leche*'.

café cortado — espresso with a smaller quantity of milk; stronger than a flat white.

café Americano — an espresso shot diluted with hot water (can also be *con leche*)

Café can also be *carajillo* (with brandy or another spirit), *bombón* (with condensed milk) or *con hielo* (con **yay**-lo — iced — you'll be given a hot espresso and a glass of ice, and milk if you ask for it). Decaffeinated (*descafeinado*) coffee is also available, but while it will be properly made (*de máquina*) in coffee shops, in most bars the only option is '*de sobre*' (from the packet, i.e. instant). The number of permutations in which Spaniards will drink their coffee and milk is almost infinite (hot milk, cold milk, in a cup, in a glass, differing ratios of milk to coffee, etc.).

You and I may both order a *café con leche*, but you may want a touch more coffee while I will prefer a touch more milk. Fed up with wasting cups of coffee not precisely to a customer's taste at a time when coffee, milk and sugar were extremely expensive, the owner of Málaga's Café Central in the 1950s, José Prado Crespo, devised nine ways to order a coffee. The clientele got used to it and years later they were captured in tiles by the artist Amparo Ruiz de Luna, who added a humorous tenth option for reasons of artistic composition (see p. 188). These names are used throughout Málaga, though if you try to order an '*entre corto*' anywhere else in Spain, you may receive an old-fashioned look. And if the coffee-ordering vocabulary of Málaga wasn't already complicated enough, *malagueños* tend not to go out for café, but for a *cafelito* (*lit*. a 'little coffee'). Spaniards love diminutives!

	Name in Málaga	Translation	Coffee	Milk	Similar to:
	Solo	'just' coffee	100%	0%	*espresso, lungo*
	Largo	long	90%	10%	*macchiato*
	Semi Largo	half long	75%	25%	*macchiatone*
	Solo Corto	short 'solo'	60%	0%	*ristretto*
	Mitad	half (& half)	50%	50%	*cortado*
	Entre Corto	inter–short	40%	60%	'flat white'
	Corto	short	30%	70%	*caffè latte*
	Sombra	shadow	20%	80%	
	Nube	cloud	10%	90%	
	No me lo ponga	'Don't give me any'	0%	0%	

So beloved was the tiled illustration created for the Café Central, that when the café closed in 2022, the Mayor of Málaga, Francisco de la Torre, assured people that he would find a public location 'so that it can be viewed by Málaga residents and visitors'. It will also be preserved on the package design of the *malagueña* coffee company 'Santa Cristina'.

Every cup of coffee in Spain (at least in traditional bars and cafés) will come with a sachet of sugar that contains up to three or four teaspoons of sugar. If you want artificial sweetener, the word is *edulcorante* (**ay-dool-ko-ran-**tay). The word *sacarina* is also widely used.

☕ Chocolate

Spain was the first place in Europe where chocolate was consumed (as a beverage). Although Columbus brought cocoa beans back to Spain in 1504, it was not until Spanish settlers in what are now Mexico and Guatemala developed a taste for drinking chocolate that it began to be consumed in Spain. When solid chocolate was perfected in 1847 (by Fry and Sons in Bristol) that, too, would take Spain by storm. In 1865, four million kilograms of chocolate were being manufactured annually in Spain, more than doubling to ten million a decade later. Málaga's own chocolate factory, La Riojana, opened in 1857 on Calle Mármoles, near the Zamarrilla hermitage. The factory closed not long after the Civil War, but in the 1930s it was producing 2,000 kg of chocolate per day.

Drinking chocolate (*chocolate a la taza*) is powdered bitter-sweet dark chocolate that is mixed with hot milk and sugar and, usually, thickened with cornflour. Its consistency varies from single cream at the runnier end all the way to thick custard that can only decorously be eaten with a spoon (or, more authentically, *tejeringos*). In fact, it tends only to be sold in those *cafeterías* that also serve *tejeringos* (*churros*). The best-known brand is Valor from Villajoyosa near Alicante, but you may also come across Lacasa (Huesca) and Zahor (San Sebastián).

More widely available, including in many bars, is Cola Cao: a chocolate drink made by Idilia (formerly Nutrexpa, Barcelona). It is mild and sweet, somewhat like chocolate Nesquik®, and loved by generations of Spanish children (and nostalgic adults). If you order it, you will be brought a glass of milk (usually hot, but you can specify cold if you wish) and a sachet of Cola Cao powder to mix yourself. This being Spain, you will also be given a sachet of sugar, because with 21 grams of sugar per sachet, it's clearly not sweet enough already.

🍷 *Vino* (Wine)

> *'The real wealth of Málaga is the produce of the soil, wine and 'fruit'; the latter, a generic term, like figs at Smyrna, is the all-absorbing topic of the Malagenian mind and tongue, a theme of pleasure and profit. The sweet Muscatel wines are well-known; they grow on the vine-clad heights which slope down to the sea. The richest are called Las Lagrimas like the Lacryma Christi of Naples ; they are the ruby tears which drop from the grape without pressure.'* (Hand-book for Travellers in Spain, *Richard Ford, 1845*)

A greater proportion of Spain by area is under vine than of any other country in the world (around a million hectares). Spain has been the world's third largest wine producer for decades and occasionally edges into second place. Despite the domestic popularity of wine, Spain is only the fifth-largest consumer (at 36 litres — 48 bottles — per capita per annum) but is the world's biggest exporter of wine (by volume), selling 2.3 billion litres (around 20%

of world volume traded). The most telling statistic is how much (or rather how little) wine Spain imports. While Germany and the UK both import some 1.4 billion litres of wine annually, and France 773 million litres, Spain does not even make the FAO league table of the world's top twenty importers, lagging behind Brazil (in 20th position at 92 million litres).

Spanish Wine Classifications

Spanish wines are still frequently described as coming from a particular '**DO**' (*denominación de origen* — 'designation of origin'). The term is still used, but in 2016, Spain began using the EU system of designation based on the '**DOP**' – (*denominación de origen protegida* — 'protected denomination of origin'). This designation covers not only wine but fruit, ham, cheese, honey, seafood, rice, and much more.

In the case of wine, a **DOP** may be **DOCa/DOQ** (denomination of qualified origin, *viz.* Rioja and Priorat), **DO** (*e.g.* Málaga), **VP** (*vino de pago* or 'estate wine') or **VC** (*vino de calidad*, quality wines with a geographic indication). Below the **DO** level are **IGP** wines (*indicación geográfica protegida*, protected geographical indication), and many of these are excellent quality. The lowest classification is **VdM** (*vino de mesa*, that is, table wine) — usually blended bulk wine, but occasionally it could be a very fine wine that simply does not satisfy the rules of the DO (because of the use of an unapproved grape variety, for example). This complex hierarchy of classification can be confusing, to say the least.

Viticulture has been practised in Spain for what seems like forever, and this is not much of an exaggeration. There is evidence to show that vines grew in the Peninsula as far back as the so-called Tertiary Period (which ended 2.6 million years ago), and that these grapes were cultivated sometime between 4000 and 3000 BC, long before the Phoenicians founded Cádiz around 1100 BC. It is thought that grapes for wine were first grown in the Province of Málaga in the sixth century BC. The Carthaginians, armed with the Punic texts of the agriculturalist Mago, improved on the wine-making techniques of the Phoenicians, but real wine history and culture began after the Romans won the Punic Wars against the Carthaginians and the Peninsula became 'Hispania'. Indeed, the oldest archaeological evidence of winemaking is from the late second century AD — a fermentation tank uncovered in the town of Cártama, about 25 miles from the city of Málaga.

The time Hispania spent under Roman rule was the first golden age of Spanish wine. Exports increased year on year, and Iberian wine was highly prized throughout the empire. The two main production areas were Tarraco near Barcelona in the north and Baetica in the south (modern Tarragona and Andalucía respectively). After the decline of the Roman Empire, the beer-drinking Visigoths arrived, and there is little evidence of viticulture during this period.

Things picked up again, ironically enough, when the Moors conquered the Peninsula. Even though Sharia Law forbids drinking any kind of alcohol, wine culture was somewhat revived under Muslim rule due to two coincidental and accidental factors. The Arabs were very fond of grapes — eaten both fresh and as raisins, and they introduced the science of distillation. Distillation was almost certainly first practised in the Gandhara civilization of the Indus Valley and was known to the Greeks (in Byzantine Egypt), but in the form that the Moors introduced, it came from 9th-century Iraq. The Moorish culture of Spain oscillated between tolerant cosmopolitanism and repressive fundamentalism, and in more liberal periods, wealthy Muslims would consume alcohol for permitted (cough) 'medicinal' purposes.

The Early Middle Ages brought the Benedictines and other monastic orders, and they played an important role in re-establishing and promoting viticulture. In fact, many of the current DOs had their origin around this time. Villages would grow up around a monastery and winemaking became embedded in the local economy. One of the oldest DOs — Priorat — dates from the late 12th century, when the monks of the Carthusian Monastery of Scala Dei, founded in 1194, reintroduced the art of viticulture to the area. The prior of Scala Dei ruled as a feudal lord over seven villages in the area, which gave rise to the name Priorat. The monks tended the vineyards for centuries until 1835 when their lands were expropriated by the state, and distributed to smallholders.

Monks also brought new varieties of vine and new techniques from France and Italy. The *reconquista* also revived Spanish winemaking and thus the wine export trade. Many of the wines sold at this time went to the English market, where they were at least as highly valued as French wines. 'Sherris Sack' and 'Malago Sack' wines were enormously popular in Britain, as any survey of the drinking habits of the characters of Renaissance drama will show.

The 'discovery' of the New World by Cristóbal Colón (Christopher Columbus) opened up further opportunities for export, and the Spanish conquistadores took Spanish vines with them in order to begin wine production in the new Spanish colonies. These transplanted Spanish vines would later become crucial to the effort to repopulate Spanish vineyards after various epidemics of blight and disease. In the 16th century, Spanish wines were the most famous and most exported wines anywhere in the world. Also, wine production in the colonies was so common that it started negatively affecting Spanish exports, which is why Felipe III banned the expansion of vineyards in Chile (a decree that was largely ignored).

The 15th and 16th centuries saw a huge rise in the popularity of Spanish wines, which were being produced in almost every area of the Iberian Peninsula. The Canaries had just been conquered and wine production there had also started to become popular, mainly thanks to the islands' strategic location in terms of trade and climate. Canary wines, as they were called, made a name for themselves around the world for their excellent quality. Their downfall began with Oliver Cromwell's protectionist Navigation Acts (1660–1661) and the creation of the 'Canary Company' in 1665, through which the English (virtually a monopsony) traded Canary wines at low cost, successfully establishing a monopoly as well.

Spain's decline after the Golden Age saw its wine trade overtaken by suppliers from the rest of Europe. A second blow was the Industrial Revolution which led to advances in the machinery of wine-making (presses, mash-tuns, etc.) and transportation, not least the railways. Spain came late to industrialization and saw a precipitous decline in wine exports. There was a brief respite when the phylloxera blight destroyed swathes of European vineyards during the 19th century. It was a dire time for Europe, and even though Spain did not entirely escape later on, it was also European viticulture's salvation. Many French vineyards were replanted with Spanish vine stocks. The plague was slow to reach northern Spanish vineyards (though Málaga was devastated), so there was plenty of wine to export. During this time, Spanish wines reached every corner of Europe and enjoyed something of a Renaissance.

Some French winemakers crossed the Pyrenees and arrived in the north of Spain, bringing with them new tools, methods and, of course, varieties. The north of Spain, especially Navarra and the Basque Country, benefited and their wine tradition became much richer during this time than the rest of Spain's because they had access to French wine-making culture. It was during this period that north-eastern Spain turned its hand to *cava* (sparkling white wine) — thanks to the damage to red wine grape varieties and learning the *méthode champenoise* from the French.

However, the protection offered by the Pyrenees did not last long, and the phylloxera aphid arrived in Spain later that century, a pincer movement from the north over the mountains and from the south via the Port of Málaga. Due to the country's geography (and poor transport infrastructure), the plague took longer to spread, so when things started to look really dire (the plague only reached La Rioja in 1901) the cure had already been discovered. It consisted in grafting tougher vines, the ones that could resist the bug, onto weaker vines, to create hybrids that could withstand the epidemic. This saved the Spanish vineyards, and the first Spanish 'Designation of Origin' was established in La Rioja in 1926.

The winemaking industry would go through still more difficulties before achieving its modern-day prestige. World War I paralysed the European market, which made exporting almost impossible. Then the Spanish Civil War froze the country, and while the different sides were fighting each other, the vines (particularly those near the cities) were left untended, and some of them were torn up to plant wheat and other cereals to feed a starving population. But even when the war was over, the difficulties did not end: World War II immobilized the European market once more and made it challenging for the industry to take off again until the 1950s. It was at this time that some of the vineyards were replanted and the wine tradition began to be restored in some parts of Spain.

With the 1960s came the international rediscovery of Jerez (sherry) and Rioja; but the real resurgence came only after the death of General Francisco Franco in 1975 and the transition to democracy. Spain had never been a bastion of free trade aside from local exceptions like the mercantile cities of Barcelona, Bilbao, and Málaga. Even when Sevilla was awash with gold and Spain was the richest, most powerful nation on earth, the Crown was firmly in control of every detail of commerce. The State eventually replaced the Crown but remained largely protectionist and stultifyingly bureaucratic. Franco toyed with neoliberalism when advised by economists associated with the Catholic lay organization Opus Dei, but he never fully embraced economic liberalism because he realized that it would threaten his political power. State capitalism is not the Free Market.

But as Spain's economic outlook improved during the last decades of Franco's rule, the growing middle classes (and increasing numbers of tourists) led to a mini-revival of wine-making. Things really took off, however, when Spain joined the (then) EEC (now EU) in 1986. This brought economic aid to the Spanish wine sector, but far more importantly it opened up new markets. The advent, in 1993, of Margaret Thatcher's proudest creation, the Single Market, signalled the beginning of a new phase for Spanish wine exports, coinciding with a decade-long boom under the pro-market Prime Minister José María Aznar (in office 1996–2004).

Long-overdue labour market liberalization and a programme of deregulation helped make the Spanish economy one of the fastest growing and most dynamic in Europe (admittedly from a very low base). The 1990s gave way to an acceptance of using 'new' varieties of grapes like Cabernet Sauvignon and Chardonnay, and the ban on watering (which had been imposed during a drought period) was lifted in 1996. This meant new places to plant, more grape varieties and more profitable methods of production.

Spain joined the Eurozone in 1999 and for a while, the economic miracle continued, carrying wine production along with it. Until the mid-1980s, a great deal of the wine produced in Spain had been bound for the domestic market, sold in polypins and decanted into refillable bottles in grocery stores (*bodegas* and *vinotecas*). Production values improved, often due to the input of winemakers from France, Italy and the New World, and once again Spanish wines regained a reputation for quality. Also, thanks to devaluations of the peseta in the 1990s, they were highly competitive. Once the economic crisis of 2008 hit, however, the instrument of devaluation was no longer available because Spain was by then using the Euro.

Even so, along with tourism, fruit and vegetable production, clothing (*e.g.* Zara, Mango, etc.) and to an extent automotive manufacturing, wine production is one of the sectors that has managed to weather recent economic storms reasonably well. Spain still produces a fair amount of plonk, but unless you buy your wine in bulk from a corner shop or in a Tetra Pak® you should be able to avoid it. Because of the relatively recent revival of Spanish winemaking, there are few quasi-mythical *grand cru* wines able to command exorbitant prices.

Spanish VAT (IVA) is similar to the UK rate at 21%, but alcohol duty is far lower. Duty on a pint of beer (roughly equivalent to three '*cañas*') is roughly 4p, compared to 54p in the UK. Duty on a measure of spirits is 12p rather than 48p in the UK. On wine, there is no duty levied at all, compared to almost £3 per 75cl bottle in the UK. On-sales mark-up on wine tends to be around 100% in Spain, as opposed to 200% in the UK. In other words, a bottle of wine in a Spanish restaurant which costs you €21 would have a retail price of €10.50. 21% of that (€1.82) is IVA which means that the actual cost of the wine is €8.68. A €21 (£18.20) bottle of wine in a UK restaurant, by contrast, might have a retail price of, say, £7. After VAT at 20%, (£1.40) that leaves £5.60, of which £2.67 is duty. Thus, the actual cost of your wine is £2.93 — a third of what the Spanish wine is 'worth'.

🛢️ Sherry

There are sixteen named *Indicación Geográfica Protegida* (roughly equivalent to *Vins de Pays*) wine-producing regions in Andalucía and eight *Denominación de Origen Protegido* (DOP) regions. Of the latter, the best-known is undoubtedly that of Jerez-Xérès-Sherry, a region surrounding a triangle of towns south of Sevilla (Jerez de la Frontera, El Puerto de Santa María, and Sanlúcar de Barrameda) using grapes grown in soil that is arid and chalky but has excellent water retention. The unique soil is actually three kinds of soil, already noted in the Roman era (Lucius Junius Columella [*fl.* 60 AD] wrote about *cretosi*, *sabulosi* and *palustres*) for their extraordinary properties.

It comes as a surprise to many British visitors to Spain to discover that the vast majority of sherry produced is dry. Sherry is basically an aged and slightly fortified white wine. Even the dark, sweet and sticky Pedro Ximénez is made from (dried) white grapes. Within the dry sherry category, there are two major styles: those that are biologically aged under a layer of *flor* (yeast), *viz.* Fino and Manzanilla; and that which is oxidatively aged in the absence of *flor* — Oloroso. Two intermediate styles exist (Amontillado and Palo Cortado), and both start as biologically aged wines but lose their layer of *flor* at some point and continue their maturation in the oxidative way. All of these wines are made from the Palomino grape (though the 'Fino' produced in Málaga is made from Pedro Ximénez grapes).

When it comes to sweet sherry, the most important difference is the fact that it can be naturally sweet, or 'artificially sweetened' by blending dry styles of sherry with sweet wines or grape syrup. Naturally sweet sherry is called *vino dulce natural*. It can be produced from Pedro Ximénez or Moscatel grapes that are harvested late and usually dried in the sun before being pressed. A blended sweet sherry, on the other hand, is called *vino generoso de licor* — and all types start from a base of dry Palomino wine, to which is added PX or Moscatel wine, or (in the Málaga analogue) *arrope*: a syrup made of grape juice that is boiled and highly concentrated.

The pale, dry sherries called Fino and Manzanilla are mainly drunk as *apéritifs*. Fino pairs well with seafood, *jamón*, chilled soups, and spicy or fried dishes. Manzanilla means 'chamomile' and is made in only one of the Sherry towns — Sanlúcar de Barrameda (which also has its own DOP) where proximity to the sea allows a slightly different *flor* to develop leading to a saltier, lighter palate. It pairs especially well with fish, seafood, sushi and sashimi.

Amontillado (*lit.* in the style of Montilla — see below) is an oxidized and mature Fino: brandy-coloured, with nutty aromas of tobacco, aromatic herbs and often ethereal, polished notes of oak. It is difficult for British people to appreciate because it is frequently the base of sweet blends, so when we taste the pure, dry, and complex version in Spain we tend to think about sherry trifle and assume that it is sweet. It is not. Your taste-buds are deceiving you. It pairs well with white meat, beef-based soups, medium-strength cheeses, and *pâtés*.

Oloroso ('fragrant') is aged like an Amontillado but begins with a stronger must than Finos and Amontillados, often involving two pressings. Oloroso is similar in colour to Amontillado and has nuts (especially walnuts) on the nose, combined with polished/balsamic notes, subtle dried fruits, and tobacco. There are noticeable spicy notes in older examples. Often one also detects meaty hints, truffle and leather. It pairs perfectly with dark meat, game, and mature cheeses.

Palo Cortado (*lit.* 'cut stick') is only made by accident — it begins life as a Fino but for some reason, the surface *flor* dies back and it begins to oxidize. The name comes from the vertical line chalked on a Fino barrel (the 'stick'); if the *flor* dies, the line is intersected with a diagonal chalk mark and the 'stick' is 'cut'. It should have the aromatic refinement of Amontillado combined with the structure and body of an Oloroso. In short: Amontillado on the nose, Oloroso in the mouth. Compared to an Amontillado, it will have spent less time under *flor* (traditionally up to three years, but in fact, modern Palo Cortado rarely ages under *flor* for any time at all). It pairs perfectly with cured meats, soft blue cheeses, *foie gras* and nuts.

As the well-known Spanish adage advises, '*Si nada, fino o manzanilla; si vuela, amontillado; si corre, oloroso*' ('If it swims, Fino or Manzanilla; if it flies, Amontillado; if it runs, Oloroso'). This may be a huge generalization, but it's a handy, fairly reliable, rule-of-thumb. Sherry is of course on sale in Málaga, but it is also on sale in every British supermarket. A visit to Málaga is instead a wonderful opportunity to sample Spain's other, less well-known, sweet wines.

Condado de Huelva

The wines of Spain's south-westernmost DOP (1963) are broadly made in the same styles as Sherry, though from different grape varieties. It was almost certainly wines from Huelva that were the first Old World wines to be exported to the New World, on the voyage of 1502. An unusual product of the Huelva region is *vino naranja* — an aged (10 years old) sweet Oloroso-style wine further macerated with bitter orange peel for 2 years (see p. 153). It is drunk as a dessert wine or *digestivo*.

Montilla–Moriles

This region south of Córdoba produces sherry analogues, though it would not be fair to say that they are simply copying the products of Jerez. Amontillado means 'in the style of Montilla', so Jerez copied Montilla, at least with regard to that variety. Rarely encountered outside Spain (or outside Andalucía), the different terroir and grape varieties (Pedro Ximénez, Moscatel, Airén, Baladí-Verdejo and Montepila) mean subtle differences from the more famous Sherry versions. Like Jerez-Xérès-Sherry, Montilla also produces vinegar and brandy.

Tinto, Blanco, Rosado

Before looking at the sweet wines of Málaga, it's worth mentioning that plenty of 'regular' (or 'table') wine is produced in Andalucía. The DOP of Granada produces red, white and sparkling wines from a range of grape varieties: all the usual suspects (Garnacha, Tempranillo, Sauvignon Blanc, Palomino) plus a few interesting local ones like Vigiriega. The Lebrija DOP in the Province of Sevilla produces sweet wines, but also reds (mainly Tempranillo and Cabernet Sauvignon) and whites (Moscatel de Alejandría and Vidueño).

All sixteen *Indicación Geográfica Protegida* regions and three of the DOP regions make wines in non-sherry styles. The following table indicates the permitted grape varieties and the styles of wine produced: **T**into (Red), **R**osado (Rosé), **B**lanco (White), **G**eneroso (Sweet or fortified) and **E**spumoso (Sparkling).

Region and date of formation	Styles	Main authorized grape varieties
Granada (DOP, 2009)	T R B E	(T/R) Tempranillo, Garnacha Tinta, Cabernet Sauvignon, Cabernet Franc, Merlot, Syrah, Pinot Noir, Monastrell, Romé, Petit Verdot (B/E) Vijiriego, Chardonnay, Sauvignon Blanc, Torrontes, Moscatel de Alejandría, Moscatel de Grano Menudo
Lebrija (DOP, Sevilla, 2010)	T B G	(T) Cabernet Sauvignon, Syrah, Tempranillo, Tintilla de Rota (B/G) Moscatel de Alejandría, Palomino, Vidueño
Sierras de Málaga (DOP, 2001)	T R B	(T/R) Romé, Cabernet Sauvignon, Merlot, Syrah, Tempranillo (B) PX, Moscatel, Chardonnay, Macabeo, Sauvignon Blanc

Region and date of formation	Styles	Main authorized grape varieties
Altiplano de Sierra Nevada (IGP, Granada, 2005)	T R B	(T) Garnacha Tinta, Monastrell, Cabernet Franc (B) Baladí Verdejo, Airén, Torrontés
Bailén (IGP, Jaén, 2004)	T R B	(T) Molinera, Tempranillo, Cabernet Sauvignon, (R) Molinera, Tempranillo (B) Molinera, Pedro Ximénez
Cádiz (IGP, 2005)	T B	(T) Syrah, Monastrell, Merlot, Tintilla de Rota (B) Garrido, Palomino, Chardonnay, Moscatel, Mantía
Córdoba (IGP, 2004)	T R	Pinot Noir, Syrah, Cabernet Sauvignon, Cumbres de Guadalfeo Granada (Granada, 2004)
Desierto de Almería (IGP, 2003)	T B	(T) Garnacha Tinta, Monastrell, Syrah (B) Chardonnay, Moscatel, Macabeo
Laderas del Genil (IGP, Granada, 2003)	T R B	(T/R) Garnacha Tinta, Pinot Noir, Syrah (B) Vijiriego, PX, Chardonnay, Viognier, Verdejo, Gewürztraminer, Riesling
Laujar-Alpujarra (IGP, Almería, 2004)	T R B	(T) Garnacha tinta, Monastrell, Syrah, (B) Jaén Blanco, Macabeo, Vijiriego, Moscatel de Grano Menudo
Los Palacio (IGP, Sevilla, 2003)	B	Airén, Colombard, Sauvignon Blanc
Norte de Almería (IGP, Almería, 2008)	T R B	(T/R) Cabernet Sauvignon, Merlot, Monastrell (B) Airén, Chardonnay, Macabeo
Ribera del Andarax (IGP, Almería, 2003)	T R B	(T/R) Cabernet Sauvignon, Merlot, Syrah
Sierra Norte de Sevilla (IGP, Sevilla, 2004)	T R B	(T/R) Garnacha Tinta, Tempranillo, Cabernet Sauvignon
Sierra Sur de Jaén (IGP, Jaén, 2003)	T B	(T) Garnacha Tinta, Pinot Noir, Syrah
Sierras de Las Estancias & Los Filabres (IGP, Almería, 2008)	T R B	(T/R) Cabernet Sauvignon, Merlot, Monastrell, Tempranillo (B) Airén, Macabeo, Moscatel de Grano Menudo
Torreperogil (IGP, Jaén, 2006)	T B	(T) Garnacha Tinta, Syrah, Cabernet Sauvignon, Tempranillo
Villaviciosa de Córdoba (IGP, Córdoba, 2008)	B G	(B) Baladí Verdejo, Calagraño, Palomino Fino, Verdejo (G) Palomino, Pedro Ximénez

⚔ Málaga Wines

If a viticulturist in the Province of Málaga wants to join an appellation (DOP), he or she has several options. They could join DOP Málaga by following its regulation. Another option would be to join DOP Sierras de Málaga (Málaga Mountain Ranges DOP) which has a different regulatory structure. These two wine regions overlap, so the regulation differs while the geographical area is exactly the same. In the subzone of Manilva or Axarquía, a viticulturist could join the DOP Pasas de Málaga (Málaga Raisins DOP) though this focuses on table grapes, not grapes for winemaking. Yet another option would be to join two DOPs (or even all three of them) by registering different vineyard plots to different appellations. This means that the Regulatory Council that controls the three DOPs will supervise each plot depending upon to which DOP it has been assigned. The two wine DOPs cover 3,800 ha (9,390 acres) and produce almost 2.5 million litres annually. The main varieties cultivated are still Moscatel de Alejandría and Pedro Ximénez (often known as Pero Ximén in the Málaga region), reflecting the historical importance of sweet wines.

When it comes to wine, not raisins, DOP Sierras de Málaga makes more conventional table wines (reds, rosés, whites; *tintos, rosados, blancos*) whilst DOP Málaga makes sweet and fortified wines or *vinos generosos*. The traditional wine style of Andalucía is the sweet or dessert style, and the familiar red/rosé/white styles are more recent, with a number of *bodegas* (wineries) switching to table wines in recent years. Though if we go back even further, the wines of the area were probably lighter and drier than those produced now, with the fortified style being developed because it maintained its quality for export (a long sea voyage) and appealed to British tastes (a big export market). The possible derivation of the English word 'sack' from '*sec*' (dry) may be a clue that Málaga wines were not always especially sweet (for a more likely origin, see p. 152).

History

After the *reconquiſta*, the Brotherhood of Viñeros de Málaga was created in 1487, as described by Cecilio García de la Leña in his book *Conversaciones históricas malagueñas* (1780):

> 'The first thing our Catholic Conquering Princes did to make this city happy, rich, and prosperous was to establish a Fraternity of Vintners (**Hermandad de Viñeros**), to watch over the production of the local wines, which even during the times of Moorish domination, played no small part in commerce and in the prosperity of the subjects. They understood that the vineyards, in addition to increasing the contentment and prosperity of their beloved city, would also contribute in no small manner to the Royal Treasury, due to the quantity of merchandise that would be exported to other dominions.'

Some years later, on 12 January 1502 in Seville, the *Reyes Católicos* confirmed the creation of the Fraternity of Vintners by Royal Decree. The guild privileges were confirmed again by their daughter Queen Juana (of Castilla) in 1513.

Although soon eclipsed by Sherry, Málaga wine was once hugely popular in Britain and throughout Europe. In 1791, Miguel de Gálvez y Gallardo, the Spanish ambassador to Moscow, presented Catherine the Great with some cases of Málaga wine, and we assume that it met with her approval because all shipments of wine controlled by the Fraternity of Vintners were soon afterwards exempted from Russian tariffs. One assumes, too, that Málaga wine enjoyed some popularity in Russia generally because it is mentioned by Fyodor Dostoevsky in his novella *The Dream of a Ridiculous Man*. Throughout the 18th century, Málaga wine grew in popularity, while Sherry declined. In the 19th century, the situation was reversed, largely due to the commercial preferences of British merchants. It was not Málaga wine that filled colonial decanters in Madras, Melbourne and Mombasa, but Sherry wine.

In 1806, by Royal Decree, the Málaga Vintners' House and Company of Commerce (*La Casa & Compañía de Comercio de Viñeros de Málaga*) was created, whose duties were 'to prevent the adulteration of the merchandise expedited by the Company, by means of placing difficult to falsify marks on all vessels, casks or containers used to ship wine'. This came just as Málaga's wine trade went into decline. And in 1878 phylloxera reached Málaga, marking the beginning of the agricultural, economic and then political crisis of the early twentieth century. The huge Russian export market collapsed with the 1917 Revolution, and then came the calamitous Spanish Civil War during which fighters on both sides helped themselves to wine from *soleras* (the system of stacked barrels used for blending to achieve consistency). Between 1878 and 1978, the total area covered by Málaga vineyards shrank by 90%: nine times worse than a decimation.[36] When other makers (in La Rioja, for example) began to recover, Málaga fell victim to changing tastes which eschewed 'sweet' and fortified wines.

More recently, there has been a modest resurgence of sweet wine and Málaga wines are beginning to rediscover their position in the world. Twenty years ago, many were convinced that the most traditional bars in Málaga would have to shut their doors as the thirst for sweet wine declined. So far, this has not happened. If anything, there has been a (modest) revival.

🔲 Subzones

There are five geographical sub-areas within the Málaga, Sierras de Málaga, and Pasas de Málaga DOPs (remember that they overlap): Axarquía, Costa Occidental-Manilva, Montes, Norte and Serranía de Ronda.

Axarquía

Axarquía (from the Arabic, *al-sarqiyya*, 'the east') is located in the eastern part of the province and it extends from the coast up into the mountains. Therefore, vineyards are often found on very steep slopes where machinery is unable to function. It is not unusual, even now, to

---

36   Julian Jeffs, *The Wines of Spain* (Mitchell Beazley, London, 2006) p.337

see mules bringing the grapes from the vineyards to the wineries. Despite these topographical challenges, Axarquía is the second-largest wine-producing subzone within the Province of Málaga. Here, Moscatel de Alejandría (Alexandria Muscat) has been grown for more than two thousand years. Another high-profile grape is the indigenous Romé (used to make *blancos* and *tintos*) which is well adapted to the subtropical conditions of mild weather and little rainfall alongside considerable moisture due to proximity to the sea. The whole area is famous for its raisins (*pasas*).

Costa Occidental-Manilva

The wines from the western coastal area have had to compete with bricks and mortar as the growth of the tourist resorts along the Costa del Sol forced vineyards to move inland and uphill when roads, golf courses, and shopping centres occupied the flatter areas near the coast. Nonetheless, wine varieties, table grapes and raisins are still produced here, facing the sea at a higher altitude or deeper inland. The main variety is (as usual) Moscatel de Alejandría, but Cabernet Sauvignon, Merlot, Syrah and Tempranillo also have an increasing share.

Montes

Málaga's municipality is surrounded by a steep hill range with very diverse vine-growing conditions, which allows wineries to make a wide range of table wines (*tinto*, *rosado* and *blanco*), sweet wines, and liqueur (fortified) wines. Two famous local *bodegas* are Antigua Casa de Guardia (also the name of a tavern on the Alameda Principal in Málaga) and Quitapenas. The main varieties are Pedro Ximénez (or Pero Ximén as it is known here) and various varieties of Moscatel (Muscat). In its heyday, Montes was known for producing the finest examples of Málaga wine and in the 18th century many British decanters had silver labels engraved with the name 'Mountain'. Dark (*tinto*) wines were anglicized as 'Tent'.

Norte

The little-known Doradilla grape variety is indigenous to this subzone, although Pero Ximén is also very common. Unlike areas such as Axarquía or Montes, the vineyards are planted in fertile soils and on largely flat ground. The climate is continental, rather than subtropical.

Serranía de Ronda

Located near Ronda are the ruins of a Roman city called Acinipo, which may be derived from the word for 'wine region' in a Celtiberian language. No one knows for sure, but it seems likely that Ronda has been a centre of wine production since the very earliest times. Almost half of the wineries belonging to the DOP Sierras de Málaga are situated in the Serranía de Ronda ('Ronda mountain range'). At an altitude of over 700 m, the focus in this zone is more on table wines than on traditional sweet and fortified wines. As a result, 'new' (to Spain, or to the region) varieties like Chardonnay, Cabernet Sauvignon, Merlot, Syrah and Tempranillo have become more and more common. Some of Málaga's best quality wines come from here.

DOP Sierras de Málaga

Types Of Wine

DOP Sierras de Málaga covers 'still wine' production with an alcohol content between 10 and 15.5% ABV and a sugar content of less than 12 g per litre. Red, Rosé and White (*tinto*, *rosado* and *blanco*) types are produced.

The authorized white grape varieties are Pero Ximén (Pedro Ximénez), Moscatel de Alejandría (Alexandria Muscat), Small Berry Muscat (Morisco), Chardonnay, Colombard, Doradilla, Airén, Gewürztraminer, Macabeo (Viura), Riesling, Sauvignon Blanc, Verdejo and Viognier.

The permitted red varieties are Romé, Cabernet Franc, Cabernet Sauvignon, Garnacha (Grenache), Graciano, Malbec, Merlot, Monastrell (Mourvedre), Petit Verdot, Pinot Noir, Syrah, Tempranillo and Tintilla (Tintilla de Rota).

Classification according to the ageing process is the same as for all Spanish table wines:

- **Crianza** ('ageing'): At least 2 years ageing between both oak barrel and bottle. The barrel ageing should last for at least 6 months.
- **Reserva**: At least 3 years ageing between both oak barrel and bottle. The barrel ageing should last for at least 12 months.
- **Gran Reserva** (for red wines): At least 5 years ageing between both oak barrel and bottle. The barrel ageing should last for at least 24 months.
- **Gran Reserva** (for white and rosé wines): At least 2½ years ageing between both oak barrel and bottle. The barrel ageing should last for at least 6 months.

DOP Málaga

DOP Málaga (designated in 1932) produces both 'liqueur wines' and what, to most British palates, seem like 'sweet' wines, even if some are officially 'dry'. There are multiple ways of classifying and describing wines of this DOP, reflecting its very long history of winemaking.

Classification according to level of fortification:

First are *vinos de licor* ('liqueur wines') including *vinos dulces naturales* ('natural sweet wines'). These wines are made from Pero Ximén (Pedro Ximénez) and/or Moscatel de Alejandría, but up to 30% Doradilla, Airén and Romé varieties (in total) are permitted. Due to a shortage of Pero Ximén grapes in the Málaga DOP, it is permissible to use grapes from some areas of the Córdoba Province. *Vinos de licor* ('liqueur wines') are fortified wines of between 15% and 22% ABV. 'Natural sweet wines' (*vinos dulces naturales*) are fortified sweet wines (that is, their sweetness is natural, but not their alcohol content, because they are fortified). Fortified semi-sweet, semi-dry or dry wines are also produced and all categories are included under the main *vinos de licor* heading.

Second, come the different, but confusingly similar-sounding, unfortified *vinos naturalmente dulces* ('naturally sweet wines'), which are at least 13% alcohol by volume. They are made from over-ripened grapes (*uvas sobremaduradas*) and the resulting alcohol content must come exclusively from the fermentation process, not fortification. They can also be made from raisined grapes (*uvas pasificadas*).

Third, are unfortified *vinos secos* (dry wines).

The official description of character is as follows:

- **Dry liqueur wine:** clear, bright, with an intense and characteristic nose, with obvious but integrated alcohol; on the palate, it can be dry or slightly sweet, with moderate acidity, being powerful, warm and persistent.
- **Sweet liqueur wine:** clear, bright; intense on the nose, obvious but integrated alcohol, honeyed, complex; Sweet or very sweet entry into the mouth, fair acidity, power-

ful, unctuous, very persistent. If it meets the conditions required, it can be identified with the specific name 'natural sweet wine'.

- **Wine from overripe grapes:** clean, bright, pale yellow to golden; fresh, complex, aromatic and characteristically fine on the nose. On the palate, its contrasted acid-sweet balance stands out; fresh, lively, unctuous and persistent. If it meets the conditions, it can be identified with the specific name 'naturally Sweet Wine'.

- **Wine from raisined grapes:** clean, bright, from pale yellow to old gold; complex, aromatic and characteristically fine on the nose, with nuances of raisined grapes and a clear expression of the preferred varieties, which are the only ones that can be used for its production; In the mouth, its concentration, acid-sweet balance, great smoothness, aromatic aftertaste and persistence stand out.

- **Dry wine:** Yellow to amber in colour depending on age; penetrating aroma, powerful, round and dry on the palate.

The three basic types of sweet liqueur wines:

- **Natural Sweet Wine:** obtained from musts from the Pero Ximén and/or Moscatel varieties, with a minimum initial natural richness of sugars of 212 g per litre, and with a natural alcoholic strength of not less than 7% ABV.

- **Vino Maestro:** ('Master Wine') natural sweet wine obtained from musts from the Pero Ximén and/or Moscatel varieties, from a very incomplete fermentation, because before it begins the must is topped with 8% alcohol. With this method, fermentation is very slow and stops when the alcohol content is 15–16% ABV, leaving more than 100 g/l of unfermented sugars.

- **Vino Tierno:** ('Soft Wine') obtained from musts from the Pero Ximén and/or Moscatel varieties, from ripe grapes, which give rise to a must with a sugar content of more than 350 g/l.

Other permitted ingredients:

- **Dry wine and concentrated grape must** from the varieties Doradilla, Lairén (as Airén is known in Córdoba) and/or Romé (up to 30%).

- **Grape must**, **grape must quenched with alcohol**, or **concentrated grape must**.

- **Must of raisined grapes** to which neutral alcohol of viticultural origin has been added to prevent ('quench') further fermentation.

- *Arrope* (boiled grape syrup): grape must concentrated to one-third of its initial volume (used to sweeten liqueur wines). *Arrope* is only used in winemaking in the Málaga DOP (elsewhere in Spain it's a popular dessert ingredient).

- *Pantomima: arrope* further reduced to half of its volume (used to sweeten liqueur wines).

- *Vino borracho* ('drunk wine'): equal parts wine and wine alcohol used to fortify wines and retard or slow fermentation.

Classification according to ageing in oak:

- *Málaga Pálido* ('Pale Málaga'), up to 6 months, but usually unaged.
- *Málaga* from 6 to 24 months.
- *Málaga Noble* ('Noble Málaga'), from 2 to 3 years.
- *Málaga Añejo* ('Old Málaga'), from 3 to 5 years.

- *Málaga Trasañejo* ('Very Old Málaga'), over 5 years.

Classification according to the sugar content:

- *Dulce* (sweet) sugar content > 140 g per litre
- *Semidulce* (semi-sweet) 75–125 g per litre
- *Abocado* or *Semiseco* (semi-dry) 45–125 g per litre
- *Seco* (dry) < 45 g per litre. Although this satisfies the regulator for Málaga wines, it cannot be exported as '*seco*' because the EU definition of dryness is different. Once again, it is a historical descriptor.

Classification according to varietal:

- **Pero Ximén** (Pedro Ximénez)
- **Moscatel** (de Alejandría)

Classification according to must:

- *Lágrima* ('Tear'): Made from the first treading (pressing) of grapes, without mechanical extraction. If it is aged for more than 2 years then it is known as '*Lacrimae Christi*'.
- *Vendimia Asoleada:* made from musts obtained entirely from sun-dried grapes, exclusively of the Moscatel and/or Pero Ximén varieties.

Classification according to colour:

Wine becomes darker the longer it is aged in the barrel, but also the more *arrope* is added.

- *Dorado* or **Golden**: A liqueur wine made with no addition of *arrope*, or else an unfortified naturally sweet wine that has been oak-aged. (Both the Spanish and the English names are recognized by the DOP due to the important historical trade of these wines with the British Isles.)
- *Rojo dorado* or **Rot Gold**: A liqueur wine made with less than 5% *arrope* added by volume and subjected to an ageing process. (The German term is recognized by the regulator, again for historical reasons.)
- *Oscuro* or **Brown**: A liqueur wine made with 5–10% *arrope* added by volume and subjected to an ageing process.
- *Color:* A liqueur wine made with 10–15% *arrope* added by volume and subjected to an ageing process.
- *Negro* or **Dunkel**: ('dark'): A liqueur wine made with more than 15% *arrope* added by volume and subjected to an ageing process.

Classification according to style:

- **Dry Pale** or **Pale Dry**: a liqueur wine without *arrope* that contains less than 45 grams of sugar per litre.
- **Pale Cream:** Either a liqueur wine without *arrope*, a wine of natural sweetness, or a naturally sweet wine (unfortified) that contains more than 45 grams of sugar per litre.
- *Pajarete* ('Little bird'): This is an amber fortified liqueur that has a total sugar content of between 45 and 140 g per litre. It is an oak-aged wine made without any addition of *arrope* (concentrated grape syrup).
- *Dulce Crema* or **Cream**: An amber oak-aged liqueur wine that contains between 100 and 140 grams of sugar per litre.

- **Sweet:** An oak-aged liqueur wine that contains more than 140 grams of sugar per litre. The colour ranges from amber to almost black.

Classification according to mode of ageing:

With the exception of *pálido*, all Málaga wines are aged for at least 6 months. Some wines are aged as *añadas* or vintages; that is, the wine is put in a barrel and left to mature (usually with older wine from another barrel). Some Málaga wines, however, use the dynamic *solera* system also employed in the ageing of sherry, sherry vinegar, and brandy (and some Madeira and Port). This method of ageing and blending is explained further below.

The multiple and often overlapping ways of categorizing and naming Málaga wines is rather confusing for the consumer, with very similar wines from different *bodegas* often using completely different names. You may find the list of wines kept by the Antigua Casa de Guardia (p. 197) a useful guide.

🛢 The *Solera* System

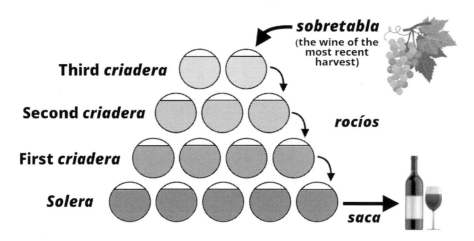

The *solera* system of maturation and fractional blending is used in the production of all sherries and Spanish brandies as well as some Málaga wines (which will often have 'solera' as part of their name or description). Invented, as far as we know, in Sanlúcar de Barremeda in the mid-18th century the method organizes and simplifies the blending process. Prior to this, new wine was added to a barrel containing residual older wine. While this would impart character and a measure of consistency to the wine at the end of ageing, the *solera* system achieves near-perfectly consistent results year on year.

It works by stacking barrels vertically. Barrels in a *solera* are arranged in different groups or tiers, called *criaderas* or 'nurseries'. Each tier contains wine of the same age. The oldest tier, at the bottom (confusingly called *solera* as well) holds wine ready to be bottled. When a fraction of the wine is extracted from the *solera* (in a process called the *saca* — the most likely origin of the English term 'sack'), it will be replaced with the same amount of wine from the first *criadera*, *i.e.* the one above that is slightly younger and typically less complex. This, in turn, will be topped up with wine from the second *criadera* and so forth.

The last/top *criadera*, which holds the youngest wine, is topped up with the wine from the latest harvest, named *sobretabla*. Taking away part of the wine and replacing it with the contents of other tiers, is called *rociar* or 'to wash down'.

The *saca* (bottling of the old wine) and *rocía* (replenishing the casks) will usually take place several times a year, but the actual number may vary and specific figures are rarely disclosed. It is impossible to give the exact age of a wine that has been aged in a *solera*, as it is a blend of many vintages. It is only possible to give an approximate or average age of the wine. This is determined by the number of *criaderas*, the typical percentage of each *saca*, and the frequency of the *saca*. The combination of these factors defines the rotation of the total stock of wine and allows us to estimate the average age.

A wine bottled from a *solera* that was started ten years ago will contain wine that is ten years old blended with wine that is nine, eight, seven... possibly up to the wine of the latest harvest. Some very ancient *soleras* could in theory contain molecules of wine hundreds of years old, although scientific testing suggests that around 80 years old is about the limit.

Sparkling Wine

A number of *bodegas* in the Málaga DO areas produce sparkling wine (*blancos* and *rosados*); mainly sweet or semi-sweet, but with an increasing number of dry styles appearing in recent years. However, although these wines are made in the Málaga region from locally grown grapes, they are not Málaga DO wines because neither Málaga wine DOP authorizes sparkling wines (*vinos espumosos*)... at least not yet.

Orange Wine

The 'orange wine' that has grown in popularity in the UK in recent years is essentially a version of rosé, but made with white grapes. Whereas contact with red grape skins produces either red (long contact) or rosé (short contact) wine, contact with white grape skins can result in a wine with an orange hue. By contrast, Spanish '*vino naranja*' actually contains orange. The best-known, '*Vino Naranja del Condado de Huelva*', is a fortified sherry-type wine matured in the *solera* system, where bitter orange peel is macerated in young wine. The (accidental) dark orange colour is due to the use of sun-dried grapes.

A version of *vino naranja* is made in Málaga, albeit by a different method. Dried bitter orange peel is macerated in grape spirit that is then added to sweet Moscatel wine. Málaga's *vino naranja* is almost clear in appearance, and far lighter on the palate than the version from Huelva. The orange adds an additional layer of flavour and perfume to an already fruity and fragrant Moscatel. If you see it on a menu, it makes a wonderful dessert wine to accompany any creamy or chocolatey pudding.

Cartojal

Cartojal, a sweet white wine made by the venerable Bodegas Málaga Virgen, is the party drink of Málaga, If you are not in the city during the *feria* (the annual fair held in August) then you may not encounter it. If you are in Málaga for the fair, you cannot miss it. Almost every adult will be clutching a full or half bottle (or carrying it in a jaunty pink cool pouch attached to a lanyard), and some hardcore party-goers will be dragging wheeled cool boxes full of bottles.

Every *feria* in Spain has its own *bebida típica* (signature drink). In Jerez it is Fino sherry, and in Sanlúcar de Barrameda it is Manzanilla. In Logroño (La Rioja) it is, naturally, red wine (they even fill the main city fountain with red wine). In Sevilla it is *rebujito* — a punch made by mixing *gaseosa* (sweet soda) and Fino sherry, with lime and mint. The Málaga tipple is Cartojal — sweet white wine, served chilled. It is sold in PET (plastic) bottles, and the labels and screw tops are a garish shade of pink with polka dots. So far, so naff, but the plastic bottles are necessary because drinking from glass bottles in the street is illegal under a Málaga by-law, and during the *feria*, there is a lot of drinking in the street.

The production of Cartojal originally began when some winemakers noticed that huge quantities of sweet white wine were being consumed during the Feria, yet none of it was locally produced. It is made from the Moscatel de Alejandría grape, a grape native to Málaga and mainly grown in the Axarquía region. The other grape used to make Cartojal is the Moscatel Morisco grape which is grown in the Montes zone. The harvest of these grapes traditionally takes place at night, to avoid the intense heat of the day.

The name of the wine is taken from the slightly differently spelt Cartaojal, a village located near the vineyard, where the grape dehydration process, or *paseras*, takes place. The grapes are spread out and dried under the sun, in order to increase sugar levels in the fruit, contributing to the wine's unique flavour and aroma. It is light yellow with shades of pale green, a delicate floral aroma and hints of honey and citrus, which makes the wine perfect to drink when chilled. Some good noses claim to detect hints of smoke.

Every year the Málaga Virgen *bodega* produces about half a million bottles of Cartojal which will appear during the festivities in Málaga and other places across Andalusia; the pink-capped bottle is always accompanied by small, pink plastic cups.

🛢️ ☂ Guided Tours and Tastings

The oenotourism (*enoturismo*) scene in Spain has developed considerably over the last couple of decades. Guided tours of wineries in La Rioja have helped draw tourists to the region for many years, and in Catalonia they have become a way of tempting tourists away from the attractions of Barcelona and into the countryside. In the case of the sherry towns — Jerez, El Puerto de Santa María and Sanlúcar de Barrameda — tours of sherry houses are one of the main draws for foreign tourists.

There are only two wineries left in Málaga city, but there are many others scattered throughout the province, producing wines with the *Denominación de Origen* of Málaga and Sierras de Málaga. For suggestions of wineries that can be visited using public transport (*i.e.* a mix of bus/train and taxi) see p. 476ff.

Other Drinks
🍷 Brandy

The most common Spanish word for brandy is *coñac*, but it has been illegal to market Spanish brandy as *coñac* since 15 June 1989 when French cognac received its Protected Designation of Origin. The word 'brandy' is an *anglicismo* (the *Real Academia Española* spells it '*brandi*') and derives from the Dutch word *brandewijn*, meaning 'burnt wine'. In defiance of EU trade law, the Real Academia still prefers the term '*coñac*' (an analogous case is *roquefort*, which in Spain refers to any creamy blue cheese, not only that made in the French town of Roquefort.

Spain was probably the first country to produce brandy as it was the first to learn about distillation from the Moors in the 8th century. Although the first written reference to Spanish brandy only comes in the 16th century, circumstantial evidence indicates that distillation was already well established by the 13th century, and very likely even earlier.

Today, Spain produces about 80 million bottles of brandy per year. Three-quarters is consumed domestically; the rest is exported around the world. Mexico and the Philippines are the largest foreign consumers of Spanish brandy. Most British supermarkets stock at least one brand of Spanish brandy (even if under their own label) but due to the long tradition of Cognac and Armagnac in the UK, the Spanish variant is largely unknown to most consumers. This is a pity, as Spanish brandy represents exceptional value and quality. It tends to have caramel notes and is intense, fruity and sweet in comparison to its French counterpart.

Spanish brandy is primarily produced in Jerez (Andalucía, 95%) and Penedès (Catalonia, 5%). In Jerez, there are 30 producers, or *bodegas*, producing brandy in the 'sherry triangle' formed by the towns of Jerez de la Frontera, El Puerto de Santa María and Sanlúcar de Barrameda. A small amount of brandy is also produced in Málaga (see p. 156), and it is worth looking out for this because you are unlikely to find it outside Málaga, let alone outside Spain.

To be called a Brandy de Jerez, the brandy needs to be matured within the sherry triangle in casks that previously held sherry and utilize a *solera* system (see above) for ageing. It does not, however, need to be distilled in Jerez or use grapes grown there.

Spanish brandy is mostly based on the Airén grape; a rather bland variety with a high tolerance of heat and drought. It is mostly grown for brandy production in La Mancha and Valdepeñas in central Spain. Palomino, a grape variety used in sherry production, is also used for producing Spanish brandy. In Penedès brandy producers use Macabeo, Xarel-lo and Parellada, the same grape varieties used to produce Cava. They also use Ugni Blanc, the same grape variety used in Cognac.

Distillation utilizes both a traditional pot still as well as column stills. The pot still is called an *alembique*. It is derived from the '*alquitara*' stills introduced by the Moors in the 8th century. They are the predecessor of the Charentais stills used in Cognac production — suggesting that Spanish brandy production predates French production. Pot still produced spirit must have an alcohol content (ABV) of between 40% and 70%. This spirit is known in the brandy trade as 'holandas'. It is usually only distilled once, although there are a few producers who double-distil. Spirit produced from column stills has to be between 70% and 94.8% ABV, and is termed 'aguardiente' (literally 'fire water').

Brandy de Jerez is classified into three categories: Solera, Solera Reserva and Solera Gran Reserva. Solera is typically a mix of 50% holandas and 50% aguardiente and is aged on average for one year (with a minimum of three months). Solera Reserva is a mix of 75% holandas and 25% aguardiente and is aged for an average of three years (minimum of one year). Solera Gran Reserva is 100% holandas and is aged for an average of 10 years (with a minimum of three years).

The sherry barrels used for ageing must be at least three years old. This ensures that the wood is largely neutral and has little impact on the maturing spirit. In practice, the sherry casks used are much older. At Osborne, for example, one of the major producers in the region, the sherry casks used for maturing Brandy de Jerez have an average age of 60 years.

In Jerez, the 'age' of a bottling refers to the weighted average of the spirit in the solera. A Spanish brandy labelled as a 20 YO, for example, would typically incorporate brandies ranging from 4 to 50 years in age. 20 years is the weighted average of the age of the different brandies in the solera.

Each age statement requires its own unique solera. You cannot produce different age statements from the same solera without dismantling that solera. In a solera system, blending takes place prior to maturation and continues over that maturation process, whereas in many other spirits, at least those that don't use a solera system, maturation takes place before blending so there is more flexibility with how to utilize warehouse stocks. Once a solera has been established the average age will remain constant, as long as the sacas are extracted on the same schedule.

This differs from, say, the Scotch whisky system where the stated age on a bottling is the youngest component of the blend. Likewise, with Cognac, the different classifications are based on the youngest component of the blend, even though those blends could incorporate spirits that are far older.

Much of the branding of Spanish brandy revolves around 'great men' in Spanish history, like Carlos I or Pedro Cardinal González de Mendoza, or commemorates important Spanish events, like the naval victory of Spain and its allies over the Ottoman fleet at Lepanto in 1571. While this focus underscores its uniquely Spanish character and plays well with a conservative home market, it also fails to resonate with export markets (rather like the Scotch whisky industry's preoccupation a generation ago with kilts and bagpipes). For those in the know, however, Spain represents some of the best value high-quality brandy available. If you enjoy brandy but have been put off the Spanish version by brands like 'Fundador' — basically a cooking brandy — then Spain is the place to sample the quality stuff.

Some of the best Spanish brandies:

Bodegas Málaga Virgen Brandy Gran Reserva 1885, Solera Gran Reserva (Málaga, 36% ABV)

Do look out for this brandy, as it is the only one produced in the province of Málaga. Produced from selected DO Málaga wines, this brandy is aged in American oak casks which have contained sweet Pedro Ximénez wines. Dark amber, with faint green highlights; powerful and complex aromas, with highlights including nuts (walnuts and hazelnuts) against a sweet background of ripe plums, dates, and a hint of vanilla.

Osborne Brandy 1866, Solera Gran Reserva (originally Málaga, 40% ABV)

This is probably the best-known *malagueño* brandy, except that it is nowadays distilled and aged in the sherry town of El Puerto de Santa María. Over the years the Osborne winery has accumulated a whole range of brandy brands. Osborne are perhaps best-known for their basic brands Veterano and Magno, but many labels were taken over from other *bodegas*, such as Domecq or Agustín Blazquez. Although the company was founded by the English merchant Thomas Osborne Mann in 1772, the name is pronounced in the Spanish fashion: oss-**bor**-nay.

Brandy 1866 was originally created by Bodegas Jiménez y Lamothe in the late 19th century. As one of the biggest distilleries of Spain at the time, they exported brandy, triple sec, anise and other liqueurs all over the world, holding a warrant from the Royal House of Spain. The *bodega* was acquired by Larios in 1918, then by Pernod Ricard and most recently — with the dismantling of the Domecq brand — by Osborne in 2008 (picking up Carlos I, Carlos III, Felipe II and others at the same time).

It is produced from Airén grapes harvested, fermented and distilled in La Mancha and then aged in *soleras* in El Puerto de Santa María. The average age is around 12 years. Lighter in colour than most other brandies from the sherry region. On the nose, it is rather oaky, with pencil shavings and peppery notes. There are hints of vanilla, orange peel and brown sugar.

In the mouth it has medium body, and is fairly sweet and oaky. There's a vague fruity note (slight orange or peach), light hints of Oloroso (dried fruits, raisins, light nuts) and plenty of caramel and cocoa. There are hints of mint from the wood as well.

Conde de Osborne, Solera Gran Reserva (Jerez, 40.5% ABV)

This brandy is produced from wine made with 100% Airén grapes that has been matured in sherry casks that previously held Pedro Ximénez sherry. The average age is over 10 years. On the nose, there are notes of beeswax, honey, dried fruit and marzipan. On the palate, this is a thick, viscous brandy, with pronounced flavours of raisins, fig and prune, along with some caramel and even some surprising meaty notes. The finish is long, featuring sweet dried fruit and a hint of bitterness at the end.

Sanchez Romate 'Cardenal Mendoza', Solera Gran Reserva (Jerez, 40% ABV)

Cardinal Mendoza is aged for an average of 15 years in a combination of Oloroso and Pedro Ximénez sherry casks. The brandy is named for Pedro Cardinal Gonzalez de Mendoza, Primate of Spain and an adviser to Fernando and Isabel who was instrumental in persuading the Spanish monarchs to support Christopher Columbus's first voyage to the new world.

On the nose, there is an intense sherry cask aroma of raisin, prune and sweet almond. The palate has pronounced weight with dried fruit, along with notes of coffee, orange zest and cinnamon. The finish, which is very rich and silky smooth, emphasizes roast almond and marzipan, with a slight hint of bitterness at the end.

Pedro Domecq 'Carlos I', Solera Gran Reserva (Jerez, 40% ABV)

The brandy is aged in casks that previously held Oloroso and Amontillado sherry from a *solera* that is more than 100 years old. The average weighted age of the brandy, however, is probably around five years. The nose is very pronounced, with Christmas cake notes of cooked pastry and dried fruit, along with vanilla, cinnamon and some oak. On the palate, the brandy is smooth, with notes of sweet dried fruit, especially golden raisin and fig, some caramel, hints of vanilla and licorice and a touch of smoke. It's a brandy of impressive complexity with every sip uncovering new flavours.

Gonzales Byass 'Lepanto', Solera Gran Reserva (Jerez, 40% ABV)

Lepanto is the only brandy distilled in the city of Jerez from locally grown Palomino grapes, the same variety used to produce sherry. The brandy is double distilled in Charentais pot stills, originally from Cognac, and is aged for an average of 12 years: the first nine years in barrels that previously contained Tío Pepe and a further three years in casks that previously held 30 YO sweet Oloroso Matusalem sherry.

The brandy is very smooth, dry and delicate, offering notes of caramel, almonds and vanilla. There is also a version finished in dry Oloroso casks (Lepanto Oloroso Viejo), and a version finished in Pedro Ximénez casks (Lepanto Pedro Ximénez). The latter is somewhat sweeter.

Williams & Humbert 'Gran Duque D'Alba', Solera Gran Reserva (Jerez, 40% ABV)

An aromatic brandy that has been aged for 10 to 12 years in butts that previously held Oloroso sherry. It delivers notes of prunes, raisins and dates, along with hints of roasted nuts and old leather. The brandy is smooth, with a pronounced palate weight, with flavours of dried fruit, caramel and vanilla. There is also an 18 YO XO version that is finished in sweet PX sherry casks and a 20 YO 'Oro' version matured in dry Palo Cortado sherry casks.

 *Cerveza* (Beer)

Beer in Spain is a near-universal beverage, enjoyed by men and women, young and old, rich and poor. Although beer made from malted barley was almost certainly introduced to Iberia by the Phoenicians, and beer from malt and hops was made in medieval monasteries, it was not a beverage that was on sale widely, unlike wine. When the 16-year-old son of Queen Juana of Castilla came to Spain to rule as co-monarch (Carlos I), he imported Mechelschen Bruynen beer from Flanders, where he had been born. When, 40 years later, he abdicated his 23 thrones and titles and withdrew from court to retire to the Monastery of Yuste, he installed a microbrewery and brought Henry Van der Hesen from Flanders to run it. Despite frequent references to taverns in 16th-century picaresque novels, none mention beer. Lope de Vega, in his comedy *Pobreza no es vileza* ('Poverty is No Disgrace' 1620–1622) has his protagonist Panduro admit to drinking beer, but only in the absence of Spanish wine — a single reference to the drink in more than 2,000 plays by Spain's most prolific Golden Age playwright.

The story of Spain's transformation into Europe's fourth-largest producer and eighth-biggest consumer of beer didn't really begin until the late nineteenth century, when beer started to become popular among urban industrial workers, having previously been the preserve of the bourgeoisie. Even nowadays, the overwhelming majority of beer consumed by Spaniards will be one of six brands, made by four companies. Where other beers are available, they are bottled and usually Pilsner-style. However, this is changing, with a growing number of bars beginning to widen the range of beers served, especially of the 'craft' variety.

There are a few things to note about beer in Spain. First, because Spain is a warm country and beer is a cold drink, people drink it in small measures so that it stays cool. The most common measure in every region of Spain is a *caña* (*lit.* 'cane' — **kan**-yah). However, it is not a standard measure by volume like a half-litre or a pint. Quite how much, or how little, beer you will get depends upon where you are. In Madrid (and Málaga) it will be around 200ml, or perhaps a little less, whereas in the Basque Country, you will get about 350ml, which is closer to what would be called a '*doble*' ('double' — **doh**-blay) in Madrid. The Basques have a sub-*caña* measure called a *zurito* ('little dove'), and if you want a Madrid *doble*, then you'd need to order a *cañón* ('barrel' — kan-**yon**). Another popular way of consuming beer in hot weather is as *una clara* (a shandy), a mixture of beer and lemon Fanta, or a not-too-sweet kind of lemonade known as *gaseosa*.

In Málaga, every bar will offer the basic *caña* measure, although it could vary in size from place to place. Every bar will also offer a larger measure, which might be double the size of a *caña*, or only 50% larger. The name of this larger measure varies, however. It might be called a *maceta* (ma-**THay**-tah), a *media* (**may**-dee-ah), a *copa*, a *tubo* (**too**-boh) or even a *doble* (**doh**-blay), though *maceta* and *copa* are most common. Some establishments also sell a tankard measure of 500ml or more, which is usually called a *tanque* (**tan**-kay), but sometimes a *grande* (**gran**-day) or even a *copón* (koh-**pon**). If you stick to *cañas*, then you will be understood everywhere. In Málaga, a bottle of beer is called a '*tercio*' ('third' — **tair**-THyoh) and not a '*botella*'.

A You may also hear people refer to a *cañita*. This literally means a 'small *caña*', but Spaniards love diminutives almost as much as the Dutch, so it is just a cutesy way of saying *caña*. Similarly, you may be told the price in '*euritos*'. This is not an alternative currency, but a way of implying that it is a good price, *e.g.* 'only three little euros!'.

Second, unless you visit a bar that specializes in beer (a *cervecería* or craft beer brew-pub), you will find only one brand of beer on draught. They might have three versions of the beer — a standard beer, an alcohol-free version (usually known as *cero* ('zero') or *sin* ('without'), and a '*radler*' (draught *clara*/shandy) — but they will all be from the same brewery. If you want the regular beer, you only need to specify the size (*caña*, *media*, *tanque*, etc.) because the compliment '*de cerveza*' is understood. (Similarly, one rarely uses the word *vino* when ordering wine in a bar. It is enough to mention the colour: *blanco*, *tinto*, *rosado* or if there is a choice, the name or region of the wine: Rioja, Rueda, Penedès, Gran Vos, etc.)

Third, Spanish beer is frankly not very exciting. It is crisp, refreshing and pleasant to drink, but on the whole, it's pretty unremarkable Pilsner-style lager for which one would struggle to write tasting notes. The big brands nationally are **Mahou** (pronounced 'Mao', as in the Chinese leader) which predominates in about 50% of the country, **Amstel** leads in the east and west, **San Miguel** in the Basque Country, and **Cruzcampo** (brewed in Sevilla) in Andalucía. Worth looking out for, though, are beers made by **Cervezas Alhambra** from Granada. Their bottled **Reserva 1925** is a quite exceptional amber Pilsner brewed from Saaz hops, making it fruity, lightly spiced and refreshingly bitter.

Málaga's local brewery, **Cerveza Victoria**, has also enjoyed a spectacular Renaissance in recent years. The Victoria brewery is named after *Santa María de la Victoria* (Our Lady of Victories), co-patroness of the city of Málaga, having been founded on her feast day (8 September) in 1928. The first brewery was located in the El Perchel *barrio* near where the rail and bus stations are found nowadays. The inaugural master brewer was the German Henrich Dietz. Before the Civil War, there were several breweries in Málaga, but by the 1950s, only Victoria remained.

The beginning of the tourist boom on the Costa del Sol led to a period of sustained growth. In 1952 they began using the slogan '*Malagueña y Exquisita*' ('From Málaga, and Exquisite'), and in 1958 they began featuring on their advertising posters '*El alemán de la Victoria*' ('the German of Victoria') — a cartoon depiction of a portly German tourist enjoying a glass of Victoria beer while mopping his brow in the summer heat. Both the slogan and the image are still used today.

In 1968, the Alameda Principal was effectively extended westwards across the river and the brewery moved to the Intehorce industrial estate farther west. Under the anti-market policies of the Franco regime in 1970, it was deemed to be producing too much beer and was forced to reduce its production capacity by 50%, being bought out by Cervezas Santander in 1972. In the early 1990s the company was sold to Cruzcampo (Sevilla) and the Málaga brewery plant was closed in 1996, the brand almost disappearing entirely. In 1999 it was taken over by Heineken, who were forced in 2001 to sell it on by the National Competition Commission. Its purchase by the Damm Group (based in Barcelona) proved to be its salvation.

Having all but disappeared from sale, Victoria beers reappeared in supermarkets and, in 2007, they returned to bars both on draught and in bottles (*tercios*). On 7 September, 2017, on the eve of the company's 89th anniversary, Victoria inaugurated a vast new factory in the Guadalhorce Industrial Park near the Atlético Malagueño football stadium and not far from the airport. They now brew a number of styles. The big seller is their regular Pilsner — bright gold in colour, with dense notes of toasted cereals, decent body and a refreshing texture (4.8% ABV). But they also make:

Victoria Sin Alcohol — A de-alcoholized (through a centrifugation process) version of their standard Pilsner. 0% ABV.

Victoria Pasos Largos — Beer with lemon (shandy). The name refers to the last true Spanish bandit, Pasos Largos, who was finally apprehended and killed in 1934 in the Serranía de Ronda. 3.2% ABV.

Victoria Marengo Negra — A dark malt beer. Marengo is the word by which people engaged in the trades of the sea are known in Málaga. 5.6% ABV.

Victoria Malacatí — Wheat beer. Its name means a native of Málaga but is also used to describe a brave or daring person. The label shows a climber on the Caminito del Rey. 5.0% ABV.

Victoria IPA — An American IPA-style beer with fruity notes of mango and citrus, and moderately bitter, inspired by the fruit-growing Axarquía region. 5.2% ABV.

Victoria Brewery Guided Tour and Tasting

If you are interested in beer and would like to explore what is probably the most modern brewery in Spain (if not Europe) then the Victoria Brewery offers 90-minute guided tours, including tastings of their beers. Tours are conducted in Spanish or English (though there are more dates for Spanish tours available) here: bit.ly/VictoriaBeerTour. The brewery is very easy to get to from the city centre: 🚌 9, 5 or 10 / Ⓜ L2. Book as early as possible!

🍺 *Cerveza Artesanal* (Craft Beer)

Until relatively recently, if you wanted to drink beer in Spain, your choice was essentially between Pilsner-style beer 'A' and Pilsner-style beer 'B'. A handful of microbreweries and brewpubs were in existence in the early 2000s, mainly in Madrid and Barcelona, and although they had a small but committed clientele, they were seen as something of a fringe novelty. Whereas 'real ale' and 'craft beer' began to take off in Britain and the United States in the 1980s, the explosion came much later in Spain. In fact, the global financial crisis played a significant role, with people setting up small-scale brewing businesses after finding themselves unable to find work in their former professions.

But as far as the growth in popularity of craft beers among consumers is concerned, other factors have played a role. One is the fact that Spaniards have travelled more widely in recent decades. Labour mobility in the European Economic Area has meant, at least since 1992, many more Spaniards living and working in European countries with a more varied beer-drinking culture. In Spain, there has been a gradual realization that beer is actually an alcoholic drink. Formerly it was treated more or less like a soft drink; simply something crisp and refreshing to consume with *tapas*. People tended to accord it no more thought than lemonade or mineral water. As long as it was cold, fizzy and wet, it would do. More recently, though, people have begun to understand that beer — good quality beer — can have a complex flavour profile and that it can be enjoyed for its own sake, not just as lubrication and hydration.

In the year 2000, there were six microbreweries operating in Spain. By 2010, there were fewer than 50, whereas in 2020 there were 420; an increase of 740% over a decade. According to the *Asociación Española de Cerveceros Artesanos Independientes* (AECAI)[37], total production increased from 1.79 million litres in 2011 to 22.4 million litres in 2019; an increase of over 1000%. A recent AECAI report identified some 3,856 distinct product lines — a huge change in a country where, twenty years ago, the beer market was dominated by three companies offering half a dozen more-or-less identical beers. That said, the craft beer sector still only represents 1.1% of the total Spanish beer market by value and 0.5% by volume.

For several years, large brewing groups such as Molson Coors, AB InBev, Heineken and Mahou have entered the craft beer market, and they have largely done so through the acquisition of percentage shares in some of the best-known Spanish microbreweries (Cerveza La Sagra, La Virgen, La Cibeles and Nómada, respectively).

'We can contribute our experience and knowledge when it comes to quality control and product consistency, but we also gain from what they bring to us in terms of creativity, knowledge of this new movement, and in terms of recipes,' explains Benet Fité, director of the New Business Unit of Mahou San Miguel.[38] He adds that during the three years they have been working with Nómada they have prepared more recipes (30 or 35) than Mahou has produced as a company over the last 40 years.

Fité says that the fact that large companies like Mahou San Miguel compete in the craft beer sector helps 'speed things up' and is 'a boost for microbrewers.' Javier Donate, president of the AECAI, thinks that two things are happening: 'On the one hand, the big breweries have become aware of what we are doing and it helps in spreading the word because they have more communicative power. And, on the other hand, it is true that when it comes to competing they exert more pressure because there is inequality in budgets.'[39]

Some *Malagueño* Craft Breweries

It would be pointless to list the names of individual beers because craft breweries tend to bring new beers to market in quick succession and often brew seasonally. However, the following are some of the main producers:

Cerveza La Axarca is a brewery in Frigiliana which claims to 'have captured the essence of Axarquía' (whatever that is). Their beers are very good, though the brewers themselves are fond of purple prose, describing a recent creation as, 'a Picassian experiment, an Arabic love poem, the murmur of the sea on summer nights...'

Cervezas Gaitanejo is located in Ardales. Gaitanejo has been operating since 2014. Each of their beers pays homage to places in the interior of the province of Málaga.

---

37   aecai.es
38   'El fenómeno de la cerveza artesanal se asienta en España', *El Pais*, 16 May 2019
39   *ibid*.

Cervezas Malnombre 'Bad Name Beers' is located in Villanueva del Rosario, in the mountains north of Málaga (Mal Nombre is the name of a famous cave near the town).

Trinidad Cerveza Artesana de Málaga brew their beers in Alhaurín el Grande and you will find their quite extensive range of beer both on draught and in bottle in most of the Málaga bars specializing in beer.

Cerveza Puente Nuevo produce a Blonde and Pale Ale in a very unusual manner: for four months the beer remains submerged at 16 degrees in a marine plot near a beach in Estepona, which achieves a completely natural carbonization and, they say, also enhances its flavour.

3Monos — *Tres Monos* or Three Monkeys is a small brewery located in Málaga city itself. Using only water, malt, hops and yeast as ingredients, their growing range of beers are highly fermented and neither filtered nor pasteurized. **3monoscraftbeer.com**

BenalHop Beer was born in a brewpub called La Caravana in Benalmádena. They began with three beers — an unfiltered lager, an APA and an IPA. While there are clear Anglo-American influences, there is also a nod to the Belgian tradition as far as strength is concerned.

La Catarina Craft Beer is a microbrewery that emerged in 2012, attached to a bar and restaurant in Estepona and has become one of the best-known craft breweries in Andalusia, producing a wide variety of styles with multi-award winning beers.

84Brewers have created a beer that is aged for a fortnight in Pedro Ximénez French oak barrels.

Bonvivant Beer is an independent craft brewery located in Málaga city that, in addition to having its own variety of beers, has a lively taproom (📍 **Calle Diderot 11** ⊕ **bonvivant.beer**) with 12 beers on tap and food served — check social media for hours). It's a bit of a trek from *centro* (about 40 minutes: 🚌 1), but if you are a beer fan who wants to enjoy genuine *cervezas malagueñas* brewed by an independent brewery alongside some good value food in a friendly atmosphere, it's well worth a visit.

For bars that have a good selection of craft beers, see the '*cervecerías*' listing from p. 194.

 *Vermú*

Vermouth is known as *vermú* (baiRR-**moo**) in Spanish. You will often see it spelt (and hear it pronounced) as *vermut* (the Catalan word) because Reus in Catalonia is a major centre of its production. Although the Spanish Royal Academy insists that the Spanish word is *vermú*, the Catalan word *vermut* is also listed, but to describe a theatre or cinema show held in the afternoon, *i.e.* a matinée. However one spells it, *vermú(t)* is one of the most *castizo* (authentic) fixtures of Spanish *aperitivo* culture, and yet one that few visitors ever bother to try (despite being rather pleased with themselves at how authentically they have embraced '*tapas* culture'). In fact, the drink gives its name to the pre-lunch aperitif, which is known as '*la hora del vermú*' (roughly 1 pm–2 pm) whether or not vermouth is being consumed.

We tend to think of vermouth as, at best, a cocktail ingredient, or at worst a bottle grasped in desperation at the tail end of a party that's run out of booze. So what you absolutely must do is banish any thought of Martini or Cinzano. Think instead of Cynar, or Punt e Mes. Although you'll find dry and *blanco* vermouths in Spain, sweet red vermouth is what the locals drink. Overall, these sweet red Spanish vermouths are quite different from their Italian cousins. Spanish reds are lighter, somewhat less bitter and slightly sweeter (even though they typically contain 25 to 30 per cent less sugar than Italian *rossi*) with flavours of sweet orange and Mediterranean herbs predominating. You will detect cinnamon, mace and dozens of other, less easy to identify, botanicals: gentian root (which gives bitterness), fennel, wormwood, walnut bark, bitter orange peel and many others. Spanish *vermú* may not have the intensity of, say, Carpano's spicy *Antica* formula, but the classic style is perilously easy to drink. It is made all over Spain, though Reus (near Tarragona), La Rioja and Madrid are where the biggest brands are produced.

A decade or so ago, *vermú* was regarded as a dated drink, consumed only by elderly men hankering after the days of the *Caudillo* (General Franco). In recent years, however, it has once again become a fashionable tipple and Andalucía is now home to several artisan producers. It is common to see it, on tap, referred to by origin (Reus, Madrid, La Rioja) or simply as *del mes* or *del tiempo* (of the month or season).

Spaniards drink it neat on ice, sometimes with *sifón* (soda). If the barman unscrews a plastic bottle of what looks like lemonade when you ask for *sifón*, that's *La Casera* — a peculiarly Spanish variety of sweet soda that is frequently mixed with red wine to make *tinto de verano* (summer red wine punch). It's not as sweet as lemonade, but sweeter than club soda. Because *vermú* is the *aperitivo* par excellence, you will sometimes be given a very modest *tapita* with each glass — usually crisps, olives or a mixture of cornichons and cocktail onions. A common *tapita* is the '*gilda*' — an olive, cocktail onion, anchovy and cornichon threaded onto a cocktail stick to form a tiny kebab. It is named after the character played by Rita Hayworth in the eponymous 1946 film. The reason for the name, it is said, is that like Ms Hayworth, these little cocktail bites are 'spicy' and make a man feel hungry.

Jerez is, after Catalonia, the oldest vermouth-producing area of the country and its style is still alive and thriving. Vermouth coming out of Jerez is essentially aromatized sherry, made from a base of Amontillado or Oloroso sweetened with PX. And, like Sherry, *andaluz* vermouth is aged in the *solera* system. This style of vermouth also exists outside of the Sherry Triangle, in nearby Montilla-Moriles and Huelva, as well as in Málaga.

Some brands to look out for:

Lustau Vermut (Jerez)

The prestigious sherry producer launched an excellent vermouth in late 2015, made from a base of Amontillado and PX wines. It is available in *tinto*, *blanco* and *rosado* versions, and while all are excellent quality, I think that the *tinto* is the most 'traditional' and the other two really need to be mixed in a cocktail to shine.

Cruz Conde Rojo Reserva 1902 (Montilla–Moriles)

Made with *solera*-aged Oloroso, this vermouth is rich and spicy. Probably the best example of Montilla-Moriles vermouth.

Roberto Amillo Vermut (Jerez)

A boutique maker, Amillo linked up with a Jerez house to produce an impressive vermouth, based on 18-year-old Oloroso and younger PX.

Vermut Dimobe A. Muñoz Cabrera (Málaga)

Produced in the Axarquía region of Málaga, this light red/amber *vermú* is intensely herbaceous and achieves an excellent balance between bitterness and sweetness. From a base of Moscatel de Alejandría and PX.

VRMTH Cásser (Álora, Málaga)

Made by Bodegas Pérez Hidalgo in the beautiful *pueblo blanco* (white town) of Álora, high up in the Guadalhorce Valley. It is mahogany in colour with an intense orange meniscus. Bright and clear. Aromas of fresh grass and ripe fruit mixed with citrus, cinnamon and toasted wood. Very soft, velvety, sweet and round on the palate. The finish is gently bitter with notes of almonds. It has excellent length and a good ripe fruit aftertaste.

Look out, too, for other *malagueño vermús* made by the big producers such as **Antigua Casa de Guardia**, **Quitapenas**, and **Málaga Virgen**, as well as those from newer wineries around the Province of Málaga such as **Niño de la Salina** (Almargen) and **Antakira** (Antequera).

Some Good Spots for Vermú in Málaga

Bodega–Bar El Pimpi (p. 196)
Casa Lola (p. 206)
La Odisea Tienda de Vinos (p. 213)
La Tranca (p. 204)
Antigua Casa del Guardia (p. 197)
Bodeguita El Gallo (p. 205)
La Pechá (p. 216)
Más Vermut (p. 217)
Vermutería La Clasica (p. 207)

🍸 Ginebra (Gin)

The *Real Academia* has long included in its dictionary the compound noun 'gin-tonic' (though it caused something of a storm on social media several years ago when it appeared to propose 'yintónic' instead). It is pronounced as in English ('voz inglesa'), with a soft-g, 'un gin-tonic, por favor' (oon jeen **toh**-neek poRR fah-**boRR**).

Spain is the largest consumer of gin (30 million litres a year) in Europe and the third largest in the world (after The Philippines and the USA). When it comes to per capita consumption, Spain outdrinks everywhere else at a fraction under 70 centilitres per person annually, with the UK (48 centilitres) and even the world's biggest gin market of The Philippines (39 centilitres) trailing considerably behind. More importantly, however, the standard bar-poured gin and tonic in Spain is the best in the world. No contest.

When you consider gin's close association with England; our lukewarm and over-diluted version served in a highball glass is shameful by comparison. In Spain, you will get a big glass, either a half-litre *chato* (like a squat Guinness glass) or a big goblet like a Belgian beer glass, into which a great scoopful of enormous ice cubes is placed. Then comes the citrus. Usually, it's a band-aid-sized piece of zest from a lemon (sometimes lime or, best of all, orange) which the bartender ruffles with tongs to spray the ice with citrus oils. That piece of zest is often discarded and a fresh piece is dropped into the glass. He (or she) then begins to pour a stream of gin from the bottle. And pours, and pours. (We have all tried to engage the bartender in conversation at this moment, or affect nonchalance, in the hope that he will become distracted and give a more generous measure, but Spanish bar staff are very skilled at measuring by eye.)

All Spanish gin-tonics are comfortably doubles, and usually trebles, so more like home measures. Your G&T might then be stirred with a bar spoon. The tonic is often Schweppes, but it doesn't seem to be quite as sweet as the version available in the UK. Other premium tonics are becoming popular. The result is pretty much perfection — the massive rocks of ice ensure that the drink is ice cold and tastes of gin. A number of bars now make a feature of their gin-tonic, treating it as a cocktail by using artisanal tonics, premium gins and adding herbs, pink peppercorns, star anise and other embellishments.

The main British gin varieties are all available in Spain; indeed it's the second-largest export market for British gin after the USA. Most popular are Gordon's (which here is export strength, 40%), Beefeater, Bombay Sapphire and Tanqueray. If you order a G&T, you will probably be offered a choice of gins, with the more expensive imported brands being pushed. Ask instead for a *nacional* (nath-yoh-**nall**, *i.e.* Spanish) gin — slightly cheaper and just as good, or better quality. There are over 40 widely available Spanish *marcas* (brands), the most popular of which are originally from Andalucía: **Larios** (once, but no longer, distilled in Málaga) and **Rives** (from El Puerto de Santa María). Their export strength lines are, respectively, **Larios 12** (**la**-ryoss **doh**-THay) and Rives Special (**ree**-bess speTH-**yall**). There is also a Spanish gin made from grape spirit (rather than the usual grain spirit) which comes from, and is called, **Mahon** (in Menorca). In the eighteenth century, Menorca was (briefly) a possession of the British who left behind a fondness for sash and bay windows, and gin.

If you want to bring back a bottle of 'Duty-Free' from the airport, then Spanish gin is a very good option. The selection of wine on sale in most airports is not very exciting, and comparatively overpriced, whereas local gin is excellent quality (certainly better than Gordon's) and competitively priced by British standards. The range is larger and the prices lower in supermarkets, so stick a bottle in your hold luggage if you can.

Gins produced in the Málaga Province

Simbuya (Cuevas Bajas) The '*morá*' carrot grown on the banks of the Genil has inspired one of the most unusual gins made in the province of Málaga. The company ESALI, has created 'the only gin in the world made with the purple carrot'. There are two versions: **Simbuya Classic** (more classic in style) and **Simbuya Purple** (sweeter on the palate).

Gin Ballix (Vélez-Málaga) is a premium gin that has Osteen mango as an added element, together with juniper, coriander and angelica.

Gin 1895 (Ronda) is made by El Tajo Distilleries, located in Ronda. They also make seasonal and limited edition gins with hints of strawberry, cinnamon, blackberry or mint, as well as **Tagus**, a non-premium (*i.e.* < 40% ABV) London Dry-style gin.

Malaka Gin (Málaga) Carlos Villanueva, owner of the Gin Tonic Bar chain makes 2 gins under the name **Malaka**. One of them is a traditional 'London Dry' for those looking for the most classic flavours. The other has 'a Mediterranean touch with a faint undercurrent of jasmine.'

Oxén Spiritus London Dry Gin (Ojén) The Sierra de las Nieves inspired this gin made in the town of Ojén. The botanicals are coriander, cardamom, and angelica, as well as other plants grown in the Sierra de las Nieves, such as juniper, thyme, rosemary, bitter chamomile and apple mint. A hint of citrus comes from dry lime and tangerine peel. One of the most interesting Málaga gins, to my mind.

Alborán Gin (Almáchar) In addition to a classic gin, where juniper predominates with touches of citrus and some spices, this range also includes 'Orange', 'Lemmon' [sic], 'Strawberry' and, more recently, 'Exotic' (with watermelon and melon).

✒ *Licores y Digestivos*

Whereas we often drink gin before dinner, Spaniards drink it after. This is perhaps because in the summer, when it can still be over 30°C in the early evening, strong mixed drinks and cocktails before dinner are likely to fell the drinker. Before lunch and dinner, Spaniards drink beer (or *clara*), wine (especially Sherry wines) and *vermú*.

Spanish after-dinner drinks:

Pacharán — This is basically anisette flavoured with sloes, coffee beans and vanilla. Spaniards drink seven million litres of this annually, well chilled. It is often spelt *patxaran* reflecting its Basque origins. It is somewhat like sloe gin but without the syrupy sweetness. There is a version made in Ronda called '*Licor de endrinas*' (see below).

Aguardiente or **Orujo** — This is marc or any spirit made from grape pomace — essentially Spanish *grappa*. As with *grappa*, there are some pretty rough and ready varieties available, but the best-known is the **Rua Vieja** brand. They produce a herb liqueur, **Licor de Hierbas**; a coffee liqueur, **Licor de Café**; a grape-marc liqueur, **Licor de Orujo**; and a grape-marc brandy, **Aguardiente de Orujo**, which together account for 35% of the Spanish grape-spirit market.

Licor 43 — A rather pedestrian name (*licor cuarenta y tres*) for rather a nice drink — golden in colour and flavoured with vanilla, citrus and 41 other ingredients. It is Spain's biggest-selling liqueur and is usually drunk on the rocks, as well as in cocktails.

Anís — Unlike in France, Spanish *anís* is flavoured only with aniseed, not aniseed and liquorice. But as in France, it is usually drunk mixed with water — you are supposed to tip the whole measure into a glass of iced water, not pour from the bottle, as this is reckoned to produce the best *palomita* ('little dove', as the resulting cloudy mixture is known). Aniseed-based liqueurs are still the most consumed spirits in Europe, and Spain is no exception.

It is fairly strong, having an alcohol content between 30% and 50% - and comes in *dulce* (sweet), *semiseco* (medium dry) and *seco* (dry) varieties. It is, believe it or not, a common tipple at breakfast. A quintessential *andaluz* drink is *sol y sombra* made from mixing *anís* and brandy, giving a layered effect of the dark brandy (*sombra* - shade) and the clear anís (*sol* - sun).

Anís is produced in a number of towns in Andalucía, the most famous being those made in Rute, in Córdoba province, and Cazalla de la Sierra in Sevilla province, where there is an interesting variant, *aguardiente de cereza* made from cherries. Miura in Cazalla also makes cherry/aniseed brandy. It is also produced in Zalamea and Cortegana in Huelva province. In Málaga Province, the main producer is the El Tajo distillery in Ronda which produces sweet and dry versions.

Ponche Caballero — This 'gentleman's punch' is a liqueur brandy flavoured with oranges, plums, sultanas and cinnamon. Usually drunk *con hielo* (with ice) in a brandy balloon, its distinctive silver bottle is supposed to recall a punchbowl. The **El Tajo** distillery makes a version of their own simply called **Ponche**.

Ron de Motril — Rum is popular in Spain, but almost all is imported from the Caribbean. The main domestic producer is in Motril, near Granada. Rum was first made in Spain (sugar cane having been introduced by the Moors) and then introduced to the New World rather than vice versa. Rum is also made in Málaga by the **El Tajo** distillery, and Carlos Villanueva recently launched **Ron Malaka**, a 5-year-old amber rum matured in Málaga with hints of orange peel.

Málagueño after-dinner drinks:

Resoli and **Mistela** — are two liqueurs that have been popular for centuries in some of the villages in Málaga province. Although they can be drunk at any time of year, autumn and winter (and especially Christmas) are when they really come into their own.

In the case of *resoli*, this is an *anís*-type drink that is mainly made in the villages of Alfarnate, Cuevas de San Marcos and Cuevas Bajas. In Alfarnate, the Arrebola family (Ana Belén and her brothers Javier and José Manuel) created the **De la Abuela** ('Grandmother's') brand in 2014. Made to a traditional recipe, it is flavoured with coffee, dry *anís*, star anise, sugar and cinnamon. As well as resoli, the Arrebola family business also makes juniper, mango, quince and raspberry liqueurs, among others.

Resoli originated in the province of Cuenca. How did a recipe come from Cuenca (in La Mancha) to Málaga and elsewhere in Andalucía? The most logical explanation is that it dates from the re-population of Andalucía by Christians which took place over 500 years ago when, following the *reconquista*, people from all over the Iberian peninsula settled in the south, bringing their customs and traditions with them. Although the recipe differs depending on where it is made, most of the ingredients and the method of making it tend to be the same.

The other traditional drink, **Mistela**, comes mostly from the Serranía de Ronda, especially Pujerra, Igualeja, Montejaque and Arriate. This is another aniseed drink, and the most famous one these days is made in Arriate, where it is bottled and sold by Miguel López. The ingredients are saffron, aniseed, cinnamon, cloves, lemon verbena, orange and lemon peel and sugar, and the brand name is **La Tradición de Arriate**. Another version, with citrus flavours to the fore, is known as *Licor de limón y hierba luisa de Montejaque*.

Mistela is made all over Spain, but the version produced in Arriate can boast of being part of the heritage of Andalucía. Miguel López has been making it for the past 16 years 'to [his] great-grandmother's recipe,' and he says it started off as a herbal tonic to which alcohol and sugar were added to preserve it for longer. Its name means 'mixed' as it is produced by arresting the fermentation of wine by the addition of spirit or brandy, thus retaining more of the flavour of grape must. It is a sweet, smooth, aniseed-tasting drink which is just 13% ABV.

Licor de higo chumbo — (Prickly Pear Liqueur) is an amber-coloured fruit brandy served cold with a slice of orange. In the Málaga Province, it is made in the town of Ojén, in the mountains north of Marbella.

Hidromiel — Though usually translated as 'mead', this is actually 'honeyed wine' (*vino melado*) made with Moscatel wine in the village of Árchez in the Axarquía region of Málaga.

Crema de Mango — is a creamy fruit liqueur made in Vélez-Málaga from organic Osteen mangoes with the addition of honey and alcohol. A little rich to drink on its own, but a fabulous base for summer cocktails. The main brand is called **Mangou Cream**.

Licor de Pasas — is a brandy flavoured with Málaga raisins (*pasas*). There are many brands, mostly originating in the Axarquía region. Most bottles contain whole raisins.

Licor de endrinas — this is basically *pacharán*, but it cannot be called by that name as it is made in Málaga, not Navarra. The best-known brand is **El Tajo** which uses sloes from the Serranía de Ronda.

Licor de cereza — also from the Axarquía region of the province, this cherry liqueur is one of the most popular, but similar drinks are also made from *membrillos* (quince), *frambuesas* (raspberries), *ciruelas* (plums), *albaricoques* (apricots), *bellotas* (acorns), and *castañas* (chestnuts).

Comer y Beber (Eating and Drinking)

Although Málaga is the fastest-growing tourist destination in Spain, no establishment can survive simply by serving chicken nuggets to unsuspecting foreigners; at least not in the centre where rents are high. The happy result is that there are remarkably few duds.

Part of the pleasure of travel is finding places to enjoy food and drink, and not just working one's way through the TripAdvisor top ten. The following suggestions are precisely that — suggestions. One of my favourite places to eat in all of Spain is a tiny, scruffy, usually standing-room-only bar in Madrid that serves excellent grilled sardines; but that's no good to someone who doesn't like sardines, or who wants to sit down to eat.

Regarding the following suggestions, nothing should be read into the order in which they are listed. If you would like to check recent reviews, then have a look on Google (or TripAdvisor, bearing in mind the advice on p. 109ff.) but, for any establishment, on this list or not, make your own judgement. Look at the menu, take a look inside, observe the other customers, and decide whether it's your sort of place.

🗺 Map

Because the centre of Málaga is fairly compact and walkable, I have listed bars and restaurants only very loosely by location. The companion map will help to show where the places are. Visit **bit.ly/MalagaMap** to consult it (on a mobile device you will need to click on **LEGEND** or the map name at the bottom of the screen to choose which POIs to display).

⚠ *Caveat Lector*

Between writing the first draft of this book and preparing it for publication, six of the establishments I had recommended closed. One was a lovely fine dining vegan restaurant (Fonzo), while another was a long-established vegetarian cafe (Lechuga). The others were thriving bars and cafés where I had spent many happy hours over the years. It's quite likely that the owners simply retired, but it's a useful reminder that in the world of hospitality, things change quickly. In 2022, the iconic Café Central closed its doors after 100 years, so nowhere is immune. Málaga is a city on the move and the pace of change is fast. Some of the restaurants and bars listed below may not survive, but others will open in their stead.

✗ Symbols

Most of the symbols relating to food and drink are intended to give a quick impression of a particular establishment, so are **not comprehensive**. Every bar in Spain serves 🍺 beer and 🍷 wine, but not all offer much of a choice. You can order a glass of Málaga wine in most bars in the city, but only a few have a choice of wines drawn from barrels behind the bar. Similarly, every restaurant will have meat, fish and probably rice dishes on its menu, but 🍖🐟 and ⊚ symbols denote a particular speciality. Likewise, when it comes to 🍨 puddings, you might be offered the ubiquitous flan or a modest choice of ice cream after any meal, but only a few restaurants are able to offer good quality homemade sweet dishes. Whilst croissants are available in some cafés, *tejeringos* (*churros*) or *tostadas* (toasted bread with crushed tomato, cheese, ham or paprika-infused lard) are far more ubiquitous. Thus, the 🥐 croissant symbol is used to indicate 'breakfast' in general, rather than 'croissants' *per se*, etc. Hence:

✖	restaurant/*comedor*	🗏	traditional dishes
🍷	bar	🌍	world/fusion cuisine
🥄	tasting menu ('*menú degustación*')	🍖	steaks or grill
📖	reservations	🌱	vegetarian options
🍴	reserve on www.thefork.co.uk	🥗	salads
G	reserve on Google	🐟	fish
🎏	*menú del día*	🦐	seafood
👫	children's menu	🥪	sandwiches/*tostadas*
🌶	*tapas*	🥚	egg dishes
◐	*raciones/medias raciones*	🧀	cheese
🍶	wine list	🍲	soup/stews
🍶	Málaga wine/*vermú*	⊚	rice dishes
🍸	cocktails	🍨	puddings
🍺	beers	🍟	fast food
☕	coffee	🥐	breakfast/*almuerzo*
🥤	take away food or drink	🍰	sweet bakery/*merienda*
🛵	delivery	🍦	ice cream

📅 Eating on Monday

Like anywhere else in Europe, Monday is not a good day for fresh fish (*bacalao* is fine because it is dried and salted, ditto '*rosada*' which is mainly frozen). And if fish is on as a 'special' on a Monday then avoid it because it is likely to be 'on the turn' and they are trying to get rid of it.

In fact, Monday is not a great day for eating full stop. Traditionally it is the weekly holiday for the tourism and hospitality sectors. Museums and galleries are mostly closed, and many bars and restaurants preserve the Monday closure 'por descanso del personal' ('to give the staff a rest'). A few top-drawer restaurants with an eye on Michelin stars, bib gourmands and so forth, will be at the top of their game whenever you visit. Other restaurants, less so. For places that do stay open on a Monday, it's likely to be the Head Chef's day off, so the 'B Team' will be cooking for you. This is often the case on Sunday evening, too — the second quietest night of the week for eating out. Choose a simple *tapas* place instead and leave the sit-down (or more expensive) meals for other days of the week.

🕮 Prices

Price categories can be pretty meaningless. One can eat cheaply or expensively in most establishments. For example, at La Taberna de Monroy (p. 177), a solid 'foodie' place, the cheapest starter and main course (together) might set you back, say, €15, whereas the most expensive choices would come to almost €50. Meanwhile, a bar where no dish costs more than €10 might sound cheap, but if it's a *tapas* bar, then that would put it at the pricier end. I have used a jasmine flower (the symbol of Málaga) to give a rough guide to price/value:

❀	Cheaper than average for its type
❀❀	About average for its type
❀❀❀	A little more expensive than average, but reflecting superior quality
❀❀❀❀	Top-end, luxury dining, a special treat

✘ *Restaurantes* (Restaurants)

The following is a list of what I call 'tablecloth restaurants', viz. establishments with waiter service where it is usually possible to book, and where you will dine at a table using cutlery from a menu on which dishes are (broadly) categorized by course. However, in choosing somewhere to dine, do not forget that many bars are also effectively restaurants, and vice versa. The most formal restaurants are only restaurants, and the lowliest bars are only bars, but the vast majority of establishments are part-bar and part-restaurant, so also check the 'Bars' section (pp. 195ff.) when looking for places to eat.

There are many places to eat and drink on the quayside and it is the location of the first restaurant in Málaga to be awarded a Michelin star, but remember that you are paying a premium for the setting and the view. It's a popular spot with families who want to enjoy something a bit different as a novelty or treat, so non-Spanish cuisine is well represented (Argentinian, Italian, Indian, Burgers, etc.).

Muelles

Cambara ❀❀❀
🍴 MUELLES ◉ Muelle Uno, Local 65 ⊕ 🕮 cambara.es 🕐 Mon–Thu 1200–0100; Fri–Sat 1200–0200 ✘ 🍷 ♈ 🍸 🥂 🍗 🍹

This is a luxuriously decorated restaurant and cocktail bar serving 'elevated' Spanish classics. Service can sometimes seem a little slow to foreigners, but it is friendly and attentive. It's the same story for most of the quayside, even the branch of 100 Montaditos is relatively laid back. Muelle Uno is a place where people come to relax and enjoy a treat, not to have a hurried snack on the go.

Amigos Grill Muelle Uno ✿✿

🍴 MUELLES 📍 Muelle Uno, Local 59 🌐 amigosmuelleuno.com
🕐 1200–1800; 2000–2230 🍴 📖 🍴 ♿ 🌐

A somewhat gaudily decorated restaurant that serves Indian, Mexican, Greek and Argentinian food and therefore normally the sort of establishment that I would advise you to run a mile from. However, the food is actually not bad, the service is warm and there is a lovely family atmosphere. The Greek options are the weakest part of the offer in my opinion, but the Indian and Mexican dishes are very tasty (though British curry lovers will find them a little bland). They will throw in a free children's menu for every two adults in your party (as long as you have children with you, of course).

Gaucho Grill ✿✿

🍴 MUELLES 📍 Muelle Uno, Local 61 🌐 gauchogrillmalaga.com/en
🕐 1200–1800; 2000–2230 🍴 🌐 🐌

This Argentinian *parrilla* (grill) is owned by the same group as the Amigos Indian/Mexican restaurant, with which it shares a kitchen. There are probably better places to eat grilled meat in Málaga, but if you want to eat on Muelle Uno, this is not a bad choice. The owner, Jaydeep Singh, opened his first restaurant just before the financial crisis of 2008 and now has a chain of seven eateries in Málaga and Benalmádena Costa.

Angus ✿✿

🍴 MUELLES 📍 Muelle Uno, Local 55 🌐 📖 angusmuelleuno.com
🕐 1300–0000 🍴 📖 🌐 🐌

Another Argentinian *parrilla* with good (if somewhat relaxed, even slow) service. As far as the quality is concerned, Angus probably just edges it over Gaucho.

✿ Restaurante José Carlos García ✿✿✿✿

🍴 MUELLES 📍 Muelle Uno, Plaza de la Capilla 🌐 restaurantejcg.com
🕐 Tue–Sat lunch & dinner 🍴 🍷 📖 🥄

Although Marbella (in the Province of Málaga) has a handful of Michelin-starred restaurants, 'RJCG' was the first restaurant in the city of Málaga to gain a star (it was joined by Kaleja in 2022). The menu is a tasting menu as one might expect (in the summer there is a choice of two — a 'light' option of fifteen passes, or the full twenty-plus experience). The inclusion of fried food and chilled soups is traditionally *andaluz* and throughout the menu there are constant nods to tradition and showcasing of local products. But this is real *alta cocina* where venerable *malagueño* dishes are elevated by fine cooking rather than radical reinvention. We find dishes such as pigeon breast with pasta and a tender stew of its legs; 'sea foie' made with monkfish liver accompanied by sweet tomato and miso soup; a veal tenderloin with roast aubergines and peppers; a mackerel 'escorted' by cucumber and mustard; a *mojama* (salt cure) of red mullet with black garlic and pomegranate, and puddings as surprising as the algae biscuit with yoghurt and the shortbread of sunflower seeds, presented in the typical wrapping of the sunflower seed snacks sold at the bullring.

Centro Histórico

L'Expérience ✹✹

🍴 CENTRO HISTÓRICO 📍 Plaza del Obispo 4 ⊕ plazadelobispo.com ⏰ Mon–Thu 0830–0000, Fri 0830–0030, Sat 1030–0100, Sun 1200–0000

To kick off the *centro* listing, I'm including an establishment that, at least at the time of publication, is **not** a recommendation, but rather a cautionary tale that illustrates why one should be suspicious of any recommendations, even the thoughtful ones in this book!

A few years ago, L'expérience was one of my favourite places to eat in Málaga. Its location in the picturesque and lively Plaza del Obispo in front of the Cathedral could hardly be bettered. They had friendly waiting staff, a great wine list and a menu of Spanish classics (like *croquetas* and *huevos rotos*) alongside 'international' dishes like burgers and club sandwiches. The vibe was relaxed and the food was top-notch.

A few months ago I visited with a friend to be welcomed (if that is the word) by an offhand, smirking *maître* (*maîtresse*?) *d'* who seemed relieved to hand us over to an admittedly lovely waiter. We ordered a couple of fairly straightforward dishes and… the food was sloppily prepared and both underseasoned and oversalted. It was, without doubt, the worst meal I've ever eaten in Málaga. Admittedly it was a Monday evening; traditionally the head chef's day off, so I was prepared to give them the benefit of the doubt. We complained, and our friendly waiter knocked the wine off our bill and brought free *digestivos*.

Passing by on subsequent evenings, I noticed that it wasn't as busy as it used to be. In the months since, it has attracted some decent (and even glowing) reviews, among a smattering of poor ones. For all I know, it may already have recovered from what was just an unfortunate blip, but at the time of writing, I cannot recommend it with much confidence. I hope it returns to form.

La Reserva 12 ✹✹✹

🍴 CENTRO HISTÓRICO 📍 Calle Bolsa 12 ⊕ lareserva12.com ⏰ 1300–2330 🍴 🍷 🍽 🥘 🍤 🍹 🍸 🥂

A few metres west of the Calle Larios, this restaurant has an excellent location in the city centre and a terrace from which to enjoy the view of one of the busiest areas of the city. La Reserva 12 specializes in typical *andaluz* cuisine. The menu is extensive and fairly pricey, but no more than the equivalent (mid-range) restaurant in London, and average for the area around Larios. It's pretty representative of popular tourist restaurants in the centre of Málaga — unlikely to disappoint but pretty unexciting. '*Ni fu ni fa*' as one might say in *castellano*.

Buenavista Gastrobar ✹✹✹

🍴 LA GOLETA 📍 Calle Gaona 8 ⊕ 📖 buenavistagastrobar.es ⏰ Thu–Mon 1300–1600, 1930–2330 🍴 🍽 🍹 🍷 🥘 🍤 🍹 🍸 🥂

Opened a few years ago by the chefs Juan Molina and Marco Silva, both of whom have experience working in Michelin-starred kitchens, with Yolanda Muñoz running front-of-house. Alongside the Spanish classics, they also have a reasonable selection of dishes suitable for vegetarians. This hidden gem is well worth seeking out in the back streets in the north of the city centre. Typical dishes include sea bass ceviche with avocado, coriander and mango, or confit cod with cauliflower purée, and there is a good choice of well-cooked traditional *paella* and *fideuà/fideos* dishes. The dishes mainly come as *raciones* or *medias raciones* so not really a place to dine alone!

Andino Gastrobar ✹✹

🍴 CENTRO HISTÓRICO 📍 Calle Calderón de la Barca 3

🌐 📖 andinorestaurante.wordpress.com 🕐 1300–0000 ✗ 🍷 📖 🍸 🌐

Something a bit different. Latin American *tapas* and *raciones* and, unusually for Spain, plenty of vegetarian and even vegan options. Very good cooking.

Vegetariano El Calafate ✹✹

🍴 CENTRO HISTÓRICO 📍 Calle Andrés Pérez 6

🌐 📖 vegetarianoelcalafate.es 🕐 1300–1600, Fri–Sat 2000–2200
✗ 📖 🥗 🌱

It is not a crowded field, but El Calafate is considered by many to be Málaga's most interesting and reliable vegetarian restaurant. The price of the *menú del día* is good value with starters of Spanish classics and slightly more exotic main courses like couscous etc. — and yes, couscous is exotic for Spain; why eat Moroccan food when you could be eating *gachas* (wheat porridge) instead?

El Gastronauta ✹✹

🍴 CENTRO HISTÓRICO 📍 Calle Echegaray 3 🌐 elgastronauta.es

🕐 Wed 1900–000, Thu–Mon 1230–1630, 1930–0000 ✗ 🍷 📖 🎣 ◐ 🍖 🌐
🥗 🍷 🍴 🍵 🍺

The food at El Gastronauta manages to be traditional and modern. Most of the dishes are traditionally Spanish (and, unusually, even the *paella* is good here), but with some interesting flourishes. More 'reimagined' and updated than 'reinvented'. Simple, tasty, well-cooked food and excellent friendly service. El Gastronauta has a lovely *ambiente*.

✿ Kaleja ✹✹✹✹

🍴 CENTRO HISTÓRICO 📍 Calle Marquesa de Moya 9

🌐 📖 restaurantekaleja.com 🕐 Tue–Sat Lunch & Dinner ✗ 🍖 📖 🍖

Kaleja — the Ladino (Judaeo-Spanish) word for 'alley' — is the latest venture of the former ElBulli chef Dani Carnero and won him his first Michelin star in 2022. There are 13 and 15-course tasting menus which can be eaten in the 'Living Room' (the traditional dining room) or the 'Kitchen' (next to the open kitchen, a sort of chef's table). Both take 2½ hours to serve. You can opt for a wine pairing if you wish, or simply take advantage of expert the advice of the sommelier, Juan Pérez, as you make your way through the 'passes'. Kaleja's use of a Coravin® machine means that it's possible to enjoy a very wide selection of different wines by the glass.

Carnero is a fan of legumes, using beans in ways normally associated with pasta, and many of the dishes are slow-cooked. The menus feature a lot of fish and seafood and the meat is often game. Popular dishes are reimagined, like a curious *pringá de puchero* sandwich that includes the touch of a few slices of ling. Also striking are the mackerel tacos with mushroom sauce; the squid presented in threads of hazelnut butter, the Norway lobster in garlic chicken sauce or some fresh lettuce hearts that acquire substance with a few brush-strokes of prawn butter. Carnero simplifies and elevates, rejecting the temptation to multiply flavours but instead showcasing the key elements in a dish. For example, a traditional '*esparragao*' (a dish of fried bread, asparagus and garlic) is transformed into a soft pillow of intensely flavoured mousse, topped with lightly steamed leaves of spinach and crowned with a torched and butterflied fat anchovy. One is left wondering how it is possible to deliver such incredible flavour from so few ingredients. The answer, to quote the late Julia Child, is 'good cooking'.

Dani Carnero: Master of 'Candle Cooking'

Carnero's first Michelin Star, awarded for his second Málaga restaurant Kaleja in 2022, had long been anticipated by critics. What was notable when the announcement came, however, was the enormous pride felt by ordinary *malagueños*. Social media fizzed with posts about the award, noting how Carnero had done so much to put Málaga on the gastronomic map.

Like José Carlos García, the first chef to win a Michelin Star for a restaurant in Málaga city, Daniel Carnero Sierra was born in Málaga (1973). Son of a chef, Dani began cooking in professional kitchens in the 1980s, first at Mar de Alborán, then one of Málaga's best restaurants, before stints with Martín Berasategui, Manolo de la Osa, and Ferran Adrià. Most people have heard of Adrià, but Martín Berasategui remains little known outside Spain, or beyond foodie circles. However, he is a culinary superstar in Spain, holding more Michelin Stars (twelve) than any other Spanish chef. As Carnero put it in an interview with the 'Great British Chefs' website, 'My generation of Andalusian chefs, we grew up thinking that the best of Spain was in the North' and in the 1990s and early 2000s, it probably was.

Carnero's brilliance lies not only in his skill in the kitchen but also in his passion for the traditional cuisine of Andalucía in general and Málaga in particular. Just as the *malagueño* lawyer Enrique Mapelli made his contribution to Málaga's gastronomic patrimony by collecting traditional recipes in the 1980s, so Carnero has (like many others) made it his mission to allow diners the opportunity to experience 'traditional *malagueña* cuisine'. As he puts it in his own idiomatic phrase, '*Guisa que te guisa*' which is perhaps best, though clumsily, translated as 'A way of cooking that shapes you'.

Returning to Málaga in 2010 he opened La Cosmopolita explaining, 'Ferran Adrià said that chefs need to open places that offer diners something different and what we did with La Cosmopolita was open one of the first classic food restaurants in the city.' Kaleja, the restaurant that won him his first Michelin Star opened in December 2019, on the eve of the COVID pandemic, with La Cosmo opening in 2022.

Dani's favourite vegetables to use across his restaurants are always local and include the Huevo de Toro tomato from Coín, lettuce from Alhaurín el Grande and leeks from Cártama, while the olive oil he uses is Aceite Oro Bailén from Jaén. 'It took us a few years,' he explains, 'but we learned to seek out and appreciate our own produce and our own wine, which in turn enabled more producers to make better produce.'

His style of cooking is modern and inventive, but a long way from the molecular gastronomy of Adrià. His food involves few foams, gels or pipettes. In an interview with the magazine *Bon Viveur*, he decried 'circus' elements in cuisine, saying that food did not need to have 'smoke understood as paraphernalia for the circus, not from the point of view of smoke as such, which we already know is awesome. What it doesn't have to have is smoke, what it doesn't have to have is circus nonsense.' It is thus the 'circus' of smoke that he criticizes, not smoke *per se*, because his cooking often makes use of smoke.

Visit any of Carnero's restaurants and you will see many items cooked '*a la candela*' which, by its nature, imparts a certain smokiness. '*A la candela*' (literally 'to the candle') can refer to food which has been blow-torched or cooked over fire or embers. In Carnero's restaurants, it is the latter.

However, Dani Carnero describes his approach to food best himself. He summarizes it as 'Taste, depth, memory and fire'. That may sound like highfalutin nonsense, but when you eat his food, you will understand. Carnero's simple description of his perfect morning tells us a great deal about his approach to food:

> *A good breakfast of a good Antequera muffin with tomato and oil … a good amontillado aperitif at a friend's house and wait for half past one to sit down [to lunch]*

And finally, his advice about how to be a gourmet:

> *Many hours at the table and not on the phone screen*

Who could possibly argue?

La Cosmopolita Malagueña ✳✳✳

🍴 CENTRO HISTÓRICO 📍 Calle José Denis Belgrano 3
🌐 📖 lacosmopolita.es 🕐 Mon–Sat 1330–1600, 2000–2330 ✗ ⛶ ◑ ⬥

La Cosmopolita is Dani Carnero's original Málaga restaurant (it opened in 2010). It calls itself a 'Casa de Comidas' which roughly translates as 'canteen'. To call La Cosmopolita a 'canteen' is rather like calling Wiltons a 'fish and chip shop' or Simpson's in the Strand a 'carvery'. The message conveyed by this tongue-in-cheek description, of course, is that this is what Gordon Ramsay would no doubt call 'good, honest food' while doing that weird hand-slapping gesture. But make no mistake, this is stellar cooking.

Mar y montañas (sea and mountains) combine in deliciously inventive ways. Pairing a tartare of fat, sweet prawns with roasted bone marrow is inspired. His remarkable spider crab omelette accompanied by sweet onion and Palo Cortado sherry reduction is an opportunity to enjoy a crustacean (almost certainly Cornish) that few British restaurants have the skill or patience to prepare. Even the Russian salad — the ubiquitous staple of every bar in Spain — is served slightly warm and crowned by tiny tacos of ham, taking it to entirely another level. While La Cosmopolita's most famous dishes (like the crab omelette and *ensaladilla rusa*) are almost always available, the *carta* changes daily reflecting seasonal ingredients.

La Cosmo ✳✳✳

🍴 CENTRO HISTÓRICO 📍 Calle Císter 11 🌐 📖 lacosmo.es 🕐 Mon–Sat 1330–1530, 2000–2330 ✗ ⛶ ◑ ⬥

La Cosmo is Dani Carnero's latest venture, opening in 2022, and is clearly intended to be a more relaxed version of Kaleja. The décor is bright and plain, even a little cool, and the *carta* is concise, running to half a dozen starters, ten mains and three puddings. The cooking is faultless, bearing all the hallmarks of Carnero's signature style with no unnecessary over-complication, allowing the individual elements of a dish to sing. The menu changes regularly, reflecting seasonal availability.

Few dishes demonstrate that approach so clearly as one of the most popular starters, called simply '*la ensaladilla*' (the little salad) — a warm salad of broken confit potatoes with shaved green beans and hake with a mayonnaise emulsified with a rich stock prepared using hake heads. It sounds simple. Similar dishes of potato, fish, beans and mayonnaise are served in countless *tapas* bars the length and breadth of Spain, but Carnero's version is sensational. It is warm and comforting, while rich and bursting with flavour, the essence of the freshest hake — the fish so beloved by Spaniards — so that one feels that one is tasting it for the first time.

The prices are no higher than those of the touristy restaurants between Larios and the Cathedral and twenty wines are available by the glass, so a meal here can be a relatively affordable way to enjoy some of the best cooking in Andalucía.

Restaurante Mesón Mariano ✱

🍴 CENTRO HISTÓRICO 📍 Calle Granados 2 🅕 Mesón-Mariano
🕐 Mon–Sat 1300–1630; Tue–Sat 2000–0000

A very traditional place where they know how to treat an artichoke. The founder and chef-patron, Mariano Martín was recently awarded the 'Antonio Espinosa Award for A Life Dedicated to Tourism and Gastronomy' by the Málaga Academy of Gastronomy after notching up an incredible 50 years of professional cooking. He still runs the kitchen, while his daughter Laura runs front-of-house. If you want to experience classical *cocina malagueña* without 'fusion' or fripperies, this is one of the best places to come. The fish is simply prepared and the meat dishes perfectly cooked. If you order one of the house specialities — for example *chivo lechal al ajillo* (suckling kid with garlic) — that is what you get; beautiful ingredients skilfully cooked, not hiding behind gels, foams or modish additions. And if you like artichokes (*alcachofas*), then Mesón Mariano is a temple dedicated to *Cynara cardunculus*. Mariano's *sous chefs* must have incredible patience because every day around 50kg of globe artichokes are prepared to be served: fried, grilled, breaded, confited or stewed in Montilla wine. Almost all 'main' dishes are served as *raciones* and *medias raciones* with about 20 *tapas* as well. Puddings are pretty traditional, but if you see '*gachas malagueñas*' — sweet wheat porridge (more like a custard) flavoured with anís, brandy and molasses and topped with sweet croutons — give it a try! For the quality of the cooking, the prices are bargain-level.

Restaurante Balausta ✱✱✱✱

🍴 CENTRO HISTÓRICO 📍 Calle Granada 57–59
🌐 📖 restaurantebalausta.com 🕐 1230–0000

This is the restaurant for the Palacio Solecio Hotel. The head chef is Marcos Granados and José Carlos García acts as consultant. The restaurant makes a great deal of its location in an 'eighteenth-century palace' which is technically accurate, although the *palacio* was in such a woeful state by the turn of the century that it was pretty much demolished in 2006 (though the façades and most of the central patio were preserved). This practice of keeping the exterior walls and gutting the interior is a common planning condition in Spain and is called by its detractors '*fachadismo*' (the similarity with *fascismo* is not accidental) and Málaga and Madrid appear to be among the worst offenders (or the best examples, depending upon your view of this approach to urban regeneration).

The restaurant is listed in the Michelin Guide, though it does not hold a star or bib gourmand. The setting is stunning and the service is of the standard one would expect at this price. The food is undoubtedly *alta cocina*, but the restaurant suffers from the 'Curse of Michelin' — that is, because it is listed in the guide, some customers come expecting three-star food and judge it very harshly for not being the best-restaurant-in-the-world. There is an *à la carte* menu and usually a tasting menu which is rather cheaper (though less extensive) than that at Restaurante José Carlos García.

La Taberna de Monroy ✶✶✶

🍴 CENTRO HISTÓRICO 📍 Calle Moreno Monroy 3
🌐 latabernademonroy.com 🕐 Tue–Sat 1300–1600, 2030–2300
✗ 🍷 🍴 ⟡ ⧓ 🌐

Owned by Carmen Pozo, as head chef, and her husband Alejandro Fernández, the Taberna de Monroy is a relative newcomer to the *malagueño* dining scene, despite its traditional atmosphere. Carmen and Alejandro are from Córdoba and the food reflects that tradition with *salmorejo* and oxtail in the *cordobés* style always on the menu. Many of the ingredients are carefully sourced from specific producers: extra virgin olive oil from the *Cooperativa La Aurora de Montilla*, and acorn-fed Iberian ham from the Los Pedroches Valley. But even simple dishes are elevated above the merely rustic, like the exquisite morsels of artichokes which accompany the *salmorejo* and a reduction of sweet Moscatel de Alejandría wine.

Mesón Antonio ✶✶✶

🍴 CENTRO HISTÓRICO 📍 Calle Fernando de Lesseps 7
🌐 mesonantonio.com 🕐 Mon–Sat 1300–2330 ✗ ⧆ ⟡ ⧓ 🍴 ✎ 🦐 ◖

This venerable institution is tucked away down an alley off the Calle Nueva and has been serving classic *cocina malagueña* for over 40 years. Paco Viñolo ran the restaurant for over 20 years and recently handed over the reins to his son Raúl, while Juan Miguel and Ana look after the family's well-regarded steak house (Asador Viñolo) beyond the airport in Churriana. Mesón Antonio could hardly be more 'traditional' if it tried — square tables and wooden chairs with woven *esparto* seats, plus a *carta* featuring every classic *malagueño* dish that you can imagine (including goat, both chops and leg, the latter to order only). Fish, seafood, meat and eggs (*revueltos*) are all well represented. The place brims with *ambiente* and the service, like the food, is faultless. The large portions make it good value eating so it is a place best visited when hungry.

Terraza de las Flores ✶✶

🍴 CENTRO HISTÓRICO 📍 Plaza de las Flores 4
🌐 📖 terrazadelasflores.com 🕐 1200–1600, 1900–2300 ✗ 🍷 📖 ⚐ ⧆

There are plenty of decent eateries in this square and nearby, but the Terraza de las Flores is always reliable. The prices are fair for the heart of the city centre (in an attractive square) and the food is tasty and well-prepared.

Restaurante El Jardín 1887 ✶✶

🍴 CENTRO HISTÓRICO 📍 Calle Cañón 1 🌐 eljardinmalaga.com
🕐 Mon–Fri 0900–1600, 1900–0000; Sat 1000–1600, 1900–0000
📱 📖 +34 635 539 284 ✗ ⧆ 🍵 ▬ 🍸

Founded in 1988 by Dolores Gómez de Cisneros and Miguel Trugillo Giménez and occupying a beautiful building designed by the *malagueño* architect Gerónimo Cuervo, this is a cosy and somewhat quirky (the tablecloths are literally chintzy) restaurant overlooking the Cathedral Gardens. It has a small *carta* and specializes in *paella*, which is prepared well, though they can be a little heavy-handed with the salt. I am including it in this section due to its moderately priced *menú del día* (not including a drink). Be warned that service can often be slow at busy times, though this is a consequence of the fact that the food is all freshly prepared.

Marisquería Casa Vicente ✴✴

🍴 CENTRO HISTÓRICO 📍 Calle Comisario 2 🕐 Wed–Sun 1230–1540, 2015–2300 🍴 🛵 ⊙ 🍷 🖐

This is a no-frills fish and seafood restaurant almost hidden down a narrow side street near the Atarazanas market. The service is good (though it can be a little slow when busy) and the food is well cooked and reasonably priced (though excellent quality fresh fish is never 'cheap'). Most dishes are offered as *raciones* and *medias raciones*. The *gambas a la plancha* (grilled prawns), *gambas al pil pil* (prawns in oil with garlic and chilli) and *navajas* (razor clams) are especially delicious, and the *conchas finas* are good value too. Come early if you want a seat, because it's a popular place and there is often a queue. As a restaurant serious about fresh fish, it's closed on Monday and Tuesday.

Taberna Los Hidalgos ✴

🍴 CENTRO HISTÓRICO 📍 Calle Duque de la Victoria 8
🌐 loshidalgos.es 🕐 Tue–Sun 1230–1630, 2000–0000 🍴 🍷 ⊙ 🎱

This local favourite makes it into the 'restaurant' section, even though it calls itself a *'taberna'*, because the *carta* is composed of *raciones* and *medias raciones*, not *tapas*. Most people come here to eat a meal, though the way of eating tends to be the usual Spanish sharing of a few plates, rather than three courses per person. '*Los Hidalgos*' basically means 'the noblemen' — the word *hidalgo* is a contraction of '*hijo de algo*' i.e. 'son of someone' — though *hidalgo* can also mean to down a drink on one, so that's a possibility in this case.

Los Hidalgos has been feeding *malagueños* since 1968, though not always in its current location. It's not much to look at — a plain whitewashed room with a bar in the corner and a few rows of plain tables and chairs — which is why thousands of tourists walk straight past it every day without giving it a second look. It is therefore also a place which is '*muy malagueño*' — I don't think I've ever seen another tourist in here. But there is nothing to fear — the owner, Antonio, is warm and friendly and the excellent, reasonably priced food makes it well worth the potential discomfort of feeling that one is encroaching upon *terra incognita*.

As the signage outside proclaims, Los Hidalgos 'specializes in snails' and here they serve them in a delicious piquant almond sauce. Their other speciality is fish and seafood, rather than meat (though the *pajaritos* — fried quails — are a popular choice). Also popular is the avocado and apple salad. This is an excellent place to try the traditional fisherman's stew from Málaga — *caldillo de pintarroja*. *Pintarroja* is a kind of dogfish/shark often used in stews, and the *caldillo* (little broth) is a spicy, rich fish soup flavoured with almonds, cumin, chilli and paprika, traditionally eaten by fishermen to warm up after a cold morning at sea. Another curiosity on the *carta* is '*arañas fritas*' which Google will tell you means 'fried spiders' but are actually fried *goujons* of weever fish.

Kortxo ✴✴✴

🍴 CENTRO HISTÓRICO 📍 Calle Salinas 3 📘 kortxomalaga 🕐 Tue–Sat 1230–1600, 2000–0000 💬 📱+34 951 697 209 🌱 📖 bit.ly/KortxoFork
🍴 🍷 🐚 📖 🛵 ⊙ 🍸 🎱 🌍 🍹

A clue to the style of this lovely restaurant is its name, which is the Basque word for 'cork'. This is a place that prides itself on its wine list and the high quality of its *tapas* or, more precisely *pintxos donostiarras* (the owners Jorge and Lola have recreated a typical San Sebastián bar). *Pintxos* here have intriguing but non-descriptive names, like '*Delerium*' and '*Kaos*' so you will probably need to ask for clarification from the helpful staff (most of whom speak good English). The food menu changes frequently and the quality is consistently high. San Sebastián arguably has the best food in Spain, if not Europe, so expect something slightly above the usual standard here.

El Descorche de Cervantes ✹✹

CENTRO HISTÓRICO ⚲ Calle Álamos 8 📷 descorchemalagawinebar
🕐 Tue–Sun 1300–0100 📞 +34 689 586 795 ⚭ 📖 bit.ly/DescorcheFork
✗⚑⚡☉⚬☰

Descorche ('uncorking') is a beautiful wine bar-restaurant and a temple to the produce of Málaga, both edible and potable. The food is exquisite, highlighting the very best of the Province's produce, and the wine list is a showcase of local wine. A real treasure.

El Mesón de Cervantes ✹✹

LA MERCED ⚲ Calle Álamos 11 ⊕ elmesondecervantes.com
🕐 Wed–Mon 1900–0000 ✗📖⚡☉⚬☰⚭✿⚑✤⚘☕

In Spain, a '*mesón*' is always a traditional kind of place and this is no exception, although this example is a relatively recent addition to the Málaga gastronomic scene. The Argentinian restaurateur Gabriel Spatz opened a *tapas* bar (El Tapeo de Cervantes) in 2008, and a few years later, this restaurant. It serves mostly *tapas* and *raciones* that are well executed under the direction of head chef Jesús, and keenly priced. This is a very reliable choice.

Alameda & Soho

Mesón Ibérico ✹✹

SOHO ⚲ Calle San Lorenzo 27 ⊕ 📖 mesoniberico.net
🕐 Mon–Fri 1300–1700, 2030–0000; Sat 1300–1700 📞 +34 952 603 290
✗📖⚬☰⚭⚘✤⚘⚓

A very traditional *mesón* serving a huge range of *raciones* and *medias raciones* as well as *tapas* in the form of '*mini bocadillos*'. Tucked away in the south-western corner of Soho, this place is slightly off the tourist radar, but it is very popular with locals and there is often a queue outside before it opens at 8.30 pm. Phone ahead to book, or call in ahead of time to book in person. The food is excellent and the service is faultless. A lovely touch is that they usually give you something sweet (like profiteroles) when they bring you the *cuenta* (bill).

Restaurante La Marina ✹✹

ALAMEDA ⚲ Alameda Principal 11 ⊕ 📖 lamarinamalaga.com
🕐 Mon–Fri 0700–2330; Sat–Sun 0800–2330 📲 📖 +34 652 841 336
✗⚑📖🛏🍴☰⚭✤⚘

This bar-restaurant is one of the most popular and economical places to eat well on the Alameda Principal. Its relaxed atmosphere and friendly service mean that it's a favourite with *malagueños* of every stripe, making it a fascinating place to people-watch. You'll see young mums meeting for lunch, retired couples enjoying a day out, couples, suited professionals doing business, manual workers — a whole cross-section of Málaga, though few tourists. There is an extensive *carta* of well-cooked and reasonably priced food, but one of the main reasons for its popularity is its two *menús del día*. One (the '*Ejutivo*') is served Monday to Friday and includes many dishes not normally included in *menús* like *secreto ibérico* (the most expensive pork cut) and veal rib-eye steak. There is also a cheaper *menú* ('*Clásico*') served every day (although it does not include a drink on Friday, Saturday or Sunday). Lunch is served from 1.30 pm at the earliest, and you should arrive before 2 pm to get a seat — but even if it looks packed, it's worth asking if there is a table because there is an upstairs *comedor* that they open at busy times.

La Deriva ✸✸✸

🏍 SOHO ♀ Alameda de Colón 7 ⊕ 🕮 laderiva.es ⊙ Daily 1200–0130
✗ 🍷 🕮 🚬 ⊙ 🔖 🍴 🎵 🚐 🍹

La Deriva is a stylish restaurant in Soho, close to the river and the Alameda. It has a few tables outside and as with most of the restaurants in this section, booking is strongly advised. The food is 'modern Spanish' — well cooked and beautifully presented, making good use of quality ingredients. The chef has clearly decided that puddings must be '*deconstruidos*'. However, the deconstruction is thoughtfully done and to good effect, rather than simply for the Instagram clicks, so a *tarta de queso* (cheesecake) has all the required elements — biscuit, fresh fruit, a scoop of intensely rich fruit ice cream and cream cheese — but the 'cheese' takes the form of a custard poured around everything else. It's delicious, but it's not technically a *tarta*. Their *ensaladilla rusa*, swathed in a cool fish mousse and topped with a juicy flake of bonito is a thing of beauty, as is their delicious beetroot hummus served with shards of *torta de aceite* wafer. They serve 'Joselito' *jamón*, a brand reckoned by some to be the best in the world.

The main courses are simple, but beautifully cooked, with a few carefully measured accompanying flavours chosen to showcase the meat or fish. So do not expect a plate groaning with food — most main courses are the same sort of size as the starters — a neat slab of suckling pig comes with pillowy potato puree rich with olive oil and pork fat, a few lightly pickled and roasted shallots and a lip-smackingly rich sauce. The wine list is excellent and extensive.

It is one of my favourite restaurants in Málaga, but La Deriva is not a place in which to enjoy a 'quick bite'. The service, though always in my experience friendly, can be relaxed (some might say slow). You might even wonder at times if they've forgotten about you. So if you enjoy lingering over a good meal without hovering waiters, this is the place for you. If you need to be in and out in an hour, not so much.

Óleo ✸✸✸

🏍 SOHO ♀ Edificio CAC (Centro de Arte Contemporáneo) Calle Alemania ⊕ 🕮 oleorestaurante.es ⊙ Mon–Sat 1130–1630, 2030–0000
✗ 🕮 🚬 ⊙ 🔖 👁 🍴 🎵

This '*malagueño*–sushi' fusion restaurant is a triumph that makes perfect sense. Japanese and Asian flavours meet traditional *andaluz* meat dishes while Spain's love affair with seafood makes sashimi and nigiri obvious choices. There are stewed beef croquettes and shrimp omelettes, Vietnamese rolls of suckling goat, a false tempura maki of boletus, asparagus and tartufata and a salmon tataki salad with seaweed and sesame vinaigrette.

The meat dishes are classic, such as Galician blond veal loin with chips and a herb mayonnaise, or closer to the flavours of Andalusia, for example, a sweet *ibérico* pig cheek stewed with lemongrass and vanilla. In addition, Óleo proposes a complete sushi menu featuring simple nigiris such as eel, scallop or tuna belly. More complex is the salmon, coconut milk and passion fruit flambé uramaki with avocado, cucumber and salmon topped with coconut and passion fruit sauce, the gunkan hotate with scallops and roe or the unagi roll with eel, avocado, and teriyaki sauce sprinkled with sesame.

Rather than turning into the sort of muddle that one often finds in 'fusion' restaurants, Óleo avoids this with two head chefs. The Brazilian Rui Da Mata looks after the sushi section, while Sergio del Río (who has cooked under Martín Berasategui and Andrés Madrigal) looks after the *andaluz* parts of the menu.

Cávala ★★★★

🍴 SOHO 📍 Alameda de Colón 5 📱 +34 628 021 363 🕐 Daily 1330–1600, 2000–0000 ✕ 🍷 🐚 🦞 🌿

This is a fairly new restaurant opened within the Soho Boutique Colón Hotel with Juan José Carmona as head chef. It is not cheap (there is a twelve-stage tasting menu and an *à la carte* menu), but it is excellent, particularly if you enjoy seafood.

The first breeze from the sea comes in the form of some Carril clams, finished with extra virgin olive oil and salt and roasted on the robata (Japanese grill) which Carmona claims to have introduced to Málaga, using it to cook shrimp, crayfish, Sanlúcar prawns, squid, red prawns and *percebes* (goose barnacles). For starters, a balanced and silky cream of peas with *cañaíllas* (*murex* sea snails) followed by a seaweed croquette with confit garlic *alioli*. The spicy *gazpacho*, shrimp with its roe and fried heads is a fantastic dish. A fat oyster, first sealed on the grill to contain the juice and then covered with a sour *béarnaise* is another achievement of a chef who works with very high-level products and respects them without unnecessary artifice. An illustration that a well-dressed humble product can be the star is evident in the case of the omelette with poultry juice and crisp skin (the first, tentative appearance of meat in the tasting menu) with prawns and caviar.

Next, some sautéed *boletus* (cèpes) with pepper sauce and white truffle. The smooth and delicate sauce envelops well-cooked, meaty cèpes. In the last savoury pass, a citrusy, garlicky fish grilled with potatoes and crisp pickled garlic. The fish, cooked to perfection, coated with a *demi-glace* that gives another nod to meat with its poultry base notes, evokes memories of garlic chicken, with the perfume of lemon grass, creating a game of sea and mountain.

One gets a sense here that Carmona is somehow both constantly pushing at the boundaries, and holding back within the tradition, letting the ingredients speak for themselves. The result is cooking of an extremely high standard to delight any lover of fish and seafood.

La Malagueta

From the city centre, the *barrio* of La Malagueta (between the bullring and the Malagueta beach) is a pleasant 15-minute walk through the Parque de Málaga, so there's no excuse not to explore this part of the city. You are likely to eat far better here than in the tourist traps between Calle Larios and the Cathedral and there are lots of good quality restaurants to choose from.

Cal y Mar ★★

🍴 LA MALAGUETA 📍 Calle Fernando Camino 17
🌐 restaurantecalymar.com 🕐 Tue–Sat 1200–0000; Sun 1200–1630
✕ 📖 🍷 🅖 🍽 🍴 🐚 🍫 🦞 🍹 🥂 🍸

Despite the rather clunky name (a pun on squid, one assumes), this is one of Málaga's best restaurants and is very popular with local families. Ecuadorian head chef Jairon Rodríguez delivers consistently excellent food. The dishes cover the traditional bases — seafood, salads, seafood, fish, tartars, steak, pork and so forth — marrying them with more unusual flavours. Thus, steamed mussels are served in a light sauce of coconut, mint and saffron, while salmon tartar (with mango and avocado) is accompanied by red pepper sorbet. The often rather rustic dish of braised pork cheeks is served not with the usual mashed potato, but a creamy pillow of parsnip purée. Touches of orange and lime make an appearance in the *tiramisù*, transforming an often cloying pudding into something lighter and more subtle. The lunchtime '*menú gourmet*' allows you to enjoy many of the *à la carte* dishes at a bargain price.

Divinno ✦✦

🍴 LA MALAGUETA ♀ Paseo de la Farola 8 ⓞ divinno.malaga ⏱ Sun–Thu 1200–2300; Fri–Sat 1200–2330 📞 +34 627 142 638 ✗ ⊙ ⚲

Divinno is situated on the street that runs behind and above Muelle Uno, meaning that from the *terraza* there is a fine view across the port. It's a beautiful restaurant with clean, modern decor, a young and friendly front-of-house team, and a relaxed, local vibe. It is also one of the best restaurants in Málaga, producing perfectly executed Spanish classics albeit in a light and modern style. Most of the 'starters' are available as *raciones*, *medias raciones* and *tapas* and range from light salads and seafood to more hearty staples like *fabada* and *callos* (tripe). A few of the 'mains' are available as *medias raciones* too, with vegetarian (and vegan), fish, seafood and meat all well represented.

There are so many dishes that one could recommend, but if I had to choose only one it would be the *confit* '*secreto ibérico*' with Lyonnaise potatoes, which is exquisite. '*Secreto*' is a cut which is hidden (hence the name) behind the shoulder of the Iberian *pata negra* (black-hoofed) pig —it is effectively the pig's armpit, but that description is hardly alluring. It is richly marbled, incredibly juicy and tender, and with a mild, nutty flavour. If you haven't eaten pork from Spain's acorn-fed native pig breed, this is the cut to try.

Aire Gastrobar ✦✦✦

🍴 LA MALAGUETA ♀ Avenida de Príes 16 ⊕ ▥ airegastrobar.es ⏱ Wed–Sat 2000–2330; Thu–Sat 1330–1700 ✗ ⊞ ⚫ Ⓖ 🎏 🍴 ⊙ ⚲ ♈ ⇌

Almost opposite the English Cemetery, Aire Gastrobar is one of Málaga's most innovative small restaurants, with a beautiful, constantly evolving menu and a magnificent wine list. The chef-patron, Pepo Frade, uses local products and plays with traditional dishes, elevating and reimagining them. He is known for serving a savoury version of the '*pionono*' — the syrup-drenched sponge cake from Granada. Fade's riff has a savoury sponge, cream cheese and *chorizo* with just a touch of sweetness from honey. He worked the same magic with the '*torta loca*', a simple biscuit consisting of two circles of puff pastry sandwiched with custard and iced with vivid orange icing. Frade's take stacks discs of duck *foie gras* with *turrón*, 'iced' with an apricot gel. Part of the humour is that the *torta loca* is a very ordinary thing, created to bring a little colour to the lives of poor *malagueños* in the dark days of the 1950s, whereas Don Pepo's *foie* version is very much *alta cocina*. Another signature is a '*biznaga*' (Málaga's famous jasmine flower corsage) made from white chocolate alongside three ingredients very typical of Málaga: sweet wine, mango and *garrapiñadas* (caramelized almonds). Fish, seafood, meat and *guisos* (stews) receive the same careful attention. Front-of-house is managed by co-owner and *sumiller* (*sommelier*) María Schaller. Service is unobtrusive, but warm and efficient and the wine recommendations can be relied upon to complement the dishes perfectly. A reasonably priced tasting menu is available (except on Friday and Saturday evenings) and the *carta* includes a (beautifully prepared gourmet) hamburger option for children.

El Perchel

La Alacena de Francis ✹✹✹

🍽 EL PERCHEL 📍 Calle Montalbán 1 🌐 laalacenadefrancis.com
🕐 Tue–Sat 1300–1600, 1930–2300 🍴 🍷 🎐 🛵 🗺 🌍 🍦 🐚 🥄 🥢 🦐

I don't know how many Spanish–Russian fusion restaurants there are in Spain. Not many, I suspect. But this one, run by Spaniard Daniel and his Russian wife Natalia is probably the best. The Russian love of cured and smoked fish fits well with the *malagueño* love of fresh seafood and the resulting 'fusion' is delicious. One of the specialities of the house is the platter of fish smoked by Daniel himself, featuring salmon, trout and bream. We've probably all had the first two, but when did you last have smoked sea-bream? It's a beautifully delicate delight.

What makes La Alacena one of Málaga's best restaurants, however, is the exquisite service. A tiny place with just over half a dozen tables, it has an intimate feel and Daniel's warmth and enthusiasm soon make you feel like a house guest rather than a paying customer. There is an infectious esprit de corps among diners when you express an interest in a shot glass of iced vodka accompanied by slices of gherkin and other diners decide that they fancy trying this too. Daniel instructs you how to enjoy both perfectly.

La Alacena de Francis is not the most traditional, nor the most *malagueño*, restaurant in Málaga, but it is one of the loveliest. Reservations are best made by telephone or in person.

Beyond Centro

Restaurante Tita Ché ✹✹

🍽 CARRETERA DE CÁDIZ 📍 Calle Francisco de Salinas 17
📘 titache.restaurante 🕐 Tue–Sat 1330–1600, 2000–2330; Sun 1330–1700 📱+34 647 190 496 🍴 🍷 🛵 🕐 🐚 🗺

This restaurant near the Parque del Oeste combines excellent cooking with great service. Well off the tourist drag, this place is popular with locals who regularly pack out the large terrace.

Pórtico Puerta del Norte ✹✹

🍽 CARRETERA DE CÁDIZ 📍 Avenida de Sor Teresa Prat 76
🌐 porticopuertadelnorte.com 🕐 Mon–Tue & Thu–Sat 1200–1630, 2000–2330; Sun 1200–1630 📱+34 952 657 337 🍴 🍽 🐚 🕐 🥄 🍷

This restaurant may be in Málaga (east of the Parque del Oeste), but the cooking style is from Castilla–León. Well-cooked food and friendly service. They offer a very reasonably priced *menú del día*.

Taró ✹✹✹

🍽 HUELIN 📍 Calle Tomás Echeverría 15 🌐 tarorestaurante.com
🕐 Wed–Mon 1300–0000 🍴 📖 🐚 🗺 🍷

The *taró* is the low mist that forms in the Bay of Málaga on the hottest days of the year when the cold waters of the Atlantic meet the warm air from Africa. It is a very *malagueño* phenomenon, and Taró is a very *malagueño* restaurant, where local products and dishes dominate the menu. It is a modern restaurant in the *barrio* of Huelin and the cooking is as refreshingly modern as it is reassuringly traditional. Thus, a chilled *ajoblanco* is served with creamy mango, and *porra* (Antequera's version of *gazpacho*)

— a dish that can sometimes be cloying, is made sharp and refreshing with the addition of green tomatoes.

The chef patron is the *malagueño* Pachu Barrera who brings an impressive CV of experience in some of Spain's finest restaurants. His local claim to fame is the invention of *'Tartar de salchichón de Málaga'* — a riff on steak tartare made with Málaga's lightly cured local sausage. Although now much copied throughout the city, the version at Taró still surprises, with the addition of a touch of *miel de cana* and some marinated raisins.

The decision to locate Taró outside the historic centre was deliberate. Barrera wanted his restaurant to be in the 'real Málaga', bringing *alta cocina* to the very untouristy environs of Huelin, a historically working-class suburb. Taró is not yet on the tourist radar, and even if it were, few would bother to make the journey. They are missing out. On a balmy evening, it's a pleasant 30-minute walk from the centre to Huelin and the quality of the experience that awaits you, in terms of food, drink and *ambiente*, will make it more than worth your while.

Cafetería Vanessa ✹✹

🍽 CARRETERA DE CÁDIZ 📍 Camino de la Térmica 10
�textf bit.ly/CVanessaMLG 🕐 Mon–Fri 0800–1600 🍴 🍷 🍲 🛵 🕐 💲 ☷

This unassuming café-bar near the Parque del Oeste serves an excellent (and very cheap) *menú del día* Monday to Friday as well as doing a roaring trade in the morning for *desayuno* and *almuerzo*. If you don't fancy the *menú*, they have an extensive range of *platos combinados*. Guidebooks too often talk about 'secret spots that only the locals know about', but Vanessa is pretty much that. As far as TripAdvisor is concerned it closed long ago after mustering only three reviews. In fact, not only is it very much open and thriving (at the time of writing at least!), it is one of my favourite *cafeterías* in Málaga. It's not at all a touristy place so don't expect menus in English (or English to be spoken), but you'll receive super-friendly service and delicious home cooking at an unbeatable price.

🍴 *Comida Rápida* (Fast Food)

The following are a few suggestions of 'non-traditional' eateries serving fast food and/or non-Spanish food. These recommendations might be useful to families with children or teenagers.

Carl's Jr. ✹✹

🍽 EL PERCHEL 📍 Explanada de la Estación, Centro Comercial Vialia, María Zambrano Station 🌐 🛵 carlsjr.es 🕐 1200–2300 🍴 🚭 🛵 ☷ 💲

If you, or your children, are hankering after a McDonald's or Burger King, why not try Carl's Jr. instead? Okay, it's also an American chain, but it doesn't operate in the UK, so it's something a little bit different (and it's also somewhat better than the usual suspects). In the same commercial centre of the station is Foster's Hollywood, Spain's best-known 'American' restaurant, and VIPs, another vaguely US-style eatery.

100 Montaditos ✹

100 Montaditos is always a good bet for a refuelling pit stop when you need something to keep you going, especially on Sundays and Wednesdays when everything on the *carta* is €1. On these 'Euromania' days, you can build quite a filling sandwich lunch, including beer or wine, for a few euros (see p. 116).

🍃 *Empanadas*

The *empanada* is the Spanish member of that culinary family which also counts the Cornish pasty, samosa, calzone and brik among its members. In Spain, it takes various shapes and forms, but always involves some kind of filled pastry. However, the little shops that have sprung up around Málaga in recent years sell Argentinian *empanadas*, which look like tiny Cornish pasties and tend to have rich fillings involving meat or cheese.

The stores are small, so take your purchase to a nearby square or park to enjoy (ask for extra napkins as *empanadas* can be quite greasy). Most of the shops have promotions if you buy more than one *empanada* and all sell a selection of drinks, including beer (in cans — drinking from bottles in the street is not permitted in Málaga city). The main outlets are **Malvón (Calle Cisneros 7 & Avenida de las Américas 1, near the Railway Station)**, **Las Muns (Calle Tomás Heredia 4 in Soho)**, **El Ombú (Calle Carretería 4 & Calle Victoria 65)**, and **Panaditas (Calle Granada 23)**. All are indicated on the companion Google map.

🍔 *Hamburguesas*

Hamburgers in Spain are generally an excellent, even gourmet, option. Even quite modest bars will produce something somewhere between 'acceptable' and 'excellent'. In short, if an establishment serves good grilled meat (and Spaniards tend to be very skilled at working the *parrilla*), then they'll make a good burger. You are very unlikely to be served anything that has been frozen. The growing popularity of 'smash' burgers (where a ball of minced beef is placed on the griddle and 'smashed' with a spatula to make an irregular patty) demonstrates that most burgers are not made from pre-shaped patties, but hand-formed meat.

However, if you want not only a burger, but a good choice of burgers made from prime cuts of a range of meats, plus a choice of toppings, fillings and sauces as well as onion rings etc., then that means going to an '*hamburguesería*' or burger restaurant. A few notable ones are:

Kanival Burger ✳

🍴 HUELIN 📍 Calle Alfredo Catalani 2 🌐 📖 🔧 kanivalburger.com
🕐 Wed–Sun 1300–1600, 2000–0000 📖 🍺 🔧 🍷 🧆 🍹 🍽

Hands down the best and friendliest burger restaurant in Málaga, but one which will require you to leave the centre to enjoy it (it's situated a few blocks north of the Museo Ruso, in Huelin, though they also deliver). Raúl Retamero and Juan Fernando Duque opened their small but stylish burger joint in the uncertain post-COVID landscape, but it has deservedly gone from strength to strength. Their secret is an absolute commitment to top-quality fresh and local ingredients. Burgers are made from prime cuts of beef from a farmers' cooperative in the Los Pedroches Valley north of Córdoba with the addition of fat from the same animals to ensure rich, tasty burgers. The bacon and pulled pork are from *ibérico* pigs from the same region, marinated in artisanal dark beer from Ardales. The brioche buns are from a bakery in Marbella, the cheese is from the provinces of Málaga and Cádiz (mainly goat's cheese), the *tapenade* is made from olives from Álora, sweet Málaga wine finds its way into marinades and dressings, and even the avocado for the garnishes is grown in Axarquía.

Here, absolutely everything is homemade, right down to the mayonnaise, ketchup, relish, and pickled gherkins. And although Kanival is very much in 'gourmet' territory, prices are competitive, and no more expensive than the local chains listed below. The most expensive option, 'La Roma' comes with roasted bone marrow, roasted garlic mayonnaise and a meat *jus* and tomato broth reduction. Most burgers are available as 100, 150 or 200-gram patties and come with delicious twice-cooked fries, or coleslaw. There is a simple burger available as a kid's option and they also make a vegan version. If you want to augment what's on offer on the menu, you can choose from eight sauces and add up to fifteen toppings, including extra patties and even bone marrow, although as this needs to be roasted to order, you'll have to wait.

Burgers at Kanival tend to be cooked *'en punto'* (medium rare). To check how to ask for other grades of 'doneness' see the information on p. 136. There are homemade puddings on the menu — currently a goat's cheese cheesecake, a lemon pie and a chocolate and pistachio carrot cake, all homemade. There is Victoria beer on draught and craft beer from the Gaitanejo brewery in Ardales by the bottle.

Dak Burger ✹✹

🍴 El Perchel 📍 Calle Héroe de Sostoa 14, Local 1 ⊕ 📖 ⏱ dakburger.es
🕐 1200–2230 📖 ☕ 🖥🐾 🪑

Dak Burger is a Málaga burger company based in La Cala de Mijas with a branch in the city centre. It's an excellent choice if you really like meat because the burgers are intensely 'beefy' with lots of umami in the toppings. Anyone used to the insipid offerings of US fast food chains may find their senses overwhelmed!

Gottan Grill Centro ✹✹✹

🍴 LA MERCED 📍 Calle Álamos 12 ⊕ 📖 ⏱ gottangrill.com 🕐 1300–1600, 2000–0000 📖 🍽 🍷 ☕ 🖥🐾 🪑

Gottan (*i.e.* 'Gotham') Grill offers a children's menu (drink, hamburger/nuggets, fries/potatoes and a fruit yoghurt dessert) but this is only shown on the Spanish menu, so ask for a *'menú infantil'* (men-**oo** een-fan-**teel**). They also claim to offer (pre-order necessary) the world's most expensive burger costing almost €2,000 and made with Premium Galician blonde rib-eye beef, crispy Kobe beef *cecina*, edible 22-carat gold, poppy seed brioche bread, red onion in imperial rose Moët tempura, imperial beluga caviar, *foie gras*, Payoyo cheese sauce and black winter truffle. I cannot decide whether this is a joke or not, but the (regular) burgers are good. They also have a branch in Huelin (**Calle Antonio Soler 5**).

Black Label Urban Grill ✹✹✹

🍴 LA MERCED 📍 Calle Álamos 22 ⊕ 📖 ⏱ blacklabelurbangrill.com
🕐 Wed 2000–1200; Thu–Mon 1300–1630, 2000–0000 📖 🍽 ☕ 🖥🐾 🪑

This is on the same street as Gottan Grill. Their proximity keeps their game up and their prices competitive. This is another good option in the centre. The reason for their perfectly cooked, juicy burger is, they say, their prized Josper Grill (a kind of combined charcoal grill and oven developed in Barcelona in the 1960s).

La Calle Burger Málaga Centro ✹✹

🍴 CENTRO HISTÓRICO 📍 Calle Mosquera 3 ⊕ 📖 ⏱ lacalleburger.com
🕐 Mon–Thu 1300–1630, 2000–2330; Fri–Sun 1230–1630, 2000–0030 (Sun 0000) 📖 ☕ 🖥🐾 🪑

'The Street Burger' is an *andaluz* chain with a few franchises in greater Málaga. The city centre branch is on Calle Mosquera, and there are other branches near the Larios shopping centre (**Avenida de las Américas 9**) and the Parque del Oeste (**Calle Diamantino García Acosta 1**). The meat for the burgers comes from the company's own 1,300-hectare farm in the Serranía de Ronda where they raise Black Angus, Red Angus and Wagyu cattle.

Burguer Parrilla ✤

🍴 SAN FELIPE NERI 📍 Plaza de Montaño 3
🌐 burguerparrilla.eatbu.com 🕐 Mon, Wed–Fri 1930–0100; Sat–Sun
1300–1700, 1930–0100 🍴 ⏲ 🍵 🚬 🐾 🦮 ♿ 🍺 📶

Located on the Plaza de Montaño, Burguer Parrilla is a no-frills burger bar a block north of the *centro histórico*. Hugely popular with locals but rarely on the tourist radar, the burgers are homemade and delicious (the prime burgers are called *hamburguesas de buey*) and the chips are hand cut rather than the more usual frozen fries. They also offer a range of homemade salads, *bocadillos* and *platos combinados*, but one of their main claims to fame is the big range of *camperos* (warm sandwiches in an Antequera *mollete*). Burguer Parrilla offers some of the most reasonably priced food in the city, so don't be surprised to find it packed out. The service is excellent but can be a little slow at very busy times.

Bocatería Los Delfines ✤

🍴 CAPUCHINOS 📍 Alameda de Barceló 16 🕐 Thu–Tue 0800–2300
🍵 📶 🍽

Bocatería means 'sandwich bar', but not of the egg and cress variety. This bar — 'The Dolphins' — serves hearty *camperos* (toasted *mollete* muffins filled with ham — or any number of other fillings — cheese, tomato, lettuce, garlic mayonnaise and ketchup), *hamburguesas*, *perritos* (hot dogs), *pepitos* (hot pork baguettes), *crestas* (paprika-spiced hamburgers) and their own '*delfipollos*' (hot chicken sandwiches). The *carta* lists 40 combinations, but as everything is prepared freshly to order and customizable, the total number of sandwiches available is almost infinite. Making all the sandwiches to order also means that at busy times it can take a while for your order to arrive. Unusually, there is no draught beer or wine here, but beer and soft drinks are sold by the bottle or can, and they make really good coffee. Los Delfines make some of the cheapest *camperos* and burgers in Málaga, and certainly some of the best. They only take cash.

 Pizza

Like most cities, Málaga has some decent Italian restaurants that serve good pizza. It also has plenty of pretty dreadful small pizza shops with lukewarm slices of pizza made who-knows-when, covered in rubbery cheese. There is, however, one rather magnificent exception to this somewhat dreary collection...

La Pizza de María ✤

🍴 SOHO 📍 Calle Alemania 21 🌐 🦮 lapizzademaria.com 🕐 Wed–Mon
1930–2330 📞 +34 651 687 822 🍵 📶 🍽

If you want a freshly made, tasty, reasonably priced and authentic pizza, then Pizza de María ticks every box. Run by Javier and Bea from Córdoba whose family has been in the pizza business for many years. Their '*Cinco Países*' (cheeses from five different countries) pizza, German pizza with frankfurters and gherkins, and English Breakfast pizza with bacon, sausage and mushrooms (let alone the sweet pizza options) will shock Italians to their Salvatore Ferragamo loafers, but they could go for the classic Margherita or Pepperoni options if they wished. The toppings are inventive and fun, the quality of the ingredients is exceptional and the pizzas themselves are note-perfect, made with an artisanal sourdough crust. The icing on the cake is the warm and friendly service one receives here. You can phone your order ahead so that it is ready for you to collect (a couple of tables are available inside if you want to dive in immediately).

187

Única

There is another pizza restaurant in Soho called Única (**unicasoho.com**) which opened in 2023 to rave reviews. The owner is a former hotel manager from Verona called Francesco Bernardinelli and the quality and authenticity of the product are beyond reproach (in its first month of trading it didn't receive a single Google review of less than 5 stars). However, it is pretty pricey for a pizza place, with the average price of a pizza around €20 when it first opened. Unusually (and, in my view, regrettably), it is a restaurant where children are not welcome. One of Única's starters is 'focaccia served our way'. A photo on their website shows that 'our way' means serving it on a skateboard(!). That may be their way, but it's not mine. Still, if you're a huge pizza fan, I dare say you could overlook such nonsense.

☕ *Cafeterías* (Cafés)

Casa Aranda ✵✵

🍴 CENTRO HISTÓRICO ⚲ Calle Herrería del Rey 3 ⊕ casa-aranda.net
🕐 0800–1230, 1700–2100 ☕♨️🍵

Founded in 1923 by Antonio Aranda and his sister Lolita, this is one of the best and most popular places in the city centre to eat *churros* (or, rather, *tejeringos*), Casa Aranda is popular for *desayunos*, *almuerzos* and *meriendas*.

Byoko ✵✵

🍴 CENTRO ⚲ Calle Strachan 5 🕐 0900–1630
🍴 MERCED ⚲ Plaza de La Merced 22 🕐 Sun–Thu 0900–2230; Fri–Sat 0900–2300 ⊕ byoko.es ✗🌱🕐🍷☕🌍🍤🍲♨️🍵🥤🍵🍽️

Málaga has a handful of vegetarian and 'health-food' joints and Byoko is an example of the latter. It is also one of the best examples, as their opening of a second branch in the Plaza de La Merced a couple of years ago shows. A lot of 'veggie' and 'Bio' restaurants tend to serve the kind of veggie dishes you can get anywhere (*ajoblanco*, tortilla, salads, etc.) plus a lot of soya-based meat substitutes. None of this nonsense at Byoko, where Lorenzo and Rémi prepare plenty of dishes with fish, poultry, meat and ham, just of the free-range organic variety; and they serve beer and spirits (though, strangely, no wine except Cava), which is unusual for restaurants of Byoko's ilk. Still, it is the sort of place that also serves 'detox smoothies' and kombucha mocktails. It remains the only place I have ever eaten avocado toast (with poached egg and béarnaise sauce) and very good it was too.

Mia Coffee Shop ✷✷

🍴 CENTRO HISTÓRICO 📍 Plaza de los Mártires Ciriaco y Paula 4
f Miacoffeeshop 🕐 Mon–Fri 0930–1800; Sat 1000–1800 ☕🍰🥪

If you're after 'normal' coffee rather than Spanish-style *solos* and *con leches* (or *mitades* or *cortos* as one would say in Málaga), then Mia's is one of the best places in Málaga to find it. They roast their own coffee (also available to buy) and sell the full range — latte, flat white, cappuccino, filter etc. — with a choice of milk, including non-dairy. They offer a good range of homemade pastries and cakes, with a choice of vegan options. It's tiny, so you'll be lucky to get a seat, but people often order coffee to go and congregate outside the hatch window that faces the church of *Santos Mártires' Ciriaco y Paula* opposite.

Los Valle Churros ✷

🍴 EL PERCHEL 📍 Calle Cuarteles 54 **f** bit.ly/LosValle 🕐 Mon–Fri 0700–1200, 1730–2000; Sat 0700–1700 ☕🥪🍩

To my mind, this is the most charming spot for *tejeringos* in Málaga. It's in El Perchel and has a bit more of an authentic, local feel. No frills, but friendly service, and on the way to the railway station (if you are walking), so a fine place to fortify yourself for a journey ahead. When I visit Málaga, I often stay in El Perchel (because it's quieter at night and cheaper than the *centro histórico*), but even when I don't, I always make a pilgrimage to Los Valle because I love it so much.

Churrería La Malagueña ✷✷

🍴 CENTRO HISTÓRICO 📍 Calle Sebastián Souvirón 6
🌐 tejeringosmalaga.es 🕐 Mon–Sat 0730–1230, 1630–2030 ☕🥪🍩

This is a modern yet traditional café specializing in *tejeringos* (aka *churros*) and busy for breakfast and morning snacks as well as for *merienda*. Most people come for the *tejeringos*, but they also serve a good range of *bocadillos* (sandwiches) and *tostadas* with a wide range of fillings/toppings, including *zurrapa* — a soft, spreadable mixture of pulled pork and lard, typical of Málaga. You can choose your bread — *pulga*, *pitufo*, or a half or whole *mollete* (a soft Antequera muffin), as well as *molde* (a slice of a tin loaf) and *rebanada* (a slice of sourdough-type bread).

La Bella Julieta ✷✷

🍴 CENTRO HISTÓRICO 📍 Calle Puerta del Mar 20 🌐 labellajulieta.com
🕐 Mon–Fri 0800–2100; Sat–Sun 0900–2100 ☕🍰🍩🥪

This is a chain, but an *andaluz* chain, started by Eva Mostazo and Carlos Pérez several years ago, now with branches throughout the south of Spain. They have other branches at **Calle Santa Lucía 9** and **Calle Córdoba 5**. La Bella Julieta offers traditional breakfast options (such as *tostada* with oil, tomato or ham) as well as pastries, waffles, salads, avocado toast, etc.

Ana La Fantástica ✷✷

🍴 CENTRO HISTÓRICO 📍 Calle Camas 3
🌐 analafantastica.eatbu.com 🕐 Mon–Thu 0815–1400, 1700–2000; Fri 0815–1400; Sat 0815–2000 ☕🍰🥪🍩🥪

This fairly new *panadería* also has tables for breakfast, *almuerzo* and *merienda*. The name ('The Fantastic Ana') hardly seems modest, but it's tongue in cheek. Although the owner is called Ana, '*La Fantástica*' is also a nickname of the glamorous Spanish actress Ana

García Obregón, once called a 'geriatric Barbie' by Victoria Beckham. Either way, the bread and pastries certainly are most certainly *fantásticos*. The Spanish iteration of croissants, although tasty enough, is often a far cry from the *vrai croissant de France*, but here they are the real deal — buttery, light, flaky and perfectly layered. Ana also bakes fantastic bread, including sourdough, Galician olive bread, and walnut bread. I'm told that she is giving more established bakeries a run for their money when it comes to the Epiphany *Roscón de Reyes*. She also prepares savoury filled croissants, *tostadas* and other brunch dishes.

La Tetería ✳✳

🍴 CENTRO 📍 Calle San Agustín 9 🌐 la-teteria.com 🕘 0900–2100 (Fri–Sun 2130) ☕🍵🍰

If the cafés above are the place to go for *desayuno* and *almuerzo* then La Tetería (which means 'teapot shop') is the perfect spot for *merienda* (the afternoon snack). It is one of the few places in Málaga where you can find a decent cup of tea, made with just boiled, rather than merely hot, water. They have 150 varieties of tea, but serve good coffee too. Where they really score highly, though, is with their wide range of cakes made on the premises. As well as the expected carrot cake and cheesecake, you could try the 'apple and ginger toffee streusel cake' or '*dulce de leche* cake'; both excellent if you have a sweet tooth.

Café-Bar El Diamante ✳

🍴 CENTRO HISTÓRICO 📍 Calle Pozos Dulces 3
🄵 📖 bit.ly/CBDiamante 🕘 Mon–Sat 0730–1230 ☕🍷🍰🍵

A great place for breakfast and, unless people buy and read this book in significant numbers, off the tourist radar. They serve *tostadas*, *pitufos* and *bocadillos* (Málaga may love its own vocabulary, but it is charmingly inconsistent) with a huge choice of fillings. Try the *pitufo de salchichón* (Málaga sausage sandwich) here. Delicious! The orange juice is especially good here (perhaps they buy a superior variety of orange?), and an unusual and popular speciality is *leche con fresa* (layered strawberry milk).

Pastelería Ñanduti ✳✳

🍴 EL PERCHEL 📍 Calle Canales 3 🌐 ñanduti.es 🕘 Tue–Sat 0900–1400, 1630–2000 ☕🍴🍰🍵🍰

Just across the river in El Perchel, this artisanal bakery/café owned by Dora Ortiz is an excellent place for breakfast (and afternoon *merienda*). The *carta* is extensive, including traditional *bocadillos* and *tostadas* as well as bagels, croissants, crêpes, waffles, and various riffs on Eggs Benedict. They also offer some good lunchtime choices, including a '*formula de medio día*' (set lunch menu).

O Melhor Croissant Da Minha Rua ✳✳

🍴 CENTRO HISTÓRICO 📍 Calle Atarazanas 13
🌐 omelhorcroissantdaminharua.com 🕘 Daily 0900–2030
☕🍵🍰🍵🍰

Twenty years ago, Spanish cafés served approximations of French patisserie. The soi-disant *pain au chocolat* was, more accurately, a *napolitana* — filled not with sticks of dark chocolate but with custard or cloyingly sweet chocolate icing. Spanish croissants (*cruasanes*) were not only enormous but usually glazed with apricot jam. In those days, if you asked for a cappuccino, even quite smart cafés would serve you an espresso with a turret of squirty UHT cream on top. Things have improved markedly since.

This Portuguese café (the name translates as 'The Best Croissant in My Street') still serves glazed croissants, but the pastry itself is excellent — light and buttery. As the name suggests, this café serves only croissants, albeit with a variety of fillings. There are some good savoury fillings (from the time-honoured ham and cheese to chicken and parsley or salmon and cream cheese) but their popularity rests upon their menu of sweet filled croissants, which are very sweet indeed — custard, Nutella®, apple and cinnamon, Kinder Bueno®, Milky Bar®, etc. They serve fruit juices and coffee too. If you have a sweet tooth, then this is certainly the place for you, though the savoury croissants are good value and quite filling, too.

La Flor Negra ★★

🍴 CENTRO HISTÓRICO 📍 Calle Santa Lucía 10 🄵 flornegravanilla
🕐 Mon–Sun 0900–2100 🍽🍶①🍵🌶🍴🍟🥖

This lovely café has tables inside and out, friendly and attentive staff and a deliciously tempting range of tarts and cakes. They serve a number of options for breakfast, as well as light savoury brunch dishes (eggs, sandwiches, focaccia, *tostadas*, etc.). They also offer a good value *menú del día*.

Desal Café ★★

🍴 CENTRO HISTÓRICO 📍 Calle Nosquera 2 🄵 desalcafe 🕐 Wed–Mon Breakfast & Brunch 📍 Calle Ollerías 24 🕐 Thu–Tue Breakfast, Brunch & Lunch 🍽🍶🍵🍴🍟🥖

Desal is a portmanteau word formed from **DES**ayuno and **AL**muerzo (breakfast and brunch). The menu is modest but offers classic options like cheese and ham as well as more 'trendy' fillings like avocado and mozzarella as *pitufos*, *tostadas* and *molletes*, as well as yoghurt, fruit and other dishes. The café is run by Violeta Rabasco and her sister Azahara and the tale behind it is not untypical of some of Málaga's newer enterprises. The sisters, then living in London and Barcelona respectively, met up at the Málaga Feria in 2016 and decided to set up their new business in the city, starting trading within six months. They pride themselves on using local produce: the fruit is from the greengrocer on Calle Peña, the bread from Alhaurín, and the oil from the Sierra de Yeguas. They recently opened a second branch on Calle Ollerías, in the former premises of the Taberna Casa Antonio and began offering a *menú del día* to extend brunch to lunch in March 2023.

Cafetería Framil ★★

🍴 CENTRO HISTÓRICO 📍 Calle Cisneros 1 🌐 bit.ly/Framil 🕐 Mon–Fri 0800–2100; Sat 0830–1500 🍽🍷🍶💸🍴🌶

This simple, modern café serves mainly coffee and soft drinks (though this is Spain, so you can order wine or beer too), a dozen *tapas* and a slightly larger choice of *pitufos* and *molletes*. They also serve *churros*, though only before lunch. There is quite a cheap (and basic) *menú del día* served from 1.30 pm Monday to Friday.

Calle de Bruselas ★★

🍴 LA MERCED 📍 Plaza de La Merced 16 🄵 bit.ly/CalleBruselas
🕐 1000–0200 🍽🍷📖🍶💸①🍴🌶🍷🍵🍴🍸🌶🍟🥖🍽

This is basically a *tapas* bar, but I am including it in the café section because it is widely held to be the place that serves the best '*pitufo mixto*' (grilled ham and cheese roll) for breakfast. The owner, Nacho Valle, is exacting, stressing the importance of good bread (Calle de Bruselas buy theirs from a local bakery, not a catering supplier), a touch of butter and just enough time under the grill.

Grand Café Gezellig ✸✸

🍴 SOHO 📍 Calle Trinidad Grund 33–35 ⊕ gcgezellig.es 🕐 Tue–Thu 1300–0100; Fri 1300–0300; Sat 1600–0300; Sun 1300–2300
✗🍺🍷🕯◊🍸🍽🥤🍽🥢🍽

It may seem odd, in a book extolling the delights of *malagueña* cuisine, to recommend a café serving *Vlaamse frites* and *Bitterballen*, but Gezellig is such a lovely place that it deserves a mention. Opened quite recently by Dutch expats Naomi Uijlenhoed and Jackie Stor, it aims to recreate a traditional Amsterdam café and it more than succeeds, except that the coffee and food are much better here than in Amsterdam. Most of the menu consists of sandwiches of various kinds, both hot and cold, though they have not yet introduced *malagueños* to the wonder that is the Uitsmijter. There are more substantial dishes too. As well as coffee, they have a good selection of beers, half a dozen well-made classic cocktails and a short list of reasonably priced wine. As for liqueurs and spirits, the menu simply reassures customers, 'We have plenty of that'. The *ambiente* is relaxed and homely and the service is bright and friendly. Board games are available to play and Formula One is shown on Sundays (a slightly eccentric choice, but one that has developed quite a local following).

La Cheesequería ✸✸

🍴 LA GOLETA 📍 Calle Carretería 44 🟦 bit.ly/LaCheesequeria 🕐 Mon 1400–2100; Tue–Sun 0900–2100 🖥🍵🍽

This is a fairly new addition to the café scene in central Málaga (they have a long-established branch in the Este district), and its offering is simple and delicious — nice coffee and a huge selection of homemade, delicious cheesecakes to eat-in or take away. The cheesecakes are prepared in the Basque style which means that they have a soft, even runny, texture.

Taybo Coffee & Bakery ✸

🍴 LA VICTORIA 📍 Calle Victoria 45 ⊕ taybo.es 🕐 Sun 0800–1300; Mon–Tue & Thu–Sat 0800–1300, 1600–1900 🖥🍵🍽

Another new addition to the Málaga café scene, opened in 2022, with Gonzo as *barista* and Dani in the kitchen. Like most modern cafés, the coffee is 'natural' rather than *torrefacto*, and the pastries are international (the *alfajores*, for example, are South American-style sandwich biscuits rather than Spanish almond fingers). Both coffee and pastries are inexpensive and utterly delicious, and Dani and Gonzo could hardly be friendlier. A lovely place a little off the beaten track.

🍦 *Heladerías* (Ice Cream Parlours)

Casa Mira ✸✸

🍴 CENTRO HISTÓRICO 📍 Calle Larios 5 ⊕ dimasmiraehijos.es 🕐 from 1030 (Take Away) 📍 Calle Císter 8 🕐 from 1030 (Eat In & Take Away) 🍦

Not a café, but an *heladería* (ice cream parlour). But what an ice cream parlour! There are broadly three kinds *heladerías* in Spain: those run by Italians, those run by Argentinians (who may also be Italians) and those run by *valencianos* (people from Valencia, specifically, *jijonecos* from Jijona/Xixona). Casa Mira is an example of the third type. At the end of the 19th century, Severino Mira left Jijona for the first time. His destination was the then-booming city of Málaga where he intended to sell his cargo of *turrón* (nougat) transported on the backs of donkeys. After the success of his first trip, he decided to return and established a sales office.

The Mira family settled in Málaga permanently, but the *turrón* only generated income in the winter season, so, taking advantage of the traditions of the *jijoneco* ice cream makers, he also began the production and sale of ice cream..To make ice cream back then he used snow that he brought in carts from the Sierra de las Nieves north of Málaga, and thus he was able to have the first ice cream parlour that could stay open in the summer. Casa Mira still makes *turrón* and other sweets, but as an ice cream parlour they are a Málaga institution. Even during the winter, their shops are busy, and many people forgo the dreary pudding options of flan or *crema catalana* in a restaurant to go for an ice cream after dinner. The closing time changes seasonally, staying open until midnight and beyond in the summer. It is so busy on summer evenings that they operate a ticket system to deal with the queue. Even at the busiest times, the wait is never too long because the staff are extremely efficient, as well as friendly and patient.

You can have your ice cream served in a small, medium or large (*pequeño*, *mediano* or *grande*) cone (*cucurucho*) or cup (*tarrina*). You can ask for at least two flavours even for the smallest servings and three for the larger sizes. All the popular flavours are available, of course, but it seems a shame to just go for (admittedly delicious) chocolate or vanilla when more exotic varieties are available. Some of the more unusual flavours include *cuajada con miel* (sheep's curd cheese with honey), *tarta de queso* (cheesecake), *milhojas* (custard *mille-feuille*), *manzana verde* (green apple), *mantecado* (the name refers to a kind of crumbly shortbread biscuit traditionally made by nuns; with subtle flavours of lemon and cinnamon), *crema tostada* (*crème brûlée*), *avellana* (hazelnut) and, not to be missed, *Málaga*. The eponymous ice cream of Málaga is the apotheosis of 'Rum-n-Raisin', but rather than the artificial tang typical of what you might find in your local supermarket, *helado de Málaga* is a sophisticated, quality product. The ice cream is flavoured with sweet Málaga wine and studded with fat, Málaga raisins that have been macerated in the same liquor. It's a very 'grown up' ice cream and manages to be rich, sweet, boozy and (almost, but alas not quite) one of your five-a-day.

In addition to ice cream and sorbet, Casa Mira also serves a range of iced drinks including *granizados* (ice slush in lemon and coffee flavours), *batidos* (milkshakes), *leche fría* (cold milk), *horchata* (tiger nut milk), *granizados ácidos* (ice slushes with a scoop of ice cream), and the hugely popular *blanco y negro* ('black and white' — a coffee ice cream float).

Helados Bico de Xeado Málaga ✶✶

🏛 CENTRO HISTÓRICO 📍 Calle Méndez Núñez 6
🌐 galimalaga.wixsite.com/misitio 🕐 1100–2300 ▼

There are *heladerías* dotted all over the city centre as well as a branch of the popular frozen yoghurt outlet **llaollao (Calle Granada 23)**. Many of these serve good quality ice cream, but of the kind you can find anywhere in Spain. Outside Málaga, keep your eyes peeled for independent *heladerías* who still make ice cream locally, like

Inma (Calle Moreti 15) in the western suburbs and **Lauri** (Calle Bolivia 117) in Pedregalejo.

For something interesting and artisanal in the city centre, Bico de Xeado is worth a visit. It means 'ice cream kiss' in the *gallego* language and while ice cream is the main business, the shop also stocks a small range of food and drink products from Galicia. The '*requesón y higo caramelizado*' (Spanish ricotta and caramelized fig) ice cream is highly recommended. While Casa Mira's ice creams are very classical and creamy, those of Bico de Xeado are slightly more intensely flavoured.

Levi Angelo Gelato & Chocolate ✳✳

🍴 SOHO 📍 Calle Tomás Heredia 11 🌐 leviangelo.com 🕐 1200–2300 🍸

Owned by the *chocolatier* Levi Angelo, the ice cream sold here is exceptional, with plenty of vegan and gluten-free options. He also makes artisan chocolates, *turrón* and pralines. Certified kosher.

🍺 *Cervecerías* (Beer & Brew Bars)

British pubs have changed a lot in the last few decades. The food offer has improved and most now serve decent coffee and have a wine selection that goes beyond Stowells of Chelsea draught Hock. Spanish bars, on the other hand, have always been places to find good food (even just *tapas*), fresh coffee and a choice of wine. What Spanish bars have never traditionally offered is a choice of beer. Most have one or two taps serving one brand of beer. Craft beer (*cerveza artesana* — see p. 160f) is still fairly new in Spain, but if you want more than Hobson's choice, then here's my list of Málaga's top five craft beer bars (note: most restrict admission to those over the age of 18).

El Rincón del Cervecero ✳✳

🍴 SOHO 📍 Calle Casas de Campos 5 🌐 elrincondelcervecero.com
🕐 Mon–Thu 1900–0000; Fri–Sat 1300–0000 ✂ 🍸

Located in the *barrio* of Soho, this craft beer bar is modern, spacious and bright with a friendly, relaxed atmosphere. Apart from enjoying the draught and bottled beer, customers can also take a variety of brewing workshops and buy materials for home-brew. David, the owner, has commissioned a handful of local brewers to produce a selection of beers which he sells under his own brand. The food offered along with the ales is a range of top-quality dried and cured meats as well as a selection of *tostas*. The selection of beers is enormous: literally one for every day of the year.

La Fábrica ✳✳✳

🍴 SOHO 📍 Calle Trinidad Grund 29 🌐 lafabricadecerveza.com
🕐 Sun–Wed 1230–0100, Thu–Sat 1230–0200 🍴 📖 🍴 ✂ 🕐 🍸

Cruzcampo is the main brewery in Seville and its beer is famously... average. However, their microbrewery in Málaga is great, and they serve some really delicious beers of all different kinds — nine resident beers and a couple of guests. La Fábrica (*lit.* 'the factory', but meaning 'brewery' in this case) is a huge, open-plan space and one of the best places to drink beer in Málaga. At weekends they often have bookable tasting visits where you can find out about how the beer is made (on-site) and enjoy a guided tasting. The main menu, though good, is slightly on the pricey side, but the *tapas* menu is good value and goes well beyond the basics. The black pudding *croquetas* with roasted apple, cinnamon and yuzu mayonnaise are exquisite. Unlike the other *cervecerías* in this section, children are welcome and there is a children's menu. The music (often live — check the website for upcoming gigs) can sometimes be a little loud, but if you're under 50, I dare say you'll manage.

La Botica de la Cerveza ❀❀

 LA VICTORIA Calle Victoria 13 laboticadelacerveza 1230–1500, 1800–0100 (Fri–Sat until 0200)

'Botica' has the same derivation (from the Greek ἀποθήκη, 'storehouse') as *bodega*. And in beer shops like this, one can see how the *bodega* (originally just a wine shop) developed into a bar. People came to buy wine, filling their own bottles from the barrels, but they also wanted to try the product. Soon, the tasting became more important than the bottle-filling and the *bodegas* morphed from shops into bars. Like El Rincón above, La Botica is first and foremost a beer shop, but it is already starting to resemble a bar, with up to ten beers on draught. The owner, Miguel Arrabal, stocks beers from around the world, but he is especially knowledgeable about the most exciting craft beers from Spain.

Central Beers Craft Beer ❀❀

 CENTRO HISTÓRICO Calle Cárcer 6 centralbeers.com Mon–Thu 1800–0200; Fri–Sat 1300–0300; Sun 1230–0200

Probably the best-known beer house in the city. It's pretty central and serves a lot of different beers, so it is true to its name. In style, it is modern, industrial and cosmopolitan with warm lighting. It offers up to 15 beers on draught and many more by bottle. The food *carta* is eclectic and international, but the food is tasty and filling. I suppose that nobody finds the fact that Wetherspoons has nachos, curry and lasagne on its menu bizarre, so perhaps the very 'pubby' fusion of Central Beers should not surprise us.

La Madriguera Bar ❀❀

 LA GOLETA Calle Carretería 73 lamadriguerabar.com Mon–Thu 1900–0100; Fri–Sat 1900–0200

Run by the brothers Manu and Ramón, this small bar (*madriguera* means 'den' or 'lair') is perfectly judged. There are eight beers on draught and almost 70 available by bottle or can. The *carta* of *tapas* and *raciones* may look basic, but Manu has worked in Michelin-starred restaurants and produces really delicious food. Like most craft beer bars in Spain the vibe is rather 'hipsterish', but don't let the waxed beards, tattoos and piercings put you off — La Madriguera is one of the friendliest bars in town.

Bares de Tapas (Tapas Bars)

Like every city and town in Spain, Málaga is well served with watering holes. The city of Málaga has well over a thousand bars: 1.84 per 1000 inhabitants. Although this is three times as many per capita than the UK it is quite a modest figure in Spanish terms. The average ratio in Spain as a whole is 2.8 bars per thousand people, but many cities punch above their weight. The university city of Salamanca has 4.22 bars per thousand, while the city of León, where one neighbourhood is known as the '*barrio húmedo*' on account of the sheer amount of drink sloshing about, boasts 5.03. However, to put Málaga's figure in context, if you wished to visit one bar per day, Tuesday to Sunday, you would have to stay for over three years to visit them all. The following list is, therefore, a mere scratching of the surface; a handful of suggestions. Be sure to check out the section covering Málaga's *mercados* (markets) as some of the best *tapas* bars are found within them.

Centro Histórico

El Tapeo de Cervantes ✷✷

🍴 LA MERCED ♀ Calle Cárcer 8 ⊕ 📖 eltapeodecervantes.com
🕐 Tue–Sun 1300–1530, 1930–2330 ✗ ♀ 🐟 📖 ✍ ⊙ ◖ ☲

A very traditional *tapas* bar, right down to the heavy wooden tables and, until a recent makeover, its gingham tablecloths. The food is even more traditional than the décor, with plenty of seafood, fish and rich meat dishes, though there are some surprises, like their delicious artichoke and goat's cheese quiche. There are always excellent daily specials. Great *ambiente*.

Cortijo de Pepe ✷✷

🍴 LA MERCED ♀ Plaza de la Merced 2 ⊕ 📖 cortijodepepe.es 🕐 1300–0000 ✗ ♀ 📖 ☲ ✍ ⊙ ☲ ⊕ 🌐 ◑ ✿ ◗

This is one of many bars in and around the Plaza de La Merced. It's a little place consisting mainly of a large bar with stools to sit on. There is a *terraza* for those who prefer to be outdoors, and upstairs there are plenty of tables for diners. Its décor is that of a typical Spanish tavern and the food is typical too: meat, fish and a handful of vegetarian options. The octopus salad is delicious, as is the avocado salad.

El Pimpi ✷✷

🍴 CENTRO HISTÓRICO ♀ Calle Granada 62 ⊕ 📖 elpimpi.com
🕐 1200–0000 ✗ ♀ 📖 ⅙ ✍ ⊙ ◖ ◍ ♈ ♀ ☲

This *malagueño* institution, set in an 18th-century house and its ancillary buildings, runs through a warren of cavernous rooms before spilling out onto a terrace and garden. With a location encircled by many historic attractions, the terrace is not to be missed for its stunning views of the Roman Amphitheatre and the Alcazaba. Inside, you get an idea of how popular it is — take note of the rash of famous autographs that cover its wine barrels. You pay slightly over the odds here because of the view and its iconic status, but it is certainly worth calling in for at least a *caña* or a glass of *vino de Málaga* just to see what the fuss is about and soak up the *ambiente*.

La Plaza ✷✷

🍴 CENTRO HISTÓRICO/LA MERCED ♀ Plaza de La Merced 18
🕐 Sun–Thu 0900–2300 (☀ 0000), Fri–Sat 0900–0000 (☀ 0030)
♀ Calle Alcazabilla 7 🕐 Sun–Thu 0830–2300 (☀ 0000), Fri–Sat 0830–0000 (☀ 0030) ⊕ laplazamalaga.com ✗ ♀ 📖 ✍ ⊙ ♀ ⊕ ◑ ☲

This *tapas* restaurant has two locations; one on the Plaza de La Merced, the other near the *Teatro Romano*. It shows many of the warning signs that I would normally advise visitors to run a mile from: it is a chain (though admittedly of only two), has a laminated menu with photographs, and offers 'international dishes'. Most of the *tapas* are good value, while some are expensive for what they are. But I am including it here because it is reliable and, as long as you don't choose the more expensive options from the *carta*, pretty good value given its prime locations in the Plaza de Merced and overlooking the Alcazaba. If all you want is a drink and a snack (from a frankly enormous choice) to keep you going, then La Plaza is a reliable choice.

Las Merchanas ✽✽

🍽 CENTRO HISTÓRICO ♀ Calle Mosquera 5 📷 lasmerchanas ⏰ 1200–0000 🍷 ✂ 🕐 🎖 🚃

This bar is dedicated to all things *Semana Santa* (Holy Week), so be prepared for walls covered from top to bottom in religious images, portraits of saints, and *Semana Santa* paraphernalia. Behind the bar, a calendar counts down the number of days until *Domingo de Ramos* (Palm Sunday), the start of the next *Semana Santa*, and even the background music consists of recordings of Holy Week drum and bugle bands. The *tapas* are classic and well-prepared at a good price. *Raciones* are the norm, with many also available as *medias* and a handful as *tapas*. They have a good range of small, warm sandwiches (*montaditos calientes*). Las Merchanas was one of the first bars to serve the local beer (Victoria) on draught following its modern revival. The tiny bar and covered yard on Calle Mosquera is the original, but there are other branches: one just around the corner (**Calle Andrés Pérez 12**), and another in El Perchel near the Carmen market (**Plaza de la Misericordia**).

Restaurante Cofrade Entre Varales ✽

🍽 CENTRO HISTÓRICO ♀ Calle Nosquera 15
🌐 entrevaralesmalaga.com ⏰ Tue–Sat 1000–1600, 2000–0000; Sun 1300–1600 ✗ 🍷 📖 🍽 ✂ 🕐 🔖 🚃 🎖 🍹 🎗

Just around the corner from Las Merchanas, this is another bar connected with *Semana Santa* ('*Entre Varales*' means 'between the poles', referring to the poles used to carry the thrones of Holy Week). The bar is owned by Holy Week brotherhoods and is a Formica tables and fluorescent strip-light sort of place, rather than a picturesque tavern unchanged since the reign of Alfonso XIII. But the staff are really friendly, the food is basic but fresh and delicious and, as this is more of a locals' haunt, the prices are quite a bit cheaper than in the very centre. The waiters can seem slightly chaotic and non-Spanish clients often bemoan the lack of 'polish', but this is because at busy times many of the staff will be volunteers from Holy Week brotherhoods, rather than professionals. It has a lovely family atmosphere and is hugely popular with its regular local clientele. There are frequent special offers on drinks and other deals. On my last visit, 50% of the proceeds from a popular sharing plate of *croquetas* and chicken strips were being donated to a children's cancer charity.

Antigua Casa de Guardia ✽✽

🍽 CENTRO HISTÓRICO ♀ Alameda Principal 18
🌐 antiguacasadeguardia.com ⏰ Mon–Thu 1030–2200; Fri–Sat 1030–1045; Sun 1100–1500 🍷 ✂ 🕐 🔖 🎖 🚃

The Antigua Casa de Guardia winery has had a tavern in Málaga since 1840, so this establishment lays claim to the title of the oldest bar in the city. The peeling custard-coloured paintwork, huge wooden barrels (which are not for decoration, but full of wine), black-and-white photographs of local boy Picasso and the all-male *equipo* of bar staff all look fittingly old-school. I have overheard more than one tour guide confidently vouchsafe that the Antigua Casa de Guardia was 'Picasso's favourite bar'. This claim is extremely unlikely to be true, not least because the great painter's family left Málaga when Pablo was 10 years old. He did return for holidays from the age of 15, but within a couple of years he had fallen out with his family and his final visit was to ask his uncle Salvador for money when he was 20. During those last visits, he painted some rather angry and not very good pictures of prostitutes, brothels, Gypsy hovels and dive bars but none of his supposed 'favourite tavern'. When Picasso was born, Antigua Casa de Guardia was situated in Calle Ollerías in the *barrio* of San Felipe Neri. During his teenage visits, it stood on the corner of Calle Alhódinga. Only during his final visit in 1901 had it found its current location. What we do know, however, is that Picasso enjoyed Málaga wine and it is entirely likely that Antigua Casa de Guardia was his favourite wine-maker.

History

We need to distinguish between the Antigua Casa de Guardia winery and the *taberna* of the same name. The winery (*bodega*) still produces wines from grapes grown in the Montes de Málaga and the *taberna* serves these same wines. In the 19th century, for wines to be called 'Málaga', they had to be matured in the city. Although this is no longer the case, much of the winemaking takes place in Olías, 20 km from the centre of Málaga near the vineyards. However, if you walk along Calle Peinado, just north of the *barrio* of El Molinillo, you will pass a huge unmarked building with grilles instead of windows. This is Antigua Casa de Guardia's city centre *bodega* and within its walls are hundreds of thousands of litres of Málaga wine maturing in the cask in *soleras* well over a hundred years old.

'Antigua Casa de Guardia' literally means 'Old Guard House' but there was never a 'guard house' on this site. The name is from the founder, José de Guardia, a *malagueño* wine and spirit merchant who established the Casa de Guardia *bodega* (winery) in 1820 and the ancestor of the current *taberna* two decades later. He began with premises on Calle Ollerías and Calle Compañía (on the site now occupied by the café of the Museo Thyssen) where he distilled liqueurs with racy names like 'Girlfriend's Kiss' (*Beso de Novia*) and 'Perfect Love' (*Perfecto Amor*). In those days, more than thirty liquor stills were operating in the city. It was de Guardia who secured the all-important royal warrant from Queen Isabel II when she visited Málaga in 1862. When the Queen appointed Don José governor of Soria, he left the business in the hands of his friend Enrique Navarro Ortiz.

Don Enrique proved to be a skilled businessman and he brought together the different elements of the business — winery, still, offices, and sales outlet — on one site. The business occupied the entire block to the east of the Atarazanas Market (bounded by Atarazanas, Albóndiga, Guillén de Castro and Herrería del Rey streets). In fact, Navarro probably has the greatest claim to have founded the *taberna*. Many Spanish bars began as wine stores where customers would bring bottles to be filled from the barrel. Naturally, people wanted to taste the wine before buying, and wine shops evolved into taverns.

In 1892, Navarro employed as a barman a young man by the name of José Ruiz Luque from Antequera who quickly proved himself as an efficient worker. Ruiz's younger brother Antonio soon joined the company and Casa de Guardia continued to innovate. They increased the range of wines on offer and took steps to make the tavern more attractive to 'respectable' families by selling soft drinks and ice cream. In 1897, the owner of the building announced his intention to sell the plot for redevelopment and in 1899, Navarro moved the *taberna* to its current location on Alameda Principal 22. The move was intended to be temporary, but the prominent position proved to be a commercial success.

Having no heirs, Navarro entrusted the business to the Ruiz brothers. They added the appellation '*Antigua*' ('old') to the name and moved the liquor store and *bodega* (housing the *soleras*) to Calle Peinado in the Segalerva *barrio* in the north of the city (where it is still located). José Ruiz and his wife Concepción were childless, and Antonio never married, but they took a keen interest in the education of their nephew José Garijo Ruiz (son of their widowed sister Virtudes). Despite a glittering career in the law beckoning, José Garijo took over the running of the business. His pronounced Republicanism led to a spell in prison during the Civil War, only returning the take up the reins in the 1940s.

The administrators had run the business into the ground and exhausted both stock and credit, so Don José faced the massive task of rebuilding a once thriving enterprise. By the 1950s, he had opened a new *taberna* at Calle Méndez Núñez 5 (now the Cafe de Indias) and a decade later he achieved his dream of becoming a true winemaker, purchasing land and a farmhouse near the *axarqueña* village of Olías in the Montes de Málaga. Before this, Antigua Casa de Guardia had purchased young wine from various vineyards, ageing it in their own *soleras*, but from 1964 it took charge of the entire process — planting, pruning, harvesting, pressing, sun-drying, fermenting and beyond — and thus one of Málaga's oldest wine 'makers' became also one of the newest.

By the 1960s and 1970s, Antigua Casa de Guardia was at its zenith, with Garijo Ruiz winning awards from the Hermandad de Viñeros, being honoured by King Juan Carlos, and the company breaking sales records. Although Don José's son José Garijo Alba looked like the heir apparent, taking a keen interest in all aspects of the business, he died unexpectedly in 1985, leaving his ailing father practically in sole charge once more. The old man would visit Alameda Principal 22 every day until the mid-1990s. His last public appearance was at the Málaga Feria in 1996 when the Regulatory Council of the DOP Vinos de Málaga made him an honorary academician.

He died in December of the same year, leaving the Alameda 22 *taberna* to his son Antonio Garijo Alba, and the vineyards and wineries to Antonio and his seven siblings. Antonio's son Alejandro now runs the *taberna* while his cousin Cayetano looks after the winery in Olías, continuing not only a venerable winemaking tradition but a family one too.

Antigua Casa de Guardia Today

The Antigua Casa de Guardia is packed shoulder to shoulder during *Semana Santa* and on Christmas Eve, but it is busy most days for the *hora del vermú*, especially at weekends, and for the early-evening round of *aperitivos*. For any visitor to Málaga, especially any wine-lover, it is practically a secular pilgrimage site, a shrine to the liqueur wines of Málaga — the 'Malago-Sack' that was once preferred to 'Sherris-Sack' throughout Europe but which is now all but unknown outside Spain. Nicknamed 'El Barril Místico' (The Mystical Barrel) locally, the *taberna* is more than an institution. It is a symbol of Málaga. It is sometimes said that Málaga has three cathedrals: the actual Cathedral of the Incarnation; La Malagueta, the 'cathedral' of the bulls; and Antigua Casa de Guardia, the 'cathedral' of viniculture.

A visit to the Antigua Casa de Guardia can feel like stepping into another age. The wooden bar and the white-shirted barmen (white-jacketed in winter) are familiar enough, but where are the beer taps, the optics, the wine coolers? There are hardly any tables and 95% of punters will be standing, thronging the bar. A lot of people are eating *tapas*, mostly seafood, but where are the menus, where are the *tapas* laid out on the bar? In fact, where is the bar? Look closely and you'll see that it's formed of a handful of narrow tables pushed together. You look around to see what others are drinking, and apart from a handful of people with 'normal' glasses of wine and a few sipping beer, everyone else has a little shot glass of amber liquid that looks more like medicine than refreshment. And then there is the aroma: a heady mix of oak, cork, sweet alcohol esters and spice, with grapy top notes of fruit and nuts — raisins, cherry brandy and a hint of marzipan. It is as if every glassful of the millions of gallons of Málaga wines that have been decanted in this bar room over the last 120 or more years has left a trace in the air.

Visiting the Antigua Casa de Guardia for a preprandial sharpener can seem daunting for the visitor, especially one without much Spanish, because it is a place that seems to use its own arcane vocabulary and traditions. However, it may be reassuring to know that even near-fluent speakers of Spanish (and even some Spaniards from outside Málaga) are unlikely to be familiar with names like '*Pajarete*' (little bird) or '*Lágrima Trasañejo*' (very old tear). Yet, ordering and enjoying a drink in this bar is such a singular experience that it is well worth taking a deep breath and taking the plunge. The bar staff may seem a bit gruff, but they are polite and efficient and well-used to dealing with clueless foreigners (and non-*malagueño* Spaniards). So here follows is a beginner's guide to ordering food and wine and enjoying your visit. Plan before your visit so that you can order with confidence!

Food

If you want to eat something, the food (all cold) is displayed in a chiller cabinet opposite the bar. *Langostinos* (tiger prawns) and *mejillones* (mussels) are served as *raciones*. *Gambas* (prawns or pink shrimp) used to be on the menu, but they seem to have disappeared lately. Also available are *búsanos*, and this is where things get confusing. Throughout Spain, '*búsano*' is the name used for the Banded Dye *Murex* (L. *Phyllonotus trunculus*) sea snail, while the closely related, slightly smaller, Purple Dye *Murex* (L. *Bolinus brandaris*) sea snail prized in antiquity is known as '*cañadilla*'. In Andalucía, however, '*cañadilla*' drops the '**d**' to become '*cañailla*'. But in linguistically non-conforming Málaga, *búsanos* are called *cañaillas*, and *cañaillas* are called *búsanos*. It probably makes little practical difference. Both are similar kinds of predatory sea snails and if you are enough of a connoisseur to tell them apart, then you will probably be able to tell at a glance which is which. *Salchichón* (sausage/salami), *chrorizo* and *queso de oveja* (sheep's cheese) also come as *raciones*, as do *piparras picantes* (pickled green *guindilla* peppers from the North of Spain). Everything else is '*vendido por unidad*' (sold by the unit), including *conchas finas* (Málaga's beloved smooth venus clams) and *colas de langosta* '*surimi*' (surprisingly realistic and rather tasty spiny lobster 'sticks').

Extremely popular at Antigua Casa de Guardia are '*encurtidos*' (pickles) — various salty and vinegary morsels threaded onto cocktail sticks to make savoury little kebabs. These are what I recommend your trying here. Have a look at the chilled display cabinets opposite the bar to make your choice, but they are all variations of the '*Gilda*' (*vide supra*, p. 163), the little '*banderilla*' (cocktail skewer) combining pickled onions, olives, anchovies, peppers, etc. Some are spicy (*picante*), some have *anchoas* (salted brown anchovies), some *boquerones* (white anchovies in brine or vinegar), and the speciality of the house combine perfect cubes of pickled *atún* (tuna) or *salmón* alternating with cubes of mature sheep's cheese.

Drinks

You can buy beer as a *caña*, *tubo* or '*quinto*' (200 ml bottle), cider, a basic range of spirits (gin, rum, brandy, Ponche Caballero, *crème de menthe*, *anís seco* from Asturias or Andalucía ['*Machaco*'], and *anís dulce* from Chinchón), soft drinks, mineral water, mixers, and '*mosto*' — unfermented grape juice. Asking for '*un blanco*' or '*un tinto*' will get you an ordinary glass of white or red table wine. Everything else on the menu is a DOP Málaga wine. The alcohol content of almost all the wines on sale is 15% or 16% ABV, so make your choice based on style.

Although the name of a single measure in this bar is technically a '*cinco*' the simplest way to order is by name (*e.g.* '*un moscatel dorado*'). If you want to try a couple of wines first, you can ask for '*una media copa*' (half glass, **oo**-na **may**deeya **koh**-pah). *Vermú* (and any of the wines here) can be served with a dash of *gaseosa* (a slightly sweet soda — add '*con sifón*' — kon see-**fon** — to your order). *Vermú* will come with a cube of ice. You can ask for a double measure by asking for '*un doble*' (oon **doh**-blay).

THE WINES OF ANTIGUA CASA DE GUARDIA

The first two premium wines on the list are from the bottle and over twice the price of anything else and you will need to make a special request.

Solera Pedro Ximén 1908

(soh-**lair**-ah **ped**-ro KHee-**men**) A very old (8 years) dark PX wine; toasted and spicy on the nose with almonds and wood and hints of figs and muscovado, full on the palate with good balance with an underlying, savoury dryness.

Isabel II Moscatel Trasañejo

(iss-a-**bell** say-**goon**-doh) Queen Isabel II visited in 1862 and was so taken with this Moscatel de Alejandría Trasañejo that it was renamed in her honour. It is aged for 7 years in oak. *Rojo-dorado* (dark amber), with a persistent nose of wood and ripe fruit; unctuous, sweet and velvety, even slightly oily, on the palate with sweetness balanced by acidity.

VERMUT

PX Vermút — Clásico

(bair-**moot class**-ee-koh) Vermouth made from Pedro Ximén. Old, sweet, aged for 36 months in American oak barrels. Clean mahogany colour, with intense aromas of clove, cinnamon and orange peel. It is served in a slightly larger glass on ice and you can ask for it '*con sifón*' (con siff-**on**) if you want a dash of sweet soda added.

PX Vermút — Especial

(bair-**moot** ess-peTH-**yall**) 100% PX, this is superior *vermú*, costing a third more. The *clásico* is made by blending PX wine with other base vermouth wines and essences, while the *especial* is pure PX wine and natural botanicals. It has the same clove, cinnamon and bitter orange peel typical of Spanish vermouths, but in a far smoother and more harmonious palate.

DULCE NATURAL

El Chavea

(el chab-**ay**-ah) A wine from the bottle, a '*natural*' (unfortified) unaged sweet wine made from Moscatel de Alejandría grapes. It is *blanco/dorado* (pale straw yellow), floral and fruity on the nose and fresh on the palate. '*Chavea*' is a Málaga dialect word for a young man. It almost certainly comes from the *Caló* (Spanish Romani) word for boy, which may even be the origin of the English slang term 'chav', too.

SECO

These are dry wines (though they are so rich and fruity it can be difficult to detect the dryness because we associate these flavour profiles with sweet things). Made from PX, as they age they become darker and more complex, but generally they are bright old gold in colour with pastry aromas and an orange background, and some wood and dried fruit. Balanced with toasted hints and a good length.

Seco Málaga (**sek**-oh **mal**-ag-ah)

Seco Añejo (**sek**-oh an-**yeh**-кно) 3–5 years in the cask

Seco Trasañejo (**sek**-oh trass-an-**yeh**-кно) More than 5 years in the cask

PEDRO XIMÉN

These are sweet, fairly dark wines made with the Pedro Ximén (PX) grape and relatively familiar to non-Spanish drinkers because they are also produced by the Sherry/Jerez DO and available in British supermarkets. It has dried fruit on the nose — always raisins, but also prunes, figs and light 'toast' in older wines — and in the mouth, generous syrup, dark fruit and a hint of spice.

Pedro Ximén (**ped**-roh кнее-**men**) 24 months in the cask

Pajarete (pa-кна-**ray**-tay) 36 months matured

LÁGRIMA

Lágrima ('tear') is made from the first pressing of the grapes, so the base wine is very pale but acquires colour in the barrel. It's sweet, but not overly so, with rich caramel notes. Aged for more than 2 years, both of these are technically examples of '*Lágrima Christi*'.

Lágrima Añejo (**lag**-ree-mah an-**yeh**-кно) 3–5 years in the cask.

Lágrima Trasañejo (**lag**-ree-mah trass-an-**yeh**-кно) 5+ years in the cask.

MOSCATEL

Made mostly from Moscatel de Alejandría with significantly different flavour profiles emerging depending upon age and elaboration (*e.g.* how much *arrope* or concentrated grape syrup has been used or how the wine has been blended).

Moscatel Dorado (mos-ka-**tell** dor-**ah**-doh) a young, golden moscatel

Moscatel 2° (mos-ka-**tell** say-**goon**-doh) aka *Moscatel Guardia* (mos-ka-**tell** **gward**-yah) Moscatel de Alejandría (85%) and Pedro Ximén (15%) aged 24 months in American oak barrels. Intense brightness, good balance between sweetness and fine acidity, mature fruit.

Moscatel 1º (mos-ka-**tell** pRRee-**maiRR**-oh) is essentially the *añejo* version of ***Moscatel 2º***. Darker, with more complexity.

Moscatel Guinda (mos-ka-**tell geen**-dah) 'Guinda' means sour cherry, and this dark Moscatel has hints of this fruit, as well as toasted aromas of coffee. Smooth and creamy palate.

OTHERS

Málaga Quina (**mal**-ag-ah **kee**-nah) A classic, fairly young, Málaga wine with the addition of quinine giving a (very) slight bitter note.

Solera (soh-**lair**-ah) A blended, semi-seco wine close to a cream sherry in flavour.

For off sales, some of the wines produced by La Antigua Casa de Guardia are on sale in sealed bottles (*viz.* Pajarete 1908, Pedro Ximén 1908, Isabel II, Moscatel Guardia, El Chavea, Moscatel Guinda, and Vermut Clásico and Especial), as well as a few not on sale from the barrel, like Málaga Garijo and the new-ish Verdiales lines:

Málaga Garijo	100% Pedro Ximén. Sweet, aged for 12 months, 16% ABV. Dark amber, persistent ripe fruit on the nose and balance palate and finish.
Verdiales con Arte	60% Pedro Ximén and 40% Moscatel de Alejandría. Sweet, aged for 48 months in American oak casks, 16% ABV. Mahogany, persistent on the nose with aromas of ripe fruit. Soft, spicy and balanced on the palate.
Verdiales Cream	100% Pedro Ximén. Semi-dry, 36 months aged in American oak, 16% ABV. Dark and bright amber. Persistent on the nose with aromas of fine wood and almost incense-like spice. Balanced with a tasty, nutty palate.
Verdiales Seco	100% Pedro Ximén. Dry, 36 months aged in American oak, 16% ABV. Bright old gold colour. Fine aroma of pastry with an orange, wood and dried fruit background. Balanced on the palate with toasted background notes and a long finish.

For other barrel wines, you can buy an empty bottle (or bring your own) and they will fill it for you (the price per litre is chalked on the front of each barrel). They also sell leather '*botas*' (wineskins) embossed with the Antigua Casa de Guardia monogram.

Antigua Casa de Guardia has not yet entered the world of PDAs and tablets, nor even POS systems. When you order your drinks, the barman will chalk your bill on the wooden counter-top. If you order further drinks, these are added, keeping a running tally (so if you want to move away from the bar and find a quieter corner, you will need to pay first, or tell the barman). This used to be the standard practice throughout Spain, but now very few bars do it — *Bodegas* Díaz Salazar in Sevilla installed cash registers during COVID, but La Venencia in Madrid is continuing the tradition of chalk. Yet another traditional touch is that whenever anyone leaves a tip, they throw it clattering into a metal bucket and ring a bell in celebration.

La Tranca ✶✶

🏛 CENTRO HISTÓRICO 📍 Calle Carretería 93 🌐 latranca.es 🕐 1230–0200 🍷 🥗 🎵

If you want to enjoy Málaga's traditional wines slightly off the well-worn tourist track, then you'd be hard-pressed to do better than La Tranca. You'll probably also be hard-pressed to find space at the bar, though. Though only a few minutes from Plaza La Merced, this tiny place is pretty much a *malagueños*-only joint. Locals enjoy vermouth or Málaga's signature sweet wines in the kiosk-like bar area or spill out onto the busy Calle Carretería, on which a couple of barrels serve as tables. Barrels also line the back of the bar and your wine comes directly from these, served by the irrepressibly-cheerful owner, Ezequiel, and his staff. It's lively, noisy and popular with a younger crowd, so it's not a place for a quiet drink. Go early if you want to eat because it is very popular — and deservedly so.

Los Patios de Beatas ✶✶✶

🏛 CENTRO HISTÓRICO 📍 Calle Beatas 43
🌐 📖 lospatiosdebeatas.com 🕐 1300–1700, 2000–0000
✗ 🍷 🎣 📖 🎵 ☀ ◐ 🍴 ⚓ ☎ 🌍 🐚 🐾 🌿 🚐 ☕

This bar-restaurant created from a pair of carefully restored *palacios* could easily have been listed in the restaurants section, and I dare say that Los Patios sees itself primarily as a '*restaurante*' (reflected in the elevated cuisine and the opening hours). The food is excellent, consisting of sensitively 'elevated' classics and there is a beautiful dining room created in the patio of one of the buildings, but I have included it under 'bars' because perhaps the principal reason for its popularity is its excellent wine list. The excellent sommelier (the Spanish word is *sumiller* but is rarely used) Julián Sanjuán is custodian of a cellar storing over 500 different wines, with a couple of dozen chosen to showcase each month. In addition, there is a regular wine list of almost 50 *tintos*, *blancos*, *rosados*, *cavas* and *generosos*, all of which are available by the glass and, in the case of still wines, half glass. So if almost €90 for a bottle of Ribera del Duero Grand Cru is outside your budget, you can order a half glass for €12. This is because they use Coravin® devices to pour wine without opening the bottle. Julián also conducts guided tours of vineyards with wine tastings (transport to the vineyard can be arranged for an additional charge).

Atarazanas Market ✶ ✶

🏛 CENTRO HISTÓRICO 📍 Calle Atarazanas 10

There are several bars in the central market, all specializing in seafood and fish *tapas*, but offering other choices as well. See the section on '*Mercados*' below (p. 225) for more details.

Gin Tonic ✶✶

🏛 CENTRO HISTÓRICO 📍 Calle Sancha de Lara 5 🌐 gintonicbar.es
🕐 1700–0000 (Thu 0200, Fri–Sat 0300) 🍷

Does what it says on the tin. This is a bar for gin and tonic. Over 100 gins (and vodkas, rums and whiskies) and 20 tonics plus botanicals for garnish.

Most bars these days (except a few old-fashioned bars known principally for beer or wine) will carry a decent selection of gins, both imported and domestic ('*nacional*'), but this is a place to sample something more unusual or niche. Note the late opening hours — gin and tonic in Spain is a postprandial, not preprandial, tipple. They also sell their own brands under the 'Malaka' label. British gin lovers who enjoy a G&T before dinner are in luck, though, because this bar only tends to fill up after dinner.

Bodeguita El Gallo ✿✿

CENTRO HISTÓRICO ♀ Calle San Agustín 19
bodeguitaelgallomalaga.com Thu 2000–0000, Fri–Sat 1300–1700, 2000–0000; Sun 1300–1700

A great *tapas* bar near the Picasso Museum that has a good wine list in addition to specializing in *vermú*. The *tapas* menu is excellent, reasonably priced, and has some unusual dishes that are well worth trying — the *croquetas* for example, where you can choose from among black pudding and pine nuts, *salɕhiɕhón de Málaga*, Payoyo cheese with raisins and almonds, *Cabrales* cheese with walnuts, ham and sherry, and more.

La Taberna del Pintxo Larios ✿✿

CENTRO HISTÓRICO ♀ Calle Alarcon Lujan 12
latabernadelpintxo-malaga.com 1230–0000

This is a very popular Basque-style bar serving *pintxos* (small *tapas* on a slices of baguette, impaled with a wooden stick — *pintxo* means 'pierced'). A few *raciones* are listed on blackboards, but most people come for the *pintxos*. There is no *carta* as such. After the Basque fashion, cold *pintxos* (savoury and sweet) are displayed on the bar. If you have particular dietary requirements, ask the bar staff for advice (the *pintxos* are labelled, but only with the main ingredient). Order your drinks at the bar, help yourself to *pintxos* and find a table. Wait staff emerge from the kitchen bearing trays of freshly made hot *pintxos*, so help yourself as they pass. When it comes to the bill, they count the skewers (and in the case of *cazuelitos* — little stews — and puddings, the small dishes). Different skewers denote different prices and a key to which costs what is displayed on various blackboards.

My advice here (and in any Basque-style bar) is not to let your eyes rule your belly. Get a drink and choose a *pintxo*, maybe two. If you want another, you don't need to summon a server and wait for it to be brought to you; just go to the bar and help yourself, as many times as you like. A common mistake is for people to load up with *pintxos* from the bar and then look on despondently as delicious hot morsels emerge from the kitchen. To complete the experience, try a glass (or a bottle) of Txakoli (**cha-koh-lee**), the crisp, light, fruity and ever-so-slightly effervescent Basque white wine. The high acidity makes it a perfect partner to rich *pintxos*, fish and seafood, and its low alcohol content (around 10.5% ABV) makes it an ideal lunchtime tipple.

Los Gatos ✿✿

CENTRO HISTÓRICO ♀ Plaza de Uncibay 9 1100–0000

This is a traditional, if slightly quirky, bar serving a large range of filling *tapas* (which they call canapés for some reason) and a well-priced selection of *raciones* if you want a more substantial meal. Los Gatos opened in Madrid over 30 years ago ('*los gatos*' — the cats — is a nickname for people from Madrid just as '*los boquerones*' — the anchovies — is a nickname for *malagueños*) and the owner, Miguel, opened this branch in his native Málaga in 2012. It is hugely popular and manages to thrive with no social media or web presence and without accepting reservations. This is a place where the un-Spanish habit of dining before 8 pm can be an advantage because it is well-nigh impossible to secure a table after that without a long wait.

Casa Lola ✿✿

🍴 CENTRO HISTÓRICO 📍 Calle Granada 46 📍 Calle Strachan 11 📍 Plaza de Uncibay 3 📍 Plaza del Siglo 3 🔳 casalolamalaga 🕐 1230–0000
🍴🍷🔌🕐👜🎵

A modern bar made to look like an old bar, the first Casa Lola opened in 2010, quickly getting a reputation as one of the best *tapas* bars in Málaga. Since then they have opened three more bars in Málaga, a bar devoted to fish and seafood *tapas* (Pez Lola at Calle Granada 42) and two branches in Marbella (both called Casa Blanca). The formula — a huge range of *tapas*, cooked with care, good *vermú*, and a fantastic, lively *ambiente* — has proved a hit with locals and tourists alike. They do not accept reservations. The most you can do is put your name down on the day and be given an approximate wait time. You might strike lucky if you are prepared to eat at '*guiri* time' (*i.e.* too early for Spaniards).

Madeinterranea ✿✿

🍴 CENTRO HISTÓRICO 📍 Plaza de Uncibay 3 🌐 madeinterranea.es
🕐 1200–0200 🍴🍷🥘🔌🕐🎵🌐🐾🐕🍽

Another modern *tapas* bar with updated classics. Ignore the 'clever' but slightly clunky name because it has consistently good food, carefully executed and beautifully presented. It has a relaxed atmosphere and kind and friendly staff. There is sometimes a good value *menú del día* (no drink included).

La Casa del Perro ✿

🍴 CENTRO HISTÓRICO 📍 Calle Hernán Ruiz 7 🌐 lacasadelperro.org
🕐 Wed–Sat 1300–1600, 2000–2300, Sun 1300–1600 📱 +34 644 698 270
🍴🍷📖🔌🕐👜🍽🌐

'The Dog House' doesn't translate well, but don't be put off by the name. This *bar de tapas* moved to new premises a few years back and is now in the narrow Hernán Ruiz street in the north of *centro*. It has rather curious decor, part shop (they sell natural, organic and additive-free wines) and, with its plain tables and red plastic chairs, part classroom. But eccentric décor aside, it's a lovely, friendly place presided over by the charming owner, Julia, serving excellent food. The *carta* changes frequently, even daily, and the cooking is some of the best in town. They describe their *tapas* as '*mordiscos y bocados*' (nibbles and bites) so it is a good place to try a selection of different things. Their puddings are popular, especially their riff on the traditional *malagueño* dessert of *baticate* (avocado custard), which here is served as a refreshing avocado and lemon fool. Do try it if it's on the menu.

La Barra de Zapata ✿✿✿

🍴 CENTRO HISTÓRICO 📍 Calle Salina 10 🔳 labarradezapatamalaga
🕐 1300–1600, 1900–2300 🍴🍷🔌🍽

A modern bar with clean, cool décor and a list of traditional *tapas* prepared with a modern twist, all beautifully presented. When you look at the *carta*, you may think it both limited and expensive, but the quality of the food means that the prices are pretty reasonable and the small selection of dishes is hardly surprising given the intricacy of their preparation. The owner, Rafael, is passionate about his food and an excellent host. The service is friendly, efficient and intimate, and the food is highly 'Instagrammable' (as well as highly edible). It is very popular with locals which, as always, is an excellent sign.

La Farola de Orellana ✹✹

∰ CENTRO HISTÓRICO ♀ Calle Moreno Monroy 5
ⓕ La-Farola-de-Orellana ⊘ Mondays ✕ ♀ ✄ ⊕ ❧ ☰

La Farola de Orellana is an old bar (1938) that received a facelift/redesign in 2013 and is just as popular as it ever was. With a *carta* of 50 *tapas*, there should be something for everyone. It is also one of the best *tapas* bars in Málaga. The only point not in its favour is that it is tiny and can get very busy, but this is also part of its charm. There are a few tables inside, some stools at the bar, and a few upturned barrels with stools outside, but unless you are very lucky with your timings, you will be lucky to get a seat here. But seat or no seat, it is well worth trying because the atmosphere is lively and fun, the service is quick and friendly, and the *tapas* are reasonably priced and delicious. Quite a few are available at *tapas, medias raciones* and *raciones*. The danger in trying to recommend a few of their best dishes is that I could end up just reproducing the entire menu. But if pushed, here are a few specialities not to be missed: *champiñones rellenos de queso* (mushrooms stuffed with cheese), *papas a la mala leche* ('grumpy' –i.e. spicy — potatoes), *costillas de cerdo* (pork ribs), *carrillada* (pork cheek), *higaditos de pollo* (chicken livers), *langostinos al pil-pil* (tiger prawns with garlic and chilli) and *cordero* (lamb — available as a *ración* or a '*pinchito*'). The *callos* (stewed tripe) and *caracoles* (snails) are also excellent here.

Taberna El Carpintero ✹

∰ CENTRO HISTÓRICO ♀ Calle Beatas 32
ⓕ ElCarpinteroCasaManzanilla ⊕ Tue–Sat 1300–1600, 2000–0000
♀ ✄ ⊕ ☰

This is another back street bar rarely troubled by tourists. It's a basic sort of place with anaglypta wallpaper and random carpentry tools hanging on the walls, but the welcome is friendly and the *tapas* (most also available as *medias* and *raciones*) are simple, classical and well executed.

Taberna El Harén ✹

∰ CENTRO HISTÓRICO ♀ Calle Andrés Pérez 3 **ⓕ bit.ly/ElHaren**
⊕ Sun–Thu 1300–1600, 2000–0000; Fri–Sat 1300–0300 ♀ ▯ ◐ ⒢ ✄ ⊕ ⛁

This attractive little bar on a quiet back street occupies an old *corralón* with the courtyard transformed into a bar area, and rooms on two levels. Formerly, there was a Moroccan tea room on this site, but it did not survive the COVID shutdown of hospitality. The current *taberna* is still finding its feet, and the service can occasionally be slow, but the food is good (and inexpensive) and the staff are friendly.

Vermutería La Clasica ✹✹

∰ CENTRO HISTÓRICO ♀ Plaza de Uncibay 1
⊕ vermuterialaclasica.es ⊕ 1200–0000 ✕ ♀ ✄ ⊕ ▯ ❧ ☰

This bar is well-named, with three *vermús* on tap and another thirteen from the bottle. It is located in '*el triangulo*' (aka the 'tourist central' triangle formed between the plazas del Siglo, del Carbón and de Uncibay) but it is popular with locals too. The service is great whilst the food is traditional and good value given the location, though their website's claim that it is '*cocina en peligro de extinción*' (cuisine in danger of extinction) has more than a touch of the hyperbolic.

Lo Güeno ✹✹

🍴 CENTRO HISTÓRICO 📍 Calle Marín García 9 ⊕ loguemo.es 🕐 1200–0000 ✗🍷📖👌🇬✒️🕐🍸🚲⊠🔊🍤🐾🥢🍵🍴🥄

Lo Güeno (an idiomatic misspelling of 'Lo Bueno', i.e. 'The Good One') is another Málaga institution, founded by José Puerto Galveño in 1967 on the Calle Marín García. Although it nowadays seems like the epitome of a traditional Spanish bar, Lo Güeno was one of the first bars in Málaga to serve 'gastro' tapas — not simply something solid to accompany a drink, but more refined dishes that would be chosen for their own sake. The founder's daughter, Lidia Puerto, and her husband Mariano, expanded into the next-door lot in 2002, making this the comedor and began serving restaurant-style dishes. They opened a restaurant, Lo Güeno de Strachan, on Calle Strachan in 2010. The Strachan restaurant is a 'white tablecloth' establishment, and its clientele seems mainly to be composed of tourists. The original bar (on Marín García) is a better choice in my view (though not if you want to eat outside). Most of the dishes available at Strachan are available at Marín García (and are slightly cheaper). It also has an extensive tapas list (⚠ not shown on the website). If you've ever wished you'd had the opportunity to eat ortolan bunting, then order the 'pajaritos' (little birds). You won't be given an ortolan, but a fried quail, so you won't need to cover your head with a napkin while eating it.

Pez Lola ✹✹

🍴 CENTRO HISTÓRICO 📍 Calle Granada 42 ⊕ pezlolamalaga 🕐 1200–0000 ✗🍷✒️🕐🍸⊠🥢🐾

This is the fish and seafood-focused sibling of nearby Casa Lola and, like most bars on the Calle Granada it is popular with tourists, and rightly so. The service is friendly and the tapas are of excellent quality (though the portions are hardly enormous). Overall, however, the prices are reasonable given the quality of the cooking. It is also a colourful, bright and modern bar, so if the outside tables are full, don't hesitate to eat indoors and enjoy the surroundings and buzz.

Puerta Oscura ✹✹✹

🍴 CENTRO HISTÓRICO 📍 Calle Molina Lario 5 🇫 Puertaoscuramalaga 🕐 1700–0100 (Fri–Sat 0200) 🍷🍸

Cocktail bars tend to fall into one of two categories. They are either cool and hip with neon lights and a suggestion of the louche, or else refined and elegant. Either Hunter S. Thompson dive bars or Ernest Hemingway cocktail lounges. Puerta Oscura ('The Dark Door'), named after one of the entrances to the Alcazaba, is an example of the latter type, with its sofas, carpets, chandeliers and, on my last visit, an exquisitely painted carved statue of the Virgin Mary. It is not terribly obvious from the street — the sort of place one might walk past because it looks a little like an antiques shop. Classic cocktails (no porn star Martinis or slippery nipples here) are prepared with skill and care. Cocktails are generally a postprandial pleasure in Spain, so British visitors who fancy a preprandial sharpener are likely to find this and other similar bars not too busy.

Background classical music (and occasional live chamber music) plays as you sip your drink and they frequently stage small art exhibitions. I dare say that some may find it a little precious and it's certainly not where the cool kids go, but when it comes to enjoying a delicious drink in surroundings that seem to give a veneer of respectability to the rather shocking reality that one is knocking back four units of alcohol before dinner, there is nowhere better.

🍸 Other Cocktail Bars

The following is a list of the best (and trendier) cocktail bars in central Málaga (most close around an hour later than indicated on Fridays and Saturdays):

Speakeasy "The Pharmacy" 📍 Calle García Briz 3 🕐 1900–0200

Chester and Punk 📍 Calle Méndez Núñez 4 🕐 1700–0200

Nusa 📍 Paseo de la Farola 6 🕐 1200–0300

Mañana 📍 Calle San Juan de Letrán 7 🕐 1700–0200

Chloe 📍 Calle Correo Viejo, 9 🕐 Tue–Sat 1800–0200

La Vida de la Gente 📍 Calle Carretería 44 🕐 Wed–Mon 1900–0200

La Destilería 📍 Calle Beatas 1 🕐 Thu–Sun 1900–0300

Ghetto 📍 Calle Gómez Pallete 4 🕐 1800–0200

Taberna Uvedoble ✷✷

🏛 CENTRO HISTÓRICO 📍 Calle Alcazabilla 1 🌐 uvedobletaberna.com 🕐 Mon–Sat 1230–0000 📞 +34 951 24 84 78 🍴🍷🏨💈🕐🥄🍸🍷🍴🍷🌐🍸

This very busy *tapas* bar near the *Teatro Romano* will appeal to anyone who loves fish and seafood. The wine list is excellent and the food is some of the best in Málaga. The *tapas* of smoked sardine on *focaccia* with rosemary and sweet tomato, and grilled razor clams with fried almond, lime and soy dressing are both highlights of the menu. It will also satisfy meat eaters tempted by cannelloni of kid, suckling lamb with couscous, or veal sweetbreads cooked in sherry. Although the menu is divided into 'starters', 'snacks' and 'mains' etc., it's basically *tapas* dining here with many dishes available as *tapas*, *medias raciones*, and *raciones*. It's therefore ideal either for a glass of wine and a *tapa* at the bar, or a full meal. The *terraza* is small and fills up quickly, but staff can often find you a table inside if you don't mind a short wait, but booking ahead, in person or by phone is strongly advised, especially at weekends or for later dining

Bar Jamones ✷✷

🏛 SAN FELIPE NERI 📍 Calle Carretería 87 📘 Jamonesbar 🕐 Mon–Fri 1200–1600, 2000–0000; Fri–Sat 1200–0000 🍷💈🕐🥄🏨🍴

Great owner, lovely staff, good food. You will sometimes receive a small *tapita* free with your first drink. What more could one want? The food, mostly available as *tapas*, *medias* and *raciones*, is delicious with the accent (as the name suggests) on pork. It's the sort of bar that one often calls into for a 'quick drink' but which then proves difficult to leave because it has such a lovely, relaxed *ambiente*.

Bar Málaga ✷✷

🏛 CENTRO HISTÓRICO 📍 Calle Santa María 4 🕐 1200–0200 🍴🍷💈🕐🍴

Bar Málaga, on Calle Santa María, dates back to 1852 . Now ably managed by Manuel, you can enjoy classics such as artichokes, octopus with *aioli*, or sirloin in sweet wine, but the obligatory *tapa* is *atún en manteca* (usually translated as 'tuna in butter', but in fact, it's in lard). On the upper floor it has a dining room for diners wanting *raciones* or *medias raciones*, and, overlooking the Calle Santa María, a pair of balconies accommodating two highly sought-after tables.

VARO ✯✯

🍽 CENTRO HISTÓRICO 📍 Calle Andrés Pérez 20 📷 varo.1960 🕐 Tue–Sat 1300–1630, 2000–0000 🍴🍷📖🦴🕐🥄🍴💺🪑

The VARO *taberna* is a happy ending to an all-too-familiar story. For decades the Varo family ran a *mercería* (haberdashery) on these premises, but when the owners José Varo and Concepción Fernández retired in 2010 they pulled down the shutters, unable to sell the business as a going concern. More than a dozen years later, their son Eduardo Varo took early retirement from the bank where he had worked and opened this bar preserving many items of furniture, objects and decorations from the original shop. He also expanded into the historic 'Velfer' stationers and bookseller next door, which his uncle had run until 2008. The result is a beautiful space which, despite being one of Málaga's newest establishments, looks as though it has been open for years.

In the last century, Calle Andrés Pérez was one of Málaga's liveliest commercial streets, with over 70 shops including the Anglada bakery, Siles the tailor, an *ultramarinos* (grocer's) specializing in *encurtidos* (pickles), a bank and three shoe shops. It was called 'Larios la Chica' (Little Larios Street) by locals. After a period in the doldrums, the street is rising from the ashes with the opening of **Las Merchanas II**, a branch of the **Astrid** bakery, a luxury **Casa Mira** ice cream parlour, various antique shops, the **Scrappiel** 'scrapbooking' and paper craft shop, and, of course, VARO. Down an alleyway, you'll find the doorway that leads to **La Invisible**, a hidden terrace that stages theatre and music performances and offers inexpensive refreshments in a rather chaotic yet strangely restful urban patio. Another narrow lane brings you into **Plaza Pintor Eugenio Chicano**, where workshops include those of a luthier and a ceramicist.

At VARO there is a small menu of *tapas* and *medias raciones*, all using local products. The essential (for Málaga) anchovy dish is accompanied by *pipirrana* (diced mixed salad) of avocados from Axarquía. There are also things *para untar* (to spread) — whipped goats cheese and olive oil served with mango jam, *pâté* of Ronda black pudding with fried almonds and apple compote, and *pâté* made from Málaga suckling kid accompanied by fig and date chutney. Filled muffins ('*molletitos*') and a handful of hot dishes, again showcasing local ingredients, complete the *tapas* offer. The cheese and cured meat available as sharing plates are also sourced from the Province of Málaga — goat's cheese from Coín, lightly cured cheese from Casabermeja, *morcón* (a type of *chorizo*) from Arriate and a *chorizo* made from goat are among what's on offer.

North and East of the Centro Histórico

As one crosses the Calle Carretería and Calle Álamos that follow the line of the medieval walls bounding the *centro histórico* to the north and east, the bars and restaurants you encounter tend to have fewer tourists and slightly lower prices. *Barrios* like La Goleta, San Felipe Neri, El Molinillo, La Victoria and Capuchinos are really worth exploring. These are where you will find local bars, well off the main tourist drag, and whilst you're unlikely to find anything listed in the Michelin or Repsol guides, you will encounter good, traditional cooking, cold beer and decent wine selections. In fact, during high season, when the bars and restaurants in the centre are rammed, leaving the boundary of the old *medina* is also your best chance of finding a table, especially on a Friday or Saturday night.

Palermo Coffee and Drinks ✱✱

🍴 LA MERCED 📍 Calle Ramos Marín 2 ⊕ palermocoffeedrinks.com
🕐 Sun–Thu 0930–0200; Fri–Sat 0930–0300 🍷✂️🍸🍺🥂🍨

This is one of Málaga's loveliest bars — elegant, comfortable, and relaxed with unfailingly friendly staff — and yet few visitors ever discover it because it is slightly hidden on a corner between the Mercado de La Merced and the Teatro Cervantes. As the name suggests, it's all about beverages — both delicious coffee and alcoholic drinks, mostly cocktails and spirits (although wine and bottled beer are available, along with soft drinks). There is a delicious range of pastries and cakes to accompany the coffee and a small list of *tapitas* to accompany the cocktails. *Empanadas* are a favourite. Palermo is a beautiful spot for coffee at any time, for preprandial cocktails and for a relaxed after-dinner drink as you wind down. There is a selection of board games for customers to borrow and play

La Polivalente ✱

🍴 LAGUNILLAS 📍 Calle Lagunillas 53 ⊕ lapolivalente.com 🕐 Mon–Sat from 1700 🍷✂️🐌🍷

A friendly local bar north-east of the Plaza de La Merced serving a small range of *tapas* alongside wine and beer. La Polivalente (which means 'multi-purpose') is primarily a community arts venue and most nights of the week there are live performances of almost anything you can imagine, from very classical flamenco to experimental performance art. There is open mike music and poetry, recitals, readings, blues, Brazilian bossa nova, theatre, jazz, rock, salsa, you name it. Entry to these events usually costs a few euros, though sometimes it's free. Alongside these evening gigs, the bar mounts exhibitions of art and photography. Upcoming events are listed on the website.

Restaurante Café Bar El Camino ✱

🍴 CRISTO DE LA EPIDEMIA 📍 Plaza Benigno Santiago Peña 3 🕐 Mon–Fri 0700–1700; Sat 0700–1400 🍷🍲✂️🕐🍽️🥂🍵

Another local bar named after a pilgrimage (to Santiago de Compostela). They serve *tostadas* etc. for breakfast and *almuerzo* and there is a very cheap weekday *menú del día* which, although basic, is tasty and filling. Their baked potatoes (a welcome change from the ubiquitous chip) are excellent.

Mesón El Picoteo ✱

🍴 CRISTO DE LA EPIDEMIA 📍 Calle Tejeros 15 📘 mesonelpicoteo
🕐 Mon–Fri 0800–1600 🍷✂️🕐🍽️🍵

A very popular spot for a good breakfast and keenly prices *tapas* and *raciones* for lunch, '*picoteo*' means picking at something, in this case, food. The food is traditional and prepared from top-quality ingredients fresh from the market and the owners and staff are friendly and welcoming.

Lorena II ✱

🍴 CRISTO DE LA EPIDEMIA 📍 Calle Manrique 15 🕐 Mon–Sat 0630–1600 🍷✂️🕐🍽️🍵

There is a chain of family-friendly fast food cafés called Lorena on the Costa del Sol, but this local bar 'Lorena Dos' is not connected. Whilst in Britain any city might easily have two or more pubs called 'The Red Lion', every Spanish bar's name is unique in its own town (unless it belongs to a chain, which is still pretty rare). Lorena II is run by Mari, a lovely woman who greets her customers as friends and serves good home-made food.

Victoria Bar ✸✸

🍽 CRISTO DE LA EPIDEMIA ♀ Calle Zenete 8 🕐 Tue–Sun 1200–0200
🍷 ⚡ ① ☲

A modern and surprisingly spacious bar off the beaten track with a live-ly and friendly atmosphere. The *tapas* are delicious, reasonably priced and come in generous portions. If you fancy being transported back to the 1970s and 1980s there is *'futbolín'* (table football) here. The owner, Antonio, is an excellent host.

Oliva Tapas ✸

🍽 LA MERCED ♀ Calle Madre de Dios 39 🕐 Mon–Fri 0800–0000; Sat–Sun 1300–0000 ✖ 🍷 ⚡ ① ☲ 🐾

The owners of this great *tapas* bar are from Linares in Jaén, so there are many dishes showcasing olives and olive oil from that region. But they have intro-duced another tradition from their home province — that of a free *tapa* with every drink, so if you order a few *cañas* you can eat quite cheaply here. If you're not feeling especially thirsty or if you don't want to drink beer, then *tapas* and *raciones* can be ordered individually.

La Goleta Bar Café ✸

🍽 LA GOLETA ♀ Calle Cruz del Molinillo 5 🕐 Mon–Fri 0700–1630; Sat 0830–1230 🍷 🎛 ⚡ ① ☲ ⛟ 🌙 🐾

This friendly neighbourhood bar is popular with people visiting the near-by Mercado de Salamanca. They offer typical Spanish breakfasts, including freshly cooked egg dishes (the scrambled eggs are delicious). At lunchtime, *tapas* and *raciones* are available, but the real bargain is the *menú del día*, which is cheap and filling. For those who find a big lunch too much in the middle of the day, there is the option to have a one-course half menu. The food is tasty and home cooked.

Molinillo 33 ✸

🍽 SAN FELIPE NERI ♀ Calle Cruz del Molinillo 33 🕐 Mon–Fri 0700–2233; Sat 0800–2230; Sun 0800–1230 🍷 ⚡ ① ☲ 🌐 🐾

This place looks like a very ordinary local bar from the outside, with its plain seating and a handful of tables squeezed onto the pavement outside, but it's an ordinary bar with a difference. The speciality here is a mix of Spanish-Mexican-Argen-tinian dishes, so as well as the expected tortilla and *croquetas*, they also serve fantastic tacos and wonderfully tasty homemade *empanadas*.

Bar Salamanca ✸

🍽 EL MOLINILLO ♀ Calle Tirso de Molina 9 🕐 Mon 0700–1230; Tue–Sat 0700–1530 🍷 ⚡ ① ☲ 🔪 🐚 ⛟ 🌙 🐾

Bar Salamanca (which admittedly looks somewhat dingy from the outside) has been serving delicious, home-cooked *tapas* to local residents and cus-tomers visiting the Mercado de Salamanca for over 35 years. As well as *raciones* (the fried fish and seafood is fresh and always perfectly cooked) there is a daily list of 15 or so *tapas* all at the same (bargain) price. The hard-boiled eggs stuffed with tuna are an unexpected delight.

La Mona Tapas ✷

🍽 CAPUCHINOS 📍 Calle Eduardo Domínguez de Ávila 2 🕐 Daily
🍷 ✿ ⓘ ⌫ ⊕ ✤

This is a friendly bar overlooking the Plaza de Capuchinos that serves classic well-executed *tapas* and *raciones*, always freshly cooked. Unusually for a neighbourhood bar outside the main tourist area, they have a very good homemade vegetarian burger on the menu, and interesting dishes like Moroccan-style *pastillas*.

La Malagueta

Casa de vinos La Odisea ✷✷

🍽 GIBRALFARO 📍 Subida Coracha 2 ⊕ casadevinoslaodisea.com
🕐 1200–0000 ✗ 🍷 📖 🍲 ✿ ⓘ ◐ ✦ 🐟 ⌫ ⊕ ✤

At the foot of the Monte Gibralfaro, this bar is almost all that is left of the long-demolished slum of La Coracha, and another excellent place to enjoy Málaga wine. By its own admission, La Odisea has, like many bars and restaurants, prioritized local customers over tourists since the COVID pandemic which, somewhat counter-intuitively, is good for visitors. Substandard restaurants kept afloat by tourists can survive far longer than places that are reliant upon locals. It's a friendly bar with a great atmosphere and the food is high quality. There is a mid-price *menú del día* if you're feeling hungry at lunchtime. At very busy times, service can be a little slow, so this is a place for lingering. Unusually for Spain, there is a decent selection of vegetarian and vegan dishes.

La Coracha — Málaga's Picturesque Lost Slum

A *coracha* is a fortified corridor between a fortress (in this case the Castillo Gibralfaro) and another point nearby. This would often be a water source, but in Málaga, it was the Alcazaba. If you look down from the Castillo, you can see the original *coracha*, in poor repair, overgrown with weeds and filled with rubble, leading down to the Alcazaba. The *barrio* 'La Coracha' grew up later, built against the fortified walls of the corridor. In the late 18th century, the Castillo's military function waned and the poor plundered stone from the *coracha* and even the Castillo itself to construct homes.

The result was a dense maze of hastily constructed dwellings, clinging precariously to the hill, lacking adequate water supply and proper sewerage. As early as 1821 the *ayuntamiento* proposed demolishing the settlement and newspapers of the day bemoaned the unsanitary conditions in which the people lived as well as the lawlessness of the area. There was even a proposal to blast away the ridge between the Castillo and the Alcazaba to create a canal for the

213

Guadalmedina River — an early attempt to address Málaga's periodic flooding problem.

Picture postcards of La Coracha at late as the 1980s showed a picturesque street of vernacular *andaluz* dwellings, whitewashed and decorated with flowers. The reality was rather different. Behind the undeniable charm of this outward-facing street was a warren of insalubrious hovels, where disease and death were never far away. Fernando Guerrero Strachan-Rosado, a member of the illustrious *malagueña* architectural dynasty, was involved in plans to improve the area, but on a site visit, he contracted typhus and died, aged only 34.

Under the Second Republic (in 1931) the art critic Ricardo de Orueta and the architects Palacios and Torres Balbás came up with a plan whereby the San Telmo Royal Academy of Fine Arts would acquire the buildings and progressively restore and preserve them, but the Civil War intervened and it would be another thirty years before work began.

During the 1970s and 1980s, local government all but ignored La Coracha and its problems. Some historical context is perhaps necessary. In 1980, Spain was the third poorest country in Western Europe after Ireland and Portugal. The idea that there were billions of *pesetas* sloshing around for capital projects is fanciful, and it would be another 6 years before Spain joined the EU (then the EC). The death knell for La Coracha came with plans for the construction of the *Túnel de la Alcazaba* between the Plaza de La Merced and La Malagueta (completed in 1999)

Various citizens' groups in Málaga have ever since denounced the final bulldozing of La Coracha in the 1990s as a criminal act of destruction of civic patrimony, and it is hard to disagree. The demolition came towards the end of a period during which, throughout Europe, there seemed to be limitless funds to build new roads and ugly modern buildings, yet little to spare to safeguard historically important locales.

One wonders how La Coracha might have fared under the tourism-aware administration of Francisco de la Torre a decade later. It seems inconceivable that this administration would have razed to the ground what was effectively a little slice of a *pueblo blanco* in the city when it could have become Málaga's own Sacromonte (a 19th-century slum *barrio* of Granada which is now one of the most picturesque and most visited parts of the city).

And then there was one...

One building in La Coracha managed to survive — No. 2 (the current Casa de vinos La Odisea), an elegant house built in 1750 (and, in truth, only ever accidentally part of the *barrio*, having predated it by a few decades). The fifth-generation owner of the property, Juan Jesús Ortega Ruiz, faced a tough struggle with the *ayuntamiento* of the time to preserve his property, even though it had been officially declared '*Patrimonio artístico malagueño*' as early as 1970.

The name of Don Juan Jesús's *taberna*, 'La Odisea', reflects this struggle. In other words, it was a task so arduous that it seemed like the trials of Odysseus, King of Ithaca. In 2007, the Ortega Ruiz family established a *taberna*, so what you can visit nowadays is a relatively new (yet 'traditional') bar in an old and historic building in a lost *barrio*.

Casa Carlos 1936 ✳

🍴 LA MALAGUETA 📍 Calle Keromnes 6
🅕 CasaCarlosRestauranteMalaga 🕐 0800–1600 ⊘ Sun 🍽🍷⚡⏱☰

Don't be put off by the rather basic and utilitarian décor — this award-winning bar-restaurant has occupied this site since its foundation by Carlos Cejas Jaén during the Civil War. Mariloli and Carmen are the latest members of the family to preside over the place. The food is simple but well cooked and very traditionally *malagueña*. Though it's very much a locals' haunt, the service couldn't be friendlier.

Anyway Wine Bar ✳✳

🍴 LA MALAGUETA 📍 Paseo de la Farola 8 🌐 📖 anywaywinebar.com
🕐 1900–0000 🍽🍷📖⚡⏱🥄🍶🍷☰🏠

Most Spanish bars are multi-purpose spaces. People go to have breakfast, drink coffee, have lunch or an afternoon tea, to enjoy an *aperitivo* or an evening meal. Some bars have a house red and a house white while others have a more varied wine list. Anyway Wine Bar, however, really is all about the wine. Created by David Camino, a *malagueño* who developed a passion for wine while working in hospitality in London, with Daniel Lopez in the kitchen, the focus is on natural, organic and so-called 'biodynamic' wines with over 100 available by the glass (thanks to our friend the Coravin® machine).

When it comes to food, the specialities of the house are chosen to accompany wine: *bellota ibérica* pork products from Extremadura (*jamón*, *cecina* or air-dried ham, *panceta*, *morcilla*, *salchichón*, *chorizo* and more) and over twenty kinds of cheese, all available as *tapas*, *medias* and *raciones*. There is a small list of 'mains' if you want something more substantial. David and his *equipo* (team) are clearly passionate about wine, and this shows in the exceptional level of service. Being enthusiastic about local olive oil isn't enough, for example — staff will happily give you an impromptu tasting so that you can become an enthusiast too.

Bar Emily ✳✳

🍴 LA MALAGUETA 📍 Avenida de Príes 30 🕐 2100–0400 🍷

Describing an unusual bar as 'unique' is a temptation that too few travel guide authors manage to resist, but in the case of Bar Emily, the adjective is apposite. There is no draught beer here, only wine and spirits (it's a late-night bar, after all) and there are no *tapas*. The décor is eclectic, to say the least. Every inch of wall is covered with paintings and photos of stars of stage and screen. A large poster of Rita Hayworth (in *Gilda*) presides over the bar (if bar is the word). The furniture is mismatched but homely and the soundtrack is music from the 50s and 60s.

This bar is basically a manifestation of the character of the owner, Emilio, who is a man one would readily describe as 'a character'. You feel that you have been invited into Emilio's living room, or study, to have a drink with him, and one gets the impression that this is how he sees it too. It also explains the rather unpredictable opening times. It may open at 9 pm, or later, or not at all. Sometimes it seems that Emilio decides the mix of customers is optimal and he'll close the door. Enjoying a quiet drink here, conversing with Emilio about life, the universe and everything, is an extraordinary pleasure. There really is nowhere else quite like it.

El Ensanche/Soho and Alameda

As an up-and-coming part of town, bars are opening all the time the El Ensanche/Soho. They are also, just as quickly, closing or changing names. Those listed below (along with La Fábrica, p. 194) are well-established, but have a stroll around and you are sure to discover others.

La Pechá Taberna ✱

 SOHO ♥ Calle San Lorenzo lapecha2020 ⏱ Mon–Sat 0930–0100
♟ ✗ ⓘ ⌷ ⊕ ♨ ⚖

This is an unusual but lovely bar in a part of Soho that few visitors explore. La Pechá seems as if it has been hollowed out from the corner of a multi-storey car park. It is not an old bar (its owner, Raúl Nieto, opened the doors in 2020), and yet it feels utterly traditional. It is also very *malagueño*, as one can tell from the name. 'Pechá' is the *malagueño* rendering of the *castellana* word *pechada*, meaning 'a lot' or 'plenty'. This bar, known for its good selection of *vermú*, has a limited but excellent *tapas* list, and you are invited to choose a '*mejilla*', '*hartá*' or '*pechá*' portion (viz. *tapa*, *media ración*, or *ración*). These words are pure *malagueño* dialect. The *ensaladilla rusa* is especially good, as are the small *bocaditos* (strangely not called *pulgas* or *pulguitas* here), black bao buns and *tostitas*. It is often packed, with customers spilling out onto the street, but the efficient and friendly staff ensure that you'll be served promptly. It was due to expand into larger premises in 2023.

Bar Atenas ✱

 SOHO ♥ Calle Tomás Heredia 7 ⏱ Mon–Sat 0630–1630; Sat 0800–1400 ♟ ✗ ⓘ ⌷ ⚖ ⊛ ⓘ ◔

This friendly, family-run bar is very popular for breakfast and *almuerzo* and is busy at lunchtime with people enjoying *tapas*. Their sandwiches (which come as *pitufos* and *vienas*) are tasty and inexpensive. The Friday special — *paella* — may not be totally authentic (it contains seafood), but it is very good and always runs out quickly.

La Barra de Doña Inés ✱✱

 ALAMEDA ♥ Alameda Principal 15 ⊕ bit.ly/LBdDonaM ⏱ Mon–Sat 1200–0200; Sun 1200–1800 ✗ ♟ ▯ ✗ ⓘ ◗ ⌷ ⊕

The name 'The Bar of Madam Inés' makes one think of a venerable institution where the descendants of a redoubtable matron called Inés (the Spanish form of 'Agnes') have been doling out Málaga wine and *boquerones* for generations. In fact, it is a bar run by Antonio Banderas's 'Tercer Acto' Group who are behind the Japanese/Spanish fusion gastrobar at the Soho theatre (hence the name 'Third Act'). They also have other *restaurantes* — an upmarket tablecloth restaurant, also called Doñainés (but all one word) and an Italian called Atrezzo — both in the Soho district, and La Pérgola del Mediterráneo in the Royal Club Mediterráneo at the end of Muelle Uno.

Of the four, La Barra is the one most worth visiting on account of its smart but relaxed *ambiente* and reasonably priced but excellent *tapas* and *raciones*. If the first item that catches your gaze is 30g of caviar for almost €80, you might initially deduce that this is a very expensive bar, but if you look more carefully you will see that there is plenty to enjoy here at more acceptable prices, like the brioche of braised bull's tail, which is delicious.

West of the Guadalmedina

Más Vermut ✿✿

🍴 EL PERCHEL 📍 Pasaje San Fernando 4 ⬛ masvermutmalaga
🕐 Mon, Wed, Thu 1200–1600, 1930–2300; Fri–Sat 1200–1630, 1930–2330; Sun 1200–1700 🍷 🍴 ⓘ 🔖 🍽

As the name suggests, this small bar located in an alleyway between Cuarteles and Salitre streets in El Perchel specializes in *vermú*. Unlike Antigua Casa de Guardia, this place is bright and modern, but their selection and knowledge of vermouths (mostly, though not solely, of the dark and fruity Spanish style) are both impressive. A small menu of tasty *tapas* dishes is available and, for my money, they serve the best *patatas bravas* in Málaga.

El Añejo Taberna ✿

🍴 LA TRINIDAD 📍 Mercado de Bailén, Plaza de Bailén 8, Stall 46
⬛ elanejotaberna 🕐 Mon–Sat 0730–1700 🍷 🍴 ⓘ 🍽 ⊑ 🥢

This is not an *añejo* (old) bar (which would be '*añeja*' anyway), but a bar named after the Málaga wine called *añejo*. I mention it elsewhere in the section about the market (p. 231), but it merits another inclusion here because it is one of Málaga's hidden gems. Eduardo and Juan Pablo are friendly and attentive behind the bar, and Marcela prepares excellent *tapas*. This is one of the best places in Málaga to sample *callos* (a stewed tripe dish, slow-cooked with trotters, snout, black pudding, paprika and tomato).

La Reserva ✿

🍴 LA TRINIDAD 📍 Calle Francisco Monje 14 🕐 Mon–Sat 0800–1800
✗ 🍷 🍴 ⓘ 🔖 ⊑ 🥢 🥢 🥢

Almost the epitome of a neighbourhood bar. It might look like the kind of place that will fall silent the moment a tourist walks in, but it's a very friendly and welcoming place, so do visit if you're in the area. The breakfasts are delicious, with plenty of choice, and there is a bargain *menú del día*. The food is traditional and cooked to order from the freshest ingredients. The fish and seafood are especially good.

La Bohemia ✿

🍴 MÁRMOLES 📍 Calle Huescar 8 🕐 Mon–Fri 0900–1600; Fri 2030–2300; Sat 1230–1600 ✗ 🍷 🍴 ⓘ 🔖 ⊑ 🧺 🏪

The surroundings of boxy commercial offices are far from picturesque, but La Bohemia is one of Málaga's most charming spots to enjoy *tapas* (or breakfast). They offer a huge range of almost 50 *pitufos* as well *tapas*, *medias* and *raciones* of *chacinas* (*charcuterie*) and cheeses. Describing itself as a '*tienda degustación*' (tasting shop), La Bohemia is a wine shop that happens to have a very good bar attached. If you want to drink wine then there is a house red and a house white which change daily and are available by the glass, but if there are a few of you, buy a bottle from the shop and order some snacks to enjoy it with.

La Despensa de Iñaki ✿

🍴 EL PERCHEL 📍 Calle Héroe de Sostoa 46 🌐 ladespensadeinaki.com
🕐 1100–2300 (Sun 1600) ✗ 🍷 🍴 ⓘ 🔖 ⊑

This is another hidden gem near the railway station, on the Huelin side. A '*despensa*' is an *almacen* ('larder', *i.e.* delicatessen) and this bar is located in a gourmet food shop (or perhaps the gourmet food shop is located in a bar?). The name of the owner, Iñaki, and the fact that they serve *pintxos* rather than *tapas* tells you that this is a Basque bar/shop, though they stock a wide range of products from the Province of Málaga. The *pintxos* display all the culinary flare one would expect of the Basque County; for example, a warm *pintxo* topped with a slice of Wagyu black pudding on asparagus with strawberry chutney, or braised duck *foie gras* on mango jam and a touch of balsamic vinegar reduction. They serve over 30 wines by the glass, many of them from Málaga. In their fairly recent addition to the gastronomic scene, Iñaki and Ángeles have created a wonderfully friendly bar in which to enjoy a glass of wine and some excellent plates and *tapas* while browsing for local gourmet gifts to take home. Serious meat lovers would also enjoy Iñaki's nearby restaurant grill (**Asador Iñaki ♀ Calle Ayala 38 ⊕ asadorinakimalaga.com**) which, though not cheap, serves some incredible cuts of beef (there is fish and seafood too).

Taberna Los 13 ✹✹

🍴 **EL PERCHEL ♀ Calle Edison 10 ⊕ 🛍 tabernalos13.com** ⊙ Mon–Sun 1300–1630, 2000–2330 🍷 🛍 🖋 🛈 🍽 🍴 🍷 ⊛

Run by *gaditanos* (people from Cádiz), this *taberna* serves an extensive *carta* of excellent dishes, many of them typical of Cádiz. This is a great option if you are near the bus or railway stations. If you only want a drink and a snack there is short *carta* of well-chosen and delicious *tapas*.

Base9 ✹✹

🍴 **EL PERCHEL ♀ Calle Salitre 9 ⊕ base9restaurante.com** ⊙ Mon–Sat 1330–1600, 2030–2300 🍷 🛍 🖋 🛈 🍽

This recent addition to the Málaga bar scene is on a street that most tourists will speed along in a taxi or on a bus, yet is only a few minutes' walk across the river from the centre. Pablo Zamudio and Cristian Fernández describe their gastronomic offer as 'Grandma's cooking for young people' and it doesn't disappoint. Everything is traditional, and yet nothing is. The *garbanzos* (chickpeas) are made into a rich broth and paired not with the expected *chorizo*, but with tiger prawns, while the *tortilla de patatas* is not the usual firm wedge, but almost French-style with a light omelette wrapped around an interior of confit potatoes swathed in a rich, yolky sauce. This is a small bar with a small menu of small dishes, but every single one is perfectly executed — absolutely stunning *tapas* and an excellent wine list.

La Pluma 'El Nido' ✹

🍴 **EL PERCHEL ♀ Paseo de los Tilos 62 🖪 La-Pluma-El-Nido** ⊙ Wed–Sun 1230–1630, 1930–0000 🍷 🖋 🛈 🍽

The Paseo de los Tilos is the street on which you find the main passenger entrance to the bus station. On this street for many years (at No. 42) stood **Café-Bar Lucy**, one of my favourite bars in all of Málaga, where Cristóbal and Lucía welcomed scores of faithful customers to drink, eat tapas and enjoy impromptu guitar recitals. A night at Bar Lucy felt like spending an evening with friends. In early 2023, Bar Lucy pulled down the shutters — which might mean a (hopefully) temporary or (sadly) permanent closure. However, less than 200 metres farther west, on the same street, is La Pluma (the feather) 'El Nido' (the nest) and although it lacks Bar Lucy's eccentricity, it's still a lovely, local bar, only 5 minutes' walk from the Bus Station. The food is *tapas*-style, with *raciones* and sandwiches too, but freshly cooked from top-quality ingredients. The service (from Antonio, José and Ana on my last visit) is faultlessly friendly.

🏛 *Azoteas* (Rooftop Bars)

You pay a premium for enjoying a drink on a hotel roof terrace, but the views across the city and the bay make it worth it. Begin your evening with a glass of sherry or even '*un gin-tonic*' a few storeys up before returning to sea level for the rest of the night. The following rooftop terraces are all open to non-guests (though the swimming pools are not).

Opening times vary, but most open in the late afternoon (1500 or 1600) and stay open until midnight during the week and 0100 or 0200 on Fridays and Saturdays. Admission is restricted to over 18s and you may be refused entry if you are not smartly dressed.

Gran Hotel Miramar ✹✹✹
◉ Paseo Reding 22

The rooftop bar (called '*Terraza* Chill Out') of Málaga's grandest (and only 5 Star '*gran lujo*') hotel is located on the top floor of the hotel. Open from 6 pm daily (see p. 73).

Hotel AC Málaga Palacio ✹✹✹
◉ Calle Cortina del Muelle 1

There are great cathedral views from this large terrace, which was the pioneer in Málaga, and remains one of the best. It's also one of the highest, which means it can get breezy, so take a jacket or shawl if it's windy. This is a popular meeting point during the Málaga Film Festival in March. It has a restaurant and swimming pool (the latter only for guests).

OnlyYOU Hotel Lolita Terrace ✹✹✹
◉ Alameda Principal 1

Despite the rather cutesy name of this hotel, it's a stylish place and 'Lolita' is a sophisticated terrace. It is also one of the most expensive, but it offers wonderful views of the Calle Larios, Alameda Principal, Alcazaba, Parque de Málaga and Muelle Uno.

If you want to enjoy the unrivalled panorama, come up for a glass of wine (about the cheapest beverage option). By the way, 'Lolita' isn't a dodgy Nabokov reference — the hotel's restaurant is called 'Lola' (a diminutive of Dolores) and Lolita is a diminutive of Lola (*i.e.* a double diminutive of Dolores).

Hotel Room Mate Larios ✹✹✹
◉ Calle Marqués de Larios 2

Popular for events and parties, this terrace overlooks the city's most famous shopping street, Calle Marqués de Larios — Málaga at its most elegant. Hip monochrome furniture, stone walls, mosaic-tiled bar and night-time entertainment with DJs make it a popular choice.

Hotel Molina Lario ✿✿✿
📍 Calle Molina Lario 22

This seasonal terrace of the stylish hotel, on the eighth floor, is more sheltered than the AC Málaga, and hosts concerts and other activities, mostly in summer.

Room Mate Valeria ✿✿✿
📍 Plaza Poeta Alfonso Canales 5

One of the newer roof terraces in Málaga, this one comes with its own pool (guests only) and great views of the Port and Muelle Dos.

Hotel Sallés Málaga Centro ✿✿✿
📍 Calle Mármoles 6

Just on the other side of the Guadalmedina River, the terrace of the Málaga Centro has a small and cosy terrace. Summer nights are lively, as it is full of lights, colours and live music.

La Terraza de San Telmo ✿✿
📍 Calle San Telmo 14

The Terrace of San Telmo, formerly known as the Oasis attic, is located near the Thyssen Museum. The terrace has lovely views of the Iglesia de los Mártires.

Hotel Soho Bahia Málaga ✿✿✿
📍 Calle Somera 8

In the heart of the newly-hip Soho *barrio*, famous for its avant-garde graffiti, this new hotel with its bold décor (it has a very colourful façade) has a new terrace called Soho, featuring a futuristic white bar and shaded tent areas. Probably not for anyone over 35, though.

Hotel Málaga Premium (San Juan) ✿✿✿
📍 Calle San Juan 12

This rooftop has great views of the city skyline and the Cathedral Tower. It is slightly more hidden than the others and, therefore, it is usually less crowded.

La7 — Hotel Soho Boutique Equitativa ✿✿✿
📍 Alameda Principal 3

Next door to OnlyYOU, this seventh-floor bar-restaurant has a lovely view up the Calle Larios. Although it is primarily a cocktail bar and restaurant, it's also a nice place for a coffee with a view in the late afternoon.

H10 Croma Málaga ✿✿✿
📍 Calle Prim 4

This hotel is one of Málaga's newest, and most controversial. Located on the east bank of the Guadalmedina, this imposing white cube stands on Hoyo de Esparteros square which, until a few years ago, was used principally as a car park. Many of the buildings were in a poor state of repair, having been bombed in the Civil War and inadequately repaired or rebuilt since.

The controversy is mainly because to construct the hotel, a building known as 'La Mundial' was demolished (in March 2019). Constructed as the residence of the Marqués de Benahavís, for many years most people assumed that the building's architect was Gerónimo Cuervo, but later research discovered that it had actually been designed by Eduardo Strachan Viana-Cárdenas, the architect of Calle Larios. It was commissioned by Isabel Loring Heredia, which accounts for the high quality of the ironwork adorning the balconies and roof.

The demolition of a historic building rarely goes ahead without opposition, though I remember La Mundial as a down-at-heel *pensión* and something of an eyesore. Many are not happy with the new hotel building, finding it too plain, angular and unsympathetic. Personally, I think it's stunning, (the architect was Rafael Moneo who also designed the breathtaking National Museum of Roman Art in Mérida). The designer Lázaro Rosa Violán also worked on the project, which brings together neo-Cubist designs and traditional *andalúz* crafts in the *azulejos* (tiles) used for the hotel's balconies.

The rooftop bar has fantastic views and a relaxed vibe (though service can be a little slow), but before you go in, have a look at the building behind the hotel. It's a handsome four-storey structure with green shutters and impressive ironwork and gently curving corners. It is, in fact, a facsimile of La Mundial, finished using the ironwork salvaged from Strachan's original.

Alcazaba Premium Hotel Málaga ✿✿✿

Calle Alcazabilla 12

This popular terrace overlooks the Alcazaba and the *Teatro Romano*.

Casa Hermandad del Sepulcro ✿

Calle Alcazabilla 5

A rooftop terrace with a difference: not a hotel, but a bar operated by the Brotherhood of the Sepulchre. When not being used for members' functions and events, they open their social club and roof terrace to the public as a '*terraza benéfica*' ('charity terrace') to help raise funds for the brotherhood's social projects. It's a modern building, so the bar area has something of a '1990s church hall' vibe, and the terrace is quite plain (no fountains, sun loungers or DJs), but the view of the theatre and Alcazaba is unimpeded and beautiful. The prices are also very competitive — just a fraction of what you would pay at a hotel roof terrace and all for a good cause (supporting a project to provide basic household goods and food for poor families in Málaga).

You should plan your visit, however, as it is not a commercial venture and it is often closed for private events. Fridays and Saturdays, when the terrace is open until 1 am, are often fully booked far ahead. If you would like to visit, send an email to **salonsocial@hermandadsepulcro.org**, or use the contact form on the website, specifying 'Salón Social' as the subject: **hermandadsepulcro.org/contacto**

When you arrive, you may sometimes be asked to buy a €10 voucher ('*gasto mínimo*') which you can then use to pay for drinks (they do not serve food beyond crisps and nuts). As you would expect of a religious organization, the *Hermandad del Sepulcro Terraza Benéfica* has quite a sedate atmosphere rather than a hedonistic party vibe, but it is far from stuffy. The members of the brotherhood (who volunteer their time to run the bar) are very friendly and hospitable. As the Secretary of the *Hermandad* told me, 'Anyone who wishes to visit us will be well received and attended to within our means'. It is one of my favourite places in Málaga to enjoy a pre-dinner drink and a lovely way in which to participate in the life of a real *malagueña* institution that stretches back over 125 years.

Other brotherhoods in Málaga (*e.g. La Cena*) also open their *terrazas* seasonally, so look out for publicity as you explore the city.

🏪 *Mercados* (Markets)

Whilst the UK boasts a few city centre covered markets with among the best-known being Borough (London), Kirkgate (Leeds), Oxford, and Grainger (Newcastle upon Tyne), pretty much every large town in Spain has a (usually) thriving municipal market. La Boquería in Barcelona has become a tourist attraction in its own right. The municipality of Málaga has 15 markets, five of them in the centre, and all are worth exploring. The quality of the goods on sale is high and the prices are low, but even if you don't have anything on your shopping list, they offer an interesting glimpse of local culture. **But please buy something!** Although fascinating places, markets are not museums charging an admission fee, but places where people try to make a living and *malagueños* do their shopping. So buy a tumbler of freshly squeezed juice or a smoothie, or a bag of cherries, almonds or raisins to snack on, or some slices of *jamón* to take home with you. Or stop by one of the market bars for a glass of something cool and a *tapa*. Markets are also great places to put together a picnic (see also p. 233).

Unless you are staying in an apartment, the butchery counters and wet fish stalls will probably be of little practical interest, but for anyone who enjoys food and cooking, they are fascinating to investigate. The meat cuts are different, for example. The forequarters of beef cattle give us blade, chuck and brisket in Britain, while in Spain this same portion yields *agruja*, *pescuezo*, *pez*, *llana*, *espadilla*, *brazuelo*, *aleta* and *morillo*. Beef cheeks, which in the UK tend to go into pies, are highly prized by restaurants and home cooks. The quality of the meat is visible in the bright vermilion flesh of mature beef and the rosier hue of *ternera* (young beef, often translated on menus as 'veal'). A few counters have massive chops of richly marbled, garnet-coloured meat that you may not have seen before. This is the meat of the 'Rubia Gallega' — Galician Blonde beef, from animals that have spent 15–18 years grazing pasture and it is, in the opinion of many, the best beef in the world. It takes skill to cook a 'Chuletón' or large chop well (fillet steak it is not), but in the right hands, it can be magical.

And then there are the fish counters. Unless you are a regular at Billingsgate, Brixham or North Shields, you will probably struggle to recognize much of what is on display. And even if you recognize the distinctive profile of a bream (and in Spain, it is most likely to be 'Dorada' — Gilt-Head Bream), can you be sure that it's not *Pargo* (Sea Bream), *Hurta* (Red-Banded Sea Bream), *Zapata* (Blue-Spotted Sea Bream), *Sargo* (White Sea Bream), *Mojarra* (Two-Banded Bream), or *Besugo* (Red Bream)? The quality is obvious in the glistening scales and shining eyes, and it's common to see fish displayed with their gills open to show that they are bright red (rather than dull and brown — the sign of a less than fresh fish). The range of seafood is dizzying. There will be cockles, clams and scallops, just like in your local fishmonger, but there will probably be two or three varieties of each. Similarly, crustaceans seem to come in every size imaginable, from tiny shrimps up to lobster-like *cigalas*, lobsters and crabs.

The city's markets are where you can pick up the basics for a picnic — some slices of *jamón*, *chorizo* or other cured meat, some marinated anchovies, a wedge of cheese, fresh bread, olives, tomatoes, a bag of cherries, some peaches, some roasted and salted almonds, for example. There is always a magnificent range of fresh fruit in season, with plenty of choice. A display of reasonably-priced plump, glossy cherries (*cerezas*) might take your fancy, but as you look more closely, there is a mound of cherries next to these for almost double the price. These could be 'Cerezas de la Montaña de Alicante' grown in the hills between Valencia and Alicante, and they really are worth the extra cost. Then you might see another type of cherry that's even pricier, perhaps 'Picotas del Jerte' from Extremadura — Spain's most famous and highly prized cherry. There might even be yet another heap of cherries labelled 'guindas' — these are sour cherries, used for compotes, jams and confections. Another stall may have plastic tumblers of freshly expressed cherry juice sitting in a trough of crushed ice. Across the aisle are yet more cherries, this time dried, candied, or macerated, from a '*frutos secos*' stall. '*Frutos secos*' (*seco* means 'dry'), strictly speaking, describes nuts whereas dried figs and prunes are '*frutas secas*', but the former is used as a catch-all term. The distinction is probably academic, given that walnuts, peanuts and almonds are not, botanically speaking, 'nuts'.

Málaga is famous for its raisins (*pasas*), which have their own 'Denomination of Origin' classification and are dried Moscatel de Málaga ('*Moscatel Gordo*') or Moscatel de Alejandría grapes. Málaga is also known for its almonds, which are sold plain for baking, or candied or roasted for snacking. However, the '*frutos secos*' stalls sell a variety of other fruits and nuts, as well as trail mix, and bar nibbles (*aperitivos*) like Bombay mix, 'Mexican' mix, rice crackers, fried beans and a peculiarly Spanish mix of sunflower seeds, chickpeas, fried corn, lupin seeds and monkey nuts known as '*Cocktail Rumba*'. Most also sell legumes, including lentils, chickpeas and a huge variety of beans. Spaniards consume pulses on a grand scale and demand high quality, so these are good things to buy to take home with you.

almonds	*almendras*	lupins	*altramuces/chochitos*
apples	*manzanas*	mulberries	*moras*
apricots	*albaricoques*	peaches	*melocotones*
blackcurrants	*grosellas negras*	peanuts	*cacahuetes*
blueberries	*arándanos azules*	pecans	*pacanas/pecanas*
Brazil nuts	*nueces de Brasil*	pine nuts	*piñones*
cashews	*anacardos*	pistachios	*pistachos*
cherries	*cerezas*	prunes	*ciruelas*
chestnuts	*castañas*	raisins	*pasas*
cranberries	*arándanos*	redcurrants	*grosellas rojas*
dates	*dátiles*	sultanas	*pasas sultanas*
figs	*higos*	walnuts	*nueces*
hazelnuts	*avellanas*	pitted/seedless	*sin hueso/sin semillas*

Also well worth buying from a market is fresh fruit. The region of Axarquía, east of Málaga, has a subtropical climate suitable for growing a variety of non-native fruits such as lychees, avocados, star fruit, persimmons, prickly pears and dragon fruit. You will also see a few fruits that are never spotted in UK supermarkets, like custard apples, lucumas and white sapotas. The following table shows the main seasons for common fruits, with most available about a month before and after these windows.

English	Spanish	High Season
apricot	*amasquillo (in Málaga)*	May-Aug
banana	*plátano*	All Year
cherries	*cerezas*	May-Jul

English	Spanish	High Season
clementine	*clementina/clemenvilla*	Dec-Jan
custard apple	*chirimoya*	Oct-Dec
dragon fruit	*pitahaya*	Oct-Dec
figs	*higos*	Jul-Sep
grapes	*uvas*	Oct-Dec
grapefruit	*pomelo*	Dec-Apr
greengage	*ciruela 'Reina Claudia'*	Jun-Aug
guava	*guayaba*	Oct-Feb
lemon	*limón*	Nov-Mar
lucuma	*lúcuma*	Oct-Dec
lychees	*litchis*	Nov-Feb
mandarin	*mandarina*	Nov-Mar
mango	*mango*	Aug-Nov
melon	*melón*	May-Sep
medlar (or loquat)	*níspero*	Apr-Jun
nectarine	*nectarina*	May-Sep
orange	*naranja*	Nov-Apr
passion fruit	*maracuyá*	Oct-Apr
peach	*melocotón*	May-Sep
pineapple	*piña*	All Year
flat peach	*paraguaya*	Jun-Aug
plum	*ciruela*	Jun-Aug
pomegranate	*granada*	Sep-Nov
pear	*pera*	Jun-Nov
persimmon	*caqui*	Sep-Nov
raspberries	*frambuesas*	Jun-Aug
star fruit	*carambola*	Sep-Jan
strawberries	*fresas*	Feb- May
large strawberries	*fresónes*	Mar-May
watermelon	*sandía*	Jun-Aug

Mercado Central de Atarazanas

🍴 CENTRO HISTÓRICO 📍 Calle Atarazanas 10 🕐 Mon–Sat 0800–1400

Built in 1879, Málaga's main indoor market stands on the site of the Nasrid shipyards, an area that, after the *reconquista* became an arsenal, then a barracks, and finally a slum. Thanks to the Málaga Academy of Fine Arts, the original gates of the Nasrid period were preserved and restored and now serve as the principal entrance to this enormous structure of wrought iron and stained glass. The building's architect was Joaquín de Rucoba who also designed the Malagueta bullring and the Parque de Málaga.

You'll find the usual mountains of fish, seafood, cured meats, fruit, vegetables and cheese that are for sale in every other city centre market in Spain (and being Spain, quite a few bars, too), though the local taste for *boquerones* (anchovies) and *sardinas* (sardines) is clearly reflected in the glistening piles of these fish. Something else that makes this Málaga market different is the large number of stalls selling *frutos secos* — dried fruit and nuts. Many of the items on sale are grown in the region (Andalucía is the only region of Europe to grow dates commercially) and most stalls offer several varieties of almonds, raisins and figs. Moscatel raisins from Málaga are unbelievably delicious, quite a revelation if you are only used to the Californian 'Thompson Seedless' variety most widely consumed in the UK.

Vendors are understandably wary of tourists asking to try this or that just to get a free snack, especially when some of the finest hams might cost up to €200 per kilogram. However, if you want to buy something and need help to decide between A and B then you shouldn't be shy about asking to taste the goods. In fact, you'll often be offered samples unbidden — a couple of cherries, a sliver of cheese, a few raisins, a shaving of *jamón*, say.

The market is organized in three sections: meat in the western part, fish and seafood in the central section and everything else in the eastern part, closest to the city centre. The central fish market is almost like a market within a market, though there are crossings in the middle. As Málaga's main municipal market, the quality of produce is generally high whichever stall you go to, but here's my pick of the best.

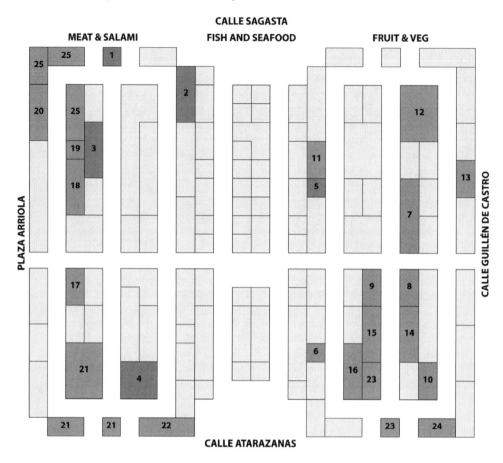

Ham, Cheese, etc.

1. Charcutería Sensi — a small but handsomely stocked deli counter selling cheese, ham, salami and other *embutidos* (cured meats) run by a friendly couple who always seem willing to take the time to help their customers make the right choice of product.

2. Charcutería Ana — a Málaga institution selling mostly ham (a huge selection from the most expensive gourmet *jamón bellota* down to the more everyday *jamón serrano*) and meat products, but with a good range of cheese too. It's often very busy, but don't be put off — the staff are very friendly!

3. Carnicería Jesús — have been selling *jamón*, *embutidos* (cured meat and sausage) and a good selection of mature cheeses since 1941. They will vacuum pack your purchase, so this is a good place to buy mature cheese, ham and other cured meats to take home with you.

4. Charcutería Armando Cuberos — has it all: a massive selection of cured meats, ham and Spanish and European cheeses.

5. Charcutería Delgado — run by Rocío and José, Delgado also specializes in ham, especially that produced in Trevelez, a village in the Sierra Nevada (Granada Province). Consumers usually tend to be most concerned about the breed of the pig and its diet (black-footed *ibérico* pigs fed on acorns is the dream combination), but what sets Trevelez jamón apart is something else — the fact that it is dry-cured with no additives, in particular no sodium nitrite or potassium nitrite, which are common preservatives.

Frutos Secos and Pickles

6. Aceite Gourmet (Oil Gourmet) — time will tell whether this stall survives because its bold USP is that it sells only one product: 'Mergaoliva' olive oil from Jaén. In a market where most stalls sell an enormous variety of products, this is a niche approach, to say the least. The olive oil, however, is delicious, and customers are welcome — in fact encouraged — to taste it. Another great product to take home with you for your own use or as an interesting gift.

7. Especias y Encurtidos El Veloz — beyond the butchers' stalls and fish counters, lines tend to blur somewhat, and El Veloz is a good example of this tendency — selling raisins and spices, but also salt cod (*bacalao*), sardine herrings (*arenque*) and the *malagueña* specialities of paprika lard (*manteca colorá*) and smooth pork *rillettes* in lard (*zurrapa*). If you develop a taste for *manteca colorá* or *zurrapa* (and you really should, because they are delicious), then it's probably more practical to buy a tub from a supermarket if you want to take some home with you, but do buy some from the market to enjoy with crusty bread for a picnic of champions.

8. Aceitunas Roldán — sells olives and is the outlet of a local producer (their processing plant is near the fairground). They carry a big range, but what makes them stand out is that they specialize in olives (and extra virgin olive oil) grown in the Málaga Province.

9. Aceitunas Bravo — a stall mainly offering dried fruit and nuts, but also local olives ('*Aloreñas*' from Álora), sweet wine from Competa (in the Axarquía region of the Málaga Province) and, like El Veloz, salted sardines known as '*arencas*' in Málaga.

10. Especias y Frutos Secos Ana Mesa — a treasure trove of dried fruits, nuts, spices, sweet wine and olive oil.

Fruit, Juices and Smoothies

11. Mr Coco — deserves an honourable mention because it was the first stall in the market to offer fresh juice and smoothies, though many fruit stalls have since followed suit. It's a very good way to use fruit that, although still fresh, doesn't look pristine, thus cutting down on waste. For the customer, it means that there are usually some interesting combinations beyond the usual, rather generic, smoothies of the banana and strawberry variety. After a night of rich food and delicious wine, a fresh fruit smoothie makes a refreshing breakfast.

12. Servi-Frutas Juani — is just one of many fruit (and veg) stalls, but it is certainly one of the biggest. It also has a lot of staff, so you never have to wait long.

13. Frutas y Verduras Marisol — is run by two women, who may be mother and daughter, aunt and niece, or are perhaps entirely unrelated. The quality of their produce, however, is excellent, and they specialize in seasonal produce.

14. Frutería Triano — has been selling fruit and veg since 1930. It is not the cheapest greengrocer in the market, but the quality is absolutely excellent.

15. Frutas y Verduras Juan y Diana — probably errs more towards vegetables than fruit, and has a devoted local clientele. Juan (if that is his name) is a big man with a bigger voice, but he is a gentle soul who treats locals and tourists with the same attentive kindness.

16. Frutería Paco e Hijos — is run by Francisco (Paco), son of Leonor who founded the stall in 1945. It can seem rather chaotic and the service is usually brisk, but the prices are some of the lowest in the market and a lot of what you will eat in Málaga restaurants is supplied from here.

Bread

17. Panadería Loli — the name suggests that this stall is a bakery, but in truth it is more of a mini-market, selling a wide variety of foodstuffs.

18. Panadería Confitería Nuestra Señora del Socorro (Bakery–Sweet Shop of Our Lady of Perpetual Succour) — has been operating in the market since 1912. The ordinary bread is nothing to write home about, but they also sell excellent 'pan cateto' which is close-textured rustic bread rather like sourdough and a speciality of the Málaga province.

19. Panadería Rafalito — is barely more than a kiosk and probably the smallest stall in the market, but it sells the best bread in traditional *malagueño* styles. The '*pan cateto*' is excellent, but to share for a picnic, try the '*lagarto*' (alligator) loaves — like flattened baguettes with a tasty, toasted crust.

Bars

20. Bar Central — is confusingly named because it is as far from the centre of the market as it's possible to be, but they have a well-deserved reputation. Their speciality is fried and grilled fish, but there are *tapas* of cheese, ham, *embutidos* and shellfish on offer too. They carry a good selection of Málaga wines, as well as still wines from the region.

21. Café Bar Mercado Atarazanas — the proprietorial name speaks a truth: this was the first bar in the market and, until fairly recently, the only one. The speciality here is seafood, as well as fried and grilled fish. There is also cold beer and refreshing, chilled Rueda wine. It can get very busy during lunchtime in high season, so don't be scared to sharpen your elbows and approach the bar. There are few better places in Málaga to drink a glass of dry white wine with a plate of raw *conchas finas* (smooth venus clams).

22. Medina Bar — a third of the market consists of fish and seafood, and the bars reflect this. Medina Bar serves great fish and seafood dishes, but what sets them apart are their excellent grilled meat dishes and their fantastic *croquetas*. It's popular and sometimes frenetic, but the serving staff are wonderfully friendly. It has some tables outside. I love all the bars in this market, but if I had to choose a favourite, it would be Medina. It has some outside tables.

23. Bar Central No.1 — is a relative newcomer and is currently probably the 'hippest' bar in the market (or so they think). Ignore the paella (which is okay, but not the real McCoy) but everything else is great. My advice is to go for the *tapa* portions here so that you can sample a bigger selection. It has some tables outside. Waiters sometimes 'oversell' and with some dishes like jumbo Carabinero prawns costing €25 **each**, make sure you study the menu and order carefully.

24. Pescaítos Fritos El Cartuchito — sells freshly fried portions of fish in a little paper cone (a *cartuchito*). It's relatively expensive as far as the market is concerned but the fried fish is fresh and tasty and it's a popular spot.

25. Marisquería El Yerno — is a seafood bar that has recently expanded into a third *puesto* (stall) so they are clearly thriving. They also have tables outside the market. Their seafood is excellent quality and the service is friendly and professional. It is also the most expensive of the market bars, so again keep a weather eye on the menu/price list.

Mercado de Salamanca

🏛 EL MOLINILLO 📍 Calle San Bartolomé 1 🕘 Mon–Sat: 0900–1400

The Mercado de Salamanca is the market serving the *barrios* of La Goleta, El Molinillo, and Capuchinos. It is small, but the building itself is handsome, built in the 1920s and designed by the architect Daniel Rubio Sánchez. It is *neomudéjar* in style, featuring a decorated horse-shoe arch (a nod to the Nasrid arch of the Mercado de Atarazanas) and incorporating glazed tiles on the exterior and interior. One of the architect's other famous designs is the Casa de Hortelano in Albacete (La Mancha), an eclectic, neo-Gothic and rather over-the-top villa that nowadays houses the Albacete Knife Museum. The market is restrained in comparison! He also designed the eye-catching Angulas Mayoz frozen fish shop on Calle Sagasta, beside the Atarazanas market.

Like the Mercado de Atarazanas, the central part of the market consists of fishmongers. There are a few vacant lots, but of the 22 '*puestos*' (stalls) that are trading, eleven sell fish and seafood. It's less busy than Atarazanas and while perhaps not worth making a special trip, do call in if you are in the area (it is very near the Jorge Rando Museum, and only a few blocks north of the Glass Museum). One of the advantages of this market is that, unlike Atarazanas, if you want to make purchases, you will usually be able to do so without feeling the weight of dozens of impatient *malagueños* in the queue behind you.

Entering from the main entrance on the Calle San Bartolomé, take the right-hand aisle. The first '*puesto*' is **Especias y Frutos Secos Juan Miguel** (spices and dried fruit and nuts). The counter makes this place look like a sweet shop, but it sells a variety of goods, including the fruit, nuts and spices (like '*pimentón*' — paprika) one would expect. However, the owner also prepares his own very popular spice mixes. Next in line is **Charcutería Campos** run by Julio, whose family have been trading in the market since 1959. He stocks a good range of ham, sausage, cured meats and cheeses, but with a couple of other interesting lines. One is *bacalao* (salted and air-dried cod) from Iceland, the other is 'Los Llanos' — an olive oil from Málaga Province (the village of Cuevas del Becerro). It is extra virgin oil mainly pressed from Hojiblanca olives (90%), with some Lechina and Marteña (10%) varieties, and comes from the first (low temperature) pressing. It is also completely unfiltered so, as a result, looks dark and cloudy, a little like cold tea. It has a rich, fruity flavour and would make a great gift because it is not available outside Spain.

Next door to Charcutería Campos is **El Rincón de Isabel** (Isabel's Corner) — a grocery stall specializing primarily in olives and other pickled goods. But, like other market stalls, she sells a lot more besides, especially seafood. Isabel herself is a lovely person who is immensely knowledgeable about the food she sells. Next in line is **Frutería Paloma**, run by the eponymous Paloma and her sister Fina (it's noteworthy quite how many stalls in Málaga's markets are owned and operated by women). Their particular USP is prepared fruit and veg, such as pomegranate seeds, or podded and peeled broad beans. Next, and the last stall before the Calle Tirso de Molina entrance, is **Frutería Alonso**, where Alonso and Maribel run a small and friendly greengrocery stall. They prepare their own '*corazones de alcachofa*' (artichoke hearts) here, as well as roasted peppers (*pimientos asados*) and roast apples (*manzana asada*).

More or less opposite Alonso is **Panadería El Artesano** (The Artisan Bakery) which genuinely is artisanal. They prepare the sourdough-like '*pan cateto*' here, baked in wood-fired ovens. 'Cateto' literally means 'yokel' or 'hick' (like the French 'paysan' or Gordon Ramsay's most overused word, 'rustic'), and one could describe the owner, José Miguel, as 'cateto' too as he's a bit of a joker. But his bark is worse than his bite and he's really quite friendly. He also speaks pretty good English. His *pan cateto*, local olive oil, some ham and some cheese, and perhaps a few olives from Isabel, would make a lovely gourmet picnic. On the other side of the market is **Frutería Antonio**, run by Antonio and his sister Ana who sell high quality (mostly organic) fruit and veg in season and are known for their friendly service.

On the outward-facing corner of the market (where Calle Tirso de Molina and Calle Salamanca meet) is one of Málaga's best-kept secrets: **Bar Los Pinchitos**. You'll notice quite how hard hospitality staff work in Spain, but Los Pinchitos takes this to the extreme. The owner, José, seems to do everything — pouring drinks, serving, mixing cocktails, cooking *tapas*, cutting ham, clearing tables, cleaning and polishing. Admittedly, it's a small bar, but the service is excellent. The *tapas* come from a limited *carta* but are good quality, often featuring seafood from the market. Unless it's incredibly busy, you'll usually be given a free *tapita* with a drink, Granada-style. Los Pinchitos is not just a great market bar, it is one of the best small *tapas* bars in Málaga.

Mercado de La Merced

LA MERCED ♀ Calle Merced 4 ⏰ Mon–Sat 0900–1400

I mention this market not because it is a great market that you really must visit, but because I hope that by the time you visit Málaga the *ayuntamiento* will have got its act together and made something of it. The original market of La Merced was built in the 1890s on a plot formerly occupied by the long-demolished Mercedarian convent. The current market dates from 1980 and, although it is a boxy and unremarkable building, its position could hardly be more convenient for anyone staying in the *centro histórico*. Less than 10 minutes' walk from the Cathedral and *Teatro Romano* and standing at the corner of the Plaza de La Merced directly opposite the house where Pablo Picasso was born, it ought to be thriving and able to attract tourists as well as locals, but it has struggled to do so.

For the first decades of its existence, the market had a branch of the Sol supermarket near the entrance, which seems a strange choice given how many complain that supermarkets are putting traditional markets out of business. Over a decade ago, with the market struggling, the *ayuntamiento* came up with a plan to dispense with the supermarket and create a 'gastromarket', no doubt eyeing the huge success of the Mercado de San Miguel in Madrid, which after decades of lying derelict, is now one of the capital's hottest foodie destinations. Despite engaging the company behind the San Miguel revamp, it was not a success in Málaga, and after floundering it was relaunched in 2015 with over 20 'gourmet' food outlets, including one owned by the chef Diego Gallegos whose restaurant (**Sollo**) in a Fuengirola hotel holds a Michelin Star. Alas, the market failed a second time and closed after a couple of years.

Its failure was disappointing because the location is perfect and the quality of the food outlets was extremely high. Perhaps the ugliness of the building put people off visiting (the Mercado de San Miguel in Madrid, by contrast, is a beautiful wrought iron and glass construction) or it may simply have been the case that people preferred to sit on the *terrazas* in the nearby Plaza de La Merced than eat indoors. It could even have been on the 'wrong' side of the square, as tourists have little reason to explore beyond the corner of the square in which Picasso's birthplace is located. Alternatively, it may simply have been poorly advertised and under-promoted. I certainly don't recall seeing any promotional material and only discovered the food court by accident when I visited to buy some fruit.

There are still a couple of reasons not to strike this market from your itinerary entirely, however. The *malagueño* supermarket chain, **Maskom**, opened a supermarket here in 2021. In their contract with the *ayuntamiento*, Maskom gave an undertaking that the prices would be the same as in their other supermarkets, which are mostly in the suburbs. In other words, they would not charge higher prices like other city centre 'express' supermarkets. This makes it the best supermarket in which to shop in the centre, and they specialize in products from the Province of Málaga.

The market bar — **Café Bar La Merced** — is a much cheaper option if you want a beer or cup of coffee than the tourist-orientated cafés in the square. In the north-west corner of the market (accessed from Calle Gómez Pallete) there is a little-known but excellent cocktail bar called **GHETTO** (qr5500.buenacarta.com) that offers a great menu of cocktails and mocktails. The '*aperitivos*' (bar snacks) lean heavily towards '*conservas*' — tinned fish and seafood (which in Spain is considered a gourmet treat, rather than something plonked on toast when one can't be bothered to cook) but they also serve a mean hot dog. They have some of the friendliest and most knowledgeable bartenders in the city.

In August 2022 a small sliver of hope came in the form of a new cheese stall opened in the market by Lodewijk van Venetiën, a young Dutch chef. **Craxi Queso** (craxiqueso.com) is pretty niche, selling artisanal cheese from The Netherlands and Belgium, and I wish it well. Whether it thrives remains to be seen, but it sells high-quality products and delivers first-rate customer service, so I hope that it marks the beginning of a return of artisan and gourmet producers and that it will be 'third time lucky' for this market which has the potential to become a real foodie destination. In the meantime, the meat, fish, cheese, ham, fruit and so forth is just as good quality as in any other market. So if you happen to be in the Plaza de La Merced or you are visiting the Maskom supermarket, do have a wander through the market itself. You never know what you might find!

Mercado de Bailén

LA TRINIDAD ♀ Plaza de Bailén 8 ⏰ Mon–Sat 0800–1430

Across the river, the Mercado de Bailén is a not terribly pretty market serving the *barrio* of La Trinidad and the district of Bailén-Miraflores to the north-west. Built in the 1960s, it lacks the architectural distinction of Atarazanas or Salamanca (though it was due a facelift in 2023), but it offers a huge range of products at low prices. It is a genuinely 'local' market for local people, very much at the heart of the community, and while there are quite a few empty lots, the atmosphere is lively. During the COVID pandemic, the market began offering a home-delivery service, which is pretty innovative for a traditional Spanish market.

It only has a couple of bars, but both of them are good. The **Bar Mercado Bailén** is in the centre and an odd sort of building-within-a-building. This is where the market traders come for breakfast, and later it is busy with shoppers having *almuerzo* (elevenses) or *comida* (lunch). It's a very traditional sort of place, serving Málaga's own 'Santa Cristina' coffee. The *tapas* and food are all made on the premises by Ana, and many people call in simply to pick up food to take away. The other bar is **Taberna El Añejo** near the Plaza de Bailén entrance. It's quite traditional and is known for its *vermú* on draught. Eduardo and Juan Pablo greet their customers warmly and fortify them with cold beer and good wine while Marcela prepares homemade (reasonably priced) *tapas* which fly out from the bar with impressive efficiency.

The **Panadería Rafalito** sells a variety of bread, cakes and biscuits baked by Rocío, and is known for its 'pan de kilo' — a sourdough-type loaf that she will slice for you. There is a branch of the **Panadería Nuestra Señora del Socorro** bakery we met in the Atarazanas market (though the signage still says 'Panadería La Royal'). The baker here is Juana and her speciality is white bread with a fine, light crumb. More '*confitería*' than '*panadería*', **Super-Cookie Málaga** specializes in sweets, milkshakes, cookies and personalized, exquisitely decorated cakes.

As well as half a dozen stalls stocked with fresh fruit and vegetables, there is a stall selling dried fruit, nuts, legumes and spices called **Especias Mendoza**. There are a couple of delicatessens. **Charcutería Antonia** is one of the longest-established stalls in the market and is known for its old-fashioned, courteous service. It does a brisk trade in *jamón*, various kinds of sausage and salami and all the other things one would expect, like olives and olive oil, as well as specializing in 'Dulce Zahira' a sweet wine made in Montilla-Moriles (Córdoba) from PX and Moscatel grapes. The other deli, **Charcutería Alejandro**, carries a similar range, but Alejandro himself is something of a ham specialist and many people bring him legs they have bought elsewhere to have him debone them. He also stocks a decent range of *jamón cocido* (cooked ham or '*jamón York*') which is good for sandwiches and can be bought by the slice ('*loncha*' in *castellano*). He also stocks a wide selection of mature Spanish cheeses.

Mercado del Carmen

🍴 EL PERCHEL 📍 Calle la Serna 3 🕐 Mon–Sat: 0800–1430 (bars stay open until 1630)

The other city centre market that is worth exploring if you are nearby is this one in El Perchel. This *barrio* is one of the oldest suburbs of Málaga as shown by the nearby church of El Carmen (Our Lady of Mount Carmel), built in 1584 as the conventual church of the Discalced Carmelite Friars. That church was completely destroyed in 1680, substantially rebuilt and then renovated several times during the 18th and 19th centuries. Like practically every church in Málaga, it was set on fire in the '*quema de conventos*' of 1931, but not destroyed.

The original market of El Carmen was not a building, but a marketplace, and today's rather unimaginative boxy structure dates only from 2010. But like the Mercado del Bailén, this is a genuinely 'local' market. The district of El Perchel is named after apparatus used by fishermen, so it's hardly surprising that this market has a reputation for the quality of its fish counters. But as well as fish, the market stocks everything else one would expect, with plenty of greengrocery, butchery and delicatessen stalls. There are also a few bars, all specializing in fish — cheaper but just as good as those in Atarazanas. **Cocedero Victoria** (also known as **Bar Marisquería Desirée y Paola**) serves excellent fish and seafood dishes, both grilled and fried. It has an outside terrace in warm weather. **GastroGrill** attached to the **Carnes de Cholo** butchers shop serves some of the best steak and chips in town. **Bar La Esquinita de Emilio** is a small bar occupying a corner stall and there is always a crowd at its shining stainless steel counter. It's a very popular place for breakfast, and the *tapas* and more substantial dishes start to appear from noon. The meatballs (*albóndigas*) are excellent, as are the *langostino* (tiger prawn) kebabs, but my personal favourite is *Salchichón de Málaga* on toast.

Málaga's eponymous sausage is rarely eaten by foreigners (apart from the Dutch) because it seems too close to raw pork which, to be frank, is almost what it is. Two hundred years ago, a Genoese family who had moved to Cártama tried to recreate the *Salame genovese di Sant'Olcese* they had enjoyed in Italy but found that the humidity of the Guadalhorce Valley prevented the sausage from fully drying. But what they had accidentally created was also delicious, so they continued to make it, establishing the 'Prolongo' *charcutería* firm that is still trading today. *Salchichón de Málaga* is made from only five ingredients: pork, salt, garlic, black pepper and nutmeg, and it is very lightly cured (though the meat is rendered safe through fermentation). In fact, it is so lightly cured that it failed to meet new product standards for cured meat products (Spain had just joined the EU) and producers had to lobby Brussels for its inclusion. It is delicious (and safe) so if you enjoy steak tartare, give it a try. If you prefer your meat 'medium to well', then it may taste a little too 'raw' and is probably best avoided!

The final pair of bars — **Bar Mercado del Carmen** and **El Pescaíto del Gran Poder** (which literally means 'The Little Fish of Great Power', although in this case '*Gran Poder*' is the name of the image of Our Lady of Mount Carmel which is kept in the nearby church) — are owned by the same people who operate the Atarazanas Market Bar. Both are good and not particularly expensive, but they are bars for people who like fish. If you are not a lover of fish and seafood, your choices are limited to grilled chicken, fried peppers, fried aubergine, artichokes and, in summer, *gazpacho*. Even the salads, which are delicious, contain fish. Everything else on the menu (which is extensive) is either grilled or fried fish and seafood. The '*pinchos*' (skewers) of prawn, scallop and prawn, tuna, monkfish or octopus are especially good. These are priced per skewer, and most of the other dishes come in *raciones* and *medias raciones*. If you want to sample their very popular *paella*, then make sure you are there around 1 pm to enjoy it freshly prepared.

There is also the **Mercado de Huelin** (at the corner of Calle la Hoz and Calle Carpo) which is worth a look if you are walking to the **Huelin beach** or the **Museo Ruso** or **Automobile Museum**. It is just about as 'local' as a Málaga market gets and is largely undiscovered by tourists. It is housed in a spectacularly ugly building but its *puestos* (stalls) sell all the usual goods and the quality is just as high as in other markets. Spaniards do not put up with poor-quality produce! It only has one bar, but it is well-known on account of its offering the cheapest *menú del día* in the whole of Spain (it was available for an unbelievable €3 until the COVID lockdown though it went up to €5 just after; still an extraordinary bargain — see p. 77).

🍱 Picnics

As mentioned above, Málaga's *mercados* are excellent places to find the basic elements of a picnic. They are, in fact, far better than supermarkets because you can control the portions you buy; for example, just a few slices of ham, rather than a whole packet. Bars and cafés that serve *pitufos*, *molletes* and *camperos* are usually happy to sell them '*para llevar*' (to take away), wrapped in aluminium foil. Remember, however, that drinking alcohol from glass bottles in public places (other than bar and restaurant terraces) is prohibited, so unless you are planning to go somewhere like the Jardín Botánico Histórico (Botanical Garden) which has designated picnic areas, then don't include a bottle of wine. This is why many food establishments (like the popular *empanada* shops) only sell beer in tins to take away.

Other great places to buy sandwiches, cheese, ham, sausage, olives, etc. are those known as *ultramarinos* (old-fashioned delicatessens). These are often overlooked by visitors, but they are where the locals go (see p. 297ff.).

If you're staying in a hotel, ask to borrow cutlery to use for your picnic. If you're in an *hostal*, or your hotel is uncooperative, you can buy cutlery very cheaply in the Eroski supermarket in the Larios centre (less than a euro per piece).

Another good place to pick up the necessary elements of a picnic is an '*asador de pollos*' (roast chicken shop). All of them sell '*menús*' of a roast chicken with fries or some kind of potato plus a drink, and many also sell '*comidas caseras*' or '*comidas para llevar*' (homemade food, or food to go), so you can pick up sides, salads, bread and puddings too, then take your haul to a nearby park or beach to enjoy. Most establishments of this kind will give you disposable (wooden) cutlery.

Parque del Oeste and Playa de la Misericordia:

🍗 **Pollos Asados Los Malagueños** 📍 Avenida de los Guindos 29
🌐 asadordepolloslosmalaguenos.es

Los Malagueños sell roast chickens, *empanadas*, a huge range of salads (and in summer,

233

chilled soups), and even pastries and puddings. The 100% homemade dishes are prepared with pride by the lovely women who own and run this business in reassuringly spotless premises. As well as chickens, they often have other roast meats available, as well as roasted apples and their own delicious 'patatas de los montes' (seasoned roast potatoes).

Parque de Huelin and Playa de Huelin:

Asador de Pollos Papagallo ♀ Calle Héroe de Sostoa 96

This asador is very popular with people living in the neighbourhood, not just for its excellent roast chicken, potatoes and fried peppers, but for a host of other dishes (including empanadas, croquetas, albóndigas, a range of salads and, in the summer, gazpacho and ajoblanco). The food is great quality and always freshly prepared and the staff couldn't be more helpful.

Playa Malagueta:

Asador de Pollos La Cocina de Lola ♀ Calle Fernando Camino 9

Hoy Cocino Yo! ♀ Calle Fernando Camino 11

Both of these places (on the same street) sell roast chicken and a big range of 'comida casera'. Both are very good, though, in my opinion, Lola just edges it when it comes to quality and value.

Centro:

Pollos San Juan ♀ Calle Herrería del Rey 9 ⊕ pollossanjuan.es

This is the best-known asador in the centro histórico, with a few tables outside. I'm not convinced that their other 'homemade' dishes are actually made in-house, but for a simple roast chicken and potato menú, or a tasty chicken sandwich, it's a great spot. For good quality comida casera in the city centre, walk into Soho and pay Unosiete a visit:

Unosiete ♀ Calle Vendeja 9 ⓕ unoSieteMalaga

Unosiete ('one seven') is not an asador de pollos, but it sells really excellent, super-fresh and genuinely homemade dishes (the menu changes daily), making it an ideal place to shop for picnics (or for meals should you be staying in a city centre apartment). Mari and Antonio's business has recently expanded into new, larger premises; a development that came as no surprise to their hundreds of faithful customers. The new shop has microwaves for customer use should you wish to heat up food to enjoy immediately.

If you are outside Málaga city, use Google to search for an asador (bit.ly/AsadorDePollos) nearby if you fancy a juicy roast chicken or ready-made dishes for a picnic — there will be one not too far away!

Asdores are also great places to buy dishes for a meal if you are staying in an apartment. The prices are competitive and the quality of the food is excellent. The UK phenomenon of supermarket 'ready meals' is not mirrored in Spain. If malagueños want to enjoy a hassle-free meal, they will go to an asador or shop selling 'comida casera' (homemade dishes) where the food, rather than being mass-produced, will have been freshly made on the premises that day.

Hacer turismo (Sightseeing)

As with restaurants, there isn't much point in giving prices in this section as the information would be out of date almost immediately. Also, how could one compare a small museum with a couple of rooms of exhibits with somewhere like the Alhambra in Granada, arguably one of the cultural wonders of Europe? If they were the same price, the former would be a rip-off or the latter foolishly undersold. Nonetheless, I have used the ❸ symbol as an approximate guide to indicate the price based on admission charges at the time of publication:

❷   free

❸   cheap (or a voluntary or nominal charge)

❸❸   mid–price

❸❸❸   more expensive, usually reflecting popularity/extensiveness

🏛 Historic Sights

Teatro Romano

𝕄 CENTRO HISTÓRICO ♀ Calle Cilla 2 ⊕ ⓔ bit.ly/TeatroRM ⏲ Tue–Sat 1000–1800, Sun 1000–1600 ❶ ✤ bit.ly/TeatroRMinfo ❷

Probably built during the reign of Octavian Augustus (†14 AD), Málaga's is one of 19 surviving Roman theatres in Spain. It is not as impressive as the one at Mérida (which still has some of its stage columns and statues), much of the stone having been plundered by the Moors to build the Alcazaba (seen towering above it), but it is still remarkably intact. Its location, on the other hand, is stunning. Not only is it (unlike the *teatro* of Mérida) in the heart of the city but the Alcazaba rises dramatically behind and above it. It was only discovered in 1951, having lain (ironically enough) under the buildings of Málaga's then 'Cultural Centre'.

It is unusual in that it is built into a hill, like Greek theatres, while most Roman theatres were constructed on flat ground. It is a 'medium-sized' example of a Roman theatre and most of the *caveae* (seats) are intact.

What makes it especially fascinating is that it was lost for so long. Its star began to fade in the late third or early fourth century (partly as a consequence of Christian antipathy towards the theatre) and, notwithstanding a short-lived revival under the Byzantines, the area had been given over to the production of garum long before the 8th-century Muslim conquest of the city. The Moors plundered the site for stone when they built the Alcazaba.

Unlike the Alcázar of Sevilla, which became (and remains) a royal palace, the Alcazaba of Málaga was pretty much abandoned not long after the *reconquista*. The wealthy preferred to construct *palacios* in the city rather than occupy a crumbling, war-damaged citadel on the top of a hill. By the 18th century, the Alcazaba itself, and its surroundings, was pretty much a slum. Little more than a ruin, the Alcazaba was occupied by hundreds of people, living without run-

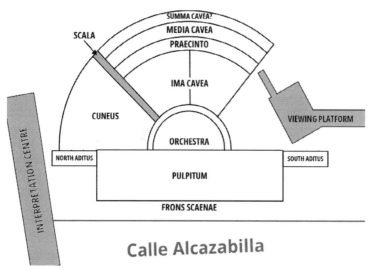

Calle Alcazabilla

ning water or a sewage system. Clinging to the slopes to the north (Alcazabilla) and east (La Coracha), were slums where conditions were no better. Epidemics were frequent and life was short.

The grand civic plan in the early 20th century was to sweep away the unsanitary housing and build a grand 'cultural centre'. This went ahead even though during the construction of that building Roman remains were discovered. But these were different times. Preservation of urban patrimony is a fairly recent concern and plenty of local politicians in the nineteenth century would gladly have demolished the entire Alcazaba in the name of slum clearance and urban regeneration (as they did as late as 1990 with the *barrio* of La Coracha). The excavation of the *teatro* began in the 1950s, but it was not until the final demolition of the *Casa de la Cultura* in 1995 that it became possible to properly open the theatre site.

The Teatro Romano is free to visit, though this fact is not advertised. So if you are passing by, there is no reason not to visit. The information leaflet published by the Junta de Andalucía (link above) that administers the site has lots of information, but the on-site interpretation centre has a great deal more. You can see it from outside of course, but nothing can really compare to venturing inside and adopting the viewpoint of a spectator. To sit on a stone seat that was once occupied by a theatre-goer 2,000 years ago is quite something.

Overlooking the theatre is the terrace of Bar El Pimpi (and yes, it means 'pimp' — a reminder of Málaga's recent history as a port city) — a bit touristy and slightly overpriced these days, but so much a *malagueña* institution that it is worth a stop for a drink over which to appreciate the view and soak up the peerless *ambiente*. Another place to enjoy an evening drink with a beautiful view of the Teatro Romano is the 'Social Salon' terrace of the *Cofradía del Sepulcro* (see p. 221)

Alcazaba

CENTRO HISTÓRICO ♀ Calle Alcazabilla 2
⊕ ✎ alcazabaygibralfaro.malaga.eu ⊙ ☁ 0900–1800; ☀ 0900–2000
⊘ **Lift closed on Monday** ⊜ (⟳ Sun from 1400)

Constructed on the ruins of a Punic fortification during the reign of Abd al-Rahman I, the first Emir of Cordoba, around 756–780 AD, the Alcazaba's original purpose was as a defence against pirates, thanks to its commanding position with views over the city, down to the sea and across to Africa. The fortress was rebuilt by the Zirid Sultan of Granada, Badis ibn Habus, between 1057 and 1063 AD, while the fortified double walls that connect the Alcazaba to the neighbouring Castillo de Gibralfaro, over the Coracha ridge, were built by the Nasrid ruler Yusuf I in the 14th century, when most of the inner palace was also refurbished. As a palace, it was home to a number of Moorish rulers.

The Alcazaba has a distinct feel in comparison to its better-known but younger neighbours, the Alcázar of Sevilla and the Alhambra of Granada. It was already three centuries old when the others were built. After the reconquest, it fell into decline, though it was considered fit for a king as late as 1675 when Felipe IV stayed here during a visit to the city. It really began to decay following the 1680 Málaga earthquake. It became, like the demolished settlements surrounding it, an urban slum, with dozens of families living within its walls until restoration work began in 1933; work that continues slowly today. Two of its original three walls remain, as well as over 100 towers and three palaces.

The fortress's entrance area, which is close to the Plaza de Aduana and the Teatro Romano in Calle Alcazabilla, forms part of the city walls. You pass through the Puerta de la Bóveda (Gate of the Vault), a typical Moorish *puerta en recodo* (a defensive castle entrance designed to delay the arrival of attackers — after entering through an arch, they come up against a blank wall, and have to make a sharp turn to gain access to the next part of the fortress). A little higher up, you pass through the Puerta de la Columnas (Gate of the Columns), which was built using Roman marble columns (from the *teatro romano*) to support Moorish horseshoe arches.

You then enter the lower precincts of the Alcazaba, via the second *puerta en recodo* under the Torre del Cristo (Christ's Tower). This was where the first mass was celebrated following the victory over the town by the *Reyes Católicos*, and it continued to be used as a chapel after this date. The lower precinct follows the contours of the hill, and you can stop and rest at the Plaza de Armas, which is now a garden with fountains and a bastion on the south side which once defended the coast.

Follow the little cobbled paths (the Alcazaba is not suitable for wheelchairs or people with mobility problems, although they can use the lift on Calle Guillen Sotelo to visit the palace complex) through the Puerta de los Cuartos de Granada (Gate of the Halls of Granada), which leads into the upper precinct where the pathway passes through attractive landscaped gardens. Inside the Nazari palace, at the top of the fortress, you can explore three courtyards: the Patio de los Surtidores (Courtyard of the Fountains), which features a row of caliphal arches leading to the Torre de la Armadura Mudéjar (*Mudéjar* Armoury Tower) with its 16th-century carved wooden ceiling. The Torre de Maldonado (Maldonado Tower), with its original marble columns and balconies, offers the best views so far. The next two courtyards in the palace are the Patio de los Naranjos (Courtyard of the Orange Trees) and the Patio de la Alberca (Courtyard of the Pool).

The palace is quite extensive with arches, towers, gates, and original marble columns. Some areas, such as the dungeon, the Patio del Aljibe (Courtyard of the Reservoir), and the Torre del Homenaje (Homage Tower), most of the original Moorish dwellings, mosque and baths (accounting for around a third of the buildings in the complex) are still the site of archaeological research and are currently closed to visitors. There is a small archaeological museum, exhibiting fragments of Roman pottery and statues of various sites around the province, including Lacipo (Casares) and Villa de Rio Verde, (Marbella). You can also see Moorish ceramics and other artefacts found on the site. Tickets used to be sold from a temperamental machine, but during COVID this was replaced by a bank of touch-screen terminals. You get the best value by buying a combined ticket to the Alcazaba and Castillo Gibralfaro together. There is an audio guide which you can access via your smartphone, but if you would prefer a human guide, a reliable company is **exploramalaga.com** which runs tours every Tuesday and Saturday afternoon (you pay for your admission and pay the guide whatever you think is fair — see p. 101 for more details about guided tours in general).

Castillo de Gibralfaro

GIBRALFARO Camino Gibralfaro 11 0900–1800 **alcazabaygibralfaro.malaga.eu** 0900–1800; 0900–2000 (Sun from 1400)

The castle was built in 929 AD by Abd al-Rahman III, Caliph of Córdoba, on an earlier Phoenician fortification and lighthouse, from which its name was derived. Yusef I, Sultan of Granada, enlarged it at the beginning of the 14th century, also adding the double wall down to the Alcazaba (La Coracha).

The castle was subjected to a three-month siege by the *Reyes Católicos*, Fernando and Isabel, which ended only when hunger forced the Moorish *malagueños* to surrender. Afterwards, Fernando occupied the site, while his queen took up residence in the town. A piece of trivia: this was the first conflict in which gunpowder was used on both sides.

The most visible remains of this historic monument are the solid ramparts which rise majestically from woods of pine and eucalyptus; inside the fortress itself, you will find some buildings and courtyards. The ramparts have been well restored and you can walk all the way around them, providing stunning views in all directions. Come here for the location and the view, and visit the Alcazaba for the architecture. Visit both to get a balance of the two.

The castle is 130 metres above sea level, so it's a fair climb to the top. The easiest way to get there is on the bus (35), a journey of about 15 minutes. There is only one bus an hour, unhelpfully leaving at irregular times past the hour, so use the Moovit app (or similar, see p. 96) to confirm. The most obvious walking route to the top is via the 'Coracha' — a paved route created in the 1990s after the demolition of the slum of La Coracha (the historic Coracha is not currently usable). But, be warned: it is steep with an average incline of 1:8. A shadier (but longer) route is the Calle Mundo Nuevo on the forested northern side of the mountain, where the average incline is only 1:16. This walking route has been created recently by the *ayuntamiento*, and includes the construction of a children's playground two-thirds of the way up (or down) and a *mirador* (viewpoint) looking eastwards along the coast.

The easiest way to find this route is to walk beneath the south side of the Alcazaba along the Paseo Don Juan Temboury. At the eastern end, you come to a little foot tunnel underneath the Alcazaba. Walk through the tunnel and take the right fork in the road. You can also reach the Calle Mundo Nuevo from various points in the *barrio* of La Victoria. **A** Google Maps is pretty useless for calculating walking routes that do not involve major roads, so I recommend you use a different (*i.e.* better) map app like **maps.me** or **osmand.net**.

To return to the city, you have the same three options: the bus, the Coracha (though downhill) and the Calle Mundo Nuevo (slower but shadier). A word of warning about the Coracha route: it is paved with stone that has become quite polished with all the footfall and as a consequence it can get very slippery when wet. Even in dry conditions, you will need shoes with a good grip.

City Walls

CENTRO HISTÓRICO 🌐 ⓘ✛ **rutasarqueologicas.malaga.eu**

A few small sections of Málaga's city walls (Phoenician, Roman, and Moorish) survive. Some are visible at street level, others are in the basements of museums, hotels, car parks and offices. The archaeology website of the *ayuntamiento* is full of information, in both Spanish and English (see p. 101). A dozen of the most accessible sections (with English descriptions) are included on the companion Google Map (**bit.ly/MalagaMap**). Click '**LEGEND**' then select '**MÁLAGA History**' to display them.

⚜ Streets and Squares

Calle Marqués de Larios

CENTRO HISTÓRICO

This is the main shopping street in Málaga's old town and the main artery of the *centro histórico*, yet it is one of the newer thoroughfares. It runs from the Alameda Principal at its southern end up to the Plaza de la Constitución to the north, with its 16th-century fountain. Inaugurated in 1891, the city established a limited company to oversee the street's construction, with the Second Marqués de Larios & Larios buying most of the shares. A fine statue of the great man stands at the end of the street on the Alameda Principal, though he has not always enjoyed a place of honour — the monument was torn down at the beginning of the Civil War and dumped in the sea. Almost all the buildings are the work of a single architect: Eduardo Strachan Viana-Cárdenas, a master of Spanish Belle Époque (one of the cross streets — Calle Strachan — is named for him). Though most of the shops are now modern chains, like Zara and Mango, some older establishments remain, such as La Casa Mira, Málaga's oldest ice cream parlour which opened 70 years ago. The polished marble paving (the street was closed to traffic and restored in 2003) and 19th-century street lamps mean that this street is perhaps even more striking at night than during the day.

More than just a shopping street, the Calle Larios is a promenade and effectively the city's Gran Vía (High Street); a place for an evening stroll to see and be seen. It is one of the main thoroughfares used by the Holy Week processions, it forms the catwalk for the Málaga Fashion Festival and it is where the red carpet is laid for the Film Festival. But it is also used for more pedestrian social interactions. In 2019, a *malagueño* by the name of José Antonio Sánchez saw a couple of French backpackers take out a chess board and begin playing. Reminded of the public chess tournaments that he enjoyed while working in Lille, he asked if he could play too. People gathered to watch, and ever since regular chess games have taken place on Tuesday and Thursday evenings (usually beginning around 5 pm or 6 pm). Dozens of people set up boards on the stone benches along the street, with all ages and nationalities represented. The local charity 'Chess Attitude' also organizes tournaments for children which take place on the Alameda Principal in the Librería Luces bookshop, and in other locations, turning Málaga into quite the 'Chess City'.

Calle Larios also has the most impressive Christmas light displays I have ever seen, con-

239

sisting not of the usual lights strung across the streets at intervals, but often entire edifices constructed from thousands of LED lights. The Christmas lights 'switch on' is a significant event in the annual *malagueño* calendar, with thousands of people gathering to witness it.

Plaza de La Merced

MERCED

This is another iconic location in Málaga's old town that was extensively remodelled in the 19th century, and before becoming a square for 'leisure and recreation' it was the site of the main market. In late May into early June, the jacaranda trees blossom, filling the square with a vivid display of pale violet blossom, and for much of the late spring and early summer one is likely to encounter *biznagueros*, Málaga's distinctively garbed jasmine bloom sellers. The *biznaga* has been a favourite adornment of *malagueñas* since before the *reconquista*, and it is made by threading jasmine blooms (collected before sunrise so that they initially remain closed) onto the stems of dried thistles. So emblematic is the *biznaga* that there is a statue of a *biznaguero* in the elegant Pedro Luís Alonso Gardens just east of City Hall.

Plaza de la Constitución

CENTRO HISTÓRICO

Under Nasrid Rule, this was already the main city square, known as the Plaza de las Cuatro Calles or Plaza Pública. Its definitive structure was subsequently formed between the 15th and 16th centuries, and a number of new municipal buildings were constructed, including the Town Hall (the large building now housing, among other things, a Nespresso 'Boutique'). At one time the mayor's residence, the court, the jail and a convent of Discalced Augustinian nuns were all found in this square.

It was renamed Plaza de la Constitución in 1812, although it subsequently changed its name many times: *de la Libertad*, *de la República Federal*, *del 14 de Abril*, and *de José Antonio Primo de Rivera*, returning to **de la Constitución** after Spain's return to democracy after Franco.

In the 19th century, with the repeated confiscations of ecclesiastical property, it underwent significant changes. Several buildings were demolished, such as the chapel of Santa Lucía and the Public Jail, where in December 1831 some of the companions of General Torrijos had been imprisoned (the others had been incarcerated in the Carmelite Convent in El Perchel, allowing them to make their final confessions). Influenced by Parisian and London commercial arcades, Manuel Agustín Heredia promoted the Pasaje Heredia for the enjoyment of the Málaga bourgeoisie in 1837, the first commercial arcade in Spain (now sadly a rather soulless cut-through, rather than the attractive shopping arcade it could be). From the same period dates the Pasaje Chinitas (originally the Pasaje de Álvarez), named after the Chinitas café-theatre, the favourite haunt of Bohemian *malagueños* of the time.

Opened as the Salón Royal in 1857, it was built upon land formerly occupied by the disentailed monastery of Augustinian nuns. The rather grand gateway to the Pasaje Chinitas is all that remains of their convent. The café was a small place with a reduced stage and six boxes at the sides reserved for the most important patrons. It also operated as a brothel from time to time and was frequently closed due to various scandals and knife brawls. Nonetheless, for a time it became one of the most popular café-theatres in Spain and an emblem of the city's musical history. It had a piano that was just below the stage and the rest of the audience settled around small tables. Its celebrity came from its famous flamenco shows, and the attendance of illustrious personalities in the years before the Civil War, including Federico García Lorca, the flamenco dancer 'La Argentinita', Salvador Dalí, Vicente Aleixandre, and Picasso's cousin Manuel Blasco Alarcón, among many others.

The café was closed on the orders of the civil authorities, never to reopen, in 1937, but its reputation lives on thanks to Lorca's eponymous poem of 1931, *En el café de Chinitas* where the bullfighter Paquiro says to his brother, '*soy más valiente que tú, más torero y más gitano*' ('I am braver than you, more of a bullfighter and more of a Gypsy'), bringing together three of Lorca's obsessions: bullfighting, *duende* and machismo. The lines are now inscribed on a plaque, put up to mark the 50th anniversary of Lorca's assassination.

Most of the city's cultural events are centred on the Plaza de la Constitución. For example, during Holy Week this is where the *tribuna* is located — the place where each brotherhood must officially seek permission to proceed (the '*venia*'). During the Málaga Fair, this is the main centre of the 'day fair', while on New Year's Eve (*Nochevieja*) it is where people gather to eat their 12 symbolic grapes.

Since the 17th century, the Genoa or Charles V fountain has stood in the square. It was carved from marble in the 16th century and brought to Málaga in the 17th. It is an Italian Renaissance-style piece and is assumed to come from the Italian city of Genoa, although there are no documents that corroborate its origin (though there is evidence that it cost the Málaga City Council 1,000 ducats). In the 19th century, it was temporarily relocated to the new Alameda Principal before being moved back. Following the advent of motor traffic, the fountain was moved to the Parque de Málaga for safety until the pedestrianization of the city centre in 2002, when it was finally restored to its original place.

Plaza del Obispo
🏛 CENTRO HISTÓRICO

The Plaza del Obispo (Bishop's Square) stands in front of the main façade of the Cathedral of the Incarnation. Its origin possibly dates back to Moorish times, but it acquired its current appearance with the completion of the Cathedral and the episcopal palace in the 18th century. In the last decade of the 20th century, the square was reformed and some of its buildings renovated, replacing old buildings of Diego Clavero and Gerónimo Cuervo, both in a poor state of repair. The works allowed the excavation of remains of the late Roman and Byzantine walls.

In the centre of the square is a fountain from 1785, the water for which was once brought via the San Telmo aqueduct (one of the most ambitious hydraulic engineering works of the 18th century bringing water into the city from 10 km north, through 30 aqueducts and over 33 bridges). The fountain is of the same grey marble as the doorway of the Episcopal Palace. Construction of the baroque episcopal palace began in 1762 and took over 30 years. It is no longer the residence of the Bishop of the Málaga though the rear of the building is still occupied by diocesan offices. The main font portion of the palace was converted into a short-lived Diocesan Museum of Sacred Art in the 1990s. In 2019, it was opened as a 'Cultural Centre' of the Unicaja (Bank) Foundation which announced an 'ambitious programme' of exhibitions of 'top-level artists'. The inaugural exhibition was of works by Joaquín Sorolla. One of the most important events held in this square is the traditional release of a prisoner on Good Friday (see p. 380ff.).

'*El Triangulo*'
🏛 CENTRO HISTÓRICO

To be clear, while I'm calling it '*el triangulo*' (the triangle) no one else does! What I am referring to is the roughly triangular area between the Plaza del Siglo, the Plaza del Carbón, the Plaza de Spínola and the Plaza de Uncibay.

There are two tourist/hospitality hot spots in the centre of Málaga. One is in the streets between the Calle Larios and the Cathedral (*calles* Moreno Monroy, Salinas, Strachan, Bolsa, etc.), and the other is this collection of small squares: the busiest part of central Málaga. To be fair, it is not quite accurate to call them 'tourist' areas. Popular with tourists, certainly, but not exclusively so (unlike some establishments elsewhere on the Costa del Sol). Indeed, one of the lovely aspects of visiting Málaga is that there isn't a sharp distinction between 'local places' and 'tourist places'. At least not yet…

Walking up Calle Molina Lario from the Cathedral, one reaches the Plaza del Siglo first. It emerged as a 'square' following the 19th-century confiscations of ecclesiastical property when the convent on the site was demolished. The convent of Santa Clara, founded in 1505 (or possibly somewhat earlier) was the oldest house of religious women in the city. For a time the square was called the 'Plaza Manuel Loring' (the son of the founders of the Málaga Botanical Gardens and a Mayor of Málaga who was assassinated near here in 1891). It was renamed soon after in honour of the turn of the century ('*siglo*' means 'century'). Since 2008 it has had a modern stainless steel sculpture ('*Panta Rei*') which is supposed to evoke a sense of rivers making their way to the sea.

The Plaza del Siglo gives way to the Plaza del Carbón, another square created after the destruction of convents in the 19th century. The name comes from a coal merchant that used to trade here, supplying nearby coppersmiths. The next square along is the Plaza de Spínola, named after Marcelo Spínola y Maestre, Bishop of Málaga between 1886 and 1896. Among the buildings in the square, Calle Sánchez Pastor 9 stands out — a work from 1886 by the architect Gerónimo Cuervo González and one of the most beautiful 19th-century buildings in Málaga.

The last point of the triangle is the Plaza de Uncibay (**oon-thi-buy**). It is a triangular 'square' filled with bars and restaurants and is one of the busiest and best-known *plazas* in the historic centre. It is named after a Basque supporter of the *Reyes Católicos*, Fernando de Anunçibay (or Uncibay).

🚶 Statues

Hans Christian Andersen
📍 Calle Ancla

The Hans Christian Andersen Statue is a bronze sculpture by José María Córdoba, inaugurated in 2005. It is located in the Plaza de la Marina and is a tribute to the famous Danish writer, commemorating the writer's visit of 1862 recorded in his book *In Spain* (*I Spanien*).

The Cenachero
📍 Plaza de la Marina

A *cenacho* is a round *esparto* (straw) basket that was filled with fish on the beaches (mainly anchovies, horse mackerel, sardines or whitebait) and carried by *cenacheros* into the city. The

Cenachero Statue is a 1968 bronze sculpture made by the Málaga-born artist Jaime Fernández Pimentel. It is located in the Plaza de la Marina and is one of the symbols of Málaga representing a popular *malagueño* character of yesteryear carrying a yoke with a pair of *cenachos*, dressed in a sash and hat; a figure that has disappeared today. The statue was inspired by one of Málaga's last *cenacheros*, Manolo '*El Petaca*'.

The Biznaguero

📍 Jardines de Pedro Luis Alonso

The Statue of the *Biznaguero* is a bronze sculpture from 1963 also by Jaime Fernández Pimentel. The *biznaga* is a characteristic floral corsage of Málaga, consisting of jasmine flowers threaded one by one onto a dried thistle stem. The statue is located in the Pedro Luis Alonso Gardens, next to the Málaga City Hall, and represents a very recognisable Málaga character: the *biznaga* pedlar, dressed in his typical costume, carrying *biznaga*s in his left hand and with his right hand resting on his face looking at the sky, as if he were announcing the sale of the *biznaga*s.

The Espetero

📍 Paseo Marítimo Antonio Banderas

The Statue of the *Espetero* (sardine *espeto* cook) is a sculpture made by Machú Harras and it was unveiled in 2006. It is to be found on the Paseo Marítimo Antonio Banderas next to the Pacífico beach, and represents another typical *malagueño* character.

The Fiestero

📍 Parque de Málaga

The *fiestero* (lit. 'the party man') is the name of a member of a verdiales gang, or '*panda*' (a group of musicians, singers and dancers who perform *verdiales*, the typical musical form from Málaga). Found in the centre of the Parque de Málaga, the statue of the *fiestero* is by Miguel García Navas and was unveiled in 1998.

The Marqués de Larios

📍 Alameda Principal

The statue of the Marqués de Larios is a bronze sculpture on a marble pedestal by Mariano Benlliure from 1899. The statue has two figures on its sides, a man with a pick and a hoe, representing work, and a woman presenting an offering to a child, representing charity. It is located on the Alameda at the entrance to Calle Larios and is a tribute to Manuel Domingo Marquess of Larios and Larios, promoter of the most important street in Málaga and its main investor. The statue of the Marquess was thrown into the sea when the 2nd Republic was proclaimed and recovered after the Spanish Civil War.

Pablo Picasso

📍 Plaza de La Merced 📍 Jardines de Picasso

The statue of Pablo Picasso is a bronze sculpture in the Plaza de La Merced by Francisco López Hernández. It represents the painter with a pensive countenance seated on a marble bench with a notebook and a pencil. Showing him with a pencil, rather than a brush and palette, is significant because Pablo lived in Málaga as a child, not as an adult. It is said that his first word was '*piz*' — a child's word for a pencil (*lápiz*). Less well-known is the Monument to Picasso in the Jardines de Picasso (an urban park just north of the Larios shopping centre). It is called '*Siéxtasis*' (a play on words, combining 'siesta' and 'ecstasy' depicting entwined male and female forms) and is the work of the *malagueño* sculptor Miguel Ortiz Berrocal.

Manuel Agustín Heredia

⚲ Avenida de Manuel Agustín Heredia

Manuel Agustín Heredia arrived in Málaga in 1901 at the age of 15 and worked as a shop assistant. He later opened a small business and ended up becoming one of the most successful businessmen in Spain with interests in the steel, textile and chemical industries. He also participated in the insurance, transport and banking trades. His statue is an iron sculpture by the sculptor José de Vílchez, made from cast iron from his steel mill, where it was initially placed. It is now located on Avenida Manuel Agustín Heredia and is a tribute to this businessman who supplied much of Spain during the early part of its industrial revolution.

Cardinal Ángel Herrera Oria

⚲ Calle Cortina del Muelle

The statue of Cardinal Ángel Herrera Oria is a bronze sculpture by the sculptor José María Palma Burgos, from 1970. Herrera Oria was Bishop of Málaga from 1947 until 1966 and is buried in the Cathedral of Málaga. He was a passionate campaigner for social justice.

Father Tiburcio Arnáiz

⚲ Calle Armengual de la Mota

The Statue of Blessed Tiburcio Arnáiz is a life-size bronze sculpture located in front of the Corte Inglés, erected by popular subscription. The so-called 'Apostle of Málaga', the Jesuit priest Father Tiburcio Arnáiz (1865–1926), rented rooms in a corralón in this part of Málaga to use as a small school where he taught local children to read, write and do maths. He is depicted with hands outstretched toward those in need in a gesture of welcome.

Parque de Málaga

There are many statues in the Parque de Málaga. Some useful background information about them (including a map) is provided on this blog about the park: **bit.ly/MParkStatues**

🏺🖼 Museums and Galleries

'Málaga has no fine arts; the chief, if art it can be called, is the making of painted terracotta images.' (Hand-book for Travellers in Spain, Richard Ford, 1845)

🖼 Centre Pompidou Málaga

🍴 MUELLES ⚲ Pasaje del Dr. Carrillo Casaux ⏱ Wed–Mon 0930–2000 ⊘ Tue ⊕ ✎ centrepompidou-malaga.eu 💶💶 (💶 under 18s & Sundays from 1600)

This is a 'pop-up' outpost of the Centre Georges Pompidou in Paris. It opened its doors in 2015 with a collection of 80 works (and 3 special exhibitions a year) The option to stay in Málaga was renewed in 2020. In the first three months after opening, it received 76,000 visitors. Works in the centre's collection include 20th-century masterpieces such as *The Frame* (self-portrait) by Frida Kahlo, *The Flowered Hat* by Picasso, a self-portrait by Francis Bacon, *The Rape* by René Magritte and *Women in an Interior* by Fernand Léger, as well as contemporary works by French-Tunisian artist Kader Attia and French conceptual artist Sophie Calle. The Pompidou Málaga will follow the example of the Georges Pompidou Centre in Paris, with works from 1905 to the present day.

🏛 Museo Picasso Málaga

🍴 CENTRO HISTÓRICO 📍 Palacio de Buenavista, Calle San Agustín 8
🕐 1000–1900 🌐 *⬦ museopicassomalaga.org* 💶💶 (*🆓 under 16s and Sundays from 1700)*

Although the Pompidou has one Picasso and most of his most famous works are elsewhere, the obvious place to see his work in the town of his birth is the museum entirely devoted to his life and work. It is housed in the 16th-century Palacio Buenavista, formerly the seat of the Condes de Buenavista, which for much of the twentieth century was the Museum of Fine Arts. The museum extends into a number of adjoining buildings that once formed part of the Judería (Jewish Quarter).

Some make fun of Málaga for its Picasso Museum when his best-known works are exhibited in Madrid and in eponymous museums in Barcelona, Antibes, Münster and Paris. The implication is that Málaga has cynically sought to capitalize on the reputation of an artist who had little connection with the city besides being born there. It is true that Picasso himself had a somewhat conflicted relationship with the city of his birth. His family left for La Coruña when he was 10 years old and he missed Málaga terribly, lamenting that in Galicia he could find 'no Málaga, no bulls, no friends, anything at all'. He returned to Málaga for holidays, but by his late teens, his relationship with his stuffy, disapproving uncle Salvador had become so strained that he had come to resent the city itself, seeing it as a place typified by bourgeois hypocrisy. His final visit was when he was 20, never once returning in the next 72 years of his life.

And yet he remained devoted to the consumption of Málaga wine and very late in life he would gaze out from his villa on the Côte d'Azur and talk wistfully of Málaga, far to the south-west. In fact, the idea of a Picasso collection in Málaga was first seriously discussed in 1953, during the Franco era. Picasso was in touch with Juan Temboury Álvarez, the Provincial Delegate for Fine Arts in Málaga and the man who probably contributed more to the preservation and development of the artistic and cultural heritage of the city than any other twentieth-century figure. Temboury had asked if Picasso would consider donating two works, and the artist had enthusiastically replied that he would send 'two trucks' instead. The negotiations came to naught, however, because the loathing between Picasso and Franco was mutual and the authorities in Málaga at the time refused to accept any donation for fear if displeasing *El Caudillo*. The works went instead to Barcelona, a city quite happy to offend Franco.

Christine Ruiz-Picasso, the widow of the artist's eldest son Paul Ruiz-Picasso, resumed contact with Málaga in 1992 on the occasion of the 'Classic Picasso' exhibition in the city and in 1994 with the 'Picasso, First Look' exhibition. In 1996, she revived the 1953 project, which finally became a reality 50 years later, on October 27, 2003, when the Museo Picasso Málaga was inaugurated in the presence of Their Majesties King Juan Carlos and Queen Sofía.

Christine Ruiz-Picasso donated 14 paintings, nine sculptures, 44 individual drawings, a sketchbook with more than 36 drawings, 58 engravings, and nine ceramic pieces; 133 pieces of art in all. In addition, Picasso's grandson, Bernard Ruiz-Picasso, donated another five paintings, two drawings, ten engravings and five ceramic pieces. The museum's collection currently features over 200 works covering 80 years of the painter's work, from 1892 to 1972, ranging from the first academic studies towards cubism to late reinterpretations of the Old Masters. The library houses an archive with more than 800 titles on the subject of Picasso, including relevant documents and photographs. Although the museum is free from 5 pm on Sundays, it is very popular (it's the most-visited museum in Andalucía) and people begin queuing up to three hours ahead of time.

🖼🏛 Fundación Picasso Museo de Casa Natal

🏛 LA MERCED 📍 Plaza de La Merced 15
🌐 🔗 fundacionpicasso.malaga.eu 🕐 0930–2000 💶 (🎫 under 18s and Sundays from 1600)

The apartment where Pablo Picasso was born in 1881 has been open to the public for over 25 years, and the displays are as much biographical as artistic, with objects, photographs and letters relating to the Picasso family as well as artworks (there is always a temporary exhibition, too). However, the collection is large (over 3,500 items), and includes less well-known Picasso works such as ceramics, family sketches and book illustrations, as well as works by around 200 contemporaries and other *malagueño* artists. This is not a museum in which to view masterpieces. Instead, it offers something more unusual, and probably of interest to Picasso agnostics as well as Picasso fans: a fascinating glimpse into the childhood and artistic development of one of the twentieth century's artistic geniuses.

🖼 Colección del Museo Ruso

🏛 EL PERCHEL 📍 Edificio de La Tabacalera, Avenida Sor Teresa Prat 15
🌐 🔗 coleccionmuseoruso.es 🕐 Tues–Sun 0930–2000 💶💶 (🎫 under 18s and Sundays from 1600)

Perhaps not top of the list for tourists (who understandably want to see Spanish art in Spain), the presence of this outpost of the Russian State Museum (St Petersburg) in Málaga is a sign of how seriously the city has gone about the project of establishing itself as a cultural centre (and the hundreds of millions of euros they have spent doing so). Before the invasion of Ukraine in 2022, the museum mounted three temporary exhibitions each year as well as frequent talks and other events. Opening in 2015, the museum attracted 107,000 visitors in its first year of operation and occupies the premises of the former Royal Tobacco Factory, south-west of the railway station, situated in the *barrio* of Huelin. Local newspapers took to referring to the neighbourhood as 'Huelingrad'.

The future of the Russian Museum was a matter of some debate following the 2022 Russian invasion of Ukraine. Bars all over the city renamed their *ensaladilla rusa* (a *tapa* as ubiquitous as *tortilla*) '*ensaladilla ucraniana*' in solidarity with Kyiv. The mayor, Francisco de la Torre, returned the 'Medal of Pushkin' he had received in 2018 (in recognition of his contribution to promoting Russian culture) from President Vladimir Putin. The question of whether the museum was subject to sanctions against Russia remained. Torre's Centre-Right *Partido Popular* was in coalition with Noelia Losada's Centrist *Ciudadanos* ('Citizens') Party, with Losada also serving as Councillor for Culture, and after some political posturing and discussions with the Minister of Culture, it was agreed that the museum would remain open.

The museum is run by the *ayuntamiento*, rather than by the Russian state. An agreement with the Russian State Museum allowed the museum to display art from its collection in return for an annual payment of (according to press reports) €400,000. The mayor, most Málaga councillors, and the Spanish State agreed that art and culture should not be included in the sanctions imposed upon the Russian state, especially as many of the artists whose work is exhibited were themselves dissidents once sent to the Gulags. However, in 2022, payments to the Russian State Museum ceased and it was decided that no new exhibitions would be staged for the time being.

The major exhibition at the time of Russia's invasion of Ukraine was entitled, fittingly, 'War and Peace in Russian Art'. This exhibition was to continue past its April 2022 end date, but as the war in Ukraine unfolded and dragged on with increasingly horrifying evidence of the shameful treatment of civilians, it was quietly packed away and replaced by exhibitions of

Spanish art. Exhibitions marking the 50th anniversary of the death of Picasso were hastily scheduled for 2023 and further assistance came when Jenny Green, a private British collector of Russian artworks lent almost her entire collection for exhibition. What the future holds for this museum will no doubt be determined by what happens in Russia in the years ahead.

🏛 Museo Carmen Thyssen Málaga

🏛 CENTRO HISTÓRICO ♀ Calle Compañía 10
⊕ ✎ carmenthyssenmalaga.org ⏱ Tues–Sun 1000–2000 ⊕⊕ (✦ under 18s and Sundays from 1600)

Another feather in the cap of the city authorities was winning the competition to secure the first museum to house works from the collection of Doña Carmen Thyssen-Bornemisza. Almost every city in Spain vied for the honour. The gallery opened in 2011 and occupies the beautiful 16th-century Palacio de Villalón. During renovations, Roman garum (fermented fish sauce) pools were discovered and a small exhibition relates to this. There is a permanent collection of almost 230 works of Spanish artists from the 13th century onwards — though most are examples of 19th-century Spanish genre paintings and there is a deeply *andaluz* feel to many of them. There are temporary exhibitions throughout the year and in recent years, there have been exhibitions featuring Matisse, Monet, Bruegel, and Gauguin.

La Buenaventura (c.1922), Julio Romero de Torres

The works permanently displayed are from the personal collection of Carmen, *la baronesa* Thyssen, widow of the late Baron Hans Heinrich von Thyssen-Bornemisza, whose artworks form the permanent collection of the eponymous museum in Madrid. She was his third wife (and he her third husband) and it was Doña Carmen who first persuaded Hans Heinrich to exhibit his art collection to the public in Madrid, which he did in 1992. This earned her the disapproval of Mrs Thatcher, who had been hoping to persuade Don Hans Heinrich (who owned a large house in Gloucestershire) to bring his collection to the UK. Carmen's native city of Barcelona was similarly displeased with her when Málaga beat them in the later competition to house (some of) her own collection.

Carmen 'Tita' Thyssen (María del Carmen Rosario Soledad Cervera & Fernández de la Guerra de Thyssen-Bornemisza) is a former Miss Spain (1961) and she began collecting art herself only after her late husband's collection went on display in Madrid. She is now the seventh richest woman in Spain and the foremost private patron of the arts. Not bad for a girl brought up in a working-class *barrio* of Barcelona. The agreement with Málaga city hall is due for renewal in 2025, but Doña Carmen's statement (in 2022), 'I want this museum to be forever. Forever!' could hardly be more emphatic. The Thyssen Gallery has helped put Málaga on the cultural map, so it seems vanishingly unlikely that the *ayuntamiento* would allow its continued presence in the city to be put in jeopardy for any reason either.

📖🏛 Museo de Málaga

🏛 ALAMEDA 📍 Plaza de la Aduana ⊕ 🄫 bit.ly/MdeMalaga ⏰ Tue–Sat 0900–2100; Sun 0900–1500 💶 (✅ EU Passport Holders)

This is another museum occupying a palace though not, in this case, an aristocratic one. The Palacio de la Aduana was originally a customs house for Málaga Port, begun in 1791 and modelled on Renaissance Italian palaces. Construction was still underway in 1810 when the building was ransacked by the French during the Peninsular War, and it was not completed until 1829. When the Paseo del Parque and the present port were constructed on reclaimed land at the end of the 19th century the building served as the Royal Tobacco Factory. In 1922 it was badly damaged by a fire that led to the deaths of 28 government employees living on the top floor. After the Civil War, the national government's Málaga provincial delegation returned. It opened as the Museum of Málaga in December 2016 after a €23m refurbishment, combining the collections of the Provincial Fine Art and Archaeological museums under one roof. For holders of non-EU passports, the entrance fee is nominal.

With so many new and unusual museums in Málaga, the municipal museum is often overlooked by visitors, who imagine a dreary collection of dusty artefacts. But they could not be more wrong. In total, the Museum of Málaga has more than 2,000 artworks of considerable value, many created by artists of importance, such as Luis de Morales, Luca Giordano, Bartolomé Esteban Murillo, Antonio del Castillo, Alonso Cano, José de Ribera, Diego Velázquez, Vicente Carducho, Francisco de Goya, Pedro de Mena and Francisco de Zurbarán. As an art gallery, it houses what is considered one of the largest collections of 19th-century art in Spain, displaying works by Joaquín Sorolla, Carlos de Haes, Federico de Madrazo, Antonio María Esquivel, Vicente López and Ramón Casas, as well as several of the most famous members of the so-called Málaga School of painting: José Moreno Carbonero, Enrique Simonet, Antonio Muñoz Degrain, José Nogales Sevilla, Bernardo Ferrándiz, etc. It also has an interesting collection of modern art from Málaga and Andalusia up to the 1950s with works by Picasso, Canogar, Barjola, Óscar Domínguez and Guinovart among others.

The other focus of the museum — archaeology — is represented by a magnificent collection. The archaeological collection has more than 15,000 pieces, covering a period from the 8th century BC to the Middle Ages: Egyptian, Phoenician, Greek, Roman, Arab, Visigothic and Byzantine. In recent decades, pieces from excavations carried out by the University of Málaga have been incorporated, as well as various finds from archaeological interventions that have been carried out in the urban area of Málaga, such as those found in the excavation of the Teatro Romano and the Tomb of the Warrior. Also on display is the Mosaic of Venus from the 2nd century AD that was discovered in Cártama in the 1950s.

An interesting piece of trivia about the building (the Palacio de la Aduana) concerns its rather odd alignment with the nearby streets, at a sort of diagonal. Remember that it was built as the Customs House, and was thus concerned with shipping and trade — well, its corners are aligned to the points of the compass.

🏛 Museo del Patrimonio Municipal

🏛 LA MALAGUETA 📍 Paseo de Reding 1

⊕ 🄫 museodelpatrimoniomunicipal.malaga.eu ⏰ Tue–Sun 1000–2000 (Sep–Jun); Tue–Sun 1000–1400, 1730–2130 (Jul–Aug) ✅

The MUPAM, as it is known, is somewhat out on a limb, near the bullring, and it deserves to be better known and appreciated. It also has the misfortune to be housed in a somewhat ugly building, reminiscent of an unimaginative 1990s office building. In fact, the glass and steel edifice visible from the street is essentially an office block, housing meeting rooms and offices. The exhibition spaces are to the rear. This rear module is divided into three rooms. Room I is dedicated to pieces from the 15th to the 18th centuries and is divided into several units dealing with the incorporation of Málaga into the Crown of Castilla, festivals and celebration, and the 17th-century painter Alonso Cano. Room II shows 19th-century artworks, mainly by *malagueño* artists. Room III is dedicated to the 20th century, in particular the so-called 'Generation of the 50s' and more recent movements.

There are usually two or three temporary exhibitions on display and these are varied, but always with some connection to Málaga. Best of all, it is free to visit, which means you don't have to worry about 'getting your money's worth'. You can call in, look at a few exhibits and move on. The staff are lovely and will do their best to answer any questions you might have about the exhibits. If you are learning Spanish in Málaga, the museum offers guided tours tailored to your own level of Spanish proficiency (✉ activities.mupam@evento.es). If you have a reasonable level of *castellano* then there are also lots of regular guided tours (and not only of the museum — a popular one ventures out to explore the sculpture in the Parque de Málaga), all of which are free.

🖼 Centro de Arte Contemporáneo Málaga (CAC)

🍴 SOHO ◉ Calle Alemania 🕐 Tue–Sun 0900–2100 (☀ 0900–1400, 1700–2130) ◉ Subida Coracha 25 🕐 Tue–Sun 1000–2000 (☀ 1000–1400, 1730–2130) ⊕ ⓒ cacmalaga.eu ⓖ

Exploring the artistic trends of the 20th century, CAC's permanent collection is particularly strong on international artists from 1950 to the present (think Damian Hirst and Thomas Ruff) and Spanish artists since the 1980s, with a focus on local, Málaga-born talent. The works — which include sculpture and installations — are displayed in futuristic white rooms and are complemented by a full events and educational calendar along with temporary exhibitions promoting Málaga's up-and-coming artists. Attached to CAC is a popular bar-restaurant serving *tapas* and full meals with more than a nod in the direction of Japanese cuisine (see p. 180).

The main museum occupies Málaga's modernist former wholesale market, designed by Luis Gutiérrez Soto and dating from the 1940s. The archive and second exhibition space (CAC La Coracha) is at the other end of the Alameda, next to MUPAM. Entry to both sites is free, so these are great places to drop into as you're passing

🖼 Málaga Arte Urbano Soho (MAUS)

🍴 SOHO ⊕ mausmalaga.com ⓖ

This is not a museum but the result of an initiative led by Fernando Francés, the director of the Centro de Arte Contemporáneo (CAC). He worked with the city council to contribute to the regeneration of the Ensanche Heredia (aka 'Soho'). A little over a decade ago, Soho was a rather scruffy and fairly typical port-side district with its fair share of flea-bitten boarding houses, dive bars, sex shops and brothels. The idea that it could be transformed into a cool cultural district seemed impossibly optimistic. And yet residents and businesses came together and it now has a theatre backed by Antonio

Banderas, new boutique hotels, some of Málaga's most exciting restaurants, its largest craft beer bar and fantastic neighbourhood bars like La Pechá.

MAUS is a project aimed at promoting street art, or 'curated graffiti'. As the London-based artist 'D*Face' explains, 'To be part of a city's growing culture and for that to be recognized … is really awesome. I think, for a lot of people, street art is still aligned with graffiti and run-down city suburbs but it's a misleading stereotype — street art is made to benefit a location, not degrade it.' The website has a map showing the locations of the artworks.

Small and Specialist Museums

Museo Unicaja de Artes & Costumbres Populares

CENTRO HISTÓRICO ♀ Plaza Enrique García-Herrera 1
⊕ ©museoartespopulares.com ⊕ Mon–Fri 1000–1700, Sat 1000–1500 € (under 14s and Tuesdays 1300–1700)

Like many Spanish museums and galleries, this museum of popular artefacts and customs is owned and operated by a bank, Unicaja, as part of its corporate social responsibility commitment. It occupies a 17th-century inn arranged, in the *andaluz* manner, around a shady central courtyard. The collection consists of artefacts documenting the everyday life of Málaga and Andalucía — equestrian tack, milling, fishing, farming, horticulture, oil pressing, winemaking, bread making, cooking, blacksmithing, dining, costume, children's games and clothes, china and decoration, textiles, popular religion and plenty more besides. Lowbrow by definition, but fascinating and charming.

Málaga Wine Museum

LA GOLETA ♀ Plaza de los Viñeros 1 ⊕ museovinomalaga.com
⊕ Mon–Fri 1000–1700, Sat 1000–1400 € ∩

It is fair to say that this museum polarizes opinion. It regularly receives grudging one-star reviews on TripAdvisor and Google, but it also receives plenty of gushing five-star reviews. I am in the latter camp. The display is modest, mostly consisting of wine labels and infographics, but if you are interested in the wines (and raisins) of the Málaga region, then you will find it fascinating. It is also the headquarters of the regulatory authority for Málaga and Sierras de Málaga wines, and for Málaga raisins, so the staff really do know what they are talking about. The audio guide is comprehensive and available in several languages (you need a smartphone and headphones to be able to use it). Visits conclude with a tasting of two wines — usually a sweet Málaga wine and a Sierras de Málaga 'table' wine, but feel free to ask to try a particular style. You are also free to ask for an additional wine to taste for a modest extra charge. There is a well-stocked museum shop selling local wines and wine-related souvenirs. The staff are knowledgeable and enthusiastic and go out of their way to be helpful.

Museo del Vidrio & Cristal

SAN FELIPE NERI ♀ Plazuela Santísimo Cristo de la Sangre 2
⊕ museovidrioycristalmalaga.com ⊕ Tue–Sun 1100–1900 ♛ guided tour only € (children under 6)

Unlike the Museum of Popular Artefacts and Customs, there is nothing particularly *malagueño* about the Museum of Glass and Crystal, and yet it regularly tops the tourist polls as the most enjoyed exhibition in Málaga. It's certainly pretty unique (this solecism is justified on the grounds that although there is a glass museum in Venice, it is not quite like this one). Yet again, this museum is housed in an 18th-century *palacio* not far from the Church of San Felipe Neri. It is run by three amateurs (in the fullest sense of the term) — the co-founders Gonzalez Fernández-Prieto, Steven Spragwe, and the former Clinical Dean of Guy's and St Thomas's, Professor Ian Phillips — all of whom live 'over the shop' for at least some of the year. Their combined collection numbers around 3,000 pieces as well as over 60 stained glass windows rescued from all over Europe (though due to limited space only a few of these are on display at any one time). They have Phoenician, Egyptian and Roman pieces on display as well as medieval glassware from Europe and Iran, among other places. The chronological collection then moves through Catalan, Venetian and Bohemian glass of the 16th and 17th centuries, Spanish glass of the 18th, British of the 19th, right up to Pop Art 20th century examples.

Simply wandering around left to one's own devices might be repetitive and confusing, but what really makes this museum so enjoyable is the fact that the only way to visit is by guided tour (offered in 5 languages) of over an hour's duration, and it is the knowledgeable and passionate commentary provided by the guide that brings everything alive; not only describing the pieces on display but explaining glass-making techniques and their contemporary significance. Señor Fernández-Prieto and his collaborators more than deserve their success. Opened in 2009, the museum has only broken even since 2014, receiving no public subsidy or sponsorship. It now occupies the 3rd spot on TripAdvisor for Málaga 'attractions' and the 2nd spot for Málaga 'museums'. While TripAdvisor may be an uncertain guide, making the top three of a list of over 210 attractions is hugely impressive for a small, private museum. If you have the slightest interest in (or curiosity about) glass, then do visit this museum — it really is *sui generis*.

🏺 Museo Automovilístico y de la Moda

🍽 HUELIN 📍 Edificio de La Tabacalera, Avenida Sor Teresa Prat 15 ⊕ 🎟 museoautomovilmalaga.com 🕐 Mon–Sun 1000–1430, 1600–1900 €€

In the same complex as the Museo Ruso, the Automobile and Fashion Museum has 10 rooms with 90+ classic cars from the 19th century to the present day and, curiously, an enormous collection of *haute couture*, hats and handbags (the unifying theme seems to be 'style'). With classic Spanish disregard for political correctness, I have seen promotional materials proudly boasting that it, therefore, has something for 'him and her'! According to online reviews, it has made the top three of Málaga's museums, though it may not appeal to visitors without some interest in either cars or fashion. Like the Glass Museum, it is privately owned.

🏺 OXO Museo Videojuego

🍽 CENTRO HISTÓRICO 📍 Plaza del Siglo ⊕ 🎟 oxomuseo.com 🕐 Mon–Thu 1100–2100; Fri 1100–2200; Sat 1000–2200; Sun 1000–2100 €€€ (🎟 children under 6) 🎧

Promoted by the Málaga Provincial Council and managed by Kaiju Group (an events and technology company based in Málaga), the OXO Videogame Museum is 'a unique space in Europe where the past, present and future of the video game industry converge'. Only inaugurated in early 2023, it welcomed over 11,000 visitors in its first month of operation. Over several floors, the permanent exhibition covers the history of video games from the 1950s to the present day, but what is presented is far more than a display of obsolete handsets and controllers. Many of the 'exhibits' are available to play and the visitor experience is intended to be 'immersive'.

Temporary exhibitions feature particular games looking at their design and going, as it were, 'behind the scenes'. Other exhibits focus on the latest trends and developments in the industry. The language of the museum is Spanish, but all information is also provided in English, and there are audio guides in Spanish and English, with other languages to follow. On the top floor of the museum is a bar-restaurant (**terrazacatedral.es**) which serves excellent food. The restaurant main menu prices reflect the roof terrace location but *tapas* are fairly reasonably priced.

🏛 Museo Jorge Rando

🚇 La Goleta 📍 Calle Cruz del Molinillo 12 🌐 **museojorgerando.org**
🕐 Mon–Fri 1000–1400, 1600–2000 (☀ 1700–2100); Sat 1000–1400 🎟

The Jorge Rando Museum was inaugurated in 2014, occupying the space once occupied by the Nuestra Señora de La Merced y Santísima Trinidad school, an annex to the Mercederías convent (1893). It is a museum dedicated exclusively to the *malagueño* neo-expressionist painter Jorge Rando (b. 1941), although there are also exhibitions by other artists. Made up of 10 rooms over two levels around an irregular patio, the museum is well-planned and missing a room is practically impossible. Its small size makes any visit an intimate and immersive experience. The staff are friendly and helpful, and very happy to give (free) guided tours upon request, either to the whole museum or some room or theme of it.

After completing his philosophy studies, Jorge Rando moved to Cologne, and he has remained deeply linked to Germany, with his work strongly influenced by Central European art and culture. Along with his wife, Margit, Rando returned to Spain in 1984, alternating his residences between Málaga and Hamburg ever since. Rando's painting is characterized by the distortion of the form, an emotional use of colour and the importance of gesture and line. He works mainly by series. Since the late sixties and early seventies, he has highlighted themes such as Prostitution, Maternity, Sorrows, Animals, Landscapes, Africa, etc. Another important aspect of his work is religious themes and the scenes of *Semana Santa* in Málaga have been an important inspiration.

✈ Museo Nacional de Aeropuertos y Transporte

🚇 AEROPUERTO 📍 Aeropuerto de Málaga (next to 'Aviación General')
🌐 📧 **aeromuseo.org** 🕐 Tue: 1000–2000; Wed–Sat 1000–1400 🎟

Run by the company that operates the airport — AENA–Aeropuerto de Málaga — this museum of civil aeronautical heritage is more an 'airport museum' than an 'aeronautical museum'. Its exhibition halls cover about 3,000 metres in total and visitors can see historic aeroplanes and items related to the world of aviation collected from airports around Spain. There is also an Aeroplane Observatory located inside the old control tower looking out onto the current runways.

On the way around the exhibition, visitors will be able to see some of the old marketing posters that were used to publicize the airport as well as having the chance to sit inside the cockpit of an Iberian Airlines DC-9. There is also an important collection of models, uniforms, and many other items related to the evolution of the aviation industry and see the technological development the industry has undergone over the years: there are motor engines, runway design models, radio-operated lighting, radio control systems, and much more.

Visits are free and can be guided if desired. The museum can be reached by the 🕑 *Cercanías* train to the Airport, or by city buses 10 or 19.

🖼 Ateneo de Málaga

🍴 CENTRO HISTÓRICO 📍 Calle Compañía 2 🌐 ateneomalaga.org
🕐 Mon–Fri 1200–1400, 1730–2100 🈯

Next door to the church of Santo Cristo de la Salud, the Athenaeum of Málaga is a cultural association founded in 1966 which occupies part of the old Jesuit Novitiate College of San Sebastián, built between 1578 and 1599 (the other part of the college is now a primary school). It holds an important collection of contemporary art by Málaga artists and temporary exhibitions are continuously staged featuring a range of artists working in a variety of media, but there is always something to see, and entry is free.

🖼 Museo Revello de Toro

🍴 CENTRO HISTÓRICO 📍 Calle Afligidos 5 🌐 museorevellodetoro.net
🕐 Tue–Sat 1000–2000; Sun 1000–1400 💶 (🈯 under 18, over 65 and all day Sunday, with a small charge for audio guide)

Another museum honouring a *malagueño* artist, in this case, the figurative painter Félix Revello de Toro (b. 1926). Revello de Toro's interest in art was obvious from a young age, and at eight years old he made a stunning sketch of the image of the Cristo de Mena, destroyed a few years earlier. His first exhibition took place in 1938 when he was 12 years old, and at 16 he received his first professional commission from a local brotherhood. The following year he received a scholarship to study at the Royal Academy of San Fernando in Madrid. He was a professor of Fine Art in Barcelona (Escuela de la Lonja) and has been an honorary member of the San Telmo Royal Academy of Fine Arts (Málaga) since 1987.

In 2010, the museum dedicated to him opened with 117 works donated by the painter. The museum is housed in a residential building dating back to the 17th century and which was once the home and workshop of the sculptor Pedro de Mena. It is one of the very few buildings from that century remaining in the city. The museum was founded with three main goals: to display the works of Félix Revello de Toro and other local artists; to give visibility to the home and workshop of Pedro de Mena; and demonstrate the latter's knowledge, development, life and works. In addition to the six rooms displaying Revello de Toro's work, the museum also has two additional cultural spaces. One for temporary exhibitions and another dedicated to the memory of Pedro de Mena.

🖼 Centro Cultural La Malagueta

🍴 LA MALAGUETA 📍 Plaza de Toros La Malagueta, Paseo de Reding 8
🌐 ⓒ cclamalagueta.com 🕐 Tue–Sun 1000–1400, 1500–1900 💶/🈯

Like many others of its kind in Andalucía, this museum, which opened in the Malagueta Bullring in 1999, was initially an exhibition of bullfighting objects and memorabilia, offering the visitor a glimpse into the world of Spain's national festival. It included matadors' costumes, photographs, posters and other valuable bullfighting items. However, in 2020, as part of a considerable restoration of the Malagueta bullring, a new cultural centre opened, devoted to exhibitions mostly of art and photography.

☷Ifergan Collection — Ancient Art

⋈ CENTRO HISTÓRICO ♀ Calle Sebastián Souvirón 9 ☻☻

Owner Vicente Jiménez Ifergan established this gallery to share his hobby and collection with others. The focus is on the cultures and civilizations of the Mediterranean: from Mesopotamia, Canaan, Egypt, Greece, Rome, Persia, and Byzantium, to Moorish Spain. Among many important pieces in this collection is an Egyptian mummy head from the Eighteenth Dynasty (1500–1200 BC), the 'Kudurru', which is a Babylonian stone stela from the era of Nebuchadnezzar I. There are only three in the world: in Beijing, in the British Museum and in Málaga. Also, a bust of one of the Roman Emperor Antoninus Pius (2nd century AD) found in Málaga in 1904 close to the Cádiz Highway — without a doubt, one of the most important archaeological discoveries in the history of Málaga.

The jewel of the collection is the unique Malaka Room. It is a repository of treasures which lay at the bottom of the sea for almost 2,500 years as a result of a ship which sank fleeing a siege by troops of Alexander the Great in 332 BC comprising more than 100 votive terracotta figures (dated to between the 6th and 4th centuries BC) from the Temples of Melkart and Astarte. The gallery is part museum and part fine art dealership, with some items available to buy (if you happen to be a 'high-value individual').

☷Casa Gerald Brenan

⋈ CHURRIANA ♀ Calle Torremolinos 56 **f** bit.ly/CasaGB ⏱ Wed–Thu 1600–2100; Fri 1100–1400, 1700–2100 ☻

This is probably one for the Hispanists. Opened in 2014, this museum ('cultural centre' might be more accurate) occupies the house lived in by the Anglo-Irish writer Gerald Brenan and his American wife, Gamel Woolsey. It is found in the *barrio* of Churriana, the other side of the airport, though it can be reached fairly easily by bus (🚌 10 or C8).

Edward Fitzgerald Brenan was born in Malta in 1894, and dragged by his family through South Africa, England, Ireland, Malta (again), India and Ireland (again), Gerald Brenan was a fundamentally restless man (at 18 he tried to walk to China, though only got as far as Bosnia). He fought in the battles of Yprés and the Somme, and the second battle of the Marne, and in 1918 he won the Military Cross and the Croix de Guerre. He was introduced to the Bloomsbury Circle and had a brief but intense romance with Dora Carrington before breaking it off, frustrated by her doomed love for Lytton Strachey. An inheritance gave him the economic means to travel to Granada, where between 1919 and 1936 he lived for long periods.

In the early 1930s, he conceived the project of writing a biography of San Juan de la Cruz (St John of the Cross) and spent the following years visiting the places associated with the saint. In 1935 he settled in a new house, in the town of Churriana, Málaga, next to what was then a small airfield. He was a perplexed witness to the Spanish Civil War and in 1943 he published *El Laberinto Español* (The Spanish Labyrinth), a study of the social and political background of the 1936–1939 War. The work was banned in Spain but published by Ruedo Ibérico in Paris. In 1946 he wrote his article 'Spanish Scene', as well as several articles on Saint John of the Cross that he published in 1947. In 1949 he went on a tour of Spain and in 1950 published the travel book *La faz de España* (The Face of Spain) where, in its sixth chapter, he revealed his investigations into the murder of Federico García Lorca. In 1953 he returned to Churriana and published *South of Granada* — probably his best-known travel book in English.

He paints a picture of a Spain (and of Andalucía) that is now largely lost (though much is still recognisable) and he does so beautifully. Many of his attitudes will strike the modern reader as benighted, certainly sexist and, for all of his affection for Spain, slightly racist and tinged with remnants of the Black Legend. But I suppose we must remember that he was born a Victorian, and was a veteran of the First World War. He was certainly a more attractive character than the dreadful bluestockings and hypocritical prigs of the Bloomsbury Group with whom he was associated for a time.

Brenan was well aware that his neighbours, first in Yegen (Granada) and later in Churriana regarded him as 'incongruous'. In his account of his attempts to transport Lytton Strachey by mule, one detects some ironic bathos, noting that Strachey must have cut a 'strange figure to meet on a country ramble . . . bearded, spectacled, very long and thin, with his coarse red nose, holding an open sun-shade above him.' Strachey had been the obstacle to — as Brenan once saw it — happiness with Dora Carrington. It would have taken a heart of stone not to have enjoyed the great literary figure's discomfort at that moment: crucified by his haemorrhoids, suffering in the heat and repulsed by Spanish food.

It's fair to say that Brenan's fathering of a child with his maid in 1931 raised eyebrows at the time, and has done ever since, not least because the maid, Juliana Pelegrina, was 15 and Brenan 37. The standard account has been that Gerald packed the child (a girl baptized Elena but later called Miranda Helen) off to England and thereafter ignored her (it is also entirely possible that Brenan was not the natural father at all). Yet in a reminder of how much interest there is even today in Brenan, the *ayuntamiento* acquired a new cache of letters as recently as 2023, shedding new light on the relationship between father and daughter. Their letters, in fact, reveal a warm and loving relationship. Miranda would marry a French physician, Xavier Corre, in London and have two children of her own. Relations were certainly warm enough for Brenan's grandson, Stéphan Corre, to attend his funeral.

The genuinely sad part of the story is the intense sorrow experienced by Juliana, something explored by the journalist Antonio Ramos Espejo in his 1990 book *Ciega en Granada* ('Blind Woman in Granada'). He recounts the heart-rending tale of Juliana studying every young Englishwoman she saw in Granada. Her daughter, whom she had not seen since the outbreak of the Civil War, had a form of syndactyly (a pair of fused toes) as she did herself. Juliana, already losing her eyesight to diabetes, took to hanging around shoe shops obsessed with the hope of encountering someone who might be her daughter. She would die in 1980 at the age of 64, unaware that her beloved and long lost 'Elena' had died of cancer, aged 49, only two months earlier.

And yet, despite Brenan's 'incongruity' and details of his life which many find troubling, he was hugely respected by his neighbours, as a writer, and as a lover of Spain, of Andalucía and of Málaga. Famously, he bequeathed his remains to the Málaga University Medical School and there is a (perhaps apocryphal) story that students refused to dissect such a respected adopted citizen of Málaga. Whether they cut him up or not, 14 years exactly after his death, his body was cremated and interred in the Anglican Cemetery in Málaga beside his wife, Gamel, who had predeceased him. In total, he wrote some fifty books, most of them on Spanish themes, but ranging across history, social commentary, culture, travel, memoir and poetry.

The Málaga *Ayuntamiento* spent ten years and over €1 million to create the Casa Gerald Brenan as a centre to foster connections between British and Spanish writers and help promote the culture of Andalucía among the British. Given such an investment, it seems odd that the Casa does not have a dedicated website and relies on Facebook/Meta, but there we are. I love this place, but then I love reading Brenan. For visitors unfamiliar with Brenan and his works, it may feel disappointing, but for anyone with an interest in Spain or travel writing, it will be a fascinating experience.

🔔 Cofradía Museums

Practically every *cofradía* or *hermandad* (religious fraternity) in Málaga has a small museum of some kind, in which the paraphernalia of *Semana Santa* are displayed. This does not mean the statues of Jesus and Mary — they will be in the churches or 'temples' of the fraternity — but everything else: thrones, banners, costumes, candles, incense burners, veils, canopies, lanterns, dalmatics, etc. Most are not routinely open to the public, because each *casa hermandad* is run by volunteers and it would not be economically viable as public museums.

🔔 Museo del Arte Cofrade–Semana Santa de Málaga

🏛 CENTRO HISTÓRICO   📍 Calle Muro de San Julián 2
🌐 ⓔ agrupaciondecofradias.com 🕐 Mon–Fri 1000–1400, 1700–2100 ⊖

This museum is operated by the grouped Holy Week fraternities. The museum was inaugurated in 2010 in the building that housed the Old Hospital of San Julián, a building from the late 17th century built by the Brotherhood of Santa Caridad de Cristo. It is not, therefore, a collection of the patrimony of a single brotherhood, but an exhibition about Holy Week in general, explaining the art, decoration and key elements of the processions. Even two years after the relaxation of COVID measures, the museum had not reopened, but presumably it will at some point (and perhaps it already has). Opening times can be unpredictable and sporadic, so to avoid disappointment, check ahead: **museo@agrupaciondecofradias.com** 📞 +34 952 210 400

🔔 Museo de la Cofradía Estudiantes

🏛 CENTRO HISTÓRICO   📍 Calle Alcazabilla 3
🌐 ⓔ cofradiaestudiantes.es ✉ info@cofradiaestudiantes.es
📞 +34 952 221 264

🔔 Museo de la Cofradía del Santo Sepulcro

🏛 CENTRO HISTÓRICO   📍 Calle Alcazabilla 5
🌐 ⓔ hermandadsepulcro.org ✉ secretaria@hermandadsepulcro.org
📞 +34 952 602 150

These two brotherhood houses are next door to one another, just opposite the Teatro Romano. They both have museums, but opening has been sporadic since the COVID lockdowns. If you spend more than a day in Málaga, you are likely to walk past them both a few times, so if you see the door open, call in and ask if the museum is open. Or send an email.

⚱ Other Museums

Museo de la Imaginación (p. 278)
Museo Interactivo de la Música (p. 279)

Temporary Exhibitions and Entertainment

As a provincial capital, Málaga has a number of theatres and cinemas, as well as various venues for exhibitions and performances. Only Madrid and Barcelona are large enough to maintain genre-specific theatres (such as opera houses), so the theatres in Málaga stage a variety of genres, from opera to musicals, Rachmaninov to Rock, ballet to flamenco, Lope de Vega (the 'Spanish Shakespeare') to pantomime.

🎭 🎬 *Teatros & Cines* (Theatres & Cinemas)

🎭 Teatro Cervantes and Teatro Echegaray

🎟 LA MERCED 📍 Calle Ramos Marín 🌐 🔗 teatrocervantes.com

The Teatro Cervantes is Málaga's flagship theatre with a capacity of 1,171, and it is the main venue for opera performances staged by the *Orquesta Filarmónica de Málaga* and the *Coro de Ópera de Málaga* (**corodeoperademalaga.org**). Built in the 19th century, it was initially called the Teatro del Príncipe Alfonso and, later, after the abdication of the Bourbon monarchy, the Teatro de la Libertad (Liberty Theatre). By the 1950s, it was in poor condition and was converted into a cinema. In 1984, the *ayuntamiento* purchased the building and embarked upon a massive programme of restoration. It reopened on 6 April 1987, in the presence of Her Majesty Queen Sofía of Spain, a tireless champion of the arts. The Teatro Cervantes is also the main venue during the Málaga Spanish Film Festival, one of the biggest cultural events in the city.

🎟 CENTRO HISTÓRICO 📍 Calle Echegaray 6 🌐 🔗 teatroechegaray.es

With only one-third the capacity of the Teatro Cervantes, Teatro Echegaray is another recently restored theatre. In fact, built in 1932, it was originally constructed as a cinema. It was purchased by the *ayuntamiento* in 2001 and completely restored, being remodelled according to a new design intended to be faithful to the 1930s 'spirit' of the original. An interesting design feature is that the seats are attached to retractable 'bleachers', so that capacity can be increased or decreased according to the requirements of the performance. It reopened in 2009.

The theatres effectively share a website. Choose 'All Programmes' from the menu to see upcoming performances in both theatres, plus screenings of drama and opera at Cine Albéniz.

🎭 Teatro Soho CaixaBank

🎟 SOHO 📍 Calle Córdoba 13 🌐 🖼 🔗 teatrodelsoho.com

This is another theatre that began life as a cinema (Cine Pascualini), in 1907. Its owner, Emilio Pascual Martos, made a name for himself bringing big American films to Málaga until a bomb destroyed the building during the Civil War. The current building dates from 1961, re-opened as the Teatro–Cine Alameda, and at the time it was the only large-format private theatre in Andalucía. Still privately owned, it is now the Teatro del Soho CaixaBank, operated by an arts company created and promoted by the *malagueño* actor, director, producer, and now philanthropist, Antonio Banderas. It incorporates a performing arts centre and operates as a non-profit. It (re)opened late in 2019 with a première of the musical A Chorus Line.

Unlike the municipally owned theatres, the Soho CaixaBank stages only two or three productions per month, and they tend to be at the more 'popular' end of things (musicals rather than operas, contemporary dramas rather than Golden Age tragedies). Even so, operating a theatre without public money is a considerable achievement and Don Antonio deserves great credit for pulling it off. Business sponsorship is significant, mind you, with the banking giant Caixa being the chief sponsor.

🎬 Cine Albéniz

🏙 CENTRO HISTÓRICO ⦿ Calle Alcazabilla 4 ⊕ ⓔ ✎ cinealbeniz.com

The Cine Albéniz is a four-screen cinema on Calle Alcazabilla. Since 2008 it has been owned by the *ayuntamiento* and its management is delegated to the arms-length company formed to run the Málaga Film Festival. It is Málaga's main 'art' cinema, so this is a good place to come if you want to see an undubbed film ('VOSE' or '*Versión Original con Subtítulos en Español*').

🎬 Cine Yelmo

🏙 EL PERCHEL ⦿ C.C. Vialia, Explanada de la Estación
⊕ ⓔ yelmocines.es

This is a popular 'high street' cinema on the upper floor of the Vialia shopping centre in the María–Zambrano railway station. Though most films are dubbed, there are still a few VOSE screenings. Use the QR code to consult the programme.

🎬🎭 🎵 English Cemetery (Las Noches del Inglés)

🏙 LA MALAGUETA ⦿ Avenida de Pries 1 ⊕ ⊕ lasnochesdelingles.com

Beginning in 2023, the English Cemetery stages evening concerts, drama and films between July and September. Tickets are a bargain and entry is free for children 12 and under. There is also a *terraza* bar serving food and drinks.

🎵 Museo Jorge Rando

🏙 LA GOLETA ⦿ Calle Cruz del Molinillo 12 ⊕ museojorgerando.org

Before the interruption of COVID, the museum held regular free chamber concerts on Saturday lunchtimes in the chapel of the Mercederías Monastery next door. More recently, however, their concerts have been held in the evenings, and sometimes in other locations. During the summer, daytime concerts are held in the museum's central patio. Use the QR code to check the website's 'Events' section or keep an eye on their Twitter feed @museojorgerando. Concerts are almost always free, but sometimes one needs to book by email.

🎵 Sala María Cristina

🏙 LA GOLETA ⦿ Calle Marqués de Valdecañas 2
⊕ ⓔ ✎ fundacionunicaja.com

The Sala María Cristina is a music auditorium managed by the Unicaja Foundation. It is located in part of what was formerly the Franciscan Convent of San Luis El Real. After its confiscation in 1836, some of the buildings were used to house the *liceo*, a cultural society founded in 1843 on the initiative of the then mayor, Pedro Gómez Sancho, and an institution that came to have a great influence on the political and cultural life of Málaga society. At the beginning of the 20th century, the Conservatory of Music was transferred to this building, renamed for Queen María Cristina in recognition of her support of the project. After the construction in 1971 of a new headquarters for the Conservatory of Music in the *barrio* of El Ejido, the building was briefly occupied by a religious community (the Sisters of Nazareth). In 1975 it was acquired by the *Caja de Ahorros de Ronda* (Ronda Savings Bank), and rehabilitated according to a design by the architect Enrique Atencia, for use as a cultural venue.

The public parts of the complex are the Hall of Mirrors, the Salón Mudéjar, and the concert hall. The concert hall itself was originally the nave of the convent chapel and has exquisite acoustics, the Salón Mudéjar is notable for its finely decorated coffered ceiling, which had been hidden for many years but is reckoned to be one of the finest examples of *mudéjar* woodwork in Spain. The Hall of Mirrors, which forms the foyer, is filled with Venetian mirrors with beautiful gilded frames. During the Portuguese earthquake of 1755, the mirrors cracked. An unknown artist then painted flowers on the mirrors, to hide the cracks. The ceiling murals were created by Jose Denis Belgrano, Martinez de la Vega, and Jose Nogales.

In 2019, Fernando Mira (one of the owners of the Casa Mira ice cream brand) opened a café (Libo Café) on the premises, but it closed 'temporarily' in 2022 and whether it reopens remains to be seen. I hope that it does because it was one of the most elegant places in Málaga to enjoy coffee and an ice cream, particularly when accompanied by the sound of a chamber group practising in one of the nearby music rooms.

 The concerts tend in the main to be classical and 'light classical' chamber concerts, which are appropriate to the venue, but pop, rock and jazz are staged too. Unfortunately, the Unicaja website is not terribly user-friendly and often it does not even list all upcoming concerts. It is worth checking a general ticket site like taquilla.com (use the QR code).

𝄞🎬🎭🕺🖼 Centro Cultural La Térmica
🍽 CARRETERA DE CÁDIZ 📍 Avenida de los Guindos 48
🌐 ⓒ ✦ latermicamalaga.com

La Térmica is a centre for contemporary cultural creation and production, managed by the *Diputación de Málaga*. As a cultural and social space, there is room for all forms of artistic expression, from the performing arts to fashion, through cinema, plastic arts, music, design, architecture, urban planning, and landscaping. Regular (mainly classical) concerts are held in the adjoining Auditorio Edgar Neville named after Edgar Neville Romrée the Conde de Berlanga de Duero, a pioneer of Spanish cinema. Check bit.ly/EdgarNev for tickets to concerts at the Edgar Neville Auditorium.

𝄞🎬🎭🕺🖼 Centro Cultural MVA
🍽 SAN FELIPE NERÍ 📍 Calle Ollerías 34 🌐 ⓒ ✦ centroculturalmva.es

The Centro Cultural MVA (María Victoria Atencia — one of Málaga's best-known contemporary poets, born in 1931) is a cultural space operated by the *Diputación de Málaga* in the city centre. It stages a variety of concerts, classical and modern dance, plays, musicals and poetry readings as well as mounting exhibitions.

🕺𝄞Sala Joaquín Eléjar
🍽 LAS FLORES 📍 Calle San Juan Bosco 79 🌐 ⓒ ✦ maynake.es

The Maynake Cultural Collective is a non-profit association founded in 1981. They stage a variety of shows including theatre, concerts, comedy, etc.

📅 Event Listings

🌐 ⓒ ✦ mientrada.net
This is the ticket purchase portal operated by the *Diputación* for the venues they operate (Centro Cultural MVA, La Térmica, Sala Joaquín Eléjar and others). It also sells tickets for some events in Marbella, Nerja and other towns.

⊕©✦ mmalaga.es

Más Málaga is a great site to find out what's going on and what's coming up in the city of Málaga and surrounding areas. The most helpful section is the '*eventos gratuitos (o casi)*' (free or nearly free events) listing which is a good way to find out about free concerts, exhibitions, cultural events, community celebrations, food festivals, etc. It is far easier to find out from this site when the next free Sunday morning chamber recital at the Málaga Museum is taking place than it is from the museum's own website. Content only in Spanish.

⊕©✦ conciertos.club/malaga

One of the best websites for music listings, covering all genres from opera and classical to Hip Hop with flamenco in between. It is especially useful for finding out about jazz, swing, blues or folk bands playing in small venues like pubs and bars. Content in Spanish.

⊕©✦ malagadecultura.com

Málaga de Cultura is a news and reviews website about the Málaga cultural scene, but it carries a very comprehensive listing of upcoming events. Content in Spanish.

⊕©✦ visita.malaga.eu

The official *turismo* website really ought to be the most comprehensive event listing of all, but it is not. In fact, it often has no more than a few upcoming events listed. What you need to do is use the **Spanish** version of the website. Lo and behold, that short list of a handful of events suddenly grows to dozens!

💃 Flamenco

Before COVID, Málaga had a settled weekly timetable of flamenco concerts, demonstrations and *tablao* shows, but the venues were hit hard by the restrictions, both those imposed upon licensed premises and upon entertainment (*tablao* is the typical *andaluz* pronunciation of *tablado* and refers to the wooden stage on which flamenco is performed; in this case, it means a floor show in a bar or restaurant). It will take some time for a new rhythm to be re-established.

Some will tell you that Málaga is not a place in which to see flamenco, which is of course nonsense. It is certainly a far more obvious place to see authentic flamenco than, say, Madrid or Benidorm. Perhaps what these people mean is that the flamenco in Málaga is different to that seen in Granada or Sevilla, which is true. Flamenco is a hugely varied art form with countless influences, patterns of development and expressions. The *palos* (or styles) of flamenco fit into three broad categories: the most serious is known as *cante jondo* (or *cante grande*), while lighter, 'frivolous' forms are called *cante chico*. Forms that do not fit either category are classed as *cante intermedio*. Among these *cantos* there are hundreds of sub-divisions. The *siguiriyas* that first emerged in 18th Century Cádiz, Sevilla and Jerez de la Frontera, for example, are slow, majestic and tragic, the most *jondo* of *cante jondo* forms with lyrics focussing on tragedy, inconsolable sorrow, and pain.

Malagueñas are Málaga's contribution. *Fandangos de Málaga* is the name given to a broad array of flamenco forms which, taken together, seem to have little in common. Part of the confusion stems from the fact that the term *fandango* is used across the Spanish-speaking world to refer to a wide range of songs and dances. Within this division, there are *fandangos de Huelva* and *fandangos naturales*. All of these forms are related to the *verdiales*: traditional folk songs from the mountains around Málaga. It also includes the dance forms of *verdiales*, *abandolaos*, *jaberas*, *malagueñas* and *rondeñas*.

The best places to see top-quality flamenco performances in Málaga are the theatres, like the Cervantes and Echegaray, so check their programmes to see if they have any flamenco coming up. The **Museo Flamenco Peña Juan Breva (Calle Ramón Franquelo 4)** is also a good place. They used to have concerts on Thursday, Friday and Saturday evenings and perhaps these have started again, but information on their rather clunky website (**peñajuanbreva.eu**) is scant. The best thing is to pay them a visit and book in person. **MIMMA (Museo Interactivo de la Música Málaga, Calle Beatas 15 musicaenaccion.com/eventos**) also stages regular flamenco demonstrations in the afternoon — a far more suitable time for families than the late-night shows in bars. They also put on other concerts that are often free with a museum entry ticket.

The ⊕ **guiaflama.com** website (only in Spanish) is a useful source of information about flamenco performances and events in Málaga (indeed, all over Spain). They also sell tickets to some *tablaos*.

The other options for seeing decent flamenco are the aforementioned *tablaos*. A few of the best-known are:

⚔️🍴 El Gallo Ronco ✹✹

🏛️ CENTRO HISTÓRICO 📍 Plaza de las Flores 1 ⊕ elgalloronco.com

This bar (the name of which means 'hoarse rooster') has flamenco shows from Wednesday to Saturday at 1900 and 2100. You can opt for the basic ticket which includes a drink and a *tapita* or you can pay more for a drink and a *surtido ibérico* (selection of ham, sausage and cheese). The bar also has a good selection of *tapas* and *raciones* but the performance *tablao* is separate from the restaurant area. There are two other branches of the bar in town (**Calle Arquitecto Blanco Soler 3** and **Calle Álamos 1**) which also sometimes have flamenco performances, but these are not bookable online. You will need to pay them a visit and enquire.

⚔️🍴 Restaurante Tablao Alegría ✹✹✹

🏛️ MALAGUETA 📍 Calle Vélez Málaga 6 ⊕ 🎗️ flamencomalaga.com

This is a flamenco-themed Restaurant near the Port of Málaga and the Pompidou Centre. It stages shows every day at 1800, 2000 and 2200. The food is good quality if you want to go for the dining option. The duration of the show is approximately 60 minutes and features well-known artists. The basic price is just for the show, but there are set menus and *à la carte* options available. The venue is fully adapted for people with limited mobility.

⚔️🍴 Restaurante Vino Mío ✹✹

🏛️ LA MERCED 📍 Plaza de Jerónimo Cuervo 2
⊕ 🎗️ restaurantevinomio.es

Situated in front of the Teatro Cervantes, Vino Mío Restaurant has a flamenco show from Wednesday to Sunday (2000–2130). You make a booking for dinner (you can do this via their website) and pay a supplement for the show. Vino Mío is an excellent choice for children and families because it puts on a show in the early evening (most customers are tourists) and because of its informality. The musicians and dancers are not positioned on a distant *tablao* in a dark venue, but literally playing and dancing among the tables in the brightly lit restaurant. Purists might not approve, but it creates a fun, relaxed atmosphere.

🏆🕴 El Pimpi ✹✹

🏛 CENTRO HISTÓRICO 📍 Calle Granada 62 ⊕ elpimpi.com

On the first Thursday of the month, *Bodegas* El Pimpi stages a flamenco *tablao* under the name '*Jaleo en El Palomar*'. Before COVID a dinner reservation was required but more recently the flamenco has been put on as post-lunch entertainment. This may change, so check the website for up-to-date information.

🏆🕴 Kelipé Centro de Arte Flamenco ✹✹

🏛 CENTRO HISTÓRICO 📍 Calle Muro de Puerta Nueva 10
⊕ Ⓒ🖉 kelipe.net

A flamenco school run by the *bailaora* Susan Manzano, the Kelipé Flamenco Art Centre is a good place to see a serious performance of flamenco. With shows every evening between Thursday and Monday, although this is not a restaurant or bar, the entrance price includes a drink (and further drinks may be purchased).

⊕ FlamencoTickets.com

This is a useful website to find out about flamenco performances not only in Málaga city but throughout the Province of Málaga (Torremolinos, Benalmádena, Fuengirola, Ronda, etc.). The website has an English language option.

🏠 *Iglesias* (Churches)

Málaga has a lot of beautiful churches, many of which have been restored in recent years. Most churches in the *centro histórico* are open in the morning (until 1300 or 1330) and then close in the afternoon before reopening in the early evening (around 1700 or 1730) for a couple of hours. The reason for these opening hours is simple and practical. Most churches have a morning and evening Mass. They open for the morning mass, they then stay open during 'office hours' (when the Parish office is open), and reopen for the evening mass. Bear in mind, however, that churches rely upon volunteers to open and close up, so a church which is 'supposed' to be open at 10 am on a Wednesday may be closed, without warning or explanation. A good plan, therefore, is to visit a church in the morning, before starting your 'programme' for the day, and then take in another before pre-dinner drinks. If you pass a church, and it looks open, have a peek inside. There will be something of interest inside, even if it is only a statue or a ceiling. Also, apart from the Cathedral, all are free to visit (⚠ donations are necessary to keep these churches open to be enjoyed by other visitors, so please be generous).

The list below is not exhaustive by any means. It includes the Cathedral and the Sagrario (which was effectively the Pro-Cathedral and is now part of the Cathedral complex), plus a half dozen notable churches in the centre. There are many more parish churches, convent chapels, wayside shrines and hermitages, all of which have something of interest to see. If you would like to get to know the ecclesiastical patrimony of Málaga better, then the best way to do so would be to do one or more of the '*Málaga Nazarena*' walking routes planned by the Grouped Holy Week Brotherhoods (see p. 411).

Opening Times

Apart from the Cathedral, where opening times are shown on the website, opening times for most other churches are at best variable and at worst unreliable or vague. Most operate a different winter (earlier) and summer (later) timetable. Keeping churches open requires volunteers, so at those times when helpful members of the parish aren't available to keep an eye on things then the church may have to close, whatever the sign outside says. A majority of city centre churches open in the morning, until lunchtime (1 or 1.30 pm), and then open again for a couple of hours after the siesta (from 5 pm or so). A very useful, and generally up-to-date website is misas.org — it works using GPS if you happen to be near the church you wish to visit, or you can use the search function. This should tell you the times of 'misas' (masses), enabling you to visit before or after (a weekday mass usually lasts about 25 minutes). No one will object to your looking into a church while mass is being celebrated, but remain quietly at the back, don't walk about and don't take photos.

Etiquette

If you are not dressed appropriately, you will probably be refused entry to the Cathedral. In other churches, you might be asked to leave but it's more likely that you'll just arouse theatrical 'tuts' from the handful of Spanish *señoras* already in the church. Enforcing minimum standards of dress is more of an issue in the resort towns of the Costa del Sol where people are more likely to be wandering around in beach attire.

The 'rules', such as they exist, are pretty much the same for men and women: no bare shoulders or thighs. That means that vest tops and 'short' shorts are not acceptable. Men must remove their hats. Be aware of logos (*e.g.* on t-shirts) or tattoos that might be considered offensive or obscene. If you have a pentagram on your t-shirt or a tattoo of a naked woman on your forearm, it will need to be covered up.

As far as I am aware, photography is permitted in all of Málaga's churches, though not with flash (because it disturbs other visitors and worshippers). As long as you keep noise to a minimum and talk, if you need to, *sotto voce*, you are free to explore, though you should not enter the sanctuary (the area around the main altar, reached by steps). Something you should look out for is if 'adoration' is taking place. This is where the Blessed Sacrament is exposed on the altar and people come to pray before it (or, for Catholics, 'Him'). The main church where this takes place every day is Santo Cristo de la Salud, but it happens in other churches too. The signs are that the candles on the altar are lit and that there is a monstrance (a decorative gold stand used to display the Eucharistic host) on the altar. During adoration, do not talk and do not walk between the altar and the people in the pews.

La Manquita (Cathedral of the Incarnation)

🏛 CENTRO HISTÓRICO 📍 Calle Císter ⊕ ✦ malagacatedral.com
🕐 Mon–Fri 1000–1930; Sat 1000–1800; Sun 1400–1800 ⊕⊖ (✦ under 13s, people with disabilities, and Mon–Sat 0830–0900) 🎧

Málaga's Cathedral divides opinion. While some think it one of the jewels of the Spanish Renaissance, Lady Louisa Tenison felt that it could not 'boast of much architectural beauty'. Hans Christian Andersen thought its appeal lay in its sheer size, calling it a 'mountain of marble' (although its tower is only 92 metres high it was — remarkably — the second tallest non-industrial structure in Andalucía until 2012). Personally, I find the exterior rather 'heavy' and overwrought, but the interior is unexpectedly light, expansive and well-balanced. Because it is surrounded by other buildings, it is easier to grasp quite how vast it is from within. As far as the height of the nave (the body of the church) is concerned, it is taller than any British cathedral save Liverpool and around the same height as Notre-Dame in Paris.

Dedicated to the Incarnation, the *Reyes Católicos* ordered the construction of a cathedral on the site of the *aljama* (main) mosque within days of taking Málaga in 1487. Thus, Málaga followed the pattern of practically every other city in Andalucía. Supplanting the 'old religion' by building over it is symbolic because sacred space is important. Almost any significant church in southern Spain is built on the site of a mosque (nowhere quite so clearly as in Córdoba), but dig a little further and you will find that the mosque was itself built over an earlier Visigothic church. Delve deeper and you will probably find pre-Visigothic paleochristian remains, themselves on top of a pagan Roman temple. It seems likely that even those pagan Roman deities will have superseded even earlier Iberian pagan deities. And then when we look at the geographical features of the location, we usually find something nearby to explain the reason for its 'sanctity', such as a hill, cave, crag, well or stream. Sure enough, in the case of Málaga, an underground river runs beneath the Cathedral (just as in London Westminster Abbey was built next to the Tyburn and St Paul's and Blackfriars beside the Fleet River).

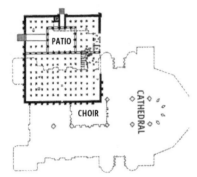

The oldest extant part of the original mosque is now the Iglesia del Sagrario (Church of the Tabernacle) which stands just to the west of the main entrance on Calle Santa María/Calle Císter. The elaborate Renaissance doorway is a subsequent addition, but some of the structure once formed the base of the minaret. No one is quite sure where the original mosque stood, but the plan on the left shows one possibility. After the *reconquista*, the mosque was simply repurposed for Christian worship but it quickly became too small for purpose. Construction of the new cathedral began in 1528 according to plans by Enrique Egas of Toledo and Diego de Siloé of Burgos who worked on several cathedrals in both Spain and the New World. The first part of the Cathedral to be constructed was the east end (the rounded part containing the altar), allowing the old mosque to continue to be used until it was ready. Work stalled for a time, beginning again under the direction of Hernán Ruiz II and Diego de Vergara, continuing until the end of the century. The Cathedral was consecrated on 3 August 1588.

With the demolition of most of the former mosque, the construction of the nave and west elevation (the left-hand side of the diagram) could begin, but this work only started at the beginning of the 18th century. To cover the enormous expense of the work, the Crown, after the War of Succession, imposed a tax to be levied at the Port of Málaga, on each *arroba* (roughly a quarter of a hundredweight) shipped. In this way, throughout the eighteenth century and especially since 1776, when trade with America began to be freed up thanks to the efforts of the Unzaga, Gálvez and Molina merchant families, work progressed rapidly. At the end of the century, the budgets to finish the work ran out because the king decreed they be sent as aid to the Americans who had risen up against the United Kingdom to gain their independence. The rest of the port tax receipts were used to rehabilitate the roads of Vélez-Málaga and Antequera, a scheme to bring water to Málaga through the San Telmo aqueduct, and a number of other infrastructure and social projects. Thus, the Cathedral was left unfinished. The south tower remains incomplete — hence its nickname *La Manquita* (The Maimed Woman). The roof, the main sacristy, the central belfry, and other sculptural ornamentation, were likewise unfinished.

The contemporary debate on the completion of the Cathedral still rages, because in addition to the non-existence of its second tower, the roof over the vaults was not completed either, which led to a serious deterioration of the fabric of the Cathedral. In 2009, the first urgent restoration of the roofs of the Cathedral was carried out by the Junta de Andalucía and in 2011, the 'Master Plan for the Cathedral of Málaga' was drafted. The *ayuntamiento*, *diputación* and the Diocese of Málaga have declared that they are in favour of the completion of the Cathedral according to the original construction plans, including the construction of the second tower. Local opinion is split. Some think that completing the Cathedral would be a powerful symbol of a resurgent, confident city, while others point out that the Cathedral's lop-sided appearance is part of what makes it unique and recognisable, arguing that completing the south tower would be like straightening the Leaning Tower of Pisa. Although the construction of the South Tower would be the most visible change, of greater importance to the structural integrity of the building is making good the roof. In 2023, the Diocese announced a 28-month programme of works costing €17 million. This would involve removing the 'brick skin' applied in 2009 and the construction of a gabled roof designed by the architects Juan Manuel Sánchez La Chica and Adolfo de la Torre Prieto.[40]

Málaga's is a Renaissance Cathedral with a baroque façade and significant Gothic elements, which makes it a bit of a muddle, but it is impressive, beautiful and well worth visiting. The audio guide is free. When I last used it, the English narrator was bizarrely unable to pronounce many of the ecclesiastical terms necessary for such a guide, but perhaps it has been updated since then. There is also an audio guide especially created for children, in Spanish, English, French and Italian.

A Something that often confuses visitors is the presence of a number of iron scroll-work structures supporting large stones (a couple are inside the building, the rest outside). These are not obscure liturgical objects but 'artworks' repurposing items left over from the restoration of the Cathedral's 12 bells in 2005. The stones represent 'absent bells', apparently.

Santa María del Sagrario

CENTRO HISTÓRICO ♀ Calle Císter

'Holy Mary of the Sacristy' is one of four churches constructed by the *Reyes Católicos* after the *reconquista*. The whitewashed interior is fairly simple (earthquakes, Napoleon and finally Republican arsonists and, later, artillery destroyed much of the original fabric of Málaga's churches), but there is an impressive plateresque retable — the work of Juan de Balmaseda, from the church of San Pedro de Becerril de Campos (Palencia). The original Gothic doorway dates from 1487 and is the oldest stonework of the cathedral complex. It was cut into the foot of the minaret of the former mosque, probably under the first post-*reconquista* bishop, Pedro Díaz de Toledo y Ovalle. The base of the original minaret is visible in the crypt. It is home to the (formerly suppressed) Brotherhood of the Mutilated Christ, now called the Brotherhood of Clemency.

Following the appearance of significant cracks in the walls of the church and an exploratory survey of the foundations, the church was closed in 2020 for both worship and tourist visits 'indefinitely'. Specialist contractors have warned that an earthquake with a magnitude of 4 or more would likely cause the structure to collapse. With Andalucía positioned between the Eurasian and African plates, earthquakes are a real risk with a significant tremor predicted to occur before the end of the century. The work necessary to stabilize the building is likely to take many years.

---

40   bit.ly/CathedralRoof

Basílica de Santa María de La Victoria

🍴 CRISTO DE LA EPIDEMIA ⊕ ⓔ santamariadelavictoria.es 🕐 0830–1300, 1830–2030 ⊘ (✞ ⓔ visit to the Crypt Tues–Sat 1000–1300*)

Some of Málaga's churches don't look much from the outside but hide fascinating interiors. The Royal Sanctuary of Santa María de la Victoria (Our Lady of Victories) is one such. The current building dates from the late 17th century, but replaced an earlier church which in turn was the expansion of a small chapel. It stands upon the spot where Fernando II camped during the siege of Málaga. During the long campaign, Fernando was visited by friars of the Order of Minims, who brought him a message from their founder (St Francis de Paola) assuring him of victory. That victory came three days later and in due course, a chapel was erected that later became the first convent of the Minims in Spain. A church and new convent were constructed in the early 16th century, then demolished and rebuilt in the late 17th century. It was raised to the status of minor basilica (that is, a papal church) by Pope Benedict XVI in 2007.

The church houses a number of important images, including that of Our Lady of Victory, patroness of the Diocese and City of Málaga, carved in Germany, a gift to Fernando II from Emperor Maximilian I. It also houses the images of the several *hermandades* that have their headquarters here, including a *dolorosa* carved by Pedro de Mena. There is also an ornate *retablo* (altarpiece) and a highly decorated dome above the crossing.

The highlight, however, is the pantheon crypt* of the Counts of Buenavista; one of the gloomiest in Spain thanks to its sombre decoration featuring skeletons and figures of death in white plaster: a Baroque discourse on death. The crypt can only be visited with a guide (see times above and note below). The guided tours are conducted by volunteers from the *cofradía* (fraternity) attached to the church.

* At the time of publication, the crypt is closed for restoration works following a devastating ingress of water from the abandoned Doctor Pascual Hospital causing considerable damage to the plasterwork. The date for it to reopen is unknown.

Santos Mártires (San Ciriaco & Santa Paula)

🍴 CENTRO HISTÓRICO 📍 Plaza de los Mártires Ciriaco y Paula ⊕ ⓔ santosmartires.es 🕐 Mon–Sat 0930–1330, 1800–2030; Sun 1100–1400

Another of the foundations of the *Reyes Católicos*, dedicated to Málaga's patron saints, martyred under Diocletian. The earliest extant documentary references to Ciriaco and Paula date only from the ninth century and some historians have suggested that they were martyred in Almería. When it comes to the Catholic idea of patron saints, geography doesn't much matter. After all, the patron saint of England was born in Asia Minor. Patronage is a matter of public devotion, and we can be reasonably certain that devotion to Ciriaco and Paula was well-established in Málaga very early on. Their cult extended throughout the Roman Province of Baetica, and the monastery of Hieronymite nuns in Sevilla, famous for their delicious jams and marmalade, is dedicated to Santa Paula. Early editions of the Roman Martyrology record the place of their execution as being beside the river Guadalmedina, a fact commemorated in the name of the *barrio* south of the football stadium: Martiricos.

The church, originally in the Gothic-*mudéjar* style, was rebuilt after the 1755 earthquake. Further rebuilding and restoration were needed after it was struck by a cannonball in 1854, and damaged by another earthquake in 1884. With each rebuilding it became more and more rococo, though it is still relatively plain on the outside. It was badly damaged in 1931 and looted in 1936. The final rebuilding began in 1945 and the most recent restoration was completed in 2022. The fact that it took 90 years to restore the church to its pre-1931 state shows quite how devastating the damage was. Five Holy Week brotherhoods have this church as their '*templo*'. (*i.e.* the church where their processional statues normally reside).

San Juan Bautista

CENTRO HISTÓRICO ♀ Calle San Juan 3

Saint John the Baptist is another of the foundational parishes erected by the *Reyes Católicos* and was originally a Gothic and *mudéjar* (Moorish style) building, but it was badly damaged in the earthquake of 1680 and was rebuilt in a more baroque style. In 1931 it was attacked by Republicans and many polychromatic wooden statues by Alonso Cano and others were destroyed, along with paintings by Murillo. In 1980, another fire destroyed the statues that had been saved in 1931. This church is the headquarters of the *Cofradías Fusionadas* — the eight ancient fraternities that merged

in 1980 in order to raise funds for the restoration of the church and its Holy Week processional images. A member of this fraternity is the actor Antonio Banderas and he has been closely involved in fundraising to pay for the church's restoration.

The plaster walls of San Juan are painted with geometric patterns. This style became popular in the early 18th century and is known as '*horror vacui*' (horror of emptiness). This mode of decoration was soon extended to secular buildings, adding *trompe-l'œil* elements like columns, sculptures, stone blocks and bricks. During the nineteenth century, these wall paintings disappeared under layers of lime whitewash applied as an anti-epidemic measure, but they have been uncovered again as a result of restoration efforts. Other mural paintings can be seen in the Church of El Sagrario, the Parish Church of Los Santos Mártires, the Church of Santiago, the Church of San Felipe Neri, Calle Carretería 23, the Glass Museum and Calle Panaderos.

Santiago Apóstol

CENTRO HISTÓRICO ♀ Calle Granada 78 ⏰ Mon–Sun 0900–1300, 1800–2100

Saint James the Apostle is another foundation of the *Reyes Católicos*. Though it has baroque elements aplenty, this church retains the clearest evidence of the local *mudéjar* architectural style. It was built on the site of a mosque, and at the time of its construction, Málaga would have looked more like Marrakesh than the Málaga of today. The *mudéjar* footprint is most clearly seen in the 16th-century bell tower. Until the consecration of the Cathedral, Santiago served as the pro-cathedral. Initially, the former mosque was used for Christian worship, but construction of the church had begun by 1505 and was

267

complete by 1545 (though the structure has been enlarged and reordered many times since). You may be told that the tower is the minaret of the former mosque. While it may be constructed on the foundations of the minaret, it is actually a new structure. The most famous Holy Week image inside the church is the 'El Rico' Christ and several fraternities are based here. Extensive restoration work has been undertaken recently and the church reopened for worship in July 2017. Picasso was baptized here.

The church is known especially for a popular local devotion centred upon praying for the souls in Purgatory and is home to the *Cuadro de Ánimas* (c.1665), a famous painting by Juan Niño de Guevara, a disciple of the *granadino* painter Alonso Cano[41]. According to the teaching of the Catholic Church, many of those who die spend a period in a state called Purgatory. This is not a place of separation and suffering (like Hell), but of purification. The souls in Purgatory are destined for Heaven, but they first need to learn to let go of earthly attachments. The painting shows two aspects of the 'Communion of Saints'. At the top of the canvas is seated the Virgin Mary, with the infant Jesus standing on an orb, as creator and redeemer. Alongside them, on the right, is the figure of St James (Santiago), the patron of the parish, and to their left, an angel. This ensemble represents the 'Church Triumphant'.

Below them is a collection of naked figures reaching upwards towards heaven. Their countenance is not marked by pain or suffering (like those terrifying and disfigured depictions of Hell by van Eyck or Bosch), but by hope, piety and serenity. These are the souls in Purgatory or the 'Church Suffering'. Above them, the Blessed Virgin intercedes for them and the Child Jesus awaits them as their just judge. The Angel reaches down to lift them upwards into heaven while Saint James, dressed in the garb of a pilgrim, pours grace upon them in the form of liquid from a ewer. But there is a third aspect of the Communion of Saints: the 'Church Militant'. That is made up of living men and women on earth. Thus the painting is 'completed' by the person or people looking at it. The three together tell the story of Salvation: life on earth, suffering in Purgatory, and joy in Heaven, with Jesus Christ at the head.

But what makes the *Cuadro de Ánimas* more than just a painting is the devotion it inspires. Praying for the dead (that is, the souls in Purgatory) is a universally popular Catholic practice and every Catholic church will have a donation box marked 'Holy Souls' (this money is used to pay for masses to be celebrated). In the church of Santiago, however, the offerings take the form of oil. Ostensibly, this is to supply the oil lamps that burn continually in front of the painting. These flames symbolize the prayers of the parishioners (the 'Church Militant'). So the dynamic of the painting is enriched. The souls in Purgatory are lifted up by Christ's grace (poured out by Saint James as his apostle or minister) and by the angel, but as well as being lifted up, they are also, as it were, 'pushed up' by the prayers of those on earth.

It takes about 10 litres of oil to keep the lamps lit for a year, but more than 3,000 litres is left in offering **every month**. This oil is distributed by the parish (or the Holy Week fraternities associated with it) to more than 30 local charities that work with the poor running social projects, soup kitchens, residential homes, children's groups and so forth.

The name of the patronal saint, Santiago, is a curiosity. In Spanish, male saints are *San* and female saints are *Santa* (for reasons of euphony, '*santo*' is used with Domingo, Tomás, Tomé and Toribio). But Santiago, uniquely, is one word. This reflects local usage in Galicia where *gallego* is spoken. The Latin *Iacobus* became Iago or Yagüe, to give Sant Iago. Its popularity as a battle cry led to it being blended as one word — Santiago — so Spanish boys baptized 'James' are called 'Santiago' (but invariably shortened to Santi, Yago, Diego, Chago, or Tiago).

---

41   *q.v.* José Domínguez Cubero, 'El Cuadro de Ánimas de la parroquia de Santiago, de Málaga' in *Boletin de Arte* (Universidad de Málaga, Departamento de Historia de Arte), No. 32–33 (2012), pp. 223–232

Santo Cristo de la Salud

CENTRO HISTÓRICO ⬤ Calle Compañía 4

This baroque church ('The Holy Christ of Health') was designed by Pedro Sánchez for his own order, the Jesuits (Society of Jesus), and opened in 1630. It is unusual in having a circular floor plan beneath the central dome (no aisles or transepts). After the expulsion of the Jesuits in 1767, the church was taken over by the civil authorities. The dome is a *trompe-l'œil* rendering of masonry, with portraits of saints, and was completely restored in 2014. In 2016, Santo Cristo was returned to ecclesiastical use after a three-year restoration project. Málaga has a rich Holy Week tradition, and like most *malagueña* churches, Santo Cristo is the headquarters of *cofradías* that carry the *tronos* (floats) during Holy Week, including the Brotherhood of Students who carry Christ Crowned with Thorns, and Our Lady of Grace and Hope.

Santo Domingo de Guzmán

MÁRMOLES ⬤ Calle Cerrojo ⊕ Mon–Sat 0900–1300, 1700–2000

St Dominic's is just across the river from the *centro histórico*, in El Perchel, and was originally the chapel of a vast 15th-century Dominican priory. It was the oldest ecclesiastical foundation to be built outside the medieval city walls, and it remains the largest city church after the Cathedral. The Dominicans were invited to establish a convent (friars live in convents, monks and nuns live in monasteries) in the city in 1489 and along with the Franciscans they were among the first religious orders to arrive in Málaga.

The convent reached its apotheosis in the 17th century with the arrival of Fray Alonso de Santo Tomás in 1656. Fray Alonso, born in Vélez-Málaga in 1631, was the illegitimate son of King Felipe IV and Constanza de Ribera y Orozco, Queen Isabel's lady-in-waiting. When Constanza got pregnant, she was hastily married off to José Enríquez de Guzmán y de Porres, the Count of Castronuevo and gentleman of the king's chamber. The product of the affair, Alonso, would become the Provincial of the Dominican Order in Andalucía and be named Bishop of Osma, then Plasencia, and finally Málaga.

So far, so typical, for 16th-century church and society in which aristocratic nepotism was rife, you might think. But Alonso was a man of genuine holiness and principle. When his half-brother Baltasar, the Prince of Asturias, died aged 16 in 1646, Felipe IV made efforts to legitimize Alonso and receive him at court. His overtures were rejected, with Alonso informing his natural father that he intended to enter the Order of Preachers (Dominicans). Admittedly, he would live a very comfortable life as a bishop, constructing a country estate in Churriana, but had he chosen to, he could well have become King of Spain.

He sent aid to Orán (in modern-day Algeria, then a Spanish possession) when it succumbed to the plague, and when that same plague reached Málaga in 1679, he brought the Brothers of Saint John of God to the city to establish a hospital. He also spearheaded relief efforts following the devastating earthquake of 1680. A gifted theologian and orator, his fame today is largely due to his patronage of the arts. In his youth, he had known Velázquez, and as Bishop of Málaga, he was patron and protector of Pedro de Mena and Alonso Cano. Alonso de Santo Tomás himself, as a novice, was the subject of one of the last portraits painted by Juan Bautista Maino (a canvas which leaves the young friar's true paternity in little doubt).

There is no sign of the enhancements made by Fray Alonso now, however. In fact, very little of the original fabric remains. The church sustained significant damage in the earthquake of 1680 and had to be rebuilt, and its riverside position means that it suffered repeated flood damage. The priory was confiscated in the 19th century, forcing the friars to leave the city, and in 1931, most of the church was destroyed by arson. The friars returned in 1988 but handed the church back to the diocese in 2012, ending a connection with Málaga that hitherto had spanned more than 500 years.

It is nowadays rather plain on the inside, though this perhaps comes as a relief after the wedding-cake baroque and rococo elsewhere. The chief reason to pay a visit, however, is that Santo Domingo houses the (life-size) crucifix statue of the *Cristo de la Buena Muerte*, originally carved in 1660 by Pedro de Mena. That image was destroyed by rioters in 1931 and the current image was carved in Málaga in 1941 by Francisco Palma Burgos. During *Semana Santa*, when it is being transferred from the church to the headquarters of the fraternity next door, this image is carried aloft by soldiers of the Spanish Foreign Legion in a display, some would say, almost as camp as it is macho...

San Felipe Neri

 SAN FELIPE NERI Calle Cabello 20 Thu 1000–1300; Tue–Thu 1800–1900

This church, from the 18th century, is the result of multiple extensions and reforms since the construction of the primitive chapel which was ordered to be built by Antonio Tomás Guerrero Coronado and Zapata, the Second Count of Buenavista. Construction began in 1720 and the first chapel opened in 1730. Several religious orders were interested in establishing a house to serve the church but the Count granted it to the Oratorians (founded by Saint Philip Neri) because he had planned to dedicate it to the same saint and he took this to be a premonition. The Oratorian Fathers took possession on 11 November 1738. At the beginning of July of the following year, the Count of Buenavista ceded the church to them, as well as a house located next to the church, and several others nearby.

The dimensions of the new chapel were modest, and Cardinal Molina Lario determined the need for an extension, with the expenses to be borne by the Count of Buenavista, but the death of both, in 1744 and 1745 respectively, frustrated the project. Work would begin in 1750, stalling many times through lack of funds. In 1771, the works resumed, under the direction of the great architects of the baroque, Ventura Rodríguez and Martín de Aldehuela. The congregation suffered two confiscations. The first, under the French, proved to be temporary, but with the establishment of the liberal regime in 1833, ecclesiastical confiscation took place through the Royal Decree of March 8, 1836, which provided for the suppression of all houses of religion, including that of the Oratorians of Málaga. The church was set on fire in 1931. On the Calle Parra and Plaza Montaño, bonfires were made with objects taken from the church. Four sculptures by Pedro de Mena and four paintings by Miguel de Manrique were stolen, burned or otherwise destroyed.

Since the 1970s, following considerable repairs and further accidental discoveries, a series of paintings has emerged that decorate part of the side of the church. These paintings have been the object of expert restoration carried out by the Ministry of Culture of the *Junta de Andalucía*. Between September 2010 and November 2011, the Church was closed for a thorough restoration, though its Baroque splendour emerged undimmed.

Nuestra Señora del Carmen

⑭ EL PERCHEL **♀ Calle Plaza de Toros Vieja**
23 ⊕ ⓔ elcarmenmalaga.es ⏱ Mon–Fri 0800–1230, 1730–2030

Our Lady of Mount Carmel is another relatively old (late 16th c.) church in the *barrio* of El Perchel. In 1584 the Discalced Carmelite convent of San Andrés was built (taking its dedication from an earlier hermitage situated near the beach). Suffering severe damage in the earthquake of 1680, the church would be extensively remodelled in the 18th century. The liberal General José María de Torrijos and his 49 companions were brought to the Convent on 10 December 1831 and placed in the chapel, ostensibly so that their confessions could be heard. They were executed by firing squad the next day on the beach of San Andrés. In 1835 the convent was disentailed and the community expelled the following year. The *ayuntamiento* took possession of the chapel, though masses continued to be celebrated.

In 1931, almost the entire patrimony of the church was destroyed, including multiple works by Pedro de Mena. Those treasures that remained were destroyed during the Civil War. The Claretian Order took possession in 1937 and the church was partially restored in the 1940s under the direction of the diocesan architect, Enrique Atencia, who designed the current altarpiece. In the current century, there have been further works to stabilize the structure and deal with a persistent damp problem.

The church has three naves with side chapels and a wide transept. The main chapel and arms of the transept are covered with half-barrel vaults with lunettes and frames for plasterwork. The Virgen del Carmen (by the Granada sculptor José Navas Parejo, 1945) is located in a niche. The church is also the *sede canónica* of the images of Jesús Nazareno de la Misericordia (carved by José Navas Parejo from Granada, 1944) and the Virgen del Gran Poder (an image of the 18th century Málaga circle, restored by the *sevillano* sculptor Álvarez Duarte).

San Lázaro

⑭ LA VICTORIA **♀ Plaza de la Victoria 19** ⏱ 0900–1300, 1800–2000

Founded by the *Reyes Católicos* in 1491, this was initially intended as a chapel for the Hospital de San Lázaro, established for the treatment of leprosy. Nowadays only the chapel remains, since the rest of the facilities suffered extensive damage during the floods of 1628. After its repair, it played an important role during the plague epidemic of 1637. Since 1706 it has been the headquarters of the Sacramental Brotherhood of *Nuestro Padre Jesús Nazareno de los Pasos del Monte Calvario* which processes with the image of *María Santísima del Rocío*, known in the city as the 'Bride of Málaga' (and the reason that the brotherhood is popularly known as '*El Rocío*').

In 1948, the church was restored under the direction of the architect Enrique Atencia, with funding from the Civil Government and the *Cofradía del Rocío* after the burning of convents in 1931 and 1936 in which practically all of its patrimony was lost. It is a popular church for the celebration of marriages on account of its beautiful altarpiece and association with the 'Bride of Málaga'.

San Agustín

📍 CENTRO HISTÓRICO ♀ Calle San Agustín 7 ⏰ Sun 0930–1230; Mon–Fri 1730–1930

Until the disentailments and confiscations of the nineteenth century, Málaga was full of friars — Augustinians, Franciscans, Dominicans, Capuchins, Mercedarians, Minims, Trinitarians and Carmelites. Although the Carmelites have returned to the city (they look after the church of Stella Maris on the Alameda Principal), only the Augustinians still occupy their original location.

Construction of the complex (consisting of a convent, church and former school, with the first two visible from Calle San Agustín, next to the Picasso Museum) began in 1575 following the purchase of land on what was then called the Calle de los Caballeros. In 1843, after Mendizábal 's confiscation, the buildings were seized by the State and ceded to the Málaga *Ayuntamiento*. They were later commandeered to serve as a hospital during the African War of 1863–1865. The buildings were put to various different uses until the friars re-founded a school in 1918. In 1931, it was set on fire during the burning of convents under the Second Spanish Republic, but with a hiatus during the Civil War, the school functioned until 1972, when it moved to the outskirts of the city, where its current school (Los Olivos) is still located.

The church consists of three luminous naves, with a main chapel where there is a fine altarpiece designed by the *turolense* (viz. from Teruel, Aragón) architect José Martín de Aldehuela in 1798 housing a monumental sculpture of San Agustín, carved after the Civil War by Father Félix Granda. Several canvases are of interest: in the chancel a San Juan de Dios by Juan Niño de Guevara, and in the transept an Immaculate Conception from the early 17th century.

The altar and the pulpit are of some interest, both made of red marble (17th century). The church opens onto an attractive courtyard with a baroque doorway, also the work of Aldehuela. In 2004 the fabric was significantly restored. In one of its chapels, Saint Rita de Cascia — an Italian Augustinian saint from the 15th century, patroness of marriage and the family and 'advocate of the impossible' — is venerated. On her feast day (22 May) there is a tradition of blessing and distributing thousands of roses. At the time of publication San Agustín, which is not a parish church, is the only church in Málaga where on Sundays and feast days the extraordinary form of Mass (the so-called 'Old Rite' in Latin) is celebrated.

La Aurora y Divina Providencia

📍 CENTRO HISTÓRICO ♀ Calle Andrés Pérez 15 ⏰ Mon–Sat 1100–1300; Mon–Fri 1700–1900

The Church of Our Lady of The Dawn and Divine Providence was constructed in the 18th century (1787). A schoolteacher from El Perchel, Juan Sanchez, established a group of laypeople that came together at daybreak to pray the Rosary. This *hermandad de gloria* grew in popularity and came to the attention of the Dominican friars, traditionally promoters of the Holy Rosary. A married couple, Manuel Francisco de Anaya and Margarita del Villar, bequeathed their property (a number of houses) to the Dominican nuns provided they were able to build a monastery and chapel within eight years.

For the next two hundred years or so, this church was the sisters' chapel and was adopted as the '*sede canónica*' of the Fraternity of the Vintners (*Hermandad Sacramental de Viñeros*) in 1950. The nuns withdrew from their monastery in 2006 and in 2013 the Diocese of Málaga handed the chapel to the *hermandad* to use as their *templo* (canonical seat or church), on the understanding that they would care for the fabric and ensure its upkeep. They subsequently embarked upon an ambitious programme of restoration costing hundreds of thousands of euros (when they took possession, the chapel was not even supplied with electricity).

The church is in the Baroque style, with some elements of austere Rococo. It has a neoclassical doorway of white limestone, with a semicircular arch, topped with a niche that houses a sculpture of Divine Providence. On the façade, there are several mosaics, such as the *Nazareno* (Alfonso Chaves Tejada and Ramos Rejano, Seville, 1950s). The nave has a box plan and culminates with an 18th-century altarpiece, which was restored in 1951 by Cristóbal Velasco, presided over by an image of the *Nazareno de Viñeros* (a carving of Christ carrying his cross).

Basílica de María Santísima de la Esperanza

🍴 Mármoles ⚲ Calle San Jacinto 1 🕒 Mon–Sat 0930–1300, 1800–2100; Sun 1100–1300

This is another brotherhood temple (The Archconfraternity of *El Paso y La Esperanza*) of recent construction. Built in 1988 and raised to the status of a minor basilica the same year, the single nave is fairly plain, but a richly gilded apse above the high altar forms the *camarín* ('dressing room' or niche) for the images of the brotherhood. These are the Sweet Name of Jesus 'El Paso' by Mariano Benlliure (1935, replacing a 17th c. image that was destroyed in 1931) and Holy Mary of Hope, a 17th-century carving restored by Luis Álvarez Duarte. The ceiling is decorated with depictions in oils of Marian allegories and portraits of the major prophets respectively by García Ibáñez.

Oratorio de Santa María Reina y Madre

🍴 CENTRO HISTÓRICO ⚲ Plazuela Virgen de las Penas 🕒 Mon–Sat 1100–1300

This chapel, which is the *sede canónica* of the Holy Week Brotherhood of Sorrows (*Las Penas*) has a fine baroque façade very similar to that of the Episcopal Palace (1762) and one might assume that it is of a similar vintage. This oratory, however, was only built in 2008, making it the newest place of worship in the city. In the view of some it is thus an unimaginative pastiche of the baroque, while others hold it up as an example of a new ecclesiastical building that blends sensitively with its environment and history.

Perhaps the chief reason to visit, though, is to see the extensive murals that cover the entire ceiling of the chapel, some 140 m². These murals represent six years of work by the *malagueño* artist Raúl Berzosa Fernández who completed them in 2014. Raúl, whose secular works are reminiscent of those executed by Joaquín Sorolla, has also completed commissions for other brotherhoods and designed a number of Holy Week posters.[42]

---

42   raulberzosa.com

Málaga con niños
(Málaga with Children)

Once a country of large families, Spain is not as fecund as it once was (though families with 3 children or more can still get travel discounts of up to 50 %). The fertility rate is now lower in Spain than it is in the UK (though the statistics fail to take into account the relative contribution of immigrant populations, in which family size tends to be larger). Yet, despite this, Spain remains a very family-friendly and child-friendly culture. In 2021, the decision of a restaurant in Bilbao to ban children made the national news. There was even talk of challenging the policy in the courts.

Children are welcomed in the vast majority of eating (and drinking) establishments in Spain, and Málaga is no different. The obvious exceptions are places which are about 'grown-up drinking' — nightclubs, cocktail bars, rooftop hotel bars, and the like. If you are in any doubt, just have a look around you.

The legal drinking age in Spain has been set at 18 since a change in the law in 2009, however, as in the UK, minors of 16 and 17 may consume alcohol with a meal in a restaurant when accompanied by an adult. Spanish bars are generally welcoming to families with children (of any age, from babes in arms upwards), and it is usual to see well-behaved groups of teenage friends in those establishments that are not primarily devoted to the consumption of alcohol such as *cafeterías* and fast food places — they just cannot order alcohol (McDonald's and Burger King both serve draught beer in Spain). Hotel rooftop bars, cocktail bars and craft beer *cervecerías* generally operate a strict 'over 18s' policy.

🏃 For Older Children and Teens

Regarding things to do and see, teenagers should be able to flick through this guide or, more likely, do their own research online and suggest the sort of activities and sightseeing that would appeal to them. Give them a day for which they can choose the itinerary themselves, including the choice of where to eat. They may be fascinated by the CAC and bored to tears by the Thyssen, or vice versa. If you are planning to take secondary school-age children to Málaga, a good way of involving them in the experience is asking them, tech-savvy as they no doubt will be, to help with the planning and booking of the trip: letting them organize the transport links in Málaga, working out which smartphone apps are required, and encouraging them to post on their preferred social media sites.

While French just about retains its place as the most widely studied foreign language in UK schools, Spanish is nipping at its heels, having long since displaced German in the number two slot. If your school-age child is studying Spanish, then researching and planning the trip, and taking a lead in communicating in Spanish while in Spain, will help them considerably with the language. There is a world of difference between role-playing ordering breakfast in a classroom, and actually ordering breakfast in a Spanish *cafetería*, from a Spaniard — especially one speaking with a slightly incomprehensible *andaluz* accent and all sorts of *malagueño* vocabulary that not even other Spaniards understand.

⚽ Spectator Sport

The **Málaga CF** soccer team played in the top division but was relegated in 2018, only five years after reaching the Champions League quarter final in 2013. After a long period of decline and a disastrous 2022/23 season, it was relegated again to the Primera Federación (the third tier of the Spanish league system). The **Unicaja Baloncesto Málaga** team plays in the Premiership basketball league. You can check fixtures and buy tickets for football matches here: **malagacf.com**, and, compared to UK tickets, you won't have to take out a mortgage to take the family. Their ground, **Estadio La Rosaleda**, is a 15 minute walk from the centre of Málaga. It is also possible to visit the stadium and see the stands, presidential box, VIP area, pitch, changing rooms, press room and museum. The tour runs daily, Monday to Saturday (match days excluded), in English and Spanish, at 1100, 1300, 1630 and 1800: **malagacf.com/en/museum**. There is no booking form on the website, so contact the club by email or phone to arrange. Tickets for Unicaja basketball games can be purchased here: **venta.unicajabaloncesto.com/en/next-games**. They play at the **Palacio de Deportes José María Martín Carpena** (Ⓜ Line 2 or 🚌 16).

🏃 Physical Activities

An alternative to exploring the streets of Málaga on foot is doing so on a bicycle or Segway®. There are several companies that hire bikes, with **bike2malaga.com** and **biketoursmalaga.com** being two of the best-known (see also p. 100f.). Both will hire out bikes if you want to go off to explore on your own, and Bike Tours Málaga offers 3-hour-long city bike tours twice a day at reasonable rates (with the option to extend the bike hire until the close of business for a few euros extra). Children's bikes are available, and for very young children, they can supply and fit child seats. Booking ahead online is strongly advised, especially with children.

Bike tour companies have agreed their routes with the *ayuntamiento*, but if you hire a bicycle for your own use then you must obey the laws of the road as they apply to cyclists in Spain in general and Málaga in particular. New regulations came into force in February 2021 imposing fines ranging between €60 and €200 for infractions. Bicycles may use the road, cycle lanes and '30 lanes' (where motor vehicles are limited to 30 kph and 'VMPs' — personal mobility vehicles — have priority). Bicycles are strictly prohibited on pavements, pedestrianized streets, part-pedestrianized streets in the historic centre, bus lanes (except where indicated) and some seafront promenades.

In the *centro histórico* in particular, signage is poor. Signs indicating 'no cycles' (with a red border, as in the UK) are often small and easy to miss, while bicycle paths are poorly marked. Ask the bicycle hire staff for advice about where to cycle (and not to cycle). Except on the main road, the speed limit for bicycles is 30 kph (18 mph). Riders under 16 must wear a helmet.

There are few companies offering Segway® tours (which can provide a more relaxed means of getting up to the Gibralfaro Castle). Two well-established agencies are **segwaymalagatours.com** and **topsegway.es**, both of which offer guided tours lasting from just 30 minutes up to 3 hours for adults and children aged nine and above. Booking ahead is also recommended. I suggest you do your own research online as Segway ceased production of its 'self-balancing personal transporter' in 2019, so it's possible that companies will adapt and begin to use other forms of transport, such as e-scooters, in the near future.

And talking of e-scooters, there are currently several companies hiring e-scooters (*patinetes eléctricos*) in Málaga, available to pick up from a number of points in the city after booking using an app. E-scooters began appearing in Málaga in 2017 and it is fair to say that their arrival was not universally welcomed. Pedestrians found themselves having to dodge often inexpert riders as they sped along the pavement at 20 kph. Many of those hiring the scooters were tourists unfamiliar with the city and with little or no understanding of the Spanish Highway Code, and e-scooters casually abandoned on pavements were a serious headache for the blind and disabled. **A** Although the Spanish word '*escúter*' sounds like it should mean electric scooter, it is in fact the word for a moped

There are multiple e-scooter hire providers operating in Málaga, so to provide a list here would not be helpful because it would very quickly become out of date. Companies arrive and depart quickly. One of the first to market was the Spanish company UFO, which began in Madrid before expanding into other Spanish cities. Despite being the market leader in 2018, by early 2019 they had only 50 e-scooters for hire in Spain, all of them in Málaga. By mid-2019 they had ceased to trade. Other companies move in the opposite direction. One of the first commercial enterprises to move into Málaga after the *ayuntamiento* ended their municipal bike hire scheme was Dott, but they soon switched from bicycles to scooters.

At the time of publication, the big names (Dott, Voi, Lime, Tier, Wind) are either operating in Málaga, or have had a presence recently, and you may find Helbiz and Spin (which until not long ago was known as Jump) too. A fixed unlock fee and then a per-minute tariff seems to be the normal charging structure. Your best bet is to find a rank of e-scooters first (there are several around town) and then download the relevant smartphone app (scooters have a QR code which will open the Google or Apple app store). None of these parking stations are in the historic centre because scooter use is forbidden (except for residents or those making deliveries of medicine). Quite a few stations are positioned along the seafront (both west and east of Málaga) and at the boundaries of the historic centre. The María Zambrano railway station, Soho, Plaza de La Merced and Muelle Uno usually have stations with scooters available.

Scooter Regulations

After spending some time catching up, the *ayuntamiento* brought in new regulations for bicycles and e-scooters in 2021. The rules for e-scooters are similar to those for bicycles, with a few specific additions:

Minimum age: 16 years (however, check the terms and conditions of the relevant app for the scooter you wish to hire as some set a limit of 18 years). The scooter and driver together must have a minimum height of 1.40 meters.

Maximum capacity: one person.

Lights: must be on at any time of the day for easy visibility.

Use of the helmet and 'hi vis' vest: Is mandatory only when using '30 Lanes' (see above).

Civil liability insurance: is mandatory for scooter rental and tour guide companies, so you will be covered.

Pedestrian areas: the use of e-scooters on pavements and other areas intended for the exclusive use of pedestrians is prohibited. Most e-scooter hire apps indicate the areas where scooters may not be ridden on a map (basically the historic centre and Muelle Uno/Dos).

Permitted routes: bike lanes, 20 kph zones ('*Zonas 20*'), residential streets or 'single-platform' roads (those with no kerbstones, only bollards, and where pedestrians have priority) at a maximum speed of 20 kph, and in 30 kph zones ('*Zonas 30*'), at a maximum speed of 25 kph. E-scooters may use the road as long as there is no alternative cycle path alongside. They may not use the 'Basic Road Network' of the city of Málaga (*Red Viaria Básica de la ciudad de Málaga*), except for signposted sections that are limited to 30 kph, in the right lane, at  a maximum of 25 kph. The 'basic road network' of Málaga consists of what, in the United Kingdom, would be city centre 'A-roads' — the main transport arteries of the city (such as the Alameda Principal) indicated with a blue lozenge-shaped sign. 'Zona 30' sections are indicated by road markings, often with the bicycle symbol.

Parking: exclusively in the reserved space indicated for this purpose. Consult the app to find permitted locations.

Most common fines (2023)

- Riding on the pavement, promenades and other pedestrian areas: bicycle €60, e-scooter €200

- Parking outside the permitted areas: bicycle €60, e-scooter €200

- More than one person on an e-scooter: €90

- Riding an e-scooter under 16 years old: €60

- Using an e-scooter without lights or without helmet and vest in '30 Zones': €90

- Riding an e-scooter at more than 25 kph: €200

- Riding a bicycle or e-scooter recklessly, competitively, or under the influence of alcohol or drugs: €500

⚠ The regulations are subject to change at any time, so please refer to the information section of the e-scooter hire app that you are using to consult the current rules.

Other Activities

Kart & Fun

🍽 CARRETERA DE CÁDIZ 📍 Calle Victoria de los Angeles 1
🌐 💬 kartfun.es 🕐 1100–2100 😊😊

Next to the 'Plaza Mayor' out-of-town shopping centre, 'Kart & Fun' operate two floodlit go-kart tracks — one of 840 m, and a smaller children's course, with circuits supervised by qualified staff. 'Extreme Kart' is for drivers over 15 years old (and over 1.60 metres tall) in 270 cc karts, and 'Junior Kart' allows 10 to 14-year-olds (1.45 to 1.60 metres tall) to race 160 cc karts. 5 to 10-year-olds (1.20 to 1.45 metres in height) can race 35 cc karts on the children's track. Two-seater karts allow kids under 5 (or under 1.20 metres) to race with an adult. You can either take the 🚆 *Cercanías* (local) train to the Plaza Mayor stop just after the airport or the No. 5 bus from the centre.

Skate Park

🏙 BAILÉN–MIRAFLORES 📍 Calle Camino Cuarto
🌐 ⓒ skateparkmalaga.info 🕐 Daily (consult website for times) 💶

In the suburb of Camino Cuarto, north-west of the centre, near the University Hospital, the Rubén Alcántara Skatepark has a number of installations (bowl, mini-ramp, halfpipe, street zone and dirt track) for BMX, skateboarders, skaters and scooter users. The courses were designed by the twice-world-champion BMX star Rubén Alcántara, who is from Málaga. The park is easily reached by bus from the centre (🚌 C1 ⓦ 923 **Magistrado Salvador Barberá**). However, although the skatepark's website has a link marked '*Alquila tu material*' (rent your equipment), it does not seem to lead anywhere. Plans to offer equipment hire were delayed and complicated by the COVID pandemic, but it may be a service offered in the future, so it is worth dropping them an email to enquire.

Caminito del Rey

Adventurous teens (and children aged 8+) with a head for heights are sure to enjoy the Caminito del Rey: a 3 km walkway pinned to the rock of a narrow gorge, 100 metres above the river. See the entry on p. 548f.

🏛 Museums

If the more traditional art galleries and museums fail to elicit much enthusiasm from your adolescents, there are still a few unusual exhibition spaces and collections that may pique their interest.

Museo de la Imaginación

🏙 SOHO 📍 Calle Martínez Campos 13 🌐 museoimaginacion.com
⊘ Wednesdays 💶💶

This is one of Málaga's newer museums/exhibitions, having opened in 2018. It is also one of the most popular, attracting 5,000 visitors in its first four months of operation. The 'Museum of the Imagination' is small (only three large rooms), but there is plenty to see and experience. Essentially an exhibition of optical illusions, this is far more than a collection of curios. There is a wealth of information (in Spanish and English) which explains how the toys and exhibits challenge reason and visual perception.

The Museum's exhibition is divided into three rooms, each one dedicated to different kinds of effects — optical and visual illusions; playing with light, shade and colour; and the use of photography and videography in creating visual effects and confusion. Though clearly the sort of museum that would be of particular interest to inquisitive children and teens, I defy anyone not to be fascinated and captivated by this place. This is not a 'children's museum', but it is most certainly a place where even the most jaded adults can feel like children.

Such a museum is a perfect addition to Málaga's museum and gallery offer. Most visitors to Málaga are likely to spend several hours looking at paintings, religious art and architecture, whereas the Museum of the Imagination explores more fundamental questions of perception and visual interpretation. For young people in particular, it will be the source of multiple 'Instagrammable' moments. But remember — it is primarily interactive. To get the best value from your visit, you need to get involved in the exhibition. This is not a 'look and see', but a 'look and do' museum.

Principia Centro de Ciencia

🎪 LA ROSALEDA 📍 Avenida de Luis Buñuel 6 (near the La Rosaleda Football Stadium) 🌐 principia-malaga.com 🕐 Mon–Sat 1700–2000

This is undoubtedly one of the best science museums anywhere, though it is mainly about labs, workshops and demonstrations as opposed to static exhibits. Situated near the home ground of Málaga FC, it was founded by local science teachers and school groups make up the majority of visitors. However, they are open for visits by the general public of all ages, both on green days (school days) and blue days (non-school days). Families and tourists are always welcome, and they regularly receive visitors from different parts of Spain and from around the world. The experiment session for groups can be carried out (upon request) in English or French, and during visits to the interactive modules room, staff can answer your questions in both Spanish and English. Throughout the year they organize a large number of free events and workshops (building robots, astronomy, 3D design, family events, microscopy, biology and botany, etc.) which are advertised on the website. Helpful staff will do their best to answer any queries you have by email.

See also the National Airports Museum (p. 252)

👨‍👧 For Younger Children

🏛 Museums and Exhibitions

One of the museums that seems particularly to appeal to primary school-aged children is the **Artes y Costumbres** (p. 250) because its collection is of everyday objects from typical homes — things that any child can recognize and compare to their modern (or British) equivalents. The **Centre Pompidou** (p. 244) goes out of its way to welcome children and there is almost always an exhibition curated with younger visitors in mind. In July (the first full month of the school summer holidays) the **Centre Pompidou** and **Museo Casa Natal Picasso** (p. 246) often organize activities and workshops aimed at children. The **Museo Casa Natal Picasso** has events for families with children aged 3–12 almost every Saturday. In recent years, some of these sessions have been conducted in English. Check the websites for details. Even where the event or workshop is not specifically advertised as being suitable for English-speaking children, there is no harm in sending an email to ask whether it might be suitable (most of the activities are rather more about 'doing' than 'listening').

The **Museo de la Imaginación** (p. 278) has plenty to interest primary school age children. Also not to be missed is 'MIMMA' — the Museo Interactivo de la Música Málaga, or Interactive Málaga Museum of Music:

Museo Interactivo de la Música

🎪 CENTRO HISTÓRICO 📍 Calle Beatas 15 🌐 musicaenaccion.com 🕐 Mon 1030–1600, Tue–Sun 1030–1930 💶

This fascinating and highly enjoyable museum first opened in 2002 but was little known thanks to its occupying a subterranean space under the Plaza de la Marina. But in 2013 it moved to the Palacio del Conde de las Navas in the historic centre. The *palacio* is fairly modest in comparison to some, built in the 1770s for Juan Gualberto López-Valdemoro de Quesada, from Málaga, Count of Las Navas and full academician of the Royal Spanish Academy, who in 1893 was appointed chief librarian of King Alfonso XIII. In 2010 the *ayuntamiento* purchased the property and restored it to provide a permanent home for the Music Museum.

The museum itself has a collection of some 1,000 musical instruments, of which around 400 are on display at any given time. These 'primary sources' are augmented by audiovisual exhibits that explore the nature of sound and music. The entire museum is designed with younger visitors in mind and perhaps what will appeal most to children (and to the 'inner child' of older visitors) is the museum's motto, '*Se ruega tocar*' — 'Please play'. Video displays function as 'virtual teachers', guiding visitors as they try their hand at playing stringed, keyboard and percussion instruments.

The exhibition is nothing if not comprehensive and is divided into nine rooms exploring the origins of music, the physics of sound, the chronology of music and world music, the importance of music as sensation, ethnomusicology, the music of Andalucía in general and of Málaga in particular (the city was once home to two famous piano makers, Juan López and López y Griffo), and an opportunity to see how guitars are made in a display donated by the Bellido family of luthiers, who have their workshops in Granada. The remaining rooms have various different kinds of instruments: chordophone (from cellos to pianos), aerophone (woodwind and brass), percussion, electronic, and recorded sound.

The museum also stages frequent flamenco concerts, which are ideal for families with children. They are reasonably priced (you will not be required to spend money on drinks and dinner), last 45 minutes (so will not put too much strain on a child's attention span), and usually take place at family-friendly times in the afternoon. Consult the website to see what's coming up and buy tickets from the ticket office at the museum.

The English Cemetery

◆ MALAGUETA ♀ Avenida de Pries 1 ⊕ cementerioinglesmalaga.org
⊙ Tue–Sun 0900–1400 € (✿ if attending church services or visiting a family grave)

A family 'fun day' in a cemetery? As strange as it may seem, yes. The English Cemetery in Málaga is the oldest non-Catholic cemetery in Spain, having been established in 1831 to provide a decent burial place for British subjects who died in Málaga. Previously, Protestants were buried on the beach, at night, in an upright position. When the cemetery opened, the locals, who had only a vague grasp of Reform Christianity, were surprised to see a cross at the entrance, having been unaware that 'these Jews' *[sic]* worshipped under the same symbol that Catholics did. The new cemetery began to fill up towards the end of the 19th century because by then Málaga had become popular as a winter destination for recuperating invalids, although the writer Augustus Hare wondered why such a dusty city should be so attractive to convalescents.[43] By the end of the 20th century, with no source of stable funding, it was in a sad and run-down state, but since 2006 it has been operated as a charitable foundation, so while the admission price may seem a bit steep to visit a small, albeit peaceful and beautiful, graveyard, entrance fees are a vital source of revenue that go towards the cemetery's restoration and upkeep.

Family Visits take place on Saturdays throughout the year. There is an email booking form on the website (click on 'VISITS') and the entrance fee is payable upon arrival. Choose your arrival time (between 10.30 am and 1.30 pm, though remember that the cemetery closes at 2 pm). The cemetery provides you with the materials you need to take part in the self-guided activities — maps, quizzes and games, in English and Spanish — which help children learn about the history of the cemetery itself, discover the stories of some of the people interred there and find out about the history of Málaga in the 19th and 20th centuries.

---

43   Augustus Hare, *Wanderings in Spain* (London, Strahan & Co., 1873)

The Alcazaba and Castillo Gibralfaro

Children who may be too young to appreciate the history or Moorish architecture of these monuments will still enjoy exploring their battlements and nooks and crannies. Keep a close eye on them, though — the Spanish attitude to 'Health and Safety' is somewhat more relaxed than that in the UK, so you cannot assume that there will always be a safety railing to prevent a small adventurer from climbing over the top.

🏖 Beaches

Málaga's beaches are likely to be a draw for most children, as are boat trips. During the 'beach season' (roughly from Easter until mid-September), beach-side kiosks sell bucket and spade sets, beach games, cold drinks and ice creams. During the same period, both of the city's 'blue flag' **Malagueta** and **Misericordia** Beaches have lifeguards. The safest places for children to swim are either at the far end of the Misericordia Beach near the spit ('Espigón de La Térmica'), or in the sheltered bays along the **Pedregalejo** Beach, but keep an eye on the flags on any beach. Green means safe to bathe, yellow advises caution (for strong swimmers, and keep close to the shore), and red indicates danger. Both beaches are journeys of around 20 minutes from the city centre by bus.

🛝 Play Parks

Who doesn't love climbing up something and sliding down something? Málaga has lots of play parks for kids, though most are in residential areas where they are often situated in squares so that parents can enjoy beer and *tapas* in a bar while their children play within sight. The play parks in the centre are more suited to younger children or toddlers (see below, p. 285), so if it's big slides and zip-wires you are looking for, then head to the beach. You can find abundant play parks in both directions — going east of the city to the Malagueta, Caleta and Pedregalejo beaches, and west to the Huelin and Misericordia beaches.

Of the two options, I would recommend travelling west. This takes you into the working-class Carretera de Cádiz *barrio*, one of the most densely populated neighbourhoods in Europe and a taste of real, 'local' Málaga. As these are the areas where *malagueña* families actually live, you will find plenty of parks and attractions for children. You can take the bus (e.g. 🚌 3 or 7) from the city centre, or with plenty of stops for playing, eating and enjoying the beach, it's a pleasant 4 km walk from María Zambrano Railway Station to Sacaba Beach, the last beach before the Guadalhorce estuary nature reserve and the airport. The closest western beach, Huelin, is only 1.4 km away.

If you choose to walk (you can always hop on a bus if you get tired), then there is a shady promenade all the way from the Port to the Guadalhorce Nature Reserve. En route, you will pass the Parque de Huelin, which has a children's play park. On your walk along the promenade, you will come across three chimneys, standing like obelisks on the seafront. The first, by Burger King at the end of Huelin Beach, is the smallest of the three, and was once part of La Trinidad Fertilizer Factory, belching out sulphuric acid fumes until the 1990s. The last of the three, very close to the mouth of the Guadalhorce River, is the chimney of the La Misericordia thermal power plant, known as 'La Térmica'. The tallest and most iconic chimney, however, is the one in the middle, level with the San Andrés beach. This is the **Los Guindos** Chimney, also known as the 'Mónica Tower'. Built in 1923 to carry away the toxic fumes of the Los Guindos lead smelting works, it was once the tallest structure in Spain and though the lead works closed in 1979, the chimney remains as a reminder of Málaga's industrial past.

281

Its local name has a rather lovely story behind it. In September 1992, 17-year-old José Carlos Selva proposed to his 15-year-old girlfriend, Mónica Vallejo. She accepted, but about a year later they quarrelled one Friday evening. Meeting the next day, they resolved their disagreement, but José wanted to make a statement. He climbed to the top of the chimney with two 5-kilo cans of white paint. Lowering himself on ropes, between 10 pm on Saturday night and 2 am on Sunday morning, he set about painting '*Mónica, te amo*' ('Monica, I love you') in letters several metres high, but ran out of paint and only managed to write 'Mónica'. Somewhat unromantically, the graffiti was removed by the *ayuntamiento* in 2007, but José and Mónica, now married and living in Tenerife with their three children, still make an annual pilgrimage to what locals to this day know as the 'Torre Mónica'.

If you turn right (*i.e.* north) at the chimney you will find the huge Parque del Oeste, with play parks, lakes, and modern sculptures (and lots of cafés nearby). Further west is the Misericordia beach, which has a play park (with zip-wire) at its eastern end and good swimming for children at the sheltered west end next to the spit (Espigón de La Térmica). Beyond the spit is the small Sacaba Beach, and just inland from here is one of the best play parks in town — Parque Litoral, which has play parks for younger children and, as its centrepiece, an artificial mound with three precipitous slides and rope webbing to grapple your way back to the top. You are in a residential district, so there is no shortage of family-friendly restaurants if you want to have some lunch and make a day of it.

A bus ride away from the centre in the Teatinos neighbourhood is the Parque del Cine (Cinema Park) — a 10,000 m² landscaped space inspired by the world of cinema, and where you can also find corners dedicated to the universe of books. Walks drawn like a reel of coloured film, yellow brick roads like in *The Wizard of Oz*, or a walk of fame as in Hollywood are some of its features. The largest structure rests on a giant rubber book, and it has a large sports area and several children's areas designed for kids of different ages. It has a fun zip line, swings in the shape of a whale and a rhinoceros, a trampoline, a climbing structure, revolving games and a ping-pong table.

Chiringuitos

Eating at the beach is always fun, so have lunch at a *chiringuito*. If a skewer of delicious sardines (heads, fins, scales and all) is a step too far, most *chiringuitos* have non-fish options, even if they are not terribly exciting. French fries are pretty ubiquitous, and some places even offer burgers and pizzas.

Along the almost two-mile stretch of the Huelin, Misericordia and Sacaba beaches, there is a wealth of places to eat and drink. You will find more than a dozen *chiringuitos* serving barbecued fish and seafood, most with seating indoors and outdoors, at least in the warmer months. Litoral Pacífico and Gutierrez Playa, both at the west end of San Andrés Beach, are very well known and reliable, but with so many competing outlets in such a compact area, you should be able to dine pretty well wherever you go. Find one that you like the look of; preferably one with plenty of customers eating, rather than twiddling their thumbs as they wait for food from an overwhelmed kitchen. If grilled sardines do not appeal, then there are plenty of other seafront options — pizza, burgers, *tapas*, and fast food (KFC and Burger King), including a branch of **100 Montaditos** (next to the Torre Mónica). There is also a handful of ice cream shacks and, between the Litoral Pacífico and Gutierrez Playa *chiringuitos*, '**Mums Cafetería**' — a friendly, relaxed spot for breakfasts, coffee, ice creams and the filling sandwiches known in Málaga as *camperos* (soft, muffin-like *mollete* rolls filled with tomato, lettuce and mayonnaise plus a 'main' filling of bacon, ham, cheese, chicken, omelette or tuna).

🏊 Beaches (City Centre and East)

The city centre beach, east of the bullring on the other side of Muelle Uno is the Malagueta Beach which extends as far as the 'Espigón de la T' spit, where it becomes the Caleta Beach. There is a small children's playground between the two beaches and plenty of bars and *chiringuitos* for refreshments. A little further east are the beaches of Pedregalejo and El Palo which, like the *barrio* of Carretera de Cádiz, have their own distinctive characters. The beginning of the Playa de Pedregalejo is only about half an hour's walk from the centre of Málaga, but you can preserve your energy for a morning or afternoon at the beach by taking a bus (🚌 3 or 8, towards El Palo) from the city centre. Get off at **Baños del Carmen** (Ⓑ1111).

The **Baños del Carmen** ('Carmen Baths') were constructed in 1918 as a state-of-the-art bathing station for well-heeled visitors. After beach-going tourists migrated westwards to the resorts of Torremolinos, Fuengirola and Marbella, it fell into near ruin but is nowadays the site of a bar and restaurant, '**El Balneario**' ('The Spa' elbalneariomalaga.com). The prices are fairly reasonable given the prime location and the service is first class.

A little farther on from the Baños del Carmen are the **Astilleros Nereo** (Nereus Shipyards astillerosnereo.com), a working boatyard making, repairing and restoring wooden boats. They have a small but fascinating museum and offer guided tours of their workshops for groups of 4 or more. Contact them to book: ✉ info@astillerosnereo.com 📞+34 952 291 198

Continuing to walk eastwards, you'll follow the promenade to the four sheltered bays of Pedregalejo Beach, where there are a number of smart *chiringuitos* that seem to be busy all year round. Looking at the calm waters of the Mar de Alborán, it is hard to believe that in the 1970s this beach was the birthplace of surfing in Spain and the first Spanish surf club was established here in 1974 (before Los Baños del Carmen was rescued from picturesque ruin to become an elegant restaurant, it served as a second-hand market for surf gear). The giant waves have since been calmed by the breakwaters and the surfers have moved eastwards towards Vélez-Málaga and Torrox.

Leaving the Pedregalejo beach, the esplanade crosses the Arroyo Jaboneras ('Soapmakers' Stream') and you come to the district of El Palo, which has a real 'seaside' feel to it. You are only 3 km from the centre of Málaga, but it feels further away. There are very few, if any, tourists here (though it is a popular spot for city-dwelling *malagueños* at weekends) but it is well-served by bars and restaurants. There are *chiringuitos* on the beach itself, another strip of restaurants and bars along the promenade (Calle Quitapenas and Calle Banda del Mar), and even more options as you venture into 'town' from the beach (north of the Avenida Salvador Allende). The dining options here are a bit more rough-and-ready than those in Pedregalejo, but the food is just as good and the bill will be much, much less. To take the bus directly to El Palo, get off at Avenida Juan Sebastián Elcano–Iglesia (Ⓑ 1131).

🍴 A Few Eateries in El Palo

 🍴 Ohana Poké & More (📍 Avenida Salvador Allende 21) marries the *malagueño* love of fish with the raw fish speciality of Hawaii called 'poké' (though they serve salads, burgers and kids' menus too). Dishes are served in plastic pots with disposable cutlery which makes this an ideal place to buy food to take to enjoy on the beachfront. They also operate a home-delivery service (useful if you are staying in an apartment in Málaga) and there is a city centre branch at Calle Muro de Puerta Nueva 3.

 🍴🐟 Casa Manuel de La Lonja (📍 Calle Banda del Mar 19) is a long-established restaurant serving — you guessed it — fish and seafood. Excellent cooking, friendly service and a relaxed 'local' atmosphere.

 🍴🐟 Tintero (📍 Avenida Salvador Allende 340) is another fish and seafood favourite but with a slight twist. Rather than ordering from a menu, you stop waiters as they pass. As in the *tapas* (*pintxo*) bars of the Basque Country, waiters emerge from the kitchen with hot, fresh food, shouting the names of the dishes. If you want it, call them over. If you don't speak Spanish, then this puts you at a slight disadvantage, but if you are not too picky and enjoy most fish and seafood, then it is a fun way to eat. Needless to say, this is not a place for a quiet meal. The *ambiente* is noisy but friendly, even theatrical!

 🍦 Helados Cremades (📍 Pedregalejo: Calle Cenacheros 34 📍 El Palo: Avenida Salvador Allende 256) Like most ice cream makers in Málaga, Cremades make and sell *valenciano* ice cream. They offer all the usual Spanish flavours (including, of course, 'Málaga'), as well as seasonal specials. Their sundaes are immense.

 If you fancy hiring kayaks or paddle boards (or bicycles), then **Kayak y Bike** (📍 Calle Quitapenas 7), just after the bridge over the Arroyo Jaboneras, will be able to help you. Paddle-boards, kayaks, and bikes are all available to hire and the prices are probably the cheapest in Málaga. They offer beginners' courses and will hire neoprene wetsuits in colder weather. Staff are extremely friendly and helpful, so just contact them to discuss your requirements: ✉ reservas@kayakybike.es 📱 +34 662 050 713

Out of Town

Bioparc Fuengirola

Bioparc Fuengirola is perhaps the epitome of an urban zoo, occupying an even smaller space than London Zoo. Run by committed, friendly staff. Take the *Cercanías* train from Málaga to Fuengirola.

It is worth looking through the information about the Costa del Sol in the Day Trips section (p. 490ff.) as there are lots of other attractions suitable for children in Benalmádena and Fuengirola.

Sealife

Sealife is an impressive aquarium in nearby Benalmádena — just under an hour by bus (**M-110**) from the Muelle Heredia, or take the local train (**C1 to El Pinillo**).

Toddlers

As much as Málaga might be about bars, restaurants and museums, it is still a welcoming place for families with very small children. Save for the most exclusive locations, most bars and restaurants will be used to (well-behaved) children of all ages. There is a decent play park in the historic centre in the **Plaza Enrique García-Herrera**, lots of smaller playgrounds dotted about, and plenty of other parks on the beaches that stretch west and east from Málaga city (see above). The main bike hire shops will hire bikes with children's seats (best to give them a bit of notice to be sure of availability).

The play parks west of Málaga should appeal, as should the **Parque del Oeste** with the added attractions of a resident wallaby, emus and terrapins. In the centre, the **Parque de Málaga** is fun for small children to explore and can seem deceptively expansive despite being sandwiched between two busy roads. Lots of trees and pathways provide endless opportunities for playing *el escondite* (hide and seek). There is a small play park near the auditorium as well as a kiosk for refreshments (seasonal). Next to the park is **Muelle Dos**, which is a wide, open promenade where children can safely run around. The glass barrier prevents them from falling into the water and there are play parks to enjoy.

The **Gibralfaro Castle** and the **Alcazaba** both have plenty of interesting corners to explore, though you will need to keep a watchful eye on very young children. The Spanish approach to 'Health and Safety' is not quite as belt-and-braces as that followed in the UK. Generally speaking, the expectation is that parents will see to their children's safety rather than a multiplicity of railings, barriers and striped hazard tape. If you go up to the Gibralfaro Castle on foot, take the **Calle Mundo Nuevo** route, which is not only shadier but has playgrounds to break up the walk (see p. 238).

Some of the attractions listed in the sections above should be sufficient to entertain younger children, particularly the beaches, Fuengirola **Bioparc** and Benalmádena **Aquarium** (which is free for children under 3). The 'hands-on' section of the **Music Museum** (p. 279) would be fun, too.

El aire libre (The Great Outdoors)
🌳 Parks and Gardens

Jardín Botánico de la Concepción

📍 Camino del Jardín Botánico 3 ⊕ laconcepcion.malaga.eu ⏰ Tue–Sun 0930–1930 💶

Continually rated as one of the best botanical gardens in Europe, La Concepción is a subtropical paradise that features formal gardens adjoining lush green forest. Created in the mid-19th century by an aristocratic couple, Jorge Loring Oyarzábal and his wife Amalia Heredia Livermore, the gardens fell into decline in the 20th century but have been restored to their former glory by the *ayuntamiento*. Following the basic route takes around an hour and a half, but you could easily spend all day there. There is a *cafetería* and 7 picnic areas if you want to bring your own food. It has a route designed for wheelchair users and those with limited mobility. They also stage frequent art exhibitions and lay on fantastic family activities around Christmas time.

The gardens are on the northern edge of Málaga, too far to walk, but one can take a local bus. It is exceptionally well curated, and arranged as a number of walks and collections. Geologically, you are practically in North Africa, so expect to see a great number of subtropical plants and cacti. If you visit in May, then you will also see a riot of jacaranda, a tree with bluish-purple blossom which is common in the Caribbean and Central and South America, but almost unknown north of the Spanish Sierra Nevada. (You will see jacaranda not just in the Botanical gardens, but all over Málaga.)

How to get there:

(A) The Number 91 Tourist Bus (5–7 buses per day) from the *Centro histórico*, direct.

(B) The Number 2 bus (every 12–15 mins) from the *Centro histórico*, plus a 15-minute walk.

Bus No. 91

The departure stop closest to the *centro histórico* is **Pasillo de Santa Isabel** (🚏 202), though you can also catch it from in front of the María Zambrano railway station. 🚌 91 is operated not by the EMT Málaga bus company, but by the same firm that runs the open-top tourist buses. Thus, the '*bonobús*' card is not valid, but there is a special return fare. The timetable changes seasonally, like the opening hours of the gardens. Search for *linea* (line) 91 on the EMT app (QR code left) and you will be directed to a link showing a special timetable. This link is blocked for IP addresses outside Spain but should work locally. As the information on the website/app is not always up-to-date, I advise you to check with the *turismo*, or at the EMT office (**Alameda Principal 47, Mon–Fri 0900–1330, 1700–1900; July–August: Mon–Fri 0830–1430**).

Bus No. 2

The departure bus stop is called **Pasillo de Santa Isabel (Ⓑ 202)** which is behind the Museum of Popular Arts and Customs (p. 250), that is, facing the river. Get off at the final stop, which is called **San José (Ⓑ 251)**, and then walk to the garden entrance.

To take the bus back towards the city, retrace your steps and catch the 🚍2 from the same stop at which you got off (**Ⓑ San José: 251**).

On the return journey, the bus route takes you on the west side of the river, past El Corte Inglés, and then turns east along the Alameda. The final stop is near the Atarazanas market.

University of Málaga Botanical Garden

This is probably a place that will appeal to those with a particular interest in the flora of Spain, rather than people simply looking for a shady walk. Málaga's second botanical garden is not only far newer than La Concepción, but very different. For one thing, its setting is urban, being located in the middle of the Teatinos University campus. The garden covers 1.5 hectares and is laid out taxonomically in 54 beds. It can be reached easily from the city centre by Metro or bus and is open, and free to visit, Monday to Friday between 10 am and 6 pm. It is occasionally closed for university events, so consult the website before setting out. Given its location, there aren't any nearby eateries or bars nearby, but there is plenty of choice just north of the hospital, on either side of the Avenida Plutarco.

Parque de Málaga

At the eastern end of the Alameda Principal, south of the Cathedral and Alcazaba, this park is a cool oasis in the centre of the city. In 1876, the engineer Rafael Yagüe oversaw a project to reclaim land from the sea in order to extend the Alameda Principal (and thus creating Muelle Dos as it is today). The project had been the brainchild of the *malagueño* Antonio Cánovas del Castillo who, between 1875 and 1897, served six non-consecutive terms as Prime Minister of Spain. Rubble from demolished slum housing surrounding the Alcazaba and from dredging the Guadalmedina river bed was used for infill, and thousands of tonnes of rocks from quarries near El Palo arrived by barge.

Behind the preliminary project were names already familiar to us: the Marquess of Larios and architects such as Manuel Rivera Valentín, Eduardo Strachan Viana-Cárdenas, Manuel Rivera Vera, Fernando Guerrero Strachan and Joaquín de Rucoba, the latter being the main designer of the gardens. Planting began in 1899, though it would take another 20 years to achieve its current appearance. Since then, the park has undergone several renovations, the last time in 2007, when its biodiversity was expanded to 300 species.

 The Parque de Málaga is not large (1.5 hectares) and occupies a seventy-metre-wide space between two busy roads (the Paseo del Parque and the Paseo de los Curas), but the plentiful vegetation and mature trees shield visitors from the noise of the city to create a *'rus in urbe'*. The 'main' park is known as the *'banda exterior'*, but across the Paseo del Parque, in the shadow of the Museo de Málaga, is a small triangular section known as the *'banda interior'*. The hundreds of mature trees in the park come from six continents and include many tropical and subtropical species making it one of the most important subtropical flora gardens in Europe. The website of the *ayuntamiento* has a wealth of information about some of the most interesting arboreal species, but only in Spanish: **bit.ly/parquedemalagaspecies**.

The Parque de Málaga is also home to many works of sculpture, mainly in the form of monuments topped with busts of illustrious men (and they are all men) — poets, composers, politicians and soldiers — associated with Málaga. There are also more 'cultural' and poetic representations, like the *Ninfa del Cántaro* (Pitcher Nymph) and *Ninfa de la Caracola* (Conch Shell Nymph) fountains, and the *Burrito Platero* (Little Silver Donkey). This latter work celebrates a character in the lyrical poem *Platero y yo* (subtitled *An Andalusian Elegy*) by the Nobel Prize winner Juan Ramón Jiménez, and you will find it in the children's play area in the centre of the park, next to the amphitheatre and café. You will also notice frequent use of *azulejo* (painted) tiles, typical of *andaluz* architectural decoration. You can find information about a lot of the sculpture and flora of the park (in English) on the British horticulturist Simon Needham's excellent personal blog: **parquedemalaga.wordpress.com**.

Cemeteries

Málaga has two 19th-century cemeteries worth exploring. The more famous among visitors is the Anglican Cemetery near the bullring (p. 71 and p. 280), but there is also the city's large Catholic cemetery north of the city, about half an hour's walk from the centre, or a fifteen-minute bus ride (🚌 1, 2 or C2) from the Alameda or Plaza de La Merced. The **San Miguel Cemetery** is of interest due to the numerous mausoleums that the 19th-century bourgeoisie had built there. It is currently being restored for the construction of gardens, recreation areas and other facilities, having been closed to new burials for some years.

 The San Miguel Cemetery was consecrated in 1810, at a time when the city was occupied by Napoleon's troops. Nevertheless, it would be a couple of decades before it took on its current aspect. The wall around it was not built until 1827 and it would be another two years before it was considered completed, a fact that is commemorated in the inscription on the triangular plaque above the entrance arch. The address is **Plaza Patrocinio 8**.

Parque del Oeste

 The 'Eastern Park' is a relative newcomer among Málaga's green spaces, only inaugurated in 1992. It is the largest park in the suburbs, in the *barrio* of Carretera de Cádiz between the railway station and the airport. If you are visiting Málaga as a family with children, then the Parque del Oeste should be on your list of places to visit, but even *sans enfants*, it is a pleasant and diverting place. If you are taking a walk along the beaches that run south-west of the city then take a detour, or if you are travelling from the centre by bus (🚌 16) then alight at **Luis Barahona Soto/Parque del Oeste** (Ⓑ1523) and make your way to the seafront through the park. Surrounded by blocks of flats, it is not the most beautiful setting for an urban park, but it still manages to feel like an oasis. It has a lovely *ambiente*, is well used by locals (especially families) and is surrounded by good cafés and bars.

You'll have noticed that housing in Málaga is fairly dense, and the *barrio* of Carretera de Cádiz is the third most densely populated in Spain. People live in apartments and flats, rather than in houses with gardens. Outdoor space is public and shared, which helps to account for (or is perhaps explained by) the almost obsessively sociable nature of the Spaniards. This park, then, is effectively the 'garden' of the thousands of people living nearby. It certainly packs a great deal into a fairly small space with over 800 trees, areas for basketball and football, an open-air gym, a huge lake with an impressive fountain, dozens of surreal modern sculptures (by the German sculptor Stefan von Reiswitz, an adopted son of Málaga), a couple of children's play parks, wildfowl and other animals including a wallaby, emus, a tortoise and a chameleon. There are even two examples of that rarest of features — a public lavatory.

🦅 Birding

David Lindo (aka **@urbanbirder**), known from UK TV programmes like Springwatch and Countryfile recommends Málaga as one of the best urban birding locations.[44] Even in the city centre, you will see birds that are rarely seen in urban spaces in Britain. There are the squawking escaped parakeets, of course, but also starlings and sparrows in abundance. You will also see Lesser Kestrels, and even Peregrine Falcons, flitting around the towers of the Cathedral and other churches, as well as Black Wheatears and Blue Rock Thrushes around the *Teatro Romano* and Alcazaba. The prime spot for birdwatching, however, is the Parque del Guadalhorce (Guadalhorce Natural Park) near the airport

Located at the delta of the Guadalhorce River, this 67-hectare wetland reserve has a wealth of bird life at any time of year. The Booted Eagle, Black-winged Stilt, Purple Swamphen, Sardinian Warbler, Zitting Cisticola and European Serin can be seen year-round and the reserve is also home to the endangered White-headed Duck. Winter brings more duck species onto the lagoons as well as the Greater Flamingo. The reserve really comes alive during migration and especially in spring, when it's possible to find Osprey, Bluethroat, Great Reed Warbler, Little Bittern and Purple Heron, as well as storks, hirundines and plovers. Near the sea, keep an eye out for Audouin's Gull and Slender-billed Gull.

For more information about this and other birding sites throughout the province, consult the excellent website of the *Diputación* (Provincial Government) **birdingmalaga.es** and also **wildandalucia.com/bird-watching-in-malaga**.

To combine some birdwatching (at Europe's second largest colony of flamingos) with a visit to a winery, have a look at the information about Fuente de Piedra (p. 481).

🚶 Walking and Hiking

The possibilities for walking and hiking in the city and province of Málaga are extensive. You are limited only by your energy, time and shoe leather. Walks around urban areas are one thing, but in the countryside and mountains, then you need to make adequate preparations. The terrain can be tough, particularly in the summer heat, but if you are an experienced hiker, there are lots of possibilities. You could combine a rural walk with almost any of the locations in the Day Trips section (p. 467ff.) by, for example, studying the train or bus time-

44   David Lindo, 'Six cities that are unexpected havens for birdwatching', *The Daily Telegraph*, 13 February 2018 archive.ph/UuidF

table and walking part of that route (between two or more stops). If you are an experienced hiker then I do not need to tell you that Google Maps is not a suitable app for planning hiking routes because it will try to send you along roads that are prohibited to pedestrians (highways and expressways), but also because its level of detail is very poor outside cities.

To find suitable routes outside Málaga city, begin with the website of the local *turismo* as many of them will have a section about walking and hiking routes, as well as maps. If you can't find anything, send an email in advance of your visit. Most tourist offices are good at responding to queries. Other good places to find tried and tested routes are **komoot.com**, **alltrails.com**, **hiiker.app**, and **wikiloc.com** (the site/app that the *Diputación de Málaga* has chosen to partner with). It is also worth searching online more generally, and you may find that using Spanish delivers more relevant results (*ruta* = route, *camino* = path, *senderismo* = hiking, *a pie* = on foot).

Gran Senda

This is the official hiking route through the Province of Málaga — 650 km and 35 stages of the *Gran Senda* (Great Route) *de Málaga* covers 9 regions and 50 towns going through, or around, 13 protected natural areas. On foot and by bicycle (or on horseback) along its trails, paths and tracks, through river basins and around lakes, crossing steppe areas, mountain areas and coast-land, you will have the chance to see and enjoy the essence of the Province of Málaga: **gransendademalaga.es** (there is also a smartphone app). A number of PDF guides (to trees, birdlife and more) are available to download, though most are in Spanish. However, there are a couple of comprehensive guides in English that you can download for free:

 Sierra de las Nieves Path

 The Great Málaga Path

If the links are broken, consult the main page at: **malaga.es/en/laprovincia/publicaciones**

Senda Litoral

The *Senda Litoral* is the coastal path of the Province of Málaga, a project of the *Diputación de Málaga* in cooperation with the coastal municipalities. Although unfinished, the eventual aim is to allow a person (on foot, on a bicycle or in a wheelchair) to travel from Nerja in the east to Manilva in the west, some 160 km to 180 km, depending upon the final route. The *kilometro cero* (Km 0) starting point will be the Balcón de Europa in Nerja and the finish was to have been the Castillo de la Duquesa in Manilva but that has now been extended to Punta Chullera, the provincial border with Cádiz. Some sections are complete, either using existing infrastructure (*e.g.* promenades) or new walkways, while other sections are in progress and some yet to be started. There are considerable challenges to be overcome in places. Despite its image of an endless strip of hotels, the Costa del Sol is not one continuous beach development. In much of the east of the province (*Costa del Sol Oriental*), there are places where farmers' fields extend to the beach, with the principal road far inland. Here, new boardwalks will be constructed. In other places, cliffs are the challenge.

The path has the reference GR92. 'GR' footpaths are a network of long-distance walking trails in Europe, mostly in France, Belgium, the Netherlands and Spain, where the network is called '*Sendero de Gran Recorrido*'. The *Senda Litoral* will form a stage in the long coastal route from Catalonia to Tarifa. There is a website with information at **sendalitoral.es** and

Chris Chaplow at **andalucia.com** is maintaining a very useful map showing the current state of play vis-à-vis the progress of construction (GREEN — complete; ORANGE — port or marina; BLUE — beach with no boardwalk; RED — you need to make a diversion to reach the next section). Use the QR code to view the map, or go to: **bit.ly/SendaLit**

🏖 Beaches

 The main tourist beaches are west of Málaga (Torremolinos, Fuengirola, Mijas, Marbella) or to the East (the many small resorts along the coast as far as Nerja). However, Málaga has beaches of its own within walking distance of the city centre, or a short bus ride away. They are used almost exclusively by residents of Málaga and the only tourists will be Spaniards. The 'bathing season' is reckoned to be between 15 June and 15 September (with July and August the peak), so although the beaches are open and accessible from mid-September to mid-June, the showers, bathrooms and some of the beach bars won't, there will be no lifeguards and you will not be able to hire deckchairs or parasols.

The beach nearest the city centre is the Malagueta Beach, just east of the bullring and the other side of Muelle Uno. But to the west, close to the working class district of Huelin, there are a couple of very good and popular beaches, full of *malagueña* families enjoying an afternoon out. To find beaches beyond the Malagueta, then check the section on activities for children beginning on p. 283, and consult the following websites for the most up-to-date information, including occupancy and flag status:

 bit.ly/MalagaCityBeaches — use the 'map' view

 playas.malaga.eu — the official town hall site (in *castellano*)

 aforocostadelsol.es/aforo — live information about beaches in the Province of Málaga (in *castellano* and only updated during the June-September bathing season)

Beach Rules

Foreign visitors are often caught out by local laws regarding the use of the beaches in the Málaga municipality, which are a mixture of national and local legislation. A sensible approach is not to do anything that you don't see others doing. For example, smoking is prohibited on some beaches despite their being 'open spaces', and on any beach, the disposal of cigarette butts anywhere other than refuse bins could attract a large fine (of between €300 and €3,000). The use of soap or shampoo in the showers is also prohibited.

Nudity is forbidden on any beach that is not a '*playa nudista*', though topless bathing is generally permitted. On the other hand, beachwear (bikinis, trunks, swimsuits, etc.) is for the beach, not the town. Other prohibited activities include playing music that might annoy others, leaving litter, camping, lighting fires and cleaning anything other than your own body in the showers. 'Litter' covers anything left behind on the beach, including organic matter such as peanut shells or cherry pips.

🚤 Boat Trips

A fun sightseeing option in Málaga is to take a boat trip around the bay. The basic trip lasts an hour and the rates are standardized between the three operators. Remember that children aged 14 and over count as adults. The standard trip takes you out into the open sea — just — but you get a different, and beautiful, view of the city of Málaga (as long as you can filter out the heavy industrial plant of the port). All three operators embark at the intersection of Muelle Uno and Muelle Dos. ⚠ 'cruise' (*paseo*) and 'bathing' (*baño*) don't translate well on websites, so don't be confused about references to a 'walk around the bay' or a 'walk' that includes a 'bath'!

CitySightseeing Spain Boat Tour

This is operated by the 'CitySightseeing' tour bus franchise based in Sevilla whose open-top buses you see in almost every city in Europe. The boat uses the same gaudy red livery, so is easy to spot. Booking online is advised.

Fly Blue

With this company, which appears to be the most popular, you have a choice between the standard 1 hour excursion or, for a higher ticket price, a 90-minute sailing at sunset.

Catamarán Mundo Marino

This company offers the most choices. You can choose the standard 1-hour cruise or the 90-minute sunset cruise as above, but other options include a sunset cruise with music, a 90-minute trip including half an hour's swim, a 3-hour excursion further along the coast, etc.

Outside Málaga

Costa Sol Cruceros operate a regular cruise launch between Benalmádena and Fuengirola (an hour each way), as well as a separate 2-hour dolphin-spotting trip.

🧖 Hammams

In Moorish times there would have been dozens of bath houses in the Medina of Málaga, as there were all over Andalucía. For some time now there has been a modern hammam in the

Plaza de los Mártires, where a pair of narrow doors open into a 1,300 square metre facility, that opened in 2013. It's not original, of course, but hammams are popular in Andalucía and the same company operates in Madrid, Granada and Córdoba. I suspect it's all aromatherapy oils and organic fair-trade cotton towels, but the reviews are good. You can book online. What is interesting is how 'authentically' the place has been created/restored — a sign of how much the contemporary arts of Andalucía still owe to the Moorish period. The coloured tiles, for example, seem to 'fit' with a Moorish bath house, and yet they can also be found in practically every bar in southern Spain. More recently, another hammam has opened near the Cathedral.

Hammam Al-Andalus Málaga

🏛 CENTRO HISTÓRICO 📍 Plaza de los Mártires Ciriaco & Paula 5
🌐 malaga.hammamalandalus.com 🕐 Mon–Sun 1000–0000

Hammam Open Space and Spa

🏛 CENTRO HISTÓRICO 📍 Calle Tomás de Cózar 13
🌐 elhammamspa.com 🕐 Mon–Sun 1100–2200

🚻 Lavatories

Visitors to Spain often remark upon how few public lavatories there are. Whilst old-fashioned municipal public conveniences are few and far between, these have mostly disappeared from UK town centres, too. As a visitor to Málaga, spending most of the day out of your hotel or accommodation, it's worth engaging in a little forward planning regarding your 'comfort breaks'. Try to use the loo before setting out for the day, whenever you visit a museum, and every time you stop to eat or drink — 'whether you need to or not' in the manner of Queen Elizabeth I's monthly bath.

As in English, the *castellano* words for the loo are all euphemisms: *baños* (bathrooms), *servicios* (services), *aseos* (washrooms) and, less commonly, *lavabos* (washrooms). If you need to ask for directions ask, '*Dónde están los servicios*' (**don**-day ess-**tan** los sair-**beeth**-yoss).

Museums all have lavatories, but these tend to be the other side of the entrance barrier (though one or two can be accessed from the separate *cafetería*). The larger hotels (the sort with a bar in the foyer) have lavatories in the lobby, but they are for guests and customers only. Whether you want to chance your arm and sneak in will rather depend on your level of confidence or chutzpah. Bars, restaurants and *cafeterías* all have lavatories for the use of customers, and as one can barely walk more than a few metres in Spain without encountering a bar, you will always be able to find somewhere to relieve yourself if you are desperate.

Some establishments will not object to your using their facilities if you ask politely (*¿Puedo usar el baño?* **pway**-doh oo-**sar** el **ban**-yoh), though those near the tourist hot spots can understandably be less accommodating. It would probably be good form to buy a drink, in which case you have every right to use their facilities. A coffee or a glass of mineral water (or a small bottle of chilled water to take away) is less than €2 pretty much everywhere, which is what one might pay in some cities for admission to 'public' conveniences. Facilities in bars can range from modern and immaculate to, well, somewhat basic (especially in smaller and older bars). Provision can also be unpredictable. A tiny dive of a bar might have pristine and palatial loos, while a chic cocktail bar could have facilities with slippery floors, overflowing bins and absent soap. Very often there is a single cubicle for men and a single cubicle for women (and do not be surprised if the ladies' is locked and you need to ask for a key). When you switch on the light, remember where it is! Most lights are on timers and you may find yourself suddenly plunged into darkness.

Lavatory paper and paper towels (or a working hand dryer) are also something of a lottery, so make sure you are prepared. The supermarket Mercadona (branches in the main railway station and on Paseo de Reding, 500 metres beyond the bullring) sells biodegradable moist wipes, including in a pocket size (15 wipes) for around a euro. Do not be surprised if there is no loo seat — Spaniards are adept at 'hovering' when using a public lavatory. Also, if there is a bin next to the pan, this is where you should deposit your lavatory paper. Although this mode of disposal is far less common than in the past, there are still areas where it is necessary due to ancient plumbing.

You can find public lavatories at the following locations:

Beaches — there are basic facilities at most of Málaga's beaches (though generally only open during high season)

Parque del Oeste — rather unusually, this urban park has two sets of public conveniences

María Zambrano Railway Station — there are two sets of free facilities in the Vialia shopping centre, one on the ground floor and one upstairs next to the cinema. Both are fully accessible, modern and clean.

Málaga Bus Station — two very basic, but free, facilities at either end of the concourse.

Shopping Centres — in Málaga city this means the **Centro Comercial Larios**, near the bus station. The facilities are clean and accessible. There are also loos in the **Mercado Atarazanas**.

Muelle Uno — there are public lavatories on Muelle Uno which are very clean and fully accessible.

Turismo — the main office at Plaza de la Marina has a single-cubicle loo.

Department Stores — in other words, El Corte Inglés on the El Perchel side of the river. There are toilets on every floor. These are for the use of customers, but even if you are only browsing, you are at least a potential customer, right?

CAC — the toilets in the **Centro de Arte Comtemporáneo de Málaga** are for the use of patrons, but they are accessible (go through the main entrance and they are downstairs on the right) and admission to the gallery is free in any case.

Car Parks — walking around Málaga, you may wonder where all the multi-storey car parks are. The answer is that they are underground. Under the Plaza de la Marina, under Muelle Uno, under the rail station, under El Corte Inglés, and so forth. There are lavatories in the subterranean car parks at Muelle Uno, Plaza de la Marina, Alcazaba and Calle Salitre, situated near the pedestrian access point and ticket machines.

Municipal Automatic Cubicles — the *ayuntamiento* is spending almost €760,000 installing five free, automatic and self-cleaning public conveniences in different areas of the city. The first appeared in the Plaza de la Marina in October 2022, and the others are planned for south of the Cathedral, near the statue of Cardenal Herrera Oria; on the Avenida Cervantes in front of the Jardines Pedro Luis Alonso; near the Plaza de La Merced; and near the Playa de Pedregalejo. All are (or will be) fully accessible.

Portaloos — during *Semana Santa* and the *feria*, extra loos are provided by the *ayuntamiento*.

De compras (Shopping)

Most of the big-name Spanish stores (Mango, Massimo Dutti, Bimba & Lola and Zara) are on, or near, **Calle Larios**. **Calle Nueva** (the parallel street to the west) is also a busy shopping street. The **Calle San Juan** has a number of local, independent stores, and **Calle Especería** (running west from the Plaza de la Constitución towards the river, becoming **Calle Cisneros**) is the street for typically Spanish clothing — flamenco dresses, shawls, and *sombreros* (hats).

🛒 *Supermercados* (Supermarkets)

For everyday items, there are a few 'express' type supermarkets around the *centro histórico*:

🛒 **Carrefour Express** 📍 Calle Atarazanas s/n 🕐 Mon–Sat 0830–2200

🛒 **Preba** 📍 Calle Fernán González 4 🕐 0900–1430, 1700–2100

🛒 **Carrefour Express** 📍 Calle Tejón y Rodríguez 1 📍 Calle Especería 7 🕐 0900–2130

🛒 **Día** 📍 Calle Carretería 105 🕐 0900–1500, 1700–2100

Outside these times, or for basics and/or emergencies, there are plenty of small corner shops in the centre, mostly run by Chinese families and known colloquially as '*chinos*'. Like corner shops in the UK, they sell snack foods, milk, soft drinks, alcohol etc., and like UK corner shops, you pay over the odds for convenience. Most are open from mid-morning until late (usually midnight or even later). Currently, convenience stores cannot legally sell spirits after 6 pm, nor alcohol after 10 pm.

Although fairly small, the best-stocked supermarket in the city centre is **Maskom** (**Calle Gómez Pallete 2**) which occupies space in the **Mercado de La Merced**, just off the plaza of the same name. Open from 0900–2130 daily and 0930–2100 on Sundays and holidays.

A lot of the small Spanish supermarkets are being taken over by **Carrefour**, so some on the list and on the companion map may have changed! For more choice, take a 20-minute walk or bus ride from the centre to **El Corte Inglés**, Eroski (Larios Shopping Centre) or **Mercadona** (María Zambrano railway station).

El Corte Inglés

🚇 Mármoles 📍 Centro Comercial Málaga, Avenida de Andalucía 4–6
🕐 Mon–Sun 1000–2200

El Corte Inglés is the Selfridges of Spain and although it is not the cheapest place to shop, it is a useful place to know about. Food in the basement supermarket is not the cheapest either, but it is still reasonably priced by UK standards (the most expensive lines are stocked in '**Gourmet Experience**' on the top floor: see the section on Mármoles for more details, p. 79) — more expensive than local *supermercados* like Día or Mercadona, but no more expensive than 'express' supermarkets or corner shops, and with a huge range of products. For other goods, it has the great advantage of stocking almost anything you might need all under one roof. It is useful to know that there is a branch of **Mister Minit** here. This is the continental equivalent of Timpsons and is very useful if you need your shoes or watch repaired.

🏬 *Centros comerciales* (Shopping Centres)

Centro Comercial Larios

🍴 EL PERCHEL 📍 Avenida de la Aurora 25 🕐 1000–2200

In Spain, a *centro comercial* is a shopping centre in the UK sense, a mall in the US sense — *viz.* chain stores and a few basic eateries. Larios Centro is the nearest such shopping centre to the *centro histórico* and while it is never going to feature on any visitor's sightseeing itinerary, it is handy to know where it is should you need it. In the basement, there is a very large, low-cost but good quality supermarket called Eroski. And like El Corte Inglés, there is everything else that you might need here, though at more competitive prices. It is also where Málaga's branch of Primark is located. It's barely a 5-minute walk from the rail and bus stations.

Centro Comercial Vialia

🍴 El Perchel 📍 Explanada de la Estación 🕐 1000–2200

If you happen to be passing through (or near) the railway station (María Zambrano) then remember that there is a good supermarket on the upper level (Mercadona) that not only has a wide selection of groceries (although the wine section is pretty limited) but also a wide range of toiletries. Picking up some essentials here when you arrive in Málaga could save you from having to make a special journey later on.

Plaza Mayor

🍴 CARRETERA DE CÁDIZ 📍 Calle Alfonso Ponce de León 🕐 1000–0100

Plaza Mayor is a large, out-of-town shopping centre just past the airport. It can be easily reached by the 🚆 *Cercanías* train (the Plaza Mayor station is just over the road from the shopping centre entrance). It has 79 stores, a **Mercadona** supermarket, 33 eateries, all the major Spanish brands and a few international ones too (there is an Adidas 'outlet', for example). But the international brands are 'high street', rather than designer, brands — no Louis Vuitton or Gucci here. It is rather more Westfield than Bicester Village.

🛍 Independent shops

Espadrilles

If you are in search of traditional (and cheap) *alpargatas* (as espadrilles are known in *castellano*), you will need to shop around. Old-fashioned, independent shoe shops are your best bet. In 2023, Málaga's longest-established and most traditional shoe shop, Calzados Hinojosa, closed when the owners Alberto and Javier Hinojosa decided to retire.[45] Their father José came to Málaga as a boy, travelling on a donkey, and was apprenticed at 'Alpargatas La Comba'. He acquired it in 1920, changing the name. In that incarnation, it shod generations of *malagueños* and summer visitors. For those of us who know Málaga well, the Calle San Juan

---

45   C. Clavijo, 'Calzados Hinojosa, la meca de las alpargatas del Centro de Málaga, cerrará en junio', in *Málaga Hoy* (newspaper) https://archive.ph/4wfTW

will never seem quite the same again. To find '*alpargatas básicas*', shoe shops in the suburbs are your best bet, or **Merkal** in the **Centro Comercial Rosaleda (Avenida Simón Bolívar)**. Buy the smallest size you can (uncomfortably) wedge your foot into because they stretch. A lot. For modern fashion *alpargatas*, try **Toni Pons (Calle Nueva 22)**, and for eye-catching, stylish colourful trainers visit **Hoff (Plaza de la Constitución 2)**, a footwear company based in Elche (Alicante).

Corcel (Handbags)

MÁRMOLES ⚲ Calle Hilera 6 🕒 Mon–Sat 1000–1400, 1730–2030

A very small shop opposite El Corte Inglés (on the north side).

Zerimar-Málaga (Handbags and leather goods)

CENTRO HISTÓRICO ⚲ Calle Granada 12 🕒 Mon–Sat 1000–2030; Sun 1100–1900

The Málaga store of a company based in Campillos (between Málaga and Córdoba). The shop is 50 metres north-east of the Plaza de la Constitución. They have branches in Torremolinos, Benalmádena and Fuengirola

Misako (Fashion Bags)

CENTRO HISTÓRICO ⚲ Calle Nueva 29 🕒 Mon–Sat 1000–2130

Misako is a very popular brand of handbags (they also make bags for men, backpacks and purses) based in Barcelona. They are faux leather, but good quality and sold at amazingly low prices.

Souvenirs

Temporánea Concept Shop

CENTRO HISTÓRICO ⚲ Calle Santos 4 🕒 1030–1330, 1700–2100

If you want to avoid the usual mass-produced tat then this little shop selling tasteful and high-quality products is a good start. Also worth looking out for is anything made by malagapatterns.com and lamalagamoderna.com though currently both stores are on-line only.

 *Ultramarinos* (Delicatessens)

An *ultramarinos* is a traditional Spanish grocer's shop. The name was originally due to their stocking of 'exotic' products that have come 'across the seas', but nowadays they are valued more for selling local delicacies. They have an old-fashioned set-up with a shopkeeper behind a counter, rather than supermarket-style self-service. They are excellent places to buy local products as gifts and souvenirs.

If you don't speak Spanish, you may

feel nervous about shopping in an old-fashioned establishment where communication with an employee is unavoidable (rather than in a more comfortably anonymous supermarket). However, I would urge you to take a deep breath and give it a go. First-rate customer service is the USP of *ultramarinos* these days, so you can be sure of a warm welcome. Also, they will be glad of your custom. What a shame it would be if these beautiful, traditional grocers went the same way as Café Central and Calzados Hinojosa, only to be supplanted by those garish chain stores selling nougat and chocolates exclusively to tourists.

Zoilo

🏛 CENTRO HISTÓRICO ♀ Calle Granada 65 (near Plaza de La Merced) ⏱ 0900–1430, 1630–2100; Sat 0930–1430; ⊘ Sun

Founded in 1956, Zoilo carries a huge range of products, many of them from the Province of Málaga. It also sells a small range of *empanadas* and delicious, freshly made *pitufos* (small sandwiches). The staff are very friendly and good at making helpful recommendations.

In the 1940s, at the age of 14, the eponymous Zoilo Montero left his small *sevillano* home town of Herrera and came to Málaga to work for his uncle, first in Pedregalejo and later on Calle Granada in Ultramarinos Álvarez, which he would inherit. He got to know Mari Carmen Rodríguez who worked in the egg shop next door. Zoilo and Mari Carmen later married and established Ultramarinos Zoilo. Now retired, Don Zoilo is often seen in the shop, keeping an eye on his children Ginés and Luisa who run the shop nowadays.

Zoilo sells all the usual staples and delicacies: Málaga *salchichón*, Ronda *chorizo*, local cheese, sweet and table wines, ham, *borrachuelos*, carob and almond cakes, homemade jams, raisins, fig bread, olive oil, vinegar, cane honey, olives and the rest. It is probably most famous, though, for its sandwiches (fillings include jamón, cheese, *tortilla*, pork belly, *salchichón* and turkey); the biggest selling item. Indeed, in Victoria Sotorrío's crime thriller *Nassricht* (2020) set in 1990s Málaga, the protagonist buys a sandwich each day from Zoilo.

Another big seller is oil, but not all of it is destined for the kitchen. Instead, it is taken across the road to the church of Santiago Apóstol to be left as a votive offering for the souls in Purgatory (see p. 267 for an explanation of this *malagueña* tradition).

Juan de Dios Barba

🏛 CENTRO HISTÓRICO ♀ Calle Martínez 10 ⏱ Mon–Fri 0930–1400, 1700–2030; Sat 0930–1400; ⊘ Sun

This traditional shop is known for its excellent quality *bacalao* (dried salt cod), great rolls of which fill the window, but it stocks a huge range of gourmet products from salted Málaga almonds to La Torre olive oil, acorn-fed *jamón* and local cheeses. It is now run by Javier and Carlos Crespillo, great-grandsons of the founder.

El Almacén del Indiano

🏛 CENTRO HISTÓRICO ♀ Calle Cisneros 7 ⏱ Mon–Sat 1130–1500, 1800–2100; ⊘ Sun

Although it is not particularly old (the owner admits that he set out to create a 'time machine' to recreate a traditional grocer), this is a typical *ultramarinos* where you can taste and buy an exquisite selection of wines, craft beers, hams, cured meats, cheeses, oils and pickles from Andalucía and other parts of Spain. You can also purchase traditional and typical sweets, as well as high-quality preserves. On Thursday evenings it often organizes wine tastings, and look out for olive oil tastings too. It's primarily a shop, but the 'tasting' element means that it's also an intimate *tapas* bar. A good plan (for two or more people) is to order a glass (or a bottle) of the excellent house wine and the '*surtido malagueño*' — a selection of cured local meats and cheeses.

La Princesa Pastelería

🍴 La Merced 📍 Calle Granada 84 🕐 1000–1430, 1700–2100

Strictly speaking a *pastelería* (confectioners or patisserie) rather than an *ultramarinos*, but it is one of the most traditional shops in Málaga having chalked more than 80 years of serving customers. María Ángeles Guerrero, daughter of the founder, is to be found behind the counter and she does a good trade in traditional sweets and biscuits from the region. Doña María's meringues are much loved by *malagueños*.

La Mallorquina

🍴 CENTRO HISTÓRICO 📍 Plaza de Félix Sáenz 7 🕐 Mon–Sat 0900–1400, 1730–2030, Half Day Sat)

Every city in Spain seems to have an establishment called 'La Mallorquina' (the Mallorcan). In Sevilla it's a traditional shoe shop, in Madrid it's a very traditional café on the Puerta del Sol, and in Málaga, it's an *ultramarinos*. It was founded in 1943 by Salvador Postigo, who ran it until 1982 when it was acquired by José Palma Aguilar. Now run by José's son, José Palma Medina, this is another lovely little deli that's perfect for loading up on Spanish delicacies to take home. Its range of interesting jams is especially noteworthy and includes plenty of unusual (and local) varieties like chestnut or Pedro Ximénez. Don José has recently moved into online commerce with an excellent website, but in the shop the service is as kind and professional as it ever was.

La Despensa de Iñaki (see p. 217)

Crespillo Innova

🍴 MALAGUETA 📍 Calle Cervantes 10 🕐 Mon–Fri 0930–1400, 1730–2100; Sat 0930–1400

Only established in 2004, this is an Aladdin's cave of gourmet delights behind the bullring, selling the finest products from all over Spain — wine, oil, vinegar, ham, chocolates, *conservas* (tinned seafood) and preserves, Málaga honey, etc. It is run by the Crespillo brothers who also own Juan de Dios Barba.

Jamones y Embutidos Melgar

🍴 CENTRO HISTÓRICO 📍 Calle Martínez 2, local 1 🕐 Mon–Sat 0930–1500, 1700–2100

Melgar is a butcher based in Arriate, a village not far from Ronda. As well as ham and sausages, it also stocks cheese and other artisan products from the Serranía de Ronda, including some of the best *bocadillos* (sandwiches) *de jamón* in town.

Frinsa La Conservera Market

🍴 CENTRO HISTÓRICO 📍 Calle Martínez 2, local 2 🕐 Mon–Fri 1000–1500, 1700–2000; Sat 1000–1500

This is not a traditional *ultramarinos*, but an interesting shop nonetheless. Strange as it might seem to many foreigners, tinned fish and seafood is a premium product in Spain, and many go out of their way to visit bars that serve *tapas* of tinned fish and seafood. The logic is impeccable — tinned seafood is canned within minutes of being landed, whereas the 'fresh' fish is likely to be a few hours old at the very least. Frinsa is a well-known fish and seafood company from Galicia and produces gourmet products at reasonable prices. If you like tuna, then the beautiful hand-cut fillets of Bonito del Norte (Albacore Tuna) in oil are a must-buy — a far cry from the greyish sludge we often encounter in UK supermarkets.

Manzana de Oro (Golden Apple)
🏙 MALAGUETA 📍 Paseo Reding, 16 🕐 0900–1400, 1700–2100

The shelves of this charming *ultramarinos* are meticulously stocked with great attention to detail. At Manzana de Oro, you will find only local products from Málaga and the surrounding region; among them some of the highest-quality wines in the province. Friendly, knowledgeable staff.

📕 Books

Mapas y Compañía
🏙 CENTRO HISTÓRICO 📍 Calle Compañía 33 🕐 Mon–Fri 1000–1330, 1700–2000; Sat 1000–1400

This is a lovely bookshop that focuses on travel. The English section isn't huge, but it is well worth a visit just for the experience. The closest that Málaga has to Daunt or Stanfords bookshop in London. A delightful place.

Librería Luces
🏙 ALAMEDA 📍 Alameda Principal 37 🕐 Mon–Sat 0930–2030

This much-loved independent bookshop is an important cultural landmark in Málaga (they organize the regular chess tournaments for children on the Alameda Principal). They stock a modest range of books in English.

Librería Rayuela
🏙 CENTRO HISTÓRICO 📍 Calle Cárcer 1 🕐 Mon–Fri 1000–2000; Sat 1000–1400)

Another independent bookshop with a decent range of books in English.

🛍 Others

Tea and Coffee: Golden Tips
🏙 CENTRO HISTÓRICO 📍 Calle Especería 26 🕐 Mon–Sat 1000–1400, 1700–2030

A lovely boutique shop specializing in teas, coffees, chocolates and all related accessories.

Accessories: Ten to Nine
CENTRO HISTÓRICO 📍 Plaza Constitución 7 🕐 Mon–Sat 1000–1400, 1700–2030

This is a *'bisutería'* — *'bisu'* being a Spanish mangling of the French *'bijou'*. In other words, a place selling pretty little things. This small independent shop sells goods made in Málaga — hats, costume jewellery, baskets for the beach, tunics, shirts, etc. The clothes are marketed under the 'Smach' brand and the accessories under the 'Boho' brand.

Jewellery: Calamita

🍴 CENTRO HISTÓRICO 📍 Calle Cárcer 1 🕐 Tue–Sat 1100–1400, 1730–2030

This jewellery shop was started by Nora Zurita (with her partner Ale) and specializes in simple items made with silver, crystal and leather. For hand-made artisan pieces, the prices are reasonable.

Ceramics: Alfajar Cerámica Artesanal

🍴 CENTRO HISTÓRICO 📍 Calle Císter 1 🕐 Tue–Sun 1000–1330, 1600–1830; Mon 1000–2030

Run by husband and wife team José Ángel Ruiz and Lola Díaz, this store sells pottery and ceramics with vaguely 'cubist' designs. The goods are excellent quality but given the unique style, it's one of those places that is either going to be your cup of tea or not.

Records: Discos Candilejas

🍴 CENTRO HISTÓRICO 📍 Calle Sta. Lucía 9 🕐 Mon–Sat 1030–1330, 1730–2030

Some families go to Discos Candilejas on Saturdays to teach their children what music is 'really' about. They introduce them to the world of CDs, vinyl and tapes, while the kids watch in wonder (and perhaps disbelief).

Wine

The better supermarkets carry a decent selection of wine. But if you want to buy a bottle of local wine to enjoy during your stay, or want to take a bottle or two home while avoiding the airport offerings, try an *ultramarinos* or the following:

Málaga Wine Museum

🍴 La Goleta 📍 Plaza de los Viñeros 1 🕐 Mon–Fri 1000–1700, Sat 1000–1400

The museum's shop carries a good selection of the best wines from the region, with knowledgeable staff to tell you about the wine, its region and *bodega*.

El Templo de Vino

🍴 CENTRO HISTÓRICO 📍 Calle Sebastián Souvirón 11 🕐 1030–1400, 1800–2130

The aptly named El Templo de Vino is one of the newer wine shops in Málaga, having opened its doors in 2011. It carries a very well-chosen selection of Spanish and lesser-known international wines, many of which are available to try by the glass. The passionate, knowledgeable staff speak Spanish, English, French, Italian and German.

🧂 *Dulces de Convento*

One of the more unusual purchases one can make in Spain is confectionery made by local nuns. These sweetmeats (mostly rich or crumbly biscuits) are sold from the convent door. Again, this is one of those times when visitors need to take a deep breath and go for it. Ring the bell and wait for the voice behind the wooden *torno* (a kind of enclosed lazy susan) to say, 'Ave María purísima!' ('Hail, purest Mary!') to which you respond, 'Sin pecado concebida!' ('Conceived without sin!' sin peh-**kah**-doh con-thay-**bee**-dah) and give your order. Next to the *torno* will be a list of products, all with extraordinary and ancient names: *roscos de vino, mantecadas, borrachuelos, roscos de vanilla, paſtitas de almendras, clarinas, pujaldrinas, hortolanas, hugolinas, yemas,* and many more. Place your money into the lazy susan and after it turns back and forth, retrieve a box of sweet biscuits, wrapped in tissue paper.

It is possible to buy similar biscuits and sweets in almost any supermarket or gift shop, and even in the airport, but these might have been made anywhere, and by anyone. Contemplative nuns support themselves by making sweets and it is also one way in which they can share their secluded life with 'the world'. As the Mother Superior of the Minim Nuns in Archidona puts it, 'What we intend with these sweets is that they provide the flavour of heaven, that when tasting the sweets you will experience the sweetness of God.'

🍴 La Trinidad 📍 Plaza Zumaya 5 🕐 Mon–Sat 1030–1330, 1600–1830; Sun 1200–1330, 1600–1830

In Málaga, sweets are made and sold by the Poor Claire Sisters at the **Monasterio de Nuestra Señora de la Paz y Santísima Trinidad** (Monastery of Our Lady of Peace and the Holy Trinity). Each sweet biscuit is sold in boxes of 250 g, 500 g or 1 kg, and you can also buy selection (*surtido*) boxes in the same weights.

In the city centre, one can also buy sweets and biscuits made by nuns from the Province of Málaga (Málaga, Antequera, Ronda, Coín, Archidona, etc.) in most *ultramarinos*.

🎁 Gift Ideas from Málaga

*'All who are wise will bring from Málaga a good hamper of eatables,
a bota of wine, and some cigars...'*
(Hand-book for Travellers in Spain, *Richard Ford, 1845*)

The best places to find the food and drink items in this section are the *ultramarinos* listed above (p. 297ff.), any of the city *mercados* (markets) or larger supermarkets (El Corte Inglés has the most choice and a better selection of premium and gourmet products).

Goat's Cheese

Cheese-making in Spain is still very localized. *Manchego* is made in La Mancha, *Torta del Casar* is from Cáceres and the fantastically piquant blue *Cabrales* is made in Asturias. Málaga is famous for its goat's cheese. Most goats from Málaga are descended from two ancient goat breeds. The first type was the Pyrenean mountain goat, which came from the north of the Peninsula, and the other was the Maltese goat, originally from North Africa. Another common goat is the Payoya (or Montejaque), originally from the Sierra de Grazalema, located on the border between the provinces of Cádiz and Málaga.

The cheese produced is exceptionally buttery and creamy. To take some home with you, the best kinds are *curado* (mature) or *semi-curado* (medium mature) as the fresh cheese (*queso fresco*) has a short shelf life. Award winning brands include **Santa María del Cerro** (from Torcal), **El Pinsapo** (a cooperative in the Sierra de las Nieves), **Agamma** (Montes de Málaga), **Argudo** (using raw milk in Campillos), and **El Alcornocal** (made on a farm in Cortes de la Frontera) but there are hundreds of producers. Look out too for *Crema* (or *Pâté*) *de Queso* — goats cheese whipped with olive oil to make a very grown-up cheese spread. It is sold in jars.

Jamón Ibérico y de Castaña

Some slices of good ham (*jamón ibérico* is the best) is an obvious food to take home with you. Supermarkets sell a huge range, all the way from the basic (but still very good) *serrano* right up to the eye-wateringly expensive top brands. If you want to try before you buy, quite a few market traders will now vacuum pack your purchase (such as **Charcutería Delgado** in the Atarazanas market).

A unique local product is *jamón de castaña* (chestnut ham). The main difference between this and traditional *ibérico* ham is that the pigs have been fed with chestnuts, alongside acorns and cereals. The final cured ham has its own distinct flavour profile and is rich and soft in texture. Production takes place mostly in the Alto Genal, an area of Serranía de Ronda with an ideal environment both for the breeding of pigs and the curing of hams. The rough, steep terrain makes pigs move in their search for food, which allows for better fat infiltration into the meat (marbling). The main producer is '**Melgar**' from Arriate, near Ronda, but it is on sale in Málaga in their own shop (see p. 299). As well as *jamón de castaña*, the shop sells their own range of cured pork products (varieties of ham, cured shoulder, sausages, salami, black pudding, etc.) plus a huge range of gourmet products from the Ronda area (wine, cheese, jam, honey, etc.). The shop also sells delicious ham rolls to take away.

Embutidos (Charcuterie)

A well-known Spanish expression is '*del cerdo hasta los andares*', which is best rendered in English as 'everything by the squeal' (*i.e.* no part of the pig is uneaten). If you have visited a few bars and enjoyed some *tapas*, you will likely have tasted a variety of local *embutidos* already — *chorizo, salchicha, salchichón, morcilla, morcón*, etc. ('*embutido*' means 'something that is stuffed'). Most emblematic of all is the *Salchichón de Málaga*, a very soft, lightly cured (and fermented) sausage that is soft enough to be spread on toast. Supermarkets will stock all the typical Spanish *embutidos*, but they might come from anywhere in Spain. They are excellent, no doubt, but if you want to take something locally produced, then go to an *ultramarinos* or a market stall like **Charcutería Delgado** or **Carnicería Jesús**.

Snails and 'Caviar'

Málaga has its own variety of snail — the *Helix aspersa* — which is used in recipes in preference to the larger *Helix lucorum* or the French favourite, *Helix pomatia*. If you want to take some home, they are available in tins. But the Málaga snail is also the source of another highly prized delicacy. If the Málaga snail meat is coveted, even more so are its eggs, nicknamed white caviar or earth caviar. Snail eggs provide an intense flavour and aroma. If the idea of pure white 'caviar' from mountain snails appeals to you, then your best bet would be the top floor of El Corte Inglés where their '**Gourmet Experience**' food shop is located.

Alcohol

If you have checked-in bags on your return journey, then you have lots of options. It seems a waste to carry home a bottle of Rioja or a bottle of Bombay Sapphire when both are available at home (admittedly at higher prices). Take some DOP Málaga or DOP Sierras de Málaga wine, or some Resoli or Mistela (see p. 167), or even some local (or at least Spanish) gin.

Olive Oil

Another delicious bottled liquid that is worth taking home is extra-virgin olive oil. Spain is the world's biggest producer of olives and olive oil and produces some gourmet varieties of stunning quality. The non-profit organization 'World's Best Olive Oils'[46] chose a Spanish olive oil (from Córdoba) as the best in the world in 2022 (in a blind tasting), with a further six Spanish oils making it into the top ten. If you taste a particularly good olive oil in a restaurant (and some are stunning, with an almost wine-like complexity of flavour) then do ask what the type and brand is and try to find a bottle to take home. In the markets, keep your eyes peeled for stalls where they have open bottles for tasting. Useful vocabulary is:

- Olive oil — *aceite de oliva* (ah-**thay**-tay day oh-**lee**-bah)
- Which do you recommend? — *¿Cuál me recomienda?* (kwal may reko-**myenn**-da)
- Could I try it? — *¿Podría probarlo?* (poh-**dree**-ah proh-**bar**-loh)

Tasting Olive Oil

Don't consider buying anything other than Extra Virgin Olive Oil (AOVE) as this is made from young, recently harvested olives and will give you the purest 'olive flavour' (virgin and regular olive oils are best kept for cooking and not worth paying a premium for). You should also ignore terms like 'cold-pressed', 'first-pressing', 'zero cholesterol', 'natural', 'unrefined', 'additive free', or 'preservative free' because ALL extra virgin olive oil must legally be made from a cold first pressing, and be natural, unrefined and additive free, Furthermore, vegetable products don't contain cholesterol (though they do contain, and in fact are, fat). Also beware of descriptions like 'heirloom', 'organic', 'handmade' or references to 'ancient olive trees' and the like. These may be, *prima facie*, desirable traits, but they are no guarantee of quality or flavour.

When it comes to tasting, the colour may tell you a little. Opaque oils are often young, and green oils tend to be more bitter than yellow oils. A deep golden colour may be a sign of rancidness. The bouquet should be grassy, fruity or almond/nut-like, but not excessively 'olivey'. Taste it like wine, from a glass or spoon (not bread, if possible) and taste it like wine by taking a mouthful (about a dessert-spoonful). Roll it around your mouth, and if you are able, aspirate it by pursing your lips as if you were about to whistle then drawing some air into your mouth, exhaling through your nose (don't attempt this without practising first!). Don't hurry. Think about the flavours in your mouth before swallowing. As with wine, you are interested in texture or consistency, 'mouthfeel', taste on the palate, and then 'length' (what you taste after swallowing).

Tastes to look out for in the palate are fruitiness — a kind of lively, fresh flavour; grassiness — a grassy or herbaceous taste; nuttiness — most often a hint of almonds, but sometimes hazelnuts or peanuts (*i.e.* beans) which are associated with oil made from more mature ol-

---

46   wboo.org

ives or an older oil; and you may also get hints of artichokes, citrus, tomatoes, apples, dried fruit, pears, figs, tropical fruits and even bananas. Then, after swallowing, pay attention to the 'length' — this is where you detect pepperiness and bitterness. These are part of an oil's flavour profile and are neither good nor bad in themselves. It depends upon your personal taste and what you want to use the oil for (*e.g.* an oil to drizzle over grilled sardines will probably need to be more strongly flavoured than one used to make mayonnaise). In general, people who love olives will prefer more bitter and peppery oils, as will those who prefer their coffee black and their tea unsweetened and strong.

But look, too, for the flavours and odours that you don't want — any hint of rancidness, notes of wine or vinegar (a sign that fermentation has taken place), mould, 'muddiness' or anything that tastes dull, flat or metallic. And while a lively, fresh 'green vegetable' taste is a good sign, anything reminiscent of cooked or boiled green vegetables is usually a sign of poor extraction.

If you buy a bottle of excellent AOVE to take home (and the best brands will cost between €3 and €30 for 500ml), then please look after it. Olive oil does not improve with age but begins to deteriorate from the moment it is pressed. Store it in a dark cupboard in the coolest part of your kitchen. An opened bottle of extra virgin olive oil kept on a sunny window sill or close to your hob will not simply decline in quality, but could easily turn rancid within a few weeks. It's understandable that one might want to display interesting bottles of gourmet oils picked up on your travels as a 'talking point', but the way to do this is to clean out the empty bottles with warm water and washing soda to completely remove any trace of the old oil, and then refill with your everyday mild cooking oil. Keep the good stuff in the cupboard!

Dried Fruit

> 'The fruits of Málaga, are unequalled. The yellow plains, girdled by the green
> sea, bask in the sunshine, like a topaz set around with emeralds.' (Hand-
> book for Travellers in Spain, *Richard Ford, 1845*)

Málaga is world-famous for its Moscatel raisins (*pasas de Málaga*). These are sold either *con* (with) or *sin* (without) *semillas* (seeds). Markets and *ultramarinos* are the best places to buy (and try) these. Alongside the raisins will be the almonds (*almendras*), another typically *malagueño* product. The main varieties grown in the Province of Málaga are Marcona, Largueta and Comuna, although in recent years the Guara has started to be cultivated. You can buy them plain, roasted, fried, salted, caramelized and even spiced. They are one of the leitmotif fragrances of the city of Málaga thanks to the vendors of roasted and caramelized almonds (*garapiñadas*) on the streets. However, beware — although they are rich and full of flavour and probably like no almonds you have ever tasted before — those you buy in a Málaga market are a natural product without preservatives, so their shelf-life is short. If you take a bag home with you, consume them within a few weeks at most. To keep for a special recipe (like Christmas Pudding), you should freeze them.

> 'Other exports comprise grapes, raisins, figs, oranges, almonds, lemons, olive
> oil... About 1½ million boxes of muscatel raisins are sent to England yearly,
> and nearly as much to the United States.' (Bradshaw's Illustrated Hand-
> book to Spain and Portugal *by Dr Charnock FSA, FRGS, &c. 1897*)

Also in the 'dried fruit and nuts' (*frutas secas/frutos secos*) category is the fig. The province is a significant producer of figs and because the season for fresh figs is short (August to October), most of the crop is dried and therefore available all year round. A typical product made from figs is *pan de higo* or 'fig bread'. It is not bread (it contains no flour) but rather a pressed cake of dried figs, sometimes with nuts and other fruit, and it is a delicious accompaniment to cheese. The best-known kind is from Coín.

Another fig-based treat is the *rabito* ('little tail'). *Rabitos* are figs soaked in liqueur, stuffed with praline truffle, and dipped in chocolate. I am generally not a huge fan of chocolates (as in, boxes of), but I cannot resist these. They are fairly expensive, but they are a very grown-up chocolate indeed.

Turrón

In the last few years, a number of touristy, faux-olde-worlde shops selling *turrón* (nougat) have sprung up throughout Málaga. *Turrón* is originally from the Valencia region, but has been made in Málaga for so long that it can now be considered 'local'. It comes in two kinds: hard (*duro* from Alicante), or soft (*blando* from Jijona/Xixona). The hard kind can be tooth-shatteringly hard, and the soft kind can be very chewy. If you like it, then fill your boots and buy great ingots of the stuff. But if you're more of a mind that it's an interesting local sweet and an unusual gift, then go for a selection box or chocolate coated *turrón*. That tiny morsel of orange and chocolate *turrón* may have tasted delicious in the shop, but being faced with a kilogram of the stuff may be too much of a good thing. As always, try to buy it from an *ultramarinos* or from Casa Mira and not one of the new chain stores that seem to be proliferating lately.

Paprika and Saffron

Neither paprika (*pimentón*) nor saffron (*azafrán*) are cultivated in the Province of Málaga, but both make good gifts to bring home from Spain. Saffron is mainly produced in La Mancha (though some comes from Valencia, Catalonia and Aragón) and will be slightly cheaper (and certainly fresher) than what you can buy in the UK. Paprika — *pimentón* — comes in two kinds and three intensities. Produced in two geographical 'denominations of origin', *Pimentón de Murcia* is unsmoked, and *Pimentón de la Vera* (from Extremadura) is smoked. There are also three grades of heat (though no one who has eaten at an Indian restaurant in the UK would consider any of them especially 'hot') — *dulce* (sweet), *agridulce* (medium), and *picante* (hot). One of the reasons why *pimentón* makes a lovely gift or souvenir is that it is often packaged in a beautifully decorated tin.

 ## Other Products from Málaga

The Diputación has created the '*Sabor a Málaga*' (Taste of Málaga) brand to bring together local producers in order to showcase and promote their products. Have a look at their website to discover the full range (the translation link for English is in the top right-hand corner). *Sabor a Málaga* also organises food fairs all over the Province, including a huge event in the Paseo del Parque in Málaga city during December (**saboramalaga.es/categoria/ferias**).

Religión (Religion)
🏆 Catholicism

Spain is culturally, though not officially or constitutionally, a Catholic country, and the Queen, as the spouse of a 'Catholic Monarch' is still accorded the *'Le privilège du blanc'* at the Vatican, meaning that alongside the Queen of the Belgians, the Princess of Monaco, the Grand Duchess of Luxembourg and the Duchess of Savoy, she is permitted to wear white, rather than black, for a Papal audience.

There are hundreds of Catholic masses celebrated in Málaga city every Sunday, and dozens every day. Anyone is welcome to attend Mass in a Catholic church (although only baptized Catholics are able to receive communion), so if you'd like to experience a Spanish liturgy, you certainly can, whatever your personal religious beliefs (or lack thereof). Most churches have a morning or lunchtime mass, and an evening mass, but please check locally. Mass times change seasonally so it would not be helpful to try to provide a timetable here, but the 🌐 misas.org website may be useful (if you access this site on a mobile device, it will use GPS).

The busiest city-centre church is also the least beautiful — Stella Maris on the Alameda Principal — a huge brick-built box served by the Carmelite Friars. There are five daily masses and seven Sunday masses 🌐 stellamarismalaga.es.

Mass is celebrated in the extraordinary form (*aka* the Tridentine Rite) at the **Iglesia Conventual de San Agustín** (Augustinian Canons) at 10 am every Sunday. For other masses, check the Una Voce blog: bit.ly/UVMalaga

Mass is celebrated in the ordinary form in Latin in the Cathedral on Sundays at 10 am.

Mass is celebrated in English at the **Parroquia de Cristo Rey** (Avenida Santiago Ramón y Cajal 5) at 11.30 am on Sundays. For information about masses (and confessions) in the greater Málaga area, it's best to search online for up-to-date information: bit.ly/MisasMalaga

Most of the 75,000 non-Latin Catholics in Spain belong to Byzantine Rite churches (Ukrainian and Romanian), with a tiny number of Syro-Malabar worshippers. They are cared for by the 'Ordinariato para los fieles de ritos orientales en España' (Ordinariate for the Faithful of Eastern Rite in Spain). There are no established churches or congregations in Málaga.

✝ Other Christian Denominations

St George's Anglican Church (in the English Cemetery) has a sung Eucharist each Sunday at 11 am. **stgeorgeschurchmalaga.org** (p. 71)

There are many Baptist and Evangelical churches in Málaga, which a Google search will quickly uncover. A rough rule of thumb is that when the name (and website) is in Spanish (*e.g.* 'Iglesia evangélica la puerta Málaga') then services will be in Spanish with a mostly Latino congregation, and when in English (*e.g.* 'The Worship Place') then the congregation will be almost entirely composed of ex-pats.

There is a Romanian Orthodox Church in Mijas (Costa), and there is a small Moscow Patriarchate congregation in Málaga city (**Русская Православная Церковь в Малаге** 🅕 **russkayapravoslavnayatserkov**). They use rented office space but hold regular liturgies and seem to have a resident priest. Consult the Facebook/Meta page for details. The largest orthodox community is in Marbella.

✡ Judaism

A service in a Spanish synagogue, from the Sister Haggadah (c. 1350)

Spain, like most of Europe, has a rather shameful record with respect to Jews. The period of Moorish rule is often held up as a time of tolerance and even flourishing for *sefardíes* (Sephardi or Hispanic Jews), yet in this period there were pogroms, expulsions and even crucifixions. After the *reconquista*, Jews fared little better and, arguably, much worse, in part due to their reputation for having 'collaborated' with the Moorish 'enemy' (in other words, for their simply having lived according to their *dhimmi* status under the Caliphate). Worse was to come, with the edict of expulsion in 1492.

And yet Spain's connection to Judaism runs deep. Much of what we take to be 'Spanish cuisine', and even that often assumed to be 'Arab', is almost certainly Jewish in origin. Ironically perhaps, the food now most associated with Lent, Easter and Christmas (*torrijas, tortas de aceite, buñuelos, bizcochos*, etc.) has a clearly Jewish origin.

Laws were passed in 1924 under the dictatorship of Primo de Rivera to grant citizenship to Sephardi Jews, leading to an increase in the Jewish population from 1,000 in 1900 to 7,000 in 1936.[47] Another influx came during and following the Second World War. In 2014 it was announced that the descendants of Sephardi Jews who were expelled from Spain by the Alhambra Decree of 1492 would be offered Spanish citizenship, without being required to move to Spain or renounce any other citizenship they may have. The law lapsed on 1 October

---

47   Gonzalo Álvarez Chillida, 'Presencia e imagen judía en la España contemporánea. Herencia castiza y modernidad' (2011) in Silvina Schammah Gesser *El otro en la España contemporánea / Prácticas, discursos y representaciones* (Sevilla: Fundación Tres Culturas del Mediterráneo) pp.132

2019 and has been much criticized for the mealy-mouthed way in which it has been implemented. It is thought that the current Jewish population of Spain is about 50,000.

The Jewish quarter of Málaga is the sector of the historic centre where the Jewish *aljama* lived during the Middle Ages (*viz.* even in the so-called 'Golden Age' they were concentrated in ghettos to keep them under surveillance and control). It is known that, at the time of the *reconquista* of Málaga, there were some 450 Jews in the city and any who refused to convert were deported in October 1487. But despite this, the remaining *conversos* (those who publicly converted to Christianity) remained for a time in the Jewish quarter. But this time of rebirth was short-lived, ending with the Alhambra Decree (of expulsion) in 1492. This ordered that all observant Jews and suspected 'crypto-Jews' ('*marranos*') be expelled. Following that came the practical disappearance of everything that could preserve the memory of a once significant and vibrant Jewish presence in the city.

From Calle Alcazabilla to Calle Cárcer, and running along the medieval wall that reached the current Plaza de La Merced, Calle Granada, Calle Santiago and Postigo de San Agustín, the area still preserves, in some of its enclaves, the typical architectural configuration (narrow and winding streets) of a Jewish quarter. A Jewish cemetery on the slopes of the Gibralfaro Castle has been discovered in recent years. The old synagogue is presumed to be partially located in what is now Bodegas El Pimpi, on an alley that ran between Calle Redes (now the Postigo de San Agustín) and Calle Real (now Calle Granada).

Since 2004, works have been carried out for the recovery and rehabilitation of the Jewish quarter. The so-called 'Plan of the Jewish Quarter' of the *ayuntamiento* has seen the restoration of a *mudéjar* tower (the Centro Ben Gabirol) which houses on the ground floor a tourist information office with, on the top floor, a kind of covered terrace and small exhibition space. It stands in the former Plaza de la Nieve, recently renamed the 'Plaza de la Judería'.

On the Calle Alcazabilla, facing the Teatro Romano, there is a rather beautiful, yet sad-looking, statue of Solomon Ibn Gabirol, the Jewish poet and philosopher born in Málaga around 1021. Gabirol's gaze might well be downcast and his countenance sorrowful, for so was his life, afflicted with some unknown malady which left him unable to work and caused him great pain. His parents had moved to Málaga after falling out with the Moorish ruler of Córdoba and then had to move again, to Zaragoza, taking the young Solomon with them. He lost his father in his teens and his mother a few years later and his poetry, although beautiful, tends towards the elegiac and maudlin. His philosophy was, as far as we can tell, entirely ignored by Muslim thinkers, and mostly ignored by Jewish ones, but to the medieval Christian world he was known as Avicebron and his writings were assumed (by William of Auvergne at least) to be the work of an Arab Christian.

The **Comunidad Judía de Málaga** is currently situated in the Soho district (⊙ **Calle Duquesa de Parcent 8** ⊕ cjmalaga.org) and occupies an unremarkable office block. There is a shul (and mikvah) but many visitors complain that they have been unable to find it. Sadly, in common with many Jewish places of worship around the world, security is necessarily tight and the community does not advertise its presence, so if you want to worship during your visit to Málaga, I suggest you get in touch by email first: ✉ rabinocjma@gmail.com, ✉ info@cjmalaga.org.

There are no kosher restaurants in Málaga city, though there is a kosher supermarket in Huelin **(La Makolet, Calle Góngora 20)**. Where Jewish visitors wanting to keep kosher will have to be careful is in dealing with the Spanish obsession with 'garnishing' all kinds of dishes with *jamón* or *chorizo*, and also understanding the distinction between '*pescados*' (fish) and '*mariscos*' (seafood), with the latter often finding its way into dishes that appear to contain only the former. Apart from clams and prawns, most of the best-loved local dishes are fish (not seafood) based, but the phrase '*¿lleva mariscos?*' ('Does it contain seafood?' – **yay**-bah ma-**riss**-koss) may be useful. Remember that even a chickpea stew is almost certainly going to be cooked in meat stock. The easiest way forward is probably to be a 'vegetarian' for the duration of your visit. For other links and information about the Costa del Sol more generally, use the QR code link or visit: **totallyjewishtravel.com**

☪ Islam

Despite the ubiquity and prominence of alcohol and pork in Spanish gastronomy, Muslim visitors to Málaga should not encounter too many difficulties. The Province of Málaga is home to 50,000–60,000 Muslims, most of them of Moroccan descent, though there are significant numbers of Muslim immigrants from Pakistan and various African countries. When Morocco knocked Spain out of the 2022 World Cup, *malaguenõs* of Moroccan heritage celebrated openly in the centre of Málaga without difficulty, unlike those in Paris, Brussels or Amsterdam (though there are also poorly-integrated immigrant communities in more far-flung suburbs, so the picture isn't entirely rosy). As far as eating is concerned, it is far easier to avoid meat than fish which, for all bar Hanafis, makes it relatively easy to eat halal in most bars and restaurants. Muslim visitors should remember that biscuits and pastries in Spain are often made with lard (pork fat) and that some traditional stews and soups, while apparently 'vegetarian', will be made with meat stock.

The large Moroccan population means that it is also relatively easy to find fully halal restaurants in which to eat (quite a few are found north of the railway and bus stations near the Larios Shopping Centre).

The city's largest mosque, and the closest to the *centro histórico*, is part of the Saudi-funded **Centro Cultural Andalusí de Málaga (**♀**Calle Ingeniero de la Torre Acosta 3** ⊕ **ccandalusi.org)**, and there are numerous smaller mosques in the western

part of Málaga. **HalalTrip** has produced a free guide to Málaga for Muslim travellers: ❶ **bit.ly/HalalMLG**.

The main mosque has a most interesting and sensitive design. In the wake of a *reconquista*, the *mudéjar* (neo-Moorish) architectural style became hugely popular, incorporating horse-shoe and multi-lobed arches, brickwork, carved wood, glazed ceramic tiles, stucco work, etc. The Málaga mosque, on the other hand, owes something to typical Spanish ecclesiastical architecture.

Agenda (Málaga Through the Year)
📅 National and Local Holidays

When you look at the '*horarios*' (timetable) for a bar or museum in Spain you are likely to see different opening times for '*laborales*' (weekdays), '*fines de semana*' (weekends), '*domingos*' (Sundays), etc. as well as for '*festivos*', which can occur on various days of the week and are public religious or civic holidays. In Málaga, these are as follows:

1 January:	**New Year's Day**
6 January:	**Epiphany**
*28 February:	**Andalusia Day (*Día de Andalucía*)**
March/April:	**Holy Thursday (Thursday before the moveable feast of Easter)**
March/April:	**Good Friday (Friday before the moveable feast of Easter)**
1 May:	**Labour Day**
15 August:	**The Assumption of the Blessed Virgin Mary**
*19 August:	**Incorporation of Málaga to the Crown of Castilla**
*8 September:	**Feast of Our Lady of the Victory (*La Virgen de la Victoria*)**
12 October:	**National Day of Spain (*Fiesta Nacional de España*)**
1 November:	**All Saints Day**
6 December:	**Constitution Day**
8 December:	**The Solemnity of the Immaculate Conception**
25 December:	**Christmas Day (Navidad)**

If any of these dates falls on a Sunday, then the public holiday is transferred to the Monday in the same way that people in the UK get a holiday on 2 January when New Year's Day falls on a Sunday. *All of the dates above are holidays throughout Spain save three: 28 February, 19 August, and 8 September.

Spanish Virgins

Four of the festivals in Málaga's annual calendar are celebrations of feasts of the Blessed Virgin Mary (the Mother of Jesus). Three are Marian feasts — the Assumption (15 August), Immaculate Conception (8 December) and her title of 'Virgin of the Victory' (8 September). The National Day of Spain, meanwhile, is celebrated on 12 October because it is the feast day of Spain's patron saint, Our Lady of the Pillar.

But surely St James is the Patron Saint of Spain? Indeed he is, but he is closely associated with Our Lady of the Pillar (*Nuestra Señora del Pilar*). According to pious legend, when the Apostle James was preaching the Gospel in Roman Spain in the year 40 AD, facing difficulties and greatly discouraged, Mary the mother of Jesus appeared to James beside the Ebro river (at Zaragoza) where he was praying. The thousands of angels who accompanied her fashioned a marble pillar that is preserved to this day in the *Seo* (seat or cathedral) of Zaragoza, giving off the sweet odour of rose petals.

And just as the nation of Spain has two patron saints, so do many of its towns, cities and regions. Even Zaragoza, the custodian of '*El Pilar*' has as co-patron St Valero of Zaragoza, bishop and martyr. The city of Santander may be named after St Andrew, but its patron is '*La Virgen de la Bien Aparecida*'. The patron saint of Málaga is Our Lady of the Victory (*Santa María de la Victoria*), the victory in this case being over the Moors in 1487, while the city's co-patrons are the Roman-era martyrs Ciriaco and Paula. Trujillo, in Extremadura, also has 'Our Lady of the Victory' as patron, but that refers to a different victory in 1232, two and a half centuries before that in Málaga.

In case you are wondering, the churches of Our Lady of the Victories in Kensington (London) and Santa Maria della Vittoria in Rome are both dedicated to yet another victory attributed to the intercession of the Blessed Virgin, this time over the Ottoman fleet at Lepanto in October 1571.

So why doesn't the Virgin Mary just have one feast day, like St Mark, St Francis and St Mary Magdalene? There are a few interconnected reasons. The first is the huge popularity of Mary among Christians (we tend to think of the rich tradition of Marian devotion among Catholics, but it is a similar story in the Orthodox East, too). Connected to this is the understanding that while other saints are patrons of particular groups of people, places and professions, the Virgin Mary has a kind of 'universal' patronage because, as the mother of Jesus, she is mother of us all. Her titles and epithets are legion: Virgin of Virgins, Mother of God, Health of the Sick, Perpetual Help, Star of the Sea, and hundreds more. Thus, a hospital might be dedicated to Our Lady Health of the Sick, while a church in a fishing village would be dedicated to Our Lady Star of the Sea.

Finally, because according to Catholic and Orthodox doctrine, Mary has no tomb (because when her earthly life was ended she was taken body and soul into heaven), there is no single site of pilgrimage. The shrine of St Peter is in Rome, the shrine of St James is in Santiago de Compostela, the shrine of St Cuthbert is in Durham, etc. But Catholics also believe that Mary has appeared to the faithful at various times and in various places to comfort and encourage them and to urge them to have faith in her son Jesus. So Mary is closely associated with particular times (the victory of 1487 in Málaga, or of 1571 in Lepanto, etc.), and particular places (Zaragoza, Walsingham, Lourdes, Fatima, etc.).

Where (Almost) Everyone is Called Mary or Joseph

Spanish given names have changed a great deal in the last few decades. Until the end of the 20th century, almost all babies (born to at least nominally Christian families) were baptized with 'Christian' names, *i.e.* those of saints or biblical figures (Marta, Teresa, Magdalena, José, Martín), or classical names (Irene, Laura, César, León). In recent decades, 'international' names have become more popular — Lisa, Kayla, Ryan, Liam, etc. For example, in 2023, one of the most popular boy's names was 'Timothée', presumably because of the actor Timothée Chalamet, even though the standard spelling of the name 'Timothy' in Spanish is 'Timoteo'.

What many people do not realize is that Spanish women called 'Dolores', 'Paz', 'Mercedes', 'Inmaculada' etc. are also called 'María' (Mary). Girls are often named María, honouring the Virgin Mary, by appending either a shrine, place, or epithet to María. In daily life, such women omit the 'Mary of the...' nominal prefix and use the suffix portion of their composite names as their usual name. Hence, women with Marian names such as María de los Ángeles (Mary of the Angels), María del Pilar (Mary of the Pillar), or María de la Luz (Mary of the Light), are normally addressed as Ángeles, Pilar, or Luz; however, each could also be addressed as María. Nicknames such as *Maricarmen* for María del Carmen, *Marisol* for 'María (de la) Soledad' ('Our Lady of Solitude'), *Dolores*, *Lola* or *Lolita* for María de los Dolores ('Our Lady of Sorrows'), *Merche* for María de las Mercedes ('Our Lady of Mercy'), etc. are often used. Also, parents can simply name a girl María, or Mari without a suffix.

It is not unusual for a boy's formal name to include María, preceded by a masculine name, *e.g.* the former Prime Minister of Spain, José María Aznar (Joseph Mary Aznar). Equally, a girl can be formally named María José (Mary Joseph), and informally named *Marijose, Mariajo, Majo, Ajo, Marisé* or even *José* in honour of St. Joseph. It is unusual for any names other than the religiously significant María and José to be used in this way except for the name Jesús which is also common and can be 'Jesús María' for a boy and 'María Jesús' for a girl, and this can be abbreviated as *Sus, Chus* and other nicknames.

A Rose By Any Other Name

While we are on the subject of names, Spanish surnames can seem like a minefield. They are actually fairly straightforward, and everyone has (at least) two. The first is the patronymic, the second is the matronymic. Thus if Antonio García González and María Martínez Morales have a child called José Antonio, then his full name — when it comes to official form-filling — would be José Antonio García Martínez (his Mum, incidentally, remains 'María Martínez Morales', though she might choose to call herself 'María Martínez *de* Garcia' if she chooses. Conventionally, only the patronymic portion (García) would be carried on to young José Antonio's offspring, but since 1999, couples (and their children upon reaching the age of majority) have been permitted to reverse the surnames to put the mother's first. This tends to happen if the mother's first surname is considered rather more upper crust or unusual than the father's — the reason why, among English speakers, the surname Smith is so often 'double-barrelled'. A famous artist from Málaga named Pablo famously took his mother's unusual (part-Italian) surname 'Picasso' in preference to his father's very common surname 'Ruiz'.

But how would José Antonio be addressed? This is where it becomes interesting and complicated. Formally, he would be called *señor* García Martínez, or *señor* García. A formal address using only his forename would be Don José Antonio. And his legal forename (singular) is 'José Antonio'. While Brits and Americans might have two forenames and one surname, Spaniards have one or more forenames and two surnames. Informally, you can take your pick:

- José Antonio
- José
- Pepe (nickname for José)

- Antonio
- Toño (nickname for Antonio)
- Joselito, Josito, Joselillo, Josico or Joselín (diminutives of José)
- Antoñito, Toñín, Toñito, Ñoño or Nono (diminutives of Antonio)
- Joseán (an 'apocopation')

Why, incidentally, is 'Pepe' a nickname for José? Well, José is 'Joseph', and Joseph was not the natural father of Jesus, only his 'putative' father. The initials of *'padre putativo'* (or in Latin *'pater putativus'*) are 'P.P.' which, in Spanish, is pronounced, 'Pepe'!

If you've ever wondered why so many Spanish surnames end in -ez, it's because this is the Hispanic form of the suffix 'son' or the prefix 'O' or 'Mac'. Thus, 'Fernández' and 'Hernández' mean 'Son of Fernando' and 'Díaz' means 'Son of Diego'. 'García' — the most common Spanish surname — is also a patronymic, but from a now-extinct medieval forename which probably originated in the Basque Country. Non-patronymic surnames like 'Iglesias' (Churches) or 'Cruz' (Cross) were names given to foundlings, often raised in church-run institutions. Similarly, the surname 'Blanco' does not mean 'white' but 'blank' — in the rather sad sense of having no papers. Before 1921, many Spaniards had the surname 'Expósito' (*lit.* 'exposed', abandoned) but due to the stigma associated with the name, a law was passed to allow people to choose a new surname.

🌼 A Floral Calendar

The scent of unseen jasmine on the warm night beach.
The tram along the sea road all the way from town
through its wide open sides drank unseen jasmine down.
Living was nothing all those nights but that strong flower,
whose hidden voice on darkness grew to such mad power
I could have sworn for once I travelled through full peace
and eve love at last had perfect calm release
only by breathing in the unseen jasmine scent,
that ruled us and the summer every hour we went.

(Pearse Hutchinson, 'Málaga' in Tongue Without Hands, *1963)*

The Mediterranean climate and mild winters of Málaga mean that there are flowers in bloom all year round. The best places to see these displays of colour are the Parque de Málaga, the Jardines de Pedro Luis Alonso and Puerta Oscura opposite, and around the Alcazaba and Cathedral. But for the biggest variety, the Botanical Gardens cannot be beaten. Use the QR code link for a calendar of trees and shrubs in bloom and/or fruit (in Spanish with Latin botanical names).

All Year Round: Bougainvillea (Jardines de Pedro Luis Alonso, English Cemetery)

February to April: Seville Orange blossom (Paseo del Parque, Jardines de Pedro Luis Alonso, Cathedral); Judas Tree (*Cercis siliquastrum* — Avenida de Andalucía)

May to June: Jacaranda (Jardines de Puerta Oscura, Plaza de La Merced); Jasmine

Spring to Autumn: Roses (Jardines de Pedro Luis Alonso); Hibiscus (Cathedral, Alcazaba, Paseo del Parque); Jasmine

November to December: Silk Floss Tree (*Chorisia speciosa* — Cortina del Muelle, Parque de Málaga, Plaza del Poeta Alfonso Canales, Avenida Andalucía)

December: Seville Orange fruit (Paseo del Parque, Jardines de Pedro Luis Alonso, Cathedral); Poinsettia (Ayuntamiento, Plaza del General Torrijos); Crane Flower (*Strelitzia Reginae* — Paseo del Parque, Cathedral)

January

❦ *Nochevieja* (31 December–1 January)

In Spanish, New Year is called *Nochevieja*, which means 'old night' (*i.e.* the last night of the old year). It has been marked on 1 January in Spain since 1555, 200 years before the UK marked it on this date. New Year celebrations are fairly similar to those found in other European and world cities — either observed at home with family and friends, with special programmes on the TV, or publicly in the main squares. In Málaga, that means the Plaza de la Constitución, where celebrations get going around 10 pm, with live music from 11 pm.

If you are lucky enough to find room in the square (and remember, if you want to eat dinner in a restaurant beforehand, booking is essential and prices will be inflated), then you may find that someone hands you one or more little paper bags. These bags contain either 12 grapes or a handful of confetti. The event organizers distribute around 3,000 of each. Don't throw the confetti (yet) because it is for midnight. The grapes too. When the hush descends just before the stroke of midnight, have your grapes ready. With each chime of the clock bell, you are supposed to eat a grape — one grape for each month of the year to come. When the chimes stop and you've eaten your grapes, you throw the confetti and hug and kiss your neighbours. The music then begins again and continues until 2 am.

It would be nice to think that the eating of the twelve grapes is an ancient Spanish custom. It would be fitting, after all, in a country that has more land under vines, relative to its size, than any other. However, as far as we can tell, it began in the late nineteenth century among the middle classes, only taking root among the general population in 1909. The reason for this was a bumper harvest of grapes that year in the Alicante region and a glut of cheap fruit in the markets.

⁙ *Los Reyes Magos* (6 January)

The Feast of the Epiphany, known as *Los Reyes Magos* (The Magi Kings), is the major celebration connected with the birth of Jesus in Spain. For all that Spanish cities have Christmas trees and lights, and even Santas and reindeer in shop windows, Christmas Day itself is not the main celebration of the season. The big day, especially for children, is *Los Reyes Magos*, mainly because they are the bringers of gifts. Spanish children write their letters full of wishes not to Santa Claus, but to 'The Kings'.

Nowhere in the Bible does it call the visitors to Jesus on Twelfth Night 'kings', and they are never enumerated as 'three'. Pious tradition, on the other hand, has concluded that it would be fitting for the King of Kings to be worshipped by earthly kings. The fixing of their number at three is inferred from the three gifts of gold, frankincense and myrrh, but based on the account in Saint Matthew's Gospel, all we know is that there were at least two of them. Spain has also followed extra-biblical tradition in calling them Gaspar, Melchor and Baltasar (supposedly representing Europe, Asia and Africa), though whereas many traditions have them arriving, respectively, on a horse, a camel and an elephant, in Spain they all ride camels.

The celebration begins on 5 January (Twelfth Night) with the sharing of the *Roscón de Reyes*, a large doughnut-shaped cake made of sweet dough studded with candied peel, often dusted with sugar and, in these decadent times, filled with cream or ganache. Although its origin is pagan and Roman, the ring shape is now meant to suggest a king's crown — the baked dough is the gold, and the pieces of fruit and peel are the gemstones. So many traditions surround it that the *roscón* varies from family to family. Some are baked with small clay or metal trinkets (thimbles, rings, coins, etc.) inside — the equivalent, perhaps, of Christmas cracker toys — but they all normally contain a broad bean. The one who finds this in his or her portion is proclaimed the 'King of the Bean'. This honour is a mixed blessing given that, as king, paying for the *roscón* (or next year's *roscón*) becomes their responsibility.

When the children go to bed, they leave a plate of biscuits and three glasses of sweet wine for the three kings and their camels. The following morning, the plate is empty, the wine drunk and a pile of presents has been left. In some parts of Spain, and in some families, the Magi begin to leave small gifts even earlier and children leave their shoes out on the nights leading up to Twelfth Night, much as Dutch children do in the days before the Feast of St Nicholas.

The Eve is also when the public celebrations take place. 6 January itself is a day for family celebrations and also a public holiday. If you happen to be in Málaga for 'The Kings', search on the web to find the exact programme, because the precise timings sometimes change. (Searching for '*cabalgata de Reyes de Málaga*' **bit.ly/3KingsMLG** should come up with the information from a newspaper website).

In recent years, however, the programme of celebrations has been extensive. A few days before Los Reyes, the '*concejal de Fiestas*' (and who would not want to be, literally, the 'councillor for parties'?) announces the programme, alongside a representative of 'Their Majesties the Kings'. Remember, to Spanish children, the Kings, and their gift-giving abilities are as real as Santa is to British children. On the evening of 5 January, in a piece of slightly questionable orientalism, '*Sus Majestades de Oriente*' (Their Majesties of the East) emerge from the Alcazaba and walk down to the Town Hall.

On the steps of the Town Hall, they are received by the mayor, the Councillor for Fiestas, and the members of the Corporation to the sounds of the Municipal Band of Málaga. After the greeting, the Kings go up to the balcony of the Town Hall, where a child chosen to represent all the boys and girls of Málaga reads a letter addressed to 'Their Majesties', the end of which will be the signal for the beginning of the Parade. At around 6 pm the procession begins, parading down Avenida de Cervantes, and when the royal carriages arrive at the City Hall, Melchor, Gaspar and Baltasar occupy their respective places. In recent years the parade has been made up of a total of 16 floats: three royal floats and 13 accompanying ones.

The people who play the three Wise Men during the parade in Málaga are carefully chosen. One is normally a media personality, another an *hermano mayor* of one of the Holy Week brotherhoods, and the third a representative of the municipal corporation. At least one of the kings is often a queen. They wear costumes specially designed for the event, usually by a well-known local *modisto* (couturier).

The procession heads towards the river along the Alameda Principal and then, after a short incursion into the centre, makes its way back to City Hall. On the way back to, passing the

Plaza de La Marina, The Kings and their entourage will get out of their carriages and walk towards the Cathedral. On the main steps Melchor, Gaspar and Baltasar will make their symbolic offering before a *Belén* (Nativity scene) accompanied by the University choir.

The Kings are gift-givers, and the parade is no exception. In 2023, the floats distributed 1.44 tonnes of *mantecados* (very crumbly shortbread biscuits often eaten around Christmas), and almost 20 tonnes of jelly babies and assorted sweets.

February/March

 *Carnaval*

Carnaval (Carnival) has been celebrated in Spain since at least the Middle Ages and is a festival of two dimensions. It is held in the days before the season of Lent — forty days of self-denial in preparation for Easter. Lent is still supposed to be penitential, with fasting on the first and last days (Ash Wednesday and Good Friday) and abstinence from meat on Fridays, but in former times it essentially meant 40 days of veganism (and abstinence from sex). *Carnaval* is thus both putting away the pleasures of the flesh and a kind of celebration of them. Food, drink and sex are not bad, after all. Indeed, they are gifts from God, but laid aside in the pursuit of something greater (God himself). The origin of the term is probably not a farewell ('*Vale!*') to meat ('*carnis*') as commonly supposed, but from '*carnem levanem*' (*lit.* 'meat dismissal') or '*carnualia*' ('meat feast').

The biggest *carnavales* in Spain are those held in Cádiz, Santa Cruz de Tenerife and Murcia and they traditionally begin in time for 'Fat Thursday' (*jueves lardero*, the week before Ash Wednesday) and run until Shrove Tuesday (the day before). *Carnaval* in Málaga begins even earlier, traditionally two Fridays before Ash Wednesday, running until the Sunday before Ash Wednesday, with preliminary events starting even earlier, in January. Despite the historic connection with preparations for Lent, *carnaval* is almost entirely secular these days. For over a week, centred around the specially decorated Calle Larios and Plaza de la Constitución, there are lots of events and competitions for children, parades, and evening concerts. The last Friday of *carnaval* sees the biggest parade of all in the late afternoon (from 6 pm), then *La Batalla de las Flores* (Battle of the Flowers) on Calle Larios (at 8.30 pm or thereabouts) which involves throwing confetti and being showered with petals. Later in the evening, there is a competition in which Málaga drag queens compete for the carnival crown.

On the last Sunday (before Ash Wednesday), the very non-Christian parade of 'gods and goddesses' sets off from the Plaza de la Constitución at noon, processing through the old city before arriving back at the plaza (via Calle Larios) for the *Gran Boqueroná* — a huge (and free!) feast of fried anchovies (from 2 pm). Grab a paper cone from one of the stalls and tuck in!

Málaga's anchovy obsession is in evidence at the last event of *carnaval* held later in the afternoon. Throughout Spain, a curious *carnaval* tradition is *El Entierro de la Sardina* (The Burial of the Sardine). In Britain, the medieval custom of bidding farewell to animal products (*viz.* eggs, milk and butter) persists on Shrove Tuesday in the preparation of pancakes. Yet the sardine, as a fish, has always been permitted during Lent. What it represents, rather, is celebration and enjoyment. That is what is being bade farewell to. For all their love of *jamón*, *chorizo* and *rabo de toro*, what Spaniards love above all are fish and seafood. Sardines are party food.

Malagueños love sardines, but they love anchovies even more, so rather than burying a sardine, they bury an anchovy. In fact, they 'bury' a gigantic papier mâché model of an anchovy, setting off from the Plaza de la Constitución (usually around 5 pm) in a mock funeral procession to the Malagueta beach where the symbolic anchovy is not interred, but cremated on a bonfire.

The events leading up to and during *Carnaval* are coordinated (with the *ayuntamiento*) by the *Fundación Ciudadana Carnaval de Málaga* (Citizens' Foundation for the Málaga *Carnaval*). Preliminary events (*La Previa*) begin in mid-January, four weekends before Shrove Tuesday. These consist of gastronomic and musical celebrations held in different *barrios* of the city. A full week before, *murgas* (street musicians) and *comparsas* (*Carnaval* troupes) perform as part of a singing competition, the final of which is held in the Teatro Cervantes. The earlier heats take place in the **Teatro Esad** in the Teatinos (university) district. Tickets go on sale at **malagaentradas.com** around the end of December. To see the full programme, consult the FCCM website (Spanish only): **carnavaldemalaga.es**

March

🎬 *Festival de Málaga* (Málaga Film Festival)

The biggest and most famous film festival in Spain is held in San Sebastián in the Basque Country each September. Whereas the San Sebastián festival is 'international', the Málaga film festival, held in March, focuses more on Spanish and Spanish language cinema. There might be a film or two which is indicated as 'VOSE' (*versión original subtitulada en español*) i.e. subtitled rather than dubbed, the latter being the norm in Spain. This does not mean that it is in English, though. It could be in French or Farsi!

The red carpet is laid out along Calle Larios and all the events, celebrity arrivals and awarding of prizes can be viewed on huge screens erected in the Plaza de la Constitución. The lavish closing gala takes place at the Teatro de Cervantes.

Hundreds of films are shown during the festival at multiple locations, including all the main theatres and cinemas in the city centre. These range from full-length feature films to shorts and documentaries. Tickets can be purchased from the relevant box office(s), including online. Around twenty films form the 'official' festival and are in line for the prizes (gold and silver trophies in the form of '*biznagas*'). Tickets for these are more expensive.

Consult the festival website for the programme and to buy tickets: **festivaldemalaga.com** (Spanish only).

'VinomaScope'

Running alongside the Film Festival, the *Consejo Regulador Denominaciones de Origen* (the Málaga DOP wine and raisin regulator) arranges a *tapas* and wine route around the city centre. Dozens of bars and restaurants participate in VinomaScope, offering *maridajes* (pairings) of a signature *tapa* with an especially selected Málaga or Sierras de Málaga wine for a few euros. You can find the details here: **vinomascope.es**.

March/April

A major event in Málaga's calendar is *Semana Santa*, or Holy Week, taking place in late March or during April. For a detailed guide, look at the '*Semana Santa*' chapter beginning on p. 334.

May/June

 *Noche en Blanco*

The 'White Night', loosely tied to midsummer, is usually celebrated in late May (search online to find the dates of the next *Noche en Blanco* — in 2022 it took place, exceptionally, in October). *Noche en Blanco* has been marked in Málaga since 2008 and each year there is a different theme, chosen by popular vote since 2016. Recent themes have been 'The Sea' (2015), 'The Stars' (2016), 'Dreams' (2017), 'Around the World in One Night' (2019) and 'The Four Elements' (2022). Beginning around 7 pm, it is probably the most concentrated cultural festival anywhere in Europe, with almost 200 events taking place within five or six hours.

Almost every cultural and municipal institution in Málaga takes part. There are public concerts (*e.g.* classical piano recitals in front of the Teatro Romano), museums open after hours for special tours, there are magic and circus performances, street art, dance, and more. The vast majority of the programme is free, and at only nominal cost to secure a place if not. Comprehensive programmes are available from the turismo, but these are only in Spanish. lanocheenblancomalaga.com

Corpus Christi

The Feast of Corpus Christi (The Solemnity of the Most Holy Body and Blood of Christ) is celebrated 60 days after Easter (the Thursday after Trinity Sunday), so it is a moveable feast, occurring in the last week of May or the first half of June. It is a feast that celebrates and promotes the Catholic belief in the real presence of Jesus Christ in the Eucharist or Blessed Sacrament (the transformation of bread and wine). Holy Thursday is the pre-eminent feast of the Eucharist, but what with the foot-washing, the blessing of the Holy Oils and the impending crucifixion of Christ, there is a lot more going on besides. Hence a second feast was established. It began as a local celebration in the Diocese of Liège (Belgium) in the early 13th century, before being extended to the whole Church by Pope Urban IV in 1264.

From its inception, a key part of the liturgical celebration has been a procession, either around a church or through the streets. In Spain, most municipalities have public processions and in some cities, it is a huge event, most notably in Toledo, Valladolid, Cádiz, Barcelona and Granada (which holds its annual *feria* to coincide with it). Until 1989, the public festivities took place on a Thursday, which was a national public holiday, but the government succeeded in persuading the Bishops to transfer the feast to the following Sunday and the public holiday was dropped.

In Málaga, there is a public procession on the Sunday morning. The previous evening, there is a Vigil Mass (usually around 6.30 pm) followed by Vespers (evening prayer) and then a concert in the Plaza del Obispo. When this concludes, the church of Santo Cristo de la Salud remains open for Eucharistic Adoration Vigil until 1 am (in previous years, nocturnal adoration has been at the Cathedral).

The procession begins from the Cathedral at 10 am on Sunday (it seems to vary between 10 and 11 every few years). The Holy Week Brotherhoods set up altars along the route, most having brought their titular image in procession earlier in the morning or the previous evening. These street altars are decorated with flowers and a carpet of fragrant herbs like juniper and rosemary are spread across the road. Members of the various brotherhoods distribute holy pictures, prayer cards and ears of wheat (symbolizing the Bread of Life) to onlookers.

In the first public procession following the COVID restrictions, only three brotherhoods set up roadside altars, but in the past, there were more than a dozen, so numbers will no doubt increase again.

For the procession, the Blessed Sacrament (in the form of a host or 'wafer') is placed in a gold and silver '*custodia*' (a vessel designed to hold and display the Eucharistic host, called a 'monstrance' in English). This, in turn, is placed into a larger *custodia* of silver and gold which looks like a miniature temple — four pillars supporting a domed *baldaquino* (canopy). The version used by the Cathedral was made in the 1950s by the famous ecclesiastical gold-smith 'Granda' in Alcalá de Henares, near Madrid. This is supported on a throne, again of hand-worked sterling silver, made in the first decade of the 21st century by apprentices at the Molina Lario de la Catedral workshop school. Unlike the *Semana Santa* thrones, it is not carried but is on wheels (hidden by a brocade curtain).

It leaves the Cathedral through the door of the Patio de los Naranjos, then continues along San Agustín, Echegaray, Granada, Plaza del Siglo, Plaza del Carbón, Plaza de Spínola, Granada, Plaza de la Constitución, Larios, Strachan, and Molina Lario, returning to Plaza del Obispo and Cathedral. It is accompanied by the Royal Fire Department and the Municipal Band, with the music band *Nuestra Señora de la Soledad*, from the Congregation of Mena, playing at the altar stations.

🏠 Semana Popular de los Corralones

At the end of May and/or the beginning of June dozens of *corralones* (a traditional form of housing arranged around a shared patio) in La Trinidad and El Perchel are opened to the public. Some patios in Capuchinos, Cruz Verde–Lagunillas and Ollerías also participate. See p. 83 for more details.

🔥 San Juan

San Juan is usually celebrated on the night of 23 June, which is the Eve of the Feast of the Nativity of St John the Baptist (on 24 June). Although the name is religious, it is nowadays pretty much a secular celebration, more linked to Midsummer (21 June). Although celebrated all over Spain, it is primarily a beach festival, so very popular along the Málaga coast. Traditionally, huge bonfires (*hogueras*) are lit on the beach and the party continues into the small hours. Throughout the province of Málaga, there is also the custom of burning what are known as *júas*: effigies made out of old clothes stuffed with sawdust and paper that are put on the bonfire when the clock strikes midnight. It is said that jumping nine waves with your back to the sea brings fertility. Jumping over the bonfire seven times will bring you good luck for the year ahead, provided you can avoid third-degree burns. People also write down their wishes (or regrets) and burn them on the bonfire.

Almost all the coastal towns of Málaga host special events for the Fiesta de San Juan. In Málaga city, the party centres around La Malagueta, where there are usually concerts, a huge bonfire, and fireworks. The party atmosphere also spills over to La Misericordia and El Palo. If you are close to Torremolinos or Benalmádena, then head to La Carihuela or Bil-Bil beach, respectively. But wherever you are on the coast, if there's a decent-size beach, there will be a bonfire.

June-August
 *Cine Abierto* (Open Cinema)

 An extension of the (Film) *Festival de Málaga*, this is a programme of (mostly free) film screenings throughout June, July and the first half of August in different locations around the city. Most of these locations are not in the city centre, but in suburban parks and on various beaches. The main central location for *Cine Abierto* is the Cine Albéniz, the main 'art' cinema near the Teatro Romano on Calle Alcazabilla. **festivaldemalaga.com/cineabierto**

July
🗽 *Virgen del Carmen*

The *Virgen del Carmen* or *Nuestra Señora del Carmen* is how *Santa María del Monte Carmelo* (Our Lady of Mount Carmel) is usually known in Spain, one of the various invocations of the Virgin Mary. Her title comes from veneration of her on Mount Carmel (in the Holy Land) by the friars who came to be known as Carmelites. According to Carmelite tradition, on 16 July 1251, the image of the Virgin appeared to Saint Simon Stock, Superior General of the Order, giving him the scapular, (a garment that forms part of a religious habit) and promising to protect him. Devotional scapulars were worn by lay people and members of brotherhoods who wanted to share in Carmelite spirituality, which helped foster the cult.

Spain is one of the countries where this dedication is most deeply rooted. She is the patron saint of sailors and fishermen. On April 19, 1901, the Regent María Cristina and the Minister of the Navy Cristóbal Colón de la Cerda, Duke of Veragua, endorsed with their signatures the Royal Order by which the Blessed Virgin of Carmen was proclaimed Patron of the Spanish Navy.

In the General Chapter of the Carmelites held at London (1254), the order was given to found houses in Spain and as a consequence, around 1270, the first foundations were made in some of the most important cities under the Crown of Aragón. Its spread was rapid throughout the Iberian Peninsula, reaching Seville in 1358, and establishing 'Betica' (Andalucía) as a separate province of the Order in 1499. At this time the first female communities of Carmelite nuns began to emerge. Saint Teresa of Jesus (of Ávila) and Saint John of the Cross, during the 16th century, introduced reforms within the Order giving rise to the 'Discalced' (barefoot) Carmelites, a new, more austere congregation that separated from the parent order, which was thereafter called the 'Calced' or 'Ancient Observance' Carmelites. The Discalced Carmelite friars established themselves in Málaga in 1584, with the Discalced nuns following in 1585.

The Carmelites built the convent of San Andrés and a church in the *barrio* of El Perchel. During the Disentailment of Mendizábal, the assets of the Carmelites and the convent were requisitioned and their members expelled from Málaga in 1836. The Carmelite Order left Spain until its return in 1868 and did not return to Málaga until 1943. They currently care for the busy, but rather plain and modern, church of Stella Maris (Star of the Sea).

Even though the Carmelites themselves were banished, they left behind them strong popular devotion to Our Lady of Mount Carmel, especially in areas where people made their living from the sea. Practically all Spanish coastal towns and cities celebrate the feast of the Virgen del Carmen on July 16 and Málaga is no exception. The processions that take place are real demonstrations of community devotion — less solemn or tightly choreographed than those of *Semana Santa*, but just as moving. People carry the image of the Virgin on a small litter, surrounded with flowers and candles, from the church to the sea. Not just the seashore, but the sea, carrying the throne into the water. People watch from the shore, or from boats, and many wade into the water.

Where to watch a procession

A Please check the timings of these celebrations online (you will probably see posters around town) as they do not always take place on the feast itself (16 July) but a day earlier or later, or are transferred to a weekend.

One of Málaga's largest *Virgen del Carmen* processions, and perhaps the most famous, is held in **El Palo** district. The district is decorated for the festivities with the image leaving **Nuestra Señora de las Angustias** church **(Calle Villafuerte 1)** around 5.30 pm and carried along **El Chanquete** beach.

Beginning around 6 pm, the streets and waters of **Pedregalejo** hold their *Virgen del Carmen* procession. The image sets off from **Corpus Christi** parish church **(Calle Ventura de la Vega 8)** and is then placed aboard a fishing boat moored at the mouth of the Pilones River.

In **Huelin**, the *Virgen del Carmen* procession usually starts at 5 pm from **San Patricio** church **(Calle Abogado Federico Orellana Toledano 2)**.

There is an earlier start for the procession from **El Perchel**, which includes a blessing of the waters and a commemoration of all those who have perished at sea. The image of the *Virgen del Carmen Coronada del Perchel* leaves the parish church in El Perchel **(Plaza de Toros Vieja 23)** at 8 am and is taken in procession to Muelle Dos. At 10 am, the image embarks on a two-hour boat journey from the port to the **Playa La Malagueta**, after which it moves to the **Cathedral** for an afternoon mass, before returning to El Perchel in the evening. In **Fuengirola**, the *Procesión Triunfal de la Virgen del Carmen* takes place in the evening.

Many other Virgen del Carmen processions take place along the Málaga coast: **Marbella, Nerja, Los Boliches, Benalmádena, Rincón de la Victoria, Estepona, Manilva** and **La Carihuela** to name just some.

August

👯 🐂 The *Feria* and The Bulls

Please see the section about the *feria* beginning on p. 416, and about the bulls from p. 437.

September

🍸 Málaga Fashion Week

Also known as '*Pasarela Larios*', Málaga's annual fashion show takes place in the first half of September. The trade event lasts almost a week, but the catwalk shows happen on the Friday and Saturday evenings. In recent years the first show has been as early as 2 September or as late as 17 September. There is an exhibition area set up in the Plaza de la Constitución and the Calle Marqués de Larios is transformed into a 300-metre catwalk (*pasarela*) with the addition of a turquoise carpet — a nod to Málaga's maritime position and heritage. The shows begin at 8 pm. There are no tickets on sale and most of the chairs are set aside for buyers, journalists and fashionista hangers-on. However, if you can find a spot, the event is free to watch. You will need to arrive early to bag a perch on a stone bench (or one of the public seats if you are lucky) or find a place to stand behind the official seating.

🕯 *Virgen de la Victoria* (8 September)

Our Lady of the Victory is the Co-Patron of the Diocese and City of Málaga (along with the Cristo de la Salud and Saints Ciriaco and Paula). Her feast day is a public holiday in the Málaga municipal area.

On the Saturday afternoon before 30 August, the image (statue) of Santa María de la Victoria is lowered from her place above the high altar to the transfer throne. Early on Sunday morning, the image is transferred from the Basilica of La Victoria (Plaza Santuario) to the Cathedral Basilica. This is done simply, by the most direct route, while reciting the Rosary. Santa María de la Victoria later presides over the main altar of the Cathedral under a red canopy and is enthroned in a small temple, accompanied by candles and flowers.

In the Cathedral, between 30 August and 7 September a 'novena' is celebrated. A novena is nine consecutive days of prayer and devotions recalling the nine days that the disciples spent in prayer between the Ascension and Pentecost. Each year a preacher is invited to deliver a daily homily. He will usually have a theme that is explored over the days. The novena begins on 30 August at 7.30 pm with novena prayers and solemn vespers (evening prayer) and on subsequent days a similar pattern is followed: novena prayers at 7.30 pm, Mass at 8 pm, concluding with a hymn to the Virgin. The anniversary of the consecration of the Cathedral also occurs within this period (31 August). Various other elements occur during the week. On one of the days (usually a Saturday), children visit the image and people pray that the Virgin Mary will protect them throughout their lives. On another day, those wishing to be admitted to the brotherhood are welcomed and presented with the medal of the corporation (*Real Hermandad de Santa María de la Victoria*). Each day, musical accompaniment for the Mass is provided by choirs from different churches in Málaga. The precise programme (in Spanish) is usually posted on the Cathedral website (**bit.ly/MCatVictoria**) in early August.

On September 8 (usually at about 11.30 am), the Municipal Corporation, as well as the Málaga Provincial Council, the Sub-delegation of the Government of Spain, and the Delegation of the *Junta de Andalucía* attend a Mass presided over by the Bishop. Before the Eucharistic celebration, they make a traditional floral offering. The banner of the City of Málaga is placed on the altar of the Cathedral. At the end of the Solemn Mass, the '*Salve Malagueña*' is sung in honour of the Patron Saint (composed by D. Manuel Gámez in 1985, it is a version of the traditional hymn '*Salve Regina*' or 'Hail Holy Queen'). After the Mass, an offering of flowers by the people of Málaga is made in the atrium of the Main Gate in the Plaza del Obispo, organized by 'La Coracha', an association dedicated to the preservation of *malagueña* culture and heritage. While the floral offering is made, people dance *malagueñas*.

In the evening, beginning around 7.30 pm, the triumphal procession takes place, from the Cathedral to the Basilica and Royal Sanctuary. The image is carried on a throne carried by one hundred and fifty members of the Brotherhood of Our Lady of the Victory, and adorned with the flowers from the various offerings. This brotherhood (**santamariadelavictoria.es**) is an example of an important and popular Málaga brotherhood that does not take part in the ceremonies of *Semana Santa*. They are a brotherhood *'De Gloria'* — committed to the promotion of devotion to a cult or saint, in this case, the Virgin of Victory.

The image of *Santa María de la Victoria* corresponds to a type of Marian image of the 'Theothokos' ('God-Bearer'), the origin of which is the Council of Ephesus of 431, spreading the cult of the Mother of Jesus, a cause taken up by the Cistercian order since the 10th century. The statue of Santa María de la Victoria is made of polychrome and gilded wood. From an anonymous *imaginero*, various scholars attribute it to different craftsmen or schools. Some suspect a German or Austrian origin (it was a gift from the Habsburg emperor Maximilian I to his in-laws, the Catholic Monarchs); others consider it an image of the circle of the *sevillano* sculptors Pedro Millán, Juan de Figueroa or Jorge Fernández 'El Alemán', made at the end of the 15th century. The image was originally part of an altarpiece and it is hollow inside. It escaped damage and destruction in the events of 1931 because the nearby military hospital meant troops were able to defend the basilica. The throne, however, was entirely destroyed. The Child Jesus is a work by the sculptor Adrián Risueño Gallardo, made in 1943 for the Canonical Coronation of Santa María de la Victoria, replacing a previous one from the 19th century. It follows the artistic lines of the Virgin. The canopy and many of the banners and other fabric decorations have recently been restored or renewed as, since 2019 the brotherhood has operated its own embroidery workshop, under the direction of Sebastián Marchante.

The current throne, re-silvered in 1998, dates from the 1980s, having replaced an earlier version made in the 1960s. Its corners are decorated with hundreds of tuberoses (*polianthes*). In the middle of the front of the throne are miniatures of the Catholic Monarchs and the Minim Friars depicted during the *reconquista* and the establishment of the friars in the kingdoms of Castilla and Aragón. The crown that the Virgin wears in the procession was donated by the people of Málaga on the occasion of her canonical coronation in 1943 (and in 2020, sufficient funds were raised to commission a new version, designed by Don Juan Antonio Sánchez López, Professor of Art History at the University of Málaga, and fabricated in the Montenegro Goldsmith Workshops). The procession is again made up of the corporate representation of brotherhoods and brotherhoods, clubs, the University, institutions, City Hall, Provincial Council, Sub-delegation of the Government of Spain, Delegation of the *Junta de Andalucía*, as well as various public and private entities.

The procession begins inside the Cathedral, going out into the street through the Puerta de las Cadenas (into the Patio de los Naranjos). At that moment, all the church bells throughout the diocese ring, paying homage to their Patroness. The procession moves through the city centre along the following streets: Santa María, Molina Lario, Plaza del Obispo, Molina Lario, Strachan, Torre de Sandoval, Bolsa, Marqués de Larios, Plaza de la Constitución, Granada, Calderería, Plaza de Uncibay, Casapalma, Cárcer, Madre de Dios, Plaza de La Merced (west and south side), Plaza de María Guerrero, Victoria, Plaza de la Victoria, Compás de la Victoria, and Plaza del Santuario with confinement in the Sanctuary (around 11.30 pm).

At several points on the route, people make offerings of different kinds — songs, dances and *'petaladas'* (showers of rose petals). In the Plaza de la Constitución, the Municipal Music

Band will play the national anthem to announce the departure of the authorities from the procession. The procession itself is accompanied by the Maestro Eloy García Music Band of the *Archicofradía de la Expiración*.

October

 ## *Fiesta Nacional de España* (National Day of Spain)

October 12 is a national holiday and most shops are closed. It is also traditionally and commonly referred to as the *Día de la Hispanidad* ('Spanishness Day'), commemorating Spain's legacy worldwide, especially in Hispanic America. The National Day of Spain commemorates the 'discovery' of the Americas by Christopher Columbus on 12 October 1492. It is also the official Spanish Language Day, the Feasts of both Our Lady of the Pillar (Zaragoza) and the Virgin of Zapopan (Mexico) as well as the National Day of the Spanish Armed Forces.

Events are usually held in which the Latin American communities resident in Málaga share their culture, traditions, gastronomy and handicraft products. There are events for children such as plays or contests, as well as parades, Latin dance classes and many more activities. These activities have been held for years in **Parque de Huelin (Calle Orfila)**, a ten-minute walk from María Zambrano railway station starting around noon and continuing into the evening.

 ## Halloween (31 October)

The fact that this celebration is called 'Halloween' and not '*Noche de Brujas*', '*Víspera de Difuntos*', '*Víspera de Todos los Santos*', '*Noche de los Muertos*', or '*Noche de Difuntos*' tells you all you need to know about this recent addition to Málaga's cultural agenda. Indeed, one listing of events in Málaga rather sniffily explains that it takes place due to '*contagio cultural*' from the '*angloesfera*' ('cultural contagion from the Anglosphere')! However, *malagueños* are not ones to miss an opportunity to have fun, so one suspects that Halloween in all its trashy American awfulness is here to stay.

During the last few years, a so-called 'Zombie March' has taken place with a large number of young people in 'living dead' fancy dress taking to the streets of the centre in a march that leaves from the Plaza de la Constitución around 10.30 pm. Events for children are held at the Botanical Gardens (treasure hunts for children in the day and a scary tour for adults in the evening) and the English Cemetery (in Spanish). Booking is essential for both, so check websites for times and information. Between 5 and 9 pm, events for children are organized in the Soho district (around the pedestrianized portion of Calle Tomás Heredia) and on Muelle Uno, both featuring fancy dress competitions, face painting, music, dancing, sweet treasure hunts and games.

November

✝ *Todos Los Santos* (All Saints)

The feast of *Todos Los Santos* (often shortened as '*Tosantos*') on 1 November is a public holiday in Spain, but most of the 'celebrations' are private and observed within families. The reason is that the following day, *La Conmemoración de Todos los Fieles Difuntos* (The Commemoration of the Faithful Departed, or All Souls) is the day when people pray for their dead loved ones. Today is a busy day for florists as people flock to cemeteries to lay flowers and tend graves to make them ready for the 'Day of the Dead' the next day. Particularly busy is the beautiful

Cementerio Municipal de San Miguel (♀Plaza del Patrocinio 8, p. 288) in the north of the city, established in the 19th century. Spanish cemeteries tend to be quite compact thanks to the custom of interring remains (usually ashes nowadays) not in dug graves but in *columbaria* or funerary niches (rented for a certain number of years). Thus, many have the appearance of 'cities of the dead' with streets of niches stacked six or more high.

As for any Spanish feast day, certain sweets are associated with this day. We are well into the season for roasted chestnuts by this point, and street vendors will be busy. Other typical treats eaten today are *buñuelos*, *borrachuelos* and '*huesos de santo*'. The deep-fried fritters or doughnuts called *buñuelos* are a popular snack at the time of any feast or celebration (especially *Semana Santa* and the *feria*). *Borrachuelos* (which means 'drunken ones') originate in Málaga (probably) and are closely related to *pestiños*. They are also popular at Christmas and during *Carnaval*. Made from dough enriched with wine, brandy (or anisette), orange, cloves and aniseed (known as '*matalahuga*' in Andalucía), they are stuffed with '*cabello de ángel*' (a sweet jam made from a kind of pumpkin), deep fried then dusted in sugar or rolled in honey. *Huesos de Santo* are only made and eaten at this time of year — the name means 'bones of a saint'. They appear in *panaderías* towards the end of October and remain on sale for only a week or so. They are tubes of marzipan filled with a rich egg yolk custard (or *cabello de ángel*, jam, chocolate, or other filling). The marzipan is the 'bone', and the custard, or jam, is the 'marrow'. Like many limited edition Spanish '*dulces*' (sweets), they are very, very sweet.

An old tradition on *Todos Los Santos* was to see a production (or the film) of the play *Don Juan Tenorio*, a play of 1844 by José Zorrilla. Subtitled a '*Religious-Fantasy Drama in Two Parts*', it is one of the more romantic treatments of the Don Juan myth. The great womanizer Don Juan, having already bedded thousands of women in Sevilla, from serving girls to countesses, is eager to seduce a religious novice (an aspirant nun). He tries his luck with the saintly Doña Inés de Ulloa and in a tender scene it seems that he approaches something like real love rather than lust. However, after shooting her father dead, he flees Sevilla, only returning after 10 years to find that, unsurprisingly, Doña Inés has died of a broken heart.

This play is one of the most lucrative in Spanish history and has been performed continually ever since it was written and there have been nine film versions in the last 100 years. While it does not sound like the most edifying tale for a religious feast, it was once performed in auditoriums and parish halls throughout Spain on All Saints' Day. The reason? The end of the work takes place on the night of All Saints and is a meditation upon the nature of death, forgiveness and redemption. In a dreamlike scene, Don Juan has been killed in a duel but, as if still living, he meets the ghost of Don Gonzalo, Inés's dead father, whom he murdered. Gonzalo reaches out to lead him to hell, but Don Juan cries out to heaven for mercy and Doña Inés appears, leading him to heaven — her Christlike love, purity and forgiveness redeems even the most base of sinners. In recent years this play has begun to be staged again (including at the English Cemetery), though it now seems more usual to mount the productions on Halloween, rather than the Eve of All Souls.

🎷 Málaga International Jazz Festival

This festival has been running for over 30 years and usually takes place in the first or second week of November. The main concerts are held at the Teatro Cervantes, so consult their website for the programme (⊕ teatrocervantes.com), which includes details of other performances mounted in other venues.

🐛 *Luces de Navidad* (Christmas Lights)

The switch-on of the Christmas lights in Málaga usually takes place on the last (or penultimate) Saturday in November. Search for '*¿Cuándo se encienden las luces de Navidad en Málaga?*' (🌐 bit.ly/46DYABQ) to find the schedule. The precise dates are often not fixed until October or even early November. Christmas lights begin to appear in the streets of Málaga during October, but the big displays are in the Plaza de la Constitución, the Plaza de la Marina and, par excellence, along the Calle Marqués de Larios.

The display on Calle Larios was traditionally one of the most lavish and beautiful (and expensive) in all of Spain. Following the Russian invasion of Ukraine and the rise in energy costs, coupled with the rise in the cost of living, the Larios spectacle was scaled back in 2022, but other streets were lit and decorated. The official 'switch on' is always a big event, however, with live bands and a DJ in the Plaza de la Marina to provide entertainment before and after the illumination. There are also drone displays in the Port area.

December
🏃 *Maratón de Málaga*

The Málaga Marathon (and Half-Marathon) takes place in December, usually on the first or second Sunday. Registrations close about a week before the race takes place. To find out more, search online for '*maratón de Málaga*' (🌐 bit.ly/3O7sGGM — there is no point giving a web link because the address changes each time there is a change of sponsor).

🕯 *La Inmaculada Concepción* (The Immaculate Conception 8 December)

The winter holiday season kicks off in Spain in early December with two national holidays falling only a day apart: *Día de la Constitución* (Spanish Constitution Day) on 6 December and *La Inmaculada Concepción* (The Immaculate Conception, also known as *La Purísima*) on 8 December. While you will not see public celebrations of either, these days are eagerly anticipated by many for the opportunity to plan a long, much-needed (hopefully) weekend getaway.

The Immaculate Conception, of course, is not about the Virgin Birth of Christ. Many often incorrectly assume that it refers to the virginal conception of Christ in Mary's womb. It doesn't. That's a different feast day: the Feast of the Annunciation, which falls on March 25 (nine months before Christmas Day). It commemorates the day the Archangel Gabriel announced to the Virgin Mary that she would give birth to the Son of God.

'*La Purísima*' is actually a dogma of the Catholic Church that asserts that Christ's mother, Mary, was herself conceived free from original sin in her own mother's womb. However, to dip into some theology here, this was not because of any superhuman qualities on the part of Mary. Like any human being, she is saved by Jesus Christ. It is just that in Mary's case, she is saved by the 'foreseen' merits of her Son.

On this day, a lot is going on in Málaga, but not on the streets. There is no obvious partying today. Nonetheless, all the Holy Week brotherhoods, and many others, observe the feast in their canonical seats, or temples. The images of the Virgins are usually enthroned on the eve of the feast (7 December) and a solemn Mass celebrated on the feast day itself (8 December). Try an internet search for '*la Inmaculada*' and '*Málaga*' to find this year's programme.

Besamanos (18 December)

18 December is the Feast of the 'Expectation of the Blessed Virgin Mary' (*Nuestra Señora de la Expectación*) celebrated primarily in Spain, Portugal, and parts of Italy and Poland. The 'expectation' is the expectation of a child, and the feast is closely linked with the virtue of Hope, and thus the *Virgen de la Esperanza*. In Málaga, there are five virgins with this dedication: *La Esperanza del Perchel* (Archicofradía del Paso y Esperanza), *Nueva Esperanza* (Hermandad de Nueva Esperanza), *Gracia y Esperanza* (Estudiantes), *María Santísima de la 'O'* (Gitanos) and the *María Santísima de Dolores y Esperanza* (Humildad y Paciencia).

On the feast, and over the day or two beforehand, there is a tradition of visiting these images to 'kiss the hand' (*besamanos*) in their various 'temples'. Many of those who make this small pilgrimage are mothers, expectant mothers and families with very young children. They come to ask for the prayers and blessings of the expectant mother of Jesus upon themselves and their families. There are also processions — for example, in the north-western suburbs, the *Virgen de la Esperanza y Refugio de los Ancianos* is taken to a care home for the elderly, her route accompanied by a band.

For the last few years around 30 of the Málaga brotherhoods have used this feast as an opportunity to collect food, household products and money to assist poor families in the city. Volunteers from the *cofradías* (brotherhoods) volunteer in supermarkets during the week leading up to the feast, inviting donations of food and, although the many concerts and recitals over the '*triduum*' (three days of celebration) are technically free, the 'entrance price' is a donation of food or a child's toy. To find the programme of events, search online for '*festividad de la Esperanza*' and '*besamanos*' in the days before 18 December.

🏠 *Navidad* (Christmas)

Christmas Day is largely a day enjoyed at home by families, so there are no big events in Málaga on this day, and no grand religious processions or street parties. However, Christmas is an increasingly popular time to visit Málaga due to the pleasant weather. The average daytime temperature is 17° or 18° Celsius (rarely dropping below 14°C) and night-time lows are around 8°C, which is basically as cold as Málaga gets. More importantly, the weather is often sunny, so if you find a nice spot it can feel significantly warmer than the temperature in the shade.

If you are going to be in Málaga for Christmas Day itself (a public holiday, as in the UK), then make sure you have your meals sorted ahead of time. Most of the big hotels, as in Britain, serve meals on Christmas Day, but some only have snacks available. Smaller and independent hotels may close their kitchens after breakfast, so please check in advance. If you are staying in an *hostal* then you will need to make other arrangements. A few restaurants will be open for lunch and dinner (including hotel restaurants open to non-guests), so even if you are staying in accommodation which does not offer meals, you should be able to find somewhere. Many of the places offering meals are near the top end, however, so expect to pay over the odds! Try this web search to find information: bit.ly/MLGXmasOpen. However, always check with the restaurant itself as booking is essential, and remember that there will be much reduced public transport so either choose somewhere within walking distance or factor in the cost of a taxi on its maximum tariff. Bear in mind, too, that the main Christmas meal in Spain is on the evening of Christmas Eve.

During the run-up to Christmas, though, there is plenty going on. Here are a few suggestions:

Ice Skating

A modestly sized rink (35m x 15m) has for a number of years been set up on Avenida de Andalucía, next to the entrance to El Corte Inglés, which offers children the opportunity to enjoy ice skating during the Christmas holidays (from the end of November until 6 January). There are other ice-based attractions such as a toboggan, a small train and various rides.

The MIMA children's fair (**⨍ mimamalaga**) takes place every year at the Palacio de Congresos, near the fairground (**Avenida de José Ortega y Gasset 201**). It runs from 26 until 30 December and then from 2 to 4 January. Covering an area of 1,850 m², there are more than 60 activities and rides for children, and some years there has been an ice rink. It's more like a UK fair, but with zip wires and climbing walls as well as rides and dodgems.

Belénes (Nativity Scenes)

The Crib or Nativity Scene celebrated its eight hundredth anniversary in 2023, having first appeared in 1223, designed by St Francis of Assisi (though he used only animals rather than figurines of people). Although promoted by the Franciscan Order, the Christmas Crib remained a largely Italian custom and only came to Spain in the mid-18th century when King Carlo VII of Naples became King Carlos III of Spain. He popularized the '*Belén*' (Bethlehem) among the aristocracy, from whence the custom spread to the populace. The Spanish nativity scene is usually something rather more impressive than a collection of mass-produced figures on a bed of straw. There are numerous workshops throughout Spain that produce high-quality carved or plaster figures that can approach the quality of *Semana Santa* images at their best. Families often build their own collections of figures and decorations over years.

Just like many great religious artworks, artists and patrons find ways to insert themselves into a *Belén*, so if you look carefully, perhaps one of the shepherds looks like the artist who created the scene, or you may be able to spot the banner of a Holy Week brotherhood hanging in the corner of the cave (Jesus being born in a stable, though not unknown in Spanish Nativities, is more of a Protestant tradition — in Spain his manger is usually depicted as being in a house or, for those who follow the 2nd-century theologian Justin Martyr, a cave). Something similar happens in Catalonia, where any self-respecting *Belén* has a '*caganer*' (lit. 'defecator'): a figure of a peasant with his trousers down who defecates in a corner. He almost certainly has a pagan origin, but also serves as a reminder of the 'earthiness' of the Incarnation and Nativity. Jesus Christ was not born in a palace but in a rented room in a small Judaean city surrounded by a great mess of humanity and defecating cattle. In recent years, the *caganer* is often a public figure that people wish to ridicule, so defecating politicians often feature. But such is the affection in which the *caganer* is held (as a symbol of fertility and a good harvest), it can also be an honour to be a figure. Hence the headline in the British newspaper, The Telegraph, in 2009 about the late Queen Elizabeth II. The artist who produced the hand-painted figure of her late Majesty attending to the call of nature explained,

> *It is not making fun but quite the opposite, it is a tribute to the person and*
> *the office or activity they represent. This year we decided to include Queen*
> *Elizabeth II because she is such an important figure.*[48]

The *Belénes* of Málaga, however, are rather more decorous.

The *Diputación de Málaga* (**🚌 Carretera de Cádiz 📍 Calle Pacífico 54**) stages a monumental nativity from the end of November. It is free to visit and covers over 250 m² featuring almost 15,000 figures. In addition, it also features caves, gorges, cliffs, rivers, lakes and even the

---

48   Fiona Govan, 'Queen "honoured" with Spanish Christmas tradition', in *The Telegraph*, 20 November 2009, archive.ph/kp15K

sea, all depicting real places in the Province of Málaga. It contains streets, squares and more than a hundred buildings. Moreover, it includes 19 biblical scenes, such as the Annunciation of Mary and the return of the Holy Family to Nazareth after the death of Herod. In the other direction, the *barrio* of La Mosca (north of El Palo) has a large and impressive *Belén* built into the side of a mountain that attracts visitors from all around **(Calle Escritor Manuel Solano 93)**. It is a 30-minute journey on the bus (🚌 34) from the Alameda Principal.

In the city centre, some of the most impressive Nativity scenes in Málaga are the one show-cased at Málaga City Hall, outside the Cathedral, and those created by the brotherhoods (naturally, they all claim to have the most impressive *Belén* in Málaga). There is an official nativity scene route with a 'passport' showing the location of all the main ones in the city — ask for a copy at the tourist office, or try this search: ⊕ **bit.ly/RutaBelenesMLG** — the programme usually hits the press around the beginning of December).

Christmas Markets

Like more or less any large city in Europe, Málaga has a Christmas Market, usually opening at the end of November and continuing until Christmas. Some stalls are found at the Plaza de la Marina end of the *Paseo* del Parque, and another collection pops up on Muelle Uno. Similar markets operate in Torremolinos, Benalmádena and Fuengirola. The Málaga Christmas Market is not an approximation of a faux-German Weihnachtsmarkt selling Glühwein and sausages as in the UK, but a high-quality local crafts and food market. As well as the usual handicrafts and jewellery, you can also find typically Spanish Christmas goods such as nativity scenes and figures, children's Christmas costumes, stocking-filler toys, tambourines and seasonal foods and sweets.

Botanical Gardens Light Installation

From the end of November until the first week of January, the Jardín Botánico Histórico–La Concepción is illuminated with dozens of beautifully curated light installations covering a 2.2km route, recreating elements of the Christmas story such as 'Bethlehem', 'Persia of the Kings' or 'The Star'. There are food and drink stalls and admission is between 6.30 pm and 9 pm (with buses running later than usual). It is a stunning and extremely popular display attracting over 100,000 visitors.

La Misa del Gallo (Midnight Mass)

There are four Masses of Christmas. The first is known as the Vigil Mass, and it takes place in the afternoon or early evening of 24 December. In it, the text of Matthew 1:18–24 is read, where the virginal conception of Mary is recounted, as well as the doubts of Joseph her betrothed. The second is the *Misa del Gallo* (Mass of the Rooster, because of a tradition that the first animal to witness the newborn Jesus was the rooster at cockcrow). This celebration is traditionally at midnight, although in recent years it has been moved earlier in the evening in most parishes. In this Mass, the reading of Luke 2:1–7 is proclaimed, in which the journey of Joseph and Mary to Bethlehem to register in the census and the birth of Jesus in a manger is recounted. The third Mass is the Dawn Mass, and the reading that follows is the one immediately after the *Misa del Gallo*, in which the adoration of the shepherds of the child Jesus is related. Finally, there is the 'Mass During the Day' when John chapter 1 is read ('In the beginning was the Word…').

Midnight Mass, once a mainstay of Catholic worship, is becoming a rarer occurrence in Europe, and Málaga is no exception. The following list shows the usual times of 'Midnight Mass' in Málaga *centro*, though as always, please check before making plans to attend.

Santa Iglesia Catedral Basílica de la Encarnación: Advertised as 23.55 for 00.00, preceded by an organ concert starting at 23.20. This is a combined celebration for the Cathedral and the city centre parishes of Santos Mártires (Ciriaco and Paula), San Juan, San Felipe Neri, and Santiago Apóstol.

Nuestra Señora del Carmen (El Perchel): 00.00

San Carlos y Santo Domingo de Guzmán (Perchel Norte): 19.00

La Divina Pastora y Santa Teresa de Jesús (Capuchinos): 00.00

Santa María de la Amargura (Mármoles): 19.00

Santa María de la Victoria (Victoria): 00.00

Stella Maris (Alameda): 00.00

Dulces (Christmas Sweets)

A number of sweets and biscuits, while not exclusively consumed at Christmas, are associated with it.

The *borrachuelo* is a very typical sweet in the Province of Málaga. It is similar to the *pestiño*, and is usually eaten at Easter and Christmas. This delicacy is prepared from a dough made with flour and olive oil flavoured with lemon or orange peel, aniseed and sesame seeds, so that it takes on a variety of flavours. Finally, a glug of Málaga wine from which it gets its name ('*borracho*' means 'drunk'). Next, the dough is cut into circles, filled with angel hair (a kind of confit pumpkin) or sweet potato, then folded and fried. Finally, they are covered in sugar or rolled in honey syrup.

Pestiños are very similar but unfilled.

Yemas del Tajo are a typical sweet from the municipality of Ronda and widely consumed at Christmas time. They are basically candied egg yolks, like little bombs of custard.

Roscos de Vino (ring-shaped biscuits flavoured with wine), another of the typical Christmas sweets of Málaga, are a typical Christmas product throughout Spain, But Málaga has its own version flavoured, naturally, with Málaga wine. These delicious morsels are made with flour, sweet Moscatel wine, sugar, olive oil, sesame seeds, lemon zest and brandy. Once baked, they are covered with icing sugar. Many *panaderías* and *confiterías* make their own version, or sell the famous brands of **Hermanos Montañez** (located in El Palo), or those made by **Framancha** in the mountain village of Monda. However, for the real Málaga version, you should visit the **Nuestra Señora de la Paz y Santísima Trinidad Monastery** (📍 Plaza Zumaya 5, 1000–1330, 1600–1830) and buy a box from the nuns. The sisters also sell *mantecados* (see below) and *borrachuelos*.

In Spain, it is traditional to eat *mantecados*, *polvorones* and *alfajores* at Christmas. The first two are very similar and both usually translated as 'shortbread' in English. The big centres of production in Andalucía are the Seville municipality of Estepa, and the Málaga municipality of Antequera, and both love to argue about which version is the most 'authentic' (though all sources indicate that the recipe for *mantecados*, at least, originated in Antequera). For this reason, *mantecados* are considered the most typical Christmas biscuits in Málaga.

Polvorones are either a variant of *mantecados*, or vice versa, and the differences are slight. Roughly speaking, *polvorones* are oval and dusted with icing sugar, and *mantecados* are circular and (sometimes) topped with sesame seeds. *Mantecados* are slightly richer, eaten all year round and can come in different flavours, while *polvorones* are not made in different flavours, are powdery ('*polvo*' means 'dust') and only eaten at Christmas.

A few Málaga bakeries (such as **Confitería Aparacio** on **Plaza Capuchinos**) make their own *polvorones* and *mantecados*, but in the main, they come from Antequera. Well-known brands include **La Antequerana, Nuestra Señora del Carmen, D. Sancho Melero, Delicias de Antequera, Torcadul, La Perla de Antequera** and **Convento de Antequera.**

Alfajores are also associated with Christmas in Andalucía. In its basic form, the *alfajor* consists of ground almonds and other types of nuts that are combined with honey and various spices (especially cinnamon) before they are shaped into cigar shapes, baked and dusted with sugar. It is believed that the *alfajores* were developed under the Moorish influence and that they reached American soil during Spanish expeditions, which eventually led to the creation of South American sandwich cookies which are also known as *alfajores*, but which are now completely different.

Often, during December, the **Brothers of Saint John of God (Plaza de San Juan de Dios 2, 1030–1330, 1700–1930)** operate a pop-up store selling Christmas biscuits and candies made by nuns from various monasteries in the Province of Málaga (Cistercians, Poor Clares, Minims, and Carmelites). The profits go to the San Juan de Dios Brothers' Shelter, which cares for homeless and socially excluded people: 12 teenagers in rehabilitation programmes, 45 people living in the shelter and dozens of people who come to use the dining room service at noon and at night, to use showers or to receive clean clothes.

Another appropriately festive sweet treat is sparkling ('*espumoso*') wine from the Málaga region, which is increasing in popularity. A fairly new entry is **Botani**, which was first released onto the market in 2014. This sparkling wine, made by Jorge Ordoñez, is produced with Moscatel grapes from the Axarquía region of Málaga. It is more 'off-dry' than sweet

Another of the Málaga wineries that has opted for the production of sweet sparkling wine is the **Tierras de Mollina** winery. They produce **Apiane** (in both *blanco* and *rosado*, in dry and off-dry/sweet versions) with Moscatel grapes in the municipality of Mollina, north of Antequera.

The **Quitapenas** wineries also make their own sparkling wines, both sweet and dry. These wines, called **Florestel**, are made from the Muscat of Alexandria grape. Look out too, for **Las Olas del Melillero**, from **Bodega Victoria Ordóñez**, or **Tartatros** made by **Bodegas Dimobe** in Rincón de la Victoria.

🎺 *Día de los Santos Inocentes*
(Holy Innocents – 28 December)

The Feast of the Holy Innocents (the commemoration of the slaughter of children under two years of age born in Bethlehem, ordered by King Herod the Great) is the Spanish equivalent of April Fools' Day. People play tricks on one another and the media report on fantastical (and invented) stories. This tradition is very old and in pre-Reformation Britain something similar took place with 'boy bishops' enjoying their final day of 'authority' on the Feast of Holy Innocents. They would be elected on 6 November (Feast of St Nicholas, patron saint of children) when the adult bishop would symbolically step down at the words '*deposuit potentes de sede*' in the Magnificat ('he has put down the mighty from their seat'), and the boy would take his seat at '*et exaltavit humiles*' ('and has exalted the humble and meek').

After the election, the boy (usually a chorister) dressed in bishop's robes with mitre and crozier and attended by other boys dressed as priests, made a circuit of the town 'blessing' the people. Typically the boy Bishop and his minions took possession of the Cathedral and performed all the ceremonies and offices (except Mass). There was, of course, a serious point to this and to related spectacles like the Feast of Fools and the Feast of Asses (also in January).

These were topsy-turvy illustrations of the cataclysmic event of the incarnation, the coming into the world of God himself — not in majesty and pomp, but as a helpless baby.

There are no special municipal celebrations on this day, but if you watch the Spanish news or buy a newspaper, don't believe anything you hear or read!

🎸 *Fiesta Mayor de Verdiales* (Verdiales Festival)

This is the big annual competition of *verdiales* '*pandas*' (see p. 425ff.) and it has been held on the Feast of Holy Innocents for more than 60 years. It brings together more than a dozen *pandas* (troupes) representing the three traditional styles: Montes, Almogía and Comares. The members of *verdiales* troupes are called *fiesteros* (party men) or *tontos* (fools), hence the link with the Feast of Holy Innocents. It takes place in the **Parque de Andrés Jiménez Díaz** in the Puerto de la Torre district of north-west Málaga starting around 1 pm. It's a 30-minute journey taking the bus (🚌 **21**) from the Alameda Principal — get off at the **Lope de Rueda – Correos** stop (🅑 2108).

If you want to see genuine, local folk music performed to the highest standard, then this event is not to be missed. The atmosphere is joyful and friendly, and there is a busy bar serving drinks. There is plenty of food in the form of *paella* (or a *malagueña* approximation of it), so if you're not a rice and/or seafood fan, take a sandwich with you or have an early lunch before leaving the city centre.

Semana Santa (Holy Week)

The colourful spectacle of *Semana Santa* (Holy Week) in Spain is familiar to foreigners from tourist posters and picture postcards — the processions of ethereal figures in tall pointed hoods, and the hyperrealistic statues of Christ in agony or the weeping Virgin Mary making their slow progress through the streets. Everyone, it seems, is aware that *Semana Santa* is marked with great solemnity in Sevilla and every year, numerous tourists flock there for it, but few know that almost every other city in Spain will be holding lavish celebrations of their own. Some of the most beautiful and venerable take place in towns that many foreigners have never heard of, still less visited: Ferrol, Cuenca, Orihuela, Teruel, and Zamora. There are other cities in Spain that more than rival Sevilla for the sheer scale of *Semana Santa*. One is the former royal capital of Valladolid, another is Zamora, and the third is Málaga.

Semana Santa in Málaga is a huge affair, and it involves so many processions and public acts of worship that it lasts more than a week, with smaller processions known as 'translations' beginning before Palm Sunday. It takes over the city centre to such an extent that if public religious observance is not your cup of tea, it would probably be best to avoid Málaga during Holy Week. But if it interests you — culturally, artistically or religiously — then there are few more beautiful and fascinating places in Spain in which to spend this 'Great Week' as the Eastern Christians call it.

Semana Santa is a vivid and beautiful spectacle which, like flamenco and the bulls, is deeply interwoven with *andaluz* culture and history. Fundamentally, it is a Christian (Catholic) event, but for many lapsed Catholics and agnostics, it nonetheless retains a profound significance. The sort of hard-line atheist who believes that religion in the root of all evil might find the processions ludicrous, and iconoclastic Protestants or Biblical Fundamentalists would probably judge it all to be 'a fond thing vainly invented, and grounded upon no warranty of Scripture, but rather repugnant to the Word of God.'[49] As with any relatively unfamiliar cultural phenomenon (and the *Semanas Santas* of Spain would be pretty confusing even to a lot of non-Spanish Catholics), it is helpful to be able to understand something of the history and principles that lie behind it. Many guidebooks and tourist websites simply mention *Semana Santa* as if it were a quaint historical relic, rather than a living tradition that is of huge importance to many people. The following sections are an attempt to explain this in more detail, but flick forward to p. 344 if you want to get to the practical information

The Origins of Holy Week

The first Christians — the Apostles and other disciples of Jesus of Nazareth — were Jews who continued, for a time, to worship in the synagogue on the seventh day of the week,

---

49   Article XXII ('On Purgatory'), *Book of Common Prayer*

or Sabbath (Saturday). In addition, they also kept 'The Lord's Day' (Sunday) which they came to understand as both the first day of the week (according to the account of Creation in Genesis), but also as a kind of 'eighth day', because it represented the 'New Creation' ushered in by the Resurrection of Jesus from the dead.

The Christian celebration on Sunday was not initially marked by rest from work like the Jewish Sabbath but was primarily about the liturgy of the 'Lord's Supper': the offering of bread and wine to be received as Christ's body and blood according to the commandment he gave at his own Last Supper. Two thousand years later, it is easy to forget that in these very early days, there was not yet any 'liturgical calendar' (just as there was no New Testament). Even in our own very secular, 'post-Christian' society, most people are dimly aware of the times and seasons of the Christian liturgical year ('liturgy' comes from the Greek word for 'public service' and was adopted by the Early Church to mean 'religious service'). Most people know the difference between Christmas and Easter, many talk about giving something up for Lent and could tell you when Halloween is, even if they are unaware that it was originally a Christian celebration.

In the Early Church, there was initially no seasonal variation, just a procession of Sundays. By the end of the first century, Easter and Good Friday were celebrated as annual commemorations and celebrations, but not with the particular liturgical acts that we know today. Fittingly enough, the story of how Holy Week came to be marked as a season of the Church's worship involves a Spaniard (or someone from the place we now call Spain). That person was a consecrated virgin or female hermit called Egeria. We know little about her, but it is probable that she was a Roman citizen living in 4th-century Hispania. Clearly a woman of means, she spent three years travelling in Egypt, the Middle East, and the Eastern Mediterranean while either keeping a diary or sending letters home.

Fragments of her first-hand accounts were only discovered in 1887, prompting scholars to identify her with a saintly woman by the name of 'Aetheria' who was mentioned by a seventh-century Spanish monk. The reason that she is important is that she witnessed and described the local Christian celebrations in Jerusalem during 'Holy Week' (which, like the crucifixion itself, was observed around the time of the Jewish Passover). What she described was not simply a liturgy but also a 'dramaturgy' — a dramatic recreation of the events of the last week in the life of Jesus. The 'triumphant' entry into Jerusalem on a donkey is thus re-enacted, with the Bishop on a donkey and the people carrying palms and olive branches. On what we now call Good Friday, she provides the first account of the Veneration of the Cross.

> *'A throne is set up for the bishop on Golgotha behind the Cross, which now stands there ... The gilded silver casket containing the sacred wood of the cross is brought in and opened ... It is the practice here for all the people to come forth one by one, the faithful as well as the catechumens to bow down before the table, kiss the holy wood, and then move on.'*

These practices spread throughout the Church and the liturgies of Holy Week became a dramatization of the Gospel stories, playing out in real time the events leading up to the death and Resurrection of Jesus.

A second significant moment in the history of Holy Week in Spain would be in 1519 (though many much-copied sources online incorrectly say 1521), when Don Fadrique Enríquez de Ribera, the First Marquess of Tarifa returned to Spain from extensive travels, including to the Holy Land. After his trip, he helped popularize the *Via Crucis* (the Way of the Cross) in Spain, and from that moment this was celebrated with a procession. Over time, the practice of the *Via Crucis* was divided into different scenes of the Passion, with the addition of crosses and portable altars. This would lead to the processions we see nowadays, spanning not just one day — Good Friday — but telescoped to extend over an entire week.

Cofradías y Hermandades
(Brotherhoods and Brotherhoods)

'I'll tell you what that is, Julie. It's a bus garage!' I overheard this example of 'mansplaining' on the Calle Victoria, near the Plaza de La Merced. 'Julie' had wondered aloud about the enormous black door of the building opposite — 5 metres wide and 5 metres high — and her male companion had made a pretty plausible guess about its purpose, passing it off as an authoritative explanation. The building, in fact, is the headquarters of the 'Royal, Most Excellent, Very Distinguished and Venerable Brotherhood of the Cult and Procession of Our Father Jesus of Nazareth called 'El Rico' and Most Holy Mary of Love'. Their Holy Week floats are carried through the door on Wednesday of Holy Week. In the rest of Spain, these processional floats are called '*pasos*', but in Málaga, which has its own terminology for sandwiches and coffee, a different term is used. They are called '*tronos*' (thrones). The *trono* of the *Cristo* 'El Rico' weighs 3,200 kg, and that of the *Virgen* weighs 3,600 kg, each carried by 220 men. The fact that the door is black accounts for the nickname of this particular image of the *Virgen* — '*La Niña de Puerta Oscura*' (The Girl from the Dark Door).

There are forty-five such brotherhoods in Málaga, and many of them have similarly large-doored headquarters to those of '*El Rico*'. You will see these enormous, two-storey doors all around the city. The processions of *Semana Santa* may be liturgical acts of the Catholic Church, but they are staged and organized by the laity — organized into fraternities — rather than by the local bishop and clergy. The brotherhoods (most of which have women members and associates) are most visible during *Semana Santa*, but they are active all year round: praying, studying and enjoying fellowship together, performing works of charity, running social action projects, preaching the Gospel in their daily lives in 'the world', and supporting the life and work of the Church locally and more widely. It would be a mistake to see such brotherhoods as a medieval relic, though, as some of the Málaga brotherhoods were founded (or refounded) within the last 20 years. However, to understand where brotherhoods came from, we do need to go back to the Middle Ages.

The Rise of Penitential Brotherhoods

The first thousand years of Christianity were dominated by monasticism (monks) — first solitary hermits and later communities that withdrew from 'the world' to devote themselves to prayer and contemplation. The towering 6th-century figure of St Benedict, known as the 'Father of Western Monasticism', wrote perhaps the most influential monastic rule of life. From the year 600 AD until 1000 AD, monasticism was the dominant form of 'consecrated' (*lit.* 'set apart') religious life, mainly lived outside the towns and cities. Pastoral care of the people in urban centres was left to 'secular' (*viz.* not 'set apart') priests.

The eleventh century would see significant reforms and reimagining of traditional (mostly Benedictine) monasticism — the Cluniacs in 910, the Camaldolese and Carthusian hermits and contemplative monks (1050–1150), the Cistercians (1098) and the Norbertines (1121). The Norbertines (also called the Premonstratensians) were a watershed. They lived a common life, but were 'Canons Regular' meaning that unlike monks they established their houses in cities, ministering to the people. They were also the first religious order to have a 'Third Order' of associated lay people. These 'tertiaries' were engaged in secular occupations, but they cooperated with the Norbertine Canons by praying for them and with them, and sharing in their social outreach.

The thirteenth century saw the rise of the 'mendicant' (begging) orders — the Dominicans, Franciscans, Carmelites, Trinitarians, Mercedarians, Servites, Minims and others. Unlike the monks, their houses were all in the cities, and lacking farms and vineyards to yield income they needed to beg ('mendicant' is from the Latin *'mendico'*: 'I beg'). All of the orders mentioned above had houses in Málaga following the *reconquista*. This 'mendicant revolution' had a number of effects, the most striking of which was to make parishes more distinct, because each order had its own 'charism' or spiritual focus. The Franciscans followed a path of radical poverty, the Dominicans were devoted to preaching the truth of the Faith against heretics and were popularizers of the Rosary, the Carmelites came from the hermit tradition of the Middle East and had a special devotion to the Virgin Mary, the Mercedarians and Trinitarians were founded to ransom captives from Muslim slave traders, and so forth. As a result, some people no longer simply went to Mass at their nearest church but began to seek out a place of worship where they felt some fellow feeling or sympathy.

All of these mendicant orders had 'tertiaries' who would share in some element of the religious order's charism with the professed friars. This would take a different form depending upon the order. Franciscan tertiaries might be attracted by radical, evangelical poverty; Dominican tertiaries might be drawn to the intellectual life or the Rosary, and Mercedarian tertiaries would be at the forefront of raising funds to redeem captives from Berber pirates. But tertiaries were also closely involved in the life of the local parish. In medieval Europe, it is easy to forget, there was no welfare state, no state education, and no universal health care. The 'safety net', such as it was, was the Church (as Professor Eamon Duffy memorably demonstrated in his book about the impact of the Reformation on one English parish: *The Voices of Morebath: Reformation and Rebellion in an English Village*).[50] The distinction between health and social care was not clear in the Middle Ages, as the etymology of the word 'hospital' suggests. In English, the Norman 'hospital' (meaning guest house) displaced the more specific Old English 'læcehus', which meant 'doctor house'. St Benedict has an entire chapter

---

50 (Yale, 2003)

in his *Rule* about how guests should be received and treated, and the first 'hospitals' were monastic guest houses that welcomed pilgrims.[51] The mendicant orders established 'hospitals' in cities that served variously as orphanages, convalescent homes and refuges for the poor and the sick. Additionally, parishes collected alms for the assistance of the poor and encouraged the wealthy to give generously as a religious duty. The brotherhoods were key to these endeavours, as co-workers with, and supporters of, the friars and the nuns (who were engaged in the education of girls and the care of women).

There was considerable overlap between the brotherhoods attached to a particular church or religious congregation and the trade guilds, which coalesced primarily due to a shared trade or occupation but would still attach themselves to a particular church. One example is '*Los Viñeros*' (The Vineyard Owners) founded in 1615 as a trade guild. Just as the various brotherhoods would have 'their' own church or convent, so they would also have their own image — a statue of Christ, the Virgin Mary or another saint as a focus of particular devotion. To this day, residents of a particular *barrio* will show great proprietary devotion to 'their' *Virgen*.

The High Middle Ages, which saw both the rise of mendicant orders and the birth of the brotherhoods, was also a time of profound theological reflection on the nature of sin and forgiveness. In the Early Church, there was a view that 'conversion' — turning away from sin and receiving God's forgiveness — could only really happen once and so penances (the acts prescribed for those becoming Christians) were usually public and arduous. However, following the practice of Irish monks, a pattern of regular confession became the norm. But the need for penance remained. Forgiveness ('absolution') is only part of the story. The harm done by sin needs to be repaired, and sometimes that involves restitution (*e.g.* paying back the money I stole), but it always requires spiritual 'repair' to oneself, because sin damages the sinner most of all. The Church teaches that the most effective ways to heal the damage inflicted by sin are prayer, fasting, almsgiving, spiritual works of mercy (like forgiving those who injure us) and corporal works of mercy (like visiting the sick). Many brotherhoods developed a decidedly penitential character. These would become the *Cofradías Penitenciales*, and these are the ones that take to the streets in the processions of *Semana Santa*.

There are also two other kinds of brotherhoods: *Cofradías Sacramentales*, which promote devotion to the Blessed Sacrament, and *Cofradías de Gloria*, which promote devotion to The Blessed Virgin or some other saint. In the Málaga municipality, there are almost one hundred brotherhoods whose constitutions have been officially recognized by the Church and a full list may be found here: 🔗bit.ly/MalagaCofradiasList. The confraternities *de Gloria* have their own association: 🔗gloriasdemalaga.org. It would be wrong to suppose, however, that all the penitents one sees during *Semana Santa* in their hooded robes are atoning for some terrible sin they personally once committed. While they are doing penance for their own sins, they are doing it for others too.

The reason that it is thought possible to do penance for others is because of an idea expressed most clearly in the practice of gaining indulgences, which were not, as many suppose, something quietly dropped by the Catholic Church after the Protestant Reformation. An indulgence is **not** to do with the forgiveness of sins. Sins are dealt with by the sacrament of confession, and forgiveness is a free gift. But what remains is the need to repair the **damage** that sin does; what the Catholic Church terms 'the temporal punishment due to sin'. An analogy may help. Let's say that a boy enjoys sledging cricket balls in his backyard, and his parents tell him not to. Nevertheless, the boy continues and soon breaks a window. The 'sin' here is really the boy's disobedience to his parents, not the breaking of the window, which is

---

51   *q.v.* James Brodman, *Charity and Welfare: Hospitals and the Poor in Medieval Catalonia* (University of Pennsylvania Press, 1998), Ch. 1, 'Hospitals and The Poor' archive.ph/5X8B

just the effect of the disobedience. The boy, full of regret, goes to his parents and says that he is sorry. His loving parents forgive him immediately and unconditionally (this is the analogy with sacramental confession), but the window is still broken. The boy is unable to pay to repair the damage. So a nominal 'punishment' is imposed. Perhaps a temporary reduction in pocket money, or a restriction on time spent playing computer games, or a requirement to sweep the yard once a week. This is the analogy with 'partial or total remissions of the temporal punishment due to sin'.

Now let's say that the boy's older brother, (aware that he has himself behaved foolishly in the past) chooses to help his younger sibling; for example by sharing his pocket money, or helping sweep the yard. Some might think that this is letting the younger boy 'off the hook', but one could equally see it as a very natural exercise of fraternal charity. And this analogy helps shed light upon another aspect of the 'Theology of Grace' that was developing in the Middle Ages — the idea of the 'Treasury of Merit'. At its root is the notion that because Christians become one body in Christ through baptism, it is fitting that they share one another's joys, sorrows and, indeed, penances. This is the analogy with indulgences.

In other words, the works of spiritual and corporal mercy that gain indulgences and bring spiritual help to us ourselves can also be applied to others; particularly to the souls in Purgatory. The Protestant reformer John Calvin famously called Purgatory 'a pernicious fiction of Satan', but Catholics believe that it is the state enjoyed by those who, although they die forgiven from their sins, still need to undergo temporal punishment for those sins, and cleansing from the attachment to sin and to the world. Purgatory, in the Catholic view, is not a destination, but a waiting room or, still better, a 'recovery room'. When we die we retain an attachment to the things of this world, both good and bad, even if we are destined for the things of heaven. To paraphrase the theologian Herbert McCabe, Purgatory is about 'learning how to be dead' so that we are ready to accept the gift of eternal life.

When you witness the ceremonies of *Semana Santa*, then, you are witnessing something that operates at many levels. Partly it is a sort of Passion Play — the events of the last week of the life of Jesus Christ staged again in our time and place. But what we also witness is a demonstration of what it means to be part of the Catholic Church, to be 'in communion'. The brotherhoods bring images of Christ and the Virgin from many churches into the city centre, following the main thoroughfares on their route to the Cathedral. *Semana Santa* is thus also a pilgrimage of individual parishes and *barrios* to the 'Mother Church' of the Cathedral, where the bishop, the successor of the Apostles, has his seat. This recalls the fact that Jesus and his disciples had gone to Jerusalem, the city of the Temple, to celebrate the Passover.

It is also a display of 'popular piety' (*i.e.* the religious expression of lay people, rather than the formal liturgy of the Church). The 2001 *Directory on Popular Piety and the Liturgy* published by the Vatican notes that 'a form of celebrational parallelism has arisen in the Rites of Holy Week, resulting in two cycles each with its own specific character: one is strictly liturgical, the other is marked by particular pious exercise, especially processions.'[52] This is an apt description. Another way to see the processions of *Semana Santa* is as an expression of '*Ecclesia in Urbe*' (the Church in the city) — during this most solemn of weeks, not hidden behind the walls of churches but in the streets. It is a public act of faith and witness.

Most of all, *Semana Santa* has a penitential character. It invites the people who witness it to feel sorrow for their sins by confronting them with depictions of the sufferings of Jesus, whom Christians believe died for those very sins, and depictions of the sorrows of Mary, his mother. Mary is not simply a witness to Christ's suffering and death, but the model of

---

52   *Directory On Popular Piety And The Liturgy: Principles And Guidelines*, Congregation for Divine Worship and the Discipline of the Sacraments (Vatican City, December 2001), § 138

a witness. Yet while *Semana Santa* is marked by sorrow and penitence, it is also about hope, and part of that hope consists in the understanding that we are 'in this together' as brothers and sisters. The *nazarenos* (the hooded and masked figures) are doing penance, not only for themselves but for their fellow men and women.

The great anchor of hope for participants in the solemn processions of *Semana Santa* is a certainty that the first companions of Jesus did not possess. Unlike St Peter, who denied even knowing Jesus, or St Matthew who lashed out with his sword at the High Priest's servant, or Mary Magdalene who thought that the body of Jesus had been stolen, we know the next part of the story. And Christians believe it. They believe that after that week of suffering, pain and sorrow, Jesus rose from the dead.

Semana Santa in Málaga

After the *reconquista* in 1487, the first brotherhoods were created, under the protection of the newly established religious orders in the city. In the first half of the 16th century, at least six Passion brotherhoods already existed in Málaga: *Vera✠Cruz* (True Cross), *Sangre* (Precious Blood), *Ánimas de Ciegos* (Souls of the Blind), *El Paso* (The Passion), *Monte Calvario* (Calvary), and *Soledad* (Solitude); all of them linked to religious houses. The Council of Trent (1545–1563) encouraged demonstrations of popular piety. Religious Orders, brotherhoods and their patrons began commissioning artworks, mainly statues of Christ and the Virgin, to be carried in these processions. Until the second half of the 17th century, the works and sculptural models of *granadino* and *sevillano* (*i.e.* from Granada and Sevilla) sculptors of the school of Andalucía predominated.

The arrival of the sculptor Pedro de Mena in Málaga in 1658 inaugurated an authentically local style. It would be under his influence, and that of José Micael Alfaro, that the *malagueño* style was born. In the 18th century, Fernando Ortiz was the greatest exponent of this style, adopting Italianate influences from Juan Domingo Olivieri. Also of note is the work of artists such as Francisco Gómez de Valdivieso and Salvador Gutiérrez de León. In the 19th century, the main sculptor from Málaga was Antonio Gutiérrez de León, (grandson of Salvador), who continued the tradition. With the arrival of the 20th century and despite the existence of a number of sculptors in the city, the *malagueña* school declined, and as commissions from *sevillano*, *granadino* and *valenciano* sculptors increased, the so-called *malagueño* style definitively vanished.

Many of the Málaga brotherhoods can trace their lineage back centuries and the city was a centre of religious image-making between the 16th and 19th centuries. It might seem surprising, therefore, that many of the brotherhoods were apparently founded in the 19th or 20th (or even 21st) century, and many of the sculptures of Christ and the Virgin were made in the last couple of decades. Many, indeed, were carved within the last few years. There are a couple of significant historical events that explain this apparent anomaly.

The first was the wave of confiscations of property deemed to belong to the *Ancien Régime* that began in the 18th century. By this point, Spain had gone from being one of the richest countries on earth in the 16th century to an indebted backwater with an urgent need for money. In 1798, the so-called 'Confiscation of Godoy' took place, seizing one-sixth of ecclesiastical property. After Joseph-Napoléon Bonaparte was installed as King of Spain by his younger brother, he appropriated all property belonging to religious orders and further confiscated the income of all ecclesiastical property to help fund the French side in the Napoleonic Wars. A further five confiscations took place, of which the most significant and catastrophic was that which took place under Juan Álvarez Mendizábal, Prime Minister in the time of the Queen Regent María Cristina. Full of the zeal of a Liberal Revolutionary de-termined to smash old vested interests and create a new liberal bourgeoisie, Mendizábal issued a succession of decrees confiscating property and land belonging to religious orders. Joseph Bonaparte had effectively transferred ownership to the State. Now the State was tak-ing possession, demolishing the monasteries and convents and selling the land.

Mendizábal's confiscation, however, was a disaster that failed to achieve what was intended, if anything worsening economic inequality in Spain. The land released by the confiscation was to be sold, but the division of lots was entrusted to municipal commissions that took advantage of their power to manipulate and configure the land into larger lots that were un-affordable for most people but well within the means of wealthy oligarchs who brought their considerable influence to bear upon the whole process. Small farmers and entrepreneurs could not enter bids of sufficient value and the land was bought by wealthy urban nobles and the old bourgeoisie, so the opportunity to create a true bourgeoisie or middle class that might have helped get Spain out of its stagnant economic situation, was missed.

The second event that had a massive impact on the tradition of Holy Week in Málaga was the so-called 'Burning of Convents' of 1931 in which a great many of the buildings that had survived Godoy, Napoleon and Mendizábal were damaged or destroyed, along with a huge quantity of artistic patrimony. By the end of the Civil War, most of the brotherhoods of Málaga were in a parlous state. The religious Orders that they had been attached to had seen their houses confiscated and most had been expelled, some never to return. The images of Christ and the Virgin that they had treasured, in some cases for centuries, had been burned. *Semana Santa* itself had, for a time, been seen not as a coming together of the whole people of Málaga, but a provocative act bound up in the political 'culture wars' of the time.

1931 Quema de conventos

In May 1931, during the first months of the Second Spanish Republic (1931–1939) tem-pers in Spain ran high following the proclamation of a new constitutional order that promised to protect freedom of conscience and develop a process of secularization that would dismantle the traditional relationship between the State and the Catholic Church. The Papal Nuncio (Vatican Ambassador) sent a letter to the Spanish Bish-ops which conveyed to them the 'wish of the Holy See' that they 'recommend [their] priests, religious and faithful of their diocese[s] that [they] respect the constituted powers and obey them for the maintenance of order and for the common good.' Most of the Metropolitan Archbishops were similarly conciliatory. However, Pedro Cardi-nal Segura, Archbishop of Toledo and Primate of Spain, was less accommodating, declaring that the Republican regime was the work of the 'enemies of the Church and the social order', and urging the formation of a 'compact united front' in defence of the monarchy and the Catholic Church. In his first intervention from the pulpit, he referred to the Republic as a 'divine punishment', which unsurprisingly raised the ire of the republican press, pointing to it as evidence of monarchical clericalism.

The deposed former King, Alfonso XIII, in exile in London, gave an interview with the pro-monarchist ABC newspaper. His erstwhile Majesty's words were measured and pacific, calling upon monarchists to organise themselves to participate peacefully in public life, supporting the legitimate government 'in everything' in defence of the or-der and the integrity of the country. ABC, however, appended a belligerent editorial to the King's interview, describing Spain as a 'monarchy'. This was followed by an appeal to monarchists to enrol in an 'Independent Monarchist Circle' to promote the monarchist cause ahead of the forthcoming constituent elections. Two days after this call to action, on Sunday 10 May 1931, a Monarchist Circle was inaugurated in Madrid.

Monarchist slogans were shouted, the former national anthem, the '*Marcha real*', was played on a gramophone, and scuffles broke out when a taxi driver retorted with Republican rallying cries. One of the monarchists struck the taxi driver with his cane, and passers-by who came to his aid were beaten. Within minutes the (false, as it turned out) rumour spread that the taxi driver had been killed, and when news arrived that the former monarchist Prime Minister General Dámaso Berenguer had been released from prison, it triggered a wave of violence and riots throughout the city.

The belligerents were predominantly the Monarchists, whipped up by the ABC newspaper, and this was at its root, a struggle between Monarchists and Republicans. However, with the monarchy overthrown and the King and Queen in exile, there were few 'monarchist' targets for the rage of the protesters. Instead, ire was directed towards the Church and her institutions. The link between the Church and the Monarchy was age-old and deeply ingrained in Spanish history, and the ill-judged intervention of Cardinal Segura had effectively restated that connection. Nonetheless, the fact remains that the '*Quema de conventos*' (Burning of the Convents) of 1931 was not, primarily, an anti-clerical protest, but an anti-monarchist, or anti-aristocratic one.

Relative to its size, Madrid got off lightly, with only nine religious buildings destroyed, even though the losses went far beyond bricks and mortar. When the Jesuit House of Studies was set alight, its entire library of over 80,000 books was destroyed, including irreplaceable incunabula and first editions of Lope de Vega, Quevedo, and Calderón de la Barca. In Málaga, the destruction was far worse. According to the Socialist Re-

publican Deputy Juan Simeón Vidarte, the 48 hours of violence in Málaga were the ones that caused 'the greatest destruction and greatest artistic loss for Spain'. It was also a catastrophe for the cause of the Republic in Málaga since it damaged their credibility and lost them the esteem of moderate citizens, who were appalled by the wanton excess of the demonstrators, and eager instead for reforms to be carried out in a democratic and civilized manner.

When the news of the events in Madrid reached the city, mobs took to the streets on the night of May 11 and the assaults began, first of all on the Jesuit Residence and the Bishop's Palace. The incidents lasted during the early morning and throughout the day of May 12. A journalist in his car on the Colmenar highway described the city:

> *The panorama that we witness from there will not be easily erased from our retina. It was truly terrifying, Dantesque, it produced chills in the*

> *body and an intense bitterness in the spirit. The city was silent and gloomy. The sky looked red, black columns of smoke ascended towards him. It was the glow of the tremendous bonfires, which from various places in the capital, raised their intense flames towards infinity.*[49]

Málaga witnessed not only the total or partial destruction of many of its buildings but also the loss of extremely important historical archives, pieces of precious metalwork, embroidery, priceless carvings, paintings, libraries, etc. Among the works that were completely destroyed were many formerly used during *Semana Santa*, for example, the sculptures of the Nazareno of the Holy Name of Jesus of the Way, the Crucified Christ of the Good Death and the Virgin of Bethlehem (from the Church of Santo Domingo); all peerless examples of the Spanish Baroque and works of Pedro de Mena. Fernando Ortiz's full-size sculpture of Jesus Praying in the Garden, and the recumbent Christ in the Holy Sepulchre from the Church of San Agustín were both thrown onto a bonfire in front of the church of the Merced. The famous carving of the *Nazareno*, known as '*El Chiquito*' of the Brotherhood of Mercy in El Perchel by the sculptor José de Mora, was also destroyed.

Attacks on Church property, including churches and convents, had long been part and parcel of anti-clerical uprisings, and religious artworks had often been collateral damage. However, what shocked the populace of Málaga was the way in which the protesters not only burned and vandalized buildings but targeted religious objects. Even those critical of the power, wealth and prestige of the Church, and angry about its tacit or explicit support for the monarchy and the *Ancien Régime* were still believing Catholics. Seeing religious images thrown on a bonfire was profoundly shocking. In a macabre parody of a *Semana Santa* procession, the statue of '*El Chiquito*' was carried all the way to the Plaza de Riego (now the Plaza de La Merced) where a pyre was built around it, making it look as if Jesus were being burned at the stake. Burning actual priests might have been excused, but burning statues of Christ was unforgivable.

In addition to these deliberate acts of vandalism, several dozen tombs were desecrated in the crypts of the churches of San Pablo, San Lázaro and the Monastery of the Immaculate Conception. Moreover, many of the buildings put to the torch were nurseries and schools that educated the poor of the city. The school of San Agustín was a residential school and had it not been evacuated earlier in the day, the conflagration would likely have caused the deaths of dozens of boarding children. But the act which was most shocking to *malagueños* was the destruction of the *tabernacle* of the Cathedral (the *tabernacle* is the place where the Blessed Sacrament — the bread which Catholics believe is transformed to become Christ's Body — is reserved). To desecrate the Sacrament would be considered by many Catholics to be not merely heretical, but Satanic.

All these aspects of the *quema* seemed to go far beyond a political expression of anti-clerical sentiment. They were seen by many contemporary witnesses as acts committed in *odium fidei* — in hatred of the faith itself — a faith in which most *malagueños*, including most Republicans, still believed. There was also a sense in which people viewed the destruction of the *Semana Santa* images not as the destruction of the property of the Church, but of the property and patrimony of the people of Málaga.

---

49 'La Quema de conventos en mayo de 1931', *Revista Jábega* No. 7, p.68 (*Centro de Ediciones de la Diputación de Málaga*, 1974)

After the destruction of 1931 and to a lesser extent, of 1936 (in the Civil War), a process of gradual reconstruction began, with new images commissioned from artists such as the *malagueños* Francisco Palma Burgos, Pedro Pérez Hidalgo, Pedro Moreira and Adrián Risueño, the *granadinos* José Gabriel Martín Simón, José Navas Parejo and Nicolás Prados López, the *sevillano* Antonio Castillo Lastrucci, and the *valenciano* Pío Mollar Franch. The fire damage to the churches and buildings remained visible for decades after, and some city centre churches have only been properly restored in the last dozen or so years. Yet the backdrop of the events of 1931 has, in a curious way, deepened the experience of *Semana Santa* for *malagueños*.

The mood of the week is sombre, even mournful. There is a powerful sense that, for the disciples at least, the events must have seemed like the end of hope. The man, Jesus of Nazareth, whom they had thought was the Messiah, ended up being executed by the Roman authorities in a cruel and shameful manner. It is a sequence of events that ends with the fading of the light on Calvary and the utter darkness of the tomb. But then with the Resurrection comes new light, new hope, and a new beginning. The world is made new. It may be just a folk memory nowadays, but the people of Málaga are keenly aware of the legacy of the *Quema de conventos*. The fact that what once seemed irrevocably lost has, over many decades, been lovingly restored and remade, must give added poignancy to the message of the Passion and Resurrection.

So one can understand why a particular brotherhood can apparently be so old and yet so recent. The oldest extant brotherhood in Málaga is the *Archicofradía de la Sangre* (Archconfraternity of the Precious Blood). It began in 1499 and was formally established in 1507, yet its *Cristo* only dates from 1941 and although it managed to preserve an 18th (or possibly 17th) century *Virgen*, almost all of the sculptures one can see on the *tronos* were carved between 1978 and 2019. The brotherhood's *casa hermandad* was constructed in 1990. Moreover, another reason why it has taken many brotherhoods decades (in some cases more than seventy years) to replace the images and thrones destroyed in 1931 or earlier is the expense. The painted wooden carvings of Christ, the Virgin and the Saints are works of considerable craftsmanship that take thousands of hours to execute, and the thrones which carry them are the work of specialist silversmiths and goldsmiths. The artworks that you see carried through the streets of Málaga today are the fruits of decades of fundraising.

Dramatis Personœ et Res

The main players are drawn from the brotherhoods or confraternities. An individual brotherhood may be called an '*hermandad*' or a '*cofradía*'. Both words are translated as 'brotherhood'. Historically, a '*cofradía*' was a brotherhood based on a profession (vintners, students, fishermen, etc.) or other shared identity (knights or noblemen), while an '*hermandad*' integrated people of different professions or social status. Nowadays there is no legal difference between the two. The 'law' in question is the Canon Law of the Catholic Church and all brotherhoods are officially 'lay associations of the faithful', governed by Church law and approved by the diocesan Bishop. Some have titles like '*ilustre*' (illustrious) or '*real*' (royal) as part of their name. This is because these designations have been historically awarded by either the Pope or the Spanish crown. The most ancient confraternities are called '*archicofradías*' (archconfraternities), which is a title that can only be conferred by the Pope.

Cruz de Guía

At the head of the procession comes the 'guide cross' — what would usually be called a processional cross in English. Like the entrance procession at a solemn Catholic Mass, the entire procession is led by a large cross flanked by torches (candles or lanterns). These are often carried by *nazarenos* or else by acolytes (altar servers) some of whom may be wearing brightly coloured, tabard-shaped vestments called dalmatics (though technically they are tunicles). Other servers may be carrying *incensarios* burning incense. Incense is a mixture of frankincense (*olibanum*) and other aromatic tree resins with the addition of aromatics such as cinnamon, orange peel, rose petals and jasmine, and each brotherhood will use its own recipe (most are available to buy from **F. Ojeda ♀ Calle San Juan 8**).

Penitentes

The most recognisable participants of the drama are the *nazarenos* or *penitentes* — the brothers who accompany the *tronos* during the course of the processions. They are usually dressed in a tunic (in Málaga called an *equipo* — the 'equipment') gathered with a girdle made of fabric, like a cummerbund, or of woven grass, a hood (*capirote*) and gloves, and some may wear a cape, although each brotherhood has established in its constitutions the characteristics of their clothing, in terms of colour, insignia and accessories. While the term *nazareno* is a general term understood throughout Spain, they are mainly called *penitentes* in Málaga (in the rest of Spain, *penitente* is used to refer to those in the procession who are **not** wearing the *capirote*). By contrast, *Nazareno* (with a capital letter) is the name given to figures of Christ carrying the cross (Jesus crucified or dead is called *Cristo*).

Some *penitentes* carry insignia of the brotherhood. Many hold a copy of the *Libro de Reglas* (Rules and Constitutions of the Brotherhood) while others carry banners of various kinds. One is the teardrop-shaped *guión*, embroidered with the arms of the brotherhood in gold on velvet. The unusual shape is meant to represent a folded flag. Serendipitously, it also looks rather like the pointed hood of a *penitente*, and they are a common sight in Spanish churches throughout the year. Another is called the *senatus*: the emblem SPQR (*Senatus Populusque Romanus* — The Senate and People of Rome) recalling the historical period of Christ's Passion. Another is a vertical swallowtail or pennon flag called an *estandarte* which is the standard of the brotherhood; usually embroidered in gold and bearing an image of the *Cristo* or *Virgen*.

The *penitentes* are easy to spot on account of their pointed hats and hoods (though a couple of brotherhoods wear a slightly different design of headgear). The word *capirote* is derived from the Latin *cappa* meaning hood and is used to describe the whole ensemble. A coloured cloth hood with holes cut out for the eyes is worn over a tall conical hat such that it falls over the face and onto the shoulders. Until the 1990s the conical hat (*cucurucho*) was made from cardboard but nowadays is formed from more rigid and breathable mesh.

The reason for the shape is much discussed. The most likely reason is that it recalls the cone-shaped hats that those condemned by the Inquisition were made to wear at *autos de fe* — in other words, it is the mark of public humiliation. Another suggestion is that it is also intended to point away from the penitent towards God. If the shape of the hat speaks of humiliation, the face covering is about humility. The *penitentes* are members of brotherhoods that spend much of their time voluntarily performing charitable works, and during *Semana Santa*, as we saw above, they do public penance not only for their own sins but for their fellow men and women too. Covering their faces is a way of guarding against being like the Pharisees of the New Testament of whom Jesus observed his disciples, 'Everything they do is done for people to see.'[53] The costume of the *penitente* may be eye-catching, but its purpose is the draw attention to the act of penance, not the person of the penitent. The *equipo* (tunic) and cape (if worn), though often made from fine fabric, is also a sign of humiliation because it is meant to recall the robe that Jesus was dressed in while being mocked before his crucifixion, described variously as 'scarlet', 'purple' (the colour of royalty), or 'splendid'.

---

53   Gospel of St Matthew, 23:5

Trono

The *trono* (throne) is the float or litter which is carried in procession. Most brotherhoods have two thrones; the first is of the *Cristo*, on which the image is a *Nazareno* (Jesus carrying his cross), a *Crucificado* (Jesus on the Cross), or a *Misterio* (a representation of another scene from the Passion, such as Christ in Gethsemane), and the second throne of the *Virgen*, on which the image of Mary is usually placed under a canopy. Often, the *Virgen* is accompanied by Saint John the Evangelist. The lightest *Cristo* is 1,950 kg (*Expiración*) and the heaviest 4,550 kg (*Nazareno del Paso*). The lightest *Virgen*, that of *Las Servitas* is only 400 kg, whereas the heaviest — the *Esperanza Coronada* — is a whopping 5,700 kg, roughly the weight of an adult elephant or four Nissan Micra cars.

Hombres de Trono (Portadores)

In the rest of Spain, the *tronos* are called *pasos* and are carried by *costaleros* on the neck, but the *tronos* of Málaga are carried by *portadores* (bearers) properly called *hombres de trono* (throne men, and in recent years, *mujeres de trono*: throne women), who put their shoulders under the *varales*: long beams of metal or wood that protrude from the front and rear of the *cajillo* (the main rectangular frame of the *trono*). Again, because Málaga is different, in the rest of Spain the *varales* are the vertical posts that support the canopy of the throne, not the horizontal beams. The smaller *tronos* have four *varales*, and the larger have eight, some requiring more than 250 *hombres* to lift them. The throne men who spend the entire procession hidden underneath the *trono* are sometimes called *submarinos* — submariners.

Mayordomos de Trono

The throne men raise or lower the *trono* according to the signals indicated by the bell at the front. This bell is rung by the *mayordomos de trono* (throne stewards). Different patterns and numbers of rings indicate to the *hombres de trono* when to raise or lower the *trono* as well as setting the pace and rhythm. Apart from those at the front and on the sides of the *trono*, most of the bearers are unable to see their surroundings, so they are totally dependent upon the signals from the bell. It is not uncommon to see some *hombres de trono* also wearing actual blindfolds (*vendas*). There are different styles of carrying a throne. Some thrones are carried so that they seem to glide, whereas others are made to 'rock' gently from side to side in time with the music, even inclining in places to make it seem that the images are blessing onlookers or acknowledging landmarks being passed.

Capataz

A *capataz* is a foreman, and each procession has at least four *capataces*, one at each corner of the *trono*, and sometimes more. The job of each *capataz* is to observe the progress of the procession, ensure that it is orderly and that the various sections do not straggle.

Mantilla

The *mantilla* is the dress worn by the women who accompany the *tronos*, usually in front. It is mourning dress for the death of Christ. The clothes that make up the *mantilla* not only consist of the *mantilla* (veil) itself, which is made of lace worn over a high tortoiseshell comb, but also a knee-length black dress, black tights, shoes and gloves. They parade during the most solemn processions, *i.e.* Holy Thursday and Good Friday.

Bands and Music

Most processions are accompanied by music. Processions consisting of two *tronos* (Christ and the Virgin) usually have two or three bands. A band of *cornetas y tambores* (bugles and drums) processes behind the '*Cruz de Guía*' (lead cross). These bands originated in Málaga. Behind the *trono* with the image of Christ comes the second band — either more bugles and drums, a military-style marching band, or a concert band with varied instruments including woodwind, brass, and percussion. Finally, the *trono* of the Virgin is accompanied by a concert band.

Many of these bands are attached to the brotherhoods themselves, with others drawn from the Armed Forces, Fire Brigade or Civil Guard. Some bands come from outside Málaga. For such bands, *Semana Santa* is the biggest week of the year, so those that find themselves with a 'free day' in their own city will often travel to provide their services somewhere else. Thus, it is not unusual to find bands from other towns in the Málaga Province and from as far away as Sevilla, Cádiz, or Jerez.

The bands play processional marches, all of which have been composed specifically to accompany the movement of the thrones. Particular marches are associated with particular brotherhoods and particular images, and new ones are being composed every year. It is a tradition that the *Marcha real* (Spanish National Anthem) is played at the *salida* and *encierro* (departure and enclosure) of the *tronos*, and you will see current and former armed forces and police personnel saluting. You will not hear anyone singing, of course, because the *Marcha real* has no lyrics (a fact of which the Ulster politician Lord Kilclooney was evidently unaware when he criticized the Spanish national soccer side for remaining mute at Wembley during the 2020 euros[54]).

The music played can sound rather strident to an ear more used to the soft harmonies of a brass band, but the effect is intended to be dramatic, moving and enlivening. Another element of musical accompaniment is the '*saeta*' (*lit.* 'arrow') — a religious song, generally improvised and unaccompanied, sung in the '*cante jondo*' ('deep song') style typical of the flamenco musical tradition. These songs are theoretically spontaneous — occurring when a spectator is so moved by the spectacle that he or she bursts into appreciative song (in reality, they are almost all carefully positioned and planned).

Semana Santa Today

Much about *Semana Santa* will strike the foreign visitor as odd, or even distasteful — not least the playing of the national anthem, the saluting, and the military bands, let alone members of the Spanish Foreign Legion armed and in full training uniform carrying the huge crucifix of the Mena ahead of the procession. While the Catholic Church has no constitutionally protected status and Spain is officially a secular state, it remains a majority Catholic country (though only just, with practising Catholics accounting for more than a quarter but less than a third of Spaniards and Catholics of any stripe only accounting for 56% of the population).

The truth is that Spain is still largely culturally Catholic, just as the UK is still largely culturally Anglican. The mixed (*i.e.* ecclesiastical, lay, municipal, military, etc.) nature of *Semana Santa* is a reminder of this. For many people, probably including a few members of the brotherhoods, *Semana Santa* represents a link with a baptismal faith they do not regularly practise. This might seem hypocritical to some, but it is not dissimilar to the British approach to Christmas. The liturgical feast of Christmas begins on 25 December and lasts for

---

54 'Lord Kilclooney mocked on Twitter for criticizing Spanish players for not singing national anthem', *Belfast Telegraph* (7 July 2021) archive.ph/o1bFW

eight (formerly twelve) days. The 'secular feast' of Christmas, however, seems to begin in November with an endless round of parties and celebrations and ends on 25 December, just as the religious feast begins. Plenty of people who are not practising Christians celebrate Christmas in some way, including many who adhere to other faiths or none. They value the togetherness is brings, they enjoy giving and receiving gifts, they like singing carols and enjoy making time for their families. They do not need to believe that the baby born in Bethlehem is the Son of God to appreciate the message of hope that a new birth brings. Christmas, to borrow a theological term, is a 'public cult'.

In Spain, by contrast, Christmas is celebrated in a fairly low-key way, and *Semana Santa* is Spain's great national expression of popular religion. Some mark it with solemnity and religious fervour. The Passion of Christ touches them deeply and they enter into the spirit of penitence wholeheartedly. For others, it is a week in which they connect with a church they no longer regularly attend and reconnect with a faith that has grown lukewarm. And for some, there may be no religious aspect at all. They may find some secular message in the theology of Holy Week — the themes of suffering, hope and renewal — or perhaps they enjoy the way that the rituals bring people together. For some, *Semana Santa* is an aesthetic experience, a delight taken in the beauty of the *tronos*, the music and the ceremonial. In other words, the reasons that Spaniards celebrate *Semana Santa* are as many and as varied as the reasons that people in Britain celebrate Christmas. After all, even the avowed atheist Richard Dawkins once admitted that he marked Christmas at home and enjoyed singing carols.

Are There Any Sisterhoods?

The short answer is no. Or, 'No, but...' Málaga has only brotherhoods. All brotherhoods have traditionally admitted women as associates and women take part in the processions. Some brotherhoods admit women as full members, some do not. Indeed, in the last few years, two brotherhoods (*Sangre* and *Las Penas*) have elected women to be 'Hermanas Mayores' (Elder Sisters). To have women occupying the most senior roles in only two out of 41 brotherhoods may seem like a vivid example of the most reactionary sexism. The male domination of *Semana Santa* is just par for the course, you might think, in a Church with an all-male priesthood, but the reality — as usual — is slightly more complex.

La Sangre ('Blood') is the oldest brotherhood in Málaga. It took them 510 years to elect a woman as *hermana mayor*. What is interesting is that in the election of Laura Berrocal, almost all the electors were men. In the election two years later for *Hermano* or *Hermana Mayor* of *Las Penas*, the successful female candidate Ángela Guerrero (again facing a majority male electorate) stood against two male candidates and secured a total of 64% of the vote. Neither sounds like a case of a bastion of male privilege determined to keep women out at all costs.

Historically, brotherhoods were founded by groups of men and had male members, and that is now changing. Quite a few of the Málaga brotherhoods were founded or revived in the last few decades, and there is every reason to expect that as some will decline, others will be founded in the future. There is no reason why a group of women could not found an all-female sisterhood if they wished, and they would have every right to exclude men from membership.

What is less recognized, however, is the role that male or majority male-membership brotherhoods play in the life of the Church. For all that the Catholic Church is often criticized for preserving an all-male priesthood and being 'run by men', in other ways it can be said to be run by women. It is generally the female members of congregations who keep parishes going — fundraising, dealing with finances, organizing social outreach and social events, catechizing children, looking after the fabric of the buildings, welcoming new members, and so on. And this is reflected in the composition of congregations, which usually have far more women as regular attenders than men. Boys might be altar servers when they are young, but once they have their own families they are more likely to stop practising than women, only returning in retirement. There is an argument, then, that the brotherhoods that one finds all over Spain provide laymen with a role, a way of practising their faith, that helps to keep them connected to the Church. This is not, by itself, an argument in favour of preserving the mainly male make-up of the brotherhoods, but perhaps it is an argument against too hastily sweeping them away and losing something that has enriched the Church and gives meaning to people's lives.

The Route

Almost all the brotherhoods in Málaga are incorporated in the *Agrupación de Cofradías* (Association of Brotherhoods) which was founded in 1921, making it one of the oldest such bodies in Spain. Its officers are elected every four years by the senior brothers of the constituent brotherhoods and it is in charge of overseeing the planning and organization of *Semana Santa*. The *Agrupación de Cofradías* liaises with the *ayuntamiento*, police and other public bodies and is responsible for the provision and rental of seating (20,000 chairs and several large stands) as well as determining the official route (*recorrido oficial*) of the processions.

Because each procession begins from a different brotherhood house (*casa hermandad*), or church (*templo*), every route is unique. Some begin and end in the north of the city, some across the river in the east, while others begin in the centre itself.

The Historic Route

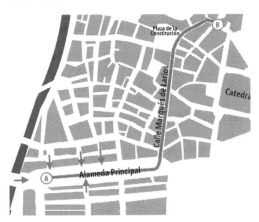

The original route, agreed in 1921, was followed for 95 years by all brotherhoods. Some processions would have been going for hours by the time they reached the official section, with hours left to process after they finished it. It began in the Alameda Principal, with five points of entry — one from the east, one from the south and three from the north. Then it turned left to continue up the Calle Marqués de Larios to the Plaza de la Constitución, where the official seating (*tribuna*) for dignitaries was located, continuing into Calle Granada. From there, some processions continued to the Cathedral while others returned to their *casa hermandad* or *templo*.

The 2016 Route

In 2016, the official route was revised due to roadworks on the Alameda Principal for the construction of a new metro station. The direction was reversed, with all processions entering the Plaza de la Constitución from Calle Granada and travelling southwards down the Calle Marqués de Larios, turning off towards the Atarazanas market. After a truncated section on the Alameda Principal, the processions would then re-enter the Calle Marqués de Larios — in the opposite direction — turning right onto Calle Bolsa and thence to the Cathedral. It was generally agreed, that splitting Calle Marqués de Larios in two, and having processions going in different directions, was not a successful experiment, and a revised route was sought.

349

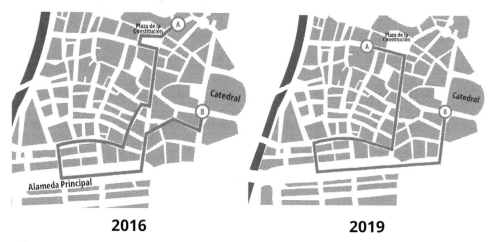

2016   **2019**

The 2019 Route

In 2018 a slightly amended route was agreed, extending the Alameda section of the processions further east as far as the Plaza de la Marina before turning left (north) towards the Cathedral. This route was used in 2019 for the first time, and after a two-year hiatus during the COVID pandemic, with some modifications in 2022 and after. Many *malagueños* were quoted in the local media expressing their dissatisfaction with the new route. A couple of issues were raised. First, having one point of ingress onto the Alameda Principal (rather than five for the old route) created bottle-necks in the busy streets around the Atarazanas market. Second, another bottleneck occurred in the vicinity of the Cathedral now that all processions were routed past it (in the old route, some processions did not pass the Cathedral at all, helping to thin the processions out). It was also suggested that the new route created a zone in the city where people were effectively 'kettled'.

The Cathedral Penance Station

Some brotherhoods (if their thrones are sufficiently manoeuvrable to get through the doors) have an *estación de penitencia* (penance station, or stop) inside the Cathedral and, since 2022, all other brotherhoods have made a stop outside, at the south (unfinished) tower. This is done for a number of reasons, not least as an expression of communion with the whole Church (the Cathedral being the 'mother church' of the city and diocese). Penance stations have always been a feature of the Holy Week processions and in the past stops were made in many churches.

All the brotherhoods in Sevilla have made an obligatory penance station at the Cathedral of Santa María de la Sede (Mary of the See) since 1606, but this was not always the case in Málaga. A growing number of brotherhoods began entering the Cathedral from the 17th century onwards, but the revolutions and disentailments of religious property in the 19th century sent the public cult of *Semana Santa* processions, and thus stations, into a decline. The practice was revived in 1949 by the *Viñeros* brotherhood and has grown ever since.

Another reason for processions to make stations (stops) is as an expression of penitence. One of the many ways in which an indulgence can be gained is by a visit to a cathedral, basilica, church, altar or shrine to pray the Our Father and make a profession of faith. The brothers and sisters who make a cathedral station are performing an act of penitence, but also uniting their act of penitence (which is the procession) to the whole church. This is especially the case because the Cathedral of Málaga is a minor basilica and hence a Papal church. Incidentally, you will often see the abbreviation 'S.I.C.B.' used to refer to the Cathedral. It stands for '*Santa Iglesia Catedral Basílica*'.

The Current Route

To avoid relying upon out-of-date information, the best plan is to download the itinerary for the upcoming *Semana Santa*. It should be available a month or more before Palm Sunday (which is a moveable feast occurring between 15 March at the earliest and 18 April at the latest). The official itinerary can be downloaded from the website of the Association of Brotherhoods: **agrupaciondecofradias.com/horarios-e-itinerarios**. Their website also features a map that shows the location of the brotherhood houses **agrupaciondecofradias.com/hermandades** (click the drop-down menu at the top of the map to choose the day).

The *Agrupación de Cofradías* once had its own smartphone app but it was rarely updated and often crashed. However, the **El Penitente app,** which covers Sevilla and Málaga, is excellent and contains all the information you might need, including route maps for each brotherhood, though it is only available in Spanish. In 2023, the Málaga brotherhoods adopted El Penitente as their official app.

To plot the route of a particular procession, you can work from the information provided by the official itinerary. Here we can see the example of the *Cristo* of 'Humiliation and Forgiveness' and the *Virgen* of the Star from 2023:

MARTES SANTO

COFRADÍAS Y HERMANDADES	SALIDA	TRIBUNA	TORRE SUR	CATEDRAL	ENCIERRO
ILUSTRE Y VENERABLE HERMANDAD DE LA ORDEN DE SANTO DOMINGO DE GUZMÁN DE NUESTRO PADRE JESÚS DE LA HUMILLACIÓN Y PERDÓN Y MARÍA SANTÍSIMA DE LA ESTRELLA					
Parroquia de Santo Domingo (Barrio del Perchel)					
Itinerario: Iglesia Santo Domingo Guzmán, Plaza de Fray Alonso de Santo Tomás, Plaza Legión Española, San Jacinto,Huerta del Obispo, Agustín Parejo, Llano de Doña Trinidad, Álvaro de Bazán, Mármoles, Puente de la Aurora, Pasillo de Santa Isabel, Cisneros, Especería, Plaza de la Constitución, **Tribuna Principal**, Marqués de Larios, Martínez, Atarazanas, Torregorda, Alameda Principal, Plaza de La Marina, Molina Lario, **Torre Sur**, Plaza del Obispo, Molina Lario, Plaza del Siglo, Plaza del Carbón, Granada, Plaza de la Constitución, Especería, Nueva, Plaza de Félix Sáenz, Sagasta, Plaza Arriola, Atarazanas, Prim, Puente de la Esperanza, Pasillo de Santo Domingo, Plaza de la Religiosa Filipense Dolores Márquez, Padre Jorge Lamothe y **Casa Hermandad**.	17.45	20.20	22.25		02.15

Remember that the route may change in 2024 or beyond, but the basic principles of reading the itinerary should still be helpful. Several processions take place each day, with staggered starting times to prevent sacred traffic jams. On *Martes Santo* (Holy Tuesday), there are six

351

processions. The first sets off at 1500, the last at 1900. The shortest procession takes 6 hours and 45 minutes and the longest procession takes almost 14 hours. The one we are using as an example takes just shy of 9 hours, covering just under 4 km.

The brotherhood is *La Ilustre y Venerable Hermandad de la Orden de Santo Domingo de Guzmán de Nuestro Padre Jesús de la Humillación y Perdón y María Santísima de la Estrella* (The Illustrious and Venerable Brotherhood of the Order of Saint Dominic Guzmán of Our Father Jesus of Humiliation and Forgiveness and Holy Mary of the Star). Next is listed the *templo* — the church or chapel serving as the official home of the image or images. In some cases, the procession will set off from the *templo*, while in others the starting point is the *casa hermandad*. So we need to look at the itinerary (*itinerario*).

Looking at the columns on the right-hand side of the table, you will see five headings: *salida*, *tribuna*, *torre sur*, *catedral* and *encierro*. These have timings listed, so think of these points like bus stops on a bus timetable. 'Salida' means 'departure' or 'exit', so this is where the procession begins, at 1745. Then comes a list of streets ('*calle de*' — 'street of' — is implied, though other types of thoroughfare, like '*plaza*' or '*avenida*' are usually specified for the sake of clarity). You can find these streets by searching Google Maps or other mapping app to sketch out the route, which will look like the figure below.

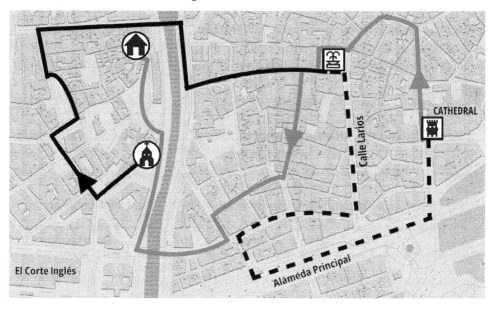

So, beginning from the '*salida*' [🚶] (exit) the procession (dark line) sets off south-west from the Plaza Fray Alonso de Santo Tomás, heading north through the north-western part of the *barrio* of Perchel, along Calle Mármoles, crossing the bridge Puente de la Aurora, heading south before turning left/east onto Calle Cisneros and Calle Especerías to the Plaza de la Constitución. This is the next 'stop' — *tribuna* [🏛], reached two and a half hours after departure. This is the official stand and all processions pass this point. It is also where the '*venia*' is made. Venia is a term and practice borrowed from monasticism where it can variously be an act of obedience, penance, humility or welcome. In the context of *Semana Santa*, it is 'permission to proceed' granted to a brotherhood near the start of the official route. One of the *penitentes* approaches the *tribuna* and requests leave to continue from the official delegated to preside over *Semana Santa*. The first, highly symbolic, venia of *Semana Santa* is requested by the *Pollinica* Brotherhood and permission is granted by the Bishop of Málaga and the President of the *Agrupación de Cofradías*. At other times, other officials will be present in the tribuna, including representatives from the city and provincial governments, the Civil Guard, etc. After the *venia*, the procession travels down the Calle Marqués de Larios, turning right towards the Atarazanas market then left to reach the Alameda Principal, where there are more stands of tiered seating. This is the official route (indicated by a dashed line).

After the Plaza de la Marina, another left turn takes the procession north towards the Cathedral. Just over two hours after passing the *tribuna*, the procession reaches the *Torre Sur* [⬚] at 10.25 pm. This is the South Tower of the Cathedral (the unfinished one). Processions that have a station inside the Cathedral have a time indicated under '*Catedral*', not '*Torre Sur*'. The door by which brotherhoods enter the Cathedral has changed in recent years, but it is never any of the large West Doors on the Plaza del Obispo. Traditionally, the door on the south side of the building, on the Calle Postigo de los Abades, was used, requiring huge ramps to be constructed. In other years, the corresponding door on the north side (reached via the *Patio de los Naranjos* on Calle Císter) has been used.

Our procession, however, continues north past the Cathedral, through the Plaza del Carbón and along the Calle Granada to reach the Plaza de la Constitución for the second time. It passes close to the Atarazanas market once again, before crossing the river and heading north. The location of the '*encierro*' [⬚] (enclosure) is not the church, but the brotherhood house, which is nearby. Some *casas hermandades* are some distance from the *templos* where the images officially reside, so do not assume that the beginning and the end of the procession will always be in the same location!

⚠ The timed points on the route are likely to change if the route changes. Note, too, that '*tribuna*' and '*venia*' may be used interchangeably.

Watching the Processions

It is theoretically possible to rent seats in the stands set up for *Semana Santa* (ventanillavirtual.agrupaciondecofradias.com) from three weeks before Palm Sunday. In reality, however, it is very difficult to find seats to rent because demand is huge. Also, many people renew their rental annually (this is called an '*abono*' or season ticket). A week or so before Palm Sunday (usually from noon on the Friday ten days before) a small number of non-renewable *abonos* go on sale, and they sell out quickly.

The so-called *Tribuna de los Pobres* (Tribune of the Poor) is a traditional spot to watch the processions, almost all of which pass by. It is a fan-shaped set of stone steps descending from the eastern end of the Puente de la Aurora bridge to the Calle Carretería. It is always extremely busy, but it is worth checking out, especially if you are willing to bag your place early. Other places to get a good view are at the churches and brotherhood houses where the processions begin and end, especially those situated in large plazas with plenty of room for onlookers. The example we looked at above (which begins in the Plaza Fray Alonso de Santo Tomás and passes by again a few minutes before the *encierro*) is one such. But if you want to see all the processions, you'll need to find a vantage point on the official route.

There are lots of hotels and *hostales* on the official route (and on other streets used by multiple processions), so another possibility is to rent a room that has a street-facing balcony. Some residents even rent their balconies — not apartments, just the balcony — to people who want an elevated view of proceedings (many advertise on the Spanish equivalents of Gumtree, such as milanuncios.es and vibbo.com). However, demand is high and prices skyrocket because large numbers of Spaniards come to the city for the week. For example, booked through booking.com, a one-bedroom apartment (with balcony) on the Calle

Marqués de Larios costs on average six times as much per night during Holy Week as it does the previous or following week. If you are prepared to book months, or even a year, ahead then you may find something reasonably priced, but it is important to double-check that the room has a view onto the correct street. Even if the description indicates a balcony, that balcony may overlook a *callejón* (narrow alleyway) or *patio* (interior courtyard).

If you are willing to stand, then you will always be able to find a vantage point in the city centre, especially if you are prepared to stray beyond the official route, which can be very busy indeed. Wider thoroughfares and squares are better than narrow streets as you may be moved on from the latter to allow the *tronos* to pass. Be prepared to wait, though. Even outside the official route, if you try to find a place mere minutes before a procession, you are likely to be disappointed.

Many of the brotherhoods are associated with the historic churches in the centre, several dating from the time of the *reconquista*, but other *templos* and brotherhood houses are located in the residential districts outside the line of the medieval walls. There is certainly something especially dramatic about seeing a procession gently swaying through the narrow streets of the historic centre, and a powerful intimacy to the experience, but there is much to be said for venturing further afield. The Brotherhood of Humility and Patience, for example, begin their peregrination at around 2.45 pm on Palm Sunday. Their *casa hermandad* is in the Cruz del Humilladero district, beyond the railway station. It is a modern building next to a primary school and playground set among residential apartment blocks. That may not sound especially picturesque, but there is plenty of space around about and you will be guaranteed an excellent view. But there is something else, too. You will get to witness the locals taking part in *Semana Santa*. The images that emerge — Christ of Humiliation and Patience, and Our Lady of Sorrow and Hope — belong to these people. When they go to mass or drop into their parish church to say a prayer, they see these images and have a connection with them. To see the pride of local residents as 'their' Jesus and Mary begin the *Semana Santa* procession can be very moving.

Consult the weather forecast and come prepared. Holy Week in Málaga can be scorchingly hot, but it can equally be chilly or wet or a mixture of all three. The brotherhoods will always process if they can, but you may find that *salidas* are delayed or processions are truncated with *encierros* brought forward if heavy rain is forecast. In the case of heavy rain lasting all day, then processions may be cancelled entirely.

Once you find a place, you cannot pop into a nearby bar for refreshments without losing it (though if you are in a group, one person can be sent to find victuals). So come prepared with some water and snacks. Almonds, dried fruit (like raisins) or trail mix are good sources of energy to keep you going, so pick some up in the morning from the Atarazanas market (though remember that Thursday and Friday are public holidays). Take a leaf out of the book of Spaniards going to the football ground or bullring and pack a couple of sandwiches. Most cafés or bars that sell sandwiches will usually wrap them up in tin foil as take-away (*'para llevar'* — para yeh-**bar**) and they will be far better than the wet cardboard offerings sold in the chilled section of supermarkets that still lag far behind UK supermarket sandwiches in quality. *Ultramarinos* are also good places to buy sandwiches. Proper sandwiches (*'bocadillos'*) are filled bread rolls and known as *'pulgas'*, *'pitufos'*, and *'vienas'* in Málaga, going from smaller to larger (*i.e.* a palmful, a handful, and more than a handful). There are also *'camperos'* which are filled, toasted muffins and very tasty and filling. Bear in mind that Good Friday is a day of fasting and abstinence (*i.e.* two snacks are permitted, and no meat), so while snacking might not be offensive to others, engaging in conspicuous sausage eating or face-stuffing is at best poor form and at worst marks you out as a *guiri*.

For all its solemnity, *Semana Santa* is a slightly more relaxed affair in Málaga than in Sevilla. You will often hear applause and cheering as people get their first glimpse of a particular *trono*, and there will usually be applause at the conclusion of a particular piece of music, especially if it is a new piece (new marches are composed and premièred every year). *Saetas* are almost always acknowledged with applause and cries of '¡*Otra!*' and '¡*Bis!*' (encore). However, don't get carried away. Some processions are observed in almost total silence, especially those on Good Friday.

Lastly, do not push to the front. It is first come, first placed. Spaniards are usually pretty tolerant about young children coming to the front, but when people may already have been waiting for a couple of hours, expect positions to be jealously guarded! If it rains, umbrellas (at least while the procession is actually passing) are frowned upon because they obscure the view of others. Folding chairs (*e.g.* deckchairs) are prohibited because people often try to use chairs as placeholders to 'bag' a spot (like putting towels on sun loungers) and they can cause problems for street cleaners if abandoned. People who are obviously elderly or infirm could probably get away with using a small camping stool (the folding three-legged kind with a fabric seat) or a walking stick seat (such as a 'Flipstick').

Traslados (Transfers)

Even if you are not in Málaga for *Semana Santa* itself, you can still appreciate something of its flavour (and without such dense crowds) during the week or so before by observing the ceremonies known as *traslados*, or transfers, of the images. These are necessary because only a handful of the churches and chapels that serve as the canonical seats of the images have doors large enough through which to carry a fully laden throne. Some thrones are carried on the shoulders of almost 300 men and women and take up more space than a bus. Brotherhood houses, however, are specially constructed to allow the egress and ingress of the thrones.

For most of the year, the images of Christ and the Virgin carried during *Semana Santa* are displayed in their *templos*, usually above an altar or in a side chapel. Sometime before (and in some cases during) *Semana Santa* they need to be taken from the *templo* to the *casa hermandad*. This is usually done by placing the images on a small platform (called an *anda*), or pair of platforms, and processing to the brotherhood house. Although not as grand as the *Semana Santa* processions, with no retinue of *nazarenos* wearing *capirotes*, these transfers are still carried out with considerable solemnity and often accompanied by a band.

In cases where the images leave from their own *templo*, what is known as a 'cloister transfer' (*traslado claustral*) takes place. This is a procession inside the church, with the images carried, often during the praying of the Stations of the Cross, before being solemnly and publicly enthroned. Return transfers, from the *casa hermandad* to the *templo*, also take place, but these often happen shortly after the closure of the procession, without much ceremony. Others (such as the Garden, Students and Expiration) are held on another day to generate expectation. A couple, like the Star and the Captive, make the return transfer with considerable solemnity and musical accompaniment. Return transfers take place until the middle of Easter Week.

The first transfers happen on the Fifth Friday of Lent (*i.e.* ten days before Palm Sunday) and most happen in the week preceding Palm Sunday (known as 'Passion Week'). The busiest day for transfers is the Friday before Palm Sunday which is known as *Viernes de Dolores* (Friday of Sorrows). Although transfers tend in the main to be simpler than the processions proper, some are carried out with great solemnity and are the objects of considerable popular devotion. For example, the translation of *Jesús Cautivo* (Jesus the Captive, called 'The Lord of Málaga) and Our Lady of the Trinity in the *barrio* of La Trinidad on Passion Saturday is a huge event.

Although the *casa hermandad* isn't far from the church of San Pablo where the images reside, they are taken via a much longer route, accompanied by two bands after the bishop has celebrated mass. First, they are taken to the Civil Hospital to allow staff and patients

to participate, and they make a courtesy call at the *casa hermandad* of *Santo Traslado* — an expression of communion and solidarity between brotherhoods. A number of *saetas* are sung and bystanders in the street and residents on their balconies throw red and white carnations onto the *anda*. In fact, so many thousands of carnations are thrown that the procession has to halt several times to allow the flowers to be cleared.

There is no point in giving a list of transfers here because the days and times of a particular brotherhood's transfer often change year by year. Once the official programme is fixed, you can usually download the timetable of transfers from the website of the Association of Holy Week Brotherhoods: **agrupaciondecofradias.com**, although in 2023 they did not publish this information. The most reliable source of information, therefore, is the El Penitente app (see p. 351).

⚠ Links (as QR codes) are given below for *cofradía* websites. When elections are taking place, some will temporarily display a simple page in the manner of the 'Sede Vacante' ('the chair being vacant') notice displayed by the Vatican after a Pope's death or abdication.

Semana Santa Day by Day

The following is an outline of the usual programme of *Semana Santa* processions. For precise information about routes and timings, you should consult the official itinerary published by the *Agrupación de Cofradías* ahead of *Semana Santa*. When you are in Málaga, you will find no shortage of information available in the form of leaflets and posters (illustrating the different colours of tunics and hoods worn by the *penitentes* and *hombres de trono* and providing maps of the various routes taken). The local newspapers (*e.g. Diario Sur, La Opinión de Málaga*, and *Málaga Hoy*) usually provide daily information on their websites and illustrated pages in their print editions.

Key to Symbols

 Templo — the church, oratory or chapel which is the '*sede canónica*' (official seat) of the Holy Week image(s).

 Casa Hermandad (brotherhood house) — the headquarters of the brotherhood. Many processions leave from the *casa hermandad* because the throne is too large for the church door.

 Tinglao — some brotherhood houses are not large enough for the thrones, so a temporary marquee is erected nearby ('*tinglado*' means 'shed' in Spanish and, as is usual in Andalucía, the 'd' is dropped).

 Tribuna — the tribune is the public stand in the Plaza de la Constitución, just in front of the fountain, where each brotherhood requests permission (*venia*) to join the official route (*recorrido oficial*).

 Catedral — some brotherhoods are given the honour of making a penance station (*estación de penitencia*) inside the Cathedral ('S.I.C.B'). In reality, many thrones are simply too large to take inside the Cathedral.

 Torre Sur — those brotherhoods that do not enter the Cathedral make a stop at the south (unfinished) tower of the Cathedral.

 Cristo (*Nazareno*) — an *imagen titular* (title image, or statue) of a brotherhood depicting Jesus carrying his cross.

 Cristo (*Ecce Homo* ('Behold the Man') / ***Azotado*** (Scourged) / ***Cautivo*** (Captive)) — a titular image depicting Jesus before Pontius Pilate The three gold or silver decorations often seen on top of Christ's head are called '*potencias*' (powers), a Spanish version of a halo. Another version of this image (as captive) depicts Jesus scourged, wearing a crown of thorns.

 Cristo (*Crucificado*) — a titular image depicting the Crucified Christ. A subset of this class of image is the 'dead Christ' (Jesus in the tomb).

 Cristo (*Resucitado*) — a title image depicting the Risen Christ.

 Virgen — a title image depicting the Blessed Virgin Mary. Broadly, these fall into two categories: a '*dolorosa*' (sorrowful or pained) shown weeping and sometimes with a sword in her breast, or a '*soledad*' (solitary) shown with a more reflective , less anguished countenance.

 Música — the bands of bugles and drums, ensembles and marching bands that accompany the procession. There are usually two; one after the *Cristo* and one after the *Virgen*, and sometimes a third after the *Cruz de Guía*.

Domingo de Ramos (Palm Sunday)

The Sunday before Easter Sunday, all four Gospels recount the triumphal entry of Jesus into Jerusalem. According to the Gospels, Jesus rode on a donkey (a colt, the foal of an ass), and the people there laid down their cloaks and palm branches in front of him, singing part of Psalm 118 — 'Blessed is He who comes in the name of the Lord.' You will see people carrying large palm branches, some woven into elaborate designs. Many of these will be fixed to balconies and over doorways where they will remain until next Palm Sunday. You will also people admiring one another's new clothes, because as a Spanish proverb has it, '*Domingo de Ramos, quien no estrena algo, se le caen las manos*' ('On Palm Sunday, the hands drop off of those who fail to wear something new').

Pollinica (Little Donkey)

The origins of this brotherhood (the name means 'Little Donkey') are in the 17th century. Everywhere else in Spain, this devotion is called the '*Borriquita*'. The procession of the *Pollinica* of Holy Week in Málaga has a retinue of children dressed as the people of Jerusalem in white tunics and purple head-dresses, carrying bouquets. The image of the *Cristo* is accompanied by images of three children, Saint John, a woman and two donkeys, hence the name of one of the happiest Holy Week processions and brotherhoods in Málaga.

 Real Cofradía de Nuestro Padre Jesús a su Entrada en Jerusalén y María Santísima del Amparo

Royal Brotherhood of Our Father Jesus at his Entry into Jerusalem and Holy Mary of Refuge

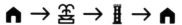

🏠 Convento de San Agustín (Calle San Agustín)   🏠 Calle Parras 20

🚶 Our Father Jesus at his Entry into Jerusalem. The throne of the *Pollinica* represents the moment in which Jesus enters Jerusalem on the back of a colt. Jesus and the colt by Juan Martínez Cerrilo (1943). The Samaritan woman, two children and St John the Evangelist by José Antonio Navarro Arteaga (1990).

🎺 *Cruz de Guía*: Band of Bugles and Drums 'Our Father Jesus of Nazareth' (Almogía, Málaga). *Cristo*: Musical Group 'Most Holy Christ of Clemency' (Jerez de la Frontera, Cádiz)

🏛 Holy Mary of Refuge by Castillo Ariza (1947)

🎺 Municipal Music Band of Lora del Río (Seville)

Lágrimas y Favores (Tears and Favours)

This is the procession of the titular Marian image of the 'Merged Sacramental and Royal Brotherhoods' (*Fusionadas*), which brings together four ancient *malagueño* brotherhoods.

This is one of the most photographed processions because the actor Antonio Banderas is a member and is often one of the *mayordomos* or stewards of the procession (the Brotherhood itself describes him with admirable discretion as 'a well-known artist from Málaga who is highly respected internationally').

 Primitiva Hermandad Sacramental y Reales Cofradías Fusionadas de Nuestro Padre Jesús de Azotes y Columna, Santísimo Cristo de la Exaltación, Santísimo Cristo de Ánimas de Ciegos, María Santísima de Lágrimas y Favores, e Ilustre Archicofradía de la Santa Vera✝Cruz y Sangre, Nuestra Señora del Mayor Dolor y San Juan Evangelista

Primitive Sacramental Brotherhood and Royal Fused Brotherhoods of Our Father Jesus of Scourges and the Column, Holy Christ of Exaltation, Holy Christ of Souls of the Blind, Holy Mary of Tears and Favours, and The Illustrious Archconfraternity of the True Holy Cross and Precious Blood, Our Lady of Great Pain and Saint John the Evangelist

⛪ → 🏛 → 🏛 → ⛪

⛪ Iglesia de San Juan Bautista (Calle San Juan 3) ⛪ Pasillo Santa Isabel 11

🖼 Holy Mary of Tears and Favours by Antonio Dubé de Luque (1982). It represents the Virgin Mary as a young woman, with a sorrowful face, and five crystal tears.

🎺 Municipal Music Band of Arahal (Sevilla)

Dulce Nombre (Holy Name of Mary)

This is a fairly recent foundation, begun by students studying at a Salesian college in 1987. This procession stands out for the high quality of its sculpture, which depicts the scene of St Peter's denial. It is one of the few corporations that comes out of a temporary marquee because neither the *templo* nor the *casa hermandad* has doors large enough. The *trono* of the *Cristo* features a dog that is not mentioned in the Gospel story. It is intended, rather, to represent Saint Francis of Assisi (the brotherhood is based in the Capuchinos district, named after the Capuchin Franciscan Friary that once stood there).

Antigua, Venerable Hermandad y Cofradía de Nazarenos de Nuestro Padre Jesús de la Soledad, Negaciones y Lágrimas de San Pedro, María Santísima del Dulce Nombre y San Francisco de Asís

Ancient, Venerable Brotherhood of Nazarenes of Our Father Jesus of Solitude, The Denials and Tears of Saint Peter, The Most Holy Name of Mary and Saint Francis Of Assisi.

🔺 → ♒ → 🏰 → 🔺

⛪ Parroquia de la Divina Pastora (Plaza de Capuchinos 5) 🏠 Calle Juan del Encina 39

🔔 Our Father Jesus of the Solitude, by Antonio Bernal (2000). The *trono* represents the scene of the denials of Saint Peter. The image also features four Jewish soldiers, Saint Peter, the accusing woman, the rooster and a dog.

🎺 Musical Ensemble 'Virgin of the Olive' (Vejer de la Frontera, Cádiz)

🎭 The Most Holy Name of Mary, by Antonio Bernal (2005)

🎺 Symphony Band 'Virgin of the Trinity' (Málaga)

Salutación (Salutation)

This is another recent foundation, or rather a revival of an extinct eighteenth-century brotherhood that re-emerged in 1984 when a group of young people decided to resurrect it. They appeared during *Semana Santa* for the first time in 1990. The 'salutation' is the meeting between Veronica and Jesus as he carried his cross to Calvary. This event is not recorded in any Gospel but is a matter of Christian tradition (just as nowhere in the Gospels does it say that there were three wise men, or that Jesus was born in a stable). The story recounts how a woman of Jerusalem, moved by Jesus' suffering, wiped his face with her veil which then bore an imprint of his face. 'Veronica' is actually derived from the Greek name meaning 'bringer of victory' (*phero-nike*), but the Latin Church popularized the co-etymology '*vero icon*' or 'true image'. The image on Veronica's veil is painted by a different artist each year.

 Fervorosa Hermandad y Antigua Cofradía del Divino Nombre de Jesús Nazareno de la Salutación, María Santísima del Patrocinio Reina de los Cielos, San Juan Evangelista, Santa Mujer Verónica y de la Santa Faz de Nuestro Señor Jesucristo

Fervent and Ancient Brotherhood of the Divine Name of Jesus the Nazarene of the Salutation, Holy Mary of Patronage, Queen of Heaven, Saint John the Evangelist, The Holy Woman Veronica and of the Holy Face of Our Lord Jesus Christ

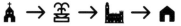 ⛪ → ♒ → 🏰 → 🏠

⛪ San Felipe Neri (Calle Guerrero 6) 🏠 Calle Cabello 21

🚶 Our Father Jesus of the Salutation by Antonio J. Dubé de Luque (1988) and restored by Salomé Carrillo Becerra (2002). The scene is made up of the images of the holy woman Veronica, the pious women of Jerusalem and a Roman centurion; all the images were carved by Antonio J. Dubé de Luque, except the centurion, which is by José Antonio Navarro Arteaga.

🎺 Musical Ensemble 'Saint Laurence the Martyr' (Málaga)

🪦 The Virgin of Patronage by Antonio J. Dubé de Luque (1985) with Saint John the Evangelist by José Antonio Navarro Arteaga (1999).

🎺 Music Band 'Our Father Jesus of Nazareth' (Almogía, Málaga)

Humildad y Paciencia (Humility and Patience)

This brotherhood was established in 1634 as a subsidiary of the Brotherhood of The Clean and Pure Conception. According to the legend cited in the Statutes of Humility and Patience, the image of Christ was made by two unknown sculptors who appeared out of nowhere and then disappeared without charging for their services. The brotherhood disappeared in 1835 and the image was lost during the burning of convents in 1931. In 1987 the brotherhood was restructured adding the invocation of the *Dolorosa* (Sorrowful Virgin), and its canonical seat was definitively established in the parish of San Vicente de Paul. The procession begins in the neighbourhood of Cruz de Humillidero beyond the railway station, taking 10 hours in total. The *trono* of the *Cristo* represents the moment before the crucifixion in which Jesus retires to pray. '*Cruz de humilladero*' — named after a 16th-century wayside cross that once stood in the area, refers to the Cross on Calvary.

 Venerable Hermandad Carmelita y Cofradía de Nazarenos del Santísimo Cristo de la Humildad y Paciencia, María Santísima de Dolores y Esperanza y Nuestra Señora de la Aurora.
Venerable Carmelite Brotherhood of Nazarenes of the Holy Christ of Humility and Patience, Holy Mary of Sorrows and Hope, and Our Lady of The Dawn

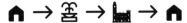

⛪ Parroquia de San Vicente de Paúl (Calle La Unión 83) 🏠 Plazuela María Santísima de Dolores y Esperanza 1

🔔 Most Holy Christ of Humility and Patience. On 15 October 2022, a new image by the *imaginero malagueño* José María Ruiz Montes was blessed, replacing an earlier Christ made by Manuel Ramos Corona (2007). The figures of the three Roman soldiers and two executioners, by Manuel Ramos Corona were made in 2011.

🎺 Band of Bugles and Drums 'Our Lady of Mount Carmel' (Málaga)

🪦 Most Holy Mary of Sorrows and Hope — an anonymous 19th century carving (attributed to Antonio Marín).

🎺 Music Band 'Cruz del Humillidero' (Málaga)

Humildad (Humility)

In 1694, a group of people with a special devotion to the Passion of Our Lord met in the Convent of La Merced to found the brotherhood of Humility, with 72 members. They first participated in *Semana Santa* in Málaga on Holy Thursday night when they toured the altars of repose (special *tabernacles* where the Blessed Sacrament is reserved for distribution on Good Friday, one day of the year when the celebration of Mass is not permitted). Its participants wore unbleached linen tunics, went barefoot and had a rope around their throats and waists. On their heads, they wore crowns of thorns and each carried a candle and a rosary.

In 1980 the brotherhood was reorganized in the Sanctuary of Victoria on the initiative of Juan Casielles del Nido and Juan Antonio Quintana Urdiales. On 23 April 1983, the newly carved images were blessed in the Sanctuary and the following year the Brotherhood went out in procession for the first time. The brotherhood is still popularly known as the *'servitas blancos'* (white Servites) for their seriousness and composure and they begin their procession from the Sanctuary of Santa María de la Victoria. The image represents the moment at which Pontius Pilate utters the words *'Ecce homo'* ('Behold, the man') when he presents the scourged Jesus, bound and crowned with thorns, to a hostile crowd.

 Antigua Hermandad y Real Cofradía de Nazarenos del Santísimo Cristo de la Humildad en su Presentación al Pueblo (Ecce-Homo), Nuestra Madre y Señora de La Merced y San Juan Evangelista

Ancient and Royal Brotherhood of the Nazarenes of the Holy Christ of Humility in his Presentation to the People (*'Ecce Homo'*), Our Mother and Lady of Mercy and Saint John the Evangelist

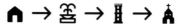

🏛 Basílica y Real Santuario de Santa María de la Victoria (Plaza Santuario)
🏠 Calle Agua 4

🔔 Holy Christ of Humility. The *'Ecce Homo'* was made in 1983 — begun by Francisco Buiza and completed by Francisco Berlanga after Buiza's sudden death. The remainder of the figures are two Roman soldiers, Pilate, Caiaphas, Barabbas, and Claudia Procula (Pilate's wife) — all carved by Elías Rodríguez Picón (2012).

🥁 Band of Bugles and Drums of the Archconfraternity of the Passion and the Hope (Málaga)

🏛 Our Mother and Lady of Mercy by Luis Álvarez Duarte (1982) with Saint John the Evangelist by the same sculptor (1986).

🥁 Music Band 'Maestro Eloy García' of the Archconfraternity of the Expiration (Málaga)

Salud (Health)

The Brotherhood of Health is a corporation founded in 1979 by a youth group associated with the Cistercian Convent. The brotherhood was formed around the image of Christ of the

Great Love by the *imaginero* Luis Alberto Duque, and later they acquired the Marian image to which they decided to add the dedication 'Health' to reflect their social outreach projects that were, and continue to be, concerned with the care of the sick. The procession begins in the *barrio* of La Trinidad, and is characterized by its sobriety and faultless 'choreography'. The *Cristo* represents Jesus at the moment of his crucifixion.

 Hermandad del Santísimo Cristo de la Esperanza en su Gran Amor y María Santísima de la Salud
Brotherhood of the Holy Christ of Hope in his Great Love and Holy Mary of Health

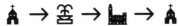

A Parroquia de San Pablo (Calle Trinidad 35) **A** Calle Trinidad 5

† Holy Christ of Hope in his Great Love — figure by Luis Álvarez Duarte (Sevilla, 1991) and throne of carved gilded wood by the workshop of the Caballero González Brothers (completed in 2016).

🎺 *Cruz de Guía*: Band of Bugles and Drums of the Brotherhood of the Gypsies (Málaga). *Cristo*: Musical Group 'Vera✠Cruz', (Campillos, Málaga)

🏛 Holy Mary of Health also by Luis Álvarez Duarte (Sevilla, 1988). The elaborate canopy is embroidered gold lamé and burgundy velvet by Jesús Ruiz Cebreros and brothers of the Corporation.

🎺 Music Band 'Our Lady of Peace' (Málaga)

Huerto (Garden)

This brotherhood was formed by the merger between two brotherhoods that occurred in 1920: the Brotherhood of Our Father Jesus Praying in the Garden and the Brotherhood of the Conception. The first was founded in 1735 in the convent of San Luis '*El Real*' and in 1756 it was reorganized by the olive growers' guild. In 2020, the Brotherhood received the title of 'Royal' from His Majesty Felipe VI, who also gained the title of '*Hermano Mayor Honorario*' (Honorary Elder Brother) of the archconfraternity.

Pontificia, Real, Muy Ilustre y Venerable Archicofradía Sacramental y Seráfica de Nuestro Padre Jesús Orando en el Huerto, Nuestra Señora de la Concepción, San Juan Evangelista y Nuestra Señora de la Oliva

Pontifical, Royal, Very Illustrious and Venerable Sacramental and Seraphic Archconfraternity of Our Father Jesus Praying in the Garden, Our Lady of the Conception, Saint John the Evangelist and Our Lady of the Olive

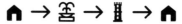

🕊 Parroquia de Los Mártires San Ciriaco y Santa Paula (Plaza de los Mártires Ciriaco y Paula 1) 🏠 Plazuela Virgen de la Concepción 1

👤 Our Father Jesus Praying in the Garden of Olives by Fernando Ortiz (Málaga, 1756) restored by Manuel Carmona (2006) who carved a new corpus (i.e. body; the previous one having disappeared in 1931). The Comforting Angel is by Antonio Castillo Lastrucci (1940).

🎺 Musical Ensemble 'Our Father Jesus, Captive' (Estepona, Málaga)

👤 Our Lady of the Conception (anonymous, 18th c. attributed to Fernando Ortiz) restored by Antonio Eslava Rubio, who gave it new hands (1978). Saint John the Evangelist and the Virgin of the Olive are by Juan Manuel García Palomo and Juan Ventura, respectively.

🎺 Vera✠Cruz Music Band, from Almogía (Málaga)

Prendimiento (Arrest)

This brotherhood's *Cristo* shows the moment at which Judas Iscariot kisses Jesus and his arrest takes place. Its *templo* is, like the Dulce Nombre, the Church of the Divine Shepherdess (Divina Pastora). The *Cristo* is accompanied by the Virgin of the Great Forgiveness, on one of the largest and most impressive thrones in the city.

 Fervorosa y Muy Ilustre Hermandad de Nuestro Padre Jesús del Prendimiento y María Santísima del Gran Perdón

Fervent and Very Illustrious Brotherhood of Our Father Jesus of Arrest and Holy Mary of Great Forgiveness

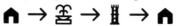

🕊 Parroquia de la Divina Pastora (Plaza de Capuchinos 5) 🏠 Calle San Millán 23

👤 The images of the Lord of the Arrest and Judas Iscariot are by Antonio Castillo Lastrucci (1961). The other images (Saint Peter and Malchus) are by Juan Manuel García Palomo (2005–2007). The trono itself was made by the goldsmiths Villarreal (Sevilla, 1965).

🎺 *Cruz de Guía*: Band of Bugles and Drums of the Royal Fire Department

(Málaga). *Cristo*: Musical Ensemble 'Our Lady of Anguish', (Alcalá la Real, Jaén).

🏛 Holy Mary of the Great Forgiveness by Andrés Cabello Requena (1957) on a trono by Villareal (Sevilla, 1975)

🎺 Music Band 'Our Lady of Solitude' (Málaga)

Lunes Santo (Holy Monday)

Traditionally this is reckoned to be the day on which Jesus drove the moneylenders out of the Temple. During Mass on this day, the Gospel that is proclaimed recounts the story of the Anointing at Bethany in the house of Lazarus and his sisters Martha and Mary (John 12:1–11). Mary anoints the feet of Jesus with costly perfumed oil. She is upbraided by Judas (the treasurer of the Twelve), but Jesus explains that she is preparing him for his burial. This Gospel, which shows an example of the Virtue of 'Magnificence' (*i.e.* doing great things for the love of God) might be read as a response to those who would criticize the lavish grandeur of the *Semana Santa* ceremonies.

Crucifixión

This is a modern foundation, established in 1977 in the *barrio* of Parque Victoria Eugenia by a local woman, Antonia Hernández, to provide a free dispensary and medical services to the needy. It received its title in 1983 and made its first official outing during *Semana Santa* proper on Holy Monday, 1993. The sculptures are Christ of the Crucifixion, showing the moment when the Roman soldiers cast lots for his robe, while the thieves Dismas and Gestas await their execution and Holy Mary of Sorrow is depicted in her solitude.

 Fervorosa Hermandad de culto y procesión del Santísimo Cristo de la Crucifixión y María Santísima del Mayor Dolor en su Soledad

Fervent Brotherhood of the worship and procession of the Holy Christ of the Crucifixion and Holy Mary of Great Pain in her Solitude

🏠 → ⛪ → 🏛 → 🏠

⛪ Parroquia del Buen Pastor (Calle Carrión 12)   🏠 Calle Diego de Siloé 8

✝ Most Holy Christ of the Crucifixion by José Manuel Bonilla Cornejo (1993) on a neo–baroque throne by Manuel Toledano Vega with goldsmithing by Antonio Rodríguez.

🎺 Band of Bugles and Drums 'Saint John the Evangelist' (Las Cabezas de San Juan, Seville)

🏛 Most Holy Mary of the Greatest Pain in her Solitude by Antonio Dubé de Luque (1988) on a throne made in the Orovio de la Torre workshops (2008–2009).

🎺 Musical Ensemble 'Our Father Jesus the Nazarene' (Almogía, Málaga)

Pasión

Founded in the parish of San Felipe Neri in 1934, this brotherhood made its first processional outing in 1942 from the now-demolished church of San José, Nowadays it leaves from the nearby church of the Martyrs Ciriaco and Paula. The sculpture of Jesus of the Passion represents Jesus carrying the cross helped by Simon of Cyrene and is one of the most notable pieces by the 20th-century *imaginero* Luis Ortega Bru.

 Real, Muy Ilustre y Venerable Archicofradía de Nazarenos del Santísimo Sacramento, Nuestro Padre Jesús de la Pasión y María Santísima del Amor Doloroso

Royal, Very Illustrious and Venerable Archconfraternity of Nazarenes of the Blessed Sacrament, Our Father Jesus of the Passion and Mary Most Holy of Sorrowful Love

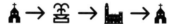

🏛 Parroquia de Los Mártires San Ciriaco y Santa Paula (Plaza de los Mártires Ciriaco y Paula 1) 🏛 Calle Convalescents 7

🏃 Our Father Jesus of the Passion Luis Ortega Bru (Cádiz, 1976). The figure of Simone of Cyrene is by Darío Fernández Parra (2010). The throne is by the goldsmith Seco Velasco (1946).

🎺 *Cruz de Guía*: Band of Bugles and Drums 'Our Father Jesus the Nazarene' (Almogía, Málaga). *Cristo*: Band of Bugles and Drums of the Archconfraternity of the Passion and the Hope (Málaga).

🖼 Holy Mary of Sorrowful Love (Anonymous, 18th c., attributed to Antonio Asensio de la Cerda and restored by Ortega Bru in 1977)

🎺 Municipal Music Band of Arahal (Seville)

Gitanos/Columna (Gypsies/Column)

The Brotherhood of the Gypsies is a very old brotherhood. The first historical reference to it appears in a document of 1682 as the Brotherhood of 'the Holy Christ of the Column' (the 'column' being the pillar to which Jesus was chained as he was scourged) at the church of La Merced. Historically, it was linked to the blacksmiths' guild in which Gypsies also participated. Its ostensible purpose was to provide assistance with the burial of brothers.

In the early years of the 20th century, the Gitanos transferred the canonical seat from the church of La Merced to the Santos Mártires parish church, and they incorporated the title *María Santísima de la O* ('Our Lady of the "O"'). The *Virgen* holds a relic of the *Lignum Crucis* (True Cross) in her right hand.

Our Lady of the 'O' is a Marian title closely associated with Gypsies in Spain. One of the principal churches in the traditionally Gypsy *barrio* of Triana in Sevilla is dedicated to her. Hers is an invocation of the Virgin Mary celebrated on 18 December commemorating the expectation of Mary's being delivered of her son, Jesus. The title 'of the "O"' came about because on the Eve of the feast, and every evening until 23 December, the antiphon (introductory verse) at vespers (evening prayers) is one of expectation, beginning with an invocation: '*O Sapientia!*' (O Wisdom!), '*O Adonai!*' (O Lord!), '*O Rex Gentium!*' (O King of the Nations!), etc.

Many Romani people come to Málaga for this procession, and it is one of the most dramatic and moving of the week, with a great deal of singing and even dancing. English-speaking readers may be shocked by the use of the term 'Gypsy' in this text, given that 'Roma' tends to be preferred. However, while '*gitano*' (having the same faulty etymology, *viz.* 'Egyptian') does sometimes have negative connotations in Spain, it is not generally regarded as a slur, especially as many of the most treasured Spanish traditions — *Semana Santa*, pilgrimages, the *feria*, flamenco and bullfighting — would be unimaginable without '*los gitanos*'. Moreover, '*los Gitanos*' is the name that Romani members of the fraternity use themselves.

 Excelentísima, Muy Ilustre y Venerable Hermandad y Cofradía de Nazarenos de Nuestro Padre Jesús de la Columna y María Santísima de la O

Most Excellent, Very Illustrious and Venerable Brotherhood of Nazarenes of Our Father Jesus of the Column and Holy Mary of the 'O'

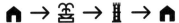

🏛 Parroquia de Los Mártires San Ciriaco y Santa Paula (Plaza de los Mártires Ciriaco y Paula 1) ⛪ Calle Frailes 17

🔔 Our Father Jesus of the Column by Juan Vargas Cortés (1942)

🎺 *Cruz de Guía*: Band of Bugles and Drums 'Crowned Sorrowful Virgin' (Álora, Málaga). *Cristo*: Band of Bugles and Drums of the Brotherhood of the Gypsies (Málaga).

🎗 Mary of the O by Francisco Buiza (1970) with a canopy and mantle embroidered by Juan Rosén (Málaga).

🎺 Band of the Brotherhood of Zamarrilla (Málaga)

Dolores del Puente
(Our Lady of Sorrows of the Bridge)

At the end of the 18th century, a street chapel was built beside the Guadalmedina River to house the 'Christ of Forgiveness' ('*Cristo del Perdón*'). Devotion to the *Virgen de los Dolores* (Virgin of Sorrows), was popularized by a parishioner of the church of San Juan, who in 1747 initiated a nocturnal rosary, popularly known as the 'Brotherhood of the *Tiñosos*' (they prayed for those suffering from '*tiña*', *i.e.* ringworm). Lacking a place to deposit the image and its accoutrements, he requested permission to settle in the chapel of *Cristo del Perdón*.

In 1927 the chapel was demolished, and the Virgin was moved to the other bank of the river, to a chapel built by the Archconfraternity of Hope, which housed the image until 1992, when it was demolished and the current chapel was built into the walls of the Church of Santo Domingo. The Brotherhood was reorganized by Jesús Castellanos in 1982, and in 1987 it was accepted into the Association of Brotherhoods and the new image of the *Cristo del Perdón*, the work of the *gallego* sculptor Suso de Marcos, was blessed.

Antigua Cofradía del Santísimo Cristo del Perdón y Nuestra Señora de los Dolores

Former Brotherhood of the Holy Christ of Forgiveness and Our Lady of Sorrows

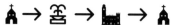

🅰 Parroquia de Santo Domingo de Guzmán (Calle Cerrojo 1) 🏠 Plaza de la Religiosa Filipense Dolores Márquez 1

✝ Holy Christ of Forgiveness (representing the moment at which Jesus forgives the Repentant Thief) by Suso de Marcos (1987). He is accompanied on the throne by the images of Gestas and San Dimas (1986), and San Juan Evangelista (2000) — all by Suso de Marcos. The group is completed by the Virgin of the Incarnation (Anonymous, 17th c., possibly by Antonio del Castillo)

🎺 *Cruz de Guía*: Band of Bugles and Drums of the Royal Fused Brotherhoods (Málaga). *Cristo*: Music Band 'Maestro Eloy García' of the Archconfraternity of Expiration (Málaga).

🔔 Our Lady of Sorrows — *Virgen de los Dolores del Puente* (Anonymous, 18th century, attributed to Pedro Asensio de la Cerda). She processes on a gilded wooden throne made by Virginia Jiménez (2005).

🎺 Music Band of the Archconfraternity of The Way and the Hope (Málaga)

Cautivo (Captive)

The brotherhood of *El Cautivo* has as its titular *Cristo* one of the most revered in Málaga and it is one of the largest brotherhoods (with more than 3,600 members) and most anticipated processions. The image is an '*Ecce Homo*' known as 'The Lord of Málaga'. The brotherhood was founded in 1934 in a classroom of the former Trinitarian school under the invocation of *María Santísima de La Trinidad* (Holy Mary of the Trinity). They began with an image of the Virgin that they saved from the destruction of the War Civil by hiding it beneath the patio of the founder's house in the Pasaje Zambrana. Its canonical seat is in the Parish of San Pablo in the *barrio* of La Trinidad. The titular image of the Captive is a sculpture from 1939, in which Jesus appears with his head slightly bowed, hands bound, wearing the scapular of the Trinitarian Order (a scapular part of the religious habit, and this is a devotional version). The Trinitarians were founded in the 12th century to ransom those taken captive by Barbary pirates.

On the day before Palm Sunday (Passion Saturday), both images — Jesus Captive and Our Lady of the Trinity — are taken during their *traslado* to the nearby Civil Hospital so that staff and patients can participate in *Semana Santa*.

Real, Muy Ilustre y Venerable Cofradía de Nazarenos de Nuestro Padre Jesús Cautivo, María Santísima de La Trinidad Coronada y del Glorioso Apóstol Santiago

Royal, Very Illustrious and Venerable Brotherhood of Nazarenes of Our Father Jesus Captive, Holy Mary of the Crowned Trinity and of the Glorious Apostle Saint James

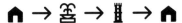

🏛 Parroquia San Pablo (Calle Trinidad 35) 🏠 Calle Trinidad 95

🔔 Our Father Jesus Captive by José Martín Simón (1939). The *trono* is of mahogany and embossed silver (1953).

🎺 *Cruz de Guía*: Band of Bugles and Drums of the Royal Fire Department (Málaga). *Cristo*: Band of Bugles and Drums 'Our Father Jesus Captive' (Málaga).

🔔 Holy Mary of the Trinity by Francisco Buiza (1963, replacing the 19th c. image hidden during the Civil War). The gold–work *trono* is by Villarreal (1971). The mantle was embroidered in the workshops of Joaquín Salcedo (2008).

🎺 Symphonic Band 'Virgin of the Trinity' (Málaga)

Estudiantes (Students)

This began in 1943 when a group of students from the San Agustín school obtained the endorsement of the Bishop to form a brotherhood. He asked them to 'resurrect' a historic fraternity and they chose the 18th-century 'Christ Crowned with Thorns and Our Lady of Hope and Saint Joachim' that had cared for plague victims (possibly the reason why they, literally, died out). Closely linked to the University of Málaga, it is one of the largest brotherhoods in terms of membership, and one of the biggest processions. Unusually, the bearers of both thrones sing as they process, in this case the traditional student song, '*Gaudeamus igitur*'.

 Hermandad del Santo Cristo Coronado de espinas y Nuestra Señora de Gracia y Esperanza

Brotherhood of the Holy Christ Crowned with Thorns and Our Lady of Grace and Hope

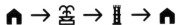

🏛 Iglesia del Santo Cristo de la Salud (Calle Compañía) 🏠 Calle Alcazabilla 3

🔔 Holy Christ Crowned with Thorns by Pedro Moreira (Málaga, 1946) on a gilded wooden *trono* (1955–56).

🎺 *Cruz de Guía*: Band of Bugles and Drums 'Holy Christ of the Redemption', (Benalmádena, Málaga). *Cristo*: Music Band 'Our Lady of Solitude' (Málaga).

🔔 Our Lady of Grace and Hope by Manuel Caderot (Madrid, 1948). The Trinitarian nuns in Málaga embroidered the canopy in 1952.

🎺 Music Band 'Our Lady of Solitude' (Cantillana, Sevilla).

Martes Santo (Holy Tuesday)

This day is traditionally associated with Jesus cursing the fig tree (Mark 11:12–25, Matthew 21:18–22). In the Gospel reading at Mass on this day, the betrayal by Judas and Saint Peter's denials are anticipated (John 13:21–33, 36–38)

Rocío (Dew)

The brotherhood of El Rocío dates back to 1706 when the Brotherhood of '*los Pasos*' (*lit*. 'the steps' though here it refers to the path to Calvary and to the three 'falls' of Jesus during the traditional Catholic devotion known as the *Via Crucis* or Way of the Cross) was established in the chapel of the San Lázaro hospital under the patronage of Christ of Mount Calvary. This brotherhood was originally attached to the Order of the Minims, who established the Royal Convent of Our Lady of the Victory in Málaga as early as 1493, and by the end of the 18th century had over forty foundations in Andalucía.

The Order did not survive the exclaustrations and disentailments of the 19th century and its associated brotherhood became inactive. It was revived in 1922 and was admitted within the group of brotherhoods in 1925. In 1926, it was granted the title 'Royal' by King Alfonso XIII, who accepted the title of Honorary Elder Brother. In March 1931 they acquired, as their Marian title, an image of the *Virgen del Rocío* — an enormously popular devotion in Andalucía — made by the *imaginero valenciano* Pío Mollar Franch. Only nine weeks later, this image was lost in the burning of convents, but they were able to have a replica made as they had preserved a clay mould of the original. This replacement image was blessed in 1935 and was saved from the second burning of the convents in 1936. The Virgin wears a dazzling white mantle and is known by all as the 'Bride of Málaga'. Her great popularity and the esteem in which she is held in Málaga is the reason that the brotherhood is called '*del Rocío*' rather than '*de los Pasos*'.

Real, Ilustre y Venerable Hermandad Sacramental de Nuestro Padre Jesús Nazareno de los Pasos en el Monte Calvario y María Santísima del Rocío Coronada.

Royal, Illustrious and Venerable Sacramental Brotherhood of Our Father Jesus of Nazareth of the Steps on Mount Calvary and The Crowned Holy Mary of Rocío

🏠 → ⛪ → 🗼 → 🏠

🏠 Parroquia de San Lázaro (Plaza Victoria 19) 🏠 Calle Circo 3

🏃 Our Father Jesus of Nazareth of 'the Steps' on Mount Calvary by Antonio Eslava Rubio (1977 from the remains of an older image).

📯 *Cruz de Guía*: Band of Bugles and Drums of the Royal Fused Brotherhoods (Málaga). *Cristo*: Musical Group 'Vera✠Cruz' (Campillos, Málaga).

🎗 Holy Mary of the Rocío by Pío Mollar Franch (Valencia, 1935). The Virgin is depicted with a slight inclination of her head to the left side with no visible tears on her face; an attempt to represent a middle ground between serenity and anguish.

📯 Music Band of the Archconfraternity of The Passion and the Hope (Málaga).

Penas (Pains)

The brotherhood of *Las Penas* was founded in 1935 in the chapel of San José that once stood on the Calle Granada and was damaged in 1931 (eventually being demolished in the 1960s). They made their first appearance in the *Semana Santa* of 1943. The following year, having insufficient funds to commission an embroidered cloth mantle, they decorated the Virgin's train with flowers. Although this was meant to be a temporary measure, it was so well received by the people that it became a tradition. In fact, the Virgin later had her own cloak made in green velvet and wore it in 1949 and 1950, but the people of Málaga wanted to see her wearing the mantle of flowers, which she has done ever since. The velvet cloak was sold. Every year, gardeners working for the municipal parks department of the *ayuntamiento* produce an elaborate floral design comprising thousands of freshly cut flowers.

What is unusual about the *Cofradía de las Penas* is that their *templo* and *casa hermandad* are in the same place (and the *templo* is the more recent construction). For 42 years, the canonical seat of the titular images was the church of San Julián on the Calle Nosquera (now the Historical Archive and Museum of the *Agrupación de Cofradías de Semana Santa*), but in 2008 they transferred to the *Oratorio de Santa María Reina y Madre* (The Oratory of Holy Mary Queen and Mother) a few streets to the north. If you visit this oratory (it is open Monday to Saturday between 11 am and 1 pm) you will encounter a handsome Baroque chapel (reminiscent of the Bishop's Palace in front of the Cathedral) with a richly decorated ceiling.

What you may not realize at first is that the foundation stone of this chapel was only laid in 2004 and it was completed and consecrated in 2008. The frescos that decorate the vault (an area of some 140 m²) and depict the Coronation of the Blessed Virgin were begun in 2008 and completed in 2014. They are the work of Raúl Berzosa Fernández, a member of one of the Málaga brotherhoods and a well-known artist. Many Málaga brotherhoods have built new, and often grand, brotherhood houses in recent years, but not many have built their own *templo* too. Such is the significance of this new construction that the portion of the Calle Arco de la Cabeza where it stands has been renamed the 'Plazuela Virgen de las Penas'.

Venerable Hermandad de la Caridad en Cristo Nuestro Señor y Cofradía de Nazarenos del Santísimo Cristo de la Agonía, María Santísima de las Penas, Reina y Madre, y Santo Domingo de la Calzada

Venerable Brotherhood of Charity in Christ Our Lord and Brotherhood of Nazarenes of the Holy Christ of Agony, Holy Mary of Sorrows, Queen and Mother, and Saint Dominic of the Camino

⛪ Oratorio de Santa María Reina y Madre (Plazuela Virgen de las Penas)
🏠 Plazuela Virgen de las Penas

✝ Holy Christ of Agony by Francisco Buiza Fernández (1971) on a *trono* of gilded wood from the workshop of Antonio Martín (1982–1987).

🎺 Band of Bugles and Drums of the Archconfraternity of The Way and The Hope (Málaga)

🖼 The Virgin of Sorrows — the only Marian image by Antonio Eslava Rubio in the city (1964). The gold-work throne was designed by Juan Casielles del Nido and executed by Manuel Villarreal (1964).

🎺 Music Band 'Our Lady of Peace' (Málaga)

Nueva Esperanza (New Hope)

The home of this fairly new brotherhood founded in 1976 is, appropriately enough, in the north-western suburb of 'Nueva Málaga'. The idea for its foundation took shape over lunch among a group of members of the *Peña Nueva Málaga* (a social action club) who were volunteering at the Los Ángeles Home for the Elderly. They first obtained an image of the *Nazareno* and the following year a *Dolorosa* from the town of Peñarrubia (abandoned in the 1970s during the construction of the Guadalteba reservoir). They tried to secure inclusion in the official programme of *Semana Santa* a number of times, but as a new and inexperienced brotherhood attempting a long route (almost 7 km, taking 13 hours), they struggled. They finally fulfilled their dream of being admitted in 1997.

Venerable Hermandad de Culto y Procesión de Jesús Nazareno del Perdón, María Santísima de Nueva Esperanza, Santa Ana y San Joaquín

Venerable Brotherhood of Worship and Procession of Jesus of Nazareth of Forgiveness, Holy Mary of New Hope, Saint Joachim and Saint Anne

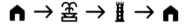

🕇 Parroquia de San Joaquín y Santa Ana (Camino Castillejos 4) 🏠 Camino de los Castillejos s/n

🕯 Our Father Jesus of Nazareth of Forgiveness by Juan Manuel García Palomo (Málaga, 1999) The *trono* is by Manuel Toledano Vega and notable because all the '*Nazarenos*' (processional images of Christ carrying his Cross) of Málaga are represented in the carvings.

🎺 Musical Ensemble '*Ecce Mater*' ('Behold Your Mother') (Cádiz)

🖼 The Virgin of New Hope by José Navas-Parejo (pre-1950) was donated to the brotherhood by the Diocese of Málaga in 1977 after its former home, the village of Peñarrubia, was flooded during the creation of the Guadalteba Reservoir. The *trono* was made in the workshops of Diego Martín and Sons (2002-2004).

🎺 Music Band of the Brotherhood of Zamarrilla (Málaga).

Humillación y Estrella (Humiliation and Star)

The Brotherhood of Humiliation and Star was founded in 1919 in the *barrio* of El Perchel, reviving an earlier brotherhood from the 17th century called the Brotherhood of the Christ of Forgiveness. It is widely regarded as one of the most traditional brotherhoods, dedicated to preserving the 'authenticity' of the *Semana Santa malagueña*. The titular image represents the moment when Jesus is taken from Herod's court to Pilate's palace.

 Ilustre y Venerable Hermandad de la Orden de Santo Domingo de Guzmán de Nuestro Padre Jesús de la Humillación y Perdón y María Santísima de la Estrella

Illustrious and Venerable Brotherhood of the Order of Saint Dominic de Guzmán of Our Father Jesus of Humiliation and Forgiveness and Holy Mary of the Star

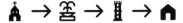

🕇 Parroquia de Santo Domingo de Guzmán (Calle Cerrojo 1)
🏠 Calle Cañaveral 3

🔔 Our Father Jesus of Humiliation and Forgiveness by Francisco Palma Burgos (Málaga, 1942).

🎺 *Cruz de Guía*: Band of Bugles and Drums of the Royal Fire Department (Málaga). *Cristo*: Band of Bugles and Drums 'Our Lady of Mount Carmel' (Málaga).

🖼 Holy Mary of the Star (Anonymous, 18th c.). Mahogany and silver *trono* by Francisco Díaz Roncero (1971-1972).

🎺 Music Band 'The Swallows' (Vélez-Málaga, Málaga)

Rescate (Rescue)

The Brotherhood of the Rescue was closely linked with the Trinitarian Order from its birth at the end of the 17th century right up until the friars in Spain were disentailed. This connection to the Trinitarian Order began in 1682, with the ransom of the image of *Jesús Nazareno Cautivo* from the Moroccan city of La Mamora (nowadays called Mehdya), where it has been taken by pirate raiders. When the Trinitarian Friars were relieved of their property in 1835, the now-homeless brotherhood moved to the church of San Juan, and later to Santo Domingo.

The image of Christ, which had been recovered at great financial cost and considerable risk to life from North Africa by the people of Málaga, did not survive the events of 1931 and the collapse of the brotherhood seemed inevitable. However, after a number of attempts it was reorganized, finding a new home in the Parish of Santiago with a titular image of *Jesús Nazareno* donated by the Cistercian Nuns of the convent of La Encarnación in Córdoba, before a replacement by Teodoro Simó Carrillo was commissioned. The image was transferred to its new (and current) *templo* — the small street chapel on the Calle Agua in 1951, and in 1956 the brotherhood acquired an image of the Virgin of Grace.

Both of the *tronos* are extremely heavy (that of the *Cristo* has nine carved figures) so the *varales* (poles) are very long to allow large numbers of *hombres de trono* to bear the weight.

Real, Piadosa y Venerable Hermandad de Culto y Procesión de Nuestro Padre Jesús del Rescate y María Santísima de Gracia

Royal, Pious and Venerable Brotherhood of Worship and Procession of Our Father Jesus of the Rescue and Holy Mary of Grace

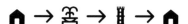

🛕 Capilla de Calle Agua (Calle Agua) 🛕 Calle Agua 15

🔔 Our Father Jesus of the Rescue with Saint John, Saint Peter, Saint James, Judas Iscariot, two Romans and two executioners by Antonio Castillo Lastrucci (Sevilla, 1957). The *trono* is neo–baroque by Antonio Martín Fernández with twenty-four cherubs by Francisco Buiza. Note the replica of the '*Virgen de la Victoria*' (Patron Saint of Málaga) on the front of the throne.

🎺 *Cruz de Guía*: Band of Bugles and Drums 'Holy Christ of the Vera ✠ Cruz' (Almogía, Málaga). *Cristo*: Musical Group 'Saint Laurence the Martyr' (Málaga).

🔔 The Virgin of Grace is also by Antonio Castillo Lastrucci (Sevilla, 1956). The *trono* is neo–Gothic in style (unique in Málaga) from 1985. The canopy is embroidered in silk by the workshops of Joaquín Salcedo Canca (2010), designed by Fernando Prinis Betés.

🎺 'Vera ✠ Cruz' Music Band (Almogía, Málaga)

Sentencia (Sentence)

The Brotherhood of Sentence was founded by a group of young worshippers in the Church of Aurora María, in 1928. Like most brotherhoods it suffered enormous losses during the burning of the convents of 1931, including their titular image, which had been carved by José Rius only a year earlier. The brotherhood regrouped in 1932 in the parish of San Pablo and commissioned a replacement *Cristo* from Rius that turned out not to be to everyone's liking, and José Martín Simón was asked to reform it in 1935. The result is a Christ that stands out for the beauty and serenity of its face.

The brotherhood was reorganized again in 1937, in the parish of Santiago located in the historic centre, where it still has its canonical headquarters. In 1938 they incorporated an image of Holy Mary of the Rosary in her Sorrowful Mysteries that had been donated by Emilia Villegas, a wealthy *malagueña* widow. Originally it was an 'Immaculate Conception' of the 19th century, but was changed into a '*Dolorosa*': her hands were separated and some tears were added. This image processed for the first time during Holy Week in Málaga from 1940 and is currently accompanied by 15 banners with the mysteries of the rosary. The *Cristo* represents Jesus at the moment Pilate condemns him.

 Muy Ilustre, Venerable y Fervorosa, Hermandad Sacramental y Cofradía de Nazarenos de Nuestro Padre Jesús de la Sentencia, María Santísima del Rosario en sus Misterios Dolorosos y San Juan Evangelista

Very Illustrious, Venerable and Fervent, Sacramental Brotherhood and Brotherhood of Nazarenes of Our Father Jesus of the Sentence, Holy Mary of the Rosary in her Sorrowful Mysteries and Saint John the Evangelist

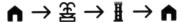

🕭 Parroquia de Santiago Apóstol (Calle Granada 78) 🏠 Calle Frailes 15

🔔 Our Father Jesus of the Sentence. The original image was by José Rius (1930), but was lost the following year in the *Quema de conventos*. In 1932 Rius created a new image that would be restored by José Gabriel Martín Simón (1935). It was reformed again by Pedro Pérez Hidalgo (1961) and again by Juan Manuel Miñarro (2008). The gilded wooden *trono* is by Pedro Pérez Hidalgo (1958).

🎺 *Cruz de Guía*: Band of Bugles and Drums 'Our Father Jesus of Nazareth' (Almogía, Málaga). *Cristo*: Musical Ensemble 'Arroquia Martínez' (Jódar, Jaén).

🔔 Holy Mary of the Rosary in her Sorrowful Mysteries is the work of the circle of a *malagueño* sculptor, Gutiérrez de León, from the 19th century. It was donated in 1938 by a *malagueña* woman, Emilia Villegas, and has undergone various restorations, first by Antonio Nadales and then José García Rodríguez who replaced the original eyes, that had been painted in the 19th century on eggshells, with glass ones.

🎺 Music Band 'Our Lady of Solitude' (Málaga)

Miércoles Santo (Holy Wednesday)

Holy Wednesday is, according to tradition, the day when the Sanhedrin — the Jewish religious tribunal — met with Judas Iscariot to condemn Jesus and arrange for him to be handed over to their authority (Matthew 26:14–25). It is officially the last day of Lent.

Mediadora (Mediatrix)

Another brotherhood with a recent origin, founded by a group devoted to the image of the *Virgen de los Dolores* in the parish of San Antonio de Padua in the neighbourhood of Portada Alta (in the western suburbs) who met for several years from 1989. In 1997, the Sisters who owned the image, requested its return and a new titular image to be called *Mediadora de la Salvación* (Mediatrix of Salvation) was commissioned from a young *malagueño* sculptor, Juan Manuel García Palomo. The brotherhood also sought a new *templo*, settling upon the parish of Santa María de la Encarnación, near the Misericordia Beach.

The brotherhood moved again when the parish of Santa María was closed, moving to the church of San Patricio (Saint Patrick), a few blocks to the west in the *barrio* of Huelin. The Patrick to whom this church is dedicated is not the Romano-British saint who ministered in Ireland, but a Hispano-Roman 4th century Bishop of Málaga. In 2017, the brethren approved a plan for a new *casa hermandad* designed by Eduardo Guerrero-Strachan Kerr. An interesting detail on the trono of the Virgin is that she carries in her left hand a model of a *jábega* — a typical fishing boat of Málaga and Huelin. Made of gilded sterling silver by the Sezar goldsmiths (Madrid), it represents the Church as a Ship of Salvation that sails towards Heaven.

 Venerable Hermandad de Nuestro Padre Jesús Nazareno Redentor del Mundo y Nuestra Señora Mediadora de la Salvación
Venerable Brotherhood of Our Father Jesus of Nazareth Redeemer of the World and Our Lady Mediatrix of Salvation

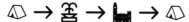

🕆 Parroquia de San Patricio (Calle Abogado Federico Orellana Toledano 2)
🏠 Calle Ayala 34

🧍 Our Father Jesus of Nazareth Redeemer of the World by José Antonio Navarro Arteaga (Sevilla, 2013). The image depicts Christ at the moment of embracing the Cross before beginning the path to Calvary. This symbolic embrace of a heavy burden represents the surrender of his own life for our salvation.

🎺 Band of Bugles and Drums of the Brotherhood of the Gypsies (Málaga)

🎑 Our Lady Mediatrix of Salvation by Juan Manuel García Palomo (Málaga, 1997). The carving has large dark eyes, a 'Greek' nose and a half–open mouth as if gasping for breath from crying. The crying is evident on her cheeks which show five crystal tears, a number that represents her salvation and mankind's salvation, recalling Christ's five wounds.

🎺 Municipal Music Band 'Villa de Osuna' (Osuna, Sevilla).

Salesianos (Salesians)

The origin of the Salesians dates back to 1985 when a group of former students of the Salesian College of San Bartolomé in Málaga decided to create a brotherhood of penance. The canonical seat is effectively the chapel of the Salesian College (a secondary school). They decided to place the new brotherhood under the patronage of '*Santo Cristo de las Penas*' (Holy Christ of Sorrows), in order to make explicit a link with an extinct fraternity that had existed in the Church of San Pedro in the 17th century. An interesting detail about this brotherhood is that their *trono* bears the images of the *Cristo* and the *Virgen* as they are brought together in the same Gospel scene.

 Hermandad Salesiana y Cofradía de Nazarenos del Santo Cristo de las Penas, María Santísima del Auxilio, San Juan Evangelista y San Juan Bosco

Salesian Brotherhood of Nazarenes of The Holy Christ of Sorrows, Our Lady Help of Christians, Saint John the Evangelist and Saint John Bosco

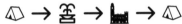

🯊 Santuario de María Auxiliadora (Calle Eduardo Domínguez Ávila 13) 🏠 Calle Eduardo Domínguez Ávila 26

✝ 🪕 The trono presents a sculptural group, including both the *Cristo* and the *Virgen*: Holy Christ of Sorrows by Manuel Carmona Martínez (1989), Our Lady Help of Christians and Saint John the Evangelist (1990), Mary Magdalene (1991) and Mary of Clopas and Mary Salome (1995). The scene represents the moment in which Jesus entrusts the beloved disciple and the Virgin Mary to one another. The processional throne is varnished cedar wood by Caballero González Brothers (1997–2000). In addition to the principal figures, four young angels hold various instruments of the Passion.

🪕 Band of Bugles and Drums 'Our Father Jesus Captive' (Málaga)

Fusionadas (Fused Brotherhoods)

The Royal Merged Brotherhoods process on Palm Sunday, Holy Wednesday and Holy Thursday. They are the union between the brotherhoods of *Santa Vera ✠ Cruz* (Holy and True Cross), *Nuestro Padre Jesús de Azotes y Columna* (Our Father Jesus of Scourges and the Column), *Cristo de Ánimas de Ciegos* (Christ of the Souls of the Blind) and *Santísimo Cristo de la Exaltación* (Holy Christ of Exaltation).

The Merged Brotherhoods have the peculiarity of being the only ones that, during *Semana Santa*, take out three *Cristos* and a *Virgen* in procession on the same day. The first *Cristo* is the *Santísimo Cristo de la Vera ✠ Cruz y Sangre* from the 17th century, the second is *El Santísimo Cristo de Ánimas de Ciegos* from 1649, and the last is the *Santísimo Cristo de la Exaltación* from 1982. The last two are accompanied by sculptural groups. In total, there are six thrones that the Fused Brotherhoods carry in procession during the week. The first outing is on Palm Sunday, behind the *Pollinica*, the second is today, and the final departure is on Holy Thursday.

Primitiva Hermandad Sacramental y Reales Cofradías Fusionadas de Nuestro Padre Jesús de Azotes y Columna, Santísimo Cristo de la Exaltación, Santísimo Cristo de Ánimas de Ciegos, María Santísima de Lágrimas y Favores, e Ilustre Archicofradía de la Santa Vera ✠ Cruz y Sangre, Nuestra Señora del Mayor Dolor y San Juan Evangelista

Primitive Sacramental Brotherhood and Royal Fused Brotherhoods of Our Father Jesus of Scourges and Column, Holy Christ of Exaltation, Holy Christ of Souls of the Blind, Holy Mary of Tears and Favours, and The Illustrious Arch-confraternity of the True Holy Cross and Precious Blood, Our Lady of Great Pain and Saint John the Evangelist

🜨 *(penitentes)* 🏠 *(tronos)* → ⚒ → 🏛 → 🏠

🜨 Parroquia de San Juan Bautista (Calle San Juan 3) 🏠 Pasillo Santa Isabel 11

🔔 (*Cristo I*) Our Father Jesus of Scourges and the Column (Anonymous, 18th c. modified by Mario Palma, 20th c.). Christ is accompanied on the throne by a sculptural group formed by two executioners who flagellate him, one Roman soldier and one centurion by Juan Vega (2012). As an example of the incredible detail of these hyperreal sculptures, on the table where the legionnaire is leaning is an unrolled parchment reading (if one were able to get close enough): 'REVM IESVM VOCATVM DE QVO DICITVR ESSE REGE IUDEOR-VM PRAECIPIMVS VERBERIBVS FLAGELLARI VSQVE AD OSSA NVDATA ROMANAE LEGIS MORE POSTEAQVE AD NOS RESTITVVM ESSE. PONTIVS PILATVS GVBERNA-TOR' ('I order that the criminal Jesus, who is said to be the King of the Jews, be flogged until his bones are exposed according to the law of Rome and then returned to my presence. Pontius Pilate, Governor'). The *trono* is by Juan Carlos García (2012).

🎺 *Cruz de Guía*: Band of Bugles and Drums of the Royal Fused Brotherhoods (Málaga). *Cristo*: Musical Group 'Our Captive Father Jesus (Estepona, Málaga).

✝ (*Cristo II*) Most Holy Christ of Exaltation by Francisco Buiza (1982) with sculptural group by Antonio Dubé de Luque (1980). The *trono* is by Guzmán Bejarano (1972).

🎺 Band of Bugles and Drums 'Coronación' (Campillos, Málaga)

✝ (*Cristo III*) Most Holy Christ of Souls of the Blind (1649, attributed to Pedro de Zayas) on a *trono* designed by Jesús Castellanos and carved by Antonio Ibáñez and García Díaz (1996).

🎺 Band of Bugles and Drums of the Paratrooper Brigade (Paracuellos del Jarama, Madrid).

🖼 Our Lady of Great Pain and Saint John the Evangelist by Dubé de Luque (1980, restored in 2007).

🎺 Music Band of the Archconfraternity of The Passion and The Hope (Málaga)

Paloma (Dove)

The Brotherhood of the Dove dates from the beginning of the 17th century as a dependent of *Santo Cristo de la Columna*. It remained active until the latter part of the 19th century, receiving the title 'Royal' from Queen Isabel II in 1868. After a period of lethargy, the Paloma was revived again in the 20th century, acquiring the *Virgen de los Dolores* in 1909. In 1921 it was a founding member of the group of Holy Week brotherhoods.

Until recently, La Paloma was the only one of the *Semana Santa* brotherhoods dedicated to the 'Lord of the Kidron Bridge'; a mystery that represents the moment when Jesus, captive and handcuffed, crosses the Kidron stream on the way to Calvary. The Kidron separates the Temple Mount from the Mount of Olives, and it was the brook crossed by King David when fleeing from Absalom. Jesus is accompanied by a Roman soldier and an executioner called 'Verruguita' ('the one with warts'). The *malagueño* freedom with language renders this as '*El Berruguita*' and this exaggeratedly ugly figure, with his bulbous eyes, hooked nose, sunken cheeks, an evil sneer and missing teeth (as well as the eponymous warts) is regarded as a sort of 'bogeyman' of *Semana Santa*. He is also modelled on a historical person — Vicente González Moreno, known as 'The Executioner of Málaga' after he betrayed General Torrijos, an act that led the latter to the firing squad on the beaches of San Andrés.

The Brotherhood of the Dove has constructed a combined *templo* and *casa hermandad* (an interesting part neo-baroque and part neoclassical building). It was designed in 1991 by the architect and brother Antonio Valero del Valle on the site of the former College of San Pedro and San Rafael and was completed in 2009.

 Real, Muy Ilustre, Venerable y Antigua Hermandad y Cofradía de Nazarenos de Nuestro Padre Jesús de la Puente del Cedrón y María Santísima de la Paloma

Royal, Very Illustrious, Venerable and Ancient Brotherhood of Nazarenes of Our Father Jesus of the Kidron Bridge and Holy Mary of the Dove

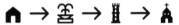

🏛 Capilla de María Santísima de la Paloma (Plaza de San Francisco) 🏠 Plaza de San Francisco

🔔 Our Father Jesus of the Kidron Bridge by Juan Manuel Miñarro (1988) with a Roman soldier and executioner by José Navas–Parejo (1939). The gilded wooden *trono* is by Guzmán Bejarano (1978).

🎺 Band of Bugles and Drums 'Our Lady of Mount Carmel' (Málaga)

🎐 Holy Mary of the Dove is by Luis Álvarez Duarte (Sevilla, 1970). It parades on a golden *trono* made in the workshops of the Caballero Farfán Brothers (2018). It has further decoration added by Juan Vega Ortega with gemstones set by Obrador Montenegro and paintings by Raúl Berzosa. The Virgin's mantle is embroidered in gold on blue velvet and the work of the 'Adoratrices' (Handmaids of the Blessed Sacrament and of Charity, 1958), since restored by Manuel Mendoza (2002).

🎺 Musical–Cultural Ensemble '*Santa Vera ✠ Cruz*' (Alhaurín el Grande, Málaga)

El Rico (The Rich One)

The brotherhood of Jesús El Rico was a founding member of the group of Holy Week brotherhoods in Málaga. The first historical data that we have appears in 1584 when the Brotherhood of *Vera ✠ Cruz* moved to the Franciscan Convent of San Luís El Real. Among the images of this brotherhood was one of 'Our Father Jesus with the Cross on His Back' that gave rise to the constitution of the Brotherhood of *Jesús Nazareno*, according to documents dated 1658. It was then composed of 72 brothers and in 1756 obtained Royal approval as an independent Brotherhood taking the name of *Jesús El Rico*. In 1938 it was reorganized again.

The first curiosity is the name — Jesus 'the Rich Man', or 'the Rich One'. This at first seems an odd, even offensive, title for someone who said that it was easier for a rich man to pass through the eye of a needle than to enter heaven, and who urged the rich young man to sell all that he had. Before the Crucifixion, Jesus is stripped of his garments and dies, naked, on the Cross. His body is then laid to rest in a tomb belonging to someone else, fulfilling his own statement that 'Foxes have holes, and birds of the air have nests, but the Son of Man has nowhere to lay his head.'[55]

The riches of Jesus are not worldly, though. As he urges his disciples, 'Lay up for yourselves treasures in heaven, where neither moth nor rust destroys and where thieves do not break in and steal.'[56] But in this case, something more is suggested. This is an image of Christ who bestows his 'riches' upon us in the form of grace and forgiveness, in keeping with the penitential tenor of *Semana Santa*. This is summed up perfectly in the Letter to the Ephesians: 'God, being rich in mercy, because of the great love with which he loved us, even when we were dead in our trespasses, made us alive together with Christ … and raised us up with him and seated us with him in the heavenly places in Christ Jesus, so that in the coming ages he might show the immeasurable riches of his grace in kindness towards us in Christ Jesus.'[57] This understanding helps makes sense of the second curious detail of the procession of '*El Rico*' — the release of a prisoner. This is not a tableau, nor an actor playing a part, nor a representative of a prisoner, but an actual prisoner. A judicially incarcerated criminal is set free.

According to the legend, in 1765 there was a terrible outbreak of cholera in Málaga, in which many perished. Such was the virulence of the epidemic that, when Holy Week arrived, there were insufficient healthy men to carry the images in procession. Nobody dared go out more than necessary for fear of infection and almost certain death. The news that there would be no processions that year penetrated the prison walls. No processions meant that the revered and much-loved image of Jesus '*El Rico*' would not appear — the Jesus of the imprisoned, the Jesus who cared for the bodies and souls of the prisoners would not go out into the streets of Málaga that year because of the plague.

The news spread through the entire prison like wildfire, and a strange mixture of pain, indignation and religious fervour took possession of the people detained within the walls. Spontaneously, and without prior agreement, the inmates, as if moved by a common feeling, rioted, overwhelmed the guards, breached the gate of the prison and made for the temple of Jesus '*El Rico*' which they carried in procession that night. But, after the procession, everyone returned quietly to jail.

Another anecdote is linked to this popular belief. It is said that not all of them returned to the jail. There was one who did not — an inmate who stayed out all that night, taking care of a relative infected with cholera. To this relative, he brought the carved head of Saint John the

---

55 Matthew 8:20

56 Matthew 6:20

57 Ephesians 2:4–6

Baptist '*degollado*' ('decollated' or beheaded) that had long been venerated by prisoners and which, at that time, was displayed at the foot of the image of Jesus '*El Rico*'. The relative was duly and miraculously cured and the jailers were greatly surprised when, the next morning, the fugitive returned voluntarily to jail like all those who had left the previous night.

It is said that to recognize the extraordinary gesture of these men, King Carlos III signed a decree granting the Justice of Málaga the right to free one prisoner each year. This prisoner would leave prison on Holy Wednesday and go out in procession with the titular brother-hood of *Nuestro Padre Jesús 'El Rico'*. Afterwards, he would return, not to prison, but home to his family, freed from his sentence. Naturally, any pardoned prisoner should have expressed contrition and exhibited the kind of good behaviour shown by those prisoners in 1765.

This '*indulto*' or pardon has been given each year ever since, at least in peacetime. Nowadays the process is more complicated, with multiple levels of municipal and judicial bureaucracy to navigate (right up to and including the *Consejo de Ministros*, or cabinet, in Madrid), but the liberation happens in much the same way as it always has. The prisoner approved for release waits on the steps of the Cathedral, dressed like a *penitente*, but all in black and, though hooded, without the pointed *capirote*. The *trono* with the figure of '*El Rico*' draws near, the *capataz* cries out, '*¡Quieto ahí!*' (Stay there!) and after two rings of the bell, the throne is low-ered. The band plays the *Marcha Real* (national anthem) and the document to be signed is presented to the Delegate of the Government, the President of the Provincial Court, and the Bishop of Málaga. With them stand the Director of the Provincial Prison, the Mayor, and the *Hermano Mayor* of the Brotherhood. When the release is signed, the moment of blessing arrives and the figure of Christ on the throne is made to raise its mechanical arm in bene-diction. The *hermano mayor* of the brotherhood approaches the freed prisoner and embraces him. The man (or, nowadays, woman) then joins the procession with the other *penitentes*, though barefoot.

The tradition is not lacking in critics. Some feel that it risks weakening the separation of powers that exists between the judicial and executive branches, with ministers, delegates and prison governors making decisions that belong to the courts (though Spain already has a parole board in the form of the *Junta de Libertad Condicional*). Others think it unacceptable in a secular state to appear to involve the Church in questions of justice or to apparently 'spiritualize' what should be a purely judicial decision. The *Fundación Civio* (Spain's equiv-alent of Britain's National Secular Society) actively campaigns to end the practice of Holy Week pardons altogether. And then there are those who are unhappy about the kinds of prisoners who are released and keen to ensure that only those who have committed very minor misdemeanours and are nearing the end of their sentences should be considered.

The Brotherhood itself sees the matter clearly, however. 'This is not a pretence. We want real pardons, freeing a prisoner with a major sentence, not people with minor crimes or who are about to be released, because otherwise what we do is kill a tradition that we have inherited almost intact from the reign of Carlos III,' said the former *Hermano Mayor* (2004–2012) José Rivas in a 2018 newspaper interview.[58] Brother José certainly has the Gospel on his side. When Jesus stated his mission early in Saint Luke's Gospel, he quoted Isaiah saying, 'He has sent me to proclaim release to prisoners and recovery of sight to the blind, to let the oppressed go free.'[59] He did not proclaim 'early release to prisoners' or commit to the release of only petty crooks or the wrongly imprisoned. The forgiveness and liberation of Christ in which Christians hope and believe is something far more radical and revolutionary. And whilst the Common Good of society would not be served by simply unlocking all prison

---

58 'Las cofradías defienden sus indultos: 'Es una tradición desde Carlos III y no un paripé', *El Confidencial*, 29 March 2018, archive.ph/h0CsG

59 Luke 4:18

gates, the *indulto* of *Semana Santa* serves as a powerful reminder that, with due repentance, forgiveness is within reach of all people, even those who have committed terrible crimes. Christ died not for the righteous, but for sinners.

So for all that the tradition has its opponents, for the populace of Málaga it remains a powerful witness. It is something that bridges the gap between the ceremonial and the concrete. Though no one is able to produce a copy of the decree from Carlos III, the release of a prisoner on Holy Wednesday now relies upon a much more powerful authority than royal writ — popular acclaim. The whole of *Semana Santa* is about penitence and forgiveness. One of the chief images is a condemned man, handcuffed and in chains, ready to face an unjust punishment. Pilate presents this prisoner with the words 'Ecce Homo' — 'Behold the Man', yet the 'turba' (mob) bay for his blood and even when Pilate offered to release Jesus, they cried, 'Crucify him!' Almost 2,000 years later the 'turba malagueña' gathers in the Plaza del Obispo and before them a man stands barefoot, dressed as a penitent. They believe in the forgiveness of Christ, and on their behalf, the Elder Brother of the Brotherhood embraces the prisoner as if to say once again, 'Ecce Homo', for this, too, is a man. This time, their response can be different. Not 'Crucify him!' but in the words of Christ himself, 'Neither do I condemn you; go, and sin no more.'

Real, Excelentísima, Muy Ilustre y Venerable Cofradía de Culto y Procesión de Nuestro Padre Jesús Nazareno Titulado 'El Rico' y María Santísima del Amor

Royal, Most Excellent, Very Illustrious and Venerable Brotherhood of Worship and Procession of Our Father Jesus of Nazarene Entitled 'The Rich Man' and Holy Mary of Love

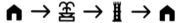

🏛 Parroquia de Santiago Apóstol (Calle Granada 78) 🏛 Calle Victoria 12

🏃 Jesus 'El Rico' by José Navas-Parejo (1939) on a *trono* of carved, gilded and polychrome wood by Nicolás Prados (1942).

🎺 *Cruz de Guía*: Band of Bugles and Drums 'Holy Christ of the Redemption' (Benalmádena, Málaga). *Cristo*: Symphonic Band 'Virgin of the Trinity' (Málaga).

🖼 The Virgin of Love by Nicolás Prados (1981). The gold work of the *trono* comes from the workshops of Manuel de los Ríos, Orfebrería Triana, and Antonio Santos Campanario. The embroidery, on both the mantle and the octagonal canopy is gold on blue velvet by Leopoldo Padilla (1952).

🎺 Music Band 'Our Lady of Solitude' (Málaga).

Sangre (Blood)

The Archconfraternity of the Blood is one of the oldest in Málaga. In the Middle Ages, the cult of the Most Precious Blood arrived in Málaga with the Order of Mercy (Mercedarians), which was established in the city in 1499. Between 1507 and 1509, the Order built its own church, and the Brotherhood of the Blood of Málaga was founded, and for centuries was connected to the Mercedarian community (at the now demolished church of La Merced) until the exclaustration of the Order.

The brotherhood popularized devotions around an anonymous, primitive carving of a '*Santísimo Cristo de la Sangre*', probably made in the 15th century judging by its characteristics: head bowed to the right, crowned with thorns, wearing a loincloth and fixed to the cross with three nails, with the right foot mounted on the left.[60] During the seventeenth century, the Brotherhood received numerous privileges from successive Popes. Their image represents the moment in which the body of Christ is pierced by a spear, the mystery of the so-called '*sagrada lanzada*' (Holy Spear Thrust). After a relatively moribund period in the second half of the 19th century, the processions began again in 1919.

In 1929 it incorporated the title of '*María Santísima de Consolación y Lágrimas*' (Holy Mary of Consolation and Tears), a carving from the 18th century. But in the wake of the events of 1931, 'The Blood' had to be reorganized again in 1940, acquiring a new image of the Most Holy Christ of the Blood on the Cross, to which was added a sculptural group composed of Saint John the Evangelist, the centurion Longinus (on horseback), an executioner, Mary Magdalene, Mary of Clopas and Mary Salome.

In 2017, the brotherhood elected as *Hermano Mayor* (Elder Brother) a secondary school teacher called Laura Berrocal Montañez. She thus became the first *Hermana Mayor* (Elder Sister) in the 500-year history of the Málaga brotherhoods (the Brotherhood of Las Penas also elected an Elder Sister, Ángela Guerrero, in 2019). Doña Laura's father, Ricardo, was *Hermano Mayor* of the same brotherhood from 1981 to 1993.

 Pontificia, Real, Muy Ilustre y Venerable Archicofradía del Santísimo Cristo de la Sangre, María Santísima de Consolación y Lágrimas y del Santo Sudario

Pontifical, Royal, Very Illustrious and Venerable Archconfraternity of the Holy Christ of the Blood, Holy Mary of Consolation and Tears and of the Holy Shroud

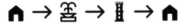

🜨 Parroquia de San Felipe Neri (Calle Guerrero 6) 🏠 Calle Dos Aceras 10

✝ Most Holy Christ of the Blood by Francisco Palma Burgos (Málaga, 1941) accompanied by a Virgin by Antonio Gutiérrez de León (1858). The other images in the sculptural group include Saint John the Evangelist by Amadeo Ruiz Olmos (1943) and Mary of Clopas, Mary Salome, Mary Magdalene, the centurion Longinus on horseback and an executioner by Rafael Ruiz Liébana (1997). The *trono* of gilded wood is by Rafael Ruiz Liébana (1995)

🎺 *Cruz de Guía*: Band of Bugles and Drums of the Royal Fire Department (Málaga). *Cristo*: Musical Group 'Vera ✠ Cruz' (Campillos, Málaga).

🖼 Holy Mary of Consolation and Tears by the school of Fernando Ortiz (18th century) restored by Luis Álvarez Duarte (1972). The *trono* is by Rafael Ruiz Liébana (2008).

🎺 Music Band 'Our Lady of Peace' (Málaga)

---

60   Juan José Salinas, *Archicofradía de la Sangre. Cinco siglos de historia y devoción en Málaga* (Málaga 2007) pp. 9–28

Expiración (Expiration)

The Expiration is a brotherhood from the 17th and 18th centuries that was founded to promote devotion to Our Lady of Sorrows. At the end of the 19th century, all traces of its activity were lost until it was reorganized in the 20th century. The iconography of the brotherhood represents the moment at which the crucified and dying Christ cries out to heaven, witnessed by 'La Dolorosa' — his sorrowful mother who feels the suffering of her son.

In 1931, the brotherhood lost almost all of its religious patrimony, forcing it to wander through several *templos* until it returned again to the church of San Pedro, its current canonical seat. In 1938 the Civil Guard joined the brotherhood as a corporate honorary *Hermano Mayor* (Elder Brother). Its thrones are famous for their fine craftsmanship, with the *trono* of the Virgin, in particular, held to be one of the finest in Spain. Weighing 4,900 kg, it is also one of the heaviest and requires 250 throne men to carry it.

 Pontificia, Real, Ilustre y Venerable Archicofradía Sacramental de Culto y Procesión del Santísimo Cristo de la Expiración y María Santísima de los Dolores Coronada

Pontifical, Royal, Illustrious and Venerable Sacramental Archconfraternity of Worship and Procession of the Holy Christ of Expiration and Crowned Holy Mary of Sorrows

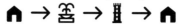

⛪ Iglesia de San Pedro (Avenida de la Aurora 8) ⛪ Plaza de Enrique Navarro 1

✝ Most Holy Christ of Expiration by Mariano Benlliure (Valencia, 1940). The *trono* is especially fine, made of mahogany, bronze and silver all in the plateresque (silver–work) style. The lower part is decorated with the prophets who foresaw the coming of Christ, while the upper part has bas–reliefs of the stations of the Cross.

🎺 *Cruz de Guía*: Band of Bugles and Drums of the Duque de Ahumada College of Civil Guards (Valdemoro, Madrid). *Cristo*: Vera ✠ Cruz Music Band (Almogía, Málaga).

🖼 Most Holy Mary of Sorrows (Crowned) attributed to Antonio Asencio de la Cerda, (18th century). The *trono* is of silver and was made by Manuel Seco Velasco (1955) with a canopy embroidered by the famous *sevillana* artist Esperanza Elena Caro. It has 5 'chapels' with different Marian dedications: The Virgin of Pilar (Patron Saint of the Civil Guard) at the front, and on the right side, Our Lady of the Victory (Patron Saint of Málaga) and the Immaculate Conception. On the left side is Our Lady of Mount Carmel and Our Lady of Fatima. The lower part of the throne is decorated with scenes from the life of Christ: the Presentation of the Child in the Temple, the Flight into Egypt, The Child Jesus lost and found in the Temple, The Way of the Cross and the encounter of Jesus with the women of Jerusalem, The Crucifixion, and The Descent from the Cross.

🎺 Music Band 'Maestro Eloy García' of the Archconfraternity of the Expiration (Málaga).

Jueves Santo (Holy Thursday)

This is the first day of the Paschal Triduum (*'triduum'* means 'three days'), the holiest time in the Church's liturgical year. It commemorates the Last Supper that Jesus ate with his disciples and is therefore also the commemoration of the institution of the Eucharist (the bread and wine which become the Body and Blood of Christ) and the commemoration of the institution of the priesthood (because Jesus said, 'Do this in remembrance of me'). In Saint John's Gospel we read that, during supper, Jesus began to wash the feet of the disciples, telling them that he was giving them a 'new commandment' (*'mandatum'*, from which the English word 'Maundy' is derived) to love one another as he had loved them. After the meal, he goes to pray in the Garden of Gethsemane and while he is there Judas arrives with soldiers and betrays him.

In the liturgy of the Church today, Mass is celebrated in the evening (though in the morning the 'Chrism' Mass takes place in the Cathedral to consecrate the sacred oils for use in baptism, confirmation, ordination and for the sick and dying). The Gospel reading tells the story of Jesus washing his disciples' feet (John 13:1–15) and afterwards, the celebrant washes the feet of twelve men (or men and women) from the congregation who symbolize those disciples. In religious houses, the Abbot or Prior may wash the feet of his monks or friars, and in a cathedral, the Bishop traditionally washed the feet of the Canons (the honorary clergy of the Cathedral). The symbolism of washing, though it speaks of humility and love, is also palpably associated with a 'preparation for death'.

At the end of the Mass, the altars are stripped. All linens and paraments (hangings, decorations, candlesticks, etc.) are taken away. This symbolizes Christ being stripped of his garments before his crucifixion. At the same time, the Blessed Sacrament is taken to a specially decorated altar in the church known as the 'altar of repose'. This recalls the time that Jesus spent praying in the Garden of Gethsemane. People are encouraged to spend time praying 'with Jesus' at this altar, at least until midnight.

Sagrada Cena (Last Supper)

The 'Sacred Supper' has its origin in a 17th-century brotherhood. In 1924 it was reorganized again in the Sanctuary of Santa María de la Victoria, thanks to a group of workers from the old *Compañía de Ferrocarriles Andaluces*, (Rail Company of Andalucía) giving rise to the nickname of the brotherhood — *Los Ferroviarios*, or The Railwaymen.

The images of Mary of Peace (by José Gabriel Martín Simón) and Christ and the Apostles (Pío Mollar Franch) were damaged, but not entirely destroyed in 1931. However, on December 28 1969, the chapel of the brotherhood (then situated next to the railway station) caught fire (accidentally this time) and both images and thrones were completely destroyed. Following this loss, new images were commissioned from the then twenty-year-old *sevillano* sculptor Luis Álvarez Duarte. Holy Mary of Peace is his first known work, and the figure of Jesus his first *Cristo* (he would go on to become one of the most famous *imagineros* of the late 20th century). The figure of St James the Less in the Last Supper group is a self-portrait.

For many years, the *templo* of the brotherhood was the church of the Holy Martyrs Ciriaco and Paula, but when it was closed for restoration they moved to Santo Domingo across the river. In 2020, the council of the Brotherhood voted unanimously to make the move permanent (joining the *Dulce Nombre* and *Esperanza* brotherhoods) and this decision was subsequently approved by the Bishop of Málaga in June 2022.

Real y Muy Ilustre Hermandad de la Sagrada Cena Sacramental de Nuestro Señor Jesucristo y María Santísima de la Paz

Royal and Very Illustrious Brotherhood of the Sacred Sacramental Supper of Our Lord Jesus Christ and Holy Mary of Peace

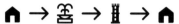

⛪ Parroquia de Santo Domingo de Guzmán (Calle Cerrojo 1) 🏠 Calle Compañía 44

🕍 The Lord of the Sacred Sacramental Supper (and Apostolic group) by Luis Álvarez Duarte (1971), on a *trono* by Guzmán Bejarano in carved and gilded wood, with images by Luis Ortega Bru and Rafael Barbero. It is one of the heavier thrones (4,100 kg) and is carried by 260 men.

🎺 *Cruz de Guía*: Bugler squadron of the Royal Fused Brotherhoods (Málaga). *Cristo*: Musical Ensemble 'Our Father Jesus of Redemption' (Córdoba).

🕍 Holy Mary of Peace by Álvarez Duarte (1970) on a *trono* of chiselled silver from the workshops of Villarreal, with images by Rafael Barbero and a canopy and mantle embroidered by the Reverend Mothers of Adoration (a religious order in Málaga), all designed by Juan Casielles del Nido (1957–1958).

🎺 Music Band 'Our Lady of Peace' (Málaga)

Viñeros (Vintners)

The *Viñeros* brotherhood has its roots in a 17th-century trade guild formed by vintners. It began its participation in *Semana Santa* in 1615 with the church of La Merced as its canonical seat. In the 20th century, the *Viñeros* brotherhood was reorganized again and in 1962 merged with the brotherhood of the *Virgen del Traspaso* and *Soledad de Viñeros* (the *Virgen del Traspaso* is a depiction of Mary meeting her son on the Way of the Cross, an extra-biblical Catholic tradition). The Brotherhood also organizes the ceremony of blessing of grapes and must each September.

The Brotherhood now has its canonical headquarters in the Conventual Church of Aurora María and Divine Providence (also known as the church of Santa Catalina, or 'Las Catalinas'), the conventual church of a former monastery of Dominican Nuns. Since the nuns left Málaga in 2003, the Brotherhood has set about the restoration of their former church as a brotherhood chapel, keeping it open to the public as a place of prayer. The image of the *Cristo* (a 'Nazareno') carries the cross on his left shoulder while lifting his right foot as if walking. In his right hand, the carving carries the keys to the *custodia* (tabernacle) of the church of Santa Catalina — a privilege granted to the Brotherhood in the 18th century by Pope Pius VI.

The web address of the Brotherhood — 'correonistas' — is a reference to the bandolier-like straps ('correas') that were once used to lift the *tronos* in Málaga (in the days when they were far smaller and lighter than today).

Muy Ilustre, Antigua y Venerable Hermandad Sacramental de Nuestro Padre Jesús Nazareno de Viñeros, Nuestra Señora del Traspaso y Soledad de Viñeros y San Lorenzo Mártir

Very Illustrious, Ancient and Venerable Sacramental Brotherhood of Our Father Jesus of Nazareth of the Vintners, Our Lady of Transfer and Solitude of the Vintners and Saint Laurence the Martyr

⌂ → ⚱ → ⛪ → ⌂

🏛 Iglesia de la Aurora y Divina Providencia, Calle Andrés Pérez 15 ⌂ Plaza de los Viñeros 5

🕯 Our Father Jesus of Nazareth by Francisco Buiza (Sevilla, 1975). The *trono* of polychrome and gilded wood in the traditional 'reel' style (i.e. shaped like a cotton-reel or bobbin) is by Francisco Pineda and Gonzalo Merencio, with gold work by the *sevillano* goldsmiths Manolo and Antonio Doradores (2012). The Guardian Angel is by José María Ruiz Montes (2014).

🎺 Musical Ensemble 'Saint Laurence the Martyr' (Málaga).

🛕 Our Lady of the Transfer and Solitude by Francisco Buiza (Sevilla, 1969). The *trono* is of carved and gilded cedar wood by Eloy Téllez Carrión (2004). The carving is by Francisco Pineda and the gilding by Manolo and Antonio Doradores (2005–2010).

🎺 Music Band 'Saint Cecilia' (Sorbas, Almería).

Vera ✠ Cruz (True Cross)

The brotherhood of *Vera✠Cruz* is the oldest extant Holy Week brotherhood in Málaga, and although the year of its foundation cannot be known for certain, it is generally thought to be 1507. At first, it was a brotherhood of penance whose cult centred around the worship of the *'Lignum Crucis'* (The Wood of the Cross). It is one of the Royal Merged Brotherhoods.

As a member of the Royal Merged Brotherhoods, is has often participated in *Semana Santa* by carrying out the last Holy Thursday procession. But in recent years it has taken an earlier slot on Thursday, as well as processing on Good Friday. Its titular image is a heavily restored *Cristo* of 1505, making it the oldest carving that is processed during Holy Week in Málaga. This image was partially destroyed during the burning of the convents, so it was archived for many decades until 1991 when its restoration was completed. The image of the Virgin and Saint John the Evangelist who accompanied her were destroyed in a fire in 1980.

 Primitiva Hermandad Sacramental y Reales Cofradías Fusionadas de Nuestro Padre Jesús de Azotes y Columna, Santísimo Cristo de la Exaltación, Santísimo Cristo de Ánimas de Ciegos, María Santísima de Lágrimas y Favores, e Ilustre Archicofradía de la Santa Vera+Cruz y Sangre, Nuestra Señora del Mayor Dolor y San Juan Evangelista

Primitive Sacramental Brotherhood and Royal Fused Brotherhoods of Our Father Jesus of Scourges and Column, Holy Christ of Exaltation, Holy Christ of Souls of the Blind, Holy Mary of Tears and Favours, and The Illustrious Archconfraternity of the True Holy Cross and Precious Blood, Our Lady of Great Pain and Saint John the Evangelist

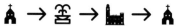

🜨 Parroquia de San Juan Bautista (Calle San Juan 3) 🏠 pasillo Santa Isabel 11

✝ Holy Christ of the True Cross (anonymous, 16th century) renewed by Óscar San José (1991) and restored by Juan Manuel Miñarro (2011–12). It is the oldest image of all those that take part in the procession during Holy Week in Málaga. Carried on a varnished wooden *trono* (1950s).

🎺 Music Band 'Maestro Infantes' (Los Barrios, Cádiz).

Santa Cruz (Holy Cross)

In 1980, a group of young brothers belonging to the Brotherhood of *La Pollinica* met to form the brotherhood of *Santa Cruz*. Originally a private association of the faithful, in 1995 it was assigned a canonical seat in the Parish of the Holy Cross and San Felipe Neri. Since its foundation, the brotherhood had based its worship around the image of the Virgin of Sorrows in her Protection and Mercy, and the Holy Cross, the latter being incorporated as head shortly after her. In 2001, the Holy Cross became an official member of the grouping of Holy Week brotherhoods and since then its official route has taken place on Holy Thursday (they formerly processed on Friday).

The brotherhood comes out with only one throne bearing Our Lady with the Holy Cross, a work made in 1986 by José Ortiz. The iconography thus represents the Virgin at the foot of the empty Cross, after the body of her son has been taken down.

Seráfica Hermandad de la Santa Cruz, Santísimo Cristo de la Victoria y Nuestra Señora de los Dolores en su Amparo y Misericordia

Seraphic Brotherhood of the Holy Cross, Holy Christ of Victory and Our Lady of Sorrows in her Protection and Mercy

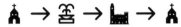

🕍 Parroquia de San Felipe Neri (Calle Guerrero 6) 🏠 Calle Julio Mathias 9

🖼 Our Lady of Sorrows in her Protection and Mercy by Antonio Dubé de Luque (1984). A *trono* of varnished mahogany in the typical Málaga 'reel' throne style by Juan Antonio García Casas and Julián Sánchez Medina (2005) to a design by Antonio Joaquín Dubé de Luque with relief works by José María Leal Bernáldez (2010–2011).

🎺 *Cruz de Guía*: *'Caeli'* Musical Ensemble. *Virgen*: Music Band 'Maestro Eloy García' of the Archconfraternity of the Expiration (Málaga).

Mena

This procession is one of the most famous, moving and beautiful of *Semana Santa*, in part due to the rather dramatic involvement of the Spanish Foreign Legion, but also due to the exquisite carving of the *Cristo*. And is so often the case, the very reasons that make this procession unique are also the reasons why critics of *Semana Santa* are especially unhappy with it (defenders of secularism are not the only ones to have difficulties; plenty of Catholics find the involvement of the military, police and civic authorities problematic).

The Congregation of Mena is the result of the merger, in 1915, of the Old Brotherhood of Our Lady of Solitude with the Brotherhood of the Holy Christ of a Good Death and Holy Souls. The Brotherhood of Our Lady of Solitude had been founded in the middle of the 16th century in the then Convent of Saint Dominic. The Dominican Order ceded the necessary land for the chapel and pantheon to be built in 1579. Much more recent and humble in its origins was the Brotherhood of Holy Christ of the Good Death, created in 1862.

Our Lady of Solitude is closely linked with the Spanish Navy (*Armada Española*) In March 1756 in the bay of Málaga, in front of the mouth of the Guadalmedina River, 'A horrific storm' was unleashed that surprised a frigate of the Spanish Navy, according to the story related by Father Federico Gutiérrez in his work *Holy Week in Málaga*.[61] The boat was about to capsize and a shipwreck seemed certain as the beaches near the mouth of the river are very rocky. Visibility was almost zero, but despite this, the desperate sailors spotted the tower of a church and a belfry through the mist. Knowing that there would be a Virgin there, they entrusted themselves to her protection without ever having seen her.

The storm subsided and the frigate was able safely to enter the port of Málaga. The sailors attributed their survival to the miraculous intercession of the unknown Virgin venerated in the church they had glimpsed. With their commanders, they decided to go to the church to thank her personally and thus they arrived at Santo Domingo where they found the Virgin of Solitude. The sailors, grateful for the protection, asked the parish priest to celebrate a

---

61   *Semana Santa en Málaga*, Federico Gutiérrez, (Alpuerto, 1976)

thanksgiving mass, but this was not possible because it was Holy Saturday and masses are prohibited by the Church until sunset on that day. Soon after, the then bishop of Málaga, José Franquis Lasso de Castilla, requested the privilege of celebrating a thanksgiving mass from Rome. After some time, Pope Benedict XIV granted the Brotherhood of the Soledad the title of 'Pontifical' and issued a bull according to which, at noon on Holy Saturday each year, a solemn mass of thanksgiving could be celebrated. This privilege is almost certainly unique in the entire Church. Since then, the Spanish Navy has been forever linked to the *Virgen de la Soledad*. A painting of the Málaga *Soledad* is found on every Spanish ship, and sailors accompany her in her procession during *Semana Santa*.

During the Burning of the Convents, the brotherhood only managed to save the image of Our Lady of Solitude. The *Cristo*, carved by the *granadino* master *imaginero* Pedro de Mena (1660) was not spared. Considered one of his finest works, and sculpted larger than life-size (a rare feature in de Mena's carvings), it suffered several attacks and mutilations before being almost completely destroyed. Of the original carving, only part of a leg is preserved, rescued during the burning by the artist Francisco Palma Burgos (it was exhibited for a time in the Episcopal Palace), and a foot, which is guarded by the Congregation of Christ of Mena. The replacement image, by Francisco Palma Burgos (1942) is, unusually, almost a facsimile of the Mena original, though not quite identical. Palma's has slightly larger proportions, the left leg rests on the right (in de Mena's it is the opposite), the hair is different in shape and the knot of the loincloth is on the right side, while de Mena carved it on the left. But in general terms, the plasticity of the sculpture and the size of the arms coincide, which are shorter with respect to the rest of the image. Despite all this, the *Cristo* continues to be called '*Mena*', remembering the one that was lost.

Before 1931, and since, the 'Christ of the Good Death' has had a close association with both the Spanish Navy and the Foreign Legion. One of the reasons that this procession is especially well-known is not due to the procession itself, but because of the '*traslado*' (transfer). The image of the Christ of the Good Death resides in the church of Saint Dominic and is transferred to the Brotherhood House a short distance away by members of the Spanish Legion on the morning of Holy Thursday. Normally, transfers make use of a small throne, but the Christ of the Good Death (which is a large crucifix) is held aloft by the legionaries in a manner which might either be described as noble and moving, or ostentatious, depending upon your point of view.

The ceremony of transfer normally takes place around noon, the legionaries having arrived earlier that morning, disembarking a ship from Melilla, one of Spain's exclaves in North Africa, and marching through the city. It is a widely anticipated event watched by thousands of *malagueños* and is broadcast live on local TV. About 200 legionnaires come from Melilla to honour their patronal image and whilst it can strike foreigners as odd or distasteful to see soldiers — in formation uniform with side arms — parading with a Cross bearing the 'Prince of Peace', it is certainly a dramatic spectacle. The legionnaires refer to themselves as the 'Bridegrooms of Death' because the ever-present danger of death in military service makes it more like a lover or spouse than an enemy. They also sing a hymn of the same name, '*El Novio de la Muerte*'. The song began life in 1921 in the music hall and had its first performance in the (long since disappeared) Teatro Vital in Málaga. Originally it was a romantic, if overblown, song about a young corporal who died of his wounds at Beni Hassán in the Rif campaign. In his pocket was found a letter written after the recent death of his girlfriend expressing his desire to be reunited with her in the afterlife. In 1952, Emilio Ángel García Ruiz, director of the Legion's music band, adapted it to be performed as procession music.

Pontificia y Real Congregación del Santísimo Cristo de la Buena Muerte y Ánimas y Nuestra Señora de la Soledad Coronada (Mena)

Pontifical and Royal Congregation of the Most Holy Christ of a Good Death and Holy Souls and Our Lady of Crowned Solitude (Mena)

♠ → ☖ → ▮ → ♠

♠ Parroquia de Santo Domingo de Guzmán (Calle Cerrojo 1) ♠ Pasillo de Santo Domingo 16

† Holy Christ of the Good Death by Francisco Palma Burgos (1942). It is accompanied by an image of Mary Magdalene by the same *imaginero* (1945). The carved, gilded and polychrome wooden throne is in a neo-baroque style. On the sides there are busts of St Dominic of the Camino (Santo Domingo de la Calzada) and the Sorrowful Virgin, and at the front there are the shields of the Congregation and, at the back, of the Spanish Foreign Legion.

🎺 *Cruz de Guía*: Muffled drums of the Legion. *Cristo*: the Duke of Alba 'War Band' of the Legion (Ceuta) with the Music Band of the 'King Alfonso XIII' Brigade of the Legion (Almería) (⚠ these bands tend to change from year to year.)

🏛 Our Lady of Solitude (Crowned) is an anonymous 18th century image acquired from a defunct brotherhood of Antequera. The *trono* of gilded oak is by Antonio Ibáñez (2006).

🎺 Music Band 'Our Lady of Solitude' (Málaga)

Zamarrilla

In 1788 there began a regular recitation of the Holy Rosary around a wayside cross called the 'Cruz de Zamarrilla' located on the road to Antequera (the current Calle Martínez Maldonado) and later, a hermitage was built, presided over by a crucified image (*Santo Cristo de Zamarrilla*). In 1792 the first Marian dedication was incorporated. After a period of decline at the end of the 19th century and the beginning of the 20th century, the brotherhood was reorganized in 1921, making its first processional outing with the Virgin of Sorrows (whose dedication would later be changed to 'of Bitterness'). In 1925, the image and sculptural group of Our Father Jesus of the Holy Torment was made by the *imaginero sevillano* Antonio Castillo Lastrucci. With the burning of convents of 1931, the Brotherhood lost practically everything. In 1935 a *'Dolorosa'* — the *Virgen del Amparo* — was acquired from the town of Álora, and the *imaginero* from Málaga, Francisco Palma García, was commissioned to make an image of the crucified *Cristo*. He died before beginning work and the piece was executed by his son Francisco Palma Burgos. In 1985 the Brotherhood blessed a third title, *Nuestro Padre Jesús del Santo Suplicio* (Our Father Jesus of the Holy Torment) to commemorate the one that was lost in 1931. It too was made by Francisco Palma Burgos (and was his last work).

The Brotherhood has primarily spiritual and religious objectives, rather than being engaged in social projects like other Málaga brotherhoods. While the public witness of penitence on Holy Thursday is its most visible act, throughout the year the Brotherhood holds weekly masses and promotes devotions such as the Rosary, the Stations of the Cross, Exposition of the Blessed Sacrament, etc. Its history is also linked, inevitably, with the legend of the bandit Cristóbal Ruiz, called 'El Zamarrilla'. Born in 1796 in Igualeja, he led a gang of bandits dedicated to highway robbery. El Zamarrilla owes that nickname to the cross that the first inhabitants of the Trinidad neighbourhood had built at the end of Calle Mármoles, in a large uninhabited area where a medicinal herb called zamarrilla grew in abundance. El Zamarrilla, pursued by agents of the Crown, had a girlfriend in the barrio of La Trinidad whom he visited in order to obtain some food. He confided to her his intention to lie low for a while and asked her to take an oath of fidelity. She did so, giving him the white rose she wore in her hair.

However, he had been spotted visiting her house and someone tipped off the agents. With his escape from the city blocked, he sought refuge in the hermitage and approached the Virgen de la Amargura. The irony of the situation should not be lost on us. This hermitage was the place where people undertaking the long, and then dangerous, journey to Antequera would come to pray for protection — protection from bandits like El Zamarrilla. Yet now that same bandit implored the Virgin's protection for himself, hiding himself under her cloak.

The Civil Guard made a thorough search including, it is said, the Virgin's mantle, but they could not find him anywhere. He seemed to have vanished as if the earth had swallowed him. Zamarrilla, when certain that the members of the guard had left, came out of his hiding place to stand before the Virgin. He took the white rose and, placing it against the breast of the image, used his dagger to attach it, and then watched it slowly turn red, as if dyed with blood. It is said that El Zamarrilla believed that the Virgin had changed the white colour of the rose for a bright red colour to lead him also to participate in the forgiveness of sins by the death of Christ on the Cross, because that colour red was the symbol of his redeeming blood. Thereafter, he gave himself to prayer and the assistance of the poor.

One afternoon, many years later, when the day was almost dark, Zamarrilla was walking along the path that took him, as it did every year, to the Virgen de la Amargura, and he was set upon by robbers. Finding no money or valuables, they stabbed him to death. In his hands, he held a red rose — his annual offering to the Virgin. As he died, it miraculously changed from red to a white so dazzling that not even his blood stained it. To this day, the image of the Virgin in procession wears a corsage of scarlet roses above her heart.

 Real y Excelentísima Hermandad de Nuestro Padre Jesús del Santo Suplicio, Santísimo Cristo de los Milagros y María Santísima de la Amargura Coronada (Zamarrilla)

Royal and Most Excellent Brotherhood of Our Father Jesus of the Holy Torment, Holy Christ of Miracles and Holy Mary of the Crowned Bitterness (Zamarrilla)

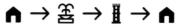

⛪ Ermita de Zamarrilla (Calle Martínez Maldonado 7) 🏠 Calle Martínez Maldonado 5

✝ Holy Christ of Miracles by Francisco Palma Burgos (1939) on a *trono* of varnished wood (Workshops of the Caballero Brothers, 2006).

🎺 Band of Bugles and Drums 'Our Lady of Mount Carmel' (Málaga)

🏛 Holy Mary of the Crowned Bitterness by Antonio Gutierrez de Leon y Martínez (19th century) on a gold throne by Manuel de los Ríos (2003). The Reverend Mothers of Adoration embroidered the canopy between 1978 and 1988 restoring previous work by the Trinitarian nuns. The mantle was embroidered in 1977 in the workshops of Esperanza Elena Caro.

🎺 Music Band of the Brotherhood of Zamarrilla (Málaga).

Misericordia (Mercy)

This Brotherhood is known among *malagueños* as 'El Chiquito' ('The Kid'), because the life-size *Cristo* is carried on such an enormous gilded throne that it consequently looks very small. Like many in Málaga, the Brotherhood is a Fusion of Brotherhoods starting with that of the *Cristo de la Misericordia* (Christ of Mercy), founded in 1864. After the decline of the brotherhoods of Málaga at the end of the 19th century following repeated disentailments and exclaustrations of ecclesiastical property and patrimony, it was reorganized in 1919 and merged with *Nuestra Señora de los Dolores*, and the *Santísimo Cristo de Ánimas*, an 18th Brotherhood from the neighbouring parish of San Pedro that had closed and merged with El Carmen. The dedication of the Virgin was changed to 'Gran Poder' (Great Power).

In the events of 1931, the Brotherhood lost their *Cristo* which had been the work of the 17th-century master *imaginero* José de Mora. His great altarpiece in the Church of the Carmen was also destroyed, though the Marian image itself was saved. The *encierro* (return to the *Casa hermandad* and enclosure) is a spectacle watched by large crowds in the *barrio* of El Perchel. The *hombres de tronos* turn to make the images — Christ and his mother — face one another, lifting the thrones aloft (a move known as a '*pulso*').

 Real Ilustre y Venerable Cofradía de Nuestro Padre Jesús de la Misericordia, Santo Cristo de Ánimas, Nuestra Señora del Gran Poder y San Juan de Dios

Royal, Illustrious and Venerable Brotherhood of Our Father Jesus of Mercy, Holy Christ of Souls, Our Lady of Great Power and Saint John of God

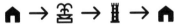

🏛 Parroquia de Nuestra Señora del Carmen (Calle Plaza de Toros Vieja 23)
🏠 Plaza de la Misericordia 8

🚶 Our Father Jesus of Mercy by José Navas–Parejo (Málaga, 1944) on a *trono* of carved and gilt wood by Cristóbal Velasco (1966). The iconography shows Jesus falling under the weight of the Cross.

🎺 *Cruz de Guía*: Band of Bugles and Drums of the Royal Fire Department (Málaga). *Cristo*: Band of Bugles and Drums 'Our Father Jesus Captive' (Málaga).

🖼 Our Lady of Great Power (Anonymous, 18th century) restored by Luis Álvarez Duarte (1979) on a goldwork throne by the Angulo workshops (1966)

🎺 Music Band 'Maestro Paco Tenorio' (Arriate, Málaga)

Paso y Esperanza (Passion & Hope)

The origin of this Archconfraternity is related to the arrival in Málaga of the Dominicans (Order of Preachers), who founded the convent of Santo Domingo and San Carlos in 1494, seven years after the *reconquista*. The Dominican friars had the papal mandate and privilege (granted by Pope Gregory X in 1274) to venerate and promote devotion to the Holy Name of Jesus, so they erected altars dedicated to the 'Sweet Name of Jesus' in all churches of the Order. The foundation of the Brotherhood of the Name of Jesus probably dates from 8 May 1567, when an agreement between the friars and the penitential brotherhood for the transfer of the first chapel was signed. The first reference to the Brotherhood of *El Paso* is found in a papal bull of 1561, while the Brotherhood of Hope was founded in 1641.

In the 19th century, two political events greatly affected the Archconfraternity: the Napoleonic invasion, during which they lost the images of Saint John and Saint Veronica; and the disentailment of Mendizábal (1836), which led to other losses and instability in the daily life of the members. The fraternity revived at the beginning of the 20th century, but during the Burning of Convents in 1931, rioters entered the parish of Santo Domingo and destroyed the images of Our Lady of Solitude, the Virgin of Bethlehem and the Christ of Mena. When they arrived at the Chapel of Hope, the images had already been hidden in the crypt and although the entrance was hidden, they began to smash the altar and discovered it. The image of the *Dulce Nazareno del Paso*, an object of almost 400 years' fervent devotion in the town, disappeared without a trace and a large part of the patrimony of the archconfraternity went up in flames. The same fate would have befallen the *Virgen de la Esperanza* had it not been for the brave actions of the 16-year-old Esperanto brothers who managed to sneak into the church and, gathering up what they could, took their haul to hide it in an apothecary shop on the Calle Cerrojo.

Since the 1940s, when the *Dulce Nombre de Jesús* and *María Santísima de la Esperanza* process, a rosemary carpet is laid out so that they 'bless' it as they advance. In the Plaza de la Constitución, the *Dulce Nombre de Jesús Nazareno del Paso* has blessed the people of Málaga with its articulated arm (like that of *El Rico*') for more than 400 years. The Infanta Elena (eldest sister of King Felipe VI) was named Maid of Honour to the Blessed Virgin in 1993 and deposited the Sash of Captain General of the Armed Forces of her father King Juan Carlos to replace that of Alfonso XIII which had disappeared in the events of 1931. This sash is worn by the Virgin in her procession — another explicit link with the military that not all are happy with.

The brotherhood's music band and band of bugles and drums are both prominent throughout *Semana Santa*, accompanying not only *Paso y Esperanza*, but other brotherhoods too. They make an appearance every day. The vast *trono* of the Virgin is the heaviest in *Semana Santa*, weighing 5,700 kg and requiring 257 *hombres de trono*.

The *templo* of the Brotherhood has, since 1988, been a chapel built by the brothers themselves, next to their *casa hermandad* on the El Perchel side of the Puente de la Esperanza bridge. Despite its very recent vintage, the chapel is one of the most striking religious buildings in Málaga. When the structure was first 'completed' it was little more than a bare shell — an apse (the large arch over the altar) and a barrel vault rectangular nave (the main body of the chapel) but over the years it has been beautifully decorated with gilding and frescoes, and a large stained glass window of the Annunciation (by Mauméjean of Madrid). The barrel vault that covers the main nave is painted with a scene entitled 'The Apotheosis of the Virgin Mary', painted in oils by García Ibáñez (1992–93). Bespoke tapestries were woven in Brussels; alluding to the Litany of Our Lady.

In accordance with the original principles of the Archconfraternity, the church has a *columbarium* under the main altar where the remains of deceased brothers rest. The bell tower was completed in 1991 and has five bronze bells whose names correspond to significant dedications in the city. In increasing order of size, they are *Santo Tomás* (Aquinas), due to the link with the University; the *Virgen del Carmen*, the *Virgen de la Victoria, María Santísima de la Esperanza* and *Dulce Nombre de Jesús*. The exterior of the *templo* is decorated with six *andaluz* tile murals that show various scenes from the Gospels: the Incarnation, the Visitation, the Nativity, the Wedding at Cana, the Coronation of the Virgin, and Mary next to the Cross. In all of them, the figure of Our Lady wears green, like the titular image of Holy Mary of Hope.

On May 28, 1998, the chapel was raised to the dignity of a minor basilica by Pope John Paul II, by virtue of the papal brief '*Dulcis Nomen Jesus a Sanctitatis*'. The other minor basilicas in Málaga are the Cathedral and the Sanctuary of Our Lady of the Victory.

Pontificia y Real Archicofradía del Dulce Nombre de Jesús Nazareno del Paso y María Santísima de la Esperanza Coronada

Pontifical and Royal Archconfraternity of the Sweet Name of Jesus of Nazareth of the Passion and Crowned Holy Mary of Hope

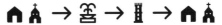

♠ Basílica del Dulce Nombre de Jesús (Calle San Jacinto 1) ♠ Calle San Jacinto 1

⚔ Our Father Jesus of Nazareth of the Passion by Mariano Benlliure (1935) on a *trono* designed by the architect Fernando Guerrero–Strachan and made of gilded wood by Francisco Palma Burgos.

🎺 *Cruz de Guía*: Band of Bugles and Drums of the Archconfraternity of 'Paso y la Esperanza' (Málaga). *Cristo*: Youth Music Band 'Miraflores–Gibraljaire' (Málaga).

🏛 Crowned Holy Mary of Hope (Anonymous, 17th c., but often attributed to Pedro de Mena) restored by Adrián Risueño after the events of 1931 and later by Luis Álvarez Duarte, on a gilded wooden *trono* by Adrián Risueño, Andrés Cabello Requena and Luis Ramos Rosas (1943–1949). The very large (7.5 metre) green procession mantle was embroidered by the Reverend Mothers of Adoration (1953).

🎺 Music Band of the Archconfraternity of 'Paso y la Esperanza' (Málaga)

Clemencia (Clemency)

⚠ This Brotherhood does not currently have a public procession during Semana Santa but has established a procession on Passion Saturday (the day before Palm Sunday). It is included in this section, however, because it always used to appear on Holy Thursday, and may do so again in the future. It was a brotherhood established in response to the burning of the convents of 1931 and was formerly known as the *Cofradía del Santísimo Cristo Mutilado* (the Most Holy Mutilated Christ) — details that are pertinent to its loss of status and subsequent rehabilitation.

At the end of the 17th century, Jerónimo Gómez de Hermosilla was commissioned to create a crucifixion image to preside over the High Altar of the Parish of the Sagrario in the Cathedral precinct. Between July and September 1936, the Sagrario was attacked by Republicans during the second Burning of Churches and Convents that took place during the Civil War. The attackers were unable to destroy the image due to its height above the altar, but they were able to damage the left foot and hack off the right leg.

The desecrated image was devoutly collected by a group of injured former fighters on the Nationalist side with the intention of founding a military, penitential and processional brotherhood. Due to the state of the image, the brotherhood had to obtain permission from the Holy See to worship the Mutilated Christ. On February 16, 1939, at the initiative of Fernando Roldán Andreu, a brotherhood was erected under the title of 'Brotherhood of the Holy Mutilated Christ'. That same year they entered the Association of Brotherhoods and had their first processional outing on the night of Holy Thursday.

From its creation until the 1970s, the Brotherhood experienced a continuous boom, reaching more than 15,000 brothers, many of them ex-servicemen. On Holy Thursday in 1976, the image was paraded for the last time on a temporary mahogany wooden litter. General Francisco Franco had died the previous year and due to the presumed closeness between the brotherhood and the regime, it was thought prudent to cease the external cult.

In the 1990s, the brotherhood requested permission to participate in the processions, but this was denied because the image was considered tantamount to a Francoist symbol of the past that could cause hurt to people who did not feel represented by it. For a time, the Brotherhood stood their ground and refused to renew the image (i.e. restore it to the state it was in before being vandalized) and so their participation in *Semana Santa* was limited to a procession of the Stations of the Cross inside the Cathedral. The first decade of the 21st century, however, saw a change of heart on the part of the brothers of 'El Mutilado', and a new spirit of reconciliation and humility.

They adopted, in March 2016, a Marian image under the title of 'Santa María Madre de la Divina Providencia'. The Mutilated Christ was withdrawn from worship in June 2016 and sent to Sevilla for restoration by Juan Manuel Miñarro López, Professor of Sculpture at the School of Fine Arts. Significantly, this was not a repair, but a restoration to its pre-1936 state which was achieved using 3D-imaging technology.

In 2020 the Virgin of Divine Providence was transferred to the convent of the 'Hermanas de la Cruz' (Sisters of the Cross, near the Atarazanas Market) due to the closure of the Sagrario for restoration. At the end of September of that same year, the restored image of the (no longer) Mutilated Christ was approved by the Brotherhood council and rededicated as 'The Christ of Clemency'. On October 4, 2020, with the Sagrario still closed, the image of the *Santísimo Cristo de la Clemencia* was placed in the Cathedral, symbolizing a significant rapprochement between the Diocesan authorities and the Brotherhood.

In 2022, on the afternoon of Passion Saturday (the day before Palm Sunday), the Brotherhood left the church of the Sacred Heart (Iglesia del Sagrado Corazón, Calle Compañía) in procession to make its first Penitence Station in the Cathedral for forty-seven years, accompanied by the Band of Bugles and Drums of *Paso & Esperanza*. There had been no time to make tunics and capirotes, so the penitentes wore black suits. The quasi-military garb of the heyday of the Franco regime was conspicuously absent. The progress was serious — the *capataz* called for silence and gave instructions that the throne not be 'rocked'. The floral carpet beneath the Cross was made up of 1,500 purple orchids (the colour of Lenten penance) and a tangle of thorns (the symbol of evil) was placed at the foot of the Cross as if trampled under Christ's feet.

In many ways, the procession was a perfect example of the nature of penitence during *Se-*

mana Santa. For all that the Brotherhood of the Mutilated Christ had been born out of devotion to the Crucified Lord, it had also been born out of anger and sustained by vengeful pride (against those who had mutilated the image). Christ himself — the real, flesh and blood Jesus — forgave those who condemned, scourged and crucified him, yet for years, the '*mutilados*' were unable to forgive those who had damaged a 'mere' wooden statue, and for this, they were effectively placed under an interdict. The Risen Christ still has his wounds, but they have become part of his glory. Eventually, the Brotherhood grasped this and were able to look beyond the mutilated figure on a Cross towards the deeper mystery to which he points: the mystery of new life.

Viernes Santo (Good Friday)

This is the commemoration of Christ's Crucifixion, the most solemn day of the Church's year. Catholics are bound to fast (which in effect means eating no more than two modest snacks) and abstain from meat. Mass is not, and cannot be, celebrated on this day. Instead, the 'Liturgy of the Passion' is celebrated.

The churches are empty, with no cross or candles on the altar. Instead of a simple Gospel reading, the entire Passion from Saint John's Gospel is read, with different people reading (or singing) the different 'parts'. A veiled wooden cross, or crucifix, is brought into the church. Three times, the veil is partially removed and the verse '*Ecce lignum Crucis, in quo salus mundi pependit*' ('Behold the wood of the Cross, on which hung the salvation of the world') is sung, and the people genuflect (drop to one knee) and reply, '*Venite adoremus!*' (Come let us adore!). After this, the congregation come forward to venerate the Cross individually.

Because no Mass is celebrated today, the Blessed Sacrament consecrated the previous evening is distributed. At the conclusion, all depart in silence, without ceremony.

Monte Calvario (Mount Calvary)

The Hermitage of '*Monte Calvario*' (Mount Calvary — the name also given to the hill behind the Sanctuary of Santa María de la Victoria, below the Gibralfaro Mountain) was erected for the first time by the *Mínimos* friars as a wayside shrine in 1495. On 25 May 1656, the property and the use of it were donated forever by the Minims to their 'Third Order' (associated lay brotherhood) which is known today as the Brotherhood of Mount Calvary. The brotherhood helped to popularize the devotion known as the 'Stations of the Cross' each Friday, walking the steep, narrow path between the Hermitage and the Sanctuary. This cult continued to be celebrated throughout the 19th and 20th centuries. Like so many places, the hermitage was looted and burned during the Civil War (the so-called 'Second Burning of the Convents'), although the chapel was by then already in a poor state of repair.

In 1970, an image of the Recumbent Christ (*Cristo Yacente*) of Peace and Unity was acquired, as were images of the mystery of the Sacred Shroud. In 1977 a group of young brothers gathered around the image of the Recumbent Christ of Peace and Unity and Santa María del Monte Calvario with the intention of reorganizing the Brotherhood of Monte Calvario. For over a decade, they processed unofficially (before *Semana Santa*) from the Sanctuary of La Victoria, using thrones and other items lent to them by established brotherhoods. In 1981 their rules were approved and the brotherhood canonically (re)erected. In the same year, they joined the Association of Brotherhoods and they followed the official route for the first time in 1982.

In the early hours of 26 February 2006, a fire broke out in the Hermitage of Calvario, causing significant damage to both images. The *Cristo* was partially burned and only the head of the Virgin remained (saved because it was made of terracotta, not wood). In 2007 the restored sacred images of the Most Holy Recumbent Christ of Peace and Unity and Our Lady of Faith and Comfort were presented. The restoration was carried out by the *imaginero* and academic Juan Manuel Miñarro (who would later restore the *Cristo Mutilado*).

The image of the *Virgen* is translated a week before Good Friday, while the translation of the *Cristo* occurs immediately before the start of the procession proper, taking the form of the Stations of the Cross prayed between the Hermitage and the Sanctuary. The *Cruz de Guía* is a reproduction of the cross-reliquary venerated in the chapel of the Santuario de la Victoria and bears a splinter of the relic of the True Cross (*Lignum Crucis*) and a relic of Saint Francis of Paola. Therefore, the brother who carries it wears a humeral veil as a sign of respect, and the Cross is continually incensed by a server who walks backwards to do so.

 Muy Antigua y Venerable Hermandad de Via Crucis del Santo Cristo del Calvario y Señor San Francisco de Paula y Cofradía de Nazarenos del Santísimo Cristo Yacente de la Paz y de la Unidad en el Misterio de su Sagrada Mortaja, Nuestra Señora de Fe y Consuelo, Santa María del Monte Calvario y San Manuel González

Very Ancient and Venerable Brotherhood of the Way of the Cross of the Holy Christ of Calvary and Lord Saint Francis of Paola and the Brotherhood of Nazarenes of the Most Holy Recumbent Christ of Peace and of the Unity in the Mystery of his Sacred Shroud, Our Lady of Faith and Consolation, Holy Mary of Mount Calvary and Saint Manuel González

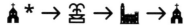

* The *Cristo* leaves the *templo*. Both images then leave The basilica of Santa María de la Victoria for the procession proper.

🏛 Ermita del Monte Calvario (Calle Amargura) – Calle Fernando el Católico 28

✝ Holy Recumbent Christ by Antonio Eslava Rubio (1970), restored by Juan Manuel Miñarro (2006). Other figures in the sculptural group are Mary Magdalene (Anonymous, 19th century), Mary Salome, Joseph of Arimathea and Nicodemus by Juan Manuel García Palomo (1993–1995), and Mary of Clopas by Juan Ventura (1980). The image of the Virgin of Faith and Consolation is anonymous (1770-1771). The throne is by Antonio Martín (2007–2010) with imagery by Manuel Carmona . The *cajillo* represents the Stations of the Cross and other moments from the Gospels.

🎺 Music Band 'Our Lady of Solitude' (Málaga)

🖼 Holy Mary of Mount Calvary (Anonymous, Granada, acquired by the Brotherhood in 1941). In 1972 it was completely remodelled by the *imaginero* Luis Álvarez Duarte and re-polychromed by Juan Manuel Miñarro (2001). Saint John the Evangelist is the work of Antonio Eslava (1965).

🎺 Music Band 'Our Lady of Peace' (Málaga)

Descendimiento (Descent)

This brotherhood traces its history back to an old Augustinian brotherhood of the 16th century that venerated the *Virgen de las AnguStias* (Our Lady of Anguish), and over the centuries a number of subsidiary brotherhoods have flowed from it. At the beginning of the 20th century, the brotherhood was refounded in the Santuario de la Victoria, under the invocation of the Sacred Descent and Holy Transfer of his Divine Body to the Sepulchre. During the burning of convents, it lost its images, so it had to be reorganized again in 1977.

The brotherhood is the only one that approaches the *recorrido oficial* from the east and processes along the Paseo del Parque (actually parallel to it on the Calle Guillén Sotelo) so has the peculiarity of requesting permission from the Town Hall with a symbolic bow. Its canonical seat is located in the chapel of the Noble Hospital, a foundation that owes its existence to a legacy of Dr Joseph Noble, an English doctor who practised in Málaga and died of Cholera in 1861. His wife and children applied their inheritance to the construction of an auxiliary hospital that would be able to attend to the citizens of the Malagueta district as well as sailors that disembarked in the port of Málaga.

Fervorosa Hermandad Sacramental y Real Cofradía de Nazarenos del Sagrado Descendimiento de Nuestro Señor Jesucristo, Nuestra Señora del Santo Sudario y María Santísima de las Angustias

Fervent Sacramental Brotherhood and Royal Brotherhood of Nazarenes of the Sacred Descent of Our Lord Jesus Christ, Our Lady of the Holy Shroud and Holy Mary of Anguish

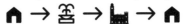

🜊 Capilla del Sagrado Descendimiento del Hospital Noble (Plaza del General Torrijos 2) 🛖 Calle Manuel Martín Estévez 6

† Descent of Christ by Luis Ortega Bru (1980) representing the moment when Jesus is taken down from the Cross by Nicodemus and Joseph of Arimathea (corresponding to the XIII station of the *Via Crucis*). The carvings of Joseph of Arimathea and Nicodemus are also by Luis Ortega Bru. Our Lady of the Holy Shroud is by his son, Luis Ángel Ortega León (1987). Saint John, Mary Magdalene, Mary of Clopas and Mary Salome are by Ricardo Rivera (1984–1985). The *trono* is by Julián Sánchez (1989).

🎺 Youth Music Band 'Cruz del Humillidero' (Málaga)

🖼 Holy Mary of Anguish by Antonio Castillo Lastrucci (acquired in 1978) renewed by Luis Álvarez Duarte (2011). The gold–work *trono* is designed by Juan Antonio Sánchez López and made by Santos Campanario (2006).

🎺 Music Band 'Maestro Infantes' (Los Barrios, Cádiz).

Dolores de San Juan (Sorrows of Saint John)

A Sacramental Brotherhood of San Juan was founded in 1487, becoming an Archconfraternity in 1540. In 1688 a brotherhood called the 'Penitential Brotherhood of Our Lady of Sorrows' was approved. In 1801, a Royal Order of King Carlos IV combined the Penitential Brotherhood and the Sacramental Archconfraternity of San Juan, creating the brotherhood as we know it today: The Sacramental Archconfraternity of Our Lady of Sorrows ('*Nuestra Señora de los Dolores*'). In 1868 it became a brotherhood '*culto interno*' (*i.e.* it no longer engaged in the public celebration of *Semana Santa*). It lost its images in the burnings of 1931 and 1936, receiving the donation of a new *Dolorosa* in 1941.

It became active again in the 20th century when a group of young people decided to reorganize it (1978). It stands out for being a sober, silent and mourning brotherhood, typical of Good Friday. The Society of Jesus (Jesuits) and Sisters of the Cross are honorary Elder Brothers and Elder Sisters and the latter sing a motet from their convent (on the Plaza Arriola, near the Atarazanas Market) as the procession passes; a tradition that began in 1978, and one of the most moving moments of the week.

 Muy Antigua, Venerable y Pontificia Archicofradía Sacramental de Nazarenos del Santísimo Cristo de la Redención y Nuestra Señora de los Dolores

Very Old, Venerable and Pontifical Sacramental Archconfraternity of Nazarenes of the Holy Christ of the Redemption and Our Lady of Sorrows

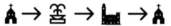

⛪ Parroquia de San Juan Bautista (Calle San Juan 3) 🚩 Pasaje de Nuestra Señora de los Dolores de San Juan 6

✝ Holy Christ of the Redemption by Juan Manuel Miñarro (Sevilla, 1987) on a *trono* designed by Fernando Prini, carved by Manuel Toledano and with imagery by José María Ruiz Montes (2013).

🖼 Our Lady of Sorrows (Attributed to Antonio Asensio de la Cerda, Málaga, 1760–71) on a *trono* by Villarreal workshops with imagery by Carlos Valle and Suso de Marcos. Her mantle is from the workshops of Manuel Mendoza and Salvador Aguilar.

🎺 Both thrones process without bands, but each set of *penitentes* is followed by a '*capilla musical*' ('musical chapel' — nowadays usually a chamber group playing woodwind instruments).

Amor y Caridad (Love & Charity)

The Brotherhood of Love is a 20th-century brotherhood that began in 1923 when a group gathered in the convent chapel of the *Agustinas Descalzas* (Barefoot Augustinian Nuns) to venerate the image of the crucified Christ and Our Lady of Sorrows. Among its founders were brothers from the brotherhoods of *Monte Calvario* and *Santo Sepulcro*.

The brotherhood was canonically erected in the Santuario de la Victoria, participating in *Semana Santa* for the first time in 1924, making its debut on Good Friday. Its titular images were saved during the burning of convents, largely thanks to the fact that the Sanctuary of Our Lady of The Victory had a military hospital nearby in those days. In 1948 they moved to the military chapel of that same Military Hospital, but it fell into disrepair and they had to move again, eventually settling once again in the Basilica of Santa María de la Victoria; the canonical seat to this day. This brotherhood had ups and downs in the last third of the 20th century, succumbing to a period of instability between the 1970s and the 1990s from which, thankfully, they now seem to have emerged largely due to the energy and tenacity of their younger members.

Real Cofradía del Santísimo Cristo del Amor y Nuestra Señora de la Caridad

Royal Brotherhood of the Holy Christ of Love and Our Lady of Charity

⛪ → ⛲ → ⛩ → 🏠

⛪ Basílica y Real Santuario de Santa María de la Victoria (Plaza Santuario)
🏠 Calle Fernando el Católico 40

✝ Holy Christ of Love (and the Dolorous Virgin at his feet) by Fernando Ortiz (Málaga, 18th century) on a gilded wooden throne by José Ávila and Pedro Román (1954).

📯 Band of Bugles and Drums of the Archconfraternity of the Passion and the Hope (Málaga).

👑 The Virgin of Charity by Francisco Buiza (1947). on a gilded wooden throne by Manuel Caballero Farfán (1987–88). The canopy was embroidered in the workshops of Leopoldo Padilla (1946) and the mantle (by the same artist) in gold thread on black velvet (1946–48).

📯 Music Band 'Maestro Eloy García' of the Archconfraternity of the Expiration (Málaga).

Traslado y Soledad (Transfer & Solitude)

The current Brotherhood of Transfer corresponds to a seventeenth-century one founded by a group of bakers that was later reorganized in 1918. Originally it venerated the Virgin of Solitude in the Church of the Aurora María, processing for the first time in the middle of the 18th century.

The Transfer suffered enormous losses during the burning of convents, so new titular images were commissioned and blessed in the 1940s. The Christ of the Holy Transfer has a sculptural group representing the scene of the body of the Redeemer in the arms of Joseph of Arimathea, Nicodemus and 'Stephen the Shepherd'. You will look in vain if you search for Stephen the Shepherd in either the canonical or apocryphal Gospels. It seems that the sculptor, Pedro Moreira López, simply invented him as a way of leaving his mark on the work. The sculptural group was renewed in 2011 by Israel Cornejo Sánchez who chose to keep the fictional Stephen, while adding the holy women Mary Salome, Mary of Clopas and

Mary Magdalene. In their procession, the section of the Roman Guard and the sandals of the *penitentes* are noteworthy. The latter is an almost lost tradition of *Semana Santa* in Málaga and only the Transfer has managed to maintain it with consistency.

 Real, Ilustre y Venerable Hermandad del Santo Traslado y Nuestra Señora de la Soledad

Royal, Illustrious and Venerable Brotherhood of the Holy Transfer and Our Lady of Solitude

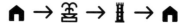

⛪ Parroquia de San Pablo (Calle Trinidad 35) 🏠 Calle Trinidad 72

✝ Holy Christ of the Holy Transfer by Pedro Moreira López (1949) with a sculptural group composed of Joseph of Arimathea, Nicodemus, Stephen the Shepherd *[sic]* and the three Marys by Israel Cornejo Sánchez (Málaga, 2011 — replacing earlier sculptures by Pedro Moreira). The gilded wooden *trono* is from the workshops of Rafael Ruiz Liébana (2008) following the model of the previous one, made by Pedro Pérez Hidalgo.

🎺 *Cruz de Guía*: Band of Bugles and Drums of the Royal Fire Department (Málaga). *Cristo*: Band of Bugles and Drums 'Our Father Jesus Captive' (Málaga).

🖼 Our Lady of Solitude also by Pedro Moreira López (1945), following the model of the previous carving once attributed to Pedro de Mena but probably by Fernando Ortiz. The gold-work trono is by the Angulo workshops (1958).

🎺 Symphonic Band 'Virgin of La Trinidad' (Málaga).

Piedad (Pietà)

The brotherhood of *La Piedad* was created in 1926 by a group of postmen in the church of La Merced. This explains its nickname — '*Los Carteros*' — 'The Postmen'. They chose as their titular image '*La Piedad*' (by Francisco Palma García) — a traditional representation of the Blessed Virgin with the body of her dead son in her lap, after he has been lowered from the cross. For this reason, while the *castellano* word '*piedad*' can be translated as mercy, pity, piety or compassion, the most accurate 'English' translation is 'Pietà' because in this case, it describes not only a virtue but an artistic representation and composition.

La Piedad joined the group of Holy Week Brotherhoods in 1928, processing on Good Friday the following year. They lost practically everything in 1931 and the brotherhood was dissolved. However, in 1940 another group of postmen reactivated the brotherhood. The commission for the new image was entrusted to the son of the original sculptor. In 1942 the Pietà returned to *Semana Santa* with a sculptural group on board and has processed ever since. The procession is noted for its calm austerity.

The Brotherhood needed to find a new *templo* after their reactivation, and after some nomadic years, they eventually settled in the Capilla de Molinillo. The Molinillo Chapel is an 18th-century street chapel located in the *barrio* of El Molinillo in the north of the city (named after the many mills — *molinos* — that once existed there). It was constructed as a chapel dedicated to the recitation of the Rosary and later became a centre of devotion to the Holy

Cross. However, by the 1940s, the chapel was walled up due to its parlous state of conservation. In 1952 it was given to the Brotherhood of Mercy of Málaga who took on responsibility for its restoration and upkeep.

What you see nowadays (and it is a beautiful building of enchanting simplicity, well worth looking into) is actually a stone-by-stone reconstruction of the original after it had to be moved (all of seven metres) from its former location in 1999. During the deconstruction, exterior geometric wall paintings were uncovered and these have now been restored.

 Real Hermandad de Nuestra Señora de la Piedad
Royal Brotherhood of Our Lady of Mercy

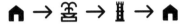

🏠 Capilla del Molinillo (Calle de la Cruz del Molinillo 29) 🏠 Calle Alderete 3

🔔 † Pietà by Francisco Palma Burgos (Málaga, 1941) following the model of his father, Francisco Palma García. The *trono* is of varnished wood designed by Antonio Téllez de Rivera and José Morales García, and fabricated by Rafael Ruiz Liébana, Francisco Martín and Carlos Castillejos.

🎺 *Cruz de Guía*: Four muffled drums of the Band of Cornets and Drums of Our Lady of Mount Carmel (Huelin, Málaga). *Trono*: Music Band of the Brotherhood of Zamarrilla (Málaga).

Sepulcro (Sepulchre)

This is the 'official' brotherhood of the City of Málaga. It was founded in 1893 by well-to-do members of the parish of the Santuario de la Victoria, though it was not until 21 October 1894 when Cardinal Spínola approved the Rules of the Brotherhood that it was officially constituted. In 1899 the invocation of Our Lady of Solitude was incorporated, and it made its first processional exit during *Semana Santa* to great popular acclaim. At a time when many traditional and older brotherhoods were in the doldrums after the disentailments and exclaustrations of the 19th century, here was a brotherhood established by middle-class professionals that processed with a certain confident grandeur. This was something that the civil authorities were keen to support, even providing financial support. To this day, all the major institutions of the city are represented in the cortège of the Holy Sepulchre.

With the arrival of the 20th century, the Holy Sepulchre seemed to enter a golden age and continued to receive an economic grant from the civil authorities. It was a co-founder of the group of Holy Week brotherhoods. In 1914 a brother donated an anonymous '*Dolorosa*' image (that would be destroyed in 1936). In 1927 the brotherhood premièred the spectacular catafalque that it still carries. This splendour was somewhat dimmed during the Civil War, but it soon raised its head again and increased the assets of the brotherhood. In 1967 it moved to the Parish of Ciriaco and Paula which it adopted as the new *sede canónica*. In 1996, and after protracted negotiations, the purchase of a plot of land on Calle Alcazabilla was concluded and an agreement reached with the *ayuntamiento* for the construction of the brotherhood house and museum. The new *casa hermandad* opened in 2002. In 2014 the canonical seat was transferred to the Abbey of *Santa Ana de Recoletas Bernardas del Císter*.

As the official brotherhood of the city, its procession stands out among the other brotherhoods during *Semana Santa*. Part of the procession is made up of the municipal corporation, with the youngest councillor carrying the city's banner. Despite its reputation as the brotherhood of '*hidalgos*' ('*hidalgo*' being a contraction of '*hijo de algo*' — 'son of someone' — in other words, a privileged person), the Brotherhood's commitment to its social action project is front and centre. As long ago as 1982 they amended their constitutions to decree that a proportion of their annual income (15% of Ordinary income, 20% of extraordinary income, and 20% of any surplus) would automatically be assigned to their charitable concerns (currently the provision of a below-market-cost commissary for hundreds of low-income families). They stole a march on other brotherhoods when it came to allowing supporters to donate to their charitable work via their website. They also raise funds by selling gift items — from pens, pins and thimbles for a couple of euros each, all the way up to official Brotherhood ties for €25. Another way in which they raise funds for their social action work is by opening their roof terrace bar (when available) to non-members. Booking is essential, but the location (overlooking the *Teatro Romano* and the Alcazaba) is one the most enviable in Málaga (see the entry on p. 221 for more details).

Real Hermandad de Nuestro Padre Jesús del Santo Sepulcro y Nuestra Señora de la Soledad

Royal Brotherhood of Our Father Jesus of the Holy Sepulchre and Our Lady of Solitude

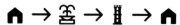

⛪ Abadía de Santa Ana de Recoletas Bernardas del Císter (Calle Abadía Santa Ana 5) 🏠 Calle Alcazabilla 5

✝ Our Father Jesus of the Holy Sepulchre by Nicolás Prados López (1938) on a *trono* made in the Granda workshops (1927) according to a design by Moreno Carbonero.

🎺 *Cruz de Guía*: Muffled Drums of the *hermandad*. *Cristo*: Municipal Music Band of Málaga.

🖼 Our Lady of Solitude by José Merino Román (1932) acquired by the brotherhood in 1938. The gold–work *trono* is by Manuel Seco Velasco (1950). The Virgin's mantle was embroidered by the Reverend Mothers of Adoration (1922).

🎺 Music Band of the Archconfraternity of the Passion and the Hope (Málaga)

Servitas (Servites)

The Venerable Third Order of Servants of Holy Mary of Sorrows (*Venerable Orden Tercera de Siervos de María Santísima de los Dolores*), known as '*Servitas*' (Servites), is a corporation that does not belong to the group of Holy Week brotherhoods in Málaga, although it is an honorary member. The Servite Religious Order was founded in the city of Florence in the early 13th century and established its first convent in Spain in 1497 (in Teruel, Aragón). Subsequent foundations of friars and nuns (the 'first' and 'second' Orders) were made in the Kingdoms of Aragón and Valencia and the, by then, Principality of Catalonia. A group of tertiaries (members of the 'third' Order of lay adherents) was established in Málaga in 1695 and in 1739 they settled in the parish of San Felipe Neri, their canonical seat to this day.

Devotion to Our Lady of Sorrows increased in Málaga during the 19th-century cholera epidemics, and regular processions were made, becoming part of the *Semana Santa* celebrations from 1920. This image of *La Dolorosa* attributed to Pedro de Mena was destroyed in the Burning of Convents of 1931, though the current titular image (Holy Mary of Sorrows) was saved. During Holy Week in Málaga in 1937, it was the only *Virgen* that went on procession (the *Cristo* being the Holy Sepulchre).

The procession of the *Servitas* on Good Friday is one of the most solemn of *Semana Santa*, processing on a modest throne carried by fewer than 50 *hombres de trono* (making it by far the smallest *trono* in the city). During the procession, the members of the Order and their companions pray the '*Corona Dolorosa*' (the Servite Rosary which has seven sorrowful mysteries rather than the more usual five) through the streets of Málaga and street lights are extinguished to give prominence to the three-wick candles used to illuminate their progress. Another detail of the procession is that the *trono* does not use a bell but rather a 'dry bell' — a sort of wooden percussion box. This mirrors the liturgical practice of the Church, where bells fall silent after the singing of the *Gloria* on Holy Thursday and remain silent until the *Gloria* on Holy Saturday evening. The *penitentes* dress all in black velvet and wear the black scapular of the Servites (the scapular is a garment that forms part of a religious habit worn over the shoulders — hence the name — and members of the third order, or 'tertiaries', wear a devotional version in the form of a large square badge).

Venerable Orden Tercera de Siervos de María Santísima de los Dolores

Venerable Third Order of Servants of the Most Holy Mary of Sorrows

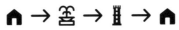

🏛 Parroquia de San Felipe Neri (Calle Guerrero 6) 🏠 Calle Cabello 20

🖼 Holy Mary of Sorrows by Fernando Ortiz (18th century) donated by the Count of Buenavista, replacing a work attributed to Pedro de Mena, paraded on a simple throne by Manuel Seco Velasco (1946).

🎺 Muffled Drums of the Band of Bugles and Drums of the Royal Fire Department (Málaga)

Sábado de Gloria (Holy Saturday)

There are no official processions on this day. Holy Saturday (Easter Saturday is a week later) is more or less a liturgical *dies non* ('non-day') insofar as during the hours of daylight Mass may not be celebrated and Holy Communion can only be received by someone in danger of death. It is a day of silent reflection because Christ lies dead in the tomb. As an ancient homily read as part of the Divine Office for Holy Saturday puts it:

> '*What is happening? Today there is a great silence over the earth,*
> *a great silence, and stillness, a great silence because the King sleeps;*

the earth was in terror and was still, because God slept in the flesh
and raised up those who were sleeping from the ages.
God has died in the flesh, and the underworld has trembled.'

Traditionally, this is the day upon which the Church reflects upon Christ's 'Harrowing of Hell', *viz.* his descent into the underworld to release the patriarchs who had waited for his coming. The Vigil and First Mass of Easter is celebrated at or after dusk, following the Jewish tradition of counting days from sunset to sunset.

Domingo de Resurrección (Easter Sunday)

This is the first day of the Easter Season, a festive period of fifty days which lasts until the Feast of Pentecost.

Resucitado (The Risen Lord)

The procession of the Resurrected has been carried out since 1915 when a Jesuit priest began the practice, but it was not until the grouping of brotherhoods that it took a definitive shape. This procession does not belong to a single brotherhood, but to them all.

Initially, the image of the Risen Christ used in the processions was loaned to them by the *Bernardas* (Cistercian) nuns who in those days had their convent on Calle de la Victoria. In the 1940s the *Agrupación* commissioned their own *Cristo* (and sculptural group) through a competition. It came out for the first time in Holy Week in 1946. This sculptural group of the Resurrected was somehow lost during the 1980s and not wanting to be left with a single image they decided to endow the parade with a Marian image during the 1990s. She appears under a canopy embroidered with the emblems of the historic parishes established after the *reconquista*. The procession is made up of 240 *nazarenos* drawn from all 43 of the brotherhoods attached to the group. They wear white tunics — like the 'young man dressed in a white robe' whom the women meet at the tomb on the first Easter Sunday (Mark 16:5) — and, because this is not penitential in character, walk bare-headed without the *capirote*.

 Agrupación de Cofradías de Semana Santa de Málaga
Association of Holy Week Brotherhoods of Málaga

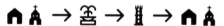

A ⌂ Iglesia de San Julián (calle Nosquera 16)

The Holy Risen Christ by José Capuz (1945) replacing an 18th century image by Fernando Ortiz loaned to the brotherhood by the Cistercian Monastery of the Assumption of Our Lady. Until the 1980s, the *Cristo* was carried together with a sculptural group formed by two Roman soldiers, but in recent decades it has appeared alone.

Cruz de Guía: Band of Bugles and Drums of the Royal Fire Department (Málaga). *Cristo*: Band of Bugles and Drums' Our Lady of Mount Carmel' (Málaga).

Holy Mary Queen of Heaven by Luis Álvarez Duarte (Sevilla, 1992).

Music Band 'Our Lady of Peace' (Málaga).

A Semana Santa Glossary

Alamares: The fringes of gold or silver yarn sewn onto the edges of the canopy over the throne of the *Virgen*.

Almohadilla: The cushion that is either attached to the poles or which the *hombres* put on their shoulder to bear the weight of the *trono*.

Alzacables: (*lit.* cable-lifter) A long stick that one of the brethren carries to lift obstacles in the way of the throne (such as electricity cables slung across the street).

Alzacola: The hidden aluminium frame placed on the rear of the *trono* of the *Virgen* for her mantle to rest upon.

Andas/Trono de traslado: The smaller throne designed for the transfer of the images between the canonical seat and the brotherhood house.

Ánforas: Silver or gold vases in which the flowers are placed on top of the throne.

Apagavelas: A candle snuffer (*lit.* 'candle quencher')

Arbotante: Literally 'flying buttresses', but in this case, a set of candle holders crowned with glass 'tulips' (very typical of Málaga) that stand at the corners of the thrones.

Báculo: (*lit.* 'staff') The insignia (depicted right) of a brother hood carried before them, like a Bishop's crozier. (Not to be confused with *'bacalao'* ('cod') — the nickname given to the brotherhood's standard (because it has the shape of a fish).

Bailar el trono: ('dancing of the throne') When the throne is caused to move (from left to right, higher and lower).

Barra de palio: The gold or silver rails that hold the canopy over the images of the Virgins (called a *'varal'* elsewhere in Spain).

Bastón: The ceremonial cane carried by the *hermano mayor* of the Brotherhood (like a military parade cane).

Berruguita: The executioner on the throne of *Nuestro Padre Jesús de la Puente del Cedrón*, so ugly that he is invoked to scare children, like a bogeyman.

Bocina: A symbolic reproduction of an ancient Roman tuba carried by the *nazarenos* in some processions.

Bola de cera: This 'ball of wax' is an important part of *Semana Santa* for children. Passing *nazarenos* allow their candles to drip onto small wax balls which steadily grow in size. Kids collect wax of different colours from different brotherhoods. These balls are treasured and added to each year and some are even bequeathed to younger siblings. A boy also might present his *bola* to a girl he likes (and vice versa) as a love-token.

Bulla: (*lit.* 'brawl' or 'ruckus') — the name given to the crowds of people that concentrate on certain streets on the processional route.

Camareras: (*lit.* 'waitresses') The group of women appointed by each brotherhood to attend to the Virgin's vesture. Only women are permitted to dress the images of Our Lady. Originally, this task was entrusted to nuns.

Campana de trono: A 'throne bell' (without a clapper) located in the centre of the front of the throne. It is struck by a hammer to indicate to the throne men when to lift, lower and move the throne.

Campanillero: The brother who rings the bell

Candelero: A rank of candles, usually on the throne of the Virgin

Caña: (*lit.* 'cane') An *alzacables* (*q.v.*)

Capirote: Alhough this word comes from the Latin '*cappa*' meaning 'hood', it has come to refer to the cone (*cucurucho*) made of cardboard or plastic mesh. The cloth hood worn over it is technically known as the '*cubrerrostro*'.

Carrete: A typical Málaga throne shape that narrows in the middle and widens at the top, like a cotton reel or bobbin.

Cartela: A 'chapel' or medallion located on the side of a throne and representing figures with meaning for the brotherhood.

Cirial: An ornate processional candlestick.

Cirineo: An ancillary figure on a *trono* who helps to hold the Cross

Corona: The crown of the Virgin as Queen of heaven.

Cíngulo: The cord or cincture worn around the waist of a *penitente*.

Cruce: (*lit.* 'crossing') The greeting between two or more thrones of the same or different brotherhoods as they pass one another (usually on the Alameda Principal or the Plaza de la Constitución or, during *traslados*, near *casas hermandades*).

Dalmática: A tabard-shaped liturgical vestment worn by the bearers of candles and by acolytes and incense bearers). Its name comes from the region of Dalmatia, from where the wool was once imported to make the garment. However, to be strictly accurate, the 'dalmatics' that one sees during Semana Santa are actually 'tunicles' ('*tunicelas*'). Lay people (like acolytes) may wear tunicles, whereas only ordained deacons (and bishops) wear dalmatics.

Diadema: The name given to the crown of the *Virgen* when it is surrounded by a 'sunburst' or halo.

Escapulario: ('scapular') A square embroidered badge worn by the *nazarenos* of some brotherhoods over the tunic.

Estación de penitencia: An act of prayer carried out by some brotherhoods inside the Cathedral during the progress of their procession.

Estampitas: The 'stamps' or small prayer cards that are distributed by the brotherhoods to members of the public as souvenirs.

Estandarte: A banner bearing the insignia of the brotherhood embroidered in gold thread and luxuriously decorated with the titular image (*aka 'bacalao'*)

Estola: ('stole') — from the Latin *stola* (and this from the Greek στολή). The stole in part symbolizes the ropes with which Jesus Christ was dragged to Calvary. It forms part of the clothing of the *penitentes* in some brotherhoods. It is usually wider than a priest's stole, more like a scarf, and is made of the same fabric as the tunic

Fajín: The red sash worn by a military general and also worn by a *Virgen* as a belt. These sashes have usually been donated by senior military officers to the image as a mark of devotion.

Faraona: Connected to the word 'pharaoh', this is the headdress worn by many throne bearers, by many of the children accompanying the procession, and by some *penitentes*.

Gloria: The decorated interior of the canopy of the throne of a *Virgen*.

Guión: The teardrop-shaped emblem of a brotherhood in the form of a folded

flag, made of velvet or satin, which has the emblem of the brotherhood embroidered in gold thread and silk

Luto: Gauze or black ribbon that is placed on the bell of the throne to mark the death of a brother or benefactor of the brotherhood.

Mantilla: Clothing worn by a 'waitress' (*camarera*) or sister of the brotherhood: all black, with tortoiseshell high comb and *mantilla* (veil), gloves and rosary.

Manto: There are two types of *manto* (cloak): the smaller cloak that the *Virgen* wears in the Church and the much larger processional cloak.

Marcha procesional: The music that accompanies each of the *tronos* on their journey to 'mark the step' and help them on their way

Matacandelas: A candle snuffer (*lit.* 'killer of candles').

Martillo: A metal or wooden hammer used to strike the bell on the front of the throne.

Mesa: ('table') The metal frame of the throne.

Moco: Drippings and jets of molten wax of the candles (*lit.* 'mucus'). The connection between nasal mucus and candle wax works the other way too — mucus hanging from the nose, especially in children, is often referred to as '*velas*', candles.

Naveta: A box in the shape of a boat containing incense grains.

Piñas: The pineapple-shaped floral arrangements in the vases of the thrones.

Potencias: A Spanish-style depiction of Christ's halo in the form of three fan-shaped decorations in silver or gold and sometimes inlaid with gemstones (shown here in the image of the Christ of Humility and Patience).

Pregón: Proclamation made by a person of relevance in the brotherhood world as an exaltation to celebrate

Holy Week. The *pregonero* or 'town crier' is appointed by the Association of Brotherhoods with the approval of the Bishop and is often from the world of politics, culture or the arts (Antonio Banderas was given this role in 2011[62]).

Procesionista: The name used to describe an individual who takes part in the processions in any capacity. A word, as far as I know, only used in Málaga.

Promesa: A person who walks behind the throne in fulfilment of a vow

Pulso: Some thrones are raised 'freehand' at certain moments of the procession. This practice consists of lifting the *varales* (poles) with the palms of the hands to raise the throne above the shoulder. The call for this manoeuvre consists of three strikes of the throne bell then a further strike to raise.

Pureza: The loin-cloth of Christ

Quitasangre: One of the large black flags that are dragged on the ground with the symbolic intention of cleaning the blood shed by Jesus during his Passion. This is a medieval tradition nowadays only observed in Málaga (in the procession of the Descent).

Recreona: A term of disapproval used to describe a brotherhood that people feel is processing too slowly in order to show off.

Saya: The dress of the Virgin with rich embroidery, sequins and beading

Sección: Each of the parts into which the processional parade is divided: i.e. the *Cristo* and the *Virgen*.

Tinglao: A marquee. A temporary structure that serves as a street temple for the processional exit. Currently, three brotherhoods use *tinglaos*: Descent, Crucifixion and Dulce Nombre.

Tintinábulo: ('bell') is an insignia of a minor basilica — a small bell on a staff that appears in solemn processions. In the Middle Ages, the *tintinábulo* had the practical function of announcing to the people of Rome the proximity of the Pope during processions.

Tocado: Lace, lamé, satin or tulle that frames the face of the Virgin.

Tren de velas: The banks of candles on the throne of the Virgin

Tulipa: A kind of glass cup that goes on the tips of the 'flying buttresses' with candles inside.

Umbela: A ceremonial umbrella in alternating panels of red and yellow. It is figuratively half-open, waiting for the Pope to take shelter beneath it. Along with the *tintinábulo* it is one of the insignia of a minor basilica.

---

62   archive.ph/hkZgV

⚲ The *Nazarena* Route

Clearly, one can only really experience *Semana Santa* during, well, *Semana Santa* (and in a limited way shortly before and after it via the *traslados*). However, the *ayuntamiento* and the *Agrupación de Cofradías* have cooperated to create 'Málaga Nazarena' — six walking routes that cover almost all of the *templos* (churches and chapels) and *casas hermandades* of the Málaga Holy Week brotherhoods, in addition to other places of interest, such as embroidery workshops and notable places on the various routes. In total, the itineraries cover 23 churches, 9 oratories, chapels, abbeys and hermitages, 38 brotherhood houses, 7 craft workshops, 6 brotherhood museums, 14 notable streets and locations and 2 other buildings of interest.

If you walk one of the routes, it is best to do so between 10 am and 1.30 pm or between 5 pm and 8 pm as you are more likely to find the churches open. The craft workshops are not open to the public, though if you are interested in visiting one then get in touch with ⊕ magnacofrade.com — a tour company that organizes guided tours relating to the *Semana Santa* tradition. But even following any of the walks on your own will enable you to visit some interesting churches and discover parts of Málaga that few other tourists ever do.

You can find out more by visiting ⊕ bit.ly/SemanaSantaWalkingRoutes. All the routes end (or begin, depending upon which direction you decide to go in) at the headquarters of the *Agrupación de Cofradías* in the former church-hospital of San Julián on Calle Muro de San Julián in the northern part of the historic centre. At each point of interest on any route, you will find an information board that displays a QR code to display more detailed information on your smartphone.

A well-written and beautifully designed 292-page guidebook has also been produced which is available as a free PDF download: ⊕ bit.ly/SSWRGuide. However, all the information is currently only in Spanish, even though English names and descriptions are provided on the information boards outside each location. Nonetheless, if you use the QR codes at each location to visit the information links, then you can use your mobile browser to translate the text. Chrome does this 'out of the box' (tap the three dots ⋮ in the top right-hand corner and select the translate option), with Safari you need to tap the 'action' button (**Aa**) on the left-hand side of the address bar, and for Firefox you will need to install a third party extension. For other browsers, you may need to do some research!

I hope that having created such a fascinating programme of walking routes and produced such excellent information, the *Agrupación de Cofradías* will soon provide information in a variety of languages. Beyond that, a smartphone app with GPS capability and commentary would really help to make 'Málaga Nazarena' an unmissable highlight of any tourist visit.

🍲 The Food of Semana Santa

Before the 1960s, which saw the Second Vatican Council and Pope Paul VI's Apostolic Constitution on the norms for fasting ('*Paenitemini*'), patterns of eating in the run-up to Easter would have looked rather different in Spain. Nowadays, the rules (for Catholics at least) are not terribly arduous. Ash Wednesday (the first day of the 40-day period of preparation for Easter) and Good Friday are days of 'fasting and abstinence' which in effect means abstaining from animal flesh and eating less (Jews, Muslims and Eastern Christians understandably find the Catholic definition of fasting somewhat bizarre given that it seems to reduce fasting to 'not eating between meals'). Additionally, Fridays of Lent are days of abstinence (from animal flesh). However, if we travel further back in time, then the whole of Lent was not only meat-free but basically 40 days of veganism.

But even as religious guidelines change and society becomes more secular, food culture has a way of remembering. Few people in Britain give up eggs and dairy for Lent as our medieval forefathers did, and not many are aware of the theological significance of 'The Lamb' as a reference to Christ, and yet the practice of eating pancakes on Ash Wednesday and roast lamb on Easter Sunday is still widespread. Similarly, in Spain, food traditions from former times survive. We should probably note that despite Spain being a generally carnivorous culture, their enormous love for fish and seafood makes abstinence from meat not especially onerous. Many of the foods on the list below are eaten all year round, but you are likely to see them cropping up on menus more often during Lent, Holy Week and Easter.

Lenten, Holy Week, and Easter Dishes

Ajoblanco/Ajobacalao

Ajoblanco is a chilled soup made from almonds, garlic, olive oil, bread and sherry vinegar that has a reasonable claim to have originated in Málaga. At its worst, it can be thin and grainy, but at its best, it is genuinely one of the megastars of Spanish cuisine — the texture of single cream with a powerful hit of garlic carried by lightly toasted almonds and a sharp edge of vinegar. During Lent and Holy Week, cod (*bacalao*) is often added, along with paprika, to make a thicker, spicier soup that can be spread on toasted bread. It is a speciality of the town of Vélez-Málaga (about 40km to the east of Málaga) and has seen a resurgence in popularity after a local firm — Lujos del Paladar — started producing a ready-prepared version. The *hombres de tronos* in Vélez-Málaga are said to sustain themselves during the processions with large quantities of *ajobacalao*.

Porra de habas

Originating in Casabermeja this is another chilled cream soup. Broad beans are pounded with bread, extra virgin olive oil and garlic to make a delicate green cream. It is usually garnished and accompanied with some whole beans and finely chopped boiled eggs just like a traditional tomato-based porra.

Ensaladilla malagueña

Oranges, cod, potatoes, spring onions, olives and extra virgin olive oil make up Málaga's signature salad. It is popular throughout the year but is consumed in still greater quantities during Lent. Although it is principally known as a salad from Málaga, there are also other local versions, such as *mojete alhaurino* or *pío antequerano*. This latter dish, typical of Antequera, does not include potatoes, which suggests that it may be the oldest version, before the arrival of the tuber from Mesoamerica.

Tortillitas de bacalao or Tortillitas de camarones

Pancakes or fritters of cod or baby shrimp are associated with Cádiz but are popular throughout Andalucía. They are made with a light batter incorporating chickpea flour for extra crispness. They should be very thin, like lace doilies, and have a satisfying crunch.

Papas con jibia

Potatoes with cuttlefish — another dish especially associated with Holy Week in Málaga, though it comes originally from Cádiz and Huelva. In Málaga, they add almonds to the broth. The rest of the ingredients are usually the same: potatoes, cuttlefish, garlic, extra virgin olive oil, water, salt and some spices, such as saffron, cloves, parsley and bay leaf.

Potaje de Semana Santa

There are many versions (again) of 'Holy Week Stew' though the main ingredients always include chickpeas (or white beans), cod and spinach (or chard). An alternative name, '*Potaje de Vigilia*', shows the association of the dish with the evening of Holy Saturday.

Hornazos

Also popularly known as '*jornazos*', these are a kind of bread dough pasty which in almost all cases have a boiled egg (complete with shell) inside. In some towns they are eaten during Holy Week, in others, they are served on Easter Sunday.

Potaje de castañas

Chestnut stew is a pudding and typical of Holy Week in Ojén. Its most significant ingredient is dried chestnuts, seasoned and cooked with cinnamon, anise, olive oil, molasses, lemon peel and sugar. The final result is usually eaten cold.

Pestiños

Pestiños are popular sweets/biscuits consumed every year during Holy Week. Many theories are advanced regarding their origin, but it seems most likely that they owe something to a number of cultural influences. Anise probably arrived with the Phoenicians, and the Romans had a very similar pastry called *frictilia*, fried in lard and drizzled with honey. Sephardic Jews had their *fijuelas* — rosettes of fried spiced pastry soaked in syrup. They were prepared at Purim, their shape supposedly representing the shape of Haman's ears (Haman being the main antagonist in the Book of Esther). Something almost identical is still made in parts of La Mancha and Aragón. And if *peStiños* are related to *fijuelas*, then they are related to the North African *shebakia*. The recipe for *peStiños* as we know it today dates back to the 16th century when they were made in convents, probably because many of the nuns were *conversos*, or converted Jews. The first mention in literature is in Francisco Delicado's *La lozana andaluza* (1528). The *peStiño* is made with a fine dough that is moulded by hand to give it its peculiar folded shape, then fried in olive oil and tossed in honey or dusted with a layer of sugar.

Buñuelos

A *buñuelo* is a fritter or doughnut. At its best, it is a beautifully light concoction, full of air (hence its common name '*buñuelo de viento*' or 'wind fritter'). That is not to say that they look especially beautiful. They are derived from the Latin word for 'lump' and, yes, the same etymology gives us the English word 'bunion'. During *Semana Santa* (and during the Feria) you will find pop-up stalls making *buñuelos*. Their origin is said to have been in the town of Almogía in Málaga, around the year 1090, shortly after the Moorish invasion (though as with many *andaluz* dishes, the origin may be Jewish). Today *buñuelos* are made from a yeast batter fried in plenty of oil. The simple kind are dusted with sugar and cinnamon, while the gourmet versions can be filled with whipped cream, custard, chocolate mousse or mascarpone. In some bars, you are likely to find a savoury version (like a gougère), made with shredded cod.

Torrijas

By any other name, French toast (or eggy bread), but in Spain, this is the quintessential dish of *Semana Santa*. There is a bar in Madrid that serves *torrijas* all year round, but in the rest of Spain, it is a genuinely seasonal treat. The basic ingredients are simple enough — a slice of stale bread, soaked in milk, and maybe some wine, then fried and dusted with sugar and cinnamon. Some versions incorporate other, often secret, ingredients — honey, cane honey, citrus zest, brandy, aguardiente (pomace brandy), dried fruit, other spices, etc.

The sports event promoter Christian Machowski (a German living in Málaga) explained the phenomenon of *torrijas* very well in a lovely article he wrote in *El Español*:

> When I asked malagueños on Twitter where you can buy the best Easter torrijas, the reaction was magnificent and overwhelming, but at the same time so typical of how I've met people. Everyone had their own opinion (and yes, Málaga people are never short of a strong opinion), but quite a few took it further. On two occasions my neighbour Manuel came to our apartment and left us torrijas that friends of his had made, who had seen the tweets and wanted me to try them.[63]

Torrijas (along with *buñuelos*, *peStiños* and *churros/tejeringos*) belong to a category of sweet treats known as '*frutas de sartén*' (fruits of the pan), or deep fried pastries. They are an ancient dish (something recognisably similar is mentioned in Apicio) and, due to their simplicity, found in almost every food culture in the world. We know that they were popular in Spain

63   Christian Machowski, 'Sobre 'malaguitas', torrijas y salchichón de Málaga', in *El Español*, 14 November 2022, (translated from the Spanish) archive.ph/SZKNE

from at least the 15th century, thanks to a reference to them by the Spanish composer, poet and playwright Juan del Encina (1468–1533) in his *Cancionero*, published in 1496. Also known as *rabanadas* or *fritas de parida*, they were probably first made in Spain by Sephardi Jews who prepared them to celebrate the birth of a child (a *parida* is a woman who has just given birth). This, and the fact that eggs and dairy would originally have been forbidden during Holy Week, suggests that *torrijas* were initially adopted by Christians as a Christmas treat (or for the Feast of the Annunciation). In modern Spain, they are an annual obsession. People swap tips on where to find the tastiest versions and speculate upon which 'secret ingredient' make those at a particular café so delicious. Málaga is an ideal place to enjoy them, not least because the local sweet wine makes a perfect ingredient and an excellent accompaniment.

During Holy Week, any *confitería* (patisserie) or *panadería* (bakery) will sell them, including chains like Canasta and Granier. Also, many *cafeterías* popular for breakfasts and *meriendas* (afternoon snacks) are likely to have them in season. The pastry shop **El Colmenero de Alhaurín (Calle Atarazanas 1)** has been making *torrijas* for over 100 years, so this is a good place to go for the traditional *malagueño* product. The best-known (and richest) version is that sold by the venerable **Confitería Aparicio** (the original shop is at **Plaza Capuchinos 15**, with another branch at **Calle Calderería 11**) that has been selling *torrijas* to grateful *malagueños* for more than 80 years.

Cascarúos

The lemon tree, introduced to Spain by the Arabs in the eleventh century, has been selectively bred ever since to produce the *cascarúo*, or sweet lemon. (Remember that, just as dogs as distinct as Dobermans and Pugs are descended from the wolf, so all citrus fruits, from the

grapefruit to the mandarin, have a common ancestor). There are references to the *cascarúo* in the town of Pizarra in the Guadalhorce Valley dating from 1751, and this remains the only region where these large, thick-rinded lemons are grown in any great quantity. During *Semana Santa*, street stalls suddenly appear hawking wedges of this lemon, usually enjoyed with salt or bicarbonate of soda. Eating *cascarúos* is especially associated with climbing the Monte Calvario on *Viernes Santo* (Good Friday).

Cañadú

This is the *malagueño* pronunciation of *cañadul*, which is itself a shortening of *cañadulce* ('sweet cane') — in other words, sugar cane. Chunks of this sweet, juicy plant are often sold by the vendors of *cascarúos*. This is an annual novelty; a 'heritage' product that harks back to the days when the area now occupied by Málaga Airport consisted of sugar cane fields and the eastern coastline of the Province of Málaga was dotted with sugar refineries (the last, in Torre del Mar, only closed in 1990). Málaga is the only place in Europe where there is commercial cultivation of sugar cane (near Frigiliana), albeit now in tiny quantities.

Palodú

Another *malagueño* vernacular word for *palodul* (or *paloduz* or *palodulce*), meaning licorice root (*lit.* 'sweet stick'). It is not often seen nowadays, but you may see the odd pile of brown twigs on a vendor's cart. Reckoned to sweeten the breath, for our forebears licorice sticks were used like chewing gum (and toothbrushes). You may also see artichokes, lupins, candied almonds and toffee apples on sale.

Feria de Málaga (The August Fair)

In the section about holidays and feast days above, we saw that holidays falling on a Sunday are transferred to a Monday. Another feature of the Spanish calendar is the *'puente'* (bridge) which occurs when a holiday falls on a Tuesday or Thursday. In such cases, people often hope (or expect) to be given an additional day off on the Monday or Friday, to make a super-long weekend. In 2012, in the teeth of the Eurozone crisis, the then Spanish Prime Minister Mariano Rajoy brought in legislation to transfer holidays falling on Tuesdays or Thursdays to the Monday or Friday. This attempt to increase productivity and wean the Spanish off of their beloved holidays has been only partly successful, and one of the reasons is the *feria* or annual fair, which in most towns and cities is held over at least a long weekend and more often, a full week.

Every city, town and village in Spain has a *feria* of some kind, mostly linked to the celebration of the local patron saint. In a village, it might mean a day or two of festivities, but in towns and cities, it will often last a week (actually nine days because many run from Friday night until the Sunday of the following week). The *feria* is always an opportunity to have fun, dance, eat and drink — a near sacred quadrumvirate of pleasures for Spaniards — but they vary from place to place. The *'semanas grandes'* (great weeks) of Bilbao and San Sebastián focus upon Basque culture with folk music, traditional games, competitive wood-chopping and processions of *'gigantes'* (giant *papier mâché* figures of characters from local legend). In most regions of Spain, there will be bullfights during the *feria*, sometimes including an *encierro* (running of the bulls through the streets) each morning. This happens, famously, in Pamplona for Sanfermines in July, but also in dozens of other towns, yet without the thrill-seeking, quasi-suicidal tourists.

🎺 Feasts and Fairs

In medieval Europe, there was no concept of a 'weekend', and besides, the majority of the poor were employed on the land meaning that the very idea of a 'day off' was a very rare thing. The feeding of animals and the sowing and harvesting of crops could not be undertaken according to a timetable of working and rest days. Even so, the year was punctuated by an annual round of liturgical seasons of fasting (like Lent) and feasting (like Easter), and days tied explicitly to the agricultural year like the blessing of ploughs in January on the Sunday after Epiphany, the Rogation Days of May when God's blessing would be sought for the growing crops, and Lammas Day ('Loaf Mass Day') in August when bread made with the newly harvested wheat would be blessed. There were also dozens of individual feast days throughout the year: feasts of the Lord (like Easter and Ascension), feasts of the Blessed Virgin Mary (like the Annunciation and the Assumption), and feasts of the saints. Some of these, such as the feasts of St Peter and St Martin of Tours, were celebrated everywhere, whereas others were national or local. In some cases, such saints might be very local indeed.

The patron saint of Madrid, San Isidro, is celebrated with a month-long programme of bull-fights and other events during May, but all but ignored in the *barrio* of La Latina (whose residents — '*los chulapos*' — consider themselves to be the authentic citizens of Madrid). There the big celebration is for the Virgin of the Dove ('*La Paloma*') which takes place in May.

A great deal of rubbish is written on the internet about medieval Europe, not least the suggestion that medieval peasants 'only worked 150 days a year'. In fact, medieval villeins 'worked' many more hours than we do, not least because simple household chores were far more time-consuming. They simply worked slightly fewer hours on some days, or were able to let their hair down now and again, or enjoy a richer meal. That latter luxury mattered when a third of the year were fast days (Lent, Advent Fridays, Ember Days, etc.).

So much for feast days. Fairs, on the other hand, although connected (at least originally) to some religious feast, were not only about enjoyment and celebration but also about trade. The earliest fairs in medieval Europe were probably the fairs of the County of Champagne, reaching their zenith in the 12th and 13th centuries. There were six Champagne fairs, each tied to a particular liturgical feast and lasting for two or three weeks, and each was largely self-regulated through the development of the '*Lex mercatoria*' (merchant law), an early form of international trade law. The fairs were engines of economic growth, trading in agricultural products, wine (though not the sparkling Champagne that we know today), textiles, leather, furs, spices and much more besides.

The first fair was held on 2nd January and the sixth began on All Saints' Day in November, each one inaugurated with the celebration of mass. The fair at Lagny-sur-Marne was held in the grounds of the Benedictine monastery. What made these fairs so significant was the wide variety of goods on sale, greater than anything an individual town market could supply. Furs and skins travelled in both directions, woollen cloth and linen were brought from the north, while silk, spices and gold came from the south and east. Wool from sheep reared in Spain and England might pass through fairs like those of Champagne twice or more, being woven into cloth in Flanders, traded again, finished and dyed in Italy, and sold a third time.

The movement of goods through Champagne was also parallel to the movement of people along the pilgrimage routes that criss-crossed Europe. At the conclusion of sales, a reckoning of credit would take place at the tables (*banche*) of the Italian money changers, who also established future payments on credit, settled bills of exchange, and made loans. To oil the wheels of trade, a common system of weights (avoirdupois) and measures was adopted. Fairs functioned as international clearing houses for paper debts and credits and the *Lex mercatoria* was initially enforced by private judges long before that function was taken over by the nation-state. However much we may think that 'globalization' is a modern phenomenon, medieval European trade fairs were an early manifestation of it.

The mercantile origin of the *feria* can be seen even today. The *feria* of Navas (Asturias) is dominated by cider, an important local product, while at the *Feria de San Mateo* of Logroño (La Rioja) wine is the star — so much so that the town's principal fountain is filled with red wine for the duration. The *feria* in Sanlúcar de Barrameda is still called the '*Feria de Manzanilla*' (the variety of sherry that is only produced in that town) and the *feria* of Jerez is not dedicated to Sherry (though a great deal of that wine is consumed) but horses, having begun as an annual horse-trading fair in the 13th century (trade was encouraged by being tax-free for a week).

Such fairs, although primarily about commerce and exchange, were obviously also opportunities for consumption, enjoyment and revelry, but these were pleasant corollaries of the main business of buying, selling and networking. The very idea of a 'leisure' activity is a rather modern one, after all. Thus, the Spanish *ferias* as we know them today are largely nineteenth-century reinventions.

The burgeoning urban working class, unlike their agricultural labouring forebears, were now able to take time off (or take less sleep, most *ferias* being in the main nocturnal). Lead smelting or sugar refining, unlike animal or crop husbandry could be suspended or slowed for a few days or a week to give the workers an actual holiday. The mystery, perhaps, is how the Spanish *feria* has managed to survive into the twenty-first century in which most people work neither on farms nor in factories, but in banks, shops and offices. One feels for health-care, law enforcement and transport workers who cannot take time off, but pretty much everyone else does. Shops close or half close, as do banks and both private and government offices, as well as many bars and restaurants, which close early to allow employees to go to the *feria*. The economic impact is not as deleterious as one might suppose because the benefit to the local economy of a *feria* is enormous. When people are off work, they tend to spend money, and they spend it on a grand scale.

Hotels are full, thousands of people from all over Spain visit the city, especially for the *feria*. They spend money on buses, trains and taxis, and in bars and restaurants during the day. At the *recinto ferial* (fairground) people spend money on food, drink and amusements. Also, as the premier social event of the year, the *feria* almost always means new clothes.

In 2022, the first Málaga *feria* since the COVID pandemic forced it to be cancelled in 2020, 76% of Málaga residents attended — an unusually low figure attributable to concerns about infection. Most said that they would attend on at least two days, and the average daily spend was likely to be over €70 per person. The predicted economic benefit for the city, partly driven by increased appetite for the first *feria* after the pandemic shutdown, was estimated to be in the region of €60m, or €8.5m per day. While modern *ferias* may now be primarily about pleasure and relaxation, they continue to be as much about trade and the economy as their medieval precursors.

Ferias in General

As we have seen, no two *ferias* in Spain are identical, but the *ferias* of Andalucía are celebrated with particular verve and intensity (though the *feria* of Murcia, and the very ancient *feria* of Albacete in La Mancha are somewhat *andaluz* in style). The most notable feature of the *feria andaluza* is the use of a *recinto ferial* (fairground) — a large area of land, usually on the outskirts of town, which although it may be used to host other events throughout the year, primarily exists to host the *feria* for one week each year (outside Andalucía, *ferias* are held in the city centre, often in the *Plaza Mayor* or municipal park). At the entrance to the fairground stands the '*portada grande*' — a monumental, but temporary, gateway with a decorated façade often illuminated with thousands of lights. These great works of craftsmanship change each year, usually showcasing the 'theme' of the *feria* for that season and reproducing floral motifs or architectural features typical of the city (so in Málaga this is often the *biznaga*, the Cathedral, Alcazaba or La Farola).

In most Spanish *ferias*, the fairground rides and games are mixed together with the bars, food stalls and hospitality marquees set up for dancing, but in Andalucía, the fairground has two distinct sections. There is the *recinto ferial* itself, where the grown-up business of socializing, drinking, eating and dancing goes on, and a separate '*zona de atracciones*' of traditional fairground rides, shooting galleries, hot dog stands and stalls selling '*algodón de azúcar*' (candyfloss).

Another typically *andaluz* feature of the *feria* is the use of *casetas* or booths, a tradition that developed at the April Fair in Sevilla. These booths are considerably more than marquees or tents, being temporary structures of some solidity. Some of the commercial *casetas* are primarily dedicated to food and drink and are reminiscent of *chiringuitos* (beach bars), while others are set up by individuals, companies, social enterprises, Holy Week fraternities, media outlets, labour unions, political parties and countless other groups. Most have food and drink available, some have live music and wooden dance floors, and nowadays the majority have lavatories (adapted for disabled use). To give an idea of the sheer scale of a typical *feria*, each *caseta* can accommodate dozens or even hundreds of people (depending upon how seating and tables are arranged), and the Málaga *feria* has around 121 *casetas* occupying some 241 'modules'. The *casetas* are arranged in an orthogonal pattern along 'streets' spread with *albero* sand (the same as is used in the bullring). The streets even have names, so it is theoretically possible to send a letter to the owner of a *caseta* during the week of the *feria*.

The distinctiveness of the *feria andaluza* is seen in other ways, too. They always involve horses, for example. The Jerez *feria* began as a horse-trading fair, but throughout Andalucía — and especially in Sevilla — the most stylish way to arrive at the *feria* in the evening is by '*caruaje de caballos*' (horse-drawn carriage). Horse riding and equestrian displays usually take place in the more sedate daytime sessions of the *feria* as the loud music at night might spook the horses. The Málaga *recinto ferial* is further from the town centre than those of Sevilla or Jerez, so rather than taking a carriage from the city, the usual practice is to hire a carriage at the fairground (during the daytime) to tour the 'streets' and view the *casetas* in style. There is something rather heartwarming about seeing a group of smartly-dressed *malagueño* teenagers excitedly climbing aboard a horse and carriage for a tour of the *recinto ferial* as opposed to clambering into a 10-metre-long 'party limo'.

The other two big features of the *feria* in Andalucía are connected: costume and dancing. Spaniards are among the best-dressed people in Europe and it is still regarded as perfectly normal to get changed or even to 'dress up' to go to a bar for *tapas* in a way that would bemuse Brits planning an evening in the pub. The sartorial standards on display at the *feria*, however, are on another level. For many, it means dressing as smartly (and expensively) as one would to attend a wedding, but for significant numbers of fair-goers it also means dressing in what is effectively the national costume of Andalucía, if not Spain. For men that means the *traje de corto* (or *traje campero*) which is the working garb of mounted cattle ranchers — leather riding boots (sometimes with spurs), high-waisted trousers, white shirt, tie, waistcoat, short jacket (in grey or navy blue), a coloured sash ('*faja*') and a broad-brimmed hat (*sombrero cordobés*).

An even greater proportion of women and girls will wear the '*traje de flamenca*' (also called the '*traje de gitana*' or 'Gypsy dress'). Commonly, this is a full (or calf) length dress in a bright colour, figure-hugging to the knee, with ruffles at the bottom of the skirt and at the elbows. Especially popular is the polka-dot design ('*traje de lunares*'). Such dresses are often worn with a tasselled silk shawl ('*mantón de Manila*'), or the dress incorporates tassels at the neckline to mimic a shawl. Women do not wear hats, but long hair is tied into a bun or ponytail and decorated with a flower and/or comb. Earrings should be large enough to have made Bet Lynch proud. Shoes are heeled, but not stilettos; rather they should have a broad heel to facilitate the vigorous footwork of the traditional dances. It is a beautiful dress — and let's be honest, there is a lot of very tight, elegant clothing on show at the *feria* — but the bright (some would say lurid) colours and bold patterns make it pretty clear that it is a costume. The *traje de flamenca* is not about smoky-eyed *femmes fatales*, but about women dressing colourfully (and slightly outrageously) and having fun.

But is it, as some suggest now, '*cultural appropriation*'? Yes and no. In the late eighteenth and early nineteenth centuries, there was a movement in Spain known as *casticismo* ('authenticity'). Though this took place at many levels, much of the movement was about dress and entertainment. It rejected the 'French' fashions imported by the Bourbons and embraced flamenco and bullfighting. This meant celebrating the most *castizo* (authentic) practitioners of those art forms — the Roma — who broadly welcomed this attention, having hitherto been a despised minority. The adoption of their typical dress by the middle and upper classes seemed to represent an acceptance that Gypsies were truly 'Spanish', and even embodied 'Spanishness'. On the other hand, the *traje de gitana* that we see today is only modelled upon the typical costume of Gypsy women of two centuries ago. Since its decisive adoption as the costume of Andalucía around one hundred years ago, it has developed and changed considerably. Hems, sleeves and necklines have risen and fallen with fashion. For example, even though the dress is also called the '*traje de flamenca*' no one could actually dance flamenco wearing it, because it is too restrictive (being gathered at the knee) — those who actually dance flamenco at the *feria* wear a version with more voluminous skirts.

Dancing is the second authentic motif of the *feria andaluza*. The first-time visitor to a *feria* in Andalucía might assume that the party-goers are dancing flamenco in the *casetas*. There will certainly be displays of high-quality flamenco in some *casetas*, but among the people, what you will see will be popular versions of the art form. The most common are varieties known as '*sevillanas*' and '*verdiales*' as well as a version of flamenco called '*pop aflamencado*'. While none of these popular forms approaches the virtuosity of professional flamenco performers, they are still recognisable as related forms and danced with great skill and beauty.

✺ The Málaga *Feria*

The *Feria de Málaga* traces its origin to the incorporation of the city into the Castilian crown in 1487. The inhabitants of Vélez-Málaga along the coast had capitulated to the Castilian crown without a fight, but in Málaga, there was a siege of over three months. Despondent, King Fernando called upon Queen Isabel to come from Córdoba to help rally the troops, who were overwhelmed with heat, exhaustion and (historians suspect) cholera. With the 'August Feast' of the Blessed Virgin (The Assumption) approaching, the King and Queen and the clergy undertook public acts of prayer and penitence to intercede for victory.

According to pious legend, the Virgin Mary appeared to Fernando in a dream, seated with Christ on her knee, both of them wearing crowns as Queen and King of Heaven, and a palm of victory in the Virgin's hand. She urged Fernando to persevere and promised that the arrival of monks at the camp would herald victory. A few days later, although no monks arrived, a group of friars did. They were a group of 'Minims', a religious order recently founded by St Francis de Paula (St Francis de Paula's namesake, St Francis of Assisi had founded an order called the 'Friars Minor', or 'lesser brothers', so this new '*Ordo Minimorum*' was the 'least of the least') who came to ask permission to establish a house in the territory.

A few days later, on August 18, the merchant custodian of the Alcazaba, Ali Dordux, surrendered the keys to the city of Málaga unconditionally. But it would be on the 19th when the royal entourage officially entered Málaga, proclaiming Fernando and Isabel as the new lords of the city from that moment. Later would come the repopulation of the city with a contingent of new settlers from the Christian territory in the hills and the Guadalquivir Valley. Two years later the first *ayuntamiento* would be constituted, and in 1491 the monarchs decreed that festivities be held on the day of the Virgin of August (the 15th). They ran '*Toros y Cañas*' (bullfights and displays of knightly combat with lances) and held a solemn procession of the Civil and Ecclesiastical councils from the old Great Mosque (today the site of the church of the Sagrario and part of the Cathedral) to the chapel of San Luis in Gibralfaro.

That same year, in March 1491, the *Reyes Católicos* handed over the 'Hermitage of Our Lady of Bitoria' and the adjoining lands to the hermit Fray Bartolomé, reserving their ownership and patronage of both the miraculous image and the chapel. Two years later, in 1493, the monarchs donated it by royal decree to the Minims as the first convent of the order in Spain. From there, and through its different foundations, the Order of the Minims would spread devotion to the Virgin of Victory beyond Málaga. The Minims still exist today, though unlike the Jesuits, Benedictines and Carthusians they have never really recovered from their near destruction following the French Revolution, and there are only around 175 friars worldwide (Paulaner München beer, named after St Francis de Paula, was first brewed by the Minims of the Priory of Neudeck ob der Au in Munich).

In 1492, bishop Pedro Díaz de Toledo, moved the date to 19 August (the feast day of St Louis of Toulouse) to commemorate the entry of the *Reyes Católicos* into Málaga. The civic-religious procession no longer went up to Gibralfaro but started from the former Great Mosque and went to the church of Santiago (the site of another mosque now in use as the pro-cathedral). There were also 'Toros y Cañas' in the Plaza de las Cuatro Calles (today the Plaza de la Cons-titución). These celebrations were intermittent throughout the years, and attempts were made to revitalize them during the 16th and 17th centuries, and in the 18th century they lost their prominence in favour of other celebrations, such as the festivities for the city's Patron Saints Ciriaco and Paula, the festivities of San Juan, and the most important celebration during this period: Corpus Christi. One must remember that during this time Málaga was growing in size, but remained a collection of parishes. When we look at the names of the old *barrios* of Málaga, it is striking how many of them are taken from the dedication of the parish, or the main convent: Capuchinos, Cristo de la Epidemia, La Merced, La Trinidad, La Victoria, Los Antonios, San Felipe Neri, San Miguel, Santa Amalia, etc. All of these would have celebrated their own feast days locally. In this or that parish, shops would be closed, religious processions would be held and there would be feasting and merry-making, while a few streets away, life continued as normal. During the nineteenth century, instability, frag-mentation of an increasingly industrialized workforce and the concomitant loss of identity militated against great city-wide celebrations. In 1884 there was an attempt to relocate the 'main' festivities of Málaga around the festivities held in honour of The Carmen (Our Lady of Mount Carmel), and the partial success of this plan led the city authorities to formulate a more ambitious plan.

For the origin of the *feria* as we know it today, we have to look to 1887, a very difficult time economically for Málaga, with the decline of industry, the scourge of numerous epidemics affecting the population and the phylloxera blight that all but obliterated the vines of the surrounding countryside. It is no accident, but rather a feature of human nature, that when times are hard, people often want to party hard. What was needed was a wake-up call to rouse a poor and sluggish people, and one that would recreate a sense of solidarity and civic identity. But in order to be of real benefit to the city, this celebration would need to appeal to people from further afield with money to spend, that is to say, tourists. The commemoration of the fourth centenary of the taking of the city was seized upon as the axis on which such a celebration would revolve.

Part of the impetus for the project arose after the declaration of Pope Pius IX, in a *brevia* (Pa-pal Brief) issued on 8 December 1867, naming Our Lady of the Victory as principal patron of the Diocese of Málaga. Not long after, the chaplain of the Royal Chapel of Granada, Cristóbal Luque Martín, wrote a letter to the Governing Board of the Brotherhood of Victory (*Real Hermandad de Santa María de la Victoria*). In it he proposed the commemoration of the fourth centenary of the reconquest of Málaga by the *Reyes Católicos*, suggesting that such a project would also serve to promote the Patronage of the *Virgen de la Victoria*, which in recent times had declined as a result of the '*Desamortización eclesiástica*' (confiscation of church property) under Queen Isabel II's Prime Minister Juan Álvarez Mendizábal, that brought with it the exclaustration of the *Mínimos* friars. He noted that the character of old Málaga had changed a great deal, both in the destruction of many religious houses of friars and nuns, but also through the gradual disappearance of the old nobility and the rise of a new class of wealthy merchants and industrialists. In 1860, came a slight sign of hope when a decree of Queen Isabel II restored the sanctuary (church) of Santa María de la Victoria to the ecclesiastical authorities (though the convent remained a military hospital and the Minims never returned).

The fraternity liked the proposal and asked Don Cristóbal to prepare a detailed plan. What he produced was a quite detailed specification carefully constructed to appeal both to Church and State by placing traditional piety, historical memory and civic pride at the centre of the plan. This project would be unanimously approved by the City Council, The Bishop and his Cathedral Chapter, and by religious, social and cultural fraternities and organizations. Undoubtedly, against the rather depressed economic backdrop of the time, they were lavish festivities that cost 55,793 pesetas (it is difficult to give a precise figure for what this would represent today, but it would probably be between one and three million euros).

The programme included religious processions, a historical cavalcade, archery competitions, nocturnal entertainments, popular dances, fireworks, bullfights, literary contests, floriculture, concerts, and regattas. These festivities also established a new 'tradition' — that of a specially commissioned '*cartel*' or poster. The 1887 *cartel* was inspired by bullfighting and very early tourism posters and it was designed by a well-known painter of the Málaga school, Joaquín Martínez de la Vega. His design featured in the upper portion a 'voussoired' horseshoe arch with the Royal coat of arms and that of Málaga on an imperial eagle to the left. Behind the arch, the Mediterranean Sea and La Farola, and a resurgent growth of vine leaves — a clear allusion to one of Málaga's most important products which was just beginning to recover from phylloxera.

The invitation extended by the poster may seem rather old-fashioned nowadays, but at the time it would have seemed rather daring and modern. Here was an important religious and civic event being advertised in language more usually encountered on posters for bullfights or circuses: 'Great Celebrations in Málaga, from the 19th to the 30th of August 1887, in Celebration of the Fourth Centenary of its Reconquest by the Catholic Kings, Don Fernando and Doña Isabel'. The iconography, too, was civic (the royal arms and La Farola) rather than religious.

🎩 The Modern *Feria*

In the guidebooks and on the tourist websites, a great deal is written about the *Semana Santa* ceremonies and the *Feria de Abril* of Sevilla. It is easy to see why, as both are extremely impressive and have inspired generations of artists and writers. But all things considered, I would advise any visitor wishing to witness either *Semana Santa* or a typical *feria andaluza* to go to Málaga, and not simply because this is a book about Málaga.

There is no doubt that the Sevilla *feria* is a glittering event of great beauty. It is hard not to be impressed by the sight of immaculately dressed *sevillanos* enjoying a glass of Fino at a venerable *sevillano* bar while their tethered horses feed from their nosebags, or by the procession of horse-drawn carriages between the Cathedral and the *recinto ferial*. The atmosphere inside the *feria* is intoxicating. So many thousands of people, so much *joie de vivre* (or *'alegría de vivir'*), the elegance of the fair-goers, the charm of the dancing, and every *caseta* seemingly more beautifully decorated than the next. But with the exception of a few *casetas* operated by the municipality, a handful of charitable organizations and left-wing political parties, almost all *casetas* are private. So unless you are lucky enough to have received an invitation from some *hidalgo* (important person), you can only really be a spectator.

In Málaga, however, all the *casetas* are open to the public, at least in principle. One still enjoys the grandeur of the *feria*, the beautifully dressed women and smartly attired men, the horse carriages, the flamenco, the music, the dancing of *sevillanas* and *verdiales*, the delicious food and plentiful drink. The difference is, that even as a visitor, you will be able to take part to some degree. And this is typically *malagueño*. As the subtitle of this book asserts, Málaga is Spain's 'most hospitable city'. Indeed, *'Muy hospitalaria'* is an official title of the city (granted by the Queen Regent María Cristina when the populace came to the aid of a sinking German ship in 1901). The friendliness and hospitality of *malagueños* is evident to any visitor at any time of year, but during the annual city-wide party that is the *feria* it is especially conspicuous.

The character of the *feria* as a welcoming event is due to a number of factors, I suspect. One is the strong local identity of traditional *barrios*, especially those to the west of the river like La Trinidad and El Perchel where the *corralones* survive. Having a *caseta* at the *feria* is an opportunity to celebrate their own local area and to show hospitality to visitors from other parts of the city, and beyond. Another factor is the large number of religious fraternities active in the city, many of whom have *casetas*. Although we tend to see these fraternities during Holy Week taking part in exotic para-liturgical ceremonies, their principal work throughout the year is charity and social action. Their presence at the *feria* is an extension of that promotion of community and work of inclusion. And then there is the determination of the *ayuntamiento* — admittedly partly with an eye upon the city's attractiveness to visitors and tourists — to make the *feria* a welcoming and inclusive event.

Although a great deal of the *Feria de Málaga* takes place in the city centre during the day (see below), the organizers try hard to ensure that everyone is able to enjoy the 'real' *feria*, which, as everyone knows, is the night-time event held in the *recinto ferial*. It would be easy to say that the disabled and elderly, for example, can 'experience' the *feria* during the day in the easily accessible city centre, or think that children will be satisfied with the fairground rides in the *'Zona de Atracciones'* and leave it at that. But organizers try to go above and beyond. Of the 120 or so *casetas*, all are accessible for wheelchair users and 50% have their own toilet facilities, all of which are fully accessible. There is a large, professionally staffed, municipal *caseta* for children that puts on free shows, plays, musicals and circus-type displays every evening from 9.30 pm. The aim is both to involve children in the 'grown-up' *recinto ferial* and allow their parents a little freedom to enjoy the *feria* by themselves.

For several years, the *ayuntamiento* has stressed the importance of the *feria* being something that all citizens of Málaga can take part in and enjoy. 'Mobility Points' have been set up in the city centre, equipped with mobility scooters, wheelchairs, crutches and walking sticks that may be borrowed at no cost. Musicians and performers also tour the city's hospitals so that in-patients are able to enjoy something of the atmosphere of the *feria*.

The biggest *caseta* of all, seating over 1,000 people, is the *Caseta 'El Rengue'* (*'rengue'* literally means 'infirm' but it also means colloquially 'a person full of wisdom and insight'). Open daily from 8.30 pm until 2 am, this *caseta* is for older people who are collected from and returned to various locations throughout Málaga by a free bus service. The aim of this *caseta* is, 'to make older people feel like the kings and queens of the *feria*,' and it is also open to the public because the *ayuntamiento* wants other *feria*-goers to see how one is 'supposed' to enjoy the *feria* to the full.

A Practical Guide to the Fair

During any *feria*, the city centre tends to be lively as people prepare to head off to the *recinto ferial*. The difference in Málaga, however, is that much of the official programme of the *feria* takes place in the city centre. This is known as the *Feria del Centro* (City Centre Fair) or the *Feria del Día* (Day Fair) and it runs from 1 pm until 6 pm every day. The *feria* that takes place at the *recinto ferial* (or *real de la feria*) is known as the *Feria de la Noche* (Night Fair), and although it gets off to a gentle start just after midday, things really liven up after dusk. The 'hinge' between the two is the *corrida* (bullfight) held at La Malagueta bullring at 7.30 pm each evening (see the bullfighting section on p. 437ff.).

If you really want to go native and throw yourself into the celebrations, you can attend the *Feria del Centro* during the day, have a brief nap and a shower, and then go to watch a bullfight at the *Plaza de Toros* 'La Malagueta' in late afternoon, all before heading out to the *Real de la Feria*, which will be in full swing by 10 pm. After enjoying a few glasses of Cartojal, eating some *tapas* and watching the *malagueños* dance *sevillanas* and *verdiales*, find your way back to the city in the small hours, briefly fortified by some *tejeringos* (*churros*) *buñuelos* (doughnuts) and *chocolate caliente*. Then put your head down for a few hours, before repeating the same itinerary later in the day. Once you have done this for a couple of days, you will begin to understand why all the banks, offices, and many of the shops are closed, and why the bars and restaurants in central Málaga close in the evenings during the *feria*. 'Going to the fair' in Spain is not simply a way to spend an enjoyable hour or two in the evening—for many, it can be a week-long commitment. The Spanish *feria* is a marathon not a sprint.

The Málaga *feria* runs for seven full days, from Saturday to Saturday, with the anniversary of the *reconquista* of Málaga occurring at some point during the festivities (*i.e.* it can start as early as 12 August, or as late as 18 August).

People begin getting in the mood on the Friday because the first event of the *feria* is the fireworks display and beach concert that takes place at midnight on Friday night. In recent years this has been preceded by drone light shows at 11.50 pm on the Malagueta and Huelin beaches, either side of the city centre. The fireworks are always an impressive display and thousands of people turn out to watch. They are set off from the cruise terminal, beyond La Farola, so they can be seen from Muelle Uno and Muelle Dos (Palmeral de Las Sorpresas). There will not, however, be much space, so be prepared to arrive early to seize your spot. Around the La Farola lighthouse is the best viewing position, but everyone in Málaga knows this and it is always packed. Another good vantage point is the Malagueta beach, but again, you will be jostling for space. Bring a picnic and your bottle(s) of Cartojal and arrive early. Another option is to go high. Málaga Cathedral sells tickets for access to the roof a week in advance (**malagacatedral.com/cultural-visit**) but there is no lift, so be prepared for a long climb up the steps. The Gibralfaro viewing terrace would give you a great view, but it also fills up quickly. Booking a late dinner for the terrace restaurant at the *Parador* is an option, but you will need to book weeks ahead and it is not a cheap option. The same goes for the various roof-top bars around Málaga. A more relaxed option would be to watch from the beaches in the west. You will miss the lower-level fireworks, but there is more room and you will still get a decent, if distant, view of the biggest pyrotechnics. Yet another option in the centre is to find a spot on the upper levels of the Jardines de Puerta Oscura, below the Alcazaba.

 The *ayuntamiento* usually publishes a map of the *recinto ferial* and the programme for the *feria* a few weeks ahead: malaga.eu/feria-de-malaga. These are PDF documents in Spanish, so if you need a translation, try searching for '*Feria de Málaga*' and '*programa*' to find a newspaper listing that you can run through Google Translate (bit.ly/MLGFeriaInfo).

On Saturday morning at 10 am, horses, carriages and people begin to gather outside the *Ayuntamiento* on the Avenida de Cervantes, where there is folk dancing and music. At 11.30 am the procession sets off along the Paseo del Parque and the Alameda, tracing the line of the medieval city walls — past the Atarazanas Market, then north beside the river, taking a right turn along Calle Carretería and Calle Álamos, through the Plaza de Merced and then to the basilica of the Santuario de Santa María de la Victoria. Unlike the liturgies of *Semana Santa*, which are liturgical and perfumed by clouds of incense, this religious act has a more civic character — the people of Málaga dedicating the *feria* to their patron saint, Our Lady of the Victory. The procession is led by an '*abanderado*' (flag bearer) who represents the people of the city and a floral offering is made before the image of the Blessed Virgin.

From about 1 pm, the *Feria del Centro* gets going. There is live music (everything from Europop to R&B, Rock to Merengue) in the Plaza de la Constitución, Plaza de las Flores, Plaza del Obispo and Plaza de San Pedro Alcántara. From midday until 3.30 pm in the Plaza de La Merced there are events for families and children — theatre, workshops, parades, magic shows, etc. In recent years there has been a 'Mini Sea Fair' organized on Muelle Uno consisting of free traditional games for younger children. This is aimed at those who will not be going to the *recinto* and runs from 8 pm until 10 pm. The Calle Marqués de Larios is where to find more traditional folk music, with different *Verdiales* '*pandas*' (gangs) performing each day, as well as folk choirs from around the city and province. Flamenco is staged every afternoon at the Peña Juan Breva Flamenco Museum (Calle Ramón Franquelo 4).

Scaramouch, Scaramouch, will you do the Fandango?

Most foreigners assume that what they see people dancing at the *feria* is flamenco (and indeed there is plenty of flamenco to be watched and seen) but those who are not professional dancers are more likely to be dancing *sevillanas* and *malagueñas*. Influenced by and with many similarities to flamenco, these are easier dances to master and far more suited to dancing in pairs. Flamenco is a particular interpretation and development of *andaluz* folk music, song and dance styles, of which there are dozens: *corríos, toná, seguiriya, fandangos, malagueñas, verdiales, jaberas, rondeñas, cartageneras, tarantas, tangos, tientos, tanguillos, cañas, trilleras, nanas, marianas, campanilleros, cachuchas, bulerías, peteneras, colombianas, jotas,* and countless others.

What are more or less unique to Málaga, however, are the *verdiales* — one of the liveliest and loveliest styles of folk music you are likely to encounter. *Verdiales* consist of a *fandango* (a triple time song/dance) sung and danced to the accompaniment of a band composed of a violin, two to four guitars, a tambourine, two or more pairs of cymbals (*crótalos*), various *castañuelas* (castanets) and, in some of its styles, a lute or *bandurria*. The ensemble, called a '*panda*', is completed with the figure of the *alcalde* (mayor) who, by holding up a *varilla* (baton or 'rule of command'), designates the singer and authorizes the beginning and end of the piece performed. There is also an *abanderado* (flag bearer), who marches with the mayor at the head of the group. The flags are used in the dances and may be Spanish, *andaluz*, *malagueña* or with the figure of the patron saint of the town or village of the *panda*. Sometimes a conch shell adorned with coloured ribbons is blown to herald the arrival of the *panda*.

The *Panda de Verdiales* is composed of *tocaores* (musicians), *cantaores* (singers) and *bailaores* (dancers). The *tocaores* are almost always men, while the *cantaores* and *bailaores* are drawn from both sexes. You can recognize a *panda de verdiales* by its members' distinctive clothing — white shirts with black trousers (and a red sash) for the men and black or red skirts for the women with white petticoats. Some of them wear hats decorated with dozens of flowers and brightly coloured streamers.

While some flamenco music or song can be foot-tappingly lively, some is meditative or melancholic. The *fandangos* of *los verdiales*, however, are generally lively (and even frenetic) whether the singer is paying a compliment to a lover or mourning an experience of loss or disappointment. The dance is simple, but beautiful, with fast footwork and movement of the body from the waist. *Castañuelas* trill constantly, almost hypnotically, such that each *fandango* sounds like a perpetual crescendo.

The *verdiales* that you see during the Málaga *feria* (both on the Calle Larios during the day and at the *Caseta de Los Verdiales* between 10 pm and 3 am during the night) are, as they say in Spanish, '*muy castizos*' (very authentic) and '*muy malagueños*'. First, they are ancient. The musicologists Hipólito Rossy and José Luque Navajas agree that *verdiales* are probably the most primitive *fandango* from Málaga and, almost certainly, from Andalucía as a whole. The scholar of flamenco Alfredo Arrebola goes so far as to affirm that the oldest *fandango* recorded in flamenco history is that of Málaga and dates from 'even before flamenco itself'. For a long time, a commonplace notion was that *verdiales* were Moorish in origin (*cf.* 'Morris', that is, 'Moorish' dances), but no serious scholar now believes this. The Muslim rulers of the *taifa*s of the Iberian peninsula were generally ideologically suspicious of music, song and mimetic art and consequently exerted little influence in these spheres. *Verdiales*, moreover, have always been a rural, rather than urban, art form and, as such, would have been preserved among the Christian peasants ('*mozárabes*') in the mountains. As the historian José Ruiz Sánchez put it, 'the [Muslim] administrators of the occupied territories were only interested in the tributary and military aspect of life, not what the locals sang or believed. Hispanics of that time didn't give a damn; that was tolerance.'

The origins of the *verdiales* are probably much older, possibly even drawing on pre-Roman influences. Professor Miguel Romero Esteo has pointed to the use of floral hats in the Minoan civilization (2800 BC), representing the exaltation of fertility. The first groups to settle Crete probably came from Anatolia around 7000 BC, and it is precisely in this area — the cradle of the Hittite culture — where archaeological excavations have found specimens of primitive tambourines and cymbals. It seems possible, or even likely, that a derivative of this culture would have accompanied the Phoenicians when they established a trading post in Málaga.

Despite successive invasions and cultural colonizations, it seems almost beyond doubt that these ancient dances survived in the rural enclaves of Málaga. There are representations of what seem to be *verdiales* gangs dating from Roman times. In a mosaic dedicated to Bacchus found in Córdoba, a woman appears playing a kind of tambourine. This instrument, also widespread throughout the Mediterranean, has long been popular in Spain. The flamenco aesthetic, however, has not adopted the use of this instrument, so we can say with some certainty that it is a pre-flamenco element.

But it is a mosaic from the so-called Villa Cicero in the ruins of Pompeii preserved in the National Museum of Naples that perhaps constitutes the strongest evidence for the antiquity and ritual connections of the *verdiales* with ancient pre-Christian Mediterranean rites. This is due to the similarity between the instruments, the representation of movement and the clothing of the current *pandas* with the group of musicians represented in the one catalogued as '*Scena comica con suonatori ambulanti*'. It is a work signed by Dioscorides of Samos (110–100 BC) and appears to be a copy of a Hellenistic painting from the 3rd century BC. The image represents a scene from the play *Theophorumene*, by the Greek playwright Menander. In the *Scena Comica* there is a group of musicians from Hellenic antiquity carrying a tambourine with decorative ribbons, some *crótalillos* or small bronze cymbals, a conch announcing the arrival of the musicians, and a double *aulós*-type flute. In addition, two of the four musicians wear headdresses with leaves and flowers on their heads similar to those that can be seen on the *verdiales* hats. All these objects are characteristic of the *verdiales* gangs from Málaga today, which suggests the existence of a continuity in the tradition.

As well as their antiquity, the *verdiales* of the Province of Málaga are also considered to be 'pure' and little changed over centuries. The somewhat 'rough' style of the *verdiales* meant that for a very long time, they were thought to be insufficiently elegant to be considered high art: merely the folk music of hicks and bumpkins. In many ways, this was the obverse of *casticismo*. Gypsies, being 'exotic' and brimming with *duende*, might be able to produce great art, but surely nothing of value could come from poor farmers from the hills? What this snooty attitude achieved, however, was to keep *verdiales* out of the salons and theatres so that it remained a relatively 'pure' genre of folk music, dance and song. This is also the source of the vitality of the *verdiales*. Other *andaluz* artistic manifestations were to some extent denatured when their cultural context disappeared and they became 'artistic' or academic, but the *verdiales* have continued to be transmitted from father to son and mother to daughter without interruption until today. There are no bars in Madrid flogging overpriced tickets for displays of 'authentic' *verdiales*, there are no 'professional' *verdiales* musicians, and no *verdiales tablaos*, which is why it is a genuine and rare example of a living folk tradition.

427

There are three styles, or schools, of *verdiales*: Almogía, Montes and Comares, depending upon where the *pandas* are based. The differences between them are rather subtle, but a rule of thumb is that the Almogía style tends to involve the dances with flags, the Montes style makes use of a larger tambourine, and the Comares style has the richest music, with guitars and lute being plucked more than strummed. The name, by the way, which means 'the green ones', comes from a variety of olive — verdial — that is grown in the Province of Málaga; so called because it remains green even when fully ripe. *Los verdiales* are most popular in the villages where this olive is grown.

Are *verdiales* the artistic equal of flamenco, then? Frankly, no. Flamenco is practised, at its best, by *virtuosi* who are often professional performers, whereas *verdiales* are performed by amateur (albeit skilled) musicians and dancers. But the purity and vitality of *verdiales* make it a joy to experience. The best analogy I can think of is the comparison between classical ballet and, say, Scottish cèilidh dancing. The former is certainly the more technically proficient and polished, but the latter can be more self-evidently joyful and more 'popular' in the literal sense.

It may not be everyone's cup of tea, but if you only have time to witness one musical performance at the Málaga *feria*, I strongly urge you to see a *panda de verdiales* in action, and defy you not to be utterly captivated and delighted by it. *Verdiales* utter the true soul of Málaga and the *feria*. As the lyrics of a well-known *verdiales* song put it:

> *Málaga has a Fiesta*
> *that stands out from the rest,*
> *there is none like the one*
> *that they call the Verdiales,*
> *as it is the oldest, ours, and the best.*

After the *Feria del Día* winds down at 6 pm, the next big event of the *feria* is the *corrida* (bullfight) at La Malagueta bullring at 7.30 pm (see below, p. 437ff.). The *Real de la Feria* gets going each day at noon with processions of carriage rides. Flamenco is performed from 2 pm, and there are equestrian displays at 4 pm and 10 pm daily. In the children's *caseta* there are films, theatre performances and other entertainment each evening from 9.30 pm. On the first Saturday evening, at 9.30 pm, the *feria* is officially opened (at the main entrance) by a local celebrity (often an actor, singer or TV presenter) and at 10 pm, the lights are turned on. From 10 pm until 3 am, *pandas de verdiales* perform in the *Caseta de los Verdiales*. From 10.30 pm on the *Explanada de la Juventud* (Youth Esplanade) there is a DJ set for young people, and concerts from 10 pm in the municipal auditorium. All attractions are free. You pay only for fairground rides, food and drink. From 11 pm each night, there is flamenco at the '*caseta municipal del flamenco y la copla*'.

To reach the *recinto*, although you could take the ◉ *Cercanías* train from the centre to Victoria Kent, by far the easiest way is to take the special bus (🚌 **F**) from the centre (Alameda Principal). This bus runs 24 hours a day during the *feria*, while a number of services covering the suburbs operate an extended service. The *bonobús* isn't valid on the special *feria* service, but you can use a contactless card to pay the fare.

A The *casetas* of the Málaga *feria* are all open to the public, but that does not necessarily mean that you will be able to enter whichever you fancy. All are free (charging for entry is strictly forbidden under a by-law) but the most popular *casetas* may be full. But with over 120 *casetas*, you will be able to find somewhere. If you need advice, visit the '*Información Feria*' *caseta* where staff from the Málaga tourist office will be able to help you. Do also tweet your experience at the *feria* using the hashtag **#FeriaMLG** and follow the official account at **@feria_malaga**.

🛡 Safety at the *Feria*

Generally speaking, the *Feria* is very safe as enormous public events go. Although there is a lot of alcoholic drink sloshing about, Spaniards rarely drink to the point of insensibility, let alone violence. Moreover, there are always plenty of people about, whatever the hour, and the buses run 24 hours a day, so there is no need to embark upon a solitary walk back to your hotel in the wee small hours. However, fairgoers still need to be vigilant, just like anyone taking part in an event that brings thousands of strangers together.

Travel to and from the *recinto ferial* as part of a group or at least with a companion, and stay together. *Malagueños* are friendly and vivacious, and like all Spaniards tend to be naturally and unselfconsciously tactile, but keep your wits about you and try to remain aware of potential dangers, particularly from 'new friends' whose interest seems to be especially eager or sets alarm bells ringing for any reason.

The *ayuntamiento* is well aware that this is the largest single annual event held in Málaga, and attracts visitors from throughout Spain as well as from overseas. The businesses, organizations and individuals operating *casetas* must go through a lengthy application and vetting process and they are inspected and scrutinized during the *feria* itself. They are also policed. For example, in 2022, three *casetas* were ordered to close after it was found that minors had been served alcohol. The local police will be very much in evidence in the city centre during the day and at the *recinto ferial* at night. If you feel uncomfortable, concerned about someone else's behaviour or in danger, find a police officer or, failing that, ask a member of staff in any of the *casetas* for help. All are trained to deal with such issues.

As part of the campaign spearheaded by the *ayuntamiento* — '*No es no*' (No means no) — alongside '*Málaga: Libre de violencias machistas*' (Málaga: Free from Sexist Violence) that works with local shops, bars and other businesses to establish and provide training for 'zero tolerance zones', there will be 'prevention teams' on hand at the *Feria*. There is a manned '*punto violeta*' ('purple point' — so called because the campaign logo is a purple circle) tent or stall, while other team members patrol the *recinto*. They hand out free drinks coasters ('*tapavasos*') which can detect GHB and other date-rape drugs.

Keep to the *recinto ferial* and the *zona de atracciones* and the official bus and taxi stand where there is safety in numbers, of course, but remember that for its scale, the *Feria de Málaga* is very safe.

The *Feria* in Numbers

To give a sense of what a monumental undertaking the *Feria de Málaga* is, here are a few statistics (from 2022, when attendance was relatively low following COVID):

- 6,092 kg of gunpowder in the fireworks display at the beginning of the fair.

- 121 *casetas*, 5 of them municipal, located in 241 modules in the Cortijo de Torres *recinto ferial*, a total area of 21,531 square metres.

- 17 special bus lines running every day from 8 pm to connect every district of Málaga with 'El Real'. 🚌F connects the city centre with fairground 24 hours a day.

- 96 fairground rides, games and attractions in the *Zona de Atracciones*. Of these, 45 are intended for all, and the rest especially for children. On the final Sunday, there is a 'Children's Day' with reduced prices.

- 247 outlets at the fairground dedicated to entertainment and the sale of food

- 4 authorized *casetas* in the city centre occupied by 35 street vendors.

- 6 defibrillators

- 80 refuse collecting vehicles — flushers, sweepers and support vehicles for cleaning tasks. An extra 321 refuse collectors and cleaners will be working during the *feria*.

- 5,000 extra rubbish bins in the city centre and the youth area, plus 1,410 bins in the *recinto ferial.*

- 730 officers of the Local Police, the National Police and the Civil Guard on duty, assisted by drones.

- 125,000 pieces of promotional material available at more than 300 locations throughout the province.

- 86% of the population of Málaga who attended at least one event of the *feria*

- 6,000,000 individual visits to the *feria*

Other Fairs in the Province of Málaga

This is not a complete list by any means, as every town and village will have a *feria*, however small. For example, in August, the village of Sayalonga holds a 'Medlar Festival' or '*Día del níspero*', while in other villages there are festivals devoted to different kinds of soup, to black pudding and to purple carrots. It is no exaggeration to say that between the *Feria de Abril* in Sevilla and the October *Feria* in Fuengirola you could probably attend well over 100 local *ferias* and *fiestas* in Andalucía. The *ferias* listed below are those held in locations mentioned in this book, or those within fairly easy reach of Málaga capital. For precise dates, please search online or check the website of the relevant *ayuntamiento* (good search terms are '*feria*' and '*programa*' or '*programación*' and the name of the location). For a comprehensive list covering the whole of Andalucía, consult:
andalucia.com/festival/summer.htm

Is there a distinction between a *feria* and a *fiesta*? The answer is, as so often, yes and no. Just as the words fair, fête, feast and festival overlap in English, so in *castellano*. '*Fiesta*' means 'festival' or 'feast', and is derived from the Latin word for the same (*festum*). It is thus used to refer to a religious celebration, like the 'Feast of St John'. It also, in modern Spanish, means 'party'. A fiesta is usually small-scale, local and often lasts a single day. A *feria*, or fair, on the other hand, lasts more than a day and operates (at least historically speaking) with royal, ecclesiastical or civic approval. Confusingly, for students of etymology, the word is derived from another Latin word (*feria*) that also means 'feast' or 'festival' and yet which, in ecclesiastical use means the opposite; *viz.* a day when there is no feast celebrated!

In the sense of 'public celebrations marked by eating, drinking and dancing', *feria*, *fiesta*, *fiestas* and *festival* are all used. Job fairs, book fairs and bridal fairs are always *ferias*, however, while birthday parties and New Year's Eve parties are always *fiestas*.

To find out what's on in the Province of Málaga during your visit, check **malaga.es/agenda** (only in Spanish). The listing is only as complete as communication from local *ayuntamientos* allows it to be, but you may spot something of interest. It's also worth asking at the *turismo* in Málaga.

February
📍 Ardales 🍴 Fiesta de la Matanza 📅 second Sunday of February 🌐 ardales.es

The 'Festival of the Slaughter' (Spaniards aren't squeamish about the realities of food production) begins at noon with the distribution of around 1,000 kg of cured pork products. These samples are free, with other local products on sale in the market. Concerts begin at 5 pm.

April
📍 Cártama 🍴 Feria de Cártama 📅 5 days including 23 April 🌐 cartama.es

The Cártama Fair is both a religious and a recreational event and has a wide range of activities on its programme. The centrepiece is the procession of the image of Our Lady of Remedies from the hermitage on the hill down into the town and the Parish church of San Pedro. There are also sports tournaments, musical and dance group performances, wine and food tastings, popular games, children's games and contests.

⌖ Fuengirola ⟡ La Feria de los Pueblos ▦ late April/early May ⊕ fipfuengirola.com

Not by any means a traditional *feria andaluza*, but great fun. Representing the international composition of the town, it's held in the main fairground of Fuengirola (between the train stations of Fuengirola and Los Boliches) and it lasts for a week. In just one day, you can visit up to 50 countries — or at least a microcosm of each one, since they are represented in full colour, flavour and sound. Each country is allocated its own *caseta*. For well over a decade now, this annual celebration has grown and become increasingly popular with local residents and visitors alike. From mini German beer festivals, to Irish dancing displays and Cuban music and dance, there is something for every taste. The typical dishes and drinks from each country are worth sampling, too. It's a very popular festival and people come from all over, making this one of the highlights of the annual events calendar

May

⌖ Coín ⟡ Fiesta de la Naranja ▦ mid-May ⊕ turismocoin.es/en

This one-day festival celebrates the end of the orange harvest (October to May) and involves tastings of orange juice, *ensaladilla malagueña* (cod and orange salad) and Coín's signature soup — *sopa hervida* (shortened in *andaluz* Spanish to 'sopa hervía'), which is a rustic soup made with chicken stock, potatoes, tomatoes, vegetables and bread. ⚠ Before COVID, the *fiesta* lasted a few days, so it may return to the older timetable in due course.

⌖ Churriana ⟡ Feria (*Fiestas Populares San Isidro Labrador de Churriana*) ▦ mid-May ⊕ churrianaweb.es

The Churriana *Feria* is a week-long event connected to the feast of San Isidro Labrador (Saint Isidore the Labourer). This *feria* is easy to get to if you are staying in Málaga because Churriana is a suburb of Málaga and there are plenty of buses (there may even be extra buses laid on). The *feria* is known for its sports events and competitions, but there are also all the usual events associated with any *feria* — music, dancing, concerts, food, drink, parades, etc.

⌖ Alhaurín el Grande ⟡ Feria ▦ mid-May ⊕ bit.ly/AEGFeria

The day fair is enjoyed on the streets of the historic centre of the town, where large numbers of people congregate to enjoy the atmosphere. This gives way to the night fair, at the fairground, where you'll find the traditional attractions of the fair — *casetas*, singing, dancing, music, food, drink, etc.

⌖ Antequera ⟡ Feria de Primavera ▦ end of May ⊕ bit.ly/AnteqPrima

This *feria* began in the late 19th century as a way of promoting local agriculture and there is still a significant overlap between the agricultural fair (farm machinery exhibitions, goat auctions, food markets) and the recreational fair (dancing, food, drink, entertainment and bullfighting).

⌖ Ronda ⟡ Real Feria de Ronda ▦ May ⊕ rondaromantica.net

This *feria* is the oldest (it has been held since 1509) and most cultured of all Andalucía's *ferias*. There is plenty of fun to be had, but the accent is upon folk culture, flamenco, music, and horsemanship. The *feria* takes place over a weekend (Friday to Sunday) with lots of daytime events in the city centre on Saturday and Sunday making it a good day trip destination from Málaga Capital.

⌖ Córdoba ⟡ Feria de Mayo ▦ late May ⊕ bit.ly/FdMCordoba

Córdoba is not in the Province of Málaga, but a provincial capital itself. I include it in this section because it is easy to get to from Málaga (an hour by train — see p. 564ff.). It is a grand affair, comparable to those of Sevilla and Málaga and, as in Málaga, entry to all *casetas* is free (that is, free in the sense of not invitation only; you'll still need to pay for food and drink). Unlike Málaga, there is no day *feria* in the city centre, with all of the events taking place at night in the *recinto ferial*, so if you want to enjoy this *feria* you will need to book overnight accommodation in Córdoba (or pull an all-nighter).

June

🍴 Granada 🍷 Feria del Corpus 📅 late May/early June ⊕ bit.ly/FerGran and turgranada.es/en

Granada (see p. 580ff.) is included here for the same reason as Córdoba. All *casetas* are open to the public and free, as in Málaga. Like Córdoba, the *feria* takes place at night, so if you want to experience it, you will need an overnight stay in the city. The week-long *feria* coincides with the Feast of Corpus Christi (the Thursday after Trinity Sunday), which can occur as early as 21 May or as late as 24 June. On the feast day itself, the Blessed Sacrament is taken in procession through the streets of the city.

🍴 Mijas 🍷 Feria Internacional de los Pueblos 📅 June ⊕ turismo.mijas.es

People of more than thirty countries come together to showcase their own cultures. Typical costumes, crafts and gastronomy are exhibited, as well as music and dance displays. Up to thirty-five clubs and associations of foreigners on the Costa del Sol participate in the event. The celebration intends to pay tribute to coexistence and tolerance.

🍴 Marbella 🍷 Feria de San Bernabé 📅 mid–June

The *feria* in Marbella is associated with the town's patron, San Bernabé (Saint Barnabas the Apostle). His feast day is 11 June, but the celebration is often transferred to the nearest Sunday, with the *feria* taking place soon after or, sometimes, before. There is a lot going on and plenty to enjoy even if you are only able to take part in the day *feria*. While the official tourism website for the *Ayuntamiento* of Marbella may boast that it is a '*Destino 5 Estrellas*' (a 'Five-Star Destination') its website is a triumph of style over substance — hard to navigate and lacking in useful information. The website of the *ayuntamiento* itself (**marbella.es/agenda.html**) is rather better. Your best bet is to search on Google to find the details of this year's *feria*. Details are usually finalised a couple of months ahead.

🍴 Puerto de la Torre 🍷 Feria 📅 late June/early July ⊕ puertodelatorre.com

A five-day *feria* in a northern suburb of Málaga featuring the usual attractions — parades, *verdiales*, flamenco, competitions, entertainment, music etc. This is a night *feria* so although you will be able to take the bus to the *feria* (about 25 minutes' journey), unless EMT schedules extra buses, you'll need to take a taxi back to your accommodation.

🍴 Cala del Moral 🍷 Feria 📅 late June/early July ⊕ lacaladelmoral.com/fiestas

Cala del Moral is on the coast, about seven miles from Málaga. There are lots of events held in the daytime — boat regattas, beach volleyball tournaments, free *paella*, music, dancing, tastings, competitions, etc., plus all the usual attractions at the night *feria*. You can reach Cala del Moral easily by bus from Málaga, though if you stay very late you will need to take a taxi back.

July

🍴 Estepona 🍷 Feria y Fiestas Estepona 📅 early July ⊕ turismo.estepona.es

The Estepona fair is lively and traditional with horse-riding, carriage driving, flamenco, dance, music, food, drink and bullfights. However, everything takes place in the *recinto ferial* and doesn't get going until after 3 pm, so it's not really a day trip option. If you want to get a proper taste of the Estepona *feria*, you'll need to stay overnight.

🍴 Caleta de Vélez 🍷 Feria 📅 early July 🌐 velezmalaga.es

East of Málaga on the coast, this *feria* is also mostly at night, but there are a few events during the day that will make a day trip worthwhile, including free sardines on the Saturday and free *paella* on the Sunday, with music and dancing.

🍴 La Cala de Mijas 🍷 Feria 📅 end of July 🌐 calamijas.com

Around July 25, the La Cala Fair takes place, in honour of its patron saint, Santiago Apóstol. This fair usually begins with parades of giants and *cabezudos* (big heads). There is a day *feria* which means that you could make a day trip from Málaga to enjoy the free *paella*, music and dance performances.

🍷 Fiestas del Carmen 📅 around 16 July

Many of the *ferias* along the coast of the Province of Málaga are associated with the Feast of Our Lady of Mount Carmel (16 July) including Rincón de la Victoria, Campanillas, El Palo, Pedregalejo, Torremolinos, Benalmádena, Fuengirola, Marbella, Los Boliches, Colonia Santa Inés, Benajarafe, La Carihuela, Nerja, Torre del Mar to name just some. In short, everywhere on the coast will mark the feast publicly in some way. These are primarily religious processions, but with elements of a traditional *feria* (music, drinking, dancing, etc.) tacked on.

August

🍴 Álora 🍷 Feria de Álora 📅 beginning of August 🌐 alora.es

A surprisingly impressive week-long *feria* for a small *pueblo blanco*, and well worth a visit if your visit to Málaga coincides (not least because Álora is very near Málaga and a lovely little town). Most of the events are at the night *feria*, but from Thursday to Sunday there are daytime events held in the Plaza Fuente Arriba, including a free tasting of 'sopa perota' — a local dish made from bread, onions, tomatoes, garlic and mint, halfway between a stir-fry and a soup.

🍴 Coín 🍷 Feria de Agosto 📅 mid–August 🌐 turismocoin.es/en

Coín's August Fair, normally concludes around the 15th of August to coincide with the feast

day of their patron Our Lady of Fuensanta. The daytime area is located in the town centre and extends from the Alameda to the Parque San Agustín, taking in the Plaza Bermúdez de la Rubia, where culinary events take place and activities such as concerts and sporting events are held. The night-time activities take place in the main fairground, where live performances and other attractions continue well into the night, but you'd need to find accommodation in Coín to make the most of these.

🍴 Antequera 🍷 Real Feria de Agosto 📅 late August 🌐 cultura.antequera.es

A five-day *feria* consisting of both a day fair and a night fair with all the usual attractions. During the day, there is music in the city centre and various competitions judging entities as distinct as 'porra' (the local, thicker version of *gazpacho*) and flamenco dress and suit designs. The annual bullfighting *feria* takes place concurrently. It is one of the oldest continuously celebrated *feria* in Spain (with its beginnings in 1748) and one of the grandest and most stylish.

🏮 Ronda 🔔 Real Feria de Agosto/Pedro Romero
📅 end of August/early September 🌐 turismoderonda.es/en

This *feria* takes place at the same time as the bullfighting *feria*. It traditionally starts on the Wednesday evening with a parade at about 7.30 pm. The highlight of the week is the procession and '*Corrida Goyesca*' bullfight that traditionally (now) takes place on the first Saturday of September at about 6 pm. Most of the *feria* takes place in the late afternoon and at night, so if you want to really enjoy this most stylish of fairs it would be worth booking a room in Ronda for the night (though you'll need to plan ahead to get a reasonable deal on a room). Take a taxi to visit a wine-making *bodega* during the day, and enjoy the *feria* in the evening!

September

🏮 Ardales 🔔 Feria 📅 first week of September 🌐 ardales.es

The main annual *feria* is in honour of Our Lady of Villaverde (feast day: 8 September).

🏮 Mijas Pueblo 🔔 Feria 📅 early September 🌐 turismo.mijas.es

The Mijas Pueblo fair takes place during the first two weeks of September in honour of its patroness, the *Virgen de la Peña*, with a varied programme of cultural, sporting, musical and festive activities. Celebrations kick off with a Parade of Giants and *cabezudos* ('big heads') through the main streets of Mijas, accompanied by marching bands and the queens of the fairs of Mijas, Las Lagunas and La Cala and their respective maids of honour. They wind up with a children's party in the municipal marquee. On the day of Mijas' patroness (8 September) and after the traditional floral offering to the Virgin, a Solemn Procession of the image of the Virgin of the Peña takes place from the parish church to her sanctuary. Most of the attractions are part of the night fair, but if you visit for the day you should still get a sense of the celebrations thanks to the day fair.

🏮 Vélez-Málaga 🔔 Real Feria de San Miguel 📅 around 29 September
🌐 velezmalaga.es

Expect the typical atmosphere of the best *andaluz* fairs: decorated streets, horse rides, people in traditional costume and the *casetas* as the main element, plus tastings of typical dishes and performances by *verdiales pandas*. There is a day fair and a night fair, so you can party at any time.

🏮 Torremolinos 🔔 Feria de San Miguel 📅 around 29 September
🌐 turismotorremolinos.es/en

The Torremolinos *feria* combines very traditional elements with the modern. It begins with a pilgrimage that attracts thousands of people, but it also involves rock concerts. Most of it takes place during the day, making it ideal if you are staying in Málaga. The afternoons are more traditional, with the rock/pop concerts later at night. A popular event is the free tasting of stewed tripe on the first day (usually in the Plaza de Andalucía from about 2 pm).

October

🏮 Fuengirola 🔔 Feria del Rosario 📅 Near 7 October 🌐 fuengirola.es

This is another *feria* where the religious and recreational are closely connected and blended. While most of the main events of the *feria* (the concerts and merry-making) take place at night, there are concerts and religious events during the day, and if you visit Fuengirola from Málaga you will at least be able to get a sense of a town '*en fête*'.

Los Toros (The Bulls)

CAUTION: This chapter includes a description (and some images) of what happens during a *corrida de toros* (or 'bullfight') which some readers may find upsetting or offensive.

In many Spanish towns and cities, a programme of bullfights is staged at the same time as the annual *feria* (fair). In Sevilla, the *feria taurina* (bullfighting fair) lasts a full month, far longer than the week-long *Feria de Abril*. In Madrid, the May *Feria de San Isidro* is now predominantly a bullfighting fair. Some places may have a week-long *feria* with one, two or three bullfights. In Málaga, the *Feria de Agosto* and the *Feria Taurina* run more-or-less concurrently.

In most of Spain, major civic celebrations (mostly linked to Christian festivals) have, for centuries, been marked by bullfights. Even in Catalonia, which famously voted in 2010 to ban the *corrida de toros* (the traditional Spanish bullfight held in a bullring), one can still find plenty of celebrations in smaller towns that involve bulls in some way. Many *aficionados* ('fans of the bulls') criticize the Catalan ban as being nakedly political, pointing across the border to Occitanian France where, if anything, the bullfight has increased in popularity in recent decades and attempts to have it banned were rejected by France's Constitutional Council as recently as 2012. But, truth be told, there are political points being made on both sides of the Franco-Spanish border. In Catalonia, the bullfight is painted as something typically 'Spanish' and so banning it is a way of demonstrating Catalonia's cultural (and, thus, political) distance from Madrid, whereas in southern France, west and east of the Pyrenees, embracing bullfighting shows their cultural (and therefore, political) distance from Paris.

I include this section on bullfighting not in order to promote it, but because this is a book about Málaga and bulls are still important in the city. You may already be *quite* certain that you have no desire ever to watch a bullfight (or even read about one), and that is perhaps a 'normal' reaction. For anyone not from the Iberian peninsula, the South of France or Latin America, bullfighting seems curious, 'foreign' and probably barbaric. But even though bullfighting is not as popular as it once was, it is still deeply embedded in Spanish culture. The red and yellow of the Spanish national flag may not actually represent the sand of the bullring and the blood of the bull, but the common folk perception is that they do.

One of Málaga's greatest admirers, the fabulist Hans Christian Andersen, was famously conflicted about the bullfight. He visited the bullring and wrote, 'It was scarcely possible to sit out this scene, and my blood tingled to the very points of my fingers.' We should remember that Andersen saw a bullfight in the days before the horses wore protective mattresses. They were old nags on their way to the knacker's yard and were frequently disembowelled in the ring (nowadays they are valuable animals and carefully protected from injury). Even so, he stayed to watch the whole spectacle, noting that there was 'something interesting and attractive in the skill and agility, the steady eye, and the dexterity with which the *banderilleros* and *espada* moved on the arena. It was like a game, or a dance upon the stage.' Most *aficionados* of the bulls would probably say that he grasped the essence of the event, *i.e.* that it is not combat, but artistry. Andersen's response is, in my experience, typical of many foreigners open-minded enough to attend a bullfight. They might be very clear that it is not something they feel comfortable with, and yet they are also able to recognize that it is not the mindless or bloodthirsty slaughter that they expected.

Just as in English, so many phrases are derived from the game of cricket (*e.g.* 'a good innings', 'a sticky wicket', 'off his own bat', 'to be bowled over', etc.), so hundreds of idioms in *castellano* come from the practice and art of bullfighting. In Spanish, one does not 'change the subject' so much as *'cambiar el tercio'* ('change the third' — because a bullfight is divided into three parts), and the expression, *'coger el toro por los cuernos'* comes word for word into English as 'to take the bull by the horns'. The first modern (and, some would say, the first postmodern) novel, Miguel de Cervantes' *Don Quixote de la Mancha* is full of references to bulls and bullfighting. Indeed, Cervantes' novel is one of the reasons we know that in the early 17th century cattle were being bred specifically for bullfighting.

The bullfight, the 'dance with death' that has been called 'indefensible but irresistible', has fascinated artists for millennia. Scenes depicting human beings and bulls together are seen in Palaeolithic paintings (that date between 15,000 and 10,000 BC) found in the caves in both France and Spain. Hercules' battle with the Nemean lion, Theseus's slaying of the Minotaur, and the vanquishing of a bull by Mithras (a scene often depicted in Hellenistic art) all share a common taurine theme. Perhaps the first *'matador'* in literature is the hero of the Epic of Gilgamesh, the most important literary text of ancient Mesopotamia. As the 4,000-year-old Babylonian legend states, 'Gilgamesh, like a huntsman, thrusts his sword between nape and horns' and slays the bull sent to destroy him. Frescoes in ancient Crete depict acrobatic dances or games with bulls, and, although these scenes do not show bullfighting as it is known today, they are noteworthy in that they show youths of both sexes vaulting over the horns of charging animals. If you want to see a very similar spectacle in the 21st century then you need to go to south-western France for a *course landaise* (though this tends to use aggressive cows rather than bulls), or to Castilla-y-León, Aragón or Madrid to witness a *recortes* with young bulls. (In 2022, an exhibition of *recortes* was staged in Málaga for the first time on the Sunday before the beginning of the *feria*.)

The art and spectacle of the bullfight have been favourite subjects for many Spanish painters, most notably Goya, who produced an extensive series of etchings in 1815–16 depicting every aspect of the Spanish bullfight. The impressionist Joaquín Sorolla produced a few paintings of bullfighting scenes and Salvador Dalí — a passionate lover of the bulls despite his wife's deep disapproval — left dozens of works. Among the best-known, however, and most fitting when talking of the bulls in Málaga, is Pablo Picasso. His first known painting is of a *picador* (a mounted bullfighter). He painted it aged only eight, after seeing a *corrida* at La Malagueta with his father, and he remained a devoted *aficionado* for the rest of his life.

The historian and literary critic, Marcelino Menéndez Pelayo (1856–1912), wrote in his *History of Aesthetic Ideas in Spain* that bullfighting 'is a terrible and colossal pantomime of ferocious and tragic beauty, in which the aesthetic elements of horsemanship and fencing are brought together and perfected, just as the opera produces together the effects of music and poetry.'[64] The philosopher José Ortega y Gasset argued that it was unthinkable to study the history of Spain without considering bullfights. The *granadino* poet Federico García Lorca expressed his open support and taste for bullfighting: 'Bullfighting is probably the poetic and vital wealth of Spain, incredibly wasted by writers and artists… I think that bullfighting is the most cultured festival in the world.'[65]

---

64 M. Menéndez Pelayo, 'Historia de las Ideas Estéticas' in *Edición Nacional de las Obras Completas*, Vol. II, p. 503

65 Federico García Lorca, *Obras completas: Prosa*. (Editorial Aguilar, 1986), p. 685

One of Lorca's most moving, tragic and celebrated poems, *Llanto por Ignacio Sánchez Mejías*, is an elegiac meditation upon a bullfight that repeats the line '*a las cinco de la tarde*' ('at five in the afternoon' — the time that the bullfight began) like a metronome.

Ortega y Gasset, like other authors, such as the academic José María de Cossío, drew a parallel between bullfighting and the very history of Spain:

> '*I affirm in the most exhaustive way that the History of Spain, from 1650 to today, cannot be well understood by anyone who has not rigorously built the history of bullfighting in the strict sense of the term, not of the bullfight that, more or less vaguely, has existed in the Peninsula for three millennia, but what we currently call by that name. The history of bullfighting reveals some of the deepest secrets of Spanish national life for almost three centuries. And it is not a question of vague appreciations, but, otherwise, it is not possible to define precisely the peculiar social structure of our people during those centuries, a social structure that is, in very important orders, strictly inverse of the normal one in the other nations of Europe.*'[66]

The bullfight has also captivated foreign writers, artists and travellers seeking to understand the Spanish 'soul' — from Édouard Manet to Raoul Millais, from George Bizet to Ernest Hemingway, from Rita Hayworth to A. L. Kennedy. Artists and academics (mainly philosophers and anthropologists) have spent years of their lives trying to appreciate, understand, and describe the bullfight. In fact, two of the most thoughtful recent studies have been penned by non-Spaniards (the Sevilla-based, Iranian-born heart surgeon Reza Hosseinpour and the French philosopher Francis Wolff), and yet a great deal about the bullfight — what it expresses and signifies — eludes description. It is, perhaps, something that can only be felt or experienced rather than explained or described. Critics sometimes draw analogies with ballet, perhaps because *aficionados* rightly insist that the *corrida* is an art, not a sport (reports of bullfights appear in the 'culture' section of the newspapers, not in the sports section).

But even this will not *quite* do, insofar as a balletic performance is choreographed and rehearsed and then repeated almost identically night after night. Yet what happens in the bullring is by its nature unpredictable and unique because it involves not only a man (and historically, it has usually been a man), but also a wild animal. So a better example might be a pass in football or rugby, even though purists will baulk at any sporting comparisons. What happens, in any pass, is that a ball is moved from one place to another. In a replay, it is possible to describe and analyse any pass, in terms of angle, velocity, direction and distance, but almost instinctively a fan of the game will just exclaim, 'Beautiful pass!' even though he or she might be hard pressed to explain precisely what made it beautiful. Any fan understands that far more is at stake than simply goals, or tries. Often it will be a goal or a try that makes one catch one's breath, but just as often it is the fluid motion of the ball between the players on the pitch, the dance-like perfection of play that is heart-stopping. For this reason, penalties and conversions are rarely as elegant as in-play goals and tries. Serendipitously, in bullfighting, one talks of the bullfighter making '*pases*' (movements) with the cape or cloth, the aim of which is to move and control not a ball, but an animal. The fact that there are no goals to be scored, nor any tally of points, does not undermine the analogy concerning the notion of the 'beautiful pass'.

---

66   José Ortega y Gasset, 'Lección primera', (1947), of 'Curso de cuatro lecciones' in *Introducción a Velázquez*, in *Obras completas. 1933–1948. Obra póstuma*, (Madrid, Fundación José Ortega y Gasset/Taurus, 2009), Vol. IX, p. 914

⏳ History

Another appropriate comparison to draw is with flamenco, though here it is less a matter of analogy than of a clear relationship, even a symbiosis. Flamenco and *toreo* (bullfighting) are inseparable. At least traditionally, the practitioners of both art forms have come from the same cultural and social milieux: working class, *andaluz*, Gypsy — occupying a liminal place between the rural and the urban. To understand the deep connection between the two traditions, we first need to explore something of the history of both.

Something akin to bullfighting has been practised in the Iberian peninsula for millennia. The Celtiberians and inhabitants of pre-Roman Tartessos (modern-day central Andalucía) almost certainly deployed bulls in warfare. The Romans brought with them a culture that featured bulls and other animals in spectacles, one such being the *contomonobolon* — an acrobatic display involving leaping over running bulls using poles (similar to that depicted in the Cretan wall paintings mentioned above). Under Visigothic rule and the Umayyad caliphate, there is evidence that a specifically Iberian form of entertainment involving bulls was developing (though for the Moors, the entertainment was for the horsemen, not for the public).

What we do know is that for some thousand years after the departure of the Romans, bulls were used in displays of horsemanship and for sport. Bulls would be hunted on horseback using lances by both Moorish and Christian knights. This, of course, was not something confined to Iberia; it was practised throughout Europe. The famous 'wild' cattle of Chillingham Park (Northumberland, UK) were probably once hunted in a similar fashion. It also tells us something about the kind of cattle used. These were not ordinary farm animals. Most farm cattle are bred to maximize meat, milk, meekness and mating. An ordinary beef or dairy farmer wants to minimize aggressiveness, which makes animals difficult, and dangerous, to handle, while maximizing flesh and milk yield and fertility and ease of calving. But in bulls bred for hunting (and now bullfights) traits like boldness and aggressiveness are important, while meat and milk are not.

The difference between domestic cattle of the kind seen on beef and dairy farms, and the fighting bulls raised on dedicated cattle ranches (*ganaderías*) is also seen in the different adjectives used. For domesticated cattle, we use the term 'bovine' which conjures an image of placid, lumbering animals moving slowly and chewing the cud. They may be enormous beasts, but they are rarely terrifying. Such a term hardly describes the pugnacious Spanish *toro*, for which the adjective 'taurine' is used. In the UK we see thousands of cows in the fields, but rarely many bulls. In Spain, the perception is reversed. Most beef and dairy production takes place in the cool and rainy north-west on the Atlantic coast. In the rest of the country, it is the fighting bull breed that is more familiar, not just in the countryside but on billboards, posters, in the decoration of bars, and even on menus. The beloved dish of slowly stewed tail is '*rabo de toro*' — the tail of a fighting bull — rather than 'oxtail'. An ox, by the way, is a steer: a castrated male. Castration reduces aggression and makes the animal easier to handle.

Both 'bovine' and 'taurine' are derived from the Latin name of the domestic cow, *Bos taurus*. Despite their Spanish name, *toro bravo*, and the fact that 'bravo' can be translated either as 'brave' or 'wild', fighting bulls are not, strictly speaking, wild. Like all European descendants of the now-extinct Aurochs, they are domesticated but have not been bred to minimize 'wild' traits like aggression and strength, and they are farmed with minimal human interaction. Unlike the feral Chillingham cattle which, apart from being fed in winter and occasionally euthanized to prevent suffering and have no contact with human beings, or even vets, the Spanish fighting bull is selectively bred in order to enhance some traits and diminish others. Even so, when a bull arrives in the bullring, that is the first time it has been confronted with a human being at close quarters (contact on the ranch is made in vehicles or on horseback), whereas most British cattle are quite used to close handling.

At least from the time of the *reconquista*, the '*corrida*' (which literally means 'running') — though still a way of practising and demonstrating horsemanship — had also become a form of public entertainment. Bulls would be chased (for example in the main square of the town) and the mounted bullfighter would incite the bull to charge, using a combination of his lance and deft horsemanship to prevent the bull from killing his mount. This is the difference between the *toro bravo* and most other animals that human beings have hunted. Pursued by huntsmen on horseback, deer and other animals flee, but bulls are different. They do not run away, even when they are dying, preferring instead to fight to the death. Bullfighting became a contest in which the most daring warriors could demonstrate their courage. But for the gentry that pursued the bulls from horseback, actually dispatching the animal after the chase and display came to be seen as rather *infra dignitatem* so the task was delegated to one of the servants who attended the mounted bullfighter. The one who dispatched the bull with a sword was called a '*matador*' (literally, 'killer') and the kill was rarely public.

The bullfight as we know it today really developed in the 18th century in Ronda, in the Province of Málaga, thanks to an extraordinary dynasty of *toreros*, beginning with Francisco Romero (1700–1763). Even before Francisco Romero, it had been common to summon the bull with a cloth, but it was he who formalized the use of the *muleta* (meaning 'crutch' — that is, the red cloth draped over a wooden stick used during the final stage of the bullfight). Francisco, his son Juan, and grandsons Pedro and Antonio introduced innovations that transformed the final stage of the bullfight (the kill) from a prosaic necessity into a display of art, skill and beauty. The *coup de grâce* itself is still — ideally — quick and clean, but it is the *danse macabre* that precedes it that has become the purest expression of the bullfighter's art and the clearest display of the bull's bravery.

At this point, we ought to get our terminology correct. What happens in a bullring is **not** a 'bullfight'. That may be the common English term, but it is a term of abuse, or at least of misunderstanding (compare someone unfamiliar with horse racing going to Cheltenham and referring to what they had witnessed as 'horse-whipping'.) The term for a bullfight [sic] in Spanish is '*corrida de toros*' (*lit*. running of bulls). The verb meaning 'to face bulls at a *corrida*' is '*torear*' or '*lidiar*'. *Torear* is a verb formed from the noun meaning 'bull' — '*toro*', whereas *lidiar* sometimes means 'to fight' but in the case of *toreo* properly means to struggle, oppose or negotiate. The man (and occasionally woman) who engages in '*toreo*' is a '*torero*' (and occasionally '*torera*') '*Toréador*' (*cf.* Georges Bizet) is an archaic Gallicism. Another, more literary, word for *toreo* is '*tauromaquia*' (from Ancient Greek ταῦρος (*tauros*, 'bull') and μάχη (*makhe*, 'battle'), from which we also derive the rarely used English term 'tauromachy'.

At the same time that the Romeros in Ronda and Costillares (Joaquín Rodríguez Costillares, 1743–1800) in Sevilla were developing and refining the physical 'vocabulary' of *toreo* (the way of holding and moving the *muleta*, the repertoire of passes through which to direct the bull, and so forth), the art form of flamenco was also developing in the same place (Andalucía). The earliest *toreros* were semi-urbanized — familiar with livestock, often servants of the landed gentry, but performing at *corridas* held in towns and cities. The entire spectacle of *toreo* is a curious mix of the rural and urban. Until the 18th century, most *corridas* took place in the main squares of towns and cities, but as they grew in popularity, purpose-built stadia — *plazas de toros* — were constructed, each one a *rus in urbe* bringing a small patch of the *ganadería* into the city. Here, animals from the countryside, the closest thing to wild cattle that we can now imagine, are tested and tamed within the city walls (at least figuratively). In many towns in Spain (not just in the most famous, Pamplona) the bulls destined for the *corrida* run from their paddocks to the bullpens (*toriles*) at the *plaza* each morning. Although the people who run behind them, and those who go to the afternoon *corrida* are largely city-dwellers, many of them will still think of themselves as 'really' coming from the countryside. Spain was overwhelmingly a rural, agricultural economy until comparatively recently, so it is not uncommon to hear a *malagueño* banker refer wistfully to 'my village' even though his great-grandfather left before the Civil War and the only family connection now is via a cousin four times removed who does not live there either but still owns a small plot of olive trees.

The *gitanos* (Gypsies) who made flamenco into the art form it is now also stood somewhat between town and country. Traditionally itinerant and involved in horse-trading, they began to settle in ghettoes in the cities of Andalucía in search of work in the 18th century. Where flamenco really came from, no one quite knows. Even the word is of contested etymology. It might refer to flamingoes, or mean 'Flemish', or be a mangling of an Arabic phrase, or be a slang term for Gypsies. As for the artistic and musical form, it could trace its ancestry to the Khattak dances of the Indian subcontinent, and the '*fandango*' dance tune may even be African in origin (perhaps via Portugal). The key period of development and consolidation of flamenco took place in the late 18th and early 19th centuries — exactly the same time that the *corrida* was developing into the art form we know today.

Between the end of the 18th and the early decades of the 19th century, a number of factors led to the rise in Spain of a phenomenon known as '*costumbrismo andaluz*' or 'Andalusian Mannerism' — that in due course became known as '*casticismo*' ('purity' or 'authenticity'). In 1783 King Carlos III promulgated a decree that regulated the social situation of the *gitanos* who, after centuries of marginalization and persecution, saw their legal situation improve substantially as a result. After the Spanish War of Independence (1808–1812), a feeling of cultural (and even racial) pride developed in the Spanish conscience, in opposition to the '*afrancesados*' — Spaniards who were influenced by French culture and the ideas of the Enlightenment. In this context, *gitanos* were seen as an ideal embodiment of Spanish culture and the emergence of the taurine schools of Ronda and Sevilla and the growing popularity of flamenco as a form of 'folk music' led to a taste for *andaluz* romantic culture which triumphed in the Madrid court (compare the taste for bucolic scenes in British painting, or Marie Antoinette's love of cosplaying as a milkmaid).

The relationship between both forms of cultural expression (flamenco and *toreo*) is bidirectional; that is, it is possible to trace elements of *toreo* in flamenco, as well as moves in *toreo* that gain their 'choreographic' character from flamenco. The presence of *toreo* in flamenco is seen in the wide repertoire of flamenco lyrics that allude to the world of the bull. It is common, for example, to trace verses in flamenco that deal with some figure of *toreo* (highlighting qualities such as courage or death), about the bull and its mystique, or about the risk and misfortunes of the profession of the *torero*. The closeness between flamenco dance and *toreo* is evident in the gestures and stances of the body, the twists of the waist and movement of the arms. Even if you have never seen real flamenco you will probably be familiar with the stance in which the *bailaora* (dancer) raises her arms above her head, turning the hands inwards slightly. This mirrors the stance of the *torero* as he stands before the bull about to place the *banderillas* (barbed sticks). Or perhaps the *banderillero* mirrors the *cantaora*? Who can say? The dancer will also often keep her hands at waist height, moving them in a broad sweeping motion, mirroring how the *torero* holds and moves the *muleta* (red cloth). The similarity between the panache and attitude of the *torero* and the pose of the dancer is evident. It is also worth noting the similarities between the *capote* (cape) and *muleta* (red cloth) of the *torero* and the clothing of the flamenco dancers. The extravagant swishing of skirts recalls the movement of the cape or *muleta*. Something else that strikes the observer the first time he or she sees flamenco, is how it manages to be fluid yet strangely static. Hips, arms, hands, fingers and feet are constantly moving, often dizzyingly quickly, but the dancer does not pirouette around the stage by any means. This is the ideal of *toreo* too. The skilful *torero* moves his body, his hands and his arms (and through them the cape or *muleta*), but the aim is to control and direct the bull while remaining still, or as still as possible, himself. Also, audiences for both use the interjection *¡olé!* liberally: to praise and encourage the artist, whether musician, singer or *torero*.

What is the 'Aim' of a *Corrida*?

What is the aim of any work of art? First, it is not about 'seeing who wins' and this is one of the many reasons why the *corrida* is not a sport or a competition. The bull, in a very few cases, is 'pardoned' with an *indulto* (that is, it is so exceptionally brave that the audience petitions the president of the *plaza* to stop the *corrida* before the final sword, to allow the bull to go back to the ranch to be a seed bull), but in over 99.9% of *corridas* the bull dies. Even if the bull manages to gore (and in very rare cases even kill) a *torero*, the bull will still be killed. The *corrida* is not something to be 'won' or 'lost'. Even if there is an *indulto*, the other five bulls faced that afternoon will be killed. The *corrida* always involves death; it is always a tragedy, and it always forces us to confront the nature of the relationship between man and beast. Perhaps a vegan or pious Jain could, with a clear conscience, denounce the *corrida* as barbaric cruelty, but those who eat meat or otherwise use domesticated animals are on a stickier wicket.

What one witnesses at a *corrida* is an encounter between an almost wild animal — and certainly one that is pugnacious and aggressive — and a man who, until the last couple of minutes of the *corrida* is not armed with any lethal weapon, but through artistry slowly tames and dominates that animal using a piece of fabric. It is an encounter between the wild and the civilized, brute nature and human reason, the rural and the urban,

the animal and the human, in which nature and culture come together, albeit fleetingly. The mounted aristocrats of the early 18th century were able to elude a charging bull and fend it off with lances and skilful riding of a horse: another animal. The contemporary *torero a pie* ('bullfighter on foot') has no such protection. He could certainly not outrun a charging bull over any distance.

When a bull enters the ring, it has never truly encountered human beings before. It may be, strictly speaking, a domesticated *Bos taurus*, but it is far from 'tame'. You will see scars on the hides of most of the bulls appearing in a *corrida*. Contrary to the claims of *The Daily Mail* (a

UK newspaper with an obsessive 'anti-bullfighting' stance) these are **not** wounds sustained in previous *corridas*, as any bull that had appeared in the ring before would be *sentido* ('aware') and therefore utterly, fatally lethal. These, rather, are wounds sustained fighting with other bulls on the *ganadería* (ranch). That is the natural behaviour of these animals. They charge and fight. The Chillingham cattle of Northumberland (UK) that, like Spanish *toros de lidia*, have not been selectively bred to diminish aggression, exhibit very similar scars.

Using, at first, a pink *capote* (cape) the *torero* creates a large shape that incites a charge from the bull, just as it might charge at another bull. At the beginning of the *corrida*, the bull simply charges, but in the space of some 20 minutes, the *torero* and his team do two things. They tire and weaken the bull and, ultimately, control it. In the final minutes, the ideal spectacle is to see the *torero* himself barely moving, while using the *muleta* (red cloth) to control the animal and direct its movement. The animal that charges (literally) wildly at the start, ends by moving almost as one with the *torero*, its lethal horns inches from his body. At first, the lure (the *capote*) is a distant target to be charged at; fifteen minutes later, it seems like the bull is connected to the lure (now the smaller *muleta*), no longer charging, but moving with fluidity and grace, immediately choreographed. The English expression 'to run rings around' (which refers to hares eluding pursuing greyhounds) is exactly wrong in this situation. Although the bull is literally running rings around the *torero*, it is the skill and dexterity of the *torero* that has tamed the unfocused urge to charge of the *toro bravo*. The bull is led in rings, in fact.

Naturally, then, the quality of the bull is of the utmost importance. A tame ('*manso*') and timid bull will not readily charge at the lure, or if incited to do so will be more like a dog chasing a ball or a kitten chasing a ball of wool. The *corrida* may be a dance of sorts, but by its nature, it cannot be choreographed or rehearsed. The jeopardy that makes the *corrida* so thrilling is that the bull is a lethal co-performer. One wrong move, one trip, one gust of wind, and the *torero* could be seriously injured, even killed. The *corrida* is a tragedy — it always involves death and the danger of death — but in the theatre, tragedy is the most sublime form of drama of which we can conceive. The deaths of Lear or Tosca move us far more, and far more viscerally and deeply than the *bons mots* of Lady Bracknell or the verbal sparring of Beatrice and Benedick ever could.

Is the *Corrida* Cruel or Immoral?

My intention, in this section, is not to convince you that you should attend a *corrida*, nor even to argue that your objections, if you have them, are misguided. All I seek to do is to try to demystify the *corrida* for those unfamiliar with it, to explain its importance in Spanish (and *andaluz*) culture and, if you want to see it for yourself, help you to understand what's going on. I know plenty of *aficionados* (followers of the *corrida*) who are vegetarians, but if you object to animals' being killed for any reason, then perhaps the *corrida* is not for you. But if you eat meat and are wondering whether the *corrida* is morally defensible, then allow me to make one or two points in its defence.

Spanish *toros bravos* are as close to genuinely free range cattle as it is possible to find anywhere in the world. They are raised on enormous ranches with almost no contact with human beings, the very opposite of intensive farming. For three to five years they spend their days unmolested by man, eating grass, rolling in mud to cool down, sparring with other bulls, mating and so forth and then, one day, a handful of them are herded onto a truck and transported to a town where they are put in an open patio of the *Plaza de Toros* known as the *corral*. The following morning, they are separated into pens from which they emerge later that day into the bullring and do exactly what they have been doing their entire lives: namely charging at what they see in front of them, and fighting for territory and dominance. For around twenty minutes they continue to do what is in their nature, charging and fighting.

They are pierced and prodded with lances and barbs, but this is nothing new as their many scars and puncture marks from horns attest. And then, high on beta-endorphins, they die, from a single thrust of a sword, severing the aorta. The *toro bravo* spends its life sparring, fighting, and charging, for much of the time jacked up on endogenous opioids. Compare this with what a placid, gentle, beef animal is likely to go through in an abattoir, and comparatively how much longer this stressful process will take.

Around 30,000 bulls are killed (and subsequently eaten) in and following *corridas* each year in Spain, compared to 2 million cattle dispatched in UK slaughterhouses. In other words, if those *corridas* took place in the UK, the animals killed would represent 1.5% of the total number of animals already slaughtered in order to keep us supplied with beefburgers, mince and the like. While we're at it, we might also want to ask about the huge number of male dairy calves slaughtered and dumped due to our taste for milk and our antipathy to veal.

If you accept the line taken by *The Daily Mail* and decide to disapprove of the *corrida* because it is a 'barbaric' practice indulged in by benighted and bloodthirsty foreigners, or if you think that it involves 'torturing' or even 'taunting' bulls, then I probably cannot persuade you otherwise. All I would say is that the best way to confirm your prejudices (or those of others) would probably be to attend a *corrida* and see for yourself. You may, as a result of watching a *corrida*, still conclude that you are right to be opposed to it in principle and resolve never to repeat the experience. But you will at least disabuse yourself of some of the claims frequently made by opponents (or perhaps also the proponents) of *toreo*.

Some *corridas*, alas, do not showcase the art in the best light (especially when, for example, the kill is badly handled or takes too long), but it should be clear to any spectator that *aficionados* do not come to the *plaza* because they take some sadistic pleasure in the death of an animal. Spectators view bulls as noble and brave and study their lineage in much the same way that racing fans can name the sire and the dam of champion mounts. A bull that is slow, or timid, might be a cause of disappointment but is never an object of blame. Blame is reserved for the human participants in the struggle — the *toreros* or the *ganadero* who sent it to the *plaza* — and it is frequently (and stridently) expressed. The honour of being able to *lidiar* with a *toro bravo* is hard won and must be earned with skill and delicacy. It may seem scandalous that these animals are bred to be killed, but that is equally true of any of the thousands of cattle you see on any farm anywhere in the world. Few farm animals die of old age after a quiet retirement.

Most of all, however, if you really want to understand the culture of Spain, then her long relationship and love affair with the bulls cannot be ignored.

Some Misconceptions

There are plenty of reasons to oppose the *corrida*, many of them concerning animal rights, but some concerning the danger to which it exposes the human participants. The latter argument was the main reason that the *corrida de toros* was condemned by the sixteenth-century Pope St Pius V. However, a number of major misconceptions exist.

Bulls are lethally dangerous. Some campaigners seek to deny this, portraying the *toro bravo* as a placid, friendly animal that only becomes aggressive when it is being 'tortured' (or even drugged) because aggression is something alien to its nature. It is certainly true that if you observe bulls at home on the ranch then they can seem rather docile. But when fighting for dominance, or separated from the herd (as happens in the *corrida*), it is anything but. A herd of dairy cows usually poses no danger to passing ramblers, but it is a different story if they are with their suckling calves. What the *torero* does, of course, is mimic the behaviour of another bull, or animal — using the cape and *muleta* to enlarge his presence beyond his puny human proportions, mimicking the horns of the bull with the pic and *banderillas*.

The obverse of the 'bulls are gentle' objection is the suggestion that bulls are in fact so dangerous that they can only be faced when they have been emasculated in some way. Oft-repeated allegations are that they have their horns filed down, their eyes rubbed with petroleum jelly, or have heavy sacks of ballast dropped on their backs to weaken them. A bull with altered horns would be just as dangerous. A blunt horn with half a tonne of force behind it could disembowel a human being just as effectively as a sharp horn. A bull with compromised vision would be far **more** dangerous than one with perfect vision because the entire *corrida* depends upon the ability of the bull to respond to even slight movements of the lure (the cape or *muleta*). A bull that has been weakened by injury would last less than a minute in the *plaza*. There is no honour in facing a weak or lame bull and it would be removed by order of the president. And if the president were slow to order its removal, you can be sure that the *plaza* (viz. the spectators) would be on their feet, whistling their displeasure).

Something else that one often hears is a statement to the effect that 'bullfights in France and Portugal are more humane because the bull isn't killed.' Considering France first, this misconception has probably arisen because in addition to the *corrida de toros* ('*course de taureaux*'), two other taurine spectacles are also very popular. The *course Camarguaise* is a bloodless display undertaken with young castrated bulls (oxen), while the *course landaise* actually uses cows, not bulls. Similar spectacles also take place in Spain. However, the *corrida de toros* in France is identical to the Spanish version, right down to the killing of the bull in the ring.

Portugal is different again. The Portuguese *corrida de touros* is somewhat different to the Spanish version in that horsemanship is far more prominent, but the bull is still killed at the end of the display. The difference is that the slaughter takes place in the bullpens, not in the view of the crowd. This may be comforting for the crowd, but in my view, it removes an important safeguard: public surveillance. When the bull is removed from the ring in Portugal, with the barbs of the '*bandarilhas*' in its neck and back, a spectator has no way of knowing whether its end will be swift, or whether the unfortunate animal will continue to suffer from its injuries for some time, while the endorphins that previously flooded its system ebb away, increasing and prolonging its suffering. One of the reasons that the kill is public (and subject to strict time limits in the official rules) is that aficionados believe that the bull deserves to die in a swift, dignified and 'noble' manner, consonant with the bravery it shows in the ring.

How to Watch a *Corrida*

First of all, which kind of *corrida* do you want to watch?

Corrida de Toros

The 'standard' and most commonly scheduled kind of *corrida* is properly called a *corrida de toros*. In this form, three *matadores* (and their *cuadrillas* or teams) face six bulls, two each, that must be at least four years old and weigh between 460 and 600 kilograms.

Sometimes two *figuras* (well-known *matadores*) will appear together, facing three bulls each. This is called a *mano a mano* ('hand to hand'). Very occasionally, a big-name *matador* might appear alone, usually facing four bulls. In both cases, an additional *matador* (called a '*sobresaliente*') must be engaged in case a scheduled *matador* is injured and has to retire. First-class rings will often have their own resident *sobresaliente* (often a retired *maestro* from the local *escuela taurina* or bullfighting school) who can pick up the *muleta* if more than one *matador* is incapacitated.

Staging a bullfight is such an expensive business that bullrings will do everything to ensure that refunds need not be given. The rules state that refunds are due only when a *corrida* is cancelled, so even in torrential rain the first unfortunate *matador* will face his first bull and only after that will the event be 'rained off'.

Corrida de Novillos

Very similar is the *corrida de novillos* (usually just a '*novillada*') in which three apprentice *matadores* known as '*novilleros*' face six young bulls ('*novillos*') of between three and four years old weighing less than 540 kilograms. *Novilleros* appearing at the most important *plazas* (including Málaga) will be far from amateur, and will already have been studying the art of *toreo* for many years. A very promising *matador de novillos* can easily outclass a jaded and average *matador de toros*. Ernest Hemingway thought that *novilladas* were the best *corridas* for a beginner to see as it is easier to understand what is going on. Whereas a '*figura*' (an experienced, top-flight *torero*) will know hundreds of tricks to disguise a wrong move or a miscalculation or to compensate for a slow or timid bull, a *novillero* has fewer places to hide. It is thus easier to see what he is trying to achieve with the bull, and how he is trying to achieve it.

Corrida de Rejones

This form, usually just called a *rejoneo*, is a *corrida* on horseback. The bulls are still put to the sword at the end, but many first-time spectators of the *corrida* find the *rejoneo* a more gentle introduction to *tauromaquia*. Whereas in *corridas* and *novilladas*, the bull is aroused mainly by the cape or the *muleta*, in a *rejoneo* it is the horse that acts as a lure. One misses the skilled work with the *muleta*, but one also gets to witness deft horsemanship of incredible skill.

In first-class *plazas* like Málaga, one afternoon of the *feria taurina* will be a *rejoneo* and another will be a *novillada*. In smaller, provincial rings one may see a *corrida* featuring two full *matadores* and one *novillero* or, more commonly a *feria mixta*, in which a *rejoneador* (mounted *torero*) appears with two *matadores*, or any other combination. Provincial bullrings that may only have one *corrida* each year might put on a *mixta* featuring a *rejoneador*, two *matadores* and a *novillero* facing a total of six *toros* and two *novillos*. *Rejoneadores* are still aristocrats, in the main.

🐂 Bullrings and Tickets

Plazas de toros are divided into three classes. First-class *plazas* should hold at least seven taurine '*espectáculos*' (shows) annually, of the which no fewer than six must be full *corridas de toros*. Following the closure of the last ring in Barcelona (once a famously '*torista*' city that boasted **two** first-class rings) there are nine first-class *plazas* in Spain, and Málaga is one. Reflecting the local popularity of the *corrida*, Andalucía is the only community in Spain to have three first-class rings (the others are Sevilla and Córdoba), though the Basque Country has two (Bilbao and San Sebastián). The others are in Madrid, Zaragoza, Valencia, and Pamplona.

For a *novillero* to proceed to the status of full *matador*, he must go through a ceremony called an '*alternativa*', traditionally in a first-class ring. He will appear with two full *matadores*, the longest serving of whom will act as '*padrino*' ('godfather') in the presence of the second, who performs the role of '*testigo*' ('witness'). Whereas the most senior *torero* would normally face the first bull, he cedes this honour to the *toricantano* (the aspirant *novillero*), ceremonially handing over the 'junk' or the 'tools of the trade' (the sword and *muleta*). Following the *alternativa*, the new full *matador* earns the right to face the bull bare-headed, setting aside his *montera* (the distinctive black hat worn by *toreros*) before the final third of the *corrida*. If the *alternativa* is the 'baptism', then the 'confirmation' is, well, the *confirmación*. This must take place (for any bullfighter appearing in Spain) at Las Ventas in Madrid. In other countries, it takes place in the premier ring, so in Mexico it takes place in the Monumental bullring in Mexico City, the largest in the world, and in France at the Arènes de Nîmes. At the end of his career, another (quasi-liturgical) ceremony takes place — the cutting of the *coleta* or ponytail. Most *toreros* wear clip-on ponytails nowadays, but the ceremony still involves cutting a lock of real hair. The allusion to Judges 16 and the cutting of Samson's hair is clear.

Málaga's main *feria taurina* is in August, running concurrently with the *Feria de Agosto*. However, there are also *corridas* in Holy Week (a *Corrida Picassiana* named in honour of Pablo Picasso that in recent years has been staged on Holy Saturday), and the *Corrida de la Prensa* (for the Press) held in June for the feast of Málaga's co-patron Saints Ciriaco and Paula, who were martyred in Málaga in 303 AD. The final *corrida* is held in September to celebrate Málaga's principal patroness, Our Lady of Victory. All are popular events, especially those held during the *feria* when the whole city is *en fête*.

At a *corrida* held during the *feria* in 2022 in which the young Peruvian phenomenon Andrés Roca Rey was appearing, signs were posted reading '*No hay billetes*' (There are no tickets) meaning that every one of the 9,032 seats was occupied. A full house is a rarity outside Sevilla and Madrid, but it shows the appeal of top-flight *toreros*. When, a few months earlier, it was announced that the slightly mysterious and reclusive — but technically magnificent — *torero* José Tomás would be facing four bulls in Jaén, every hotel room in the city was booked within an hour. Then, as the bullfighting critic Christopher North reported, because 'scalping' or reselling tickets is illegal, curious listings began appearing on eBay: 'Biro, 1500 euros, free tickets to see José Tomás included' or 'Set of car tyres, 4500 euros — plus a seat in Jaén's *plaza*'.[67]

Next, buy your ticket. You can either do this in person from the *taquilla* (ticket office) of the bullring, or online. There are a number of agencies — search for '*entradas*' '*toros*' 'Málaga'. The *empresa*, or company (in 2023) holding the contract to operate the *plaza* is lancesdefuturo.com. Online agencies will send the tickets to your hotel or accommodation. When booking, you are presented with a number of ticket options. Some seats are unavailable because many people buy *abonos* (effectively season tickets), but of the remainder, some are '*sol*' (in direct sun), some are '*sombra*' (in the shade) and some are '*sol y sombra*' (beginning in the full glare of the sun, but moving into the shade during the *corrida*).

The ring is divided into eight sectors (called *tendidos*). *Tendidos* 1, 2, 7 and 8 are *en sombra*, numbers 3 and 6 are *en sol y sombra*, and numbers 4 and 5 are *en sol*. Then you have a choice of nearer or farther away from the arena. Nearest are two rows of '*barrera*' seats, then a rank of 12 *filas* (rows) also, confusingly, called '*tendidos*'. Above the *tendidos* (in Málaga) is a row of seats called '*butacas de tendido*', and above these are a handful of rows in the lower level of the balcony called '*palcos*' (individual balconies) and '*gradas*', and then at the very top, a few rows called '*andanada*'. Simplifying things considerably, tickets are more expensive the closer you are to the sand of the ring, and in the shade. Where you sit will largely depend upon your

---

budget and tolerance of sun, but unless you are willing to splash out on *sombra* seats, I advise you to wear a hat and baste yourself in high-factor sunblock. If you sit high up, bring binoculars.

Sorteo y apartado

On the day of the *corrida*, the *apoderados* (attorneys, or managers) of the three *matadores* appearing in the afternoon come to the *corral* to inspect the bulls. There will normally be six animals from one herd (and at least two substitutes in reserve). By consensus, the *apoderados* divide ('*apartar*') them into three pairs. An apparently aggressive bull might be partnered with a more placid or timid one, or the largest and heaviest might be paired with the lightest and smallest. Once the pairings are agreed, then the *sorteo* (lottery) takes place. The names of the bulls in the pairs are written on cigarette papers and dropped into a hat. Each *apoderado* then draws the pair that 'his' *matador* will face.

In Málaga, the *apartado* and *sorteo* takes place at 12 noon and is open to the public. You do not need to buy a ticket, simply turn up in good time and make your way to the corrals (bull pens) which are on the eastern side of the bullring building. Attending the *apartado* and *sorteo* is popular with hardcore *aficionados* as it allows them to study the bulls and their behaviour at close quarters, informing their understanding of the *corrida* later on.

The bulls are then put into the pens (*toriles*) to await the afternoon's *corrida*. (A *corrida* beginning at 6 or 7 pm may feel like 'evening' to a British person, but in Spain, this is the afternoon. A *corrida* that begins after dark, under floodlights, is called a '*nocturna*'.) In Málaga, *corridas* usually begin between 6 pm and 7.30 pm, depending upon the time of year.

The *Plaza*

Arrive at the *plaza* in good time, especially if it's your first visit, as it can take some time to find your bearings. The area outside the *plaza* will be a throng of people greeting friends, seeing and being seen (this is an extension of the *paseo*). Vendors will be selling all sorts of things — cold drinks, snacks (*pipas*, or salted sunflower seeds are a favourite — the *plaza* will be littered with hundreds of thousands of discarded sunflower seed pods by the end of the *corrida*) and novelty items like flags, key-rings and postcards. Some items for sale are practical — like sun hats and rain ponchos. In the past, it was common to see people selling cigars, but this is less common these days. However, one is still permitted to smoke in the *plaza* as it is technically an outside space. A few *plazas* like San Sebastián and Logroño have roofs, but purists generally disapprove of this. The *plaza*, remember, is a '*rus is urbe*' and however much of a conceit that may seem, any '*rus*' clearly must be outdoors.

Once you have soaked up the *ambiente*, go into the bullring (your ticket should tell you which gate — *puerta* — to use). The staff on the gate will tear a corner from your ticket (though nowadays this is done electronically by scanning a QR code). Be on the lookout for people (usually attractive young women) handing out programmes. These programmes list the bulls for the afternoon — six scheduled bulls and two '*sobreros*' or understudies — their names, weights, and ages, as well as the *toreros* and their *cuadrillas* (teams). Sometimes the programmes include articles by critics and even full family trees going back to the 18th century for the bulls from that day's *ganadería*. These programmes are free, but it is polite to tip the person handing them out (whatever loose change you have, up to a euro or so).

Inside the *plaza*, in the vestibules beneath the seats, there are bars that sell a limited selection of drinks — soft drinks, water, spirits/mixers (always gin and rum, but don't presume the selection will be much wider), beer and wine. During the *corrida* (between bulls), vendors sell drinks inside the ring, carrying heavy buckets filled with ice, cans of beer and soft drinks, and miniatures of spirits. To get their attention, raise your hand and shout, '*¡Oiga!*' (**oy**-ga, 'listen'), '*¡Aquí!*' (ack-**ee** 'here'), or '*¡señor!*'/'*¡señorita!*' (sen-**yor**/sen-yor-**ee**-tah 'sir'/'miss'). Other vendors sell nuts, sunflower seeds, crisps and ice creams. You will need to pay in cash, ideally in coins ('*monedas*') or small denomination notes. Spectators in the ring are tightly packed, so money is often passed along the row(s) and then the drink, or drinks, are passed back in the opposite direction.

Before proceeding to your seat, note where the nearest lavatories are and, if you can, make use of the facilities — if you need to spend a penny during the *corrida*, you will need to wait until the *faena* (the final third of the facing of one bull) is complete before leaving your seat and you will not be permitted to return to your seat if the next bull has already entered the ring. The area beneath the bleachers is also where you will find the people who will rent you an *almohadilla*, or cushion, for a euro or two. The seating in the *plaza* is a bench made of cement, so hiring an *almohadilla* is a good idea. This is not just about comfort: the seats double as steps and can be dirty.

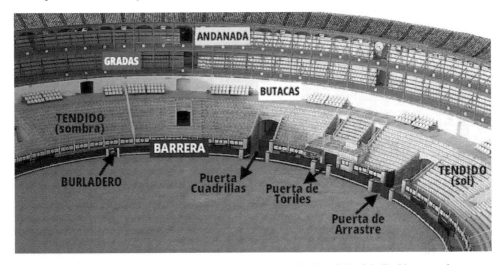

Armed with your *almohadilla*, programme and plastic beaker full of chilled beer (or beverage of choice), make your way into the ring proper. At this stage, you need to know two pieces of information: the *tendido* (sector) and whether you are seated in *barrera*/*tendido*/*butacas*, or *gradas*, or *andanada*. The first two are accessed at ground level, the other three mean climbing stairs. Someone at the entrance into the ring itself will tear another corner from your ticket (or scan the QR code). Inside the arena, staff employed by the *plaza* are on hand to help you to find your seat. Do not be afraid to ask for help — they are there to assist you and the noise and excitement of the ring before a *corrida* can be discombobulating. Having located the section where you are sitting, you now need two further pieces of information — *fila* (row number) and *asiento* (seat number). In the *tendidos*, lower *filas* will be in the *tendido bajo*, higher ones in the *tendido alto*. Climb the steps to the correct *fila* (row), and then edge your way along in order to find your seat. People are packed in and more than used to having to make way for people, so don't feel shy. If you feel lost show your ticket to someone and adopt a pleading look!

The atmosphere in the *plaza* is generally jolly and sociable. You will see plenty of families and people of all ages. In the expensive (*sombra*) seats you will see people who have dressed up as if for an evening at the opera, but even in the cheaper (*sol*) seats, many people will be wear-

449

ing their 'Sunday best'. The *feria taurina* is a big annual event and the *corridas* are important fixtures of the social calendar. Do not be surprised if the people sitting nearby offer you wine from a *bota* (a wineskin — I advise you to refuse politely unless you have practised pouring wine into your open mouth) or part of their picnic.

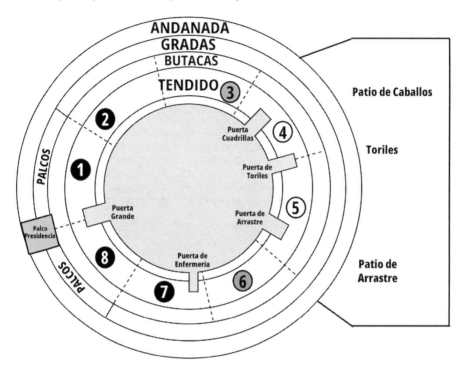

Have a look around the ring. Bullrings used to be rectangular, like the public squares where *corridas* used to take place, the first round ones being constructed in the mid-eighteenth century. The *ruedo* (ring) is covered with sand ('*arena*') or pulverized sandstone called *albero* that is quarried in the Los Alcores region of Andalucía. The *ruedo* must be at least 50 metres in diameter, but few are more than 60 metres because this would excessively tire both *toro* and *torero*. One cannot tell by looking, but the sand has a very slight camber, being higher in the centre than at the edges. You may see a group of attendants with rakes smoothing the sand and, if it is windy, dousing it with water (if it has been raining, they will be removing the tarpaulins). If a *corrida* is rained off and cancelled, you can get a refund from the *taquilla* (box office), but if it is suspended after the first bull, there will be no refunds. So if the weather looks dicey, take a waterproof (or buy a cheap polythene poncho outside the *plaza*). Umbrellas, which obscure the view of those behind you, are frowned upon!

Painted on the sand are two circles of white lime (though red clay paint is used in some *plazas*). These are called *rayas* and the outer one is seven metres from the wooden barrier, the inner one nine metres. Their significance will become clearer below. Around the ring stands the *barrera*, a wooden fence painted red (or 'ox blood'). On the inside it is 1.60 metres high, and on the side of the audience, 1.30 metres (because the *ruedo* is slightly sunken). The *barrera* is interrupted by four small gaps called *burladeros* that allow a *torero*, but not the bull, to escape the ring. A 40 cm high ledge called an *estribo* runs around the *barrera* and this also assists any *torero* who needs to vault the fence ('Exit, pursued by a bull'). On the spectators' side of the *barrera* is an alleyway called the *callejón* where the *toreros* and other employees of the *plaza* wait between bulls, as well as medics, vets, photographers, bull-breeders and journalists.

In the middle of the *sombra* section is a gate leading to a large arch. This is the *puerta grande* or 'great gate'. If any *torero* distinguishes himself by cutting two ears (awarded as trophies) from the same bull, then he will leave from this gate '*a hombros*' (on someone's shoulders). Immediately above the *puerta grande* is the *palco presidencia*, where the president of the *corrida* sits. According to the '*reglamento*' (legislation), the president should be the provincial governor, or his or her delegate. He (or she) is flanked and assisted by a vet, to advise on the bulls (especially where there is a question about a particular animal's fitness to take part) and an 'artistic advisor' to advise on the *toreros* (such as whether a particular *matador* deserves to be awarded a trophy). The latter is usually a retired *torero*, or sometimes a *ganadero* (bull breeder). The rings in Madrid and Sevilla also have a *palco real* (Royal Box), but these days any visiting royals tend to sit in *sombra*. His Majesty King Felipe VI dutifully attends a few *corridas* each year, but unlike his father Don Juan Carlos and his eldest sister Doña Elena, he is not thought to be a great *aficionado*. Her Majesty the Queen, like her mother-in-law Doña Sofía, isn't a fan either and hasn't attended a *corrida* since 2009 (when she was the Princess of Asturias).

If we imagine that the *puerta grande* and *palco presidencia* above it are at 9 o'clock on a clock face (which, if 12 o'clock is north, they pretty much are in Málaga), then directly opposite at 3 o'clock is the *puerta de toriles*. These gates lead from the bullpens and are opened to release a bull into the arena. At 2 o'clock is the *puerta de cuadrillas* and it is from this gate that the *toreros* and their teams will emerge. Those *toreros* who fail to cut two ears from at least one of their bulls will also leave the ring by this gate. At 4 o'clock is the *puerta de arraŝtre*, or the 'gate of dragging', through which the slain bulls leave the arena on their way to the butchery. By the time you leave the *corrida* in just over two hours, the carcasses of the bulls you saw in the arena will have been eviscerated and loaded onto a waiting refrigerated lorry. The destination of the meat varies. In some smaller towns, local bars and restaurants like to make a point of serving animals from the *feria*, but in most cases, it is either auctioned for charity or else distributed to care homes, night kitchens or given to charities working with the poor.

At 6 o'clock is a gate that no one (save *Daily Mail* journalists) wants to see used. This is the *puerta de enfermería*, the gate to the infirmary. The infirmary itself is a long way from a school infirmary with a first aid kit and a box of bandages. The premier bullring in Spain, Las Ventas in Madrid, has a medical team that includes a trauma doctor, three surgeons, one specialist in internal medicine, three anaesthesiologists, two nurses, and two operating room assistants. Most first-class rings will be similarly staffed and advances in emergency medicine and surgery (of which taurine surgery is a recognized branch, with its own international association and journal) have meant that deaths in the ring are far less common than they were in the past. However, bulls are powerful and aggressive animals with lethal horns from which no amount of medical expertise can save a mortally wounded *torero*. Being disembowelled by a razor-sharp horn with several tonnes of force behind it is a catastrophic injury. In 2016, Victor Barrio became the first *torero* to be killed in the ring since 1985, and in 2017 the *figura* Iván Fandiño sustained such serious injuries in the ring of Aire-sur-l'Adour (France) that even the presence of a highly experienced taurine surgeon, Dr Mathieu Poirier, was not enough to save his life.

Dramatis Personæ

Famously, *corridas* are the only events in Spain that begin on time. At the advertised time, a *clarín* (bugle) sounds and the *paseíllo* (parade) begins. First to enter the ring are a pair of mounted *alguacilillos* (sheriffs), dressed in costumes from the time of Philip IV. Their role is ceremonial now, but in the days when *corridas* took place in public squares, their job was to clear the arena of spectators and to keep order. Then come the three *toreros* (or *rejoneadores*) placed in order of seniority since they took the *alternativa*. If you were facing them, the most senior *torero* (in terms of time since his *alternativa* or, in the case of a *novillero*, the length of time since his first appearance in that class of *corrida*) is on the right, the next most senior on the left, and the most junior in the middle. Behind the row of *matadores* come the three *banderilleros* (assistants) of the first bullfighter, in the third row those of the second, and in the fourth row those of the third, respecting each one's seniority from right to left. Then the horse-mounted *picadores* follow. Sometimes there will be three pairs of *picadores* (six in all), but sometimes the three *matadores* will share four or, in a *novillada*, even two. At the end of the parade, the assistants of the *picadores* (called, somewhat rudely, '*monosabios*' or 'trained monkeys') and *areneros* (sand boys) go on foot, followed by the mules and the *mulilleros* (mule drivers).

First, the *alguacilillos* approach the *palco presidencia*, doffing their plumed bi-corn hats. The president tosses the ceremonial key to the *puerta de toriles* which they try, and usually fail, to catch in their hats. The *matadores* stop when they reach the inner *raya*. Those who are Catholics make the sign of the cross and kiss their thumbs, and many will trace the form of a cross in the sand with their right shoe. They then turn to salute the applause of the crowd. Next, followed by their *cuadrillas* (teams), they approach the *palco presidencia* and bow to the president. They then remove their ceremonial capes, which until that point have been wrapped tightly around their bodies restricting the left arm in a sling-like embrace. These capes are of silk and richly embroidered, often bearing the image of a saint, and they are either laid out on the *barrera*, or entrusted to someone in the crowd, such as the *torero*'s mother, wife, girlfriend or patron.

Note how the *toreros* (on foot) are attired. The basin-shaped hat with two fins (representing horns) is called a *montera*. It is worn throughout the *corrida*, but a full *matador* will remove it for the third part in which the bull is cited with the *muleta* and finally killed. There is considerable ceremony in this. If the first *torero* is injured and cannot kill the bull, then the task falls to the second most senior *torero*. But he will not remove his *montera* because it is not 'his' bull. A *torero* wears a white shirt with a vest underneath and a (usually red or black) *corbatín* (a ribbon-like tie). His jacket ('*chaquetilla*') is made of silk, and richly embroidered. It can be of almost any colour except red or yellow — not red because only the *muleta* and the blood of the bull are truly red, and not yellow because of an old superstition that yellow spells bad luck in the ring. Until comparatively recently it would have been regarded as bad form even for a spectator to wear yellow. You may be surprised, then, to see *toreros* attired in suits of vivid red or yellow. Any suit that actually **looks** red is **actually** called something else. The most common is '*grana*' (burgundy), but you might also see wine, crimson, and even paprika. Similarly, any yellow ('*amarillo*') suit is not truly 'yellow' but champagne, cream, lemon, old gold, straw, ochre, canary, hazel, gold, etc.

Some of the names of colours are references to specific images of the saints carried in religious processions. '*Purísima*' (sky blue) is the liturgical colour of the Feast of the Immaculate Conception, and '*nazareno*' (purple) is the colour of the cloak worn by Christ in representations of '*Jesús del Gran Poder*'. Stitched all over the silk cloth are sequins, piping, and frogging in gold thread (for full *matadores*) or silver or jet (black) for their assistants. Some full *matadores* will mix and match and occasionally wear suits embroidered with silver or jet, even though they are entitled to wear gold. The embroidered decoration catches the sun and gives the *torero*'s suit its name: *traje de luces*, or suit of lights.

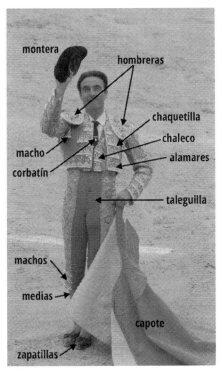

The *taleguilla* is a pair of very tight breeches extending from above the waist to the knee where they are fastened with tassels called *machos*. There are usually four pairs of machos on the suit of a *torero*: two at the bottom of the breeches and two hanging from the *hombreras* or epaulettes. And yes, the word does mean 'males'. They are in pairs because they symbolize the testicles and, therefore, *machismo*. The *machos* at the calf are the last part of the suit to be tightened so the expression '*apretarse los machos*' (to tighten the *machos*) has come to mean 'to prepare for a difficult undertaking'.

The breeches are kept up by braces and gathered at the waist with a sash (*fajín*) with an embroidered waistcoat (*chaleco*) over this. Under the breeches, *toreros* do not wear any protection of the cricket box kind, though they wear some form of long johns or other underwear. On the lower leg, they wear silk tights (*medias*) that are always pink, with white cotton tights underneath if long johns are not worn. On their feet, they wear black, patent leather, smooth-soled slippers, called *zapatillas*.

Dressing, undressing and changing dress is an integral part of the theatre of the *corrida*. The *traje de luces* is very tight (largely to avoid any loose fabric that might snag on the bull's horn) so the *matador* needs assistance in putting it on, a task that falls to his *mozo de espadas* ('sword boy') — who is effectively his valet and confidant. The preparation for the *corrida*, which takes place in the hotel room before boarding the minibus with the *cuadrilla* to go to the *plaza*, is sometimes semi-public, with close friends and acquaintances invited to have a glass of sherry and wish the *maestro* good luck (incidentally, should you bump into a *torero* on his way to a *corrida*, say, in the foyer of your hotel, then the correct greeting is, '¡Suerte, maestro!'). Then, in the ring, the richly decorated *capote de paseo* is lain aside or handed to a favourite, and the heavy pink *capote de brega* is taken up. Later, the *montera* will be taken off and handed to someone to whom the bull is to be dedicated, or else placed on the sand if the bull is dedicated to the *plaza* as a whole.

Anyone even vaguely familiar with the liturgy of the Catholic Church will recognize that what takes place in a *corrida de toros* is quasi-liturgical or at the very least, highly ritualized. It begins with a procession, in order of precedence, the sign of the cross, approaching the president and offering him obeisance. The clothing is hardly practical, but it is formal, mannered and, like liturgical vestments, coloured and decorated in ways that are traditional and meaningful. The ritual drama of the *corrida* is accompanied by music, particular moments are signalled by bugles just as moments in the Mass are signalled by bells. The people, like the congregation, make their responses with cries of '¡Olé!' going up like 'Amens'. At some points, the *montera* is worn, like the bishop's mitre or priest's biretta, while for the most solemn moment of sacrifice, it is lain aside, rather as a bishop would remove his *zucchetto* (skullcap) for the Eucharistic prayer and consecration. If an ear is awarded, the *torero* makes a circuit of the ring, holding the ear(s) aloft as a bishop might bless the faithful during the final procession, crozier in hand, or how a priest might bestow a benediction with a relic of a saint or with a monstrance containing the Blessed Sacrament. As he passes, people throw their hats into the ring. The *torero* kisses them and tosses them back. Others throw gifts, like cigars, and women throw fans. The parallels with the collection and offertory, and the ritual blessing of objects like rosaries and medals, are almost too obvious to labour. None of this is to suggest that the *corrida* is actually a religious ritual (let alone a parody of one) — the procession onto the pitch, the mascots and the singing of national anthems happens in soccer games, after all — but ritual is something very human and it is hardly surprising that in a largely Catholic country, it should at least borrow from the ritual of the Church.

The richly embroidered *traje de luces* is the costume of the *torero* on foot and their mounted assistants, the *picadores*. In a *rejoneo*, the *rejoneadores* wear the more sombre 'traje campero' — the formal garb of an *andaluz* rancher: leather boots, high-waisted grey trousers, a short jacket and broad-brimmed hat. For benefit *corridas* (*e.g.* those staged to raise money for a cancer hospital or children's charity) the *toreros* on foot wear this costume too. Even nowadays, *rejoneadores* tend to be drawn from old bull-breeding families and not for these country gentlemen are the sequins and 'bling' of mere *matadores*! Spain is a culture that, curiously, retains a fascination with the aristocracy, despite their landed gentry having even less constitutional significance than the handful of peers who remain in the UK legislature. While the pages of Britain's *Hello* magazine are dominated by pop stars, footballers and reality TV 'celebrities', Spain's *¡Hola!* magazine regularly features the Duchess of this or the Count of that, as well as *toreros*.

Preamble

Unlike many sports, which are games of two halves, the *corrida* is a drama in three acts, or perhaps six acts of three scenes each. What confuses many first-time spectators, however, is that before the 'first' third there comes a preparatory segment called the *toreo de capa*, so to the uninitiated it can seem like there are four 'thirds'. In the ring (for the first bull) are the most senior *matador* and his three assistants (*peones*) on foot, plus the other two *matadores*. *Matadores* assist one another because the *corrida* is not a sport or a competition. If all three *matadores* cut two ears from a bull, then they all become 'triunfadores' and go out from the *puerta grande*. If none do, then they all troop out of the *puerta de cuadrillas*. There can be one, two or three 'victors', or there can be none. The *corrida* is a struggle between a *torero* and a *toro*, not between *toreros*.

The first sign that the entry of the bull is imminent is a lone employee of the *plaza* walking to the centre of the ring carrying a large sign on a pole. On this is written the 'biography' of the first bull: the *ganadería* (ranch), and the bull's name, age, and weight.

The president holds a white handkerchief over the ledge of the balcony, a bugle sounds, and the *toreros* (who until now have been limbering up, moving their large pink *capotes* in front of imaginary bulls) take up their positions in the ring, apart from the most senior *torero*, who usually stands at, or behind, the *barrera*. The gate of the *toril* is opened and the bull emerges, blinking, into the sunlight. This is an exciting moment for the crowd. What are they hoping for? Ideally, a bull that comes out confidently and at some speed, with its head held high (I would normally use the masculine pronoun 'he' for the *toro*, but this might lead to some confusion when also talking about the *torero*). For some reason, bulls that have unusual colouring often raise a cheer (*aficionados* of the *corrida* are a superstitious lot). Most bulls are black, or pretty close to it, sometimes with white or other coloured patches. *Castaño* or chestnut bulls are common too, but people love to see a white (*ensabanado*) or peach (*melocotón*) coloured bull. If, however, the animal emerges slowly and seems unsure, then this might lead to (very premature) whistles and even boos from the crowd. Woe betide any bull that decides that it would rather go back to the pen and tries to return to the gate. But this is premature impatience. Bulls that seem reticent to begin with often perform magnificently, and anyone who has seen more than a few *corridas* will be all too familiar with the bull who emerges at speed, looking invincible, but runs out of fight long before the end.

Occasionally, the *matador* will choose to receive the bull alone in the ring, even dramatically on his knees ('*en rodillas*'), but it is more usual for his *peones* to '*cite*' (the Spanish verb is *citar*, which means 'invite' or 'make a date with') the bull with their capes. The *matador* watches. He is looking at the animal and studying it. The bull is around half a metric tonne of lethal force with horns that could disembowel and kill a man in seconds. Before this moment, the *torero* has never seen this bull, and the bull, to all intents and purposes, has never seen a human being, so he needs to become as familiar with it as he can, as quickly as possible. He is looking to see how readily it charges, he is also looking for any signs that it may be defective — any limp or clue that its sight is imperfect (such bulls, including bulls injured in the course of the *corrida*, breaking a horn or twisting a leg for example, will be taken off and a substitute brought on — there is no valour in facing a lame bull). He is also looking to see whether it has a tendency to 'chop' or hook with its left or right horn. Just as a human being may be left or right 'handed', bulls will tend to favour their right or left horn. Knowing this information can mean the difference between triumph and injury.

For no more than a couple of minutes, the bull charges at the *capotes*. It may do so readily, or it may need encouragement. This process is known as '*fijar al toro*' (pinning or fixing the bull) and this is something else that the *matador* is observing: how quickly does this bull learn? A bull naturally charges, but it has never been tempted by men holding large pieces of cloth before. A bull that learns quickly is likely to deliver an impressively brave display, but it can also be dangerous. A fast-learning bull will eventually, and even quite quickly, become *sentido* — aware of the *matador* himself, not just his cape. Such a bull is highly lethal.

Finally, the *matador* enters the ring and cites the bull himself. Whereas the *peones* simply invite charges, the *matador* wants to show more artistry. A common way of holding the *capote* is directly in front of the body. This is called the *verónica* because it mimics the stance of St Veronica in sacred art, holding the cloth with which she wiped the face of Jesus. When the

455

bull charges, the *torero* swings the *capote* to the left or the right, then sweeps it in the opposite direction at the last moment, sending the bull running past his body. He will do (or try to do) several of these moves (known as '*lances*' or '*suertes*') in a row, before finishing with a *lance* known as a '*media verónica*' in which, as the bull passes, he wraps the *capote* around his body, twirling dramatically.

When the president decides that there have been enough *lances*, he lets his white handkerchief drop, a bugle sounds, and the next (actually the first) third of the *corrida* begins.

Tercio de Varas

The objective of this first *tercio* (third) is to temper the bull in order to improve its behaviour, reduce the violence of its charge somewhat, and moderate its attack. The behaviour of the bull during the rest of the fight depends on the development of this third, hence its importance. This is the third of the *corrida* that new spectators tend to enjoy least because the sight of a mounted *picador* jabbing a lance into the bull's neck seems cruel, or 'unsporting' (reminder: the *corrida* is not a sport). But for the *aficionado*, this is the third that is always observed with very close attention. This is where the mettle and potential of the bull are tested and are clearly on display. When a bull is at its most aggressive, the muscles on the crest of its neck (the '*morillo*') are engorged and raised. Just behind this huge muscular mass is the *cruz* — the optimal place to place the sword for the kill. One of the aims of this *tercio*, then, is to begin to weaken the neck and lower the *morillo* (and the head).

While the *peones* keep the bull occupied on the far side of the ring (not inciting charges, but using their *capotes* to keep the bull's attention), the mounted *picadores* enter the ring. They carry long poles topped with a 29 mm long conical tip on a ferrule with a bar that prevents the barb from penetrating any deeper. It is said that the spike (called a '*rejón*' or '*puya*') mimics the sort of injury that every bull will have sustained on the *ganadería* from the horns of other bulls. The horses used by the *picadores* are trained for this function nowadays and are highly prized. In Hemingway's day, the horses used were old nags on their way to the abattoir and were frequently, and horrifically, disembowelled by the bulls. However, since 1928 horses have been required to wear a padded mattress called a *peto* (breastplate) that prevents the bull's horns from causing damage. They also wear half-blindfolds in order to keep them calm and prevent them from bolting.

Each bull (in a first-class ring) requires three *picadores*. Two enter the ring (the bull being distracted by the *peones*), and the third (which confusingly, and according to the official nomenclature is technically the second) remains in the wings, so to speak, ready to come on if one of the *picadores* (or horses) is injured and needs to retire. The first *picador* takes his position and will *lidiar* ('struggle') with the bull. The other *picador* takes up a position on the opposite side of the ring, but he will face the next bull of that *matador*. The *picador* must position his horse at or beyond the outer *vaya* (painted line on the arena), seven metres from the *barrera*.

The *peones* then use their *capotes* to draw the bull towards the lure — in this case, not a cloth, but another animal: the horse. The reason for the inner, nine-metre *raya* is that the bull must charge from within this line (*i.e.* a charge of at least 2 metres). Any less is hardly a charge at all, more of a head-butt. Much farther and a bull at full tilt would knock the horse off its feet.

When things go according to plan, the bull charges the horse, butting its horns into the horse's protected flank, and the *picador* sinks the *puya* (point) of the *vara* (lance) into the bull's *morillo* (neck hump). The number of *puyazos* (punches or 'pics') that the *picador* can make to the bull is at the discretion of the *matador*, but in the first category *plazas* it is mandatory to perform at least two punches. The second one is the more interesting. The bull has already charged once and earned a stab in the *morillo* for its trouble, so if it runs at the horse a second time, this is taken as evidence of tenacity and *bravura*, or bravery. The opposite of this trait is for the bull to be 'manso' — placid and docile.

You will notice that the *picador* wears not a *traje de luces* exactly, but a *chaquetilla de luces* — a short jacket embroidered with gold. This is a nod to the status of the *picador* as the original *torero*. Before the transformation of the *corrida* in the 18th century, the main spectacle was the mounted *torero*. Nowadays, their role is still necessary, but more formal and practical.

Quites

Once each pic or *puyazo* is done, the bull is removed from the horse through a series of moves (called *suertes* or *quites*) with the *capote*. We must distinguish between the actions carried out later by the *matador* with the red *muleta* (which are also called *suertes*) and what is erroneously called the 'tercio de quites' [sic], a third that does not exist, the correct name of these being only 'quites'. After the first *puyazo*, the next *matador* in seniority will draw the bull away. This should be done in an orderly fashion in a way that does not over-tire the bull, but it is still an opportunity for another *matador* to demonstrate his skill. The *verónica* is widely employed, but there are many other recognized ways of removing the bull, such as the *navarra* which, to an inexperienced eye looks very similar to the *verónica*, and the *larga cambiada* in which the *capote* is lifted and swirled around the body or shoulders of the *torero*. After the second pic, the next *matador* in seniority will use his *capote* in the same fashion, drawing the bull away from the horse, testing it, and allowing the *picadores* to leave the ring. There is only rarely a third pic, but it may happen for two reasons: either the bull will not stop driving its head into the horse's flank (though in this case it should be removed by passing *capotes* in its peripheral vision), or it is a very large, powerful and aggressive animal that needs to be further weakened. Even in this latter case, it is likely that the *matador* will be yelling 'Enough!' at the *picador* (though the *picador* will know perfectly well that the *matador* does not mean it). In smaller *plazas* with smaller bulls, the *matador* may petition the president (by raising his *montera*) to permit only one pic, so as not to overtire a bull that would otherwise become sluggish before the last *tercio*.

Though it sometimes happens earlier or later, it is most often in the *tercio de varas* that, if the bull is not fit to continue, this fact will become clear. The most common reason for petitioning the president to order the removal of a bull is an obvious injury (such as a broken horn); lameness being another common culprit. If you hear people whistling and shouting '¡Ya!' ('enough!') then they are protesting. I have heard plenty of foreigners at a *corrida* mistake whistling an obviously injured bull for bloodthirsty approval, but in the ring, whistling shows disapproval and disdain. It may seem strange at an event where the death of an animal is certain, but the crowd is extremely intolerant of anything it sees as cruelty towards or mistreatment of the bull.

If it looks like a bull needs to be taken off, *aficionados* will be waving green handkerchiefs. If the president agrees (and here he will take advice from his veterinary advisor), then he will signal with his green handkerchief. The bugle sounds and the ring empties, leaving a bewildered-looking bull in the middle. The next thing you see will be half a dozen *cabestros* (castrated steers) emerge onto the arena, their bells sounding. Guided by a stockman, they will lead the injured bull, a herd animal, back through the gate and into the bullpens, where it will be put down.

Tercio de Banderillas

The second third, which those new to the *corrida* often enjoy most thanks to its balletic artistry, is the third of *banderillas* (which means 'little flags' — and in a *rejoneo*, they actually are flags that unfurl). The origin of the *banderilla* dates back to the late 18th century. It is a seventy centimetre stick, adorned with coloured paper and with a small barb at one end. The purpose of this *tercio* is to enliven or stimulate the bull. But ritually, anthropologists and philosophers have described it as also being about 'adorning' or 'dressing' the bull, preparing it for its noble death. Sometimes the *matador* himself places the sticks (again in the bull's *morillo*), but it is properly the task of his assistants, who are commonly called *banderilleros*.

The *banderillero* (usually — there are several traditional ways to perform the task) faces the bull, holding the sticks above his head, mimicking the shape of the bull's horns. He may call, '*¡Toro!*', make a sound, or stamp his foot, while twisting his body or even jumping in the air to get the bull's attention. When the bull begins to charge, so does the *banderillero*, again mimicking the bull. As the two meet, he leans over the horns placing the points of the *banderillas* in the *morillo*, quickly pivoting away to the side to evade the bull as it completes its charge. The *banderillero*, if you watch closely, will tend to run in a tight arc, meeting the bull at a point at which it cannot give further chase, due to the angle. The first *banderillero* goes first and as he places his sticks, the third *banderillero* removes the bull with his *capote*. Next, the second *banderillero* places a pair of sticks, the bull is removed and the first *banderillero* returns to place a third and final pair of sticks (for the next bull that the same *matador* faces, *banderilleros* swap places). If a *banderillero* misses completely, he is usually permitted another attempt, but if it is taking too long, or the president decides that the bull is already showing signs of tiring, then he moves things on to the next *tercio* by the usual signal: a white handkerchief held over the ledge of the balcony. The 'ideal' placing of the *banderillas* is in three pairs along the *morillo* like pairs of eyelets on a shoe.

Like the colours of the *traje de luces*, the colours of the crepe paper on the sticks are significant. At a *corrida* in Málaga, for example, you are likely to see green-white-green (the colours of the flag of Andalucía), green-purple (the colours of the flag of Málaga) and red-yellow-red (the colours of the flag of Spain). If the *torero* is a native of Alicante, then some of his sticks

458

might be decorated with white and blue (the colours of the flag of Alicante). If, say, the British ambassador were present at the *corrida*, then there might be some sticks decorated with red, white and blue.

Ultimo Tercio

The last third is the most significant of the three into which the *corrida* is divided, and in it, the *torero* displays all his aesthetic and technical art. In modern times, the entire *corrida* is directed towards this last third, where the so-called *faena de muleta* ('task of the crutch') is performed and which is decisive for the bullfighter to obtain praise and trophies. Everything before this third might have been supremely beautiful, even the most perfect expression of the art of *toreo* ever witnessed, but if the *faena* is a disaster, then all of that is squandered.

Since the 18th century, and following the taurine regulations, a *matador* must dedicate his first bull to the president of the bullring. When the dedication is made, the *torero* must carry the *muleta* (a red cloth attached to a dowel) in his left hand and the *estoque* (rapier) and *montera* in the right. His second bull may be dedicated to anyone he chooses, including to the public as a whole, or to no one. If he dedicates the bull to a particular individual then he may make a short speech before handing (or throwing) them his *montera*. If he dedicates the bull to the crowd, then he salutes them from the centre of the ring with the *montera*, turning through 360 degrees before tossing it over his shoulder. Landing brim downwards is considered a good omen, landing brim upwards is considered bad luck.

This *tercio* is the only one that has a time limit laid down in the bullfighting regulations (Article 81). From the moment the *matador* lifts the *muleta*, he initially has ten minutes to complete the *faena* and kill the bull. If, after this time, the bull has not been killed, a first *aviso* (warning) will sound by means of a clarion call ordered by the president. Three minutes later a second *aviso* sounds, and two minutes later the third and last, at which, if the bull is still standing, the *matador* and *peones* return to the *callejón*. What happens next is the decision of the president. The bull is either led back to corrals (where it is slaughtered), or killed in the ring, either with the *puntilla* (short dagger used to sever the cervical spine), or put to the sword by the *matador* who is due to face the next bull.

The failure of a *matador* to complete the kill in the allotted time is often considered a failure, though not always. In 2016 the flamboyant and popular *figura* Morante de la Puebla failed to kill his bull before the third *aviso* at a *corrida* in Sevilla. The crowd took the side of the *matador* rather than the regulations, claiming that the president's decision not to allow an extension limited Morante's 'artistry'.

The *faena* is divided into two parts. The first involves a series of passes in which the objective is to dominate the bull and is called '*engaño*' ('deception'). Ideally, you will see the *matador* cover less and less distance as the *faena* proceeds. His aim is to dominate and direct the bull completely, keeping it focused on the *muleta*, bringing it ever closer to his body. In the initial charges, the bull will charge the *muleta* running through or past it. As the *matador* achieves greater mastery, the bull comes closer, the length of its charge shortened, so that the *matador* can stand almost completely still, moving only his arm and the *muleta* while the bull makes all the running, turning in increasingly tight circles around the man. In this, the *torero* shows his bravery too. A bull's horns are lethal, so the safest option would be to hold the *muleta* at arm's length, well away from the body. Bringing the animal close, because it is so dangerous, is only possible when mastery is achieved. As the *faena* goes on, individual passes give way to series of connected passes, forming a fluid unity.

The *muleta* itself is a heart-shaped red cloth ('*pico*') draped over a dowel called an *estaquillador* and is referred to in taurine slang simply as the *pañosa* ('cloth'), and the *muleta* and *capote* together are referred to as '*trastos*' ('junk'). In some passes, only the *muleta* is used, but in the early passes it is spread wider using the *estoque* (rapier). In fact, what is used for most of the *faena* is not the actual steel sword but a balsa wood replica that is lighter and easier to handle. Originally, the cloth was simply used to keep the animal's attention and to cause it to lower its head just before the kill. Using it in series of dozens of elaborate and beautiful — even balletic — passes was one of great developments of the eighteenth and nineteenth centuries.

The first passes will be wide and open because the bull is still charging without discipline. One of the aims of the *faena* is to get the bull to lower its head. The first pass you see may therefore be the *toreo de poder* — where the *matador* drops almost to one knee, extending the arm which holds the *muleta* low and far from his body, sweeping the animal around his bended knee. You will probably see *pases de la muerte* ('death passes'). In these, the *matador* stands side-on, holding the *muleta* with both hands in front of his body, at arm's length. As the bull comes near, he flicks the cloth upwards, often causing the bull to jump. This move sounds counter-intuitive when the aim is to get the bull to lower its head, but nonetheless, it is a pass that teaches the bull to follow the lure, to focus on the cloth and nothing else.

As the *matador* becomes more confident, he may attempt one or more *pases cambiados* ('changing passes'). This begins like a *pase de la muerte* but then, as the bull approaches, ready to pass in front of the *matador's* body, he swings the *muleta* behind himself, altering the bull's charge. Similar is a *péndulo*, where the *muleta* is swung back and forth in front and behind the *matador* (like a pendulum), finally directing the bull behind the body of the *matador* at the final moment of the charge.

After these initial passes, you should be able to witness (in a good *faena*) the threefold canon of *toreo*, namely '*parar, templar, mandar*'. '*Parar*' means 'to stay' or, in this case, 'to stand still'. As the *faena* proceeds, you want to see the *matador* standing his ground, his feet remaining in the same spot as the bull makes all the running. '*Templar*' ('to moderate') is a matter of rhythm and speed. The *matador* must be able to move the lure in a way that is synchronized with the bull so that the two — bull and lure — seem interconnected. When the lure is moved in time with the bull, it creates a sense that the handling of the *muleta* actually slows and controls the speed of the bull's charge. Finally, '*mandar*' ('to command') entails mastering the bull in such a way that its direction and path are totally determined by the *torero*. The other sense of the verb *mandar* (to send) helps shed light upon what is going on, too. The aim is not simply to incite or invite a charge from the bull, but also to direct where it moves after it meets the lure, or where it is 'sent'.

This is the moment when, if fluidity, skill and artistry are in evidence, the band will strike up. The rules for music vary from *plaza* to *plaza*. In Madrid, the serious 'cathedral' of *toreo*, music is only played at the beginning of the *corrida* and between bulls. In some *plazas*, music is played when the *banderillero* places *banderillas* (in Bilbao shawms are played). In most *plazas*, music accompanies impressive *faenas*, and the decision to begin playing either left to the band-master or the president. But wherever you are, expect to hear voices in the crowd demanding '¡*Música!*' if they think the display warrants it. Remember, though, that some wag will always cry '¡*Música!*' ironically when the performance is bad.

After a few more minutes of work, the passes become visibly closer; both closer in time from one to the next, but also physically closer to the *torero*, causing the bull to pass his body more closely. There are many types of pass, all with their own names, inventors, exponents and histories. But the main kinds seen in every *faena* are the '*natural*' (an open *muleta* held in the left hand, with the sword held in the right), and the '*derechazo*' ('right-handed' — the *muleta* held in the right hand and the sword supporting the cloth to maximize its size). The passes slowly build. A chain of three or four *naturales* followed by a *derechazo* can slowly develop into a long, fluid series of many alternating passes. These sequences are often brought to completion with the '*pase de pecho*' ('chest pass') in which the *muleta* is not moved out of the way, but swept upwards over the bull's head and then trailed along the length of its back, releasing the animal beyond the man. There are many other kinds of passes — *circulares*, *trincherazos*, *kikirikís*, *roblesinas*, *granadinas*, *faroles*, *molinetes*, *manoletinas*, and *bernadinas* to name just a few. If it is your first time at a *corrida* you will be doing well to identify the *natural*, the *derechazo*, and the *pase de pecho*!

La Suerte Suprema

At the end of the *tercio*, the *torero* prepares to kill the bull. If the bull, in the view of the *matador* and/or the crowd has exhibited exceptional and unusual bravery, then they may petition for an '*indulto*' — that is, for the bull to be 'pardoned'. Interestingly, the number of petitions for an *indulto* increased significantly in the wake of the COVID pandemic, but they are still rare. To request an *indulto*, the *matador* appeals directly to the president and the crowd waves orange handkerchiefs. If the *indulto* is granted (by hanging an orange handkerchief over the ledge of the balcony), the *cabestros* are called in and they lead the bull back to the bullpens. In an ideal situation, the pardoned bull is sedated, patched up by a vet and returned to the *ganadería* to be used as a seed bull, but in some cases, alas, it is put down due to its injuries.

If there is no *indulto* then, when he is ready, the *matador* goes to the *barrera* where he takes a drink of water from a silver cup and wipes his face with a white towel while two of his *peones* keep an eye on the bull, subduing it with their *capotes* if necessary. His *mozo de espadas* ('sword boy') offers a leather-covered chain-mail sheath, from which the *matador* draws a gleaming, razor-sharp rapier, a straight sword with a slightly curved tip. Once more, this is now the moment where a sublime display of the art of *toreo* can be undone by a botched kill, something the crowd rarely forgives. Until this point, the bull has been doing what is in its nature: charging, fighting, and showing *bravura*. It deserves the honour of being killed cleanly, quickly and expertly, in a way that does not cause undue suffering. Most *aficionados*, when speaking of their passion, do not say that they follow '*las corridas*' (the bullfights), but '*los toros*' (the bulls).

There are broadly three styles of sword thrusts, depending on the type of confrontation between the bull and the *torero*, that is: attacking, receiving, or a mixture of the two. The first occurs when the *torero* moves towards the standing bull ('*a un tiempo*'), the second is where it is the bull that moves towards the *torero* (called '*recibiendo*' or 'receiving') and the third is when they move towards each other at the same time ('*volapié*'). There are also intermediate styles.

Where in the ring the kill takes place is partly the bull's preference. Feral bulls (like the Chillingham Cattle) dig bull pits in the earth with their horns for reasons that zoologists do not fully understand, but it seems likely that these pits are about territory, ownership, security, or a mixture of all three. Likewise, a bull in the *plaza* will often return to a particular spot again and again, perhaps because it is especially cool, or carries the scent of another bull or animal, its pheromones, blood or urine. This is known as the bull's *querencia* ('fondness'). The bull is liable to be most calm in its *querencia*, so this is often where is it put to the sword.

Armed with the (real) sword, the *matador* will usually make a few gentle passes in order to position the bull. Hush descends upon the *plaza*. A lone idiot shouts a word of encouragement (or perhaps abuse) and everyone hisses at him (it's always a 'him') to be quiet. The *matador* stands directly before the bull, the sword in his right hand (another name for a *matador* is '*diestro*' — 'right-hander') and the *muleta* in his left. Slowly, almost imperceptibly lifting and lowering the *muleta* to keep the bull's attention he raises the sword to shoulder height, holding it horizontally. Then he simultaneously draws back his elbow, as if pulling on the string of an imaginary long bow, and twists his torso to the right at the hips. Then, he either causes the bull to charge, or he moves towards the bull, or both at once, lunging with the sword.

The target for the tip of the sword is the '*cruz*' just behind the *morillo*. When perfect, the sword plunges in cleanly, severing the pulmonary aorta (it does not pierce the heart as many suppose) causing death immediately or in seconds. However, the *cruz* is very small (about the size of a poker chip) and few spectators begrudge the *matador* a miss on the first attempt. A lunge may be a '*pinchazo*' (a puncture), an '*estocada corta*' ('short lunge', less than half the sword), a '*media estocada*' (half lunge: half a sword's length), an '*honda*' (slingshot: three-quarters of the sword), or an '*entera*' (the whole sword). Additionally, the sword might be placed too far back, too far forward or too far to the side. Again, apart from the most devoted *aficionados*, most people in the crowd do not usually seek to punish a *matador* for misplacing a sword **as long as the bull's death is swift**.

If the death is not immediate after a full thrust, then the *matador* will resort to using the '*descabello*' (*lit.* 'decapitator'). This weapon is essentially a blunt sword with a sharp, wide tip 10 cm in length and a crosspiece above it. The bull, now lethargic and immobile, is made to lower its head using the *muleta* and the *descabello* is jabbed in between the first and second cervical vertebrae. Resorting to the *descabello* is not necessarily regarded as evidence of failure. Killing a bull is not an easy task, and it is a very dangerous one for the *matador*. However, if he needs more than two attempts with the *descabello* then whatever goodwill he accrued with the crowd during the *faena* and before is likely to be greatly diminished, or erased. Although many spectators at the *corrida* feel they know better than the *torero* (just as many spectators at football matches believe they know better than the top-flight sportsmen on the pitch), most recognize that this is a spectacle rendered supremely unpredictable because it involves a dangerous animal. As mentioned above, however, what no crowd tolerates is a slow and agonizing death for the bull (if the crowd is whistling as the bull is being killed, this is an expression of displeasure at what they judge to be cruelty, rather than enjoyment of the bull's death.) To ensure the bull is dead, one of the *banderilleros* takes a dagger called a '*puntilla*' from a sheath strapped to his calf and pushes it into the top of spinal column.

Originally, the *estoque* (rapier) was used to finish off the bull, but following a fatal accident in 1834 in the ring in La Coruña where the *figura* Juan Belmonte hit bone, sending the razor-sharp rapier pinging into the crowd, killing a spectator, the *descabello* (of which only the tip is sharpened) was introduced.

Once the bull is certified as dead by the *puntillero*, the *puerta de arrastre* is opened and the *mulilleros* enter the ring with a team of mules. They secure the bull with a rope by the horns and attach it to the yoke of the mules. If the crowd in the *plaza* is silent, then they immediately drag the bull's carcass from the ring. However, if there is significant applause, then they await a signal from the president. If the crowd believes that the *matador* deserves to be rewarded for an especially fine performance, they will be waving white handkerchiefs (or their programmes or hats). If a majority of the *plaza* petitions for a trophy ('*una oreja*', an ear), then the president must award one. He indicates this by hanging a white handkerchief from the ledge of the balcony on his right. If the crowd considers that the performance has been so exemplary as to merit a second ear, then they will continue to wave their handkerchiefs and cheer. The award of this second ear is entirely at the discretion of the president, however, advised by his veterinary and artistic advisors. The award is indicated with a second white handkerchief on his left.

According to the regulations, it is possible to petition for the award of a tail ('*un rabo*'), but this almost never happens in first-class rings, though it is a frequent sight in third-class *plazas*. In premier rings, it happened most recently in Sevilla in 2023 when the *figura* Morante de la Puebla was awarded two ears and a tail during the *Feria de Abril*. Not only was he carried from the *puerta grande* '*a hombros*', but also through the streets, much to the bemusement of the tourists. It was the first time a tail had been awarded in Sevilla since 1971, a period of more than half a century.

In cases where a bull has shown exceptional *bravura*, the president can officially indicate with a blue handkerchief that a '*vuelta*' ('circuit') be awarded. In this case, rather than dragging the bull directly to the gate to the butchery, it is drawn around the perimeter of the ring so that the crowd can applaud it. Sometimes, a bull will be awarded a *vuelta* while the *matador* will not. In reality, the decision to give the bull a *vuelta* is usually taken by the *mulilleros*, rather than the president.

Permitted Trophies and Honours

Ovaciones: (ovation) applause granted directly by the public at the end of the *faena*.

Saludo desde el tercio: (salute after the final third) when a petition for an ear is strong, but not enough to convince the president, the *torero* comes back into to the ring to salute the crowd and thank them for their support (the photo on p. 464 shows the late Iván Fandiño giving a *saludo* to the crowd in the Acho bullring in Lima, Peru)..

Vuelta al ruedo: this is like the *saludo* but where the applause has been so great that the *matador* thinks it warrants his walking around the ring. This can be a risky judgment. Few things are more pitiful than a *torero* beginning a 'victory lap' where the applause dies halfway around.

Una oreja or ***dos orejas***: one or two ears. After these are cut by a *mulillero* and given to the *matador* by one of the *alguacilillos*, he makes a circuit of the ring — acknowledging applause, kissing hats thrown into the ring, and so forth.

Salida a hombros: this comes at the end of the entire *corrida*. Instead of leaving by the usual *puerta de cuadrilla*, the *torero* is carried on a man's shoulders out of the *puerta principal*. The requirements for this honour vary from place to place. In many *plazas*, any two ears are enough. In Andalucía, the two ears must be cut from the **same** bull. In Sevilla (which likes to challenge Madrid as the 'cathedral' of *toreo*), a *matador* must cut two ears from one bull and at least one from the other.

Disapproval is shown in the *plaza* in various ways. The most usual are whistling and booing, but perhaps even more effective are silence and (especially in Sevilla) distracted chatting. The *sevillanos* are expert in demonstrating disdain. Rather than whistling, booing or remaining silent, they simply turn to one another and start chatting, as if nothing were happening in front of them. This can happen very quickly. One minute, the crowd can be cheering and shouting '¡Olé!' and gasping '¡Qué *torero!*' (What a bullfighter!), their fingers already reaching for their white handkerchiefs to petition for two ears, but seconds later, after a bungled pass or a botched kill, they seem utterly indifferent to the *torero* in the ring.

The following day, a good way of 'checking your homework' (that is, seeing how much of the *corrida* you actually understood) is checking a newspaper report online and, if you need to, putting it through your browser's translate function. The critic's report of the previous afternoon's *corrida* will comment upon three essential aspects: the *toros*, the *toreros* and the *gente* (crowd). Any *corrida* is a sum of all three. Were the *toros* 'noble' and given to charging readily, or were they slow or timid? Did the *toreros* handle the bulls they faced skilfully and gracefully, or did they make mistakes? And what did the crowd think, of both *toros* and *toreros*? Even reasonably good Spanish speakers might struggle with some of the specialist terminology, and automatic translation can often mangle the words, but what should be of interest is the summary given at the end of the report.

This will normally begin with a brief description of the bulls, telling you, perhaps, that they were generally 'well-presented, serious' and '*astifinos*' (thin-horned), with the first being 'typical of its breeding ('*encastado*')' the second 'noble', the sixth noble but also 'goofy' ('*bobalicón*') and the rest '*desiguales*' or '*deslucidos*' (unequal or lacklustre). Then the performance of each *matador*, especially during the *faena* and the kill will be summarized for each of his bulls, whether he received one or more *avisos*, the crowd's reaction, and any trophies. A poor performance might be summarized, '*dos pinchazos y estocada tras aviso (silencio)*' — 'two punctures, then a sword after a warning, greeted by silence from the crowd'. A better display might be, '*estocada (ovación) dos orejas tras petición*' — 'a sword, with an ovation from the crowd, and two ears awarded after a petition from the crowd'.

♘ Other Taurine Festivals

Málaga is not the only place in the province where *corridas* are staged. Other towns celebrate *ferias taurinas* alongside their main *feria*, or stage *corridas* to mark feast days. In Spain, *corridas* are generally held in the afternoon at 6 pm or 7 pm, or even later, so with the exception of Fuengirola, unless you have your own transport, seeing one outside Málaga will almost certainly require an overnight stay. However, this will also allow you to enjoy the regular *feria* as well. Accommodation tends to be more expensive during a *feria*, but if you book ahead you will be able to find somewhere — you only need somewhere to sleep, after all — *ferias* are about late nights and partying! Booking a couple of months ahead, it is usually possible to find affordable accommodation, even in cities like Granada. The following list also includes a few localities outside the Province of Málaga, but within easy reach on public transport.

Sevilla (April)

The *toreros* of the world spend the months of October to March in South America (*i.e.* summer), but they return to Spain and France for the European Summer. The first big fixture of the *temporada* (season) in Spain is Las Fallas in Valencia, held around the Feast of St Joseph (19 March). In Sevilla, a city that fancies itself as a challenger to Madrid as the 'home of *toreo*', there is usually a *corrida* on Easter Sunday, and then the following weekend kicks off an entire month of taurine spectacles (the precise timetable varies depending upon the date of Easter — *i.e.* sometimes the *corridas* run well into May).

Málaga (March/April)

Málaga traditionally staged a *corrida* on Easter Sunday, though in recent years this has been moved to Holy Saturday with the staging of the *Corrida Picassiana*.

Córdoba (May)

Córdoba has a first-class ring, so the *carteles* (programmes) include big names. The city used to stage a *corrida* on Easter Sunday, and a full week of *corridas* during the *feria* in May. In recent years, however, there have been three *corridas* held over the first weekend of the *feria* — two *corridas de toros* and one *corrida de rejones*. Unless Córdoba stages more events, its ring may be demoted to second-class status.

Granada (May/June)

Like Córdoba, the *feria taurina* is held concurrently with the *Feria del Corpus*. Similarly, the eight-day-long programme has been reduced to four in the last few years, usually beginning on the Thursday of Corpus Christi and continuing until Sunday.

Estepona (July)

A second class ring, Estepona stages one *corrida* during the July *feria*. They usually manage to book some prominent *matadores*. Andrés Roca Rey — arguably the best and undoubtedly the most popular *torero* in the world — appeared here in 2022 and again in 2023.

Fuengirola (July)

In recent years, Fuengirola has staged a *corrida* for the *Fiesta del Carmen* (*i.e.* the weekend nearest to 16 July).

Antequera (August)

Antequera (3rd class) once had two annual *ferias taurinas* — the weekend following Corpus

Christi (May or June) and the final weekend of the *feria* (August). In recent years, *corridas* have been staged on the final Friday, Saturday and Sunday of the *Feria de Agosto* and for the *Feria de Primavera* (Spring Fair) in early June.

Ronda (September)

Again coinciding with the town's *feria*, *corridas* are held over the first weekend in September —a *corrida de novillos* on Friday, a *corrida de rejones* on Saturday and the famous *corrida goyesca* (in eighteenth-century costume) on Sunday.

Málaga (September)

In the past, Málaga has staged one or more *corridas* for the Feast of Our Lady of the Victory (8 September). In recent years, the end of the *temporada* has been in August, but it is worth checking as timetables often change.

Fuengirola (October)

In the past few years, one *corrida* has been staged during the *Feria del Rosario*.

Mijas (N/A)

No *corrida* has been staged here since 1999.

Torremolinos (?)

A decade ago, there were *corridas* staged in Torremolinos at Easter and for the *Feria de San Miguel* (September), with others in between. The last *corrida* took place for the *Feria de San Juan* (June) in 2015. It is possible that more *corridas* may be staged in the future. Much depends upon the *ayuntamiento* which can award a contract to operate the bullring or let it lie empty.

Marbella

Like Torremolinos, Marbella is another town that once staged several high-quality *corridas* each year, but in 2019 the *ayuntamiento* announced that it was going to renovate the *Plaza de Toros* as a 'cultural centre'. Opponents of the *Fiesta Nacional* (*corrida de toros*) often claim that taurine events in Spain are only kept alive by 'tourism', but if anything, the opposite is true. This seems to be what has happened in Marbella (and to an extent Torremolinos), where a large non-Spanish population has little understanding of, or interest in, *los toros*.

Benalmádena

The *Plaza de Toros* in Benalmádena tells another story of sad decline (or overdue just desserts, depending upon your point of view). The bullring closed in 2011 due to its poor state of repair and the *ayuntamiento* demolished the *corrales* (bullpens) soon after, making the staging of *corridas* effectively impossible. Twenty years ago, almost 30 *corridas* a year took place here, more than any other third-class *plaza* in Spain.

Excursiones (Day Trips)

This book is primarily a guide to the city of Málaga and anyone spending a few days in Málaga will find plenty to occupy themselves in the city. One could easily spend a week gently exploring the walkable centre of Málaga, with maybe a bus journey to the Botanical Gardens or a trip to a nearby beach for an *espeto*. However, if you are staying for longer, if you have visited Málaga before and have already 'done' the main sights, or if you simply want to get out of the city for a change, then the suggestions in the remainder of this book are for you. And they are just that: suggestions, rather than 'must-see' recommendations.

I have only included excursions that can comfortably be done in a day. This means, with the exception of Gibraltar (which, for obvious reasons, might be of particular interest to British tourists), a journey time of 2 hours or less. I also provide suggestions that do not involve hiring a vehicle, relying instead on public transport. It should go without saying that if you do choose to hire a car then many of the excursions mentioned in this section become rather more straightforward, especially visits to vineyards and small villages.

A couple of the other suggestions in this section (*viz.* Granada and Córdoba) are popular destinations outside the Province of Málaga with world-famous historical sights (the Alhambra and the Mezquita-Catedral respectively) and both are only just over an hour from Málaga by train. Although they are, unlike Málaga, well-covered by tourist guidebooks to Andalucía, I have included them as they are easy day trips from Málaga, although in the case of Granada, a day trip will only allow you to scratch the surface.

Pretty much any small town in Southern Spain is worth visiting, at least for a day. As long as you avoid Mondays (when many attractions are closed), even the smallest town will have a couple of churches to explore and perhaps a small (though probably rather eccentric and moth-eaten) museum to visit. There will be some beautiful streets and attractive architecture and it will almost certainly be set in stunning countryside (Málaga is second most mountainous province in Andalucía after Granada). Most importantly, however, there will be a pleasant *café* in which to enjoy a coffee and, later, a nice bar to have a drink and some lunch.

If you are the sort of person who enjoys soaking up the *ambiente* of a place, rather than ticking off the 'sights', then you really can't go wrong. For a country so associated with passion and emotion, Spain is also a wonderful place to slow down and just 'be'. As far as I know, the poet W. H. Davies never visited Spain, but the opening couplet of his best-known poem should be the motto of the *turismo* of every sleepy Spanish town and village:

What is this life if, full of care
We have no time to stand and stare?[68]

---

68   W. H. Davies, 'Leisure', *Songs Of Joy and Others* (1911, A. C. Fifield, London)

❦ *El Camino Mozárabe*

*To go on pilgrimage is not simply to visit a place to admire its treasures of na-
ture, art or history. To go on pilgrimage really means to step out of ourselves
in order to encounter God where he has revealed himself, where his grace has
shone with particular splendour and produced rich fruits of conversion and
holiness among those who believe.*[69]

Camino
Mozárabe
de Santiago

The Camino de Santiago (The Way of Saint James) is the
route taken by pilgrims travelling to the shrine of the Apostle
Saint James the Greater in the Cathedral of Santiago de
Compostela in Galicia, North West Spain. Saint James was
declared patron of the Kingdom of Asturias by King Alfonso II in the early 9th century and the primitive pilgrim
route began in Oviedo, 300 km away. Compostela was
razed in 997 by Almanzor (*Hajib* of Córdoba, see p. 567)
but the pilgrims continued to come. Over time, the pilgrimage grew in importance and the route was extended, beginning in the Pyrenees and entering Spain at Roncesvalles.
After the *reconquista*, Saint James was proclaimed patron of all Spain and many other routes were established, beginning in various parts of Spain, particularly port cities where pilgrims from other countries
would land (English and Irish pilgrims would traditionally walk from the port of Ferrol near La Coruña).

In 1121, the Almoravid Emir Ali ibn Yusuf passed along the road to Santiago de Compostela
while on an embassy to Leon and remarked that 'so great is the multitude of those who come
and go (to Compostela) as scarcely to leave room on the road towards the west.'[70] Geoffrey
Chaucer in The Canterbury Tales writes that the serial pilgrim, the Wife of Bath,

*… hadde passed many a straunge strem;
At Rome she hadde been, and at Boloigne,
In Galice at Seint-Jame…*[71]

Many other well-known medieval figures made the pilgrimage, including John of Gaunt, Saint Francis of Assisi, Saint
Bridget of Sweden and, just before the *reconquista*, the
Catholic Monarchs Fernando and Isabel. Their daughter,
the Infanta Catalina, made the pilgrimage on her way to
England to marry Prince Arthur Tudor. It is said that during
mass, the enormous *botafumeiro* (a swinging incense burner
suspended from the ceiling and weighing 80 kg) came de-
tached from its ropes and crashed through the window of
the Cathedral. Given Catalina's rather sad later life as 'Catherine of Aragón', the abandoned wife of Arthur's brother
Henry VIII, this has been seen by many as a bad omen.

---

69   Homily preached by Pope Benedict XVI, Cathedral of Santiago de Compostela, 6 November 2010,
     bit.ly/BXVISdC
70   E.V. Sampedro, *El Camino de Santiago: Estudio Historico-Juridico* (Madrid, 1971)
71   Geoffrey Chaucer, 'General Prologue' (466–468), *The Canterbury Tales* c. 1400

The number of pilgrims plummeted after the Protestant Reformation, and following the incursions of Sir Francis Drake (known as *El Draque* or 'The Dragon' by the Spanish) along the Spanish coast, the relics of the saint were removed from the shrine and hidden. After a modest recovery in the 17th and 18th centuries, the Camino faced a further contraction in the 19th. Strife with France made the routes via the Pyrenees difficult, and the obsession of successive liberal Spanish governments with confiscating religious property had a devastating effect. This was because religious houses (convents and monasteries) had traditionally been used as hostels by pilgrims. During the 19th century the number of pilgrims arriving in Compostela had fallen to a mere 130 per year, most of them Spaniards.

The Civil War dealt another blow, and despite efforts to promote the Camino, numbers remained low for most of the 20th century. In 1978, only 13 pilgrims were recorded. Key to its recovery was the visit in 1982 by Pope Saint John Paul II, and his return seven years later for the fourth 'World Youth Day'. In 1992, a healthy 9,764 pilgrims were recorded, and then something extraordinary happened. The following year, 1993, was a 'Holy Year' (proclaimed when the Feast of Saint James, 25 July, falls on a Sunday, the 'Jubilee Door' is opened and special indulgences granted) and both the Spanish Church and the Spanish Tourist Board promoted the Camino heavily. In the end, 99,436 pilgrims were recorded, a tenfold increase.

Since then numbers have grown steadily. The Camino has been undertaken by Catholics like Martin Sheen (who made a film about it), Mary McAleese and the King and Queen of Belgium, as well as non-Catholics (and atheists) like Angela Merkel, Stephen Hawking, Jenna Bush and Shirley MacLaine. In 2015, pilgrim numbers exceeded a quarter of a million and have continued to increase. The Holy Year of 2022 (postponed from 2021 due to travel limitations connected with COVID) saw an incredible 438,000 pilgrims.

Málaga and Almería are the traditional starting points for the *Camino Mozárabe* (The Mozarabic Way).It is one of the longest pilgrim routes, but also one of the most rewarding and beautiful in terms of natural scenery, as well as the cities, cathedrals, churches, convents, Roman and Moorish monuments and archaeological remains *en route*.

While the route from Almería is more or less complete in terms of signposting, resources and a network of official *refugios* (lodging), the route from Málaga is still being developed. It is certainly possible to walk it, but it will require some forward planning. The suggested daily sections are:

01. Málaga — La Junta de los Caminos

02. La Junta de los Caminos — Almogía

03. Almogía — Villanueva de la Concepción

04. Villanueva de la Concepción — Antequera

05. Antequera — Cartaojal

06. Cartaojal — Villanueva de Algaidas

07. Villanueva de Algaidas — Cuevas Bajas

08. Cuevas Bajas — Encinas Reales

09. Encinas Reales — Lucena

10. Lucena — Cabra

11. Cabra — Doña Mencía

12. Doña Mencía — Baena

13. Baena — Castro del Río

14. Castro del Río — Espejo

15. Espejo — Santa Cruz

16. Santa Cruz — Córdoba

The first eight of these (20 km to 25 km) stages are in the Province of Málaga, the second eight are in the Province of Córdoba. After Córdoba the route takes you north to the city of Mérida (with its wonderful Roman circus, theatre and amphitheatre). Here the *Camino Mozárabe* joins the *Camino Vía de la Plata*, which begins in Sevilla. Then it makes its way north though Cácares, Salamanca and Zamora before veering west towards Santiago.

To walk the whole 1,200 km *Camino Mozárabe–Vía de la Plata* would take up to two months if you intended to spend the odd day resting and sightseeing. But you do not have to 'do' an entire route in order to complete the pilgrimage and get your pilgrim's certificate. The minimum requirement is to complete the last 100 km (62 miles) on foot or 200 km (124 miles) by bicycle. There are people who spend years, even decades, doing the Camino — a few days here, a week there — before completing the final stage. Others do small sections of a number of different routes all over Spain (or in France and Portugal) before completing the pilgrimage. You could, for example, walk for a few days north of Málaga capital, then get the bus back to fly home. On another trip, take the bus to, say, Baena and spend four days walking to Córdoba, then take the train back to Málaga to fly home. Then, at some future date, you could begin in La Coruña and follow the *Camino Inglés* from Ferrol to complete your pilgrimage.

A pilgrimage is meant to entail some measure of hardship and a change of lifestyle. The basic accommodation, the hearty but simple food, and the fellowship with other pilgrims are all parts of the experience. In the Middle Ages — the zenith of religious pilgrimage in Europe — going on Pilgrimage, whether to Jerusalem, Rome, Santiago or even Walsingham (Norfolk) would have been a once-in-a-lifetime experience for all but the very wealthy. Modern travel has risked our losing sight of a vital aspect of any journey or quest: the journey itself. Many of those walking the Way of St James in the 21st century are not Catholics, or even Christians. Some are trying to reconnect with a faith they once had, or kindle a faith that they wish they had. Many are agnostics or even atheists. For all of these people, the reasons for going on pilgrimage are many and varied. It might be about getting to know God and his purpose for us, or about getting to know ourselves and others; or a mixture of both. It is time away from our daily routine, it is a time for reflection or 'mindfulness' — the ultimate spiritual detox.

A detailed guide to walking the *Camino Mozárabe* would fill a book by itself. Some useful websites to get you started are:

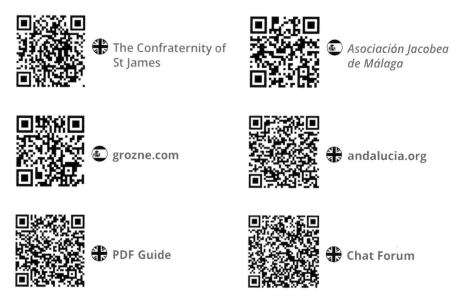

The Confraternity of St James

Asociación Jacobea de Málaga

grozne.com

andalucia.org

PDF Guide

Chat Forum

🚞 A Rail Tour of Andalucía

🎣 Luxury Train Travel

If you love train travel, the romance of an old-fashioned sleeper, and really want to push the boat out, then RENFE operates the '*Tren Al Ándaluz*' luxury train in Andalucía for ten weeks of the year between April and November. There are two routes (of six nights and seven days): one beginning in Málaga and ending in Sevilla, the other beginning in Sevilla and ending in Málaga. Sleeping, travel, and much of the dining is aboard a luxury train, with excursions in various cities en route — Granada, Linares-Baeza, Úbeda, Córdoba, Ronda, Jerez, Sanlúcar de Barrameda, and Cádiz. RENFE keeps moving its information page so the web address changes often. Instead, search for 'Al-Andalus' and 'RENFE' or use the QR code/link: **bit.ly/AndalusTrain**

The journey is marketed, accurately, as a 'luxury' option and is far from cheap. However, it is by no means poor value if luxury travel is your thing. The train itself (or rather, its carriages) once ferried the British royal family between Calais and the Côte d'Azur and retains many of its original Art Deco and Belle Époque features including bathroom fittings and marble floors. On the other hand, the en suite bathrooms now feature hydromassage showers.

Also included in the ticket price are RENFE rail tickets from your point of arrival in Spain and to your departure point. So if you fly into Málaga and take the train that terminates in Sevilla, RENFE will include a first-class train ticket back to Málaga (or to any other station in Spain).

Recreating a comparable experience on your own: staying in boutique hotels, eating in top-class restaurants and travelling by train first class could, according to my rough calculations, at least halve the cost, but it would also deprive you of the 'experience' and the luxurious ease of curated travel. Moreover, the business of taking taxis, checking in and out of different hotels and getting to grips with a new urban transport system every day would be pretty exhausting, to say nothing of booking attractions, searching for places to eat, etc. Moreover, using hotels and travelling during the day would significantly eat into your sightseeing time.

If the idea of an *andaluz* Grand Tour appeals to you, however, then you could plan and book it yourself, but one problem you will face with any 'DIY' itinerary is RENFE itself. In many ways, the Spanish railways are great: reasonably priced tickets, and lots of high-speed, comfortable trains. But they can often appear to be a law unto themselves, with tickets for some routes only going on sale a couple of weeks before travel, not to mention last-minute cancellations, timetable changes and closures due to maintenance (though remember that in Spain bus/coach travel is always a comfortable option).

If you want to plan your own tour of Andalucía by train (or train and bus), then you have many options, and the places you include will be a matter of personal choice. The provincial capitals of Andalucía (Almería, Granada, Málaga, Córdoba, Jaén, Sevilla, Huelva and Cádiz) are all connected by train, though not necessarily directly.

The main rail line, as you can see from the map on the next page, extends in an arc between Huelva and Almería, taking in Sevilla, Córdoba and Jaén (almost). Then a number of lines run south towards the coast — to Cádiz, to Antequera (and thence to either Algeciras via Ronda, or to Málaga) and to Granada via Guadix. In the last couple of years, a piece of the railway jigsaw has been completed between Málaga and Granada, but along the coast itself, train links are either local (🔵 *Cercanías*) or non-existent.

471

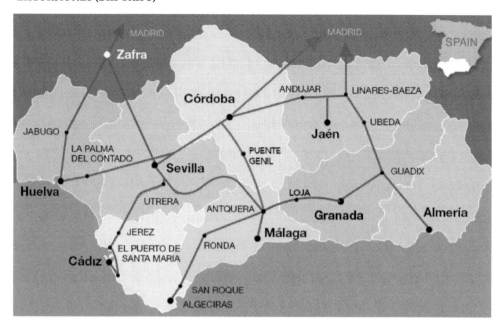

My best advice for planning a grand tour would be to try to spend more than one night in each hotel because the palaver of packing and checking in and out of accommodation is one of the most time-consuming and exhausting elements of travel. As check-out tends to be before noon and check-in after 2 pm, try to arrange travel for late morning or early afternoon. Here, by way of example, is one possibility:

Day 1: Arrive at Málaga Airport in the morning, have lunch in Málaga, and take an afternoon train to Granada. Enjoy the *tapas* scene in the evening. **Overnight**: Granada

Day 2: Visit the Alhambra and El Albaícin (on the other side of the valley) and have dinner in Granada. **Overnight**: Granada

Day 3: Lunchtime train to Sevilla. Visit the Alcázar (and/or Cathedral) in the afternoon (pre-booked). **Overnight**: Sevilla

Day 4: Morning train to Córdoba. Visit the Cathedral–Mezquita. Explore the *Judería*. Lunch in Córdoba. Return to Sevilla for dinner in Triana. **Overnight**: Sevilla

Day 5: Morning train to Cádiz, lunch in Cádiz, then take the catamaran across the bay to El Puerto de Santa María and the train back to Sevilla. (Or go to El Puerto first and tour a sherry bodega, then go across the bay to Cádiz. Jerez would be another option.) **Overnight**: Sevilla

Day 6: Late morning train to Málaga. Visit the Alcazaba and a museum. **Overnight**: Málaga

Day 7: Day trip to Ronda. **Overnight**: Málaga

Day 8: Depart Málaga.

This itinerary won't suit everyone, but it would allow you to visit seven cities while staying in only three hotels. Using different arrival and departure airports (there are also UK flights to Sevilla, Jerez, Granada and Almería) would give you even more options. Have fun planning your journey!

♦ Buying Train Tickets

The Train in Spain

Spain came late to the railways, constructing a line in its Cuban colony more than a decade before the first line in the Peninsula (1848). The relatively calm Mediterranean meant that coastal towns tended to be connected by steamer, rather than by rail. Before the First World War, there were regular ferries between Málaga and not only Sevilla and Barcelona, but London, Marseilles and Genoa. As in Britain, Spanish rail operators were nationalized in the 1940s to form a state railway (RENFE, or *Red Nacional de los Ferrocarriles Españoles*). In the 1960s, influenced by the UK's *Beeching Report*, many routes and stations were closed in a drive for 'efficiency' and profitability as people increasingly took to their motor cars.

The so-called 'Second Railway Package' of the European Union (EU Directive 2004/51) required that national rail networks be opened to operators distinct from the entity owning the infrastructure. This led to the division of RENFE into 'RENFE-Operadora' (operations) and ADIF (infrastructure) in 2005. Although RENFE is still the major carrier, at the time of publication, two other companies operate intercity trains in Spain: **Ouigo** and **Iryo**, both of which offer far cheaper tickets, albeit across a more limited range of journeys.

Whether Ouigo (pronounced 'we go' and operated by the French national railway SNCF) and Iryo ('*ir*' means 'to go' and '*yo*' means 'I' or 'me' — a joint venture by the Italian national railways and the Spanish regional airline Air Nostrum) stay the course remains to be seen.

Buying Tickets

Tickets for most RENFE (and Ouigo and Iryo) services can be booked via UK websites such as **omio.co.uk**, **raileurope.com** or **thetrainline.com**. However, not all routes or trains are always available on these sites, so it is worth consulting the operators' own websites. The **thetrainline.com** website has improved a great deal recently and sometimes gives a wider choice of journeys than the RENFE site, so it is always worth checking. For RENFE tickets, it is almost always cheaper to buy via their own website: **renfe.com/es/en**. There is also a RENFE smartphone app for iOS (**apple.co/3EMRbEg**), Android (**bit.ly/AndroidRENFE**) and Huawei (**bit.ly/HuaweiRENFE**) which saves you the trouble of printing out your tickets (keep a separate record of the ticket booking references so that you can print your tickets at a railway station if you lose or break your phone). You can also use the smartphone app to book and pay for tickets

First register with the RENFE website to make the ticket-buying process easier. The English version of the RENFE site sometimes partially reverts to Spanish, but you can easily view a translation of the page by installing a Google Translate (or similar) extension for your preferred web browser or by using a native translation function on your smartphone. The English version of the site does not seem able to deal with seat allocation, but this is a minor quibble unless you have very precise requirements regarding where you sit. After selecting your journey (or journeys if it is a return ticket), you will have to fill in personal information for each traveller (name, passport number, email address, mobile number) before proceeding to payment (and seat selection if required). You'll then be emailed PDFs of the tickets for printing, or you can download them to the RENFE app. The confirmation email has links to add the tickets to Apple Wallet or Google Wallet. The ticket number also allows you to print tickets at ticket machines in RENFE railway stations.

Rail tickets in Spain are dynamically priced, so generally speaking, the earlier you buy your ticket, the cheaper it will be. Tickets for most journeys go on sale 60 days before travel. A flexible ticket from Madrid to Sevilla purchased the day before travel is likely to cost around

50% more than one purchased 60 days before. For routes with lower demand, the price can often fall slightly after the tickets first become available, and then rise again. Based on detailed examination of the data: for high-demand routes (high-speed routes between provincial capitals) the optimal moment to buy is between 50–60 days before departure. For non-high-demand routes, the optimal moment is between 40 to 50 days before departure. For train departures in the evening, the optimal moment is 30 days before departure. But buying as far ahead as possible is not a bad general rule.

Tickets for most longer journeys are available in three classes: *Básico*, *Elige* and *Prémium* ('*elige*' means to choose).

Básico is, as the name suggests, the basic option. The cheapest fare with automatic seat allocation.

Elige offers a choice of seat, including a 'comfort' seat, usually in a carriage with rows of 2 seats on one side of the aisle and 1 seat on the other (like UK first class). For a supplement, you can also change your booking, and block a seat next to you so that you can sit alone.

Prémium is the nearest RENFE has to First Class. It allows you to choose your seat, block the seat next to you and change your booking even when you miss your train. It also means that food and drink will be served to you in your seat (when available). Another useful perk is the ability to use the RENFE '*Sala Club*' (First Class Lounge) from up to two hours before departure. *Salas Club* are available at the following stations: Alacant/Alicante–Teminal, Albacete–Los Llanos, Barcelona–Sants, Camp de Tarragona, Girona, Lleida–Pirineus, Málaga–María Zambrano, Madrid–Chamartín, Madrid–Atocha, Sevilla–Santa Justa, Valencia–Joaquín Sorolla, Valladolid–Campo Grande, and Zaragoza–Delicias. Each *Sala Club* offers free wifi, lavatories, TV, newspapers, complimentary hot and cold drinks, and light snacks.

Free ⟲ *Cercanías* Travel

Cercanías (meaning 'nearby') are local suburban commuter trains and there are networks in Asturias, Bilbao, Cádiz, Madrid, Málaga, Murcia/Alicante, Santander, San Sebastián, Seville and Zaragoza. In Valencia and Catalonia, these commuter services are called *Rodalies*. Any RENFE high-speed or long-distance (*i.e.* AVE, Alvia, Altaria, Talgo, Euromed) train departing from or arriving into any of these stations will usually include free *Cercanías* travel. So, if you are staying in Fuengirola and you book a return AVE train ticket to Córdoba, you have free travel between Fuengirola and Málaga–María Zambrano (this doesn't apply on AVANT journeys because these are already discounted). If you were travelling from Málaga to Madrid, you could use the free *Cercanías* travel option at both ends.

The scheme is called *Combinado Cercanías*, and it is easy to use when you know how. Your RENFE high-speed or long-distance ticket (printed or electronic) will have three important numbers. First is the ticket number **Num/No billete** — a 13-digit number. Then there is the booking reference **Localizador** — a 6-letter code. Finally, the number you really need: CombinadoCercanías — a 5-character alphanumeric code.

The free transfer tickets can be obtained at self-service machines showing the ⟲ *Cercanías* logo (or the **R** *Rodalies* logo in Catalonia). You'll need to enter your destination and choose the '**Suburban Trains Combo fare**' (English interface) or '**CombinadoCercanías**' (the yellow icon on the left of the screen). Depending on the machine, you'll be prompted to enter your **CombinadoCercanías** code or scan the bar-code. You'll need to do this once for each passenger. You can also go to the ticket office and present your ticket(s) to be issued with a *Cercanías* ticket. You have four hours either side of your journey to make your complimentary *Cercanías* journey.

👍 Cheaper Tickets for Older Travellers

The good news for older travellers is that if you are aged 60 or over, you can acquire a '*Tarjeta Dorada*' (Golden Card) and book and buy your rail tickets with a discount of up to 40%. The card itself is cheap (€6 in 2023) and you do not have to be a Spanish citizen to obtain it. The bad news is that you can only obtain the *Tarjeta Dorada* in person by visiting a ticket office (look for the '*Antención al Cliente*' sign) with your passport (or ID card if your country is an EU member or EEA state). However, this is well worth doing if you are likely to be spending any time in Spain and intend to book at least one medium or long-distance journey or 2 or more local (**◑** *Cercanías*) journeys, because you will recover the outlay on the card quite easily.

The card is also valid for 365 days from the date of issue, so if you are likely to return to Spain within a year, then it is a worthwhile investment. You can use the *Tarjeta Dorada* to apply a discount when you buy tickets in person, online or from machines in the station.

⚠ Unlike bus prepayment cards, *tarjetas doradas* are non-transferable, so couples will need a card each.

If you are staying somewhere without a railway station, or with only an unattended station, then search online to see if there is a local branch of '*Viajes el Corte Inglés*' (a travel agency run by the department store chain). These, as well as certain other approved '*agencias de viajes*', can issue *tarjetas doradas*, adding a small surcharge as their 'administration charge'.

Since 2022, it has also been possible to renew (though not initially purchase) your *Tarjeta Dorada* online for a further 1, 2 or 3 years using this link: **bit.ly/RenewTD**. To do this, you only need to be a registered user on the RENFE website (in order to record an associated email address and phone number). The updated pass is emailed to you as a PDF and as a passbook download for smartphone.

Discounts:

AVE and Long Distance (Larga Distancia): 25%

AVANT: Mon–Fri 25%, Sat–Sun 40%

Media Distancia and Cercanías: 40%

⚠ The discount is applied to the **base** fare, so on return journeys the reduction is applied to two single fares, not to the (already discounted) return fare. RENFE also issues other discount cards (*e.g.* for people with disabilities, or for large families), but unlike the *Tarjeta Dorada*, these are only available for Spanish residents.

🚌 Buses

Where possible I have provided links to the main bus services to each location in the following sections. Another useful website worth checking is **movelia.es/en**. Many of the journeys can also be found (and purchased) using **thetrainline.com**. However, both sites only search the large transport providers (**RENFE, Avanza, ALSA**, etc.). For smaller and local bus companies, you'll need to consult their own websites or visit a ticket office at the bus station.

The Málaga Bus Station website has a lot of useful information, though access to some sections is (unhelpfully) blocked for IP addresses outside Spain: **estabus.malaga.eu**

Enoturismo (Winery Visits)

Málaga and the Sierras de Málaga together make up one of Spain's most exciting and fast-est-developing wine regions, with around 45 *bodegas* or wineries. Many of these wineries offer tours and tastings, which will appeal to wine lovers. Most, however, can only really be visited by car thanks to their rural locations so the following is quite a short section because this book is principally aimed at people wanting a 'city break' (perhaps combined with a day trip), rather than travellers planning a road trip.

The biggest car hire companies operate from the airport and from around the María Zambrano railway station. The easiest way to find a good deal is to use a comparison site like **skyscanner.es/carhire**.

If you are going to hire a car, remember that the driver will need to remain sober. This doesn't mean not tasting the wine, but it does mean not **drinking** the wine (or, one might say, tasting it in a 'professional' manner). A few *bodegas* can potentially be visited by tourists relying on public transport, but please remember that the minimum number for any tasting or tour is usually two people, so most are not an option for single travellers. In many cases, bookings of 4, 6 or even 10 people are required. To simplify matters, I have only listed *bodegas* that accept bookings of 4 or fewer. Perhaps understandably, almost all *bodega* visits are advertised as being restricted to those aged 18 or over (*bodegas* welcoming families are marked with the 😄 symbol). For all of these brewery and *bodega* tours, I would recommend booking as far ahead as possible.

⚠ To see a list of all (or most) of the *bodegas* in the Málaga Province, check the website of the official regulator of the DOPs: **bit.ly/MalagaBodegas** or visit their dedicated *enoturismo* site: **enoturismomalaga.es**

 Breweries

Mahou-San Miguel

🍴 CARRETERA DE CÁDIZ 📍 Carretera Del Aeroclub 1 (next to the Airport) 🕐 Tue–Fri 1000, 1200

San Miguel, one of Spain's most popular and exported beers, was first brewed in the San Miguel *barrio* of Manilla, in the then colony of the Philippines, coming to Spain in 1954. It's now part of the Mahou group; a beer first brewed in Madrid by the sons and daughter of a French entrepreneur (and, in case you're wondering, it's pronounced like the 'Mao' of Mao Zedong). Its corporate headquarters moved to Málaga in 2017. Until recently, free tours lasting two hours (including tasting) were being advertised, but the website is somewhat clunky, with only the Spanish version working properly. However, these may be temporary problems, so if you are a fan of San Miguel or Mahou, then it is worth checking.

Cervezas Victoria

🍴 CARRETERA DE CÁDIZ 📍 Avenida de Velázquez 215 🕐 Tue, Wed, Fri, Sat ✉ vfabrica@cervezasvictoria.es

Victoria is Málaga's own brand of beer, born in El Perchel, almost destroyed by the economic mismanagement of the Franco regime, and recently brought back from the doldrums by the Damm group which acquired the brand in 2001 and relaunched it in 2007. It is now thriving and the Málaga state-of-the-art brewery opened in 2017.

Booking tours via the website should, in theory, be easy. However, there is often very little availability for tours in English, even months ahead. My (unconfirmed) suspicion is that the English tours may be block-booked by travel agencies. If you can't find availability on the Victoria website, you have a number of options. If you have a little Spanish, then you could book a tour *en castellano*, where there is much more availability. Or you could try a third-party agency, like tiqets.com (though even here the first available dates will probably be months ahead). Alternatively, you could try sending an email to the address given above telling them your Málaga dates and asking if they would be able to squeeze you in.

🍇 Málaga City

Bodegas Victoria Ordóñez e Hijos

📍 Calle Ciro Alegría 75 🌐 victoriaordonez.com/winetourism 🕐 days and times by arrangement

Victoria is on a mission to recover the dominant style of Montes de Málaga wines that disappeared after phylloxera: dry wines made from Pedro Ximénez grapes. In addition to her own vineyards, she buys from 30 other small growers and her winery near Málaga airport processes 60,000 kg of grapes annually. She also produces *tintos*, *blancos*, and a sparkling *rosado* (pale for a Spanish pink, with a fine mousse).

The English language version of the website mentions tastings conducted at their premises in Málaga city, though no mention is made on the Spanish language page. Vineyard tours are certainly available (your own transport is required, and a minimum of six participants). Enquire about availability by using the contact form on the website.

Bodegas Quitapenas

📍 Carretera de Guadalmar 12 🌐 quitapenas.es/en/enoturismo 🕐 Mon–Fri 1200 💶

Along with the Antigua Casa de Guardia and Málaga Virgen, Quitapenas is the 'other' big winery making sweet and fortified Málaga wines. They also operate two *tabernas* in the centre of Málaga which are great places to try Málaga wines and enjoy some relatively inexpensive *tapas*. There is also a branch in Torremolinos. It was founded in 1880, after the phylloxera plague devastated the vineyards of Ramón Suárez in the town of Cútar, and production was transferred to the Valle de las Viñas in Miraflores del Palo, in the eastern district of Málaga. Their current *bodega* is near the airport. They work mainly with Pero Ximén and Moscatel varieties but also create reds with Romé, and dry and semi-dry whites with Moscatel and Airén (including dry and sweet sparkling whites called Florestel). 'Quitapenas' is an informal word in *castellano* meaning 'comforter' and also, therefore 'stiff drink', though it can also mean 'to drown one's sorrows'.

The *Bodegas* Quitapenas tour, because it takes place in the winery, is suitable for people with limited mobility. The basic tour (minimum 2 adults) is from noon till 1 pm, Monday to Friday with three wines to be tasted. When you book, you can choose to have the tasting accompanied by cheese, or *jamón ibérico*. There are other 'experiences' available but for groups of 4, 6 or more. Unusually, youngsters between the age of 4 and 17 are able to take part in the basic tours at a reduced rate. Instead of tasting wine, they are given a small bottle of *mosto* (grape juice).

🍇 La Axarquía

Bodegas Bentomiz

📍 Finca El Almendro, Pago Cuesta Robano, Sayalonga
🌐 bodegasbentomiz.com 🕐 Wed–Sun 1230 ♿

André Both and Clara Verheij moved to the Axarquía region from The Netherlands in 1995 and began winemaking as a hobby. Soon, this interest developed into a determination to rescue and rebuild local vineyards. They make fine wines of exceptional quality, their signature *marca* (brand) being the 'Ariyanas' label (a Romé *rosado*, a Moscatel de Alejandría *blanco seco* and *blanco dulce*, and a Merlot blend *tinto*, and *dulce*). They also make a fabulous, slightly off-dry sparkling wine, and the refreshingly dry, and dryly named 'PiXél' (made from a mixture of Pedro Ximénez and Moscatel — PX + él).

On-site is a well-regarded fine-dining restaurant that offers a tasting menu. Head chef André has worked with Juan Quintanilla from Sollun restaurant in Nerja to create dishes designed to pair with the Ariyanas wines.

Booking is online and it is possible to book a single space. The tour is wheelchair accessible and the site has a stairlift. Children are welcomed at no cost (and for dining packages, a 3-course children's menu is available). The basic tour includes a tasting of four Ariyanas wines, with the option of a 'tasting platter' of snacks. If you want something more substantial, then one can combine the tour and tasting plus a 3-course *menú*.

Transport is easiest in your own vehicle, but it may — just about — be possible to find your way to the *bodega* by public transport (and taxi). Use the ALSA website alsa.com to find a bus from Málaga to Algarrobo–Costa. There are a couple of taxi firms in Algarrobo–Costa (search online to find contact details) that will be able to take you to the *bodega* (taxi pre-booking is essential as Algarrobo–Costa is a small place). If you do the simple tour (without *menú*) on a Saturday, then you may be able to return (again by taxi — +34 952 535 029 or +34 619 610 664) to Sayalonga in time to take the bus back to Málaga (timetables: loymerbus.es — click '*linea regular*'). Otherwise, book a taxi back to Algarrobo–Costa. If the times for the buses to or from Algarrobo–Costa don't quite fit with your schedule, then there is a more frequent ALSA service between Málaga and La Caleta De Vélez.

Bodega A. Muñoz Cabrera (Dimobe)

📍 Calle San Bartolomé 5, Moclinejo 🌐 dimobe.es/en 🕐 visits by prior arrangement

Founded in 1927 and now run by the fourth generation, this is one of the best-known *bodegas* in Málaga. It produces an enormous variety of wines, from both the Sierras de Málaga and the Málaga DOPs, as well as non-DOP varieties including an award-winning dry sparkling blanco, made with the earliest harvested grapes in Europe. Although the *bodega* is in the village of Moclinejo, a car is necessary to visit it because the vineyard that forms part of the tour is about 3km away. Also, buses between Málaga and Moclinejo are infrequent and at inconvenient times.

Bodega Sedella Vinos

⚲ Carretera MA–126, de Canillas de Aceituno, Km 3, 29715, Sedella
⊕ sedellavinos.com ⏰ visits by prior arrangement

This is one of the most original projects that has emerged in Spain in recent years, giving rise to one of the first mono-varietal wines of the little-known Romé grape. Its maker, Lauren Rosillo, is well-known for being the oenologist of the Martínez Bujanda group which produces wines in Rioja, Rueda and La Mancha. Sedella is located in the tiny village (pop. 400) of the same name. The wine is made from about 2.5 hectares of historic vineyard planted on steep slopes at about 750 metres above sea level. The land is worked with draught animals, Roman ploughs and ancestral techniques.

Your own transport is really necessary to visit this vineyard. There is a bus to Sedella from Málaga (**bit.ly/SedellaBus**) but it is unlikely, based on the present year-round timetable, to be suitable (*i.e.* it allows too short a time to allow for a 2-hour tour). However, if the times are updated (*e.g.* during the summer season), and if you are able to get to Sedella, then the *bodega* will collect you in their own vehicle (if pre-arranged). Remember that if you hire your own vehicle, there are a number of wineries in this region and you could easily visit a couple on the same day while seeing some stunning countryside in between.

Bodegas Almijara

⚲ Calle Canillas de Albaida, Cómpeta ⊕ bodegasalmijara.com ⏰ by prior arrangement

Bodegas Almijara is a family company founded in 1993 that has been producing DOP Málaga and DOP Sierras de Málaga wines since 2000, mainly focussing on the Moscatel de Alejandría and Romé grape varieties.

The winery should be possible to visit using public transport if you are not hiring a vehicle as it is in the village of Cómpeta (about 20 minutes' walk from the centre), as long as you are willing to make an early start. The bus timetable for the Málaga–Cómpeta route can be consulted here: **loymerbus.es** — click '*linea regular*' for timetables. The first bus from Málaga will probably not get you to Cómpeta early enough to tour the *bodega*, but you could get an ALSA bus to Torre del Mar (**alsa.com**) in time to catch the first departure to Cómpeta, (which is the stop after Sayalonga). **A** The bus to Cómpeta does not depart from the Bus Station in Torre del Mar. The stop is about 10 minutes' walk away on Calle Dr Fleming, opposite the Loymerbus office (it is marked on the '**Bodegas**' layer of the companion Google Map). If you book an early tour at the *bodega*, then you should have time for lunch in Cómpeta, which is a beautiful *pueblo blanco* with no shortage of excellent restaurants.

Bodega Hermanos López Martín

⚲ Avenida de Andalucía 2, Árchez 🛈 riberadelmudejar
☎ +34 952 553 149 ⏰ visits by prior arrangement

Just across the valley from Bodegas Almijara in the tiny village of Árchez, is this *bodega*, founded in 1988 by the López Martín brothers (Antonio and Paco). They produce traditional Axarquía fortified wines as well as their own white and red table wines, using Moscatel de Alejandría, Pero Ximén, Montúa and the indigenous Romé grape varieties. Theoretically, they offer visits and tastings, but their web presence is a little vague (at the time of publication, their website was not operational), so best to send them a message or call well in advance. There are buses from Málaga to Árchez late in the evening, and in the other direction in the early morning — exactly the wrong way around! You could get a taxi from Cómpeta, but this is really a *bodega* to try if you have your own transport.

🍇 Montes de Málaga

Bodega Antigua Casa de Guardia

📍 Carretera de Olías–Comares, Km 2.2 — scan the QR code for location 🌐 casadeguardia.com 🕐 visits by prior arrangement
✉ info@casadeguardia.com

Founded in 1840, this is the oldest (and probably the most famous) extant winery in the Province of Málaga. It is located in the Olías area, near the village of Gentilicio, in the Montes de Málaga, and has two vineyards: the La Letría and El Romerillo estates. It produces wines from the Pero Ximén and Moscatel de Alejandría varieties. It is a 40-minute or so drive from Málaga. Little information is available on the website, but tours of the *bodega* are certainly offered. You need to send an email with your request and you will need your own transport.

Bodegas Sánchez Rosado

📍 Parcela 47, Polígono 14, 29570 Cártama
🌐 bodegassanchezrosado.com 🕐 Mon–Sat 1100

A small winery producing a *crianza tinto*, a dry Moscatel de Málaga *blanco* and a Syrah *rosado*. The 2-hour tour is good value (though there is a minimum charge if the booking is for fewer than three people) including a tasting of the wines with cheese, ham, sausage, etc. Use the contact form on the website, or email directly.

The *bodega* is near Cártama and (as always) easiest to visit in a car, but if you come by train, you could take a taxi from Cártama Estación, which is about 15 minutes away. You should pre-book taxies, and there are a few firms in Cártama Estación to choose from (search online for contact details: bit.ly/CartamaTaxis).

🍇 Zona Norte

Málaga Virgen

📍 A–92 km 132, Finca Vistahermosa, Fuente de Piedra
🌐 bit.ly/MalagaVirgenMap 🌐 bodegasmalagavirgen.com 🕐 Mon–Fri 1100 ✉ enoturismo@bodegasmalagavirgen.com ♿

This is another large winery producing traditional Málaga wines. Additionally, under the Sierras de Málaga denomination, dry *blancos* are made using Chardonnay, Verdejo and Moscatel Morisco, and *rosados* and *tintos*, using Syrah. The winery also produces 'Fino' wine (under the Montilla-Moriles DOP), as well as brandy, vinegar, and *vermú*.

The *bodega* is popular with 'enoturistas', but booking needs to be done via email (or using the 'contact' form on the website) and involves making a prepayment via bank transfer. The visit takes about 2 hours and includes a visit to the vineyard and a guided tour through the winery, a tasting of 3 traditional Málaga wines (sweet and dry), pairing with local appetizers and a visit to the winery store. Families are welcome. If you want to visit, it is well worth getting in touch with the 'enoturismo' department at the *bodega* (currently looked after by the super-helpful Joana Moral).

As regards transport, this is a *bodega* for which using your own transport is recommended. A taxi from Antequera-Santa Ana is certainly a possibility, though, but should be booked in advance (there is no taxi rank). Currently, trains do not stop in the nearby village of Fuente de Piedra and, although there are (ALSA) buses, the timetable is not such that you could reach the winery in time for an 11 am tour. If that changes, then you may be able to take a taxi from Fuente de Piedra (there is only one taxi service ⊕ taxifuentepiedra.es). You could also walk from Fuente de Piedra (just under 3 km away).

Fuente de Piedra

If you have the time and are willing to hire a car then it's well worth combining a tasting at the *bodega* with a visit to the **Laguna de Fuente de Piedra** (the largest lagoon in Andalucía and home to up to 10,000 breeding pairs of flamingos as well as many other species of birds). There is comfortable and affordable accommodation in the town of Fuente de Piedra (and in the nearby towns of Humilladero and Mollina) if you want to stay overnight. With your own car, you could also visit the Bodegas Carpe Diem (see below) or the Bodega Capuchina just outside Mollina: ⊕ **bodegalacapuchina.es**. ⚠ An overnight stay in Fuente de Piedra would probably allow you to use buses and taxis (again with careful planning!).

For guided visits to the nature reserve and all sorts of helpful advice, contact Marta Luque through her excellent website: ⊕ **visitasfuentepiedra.es**. And if you do stay in Fuente de Piedra, Joana Moral (a trainer approved by all three Málaga DOP regulators) can arrange a wine tasting at your accommodation. Consult her website here: ⊕ **microcatas.es**.

Bodegas Pérez Hidalgo

📍 Avenida Virgen de Flores 15, Álora ⊕ bodegasperezhidalgo.es
✉ info@bodegasperezhidalgo.es 🕐 visits by prior arrangement

This is one of the easiest *bodegas* to visit as it is in the town of Álora, on the 🔵 *Cercanías* line from Málaga (see the Álora section for more details: p. 535). This well-regarded *bodega* was founded by local brothers Francisco and José Miguel Pérez Hidalgo in 2000. They make wonderful oak-aged *tintos*, as well as a signature *vermú* and a floral Moscatel *blanco*. They offer tours and tastings of 4 or 6 wines plus local snacks. Pre-booking is strongly advised, although they have been known to accommodate visitors on spec.

Bodegas Carpe Diem

📍 Avenida de América 35, Mollina ⊕ bodegascarpediem.com
🕐 daily, by prior appointment

This *bodega* was created in 1993 by the *Sociedad Cooperativa Andaluza Agrícola Virgen de la Oliva* (Cooperative Agricultural Society of The Virgin of the Olive), following the acquisition of the Scholz winery. The visit (45–60 mins) involves a video presentation and a tour of the oil mill and the wine cellars, ending with a tasting of oil and wine. As this *bodega* is in the urban area of Mollina (north of Antequera) it should be easy to visit using public transport but, as so often, the timings are inconvenient (⊕ alsa.com). Another option is to stay for a night or two (see the entry above for *Bodegas* Málaga Virgen).

🍇 Serranía de Ronda

Many *bodegas* can be reached by taxi from Ronda (book ahead). A reliable taxi service in Ronda is ⊕ ronda.taxi operated by Santiago López and another is ⊕ taxi12ronda.es. You would need your own vehicle to visit *bodegas* farther from Ronda. To discover them, check out: ⊕ enoturismomalaga.es (select 'Experiences' and 'Wine cellar' from the left-hand side menu).

Bodega F. Schatz

⌖ Finca Sanguijuela s/n, 29400 Ronda ⊕ f-schatz.com ⏲ bookings handled by ⊕ milamoresronda.com

Founded in 1982 by a long-established wine-making family originally from the Tyrol, this *bodega* was an early pioneer in the area, rebuilding table wine making after the disaster of phylloxera, and they produce some of the best-regarded wines of the DOP. Schatz was also the first organic winery in Málaga and the only one making 100% organic, biodynamic, natural wines without added sulphites. Four *tintos*, a *blanco* and a *rosado* are produced, all of them stunning. The white (Chardonnay), especially, is a revelation, particularly for lovers of white Burgundy who dislike the heavily oaked Chardonnays made in the New World; this one has a smack of mango and lychee but, unlike the French iteration, is crisp rather than buttery. All bookings are handled by Milamores wine tourism agency, but the winery can be reached by taxi (8 km, 10 minutes from Ronda).

Bodegas Vinos Conrad

⌖ Carretera El Burgo, km 4, Ronda ⊕ vinosconrad.com ⏲ visits by prior arrangement ◎+34 672 290 742

This boutique winery, founded in 1998 by Theo and Anne-Marie Conrad, has seven hectares of vineyards in a beautiful natural area full of oak, olive, almond and walnut trees. They make typically *rondeño*, big, fruity red wines from Cabernet Sauvignon, Merlot, Tempranillo, Cabernet Franc, Malbec and Petit Verdot varieties. Only 4 km from the city of Ronda, you can easily take a taxi here.

Bodega Vetas

⌖ Camino Nador s/n, 29350 Arriate ⊕ bodegavetas.com ⏲ visits by prior appointment ✉ info@bodegavetas.com ◎+34 647 177 620

Vetas is a small, family-run *bodega*. In fact, it is the smallest winery in the entire Sierras de Ronda, but the quality is excellent. They make *tinto* and *rosado* wines only, from Petit Verdot, Cabernet Franc and Cabernet Sauvignon. You could come by taxi from Ronda (a journey of about 10 minutes), but booking ahead is essential.

Bodega Huerto de la Condesa

⌖ Camino Huerto de La Condesa, Ronda ⊕ huertodelacondesa.com ⏲ visits by prior arrangement

The eponymous *condesa* (Countess) was María del Carmen Ábela y García (1849–1924), a prominent member of the *rondeña* gentry who received the title from King Alfonso XIII in recognition of her contributions to the town (among them the construction of the Concepción barracks and restoration of the Socorro church). The winery occupies part of what was Doña Carmen's estate, just outside Ronda. They grow Garnacha and Syrah varieties making mostly reds as well as a *garnacha rosado*. There are a few options for tastings. The simplest option (a presentation and tasting of 2 wines) is conducted at their premises in Ronda (**Calle Genal 1**, on the trading estate behind the railway station), but the minimum number of participants is four. Other options (for 2 or more people), tasting 3 or 4 wines, are offered at the *bodega* itself. This is only about 4 km from Ronda, so a 10-minute taxi journey. The vineyard is next to the *bodega*, so can be visited without your own vehicle.

Bodega Bad Man Wines

⊙ Fuente la Higuera 11, Ronda ⊕ badmanwines.com ⊙ bookings also handled by ⊕ milamoresronda.com

This *bodega* was created in 2016 by Simbad Romero and Manuel Carrizosa (Sim**BAD MAN**uel, geddit?), childhood friends from Sevilla who studied oenology and then travelled the world picking up winemaking experience. Do not be put off by the hipsterish appearance of the winemakers, or the trendy bottle design; these guys are producing some seriously exciting wines that appear on the wine lists of some of Spain's best restaurants. Apart from the Syrah-Cabernet Sauvignon *tinto* blend, they specialize in mono-varietal wines — Petit Verdot and Tempranillo *tintos*, Chardonnay and (dry) Moscatel de Alejandría *blancos*, and a Merlot *rosado*. Only 3 km from Ronda, the winery is easy to reach by taxi.

Bodega Gonzalo Beltrán

⊙ Finca Nogalera, Partida los Molinos 482, Ronda
⊕ bodegagonzalobeltran.com ⊙ visits by prior appointment

One of Ronda's oldest and friendliest family-owned *bodegas*, Gonzalo Beltrán produces five beautiful wines — two *tintos* (Petit Verdot, and Syrah), two *blancos* (Pedro Ximénez, and Viognier) and a *rosado* (Monastrell). The winery is only 1 km from Ronda as the crow flies, but it is down in the gorge. That's a pleasant 30-minute walk (take the route through the old part of town, which is more of a gentle descent). They will call you a taxi to take you back up the hill after you have sampled the four wines. The vineyards (or some of them) are next to the *bodega*, so this one can easily be visited without a vehicle of your own.

Samsara Wines

⊙ Carretera de los Molinos, 29400, Ronda ⊕ samsarawines.com
⊙ visits by prior appointment

Samsara is a fairly new *bodega* established by young winemakers (Juanma and Pablo) making red wine with French and Spanish varieties. Like Gonzalo Beltrán, it is at the foot of the gorge. Tours and tastings take place not in the *bodega* but in the vineyard, a pleasant 20–30 minute walk from Ronda (you could also take a taxi).

Bodega Cortijo Los Aguilares

⊙ Puente de la Ventilla, Carretera Ronda Campillos, Km 35, Ronda
⊕ cortijolosaguilares.com ⊙ by prior arrangement ☺

In 1999, José Antonio Itarte and his wife Victoria purchased the 800-hectare Cortijo Los Aguilares farm, which has Holm oak forests dedicated to raising the Iberian pig and grows cereals and olives. They planted 19 hectares of vineyards the following year with Pinot Noir, Tempranillo, Merlot, Cabernet Sauvignon and Petit Verdot varieties. In parallel, they set about the reconstruction of the old *cortijo* (farmhouse), as well as the construction of a new *bodega* formed of two parts: production facilities (*nave de elaboración*) and an ageing cellar (*nave de crianza*). They make mostly *tintos* of stunning quality and delicious complexity alongside a young, fruity, and bone-dry *rosado*.

Visits are for small groups only, by prior arrangement. They offer a number of 'experiences' starting with a simple vineyard and winery tour followed by a tasting of 3 wines. But there are many other options (although in some cases the minimum booking is for 4 or more people) — a more immersive tasting, a tasting followed by a picnic under a Holm oak, a 7 km guided hike through the vineyard, and a tasting followed by a private lunch with wine-pairing. The *bodega* is 8km from Ronda, so it is possible to visit by taxi.

Bodegas Lunares

📍 Carretera Ronda-El Burgo Km 1, 29400, Ronda
🌐 bodegaslunares.com ⏲ daily by prior appointment ♿

This *bodega* was established in 2003 by a *rondeño* family that purchased 4 hectares and later established a vineyard. They now make 2 *tintos*, a *blanco* (Chardonnay/Sauvignon Blanc) and a *rosado* (Merlot/Garnacha). The *bodega* is less than 2km from Ronda, so you can easily take a taxi. There are two tastings (of 4 wines) a day, every day of the year. Although the website is only in Spanish, it is very easy to book a tour and tasting. Click 'COMPRAR VISITA', then 'COMPRAR TICKETS' and then 'Comprar para mi' to reach the booking page.

🍇 Costa Occidental–Manilva

Nilva Enoturismo

📍 Calle Dr Álvarez Leiva 2, Manilva 🌐 nilva.es ⏲ Mon–Fri by prior arrangement ✉ info@nilva.es 📱 +34 609 290 370

Manilva, in the far west of the Province, is a rather overlooked zone of the Málaga wine DOP. There are still grapes (overwhelmingly Moscatel de Alejandría) grown in the area, but on nowhere near the scale of even 25 years ago. Some estimates suggest that 75% of land under vine has been lost in that period. This is the flip side of the tourism 'miracle', where coastal land could be sold for development far more profitably than if kept for viticulture.

Argimiro Martínez Moreno, a former teacher from Albacete (La Mancha), established not only a *bodega*, but also a small museum and wine 'interpretation centre' in Manilva in 2014. It is the Manilva zone's only *bodega* (other *bodegas* own vineyards and grow grapes here but make their wines elsewhere). He produces a single wine, a dry Moscatel, in small quantities — about 8,000 bottles a year — which makes his operation an example of '*Vinos de Garaje*' ('garage wines'). However, banish any notion of dodgy back-street hooch from your mind. 'Nilva' is a stunning wine — floral, mineral, and dry, with hints of citrus and liquorice. It has appeared on the wine lists of the Michelin-starred restaurants Martín Berasategui and Arzak in the Basque Country. Winemaking is more than just a hobby, or even a business, to Argimiro. It is part of a mission to preserve the winemaking heritage of Manilva.

He offers tours taking in the museum, winery and vineyards, plus tasting with *tapas*. This is only really a possibility if you have the use of a car because buses between Málaga and Manilva are infrequent and take up to 3 hours, whereas the trip in a car is just over an hour from Málaga. Also, transport is required to visit the vineyards.

🍇☂️Tour Companies

Milamores (Ronda)

📍 Calle Guadalcobacin s/n, Ronda ⊕ milamoresronda.com
✉️ info@milamoresronda.com 🟢 +34 656 543 343

In addition to being the main agent for booking visits to the Bodega F. Schatz, Milamores, run by the helpful and friendly Antonio Martínez, also organizes tours of other wineries, as well as organizing tastings at hotels and in homes. Although you can book via Milamores and they will often conduct the tour and tasting, this does not obviate the need to organize your own transport as they will meet you at the main entrance of the *bodega*. Although the website is in Spanish, tours and tastings can be conducted in English. If you have any questions about Milamores' services, don't hesitate to contact Don Antonio.

White Houses Tours

⊕ whitehousestours.com ✉️ info@whitehousestours.com
🟢 +34 634 542 355

This small company, founded by Rodrigo Romojaro and based in Benalmádena, offers tours (including transport) of Bodegas Pérez Hidalgo in Álora with a tasting of 5 wines (3.5 hours). There is also an option to combine this with a visit to the olive oil factory for an olive oil tasting (combined tour: 5 hours). The pick-up point is outside the Tourist Information Office in the Plaza de la Marina in Málaga for a 10 am departure. Tours are limited to a maximum of 7 people, so you

can be sure of personal service. They also offer visits (with transport) to a *bodega* in Ronda, a bull-breeding finca, a reserve raising the *ibérico* pig (with *embutidos* tasting), a sherry *bodega*, and more besides.

Rootz Wine Tours

⊕ rootzwinetours.com 📞 +34 644 755 966

If you want to visit a couple of *bodegas* in comfort without worrying about transport, then Rootz Wine Tours could be the answer. Run by Nicky Lloyd (who is originally from the UK), this small company offers several options for winery visits and tastings, covering four of the main five wine-growing areas of the Málaga DOPs: Manilva (Costa Occidental), Serranía de Ronda, Norte (Antequera) and La Axarquía. Nicky is a qualified guide and holds a Level 4 Diploma (DipWSET) from the Wine & Spirit Education Trust.

The tours might seem expensive, but the prices are actually pretty competitive given that the tours are kept small (between 2 and 7 people), last all day, are accompanied by a professional guide, and Rootz Tours will collect you from your accommodation in Málaga (or elsewhere on the Costa del Sol). Most tours take in two or more wineries, and all include lunch.

Oletrips

🌐 **oletrips.es** 🕐 **Consult website for availability** 💬 **+34 616 598 515**

Based in Nerja, this company is run by a young couple (Cipriano and María) and offers a range of tours and 'experiences', mainly in the Axarquía region. There are tours of *pueblos blancos*, visits to avocado and mango plantations, and olive oil tastings as well as a couple of options that offer visits (with tastings) to *bodegas*. Tours are small (no more than 8 people), include lunch, and transport is included. The pick up point can be between Torre del Mar and Nerja (you can take an early bus from Málaga).

El Colmao Wine & Experiences

📍 **Calle Real 32, Frigiliana** 🌐 **elcolmaowineandexperiences.com**
🕐 **Mon–Fri by prior arrangement**

This artisan wine bar and wine merchant in Frigiliana offers three winery tours, as well as winery tours with the optional additions of hiking, horse riding or sailing. Two are in La Axarquía (two wineries, or a winery and a raisin vineyard), and one is in the Serranía de Ronda. The prices drop if you are a group of five or more, but the tours include transport from your accommodation in Málaga (or east of Málaga).

🍷 Wine Vocabulary

If you are a wine buff, then the chances are that you will be familiar with a lot of wine-making terms in French (*cru, mousse, terroir*, etc.), but Spanish winemaking terms are less well-known to English speakers (those French terms are *pago, espuma* and *tierra* in Spanish, in case you were wondering). Even Spaniards with an excellent grasp of English often use familiar Spanish terms as anglicized 'false friends'. It's common to hear winemakers talking about 'elaborating' wines, which is confusing to English speakers, suggesting that wines are not so much being made as improved or augmented. But it just means 'to make' (the Spanish verb 'to make' is '*hacer*', but in the context of wine, '*elaborar*' is used). These 'false friends' work in the opposite direction too. English speakers wanting to say that a wine is 'clear' might say that it is '*claro*', but whilst in Spanish a glass can be '*claro*', the wine within is '*limpio*'. In both of these examples, Google Translate makes the same mistakes.

Here, then, is a short glossary of winemaking and wine tasting terms in Spanish.

In the Winery & Vineyard

English	Spanish	English	Spanish
screw-cap	*tapón de rosca*	barrels	*barricas*
cork	*corcho*	oak	*roble*
label	*etiqueta*	winemaker	*enólogo*
capsule	*cápsula*	winemaking	*elaboración de vino*
make/produce	*elaborar*	must	*mosto*
winery owner	*bodeguero*	yeast	*levadura*
vineyard	*viñedo/viña*	skins	*pieles/hollejo*
winery	*bodega*	fine/gross lees	*lías (finas/gruesas)*
production facilities	*zona de elaboración*	racking	*trasiego*
barrel cellar	*nave de barricas*	a vine	*una cepa de vid*
tanks/vats	*tanques/cubas*	pruning	*la poda*
		to prune	*podar*

vine training	*conducción de la vid*	intense	*intenso*
bush vines	*vides en vaso*	aromatic	*aromático*
trained vines	*vides en espaldera*	resinous notes	*notas balsámicas*
plough	*arar*	palate	*paladar*
fertilize	*abonar*	dry/off-dry	*seco/casi seco*
row of vines	*hilera*	sweet	*dulce*
shoot	*pámpano*	medium sweet	*semidulce*
cane	*vara*	fresh	*fresco*
young cane	*sarmiento*	acidic	*de mucha acidez*
bud	*yema*	long finish	*final largo*
flowering	*floración*	short finish	*final corto*
fruit-set	*cuajado*	complex	*complejo*
véraison	*envero*	simple	*simple*
ripening	*maduración*	balanced	*equilibrado*
pick/harvest	*cosechar/vendimiar*	citrus	*fruta cítrica*
		red/black fruit	*fruta roja/negra*

Tasting Wine

		tropical fruits:	*fruta tropical*
swirl	*airear*	stone fruits:	*fruta de hueso*
swirl the glass	*agitar la copa*	notes of spice	*notas especiadas*
sniff	*oler*	notes of oak:	*notas de roble*
sip/taste	*catar*	toasted notes:	*notas tostadas*
swallow	*tragar*	grassy notes	*notas herbáceos*
spit	*escupir*	notes of vanilla:	*notas de vainilla*
appearance	*aspecto*	...of liquorice:	*...de regaliz*
clear	*limpio*	...of nettle:	*...de ortiga*
hazy	*turbio*	...of fennel:	*...de hinojo*
pale intensity	*de capa baja*	ripe tannins:	*taninos maduros*
deep intensity	*de capa alta*	silky tannins:	*taninos sedosos*
ruby/garnet	*rubí/granate*	velvety tannins:	*taninos aterciopelados*
tawny	*teja*	harsh tannins:	*taninos agresivos*
rim	*ribete*	light-bodied:	*de cuerpo ligero*
legs/tears	*lágrimas*	medium-bodied	*de medio cuerpo*
nose	*nariz*	full-bodied	*de mucho cuerpo*

Making the Most of Day Trips

ℹ The *turismo* is your friend...

In the following few sections, I try to give a few suggestions of some interesting places to visit that aren't too far from Málaga. As well as tips about travel, I also provide some background information and make recommendations of things to see and places to eat. However, you will notice that at the start of each entry, I list first the location of the *turismo* or tourist information office, and I urge you to begin your day trip with a visit here.

Whilst we might prefer to think of ourselves as 'travellers' not 'tourists', there are excellent reasons to pop into the *turismo*. The first is that your visit helps to secure future funding — a *turismo* that no one visits will have its funding cut. But a more immediate benefit to you as a tourist (sorry, 'traveller') is that the *turismo* has the latest information — a *ruta de tapas* that's taking place today, a free exhibition at the *Ayuntamiento*, a historic building that's only open this weekend, a free lunchtime concert, or a craft or gourmet food market. Such occasional events won't be listed in a book like this one and can be hard to find out about even online, but they can often turn out to be the highlight of a day trip.

If you want to take a day trip and can't decide where, then try consulting the calendar of events (called '*Agenda*' in Spanish) on the websites of a few *turismos*. An interesting temporary exhibition, or an annual asparagus or *chorizo* festival should not be missed!

⛅ Journey Planning...

As I explained above, the following chapters are aimed at travellers who will be relying on public transport (train, bus and, in some instances, local taxis). Of course, if you want to hire a car, then the Province of Málaga — indeed, the whole of Andalucía and beyond — is your oyster. The decision of whether to hire a vehicle or not will largely depend upon what sort of day trip appeals. If you want to visit more than one of the *bodegas* listed above (or some of the more remote ones), then you'll need a car. A car is also going to be useful if you want to hike in more remote areas. But even without your own wheels, there are dozens of places that you can visit pretty easily by train or bus.

Spain's train network coverage is relatively sparse. Spain has 420 more kilometres of railway track than the UK, but for a country that is more than twice as large (though 68% is electrified in Spain versus 39% in the UK). The country is, however, very well connected by bus (intercity coach). These buses, moreover, are clean and comfortable; a far cry from the average UK experience. Outside the larger towns, however, you might find that scheduled services don't always fit with your plans, so remember that you can take (for example) the train one way and the bus the other ('return ticket' savings tend to be quite modest).

🛏️ Overnighting...

If you'd like to spend more than a few hours somewhere (to visit a *bodega*, go for a hike in the hills or enjoy a *feria*, say) or visit a couple of places in the same area, then why not spend a night out of town? It takes a little forward planning, but you could make two bookings for accommodation in Málaga leaving your luggage at your hotel in between, taking an overnight bag with you. You should message the hotel when you book to check this is okay, but most are happy to provide this service. Even if they are not, there are plenty of left luggage lockers ('*consignas*') in Málaga where you can stow your luggage pretty cheaply and safely.

Be Adventurous...

There are other attractive towns and villages not mentioned in this book that can be reached from Málaga by public transport. Archidona, for example, is a Phoenician foundation and was the Moorish capital before Málaga. Carratraca was once the location of one of the most famous sulphur spring spas in Europe. The *termas* have been closed since the COVID pandemic, but if the idea of a historic spa appeals, search online to see if they have reopened (there are buses from Málaga).

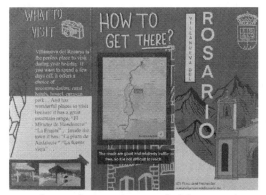

On a trip to Málaga recently, I encountered at the airport a group of polite and friendly students from the Pintor José Hernández High School in the *pueblo blanco* of Villanueva del Rosario (about 45 km from Málaga) who were handing out information about their village. They had designed their own leaflets (pictured), which listed (in English) interesting things to do in Villanueva. Presumably, this was some sort of school project. Unfamiliar with the place, I bought a return bus ticket for a few euros and spent the next day exploring. Surrounded by stunning mountain scenery (which I had expected), there were a few surprises too, like the '*Casa de Cultura*' that hosted an exhibition of works by José Hernández, a well-regarded local painter, and housed the workshops of other artisans. There was also a good choice of bars and restaurants in which to enjoy a late breakfast and, in the afternoon, a hearty lunch. It is a beautiful village about which I would have remained ignorant had it not been for those resourceful teenagers.

In other words, besides those included in this book, there are many other *pueblos blancos* and small towns in the Province of Málaga that are well worth a visit. All that limits you is transport. All are easy to reach by car, of course, but some are difficult to reach using public transport. For example, Júzcar, the former *pueblo blanco* that was painted blue by Sony to make a 'Smurf Village' in 2011, is a lovely place to visit with children (or perhaps it's of more interest to nostalgic adults?). The bus journey from Ronda is only 30 minutes. Unfortunately, however, the regular bus service only runs three days a week, and goes from Júzcar to Ronda in the morning, and from Ronda to Júzcar in the afternoon — exactly the wrong way round for day-trippers. (A seasonal service with more suitable timings does also operate — consult **autocareslara.es** for details; you may need to confirm by telephone.) However, if you are travelling with children who would really enjoy seeing the village, ⊕ **ronda.taxi** will take up to four people on a return journey (including a 30-minute stop) for quite a reasonable price.

West of Málaga
(Costa del Sol Occidental)

Over ninety per cent of the foreign visitors who arrive at Málaga–Costa del Sol Airport travel west when they leave the arrivals hall, heading along the coast to resorts like Torremolinos, Fuengirola, and Marbella. These arrivals include a good number of British holidaymakers despite Benidorm on the Costa Blanca being the most popular destination among tourists from the UK. This guide has been written for the visitor who is interested in discovering the less well-known destination of Málaga City, so I only cover these more popular resorts in brief.

If you're staying in Málaga, there are many reasons to head out of town and visit these near-by resorts. Torremolinos, for example, is known for its nightlife (and lively gay scene). But unless you are prepared to pay over the odds for a taxi home, be warned that the last public transport back to Málaga from Torremolinos is the M-110 bus at 1.25 am, which in Spain counts as 'just after dinner' and somewhat before the nightclubs get going, so book a cheap room or prepare to pull an all-nighter. During normal hours, regular local trains (RENFE ⊙ *Cercanías*) run between Málaga, via the Airport, as far as Fuengirola (a total journey of 42 minutes).

There are other attractions, many of which will appeal to families with young children, like zoos and aquariums. While the seafront between Torremolinos and Fuengirola is a wall of concrete hotels, there are also charming towns along the coast. The 'old town' of Marbella is genuinely old and rather lovely (unlike the 'old town' of Benidorm, which dates from the 1950s). Estepona, similarly, is picturesque and maintains a working fishing port. It is also home to Europe's largest collections of orchids and some of the most beautiful and impressive murals and street art anywhere in the world. Move slightly inland and you are not far from a chain of *pueblos blancos*, any of which can feel a world away from the bustle of Málaga or the all-inclusive resorts and full-English breakfasts on the coast.

However, beware of TripAdvisor and other online listings, as these can be unintentionally misleading. The charming Ermita de la Virgen de la Peña in Mijas, for example, is in the old village of Mijas (Mijas Pueblo), not the beach development, also called Mijas, with its handy train station. Likewise, many of the attractions listed as being in Benalmádena are not in the sprawling seaside resort of Benalmádena Costa, but in the historic village of Benalmádena Pueblo a few miles inland and up in the hills. Both places can be accessed on public transport, but it means another bus journey after arriving in the 'new' Mijas or Benalmádena.

Consult the '**WEST of MÁLAGA**' layer of the companion Google Map for locations mentioned in this section.

Torremolinos

⊕ turismotorremolinos.es ❶ Calle Cuesta del Tajo 1 ❶ Plaza de las Comunidades Autónomas (Bajondillo-Playamar) ❶ Plaza del Remo (La Carihuela) ⏱ Mon–Fri 0900–1400 ☎ +34 608 208 871

Before becoming an oasis of freedom and excess in the dreary days of the Franco regime, decades before the Costa del Sol became overcrowded and over-concreted, Torremolinos was the location of some of the first great tourist hotels in Andalucía.

⌛ History

An early pioneer was a Manchester-born ex-solider called George Langworthy who settled in Torremolinos after the First World War. Of modest means, he was a rich man by the standards of the Torremolinos of the time — a tiny fishing village with a handful of mills in the shadow of its more industrial neighbour, Málaga. He took up residence in the Castillo de Santa Clara, which had been constructed in 1763 to keep a lookout not only for Berber pirates who had been sending raiding parties since the *reconquiʃta* but also the British. During the War of the Spanish Succession, an Anglo-Dutch fleet commanded by the English admiral George Rooke looted and burned the houses and mills, all but destroying the village. A census of 1769, recorded a population of only 106 residents. The mills were largely rebuilt in the 19th century, but by 1924, with the paper mill and most of the 14 flour mills closed, Torremolinos petitioned to become a district of the City of Málaga. It was to remain a struggling village until the tourist boom of the 1950s.

Aware of the grinding poverty and hardship faced by his neighbours, Langworthy's habit was to give a silver peseta (enough to support a family for several days) to any poor person who came to visit. The 'castle' was the seed of the first great hotel on what we now know as the Costa del Sol. Langworthy hired several gardeners and assistants to set about surrounding the property with large gardens and providing it with viewpoints over the sea. Without realizing it, he was taking the first steps in the history of tourism in Torremolinos.

But no fortune is eternal and that of George Langworthy, whom his neighbours knew as 'Don Jorge' or '*El Inglés de la Peseta*', was soon forced to lease the property and take paying guests. Santa Clara was not the first hotel in the area — that was at the Torremolinos Golf Course, now the Parador de Málaga Golf — but it was the one that became the more famous. The poet and writer Luis Cernuda was one of the first prominent residents of the castle and his stay during the summer of 1928 inspired the story *El indolente*, set in Torremolinos.

A couple of years later, Salvador Dalí and Gala Éluard paid a visit, invited by the 'Generation of '27' — a group of avant-garde poets, many of whom were involved in the magazine *Litoral*, published in Málaga. On the beach, Gala untied the upper part of her swimsuit, exposing her breasts. This was caught on camera, making it the first topless photograph taken on the Costa del Sol and one that would later seem to sum up the freedom and hedonism of Torremolinos in the 1960s and 1970s (the bikini was only legalized in 1959, at the urging of the Mayor of Benidorm).

The toponym, Costa del Sol, was dreamt up on 16 February 1928, when a hotelier in Almería by the name of Rodolfo Lussnigg launched a promotional campaign to publicize the virtues of local beaches. The slogan 'Almería, the city where the sun spends the winter' (Almería enjoys more hours of sunshine than almost any other city in Europe) first appeared in the newspaper *La Crónica Meridional*. The name took off and, thanks to the influx of tourists, it spread to the entire Mediterranean coast of eastern and southern Spain. By the 1960s, each province wanted its own branding and portions of this 700-mile-long *costa* were renamed 'Blanca', 'Brava', 'Daurada', 'Tropical', etc. leaving the moniker '*del Sol*' for the Province of Málaga.

The Santa Clara Castle acquired the name of Hotel Costa del Sol and continued to receive guests for years. The house built for the great *bailaora flamenca*, Lola Medina, was converted into the Residencia Miami Hotel when Doña Lola fell into debt. In the 1950s, the opening of Pez Espada, the first large five-star hotel establishment and the flagship of the province's hospitality industry, led to the arrival of stars such as Brigitte Bardot, Frank Sinatra, Ava Gardner, Marlon Brando and Grace Kelly and Prince Rainier of Monaco.

There are fashions in travel just as in everything else. The grand hotels of Málaga built in the 1920s were considered *passé* after the development of Torremolinos. The smartest resort on the Costa del Sol nowadays is Marbella, but some have moved on to Puerto Banús since the TOWIE groupies colonized 'Marbs'. Eventually, they will tire of Puerto Banús and go in search of the latest 'cool' destination. Perhaps it will be Estepona, or somewhere west of Cádiz. But sixty or more years ago, the coolest place in Spain was, believe it or not, Torremolinos.

The first charter flights coming into Málaga airport in large numbers were from Stockholm, with huge numbers of Swedish tourists bringing with them attitudes to sex that were, to say the least, very different to those found in Franco's Spain. The topless bathing, the 'free love' hippies, the playboys and party girls, the tacit acceptance of homosexuality, the decadence of the nightclubs, the recreational drug use — all were unofficially tolerated by the national regime. The Spanish government needed foreign currency, and Torremolinos was a place that practically printed it (and if you ever wonder why Spain never really presses the Gibraltar issue beyond occasional sabre-rattling, the reasons are similar — namely the fact that Gibraltar is responsible for a massive economic transfer to the Campo de Gibraltar, which would otherwise be a pretty impoverished part of southern Spain).

In 1962 Toni's Bar opened its doors, the first gay bar in Spain (although not openly so). Shortly after, others such as Incógnito, Fauno and Düsseldorf opened, concentrated in the Pasaje Begoña, Spain's first 'gay village' predating Sitges and Chueca (Madrid) by decades. In 1968 the first lesbian bar in Spain — '*Pourquoi pas?*' — opened under the watchful eye of a German known as Frau Marion. The party was endless. In the discos foreign music was played, the latest from London, and rock musicians came to perform. To all this, the police turned a blind eye and Torremolinos was given the nickname 'Little New York'.

But the regime was only willing to show tolerance up to a point, and there were periodic round-ups of gay men, drug users and 'hippies'. An especially notorious one was carried out in June 1971 by order of the civil governor of Málaga, Víctor Arroyo. Two police vans were stationed at each exit of Pasaje Begoña, and all those who emerged from the clubs there were arrested, a total of 119 people, both Spaniards and foreigners, the latter being expelled from the country. Various foreign embassies protested to the Spanish government. These raids were intended to satisfy the conservatives of the regime and the detainees were usually released the next day. However, many left Torremolinos and moved onto Ibiza.

Somewhat ironically, after the death of Franco and the transition to democracy when Spain experienced a sudden liberalization, Torremolinos lost something of its cachet as a transgressive party town. The opening of the Jardín de Adán y Eva (The Garden of Adam and Eve) in Mr Langworthy's garden — Spain's first nudist hotel, rather than just a nudist beach — raised barely a whimper of protest. Towns like Fuengirola, Estepona, Torre del Mar and, above all, Marbella, took a leaf from the book of Torremolinos and ended up becoming popular summer destinations in their own right. The dominance of Torremolinos had ended and what is known today as the Costa del Sol was created. The gay clubbers and Swedish nudists gave way to '*yonquis*' (junkies) and British 'hooligans' and criminals on the run, creating a headache for the newly independent (from Málaga, in 1988) municipality of Torremolinos. But possessing the gift for hospitality that is typical of the people of the Málaga region, '*los torroles*' (as the locals are called in the *malagueño* dialect) have managed to continue to attract millions of tourists year on year.

Torremolinos Today

There is no true '*casco viejo*' (Old Town), but the most traditional neighbourhoods are El Centro, the Bajondillo area, El Calvario and La Carihuela. From east to west, the *barrios* are:

Los Álamos ('The Poplars') This *barrio* borders the Guadalmar neighbourhood of the City of Málaga to the east. In recent decades it has gained popularity thanks to its many beach bars that have evolved into 'beach clubs', a seductive combination of cocktails and light food among sun loungers, Balinese beds and live (mainly electronic) music. These have stopped operating as nightclubs open until dawn due to recent time restrictions imposed by the *ayuntamiento* following complaints from neighbours (there are still a few 'locals' who live in Torremolinos).

La Colina ('The Hill') This *barrio* is located on a hill in the eastern part of Torremolinos between Los Álamos and El Pinar. It was part of the expansion of the municipality of Málaga during the urban 'boom' of the 1960s and 1970s and is home to the La Colina Tower, the tallest building in Torremolinos.

Playamar ('Sea Beach') The Playamar area adjoins Los Álamos. Like La Colina, Playamar was built during the 70s and is dominated by the Torres de Playamar — twenty-one towers with fifteen floors each, a total of 945 apartments. Much studied by historians, these towers are taken to be efforts to put into practice Le Corbusier's idea that 'vertical elements' in the landscape would 'release' the horizontal plane. On the promenade, there are several *chiringuitos* and picnic areas.

El Bajondillo is one of the most 'typical' neighbourhoods of Torremolinos and the location of one of the most popular beaches. This beach is connected to La Carihuela by a rocky outcrop on top of which stands the Castle of Santa Clara, today adorned with beautiful gardens (no longer a nudist camp). In addition to the fact that this area is home to a number of the municipality's hotels, it is also home to some of the best bars and restaurants. In recent years it has become one of the most gay-friendly beaches on the Spanish coast. In this same area is the Casa de los Navajas (1925) noted for its (slightly gaudy) *mudéjar* architecture.

El Centro The centre of Torremolinos is located a little way from the beach, bordered to the north and west by the Calvario neighbourhood and to the south by El Bajondillo and to the east by the Playamar area. This is where we find the most important squares such as Plaza de la Independencia, Plaza Costa del Sol and Plaza de La Nogalera. In the latter, the urban complex of La Nogalera has been called 'La Chueca de Torremolinos' due to the concentration of gay bars and clubs (Chueca being, as it were, the Soho or Le Marais of Madrid).

El Calvario Since this *barrio* has somewhat withstood the tourist influences, it still has the traditional Torremolinos town style. This is where you are likely to find a handful of bars where locals drink.

La Carihuela The neighbourhood of La Carihuela is located on the shores of one of the most famous beaches on the Costa del Sol: Playa de La Carihuela. This is where the fishermen's houses used to be, and it has a magnificent promenade where one can find monuments such as the Monument to the Fisherman in the Plaza de El Remo, the famous hotels of the 1950s like the Tropicana and Pez Espada. It's one of the best *barrios* in which to eat and is the location for the *Fiestas de la Virgen del Carmen* that are celebrated around her feast day (16 July).

Montemar ('Sea Mountain') is a residential neighbourhood made up of villas and mansions built between the 1940s and the 1960s. One of the first great hotels in the city, the *Parador* de Montemar, was located in this neighbourhood. Montemar appears in novels by James A. Michener, Juan Goytisolo, William Peter McGivern, Sánchez Dragó and Antonio Pereira.

The commercial street par excellence is the Calle San Miguel, located in the 'old town' (such as it is). At the end of this street is the Torre Molinos or Torre de Pimentel, not far from the Castillo del Inglés or Castillo Santa Clara (Mr Langworthy again). Notable buildings include the Casa de María Barrabino, which was built in the 19th century and reflects the tastes of the 19th-century Málaga bourgeoisie. Other buildings of interest are the **Casa de los Navajas**, in the *neomudéjar* style, and the **Church of San Miguel**.

Although the urban development of Torremolinos, undoubtedly characterized for a long time by the disorderly and speculative growth of the Spanish coast in the second half of the 20th century, has been much criticized, a calmer analysis allows us to appreciate that not every development in this urban landscape was negative. It's important to remember, perhaps, that what was 'swept away' was not a beautiful medieval or Renaissance town, but a collection of hovels, the inhabitants of which lived in grinding poverty. Some of the buildings of Torremolinos are excellent examples of the architecture of the Modern Movement and Art Deco, such as the **Aladdin Bazaar**, a building that recalls the appearance of a ship, and also a prime example of the so-called '*Estilo del Relax*' popularized by *malagueño* architects.

The main tourist attraction of Torremolinos is, of course, its beaches. These urban beaches are accessible from the Paseo Marítimo (part of the ambitious '*Senda Litoral*' project that will make the entire coastline of the Province of Málaga, from Nerja to Estepona, fully accessible and walkable). In general, they have dark sand and moderate waves and enjoy a high level of occupation during the summer months. The most popular are the beaches of El Bajondillo and La Carihuela, located nearest to the urban centre.

If you want a change from the beach, particularly if you need to entertain children, then the **Molino de Inca Botanical Garden** is about 25 minutes' walk from the Torremolinos Ⓢ *Cercanías* station, while the **Aqualand Water Park** and the **Crocodile Park** are about 15 minutes' walk away. It's slightly uphill, so take a taxi if it is hot, and walk back.

🦅 Feria de San Miguel

The Torremolinos *feria* is in honour of the town's patron, St Michael the Archangel (feast day: 29 September) and is a mix of religious processions and liturgies and more secular merry-making. The main procession is from the town centre to the Hermitage of San Miguel up the hill. Over 200,000 people come from all over the region to join this *romería* (pilgrimage), making it the second largest in Andalucía after *El Rocío* in the Province of Huelva. The procession is a rather joyful affair with horses, ox carts, music and lots of *vino* and *jamón*. The *recinto ferial* is not far from the hermitage, near the bullring, and there are usually at least 4 nights of revelry. As in Málaga city, there is also a 'day fair' in the town centre.

As a town that has long been known for pleasure and parties, there are dozens of fairs, festivals and celebration days throughout the year. Large numbers of Irish and Dutch residents and visitors make Torremolinos one of the few places in Spain where one is able to join a St Patrick's Day Parade or celebrate '*Koningsdag*' (King's Day — the national day of The Netherlands). Other cultural events include the Lyrical Season, the Theatre Season, the Flamenco Festival, Pride on the first weekend of June, the Wonder Gay Festival, 'Mad Bear' (a well-known electronic music festival), the Los Álamos Beach Festival (celebrated in July with internationally renowned DJs), Torremolinos Fashion Weekend, the 'Tourism, Art and Culture' Fair of Latin America in Europe (EUROAL), the Torremolinos Fantastic Film Festival and a series of contests dedicated to photography, literature and contemporary painting, among many others. To see what is coming up when you are in Málaga, check the listings on the well-designed and easy-to-use turismo website: ⊕ **torremolinoscultura.es/eventos**

Benalmádena

⊕ disfruta.benalmadena.es/en ❶ Castillo de Bil–Bil, Avenida Antonio Machado 78, Benalmádena Costa ⊕ Mon–Fri 0900–1800; Sat 0900–1500

Benalmádena is the next resort along, travelling west. Also known for its sandy beaches and plentiful hotels, it never shared the slightly louche reputation of Torremolinos, being known instead for wholesome 'family tourism'. Indeed, many of the attractions of interest to children are located in Benalmádena, so if your children want a break from Málaga's museums and monuments, then it's a great nearby destination.

⧗ History

Most historians assume that the name Benalmádena is Arabic in origin, and there are a few theories about what it means (most are connected to mining activity — *al ma'din* — due to the presence of iron and ochre deposits in the area). Though settled in Palaeolithic times, little is known about the place, even from Nasrid sources, but the existence of watchtowers constructed in this period suggests that it was populated to some extent. We can be reasonably certain, however, that it was pretty unimportant. When King Enrique IV of Castilla swept through in 1456, he destroyed all in his path. Little more is heard about Benalmádena, although we know that the Moors must have rebuilt it because in 1491 King Fernando of Aragón was able to order its destruction for the second time in 40 years, forcing the Muslim residents to flee to Málaga. It remained deserted until the same king decreed that it be repopulated, a process that began with a mere thirty people. Like Torremolinos, it was exposed to pirate incursions from North Africa in the centuries after the *reconquista*, so the Torre Bermeja and Torre Quebrada, which both formed part of the Nasrid defences, were repaired and a new watchtower, Torre del Muelle, was built.

Yet, as the pirate threat retreated, other catastrophes followed. Málaga suffered droughts and epidemics, closed the port to English ships during the machinations of the Third Anglo-Dutch War, and in 1680 suffered a devastating earthquake that left every dwelling in Benalmádena uninhabitable. All of these factors paralysed the economy of Benalmádena which was almost entirely reliant upon agriculture and apiculture. In the 18th century, the Gálvez brothers won the approval of King Carlos III to establish the Royal (Playing) Card Factory in their hometown of Macharaviaya, east of Málaga. They needed a source of paper and a Genoese entrepreneur called Félix Solesio chose the Arroyo de la Miel district of Benalmádena in which to establish his paper mill (like Torremolinos, Benalmádena has a number of fast-flowing streams capable of driving water wheels). The economic recovery of Benalmádena had begun.

The English traveller William Jacob described in 1809 the richness and beauty of Benalmádena, noting the streams that powered flour and paper mills. In the mid-19th century, investors arrived in Benalmádena looking for suitable land for vines. The population increased considerably with the arrival of these new investors who leased the land and attracted a significant number of labourers. But, as in Torremolinos, the mills were unable to compete with the vast, industrial mills in the cities (including Málaga, with its port and railway) and one by one, they closed. Then the destruction of the vineyards by the phylloxera plague wrought havoc throughout the Province of Málaga. Unemployment, hunger and this viticultural plague, together with human epidemics of malaria, typhus and cholera, tore through Benalmádena like wildfires. Deaths and waves of emigration decimated the population and left the place exhausted until the great demographic boom of the 1950s and 1960s with the birth and development of tourist activity on the Spanish coast.

Benalmádena Today

The modern town is a near-conurbation of three distinct centres, though it can be hard to say where one ends and the others begin. Benalmádena Pueblo is located on the site of the Nasrid settlement, once a walled town with a modest fortress. It sits in the eastern part of town, on the slopes of Pico Mijas. Known simply as the '*pueblo*', it preserves something of the aesthetics of the *pueblos blancos* of the *andaluz* Mediterranean. In *malagueño* dialect, the locals are known as *torruscos*. Arroyo de la Miel is the intermediate area between the coast and the mountains. It is also known simply as '*El Arroyo*' (The Creek). The urban nucleus was a farmhouse where in the 18th century six paper mills were built to supply the playing card factory. The reason for its name is due to the abundance of bee hives which used to be found here (*miel* means honey). It owes its more recent urban development to the construction of the coastal ☉ *Cercanías* railway, which connects the towns of Fuengirola and Málaga capital (the Málaga–Fuengirola railway opened in 1916 but the real game-changer was the construction, in 1975, of an extension loop to include Málaga Airport). The locals are called *chichilindris*, which might sound rather rude if you know your Spanish slang, but it is not. Finally, Benalmádena Costa is the coastal area where the bulk of the hotel establishments are clustered.

Benalmádena has 12 miles of coastline consisting of sand, gravel and palm groves; a total of 17 beaches: Arroyo Hondo, Carvajal, Bil-Bil, La Morera, Arroyo de la Miel, Benalnatura, Fuente de la Salud, La Perla, Las Viborillas, Playa de Las Yucas, Malapesquera/Malapesca/Torre Bermeja, Melilleros, Santa Ana, Tajo de la Soga, Torremuelle, Torrequebrada, and Torrevigía. All the beaches are accessible from a continuous promenade (part of the *Senda Litoral*) and there are plentiful *chiringuitos*, restaurants and other establishments. The eastern beaches are wide, with breakwaters, and have public facilities (lavatories, showers, equipment hire, etc.) while the western ones are rocky, many of them calm and isolated between small cliffs.

The **Jardines del Muro** are an urban complex of gardens located in Benalmádena Pueblo on the site of the now-demolished fortress. Among its gardens stands the (17th c.) church of **Santo Domingo de Guzmán**, the oldest in the municipality. One of the attractions of the gardens is the views of the coast from its **mirador** (viewpoint). The designer of the gardens was the painter and sculptor César Manrique, from Lanzarote.

The **Parque de la Paloma** (Dove) is located on Avenida de Federico García Lorca and comprises 200,000 m² of lakes, lawns and pine forests. It has a cactus and succulent garden and there are various kiosks, bars and cafés. Other *benalmadense* attractions (which reflect the tradition of family-friendly tourism in Benalmádena rather than the transgressive hedonism of Torremolinos) include:

 The **Sea Life Aquarium** is located in the Puerto Deportivo de Benalmádena (the Marina) and is a shark conservation and protection centre that opened in 1995.

 The **Selwo Marina Dolphinarium and Penguinarium** is a marine fauna park that houses the only dolphinarium (*delfinario*) and ice penguinarium (*pingüinario*) in Andalucía. It is located in the fairground of Arroyo de la Miel, next to Parque de la Paloma.

 The **Teleférico (Cable Car)** connects the centre of Arroyo de la Miel with the summit of Mount Cálamorro, 771 metres above sea level. From the summit, you can see the Rock of Gibraltar (and even Africa) on clear days, and there is a cafeteria, shops and a bird of prey show.

 The **Mariposario (Butterfly Garden)** is the largest in Europe and is located just beyond Benalmádena Pueblo (🚌 **121 from Benalmádena, or** 🚌 **112 from Málaga**). It has around 1,500 butterflies drawn from over 150 species, mostly from Africa, South America, Asia and Australia.

 Two ferries leave the port of Benalmádena daily during high season. One is a two-hour 'dolphin spotting' cruise, and the other is a coastal ferry to Fuengirola (and back).

The user-friendly *turismo* website is a good source of information about attractions, beaches and places to eat and drink, although it is not always up to date (*e.g.* at the time of publication it was still listing the amusement park 'Tivoli World', even though it closed during the COVID pandemic and seems unlikely to reopen). As always, before embarking on a trip to Benalmádena, double-check opening times by consulting the websites of the attractions and establishments themselves, and consult Moovit for up-to-date travel information.

Mijas

🌐 turismo.mijas.es/en ❶ Plaza Virgen de la Peña 2, Mijas Pueblo
❶ Bulevar de La Cala de Mijas, La Cala de Mijas

Mijas, like Benalmádena, is a single municipality comprising three non-contiguous urban centres. Mijas Pueblo, located on the slopes of the Sierra de Mijas, is the oldest part; Las Lagunas is part of the area called Mijas Costa, and forms a conurbation with Fuengirola; and La Cala is a coastal resort some distance to the west. Inhabited since ancient times, Mijas Pueblo was a small town dedicated mainly to agriculture (the 10th-century traveller Al-Idrisi mentions in his texts that they exported their figs as far as India) and fishing until the tourist boom of the 1950s. Since then, tourist activity and the construction sector have been the engines of the local economy, simultaneously boosting the population and per capita income.

Mijas (La Cala) has some lovely beaches, but then so does pretty much the entirety of the coast of the Province of Málaga. The reason why visitors to Málaga are likely to take a trip to Mijas (Pueblo) is that it is a *pueblo blanco* within fairly easy reach (the other being Álora). The journey from Málaga takes between 80 and 90 minutes, either by bus or by a mixture of 🔵 *Cercanías* train and bus. From Arroyo de La Miel railway station, the 🚌 M-121 takes you to Mijas Pueblo, or from Fuengirola station, it is the 🚌 M-122. Check routes on Moovit or on the provincial transport consortium website: bit.ly/ctmamalaga

Mijas Pueblo may be a *pueblo blanco* in the technical sense — it has old, whitewashed buildings decorated with flowers, pretty squares, winding streets clinging to a hillside, and so forth — but it is also something of a tourist exhibit. In his magnificent tome *Andalucía* the Hispanist and art critic Michael Jacobs († 2014) is excoriating about the place, dismissing it in one sentence: 'The village is now wholly given over to tourism, and has various ridiculous museums.'[72] But Jacobs never held back in his criticism of what he sees as the disfigurement of 'España La Vieja', which is partly what makes him such an entertaining and engaging writer. Elsewhere he recounts the story of the last Republican mayor of Mijas, Manuel Cortes, who spent 30 years in hiding from Franco's forces (in his own house) before emerging in 1968, and tells of his profound shock at seeing the coastal development of Fuengirola for the first time — what Laurie Lee called a 'concrete cliff'. On the other hand, Cortes would have known Mijas at its poorest, and perhaps he realized that the 'incomer' residents and coachloads of tourists who visit throughout the season sustain the local economy in a way that smallholdings of figs, carobs and almonds never could.

The great historian of Spain, Ronald Fraser, also writes about Mijas in his 1973 book *Pueblo*[73]; or rather he writes about the fictional village of 'Tajo', which is recognisably Mijas. Fraser is an inveterate collector of oral history and one account he draws on is that of the Ital-

---

72   Michael Jacobs. *Andalucía* (Pallas Athene, London, 2013) p. 332

73   Ronald Fraser, *Pueblo: A Mountain Village on the Costa del Sol* (Allen Lane, London, 1973)

ian-American John Bertorelli who visited Mijas as a stop-off between Italy and the US and liked it so much that he stayed. As an artist and silversmith, he was able to make a living, but he found his existence in Mijas rent with paradoxes; a common expat experience. 'Incomers' (including Spaniards) move to a village partly because they are attracted by the scenery, but also because the experience of becoming part of a small, close-knit community appeals. Yet the latter ambition is more difficult to realize. They remain outsiders. Their new neighbours may be friendly enough, but true integration is impossible. This is not the case in a city where, although some residents can count their connection in generations, the population in general is more transient and one can hide behind relative anonymity. Small villages like Mijas have a love-hate relationship with incomers. On the one hand, they are 'different' and do not share a deep connection to the place stretching back centuries, while on the other, their presence is vital for the survival of the village. Spain has no shortage of isolated villages that have been entirely abandoned in recent decades.

But do not discount Mijas Pueblo. It may be 'touristy' and even twee in places, but that does not diminish the reason that so many tourists visit it in the first place — viz. it is a pretty village, easy to get to, pleasant to walk around, with some attractive churches and a handful of decent bars and restaurants. Purists may scoff at its British retirees and '*burrotaxis*' (donkeys saddled or pulling gigs and used to convey visitors through the narrow streets), but it offers a welcome change of scene after the nakedly touristic Torremolinos, and feels almost rural after a few days spent in the centre of Málaga city. During the summer there are lots of events organized by the *ayuntamiento*: padel tournaments (for adults and children), flea markets and craft markets, painting and art exhibitions, flamenco displays, al fresco (in the English sense) film screenings, theatrical performances and a '*tapas* route' where a drink and a *tapa* can be had for a bargain price at participating bars. Check the *agenda* of the *turismo* for more details (use the QR code).

There are a few sights worth seeing in Mijas Pueblo, not least the churches, which provide interesting (and refreshingly cool) places to visit. The **Hermitage of the Virgen de la Peña** is a cave excavated by a Carmelite friar between 1656 and 1682, to which an irregular stone sacristy has been added. In a niche created in the front of the façade is an image of the *Virgen de la Peña*, patroness of Mijas. According to tradition, the image was 'discovered' in 1586 by two children who were watching sheep when they were guided by the spot by a dove. The hermitage is open 24 hours a day.

The **Hermitage of Nuestra Señora de los Remedios** (also called Santa Ana) was built at the beginning of the 18th century and is a small whitewashed church with a single nave. It is the home of an 18th-century image of the *Virgen de los Remedios* (Our Lady of the Remedies — a Marian title popularized after the *reconquista* by the Trinitarian Friars, another order founded to redeem Christians held captive by Muslim pirates from North Africa). It is currently only open on Sunday mornings.

The church of **San Sebastián** is a much-photographed 17th-century chapel and is open daily. The Parish **Church of the Immaculate Conception** was consecrated in 1631 and is located in the upper area of the town. It was constructed on the ruins of the old mosque, the *mudéjar* tower of which was used to fulfil the functions of a bell tower. The largest of the older churches in Mijas, it has three naves separated by semicircular arches that rest on marble columns, covering the central wooden *mudéjar* framework. A baroque chapel was added later. During restoration work beginning in 1992, eight frescoes of the apostles were discovered, dating from the first half of the 17th century. It is open daily, all day, but if you visit on a Saturday you will probably find it being used for a wedding.

The **Hermitage of Calvary** is located in the foothills of the Sierra de Mijas and was built around 1710 as a place of retreat for the Carmelite friars from a hospice and friary that existed in Mijas until 1813. It is quite a hike and only open during the evenings of Fridays of Lent when many people follow a *Via Crucis* of 14 stations that leads up from the town. Use the link or QR code to see the route for the Stations of the Cross: **bit.ly/MijasViaX**

The **Pino Carrasco de La Muralla** (Aleppo Pine Grove of the Wall), or the **Parque de la Muralla** (Park of the Wall) are gardens built on the remains of the old Moorish fortress that protected the town. It's a very pleasant place for a stroll and has good *miradores* (viewing points). Also of interest is the tiny **Plaza de Toros** not far from the park, which is interesting because it is rectangular rather than round. Its size means that only *novillos* (young bulls) were faced here, but that is now decades ago. Even the far larger ring in Benalmádena hasn't staged a *corrida* since 2010 (though in 2000 it staged 40). Strident opponents of *toreo* (often erroneously called 'bullfighting'), such as the UK Daily Mail newspaper, like to suggest that it is only sustained in contemporary Spain thanks to tourists. In fact, the opposite is true. Tourist hotspots like Barcelona, Benidorm, Ibiza, Torremolinos and Marbella once staged some of the most notable *ferias taurinas* in Spain. Now none does.

🍴 Eating

Many of the bars and restaurants in Mijas are pitched towards the expat/foreigner market, though there is nothing that quite matches the 'Sunday Roast' carveries of Torremolinos, replete with Yorkshire puddings. A few spots are worth mentioning, however.

🍫 Mayan Monkey (📍 Plaza Virgen de la Peña 15) Not a bar, but a *chocolatería* with a *café* serving artisan chocolates, baked goods, ice cream and drinks. Off-season, when there are fewer visitors, the owners will often be happy to give you a guided tour of the 'chocolate factory', but there are chocolate-making workshops throughout the year. Experiences range from a 30-minute 'express' workshop in which you will make three bars of chocolate, up to the 90-minute gourmet masterclass. Booking ahead (minimum 2 people) is necessary, but book via their own website, not third-party websites which often charge a commission.

🍷 🍝 💃 La Bóveda del Flamenco (📍 Plaza de la Constitución 1) A café-bar in the picturesque main square that serves a light menu of *tostadas, bocadillos, tapas*, etc.

🍴 Restaurante Meguiñez (📍 Calle San Sebastián 4) A fairly traditional Spanish *taberna*-cum-*restaurante* (actually run by *argentinos*) that combines reliably delicious food with super-friendly service.

🍷 🕐 🍲 Bar La Martina (📍 Calle Málaga 19) Another restaurant-bar serving Spanish classics (mostly *raciones*), and probably my pick of the bunch. The service is friendly and attentive and the food is top-quality. The weekday *menú del día* is excellent value for two courses plus pudding or coffee. If you see *buñuelos* (sweet doughnuts; very typical of the region) on the menu, then do order some because they are homemade and excellent.

🍷 🍝 Alboka Gastro (📍 Avenida Virgen de la Peña 6) A modern — even hip — 'vinos y tapas' place delivering some of the best flavours in Mijas. A lot of the *tapas* are 'fusion', but well thought-out and finely executed. The cocktails are delicious, the wine list is extensive and the staff are warm and friendly.

🍷 🍝 Pampa Tablas y Tapas (📍 Calle Virgen de la Peña 6) Another sleek, modern *tapas* bar, giving Alboka a run for its money when it comes to high quality and innovative *tapas*.

They have an excellent wine selection and friendly, attentive staff.

Relative to its size, Mijas Pueblo has a lot of bars and restaurants, and many of them are excellent. However, some reflect the tastes of the large number of expat residents, so if you want to avoid eating pizza or chicken tikka masala, make sure you have a good look through the *carta* before taking a seat and ordering your drinks!

Fuengirola

⊕ turismo.fuengirola.es/en ❶ Paseo Marítimo 32, Plaza Teresa Zabell ❶ Paseo Jesús Santos Rein 6 ⊕ Mon–Fri 0930–1800; Sat–Sun 1000–1400

Fuengirola, yet another 'former fishing village' grown wealthy as a result of 20th and 21st-century tourism is at the end of the line (for now) on the ◑ *Cercanías* railway line from Málaga. Yet whereas Torremolinos and Benalmádena are certainly villages where fishing formerly took place, five purse-seine boats based in Fuengirola still set to sea to catch sardines, anchovies and horse mackerel, while a couple of trawlers land octopus, sea bream, red mullet, sole, squid, prawns, Norway lobsters, scallops and clams. Nonetheless, the main driver of the economy is, as elsewhere along the coast, tourism.

⧖ History

During the Roman occupation the town was known as Suel (it had almost certainly been a settlement of proto-Iberian Bastetani before the arrival of the Phoenicians). One can find Roman remains such as the baths and the Finca del Secretaria villa or the fish salting sheds found on the slopes of the castle hill. The area was occupied by the Vandals from the 5th century and later by the Byzantines (perhaps), but then the town was abandoned for some reason. It could well have been destruction by a tidal wave or the forced withdrawal of the population to the mountains due to piracy or Visigoth incursions.

During the Arab occupation it was known as Sohail (or Suhayl) and, according to legend, the name came from the star of Sohail (the *Canopus* of the Romans, which is the brightest in the southern hemisphere and a guide to desert nomads) which could only be seen from the town's castle. This is clearly a spurious back-formation because first, that particular star is not visible, and second, it is clearly an Arabizing transliteration of the former name, 'Suel'. In the late 15th century, the town was again abandoned, though historians are not sure why.

On 7 August 1485, the castle of Sohail was conquered by Christian troops. After the *reconquista*, there was an attempt to repopulate the place with 30 *mozárabes* from the surrounding hills, but the threat of invasions from North Africa and other factors, such as the scarcity of land, meant that by the time of a census in 1511, a mere 25 years later, the area appears uninhabited; nothing more than a defensive fortress and coastal surveillance.

Fuengirola would come to depend on the municipality of Mijas and, little by little, the population centre would move closer to the coast as the threat of invasion and slaving raids diminished. The new population did not settle in the same place as the Phoenicians, Romans and Arabs, but on the other side of the river where, at the beginning of the 18th century, a beach-front inn emerged. This would serve as lodging for passers-by, muleteers and sailors. A few dwellings grew up around this inn, thus forming the beginnings of a small town. During the Spanish War of Independence, the Sohail castle (occupied by the French with support from Polish units from the Duchy of Warsaw) was the scene of the Battle of Fuengirola in October 1810, one of the very few times in history that British and Polish troops have been on opposing sides.

In 1822 some residents requested the creation of an *ayuntamiento* in the town, arguing for their secession from Mijas on the basis of a census of a thousand inhabitants, a prosperous economy based on fishing and port activity, and due to the damages that they incurred in the defence of Mijas during the Peninsular War. The city hall of Mijas, for its part, sent a report minimizing the fishing activity and pointing out that the census of Fuengirola actually only recorded 409 people. The *Diputación* agreed with Mijas and Fuengirola had to wait until 1841 to set up its own town hall. Even then, the municipality of Fuengirola considered itself insulted by the small amount of territory it received and subsequently tried to expand it throughout the 19th and 20th centuries. The railway arrived in the city in 1916 and the car not long afterwards, opening the way to tourism. From the 1930s, hotels began to be built on the seafront. This trickle of tourists would turn into an avalanche in the 1960s, hot on the heels of Torremolinos.

Fuengirola Today

There are many residents who now bemoan the mass tourism and the influx of foreign (and Spanish) retirees, complaining about the damage to the environment represented by the concrete jungle that now stands where once there was a coastal village. In the 2000 study *The British on the Costa del Sol*, the sociologist Karen O'Reilly interviews both locals and incomers alike and relates a familiar story[74]. It is easy to complain now about how a quaint seaside village has been swallowed up by a tourist megapolis, but in the 1960s and 1970s, when tourism was bringing communications, infrastructure and wealth, few were complaining.

It is common to read in the guidebooks that 'Fuengirola has an attractive old town', but this somewhat overstates things. It is true that the streets around the Church of **Nuestra Señora del Rosario** (Our Lady of the Rosary) are mostly low-rise, whitewashed and pleasing, though there is little that is especially 'old'. The church, which looks baroque, only dates from 1940. Even so, the contrast with the high-rise beach-front hotels, so typical of this stretch of coast, is marked.

Like most of the Costa del Sol, the beaches are one of the main reasons that people come to Fuengirola. The beaches, from east to west, are Carvajal, Torreblanca, Los Boliches–Las Gaviotas (Las Gaviotas beach has a section especially adapted for the disabled), San Francisco, Fuengirola, Santa Amalia and Ejido–Castillo. Aside from the beaches and their associated attractions (*chiringuitos*, *cafés*, promenades, etc.) there are several sights of interest to visitors in Fuengirola. The castle (**Castillo Sohail**) is an Arab citadel built on a previous Roman fortress, built upon even earlier foundations. It is located on a small, isolated hill next to the mouth of the Fuengirola River. Most of what can be seen today is from the time of the Caliphate of 'Abd al-Rahman III, who had the castle built in 956. Phoenician and Punic remains

---

74   Karen O'Reilly, *The British on the Costa del Sol: Transnational Identities and Local Communities* (2000)

have also been found in its vicinity. It is partly ruined, but it is free to visit. The castle is not adapted for disabled visitors and although the road from the town is smooth and even, it is fairly steep. There are excellent views from the castle.

The **Finca del Secretario** (Secretary's Estate) is a Roman archaeological site dating from the 1st century and in use until the 5th. It is located next to the Pajares Stream, in the Los Pacos neighbourhood right in the middle of the town. The complex is divided in two by the N-340 coastal road and has two different areas, a salting factory and a thermal (bath) area. An arcaded room decorated with mosaics and with two *praefurnia* (ovens) for heating the baths stands out. An 'interpretation centre' opened recently and the site is free to visit. An audio guide is available to download from the *turismo* website. Not far away, the **Termas de Torreblanca** is another archaeological site discovered in 1991. This is another bath complex, but excavations are ongoing and it is not yet open to the public. A small and rather idiosyncratic **City Museum (Calle María Josefa Larrucea 3)** next to the town hall opened in 2013.

 The **Costa Sol Cruceros ferry** between Benalmádena and Fuengirola can also be boarded in Fuengirola, though the dolphin spotting cruise only leaves from Benalmádena.

 Bioparc is one of the biggest attractions in Fuengirola and a good reason to visit from Málaga, especially with children. It's generally very highly rated by its visitors and although tickets are not cheap, it is open until 10 pm and one can easily spend 2 or 3 hours here. Look at the schedule of events and make sure you arrange your visit to be able to see at least one of the 'meeting with keepers' events.

There are a couple of weekly street markets in Fuengirola. The main Fuengirola market (**El Rastro**) is held at the *Recinto Ferial* (near the bullring) on Tuesdays between 9 am and 2 pm. You will find hundreds of market stalls with items as diverse as clothing, home decoration, flowers and plants, as well as mountains of fruits and vegetables. On the same site there is a flea market on Saturdays. It's more bric-a-brac junk than artisan pottery, but if you enjoy bargain hunting, you may find something to interest you.

🍴 Eating

Fuengirola has no shortage of places to eat and drink and, like its neighbouring resorts, many tend towards the 'international' (*viz.* Indian, Chinese, Italian, and peculiar kinds of British-style eatery that I think of as 'Wetherspoons Abroad'). Indeed, of the top-ten TripAdvisor listings for restaurants in Fuengirola, only two serve 'Spanish' food, and four are Indian restaurants. The suggestions below, like most places in Spain, are suitable for a sit-down meal at a table with a tablecloth, or for *tapas*.

🍷🍴🦐 **Bar La Paz Garrido** (📍 Avenida de Mijas 1) is a venerable bar (with a *comedor* or dining room) that, for my money, is one of the best places to eat in Fuengirola, at least if you are looking for well-cooked, traditional Spanish fish and seafood. The service can sometimes be a little slow, but it is always friendly. Like all good establishments whose reputations are based on fresh seafood, it is closed on Mondays.

🍴🍽 **Restaurante Pueblo Lopez** (📍 Calle Mijas 9) is a long-established and traditional *mesón* that has indoor and terrace dining. It is not the cheapest restaurant in Fuengirola, but the food is high quality and there is a very good quality *menú del día* available weekdays.

✖ **Restaurante Tánico** (◉ Calle Blas de Lezo 2) is a sleek, contemporary restaurant serving excellent dishes — traditionally Spanish but executed in a modern style.

✖ **La Abacería de David** ('David's Grocery Store' ◉ Calle Marconi 14) is run by Teresa and the eponymous David. It's a relative newcomer to the Fuengirola bar scene, but it somehow manages to give the impression of being a very traditional place. The kitchen is open for lunch and dinner, so if you want *tapas* between 3 pm and 7 pm, order something cold. The cod confit with *escalibada* (a kind of roasted ratatouille) is a delight, as are the liver and bacon kebabs. They are known for their delicious casseroles (*cazuelas*).

✖ ❀ **El Laberinto Bistro** (◉ Calle Marbella 19) was opened by the famous chef Baltasar Díaz who has worked with culinary superstars like Martín Berasategui, Philippe Serre and the late Santi Santamaria. Baltasar's name has been dropped from the restaurant name, so he may no longer be directly involved, but he set the tone. No surprise, then, to find dishes like fennel 'risotto without rice' with smoked eel, bluefin tuna with coconut and vanilla oil; Venezuelan *arepitas* (deep fried maize buns) with roasted chicken; *ajoblanco* with raisin and rum ice cream; and wild boar's head, sardine and *piparra* sandwich. One of the great things about El Laberinto, however, is that the *carta* changes often, so don't be disappointed if the dishes mentioned no longer feature; there will be other delicious things to try.

♆ ◉ ✄ **Taberna el Callejón** (◉ Calle Francisco Cano 113) and **Tabanko el Callejón** (◉ Avenida Condes de San Isidro 55) are both owned by the brothers Juan Luis and Sergio Ruiz Jiménez. **Tabanko** is in the centre while **Taberna** is towards Los Boliches. These are among the best *tapas* bars in Fuengirola, with top-quality ingredients sourced from the nearby fish market. Their prawns are as much in demand as the oxtail hamburger, the *flamenquín*, their smoked sardines, their *jamón*, and other cured meats (*embutidos*).

✖ ❧ ❦ **Mesón de Andrés** (◉ Calle San Pancracio 16) Andrés Palacios Reino claims to serve the best *jamón* in the area, and he may well be right, as his is a restaurant known for its exceptional cooking (this is very much a 'tablecloth' restaurant, rather than a *tapas* bar with a *comedor*). Main courses are upper-end, price-wise, but good value given the quality. In a region known for fish and seafood, Mesón de Andrés has a well-deserved reputation for meat dishes, including suckling lamb shoulder and chops, Galician blonde beef burger, barbecued Iberian pork loin, and a fabulous beef sirloin with 'apple crumble', *jamón*, duck liver, truffle and a rich Málaga wine sauce.

♆ ◉ ✄ **Taberna Plaza Vieja** (◉ Calle España 21) Grilled octopus, scrambled eggs and sautéed prawn salad, Huelva prawns, baby broad beans with Iberian ham and eggs, scrambled eggs with black pudding and caramelized onions, and more. Plaza Vieja is a family-run and friendly bar offering a wide selection of beautifully prepared *tapas* and *raciones*.

✖ **Los Manueles** (◉ Avenida de Mijas 24) 'The Manuels' (Manolo and Paqui) opened their restaurant back in 1979 as a 'home-cooked food' canteen, and since then they have been growing in quality and fame. Their recipe for success is simple and is what makes Spanish food some of the best in the world: namely good ingredients and knowledge and experience when dealing with them. Steamed mushrooms with Iberian ham, *pil pil* prawns, *piquillo* peppers stuffed with seafood, and baby broad beans with ham and spring onion are some of the highlights of an extensive but well-designed *carta*. A knowing nod to tradition means that there is a good selection of Iberian hams, *chorizos*, sausages and cheeses. Both meat and fish are given equal prominence. They have a branch in Torremolinos too.

♆ ✄ ❀ ❧ **Picoteo** (◉ Calle Larga 4) Tuna tartare; salmon sashimi flower with seaweed and soy sauce; Moorish lamb skewer with quinoa tabbouleh; tomato with buffalo mozzarella, rocket and basil; roasted scallops with potatoes, asparagus, mushrooms and mushroom sauce — are just some of the dishes that make Picoteo one of the best *tapas* bars and restaurants in Fuengirola. They also offer a very reasonably priced nine-course tasting menu.

🍷 🏨 ⚓ 🦐 🐟 **Bar Los Jabegotes** (📍 Avenida Nuestro Padre Jesús Cautivo 32) The *Real Academia Española* defines a *'jabegote'* as 'one of the men who pull the ropes of the fishing net' so it comes as no surprise that this is a restaurant that seems to live, breathe and cook the seas, fish and seafood. The favourites on the *carta* are *gazpachuelo*, *ensalada malagueña*, *ensaladilla ucrania (rusa)*, shrimp *tortillitas*, garlic or *pil pil* prawns, anchovies in vinegar and cuttlefish in sauce, all beautifully cooked. They offer a good *menú del día*.

🍴 🐟 ⚓ **Restaurante El Cano** (📍 Calle Juan Sebastián Elcano 10) is a small, mostly fish and seafood bar-restaurant known for its friendly service. It is very popular with Spanish locals, which is always a good sign. The *carta* here goes beyond the ubiquitous hake, cod, sardines etc. and you will find anchovies, squid and baby squid (*puntillitas*), red mullet, pink eel, hake, turbot, roe, tuna and more. Also, grilled fish — sea bream, red mullet, gilt-head bream, sea bass, snapper, monkfish, octopus, etc. — is a speciality.

🍴 🐂 **La Taberna Gaonera** (📍 Calle Troncón 20) The *'gaonera'* is a move with the *capote* (large cape) in the *corrida* (bullfight) in which the *torero* (bullfighter) holds the cape behind his back to look like a pair of wings. Like **Plaza Vieja**, this is a taurine restaurant with beef, lamb and pork prominent on the *carta*. You can start with an assortment of Iberian cold cuts and continue with a portion of seafood — white prawns from Huelva, grilled shrimp, oysters, sautéed clams, sea anemones — or finish with meat. The roasts stand out — suckling lamb shoulder and suckling pig — as do their grilled steaks.

🏨 *Menús del Día*

If you are visiting Fuengirola from Málaga, a *menú del día* is a great option, and represents the cheapest option for lunchtime eating. The following list includes establishments known for the quality and value of their lunchtime offer — not gourmet dining perhaps, but good quality dishes made from fresh ingredients.

🍴 🏨 ⚓ **Restaurante La Esquinita** (📍 Calle Benalmádena 1) is a very popular restaurant with a varied menu but known for its excellent fish dishes.

🍴 🏨 **Restaurante La Rozuela** (📍 Calle Yunquera 1/Avenida Finlandia 2) The *menú* is also available at weekends.

🍷 🏨 **Bar Casa Gómez** (📍 Calle San Pancracio 5) is popular with locals, for good reason.

🍴 🏨 **Restaurante Bodega la Solera** (📍 Calle del Capitan 13) is at the upper end of the price range but it includes half a bottle of wine per person, not just a glass.

🍴 🏨 **Restaurante Iyudmi** (📍 Calle Martínez Catena 2) also includes half a bottle of wine.

🍴 🏨 **Bistro Michel** (📍 Edificio Cambural, Calle Orquídea 3) is rather an old-fashioned place (melon and ham, prawn cocktail and cream of tomato soup are all on the menu), but the cooking is excellent and there are plenty of traditional Spanish dishes.

🍴 🏨 **Rincón de Los Verdiales** (📍 Calle San Isidro Labrador 9) serves tasty home cooked food and very friendly, efficient service.

🍴 🏨 **Restaurante Don Julián** (📍 Calle Marbella 41) is located in a hotel. Great food.

Marbella

🌐 turismo.marbella.es/en ❶ Plaza de los Naranjos (Casco Antiguo) ❶ Glorieta de la Fontanilla (Playa del Faro) 🕐 ♨ Mon–Fri: 0800–2000; Sat–Sun: 1000–1700 🕐 ☀ Mon–Fri: 0830–2030; Sat–Sun: 1000–2100

Marbella is only around an hour by bus from Málaga. Unless you hire a car, the only way to get to Marbella is by bus as it is the largest city in Spain lacking a railway station. Buses are frequent (more than hourly) and operated by malaga.avanzagrupo.com with the last bus back to Málaga leaving the Marbella bus station at 10.45 pm. The journey takes between 45 and 90 minutes, depending upon which bus you book.

Marbella has long thought of itself as a *gran lujo* (luxury) resort, and the stars of 'The Only Way is Essex' presumably make a similar appraisal. However, with no disrespect to the cast of that TV reality show, James Argent and Gemma Collins are perhaps not quite in the same league as Orson Welles and Rita Hayworth when it comes to star quality. Decades of association with fugitive criminals, financial corruption and reliance upon Middle Eastern oligarchs have all taken the gloss off of Marbella's reputation.

Even so, if we include apartment lets, Marbella has the largest number of hospitality beds in Andalucía. It also accounts for 50% of the 5-star beds in the Province of Málaga and 30% of '*gran lujo*' (luxury 5-star) beds. The COVID pandemic and Brexit showed that while tourism is hugely important to the local economy, it is a potentially fragile source of income. While British tourists are likely to continue to visit Marbella for their holidays, fewer are now likely to invest in property or open businesses. Perhaps with an eye on the city of Málaga's careful reinvention of itself as a high-value tourism destination, the Marbella *Ayuntamiento* published a long-term tourism plan in 2022, stressing the need for a 'connected', sustainable and multi-sector approach to development

I am assuming that anyone interested in the luxury hotels and famous beaches of Marbella will actually stay in Marbella but I am including it in this section because (a) it is not far away, (b) it has an attractive and relatively unspoilt Old Town, and (c) if you are staying in Málaga, then you may wish to visit for the day to see what all the fuss is about.

⧗ History

The town's name — 'Marbella' — obviously means 'beautiful sea'; except that it doesn't. The Romans knew the town as '*Salduba*' ('Salt City'), and although the Moors called it something like '*Marbil–la*', that may have been a corruption of an earlier Phoenician or even Celtiberian word. Traditionally, the inhabitants of Marbella have been called *marbelleros* in everyday language and *marbellenses* in ecclesiastical documents. However, since the mid-1950s, they have also been called '*marbellís*' or '*marbellíes*', the only demonym that appears in the dictionary of the *Real Academia Española*. The change is due to an archaism popularized by the writer

Víctor de la Serna (1896–1958), who claimed (almost certainly mistakenly) that the term was used in the Moorish period. However, the natives of Marbella still use the word *marbelleros* to refer to themselves, and most find the word '*marbellí*' rather annoying. Most maintain the position that when they speak of '*marbelleros*' they refer to the people who were born there and when they speak of '*marbellíes*' they refer merely to the inhabitants of Marbella in general (a distinction not unlike *malaguita/malagueño*).

During the Islamic period, the city was made up of narrow streets and dwellings with large *patios*, the most notable buildings being the citadel and the mosque. The urban centre was surrounded by orchards, the most important crops being the mulberry trees to sustain silkworms, and figs. During the Battle for Granada, the town passed into the hands of the Crown of Castilla without bloodshed in 1485. The *Reyes Católicos* granted it the title of city. Very soon after this, the Plaza de los Naranjos was built, following a typically *castellano* urban design.

In the 19th century, Marbella became an industrial centre, with the Málaga industrialist Manuel Agustín Heredia opening the first blast furnaces in Spain there, producing up to 75% of the country's cast iron. In 1860 the Marqués del Duero founded what was then the most modern and important agroindustrial complex of its time, the *Colonia Agrícola San Pedro Alcántara*, for the refinement of sugar cane during the boom of the *andaluz* sugar industry. Starting in 1871, the English-owned Marbella Iron Ore Company carried out mining activity, transporting ore from the mines in Ojén for maritime transport to England. By the end of the century, thanks in part to catastrophic economic mismanagement from successive liberal [sic] governments, all these heavy industries had shut up shop and the people directly or indirectly employed by the forges returned to agriculture and fishing (if they were able).

The first decades of the twentieth century saw the inauguration of the first large hotel: the Comercial, in 1918. In 1920 the Marbella Casino Cultural and Recreational Society was founded. From the 1950s onwards, most of Marbella's income would come from tourism. In 1946 Ricardo Soriano Scholtz von Hermensdorff, Marqués de Ivanrey, acquired a farm located between Marbella and San Pedro Alcántara and constructed a tourist complex called *Venta y Albergues El Rodeo*, inaugurating luxury tourism in Marbella. His nephew, Prince Alfonso de Hohenlohe, acquired the Santa Margarita farm, the embryo of what in 1954 would become the Marbella Club and in 1975 the Puente Romano Hotel. Marbella's hotels played host to a never-ending stream of well-known European families during the fifties and sixties: Bismarck, Rothschild, Thurn und Taxis, Metternich, Goldsmith, Schönburg, Thyssen-Bornemisza, Agnelli, Onassis, Alba and Snowdon, turning Marbella into a meeting point for the international jet set. (Prince Alfonso, by the way, would eventually retire to Ronda and prove instrumental in the replanting of local vineyards at the end of the 20th century.)

From the mid-seventies, powerful businessmen and members of royal houses of the Middle East showed a marked predilection for Marbella. The then heir to the Saudi throne Fahd bin Abdulaziz had the Mar-Mar Palace built on the 'Golden Mile'. In 1981, together with his brother Salman bin Abdulaziz (who became king in 2015), he financed the construction of the Marbella Mosque. In 1983, the Saudi engineer Muafak Al Midani took ownership of the Marbella Club and Puente Romano hotels. Lebanese, Kuwaiti, Libyan and Syrian fortunes in petrodollars invested heavily in Marbella real estate which in turn encouraged a new influx of luxury tourists from the Middle East who would sometimes occupy entire hotels with their vast entourages.

In 1991, the businessman and then president of the soccer team Atlético de Madrid, Jesús Gil (1933–2004), one of the most controversial, popular and populist politicians in the history of Spain, became mayor, a position he would hold for fifteen years overseeing a massive real-estate boom in Marbella. His zeal to 'clean up' Marbella meant the persecution of drug

507

users, the removal of prostitutes from the streets (often involving beatings) and deportations of low-income foreigners, as well as bribes paid to homeless people to leave the city. He turned a blind eye to dirty money from questionable regimes and asked no questions of British fugitives from justice. Even after Gil's ejection from city hall, the corruption continued and as late as April 2006, the Government of Spain took the unprecedented step of dissolving the *ayuntamiento* of Marbella and appointing a management commission elected by the provincial *diputación* of Málaga.

🔭 Sightseeing

Unless you want to stroll along the beaches and promenades, my suggestion would be to head for the Old Town. If the 1.5km 20-minute walk from the Bus Station doesn't appeal, then you can catch the bus (🚌 2 or 6) to ⑧ Alameda–Casco Antiguo, a journey of about 10 minutes. Use the Moovit app to plan your journey, or consult the helpful Avanza local bus site: ⊕ marbella.avanzagrupo.com/en. Opposite the bus stop, locate the Calle Pedraza and follow it until you reach a small square (Plaza de la Victoria). Turn right and continue straight on to the Plaza de Los Naranjos. There is a *turismo* (Tourist Information Office) here where you can pick up a map.

Built after the Christian reconquest in 1485, the Plaza de Los Naranjos is surrounded by *andaluz*-style white houses and several historical buildings such as the Casa Consistorial (Town Hall), the Casa del Corregidor and the Ermita de Santiago — the oldest religious building in the city and the *sede canónica* of the Holy Week brotherhood *Santísimo Cristo del Amor, María Santísima de la Caridad y San Juan Evangelista*. The centre of the square is occupied by a beautiful Renaissance fountain and numerous orange trees that give colour (and a name) to this beautiful square, as well as several terrace bars where you can have a drink while you find your bearings and refresh yourself after your journey.

🔭 **Capilla San Juan De Dios** (📍 Calle Misericordia 2) dates from the 16th century and was part of the old Royal Hospital, built by the *Reyes Católicos* after the capture of the city. With a simple plan, the stone doorway of the chapel is framed by a semicircular arch and contains a door carved with the city's coat of arms and a pomegranate, symbol of the old Kingdom of Granada. Inside the chapel, the *mudéjar* coffered ceiling and the fragments of unusual frescoes in the *castellano* style stand out.

🏛 **The Castillo de Marbella** (📍 Calle Portada) also called Castillo de la Madera and Alcazaba de Marbella, is a castle in ruins with a rectangular floor plan. It dates from the time of 'Abd al-Rahman III who, following the rebellion of Umar ibn Hafsun, wished to have a defensive point on the coast. Later it was of vital importance for the defence of the Nasrid Kingdom of Granada until its surrender to the Christian troops of Fernando and Isabel. Some sources suggest a Roman origin for the castle. At the end of the 18th century a local scholar named it 'Castillo de la Madera' based on the supposed existence of a log store.

🏛 **The Bazán Hospital** (📍 Calle Hospital Bazán 10) takes its name from Don Alonso de Bazán, alderman of Marbella and warden of its castle. It is a fine example of domestic architecture of the mid-16th century in which elements of the Gothic coexist with *mudéjar* and Renaissance elements. The building currently houses the Museum of Contemporary Spanish Engraving (⊕ museodelgrabado.es 🕐 Mon–Sat 1000–2000; Sun 1000–1400 🎟)

The museum shows temporary and touring exhibitions of prints and graphic works and also arranges courses on print-making, lectures on art, concerts and drawing competitions. The museum's collection of prints and artworks covers the whole panorama of the best contemporary Spanish art expressed in a medium that has been embraced by contemporary artists and includes etchings, aquatints, lithographs, woodcuts and other examples of graphic art by artists such as Dalí, Picasso, Tàpies and Miró.

🏠 **Santa María de la Encarnación** (📍 Plaza de la Iglesia 🕐 0900–13:00, 1900–2100) is a church dedicated to Our Lady of the Incarnation. After the *reconquista* of Marbella, the mosques were converted into Christian churches and this had almost certainly been the largest mosque in Marbella (a fact also suggested by its proximity to the castle/citadel). It was canonically erected by the Archbishop of Seville in 1505. In 1618 Bishop Luis Fernández de Córdoba Portocarrero either enlarged the minaret of the old mosque or built a new one.

🏠 **Ermita del Santo Cristo** (📍 Plaza Santo Cristo) was built in the 16th century and enlarged in the 18th century. The main façade has an exposed stone doorway and the rest is finished in lime, as is traditional in many Andalusian hermitages. The bell tower is square and covered by a glazed ceramic roof. It is the headquarters of the Brotherhood of *Santo Cristo de la Vera ✠ Cruz, Santo Cristo Atado a la Columna & María Santísima Virgen Blanca.*

🏛 **Calle Ancha** ('Broad Street') During the 16th century, Marbella grew outside the Arab walls. Calle Ancha linked the city with the north, where *'alquerías'* ('farmhouses' — from the Arabic *al-qarya,* which means 'the small town') were located. This was where both arable and livestock farms were found, as well as sugar cane fields and olive presses. The Calle Ancha was a prototypical 'Gran Vía' — a demonstration of new wealth, hence its relative width and fine, aristocratic houses, many of which still bear coats of arms on their façades, have large balconies and exhibit remarkable decoration. Especially splendid is the house at No. 18, dating from 1763.

🍴 Fine Dining

Marbella has 4 restaurants with Michelin Stars, of which three are in the town itself (🌐 bit.ly/MarbellaMichelin)

Messina ✿ (📍 Avenida Severo Ochoa 12 ⊘ Sun ✗ ●) 11 and 15-course tasting menus. *À la carte* is also available.

Nintai ✿ (📍 Calle Ramón Gómez de la Serna 18 ✗ ● ⊕ ☀ only) Japanese/fusion cuisine.

Skina ✿✿ (📍 Calle Aduar 12 🕐 Daily ✗ ●) One of the most expensive restaurants in Spain.

Affordable Eating (and Drinking)

If a Michelin-starred tasting menu is not what you're looking for, then there are plenty of places in which to find reasonably priced food and drink in Marbella. Here are a few suggestions.

🍺 🍹 🦐 🕐 🍽 **Cervecería La + Fría** (📍 Edificio Parque Marbella, Calle Alonso de Bazán 1) has a very varied and quite traditional menu, with a good choice of shellfish, fresh fish and sandwiches. Dishes are available in large (*ración*) and half (*media ración*) portions.

🍷 🦐 **Bar El Estrecho** (📍 Calle de San Lázaro 12) has a long history. It was founded in the fifties and it preserves its original marble tables, with fried fish still the most popular dish. All the food is available as *raciones* and as individual *tapas.*

🍷 🍢 **Arco Tapas Bar** (📍 Calle Peral 14) has friendly staff and a wide variety of *tapas.* Arco is a small place, but the service is excellent, the price exceptional and its menu extensive, so you can try a little of everything.

🍷 🍴 **La Taberna del Pintxo** (📍 Avenida Miguel Cano 7) is another bar around the Parque de Alameda, near the marina. It operates in the Basque fashion — grab cold *tapas* from the bar and hot *tapas* as they pass by. You are charged when your skewers are tallied.

🍷 🍴 **Taberna Casa Curro** (📍 Calle Pantaleón 7) is a very popular bar and usually quite lively thanks to its excellent value for money and extensive menu. It has a wide selection of high-quality 'authentic' products like *gambas blancas* (white prawns) from Huelva and *chicharrones* (pork rinds) from Chiclana de la Frontera.

🍷 🕐 🍴 **Taberna La Niña del Pisto** (📍 Calle San Lázaro 1) is a cosy *tapas* bar with an extensive menu of traditional dishes which are mostly available as *tapas*, *medias raciones* and *raciones*. The roast goat is excellent and *cazuelas* (stews) are a speciality.

🍷 🍴 **Mia Café Tapas & Bar** (📍 Calle Remedios 7) is a friendly *tapas* bar serving well-prepared and beautifully presented food, including 'healthier' dishes like avocado toast.

Puerto Banús

ℹ️ Plaza Antonio Banderas, Avenida Julio Iglesias, José Banús Marina, Puerto Banús

If you are reading and enjoying this book, then I suspect that the glamour, glitz and conspicuous consumption of the cultural desert that is Puerto Banús (part of the Marbella municipality) may not be your cup of tea. Although the idea that the resorts of the Costa del Sol are 'former fishing villages' is often fanciful, in the case of Puerto Banús, the claim cannot be made at all. Before it was built, there was nothing here. The entire locality — port, marina, hotels and shopping complex — was designed in the late 1960s by the Swiss-Russian architect Noldi Schreck (best known for his work in Beverley Hills) and built by the property developer José Banús. That Puerto Banús is not a 'concrete cliff' of skyscraper hotels and apartments is something we have Schreck to thank for. He persuaded Banús that a 'modern *pueblo andaluz*' would be more sophisticated and attractive than yet another high-rise development.

The complex was developed by Banús, who became known as 'the regime's builder' due to his closeness to General Francisco Franco. The opening gala in 1970 was attended by, amongst others, the Aga Khan, Roman Polanski, Hugh Hefner, and Prince Rainier and Princess Grace of Monaco. A young Julio Iglesias was hired to sing for the guests and three hundred waiters from Sevilla served 22 kilos of beluga caviar to 1700 guests. The comparisons to Beverley Hills and an obsession with wealth and celebrity are clear. In a quite remarkable piece of self-promotion, the resort (the official name of which is 'Puerto José Banús') was named after its developer. Even the address of the 'Tourist Information Point' betrays this preoccupation with celebrity. It is located in a square named after a Hollywood actor, which is on an avenue named after an internationally successful singer, on a marina named after its developer, in a town also named after its developer! That's quite a chain of celebrity name-dropping.

Puerto Banús is not unattractive, in a fairly soulless way. The quality of the buildings and public facilities is high. It has a pleasant beach, and amongst the eye-wateringly expensive restaurants, there are a few slightly more affordable places to eat and drink. However, in spite of Puerto Banús's reputation for attracting a 'super-rich', rather than merely 'rich' patrons, it is interesting that out of Marbella's fifteen restaurants to hold Michelin Stars and Bib Gourmands, none is in Puerto Banús. Unless you have a superyacht (the daily mooring fee is the fourth highest in Europe, after Capri, Porto Cervo and Portofino), the other draw of Puerto Banús is the shopping. You will find Louis Vuitton, Dior, Gucci, Versace, Bvlgari, and Dolce & Gabbana all here, among many others. And they do good business. Dolce & Gabbana, for example, has seven stores in Spain, and four are in Puerto Banús.

As regards culture, Puerto Banús has a sculpture by Salvador Dalí called '*Rinoceronte vestido con puntillas*' (1956, 'Rhinoceros Dressed in Lace'). One might think that a work by one of the world's greatest surrealists would be the oddest artwork in the town, but '*El Marbellero*' (also called 'La Victoria') — a bronze and copper sculpture by the Georgian sculptor Zurab Tsereteli on a 25 metre granite pedestal — takes that prize. It was a gift from Russian expats in 1994.

You can travel between Málaga and Puerto Banús via Marbella by booking with Avanza ⊕ **malaga.avanzagrupo.com** then taking a local bus (🚌 **1 or 3**) from Marbella (use the Moovit App to plan your journey or consult ⊕ **marbella.avanzagrupo.com** for local bus times). Including transfers, allow at least 2 hours total journey time.

Estepona

⊕ **turismo.estepona.es** ❶ Plaza de las Flores

Of all the *soi-disant* 'former fishing towns' of the Costa del Sol, Estepona is the one that best retains its old character. It's a charming and attractive town and, despite a significant proportion of non-Spanish residents (around 25%), it retains a very Spanish 'feel'. Also, while it does attract seasonal tourists, many of them are Spaniards from further inland, with most foreign holidaymakers not making it quite this far west. The result is a very pleasant seaside town that doesn't feel too 'touristy'. There are regular bus services from Málaga with Avanza (**malaga.avanzagrupo.com/en**), with an average journey time of 1h 30m.

Like almost every significant settlement on Spain's southern coast, Estepona was populated during the Phoenician, Roman and Arab periods, though few Moorish structures remain. It has a beautiful cove of sandy beaches on the town's seafront, and a marina and (working) fishing port to the west. There are other beaches east and west of the town, including Spain's first naturist beach (and later resort). The main attraction for the day-tripper, though, is the pretty and well-kept old town, much of which has managed not to have become a warren of tacky souvenir shops and bars desperately touting for business (though, fear not: this is Spain, so there is no shortage of watering holes). An especially noteworthy attraction is the Orchidarium in the old town that opened in 2015 (see p. 515).

⌛ History

The name Estepona probably comes from the Arabic *Estebbuna*, though another possibility is that the name predates the Arabs and Romans, and it was once an enclave dedicated to the Celtiberian goddess Epona. In the Province of Málaga, the people of Estepona are called '*culitos mojaos*' ('little wet bottoms'). This could be due to its being a fishing village or it could be related to the figs of which Estepona was, and to some extent still is, a great producer, because when figs are placed in an oiled box (giving them 'wet bottoms'), they ripen sooner.

There is evidence of prehistoric habitation thanks to the discovery of dolmens (megalithic tombs). The Phoenician and Roman main settlement was perhaps some distance from the current town; a now silted-up port called Salduba. In the Moorish period we know of the existence of a fortress called *al-Extebunna*: the first certain record of the ancestor of today's place name. In 1342, among the campaigns of the Battle of the Strait, the naval combat of the Battle of Estepona took place, between the Moroccan Marinids and the Crown of Aragón, supported by Gil Boccanegra, a Genoese privateer. From 1344 Estepona became the western limit of the Nasrid Kingdom of Granada and its population all but vanished.

It remained the border territory of the Nasrid Kingdom of Granada until 1456 when the inhabitants of the town refused to pay taxes to King Enrique IV of Castilla, who finally authorized a Christian incursion, leaving Estepona integrated into the Lordship of Juan Pacheco, Marqués de Villena. During the Granada War of 1485, Ronda, Casares and Marbella were taken, and Estepona would eventually be placed under the jurisdiction of Marbella in 1552. As in other towns, the coastal population lived a precarious and insecure existence due to frequent slaving raids from North Africa. This led to the construction, in the 16th century, of the Guadalmansa Tower, to protect the extensive agricultural estate of Alonso de Bazán, Mayor of Marbella.

In the Chronicle of the Province of Málaga (1869) by José Bisso, the abundant fishing of sardines and anchovies in Estepona is noted. In the later 19th and early 20th centuries, forestry (for the manufacture of paper and cardboard), mineral extraction and sugar cane cultivation bolstered the local economy, with tungsten deposits discovered in the hills to the north. In the 1930s the port was developed in an attempt to increase employment in fishing (fishermen had previously had to drag their boats up and down the beach to the sea). And from the second half of the 20th century, tourism started growing, especially in the eastern part of the municipality, though it never reached the levels seen in Torremolinos, Fuengirola or Marbella.

Estepona Today

The old town of Estepona is a pleasingly picturesque place to explore. Beyond the handsome, though unremarkable **Church of Nuestra Señora De Los Remedios** (⦿ **Plaza Misioneros 13**), there are few 'must see' historic sights in the town centre, although there are a couple of interesting (and free) museums.

The bus station used to be close to the centre and the beach, but a few years ago it moved eastwards and is now on the main road into Estepona from Marbella. To get to the *turismo* on the Plaza de las Flores it's about 20 minutes' walk, although there are two local bus routes that allow you to make the walk shorter by travelling part of the way on the bus. The buses are operated by ⊕ autocaresricardo.com. However, when planning your route, I suggest using the Moovit App as Google does not currently cover the area and the timetables, even on the operator's own website, give confusing and even contradictory information. Similarly, the travel information page on the official Estepona municipal website is years out of date. Another option if you would prefer not to walk is a taxi (there is a rank opposite the bus station).

One bus used to be routed along the promenade but this is no longer the case. The best stop to get off at is ⑧Avenida Juan Carlos I (7 stops from the Bus Station). You can then walk into the Old Town from the West. If you want to go to the Fishing Port (see below), you can catch the bus from the same stop, or there is one very near the **Orquidario** ('Islas Canarias'). The stop nearest the port is ⑧Avenida Puerto del Mar. To return to the Bus Station, the buses take the same route in the opposite direction. However, one bus route (🚌L2) currently picks up on the Paseo Marítimo on the seafront — handy if you decide to finish your day trip with a walk along the promenade. But again, routes change, so consult Moovit (or a similar app).

The *turismo* is housed in the **Casa de las Tejerinas** (House of the Weavers; though in this case, nothing to do with looms and shuttles, just the surname of the last private residents) which displays artworks from the municipal collection on the first floor, as well as exhibitions. Visits are free **(Tue–Fri: 0900–2000; Sat 1000–1400, 1600–2000).**

 Estepona is often called '*El Jardín de la Costa del Sol*' (The Garden of the Costa del Sol) on account of the sheer quantity of flowers and greenery found in its streets. From the *turismo*, take a leaflet outlining the '*Ruta Rincones con Encanto*' (the 'Charming Corners Route' ⊕ **bit.ly/Estepona_Corners**) — a walking route through more than two dozen of the most beautiful streets, floral displays, squares and urban gardens of the old town. Another leaflet — the '*Ruta de las Esculturas*' (Sculpture Route ⊕ **bit.ly/Estepona_Sculpture**) shows the locations of over 50 works of sculpture in Estepona, 10 of them in the old town. Another gives information about the '*Ruta de la Poesía*' (Poetry Route ⊕ **bit.ly/Estepona_Poetry**) — a route taking you past 47 poems and extracts of poems (in various languages, though mostly in Spanish) dotted around the old town on glazed ceramic tile displays. The poems are by local poets, about Estepona, or appropriate to Estepona in some way.

🎨 The Murals

The fourth route is the '*Ruta de los Murales*' (Murals Route ⊕ **bit.ly/Estepona_Murals**) — a map and guide to 62 (and counting) urban murals all over the city, quite a few of them in the old town. Many people, when they hear 'urban murals' might nod politely as they imagine a few walls with 'street art' of questionable quality (and I would usually be one of them). But the murals of Estepona are dramatic, impressive, beautiful and, frankly, breathtaking. In many cases, they are also vast. In fact, for anyone with an interest in contemporary art, especially as it relates to urban spaces, they are not to be missed.

Urban murals are common throughout the world. A local authority has an ugly or unloved building and they hatch a plan to beautify it by commissioning an artist to paint a mural. This, indeed, is how it started in Estepona. The historic centre is charming, but outside it, much of the housing and buildings are utilitarian, to say the least. In Estepona, inviting artists to decorate such buildings is not an occasional item of minor expenditure, but a significant part of the urban development and tourism plan, with funding to match.

 Since 2012, the *ayuntamiento* (usually in collaboration with a cultural foundation — in the past they have had sponsorship from Caixa and Unicaja Banks) has staged an international competition, inviting artists to submit proposals for new murals. The competition now attracts over 100 applications, not only from Spain but from all over the world. The final short-list of 10 finalists each receive an honorarium of €1000, living expenses for the 10 days they will spend in the town, sufficient materials necessary

for a 'standard size' mural (162 square metres), and a crane (or 'mobile elevating work platform'). The first prize is €10,000.

The great strength of Estepona's 'urban art' offering lies not only in its sheer scale (the largest mural in Europe is in Estepona) but in the variety of styles and genres. An artist who manages to create great expectation and excitement whenever he is spotted in Estepona on a hydraulic platform with his paints is the sculptor and hyperrealist painter from Jaén, José Fernández Ríos. His first *obra esteponera* was a mural of a little girl watering a flowering shrub — *'Regando el Jardín'* ('Watering the Garden', see photo on previous page). Shades of Banksy, perhaps, except that the 'shrub' in this case is a living, mature tree, and the 'little girl' is 5 storeys high. The exquisite portrayal of the girl notwithstanding, the masterstroke is the tap and hosepipe (and their shadow) on the left, taking *trompe l'œil* to a new, macro level.

His other works are in the old town, near the new Orchidarium. The second is *'Día de Pesca'* ('Day of Fishing'), the largest vertical mural in Spain, spanning the walls of several six-storey apartment blocks. It shows an elderly fisherman landing a fish. In Madrid, such a mural would be a technically impressive folly, but in the fishing town of Estepona where you can smell the ozone, the hyperrealism is almost disorientating. Ríos makes it seem as if one is looking through the buildings to the sea, and the *trompe l'œil* extends vertically, into the blue sky above.

Another magnificent work of Ríos (he has 10 in total, so far) is *'Reflejos del Jardín'* ('Reflections of the Garden'), commissioned by the *ayuntamiento* to complement (and indeed compliment) the new botanical garden created as the setting for the new *Orquidario* (Orchidarium) in 2015. This monumental work shows his understanding of Estepona, his technical mastery, and his humility as an artist. The *Orquidario* houses and displays thousands of varieties of one of the most beautiful species of flower in the world, in an especially designed urban park/garden. What mural could possibly surround it? Certainly not one that stood in competition. What Ríos created, then, was a 'reflection' — hyperreal (though magnified)  depictions of the sort of flowering plants seen everywhere in the streets of Estepona as well as life-size paintings of trees seen in the gardens themselves. Depending upon the light, it is often genuinely difficult to distinguish reality from its portrayal.

🏛 Museums, Attractions and Dining

🏛 Museo Arqueológico (📍 Plaza Blas Infante 🕐 Mon–Sat 0830–1430) is housed in the Casa del Aljibe, an 18th-century palace built on top of a Moorish cistern (*aljibe*). The museum, which has a small exhibition of local finds from prehistory until the Moorish period, is free to visit, but all the information on display is in Spanish.

If you are visiting with children and are attracted by the Selwo Aventura Zoo/Safari Park, be warned: it is extremely difficult, if not impossible, to visit easily using public transport.

Do not be deceived by bus stops that include the name 'Selwo' in their name — from the main road, it is a forty-minute, uphill trek. The only practical way to visit, from Málaga, is by hiring a car (or taking a taxi from Estepona). A far better bet is to look at the sections on Fuengirola and Benalmádena above and visit the sea life centre or butterfly collection there.

Parque-Botánico Orquidario Calle Terraza 86
orchidariumestepona.com Tue–Sat: 1000–1330, 1500–1800; Sun 1000–1400 Mon

The Parque-Botánico Orquidario is a reason in itself to make the trip to Estepona for the day. Built on the site of the old *Cooperativa Agrícola Estepona* (Estepona Farmers' Cooperative — the original farmers' wholesale market which has since moved to the suburbs), it is semi-subterranean and consists of three glass domes covering a space of 1000 m² with a total area of 15000 m³ displaying 5,000 species of plants and 1,300 species of orchid, of which over 300 will be in bloom at the time of any visit. A well-planned route takes you past a 17-metre waterfall and a 30-metre intermittent waterfall with 200 m² of vertical gardens. If you want to interest children in this attraction then some may be interested in the *Cananga odorata* variety, better known as Ylang Ylang, popular with perfumers; or the *Bixa orellana*, originally from Peru and widely used in the cosmetics industry because its pigments are extracted for the production of lipstick. Budding cooks or ice cream lovers should be interested to learn that vanilla is extracted from a species of orchid. Finally, what boy (age appropriately, obviously) would not be delighted to learn that 'orchid' is the Greek word for testicle and the orchid flower is so named because of its similarity to a scrotum?

The **Puerto Pesquero** (fishing port) is located to the west of the marina. If you're lucky you might get to watch some fishing boats land their catch. Landings take place throughout the day, but generally happen early morning, mid-afternoon, and late evening. It is not possible to buy fish direct but you can watch the auction process that is followed by the packing of the fish pallets with ice and loading them into the insulated vans for distribution to local suppliers.

At the port, in the same building as the wholesale fish market is **Turismo Marinero** (turismomarinero.com), an initiative of the Estepona Fishermen's Association offering all sorts of 'experiences' connected with fishing in Estepona — sea fishing, boat trips, family activities, etc. most with food included. Booking ahead is essential, though the website is only in Spanish, so you may need to put the link into Google Translate if your language skills aren't up to grasping the detail. Their reviews are consistently excellent and, for a family, the activities are cheaper than a trip to the zoo.

Around the port, there are some good fish restaurants, but not to be missed is:

La Escollera (Calle Puerto Pesquero 10) is probably the best fish restaurant in Estepona and one of the best on the Costa del Sol. They only serve fish mains, but any non-pescatarian in your party might perhaps be persuaded to make do with a tasty salad and a plate of french fries...

The restaurants and bars in Estepona are mainly found in the lower half of the Old Town, close to the sea, around the Plaza de la Flores, and along the Calle Real and Calle Caridad. The standard is generally good and the prices more reasonable than in nearby Marbella.

Restaurante La Casa del Rey (Calle Raphael 7 lacasadelreyestepona.com) calls itself a 'gastrobar' and serves excellent food at reasonable prices. They also have an extensive and well-planned wine list as well as a children's menu.

✗ **Taberna Díez** (📍 Calle Real 68 ⊕ tabernadiez.es) is also a place for elegant dining, with excellent food and friendly service.

✗ **La Rada** (📍 Edificio Neptuno, Avenida España) has a terrace close to the promenade and they used to offer a good *menú del día* — perhaps they still do.

✗ **Restaurante ALMA de Miguel** ('The Soul of Miguel Restaurant' 📍 Calle Caridad 30 ⊕ almademiguel.com) has always been popular for its fine cooking, even when it used to be the more humble 'Taberna de Miguel'. It is at the top end, price-wise, but the food is good value given the quality. Unusually for Spain, it serves really excellent homemade puddings.

✗ 🛏 **Restaurante Sol y Mar** (📍 Calle Real 5) is a cheaper, but reliable, option, plus they offer a basic but filling *menú del día*.

🍷 🕐 🍴 **Tasca La Botica de la Cocina** (📍 Calle Santa Ana 46 ⊕ laboticadelacocina.com) is a small, friendly bar — with outdoor seating available serving excellent *tapas* and *raciones*.

🍷 🍴 **La Galería Gastrobar** (📍 Calle Caridad 48 ⊕ lagaleriabar.com) is a lively, rather garish *tapas* bar-cum-restaurant with a slight Italian spin to some of their dishes, all of which are reasonably priced, tasty and filling.

✗ 🕐 🍴 **El Típico Andaluz** (📍 Calle Caridad 59) is, as its name suggests, a typical *andaluz mesón* serving excellent *tapas* and larger dishes at good prices.

🍷 🐟 🍴 **Bar Simón** (📍 Avenida San Lorenzo 40) Don't be put off by the slightly shack-like appearance of Bar Simon — they have been serving fabulous fresh fish dishes and an amazingly cheap selection of *tapas* since 1930. 'Simonito', as the place is known, is one of Estepona's best-kept secrets.

🍷 🕐 🍴 **La Fragua** (📍 Avenida San Lorenzo 20) is another bar that doesn't look much from the outside, but produces beautifully cooked, tasty dishes at low prices.

Gibraltar

⊕ visitgibraltar.gi ❶ Customs Building, Winston Churchill Avenue ❶ Gibraltar Heritage Trust, The Main Guard, 13 John Mackintosh Square (The Piazza)

The bus (again, there is no train) from Málaga to La Línea de la Concepción takes between 2h 15m and 2h 45m. When it comes to the question of how to get to Gibraltar you might be considering driving. This is probably not the best idea, especially if you're only planning to spend a day in Gibraltar.

Gibraltar occasionally gets into disputes with Spain that can lead to delays at the border. Further delays are probably quite likely due to added friction following the UK's withdrawal from membership of the European Union. Even when everything is working smoothly, the border gets very busy at rush hour when up to 15,000 Spaniards travel to or from work. Unlike sitting in a traffic queue, getting into Gibraltar on foot by walking across the border is usually very quick. Even if you choose to hire a car to travel to Gibraltar (a 1h 30m drive), there are plenty of car parks in La Línea de la Concepción. You can park your car in La Línea de la Concepción (🌐 bit.ly/ParkLaLinea) and then walk over the border. You can also, of course, approach the border by car and go off in search of car parking if there is a queue or tailback.

📖 Practicalities

You need your passport (or EU identity card) to enter Gibraltar, and you will need it to re-enter Spain. The currency of Gibraltar is the Gibraltar Pound (GIP) which is pegged to sterling at par value. Pound Sterling is accepted everywhere in Gibraltar, but GIP is not legal tender in the UK. So do not withdraw cash from an ATM unless you are going to spend it in Gibraltar. Take some £5 Sterling notes and some coin with you if can (for small purchases and tips). Spend, or change, any GIP currency before leaving Gibraltar as UK banks won't accept it and nor will UK *bureaux de change*. Most establishments in Gibraltar accept euros, but will give change in GIP. If you have a euro-denominated currency card, remember not to use it in Gibraltar or you will have to pay conversion fees. Use your normal Sterling credit or debit card instead.

🔭 Sightseeing

The walk from the border crossing to the centre takes no more than 30 minutes. If you prefer not to walk from the border crossing you can take a bus (🚌 2).

For a small place, there is more than enough to keep you entertained for a day trip. The one thing you probably want to do if you are going to Gibraltar for the day is to explore the Rock. The 'Mediterranean Steps' is the steepest way to get to the top of the rock. Eventually, you will crest the rock at its highest point near **O'Hara's Battery**. However, this is only really an option for serious hikers as it is far from a gentle stroll. The best plan, when you only have a day, is to reach the top using the cable car.

St Michael's Caves are popular with visitors. The caves are a series of limestone chambers and tunnels that were first used when defending Gibraltar from attacks by the Moors after the reconquest of 1462. They were also once prepared to be used as a hospital during the Second World War but they were never actually used. Nowadays they also house a 600-person auditorium where concerts take place. Underneath the Rock of Gibraltar are miles of underground tunnels. The oldest were dug during the 1779–83 Great Siege of Gibraltar. No longer needed for defensive purposes, the tunnels can now be visited. Most visitors to Gibraltar want to see the Barbary Macaques, the only free-living apes in the whole of Europe. You can visit them at Apes Den on the Rock and watch as they jump around and play together. There is also a Moorish Castle, various batteries, viewpoints and a suspension bridge high up on the Rock.

Most points of interest on the Rock are part of the Nature Reserve and are included in the ticket admission price. There are four suggested paths: '**Monkey Trail**', '**History Buff**' (both medium difficulty), '**Nature Lover**' (easy) and '**Thrill Seeker**' ('challenging'), all between 2.9 km and 4.3 km (there used to be an excellent smartphone app called 'Gibraltar Upper Rock Paths' but at the time of publication this seems no longer to be available). My advice is to do some research and decide what you'd really like to visit before you visit.

 I would also advise taking the earliest bus that you can manage from Málaga, especially in the summer, so that you can explore the Rock before the heat of the day becomes unbearable (though be warned — Gibraltar is often shrouded in low cloud while Algeciras and La Línea on either side are bathed in sunshine). Have a hearty *desayuno* or *almuerzo* in La Línea and then walk across the border. When you arrive in Gibraltar, cross the runway and, if you wish, pick up a bus (🚌 **2, 3 or 10**) to the lower cable car station. There are three options (use the QR code link): Cable Car Return (if you just want to go up and down); Cable Car Return + Nature Reserve (to explore the rock a bit before taking the car down); and Cable Car Single + Nature Reserve (if you plan to walk down). To visit three or four attractions (and to walk down into town) you ought to allow **at least** three hours.

 Those with limited mobility (or simply limited time) could take a minibus tour. Leaving aside the most expensive options (that cost hundreds of euros per person), you could either book a taxi (Gibraltar taxis are used to taking visitors to the sights) or have a look at the tours offered by Blands Travel, a reputable local firm charging reasonable rates (scan the QR code link, left). John Morris has also prepared a very useful page of information on his website: ⊕ **wheelchairtravel.org/gibraltar/attractions**.

Although most of the main sights are on the rock, the Gibraltar Museum is worth a visit if you have time, not least to see the beautifully restored Arab bath house (⊕ **gibmuseum.gi**).

Back in town, the main street is conveniently called 'Main Street'. You'll find a few pubs along this thoroughfare, but many of the eateries are found on the streets running parallel, on either side. There are also some good bistros on Queensway Quay. The question is what sort of food you want to eat — Spanish, 'British', 'European', Italian, Indian, Chinese, Fish and Chips, etc. Searching on Google Maps for restaurants and specifying those rated 4+ will usually provide you with a decent list of options.

Food and drink in Gibraltar is slightly more expensive than in Spain and slightly cheaper than in the UK, but the big bargain item for visitors is tobacco (spirits are no longer significantly cheaper than in Spain). On average, 200 cigarettes (the duty-free allowance) are around one-fifth of the UK price: ⊕ **stagnettoorders.com/pricelist**

In summary, Gibraltar is a curiosity, and that is partly what makes it worth visiting (especially for British visitors). It is visibly 'British', right down to its red pillar boxes, uniformed police officers and traditional pubs serving pints of bitter and fish and chips. On the other hand, the people are ethnically (judging by surnames) mostly Spanish, Portuguese, Jewish, Genoese/Italian and Maltese. While English may be the official language, Spanish is understood and locals speak a local vernacular called *Llanito*, which is influenced by several languages, including medieval Ligurian and Maltese.

Gibraltar has a slightly old-fashioned feel and if you have travelled to countries that were once part of the British Empire, I dare say that you will notice a certain 'colonial vernacular' in the architecture. The people are generally charming — hospitable and friendly like their Spanish neighbours but with a rather British element of reserve mixed in.

East of Málaga (*Costa del Sol Oriental*)

Nerja

🌐 nerja-turismo.com ❶ Calle Carmen 1 🕐 Mon–Fri 1000–1400, 1700–2030; Sat 1000–1330

For viewers of British television, the attractive resort town of Nerja may ring a bell thanks to a 2006 episode of (Gordon) Ramsay's Kitchen Nightmares in which the eponymous sweary chef paid a visit to a failing *nerjeño* restaurant. The restaurant (La Parra de Burriana) was owned by an Englishman who wanted to tempt British tourists by offering a 'Mediterranean' menu with — wait for it — a 'twist'. To apply a 'twist' to tried-and-tested classics can be culinary alchemy in the hands of a Ferran Adrià or a Juan Mari Arzak, but in the hands of an untrained chef, such meddling usually fails. This was certainly the case at La Parra de Burriana, where the prawns in chocolate sauce and the chicken with banana failed to impress anyone except their deluded creator.

The good news is that this Spanish-British-Chinese-Turkish fusion restaurant is no longer trading and its former chef was last heard of running a Bed and Breakfast in Kent. The even better news is that Nerja is really rather lovely. It also has one of the highest concentrations of bars per capita in the whole of Andalucía, with almost 6 per 1000 inhabitants (it is narrowly beaten by Benarrabá with 6.1, nearby Frigiliana with 7.24, and the blue 'Smurf Village' of Júzcar with a whopping 8.77). Although a significant proportion of residents are non-Spaniards, Nerja also attracts plenty of Spanish holidaymakers.

Don't be misled by the tourist brochure descriptions of Nerja as a 'fishing village'. Tourism is now this town's main industry and the few fishermen still to be seen along the beach provide a picturesque scene for visitors and a slim livelihood for local families. Until a couple of decades ago the town retained a strong Spanish identity, but during recent years the influx of both northern European and Spanish retirees and seasonal visitors has somewhat eroded the genuine charm of a truly Spanish working town. But this notwithstanding, Nerja still feels far more palpably 'Spanish' than, say, Torremolinos or Fuengirola.

Nerja is still very much worth a visit. It is a quiet, charming coastal town with a central historical area that has an almost village-like feel, and the tourist mix is not exclusively British or northern European with many Spanish people visiting this resort for holidays, together with French and Italians. Unsurprisingly, the relative peacefulness of the town along with the absence of high-rise developments along the coast or noisy nightclubs means many older British people have retired here.

⌛ History

Following the discovery of the *cuevas* (caves — see below), we know that humans have inhabited the area for many thousands of years. After the Bronze Age, however, evidence of settlement is scant. Along the eastern coast of what is now the Province of Málaga, the Romans established three towns in the 2nd century BC: *Maenoba* (modern Vélez), *Claviclum* (modern Torrox), and *Detunda*. The latter was probably located where we now find Maro, the village with which Nerja forms a near-conurbation.

The defeat of the Visigoths by the Arab invaders in 711 in the Battle of Guadalete is the real beginning of the story of modern Nerja. Known by the Moors as 'Naricha' (meaning something like 'abundant spring'), Nerja became a centre of textile production, in particular silk. As well as silkworms, the Arabs also introduced sugar cane, a crop that would loom large in Nerja's history.

Following the *reconquista* of Málaga in 1487, Nerja continued for a time to be inhabited by Muslims and Jews, though this situation ended following the Edict of Granada. There is a rather sad, and probably apocryphal, story that suggests that the Playa del Salón beach is so named because it witnessed the exodus of hundreds of Jews who bade farewell to one another with the word 'shalom'.

Nerja was repopulated by relocating rural labourers from the north (especially from the historically poor regions of Galicia and Asturias), but it also suffered waves of depopulation once these incomers realized the dangers of living there. It was exposed to frequent Muslim slaving raids and the male population was routinely armed. The peaceful square now known as the Balcón de Europa was originally known as the Guards' Tower (Torre de los Guardas) and defended by cannon.

Unlike the cities, where the *reconquista* 'took root' thanks in part to the significant numbers of 'old Christians', Islam was more tenacious in rural areas and small towns. The Muslims, unlike the Jews, had not been expelled in 1492. Some had been permitted to remain as '*mudéjares*' in an almost exact mirror image of the situation that had pertained in Moorish Al-Andalus. Under Islam, Christians had been '*dhimmis*' — non-Muslims permitted to practise their religion in return for the payment of taxes and abiding by the law. Now, Muslim *mudéjar* citizens were permitted to practise their religion under Christian rule. Other former Muslims were converted and became '*moriscos*', carrying with them the suspicion of secretly maintaining their Islamic beliefs. The *mudéjar* experiment lasted barely a decade and they were required to become *moriscos*.

And yet in rural areas, they nonetheless remained in significant numbers half a century later. In 1567, in the *barrio* of Albaicín in Granada, the nobleman Hernando de Válor y Córdoba adopted the Arabic name Muhammad ibn Umayya (his Ummayad grandfather had been granted the Lordship of Válor in return for his conversion and cooperation). Hernando (or Muhammad) was 'enthroned' by his supporters as the rightful Muslim King of Granada and not long afterwards he and his fellow conspirators began their revolt, which would last for three years. The battles took place mainly in what is now the Province of Granada, but there were skirmishes in Frigiliana and Cómpeta, both within *nerjeño* territory. The *moriscos* who variously surrendered or were defeated were forcibly relocated to other Spanish kingdoms (especially Castilla). In 1609 they would finally be expelled from Spain.

Although slaving expeditions remained a threat, Nerja was now better defended and new houses and land clearing encouraged the growth of the town in the following years. The Armengol de Maro sugar mill opened in 1585, and the San Antonio Abad de Nerja sugar mill began in 1591 on the banks of the Chíllar River. Around this time, watchtowers were built along the entire Málaga coast, to spot pirate ships. They communicated with each other via a chain of beacons.

The 18th century has been described as the 'golden century' in Nerja. While the aristocracy had prospered under the Habsburgs, the reign of the Bourbons benefited the municipalities. The quasi-serfdom of manorial lordships gave way to town councils and mayors. Nerja cobbled many of its streets and enlarged its churches. Irrigation (a legacy of the Moors) improved, leading to an increase in the production of sugar cane, grapes and fruit. Most important of all, new roads linked the town to Málaga to the west and Almería to the East.

The following centuries, however, brought many setbacks and hardships. There were occasional causes for optimism, such as the purchase of the San José Sugar Mill by Martín Larios in 1873, but a devastating fire at another mill (Armengol de Maro), the arrival of Phylloxera, frequent epidemics of cholera and typhus, as well as general industrial decline, all conspired to place Nerja on a downward trajectory. Thousands of *nerjeños* emigrated to South America in search of a better life.

The uprising of the Francoist Army took place in North Africa, and across the Alborán sea in Málaga, as the people steeled themselves for what would come next, it is said that in Nerja they could 'smell the fear'. With the entry of Francoist troops into Málaga on 8 February 1937, a stream of *malagueños* sought to escape the city, taking the road to Almería. Nerja stands on that road and suffered aerial bombardment (one of the bombs fell in the Plaza de la Ermita, causing devastating loss of life). Because their own forces abandoned them in their own attempts to flee the coming danger, the *nerjeños* were left exposed and many were killed over the following weeks.

The years after the Civil War were very hard, but progress would come from an unexpected source. For centuries, the people of Nerja had made their living from what they could grow: silk, grapes, sugar cane, fruit and so forth. Their wealth came from the ground. In the 1950s, the caves of Nerja were discovered and they opened to the public in 1960. Once again, the ground (or underground) would provide a living for the locals. Nerja has beaches of course, but these were not what initially attracted tourists. Visitors first came to see the caves.

Nerja was therefore the location of a slightly different form of tourism. Lacking the miles of uninterrupted beach boasted by Torremolinos or Marbella, Nerja has not turned into a 'concrete cliff' of all-inclusive hotels full of package holidaymakers. Instead, it has attracted generally older visitors (overwhelmingly from the UK) who have come for extended periods, often in the winter and, in many cases, purchasing property locally.

Nerja Today

The town is built on a hillside with not too steep a gradient and the sprawling centre itself consists of an older neighbourhood with streets of whitewashed houses partly pedestrianized (mainly to the east of the Balcón de Europa: the natural focus of the town and the venue for *fiestas*). Beyond the 17th-century church and the Plaza Cavana, more modern development takes over.

Walking is the easiest way to get around. The centre of Nerja is small enough to explore on foot, though you will find yourself walking up or down a sometimes gradual, sometimes steep hill much of the time. As the town has no specific centre, shops, banks, bars, and eateries are scattered throughout.

The Balcón de Europa (Balcony of Europe) is a recently reconstructed promenade built atop a natural headland south of the town centre with spectacular views along the coast. Originally constructed around 1487 on the site of a former 9th-century castle, the Balcón today is the main focus for the town, with a tree-lined promenade surrounded by cafés and ice cream shops, frequented by street performers and the location of occasional concerts. It was named by King Alfonso XII who visited the town after the earthquake of 1884. Granted, for all the attention tourist guides give to this place there's not much to do except look up and down the coast, but the views are impressive. Beneath the viewpoint itself, a glass-walled restaurant (Restaurante Rey Alfonso) offers the chance to eat in a sit-down setting while taking in the scenery.

Cuevas De Nerja

🌐 Ⓐ cuevadenerja.es 🕐 ☀ 0930–1630 🕐 ☀ 0930–1900 €€€
(🎟 Under 5 years old) 🌐 ✅ entradas.cuevadenerja.es

The main reason to make a day trip from Málaga is to visit the Caves of Nerja. The caves are not a suitable place if you have mobility problems as there are 458 steps to go up and down. There are no ramps. Flash photography is not allowed inside the caves. The admission price is good value for such a spectacular attraction.

The Caves of Nerja, just south of the Sierras de Tejeda, Almijara and Alhama Natural Park, stretch for almost 5 kilometres, and are one of Spain's major tourist attractions. Concerts are regularly held in one of the chambers, which forms a natural amphitheatre. The caves were re-discovered on 12 January 1959 by five friends who entered through a narrow sinkhole known as 'La Mina'. This is one of the two natural entrances to the cave system. A third entrance was created in 1960 to allow easy access for tourists. The cave is divided into two main parts known as Nerja I and Nerja II. Nerja I includes the Show Galleries open to the public, with relatively easy access via a flight of stairs and concreted pathways to allow tourists to move about in the cavern without difficulty. Nerja II, which is not yet open to the public, comprises the Upper Gallery discovered in 1960 and the New Gallery discovered in 1969.

In February 2012 Neanderthal cave paintings were discovered. Looking oddly like DNA double helices, the images in fact depict the seals that locals would have eaten. According to José Luis Sanchidrián of the University of Córdoba, they have 'no parallel in Palaeolithic art'. His team say that charcoal remains found beside six of the paintings have been radiocarbon dated to between 42,300 and 43,500 years old. This suggests that the paintings are substantially older than the 30,000-year-old Chauvet cave paintings in south-eastern France, previously thought to be the earliest example of Palaeolithic cave art.

You can take a bus from Málaga (from the Bus Station, or Muelle Heredia in Soho) to Nerja which takes around 1hr 30m. Head off in the morning, see the caves and then take a bus back into Nerja (see below) to have lunch and see the (modest) sights, before catching your bus back into Málaga.

Also, look out for **El Puente de Aguila** (Eagle's Bridge) — a 19th-century aqueduct. It was designed to bring water to the nearby village of Maro, one of the oldest settlements in the area and it is visible on the way to the caves if you keep your eyes peeled. The **El Salvador Church**, near the Balcón de Europa, facing the plaza just around the corner from the Balcón is an attractive 17th Century church constructed in baroque *mudéjar* style. **Nuestra Señora de las Angustias** Hermitage is a 16th Century church with paintings by Alonso Cano.

Nerja has thirteen kilometres of beaches, some of which are public and some of which are private and for patrons of certain hotels only.

If you want to make a day of it and are feeling energetic, pick up the free Nerja walks guide in the Tourist Information office near the Balcón de Europa. The book details a wide variety of walks in the area, with maps and directions for where to walk, as well as interesting facts about the places you pass en route.

Getting to and from Nerja

The bus company ALSA (⊕ alsa.com) operates a regular service between Málaga and Nerja. The service from Málaga to Maro will drop you at the Caves (search for **'Nerja (Cuevas)'** as the destination). This will enable you to book a timed entrance ticket for the caves online: ⊕ entradas.cuevadenerja.es. The Caves open at 0930 with the last entry at 1530 (1800 in the Summer). Most people take about an hour to tour the cave. To return to Nerja city centre, the times of ALSA buses are liable to change seasonally, so use the ALSA website to plan your return journey carefully. Do not rely on 'Nerja Information' websites — those I checked **all** displayed out-of-date information. You can buy a ticket between Nerja (Cuevas) and Nerja on the bus and the journey takes about 10 minutes. The ALSA bus will drop you at the Nerja **Estación de Autobuses** (basically a handful of bus shelters with a sporadically open ticket kiosk). From here, it's a short walk into the main part of the old town. The Balcón de Europa is 1 km to the south.

Another option to return to the city centre from the Caves is to pre-book or call a taxi. A number of taxis have their contact numbers on display outside the ticket office, but a large and reliable taxi firm is Nerja Taxi 📞 +34 952 520 537. The taxi drivers in Nerja all speak good English due to the large number of British people (and English-speaking Germans) who live and holiday in the area.

🚂 The Tourist Train (*Cuevatren*)

This is a fun option if you are visiting the caves with children. Up-to-date timetable information can be found on this page: ⊕ cuevadenerja.es/tren-a-la-cueva-de-nerja (in *castellano* with occasional sentences in English). The train takes 30 minutes from Nerja to the Caves. The stop in Nerja is in the **Plaza de Los Cangrejos** (marked on the companion Google map). You can book a combined caves/train ticket on the website of the Caves. Reading the timetable can seem a little confusing at first, but it is simple once you get the hang of it.

Horario I (Timetable I) is the basic annual timetable that operates every day of the year except 1 January and 15 May (the day of Nerja's Fiesta of San Isidro): leaving Nerja Town at 1000/1100/1200/1003/1400/1500, and leaving the Caves at 1030/1130/1230/1330/1430 and 1630.

Horario II is the timetable for Christmas and holiday long weekends ('*puentes*').

Horario III is the timetable for Holy Week and for Summer (23 July to 11 September). During these periods trains run on the hour and half hour and continue until evening (the final train from the Caves leaves at 1900) to match the later opening times of the Caves.

To avoid confusion, just book your tickets to the Caves and the '*cuevatren*' together and the website will only offer you the train times that are actually available.

✕ Eating and Drinking

There are plenty of places to eat and drink in Nerja, including lots of Italian, Indian, Chinese and 'British' restaurants preferred by many non-Spanish visitors and residents. It is worth seeking out authentic Spanish places that make the most of local and fresh ingredients (especially fish and seafood). The following list includes the two best restaurants in Nerja (booking necessary), and a few more to get you started.

✕🍴🍽⊙☷ **Restaurante El Puente** (⊙ Calle Carretera 4) A little outside the 'historic' centre, this friendly *restaurante* offers an excellent, good value weekday *menú del día*.

✗ ✤ ⌐ **El Niño** (◉ Calle Almirante Ferrandiz 83) Spanish cuisine that is very popular with the locals

✗ ✤ ◔ ⌐ ✦ ᵛᵛ **El Pulguilla** (◉ Calle Almirante Ferrandiz 26) Amidst the bustle of shops and restaurants is this typical Spanish *marisquería* (fish and shellfish restaurant), and a place that sums up Nerja. The clientèle is usually at least 90% Spanish with the occasional adventurous holidaymaker. The drinks are cheap, the *tapas* are free (or were when I last visited) and the seafood is excellent. There is a large open-air terrace in operation during the summer.

✗ ✤ ◔ ⌐ ✦ ᵛᵛ **Marisquería La Marina** (◉ Plaza la Marina, Calle Castilla Pérez) Located on a small square in the west of town, this informal seafood *tapas* bar has a few tables inside and plenty more outside. The drinks are cheap, the language is Spanish and each drink at the bar comes with a *tapa* of seafood salad or a few *gambas*. It usually works, as you will inevitably be tempted to enjoy more fresh shellfish and seafood at a table outside. The service is a little brusque and hectic in summer, but the prices are very reasonable

✗ ⫙ ✤ ◔ ⌐ ⊕ ⊛ ✦ ♊ **Meson José y Victoria** (◉ Calle Málaga s/n) Excellent, fresh, home-cooked to order Spanish cuisine. Prepared by José and served by Victoria. Reasonably priced, great-tasting food. Try the *caldo de pescado* (fish stew), which is excellent.

❊ ✦ ᵛᵛ **Chiringuitos** (◉ Burriana Beach) There are a few *chiringuitos/merenderos* along the Burriana beach. There are all pretty good, so see which one has a free table.

✗ ⬦ ⌑ ⬱ ⌐ ⊕ ♊ **Restaurante Oliva** (◉ Plaza de España 2 ⊕ restauranteoliva.com) This is undoubtedly one of the best places to eat in Nerja (going head-to-head with Sollun for the honour). It has a great modern menu based on top-quality products from the area. The eight-course tasting menu, which takes around 2 hours, is excellent value, as is the wine pairing. Booking is essential.

✗ ⬱ ⌐ ⊕ **Mesón Patanegra** (◉ Plaza la Marina) Excellent Spanish cuisine, good *tapas* and a wine list from cheap and cheerful, through good value to expensive tastes.

✗ ⫙ ◔ ⬱ ⌐ ⬧ ✦ ᵛᵛ ⛩ **La Posada Ibérica** (◉ Calle Nueva) offers some of the best (and best value) food in Nerja. Run by an Argentinian couple who have maintained the Spanish flavour, this place is one of the most traditional you can find in Nerja. They occasionally have live music over the weekend (mainly evenings).

✗ ◔ ⬱ ⌐ ⊕ **Restaurante 34** (◉ Calle Hernando de Carabeo 34) International cuisine. Upmarket, and prices reflect this. If you want to eat something '*haute*' then I would recommend Oliva or Sollun, which although slightly more expensive, are somewhat superior when it comes to the execution of their dishes.

✗ ⬦ ⌑ ⬱ ⌐ **Sollun Restaurant** (◉ Calle Pintada 9 ⊕ sollunrestaurant.com) One of the newer restaurants in Nerja, but one of the best. The Chef, Juan Quintanilla, was previously owner of a Michelin-starred restaurant in Marbella. Great food and excellent wine. Like Oliva, there is an *à la carte* menu as well as a tasting menu.

All of these restaurants are shown on the companion Google map. Select the '**EAST OF MÁLAGA**' layer in order to see them.

Frigiliana

🌐 turismofrigiliana.es/en ❶ Calle Cuesta del Apero 10 🕐 ♣ Mon—Fri 1000–1800; Sat–Sun 1000–1400; Sat 1600–2000 🕐 ☀ Mon–Sat 1000–1430, 1730–2100; Sun 1000–1430 ✉ oficinadeturismo@frigiliana.es

The *pueblo blanco* (white village) of Frigiliana is included as a post-script to Nerja because it's a 15-minute bus ride north. However, if you want to make a day trip, you will probably have to choose between Nerja and Frigiliana. To see both (including the Nerja Caves) comfortably would ideally mean staying overnight (though outside high season, it is usually possible to find a cheap but comfortable room in either Nerja or Frigiliana). An alternative, for the committed traveller, would be to take an early bus to the Caves of Nerja in the morning (*e.g.* 8.30 am, arriving at 10.15 am) to see the Caves at 10.30 am. You could return to Nerja on the 11.45 am ALSA bus. Then take the 12.10 am bus to Frigiliana (it leaves from the bus 'station'). Bus times between Nerja and Frigiliana can be found here: 🌐 grupofajardo.es/horarios/frigiliana-nerja

The disadvantage of this plan is that you will arrive in Frigiliana just as the churches are closing, so you won't be able to include them in your sightseeing. However, if you are visiting during the Summer season (23 June to 11 September), when the Caves stay open later, then you could go to Frigiliana first. Either way, although fitting in both places using public transport is possible, it is going to involve five or six separate bus journeys and a good deal of clock watching. Of course, if the caves don't appeal, then I would suggest you catch a bus up to Frigiliana when you get to Nerja. Have a look around Frigiliana in the late morning, then come back to explore a bit of Nerja (the old centre is small). You could have lunch in either town.

There are a couple of taxi firms (by which I mean a couple of taxis) operating in Frigiliana: Taxi Frigiliana 📞 +34 696 969 469 and Frigiliana Taxi 📞 +34 625 288 811

Accessibility

It is worth saying at this point that Frigiliana, as a mountain *pueblo blanco* is hilly. Very hilly. It is the sort of place you will want to explore slowly, but walking more than a couple of hundred metres is going to involve walking uphill and downhill on some quite steep inclines and declines. Because many of the streets are stepped, wheelchair users will find quite limited routes open to them and it is unlikely to suit those with mobility issues. In recent years a rickshaw ('tuk-tuk') service has been operated by local man Raúl Hernández. Raúl is disabled himself and he began his business with the intention of allowing people with limited mobility to enjoy his town. He offers a 25-minute tour, leaving from near the bus stop. If you want to discuss your own needs and/or book ahead: 📞 +34 620 931 150 ✉ tuktukfrigiliana@gmail.com There is also a tourist 'train' that takes you around the lower portion of the town which might appeal to families with children. Enquire by phone (📞 +34 647 630 771), or wait near **El Ingenio** (marked on the companion Google map).

⧗ History

The German artist Klaus Hinkel recounts that, after having a coffee in the Jaime Bar and as he was walking up Calle Amargura, he realized that Frigiliana, a town he was visiting for the first time, was going to be his home forever. The year was 1995 and he had spent six months touring Andalucía, visiting Vejer de la Frontera, Marbella, Ronda and Casares. It was in Frigiliana, however, where everything fell into place: 'There was a quiet town and a house in ruins for sale to remodel for myself'. Today Klaus, a former pilot, has a workshop in what is often called 'the most beautiful town in Málaga' and makes his living as a watercolour artist.

Frigiliana is a small town of just over 3,000 inhabitants, perched on a rocky outcrop of the Sierra de Almijara. Its name probably comes from Roman times, since it is assumed that the word Frigiliana comes from 'Frexinius' (a personal name) and the suffix '-ana' (i.e. the villa or place of Frexinius). However, Phoenician coins have been discovered, so the settlement apparently predates the Romans.

After 711 AD, the Arabs transformed agriculture by constructing a hydraulic system of ditches and pools, some of which are still in use, and introducing new crops such as sugar cane. At the end of the 9th century, the Arab castle was built, occupying an area of about 4,000 square metres. Known during the Moorish occupation as 'Fixiana', it belonged to the Nasrid kingdom of Granada, and its economy was based on the production of oil, raisins, figs, stone fruit, sugar cane, and silk (which explains the remnants of mulberry orchards). As an isolated place, Muslims and Christians, together with a handful of Jews lived in Frigiliana for almost a century after the fall of Granada. Whether they did so happily is hard to say, just as we don't know whether the putative 'Muslims' and 'Jews' practised their religions openly, or whether they were ostensibly *moriscos* and *conversos*. The citadel was destroyed by Christian armies in 1569 after its surrender to the troops of Luis de Requesens, sent to quell one of the last Moorish uprisings in Spain. Now the story of Frigiliana's spirit of *convivencia* is much celebrated and proudly commemorated in a fountain inscribed with three symbols: the cross, the crescent and the star of David, on the Calle del Inquisidor. The fact that the fountain was only erected in 1996, plus the existence of an 'Inquisitor Street' suggests a somewhat precarious coexistence between the three faiths, rather than a multicultural flourishing.

At the end of the 16th century, the *malagueña* Manrique de Lara family, which had held the *señorío* (Lordship) of Frigiliana since 1508, built the manor house known today as the Ingenio or Casa de los Condes. This Renaissance-style building was built, in part, with materials from the Arab castle. Currently, this enormous mansion is used for the manufacture of the only '*miel de caña*' (molasses or 'cane honey') produced in Europe. The family also built the nearby Palacio del Apero, which now houses the Tourist Office, Museum and Municipal Library. On 24 May 1640, by royal decree of Felipe IV, Frigiliana was granted the title of *Villa*, thus becoming independent from the jurisdiction of Vélez-Málaga. It then numbered 160 inhabitants.

Frigiliana put up a spirited defence in the wars with the French of 1810–1812 and was punished severely by French troops who accused the townspeople of killing some of their soldiers. The end of the 19th century saw various upheavals, such as the bandit parties that sowed terror in Frigiliana and, above all, the appearance of phylloxera that devastated the vineyards and led to ruin for many families. Sugar cane survived, and the dawn of the 20th century brought the first signs of 'modern' progress to Frigiliana when power lines were connected to the municipal grid, and the first public street lighting was inaugurated with a total budget of 950 pesetas. But the constant of these first years of the last century was the economic crisis that followed on from the political instability of the previous century. Frigiliana experienced desperate poverty and there were frequent demonstrations of workers at the gates of the *Ayuntamiento* demanding 'bread and work'.

There were serious earthquakes in 1921, 1922 and 1924, followed by a devastating hurricane in 1928 that destroyed everything in its path. Mercifully, it only caused one death, but many more were injured and the destruction in the fields was almost total. Later that year, the De la Torre company acquired the San Raimundo Sugar Mill and Palace of the Counts of Frigiliana, to establish the Virgen del Carmen Sugar Mill, bringing a little hope to the village. The next decade was tumultuous for Spain as a whole, and well into the 1950s, Frigiliana remained a poor and (economically) backward village, with only one industry to speak of (sugar cane honey). Everyone else scraped a living on smallholdings augmented by seasonal agricultural labour or chased a tiny pool of public sector jobs.

Frigiliana Today

By the 1960s, however, Frigiliana was winning prizes in competitions showcasing 'Improvement and Beautification'. It is regularly spoken of as the 'most beautiful *pueblo blanco*' in Andalucía, and nowadays the atmosphere is one of prosperous gentility, rather than grinding subsistence. What changed, of course, was the arrival of 'incomers' — both seasonal tourists and those (like Herr Hinkel) who came to live in the town. Highbrow Hispanophile aesthetes who hanker after the 'unspoilt' Spain of Federico García Lorca or Laurie Lee can be very sniffy about places like Frigiliana, complaining that its orderly narrow streets, brilliant white houses and beautiful floral displays are somehow 'too perfect'. They are, they suggest, like the dressing of a film set, rather than a living town filled with 'real' inhabitants. They point out, too, that a significant proportion of residents are not from Frigiliana, or even from Spain. This is an odd criticism. I wonder if they would dare suggest that towns in the UK where immigrant communities have brought new life, new cuisine and different cultures have thereby been 'spoiled'?

Had incomers (many of whom are Spaniards) not bought property in Frigiliana, and if busloads of day-trippers off the cruises berthing in Málaga did not visit, I wonder what its fate would be today? Pretty much a ghost town, I imagine, hanging on by the skin of its teeth. There are many deserted villages in Spain, no longer viable since the young people moved to Málaga, Madrid, or Munich. The press regularly runs stories where an entire village numbering dozens of houses, a church and the remains of a medieval castle has gone on the market for less than the price of a semi-detached house in the South of England. Also, to be clear, the influx of foreigners to Frigiliana has not transformed it into wall-to-wall Full English Breakfast cafés, themed pubs and fish and chip shops. Those that have come clearly want to live somewhere more 'Spanish' than, say, Torremolinos. And even if it is part Spanish village and part living exhibition, it is still undeniably beautiful, and well worth visiting. So let's take a look around...

When you arrive on the bus, you will disembark onto an open square that is pretty much the northern extent of the road usable by motor vehicles. Here you will see the white and elongated profile of the *Nuestra Señora del Carmen* sugar cane honey factory, the only one in Europe (🌐 mieldelatorre.com). It is a reminder of the time when the Province of Málaga was a significant producer of sugar cane (now largely supplanted by mangoes and avocados), with thousands of hectares that extended to the urban area itself. The mill, near the **Plaza de las Tres Culturas**, is the beginning of the historic centre. The factory does not have opening/visiting hours, but it is theoretically possible to arrange a visit to see how the molasses is made. The email address is ✉ info@mieldelatorre.com or you can use the contact form on the website. There is a small handicrafts shop in the same building and, around the corner, a bar. Before you set off, call into the *turismo*, which is just behind you on the **Cuesta del Apero** to pick up a map. The *turismo* is also happy to respond to specific queries in advance of your visit if you contact them by email.

The streets of Frigiliana can be explored by electric rickshaw (see above), but if you are able, it is worth doing on foot. The attraction here is not so much a collection of churches, museums and 'sights', but the village itself. But be warned: the town is full of slopes, almost always with steps, so you need to watch where you're going. Once upon a time, the streets were all steep inclines, but once Frigiliana began to benefit from some inward investment, the residents decided that they preferred stepped streets as they were easier for the infirm to traverse.

If you would like to follow a guided tour, then you could not be in better hands than those of María José Caravaca who, in addition to being a local councillor looking after the tourism brief, is also the proprietor of **Frigiliana Tours** ⊕ frigilianatours.com/en. Walking tours lasting 1½ hours are conducted daily in English and Spanish. Booking (via the website) is advised. Children under 12 go free and the price for adults is a bargain (you can show your appreciation by giving María a generous tip).

As you walk up into the old town, on your left is the bar **Vinos El Lagar** (⦿ Calle Real 1) where the owner Adrián Ruiz offers sweet Málaga wines from the barrel. Your reasonably priced glass of wine can be accompanied by a *tapa* based on cold cuts, cheese and local products. Adrián is not a winemaker, but he sources his wines direct from the producers and they are bottled under his own label. Just past El Lagar is a series of brick arches. These are all that remain of the **Reales Pósitos** (Royal Granaries), an old silo built in 1767 where surplus grain was stored in good harvest years to be distributed in times of shortage. Although a granary is mentioned in 1749, it is most likely that the first was established in 1640, the year in which Frigiliana became an independent town.

In the **Barribarto** (a typically *andaluz* rendering of '*barrio alto*'), that is to say, the upper neighbourhood, thousands of clay pots decorate the façades of low, whitewashed houses with colourful wooden doors. This older part of town is also variously called *Barribarto*, the '*Casco Antiguo*' or the '*Barrio Morisco Mudéjar*'. Continuing along the Calle Real, is **El Colmao 'Wine and Experiences'** (⦿ Calle Real 32 ⊕ elcolmaowineandexperiences.com/en). This wine bar specializes in wines from the Axarquía region and has a long list of wines available by the glass. If you want the full experience, then a 5-course tasting menu with 5 wines is available (pre-booking is essential, via the website). They also offer tours of wineries (and raisin vineyards) in the Axarquía and Ronda wine areas. These are not cheap, but given that you get a tour of a couple of wineries (or a winery and a raisin vineyard) with an experienced sommelier guide, including tastings with *tapas*, lunch at a restaurant and transport from Frigiliana, Nerja or even Málaga city, they are pretty good value. Consult the 'Enoturismo' section (p. 481ff.) for general advice about visiting Málaga wineries.

A step away from the restaurant **El Adarve** (⦿ Calle Alta 3), with its exquisite aubergines drizzled with local cane honey and wonderful grilled and roasted meats, is the workshop of the aforementioned Klaus Hinkel, whose watercolours recreate the most beautiful scenes of the town. He reviewed his life and work in Frigiliana in a book he published at the end of 2021: *Ideas, arte e inspiración*, and proudly applauds how the tourist economy has given some stability to the remaining population and improved the quality of life of locals, but he also notes that the tranquillity has disappeared from the streets. He will stay, he says, but in recent decades, writers and artists who sought a creative hideaway have abandoned the place in response to increased tourism. To misquote Mallet du Pan, this sounds rather like a case of the 'revolution devouring its children'.

The church of **San Antonio de Padua** (♀ Calle Real 100), from the 17th century, has a newly recently restored façade, and next to it is the **Calle Garral**, which is especially picturesque. A small passageway reaches the (fountain) **Fuente de las Tres Culturas** (♀ Callejon de las Animas 12), the same name as the festival held here every summer to celebrate the quasi-mythical, albeit longed for, *convivencia* of Jews, Christians and Muslims. There is a surprise nearby: **La Domadora y el León** (♀ Calle Rosarico la Joaquín 26), a rather cavernous place established by Charo Barco and Javier León, who arrived in Frigiliana in 2013, also in search of a better life. They have established their own craft beer, La Axarca, but also promote another 300 brands. As Charo explains, 'We want it to be a meeting point: in addition to beers, there are exhibitions, book presentations and other proposals'. Back on Calle Real, Ana Ortiz's art gallery and antique shop **Almagra** (Calle Real 89) is a delight to get lost in.

There are plenty of places to eat and drink in Frigiliana. Prices are slightly cheaper in the Casco Nuevo (the new expansion down the hill), and you are more likely to find *menús del día* there, but a reliable bar that offers a good value set lunch menu in the old town is **El Picoteo** (♀ Calle de San Sebastián 4). If you are looking for a set menu lunch, then keep your eyes peeled for blackboards advertising a '*Menú del día*' (or sometimes just a '*Menú*'). There hasn't been a legal requirement for restaurants to offer a set lunch since 2010, and nowadays they seem to come and go on a seasonal, or even daily basis.

Other eateries (and hostelries) worth mentioning include **Punto de Encuentro** (♀ Calle Real 42) a popular bar that does a good trade in tasty (*campero*-style) sandwiches. The **Asador La Viña Nueva** (♀ Avenida Carlos Cano 4) is, as the name suggests, a traditional '*asador*' (restaurant specializing in roast meat). Many of the dishes are grilled at your table on a portable hot plate. Some dishes are quite pricey but reflect the cost of the high-quality ingredients, like fore-quarter of suckling pig. But the quality of the cooking and the generosity of the portions make this, overall, a reasonably priced option. Unusually, for a Spanish restaurant, it serves excellent homemade puddings, including a fabulous banoffee pie. **El Boquetillo Street Food** (♀ Calle de San Sebastián 8) is run by 'incomers' and burgers feature prominently on the menu. However, the quality is good and everything is home-cooked. They also have a lunchtime offer; not a *menú* exactly, but a main course plus drink. The nearby aforementioned **El Picoteo** (♀ Calle de San Sebastián 4) is authentically Spanish and serves consistently good food. **Bar la Alegría del Barrio** (♀ Calle del Chorruelo 16) is a homely, family-run bar/restaurant that is much loved by its patrons. The food is hearty, well-cooked, and keenly priced. If you would prefer to visit a café rather than a bar or restaurant, then **Cafetería Almijara** (♀ Calle Real 3) is a great option, serving a good selection of reasonably priced and freshly made sandwiches and *tostadas* as well as cakes and ice cream. Like all Spanish cafés, they also serve alcohol.

There are also a number of genuinely artisanal shops/workshops in Frigiliana (we have already encountered Herr Hinkel). One of the loveliest is **El Rincón del Esparto** (♀ Calle Conde don Iñigo 5A), owned by Lourdes Bueno, one of the foremost *esparto* artisans in Spain. *Esparto* is a coarse grass which grows in Spain and North Africa which, for at least 7,000 years has been used to weave rope, baskets, floor mats and, of course, the soles of *alpargatas* (aka espadrilles). Lourdes makes traditional baskets and household items, as well as lampshades, toys and decorative items like Christmas decorations and naïve animal heads. She has also done commissioned work for the decoration of various businesses, among them, the restaurants of the Michelin-starred chef, Dani García.

Vinos Lola y Pepe Angel (♀ Calle Real 6) is Frigiliana's main *ultramarinos* (delicatessen), stocking mainly wine, but also cane honey, bee honey, sweets, conserves, dried fruit, etc. Almost everything on sale is typical of Frigiliana or the surrounding villages. **Manos – Taller Artesanía de Cuero** (◉ Calle Real 30) produces handmade leather items, including bags, diaries, wallets and belts, among many other lines. There are many other specialist and craft shops/workshops — almost all of them on the Calle Real.

Other sites worth visiting include the **Jardín Botánico Santa Fiora** (◉ Avenida Carlos Cano/Below the Calle Real) — a small and, in its ambitions, very modest garden. Unlike, say, the Jardín Botánico–Histórico La Concepción of Málaga, the intention is not to amass a collection of exotic plants from around the world, but rather to create a more humble collection of the trees and plants that have contributed to the history of Frigiliana: grasses (used for weaving), sugar cane, palms, olive trees, mulberry trees, and traditional medicinal and culinary herbs like thyme, rosemary, oregano and rue.

The **Museo Arqueológico** (◉ Casa del Apero) is very small, having only 125 permanent exhibits, but it is beautifully curated and has information displayed in English. It charts the history of Frigiliana from 5000 BC until the 16th century. It is free to visit and keeps the same opening hours as the turismo.

🚶 Walking: Nerja and Frigiliana

There are fabulous walking routes throughout the Province of Málaga thanks to the large number of National Parks and Protected Natural Areas. Nerja makes an ideal starting point for walks because of the frequent buses to and from Málaga that run from the early morning until the very late evening. If you're a serious walker then useful guidebooks to the area are: *The Mountains of Nerja: Sierras Tejeda, Almijara Y Alhama* by Jim Ryan (⊕ amzn.to/3ojJSOw), and *Walking in Andalucia: 36 routes in Andalucia's Natural Parks* by Guy Hunter–Watts (⊕ amzn.to/403TQks), both in the Cicerone Walking Guides series. Another excellent guide is *Walk! Costa del Sol* by Charles Davis (⊕ amzn.to/41bi8dy) and the companion map (⊕ amzn.to/3MFGOGQ). You can also search for departure points (Nerja, Frigiliana, etc.) on walking route sites like **komoot**, **alltrails**, **wikloc**, etc. Steve planned his own walking holiday in the Province of Málaga and has blogged about it at 'Untravelled World' ⊕ bit.ly/UTW_Axarquia.

If you're an experienced hiker, then planning your own route is probably half the fun, but for most of us, joining a planned walk with an experienced guide is a much more attractive proposition. It is also a far more sensible option for single travellers.

John Keogh ⊕ hikingwalkingspain.com ⊙ +34 647 273 502
✉ john@hikingwalkingspain.com

John is a registered walking guide based in Nerja. He organizes short/easy (3-hour), moderate (5-hour) and serious/hard (7-hour or more) hikes in the Axarquía region. His prices are extremely reasonable and almost all hikes include lunch or dinner. Most important of all, however, is that all walks include transport from a meeting point in Nerja.

Torrox and Rincón de la Victoria

⊕ turismotorrox.es ❶ Avenida de Competa ⏲ Mon–Fri 1030–1430, 1600–2000

A few miles west of Nerja, Torrox Pueblo is also a *pueblo blanco*, and a beautiful place to visit, though it is not quite as tourism-savvy as Frigiliana. Its origins are Phoenician, it has some interesting buildings and, like every small town in Spain, some lovely bars and restaurants. In the foothills of the Sierra de Almijara, it shouldn't be confused with the larger settlement to the south: Torrox (Costa). The latter is a modern seaside resort and is to Germans what Torremolinos is to Brits. There are (infrequent) buses operated by ALSA between Málaga and Torrox Pueblo (a journey of about 1hr 25m), but if the transport timings fit, Torrox makes a very pleasant day trip (and wouldn't mean two buses like the *pueblos blancos* of Frigiliana or Mijas Pueblo). The Torrox *turismo* website is rather old-fashioned but has plenty of useful information. Another very useful resource is David Baird's 'Málaga East' website: ⊕ bit.ly/MalagaEast. David is an author and former foreign correspondent who has lived in the Province of Málaga for many years and writes extensively and knowledgeably about the region. It's well worth checking his website for information about other villages, including Nerja and Frigiliana.

 ⊕ turismoenrincon.es ❶ Avenida del Mediterráneo 140 (Antigua Estación de Ferrocarril, Paseo Marítimo Virgen del Carmen)

Rincón de la Victoria ('Corner of Our Lady of the Victory') is part of the greater Málaga conurbation. It's the most prosperous municipality in the Málaga metropolitan area and is a commuter town with few foreign tourists. It has a couple of museums and spaces which host regular exhibitions, and a large centre displaying the Roman remains of the 3rd century AD **Villa Antiopa** has recently opened to visitors (at the eastern end of the seafront). The town is the home of **Molino de Aceite de Benagalbón** producing high-quality cold pressed oil from local Verdial and Lechín olives. It also has two cave complexes — the **Cueva del Higuerón** (or del Tesoro) and the **Cueva de la Victoria**. The name of the Cueva del Tesoro comes from a legend about the last Almoravid king who supposedly shipped treasure to Andalucía shortly before his assassination (though no record of the story can be found before the late 18th c.). The Cueva de la Victoria is located within the Archaeological Park and also contains cave paintings dating from the Middle Palaeolithic period. There are at least five other caves yet to be properly explored. Neither cave is on the scale of those in Nerja, but both can be visited and are less than 30 minutes from Málaga. One can book tickets to both caves, and the Villa Antiopa, via the *turismo* website.

Rincón de la Victoria has four beautiful beaches and a number of excellent *chiringuitos*. The calm, clear waters and good facilities (in season) mean that the beaches are popular among local families. *Rinconero* bars and restaurants are of high quality, reflecting the rather prosperous complexion of the town. As luck would have it, many of the best value eateries are in the vicinity of the Tourist Information Office, both on the seafront and the two or three streets behind. There are lots of buses (operated by ALSA, Avanza and Valle Niza on behalf of the Provincial Transport Consortium) that leave Málaga from the main bus station or the Muelle de Heredia (the bus stand south of the Soho *barrio*). Use the Moovit app to plan your journey. There are also local buses run by a company called Rinconbus, which is handy for getting up the hill to the caves. The local bus is green and therefore affectionately known by local children as '*el moco*' (the bogey).

Again thanks to the prosperity of its residents, Rincón de la Victoria is a good place to search for souvenirs. There are a number of good wine shops, including **Licorería Antonio Muñoz Cabrera** (❾ Calle Frigiliana 8). They stock a good selection of local wines and have a small delicatessen section. If you have your own bottle or wineskin, they will fill it directly from the barrel (out of a selection of nine varieties made by the *bodega* of the same name located in Moclinejo). **Cerámica Gallo Negro** (❾ Avenida de la Torre 90) is a beautiful little shop selling local pottery, the perfect place to buy an interesting gift for someone (or for yourself).

North of Málaga
Álora and Other Pueblos Blancos

The *pueblo blanco* of Álora is 40 km from Málaga and the end of the 🔵 C-2 *Cercanías* railway line, making it an easy day trip destination. Before we look more closely at Álora, however, let's take a brief look at some of the other 'white villages' in the Valle del Guadalhorce (Guadalhorce Valley).

Casabermeja

🌐 casabermejaturismo.es ❶ Calle Llanete de Abajo 2 🕐 Daily 1000–1415

Casabermeja is a journey of 30–40 minutes from Málaga by bus, running frequently throughout the day, Monday to Friday. Buses also run at weekends but on a much more restricted service. You can consult the timetables here: 🌐 riosautocares.com/en/routes but pay very close attention to which days the services run on! A one-way ticket is cheap and you can purchase it from the driver when you depart Málaga bus station.

The appeal of Casabermeja is simple: it is an easily accessible *pueblo blanco* away from the bustle of Málaga. Like other villages of its kind, there isn't a huge amount to see in terms of 'attractions', but the village itself is beautiful and the journey will take you high up into the Montes de Málaga. Before the highway was completed in 1973, Casabermeja was isolated and very poor. There is an attractive church, the **Iglesia Nuestra Señora del Socorro (Our Lady of Help** 🕐 1100–1300 Monday to Saturday). Strange as it may seem, one of the reasons that people visit Casabermeja is to see its cemetery, **El Cementerio Municipal San Sebastián** (🕐 1000–1800 daily). The playwright Antonio Gala has called it 'the most magnificent necropolis [he] had ever seen', and 'necropolis' is a fitting term as it consists of a number of carefully laid out 'streets' of burial niches, pantheons and memorial pinnacles clinging to the side of the hill. It is a peaceful and surprisingly beautiful place.

Casabermeja is also known for its gastronomy. *Porra de habas*, a chilled soup made from broad beans originated here and the village is famous for its goat products. In mid-September, they hold a *Fiesta de Cabra* (Goat Festival) which runs over a weekend and involves dozens of family and child-friendly activities: feeding goats, goat meat and cheese tastings, goat's milk cheese making, tallow candle making, livestock shows and performances by *verdiales pandas*. The **Casa de la Cabra** is the headquarters of the Málaga Goat Breeders' Association and they run activities almost every weekend of the year: cabrama.com (though most take place at weekends, so take care planning transport).

As you would expect, the bars and restaurants in Casabermeja serve high-quality food and the town hall's *turismo* site 🌐 bit.ly/CasabermejaEat has a helpful listing of establishments. My own recommendation for lunch would be the charmingly friendly and family-run **Casa Caña** (📍Calle Real 27 🕐 Mon–Sat 0700–1800) which, in addition to serving fabulous '*comida casera*' (home-cooked food), offers a fantastic *menú del día* at an unbeatable price. It's almost worth the fare to Casabermeja just to enjoy this lovely restaurant.

Cártama

🌐 **cartama.es** (translation link at the top of the web page) ℹ️ Calle Rey Juan Carlos I 62 🕐 Mon–Fri 0800–1500

When you consult the timetable of the *Cercanías* Ⓒ C-2 line, you will see that there is a stop in Cártama. However, this is Cártama **Estación**. The prettier village, with the *turismo*, the museum, the churches and the lovely old bars and restaurants is Cártama **Pueblo**, some distance away up the hill. Therefore, if you want to visit Cártama, you would be better off taking the bus (🚌M-131) from either Ⓑ **Muelle Heredia** (Puerto) or Ⓑ **Vialia** (opposite the railway station front entrance): 🌐 **ctmam.es/lineas/M-131**

Cártama is a pleasant little town, although beyond the interesting **archaeological museum** and the **church of San Pedro** (with attached museum), there is not a great deal to occupy the visitor. The **Hermitage of Our Lady of Remedies** and the **Castle** are quite a steep climb up the hill: great if you like walking but not so great if you are looking for a gentle stroll. The views are lovely, though.

Pizarra

🌐 **pizarra.es** (translation link at the top of the web page) ℹ️ Camino de la Estación 1 🕐 Mon–Fri 0800–1500

Pizarra is often called a *pueblo blanco*, but it is rather different to other examples in that it is a relatively new town. 'New' is, of course, a relative term, and there are plenty of 16th century buildings in Pizarra, but nothing from the Roman or Moorish periods. At the time of the reconquest of Álora (1484), the town did not exist, but at the end of the 15th century, a place called La Pizarra appeared with some buildings on lands owned by Diego Romero (awarded to him in gratitude for supporting the assault on Álora). By the last third of the 16th century, it had become a town. This, coupled with the fact that it was built at the foot of a hill rather than on top of one, means that its layout is more regular and orthogonal than most other *pueblos blancos*.

There is a well-regarded museum, the **Museo Municipal de Pizarra**, thanks to the American painter Gino Hollander who lived in the town for many years. Beginning in the 1960s he amassed a large collection of archaeological artefacts, especially from the Roman and Moorish periods. His collection was taken on by the *ayuntamiento*, which converted a disused farm complex and turned it into a museum. This museum, however, is on the main road into Pizarra, not the village itself, so unless you are in a car, the route by foot is almost 5 km (though there are a few taxi firms in Pizarra: 🌐 **bit.ly/PizarraTaxis**).

Pizarra is very popular with walkers or, given the hilly terrain, perhaps one should say hikers. The website of the *ayuntamiento* does have a page about the hiking routes but fails to provide any decent maps. You can have a look at the main routes here: 🌐 **bit.ly/3XCHe3G**. It is probably best to avoid these routes between 8 October and 28 November because this is hunting season and, although alternative routes are signposted, getting lost could potentially be fatal.

Alhaurín el Grande

 ⊕ **alhaurinelgrande.es/turismo** ❶ Calle Real 12 ⊕ Mon–Fri 0900–1400

Alhaurín el Grande is a *pueblo blanco* (that has grown into a small town) to the west of Cártama, and the north-west of Málaga. It's a 50 minutes journey from Málaga with frequent buses (⊕ **ctmam.es/lineas/M-132**). The excellent tourism website is available in English and is packed with information (though it has a few missing links which I hope will soon be ironed out). The website even has a helpful map of restaurants and bars divided into categories. Links are also given for interurban and urban buses (you would be surprised how many *ayuntamientos* have websites that fail to tell you how to reach, let alone get around, the town they a trying to promote).

 There is a QR code to open a tourist guide on your smartphone. However, you may find it useful to call into the *turismo* to pick up some printed leaflets and maps as the rendered PDFs displayed by the app can be small and hard to read, even when magnified. But all in all, Alhaurín el Grande has one of the best tourist information offers of any town of its size.

Coín

 ⊕ **turismocoin.com** ❶ Plaza Alameda 10 ⊕ Tue–Wed 0930–1400; Thu–Fri 0930–1400, 1600–1830; Sat 0930–1400

Coín is a more typical *pueblo blanco* with Phoenician and Roman origins, but unlike many similar villages, it is fairly flat, so a good day trip destination if you don't enjoy struggling up and down hills. There are a couple of buses from Málaga every weekday morning, and a couple of buses back each afternoon (⊕ **ctmam.es/lineas/M-132**) It is the next stop after Alhaurín el Grande. Whilst there are buses on Saturdays and Sundays, the timings are impractical. This effectively means your window for visiting Coín is Tuesday to Friday, because many places, including the *turismo*, are closed on Monday. There are also four buses each day (Monday to Saturday) between Fuengirola and Coín: ⊕ **ctmam.es/lineas/M-221**.

Like Alhaurín el Grande, Coín has a good tourism website with plenty of information. However, despite presenting a good range of information (maps, historical walking routes, bar and restaurant listings, etc.) in English, the website is only partially translated, so you may have to put it through Google Translate or use the translate feature of your smartphone browser to understand news and diary posts.

If you visit Coín, don't miss the remarkable local tomato '*El Huevo de Toro*', famous throughout the Province of Málaga. '*Huevo de toro*' literally means 'bull's egg', but we all know that bulls do not lay eggs — '*huevos*' is rather a Spanish euphemism for testicles. The *Huevo de Toro* is huge, weighing on average 300—600 g, with some tipping the scales over one kilogram (the name is accurate: the testis of an adult bull is usually between 300 and 960 grams). Although grown widely throughout the region, the *Huevo de Toro* originated in Coín, where it is still grown, irrigated with spring water. British consumers might normally avoid overly large tomatoes (especially if to be eaten raw), assuming them to be watery and insipid, but this variety is a delicious revelation. It has few seeds, very little 'locular gel' (the soft jelly surrounding the seeds) and a well-developed, firm 'mesocarp' (the interior 'flesh'). If you see it on a menu, do try it. Another speciality of Coín is the fig and '*pan de higo*' — a rich 'bread' made of dried figs and often eaten with cheese and a popular item bought by visitors. It lasts for ages so makes a great gastronomic souvenir or gift.

Almogía

🌐 almogia.es (translation link at the top of the web page) ℹ Plaza de la Constitución 🕐 Mon–Fri 0800–1500

Almogía is an ancient *pueblo blanco* to the east of Álora, famous for its *verdiales pandas*, its almonds, and its olives. It is tiny (in fact the smallest municipality in the Valle del Guadalhorce), and pretty much unspoilt by tourism. There are buses from Málaga (🌐 ctmam.es/lineas/M-250) which make it a possible day trip destination Monday to Friday (in effect, Tuesday to Friday, as most monuments, bars and restaurants are closed on a Monday). The stop closest to the historic centre is called '**Lo Lomo**'. It is a beautiful little village to visit, perched on a hilltop. The *turismo* section of the website isn't great (*e.g.* it lists the village's monuments but does not provide addresses, let alone a map, and in the one case where it provides an address, no online map recognizes it). You'll find a handful of churches (marked on the companion Google Map, though most will only be open during mass), but little else. The attraction, as in so many cases, is the village itself, which is bijou and beautiful. The journey time from Málaga is about 55 minutes, so you could take an 11 am bus from Málaga, wander the streets for a while, enjoy the views and then find somewhere for lunch: **Bar–Freiduría David** (📍 Calle Carril 33–35, near the bus stop) serves excellent fish, **Bar Chiquetete** across the road is friendly, cheap and tasty, and **Bar Casa Meño** (📍 Calle Carril 8) in the centre of the village is always a lovely, welcoming spot. You could then take the 3.45 pm bus back to Málaga. Less of a sightseeing tour and more of a 'getting away from it' tour.

Álora

🌐 alora.es ℹ Plaza Fuente de Arriba 15 🕐 Mon 0900–1500; Tue–Fri 0900–1800; Sat–Sun 1000–1300, 1500–1800

The *pueblo blanco* of Álora is a great day trip destination because it is very easy to get to by train. It's the last stop on the 🚆 C-2 *Cercanías* line, with around 14 trains per day. The journey from Málaga–María Zambrano takes around 35 to 39 minutes. The railway station is down in the valley, beneath the village, but Monday to Saturday there is a local (mini) bus that will take you up to the main town square (🚏 Fuente Arriba) where the *turismo* is located. The buses are timed to coincide with the arrival and departure of the trains, and you can check the timetable here: 🌐 ctmam.es/lineas/M-341. This bus service does not run on a Sunday, so if that is the only day you are able to visit, it would be better to take the bus all the way from Málaga; although please note that the bus stop (🚏 Piscina) is 700 m from the main square: 🌐 ctmam.es/lineas/M-235.

Like most *pueblos blancos*, the main 'sight' is the village itself. My suggestion is to take a train to Álora that arrives mid-morning. Take the bus up to its terminus in the **Plaza Fuente Arriba** ('The Upper Square of the Fountain'), which is actually a triangle (and very small, so easy to miss!). Despite its diminutive size, this is the centre of the town and the Town Hall is located here (as is the *turismo*, so call in to pick up maps, leaflets and advice). The reason for the odd shape of the 'square' is that the space was created when a 17th-century convent (or Beguinage) of Franciscan nuns was destroyed during the Civil War. The stone from the destroyed convent was used in the construction of the *barrio* of Poca Agua (the more modern part of Álora that you passed through on the bus).

There are some friendly bars on the Plaza Fuente Arriba, some of which have terrace tables set out on warm days — **Restaurante Casa Romero**, **Zentral** and **Bar Madrugón**. There is also a small café, **Alegría**, and a 'café-pub', **Caballitos**. Have a drink or a cup of coffee after your journey and then set off for the **Castillo** along Calle La Parra (Vine Street). This was one of the first 'grand' streets in Álora and you will notice that the houses are relatively large. Already a sought-after address in the 17th century, the bourgeoisie that arrived with the construction of the Córdoba–Málaga railway in the second half of the 19th century quickly settled on this street, which at first was known by the name of Calle Marqués de Sotomayor. You will continue into Calla Zapata (a '*zapata*' is an archaic name for a buskin, a medieval half boot worn nowadays by bishops celebrating the Old Rite of Mass, though in this case the street it is named after a former resident, presumably a Basque). Continue onto Calle Benito Suárez and you will soon enter the **Plaza Baja de la Despedía** (Lower Square of the Farewell). This, historically, was the main square of the town.

Once it was just 'Plaza Baja' (being lower than the old streets leading up to the castle), the '*Despedía*' (farewell) was added in 1994 because during Holy Week this is where the images of Christ and the Virgin of Sorrows 'meet' (and bid farewell) on Good Friday. In this square one finds the **Parish Church of Nuestra Señora de la Encarnación**, the **Rafael Lería Municipal Museum** and a beautiful viewpoint over the Arroyo Hondo. The Monastic Hospital of San Sebastián built by the *Reyes Católicos* once stood here, but it was destroyed during the Confiscation of Mendizábal. Continue along the **Calle Ancha** ('Wide Street', though its name probably came from the fact that it was once 'wide open', having houses only on one side, the other side being the burial place of plague victims). Almost at the junction with the square you will find a glazed ceramic plate that reads (in Spanish) 'The ingenious gentleman Don Miguel de Cervantes Saavedra worked in this place from 1586 till 1593 in his job as commissioner of the king.'

Take a slow, steep walk up to the **Castillo**. It was substantively built by the Arabs, though its ultimate origins are Phoenician and Roman. Its construction was carried out in various stages and it is divided into two walled enclosures. The upper one, the base of the primitive fortress, has a square plan with six towers. The lower one, irregular in shape, adapts to the relief of the hill. Between the two enclosures is a square tower that must have been the castle's lookout tower, at the foot of which was the main mosque. From outside the castle, there are extraordinary views of the Guadalhorce Valley. The 15th-century **Capilla de las Torres** (Chapel of the Tower) stands in front of the castle, on the site of the former mosque. After the *reconquista*, it was converted into a church dedicated to Our Lady of the Incarnation. A serious earthquake in 1680 damaged the fabric, though by this time the current parish church in the Plaza Baja was under construction. That earthquake killed so many people that the old castle was used as a cemetery. We can also see the so-called **Torre del Homenaje**, which is the tallest structure of the entire upper enclosure and the only one to have been rebuilt. The *adelantado* (governor) of Andalucía, Diego Gómez de Ribera, arrived here in 1434 at the head of his troops, who surrendered before the city. According to the tale, even as they surrendered, the *adelantado* fell dead in front of the walls, slain by the Moors. These scenes would give rise to a well-known border romance, the '*Romance de Álora*', an anonymous poem that tells of Moorish treachery.

On the castle's esplanade is the *mirador* (viewpoint) of Ali Ibn Falcún 'Al-Baezi', named after the last Moorish military governor who finally handed over the keys of the castle to the *Reyes Católicos* in 1484. The tragic-romantic suggestion is that he must have stood on this spot and gazed wistfully at what he had lost, like the '*Puerto del Suspiro del Moro*' (Pass of the Moor's Last Sigh) in Granada. The view is certainly majestic. You are looking down the wide Guadalhorce Valley, with the Mountain of El Hacho to your right and the Montes de Málaga to your right. In addition to vines, the land under cultivation is mainly used to grow citrus fruits, particularly lemons (both the 'verna' mountain variety and the *cascarúo*: see p. 415), and Aloreña olives. This variety of olive, developed in the mid-18th century, was the first olive to receive a Protected Designation of Origin (DOP) in Spain. It is a fleshy, good-sized fruit, with a pit that detaches easily from the flesh, and with a low oleuproprein content (the component that makes olives bitter). All these characteristics make them extremely popular as table olives, usually brined with thyme, red pepper, garlic or wild fennel. A small quantity of oil is also produced, but it can be hard to find.

The wild vegetation that you can see from this viewpoint is typical of the valley — Aleppo pine forest, juniper groves, holm oaks and wild olives, as well as rosemary, thyme, rockrose, etc. Close to the watercourses, one finds brambles, vines, willows, poplars and eucalyptus. Remember to look upwards too as it is common to spot griffon vultures, Egyptian vultures, golden and Bonelli's eagles in this region, as well as various kinds of falcon.

When you have finished at the castle, continue in the same direction to return to the **Plaza Baja de la Despedía** via Calle Carril. The other main 'sightseeing' locations are in this square. First visit the **Rafael Lería Museum**, the sort of quirky small museum that one finds in small towns like Álora. **(Mon–Fri 0900–1500; Tue–Fri 1700–2000; Sat–Sun 0900–1400, 1700–2000)** It is located in the *Escuela de Cristo* (which may have been the chapel of the disappeared San Sebastián Hospital), a building annexed to the Church of the Encarnación. There is a small but lovingly put-together collection of archaeological pieces covering the history of Álora. The exhibits mostly have English translations, but in the numismatic displays, you may be confused by the references to 'fleece'. The Spanish word *'vellón'* does indeed also mean fleece (as in wool), but in this context, it refers to a metallic alloy of silver (or gold) and copper or zinc, borrowed from the French *'billon'*. Admission to the museum is a nominal charge and the attendant will also let you into the church, which really is well worth a look.

La Parroquia de Nuestra Señora de la Encarnación (Parish Church of Our Lady of the Incarnation) is, remarkably, the largest church in the Diocese of Málaga after the Cathedral. Its construction took almost a century, between 1600 and 1699. It has a rectangular floor plan with 3 naves separated by robust Tuscan columns. Three images stand out: the Holy Crucified Christ of the Students (the work of José Navas-Parejo); a Dolorosa (anonymous from the 17th century, in the nave of the Epistle, *i.e.* the right-hand side) titled '*María Santísima de los Dolores Coronada*' and, in the nave of the Gospel (left-hand side), a Saint Francis of Assisi, in polychrome wood. The jewel in the crown of the church was, and to an extent still is, its altarpiece. Parts of it were destroyed in the various vicissitudes of the early 20th century, but the painted and gilded wood *retablo* that remains is still impressive and stands in majestic contrast to the rather austere masonry columns of the nave.

If you are hungry or thirsty, then the **El Mocho Bar Tapería Cafetería** in the corner of the square is a lovely spot, with friendly service and excellent *tapas* (the prawn skewers are notable). If you like proper Spanish *torrefacto* (*viz.* very strong, rather bitter) coffee, then you will find it here. Return to the 'new' town centre along the Calle Atrás (Back Street). After a few metres, turn right into Calle Romero and bear left. This is the site of the **Molino Bachiller y Aljibe Árabe** (Bachiller Mill and Arab Cistern ⊕ Mon–Fri 1000–1400), still known by older *aloreños* as the *Posada de Subires*, the surname of the last owner of an inn that used to stand on the site. Hidden and derelict for many years, the mill and cistern have been restored and may be visited (though actual opening hours can be erratic). The name of the mill comes from the first owner, Bachiller Gonzalo Pérez, a very influential figure in Álora in the 16th century, which is when the mill was established.

If there is time (because it often closes around 1330), walk back to the Plaza Fuente Arriba, then continue straight on, bearing right onto the Calle Veracruz to bring you to the **Iglesia de la Veracruz**, which dates back to the 16th century, when it was built to commemorate the victory over the Moors. It is surprisingly modest for a Spanish church, with a simple beamed wooden roof, plan whitewashed walls and some modest niches to display statues of the saints. In fact, if you removed the colourful Catholic iconography then architecturally it could almost be a Welsh chapel. There are suggestions that the church's construction was partly financed by the sale of Moorish slaves. I have been unable to verify this, though given the dates this is perfectly possible and, to be honest, quite likely.

(NOTE: If you find the idea of a church being constructed using slave labour shocking (and I hope you do!), it's worth stopping to think about that for a moment. It **is** shocking, of course, but the Moorish castle of Álora, as well as the Castle and Alcazaba of Málaga, the *mezquita* of Córdoba and the Alhambra of Granada were **all** constructed using slave labour too. If we find some examples more offensive than others, then why is that?)

It will now be time for lunch, and in Álora, you have plenty of options, many of which are to be found along the **Calle Veracruz**, which becomes, after a hundred metres or so, the **Avenida de Cervantes**. But first, we should mention a couple of other attractions in the town of Álora. The first is the **Santuario Nuestra Señora de Flores** (Sanctuary/Convent of Our Lady of the Flowers), shrine of the Patroness of Álora who is represented in a 15th-century image. It is open between 10 am and 6 pm and is a 2 km walk from the centre of the town. If you want to take a taxi, a handy telephone number is 📞 **+34 952 496 424**. Just before the Santuario is the **Cruz del Humilladero**, a small commemorative structure located near the Convent of Flores that commemorates the symbolic delivery of the keys to Álora by the last *alcaide* or Muslim military governor of the city, Ali Ibn Falcún 'Al-Baezi', to the *Reyes Católicos* in June 1484.

There is also a well-regarded *bodega* (winery) in Álora called **Bodegas Pérez Hidalgo** founded by local brothers Francisco and José Miguel Pérez Hidalgo in 2000. For further details see p. 481. If you are visiting Álora in your own vehicle, then you might like to combine a visit to the Bodegas Perez Hidalgo with a tour of **Molino Aceitero La Molina**, a one-hundred-year-old olive oil producer. The guided tour of the facilities shows you the history and the extraction process of the 'liquid gold' of this region, from when they receive the olives until they bottle the oil, including the extraction and storage in extra virgin olive oil cellars. You can also take part in a tasting session of the Manzanilla Aloreña olive oil product (with additional upgrades adding a tasting of table olives, or olives and local oranges). 🌐 anvioro.es/OLEOTURISMO.

Now, for lunch! (All locations mentioned are indicated on the companion Google Map.) **El Taller** on Calle La Rampa is a real hidden gem serving an excellent *tapas* menu. The crunchy deep-fried Brie with molasses and a parmentier of crisp apple and cinnamon is a delight, as is the mini hamburger of mature blond beef from Galicia. **La Galería** is a simple bar serving cheap and delicious simple *tapas*. **La Sede** is a great concept — a *tapas* bar specializing in platters of cheese or ham/sausage, and they take both very seriously. This place is half bar, half delicatessen. **Restaurante la Casa del Abuelo** is a reliable choice, and in spite of its rather traditional Spanish menu, it also serves (rather good) pizza. **Bar El Yunque** is a textbook 'no frills' local Spanish bar, serving good *tapas* at good prices. Finally (and by no means exhausting the offerings of Álora), **La Taberna de Álora** is perhaps my personal favourite lunch spot. The service can be a little slow, and even chaotic, but it is a very friendly, welcoming place always full of local families. The menu is varied and the dishes are well cooked, from small *tapas* to hearty *raciones*. But these suggestions only scratch the surface and most bars and restaurants are pretty good. As I often observe, shockingly poor restaurants can prosper for years in the resorts by serving chicken nuggets, frozen pizza and cheap *sangria* to tourists, but in a small town like Álora, sub-standard establishments are unlikely to meet the exacting standards of the locals.

Antequera

🌐 **turismo.antequera.es** ❶ Encarnación 4A 🕐 Mon–Fri 0900–1830; Sat 0900–2200; Sun 1000–1400

If you tell your friends you are visiting Málaga, there will almost certainly be a flash of recognition (possibly mixed with incomprehension), and that would be the case even for less well-known Spanish destinations like Ronda. Mention Antequera, however, and you are likely to be met with blank stares. In fact, Antequera receives a very high number of visitors, but it tends to be used as a base for coach tours because of its lower prices and central location within easy reach of Sevilla, Málaga, Ronda, Granada and Córdoba. The city is often called '*El Corazón de Andalucía*' (the Heart of Andalucía) for this reason. It may not, quite, be the geographical heart, but as regards road and rail links, it is. Despite playing host to thousands of overnight tourists, it is not well-developed as a tourist destination in its own right, which is a great pity, because it has a great deal to offer.

Like many Spanish cities, it has a picturesque old town surrounded by somewhat less beautiful modern suburbs, but there is much to see and enjoy. It is an ideal day trip destination from Málaga as it is only an hour's journey by train. It is true that if you consult the RENFE website, you will find frequent trains to and from Antequera that take either a fraction over an hour or as little as 25 minutes on the AVE. But beware! These trains mainly stop at the new high-speed station 'Antequera–Santa Ana', 20 km outside Antequera. There is no local bus service between the city and Santa Ana, which means relying upon taxis, adding cost and losing time. The old city centre railway station was, until recently, a stop on the *media distancia* Sevilla–Almería and Algeciras–Granada lines, with only one train to and from Málaga daily.

However, in 2023 a new, subterranean railway station opened in Antequera (city) allowing some AVE and AVANT (high-speed medium distance) trains between Málaga and Granada to stop in the city centre. This has made travel between Málaga and Antequera much more straightforward and convenient. There are also plans to construct a rail link between Antequera Ciudad (*i.e.* the city centre) and Antequera–Santa Ana. It seems that the practice of building high-speed stations several miles from city centres, something repeated all over Spain, while it may have lowered initial costs for Adif (the Spanish equivalent of Network Rail) has turned out to be impractical for, and unpopular with, travellers.

Another way to reach Antequera is by bus, with ALSA (🌐 **bit.ly/ALSABus**) operating frequent services of around one hour's duration. Antequera has a good urban bus network (🌐 **urbanoantequera.es**) that covers the entire city (and all the main tourist sights) in spite of there being only two bus routes. Single tickets are inexpensive (around a euro in 2023) so travellers with mobility issues can easily use buses to reach the places they wish to visit.

The Moovit App does not yet cover Antequera, so planning journeys in the city will require some old-fashioned skills, like studying timetables. There is a local bus app (for Android only) and the download link is at the bottom of the ⊕ **urbanoantequera.es** website home-page. However, it is a basic timetable and map app, not a route planner. Even so, if you use the app (or the '**Localizar Bus**' link on the website) you will at least be able to locate the bus stops.

⧖ History

Antequera was the Roman municipality of *Anticaria* — the 'Ancient City'. The remains of previous civilizations have been found in excavations of prehistoric sites and we know it was inhabited between 3,650 and 3,750 years BC. The main evidence of flourishing during this period are the Dolmens of Menga, Viera and El Romeral, all close to the current city centre.

Under the Romans, the city was an important trading centre, known for its production of olive oil. The Roman legacy is visible in the excavated Roman baths located in the south-western part of the city, and the sculpture of the **Ephebe of Antequera**, dating from the 1st century AD. The city was more or less razed by the Visigoths. During the Moorish occupation, the city, known as 'Medina Antakira' was fortified with a citadel and a defensive wall.

From the middle of the 13th century, after the fall of Seville and Jaén, 'Antakira' began to acquire importance as a centre of military operations, due to its position on the border between Christian and Muslim kingdoms. After several unsuccessful attempts, the final assault by the forces of the Catholic Kings began on 20 April 1410 and did not end until 22 September, when the surrender of the city was negotiated.

After the conquest of Granada in 1492, the city began to develop apace, increasing its population due to the fertility of its lands and the (now) virtual absence of enemies. Under Castilian rule, the city continued to be an important commercial centre due to its location, its flourishing agriculture and the work of its artisans, who contributed to the cultural growth of the city. But it was during the 16th and 17th centuries that the city experienced the greatest demographic growth, becoming one of the most important commercial centres in Andalucía, again due to its location as a crossroads of the busiest commercial routes.

In the year 1500, the *Reyes Católicos* ceded land to the Friars of the Observance of Saint Francis to build a monastery dedicated to **San Zoilo** (martyred at Córdoba under Diocletian and a popular saint in Spain and, for some unknown reason, in medieval Chester[74]). They also founded the **Royal Collegiate Church of Santa María La Mayor**. In 1573 the first printing press appeared, Antequera being the seventh *andaluz* city to acquire it, despite the fact that it did not have a university (although it did have a professor of grammar attached to the Collegiate Church).

The eighteenth century saw the great flourishing of the city. Numerous religious congregations settled in the city and built houses, chapels and churches. The nobility also built new palaces. At this time, Antequera was one of the Andalusian cities with the highest manufacturing activity, especially in relation to the textile industry, based mainly on wool, and to a lesser extent silk and linen. In 1755 the city had 87 textile manufacturers. Due to its importance, in 1765 the title of 'Royal' was granted to the Wool and Cloth Factory.

Antequera Today

The **Royal Monastery of San Zoilo**, nowadays the municipal library, is a Gothic-style convent. Of the original work, some vaults and the front of the church are preserved. Inside, the *mudéjar* decoration of the central nave and the mannerist plasterwork of the ribbed vault stand out. Also declared a National Monument, the **Royal Collegiate Church of Santa**

---

74   archive.ph/ufVVs

María La Mayor is a transitional work with late Gothic and Renaissance elements. It was built between 1514 and 1550 and has the distinction of being (probably) the first church that was conceived in the Renaissance style in Andalucía. Its Ionic columns and *mudéjar* coffered ceiling stand out, as well as the Gothic-*mudéjar* vault of the High Altar. The ashlar façade was built with stones from the Roman remains of **Singilia Barba** (an abandoned Roman *municipium* nearby). Although the architecture is very fine, the interior is rather bare as it is nowadays mainly used for concerts. The other royal collegiate church of Antequera, the **Royal Collegiate Church of San Sebastián**, began construction in 1548, designed by the architect Diego de Vergar, although it later underwent several alterations, which is why it currently presents a mixture of styles: Renaissance and plateresque on the façade, baroque on the bell tower and neoclassical for parts of the interior.

The convents of interest are numerous. In the Province of Málaga, Antequera is the real 'city of convents'. In fact, Antequera has more churches and convents per capita than any other Spanish city. The current **Convent of Madre de Dios de Monteagudo** was built between 1747 and 1761 on the site of an old convent that had been destroyed by fire. The project corresponds to the plan of the master builder Cristóbal García, who managed to give the interior a sensation of movement by combining concave surfaces with cap vaults and other elements. Its tower is considered one of the most beautiful examples of *barroco andaluz*. As an enclosed monastery of Augustinian nuns, it is not open to the public. The **Convent of Belén** dates from the beginning of the 17th century and has a Latin cross floor plan, an austere stone and brick façade and a dome decorated with colourful baroque plasterwork. Originally a foundation of the Discalced Carmelites, it is nowadays a monastery of Poor Clares (Franciscan nuns). The sisters support themselves by selling '*dulces*' (sweet biscuits and cakes), so buy a box to take home as a gift. The **Convento de la Victoria**, constructed between 1712 and 1718, has an octagonal floor plan and was inspired by Italian Baroque models. The first community here was of the Minim Friars of Saint Francis de Paola, but they were expelled in the 19th century disentailments and the current community consists of sisters of an order founded in Antequera. The **Convent of La Encarnación**, dating from 1580, is in the mannerist–*mudéjar* style and repeats the model of a Moorish church in Granada, with a single nave covered with coffered ceilings. The Carmelite Nuns of Old Observance are here.

The **Convent of La Trinidad**, nowadays a parish church, dates from 1672–1683 and is in a classically baroque style. Also from the 17th century are the **Convento de los Remedios** (Our Lady of Remedies is the Patron of Antequera), the **Convent of Santo Domingo**, with its fine *mudéjar* central nave, and the **Convent of La Magdalena** dating from 1691 (the Discalced Franciscans were expelled in the 19th century and the convent is now a rather grand hotel on the outskirts of Antequera).

Three convents date from the 18th century. The **Convent of San José** was built between 1707 and 1734 and is considered one of the most genuine representations of the Antequera baroque. It has a two-section façade, made of carved brick and baked clay, attributed to Tomás de Melgarejo. The master builder Andrés Burgueño was also responsible for the church of the **Convent of Las Catalinas**. It has a single nave covered with a barrel vault, much repeated throughout Spain and South America. This **Convent of Santa Eufemía**, the joint patron saint of the city of Antequera, was founded in 1601 by the Minim nuns. The existing church was built between 1739 and 1763 according to the plans of the master Cristóbal García. It combines *mudéjar* and classical elements and, inside, rococo plasterwork.

From the 16th century, the group of Renaissance '*columnar*' churches (*i.e.* churches with more than one nave) made up of the churches of **San Pedro**, **Santa María de Jesús** and **San Juan Bautista** is notable. The first has Gothic ribbed vaults, possibly remains of the original church begun in 1522. Later remodelling works were directed by the architect of the Cathe-

541

dral of Málaga, Pedro Díaz de Palacios. **Santa María de Jesús** is a reconstruction since the original church was destroyed during the French invasion. It has a hexagonal floor plan and profuse decoration. The church of **San Juan Bautista** was completed in 1584. The façade is rather austere, but its interior is considered one of the jewels of the *barroco andaluz*.

The **Church of Santiago** and the **Church of El Carmen** were also built in the 16th century. Santiago was originally a hermitage, begun in 1519. It has a single nave covered with a vault. The church of the Carmen is built on an escarpment, next to the Villa River. It was part of an old convent (now disappeared) that was built between 1583 and 1633 in the mannerist-baroque style. The three large altarpieces in the main chapel, dating from the 18th century, are exceptionally fine.

⛪ Wayside Shrines and Hermitages

The **Virgen del Socorro Tribune Chapel**, also called the Portichuelo Chapel is considered one of the most interesting examples of traditional *andaluz* urbanism. The chapel was built in 1715 and is made up of two floors of open galleries with semicircular arches and three façades. The **Capilla Tribuna de la Cruz Blanca** is late baroque in style and dates from 1774, attributed to the master builder Martín de Bogas. On the other hand, the **Ermita de la Veracruz** crowns one of the highest parts of the city. It is in the Renaissance style with some mannerist elements and baroque plasterwork.

⛪ A List of (some) Visitable Churches and Convents

Entrance is free unless indicated otherwise. Naturally, the two that charge a (modest) fee for admission are among the most impressive. Some churches are only open during mass which, except on Sunday mornings, tends to be celebrated in the early morning or in the evening: not much use to a day tripper.

⚠ Smaller churches and religious houses rely upon volunteers to remain open for tourist visits, so they may not be open when advertised. Opening times change frequently, so you may simply need to cross your fingers. Even the official Antequera *turismo* website seems confused. As late as 2023, for example, on its page about the **Convento de la Victoria**, although it displayed the correct description and photo, the address and map were for a completely different Convento de la Victoria in the Province of Almería, 300 km away. The Spanish and English versions of the site also gave contradictory information. The *turismo* should be able to give you a list of current opening times when you visit.

Church/Convent	Address	Sun	Mon	Tue	Wed	Thu	Fri	Sat
Santa María La Mayor 🅖	Calle San Salvador 2		1000–1800					
Iglesia Del Carmen 🅖	Plaza del Carmen	11–14	∅	1100–1330, 1630–1745				11–14
Parroquia San Sebastián	Plaza San Sebastián		0900–1300, 1800–2000					
Madre de Dios de Monteagudo	Calle Lucena 39		(exterior only)					
Convento de Belén	Calle Belén 6		0800–1730 (church), 0930–1330, 1600–1830 (*dulces*)					
Convento de la Victoria	Carrera Madre Carmen	10–1330 17–19	0900–1400, 1630–1900					10–1330 17–19
Convento de la Victoria *museo*	Carrera Madre Carmen		1630–1900					

Church/Convent	Address	Sun	Mon	Tue	Wed	Thu	Fri	Sat
Convento de La Encarnación	Calle los Tintes 1	0800–0900 (during mass)						
Convento de San Augustín	C/ Infante Don Fernando 11	1100–1330	⊘					1100–1330
Convento de La Trinidad	Calle Cruz Blanca 25	0930–1300	1830–1930					
Convento de los Remedios	C/ Infante Don Fernando 72	1230–1400 1930–2030	1900–2000					1930–2030
Convento de Santo Domingo	cuesta de la Paz 16	⊘						1200–1400
Convento de San José	Plaza de las Descalzas	1300–1400	⊘					1300–1400
Museo de las Descalzas	Plaza de las Descalzas	0900–1230	⊘	1000–1330, 1700–1930				0900–1230 1700–1900
Convento Sta Catalina de Siena	Plaza Coso Viejo 3	0730–1830 (Wed 0730–1300)						
Convento de Santa Eufemía	Calle Belén 4	1100–1330	⊘					1100–1330
Real Monasterio de San Zoilo	Plaza San Francisco	⊘						1100–1400
Iglesia de San Pedro	Calle San Pedro 10	1200–1300, 1700–1900 (☀1800–2000)						
Iglesia de Santa María de Jesús	Plaza del Portichuelo 14	⊘	1100–1300					⊘
Iglesia de Santiago Apóstol	Plaza Santiago	check at *turismo*						
Iglesia de San Juan de Dios	C/ Infante Don Fernando 65	10–14, 16–18	⊘	1000–1400, 1600–1800				
Iglesia de San Miguel	Calle San Miguel 49	⊘	1800–1930	⊘	1800–1930	⊘		1930–2030
Convento de los Capuchinos	Plaza Capuchinos	1230–1330 1800–1900	1800–1900					

🏛 Other Monuments and Attractions

🏛 Alcazaba ♀ Plaza de los Escribanos ⏱ Daily 1000–1800 😊😊

The Alcazaba of Antequera is not as complete or as extensive as that of Málaga, let alone those of Granada and Sevilla, and really only consists of the fortified walls. However, its size and position, to say nothing of the wonderful views, make it well worth a visit. Its origins may lie in Roman times, although it is mentioned in records for the first time in the 11th-century writings of Semuel ibn Nagrella, a Jewish poet and vizier of the *Taifa* of Granada. Semuel's position as the most powerful official in the court of Badis, the third King of the *Taifa* of Granada, is often given as an example of a 'Golden Age' of tolerance and *convivencia* in Moorish Andalucía. His achievement was certainly great, and he was probably one of the most powerful Jews in Europe at the time. However, harmony and toleration were precarious. Although Semuel was fortunate to die of old age, his son Yosef, who succeeded him as vizier at the tender age of 21 was less fortunate. Perhaps jealous of his influence, he was crucified by the Muslim citizens of Granada on 30 December 1066, unleashing the 'Massacre of Granada' in which 4,000 Jews were slaughtered in a single day.

The date of Semuel's reference coincides with the Almohad domination when the two rings of walls that are still standing today were built. These walls prevented conquest by Pedro I of Castilla in 1361. Pedro (known oxymoronically both as 'The Just' and 'The Cruel') called Antequera a 'strong city'. After this event, the defences were reinforced, a barbican was built, gates were rebuilt and a '*coracha*' (a defensive wall like that between the Gibralfaro Castle and Alcazaba in Málaga) was constructed.

The city and its citadel finally fell into Christian hands during the siege of Antequera that lasted five months in 1410. The *Infante* Fernando de Trastámara, who was coregent of Castilla at the time, uttered the famous phrase "*¡Sálganos el sol por Antequera y... sea lo que Dios quiera!*" — 'The sun rises over Antequera and whatever God wants'. The fact that a King of Aragón, as Don Fernando would later become, is known by history as '*El de Antequera*' (The One from Antequera), makes very clear the importance he accorded both the city and his victory there.

In 1429 the *cortes* (parliament) of Aragón was held in the fortress under Fernando's son Alfonso V. The main tower, which is especially massive, had a smaller structure added to it in 1582 to home a bell and the city clock. It is known as the '*papabellotas*' clock because the city had to sell its own cork oak grove to cover the expenses incurred ('*bellota*' is the word for acorn). The audio tour of the Alcazaba finishes at the *mirador* (viewpoint) Plaza Santa Maria, where one can look down upon the Roman baths discovered in 1988. They were built in the first century AD and remained in use until the fifth century. Their separate rooms that maintained varying temperatures for the bathers are still visible, as are some richly detailed mosaics. The remains of a large Roman villa discovered in 1998 close to the train station are still being excavated, but several artefacts taken from the site are on display in Antequera's Municipal Museum.

The **Arco de los Gigantes** (Arch of the Giants) nearby was constructed in the 16th century to display a small collection of Roman sculptures and inscriptions, hence the oft-made claim that it is Spain's first museum. It is a good example of the humanist outlook of Antequera.

 🖼 ⚱ **Museo de la Ciudad De Antequera** 📍 Palacio de Nájera, Plaza del Coso Viejo 🕐 Tue–Sat 0900–1400, 1600–1800; Sun 1000–1400 **€**

The Museum of the City of Antequera is attractively housed in the handsome 18th-century Palacio de Nájera and contains something for everyone: historical artefacts from prehistoric to modern, textiles, silverware, religious artefacts, works by local artists, 19th and 20th-century art, all laid out in 20 large rooms. Although the museum is, by definition, provincial and cheap to visit, it has one of the most interesting and beautiful collections in the region, with frequent temporary exhibitions and even concerts. The star exhibit is the **Efebo de Antequera**, a first-century AD Roman bronze discovered by chance in a nearby farmhouse in 1955. It is a 1.43-metre-tall cast of a young man or adolescent ('*ephebus*'). It is probably the best-known and certainly one of the most beautiful works of art from Roman Hispania and it is worth visiting the museum just to see this one piece.

 🖼 ⚱ **Museo De Arte De La Diputación (MAD) Antequera** 📍 Calle Diego Ponce 12 🕐 Tue–Sun 1000–1400, 1700–2030 **€**

The Art Collection of the *Diputación* is a permanent collection of (mostly modern) artworks owned by the Provincial Government. They also stage visiting and temporary exhibitions. A similar project is located in Estepona, and in both cases these projects were conceived of as a means of saving grand houses from ruin while putting them to work for the benefit of townspeople and visitors. In Antequera's case, the house is an 18th-century mansion constructed by Don Juan Manuel Colarte y Lila. Use this link to see what the current exhibitions are: ⊕ **bit.ly/MAD_Antequera** (there is a translation link at the top of the page).

🏛 **Menga and Viera Dolmens** 📍 Carretera de Málaga 5 🕐 Tue–Sat 0900–1800; Sun 0900–1500 💶 (🎫 citizens of EU member states)

The Dolmen group is formed by three megalithic monuments (the **Tholos del Romeral** and the two Dolmens of **Menga** and **Viera**). Built in the Neolithic period, the oldest of them (and the third largest such structure in Europe) is El Dolmen de Menga, which is almost 6000 years old. Perhaps the most spectacular aspect are the huge slabs forming its walls and the blankets (ceiling slabs). The weight of the last one is estimated the be 180 tonnes. The Menga Dolmen faces the *Peña de los Enamorados*.

The **Peña de los Enamorados** (Rock of the Lovers) is an inselberg just outside Antequera which is evocative of a human face and connected with a number of overlapping legends. They all involve a Pyramus and Thisbe-style tale of star-crossed lovers. In some versions they are both Moors, from rival clans, in others they are an imprisoned Christian nobleman and his Muslim jailer's daughter, and in Robert Southey's English version (*Laila and Manuel*) they are a Muslim girl and her father's Christian Slave. In all of the stories, though, the unfortunate lovers eventually jump to their deaths from the rock. The orientation of the Menga Dolmen suggests that it was significant to Neolithic man, too.

The Viera Dolmen, a megalithic tomb built with orthostats (support slabs) and (ceiling) blankets. The fact that its entrance is orientated toward the equinoxes makes it the only one of the three dolmens that is orientated towards an astronomical event. Its construction is dated between 3510 and 3020 BC. Initially, it was known as the *Cueva Chica* ('Little Cave' in comparison to Menga), but it was later renamed Dolmen de Viera in honour of the brothers who discovered it.

The Menga and Viera dolmens are in the same location, at a distance of barely 50m apart. Both are about 1 km from the centre of the city and can be reached by foot or by bus. Romeral is about 4 km further East.

The Tholos of El Romeral, popularly known as the Dolmen del Romeral, is the most recent of the three, built as recently as 3000 or 2200 BC. Its uniqueness lies in the design of the dome, which is surprisingly intricate for the time. Its orientation is towards the El Torcal mountain range, so like the Dolmen de Menga, it has a geographical, not astronomical, focus. If you wish to visit this Dolmen then a taxi ride (or long hike) is necessary. The **Taxi Antequera** company will take you from the city centre to the Dolmen del Romeral, wait for you, and then bring you back for a pretty reasonable fee: ⊕ **taxiantequera.es/ofertas**. However, if you plan to visit this particular Dolmen, then I strongly recommend that you email the *turismo* ahead to check that it will be open (✉ **oficina.turismo@antequera.es**). You may find that they offer a free guided tour.

🥾 Eating and Drinking

Writing in the 1850s, Lady Louisa Tenison felt that Antequera was rather more refined than the den of bandits and robbers she had been led to expect. The food, though, didn't impress.:

Oil and garlic seemed to be the staple products of Antequera, and garnished the dishes to an extent even rare in this land, rendering still more unpalatable the tough, fibrous chickens.[75]

Given that Lady Louisa was a seasoned traveller familiar with the souks of Egypt, Palestine and Syria, one might have thought that she would have overcome her typical British antipathy to oil and garlic by the time she reached Spain (but then Her late Majesty Queen Eliz-

---

75   Lady Louisa Tenison, *Castilla and Andalucia: Tails from Spain* (London, 1853)

abeth II never made her peace with *Allium sativum* despite being the most widely travelled woman in the world and living to the age of 96).

The traditional and contemporary gastronomy of Antequera is pretty much the same as you will find in the rest of the Province of Málaga — the difference is that the *antequeranos* will tell you that **their** version of a particular dish is the original or the best. They have their own version of the *ensalada malagueña* which here is called *pío antequerano* ('*pío*' here does not mean 'pious' but 'piebald' — *i.e.* the salad is mainly white — cod, eggs, and onions — but with the other colours of the olives and oranges running through). The local equivalent of *gazpacho* is a thicker version called *porra* which Google Translate renders as 'truncheon' because the soup is named after the pestle with which it is traditionally made. The nearby mountainous region of El Torcal (an extraordinary, other-worldly karst landscape) is unusual in Andalucía in having a number of dairy farms. The *queso fresco* (fresh cheese) made from the milk of goats which graze the Sierra Sur del Torcal is delicious, and full of flavour, unlike the insipid *quesos frescos* found on supermarket shelves. Likewise, the butter (*matequilla*) from El Torcal is rich and luxuriously delicious.

A frequent distinction seen on Spanish menus is drawn between *mar* (sea — fish and seafood) and *montes* (mountains — meat and game). If Málaga capital is *mar* then Antequera is very firmly *montes*. You are likely to see goat and wild rabbit on menus, as well as game birds in season. The butcher **Embutidos Olmedo** makes excellent Málaga *salchichón* (salami) and an extremely rich and tasty *morcilla* (black pudding) that are famous throughout the region. They are sold in their own shop (Calle Martín de Luque 18) and in the main **Mercado de Abastos de Antequera (Plaza San Francisco, closed Sundays)**. Also in the market is an excellent *tapas* bar called **El Bar de La Plaza** which serves tasty '*manolitos*' (small rolls), as well as more substantial fish and meat dishes.

Antequera, with its profusion of religious houses, is well-known throughout Spain for its excellent traditional biscuits and sweets (*dulces*) — *alfajores, mantecados, bienmesabe, pestiños, torrijas* and *roscos* (some of which are only made seasonally, *e.g.* for Christmas or Easter). The best places to buy these sweet treats, either to enjoy yourself or for a unique gift, are from the nuns themselves. Both the Convent of the Belén and the Convent of San José sell them (open most days but closing for lunch).

Aceite (olive oil) 'SAT Labrador' is made in the nearby village of Fuente de Piedra, and well-worth looking out for. They produce several varieties, but most interesting is their 'Picual', which is intense, herbaceous, a little bitter and somewhat spicy. Staying with liquids, but more conventionally potable ones, do look out for local wines when you are eating/drinking in Antequera. The nearby area of Mollina has an excellent winery called Bodegas y Viñedos La Capuchina (see p. 481). But closer to Antequera is Bodega Gross Hermanos, which began in 2007. It is the result of a long family tradition of Málaga winemakers and exporters from the 19th and 20th centuries (Federico Gross y Compañía, Gross Hermanos and Bodegas Scholtz) who made typical (sweet and fortified) Málaga wines This new generation has moved into still wines, and the quality is stunning.

Perhaps the most typical food of Antequera, however, and that of which they are most proud, is the simplest: the '*mollete*'. As for its authenticity and origins, they have competition from Archidona, Marchena, Osuna and Écija (among many other towns), but the '*mollete antequerano*' is, without doubt, the best-known. It is very similar to what the Americans call an 'English muffin', except that it is baked, rather than cooked on a griddle, and somewhat lighter and spongier. The first mention of *molletes* can be found in a Latin-Spanish Dictionary of 1492, in which Antonio de Nebrija defines them as: 'any bread that is spongy and tender' In Latin, '*panis molliculus*' means 'soft bread', also called '*panis tenellus*' ('delicate bread'), and referred to rolls with a white and very fluffy crumb, achieved by a short bake. The culinary origin has been much speculated upon but is unknown. Some have suggested a Moorish ancestor, but as with much Spanish bakery, it is more likely that it is an embellishment of a Jewish dish — an unleavened dough, perhaps, to which milk and yeast were later added.

Because tourism in Antequera is relatively undeveloped, you can be reasonably certain that the bars and restaurants are of good quality. In other words, there are unlikely to be establishments kept afloat by serving substandard food to gullible tourists. The **Plaza Portichuelo** is an excellent spot for *tapas* with a good choice of places. **Bar Socorrilla** has several outdoor tables and more inside. A specialist in *carrillada* (braised pork cheek), this friendly *tapas* bar is often the first stopping point in Antequera for pilgrims walking from Villanueva de la Concepción on the *Camino Mozárabe* which starts in Málaga and leads all the way to Santiago de Compostela in Galicia.

It's a bit of a climb (unless you take the bus) but the **Plaza Espíritu Santo** is a pretty square where children play football and adults chat by the fountain. It's the focal point of a closeknit residential *barrio* situated high above the centre, from where you can look out over the dramatic landscapes that surround the town. Drinks and *tapas* at the friendly **Bar La Perdiz** are cheap, even by Antequera's standards, and are best enjoyed out on the square. If there's no free table, the owner will happily put one out for you, or you can sit on one of the benches indoors.

Antequera's **municipal food market** is situated on **Plaza San Francisco**, where in addition to **El Bar de La Plaza**, you'll also find **El Mercado**, a popular restaurant with a large terrace and varied menu. Standout dishes include a wonderfully tender *carrillada* (again) and the *bacalao mozárabe* — a tasty cod dish reputedly devised by *mozárabes* (Christians who lived under Moorish rule in medieval Spain). Just down the road, on **Calle Obispo**, is **Bar La Paz**, a venerable establishment plastered with Holy Week images of Jesus and the Virgin Mary.

Reckoned to be Antequera's top 'fine dining' restaurant, I should mention **Arte de Cozina**. The owner and head chef Charo Carmona specializes in rediscovering and reinterpreting ancient *andaluz* recipes, all of which are prepared in a kitchen visible from the dining room. Charo's menu changes in rhythm with seasonal ingredients but it's always focused on hearty broths and stews known as *caldosos*, *sopas* (soups) and *cazuelas* (casseroles). Next door to the restaurant, there's a smart *tapas* bar where you can enjoy smaller bites and superb wines.

As always, follow your nose and you are sure to find a great bar or restaurant almost anywhere in Antequera but other bars and restaurants I would recommend include:

♟ ✗ ≜ **Bar Machuca** (♀Plaza Santiago 4)

♟ 🏨 ✗ ≜ **Bar Carrera** (♀Carrera de Madre Carmen 18)

✗ 🏨 ⓘ ✗ **Baraka** (♀Plaza de las Descalzas)

✗ ✗ **Abrasador Bodegas Triana** (♀Calle Infante Don Fernando 20)

✗ 🏨 ⓘ **Restaurante Mesón Juan Manuel** (♀Calle San Agustín 1)

♟ ⓘ ✗ **La Cantina Antequera** (♀Alameda de Andalucía 14)

✗ ♟ 🏨 ⓘ **Restaurante A Mi Manera** (♀Calle Diego Ponce 6)

✗ ⓘ **Casa Memé – Mesón La Bombonera** (♀Calle Bombeo)

✗ 🏨 ⓘ **Bar–Restaurante Pizarro** (♀Calle Pizarro 32)

♟ 🏨 ⓘ **Bar Chicón** (♀Calle Infante Don Fernando 1)

♟ ⓘ ✗ ≜ **Bar Toral** (♀Calle Diego Ponce 27)

El Caminito del Rey

🌐 ✍ caminitodelrey.info

The 'Little Way of the King' is a 7.7 km trail through the narrow Gaitanes Gorge north of Málaga, which for around three kilometres consists of boardwalks positioned 100 metres over the river below. The route was originally constructed between 1901 and 1905 to facilitate the movement of workers between the hydroelectric power plants at either end of the gorge. It got its name after King Alfonso XIII walked it on the occasion of the inauguration of the Conde de Guadalhorce Dam (the río Guadalhorce is the river that flows, or now trickles, into the sea near Málaga Airport).

Thereafter, the *Caminito* was used by the local population who could use it as a short-cut. For many years dozens of children walked along it to get to school. But its construction from iron and primitive concrete meant that it deteriorated after several decades of use. In some places, the concrete surface completely collapsed. After two fatal accidents, the trail was closed in 2000. The boardwalks have now been remade from wood and stainless steel with due attention paid to safety (we are assured!). Cameras and guards are positioned at several locations. Access (Tue-Sun) is limited to a certain number of visitors per day. Therefore it is essential to reserve one's ticket **as far in advance as possible**. However, if you find no ticket availability it is still worth checking in the couple of days before and the day before you want to visit as they hold back a handful of tickets and release them at the last minute.

The walk is almost 8 kilometres long, mostly downhill, and will take around 2 hours — more if you take your time, stopping for pictures and enjoying the views. The first part leads from the main road to the entrance gate by a forest path. At the gate, visitors are allowed inside in tranches, so as not to overload the boardwalk. One is given a safety helmet to wear, which is collected at the exit. The portion of the *Caminito* that clings to the side of the mountains is 2.9 kilometres long and consists of a boardwalk, a forest trail, a second boardwalk, a hanging bridge, and a third boardwalk to the exit. From the exit, an unpaved path of 2.1 kilometres leads to the bus stop at El Chorro train station.

The railway line from Málaga to Córdoba also goes through the gorge. With luck, one might see a train weaving in and out of tunnels. You can preview your walk in 3D on Google maps: 🌐 bit.ly/Caminito3D.

The *Caminito* follows the Desfiladero de los Gaitanes ('The Gorge of the Flautists'), otherwise known as the Garganta del Chorro ('The Throat of the Waterfall'). Its 4 km length has sheer walls towering up to 400 metres in places, and a mere 10 metres wide at certain points. Aleppo pines, wild olive trees, junipers and holm oaks are the main trees on the hills on either side of the gorge, with undergrowth of rosemary, rock roses, dwarf fan palms, thyme and mastic. Closer to the river are rushes, reeds, tamarisk and oleander, as well as poplar, willow and eucalyptus trees. Wheeling around in the sky above the high gorge walls are Egyptian vultures, Bonelli's and golden eagles, common kestrels, peregrine falcons and griffon vultures, which also nest here. There are also red-billed choughs, crag martins, blue rock thrushes and crested tits, as well as numerous swifts in spring and summer. Spanish ibex inhabit the less accessible parts of the gorge.

The 'start' is at the northern end of the gorge, and then one walks it towards the south-east, ending at a village called Chorro. It is one way only! A shuttle bus runs on the hour and half-hour between the northern 'entrance' and southern 'exit' (and vice versa) between 8.30 am and 4.30 pm. The journey of 12km takes around 20 minutes (you can purchase a bus ticket with your admission ticket).

The easiest way to get to the *Caminito* is by car, a journey of around 50 minutes from Málaga. From Málaga take the A-357 to Ardales. Once you pass the village (on your left), turn right and follow signposts to 'Los Embalses'. This winding road takes you to the lakes/ reservoirs. Park near the restaurants and walk to a tunnel with a green sign 'Caminito del Rey 1.5km'. Go through the tunnel (which is fully illuminated) and follow the track around until you reach the start of the walk. At the 'exit' at El Chorro, catch the shuttle bus back to your parked car.

However, it is also possible, and fairly easy, to get there on public transport. Take an early train from Málaga–María Zambrano Station to El Chorro. Take the shuttle bus to the northern 'entrance' to begin the route. Allow at least three hours to complete your walk and take the train from El Chorro back to Málaga.

You can choose between a 'general' ticket and a 'guided tour' ticket. While the guide will provide interesting information about flora, fauna, geology and history, a guided group can only go as fast as its slowest member, so bear this in mind. However, 'general' slots are booked up far in advance (three months ahead in high season), and there is often a greater choice of guided tour ticket slots, so the choice may be made for you. Clearly, the more flexibility you have about dates, the more likely you are to find the best combination of tickets.

To take the hassle out of organizing transport and tickets, and to remove the worry that you may miss a connection, another option is to book through an agency. Some online travel sites will charge the earth for a 'day trip' to the Caminito, but a reliable local agency well worth considering is **Áloratur**, based in the *malagueño* town of Álora (aloratur.com). Their day tours are reasonably priced, leave María Zambrano station (outside the side entrance on Avenida Héroe de Sostoa) in the morning and include entry to the Caminito. The same company also offers excursions to the Torcal National Park and Dolmens of Antequera, and to Ronda, both including transport from Málaga.

If you are able to secure tickets and you don't suffer from vertigo, then I heartily recommend visiting the *Caminito*. The surroundings are beautiful and fascinating, the walk is exhilarating and, as things to do on holiday go, it is one of the more unusual and memorable experiences.

Ronda

🌐 **turismoderonda.es** ❶ Paseo Blas Infante 🕒☾ Mon–Fri 1000–1800 ☀ 1000–1900; Sat 1000–1700; Sun 1000–1430

Ronda is a 'city built on a hilltop', or rather two hilltops. But whereas most hilltop towns involve a great deal of climbing, Ronda is more or less flat, Jorge Luis Borges wrote:

> *It is here, in Ronda,*
> *in the delicate penumbra of blindness*
> *a concave silence of patios*
> *leisure of the jasmine and the light sound of water*
> *which summoned up memories of deserts*

having been built on the *mesas* of promontories either side of a deep gorge. A monumental bridge joins the older part (*la ciudad*) with the 17th-century expansion of the town where the railway station is situated.

> *An incomparable spot of earth, a giant of a rock which bears a small white-washed town on his shoulders.*[76]

Ronda is a great and (theoretically) easy day trip from Málaga. For years it was possible to catch a train leaving Málaga at around 10 am and be in Ronda before noon. A train back to Málaga left Ronda just before 5 pm, allowing you a couple of hours for sightseeing and a couple of hours for a leisurely lunch. By 2023, this was no longer the case, with only one direct train each way, both of them in the morning. All other trains go via the AVE station at Antequera–Santa Ana and take longer than the coach. Train schedules change all the time, so check before travelling.

At the time of publication at least, the best way to get to and from Ronda is by bus. If one travels by bus the journey time is greater than the fastest train, but there are more options. There is nothing to prevent your travelling one way by train and one way by bus. However, by bus you can leave Málaga at 8 am (arriving around 10.40 am), and then return late afternoon or early evening. Though the journey is long (1¾ to 2½ hours), it is through beautiful countryside. One of the bus companies serving the Málaga–Ronda route is 🌐 **avanzabus.com** which acquired the previous operator, Portillo, a few years ago. The Damas company (🌐 **damas-sa.es**) run a more frequent service. Lastly, Autocares Sierra de las Nieves (🌐 **grupopacopepe.com/horarios**) operates two or three services a day (buy tickets for this company at the bus station rather than online). ⚠ Bus operators change frequently. You can check which companies are serving the route and when, by consulting the Málaga Bus Station website: 🌐 **estabus.malaga.eu** ⚠ The links for 'timetables' and 'departures and arrivals' currently only work in Spain; to connect from outside Spain you

---

76 Rainer Maria Rilke (1912) in a letter to Auguste Rodin

could try using a VPN.

It takes about 20 minutes to walk from the Ronda railway station (or the bus station) to the famous bridge over the River Tajo, a walk that will take you through the 'new' part of town. Standing on the Calle Virgen de la Paz in front of the famous bullring, the *turismo* is about 50 metres in front of you, on the left-hand (south) side of the bullring. Call in to pick up maps and leaflets and find out what's on that day. After a coffee or other refreshment, head into the older part of the town to have a look at the churches (which in Spain often close during the afternoon, so on a day trip do the churches and convents first), then find somewhere nice for leisurely lunch (there is lots of choice). After lunch, you'll have time for a bit more sightseeing before a refreshing glass of wine or two and a stroll back to the station. Ronda is the centre of the Serranía de Ronda wine-producing area so there are many delicious and unusual wines to taste here that rarely get exported outside Spain, or even beyond Andalucía. The *Parador* perhaps has the most spectacular views of any in Spain (except perhaps Cuenca, in La Mancha, with which Ronda is twinned). It has a fine, though not terribly cheap, restaurant, but you can visit for a drink on the terrace and nibble a few olives or a crisp or two if you want to get a taste of the surroundings.

Most of the sights of Ronda are in the smaller old-town side of the gorge, reached by the Old (Roman) bridge, or the more impressive New Bridge. Ronda, first recorded as a city under Julius Caesar, was one of the last hold-outs of the Moors in Spain, and portions of the massive Arab walls remain. Ronda also has the best-preserved Arab baths anywhere in Spain (no longer functioning, though). There are plenty of beautiful plazas, attractive gardens, a couple of decent museums and some fine (though simple) churches.

It is a Mecca (so to speak) for *aficionados* of the bullfight (or, to avoid English terms of abuse, the *corrida*), because this is the town in which the modern bullfight was pretty much invented. The ultimate origins of *toreo* ('bullfighting') are lost in the mists of time, and something analogous was almost certainly practised by pre-Roman Celtiberians (for a more detailed account read the chapter about bulls from p. 437). The Visigoths took to it, in some form or another, but it was, perhaps surprisingly, the Moors who started to develop the bullfight as we know it today. For them, it was a pursuit of noblemen, done on horseback. Before and after the *reconquista*, it behoved Christian nobles to show that they could equal Moorish horsemanship, and this tradition is still reflected in the *rejoneo* (mounted *corrida*) that we see today. Pope St Pius V condemned bullfighting[77], and it became less respectable as a result. By the end of the 17th century, the killing of the bull was considered unseemly for noblemen, but it was such a part of the popular cultural fabric of Spain by then that the death of the bull could not be avoided (or hidden as it was, and shamefully still is, in Portugal). The solution was for the nobility to demonstrate their horsemanship and then let a common man (often

---

77   Bulla S.D.N. Pii Pape V. *Super prohibitione agitationis Taurorum & Ferarum, & annulatione votorum & iuramentorum, super eisdem pro tempore interpositorum* (Rome, Heirs of Antonio Blado, 1567)

a Gypsy) actually kill the beast (giving rise to the modern term '*matador,*' or killer, as opposed to '*torero*' or the one who masters the wild bull).

One such *matador de toros* (killer of bulls) was the *rondeño* Francisco Romero (c. 1700–1763) whose most famous innovation was the *muleta*, the 'red rag' we now think of as synonymous with matadors. His son Juan innovated still further, bringing more style and skill to the final 'third' (or act) of the *corrida*. In turn, his son Pedro was not a great innovator when it came to style, but his contribution was to codify the bullfight and to establish the bullfight on foot, with only a brief appearance by mounted *picadores*, as an art in its own right, not simply the final, bloody denouement of an equine display of aristocrats. Even in his 80s, Pedro was killing bulls in Madrid. For *aficionados*, the sand of the bullring in Ronda is hallowed. I have seen grown men kneel to kiss it.

Even for someone with no interest in bullfighting, the Ronda bullring is a beautiful 18th-century building and well worth a visit. Its cultural importance cannot be overstated. Not far from the bullring is a lovely little park (the 'Alameda' — from the word *álamo*, meaning poplar) and a stunning lookout point officially called the 'Mirador de Ronda' but known locally as the '*Balcón del Coño*' which means — and there's no polite way to say this — 'the balcony of the c*nt' — presumably because people look down into the gorge and exclaim '¡*Ay coño!*' ('F*ck me!' being the English equivalent).

> *This wonderful Roman-Moorish-Spanish town, lifted into the sky, complete with bullring and churches and palaces on tremendous cliffs sundered by a narrow chasm from top to bottom, right in the town's heart, so that one peers over the bridge and down through layers of choughs, jackdaws, raven, swallows and crows to a cascade that looks a mile below.*[78]

I think that Ronda is one of the most stunning towns in the whole of Spain, and there is plenty to see there. If the timings of your transport mean spending a whole day in Ronda (or if you are planning to stay overnight in Ronda), then you might consider visiting one of the wineries (*bodegas*) around Ronda (see p. 481ff.). A couple are close to the centre and there are a few more just outside town that you could reach by taxi (or you could hire a car, but then you would not be able to properly enjoy (drink) the wine at the end of the tour and what would be the point of that?). At the very least, do seek out the Ronda wines available in the bars or restaurants you visit.

⧖ History

A settlement near Ronda was probably founded as 'Arunda' by the Celtiberians, in the 6th century BC. Later, the Phoenicians settled in the nearby village Acinipo, and Arunda, after being conquered by the Greeks, was renamed 'Runda'. But Ronda as such was founded as a consequence of the Second Punic War, during the campaign of the Roman general Scipio the African against the Carthaginians who dominated Hispania at the end of the 3rd century BC. This was when the castle of Laurus (or Laurel) was built, and a population began to grow around it. By the time of Julius Caesar, Ronda was a Roman city, and its inhabitants Roman Citizens.

In the 5th century, with the collapse of the Roman Empire, the city was taken over by the Suevi (Visigoths) under the command of Rechila. In 711 the Muslim invasion of the Iberian Peninsula took place and, in 713, the Ronda surrendered to Zaide Ben Kesadi El Sebseki and was renamed Izn-Rand Onda (the city of the castle) becoming the capital of the *andaluz*

---

78 Patrick Leigh Fermor, *Words of Mercury* (2003) (The words themselves were presumably written soon after the Second World War when Leigh Fermor visited his wartime comrade in arms, Xan Fielding)

province of Takurunna. With the disintegration of the Caliphate of Córdoba, Takurunna became the *Taifa* of Ronda, an independent kingdom ruled by Abu Nur Hilal Ben Abi Qurra, and it was this period that saw most of the urban development of the Ronda that we see today. Ronda would later become part of the Sevillian kingdom of Al-Mutadid.

The Islamic period of the city ended when, on 22 May 1485, the *Reyes Católicos* managed to take it after a long siege. After the *reconquista*, Ronda enjoyed a resurgence that saw it expand into new neighbourhoods such as the Mercadillo (the commercial area near the bullring) and San Francisco (outside the Arab walls). As a result, the Arab nucleus became known simply as *La Ciudad* (The City). Ronda remained rebellious, with large numbers of *moriscos* (Muslims who had officially converted to Christianity, but many of whom covertly practised Islam). On 25 May 1566, Philip II decreed that the Arabic language be proscribed in his kingdom, that all front doors were to remain open on Fridays to show that no Muslim *jumu'ah* prayers were taking place, and he imposed heavy taxes on *morisco* traders. This led to several regional rebellions, including in Ronda.

In 1572 the *Real Maestranza de Caballería de Ronda* (Martial Riding School) was founded. Between the 16th and 17th centuries, the bulk of the city as it is preserved today was constructed. The old *medina* renamed La Ciudad was divided into 'Alta' (upper) and 'Baja' (lower) portions, the latter being the area around the (current) 'old bridge'. The new neighbourhoods of San Francisco and the Mercadillo experienced a construction boom, providing themselves with inns, churches and convents. In the 18th century, the city saw a series of very important constructions, including the New Bridge — the symbol of the city — and the bullring, one of the oldest and most famous in the world, both works of Martín de Aldehuela (who completed Málaga's cathedral). There is a romantic legend that Aldehuela died after throwing himself from his bridge so that he would never be asked to build one that surpassed it in beauty. In fact, he died a natural death in Málaga and was buried in the crypt of the Discalced Franciscan Convent of San Pedro de Alcántara. When it was demolished during the disentailment of 1830, his remains were not moved, so if you happen to be having a meal on the *terraza* of La Mota restaurant in Málaga (near the La Tranca bar in the north of the *centro histórico*), look for the plaque that records the presence of the illustrious bones beneath you.

Ronda's reputation for rebelliousness grew from the 18th century onwards. Partly this reputation was deserved, and partly it was confected. The mountain roads in the vicinity of Ronda were lonely, dangerous places, and banditry flourished. *Rondeños* had long had a reputation for being tough and bellicose, and now the city had a reputation as a place where men killed fighting bulls, not on horseback with a lance, but on foot, facing them head-on. But the romantic myths of banditry really took hold following the Napoleonic invasion and the subsequent War of Independence which had a special virulence in Ronda and its mountains. The Laurel castle, the Roman fortress of Ronda, was all but demolished by the French in their retreat and many of the mills and crops were ruined, leaving the area in a precarious economic state. The city was subject to the payment of high taxes and required to supply daily provisions to the invaders, which suffocated the local economy. Industrial and livestock production plummeted and a third of the orchards were left in ruins due to the large number of *rondeños* who went into the mountains to fight against the French. The resident population was reduced from over 15,000 inhabitants to 5,000 in just three years. Many of the *bandidos* were the *guerrillas* fighting the invaders, who, after the ravages of the war, were left without subsistence resources and took to robbing travellers and smuggling goods from Gibraltar. This phenomenon was exploited by romantic travellers such as Washington Irving and Prosper Mérimée, who took Ronda as a source of inspiration, mixing true history with fiction, forging the romantic image that the city still has. Hans Christian Andersen had been warned in Copenhagen that 'travellers were constantly exposed to attacks from bandits' and he had hoped that his journey north from Málaga might be protected by an armed guard. When it took place without incident, he found himself with 'a tremendous desire to experience just a little encounter with bandits'.[79]

During the 19th and 20th centuries, Ronda's economic activity continued to be overwhelmingly rural, being the meeting point for the inhabitants of the towns of the *serranía* (mountains) and it experienced a growth spike at the beginning of the 20th century with the arrival of the railway. In 1918, the city hosted the Ronda Assembly, which effectively established 'Andalucía' as an entity, and agreed upon a flag, anthem and coat of arms. Around the same time, the *Caja de Ahorros de Ronda* (Savings Bank of Ronda) was established, soon becoming a huge rural bank that significantly boosted the city's economy until its disappearance in 1990 when it merged with a number of other banks to form 'Unicaja'.

The aftermath of the Civil War dealt another blow to Ronda's economic equilibrium with the loss of one-fifth of its population. In fact, the population of the city today is only 500 more than it was in 1930. The scene in Chapter 10 of Hemingway's *For Whom the Bell Tolls*, describing the 1936 execution of Falangist sympathizers in a (fictional) village who are thrown off a cliff, is thought to be modelled on actual events of the time in Ronda. The scene is related to the protagonist Robert Jordan by Pilar, the girlfriend of the *guerrilla* leader Pablo. In her account, a number of fascists were cornered in the Plaza de España. After being permitted to confess to a priest, they were made to walk between lines of Republicans armed with clubs and pitchforks. The mayor was the first to be taken to the cliff edge and thrown into the gorge below, with a further twenty Falangists meeting the same fate. Hemingway's retelling is, if anything, understating what happened in the Ronda. According to some historians, between 200 and 600 Nationalists were killed in Ronda during the Civil War, but there is little agreement about how many met their gruesome end by being tossed into the Tajo (beyond one condemned man who committed suicide by jumping from the cliff).[80]

Ronda Today

Ronda has a small urban bus network (urbanoronda.com) and the same smartphone app that works in Antequera also works in Ronda. The download link is at the bottom of the homepage of the bus website. Be aware, however, that although the buses are comprehensive for a small town, the service tends to be more or less hourly. As all three buses service the Bus Station (♀Calle Commandante Salvador Carrasco), you shouldn't have to wait long if you want to take the bus into town. There are always taxis for hire around the railway and bus stations.

When you arrive, head for the *turismo*, either directly by bus or walk through the town centre if you want to stop for refreshments. In Ronda, an 'access all areas' ticket is called the '*Bono Turístico*' and it gets you into a fair few of the main visitor sites in Ronda. It saves you a few euros, but you also get a map that suggests a pleasant, walkable route around the most noteworthy parts of the city. The website of the Ronda *turismo* is sleek, but not terribly user-friendly (*i.e.* it has plenty of information but sometimes presents it poorly, trying to be a bit too clever, perhaps), though the *Bono Turístico* route and map are excellent. **A** Sites included in the Bono Turístico are marked with a 🏛 symbol in the text below.

Many of the main tourist sights in Ronda keep the same opening hours, *viz.* **Sun & Tue–Fri 1000–1800; Mon & Sat 1000–1400, 1500–1800.** As with all the day trips I recommend, the

---

79   Hans Christian Andersen 1975 *op. cit.*

80   For an interesting analysis of Hemingway's use of Ronda in For Whom the Bell Tolls, see 'Revolution in Ronda: the facts in Hemingway's For Whom the Bell Tolls' by Ramon Buckley in *The Hemingway Review*, 22 September 1997, bit.ly/EHinRonda

advice is the same — arrive as early as you can and get your sightseeing done by around 2 pm which, conveniently, is lunchtime in Spain.

If you visit the *turismo*, you are right next to the **Real Maestranza de Caballería de Ronda** (The Royal Cavalry Workshop of Ronda) and their arena, the **Plaza de Toros** (⊕ **rmcr.org** ◷ 1000–1800). A *maestranza* is connected to the term *maestro* (master) and is defined by the *Real Academia Española* as 'a society of knights whose purpose is to practise horsemanship; originally a school for handling weapons on horseback'. It is basically a *cofradía* or *hermandad* devoted not to a religious aim, but to horsemanship. The 'RMR' was founded in 1573 as the *Hermandad del Espíritu Santo* in response to a request by King Felipe II the previous year in which he asked all towns and cities of the Kingdom to found such a society. The RMR devoted itself to the practice of riding 'a la jineta' — a way of riding with short stirrups (*i.e.* leathers) and bent legs, as opposed to 'a la brida', with long stirrups. This former mode of riding was considered more 'noble' and is still the style employed in the mounted bullfight, though the *maestranza* these days trains riders in classical dressage. There are also *maestranzas* in Sevilla, Granada, Valencia and Zaragoza, but Ronda's is the oldest by a century.

The bullring is owned by the Real Maestranza and due to its role in the history of *toreo*, is the most famous in the world. Nowadays, three *corridas* are held over the first weekend in September, consisting of a *corrida* with young bulls (*novillos*) on Friday afternoon, a mounted *corrida de rejones* on Saturday and, on Sunday, a '*corrida de toros "Goyesca"*' for which all the participants dress in the sort of costumes worn in the time of Goya, the heyday of the Ronda ring.

Walking north, away from the *turismo* and the bullring, after about 200 metres you come to the large **Church of Nuestra Señora de La Merced** (Our Lady of Mercy). Built in 1585, the church contains some impressive artworks, but its real treasure is a First Class Relic of Saint Teresa of Ávila (her incorrupt hand in a gilded silver reliquary). If you walk down the left-hand side of the church, you come to the '*torno*' ('turn', or serving hatch) of the Convent of the Discalced Carmelite nuns, where they sell a wide variety of *dulces* (sweets and biscuits). If you would like to buy some, the transaction is conducted in the same way that it is all over Spain. Ring the bell and you will hear the portress (the nun on duty) say, '*Ave María Purísima*' (Hail, Purest Mary). You reply, '*Sin pecado concebida*' (Conceived without sin — sin pek-**ah**-doh kon-thay-**bee**-dah). The '*torno*' opens and there will be a price list for you to consult and place your order. If you don't know what to ask for then look for something that says '*surtida*' or '*surtido*' (a selection). (◷ 1000–1300, 1700–1900)

Close to the Plaza de La Merced, beside the bullring, is the **Alameda del Tajo Park** which has stunning views of the Los Molinos valley. Walk down to the **Mirador de Ronda** to appreciate the views. The Scots Hispanist and writer Alastair Boyd (Lord Kilmarnock) in recording his first visit to Ronda summed up how this small park, beside an urban street, is also a window onto a huge and dramatic landscape beyond: 'Leaving my luggage in the Hotel Royal, I walked across the street into the alameda and knew at once, as one instinctively does, that I had reached a place of great significance in my life.'[81] Boyd's first impression was prescient,

---

81   Alastair Boyd, *The Road from Ronda, Travels with a Horse through Southern Spain* (Collins, 1969)

for he went on to live most of the rest of his life in Ronda, dying there in 2009, fifty years later. Take the path that brings you to the front of the **Parador de Ronda**, which surely has one of the most dramatic locations of any hotel in this chain. Inaugurated in 1994, the building is the former town hall and the grounds were the site of the former municipal market.

Next, I suggest you walk across the famous Puente Nuevo bridge into La Ciudad. Ronda has three bridges these days, but over the years, there have been at least seven (albeit not all at the same time). The oldest is the Roman Bridge (*Puente Romano*), which is of Arab construction but on Roman foundations. Next is the Old Bridge (*Puente Viejo*), slightly higher, and built by the Arabs (though some suggest a Roman origin). It was destroyed in the *reconquista*, and King Fernando decreed in 1486 that it should urgently be rebuilt. It was replaced in 1616 after being washed away in a flood and became known as the New Bridge (*Puente Nuevo*). In 1735 the *Puente Nuevo* became the *Puente Viejo* when another bridge was built upstream (where the current *Puente Nuevo* stands). But six years later it collapsed, killing 50 people (like many bridges of the period it had cantilevered shops and taverns along its length). A new construction was begun in 1751 and funds were raised by collecting 15,000 *reales* from the Real Maestranza and taxing the May Fair. It was finally inaugurated in May 1793 and was, at that time, the highest bridge in the world. Remarkably, it kept that record for almost half a century (until 1839) when it was surpassed by the Pont de la Caille in France. In the upper part, there are rooms which in the past have been used as a jail and a tavern, but which now accommodate an 🏛 Interpretation Centre for visitors.

The official website of the *Parador* de Ronda[82] tempts potential guests promising, 'You will be staying at the edge of a cliff enjoying the amazing views of the Tagus River'. This is unlikely, to say the least, given that the Tagus River is 350 km away from Ronda. The confusion arises because the Tajo, the longest river in the Iberian Peninsula (rising in Teruel and flowing into the Atlantic at Lisbon), is called 'Tagus' in English. The bridge in Ronda does indeed span 'El Tajo', but this is not the name of a river: it means 'gorge' or 'escarpment' (from the verb *tajar* meaning to cut). The river is the **Guadalevín** (from the Arabic for 'Milk River').

On your left, as you enter the 'old town', is the plain but monumental edifice of the 🏛 **Antiguo Convento de Santo Domingo**. This convent was founded by the *Reyes Católicos* in 1485 after the *reconquista*. It was dedicated to Saint Peter Martyr and was a house of the Order of Preachers (Dominicans). It is one of the four convents founded in Ronda by the monarchs and for a while during the 16th century, it was the headquarters of the Spanish Inquisition. After the disentailments of 1836, it was used variously as a jail, barracks, market and workshop. The interior cloister dates from the second half of the 17th century and is delimited by wide semicircular brick arches supported by smooth columns and Corinthian capitals. Its church is plain (very typical of Dominican churches) and divided into three naves. Currently, the restored building is used as a *Palacio de los Congresos* (municipal conference centre) for exhibitions and also for social events. Though there is not a great deal to see apart from the architecture, the entrance price is nominal.

Detour: Turning left after the **Convento de Santo Domingo** and walking down the Calle Cuesta de Santo Domingo brings you to the **Casa del Rey Moro** (House of the Moorish King). The name is somewhat fraudulent as it was never a Moorish residence. The first documentary data on this extraordinary house–palace date back to the 18th century. It is a building of large proportions and with a rather irregular and labyrinthine floor plan, which inside has numerous stairs and corridors which serve to overcome the different slopes. It has an interesting façade that adapts to the curve of the street. It is three stories high, with a gallery at the top and two towers of different heights. The back of the house overlooks landscaped terraces leading down to the '*tajo*' formed by the Guadalevín River as it passes

---

82   archive.ph/kMFG4

through Ronda. At various points on its secluded terraces there are viewpoints located at different heights, with great views of the other side of the city of Ronda. Surrounding the house-palace are attractive gardens, also at different levels. They were designed in 1912 by the famous landscape architect Jean-Claude Nicolas Forestier to recreate an imagined (and probably rather fanciful) 'Moorish Garden'.

Though not actually Moorish itself, the house does incorporate one genuine and important relic of Ronda's Moorish occupation — the so-called 'Water Mine'. Ronda was often besieged, being in the firing line between Moorish Granada and Christian Sevilla, and the first target of any army, after bridges, is the water supply. Ronda's Moorish King Abomelek had Christian slaves cut stone steps into the cliff so that water could be brought up from the river far below. Supposedly a secret, it was clearly common knowledge in the city because as a contemporary aphorism put it, 'In Ronda, you die carrying water skins.' The palace, gardens and 'mine' have been undergoing restoration for some time, so check first with the *turismo* to find out which parts of the site are open for visits. However, be warned: the steps are steep, damp and uneven and represent a formidable descent (and more importantly, ascent — there is no other way out except to climb back to the top).

Further along the Calle Armiñán is the 🏛 **Museo Lara Coleccionismo** (⊕ museolara.org ⏰ 1100–1900). This museum is located in the *Casa–Palacio* of the 'Count of the Conquest of the Batanes Islands'. '*Coleccionismo*' means 'collecting', as in a hobby, and the collector in this case is Juan Antonio Lara Jurado who restored the *palacio* and opened the museum in 1999. The exhibitions in this privately owned museum are varied and even quirky, but with 5,000 pieces there are many genuinely fascinating exhibits, and the variety means that there is something to interest everyone. The chief themes are 18th-century timepieces, 17th-century weapons, scientific instruments, archaeology, the 18th-century *bodega*, knives and firearms, bullfighting and the history of film and photography. There are also smaller exhibition spaces devoted to 'witchcraft' and 'The Inquisition', but I am afraid that here we venture into the fanciful and ahistorical. The 'exhibits', for example, include an 'Iron Maiden' and a 'chastity belt', both of which are fanciful 19th-century inventions.

A little further on, turn right onto the Plaza del Gigante to reach the 🏛 **Casa del Gigante** (House of the Giant). The origin of the name comes from two large stone bas-reliefs that decorated the corners of the building, of which only one remains today. The house was constructed at the end of the 13th century (or the beginning of the 14th century) and is a fine example of typical Nasrid domestic architecture of the period. Unlike the Casa del Rey Moro, then, this **is** a *casa moro*. It is assumed that the house belonged to an important person, not only because of its dimensions but also because of its decorative aspects. After the *reconquista*, the house became the property of Ruy Gutiérrez de Escalante, mayor of the city. Despite having passed through so many hands subsequently and having undergone several reforms, the house has not altered its original structure too much, so we can see a fairly complete example of what a wealthy home was like in Spain under Muslim rule.

Across the square is the 🏛 **Museo Unicaja Joaquín Peinado** (📍 Plaza del Gigante ⊕ museojoaquinpeinado.com ⏰ Mon–Sat ⊘ August). The Peinado Museum is operated by the Unicaja Foundation and is located in the Palace of the Marquesses of Moctezuma (the heirs of Moctezuma II, the last Emperor of the Aztecs). It charts the different creative stages of the *rondeño* Cubist painter Joaquín Peinado (a disciple of Pablo Ruiz Picasso) through a tour of more than 190 works.

If you retrace your steps and make your way down to the Calle Tenorio, you will see the tower of the **Church of Nuestra Señora de la Paz** (Our Lady of Peace, patroness of Ronda). This church has its origin in a hermitage built by the alderman Francisco de Morales and his wife in the middle of the 16th century. The current baroque building has intense ornamentation within and above the high altar is the image of the Virgen de la Paz, profusely decorated with golden baroque plasterwork. It is rarely, however, open for visits.

On the Calle Tenorio, you will find the 🏛 **Casa Museo Don Bosco** (🌐 casadonbosco.es). This is a museum, but not a traditional one. What it offers is a glimpse into the interior of a rather grand *rondeña* house of the late 19th and early 20th centuries. The house was built circa 1850 and remodelled at the beginning of the 20th century in a modernist style by the architect Santiago Sanguinetti. The owners were an upper-class couple, the engineer Don Francisco Granadino Pérez and his wife Doña Dolores Gómez Martínez. Having no children of their own, they bequeathed the property to the Society of Saint Francis de Sales (commonly called the Salesians, founded by the Italian priest, 'Don Bosco'). In the 1940s, that congregation established a sanatorium here to help priests and students (the Order works in education) traumatized in the wake of the Civil War. The sanatorium closed in 2008 and it has now been opened to the public as a house museum. The decoration is exquisite, the garden (more of a terrace) has beautiful views and it is a delightful place to visit. Between March and June, and September and November, frequent flamenco guitar concerts are staged. Beginning at 7 pm, these are a little late for day-trippers but might appeal to those who are staying in Ronda overnight.

Walk further into the old town to find the 🏛 **Palacio de Mondragón**, the Municipal Museum of Ronda. Also known as the Palace of the Marqués de Villasierra, this palace is a *mudéjar*-Renaissance building and, although legend claims it was the residence of the kings of the Taifa of Ronda, it was almost certainly built later and in the 14th century was where the Berber King Abu Malik Abd al-Wahid ('Abomelek'), son of the Marinid Sultan of Morocco Abu'l-Hassan, resided. After his death, Ronda became dependent on the Kingdom of Granada and the palace became the residence of the Nasrid governor, its last occupant being Hamed el Zegrí. Only its layout and floor-plan, the foundations, and some underground passages that connected the garden with the old fortress remain from its Muslim period. The *Reyes Católicos* established their residence in the palace during their stay in the city in 1485, after which it passed into the hands of Captain Melchor de Mondragón, whose shield appears on the 16th-century façade with its pair of brick towers. Although it has been heavily restored (at one point it was an uninhabitable ruin) it is one of Ronda's most enchanting buildings and the Municipal Museum that it houses has some very well-curated exhibits such as the Pileta Cave reconstruction, a stone age hut, iron age technology including sword making, artefacts from the Roman period with important exhibits relating to Acinipo and Moorish Ronda (including a detailed exhibit about Arab funeral rites), as well as a very interesting display on life in Ronda's heyday, the 17th and 18th centuries.

The twentieth-century history of the Palacio de Mondragón (and the Casa de Mondragón next door) is also rather interesting. Alastair Boyd, Lord Kilmarnock, was running a language school in the *palacio* when Hilary Bardwell came to stay in Ronda after the breakdown of her second marriage, to the Classics scholar D. R. Shackleton Bailey. The story of their relationship and subsequent marriage (his second, her third) is told by Hilary's son from her first marriage, Sir Martin Amis, in his memoir *Experience* (2000). After Amis's debut novel *The Rachel Papers* (1973) won the Somerset Maugham Award (the terms of which required a period spent abroad), he came to the Casa Mondragón to work on his second novel, *Dead Babies*. Amis called Spain his 'other European country' and although he loved the dramatic scenery of Ronda he was dismissive of Hemingway's romanticization of the town.

Amis's stepfather, Alastair Boyd, had come to live in Ronda with his first wife Diana in 1957, just as the first trickle of tourists were taking day trips from fledgling resorts like Torremolinos. Nowadays, Ronda has achieved a kind of balance between its status as a tourist destination and as a relatively prosperous town at the centre of an important wine region. But in the early 1960s, the relationship was more fraught. On the one hand Ronda — devastated after the Civil War — needed tourist *pesetas*. The relative impoverishment of the town was what allowed a (then) unsuccessful novelist and English language teacher like Boyd to set up house in a palace (Boyd may have been a peer of the realm, but there was little family money and he needed to work for a living, later running a *tapas* bar). On the other hand, Ronda was jealous of her illustrious history as a town established by Royal decree after centuries as an important Roman and then Moorish centre. Boyd felt the weight of that history reflected in the Palacio de Mondragón itself:

> [T]*he locals call [the* Palacio Mondragón] Casa de Piedra, *the Stone House, a name deriving from its all-stone façade unbroken except by a great Renaissance portico and the three long windows of the saloon on the first floor. The staircase leading up to this floor has a fine plaster vaulted ceiling painted with heraldic achievements, on which three severed Moors' heads figure prominently [...] Beyond the front patio, which dates from about 1570, lies the oldest part of the house, known as the* Patio Arabe, *and beyond this again the garden hanging over the gorge.*[83]

Not far away, on the Plaza de la Duquesa de Parcent is the impressive 🏛 **Iglesia de Santa María la Mayor** (Church of Saint Mary Major), a former Collegiate Church built over the 13th-century mosque of the city, remains of the *mihrab* of which survive (adding yet another layer to a succession of sacred buildings).

The beginning of the construction of this church must have taken place very soon after the reconquest of the city by Christian troops in 1486 though the current building is mostly 16th century, having been constructed after the original church was damaged in an earthquake in 1580. The balconies at the front were added during the reign of Felipe II for the nobility and gentry of the city to watch tournaments, bullfights and other events being staged in the square by the *Maestranza*.

Across the square, known as the 'Old Plaza Mayor', is the **Convento de Santa Isabel de los Ángeles,** a 16th-century convent of Poor Clare nuns. The church is often open to visit, and this is one of the convents where you can buy '*dulces*' — the sweets, biscuits and madeleines traditionally made by religious sisters (🕐 0900–1230, 1530–1730). Also in the square, we find the **Ayuntamiento**, originally the headquarters of the old Provincial Militia. It was built in 1734, apparently on top of a row of shops with arcades built in the 16th century and of probable Islamic origin (most likely a corn exchange). After the Peninsular War (1807–1814), the barracks were left abandoned and the current building is the result of significant restoration done in the early 1970s. The **Convent of La Caridad** (Convent of Charity) was built

---

83   Boyd, *ibid.*

during the 16th century, though the building has been put to various uses since its construction. It has a church with a single nave covered with a barrel vault with lunettes. The **Church of María Auxiliadora** (Mary Help of Christians) is relatively modern, consecrated only in 1951, and built to form a complex with the Salesian school next to it. Its tall exterior façade, with classicist lines, evokes the style of Andalusian hermitages, as does the classic bichrome (yellow/white) decoration.

Continuing further south, we find a large gate in the old city walls known as the **Puerta de Almocábar**. Nearby is the gate (cut into the wall) called the **Puerta de Carlos V** (of the Holy Roman Empire, so Carlos I of Spain) which has Renaissance styling and a royal coat of arms. Just before this gate is the **Iglesia del Espíritu Santo** (Church of the Holy Spirit), built by the *Reyes Católicos* on the site of an old mosque located in the octagonal tower through which the Christian troops entered.

Construction began in 1485 and ended in 1505. Its very simple Gothic exterior gives the clear impression of being a fortified church. Above the door, you can see a small sculpture of a dove inside a niche that represents the Holy Spirit. The **Puerta de Almocábar** and its walls separate the *barrio* of San Francisco from the *barrio* of La Ciudad. It was constructed in the 13th century and consists of three gates, with three horseshoe arches between semicircular towers, (possibly where the guards once slept). Its name is from the Arabic *al-maqabi* (meaning cemetery) since it is located near the old Muslim cemetery. In the **Plaza de San Francisco**, noticeably more light and open than the old city, is the **Convento de la Franciscanas**. This monastery of Discalced Franciscan nuns is another place where one can purchase *dulces*, and they carry a huge range, including some unusual ones like *gañotes* (cinnamon and lemon twists), *cocadas* (coconut macaroons) and *batatines* (made with sweet potato, sugar and toasted almonds) as well as the usual favourites like *polvorones*. Neither *cocadas* nor *batatines* are traditional Spanish *dulces*, and reflect the international composition of religious communities in Spain, with sisters from all over the world, especially from South America and the Philippines. The nuns support their life of prayer, contemplation and social outreach by making sweets and taking in clothing for alteration and repairs (🕐 0900–1200, 1600–1900).

Heading back into the walled city, you can return to the 'new town' via the easy route by following Calle Armiñán back to the Puente Nuevo, or you can bear right and walk down the hill past the remaining sections of the city walls and into the valley, crossing over the river either by the **Puente Viejo** or the **Puente Romano**. Worth looking at on your way is the **Alminar de San Sebastián** (The Minaret of San Sebastián) — a minaret that was originally part of a mosque and later the tower of the now defunct Church of San Sebastián. Three zones can be distinguished: a lower one, built in stone with a door topped by a horseshoe arch and *alfiz* (surround); a middle zone built in brick that dates, like the previous zone, from the 14th century; and an upper portion, also made of brick, built after the Christian *reconquista* of the city, to serve as a bell tower.

If you opt to wander down the hill, then you will be able to take in the **Arco de Felipe V** and the 🏛 **Baños Árabes**. After the collapse of the first attempt at a new bridge in 1741, the need to improve the entrance to the city from the Puente Viejo arose due to the large number of people and goods that were once again forced to use it. The old '*Puerta Árabe de la Puente*' was replaced in 1742 by the current one during the reign of the first Bourbon king, Felipe V (note the Shell of Anjou and the royal coat of arms of the Bourbons on its façade). The Arab Baths are located at what was once the entrance to the Moorish city, so these were for travellers as well as residents (there would have been many other bath houses within the walls). They follow the pattern of Roman baths and consist of the same sections (cold, warm and hot rooms, hypocaust and boiler, and reception room), but unlike the Romans, who bathed by immersion in large pools, the Moorish version was largely a steam bath plus a single pool. It is a pleasant walk down to the baths, but a **very** steep climb back up. However, these are probably the best preserved Arab baths in Andalucía, if not in Spain, so well worth a visit if you feel energetic. If you think your visit might put you in the mood for enjoying a hammam yourself, then there is one just along the road (⊕ hammamaguasderonda.com/en).

🏋 Eating and Drinking

Ronda has a justly deserved reputation for the quality not only of its wines but of its food. There are myriad specialities and typical dishes of the Ronda region. Many incorporate local products like chestnuts from the Valle del Genal, pumpkin, broad beans, almonds, artichokes, goat's cheese, etc. Game is plentiful, so in season you might see rabbit, hare, partridge and other game birds on menus. Typical dishes are *migas* (fried breadcrumbs) with *chorizo*, a local *gazpacho* ('a la serrana'), served hot and more like an unblended *sofrito*, and a local variety of *tortilla* containing black pudding. There is also a local version of black pudding (*morcilla rondeña*) that finds its way into many dishes. Whereas to the east of Málaga, *chivo* (kid) is popular, in Ronda it is *cordero* (lamb) that is served more often, usually as 'cochifrito' (fried with garlic). Like most mountainous regions in Spain, stews are a firm favourite.

We are in Spain, so fish is popular, but it is not as central to menus in inland Ronda as it is in Málaga or Sevilla, preserving the distinction one often sees on restaurant menus between '*mar y montaña*' ('sea and mountain'), effectively 'surf-n-turf'. Historically, life in Ronda had meant engaging in hard agricultural work. While the 'soft' *malagueños* might crave their creamy *conchas finas* and a glass of crisp *vino blanco*, the *rondeños* demand grilled meat, blood sausage and hearty stews washed down with some gutsy *vino tinto*. Excellent white wines are made in the surrounding *bodegas*, but reds predominate. The reason is largely historical. Until comparatively recently (and bear in mind that the production of still wines in the Málaga DOP took years to recover from phylloxera) most wine in Spain was sold locally, in bulk. Thus, the wine produced in a particular area tended to be suited to the cuisine.

✗ Winemakers' Picks

The following restaurants and bar-restaurants have been recommended by local winemakers exclusively for this book as establishments where the best wines of the region can be enjoyed.

✗ 🏨 ✎ ⌱ ◈ ♁ Sensur (◉ Calle Marina 5 ⊕ sensurgastrobar.com)

A fairly new gastrobar serving fabulous food from *tapas* and sharing plates (*raciones*) all the way up to substantial main course dishes.

✗ 🏨 ✎ ⌱ Restaurante Pedro Romero (◉ Calle Virgen de la Paz 18 ⊕ rpedroromero.com)

A very traditional *rondeño* restaurant with an extensive cellar. Higher end price-wise, but they often offer a lunchtime *menú del día*.

♟ ✦ ◎ ✎ ⌱ ◈ Taberna El Almacén (◉ Calle Virgen de los Remedios 7)

An excellent *tapas* bar with lots of dishes available as both *tapas* and *raciones*, plus daily specials. They carry a large selection of wines from Ronda, about half a dozen by the glass.

♟ ✦ ◎ ✎ ⌱ ♒ ♒ Tabanco Los Arcos (◉ Calle Armiñán 6 🔲 Tabanco Los Ar)

An informal wine bar with a huge selection of *tapas* alongside more substantial dishes. An excellent place to try Ronda wines.

✗ 🍖 📖 🔪 **Bardal** ✿✿ (📍 Calle José Aparicio 1 🌐 restaurantebardal.com)

This Michelin-starred restaurant is the '*más alta*' of '*alta cocina*' in Ronda, with prices to match.

🍷 🍴 🕐 🔪 🍽 🌍 **Tragatá** (📍 Calle Nueva 4 🌐 tragata.com)

This is the *tapas* bar of Benito Gómez, providing an opportunity to sample the dishes of a Michelin Two-Star chef in more relaxed surroundings at more reasonable prices. The food here is pricey, but no more expensive than in many old-style '*mesón*'-type restaurants.

✗ 🔪 🍽 **Restaurante Tropicana** (📍 Calle Virgen de los Dolores 11 🌐 tropicanaronda.negocio.site)

One of Ronda's most popular restaurants, and for good reason. 'Elevated classics' would be a good description.

✗ 🍷 🍴 🕐 🔪 🍽 **Bar–Restaurante Almocábar** (📍 Plaza Ruedo Alameda 5)

An unassuming café-bar in the San Francisco *barrio* serving a good range of *tapas* in the bar and traditional dishes in the restaurant, accompanied by a very good wine list.

🍷 🍴 🕐 🔪 🍽 **Restaurante Casa Mateos** (📍 Calle Jerez 6 🌐 casamateos.com)

A modern, friendly bar-restaurant serving top-notch *tapas* and main dishes.

✗ 🕐 🔪 🍽 🍖 🌿 🍢 🍶 **Mesón Carmen la de Ronda** (📍 Plaza Duquesa de Parcent 10)

A traditional and always justly popular restaurant serving classic Spanish dishes.

✗ 🍷 🍴 🕐 🔪 🍽 🌍 **Restaurante Doña PaKita** (📍 Plaza Carmen Abela 🌐 dona-pakita.negocio.site)

A traditional Spanish menu with some international riffs and influences here and there. Excellent food and a friendly vibe.

🍷 🍴 🕐 🔪 🍽 🍖 🌿 🍢 🍃 ♨ 🍳 🥂 🍶 **Bar La Taberna ('del Socorro')** (📍 Plaza del Socorro 8 🌐 latabernaderonda.es)

A busy and popular bar that has a good wine list and, as far as food is concerned, covers all the bases — *tapas*, *raciones*, *chacinas* (cold cuts and cheese), *revueltos* (egg dishes), fish, meat, and puddings. Something for everyone at great prices.

🍷 🍴 🔪 🍽 **Entre Vinos** (📍 Calle Pozo 2 📘 entrevinosronda)

One of my favourite bars in Ronda, this is a tiny wine bar that serves a huge selection of *tapas* alongside a selection of *raciones*. There are a couple of tables and a few stools, but if you come here at busy times, expect to eat standing up. The *tapas* are excellent, and they know their wines, offering almost two dozen by the glass.

🍷 🍴 🕐 🔪 🍽 ♨ **Gastrobar Camelot** (📍 Calle Comandante Salvador Carrasco 2)

Another genuine *tapas* bar with an extensive *carta* of well-priced options, usually with a number of daily specials.

🏃 A Few More

🍷 📖 🍴 🕐 🍽 🍖 🍢 ♨ 🍳 🥂 🍶 🍺 **Siempre Igual** (📍 Calle San José 2 🌐 siempreigualronda.es)

Plenty of visitors to Ronda walk straight past this rather plain-looking bar and thus miss out on some of the best *tapas* in town. The service is relaxed (some would say slow) but very friendly. A perfect spot to try Ronda's own version of black pudding, or a *regañá* — a local variety of cracker with various toppings.

♀ 🥢 🕐 🍶 🥡 🍽 🍽 Bodega San Francisco (📍 Calle Comandante Salvador Carrasco)

A traditional bar serving a huge range of inexpensive *tapas* (as well as *medias* and *raciones*). Service is brisk and friendly and I love the honesty of the menu that offers not only 'homemade desserts' but also 'non-homemade desserts'.

♀ 🥢 🍽 Bodeguita El Coto (📍 Calle Virgen de los Remedios 20)

Another reliable *tapas* bar with plenty of choice at low prices brought to your table by some of the hardest-working waiters in Ronda.

♀ 🥢 🕐 🍽 Tapas Bar La Niña Adela (📍 Avenida Ricardo Navarrete 9 🌐 adelatapasbar.firnax.com)

I am including this *tapas* bar because it is 5 minutes' walk from the Railway Station, so very handy if you are watching the clock over lunch before your train's departure. It's not much to look at from the outside, and normally the laminated menus with photographs would sound an alarm, but in fact, it is a lovely bar with well-cooked food and a good range of wine

🍴 🍃 🍶 🍽 Restaurante–Bistró Casa María (📍 Plaza Ruedo Alameda 27 🕐 Lunch: Fri–Tue; Dinner: Daily)

If the 'concept' of this long-established restaurant appeals to you, then you will probably love it, because the cooking is excellent. Although they do their best to accommodate intolerances, this is not a place for finicky feeders because Casa María has no menu. There is a flat rate charge for a meal comprising several courses — two or three small plates to start, a fish dish, a meat main course and a dessert (although, like the menu, it varies from day to day), with advice on wine pairings. It's very good value for the quantity and quality of the food, but it is really only for a certain kind of diner. If the idea of a 'surprise menu' fills you with dread, stay away! Also, it is small and tends to be very popular, so if you fancy trying it, pop in when they open at noon to book a table or book ahead 📞 +34 951 08 36 63.

White in the happiness of your sleepless lime,
Ronda of the air, light and iris,
shady in the nostalgia of your orchards, I give you my song.
The water falls, or is it weeping?
and a flight of doves from the Gorge hold up in elegant stanzas;
stone and I sigh

Pablo García Baena (1923–2018)

Córdoba

🌐 turismodecordoba.org ℹ️ Plaza de las Tendillas 🕐 0900–1430
ℹ️ Plaza del Triunfo 🕐 0900–1900 (Sun 0900–1430)

Córdoba was founded by the Romans in 206 BC, soon becoming the capital of Hispania Ulterior with fine buildings and imposing fortifications. Seneca the Elder, Seneca the Younger, and the poet Lucan were all born in '*Corduba*'. In the 6th century, with the crumbling of the Roman Empire, the city fell to the Visigoths until the beginning of the 8th century when it was conquered by the Moors. Unlike other cities, it was taken by force and no deed of capitulation was signed. In 716, Córdoba became a provincial capital and, in 766, capital of the Muslim emirate of Al-Andalus which at its height (c.1000 AD) controlled two-thirds of the Iberian Peninsula.

Decline set in after the fall of the Umayyads, and the nadir came with the capture of the city in 1236 by Fernando III ('*El Santo*' — King of Castilla; the Fernando II who was the husband of Isabel was more than two centuries later and was King of Aragón). For much of its subsequent history travellers have tended to describe Córdoba as a sad, bleak and empty town, living off memories of its past. However, since the Civil War of 1936–39, 'the distant and lonely' town evoked by Garcia Lorca has developed into a thriving commercial centre and one of the major tourist centres of Spain (though even in this respect, still living off memories and myths of its past).

Córdoba is popular with tourists, who mostly come for the day (or just an hour or two) to visit the '*Mezquita-Catedral*' (the Cathedral, formerly a mosque). Therefore, if you are heading for Córdoba, I would advise you to travel as early as you can countenance and then head straight for the Cathedral (it opens at 10 am) in order to beat the coach parties. By midday the Cathedral can be really very busy, which is fine for getting a taste of what it must have been like in the Middle Ages, but less agreeable for appreciating the perfection of its architecture. Buy tickets online from the official website (see below, p. 569). Córdoba is a city where I would **not** claim that visiting the *oficina de turismo* is a must. One office is in the Plaza de las Tendillas (you could call in on your way to the Cathedral) and another is just south of the Cathedral, near the Roman Bridge. But unless they have cleaned up their act, they are among the worst, most offhand, least helpful *turismos* in Spain. They will give you a useful list of opening times of all the various attractions, but little more. As this list of '*horarios*' is available on the *turismo* website (which, curiously, is excellent), there isn't much point in visiting either office.

Most visitors come principally to see the Cathedral (or '*Mezquita-Catedral*' as it seems to be mainly known). The wonder of the building (it is a UNESCO world heritage site; actually the entire historic city centre is) is less about statues, art and decoration (because it has little of any), and more about the simplicity of the geometric forms of the Islamic architecture. On a visit, one has to 'zoom out' rather than 'zoom in' to appreciate it best. It is undeniable that this architectural monument to Moorish rule is stunning; one of the oldest mosques in the world and, when it was built, the second largest. It was, probably, built on top of a Visigothic church (dedicated to Saint Vincent, protomartyr of Spain) that was, in all likelihood, constructed on top of a Roman temple. Other Visigothic churches were plundered for stone. It was converted into a church in 1236 and was pretty much used as it was until a Renaissance chapel was constructed at its centre in the early 16th century.

Regarding the supposed basilica of San Vicente, opinion is divided. The sources for the idea that the mosque was constructed on earlier Christian foundations are the chronicles of Ibn Idari (*fl.* 1312 ad) and Al Maqqari († 1632). However, recent excavations beneath the Cathedral have failed to uncover anything conclusive (*viz.* there is evidence of older buildings, but nothing to suggest conclusively that it was a church). On the other hand, we know that Córdoba had a bishop from at least 294 AD. Bishop Osius participated in the Council of Nicaea in 325 AD and, according to some authorities, was closely involved in the drafting of the Nicene Creed. We can also be reasonably certain that Bishop Felix was martyred under the fifth Emir of Córdoba, Muhammad I (c. 853 ad). The episcopal seat of Córdoba, therefore, was more than 500 years old by the time of the Umayyad conquest and as a Roman capital city it is inconceivable that it would not have had a sizeable church building within the Roman walls. The question is, if this primitive basilica/cathedral is not beneath the mosque/cathedral then where was it?

The Córdoba 'mosque' has become totemic for Muslims, and demonstrations of Islamic piety (such as the 'spontaneous' offering of prayers) are frequent. There was a mosque on this site for 450 years, but it has now been a Christian church for almost twice as long. If one adds in the life span of the church that was (or may have been) destroyed to build the mosque, then this has been a place of Christian worship for well over a thousand years in total.

We have already encountered the disputed idea of *convivencia*, in which Muslims, Christians and Jews lived together in a kind of tolerant and enlightened paradise. The truth, as we have seen, was somewhat different. Naturally enough, it is in the interests of the city of Córdoba to reimagine its own past as a lost paradise of peaceful tolerance and high culture, but this is only possible if some unpalatable historical facts are airbrushed from the picture. A 'fact' frequently encountered on the internet is that at a time when Christian Europe had only two universities (Bologna and Paris), Andalucía alone had seven. The Islamic 'universities' of the Middle Ages were more likely to have been madrasas, devoted to the study of religious texts and law. Madrasas did begin to teach other subjects as well, but the only 'doctorate' (in the original sense of a licence to teach) available was in the field of religious law.[84]

A visitor to Córdoba is likely to form the impression that the real villains of Iberian history were the Catholic Monarchs Fernando and Isabel and, closely associated with them, the Inquisition. Their injustices are rightly laid bare (not least within Córdoba's macabre and hyperbolic Museum of The Inquisition, previously the 'Gallery of Torture') and the expulsion of Spain's Jews in 1492 is an ugly stain on her history (though hardly unique — Jews had already been expelled from France, Naples, England, Switzerland, Hungary, Austria, Bavaria and Ravenna by this time). Yet mention is rarely made of the massacre of Jews in Córdoba in 1013 when the city was supposedly at its most 'sophisticated'; nor of the Granada massacre of 1066 in which the King's Jewish vizier was crucified and 4,000 Jews were slaughtered in a single day.

Yet for all the positive revisionism of today, it is still difficult to get a sense now of the importance and magnificence of medieval Córdoba, at least within the Moorish kingdoms of Andalucía. To what extent Córdoba was 'outward looking' is subject to some debate. Its rulers

---

84 George Makdisi, 'Scholasticism and Humanism in Classical Islam and the Christian West,' in *Journal of the American Oriental Society* 109, no. 2 (1982): 176. *q.v.* George Makdisi , 'Madrasa and University in the Middle Ages,' *Studia Islamica* 32 (1970): 255–54

were engaged in failed land grabs and then endless wars with the rulers of Christian Spain to the north, so the existence of deep cultural and trading links seems unlikely. Isolated or not, there is little doubt that early medieval Córdoba was a huge city. Estimates of its population vary between 250,000 and 1,000,000 people (most authorities suggest 450,000–500,000 at most), but few historians doubt that in the year 1000 AD, Córdoba was one of the largest cities in Europe.

🛍 Shopping in Córdoba

The old *medina* (also known as the Judería) is packed with touristy shops selling a mixture of genuine local crafts and cheap tat shipped in from China. Córdoba has been famous for leather for millennia (though the centre of modern Spanish leather-work is Mallorca) so this is likely to be good quality as long as you can find a decent shop. The following are worth a look:

Zoco Municipal de la Artesanía (Calle Judíos / Plaza Maimónides)

Meryan Cueros de Córdoba (calleja de la Flores 2)

Piel Española (calleja de la Flores)

⏱ A Day in Córdoba

By far the easiest way to travel from Málaga is by train. There is a high-speed line between Málaga and Córdoba and the journey time is between 50 and 65 minutes. (There are a few buses operated by ALSA, but the journey takes 2½–3 hours.) Once you reach Córdoba, the most practical way to get around is on foot. The city centre is compact, but if you have mobility issues then you may need to take a taxi or bus. Although Córdoba has a good urban bus network, the centre of the city and the Judería are bus-free lacunæ (the streets are too narrow, though the useful 🚌3 has a route circling the old city and will get you pretty near to the Cathedral). On the other hand, most of the things you want to see are very close to the Cathedral and the streets are either pedestrianized or low-traffic.

All of the places mentioned below are shown on the companion Google map. Select the 'NORTH OF MÁLAGA' layer in order to see them. The map also shows a walking route, beginning and ending at the railway station. You will no doubt want to plan your own route, but the suggestions on the map, and in this section, are tried and tested assuming an arrival time around 10 am and a departure around 4.30 pm. It allows time to walk to the Cathedral, sightseeing in the Cathedral, a coffee/beer stop, a stroll through the Judería, a leisurely lunch, and a gentle walk back to the station. To see more, you'll need to allow more time.

The route (in red) from the railway station to the Cathedral takes you via the *turismo* on the Plaza de las Tendillas. If you'd prefer to visit the *turismo* just south of the Cathedral (near the Roman Bridge on the Plaza del Triunfo or, indeed, ignore the tourist information offices altogether then just continue walking through the park (Jardines de la Victoria). However, it's well worth consulting the agenda at **turismodecordoba.org/schedule** in advance of your visit. If there is an event taking place (*e.g.* the Festival of Patios, a *tapas* route, or a special exhibition) then the *turismo* will be able to supply you with the relevant leaflets.

My general advice is to get to the Cathedral as early as possible, before it's overrun with coach parties (any time before noon should be okay, but the earlier the better). The walk from the railway station to the Cathedral is about 1.5 km (or 2 km via the *turismo*) about 30 to 45 minutes' gentle walk. A good option is a train that leaves Málaga around 9 am. That allows 45 minutes to an hour to walk from the station to the Cathedral for entry at 11 am, before it becomes too busy.

If you follow the walking route shown on the companion map, you will pass a couple of interesting churches. The first is the **Royal Collegiate Church of San Hipólito** (📍**Plaza San Ignacio de Loyola**), part of a monastery founded by Alfonso XI, King of Castilla y León, in 1342. The monarchs Fernando IV and Alfonso XI are buried within. In Spanish terms, it's rather a plain church but worth visiting if only to see the apse, which is almost breathtaking in its architectural perfection. Next is **San Nicolás de la Villa**, founded by Fernando III after the *reconquista* of 1236 and one of the twelve so-called *Fernandina* churches. Although the original construction dates from the 13th century, it has been renovated and rebuilt a number of times. The tower dates from the time of the *Reyes Católicos*, built on a former minaret. After the *turismo*, if you visit it, is the Parish of **San Juan y Todos los Santos**, more commonly as **La Trinidad** because it is on the site of a former Trinitarian convent. Technically, this is another *Fernandina* church, but the current building only dates from the 18th century.

If you'd rather take a more direct route and miss out the *turismo*, just walk through the park. If you do, you'll pass the Mercado Victoria, a 19th-century market now reborn as a 'gastrospace' with around 20 stalls (similar to the famous Mercado de San Miguel in Madrid). Most don't open until noon, but if you want coffee and a snack, or a late breakfast, then **Panea** (a café) is open from 8 am.

Whether you walk through the park or follow the suggested route, you'll enter the Judería through the Puerta de Almodóvar, which is of Moorish origin (when it was known as *Bab al-Chawz*) and one of only three surviving medieval gates. The current structure is 14th century. Just outside the gate is a statue of Seneca, who was born in Córdoba (another famous Roman son, Lucan, is commemorated with a far more modest bust in the Plaza Eliej Nahmias). Walk through the gate and go straight ahead.

Almanzor

'Almanzor' is the Hispanicized version of the *nom de guerre* 'Al-Mansur' — 'The Victorious' or to give him his full name, Abu Amir Muhammad bin Abdullah ibn Abi Amir, al-Hajib al-Mansur, who was *de facto* ruler of the Umayyad Caliphate of Córdoba between 978 and 1002. Born near Torrox Pueblo (in what is now the Province of Málaga) of Yemeni descent, he studied in Córdoba and became a scribe. In due course, his intelligence and competence came to the notice of the Vizier and he was appointed as tutor to Prince Hisham, son and heir of the Caliph al-Hakam. When the Caliph died, Almanzor rose to a position of prominence and power as *hajib* (chamberlain) of the court of the 12-year-old Hisham. Distinguishing himself as an early fundamentalist and iconoclast, he ordered al-Hakam's library (almost certainly containing works of Greek authors preserved by Byzantine scribes) to be burned and kept Hisham a virtual prisoner in Medina Azahara, about 4 miles from Córdoba.

He was very probably also the lover of Hisham's mother, Subh, known as 'The Basque' because she was a slave captured in Pamplona. Although a *jariya* (sexual slave, or concubine), having borne the Caliph a child, she was *umm walad* and relatively powerful (she could not be sold, at least). The huge number of enslaved European concubines is one of the reasons why it is technically inaccurate to refer to the Muslim rulers of al-Andalus as 'Arab' (or even

'Moorish', though this term is used interchangeably to refer to North African ethnicity or adherence to Islam). The historian and *muhaddith* Ibn Hazm (†1064 AD) attests that all the Umayyad rulers in al-Andalus were the offspring of enslaved mothers. Even the founder of the Iberian dynasty, Abd al-Rahman I (731–788 ad) was described in contemporary sources as 'blond'. By the time we get to Hisham II (the last Umayyad), the Spanish Arabist Julián Ribera has calculated that genetically speaking at least, he would have been no more than 0.9% 'Arab'.[84]

Almanzor's military campaigns led to the capture of Coimbra (in modern-day Portugal), Salamanca and Sepúlveda. Although ultimately unsuccessful in his later campaigns, he pressed onward as far as Barcelona, Pamplona and Galicia. One of the reasons for his constant military adventures was the loot that even unsuccessful raids yielded. The most valuable share of the loot was composed of slaves, the majority of whom were children who would be assigned to work at court (the boys would be castrated so that they could work in the harem). Female slaves could be used to pay soldiers and Almanzor was said to have had a predilection for 'blonde and red-headed Galicians, Basques and Franks'.[85] Contemporary chronicles record that after destroying Barcelona in July 985, Almanzor brought seventy thousand slaves in chains to the great market of Córdoba and, after a raid on Simancas in July 983, captured seventeen thousand women. His thirst for slaves led to petitions from the people of Córdoba who complained that it had become impossible for their own daughters to find husbands because Christian slave girls were so plentiful and so cheap.

Almanzor clearly hoped to establish a great dynasty. Many of his military operations were aimed not at enlarging the territory of the Caliphate, but rather demonstrating military might and the superiority of Islam over decadent Christianity. After every battle, Almazor would instruct his slaves to remove the dirt from his clothing so that when he met his end he could be buried under the 'glorious dust'. However, he weakened the Caliphate, not only by his machinations as a usurper, but also by suppressing intellectual life. According to the chronicler Said al-Andalusi, after Almanzor's burning of philosophical texts (which were thought doubly suspect due to being pagan texts preserved by Christian scribes), the result was:

> '*Whoever had studied those sciences [philosophy] became regarded as prone to heterodoxy and suspected of heresy. Most of those who until then had studied philosophy now lost their interest in it, became terrified and kept secret the fact that they knew the subject.*'[86]

Although Almanzor was zealous in his desire to conquer (and reconquer) Christian Iberia, his martial strategy had the effect of bolstering the desire of the north to reconquer Al-Andalus. Conquest for territory was something that medieval people understood, but this was not the case with genocide. So certain of his righteousness was Almanzor that when it came to razing Christian towns, he advocated 'cutting their trees and their

84 Pierre Guichard, *Structures Sociales 'Orientales' et 'Occidentales' dans l'Espagne Musulmane* (Paris: Mouton, 1977), p.124

85 Belén Holgado Cristeto, 'Tras las huellas de las mujeres cristianas de al-Andalus' in *Actas del Congreso Conocer Al-Andalus: perspectivas desde el siglo XXI* (Sevilla: Alfar, 2010) p.110

86 Regis Blachére (*trans.*), *Said al-Andalusi: Kitab Talakat al-Umam* (Livre des Categories des Nations), (Paris: La Rose Editeurs, 1935), pp.126–27

fruits, killing their animals, and destroying their buildings and all that can be broken down.'[84]

When Almanzor died (and was buried, according to his wishes, covered in the dust of his conquests) in 1002, his son (and successor as *hajib*) followed him and effectively ruled for six years (the Caliph Hisham was still under house arrest). He was poisoned (probably) by his brother, who managed barely a year before being beheaded by the grandson of Abd al-Rahman III.

It was almost certainly Almanzor's actions, in diminishing the real power of the Caliph, that hastened the fall of the Emirate of Córdoba leading to a protracted period of Civil War, and the fracture of Andalucía into less powerful *taifas*.

84   Soha Abboud-Haggar, *El Tratado Jurídico de Al-Tafri de Ibn Al-Gallab: Manuscrito Aljamiado De Almonacid De La Sierra* (Zaragoza: Institución 'Fernando el Católico' 1999) p.231

 ## 🏛 Mezquita-Catedral de Córdoba

📍 Calle Cardenal Herrero 1 🌐 **mezquita-catedraldecordoba.es**
🕐 **Mon–Sun 1000–1900** 🔵🔵

As mentioned above, it's a good idea to book your tickets online in advance as some time slots fill up a few days ahead. Also, having a ticket will save having to queue at the ticket office. Multiple websites are authorized to sell tickets, but it's best to use the official site to ensure that you're getting the best price (some of the others are very skilled at getting you to pay for guided tours that you may not want). The entrance ticket to the Cathedral includes admission to the Fernandina Churches, which are mostly found in the western part of the city ('Axerquía'): for more details and links to smartphone apps visit **bit.ly/RutaFernandina**. Most of the churches on the route close at 2 pm (3 pm in summer) and reopen at 3 pm (5 pm in summer), so if you want to visit them you'll need to plan carefully.

The Great Mosque of Córdoba was considered a wonder of the medieval world by both Muslims and Christians. Construction began between 784 and 786 during the reign of 'Abd al-Rahman I, who escaped from Syria to the Iberian Peninsula after his family was massacred by a rival political dynasty.

The former mosque's hypostyle ('under columns') plan, consisting of a rectangular prayer hall and an enclosed courtyard, followed a tradition employed in the Umayyad and Abbasid mosques of Syria and Iraq (which were significantly influenced by, and probably constructed by, Byzantine Greek architects). The system of columns supporting double arcades of piers and arches with alternating red (brick) and white (limestone) voussoirs is unusual (though not unprecedented) and provided height within the hall. Alternating red and white voussoirs are associated with Umayyad monuments such as the Great Mosque of Damascus and the Dome of the Rock, but it was also a technique employed by the Romans ('*opus vitta-tum mixtum*'). The same goes for the double arches, also seen in the construction of Roman aqueducts, most notably that at Mérida, conquered by the Umayyads in 713 AD.

At one level, this architectural feature of the *mezquita* is a masterstroke of craftsmanship, but at another, it was a necessary short cut because they lacked the materials (or skill) to create monumental columns of sufficient height. The 856 columns, of jasper, onyx, marble, granite, and porphyry, are all reused from Roman and Visigothic buildings. You will notice that they are all different heights, and the compensation for these differences is made in the bases and capitals. The horseshoe arch, a feature we probably consider 'typical' of Moorish Spain, was introduced to the peninsula by the Visigoths.

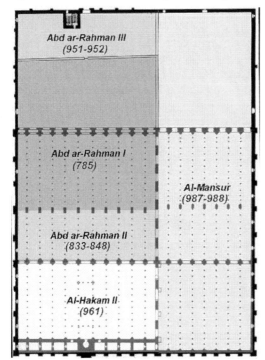

Though the mosque was expanded by later rulers (the most significant changes dating from the reigns of 'Abd al-Rahman II between 833–852, al-Hakam II between 961–976, and the *hajib* al-Mansur (Almanzor) from 987), the basic formula of arcades with alternating voussoirs was maintained in each of the additions. The resulting vistas of columns and arcades are often described as a forest of stone. The comparison is heightened by the rows of trees planted in the courtyard (*Patio de los Naranjos* or Court of the Orange Trees), which create a visual continuation of the rows of columns within the prayer hall.

The most lavish interior ornament is concentrated in the *maqsura*, the prayer space reserved for the ruler, commissioned by the Caliph al-Hakam II. The *maqsura* is visually separated from the rest of the prayer hall by screens formed of intersecting polylobed arcades, an elegant variation on the basic architectural theme set in the earliest incarnation of the *mezquita*. These screens emphasize the special status of the space, which is composed of three domed bays in front of the *mihrab*. The *mihrab* was unusual for taking the form of an entire room rather than the traditional niche, and for being flanked by two rooms whose entrances are decorated with mosaics like that of the *mihrab*. These mosaics and tesserae, as far as we know, were the work of Byzantine craftsmen.

The *maqsura* is decorated with carved marble, stucco, and mosaics. These, executed in intricate vegetal scroll forms and Kufic inscriptions, frame the *mihrab*, the two doors flanking it, and also cover the interiors of the three domes. The unusual arrangement of the *maqsura* space can be read on several levels. It may reflect the appropriation of a tri-apsidal arrangement found in local church architecture (though emptied in its new context of Trinitarian connotations). It has also been interpreted as an ideological and iconographic evocation of the Mosque of the Prophet Muhammad in Medina that served to underscore notions of Umayyad religious and political authority. A curiosity of the *mihrab* is that it is orientated towards the south and not towards Mecca (east-south-east). This is an oddity given that the purpose of the *mihrab* is to indicate the direction of Mecca (*qibla*). One theory is that the *mezquita* of Córdoba was intended to be a faithful copy of the Umayyad mosque in Damascus, which also has a south-facing *mihrab*.

After conquering Córdoba in 1236, Fernando III of Castilla had the Great Mosque consecrated as the city's cathedral. The Christian population of Córdoba used the former mosque with relatively minor changes for the next three hundred years. In the early 16th century the bishop and canons of the Cathedral proposed the construction of a new cathedral, and sought to demolish the mosque in order to build it. The opposition of the townspeople to the planned destruction of the building led to the unprecedented decision, endorsed by the

Holy Roman Emperor Carlos V, to insert an entire Gothic chapel into the very heart of the former mosque. The result is an uneasy and controversial juxtaposition: the soaring forms of a Gothic cathedral rise from the very centre of the comparatively low, sprawling prayer hall whose architectural vocabulary is rooted in the forms of classical antiquity.

When Carlos V finally set eyes on the 'renovated' *Mezquita-Catedral*, he was not impressed, and supposedly rebuked the bishop at the time with the observation that, 'You have taken something unique in all the world and destroyed it to build something one might find in any city.'

Outside the Cathedral

Before you leave the area where the Mezquita-Catedral is located, make sure to walk around the perimeter and have a look at the exterior where you will see dozens of doors and gates, each reflecting the dominant architectural style of the time of its creation (*mudéjar*, plateresque, baroque, neoclassical, etc.).

After the Cathedral

The Cathedral is on the river bank, so walk down to see the Roman Bridge (1st c. BC, but re-built in the 8th c. AD under the Ummayad Emirate). After this, you will probably want coffee or refreshments to see you through to lunch.

Puente Romano

⚲ Avenida del Alcázar

The Roman Bridge is nowadays also known as the 'Old Bridge', but until 1953 it was the only bridge across the Guadalquivir River in the city. Built in the early first century AD, it replaced an earlier wooden bridge and was part of the route of the *Via Augusta*, a spectacular feat of Roman ingenuity. The *Via Augusta* began in *Gades* (Cádiz) and ran through *Hispalis* (Sevilla), then east through *Corduba* (Córdoba), sweeping down towards *Carthago Nova* (Cartagena) and, clinging to the Mediterranean coastline, up through *Tarraco* (Tarragona) to *Narbo Martius* (Narbonne) where it joined the *Via Domitia* to continue to Rome.

The River Guadalquivir which flows beneath the bridge is the river that flows through Sevilla and joins the sea at Sanlúcar de Barrameda (where Manzanilla sherry is made). At 400 miles, it is the fifth longest river in Spain. It is the river from which Columbus set sail on his third voyage.

At the southern end of the bridge stands a defensive tower (**Torre de Calahorra**) and at its northern end the **Puerta del Puente**. This is fancifully called the 'Arc de Triomphe' by locals, but it is simply one of the gates of the old wall. The current Puerta del Puente was built by the architect Hernán Ruiz II in 1572, so vanishingly little masonry of the Roman Era can now be identified. In the centre of the bridge is the 'Triumph of San Rafael', the work of the sculptor Bernabé Gómez del Río dating from 1651. It was closed to traffic remarkably recently (1 May 2004). It has undergone reconstructions numerous times: in the Moorish era, after the *reconquista*, and at the beginning of the 20th century. In the most recent renovation (2006) a niche dedicated to Saints Acisclus and Victoria (sibling martyrs of Córdoba) was restored.

The bridge is located next to a small nature reserve, called the **Sotos de la Albolafia**. Many species of birds nest here (mostly herons and egrets, although a total of 120 distinct species have been counted), some of them endangered species, which is all the more surprising if one takes into account the fact that the area of the reserve is only two hectares. Hidden among the trees and vegetation are the remains of several defunct water mills. In 2014, some scenes for the fifth season of the TV series Game of Thrones were filmed on the bridge, which played the part of the bridge 'Volantis'.

You are in the south-western corner of historic Córdoba. If you didn't visit the *turismo* on your way to the Cathedral, there is another one at the northern end of the bridge. A short walk from here you can see a few sites in the oldest part of the city (the former Jewish Quarter, *La* Judería) and then head back past the Cathedral going east, away from the tourist throng. From here you can walk slowly back to the railway station through the old-but-not-ancient city centre, finding somewhere for lunch en route.

The most expensive places to eat and drink in Córdoba are those in the winding maze of streets in the oldest part of the city, north-west of the Cathedral. 'Expensive' is of course a relative term — for a *café con leche* in a bar or cafe, paying even half the price of a Starbucks latte would be considered exorbitant by most Spaniards. As you stand on the bridge facing the Cathedral, look to your right along the river bank and you will see a number of *cafés/restaurants*. These are likely to be reasonably priced places to grab a coffee as they are just outside the labyrinth.

♠ Fiesta de los Patios

In the first half of May (usually the first two full weeks of May) around 50 private *patios* (courtyards) of houses in Córdoba take part in a competition. During this time all these *patios* are open to the public to visit for free. This is a rare opportunity to see the inside of *cordobés* homes, so if your visit to Córdoba coincides with this festival I recommend that after visiting the Cathedral, you visit a few *patios*. Those north-east of the Cathedral are likely to be less busy than those in the heart of the Judería, so these are probably the best to visit — bearing in mind that they will close for lunch and siesta. Details of the festival, and a map, can be found here: **patios.cordoba.es**. If you visit outside the Fiesta de los Patios, there are still a number that may be visited all year round (mostly on the Calle Basilio). The list of attractions that you can download from the *turismo* website (or pick up from the *turismo*) tells you where they are.

The *patio* is a distinctive mark of *andaluz* architecture, and whilst one will often hear that it is a form 'Moorish in origin' this is not entirely true. It might be more accurate to say that its origin is simply 'oriental', for interior courtyards were a feature of Greek and Roman houses long before Islam existed (the oldest known example was in Mesopotamia and dates from around 2000 BC). It is the '*hortus inclusus*' of the Roman villa; the enclosed garden. The British may aspire to have a garden in front of or behind their houses; the Spanish like to have a garden inside the house.

Palacios might be built around more than one courtyard, and the grander houses will constitute a single dwelling around an interior *patio*, but *patios* are also a feature of more humble homes. After huge influxes during the 19th and early 20th centuries from the surrounding countryside, many *palacios* and larger houses were divided into multiple single-room dwellings to accommodate these internal refugees. The *patio* thus became a shared, but still private space. Much of the new and social housing constructed in Andalucía in the 20th century has followed the same pattern — very compact (one or two-room) flats arranged around a central courtyard, a shared urban garden (as in the *corralones* of Málaga).

Córdoba with Kids — The Zoo

📍 Avenida Linneo 🌐 zoo.cordoba.es 🕑 Tue–Sun 0930–2000 💶

If you are visiting Córdoba with children then this may be of interest, especially if they need a little reward after visiting a medieval mosque-cathedral. The zoo is only 15 minutes' walk from the Cathedral (and it is next to a large children's playground). It is small, but it has a collection of around 100 species. The animals all appear to be in good health and well cared for. Best of all, though, the ticket price is very reasonable.

Alcázar

📍 Plaza Campo Santo de los Mártires 🌐 bit.ly/CordobaAlcazar
🕑 Tue–Fri 0830–2045 💶💶

Nearby is the Alcázar — an 8th-century Moorish palace that displaced an earlier Visigothic (and later Moorish) fortress. Much later it became the Palace of Fernando and Isabel, and at one point the headquarters of the Inquisition. It has some Roman mosaics displayed in the museum. As you stand on the bridge facing the Cathedral, you are looking north and the Alcázar is to the west (slightly north west). Much of the current structure was built by King Alfonso XI in 1328 and although it is interesting and impressive in its way (it has beautiful gardens), it is perhaps not a 'must-visit' sight. If your intention in Córdoba is to explore as much of its Moorish past as you can, then do visit, but it is not the best-preserved example in Spain. Not far away, on the Plaza Campo Santo de los Mártires, are the ruins of the **Baños Califal (Royal Baths** z bit.ly/banoscalifal ⊘ Mon 💶**)**. Though little remains of the original baths, there are some informative exhibits and everything is fully accessible for wheelchair users.

👀 West of the Cathedral

San Basilio

The *barrio* of **San Basilio** is named after the convent of the monks of Saint Basil the Great that once stood here (the church of **Nuestra Señora de la Paz** (Our Lady of Peace) was their chapel). The *barrio* has three main streets running parallel to each other: **Postera, Enmedio** and **San Basilio**. Unlike the winding streets elsewhere in the city centre, they are more-or-less straight: reflecting their post-*reconquista* construction. The area was populated by Jews until the terrible pogroms of 1391 which spread throughout the country. Almost all the Jews of Córdoba were killed, and those that survived were 'converted'. From the late 14th century, then, the area was occupied by Jewish converts to Christianity ('*conversos*'). An attempt to banish them failed, thanks to mediation by the *Reyes Católicos* in 1479. However, as a result of poor sanitation, many later agreed to move to the nearby *barrio* of San Nicolas de la Villa.

At Calle San Basilio 44 is the headquarters of the *Asociación Amigos de los Patios Cordobeses* where you can see a traditional *patio cordobés* (admission free). One of the most interesting structures in San Basilio is the **Torre de Belén** (Tower of the Virgin of Bethlehem), a fine example of a former defensive gate providing access to a walled enclosure. The parish **Church of San Basilio** (and Nuestra Señora de la Paz), on the site of a monastery founded in 1590, has been rebuilt in the 17th-century Baroque style with period decoration.

The Judería

What is now called the Judería is the part of the *medina* north and west of the Cathedral (*viz.* former great mosque). Under Islamic rule, however, this was not the case. Although Jews lived in Córdoba in Roman times, when the city fell to the Muslim invaders in the 8th century, they were expelled from the walled city. In Moorish Córdoba, Jews lived in the north-east of the city, beyond the gardens of La Merced (roughly where you will end your walk if you follow the route suggested on the companion map). We know this because the only Jewish tombstone from this period, of Yehuda bar Akon, was found in this area (dated 845).

This Jewish quarter was destroyed when the city was sacked in 1013 by Sulaiman al-Mustain. Many Jews were forced into exile, but the final repression and annihilation occurred with the arrival of the Almohads in 1148 who prohibited the Jewish presence in the region by abolishing *dhimmi* status for non-Muslims. The Jews (apart from a handful of approved court employees) only returned to the city following the *reconquista* of Córdoba under Fernando III in 1236. The Judería of today was delimited by Fernando's son, Alfonso X ('The Wise') in 1272, but it was still a ghetto.

Despite a reasonably stable coexistence and the construction of a synagogue, there were sporadic (and serious) episodes of anti-Semitic violence. The pogrom of 1391 is the most infamous, but an attack of 1406 was so serious that King Enrique III intervened, fining the city of Córdoba 40,000 doublons. By this point, the Jewish population of Córdoba was distributed throughout the city, and when in 1478 the *corregidor* (royal governor) Francisco Valdés sought to corral Jews in the streets around the Alcázar, they appealed to Queen Isabel, who allowed them to stay where they were. It would be Isabel, however, who delivered a *coup de grâce* barely five years later when she gave the Jews of Andalucía six months to convert or leave (somewhat before the final edict of expulsion in 1492). This was a shocking *volte-face* from a monarch who had written in 1477:

> All the Jews of my kingdoms are mine and are under my protection and defence and it belongs to me to defend and protect and maintain justice.[85]

To find out more about the Jewish patrimony of Córdoba, you can download a beautifully designed and informative brochure (in *castellano* and English) from the '*turismo*' section of the ⊕ redjuderias.org website.

Averroes Statue

A statue of **Ibn–Rushd (Averroes)** is a hundred or so metres up Calle Cairuan. Abu l-Walid Muhammad Ibn Ahmad Ibn Rushd (1126–1198) was born in Córdoba and was one of the greatest intellectuals of medieval Europe. A staunch defender of Aristotle against the Neoplatonist tendencies of Avicenna and Al-Farabi, he was called 'The Commentator' by Saint Thomas Aquinas (even though Aquinas was a profound critic of his ideas). No other Muslim thinker has had such a deep intellectual influence on Western Christian thought.

Unlike his fellow *cordobés* philosopher, Maimonides, Averroes was, for most of his life, protected by the Almohads, but at the end of his life he fell foul of a more orthodox *ulema* (body of scholars) and he had to go into exile, while in Córdoba his books were condemned and publicly burned. We often hear (correctly) how medieval Christian scholastics (like Aquinas) encountered the works of Aristotle largely thanks to the commentaries of thinkers like Averroes. What is less well-known is that most of Averroes's extant works are nowadays available thanks to Latin translations, the Arabic originals having been 'purged' in the interests of ideological purity.

Maimonides and The Synagogue

Just after the Plaza Maimónides is a small square with a statue of **Moses ben Maimon (Maimonides)**, the 12th-century Sephardi philosopher and one of the greatest minds of the High Middle Ages. The presence of the statue is part of the celebration of '*convivencia*'. When

---

85   Joseph Pérez, *Los judíos en España* (2009, Madrid: Marcial Pons) p.174

the Almohads conquered Córdoba in 1148 they set about abolishing *dhimmi* status (*dhimmis* were non-Muslims who were permitted to live in territories under Islamic rule as long as they paid the *jizya* tax), forcing first (it has been suggested) the conversion of Maimonides's family, followed by exile. But even his own writings are clear that a genuine *convivencia* was impossible for an observant Jew. He ruled that it was sinful, for example, to enter a Muslim-owned shop, or to eat with Christians. He was clear that Jesus of Nazareth was justly condemned to death as a heretic, and elsewhere he calls the Prophet Muhammad 'the maniac', saying of the Arabs, 'Never did a nation molest, degrade, debase, and hate us as much as they.'

There is nothing especially extreme about these views, coming from a pious Jew, particularly a medieval one. 'Fair-minded' atheists must, logically, believe that Moses, Jesus and Muhammad were all at least mistaken (if not actually malevolent). The point is rather whether it is accurate to talk about a supposed *convivencia* or a golden age of inter-religious flourishing. There were certainly periods of tolerant *convivencia* in Moorish Al-Andalus, but it was not a centuries-long era of mutual flourishing. Most precarious of all was the life of Jews, first under the Muslims and then under the Christian rulers following the *reconquista*.

Synagogue

The **Sinagoga de Córdoba** (🕘 0900–1500 ⊘ Mon ⦿) was built after the *reconquista* in 1314 and is one of only four extant medieval synagogues in Spain (the others are in Utrera in the Province of Sevilla, and in Toledo). Recently re-opened after works to deal with damp, it is open Tue–Sun and is the second most-visited attraction in Córdoba. Although the building is over 700 years old, it functioned as a Jewish place of worship for less than 177 years. After the Edict of Granada it was converted into a hospital for rabies sufferers, and a century later into a hermitage dedicated to Saint Crispin and Saint Crispinian (as patron saints of shoemakers, these were important saints in Córdoba, which had been a centre of leather work from long before the Arab conquest).[86]

Four hundred years later, with no Jewish population to keep alive the memory, most people had forgotten that the church of Santa Quiteria (as it had become) had ever been a synagogue. In 1876, the parish priest was carrying out some repairs when he uncovered Hebrew inscriptions behind the altarpiece. After reporting his find to a local archaeologist, a report was made to the Monuments Commission who made a grant of 400 *reales* for the removal of later Christian murals, thus uncovering the original decoration of the synagogue. In 1885, it was declared a national monument, finally opening to visitors exactly 100 years later. Subsequent excavations have uncovered a mikvah (purification bath with running water) and the remains of what was probably a Talmudic school. An 'Interpretation Centre' is planned and was due to open in 2023 (though COVID delayed this).

Zoco Municipal

The city craft market ('souk') occupies an elegant 16th-century *palacio* built around a spacious *patio*. Originally intended to be a showcase of local art and culture, from leather-work to bullfighting and flamenco, it became the first 'artisan' craft market in Spain when it opened in 1956. After its decline in the 1970s, the bullfighting section moved to a discrete portion of the buildings to create the **Museo Taurino de Córdoba** (1983) and the new craft market opened in 1986. The products on sale are high quality and demonstrate traditional local techniques, especially in silverware, ceramics and leather. You will see leather items with *cordobán* (Visigothic) and *guadamecí* (Umayyad) techniques — both forms of decoration

---

86   Claudio Sánchez Albornoz, 'Espagne pré-islamique et Espagne musulmane', *Revue Historique* 237 (1967, Paris) p.316

involving carving, embossing, colouring and gilding.

Capilla Mudéjar: Iglesia de San Bartolomé

📍 Calle Averroes 🕐 Mon–Sat 1030–1330, 1530–1830 €

Following the attack on the Jewish quarter in 1391, and the later exodus or conversion of Jews to Christianity, the *barrio* of San Bartolomé grew up in the now empty Judería. In this district the small church of San Bartolomé — which remains unfinished — was built in the late 14th century, replacing a mosque. During the first half of the fifteenth century was added a funerary chapel dedicated to Santiago: one of the finest works of *mudéjar* art to be found in Córdoba after the Royal Chapel of the Cathedral and the Synagogue.

The word *mudéjar* comes from the Arabic term *mudayyan* meaning 'he who has been allowed to remain'. The term is used to describe those Muslims who stayed in the territories after the *reconquista* and were permitted, at least initially, to retain their religion, language and customs. *Mudéjar* art is a hybrid artistic style combining Hispano-Muslim decorative and architectural elements with other styles in vogue at the time.

The chapel preserves its original 15th-century floor of brick and glazed tiles, as well as geometric wall mosaics similar to those found in the Royal Chapel. The intricate plasterwork on the walls is decorated with latticework, the coat of arms of the 'Order of the Band' (*Orden de la Banda*, named after the band that the king awarded his most loyal noblemen) delicate *ataurique* (repeated vegetable or floral motif) stucco adornments, and kufic and *naskh* inscriptions praising Allah. Restoration work carried out in 1933 revealed an extraordinary collection of thirty-five Nazari tiles on the front of the dais leading to the altar. The tiles, depicting hunting scenes, musicians, minstrels and real and imaginary animals in what is believed to be an allegory of the senses, now form part of the Archaeological Museum's collection.

East of the Cathedral

From the Capilla Mudéjar, walk further on into the Plaza Cardenal Salazar and turn right on to Calle Romero. This is the route you took from the railway station to the Cathedral. Take the same route (right onto Calle Deanes, left onto Calle Judería) to bring you once more to the Cathedral.

The area to the east of the Cathedral has much of the charm of the Judería but with fewer tourist souvenir shops and thus, slightly fewer tourists. A popular spot for tourists to visit is the **Calleja de las Flores** (lane of the flowers) which is beautiful, but often busy. One of Córdoba's best-known leather workshops — **Meryan (Cueros de Córdoba)** — has a small shop at Calleja de la Flores 2. Most of Meyran's business is online and their creations are traditionally *cordobés*, using coloured leather and tooled designs. An old English word for a leatherworker is, of course, 'cordwainer', via the Norman French term for a native of Córdoba.

Casa-Museo del Guadamecí Omeya

📍 Plaza Agrupación de Cofradías 2 🌐 guadameciomeya.com 🕐 Mon–Sat 1030–1400, 1630–2000 €

This is a small private museum curated by Ramón García Romero and José Carlos Villarejo García exploring the techniques of Umayyad era leather work and its legacy. Perhaps a niche interest (and the display is very small) but this is one of the most consistently highly-rated museums in Córdoba.

Palacio de los Páez de Castillejo

📍 Plaza de Jerónimo Páez 7 🕐 Tue–Sun 0900–1500 💶 (🎫 EU citizens)

On the Plaza de Jerónimo Páez, reached from the Cathedral by following the Calle Encarnación, this is a Renaissance palace with an ornate façade and a cool, *patio*-dominated interior housing the town's archaeological museum. Among its most important pieces are finds from the Caliph's summer palace at Medina Azahara.

Plaza del Potro

The narrow **Plaza del Potro**, further east, is one of Córdoba's most delightful small squares and extends in a gentle slope almost to the river. The house at the top of the square belongs to the guitarist **Paco Peña** and is the headquarters of his guitar school. On the square's western side is a building which was once the Potro Inn, mentioned by Cervantes (who described it as a 'den of thieves'); built around a narrow courtyard with wooden balconies, this has now been restored to house a flamenco interpretation centre 🌐🔗**centroflamencofosforito.cordoba.es**. Opposite is the former Charity Hospital, founded by the *Reyes Católicos* and now containing the town's **Museo de Bellas Artes** and a museum dedicated to the local painter **Julio Romero de Torres**. A plaque outside the latter indicates that the building was the birthplace and home of Romero de Torres.

By now, the time has probably come for some gastronomic refreshment. At the bottom of the Plaza del Potro (towards the river) is the **Taberna del Potro**, which is reliable if unexciting. It contains a charming little shrine to St Raphael the Archangel (patron saint of Córdoba) outside the lavatories (complete with votive lamps). The other bars and restaurants nearby are reliable and popular

Slightly more up-market, but still reasonably priced, is the old *Taberna de San Francisco*, now called the **Taberna Los Plateros**, built around a glazed *patio* just off the Plaza del Potro's north-western corner (it can be entered from either the Calle de San Francisco or the parallel Calle Romero Barro).

Dating back to 1872, this was for over a century the headquarters of the *Sociedad de Plateros* (Society of Silversmiths), founded in 1868 to assist silver-workers who had fallen on hard times. The large room off the *patio* is now used as a flamenco club, attended by the likes of Paco Peña; but the place is still in the possession of the *Sociedad de Plateros*, who own some of the finest of Córdoba's old taverns, including, until recently, the nearby and exceptionally beautiful Bar Los Plateros (on the Plaza de Seneca), which has columns supporting a wooden beam ceiling. That bar is now a hotel, hence the change of name of the old *Taberna de San Francisco*. Taberna Los Plateros would be a good place to sample both the *Vinos de la Tierra* (*tintos* and *rosados*) of the Córdoba region and the sherry-style wines of Montilla-Moriles.

🍴 Some Other Places to Eat

Like any other Spanish city, there are decent places to eat everywhere. In this section I have avoided the main hotspots around the Cathedral so these suggestions, which barely scratch the surface, are mostly in the eastern part of the city. But if your exploration of Córdoba takes you to a different *barrio*, you'll have no shortage of options.

🍴🥄🕐🍽🏷🍗🎵🍷 **Taberna Los Plateros** 📍 Calle San Francisco 6
🌐 tabernaplateros.com

A cavern of place, serving traditional *andaluz* fare (see above).

✗ 🗠 🗆 ⌱ ⊕ ◔ ❧ ❦ ꙮ **La Taberna del Río** 📍 Calle Enrique Romero de Torres 7
🌐 latabernadelrio.com

Excellent food in a beautiful restaurant with a terrace overlooking the river. It is reasonably priced given the location and quality of the cooking, and there are some delicious dishes on offer ranging from very traditional (*e.g. salmorejo* and *rabo de toro*) to 'updated' versions of these dishes, like a toasted oxtail brioche with goat butter, smoked soy mayonnaise and sweet-and-sour peppers.

✗ 🗠 ◔ ⌱ ⊕ ◔ ✺ ❧ ꙮ **Restaurante La Boca** 📍 Calle San Fernando 39

A lovely restaurant with an interesting menu with plenty of vegetarian options. They usually offer an inexpensive weekday *menú del día*.

✗ 🗆 ◔ ✦ 🗠 ⌱ ◔ ❧ ꙮ ◉ ꙮ **Bodegas Campos** 📍 Calle Lineros 32
🌐 bodegascampos.com

This venerable temple of gastronomy began its existence as a wine cellar for Montilla-Moriles wines and is formed of two old *bodegas*, part of a former convent and a private house. It consists of a number of spaces and rooms and offers an extensive menu of excellent dishes. Bodegas Campos were a driving force behind the establishment of a cookery and hospitality school in Córdoba, and the high quality of the service here reflects that commitment and interest. Their puddings, including a stunning olive oil and Pedro Ximénez orange ice cream, are sensational.

🍷 ✺ ◔ ⌱ ◔ ❦ ❧ ◖ ꙮ **Taberna Regina** 📍 Plaza de Regina

This friendly little bar has plenty of tables in the square outside, beneath the orange trees. The *carta* could almost be the dictionary definition of 'typical' with all the *andaluz* favourites on offer (*salmorejo, croquetas*, aubergines with cane honey, *flamenquín, revueltos*, fried fish, etc.). Most dishes are available as *tapas, medias raciones* and *raciones*.

🍷 ✺ ◔ ⌱ ⚓ **Bar los Mosquitos** 📍 Calle Carlos Rubio 24

This is a real 'back street bar' popular with locals. The *carta* is short and simple, featuring well-known classics. Everything is available as a *tapa, media* or *ración*. The service can be a bit gruff, but it's efficient and courteous.

✗ ⌱ ⊕ ◔ ✺ ❧ ◉ ꙮ **Cocina 33 Restaurante** 📍 Paseo de la Ribera 24

A small bistro that specializes in Spanish dishes enlivened by Asian fusion elements.

✗ 🗆 ✦ 🗠 ⌱ ◔ ✺ ❧ ꙮ **El Patio de María** 📍 Calle Don Rodrigo 7
🌐 elpatiodemaria.com

This lovely restaurant (and the head chef really is called María) has indoor seating though dining extends into a beautiful small patio hidden at the rear. The *carta* is small but offers a varied selection of dishes, including a decent choice for vegetarians. Puddings are all homemade (often a reliable sign of a great kitchen).

North of the Plaza del Potro

The Calle Armas leads north from the Plaza del Potro to **Plaza de la Corredera**, a large 17th-century arcaded square inspired by Castilian examples (though it feels rather down-at-heel in comparison to squares like the Plaza Mayor of Salamanca). Once used for *corridas*, theatrical spectacles and other public entertainments (including executions), it has now been transformed into an elegant and fashionable space lined with cafés and bars. Leaving the square from the north-west corner (Calle Rodríguez Marín) will bring you face to face with the main façade of an exceptionally ugly modern Town Hall in front of which stand the much-restored columns of a Roman Temple and a section of the original Roman walls.

If you have time (allow a good half hour to reach the railway station from most points in the city) you could walk past the Town Hall and turn right (east) onto the **Calle San Pablo** and enter a fascinating but little-visited part of Córdoba. Halfway down the Calle San Pablo, on the Plazuela de Orive, is the **Palacio de Orive** (*aka* **Casa de los Villalones**), an elegant Renaissance structure crowned by a loggia. It now houses the city's Department of Culture. Though there is little to see beyond the patio, it is free to visit, so pop in for a couple of minutes if it's open (it closes for the siesta). The pleasant **Plaza San Andrés**, further down the street, features a late medieval church (again, closed in the afternoon) and another modest Renaissance house.

A five-minute walk north of the Plaza San Andrés will take you to one of the most enjoyable of Córdoba's architectural attractions. This is the **Palacio de los Marqueses de Viana (⊘Mon)**, a building constructed over several hundred years between the 14th and 18th centuries, boasting no fewer than fourteen *patios* and gardens. The interior, which can be visited, is splendidly furnished and has a well-known collection of *cordobés* leather work. ⊕⊛ palaciodeviana.com

In front of the nearby medieval Royal Church of **Santa Marina de Aguas Santas** (one of Iberia's home-grown Roman martyrs) is a monument to the bull-fighter Manolete, and a block north is a bar **(Taberna la Sacristía, Calle Alarcón López 3)** once much frequented by matadors — decorated with bull-fighting souvenirs and specializing in deep-fried *boquerones* (anchovies). West of the Palacio Viana, in the **Plaza Capuchinos**, is the **Cristo de los Faroles**: a statue of Christ crucified, behind black railings, supporting eight lanterns. The square was created after the Capuchin Convent of Santo Angél was disentailed and demolished in the 19th century.

The square is just south of the spacious **Plaza de Colón** which has, in its north-eastern corner, a 15th-century brick tower forming part of the town's original fortifications. Called the **Torre de la Malmuerta** ('Bad Death'), it was reputedly constructed as an act of contrition by a nobleman who had killed his adulterous wife and her conniving servants. Much of the western side of the square is taken up by the former 18th-century **Convent of La Merced** (now the seat of local government offices), the most important and colourful of Córdoba's baroque buildings. The railway station is to the west, on the Avenida de América (about 20 minutes' walk away).

The Alhambra (Granada)

🌐 turgranada.com ❶ Plaza del Carmen 9 🕐 ♣ 0830–1800
🕐 ☀ 0830–2000

This section is entitled 'The Alhambra' rather than 'Granada' for a couple of reasons. First, the main reason that most people visit Granada is to see the Alhambra. To go to the city without visiting it would be as contrary as visiting Córdoba without seeing the *Mezquita-Catedral*, or visiting Madrid and ignoring the Prado. Second, the Alhambra is a huge complex and to do it justice one needs to spend a few hours there (the average time spent there is three hours, according to its website), leaving little time for other sightseeing, at least on a day trip. Córdoba can comfortably be 'done' in a day, making it an ideal day trip from either Málaga or Sevilla. Granada, on the other hand, has enough to keep a visitor occupied for at least two or three days. But if your main aim is to 'do' the Alhambra, then a day trip will just about suffice.

Granada has an international airport with Vueling and British Airways currently scheduling direct flights to and from London Gatwick three times a week (Tue, Thu, Sat) during high season. So another option, allowing one to spend longer in Granada would be to travel from Málaga to Granada, stay for a night or two and fly home from there (or vice versa). However, what is suggested below is an itinerary for a day trip that will allow you to see the Alhambra, get a feel for the city and enjoy Granada's peerless *tapas* scene.

Lying in the shadow of the snowcapped peaks of the Sierra Nevada, at the eastern-most edge of the fertile plain or *'vega'* formed by the River Genil, Granada is one of the most beautifully situated of all Spanish towns, and since the early 19th century has been one of the principal tourist destinations in the Spanish interior. This town of fabled reputation was actually an obscure place in ancient and early Christian times, and even under the Moors it only rose to prominence after 1241 when Ibn Nasr, founder of the Nasrid dynasty, established the capital of his empire here following the decline and fall of Córdoba.

After its recapture by Fernando and Isabel in 1492, the town was troubled by racial and religious tensions, yet it continued to enjoy considerable cultural importance and was embellished by numerous splendid Renaissance buildings. Later the city became the main baroque centre of Andalucía after Sevilla, and among the distinguished figures of the period who worked here were the painter, sculptor and architect Alonso Cano (the 'Spanish Michelangelo'), the sculptor Pedro de Mena, the painter Sánchez Cótan and the architect Hurtado Izquierdo. Cultural decline set in during the late 18th century and coincided with the town's growth as a tourist centre. In the 1920's the poet Garcia Lorca and the musician Manuel de Falla brought new distinction to the cultural life of Granada, but both were depressed by the modern aspects of the town and preferred to dream about its distant and somewhat mythical Moorish past. By their time, much of medieval, Renaissance and baroque Granada had been badly affected by insensitive modern development. Until very recently, charming old corners of the town were being brutally pulled down and the city authorities seemed blind to graffiti and petty vandalism.

Garcia Lorca described the people of Granada as 'the worst bourgeoisie in the world', and for anyone coming to Granada from amiable, *'genial'* Málaga or vivacious Sevilla it is certainly striking how generally more dour and conservative the people here are. However, Granada also has an animated university life, and the town's almost countless lively student bars help partially to compensate for the place's inherently sober character.

The first thing you must do, as soon as you can, is buy your ticket(s) for the **Alhambra!** Two million people visit annually and numbers are strictly limited and controlled in order to protect the fabric of the site. During the summer season, many of the slots are booked weeks ahead. The Alhambra is open every day except Christmas Day and New Year's Day. ⊕ alhambra-patronato.es

The entry slot that you book for the Alhambra does not determine the time you enter the Alhambra complex itself, but the time of entry to the **Palacios Nazaríes** (Nasrid Palaces), which are just one element of a complex, albeit the most famous. So, if you think that you will get to the Alhambra at 11 am, I would advise booking a ticket for 11.30 am (or even later), to build in some latitude.

A new high-speed train route between Málaga and Granada entered into service in 2022, with the fastest trains taking just over an hour. When the trains are operating to schedule, this is the best way to travel. In the event of delays due to maintenance, the next best way to travel to Granada is by ALSA bus (journey time: 1hr 15m to 2h).

To book your travel between Málaga and Granada, consult: ⊕ renfe.es (trains), ⊕ alsa.com (buses), ⊕ omio.co.uk or ⊕ budbud.com (trains, buses and rideshares), or ⊕ thetrainline.com (trains and buses). I have used all five sites to search for sample journeys and the most surprising finding was that the most comprehensive results overall came from **thetrainline**. However, websites change all the time, so I'd advise the belt-and-braces approach of searching a handful of sites. To plan your visit and your booking the following table showing roughly how long it takes to get to the Alhambra may be helpful.

Point of Arrival	Taxi	Bus	Bus & Walk	Walk
Railway Station	15 mins	30 mins	35–45 mins	45–55 mins
Bus Station	20 mins	35–40 mins	40–50 mins	60 mins+

These are very approximate times which can of course change considerably if the taxi rank is empty, or you have to wait a long time for a bus. If you decide to walk part of the route, how long it takes depends not only upon your walking speed, but how often you want to stop and look at points of interest en route. To take the bus, use the Moovit app to plan your journey. If you take the bus all the way from either the bus or rail station, you will need to take two buses (changing, usually, at the stop opposite the Cathedral), so keep your first bus ticket because it includes a free *'transbordo'* (transfer) to your second bus.

⚓ Getting to The Alhambra

The most enjoyable and tranquil approach to the Alhambra is on foot from the lower town. I suggest you walk up by the most direct (and gentle) route. This basically follows the *Cuesta de Gómerez* (marked as a red line on the companion Google Map).

Getting off the bus at the stop level with the Cathedral (**Gran Vía 5–Catedral**), walk straight ahead, turning left onto **Reyes Católicos**. When you see the **Bar Los Diamantes** on your right, turn into the **Cuesta de Gómerez**. After just under 200 metres more you will see the **Puerta Las Granadas**, 'The Gate of the Pomegranates', erected in 1536 as the solemn entrance to the Alhambra, designed by Pedro Machuca (the same architect behind the Palace of Charles V which like this gate, is carved in stone to have 'pillow-like' appearance).

In the tympanum, we see the Imperial shield, with the allegorical figures of Peace and Abundance, crowned by the three large pomegranates, hence the name. This Renaissance gate replaced an earlier Islamic one, the remains of which can be seen to your right. Through the gate is the *bosque* (forest) of the Alhambra, dividing into three walks. We will take the central one ('The Coach Drive'), but the right fork leads around and then down the hill towards the city, while the left (a shorter but steeper route) has at its beginning a devotional marble cross (1641) and leads to the southern flank of the wall of the Alhambra and the 'Justice Gate'.

The pomegranate is a symbol that you will encounter frequently in Granada, because the *castellano* word for 'pomegranate' is *granada*. Any connection between the fruit and the place name may be serendipitous, rather than etymological. To the Romans, the place was called *Florentia* (and the paucity of Roman remains suggests that it was not a settlement of any great importance). The Moors called it *Medina Garnata*, but it is unlikely that this had any connection with pomegranates (though the 16th-century chronicler Al-Maqqari thought it did), which are called '*alrumaan*' in Arabic. It may be derived from the phrase '*gar–anat*', meaning 'hall of pilgrims'.

After 350 metres, you will see to your left the reconstructed **Puerta de Bibarrambla**, a gate that once stood at the entrance to the Bib-Rambla, the area west of the Cathedral. It was demolished in 1884, but in the 1930s the restorer of the Alhambra, Leopoldo Torres Balbás, reconstructed the gate in the Alhambra forest.

A little further on, you need to turn left onto the **Calle Real de la Alhambra**, but just ahead of this turn, also on your left, you will find a memorial to Ángel Ganivet, a writer and diplomat who wrote *Granada the Beautiful* in 1895. Suffering from syphilitic paralysis for some years, he drowned himself in 1898, at the age of 33 (after being rescued, he managed to throw himself back into the river).

The **Calle Real de la Alhambra** will lead you to the main access gate of the Alhambra, the **Puerta de la Justicia**. Pick up a map and remember that access to the Nasrid Palaces is only permitted within 60 minutes of the time indicated on your ticket, due to limited capacity. If you do not enter during this time slot, you will lose the opportunity to visit this area.

🏯 The Alhambra

The Alhambra is not merely a citadel, or a fort, or a palace. Nor is it merely a collection of palaces (though it contains such a collection). It is more like a self-contained city, consisting of palaces, defences, forts, gardens, dwellings, baths, and mosques. It was where the royalty of Moorish Granada resided, in splendid isolation from the populace in the city below. When Washington Irving visited in 1828, it was a crumbling ruin occupied by poor families (70 years later, the first edition of the *Spain and Portugal* Baedeker guide reported that the Alcazaba of Málaga was 'a confusing medley of houses, ruins and Gypsy huts'[87]).

Unlike the Alcázar of Sevilla, which is still a royal palace, and the Alcazaba of Málaga which served as an official residence for a very short time following the *reconquista*, the Alhambra was set to become the monarch's main palace in Andalucía. Indeed, one of the largest struc-

---

87   *Spain and Portugal: Handbook for Travellers* (Leipsic, Karl Baedeker, 1898) p.373

tures in the complex is the Palace of Carlos V (Carlos I of Spain). Work on this building was interrupted by the Moorish uprising in the Alpujarras in 1572 and it was never completed. So as well as the Moorish period buildings for which the Alhambra is known, in the same complex there are later additions, including a church and a convent (the latter now converted into Granada's *Parador* hotel). Visiting the Alhambra, then, is more like visiting a town than a castle or a palace and one can feel quite lost exploring 14 hectares covering several centuries of history.

Alhambra means 'the red one' and during the 'golden hour' before sunset it certainly appears to have a reddish hue. But things may not be quite this simple especially if, as many historians insist, the walls were probably whitewashed in Moorish times. There are two other theories for the name. The first is that because construction largely took place at night (the daytime summer temperature in Granada is regularly over 30° Celsius and has occasionally surpassed 40°C), people in the city below would have seen the fire of torches above them. Another possibility is that the name is connected to the founder of the Nasrid dynasty who ruled as Muhammad I (1238–1273). He was known as 'al-Hamar' ('the Red') on account of the colour of his beard.

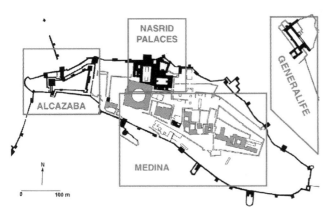

To simplify matters somewhat, the complex has four main parts. The most famous are the **Nasrid palaces**, the best-preserved Moorish buildings with their peaceful patios and fountains. The **Alcazaba** is the military zone (and the oldest part of the complex, constructed in the 11th century. The **Medina**, which is now composed of a number of buildings constructed after the *reconquista*, is the site of the old 'city' of the Alhambra complex that would have been at the service of the court. Finally, the **Generalife** is a retreat for the Nasrid royal family surrounded by orchards and gardens.

However impressive the Palace of Carlos V, the church of Santa María de la Encarnación and the Convent of San Francisco (now the *Parador*) may be, many visitors feel disappointed that the site has not been preserved in its entirety, just as many are horrified by the presence of a baroque church in the middle of the former *mezquita* of Córdoba. Something to bear in mind is that even those who constructed the magnificent buildings of the Alhambra did not expect them to last, partly because in Islam, it is sinful to seek to build anything 'eternal'. By the time that last Moorish King of Granada left the Alhambra, countless palaces and grand houses had been constructed, remodelled, demolished and rebuilt. The Alhambra's symbolic importance guaranteed the interest that Fernando and Isabel took in it, which in turn led to further construction of churches, convents and (under their grandson) a new royal palace. Yet this also ensured that much of the Moorish estate was preserved. Other Moorish citadels and palaces (like those of Antequera and Mérida) were plundered for stone leaving nothing save the defensive walls standing. In Córdoba, we may feel that the 'palimpsest' chapel in the centre of the Cathedral is out of place, but other mosques were simply demolished.

The Alhambra is a place where following some sort of guided tour is probably a good idea, if only to help make sense of such a vast complex that spans such a long sweep of history. Availability of guided tours is limited, so search online to see what's on offer (there are a few companies offering this service, one being ⊕ **alhambradegranada.org**). When booking, Check to see if the tour includes a ticket to the Nasrid Palaces (some do not). A cheaper option is to use an audio guide. Indeed, if you are able to install the app on your smartphone, then it's free. You can also pre-book a handheld set to pick up on arrival: ⊕ **bit.ly/AlhambraGuias**.

ACCESSIBILITY: Wheelchair users can access the Generalife (parts of which involve a steep incline) and the Nasrid Palace complex, but not the Alcazaba nor most of the Medina/Partal. On the other hand, tickets are available at a 33% discount. For more information visit ⊕ **bit.ly/AlhambraFAQ**

🚶 Getting back to the City Centre

After your tour of the Alhambra, there is a beautiful and surprisingly little-used footpath that will take you to the eastern end of the **Carrera del Darro** in the city below. This shaded path, known as the **Cuesta de los Chinos** or the **Cuesta del Rey Chico**, runs between the Alhambra and the Generalife and passes underneath the bridge linking the two sites.

El Rey Chico

Abu 'Abd-Illah was born in the Alhambra Palace. His name was pronounced 'a-bu-ab-di-lah' which in *andaluz* pronunciation, with its knack of cutting short every word, became 'Boabdil'. His nickname of '*el rey chico*' (the small king) did not have anything to do with his stature but referred instead to the size of his ever-diminishing kingdom.

He came to the throne in 1482, deposing his father Abul I-Hassan Ali with the help of Christian allies, and became Muhammed XII, the last Nasrid Emir of Granada. To gain more prestige, Boabdil attempted to invade Castilla but was captured and imprisoned in the castle at Lucena. His father returned to the *granadino* throne, only to be deposed by his brother, Abdullah ez Zagal, who ruled as Muhammed XIII. After three years, in exchange for his liberty (negotiated by his indomitable mother Aixa (Aisha al-Hurra), Boabdil agreed to govern Granada under the Catholic kings. Part of this deal meant his agreeing not to intervene in the Siege of Málaga of 1487.

The five years of his second period of rule saw more frequent Civil Wars and the city finally fell on 2 January 1492. Four days later, after total capitulation by its inhabitants, the *reconquista* was complete. Boabdil was granted a fiefdom in the region of Las Alpujarras and left Granada by the southern route to La Zubia. About 12 kilometres from the city he paused at a mountain pass before descending to Padul, looked back at his birthplace, his erstwhile palace and his former kingdom and sighed for what he had lost. His mother, travelling with him, is said to have been unsympathetic, telling him: 'You weep like a woman for what you could not defend like a man.' The *Puerto del Suspiro del Moro* (the Pass of the Moor's Last Sigh), around 860 metres above sea level, is the last place on that road from where the Alhambra Palace can be seen.

You access it (it's indicated in green on the **NORTH of MÁLAGA** layer of the map) from the Taxi Rank near the main entrance — look for **Restaurante La Mimbre**. Remember that you have probably exited the Alhambra complex by the Justice Gate, so you may need to take a minute to find your bearings again.

At the bottom of the hill, you will cross the **River Darro**, turning left onto the **Carrera del**

Darro and a shaded promenade popularly known as the **Paseo de los Tristes** ('The Sad People's Walk') on account of the priests who once recited their rosaries in procession to a long-defunct cemetery to the east. Containing today many of the street's numerous attractive bars, it is overlooked on the other side of the river by the verdant slopes of the Alhambra hill. If you turned right (though don't, unless you have plenty of time to explore) you would leave the boundaries of the town and eventually reach the Gypsy cave district of **Sacromonte**, much visited by tourists on account of its popular flamenco shows.

Located on the Valparaíso hillside, the Sacromonte neighbourhood is a fine place from which to gaze at the ancient Nasrid fortress. This neighbourhood is the traditional home of Granada's Roma people who have lived here in caves since the early 16th century, and for many years it has drawn romantic travellers and bohemian types searching for the legends and traditions that seem to appear on every corner.

One of these legends, regarding the alternative name for Sacromonte — *Barranco de los Negros* or 'The Valley of the Blacks' — fancifully explains the origin of the neighbourhood's cave dwellings. It is said that after the Christians conquered Granada in 1492, many noble Moors buried their treasures in the hillsides and fled with the idea of returning one day. Their slaves, many of whom were black Africans, discovered the plan and upon being liberated headed to Valparaíso intending to 'liberate' their masters' treasures. They dug large holes where nothing was found but which could at least be used as homes from that point on. According to people who believe this legend, the treasures remain here, hidden somewhere below ground. As the years passed, black residents mixed with the nomadic Romani ethnic group to eventually become the people that Sacromonte is famous for.

The truth is rather more prosaic, of course. There are many cave villages in Andalucía, and several thousand Spaniards still live in caves (for example in Guadix, on the road to Almería, where the troglodytic life even continues to attract incomers). While Iberian Roma are fairly dark-skinned, whether that is due to African antecedents is impossible to say. Whatever their genetic makeup, this is the group associated with the famous Gypsy *zambra*, a song and dance performance and possible precursor of flamenco that brings hundreds of tourists to these caves every night. Originating in an ancient pre-wedding Moorish ritual, *zambras* were adopted by Gypsies, but serious historians of flamenco consider that it is essentially now a lost art form. What is presented to tourists is effectively substandard flamenco, rather than an authentic and unbroken folk tradition.

Since the 17th century, in lonely isolation high above the narrow luxuriant valley of the Darro, the top of Valparaíso Hill has been home to **Sacromonte Abbey**, a pilgrimage destination built after the 16th-century discovery of the relics of Saint Cecil (Cecilio) and other disciples of the apostle Saint James (some legends claim that St James the Great himself celebrated mass in these caves, which rather undermines the legends about the caves being dug in the 16th century).

The first weekend in February, locals trek to Sacromonte Abbey to pay tribute to Saint Cecil, the city's patron saint. During the Holy Week, this landmark once again fills with people on Holy Wednesday as part of a procession in honour of *Cristo de los Gitanos* (Christ of the Gypsies), a *Cristo crucificado* from 1695 that is kept in the abbey's church. The Abbey can be reached by bus and can be visited if you have sufficient time in Granada: ⊕ **abadiasacromonte.com**

Continuing along the Carrera del Darro, though, note the elaborate classical plateresque façade of the **Casa de Castril**, a Renaissance house with a recently renovated interior displaying a selection of archaeological finds from the prehistoric to the Moorish period. A little farther, on your right, you will pass **El Bañuelo**, the Moorish baths (No. 31). Bath houses, as we know, were major players in the drama of the *reconquista*.

After the *reconquista*, it is true that baths (and pork and alcohol) became a touchstone of religious adherence. It is not the case, however, that public baths were an Arab import to Andalucía. In fact, the Greek-Roman culture of water and baths was already a part of the Hispano-Roman life of southern Spain, with its warm, Mediterranean climate. The Visigoths inherited the bath culture, and when the Muslims invaded they were able to take it over when they encountered it. What the Moors did was preserve the practice of bathing while in neighbouring Christian societies it began to decline due to its association with paganism and sexual immorality.

Walking on, you reach the **Plaza de Santa Ana** with the church of **San Gil & Santa Ana** (and its tall and stylish bell-tower) at its eastern end. To the south is Diego de Siloé's last known work, the **Pilar del Toro** (before 1559) — a Renaissance fountain with elegant if faded classical carvings. Beside the church of Santa Ana runs the fast-flowing stream of the Darro, which divides the Alhambra hill from that of the Albaicín. The Darro is so called because in Roman times people panned for gold (*auro*) here. Until 1990 it was still possible to find freshwater crab and trout, but these disappeared following the devastating drought that affected central Spain that year. The stream is culverted under the Plaza Nueva and eventually flows into the Genil.

Next comes the **Plaza Nueva**, surrounded by hotels and with a number of open-air bars favoured largely by tourists. At the north-western corner of the square is **Bodegas Castañeda**, a famous old bar that has now been divided into two separate establishments as a result of a family dispute. Look out for the **Tribunal Superior de Justicia** (the High Court of Andalucía, originally the Chancellery). The building, one of the finest Renaissance structures in Granada, is in a majestic Italianate style and has an elegant courtyard, probably designed by Diego de Siloé (who was certainly responsible for the two structures that dominate the eastern and southern sides of the square).

Following the route indicated on the map will bring you back to the top of the **Gran Vía**. The Gran Vía is taken by many to be evidence of the 'philistine' character of the *granadinos*. Richard Ford referred to their 'stagnating in bookless ignorance' and remarked that when the beauty of the Alhambra was mentioned, they merely shrugged. In the 19th century, every major city in Spain wanted a 'Gran Vía', and Granada was no exception. In every case, constructing a 'Great Way' necessarily meant demolishing some of the medieval footprint of a city, but this was achieved with varying degrees of success and sensitivity. Madrid's Gran Vía is a gem of Belle Époque magnificence, and Málaga's Calle Larios is one of the most beautiful streets in Europe. Granada's attempt, however, is a triumph only of insensitivity, lined with out-of-proportion shops and apartments. It was partly the Gran Vía to which Lorca was referring when he wrote that 'Granada is horrible'. He may be celebrated as Granada's foremost poet today, but Lorca's ability to speak harsh truths did not endear him to his fellow *granadinos* at the time, and few shed tears when he was assassinated in 1936. We often hear that tourism destroys the authenticity of local cultures, but in Granada's case, it has perhaps saved a city from itself, by showing what is worthy of admiration.

Albaicín

The quiet and attractive heart of the *barrio* of Albaicín (take a bus, if you have time) extends west, up the hill, from the **Casa de Chapiz**, and is an area full of beautiful villas and gardens, all with superb views of the Alhambra across the Darro. Many claim that the etymology of Albaicín is derived from the Arabic for 'Suburb of the Falconers', which is romantic but probably untrue. It was more likely named when Muslims from the town nowadays called Baeza, near Jaén, settled here after being expelled following the Battle of Las Navas de Tolosa in

1212.

One of the palaces has been converted into the **Mirador de Morayma**, a famous tourist restaurant (a mirador is a vantage point). The most renowned viewpoint is the terrace in front of the **Church of San Nicolás**, a place to which numerous people come at sunset as flamenco guitarists strum (some like *virtuosi*, others not). West of here is the 15th-century **Convent of Santa Isabel la Real**, the chapel of which has a very fine Gothic plateresque west portal, and a particularly elaborate *mudéjar* ceiling. For the *Cruces de Mayo* celebrations, held in the first week of May, the entire Albaicín hill is alight with candles.

South-west of here, returning to the lower town, the area (including at its heart the shop-lined **Caldereria Nueva**, which has now several Moroccan tearooms, small restaurants and craft shops, as well as Granada's largest mosque) testifies to recent Muslim immigration. This influx, sometimes referred to as 'the second coming of the Moors', consists not so much of Moroccans (though there are Moroccans all over Spain in reasonably large numbers) as much as European converts to Islam, many of whom were formerly part of the city's large hippy community. Known generically as 'Sufis' (now a catch-all term for non-fundamentalist Muslims, rather than used in any technical sense), these Muslims include many members of the international movement of the *Murabitun*, which is headed in Granada by a secretive Scotsman, Sheikh Abd al-Qadir, (formerly known as Ian Dallas), a one-time Beatles manager who co-authored the screenplay of Yellow Submarine.

🚶 An Alternative Route

Another route back into the city takes you through the *barrio* known as the Realejo (sometimes as 'Realejo–San Matías'). Begin from the Ángel Ganivet Statue and the Tomato Fountain walking down towards the **Hotel Alhambra Palace**. Enjoying a magnificent panorama over southern Granada, this hotel, opened in 1910, is something of an eyesore from the outside: a monstrous neo-Moorish structure in garish ochre. It would be more suited to Las Vegas (though the interior is considerably more tasteful and by all accounts it is a very good hotel). Turning left in front of the hotel, walk down the hill. Off to the left is a little street at the bottom of which is the simple and evocative home of the Spanish composer, **Manuel de Falla**, now a museum.

The route hairpins back, passing the **parish church of San Cecilio** (*i.e.* St Cecil, patron saint of Granada). San Cecilio was supposedly one of the 'Seven Apostolic Men' ordained in Rome by St Peter and St Paul and sent to evangelize Iberia. Thus he is considered to have founded the Archdiocese of Granada in 64 AD. He was martyred, possibly at Sacromonte, during the reign of Nero. Unless you happen to be passing San Cecilio church at exactly the moment that mass is taking place, you will find the church closed. And, alas, this is the case for many churches in Granada. Most remain closed when there is no liturgy taking place.

A little further on, you walk past the **Plaza Campo del Príncipe**, the lower side of which is lined by open-air bars and a favourite meeting place at night (the Nasrid dynasty held celebrations and public events on this site). It owes its name and current appearance to the *Reyes Católicos*, who in 1497 widened the square and renamed it in honour of the recent marriage of their son Juan, Prince of Asturias, to Margarita of Austria. Realejo's visitors often make three wishes (or, more conventionally, offer three prayers of intercession) at the image of **Cristo de los Favores** (Christ of Favours) that has stood in the middle of the square since 1682.

The marriage between Juan and Margarita was happy but tragically short. Contemporaries report that both had 'passionate and loving natures' and were well-matched. We might say nowadays that they couldn't keep their hands off one another. The 19-year-old Juan died six months after their marriage, officially from tuberculosis, but the standard account is that he died of 'sexual overexertion'. Margarita would give birth to their stillborn daughter two months later.

A short detour to the south is the beautiful square and early 16th-century **Church of Santo Domingo**, the façade of which features a triple-arched portico covered in frescos. West of the square, on the Calle Pavaneras, is the attractive 16th century **Casa de los Tiros**, a gorgeous building with a fortified tower that houses a modest museum and holds a collection of documents, some relating to Washington Irving — the 19th century Dan Brown. However, there are other exhibits and it is an interesting building; especially the polychromatic ceiling of the *cuadra dorada* ('golden room') and the plateresque doors. Besides, it's free for EU citizens and very cheap for everyone else. It once belonged to the Granada-Venegas family, descendants of noble Nasrids who renounced their origins (and surnames) to convert to Christianity after Granada was conquered. Behind this building, a maze of streets of Moorish houses and gardens climb up to the Alhambra Hill and gives a sense of how this area might have looked in the medieval period. You are now in the centre of Granada's **Judería**.

The city's old Jewish quarter is now an eclectic and multicultural district. Jews lived here well before the 8th-century arrival of the Moors, who called this area Garnata al-Yahud (Granada of the Jews), despite frequent expulsions (and sporadic crucifixions) of the populace. After the Jews were expelled from the Iberian Peninsula following the Christian *reconquista* of the city in 1492 and the 'Alhambra Edict', the neighbourhood remained uninhabited for a while and it was renamed **Realejo** (related to the *castellano* word *'alejar'* meaning 'to move away'). This was when the district lost most of its synagogues, which were converted into churches and modest residential palaces. The 17,000 residents of the Realejo are to this day nicknamed *'greñúos'* — a reference to the curly hair of past Sephardi inhabitants.

Realejo houses a number of tourist attractions that represent Granada's overlapping cultures throughout history. One example is the statue of the 'wise Jew' from Granada, **Judah ben Saul ibn Tibbon**, located just a few steps from **Plaza de Isabel La Católica**. Judah was a physician, translator and intellectual who was born in Granada in 1120. He fled Almohad anti-Semitic persecution and settled in Provence. The **Cuesta del Realejo** is an example of a typical street (with steps) of the Jewish quarter. The **Calle Pavaneras** leads west from the museum to the **Plaza Isabel la Católica**, a rather ugly modern square at the southern end of the **Gran Vía de Colón**. Before reaching this square you will pass near the **Casa de Vinos**, a wine bar standing next to where the gate of the old Jewish quarter once was; the bar itself — very popular with students — has an excellent range of wines and a friendly atmosphere.

Centro–Sagrario

Incongruously tucked away behind the Plaza Isabel La Católica and the Gran Vía are the **Capilla Real** (Chapel Royal) and the **Cathedral**, around which are found an extensive pedestrian and shopping district incorporating the 16th century **Plaza de Bib–Rambla** and the neo-Moorish bazaar known as the **Alcaicería** (a 19th-century pastiche largely designed to appeal to early tourists). At its southern end, the Alcaicería leads into the **Reyes Católicos**, on the other side of which is a narrow alley taking you to the Moorish **Corral del Carbón**, the only Nasrid *funduq* (caravanserai) remaining in the Iberian peninsula.

The pleasant and narrow **Calle de San Jerónimo** runs north from the Cathedral to the 18th-century **Hospital de San Juan de Dios**, passing by the shaded **Plaza de la Universidad**, close to the University's **Botanical Garden** (which is pleasant enough as a small urban park, but rather forlorn as a botanical garden). Just to the west of San Juan de Dios is the **Monastery of San Jerónimo**. Here lies, next to his wife, Gonzalo Fernández de Córdoba, who was famously known as the '*El Gran Capitán*' for his historic military actions during the war that ended the Nasrid dynasty. According to legend, he established a friendship with King Boabdil after taking him prisoner and ultimately convinced him to surrender and hand over the keys to the city. A few blocks east (the other side of the Jardines del Triunfo Park) is the **Hospital Real** (now the Rectorate of the University) — this, and San Jerónimo, are two of the most majestic Renaissance buildings in Granada.

South of the Cathedral, returning to the busy and unremarkable **Reyes Católicos** we find the **Puerta Real** at its western end. Here you enter a wide thoroughfare which splits into the **Carrera de La Virgen** and the **Acera del Darro** ('*acera*' means 'pavement', indicating that this is the paved-over course of the Darro river). To the left of the former is the 18th-century **Palacio Bibataubín** now housing the Consultative Council of Andalucía. In the same block is the **Café Restaurante Chikito** once patronized by, among others, Lorca and Falla. The **Taberna Casa Enrique**, on the Acera del Darro, is an old-fashioned establishment well-known for its hams, cheeses, and stocks of sweet Alpujarra wine known as Vino de Costa.

Granada's **Cartuja** (Charterhouse), containing perhaps the most elaborate and dynamic baroque decoration of any building in Spain, lies in the western outskirts of the town, a bus (or taxi) journey or a good twenty minutes' uphill walk from the Hospital Real. As well as its baroque decorations, it has an elegant early 16th-century cloister and a large collection of 17th-century paintings, including many technically arresting (but figuratively clumsy) works by Sanchez Cotán, a master of still life who was a monk here. It is one of 23 Carthusian monasteries that once operated in Spain (there are three extant today).

🏃 Restaurants

🍴 🥘 📖 🔥 🍲 🍷 🎗 🌳 💰 🎉 🔧 🍸 **Parador** 📍 Calle Real de la Alhambra 🕐 Lunch: 1300–1600, Dinner 2000–2300 🌐 bit.ly/MenuNazari

The restaurant of the *Parador* has a good reputation if you want to treat yourself to a meal in a stunning setting (especially if you can sit on the terrace). It is inside the Alhambra precincts so you will need to show your restaurant reservation email on your phone to be given access, unless you combine it with a visit to the Alhambra. The *Parador* serves a *menú del día* called the '*Menú Nazari*' which you can book online. It is expensive as daily *menús* go, but it is also relatively luxurious, including an appetizer, three courses and two drinks per person. Dishes are 'Moorish' style and many feature almonds, raisins and cane honey. The *Menú Nazari* does not appear to include vegetarian options, though the main *carta* does.

🍴 📖 🎗 🌳 💰 🎉 🔧 **Restaurante Jardines Alberto** 📍 Paseo de la Sabica 1 🕐 Tue–Sat 1130–2300; Sun–Mon 1130–1730 🌐 jardinesalberto.es

This restaurant, with three shady terraces, is located directly opposite the main ticket office, or 'Access Pavilion' of the Alhambra. Normally, this would set alarm bells ringing, but the quality is actually very good. The food is freshly cooked and the serving staff, ably presided over by the affable and experienced Sergio Arcas, are friendly and efficient. Though very large, it can get very busy, but it is possible to book. A significant point in its favour is the filling *menú del día* which is also available at weekends.

🍴 📖 🍷 🎗 🌳 💰 🍸 **Negro Cárbon** 📍 Puente Cabrera 9 🕐 1300–1630, 1900–2330 🌐 negrocarbon.es

Negro Carbón is an excellent restaurant, though it is not cheap. It is also not suitable for vegetarians as it not only specializes in perfectly cooked, delicious steaks, but in large steaks. If you like your meat in 'trencherman' portions, however, then you will be in your element here.

One of the best grill houses in Andalucía.

✗ 🐟 🥄 ⊐ 🍽 🐚 🥢 🌱 🍲 Asador Contrapunto ⚲ Gran Vía de Colón 20 🕐 1300–1600, 2000–2300 🌐 asadorcontrapunto.com

For a top-end meal in Granada, this would probably be my recommendation, though it has very little to offer to vegetarians. Contrapunto is a beautiful, modern restaurant serving well-executed Spanish dishes from a thoughtfully planned menu. The 6-course tasting menu is good value.

✗ 📖 🥄 ⊐ 🍽 🐚 🥀 🍤 🥢 🍩 🍜 🍲 La Cuchara de Carmela ⚲ Paseo de los Basilios 1 🌐 restaurantescarmela.com 🕐 1300–0000

Just the other side of the bridge across the River Genil, this is a traditional restaurant found-ed in 1955, but recently updated with modern twists in the kitchen too. 'Cuchara' means 'spoon' and stews and casseroles are a speciality of the house. The service is excellent and the food is prepared with love. The 'Carmela' brand now covers five restaurants (two of them serving Italian dishes). The kitchen is open all day, so ideal if you need a late lunch or early dinner to fit in with your travel plans.

✗ 🥄 ⊐ 🍽 🐚 🥢 🍲 El Mercader ⚲ Calle Imprenta 2 🕐 Mon–Tue Closed; Wed 1930–2300; Thu–Sat 1330–1530, 2000–2300 ☎ +34 633 790 440

Run by husband and wife team Cristóbal and Nuria, the food is wonderful here; very tradi-tionally Spanish with a touch of modern panache featuring dishes like lamb sweetbreads (with black garlic cream and prawns) and veal tongue (slow cooked with pumpkin puree and prunes). For the quality, it is excellent value. It is just a few metres' north of the Plaza Nueva, but they only accept bookings by telephone or in-person (call in as you pass).

✗ 🍴 ⊐ 🍽 🐚 🥢 Restaurante Albahaca ⚲ Plaza Campillo Bajo 5 🌐 restaurantealbahaca.es 🕐 1330–1530, 2030–2230

Albahaca ('basil') is a decent, traditional and reasonably priced restaurant at any time, but I include it here because they do a reasonably priced, filling and delicious menú del día Tues-day to Friday (including evenings Tue-Thu). It's rather old-fashioned in its décor but it has a lovely atmosphere and great service.

✗ 📖 🅖 🍴 🧀 🌀 🥄 ⊐ 🍽 🥀 🥢 🍜 La Vinoteca ⚲ Calle Almireceros 5 🌐 lavinotecagranada.es 🕐 1300–1630, 1930–2330

As the name suggests, La Vinoteca is primarily a wine bar, but the food stands out for its quality. The menú del día is good value and filling.

✗ 🐟 📖 🥄 Damasqueros ⚲ Calle Damasqueros 3 🕐 Tue–Sat 1300–1500, 2030–2230; Sun 1300–1500 🌐 damasqueros.com

In the Realejo district, this one makes the cut on account of their well-balanced and deli-cious tasting menu ('Menu Degustación Semanal') which changes weekly to reflect seasonal produce. The chef patron is Lola Marín who was born in Granada and has worked in some of the best restaurants in Spain, including Martín Berasategui and Arzak.

✗ 🌀 🧀 ⊐ 🌍 🐚 🍤 🥢 Casa Colón ⚲ Calle Ribera del Genil 2 🕐 1300–0000

Strictly speaking, Casa Colón is probably a tapas bar, but the quality of the tapas makes it more of a gourmet experience than your average bar. Rather too much nonsense with serv-ing food on slates rather than plates for my liking, but that's Spain for you. Spain might well be ahead of the curve in many ways, culinarily speaking, but in others, it lags a good ten years behind (balsamic glaze was de rigueur until a couple of years ago). Casa Colón is also in a lovely spot down by the River Genil, with a terrace.

✗ ⬛ ♨ 🅖 ⊙ ↘ ⚒ ✋ ✎ 🖐 **Vino y Rosas** ♈ Calle Álvaro de Bazán 12 ⊕ bit.ly/VyRGran
🕐 Tue–Sat 1300–1700, 2000–0000; Sun 1300–1700 📞 +34 958 036 520

You could easily walk straight past this little place, assuming it to be a rather twee café, and even if you go in and take a seat, the slightly eccentric decoration, simple furniture, and menu written on a blackboard, would probably not lead you to expect the food to be anything special. 'Wine and Roses', however, serves some of the best food in Granada and is one of the city's gastronomic highlights. It's extremely good value given the quality of the cooking, and it is one of the cosiest places to enjoy a meal. The staff here are rightly proud of the food and wine they serve, and that translates into faultless service.

🥢🍷 Bars

There are three places where bars (especially *tapas* bars) are concentrated in Granada. The first is around the Cathedral, north of the Bib-Rambla. There are some great places here, but it is comparatively expensive. The second is the few streets running off the corner of the Plaza Nueva — these are home to some of Granada's very best bars. The third is the famous Calle Navas. This is really 'Tapas-Central' of Granada. There is another bar-rich district in Albaicín if you happen to be in that neighbourhood. Remember that in Granada all bars hand out a free *tapa* with every drink ordered. The only exception to this rule are establishments that are primarily restaurants but which have a small bar area. As *tapas granadinas* are all free, the portions are modest. The modest sample of bars listed below serve *tapas* (everywhere in Granada does) and many have *comedores* (restaurant sections).

Plaza Nueva
Bodegas Castañeda ♈ Calle de Almireceros 1
Los Manueles ♈ Calle Reyes Católicos 61 ♈ Calle Monjas del Carmen 1
Casa Julio ♈ Calle Hermosa 5
Los Diamantes ♈ Plaza Nueva 13 (fabulous, but always packed)
Bar el León ♈ Calle Pan 1

Cathedral
Bar Soria ♈ Calle Laurel de las Tablas 3
Bar Provincias ♈ Calle Provincias 4
Más que Vinos ♈ Calle Tundidores 10
Bar Poë ♈ Calle Verónica de la Magdelena 40

Calle Navas
Almost everywhere on this narrow street is excellent

Albaicín
Casa Torcuato ♈ Calle Pagés 31
Bar los Mascarones ♈ Calle Pagés 20
Bar Aliatar 'Los Caracoles' ♈ Plaza Aliatar 4
Reina Mónica ♈ Calle Panaderos 20
Horno de Paquito ♈ Calle San Buenaventura (Plaza Aliatar)
Bar Aixa ♈ Plaza Larga 5

👀 Other Sights in Granada

If you leave Málaga early and return late (or if you decide to stay overnight in Granada; there is no shortage of cheap and basic accommodation if all you need is a bed), then you will have time to see something more than the Alhambra. Here are a few suggestions.

Monastery of San Jerónimo

📍 Calle Rector López Argueta 9 🕐 Mon–Sun 1000–1330, 1600–1930
🌐 realmonasteriosanjeronimogranada.com 💶

The Royal Monastery of St. Jerome is a former Hieronymite monastery in the Renaissance style. The church, famous for its architecture, was the first in the world consecrated to the Immaculate Conception of Mary. It was founded by the *Reyes Católicos* in Santa Fe outside the city of Granada before the last siege of the final stage of the *reconquista*. The construction of the current monastery in Granada began in 1504, and the principal architect and sculptor was Diego de Siloé. Gonzalo Fernández de Córdoba, known as the *Gran Capitán* ('Great Captain'), was thought to be buried at the crossing, along with his wife, Doña Maria de Manrique, but recent DNA testing suggests that it is not his tomb after all (the supposition being that it was plundered by the French during the War of Independence of 1808–1812).

After the monastery was sacked by the French, the Hieronymite monks were expelled and the monastery reduced to a near-ruin. The State undertook a restoration of the building in 1916–1920, hiring the architect Fernando Wihelmi for the job. The slender tower of the church had been demolished by the French, who used the rubble to build the bridge known as the Puente Verde, which crosses the River Genil, linking the *Paseo* de la Bomba to the Avenida de Cervantes. Only in the 1980s was the tower re-erected; a project completed in 1989. The star attraction is the baroque monastic church, which is breathtaking.

The Barrio of Albaicín (alto)

🌐 bit.ly/AlbaicinGranada

The upper part of the Albaicín district is picturesque and fun to explore (though, be warned — it is perched on a hill and, although one can get to and from it by bus, there is a lot of walking up and down hill required). It is probably the part of Granada that most faithfully reflects the street plan of, if not quite its Moorish heyday, then not long after..

El Bañuelo (Moorish Baths)

📍 Carrera del Darro 31 🕐 Mon–Sun 1000–1700 💶💶

Though fascinating and, unlike the modern 'Granada Hammam', a genuine Arab bathhouse (once part of the complex of the 'Mosque of the Walnut'), you might baulk at the entrance price, but the ticket will allow you to visit (on the same day) the *bañuelo* and three other historic sites: the Dar al-Horra Palace, the Casa Horno de Oro and the Corral del Carbón.

Palacio Dar al-Horra

📍 Callejón de las Monjas 🕐 ☀0900–1430, 1700–2030; 🌑1000–1700 (combined 🎟)

A Nazari palace located in the Albaicín neighbourhood and built in the fourteenth century on a former Zirid palace of the eleventh century, which was the first residence of the founder of the Nasrid dynasty, Muhammad I.

It is located on top of what was the al-Qashba Cadima, or Old Fortress, the initial nucleus of Muslim Granada. Its Arabic name means 'House of the Lady' for at the time of the *reconquista* it was the residence of Aixa, the dowager queen and mother of Boabdil.

Casa Horno de Oro

⌖ Calle Horno del Oro 14 🕐 ☀ 0900–1430, 1700–2030; ♨ 1000–1700 (combined 🎟)

The *Casa Morisca de la Calle Horno de Oro* ('The Moorish House of Golden Oven Street') is located near the River Darro, in a *barrio* once known as Axares ('Health' or 'Delight') due to its good climatic conditions and the beauty of its houses. Built in the late 15th century, the transformations of the 16th century made it an interesting example of a Moorish house that integrates Islamic and Castilian elements. The simplicity of its façade hides a striking architectural harmony inside. A rectangular patio with a pool is at the centre the building. The porticoed gallery was constructed in the Christian era.

Corral del Carbón

⌖ Calle Mariana Pineda 🕐 0900–2000 (combined 🎟)

The Corral del Carbón or Correo de los Moros is a 14th-century Nasrid *'alhóndiga'* (corn exchange) preserved almost in its entirety. It was built before 1336, and its original name was Al-Funduq al-Gidida or 'New Alhóndiga'. Located next to the silk market or Alcaicería, it served as an inn for merchants in transit, and as a warehouse and wholesale market.

Casa de Zafra

⌖ Calle Portería Concepción 8 🕐 Mon–Sun 0900–1430 €

This Hispanic-Moorish house, like others in the city, has survived because it was joined to a religious building, in this case to the convent of Santa Catalina de Zafra (see below). Its layout is like that of a typical residential house with a pool in the central courtyard, a double portico and main rooms on the two shorter sides. The changes the house has undergone reflect the urban evolution of the Albaicín district in the early 15th century, but important examples of carved ceilings and Moorish decorative painting are still well preserved. It now houses the 'Centro de Interpretación' for the Albaicín district.

Convento de Santa Catalina de Zafra

⌖ Carrera del Darro 39 🕐 Mon–Sun 0900–1430 € (donation)

A monastery of Dominican nuns ('*monjas*' in Spanish) founded in 1540 by the widow of Hernando de Zafra, the Secretary of the *Reyes Católicos*. The church may be visited and the sisters sell their homemade *dulces* from the convent door (0900–1230, 1600–1800).

Casa de Castril

⌖ Carrera del Darro 41–43 €

This grand house with its beautiful plateresque doorway takes its name from the Manor of Castril granted by the *Reyes Católicos* to their Secretary, Hernando de Zafra. It was built in 1539 by his grandson. It now houses the Archaeological Museum of Granada over two of its floors, numbering seven rooms covering several archaeological periods, from the Palaeolithic to the Roman and Arab periods.

Cuarto Real de Santo Domingo

📍 Plaza de los Campos 6 ⊘ Mon €

The 13th century 'Royal Room of St Dominic', is what remains of an Almohad Palace of Moorish Granada, located in the heart of the city, next to what was the *barrio* of Alfareros. It is the only surviving example of a true *'almunia real'* (royal summer residence) within the ancient Nasrid city.

Casa de los Tiros

📍 Calle Pavaneras 19 ⊘ Mon €

The Casa de los Tiros was built between 1530 and 1540 and is similar to other palaces of Granada at the time. It is named after the cannon ('*tiro*' means 'shot') once positioned on its battlements. It formed part of the wall of the neighbourhood of the *barrio* of Alfareros, hence its fortress-like appearance. The polychrome coffered ceiling of the *Cuadra Dorada* or main hall, stands out, as well as the plateresque doors. It is currently a museum with a fine collection of painting and sculpture.

Capilla Real (Chapel Royal)

📍 Calle Oficios ⊕ capillarealgranada.com ⏱ Mon–Sat 1000–1830; Sun 1100–1800 €€

The final resting place of Fernando and Isabel, this chapel is somewhat like a 'Royal Peculiar' in the UK and is not part of the Cathedral. It is entered separately (with a separate admission charge). It is a rather beautiful chapel, albeit somewhat austere (like the Catholic Monarchs themselves). There is a small museum of tapestries, vestments, paintings and illuminated manuscripts in the vast sacristy.

Catedral de Granada

📍 Plaza de las Pasiegas ⏱ Mon–Sat 1000–1815; Sun 1100–1815 ⊕ catedraldegranada.com €€

Like the Cathedral of Málaga, Granada's cathedral is also unfinished. Several architects worked on the structure during the almost 200 years it took to build, the most famous being Diego de Siloé. Architecturally, it is a mix of styles, predominantly Renaissance and baroque, and it is surprisingly light and open for a Spanish church, with stone, rather than polychromatic decoration, dominating.

Hospital de San Juan de Dios

📍 Calle San Juan de Dios 19 ⊕ basilicasanjuandedios.es ⏱ Mon–Sat 1000–1900; Sun 1000–1200, 1330–1900 €€

Now a private hospital run by the Order of St John of God, but it is possible to visit the chapel (a minor basilica), which is stunning, and so richly decorated and gilded that the adjective 'baroque' barely seems to do it justice.

Sevilla

This is a very short section, because I **do not** recommend that you visit Sevilla on a day trip from Málaga. Why? Because although Sevilla is one the most beautiful and vibrant cities in Spain and can be reached from Málaga in a couple of hours, trying to 'do' it as a day trip is likely to disappoint. You owe it to Sevilla to give it more than a few hours of your time. You can go to Córdoba, visit the *Mezquita-Catedral*, have a wander through the Judería and feel that you have 'done' Córdoba. Even a day in Granada will cross off the Alhambra (the main reason that people visit). But a day (effectively half a day) is simply not long enough even to scratch the surface of Sevilla. The city deserves more of your time.

If you really want to combine Málaga and Sevilla, then the only satisfying way to do it is to stay in both cities. You'll need 36 (or, better, 48) hours in Sevilla just to cover the 'essentials' in brief. I've been visiting both places pretty regularly for the last 20 years and I am still finding hitherto unknown corners. You could, for example, fly into Málaga and take a train to Sevilla, stay for a couple of nights, then return to Málaga for a night or two before travelling home (or vice versa if the flights are convenient). From most UK cities, a regional airport flight to Málaga and a Spanish train to Sevilla is likely to be a cheaper option than travelling to London to take a flight directly to Sevilla.

If you are absolutely determined to go to Sevilla for the day, then I cannot stop you. But, equally, I cannot provide you with a guide, at least not in this book, which is quite long enough already. There are plenty of guidebooks to Sevilla already available. But, just in case you choose not to follow my advice, if you start early and return late, you could probably manage to choose two options from the following list on a day trip, plus a *tapas* stop (there must always be a *tapas* stop). So, in order of 'must-see-ness':

- The Alcázar *OR* The Cathedral (pre-booking strongly advised)
- The Judería (*Barrio* Santa Cruz)
- The *Barrio* of Triana (possibly combined with your *tapas* stop)
- The Museo de Bellas Artes
- Las Setas
- The Plaza de España

But honesty, don't go. Or rather do go — in fact, go dozens of times — but go **properly**.

Appendices
Key to Symbols

barrio		breakfast/*almuerzo*	
address		sweet bakery	
restaurant		ice cream	
bar		website	
tasting menu		tickets	
reservations		Spanish	
reserve on thefork		English	
reserve on Google		date	
menú del día		opening hours	
children's menu		closed	
tapas		information	
raciones/½ raciones		price range	
wine list		entry charge	
Málaga wine/*vermú*		free	
cocktails		free audio guide	
beers		gallery	
coffee		museum	
take away		email	
delivery		WhatsApp	
traditional dishes		Android	
world/fusion cuisine		iOS	
steaks or grill		note	
vegetarian options		Facebook/Meta	
salads		phone	
fish		Instagram	
seafood		summer hours	
sandwiches/*tostadas*		off–season hours	
egg dishes		family friendly	
cheese		guided tour	
soup/stews		Metro	
rice dishes		bus	
homemade puddings		bus stop ID	
fast food		*Cercanías*	

📖 Appendix I: Bibliography

The following is a small selection of books that are interesting, well-written and can help travellers to understand Spain and Andalucía. Not all are in print, but those that aren't can often be found available second-hand, including from online retailers

⏳ History

Ghosts of Spain: Travels Through a Country's Hidden Past by Giles Tremlett

First published in 2006 and revised in 2012, this cultural portrait of contemporary Spain through snapshots of its history is a great general introduction to the country by a veteran Madrid correspondent of *The Guardian*.

Spain: A History by Raymond Carr

A concise and readable history by one of the outstanding 20th-century observers of the country.

Spain, The Root and the Flower by John A. Crow

An absorbing, well-written account of Spanish cultural history. This book spans a huge arc from prehistory through the eras of the Romans, Jews, Moors, and the Golden Age, right up to Franco and his legacy in modern Spain.

Málaga Burning: An American Woman's Eyewitness Account of the Spanish Civil War by Gamel Woolsey

A dramatic, beautiful and moving story. Through vivid character sketches and personal observations, Woolsey describes the people caught up in the bloody conflict.

The Spanish Labyrinth: An Account of the Social and Political Background of the Civil War by Gerald Brenan

Banned under Franco, this early history of the Civil War by the Hispanist Brenan was well received when finally published in Spain. The Historian of Spain, Sir Raymond Carr, called it 'a revelation'.

My House in Málaga by Peter Chalmers Mitchell

Sir Peter Chalmers Mitchell retired in his 70s from the Zoological Society of London and moved to Málaga to write his memoirs. Then came the fascist uprising of 1936. While most other British residents fled to Gibraltar, Sir Peter stayed put in order to protect his 'house and servants'.

Moorish Spain by Richard Fletcher

Perhaps the best, and certainly one of the more balanced, introductions to the history of Medieval Spain under Islamic rule.

💼 Literature and Travel

Concerning the Angels by Rafael Alberti

First published in Spain in the summer of 1929, *Concerning the Angels* (*Sobre los ángeles*) is the great Spanish poet Rafael Alberti's masterpiece, on a par with T.S. Eliot's The Waste Land, Pablo Neruda's *Residencia en la tierra*, and Federico Garcia Lorca's *Poeta en Nueva York*.

South of Granada by Gerald Brenan

Brenan is something of a literary hero in Spain and this is a charming and engaging account of his travels in Andalucía as the Civil War was brewing.

As I Walked Out One Midsummer Morning by Laurie Lee

Another Hispanophile British writer, Laurie Lee sets off for Spain on the eve of the Civil War with little more than his violin in his luggage.

A Rose for Winter by Laurie Lee

Lee's account of his return to Spain, fifteen years after the Civil War.

Two Middle-Aged Ladies in Andalucía by Penelope Chetwode

Chetwode, the wife of John Betjeman, takes a circular ride on her horse Marquesa, around the countryside between Granada and Úbeda in Andalucía in 1961. Charming and eccentric.

The Train in Spain by Christopher Howse

A modern (2013) travelogue in the form of ten train journeys (two of them in Andalucía) taken by a keen long-time observer of Spain. The result is an affectionate portrait of the country as humorous as it is erudite. Beautifully written.

Spain by Jan Morris

First published in 1964, this (almost, but not quite) universally praised odyssey through Spain has been revised and superbly illustrated. History, legend, landscape, architecture, religion, character, and anecdote are brilliantly woven together.

Cicerone Guides

If walking, hiking or trekking is your thing, Cicerone publishes a number of excellent guides (*e.g.* to the Sierra Nevada, The Mountains of Nerja, The Mountains of Ronda, etc.).

Art

Duende: A Journey in Search of Flamenco by Jason Webster

A thrilling account of Webster's attempt (and ultimate failure) to become accepted among Roma flamenco musicians, and what he learns about *duende* along the way. Beautifully written, and fascinating.

Picasso: Masters of Art by Rosalind Ormiston

A short and readable survey of the life and work of one of Málaga's most famous sons.

Gastronomy

The Food of Spain by Claudia Roden

As a Sephardi Jew born in Egypt, Roden's understanding of Spanish food and the historic influences of Jewish and Moorish cooking is deep. Few authors write so engagingly about food, though other writers to look out for are **Penelope Casas** and **Elisabeth Luard**.

A Late Dinner: Discovering the Food of Spain by Paul Richardson

An entertaining introduction to the cuisines of Spain in a travelogue format.

The Tío Pepe Guide to the Seafood of Spain and Portugal by Alan Davidson

This is the fish and seafood lover's bible. Even if you are a keen fish eater, the choice available in Spain is bewildering and Davidson lists pretty much all of them.

🐟🐬 Appendix II: Fish and Seafood

When it comes to translating menus (*cartas*), Google Translate is usually up to the task. Where it fails is with respect to names of Málaga wines — 'little bird' (for '*pajarete*') doesn't tell you much. Have a look at the sections on p. 149ff. and p. 197ff. for help. A few meat dishes tend to get mangled, too. For example, '*lagarto ibérico*' is not 'Iberian lizard' (it's many years since actual lizards appeared on menus in Extremadura) but a high quality cut of pork from between the ribs and the loin. Also, '*callos*' are not 'corns' or 'calluses' but stewed tripe.

Similarly, fish and seafood are a minefield, partly because the range of species eaten in Spain is so much more extensive than in Britain. The following is a list of fish and shellfish that may confuse or defeat automatic translation tools (it does not include common fish like cod, and some of the names are only used in Málaga):

Acedía	Sole	*Bocina*	Whelk
Agúa palá	Swordfish	*Bolo*	Warty Venus Clam
Aguacioso	Sand Eel	*Breca*	Pandora
Aguja	Gar–Fish	*Brotola*	Forkbeard
Aligote/Alijote	Bronze Bream	*Búsano*	Murex
Almeja Babosa	Venus Shell Clam	*Cabrilla*	Comber
Almeja de Perro	Furrow Shell Clam	*Caballa*	Mackerel
Almeja Dorada	Golden Carpet-Shell Clam	*Cabracho*	Red Scorpion fish
		Cadela	Furrow Shell Clam
Almeja Fina	Carpet-Shell Clam	*Camarón*	Common Prawn
Almeja Lisa	Trough–Shell Clam	*Caña(d)illa*	Murex
Almejón Briliante	Smooth Venus Clam	*Cangrejo Moruno*	Furry Crab
Almendra de Mar	Dog Cockle	*Cangrejo Real*	Shamefaced Crab
Anjova	Bluefish	*Capellan*	Poor cod
Araña	Weever	*Carabinero*	Prawn
Arbitan	Ling	*Caracol Gris*	Top-Shell
Arola	Otter Shell Clam	*Caracola*	Whelk
Bacaladilla	Blue whiting	*Caracolillo*	Winkle
Barbada	Rockling	*Caramujo*	Top-Shell
Barrilete	Fiddler Crab	*Cazón*	Tope Shark
Bejel	Tub Gurnard	*Centolla*	Spider Crab
Bertorella	Rockling	*Chaparrudo*	Goby
Besugo	Red Bream	*Cherna*	Wreckfish
Bigaro	Winkle	*Cherne **de Ley***	Grouper
Boca	Fiddler Crab Claw		

Chicharro	Horse Mackerel/Scad	*Mero*	Grouper
Chirla	Striped Venus Clam	*Mollera*	Poor cod
Chocha	Venus Shell Clam	*Muergo*	Razor-Shell Clam
Choco	Small Cuttlefish	*Nacár*	Fan Mussel
Chopito	Small Cuttlefish	*Nécora*	Swimming Crab
Cohombro	Sea Cucumber	*Oreja de Mar*	Abalone
Concha Fina	Smooth Venus Clam	*Ostión*	Portuguese Oyster
Concha Pelegrina	(Pilgrim) Scallop	*Pachán*	Red Bream
Coquina	Wedge Shell Clam	*Palometa*	Pompano
Corvallo	Corb	*Palometa Roja*	Alfonsino
Corvina	Meagre	*Palometón*	Leerfish
Datil del Mar	Date-Shell Mussel	*Paparda*	Skipper
Dentón	Grouper	*Peonta*	Top-Shell
Escorpión	Weever	*Pez de San Francisco*	Lizard Fish
Escupiña Grabada	Warty Venus Clam	*Pez de San Pedro*	John Dory
Estornino	Chub Mackerel	*Pez Limón*	Amberjack
Flaso Abadejo	Grouper	*Pez Piloto*	Pilot Fish
Galera	Mantis Shrimp	*Pintarroja*	Lesser Spotted Dog fish
Gallina	Scorpion Fish		
Gallineta	Bluemouth	*Puntilla*	Squid (usually small)
Gallineta Rosada	Slender Rockfish	*Quisquilla*	Brown Shrimp
Gamba	Prawn	*Rape*	Angler Fish
Garneo	Piper	*Rascacio*	Scorpion Fish
Gitano	Grouper	*Rata*	Star Gazer
Globito	Small Cuttlefish	*Romerillo*	Blackfish
Goraz	Red Bream	*Rosada*	see p. 130
Japuta	Ray's Bream	*Sábalo*	Shad
Jurel	Horse Mackerel/Scad	*Saboga*	Twaite shad
Lampuga	Dolphin Fish	*Salmonete*	Red Mullet
Langostillo	Cockle	*Saverina*	Smooth Venus Clam
Langostino	King Prawn	*Señorita*	Peacock Wrasse
Lapa	Limpet	*Serrano Imperial*	Comber
Longueirón	Razor-Shell Clam	*Tallarina*	Wedge Shell Clam
Luna Real	Opah	*Tordo*	Five Spotted Wrasse
Maganto	Norway Lobster	*Verdigón*	Cockle
Manolita	Sardine	*Verigueto*	Warty Venus Clam
Maragota	Wrasse	*Vibora*	Weever
Margarita	Golden Carpet-Shell Clam	*Viera*	(Pilgrim) Scallop
		Volandeira	Queen Scallop
Merillo	Brown Comber	*Voraz*	Red Bream

🍲 Appendix III: Recipes from Málaga

🥘 *Ensalada malagueña* (Málaga salad)

2 large boiled potatoes

2 oranges

2 hard-boiled eggs, peeled and quartered

a little red onion or some spring onions

200 g of flaked desalted cod, cold poached cod (or very good quality preserved tuna)

green or black olives

Extra virgin olive oil

Salt and Pepper

Chives

SERVES 4 (*tapa*)

This cod and orange salad from Málaga is very easy to prepare. Your first choice concerns the cod. The authentic version uses dried salt cod (*bacalao*) which has been desalted (soaked for 24 hours in two changes of water) and then either crumbled, or firmed up by frying in a little oil and then flaked. Salt cod is available online, in the international section of some supermarkets and from Spanish (or Portuguese/Caribbean/Brazilian) grocers. To use fresh cod, poach at a gentle simmer until just cooked (about 6–8 minutes) and then leave to cool completely before flaking.

The potatoes need to be tender but not mushy. The best way to achieve this is to boil them in their skins, leave them to cool and then slip off the skins. Of course, you can leave the skins on, or you could use baby potatoes (a waxy variety works best) and use whole or halved.

The oranges should be not too sweet (*i.e.* not clementines or mandarins), but something like a naval orange. The best way to prepare an orange for a salad is to 'top and tail' it, then use a sharp knife to remove the skin and pith, working around the sides of the fruit, top to bottom. Then, holding the orange in your hand, cut segments, leaving behind the fibrous membranes.

The 'assembly' is up to you, but there are three traditional ways of putting things together. Seen most often is the 'chunky' version. Ideally, each of the components should be a similar size — olives, cod, potatoes, with orange segments and boiled egg quarters, and then some finely sliced red onion or spring onions. Season with salt, pepper, and minced chives, then drizzle with good olive oil and lightly mix together.

Another visually pleasing way is to 'stack'. Cut your potatoes in rounds and arrange on the plate or serving dish. Season and drizzle with oil. Then top with the flakes of cod, some onion and green olives, as well as slices of peeled orange. Arrange the boiled egg quarters on top, season and drizzle with olive oil.

The third way of combining the ingredients is in an '*ensaladilla*' or 'little salad'. A 'little salad' does not mean a small helping, but finely diced. This is ideal for when you want to present the salad in a serving ring. Flake the cod more finely, dice the potato in cubes of about 10–15 mm, cutting the olives, orange and eggs to similar dimensions. Season, add chives and oil and gently stir together. Serve in a large ramekin, or shape using a serving ring.

⇔ Gazpacho

With a liquidizer (or best of all a Nutri-Bullet or equivalent), making *gazpacho* is the work of a few minutes. The precise proportions of each ingredient are a matter of taste, so do experiment. However, I suggest you start with this list of quantities (which will fit the large cup of a Nutri-Bullet) and modify according to taste.

350g vine–ripened cherry or small tomatoes (which in the UK have more flavour than the larger ones, though any home-grown variety will be superior)

½ deseeded red pepper

½ deseeded cucumber (peeled if you wish)

1–2 cloves garlic

1 bunch of spring onions (white and light green parts only)

2 tablespoons of extra virgin olive oil (the best you have — something green and grassy)

1 tablespoon sherry vinegar

pinch salt and pepper   **SERVES 3–4**

Wash and drain the tomatoes and pepper. Half the tomatoes and place in your blender. Deseed the pepper. The easiest way to do this is to place is flat on the board along its long side and slice off the top and bottom. This gives you a 'tube' of pepper. With a sharp knife cut into the pepper and 'fillet' it, cutting out the centre in a circular motion to leave just the red flesh, discarding the core of seeds and 'glands'. Roughly dice half the pepper and add to the blender goblet.

Take half a cucumber. Cut in half lengthways and draw a teaspoon along the centre to remove the seeds and jelly leaving only the firm flesh. Roughly chop and add to the blender. Remove the outer papery leaves from the onions, cut off the roots and add the white and light green parts to the blender. Peel and slice the garlic and add it. Add the oil and vinegar, a pinch of salt and grind of black pepper (or, better still, a pinch of white pepper). For the best results, it really is worth using sherry vinegar, but wine or cider vinegar will do if necessary.

Now blend, and blend again. You are aiming for a smooth liquid with the consistency of single cream, not something chunky or 'rustic'. If your liquidizer isn't highly powered you can always sieve your *gazpacho*, but 2 or 3 minutes in a NutriBullet will do the job easily. Let down with a dash of water if it is too thick. Now taste and adjust for oil, vinegar and pepper (or anything else). *Gazpacho* will keep in an airtight bottle in the fridge for up to 5 days.

Serve in bowls with a garnish of finely minced pepper, cucumber and spring onion, or in shot glasses, like a savoury smoothie. If you prefer a milder *gazpacho*, increase the cucumber and decrease the pepper (or switch for green), and if you want something more piquant, increase the pepper or add some chilli or Tabasco (not at all authentic, but quite delicious). To make *porra antequerana*, don't over-blend and add chunks of sourdough bread to the blender until you achieve the desired consistency.

Carne de lidia estofado (Fighting Bull Stew)

This rich beef stew is traditionally made with the meat of fighting bulls, which is extremely tasty but requires long, slow cooking. Use any braising steak, but if you go to a real butcher ask for skirt (though shin and flank are both good). Skirt is a cut that is very popular in Spain where it's called *'falda de res'*. It's also the cut used for *fajitas* in Mexican cuisine. This stew is popular throughout Spain, but the *malagueño* touch is the addition of salt-cured anchovies. If you've never used anchovies to add an umami kick to a savoury dish then this may be a revelation. Anchovies were an ingredient of the garum that made Málaga so

important in Antiquity, as well as Worcestershire Sauce. As well as beef and lamb, anchovies have an affinity with potatoes (*e.g.* Jansson's Temptation), tomatoes and olives (*e.g. salsa alla puttanesca*), garlic (*e.g. anchoïade*), mature cheese, and brassicas like broccoli and cauliflower.

800 g braising steak or beef skirt cut into large chunks

1 medium onion, finely chopped

1 carrot, finely chopped

½ red pepper, finely chopped

3 garlic cloves, finely chopped

2 tsp. paprika (optional)

2 bay leaves (or bouquet garni)

½ bottle gutsy red wine

250 ml beef stock

generous pinch sugar

seasoned plain flour

2 tbsp. tomato purée

olive oil

5 tinned anchovies in oil, finely chopped

200 g shallots, peeled

200 g carrots, thickly sliced (or trimmed baby carrots)

a handful of pitted black olives

Cooking time: 2 hours (oven) or 6–8 hours (slow cooker)   **SERVES 4**

First, pat the beef dry with kitchen paper or a clean tea towel. Toss in the seasoned flour and brown in a heavy-bottomed pan or casserole. Don't crowd the pan! Set aside. Over a low heat, sweat the onion, carrot and red pepper *sofrito* until soft. Mix in the tomato purée, a pinch of sugar, (paprika if using) and about ½ tbsp. of flour and mix well.

Pour in the wine and bring to a boil, stirring until very slightly thickened and glossy. Return the meat to the pan, add the anchovies, bay leaves (or bouquet garni). Bring to a simmer, cover and leave to simmer for at least 1 hour. You can also braise in the oven (140°C or 120°C fan), or cook in a slow cooker for 4–5 hours on low.

After simmering for an hour (or 4–5 hours in the slow cooker), add the peeled shallots (halve if large), olives, and carrots and cook for another hour (hob or oven) or 2 hours (slow cooker). If the meat is cooked (it should be almost falling apart) but the sauce is a little thin, then remove the meat and vegetables to a serving dish and keep warm. You have three options to thicken the sauce: whisk in *beurre manié*; bring to the boil and reduce; or liquidize (the *sofrito* will thicken the sauce, like a soup).

Serve with chips (French fries) if you want to be authentic. An alternative and delicious accompaniment would be *toſtadas de anĉhoas* — finely chop a few anchovies (or pound them in a mortar), mix with olive oil (or butter) and use this mixture to make 'anchovy toasts' with slices of French bread or sourdough just as you would prepare garlic bread. In fact, once you've tried 'anchovy bread', you may be unwilling to return to garlic bread.

❦ *Patatas a lo pobre* (Poor Man's Potatoes)

This is Málaga's version of *Pommes Lyonnaise* (potatoes cooked with onions) served alongside meat or fish, and often paired with fried egg, ham or '*ĉhacinas*' (sausages or *chorizo*).

4–6 medium-sized potatoes

1 large or 2 small onions

1 green pepper

3 cloves of garlic

olive oil

a dash of sherry vinegar

finely minced parsley

salt and pepper   SERVES 3–4

Peel the potatoes, half lengthways and cut into 3–4mm slices. Peel and half the onion(s) and slice thinly. Remove the core and seeds of the pepper (see technique above) and slice into narrow batons. Crush but do not peel the garlic cloves. In a large, heavy-bottomed frying pan or shallow casserole, heat a generous amount of olive oil (enough the cover the bottom) over a **very** gentle heat. You are going to confit rather than fry the ingredients.

Add all the ingredients and cook, stirring occasionally. You want to soften the vegetables without browning them too much. The *patatas* are ready when the potatoes are soft and cooked through. They should be no more than lightly browned in places, though the onions will be more brown, which is good for the overall flavour. Add a sprinkling of vinegar (wine vinegar if you can't find sherry vinegar), a handful of parsley and season with salt and black pepper. Remove the *patatas a lo pobre* with a slotted spoon, draining the oil. They can be kept warm in a low oven until ready to serve. If you are serving with a fried egg and ham or sausage, use the tasty left-over oil to fry these.

✍ *Gallina en pepitoria* (Chicken in Almond Sauce)

Pepitoria is a popular way of cooking meat all over Spain, involving a thick sauce of almonds and saffron. Although the etymology of the name is uncertain, its Moorish origins can hardly be in doubt (though a number of scholars point to a Jewish origin). The original version was made with *gallina* (a stewing hen), but nowadays *pollo* (a young chicken) is used.

1.5 kg chicken legs (skinless and separated into drumsticks and thighs) + seasoned flour for dusting

1 onion, finely chopped

3 garlic cloves, crushed

2 hard-boiled eggs

20 blanched almonds

1 large glass of dry Málaga wine (or sherry, e.g. Fino or Oloroso)

300 ml chicken stock

100 g stale bread torn into chunks

Salt, pepper and nutmeg

6 strands of saffron (or a teaspoon of turmeric)

A bay-leaf

Flaked almonds (optional)

Virgin olive oil   SERVES 4

Heat enough olive oil to cover the base of a heavy-bottomed pan or casserole. Brown the lightly floured chicken pieces. When golden, remove from the casserole and set aside. Set aside two tablespoons of the oil to make the '*majado*' (paste — see below). If the chicken has stuck to the pan, pour off the oil and deglaze with a glug of wine, reserving this liquid.

In the same casserole and with the remaining oil, add the onion cut into small cubes and the three crushed garlic cloves. Fry very slowly so that the onion doesn't burn. When the onion is translucent, add the chicken, mix, and season with salt, pepper and a grating of nutmeg. Add the wine or sherry and let it reduce slightly over a medium heat. Keep an eye on the main pot as you prepare the *majado*.

In a clean frying pan, toast the almonds over a low heat, making sure they don't burn, and set them aside when fragrant and golden. Next, heat the two reserved tablespoons of oil and fry the pieces of stale bread until they are crisp. In the final couple of minutes add the saffron (or turmeric) to release its full flavour. The authentic implement for making the *majado* is a pestle and mortar, but a food processor will do. Add the toasted almonds, the fried bread and saffron, and the hard-boiled egg yolks. Pound (or process) the ingredients thoroughly.

Add the *majado* to the chicken and stir briefly to mix all the flavours . Add enough chicken stock to cover the chicken pieces, toss in a bay-leaf, and mix again. Simmer over medium heat for 30–35 minutes, topping up with stock if necessary. Garnish with flaked almonds or finely diced egg whites (from the hard-boiled eggs you took the whites from). Serve with chips or rice and a salad.

🍳 *Torrijas* (Holy Week French Toast)

Torrijas, a version of French Toast, is almost an obsession in Lent and Holy Week. Newspapers publish articles promising to reveal the *panaderías* selling the best *torrijas* in this or that town while chefs at luxury restaurants compete to 'elevate' the dish to put it on their tasting menus. First mentioned almost 2,000 years ago by the Roman gourmet Marco Gavio Apio, the first mention in Spanish literature is by Juan de Encina (in 1496) who refers to 'honey and many eggs to make torrijas' in connection with the Virgin Mary who *'parió al Redentor'* (gave birth to the Redeemer). Originally, then, *torrijas* were a calorific food for postpartum mothers. How it came to be associated with Lent and Holy Week is something of a mystery, especially given that it contains eggs and dairy, traditionally renounced during Lent. It was probably first made (by Christians) for the Feast of the Annunciation (25 March). The *malagueña* version is made with wine (or wine and milk), rather than milk.

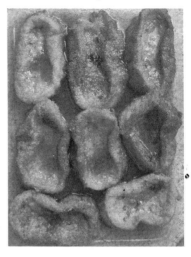

1 day-old half baguette or 'baton' (try to find one with a softish crust)

250 ml of light, sweet Málaga wine (*e.g.* Moscatel)

100 ml water

70 grams of sugar

1 cinnamon stick

the pared zest of 1 orange (without pith)

2 eggs

light olive (or vegetable) oil for frying   **MAKES ABOUT 12 *TORRIJAS***

Heat the wine, sugar, water, pared orange rind and cinnamon stick in a pan, without boiling (just below a simmer), for 10–15 minutes. Leave to cool. When cooled to room temperature, remove the orange peel and cinnamon stick.

Cut the bread into slices, about an inch thick. You want something about the size of your palm, so if the baguette is narrow, cut on the bias (diagonally). Dip each slice of bread into the wine. You want it to be well-soaked, but not sodden and disintegrating.

Beat the eggs until light and foamy and pass each bread slice through the egg, coating it well. You can cook them immediately, or leave them until you are ready. Heat a good amount of oil in a heavy frying pan and fry the slices until golden on both sides. Remove from the pan and drain on kitchen paper.

A traditional way of serving *torrijas* in Málaga is to toss them in a glaze made from honey let down with a little water (heat both ingredients in a pan until the honey 'melts'), but this gives you a very sweet final product. A very light dusting of caster sugar (mixed with powdered cinnamon if you wish) is less cloyingly sweet.

A glass of dark, sweet Málaga wine is the ideal accompaniment. If you want to make the *torrijas* into a pudding, serve them warm with cream, crème fraîche, ice cream or Greek yoghurt and maybe some fruit compote.

📷 Picture Credits

Original diagrams are the work of the author and published under a ⓒⓘ◎ licence (**creativecommons.org/licenses/by-sa/4.0**)

Creative Commons symbols are used under a ⓒⓘ licence (**creativecommons.org/licenses/by/4.0**) Other fonts used in this book are issued under the Open Font Licence (**scripts.sil.org/OFL**).

The 'Málaga' Symbol Font (created using FontForge) makes use of glyphs created by the author, henceforth licensed under a ⓒⓘ◎ licence; SVG vectors issued under an open licence (**svgrepo.com/page/licensing**); SVG vectors from **fontawesome.com** issued under a ⓒⓘ licence; icons made from **onlinewebfonts.com/icon**, Icon Fonts licensed by a ⓒⓘ licence; and glyphs from **thenounproject.com** users: Adrià Sánchez Aran (**/siqmundo**), Linseed Studio (**/linseedstudio**) infinit.space (**/infinit**), Andrew Doane (**/andydoane**), Ann Artemova (**/sunnyicons**), Lars Meiertoberens (**/lars.online**), Kick (**/kickg**), Valter Bispo (**/valterbispo**), Adrien Coquet (**/coquet_adrien**), and Abu (**/jamainabusanin7**), all licensed under a ⓒⓘ licence.

Unless otherwise attributed, all maps (and graphics with map content) were created by the author using MapOSMatic/OCitySMap (March–June 2023) with map data © 2023 OpenStreetMap contributors (**openstreetmap.org/copyright**), used here under an Open Data Commons licence (**opendatacommons.org/licenses/odbl**)

With the exception of those listed below, all other graphics and photographs in this book are either in the ⓟ public domain or the work of the author published under a ⓒⓘ◎ licence.

2   ⓒⓘ   Paolo Trabattoni flickr.com/photos/mctraba/9636914400

6   ⓒⓘ◎   Real Academia Española - Royal Spanish Academy, https://commons.wikimedia.org/w/index.php?curid=50839196

10   ⓒⓘ◎   Antonio https://flickr.com/photos/montuno/1183094952

12   ⓒⓘ◎   The Author 2023

15   ⓒⓘ   Magnus Akselvoll, https://flickr.com/photos/magnus_akselvoll/24327343590

16   ⓒⓘ   Martin Ultsch, https://flickr.com/photos/149503730@N03/31189268981

18   ⓒⓘ   Aapo Haapanen https://flickr.com/photos/decade_null/5275644988

21   ⓒⓘ   Jorge Franganillo, https://flickr.com/photos/franganillo/51901162348

25   ⓒⓘ   Hernán Piñera, https://flickr.com/photos/hernanpc/9097732121

26   ⓒⓘ   Nick Kenrick, https://flickr.com/photos/zedzap/15172070340

29   ⓒⓘ◎   Keith Williamson from Bigastro, Spain — It could be her! Project 365(4) Day 70, https://commons.wikimedia.org/w/index.php?curid=19165858

32   ⓟ   Georg Braun; Frans Hogenberg: Civitates Orbis Terrarum, Band 1, 1572 (Ausgabe Beschreibung vnd Contrafactur der vornembster Stät der Welt, Köln 1582; [VD16-B7188] Universitätsbibliothek Heidelberg http://diglit.ub.uni-heidelberg.de/diglit/braun1582bd1

42   ⓒⓘ◎   HansenBCN - Own work using: https://1.bp.blogspot.com/-6Dzff4h2l6E/WVQPBqxeVJI/AAAAAAABKPw/uThzZAbPHhAb2opeJR1G-lgcqk7GvpF5A-CLcBGAs/s1600/Málaga%2BCF.png ⓟ https://commons.wikimedia.org/w/index.php?curid=3784036

Index

Bars & Restaurants in Málaga

Made in United States
Troutdale, OR
01/06/2024

16745356R00354